Business & Society

Ethics & Stakeholder Management

EIGHTH EDITION

ANN K. BUCHHOLTZ

Rutgers University

ARCHIE B. CARROLL

University of Georgia

SOUTH-WESTERN
CENGAGE Learning

Australia • Brazil • Japan • Korea • Mexico • Singapore • Spain • United Kingdom • United States

SOUTH-WESTERN
CENGAGE Learning

Business & Society: Ethics & Stakeholder Management, Eighth Edition
Ann K. Buchholtz
Archie B. Carroll

Vice President of Editorial, Business: Jack W. Calhoun

Editor-in-Chief: Melissa Acuna

Sr. Acquisitions Editor: Michele Rhoades

Developmental Editor: Suzanna Bainbridge

Sr. Editorial Assistant: Ruth Belanger

Marketing Manager: Clinton Kernen

Sr. Content Project Manager: Kim Kusnerak

Production Technology Analyst: Jeff Weaver

Media Editor: Rob Ellington

Frontlist Buyer, Manufacturing: Arethea Thomas

Sr. Marketing Communications Manager: Jim Overly

Production Service/Compositor: MPS Limited, a Macmillan Company

Sr. Art Director: Tippy McIntosh

Internal Designer: c miller design

Cover Design: Patti Hudepohl

Photo Credits:

B/W Image: iStockphoto

Cover Image: Shutterstock Images/ SVLuma

Rights Acquisitions Specialist/Images: John Hill

Rights Acquisitions Specialist/Text: Mardell Glinski Schultz

Image Permissions Researcher: PreMediaGlobal

Text Permissions Researcher: Karyn Morrison

Printed in Canada
2 3 4 5 6 7 15 14 13 12 11

Exam*View*® is a registered trademark of eInstruction Corp. Windows is a registered trademark of the Microsoft Corporation used herein under license. Macintosh and Power Macintosh are registered trademarks of Apple Computer, Inc. used herein under license. © 2008 Cengage Learning. All Rights Reserved.

Cengage Learning WebTutor™ is a trademark of Cengage Learning.

Library of Congress Control Number: 2010939131

International Edition:

ISBN-13: 978-0-538-46676-9

ISBN-10: 0-538-46676-6

Cengage Learning International Offices

Asia
www.cengageasia.com
tel: (65) 6410 1200

Australia/New Zealand
www.cengage.com.au
tel: (61) 3 9685 4111

Brazil
www.cengage.com.br
tel: (55) 11 3665 9900

India
www.cengage.co.in
tel: (91) 11 4364 1111

Latin America
www.cengage.com.mx
tel: (52) 55 1500 6000

UK/Europe/Middle East/Africa
www.cengage.co.uk
tel: (44) 0 1264 332 424

Represented in Canada by Nelson Education, Ltd.
tel: (416) 752 9100/(800) 668 0671
www.nelson.com

Cengage Learning is a leading provider of customized learning solutions with office locations around the globe, including Singapore, the United Kingdom, Australia, Mexico, Brazil, and Japan. Locate your local office at: **www.cengage.com/global**

For product information: **www.cengage.com/international**
Visit your local office: **www.cengage.com/global**
Visit our corporate website: **www.cengage.com**

Brief Contents

Contents

PART 2   Corporate Governance and Strategic Management Issues 123

PART 3   Business Ethics and Management 227

PART 4   **External Stakeholder Issues 409**

Preface

Business & Society: Ethics & Stakeholder Management, Eighth Edition, employs a stakeholder management framework. A managerial perspective is embedded within the book's major themes of business ethics, sustainability, and stakeholder management.

The ethics dimension is central because it has become clear that value considerations are woven into the fabric of the public issues that organizations face today. An emphasis is placed on business ethics fundamentals and how ethics integrates into personal and organizational decision making. Special spheres of business ethics discussed include the realms of technology and global capitalism, where increasingly ethical questions have been arising for the past 20 years.

Sustainability has become one of business's most recent and urgent mandates. It is a new theme with this eighth edition because it has become apparent in the business world today that a concern for the natural, social, and financial environments are interrelated and that all three must be maintained in balance for both current and future generations.

The stakeholder management perspective is crucial because it requires managers to (1) identify the various groups or individuals who have stakes in the firm or its actions, decisions, and practices and (2) incorporate the stakeholders' concerns into the firm's daily operations and strategic plans. Stakeholder management is an approach that increases the likelihood decision makers will integrate ethical wisdom with management wisdom in all that they do.

As this edition goes to press, the country and world economies have been striving to recoup from one of the most perilous financial periods since the Great Depression. The world stock market collapse beginning in the fall of 2008 had devastating repercussions for economies, governments, businesses, and individuals, and we have still not resolved the uncertainty associated with what began as financial turmoil and bankruptcies on Wall Street. This major event and its consequences will be with us for many years, and we urge readers to keep in mind the extent to which our world has now changed as they read through the book and consider its content.

Applicable Courses for Text

This text is appropriate for college and university courses that carry such titles as Business and Society; Business and Its Environment; Business Ethics; Business and Public Policy; Social Issues in Management; Business, Government, and Society; Social Responsibility of Business; and Stakeholder Management. The book is appropriate for either a required or an elective course seeking to meet the most recent accrediting standards of the Association to Advance Collegiate Schools of Business (AACSB International). The book has been used successfully in both undergraduate and graduate courses.

Though the AACSB does not require any specific courses, its standards indicate that the school's curriculum should result in undergraduate and master's degree programs that contain topics covered thoroughly in this textbook. For an undergraduate degree program, learning experiences should be provided in general knowledge and skill areas such as *ethical understanding and reasoning abilities* and *multicultural and diversity understanding*. For both undergraduate and master's degree programs, learning experiences should be provided in general knowledge and skill areas such as *ethical and legal responsibilities in organizations and society* and *domestic and global environments of business.*

The book is ideal for coverage of perspectives that form the context for business: ethical and global issues; the influence of political, social, legal and regulatory, and environmental and technological issues; and the impact of diversity on organizations. The book provides perspectives on business, society, and ethics in the United States, along with examples from Europe and other parts of the world. The book has proved useful in a number of different countries outside of the United States. In previous editions, versions were published in Canada and China. Publication in Japan is under consideration. Though written from the perspective of American society, a special effort has been made to include some examples from different parts of the world to illustrate major points.

Objectives in Relevant Courses

Depending on the placement of a course in the curriculum or the individual instructor's philosophy or strategy, this book could be used for a variety of objectives. The courses for which it is intended typically include several essential goals, including the following:

1. Students should be made aware of the expectations and demands that emanate from stakeholders and are placed on business firms.
2. As prospective managers, students need to understand appropriate business responses and management approaches for dealing with social, political, environmental, technological, and global issues and stakeholders.
3. An appreciation of ethical issues and the influence these have on society, management decision making, behavior, policies, and practices is important.
4. The broad question of business's legitimacy as an institution in a global society is at stake and must be addressed from both business and societal perspectives. These topics are vital to business building trust with society and all stakeholders.
5. The increasing extent to which social, ethical, public, environmental, and global issues must be considered from a strategic perspective is critical in such courses.

New to the Eighth Edition

This eighth edition has been updated and revised to reflect the most recent research, laws, cases, and examples that would be appropriate in courses for which it is used. Material in this new edition includes:

- New research, surveys, and examples throughout all the chapters
- Coverage throughout the text on the most recent ethics scandals and their influence on business, society, organizations, and people
- Discussion of recent developments with the Sarbanes–Oxley Act and the Alien Tort Claims Act, two laws with significant importance to managers today
- Consideration of new legislation such as the Credit Card Act, which was implemented in 2010, and the Consumer Financial Protection Act of 2010
- "Spotlight on Sustainability" features in each chapter, which demonstrate how sustainability is relevant and applicable to each chapter's topics
- New "Ethics in Practice Cases" features distributed throughout the book
- Thirty-six end-of-part cases, including new cases on Goldman Sachs, the BP oil spill, the Whirlpool plant closing in Indiana, New Belgium Brewery's quest to become sustainable, and several others; twenty cases have been revised and updated

- Favorite cases from past editions included in the Instructor's Manual so that they may be duplicated and used in class
- A revised and updated Instructor's Manual

"Ethics in Practice Cases"

Continuing in this eighth edition are in-chapter features titled "Ethics in Practice Cases." Interspersed throughout the chapters, these short cases present (1) actual ethical situations faced by companies or managers or (2) dilemmas faced personally in the work experiences of our former students. These latter types of cases are real-life situations actually confronted by our students in their full- and part-time work experiences. The students contributed these cases on a voluntary basis, and we are pleased they gave us permission to use them. They provide ready examples of the types of ethical issues young people face today. We would like to acknowledge them for their contributions to the book. Instructors may wish to use these as mini-cases for class discussion on a daily basis when a lengthier case is not assigned. They can be read quickly, but they contain considerable substance for class discussion.

"Spotlight on Sustainability" Features

The "Spotlight on Sustainability" inserts in each chapter highlight an important and relevant linkage of sustainability concepts that augment each chapter's text material. The feature may highlight a pertinent organization and its activities or special topics covered in the chapter. These features permit students to explore how the sustainability theme applies to each topic covered in the text. Though the concept of sustainability began as essentially an environmental topic, it now extends to virtually all business, society, and ethics topics.

Structure of the Book

Part 1. Business, Society, and Stakeholders

Part 1 of the book provides introductory coverage of pertinent business, society, and stakeholder topics and issues. Because most courses for which this book is intended developed from the issue of corporate social responsibility, this concept is treated early on. Part 1 documents and discusses how corporate social responsiveness evolved from social responsibility and how these two matured into a concern for corporate social performance and corporate citizenship. Also given early coverage is the stakeholder management concept because it provides a way of thinking and analyzing all topics in the book.

Part 2. Corporate Governance and Strategic Management Issues

The second part of the text addresses corporate governance and strategic management for stakeholder responsiveness. The purpose of this part is to discuss management considerations and implications for dealing with the issues discussed throughout the text. Corporate governance is covered early because in the past decade this topic has been identified to be critical to effective strategic management. The strategic management perspective is useful because these issues have impacts on the total organization and have become intense for many upper-level managers. Special treatment is given to corporate public policy, issues and crisis management, and public affairs management.

   Some instructors may elect to cover Part 2 later in their courses. It could easily be covered after Part 4 or 5. This option would be most appropriate for those who use the book for a business ethics course or who desire to spend less time on the governance, strategy, and management perspectives.

Part 3. Business Ethics and Management

Four chapters dedicated to business ethics topics are presented in Part 3. In real life, business ethics cannot be separated from the full range of external and internal stakeholder concerns. Part 3 focuses on business ethics fundamentals, personal and organizational ethics, business ethics and technology, and ethical issues in the global arena. Taken together, they cover the gamut of business and society issues that require ethical thinking.

Part 4. External Stakeholder Issues

Vital topics here include business's relations with government, consumers, the environment, and the community. In each of these topic areas we see social and ethical issues that dominate business today. The business–government relationship is divided into the regulatory initiatives to monitor business practices and then a second chapter addresses business's attempts to influence government, primarily through lobbying. Consumers, environment, and community stakeholders are then treated in separate chapters.

Part 5. Internal Stakeholder Issues

The primary stakeholders covered in this part are employees. In this part, we consider workplace issues and the key themes of employee rights, employment discrimination, and affirmative action. Two chapters address the changing social contract between business and employees and the urgent subject of employee rights. A final chapter treats the vital topic of employment discrimination and affirmative action. Owner stakeholders may be seen as internal stakeholders, but we have decided to cover them in Part 2, where the subject of corporate governance has been placed.

Case Studies at the End of Each Part

The 36 cases, which are located at the end of Parts 1 through 5, address a broad range of topics and decision situations. The cases are of varying length. They include classic cases with ongoing deliberations as well as new cases touching upon issues that have arisen in the past several years. All the cases are intended to provide instructors and students with real-life situations within which to further analyze course issues and topics covered throughout the book. Many of the cases in the book carry ramifications that spill over into several areas. Almost all of them may be used for different chapters. Immediately preceding the cases after Part 1 is a set of guidelines for case analysis that the instructor may wish to use in place of or in addition to the questions that appear at the end of each case.

Some cases from previous editions have been moved to the Instructor's Manual with Test Bank. If instructors wish to use some of their favorite previous cases, they may copy and distribute them in class or contact the local representative to have a custom edition created to include the selected cases.

Support for the Instructor

Instructor's Manual

Prepared by Leigh Johnson of Murray State University, the Instructor's Manual includes learning objectives, teaching suggestions, complete chapter outlines, highlighted key terms, answers to discussion questions, suggestions for using the management and organization video, case notes, supplemental cases, and NEW group exercises. The Instructor's Manual is available only on the Web site at www.cengage.com/international.

Test Bank

The test bank for each chapter includes true/false, multiple-choice, short-answer, and essay questions. This edition's strengthened Test Bank now offers questions correlated to AACSB guidelines and learning standards, and questions are identified by the level of difficulty.

A computerized version of the test bank is also available electronically. ExamView®, an easy-to-use test-generating program, enables instructors to create printed tests, Internet tests, and online (LAN-based) tests quickly. Instructors can enter their own questions, using the software provided, and customize the appearance of the tests they create. The QuickTest wizard permits test generators to use an existing bank of questions to create a test in minutes, using a step-by-step selection process.

PowerPoint Slides

The PowerPoint presentation is colorful and varied, designed to hold students' interest and reinforce each chapter's main points. The PowerPoint presentation is available only on the Web site at www.cengage.com/international.

Video DVD

Acknowledgments

First, we would like to express gratitude to our professional colleagues in the Social Issues in Management (SIM) Division of the Academy of Management, the International Association for Business and Society (IABS), and the Society for Business Ethics (SBE). Over the years these individuals have meant a lot to us and have helped provide a stimulating environment in which we could intellectually pursue these topics in which we have a common interest. Many of these individuals are cited in this book quite liberally, and their work is sincerely appreciated.

Second, we would like to thank the many reviewers of the seven previous editions who took the time to provide us with helpful critiques. Many of their ideas and suggestions have been used for this eighth edition and led to improvements in the text:

Steven C. Alber, Hawaii Pacific University

Paula Becker Alexander, Seton Hall University

Laquita C. Blockson, The College of Charleston

Mark A. Buchanan, Boise State University

Peter Burkhardt, Western State College of Colorado

Preston D. Cameron, Mesa Community College

William B. Carper, Ph.D., University of West Florida

George S. Cole, Shippensburg University

Brenda Eichelberger, Portland State University

Jeanne Enders, Portland State University

Joshua S. Friedlander, Baruch College

John William Geranios, George Washington University

Kathleen Getz, American University

Peggy A. Golden, University of Northern Iowa

Russell Gough, Pepperdine University

Michele A. Govekar, Ohio Northern University

Frank J. Hitt, Ed.D., Mountain State University

Robert H. Hogner, Florida International University

Sylvester R. Houston, University of Denver

Ralph W. Jackson, University of Tulsa

David C. Jacobs, American University

Leigh Redd Johnson, Murray State University

Ed Leonard, Indiana University–Purdue University Fort Wayne

Timothy A. Matherly, Florida State University

Kenneth R. Mayer, Cleveland State University

Douglas M. McCabe, Georgetown University

Douglas McCloskey, A.B., Princeton University and J.D., Washington University School of Law

Bill McShain, Cumberland University

Nana Lee Moore, Warner University

Harvey Nussbaum, Wayne State University

E. Leroy Plumlee, Western Washington University

Richard Raspen, Wilkes University

Dawna Rhoades, Embry-Riddle Aeronautical University

William T. Rupp, Austin Peay State University

Robert J. Rustic, The University of Findlay

John K. Sands, Western Washington University

Valarie Spiser-Albert, Ph.D., University of Texas at San Antonio

David S. Steingard, St. Joseph's University

John M. Stevens, The Pennsylvania State University

Diane L. Swanson, Kansas State University

Dave Thiessen, Lewis-Clark State College

Jeff R. Turner, Howard Payne University

Ivan R. Vernon, D.B.A., Cleveland State University

Marion Webb, Cleveland State University

George E. Weber, Whitworth College

Ira E. Wessler, Robert Morris University

We would also like to express gratitude to our students who have not only provided comments on a regular basis but also made this eighth edition relevant with the ethical dilemmas they have personally contributed, as highlighted in the "Ethics in Practice Cases" features that may be found in many of the chapters. In addition to those students who are named in the "Ethics in Practice Cases" features and have given permission for their materials to be used, we would like to thank the following students for their anonymous contributions: Edward Bashuk, Kevin Brinker, Adrienne Brown, Bryan Burnette, Luis Delgado, Henry DeLoach, Chris Fain, Eric Harvey, Sloane Hyatt, Jensen Mast, Luke Nelson, Kristen Nessmith, Will Nimmer, Kimberly Patterson, Angela Sanders, and Nicole Zielinski.

We express grateful appreciation to all of the authors of the other cases that follow Parts 1 through 5. These individuals include Bryan Dennis, University of South Carolina, Beaufort; Joe Gerard, SUNY Institute of Technology; Jill Brown, Lehigh University; Norma Carr-Ruffino, San Francisco State University; Jonathan Bundy, University of Georgia; and Julia Merren, former student. We also thank other faculty members who contributed cases for previous editions that carried forward into the eighth edition. At the University of Georgia, we especially want to thank our departmental staff, without whose support we would not have been able to finish the book on time. We especially wish to thank Allison Davis, Ruth Davis, and Department Head Allen Amason.

Finally, we wish to express heartfelt appreciation to our family members and friends for their patience, understanding, and support when work on the book altered our priorities and plans.

Ann K. Buchholtz
Archie B. Carroll

About the Authors

Ann K. Buchholtz

Ann K. Buchholtz is Professor of Leadership and Ethics and Research Director of the Institute for Ethical Leadership in the Rutgers Business School at Rutgers University. She received her Ph.D. from the Stern School of Business at New York University.

Professor Buchholtz's research focuses on the social and ethical implications of corporate governance, in particular, and the relationship of business and society in general. Journals in which her work has appeared include *Business and Society, Business Ethics Quarterly*, the *Academy of Management Journal*, the *Academy of Management Review*, the *Journal of Management, Organization Science*, the *Journal of Management Studies*, and *Corporate Governance an International Review*, among others. She serves on the editorial boards of *Business & Society* and *Business Ethics Quarterly*.

Her teaching and consulting activities are in the areas of business ethics, social issues, strategic leadership, and corporate governance. Her service learning activities in the classroom received a Trailblazer Advocate of the Year award from the Domestic Violence Council of Northeast Georgia. She is the recipient of numerous teaching awards, including Profound Effect on a Student Leader, and was named a Senior Teaching Fellow at the University of Georgia.

Professor Buchholtz is past Division Chair of the Social Issues in Management Division of the Academy of Management. She served on the ethics task force that designed a Code of Ethics for the academy and then became the inaugural chairperson of the academy's Ethics Adjudication Committee when the code was put into effect. Prior to entering academe, Dr. Buchholtz's work focused on the education, vocational, and residential needs of individuals with disabilities. She has worked in a variety of organizations, in both managerial and consultative capacities, and has consulted with numerous public and private firms.

Archie B. Carroll

Archie B. Carroll is Robert W. Scherer Chair of Management & Corporate Public Affairs *Emeritus* and professor of management *emeritus* in the Terry College of Business, University of Georgia. He is also part-time director of the Nonprofit Management & Community Service Program in the Terry College. Dr. Carroll received his three academic degrees from The Florida State University in Tallahassee.

Professor Carroll has published numerous books, chapters, articles, and encyclopedia entries. His research has appeared in the *Academy of Management Journal, Academy of Management Review, Business and Society, Journal of Management, Business Ethics Quarterly, Journal of Business Ethics, Business Ethics: A European Review*, and many others.

He has served on the editorial review boards of *Business and Society, Business Ethics Quarterly, Academy of Management Review, Journal of Management,* and the *Journal of Public Affairs*. Professionally, he is former division chair of the Social Issues in Management (SIM) Division of the Academy of Management, a founding board member of the International Association for Business and Society (IABS), and past president of the Society for Business Ethics. He was elected a Fellow of the Southern Management Association (1995) and a Fellow of the Academy of Management (2005).

His other professional recognitions include the Sumner Marcus Award (1992) for Distinguished Service by the SIM Division of the Academy of Management; Distinguished Research Award (1993) by Terry College of Business, University of Georgia, for his work in corporate social performance and business ethics; and Distinguished Service Award (2003) by the Terry College of Business. He was named professor *emeritus* (2005) and in 2008 he received the Outstanding Ph.D. Award from the College of Business, Florida State University.

Business & Society

Business, Society, and Stakeholders

1

The Business and Society Relationship

CHAPTER LEARNING OUTCOMES

After studying this chapter, you should be able to:

1. Characterize business and society and their interrelationships.

2. Describe pluralism and identify its attributes, strengths, and weaknesses.

3. Clarify how our pluralistic society has become a special-interest society.

4. Identify, discuss, and illustrate the factors leading up to business criticism.

5. Single out the major criticisms of business and characterize business's general response.

6. Explain the major themes of the book: managerial approach, ethics, sustainability, and stakeholder management.

For decades now, the business and society relationship has generated a number of economic, social, ethical, and environmental issues. Though the business system has served society well, criticism of business and its practices has become commonplace in recent years. Perhaps this is a reflection of the natural tendency to take for granted the beneficial aspects of the relationship and to spotlight the negative or stressful ones.

The modern period of business criticism began with a rash of scandals first brought to light in late 2001 and continues today in a different form. Initially, the Enron scandal was exposed when the firm filed for bankruptcy. Gradually, the degree of fraud impacting investors, employees, and others became known to the general public. The Enron scandal did not occur in isolation. Senior officers, banks, accountants, credit agencies, lawyers, stock analysts, and others were implicated in it. Eventually, 30 states had sided with Enron shareholders in their quest for damages from investment banks implicated due to their role in the accounting fraud. The argument was that the investment banks should be held liable as participants in the fraud.[1] In 2009, the lead investigator finally articulated some of the lasting lessons from the Enron scandal. One of his main conclusions was that the board of directors was not paying enough attention to what was going on.[2]

Scandals involving Arthur Andersen, WorldCom, Global Crossing, Tyco, and Adelphia all came to light throughout 2002. The Enron debacle was an ethical tsunami that redefined business's relationships with the world. In the first decade of the 2000s, other corporate names appeared in the news for committing alleged violations of the public trust or for raising questions regarding corporate ethics: Martha Stewart, Rite Aid, ImClone, HealthSouth, and Boeing are prominent examples. As *BusinessWeek* observed, "Watching executives climb the courthouse steps became a spectator sport...."[3]

In the fall of 2008, another series of business humiliations, coupled with a collapsing U.S. stock market and worldwide recession, had a deeper and more far-reaching impact on the economy and began to raise questions about the future of the business system as we have known it. In what many have called the most serious financial collapse since the 1920s, this scandal centered on Wall Street and many of the major firms that historically had been the backbone of the U.S. financial system. As *Newsweek* pointed out, the epicenter of the financial crisis that brought about incalculable financial damage around the world was the Wall Street District and a handful of financial institutions located in what it called "the neighborhood that wrecked the world."[4]

What caused the financial collapse and the ensuing economic chaos is still being debated to this day. Unarguably, the housing bubble burst and years of lax lending standards put big investment banks and Wall Street at the center of the collapse.[5] Faced with an unprecedented financial crisis, the federal government got into the bailout business big-time as Congress approved a $700 billion rescue plan[6] for Wall Street financial firms, such as Merrill Lynch, Bear Stearns, Citigroup, Lehman Brothers, and AIG, and other notable industries, like the auto industry.

There was enough blame to go around for the financial crisis, and the finger-pointing continues to this day. Some of those named as guilty parties included greedy home buyers who took on more debt than they could handle; commission-hungry brokers; builders who conspired with crooked appraisers; and the Federal Reserve, which was accused of flooding the market with easy money.[7] But most critics pointed to Wall Street and the businesses themselves as being central to the financial collapse. Others have claimed that the Wall Street firms were just doing what the capitalist system encourages and that it is actually capitalism itself that is behind the mess. Some claim the problem has been the era of deregulation begun back in the 1980s with President Ronald Reagan's notion of "getting government off the backs of the people" and business, too. Congress has been accused of complacency in watching these developments occur.

At the same time as the financial crisis was unfolding, Barack Obama was elected the 44th president of the United States. As he took office in January 2009, it fell upon him to deal with the financial crisis as one of his first agenda items. In his inaugural address on January 20, 2009, President Obama declared, "Our economy is badly weakened, a consequence of greed and irresponsibility on the part of some but also our collective failure to make hard choices and prepare the nation for a new age." He then called for a new "era of responsibility."[8] Throughout the president's first year in office, the government increasingly got more deeply involved in the economic system, and the nature of the business and society relationship began changing. The business system and society suffered another major blow when the BP oil spill occurred in the spring of 2010. Called the worst environmental disaster in history, the ongoing challenges of the cleanup, dealing with ecological and business consequences, and assigning responsibility will take years to settle. It is against this backdrop, an era of considerable uncertainty, that we embark on our study of the respective roles of business and society in relation to the challenges facing companies and other organizations now and in the years ahead.

Aside from the financial crisis and the BP oil spill, and on a continuing basis, other serious questions arise about a host of other business issues: corporate governance, ethical conduct, executive compensation, the use of illegal immigrants as employees, fluctuating energy prices, government involvement in the economy, healthiness of fast food, international corruption, and so on. The litany of such issues could go on and on, but these examples illustrate the enduring tensions between business and society, which can be traced to recent high-profile incidents, trends, or events.

Many other familiar issues carrying social or ethical implications continue to be debated within the business and society connection. Some of these issues have included moving businesses offshore, downsizing of pension programs, high unemployment, reduced health insurance benefits, sexual harassment in the workplace, abuses of corporate power, toxic waste disposal, insider trading, whistle-blowing, product liability, deceptive marketing, and questionable lobbying by business to influence the outcome of legislation. These examples of both specific corporate incidents and general issues are typical of the kinds of stories about business and society that one finds today in newspapers and magazines, and on television and the Internet. These concerns are illustrations of the widespread interactions and tensions between business and society that capture the headlines almost daily.

At the broadest level, we discuss the role of business in society. In this book, we will address many of these concerns—the role of business relative to the role of government in our socioeconomic system; what a firm must do to be considered socially responsible; what managers must do to be considered ethical; and what responsibilities companies have to consumers, employees, owners, and communities in an age of economic uncertainty and globalization. A new mandate for sustainability has captured the attention of business leaders, critics, and public policy makers.

We are now into the second decade of the new millennium, and many economic, legal, ethical, and technological issues concerning business and society continue to be debated. This period is turbulent and has been characterized by significant changes in the world, the economy, society, technology, and global relationships. Against this setting of ongoing flux in the business and society relationship, some basic concepts and ideas are worth considering.

Business and Society

This chapter introduces and discusses some basic concepts that are central to under-standing the continuing business and society discussion. Among these concepts are pluralism, our special-interest society, business criticism, corporate power, and corporate social response to stakeholders. First, let us briefly define and explain two key terms: *business* and *society*.

Business: Defined

Business may be defined as the collection of private, commercially oriented (profit-oriented) organizations, ranging in size from one-person proprietorships (e.g., DePalma's Restaurant, Gibson's Men's Wear, and Taqueria la Parrilla) to corporate giants (e.g., Johnson & Johnson, GE, Coca-Cola, Delta Airlines, and UPS). Between these two extremes, of course, are many medium-sized proprietorships, partnerships, and corporations.

When we discuss business in this collective sense, we include businesses of all sizes and in all types of industries. However, as we embark on our discussion of business and society, we will often find ourselves speaking more of big business in selected industries. Big business is highly visible. Its products and advertising are more widely known. Consequently, it is more frequently in the critical public eye. People in our society often associate size with power, and the powerful are given closer scrutiny. Although it is well known that small businesses in our society far outnumber large ones, the pervasiveness, power, visibility, and impact of large firms keep them on the front page more of the time.

Some industries are simply more conducive than others with respect to the creation of visible, social problems. For example, many manufacturing firms by their nature cause air and water pollution. They contribute to climate changes. Such firms, therefore, are more likely to be subject to criticism than a life insurance company, which emits no obvious pollutant. The auto industry, most recently with the manufacture of sport utility vehicles (SUVs), is a particular case in point. Much of the criticism against General Motors (GM) and other automakers is raised because of their high visibility as manufacturers, the products they make (which are the largest single source of air pollution), and the popularity of their products (many families own one or more cars).

Some industries are highly visible because of the advertising-intensive nature of their products (e.g., Procter & Gamble, FedEx, Anheuser-Busch, and Home Depot). Other industries (e.g., the cigarette, toy, and fast food industries) are scrutinized because of the possible effects of their products on health or because of their roles in providing health-related products (e.g., pharmaceutical firms).

When we refer to business in its relationship with society, we focus our attention on large businesses in particular industries. However, we should not lose sight of the fact that small- and medium-sized companies also represent settings in which our discussions also apply.

Society: Defined

Society may be defined as a community, a nation, or a broad grouping of people with common traditions, values, institutions, and collective activities and interests. As such, when we speak of business and society relationships, we may in fact be referring to business and the local community (business and Atlanta), business and the United States as a whole, or business and a specific group of people (consumers, investors, minorities).

When we discuss business and the entire society, we think of society as being composed of numerous interest groups, more or less formalized organizations, and a variety of institutions. Each of these groups, organizations, and institutions is a purposeful aggregation of people who have united because they represent a common cause or share a set of common beliefs about a particular issue. Examples of interest groups or purposeful organizations are numerous: Friends of the Earth, Common Cause, chambers of commerce, National Association of Manufacturers, People for the Ethical Treatment of Animals (PETA), and Rainforest Action Network.

Society as the Macroenvironment

The environment of society is a key concept in analyzing business and society relationships. At its broadest level, the societal environment might be thought of as a **macroenvironment**, which includes the total environment outside the firm. The macroenvironment is the complete societal context in which the organization resides. The idea of the macroenvironment is just another way of thinking about society. In fact, early courses on business and society in business schools were sometimes (and some still are) titled "Business and Its Environment." The concept of the macroenvironment evokes different images or ways of thinking about business and society relationships and is therefore useful in terms of framing and understanding the total business context.

A useful conceptualization of the macroenvironment is to think of it as being composed of four segments: social, economic, political, and technological.[9]

The **social environment** focuses on demographics, lifestyles, and social values of the society. Of particular interest here is the manner in which shifts in these factors affect the organization and its functioning. The influx of illegal immigrants over the past several years has brought changes to the social environment. The **economic environment** focuses on the nature and direction of the economy in which business operates. Variables of interest include such indices as gross national product, inflation, interest rates, unemployment rates, foreign exchange fluctuations, national debt, global trade, balance of payments, and various other aspects of economic activity. In the past decade, hypercompetition and the global economy have dominated the economic segment of the environment. Businesses moving jobs offshore has been a controversial trend. Enduring levels of high unemployment have been particularly critical recently.

The **political environment** focuses on the processes by which laws get passed and officials get elected and all other aspects of the interaction between the firm, political processes, and government. Of particular interest to business in this segment are the regulatory process and the changes that occur over time in business regulation of various industries and various issues. The passage of the Sarbanes–Oxley Act continues to be a contentious issue to many businesses. Beginning in 2009, Congress ramped up its regulatory ambitions as it sought to improve the global economic system. Lobbying and political contributions are ongoing controversies. Finally, the **technological environment** represents the total set of technology-based advancements taking place in society. This segment includes new products, processes, materials, and means of communication, as well as the states of knowledge and scientific advancement. The process of technological change is of special importance here.[10] In recent years, computer-based technologies and biotechnology have been driving this segment of environmental turbulence.

Thinking of business and society relationships embedded in a macroenvironment provides us with a constructive way of understanding the kinds of issues that constitute the broad milieu in which business functions. Throughout this book, we will see evidence of these turbulent environmental segments and will learn to appreciate what challenges managers face as they strive to develop effective organizations. Each of the many specific groups and organizations that make up our pluralistic society can typically be traced to one of these four environmental segments.

A Pluralistic Society

Our society's pluralistic nature makes for business and society relationships that are more dynamic and novel than those in some other societies. **Pluralism** refers to a diffusion of power among society's many groups and organizations. The following definition of a pluralistic society is helpful: "A pluralistic society is one in which there is wide decentralization and diversity of power concentration."[11]

The key descriptive terms in this definition are *decentralization* and *diversity*. In other words, power is dispersed among many groups and people. It is not in the hands of any single institution (e.g., business, government, labor, or the military) or a small number of groups. Many years ago, in *The Federalist Papers*, James Madison speculated that pluralism was a virtuous scheme. He correctly anticipated the rise of numerous organizations in society as a consequence of it. Some of the virtues of a pluralistic society are summarized in Figure 1-1.

Pluralism Has Strengths and Weaknesses

All social systems have strengths and weaknesses. A pluralistic society prevents power from being concentrated in the hands of a few. It also maximizes freedom of expression and action. Pluralism provides for a built-in set of checks and balances so that no single group dominates. Nonetheless, a weakness of a pluralistic system is that it creates an environment in which diverse institutions pursue their own self-interests, with the result

FIGURE 1-1

The Virtues of a Pluralistic Society

A pluralistic society...

- Prevents power from being concentrated in the hands of a few
- Maximizes freedom of expression and action and strikes a balance between monism (social organization into one institution), on the one hand, and anarchy (social organization into an infinite number of persons), on the other[a]
- Is one in which the allegiance of individuals to groups is dispersed

- Creates a widely diversified set of loyalties to many organizations and minimizes the danger that a leader of any one organization will be left uncontrolled[b]
- Provides a built-in set of checks and balances, in that groups can exert power over one another with no single organization (business or government) dominating and becoming overly influential

Sources: [a]Keith Davis and Robert L. Blomstrom, *Business and Society: Environment and Responsibility*, 3d ed. (New York: McGraw-Hill, 1975), 63. [b]Joseph W. McGuire, *Business and Society* (New York: McGraw-Hill, 1963), 132.

that there is no unified direction to bring together individual pursuits. Another weakness is that groups and institutions proliferate to the extent that their goals tend to overlap, thus causing confusion as to which organizations best serve which functions. Pluralism forces conflict onto center stage because of its emphasis on autonomous groups, each pursuing its own objectives. In light of these concerns, a pluralistic system does not appear to be very efficient.

History and experience have demonstrated, however, that the merits of pluralism are considerable and that most people in society prefer the situation that has resulted from it. Indeed, pluralism has worked to achieve some equilibrium in the balance of power of the dominant institutions that constitute our society.

Multiple Publics, Systems, and Stakeholders

Knowing that society is composed of so many different semiautonomous and autonomous groups might cause one to question whether we can realistically speak of society in a definitive sense that has any generally agreed-upon meaning. Nevertheless, we do speak in such terms, knowing that, unless we specify a particular societal subgroup or subsystem, we are referring to all those persons, groups, and institutions that constitute our society. Thus, when we speak of business and society relationships, we usually refer either to particular segments or subgroups of society (consumers, women, minorities, environmentalists, senior citizens) or to business and some system in our society (politics, law, custom, religion, economics). These groups of people or systems may also be referred to in an institutional form (business and the courts, business and Common Cause, business and the church, business and the Federal Trade Commission).

Figure 1-2 depicts in graphic form the points of interface between business and some of the multiple publics, systems, or stakeholders with which business interacts. Stakeholders are those groups or individuals with whom an organization interacts or has interdependencies. We will develop the stakeholder concept further in Chapter 3. It should be noted that each of the stakeholder groups may be further subdivided into more specific subgroups.

If sheer numbers of relationships are an indicator of complexity, we could easily argue that business's current relationships with different segments of society constitute a truly complex social environment. If we had the capacity to draw a diagram similar to Figure 1-2 that displayed all the details composing each of those points of interface, it would be too complex

FIGURE 1-2 Business and Selected Stakeholder Relationships

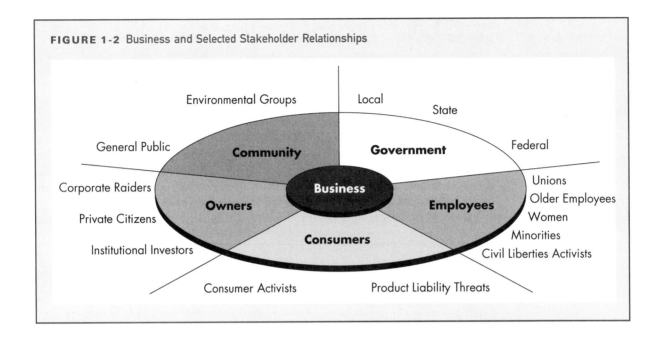

to comprehend. Today, managers cannot sidestep this problem, because management must live with these interfaces on a daily basis.

A Special-Interest Society

A pluralistic society often becomes a **special-interest society**. As the idea of pluralism is pursued to an extreme, a society is created that is characterized by tens of thousands of special-interest groups, each pursuing its own focused agenda. General-purpose interest organizations, such as Common Cause and the U.S. Chamber of Commerce, still exist. However, the past three decades have been characterized by increasing specialization on the part of interest groups representing all sectors of society—consumers, employees, investors, communities, the natural environment, government, and business itself. One newspaper headline noted that "there is a group for every cause." Special-interest groups not only have grown in number at an accelerated pace, but also have become increasingly activist, intense, diverse, and focused on single issues. Such groups are increasingly committed to their causes.

The health care debate that began raging in the fall of 2009 illustrates how a pluralistic, special-interest society works. Consider that the following special-interest groups were all active and continued to be so in the fine-tuning of the health care legislation. The major interest groups included doctors, hospitals, drug companies, insurance companies, employers, insured people, seniors, and uninsured people.[12] Each of these groups has a lot at stake in resolving this society-level issue that has significant implications for many sectors, especially business. Though the health care law was passed in 2010, it will not be implemented immediately and many controversial details still have to be worked out.

The consequence of such specialization is that each of these groups has been able to attract a significant following that is dedicated to the group's goals. Increased memberships have meant increased revenues and a sharper focus as each of these groups has aggressively sought its specific, narrow purposes. The likelihood of these groups working at cross-purposes and with no unified set of goals has made life immensely more complex for the major institutions, such as business and government, that have to deal with them. But this is how a pluralistic society works.

Business Criticism and Corporate Response

It is inevitable in a pluralistic, special-interest society that the major institutions that make up that society, such as business and government, will become the subjects of considerable scrutiny and criticism. Our purpose here is not so much to focus on the negative as it is to illustrate how the process of business criticism has shaped the evolution of the business and society relationship today. Were it not for the fact that individuals and groups have been critical of business, we would not be dealing with this subject in a book or a course, and few changes would occur in the business and society relationship over time.

Figure 1-3 illustrates how certain factors that have arisen in the social environment have created an atmosphere in which business criticism has taken place and flourished. In this chapter, we describe the response on the part of business as an increased concern for the social environment and a changed social contract (relationship) between business and society. Each of these factors merits special consideration.

Factors in the Social Environment

Over the decades, many factors in the social environment have created a climate in which criticism of business has taken place and flourished. Some of these factors occur relatively independently, but some are interrelated. In other words, they occur and grow hand in hand.

Affluence and Education. Two factors that have developed side by side are affluence and education. As a society becomes more prosperous and better educated, higher expectations of its major institutions, such as business, naturally follow.

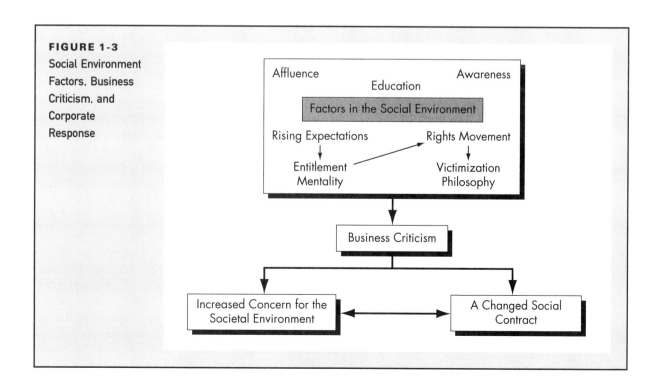

FIGURE 1-3
Social Environment Factors, Business Criticism, and Corporate Response

Affluence refers to the level of wealth, disposable income, and standard of living of the society. Measures of the U.S. standard of living indicate that it has been rising for decades, but leveling off during the past five years or so. A recent study has found that the rate at which an entire generation's lot in life improves relative to previous generations has slightly declined.[13] In spite of these effects, overall affluence remains elevated, but this could change. This movement toward affluence is found in many of the world's developed countries and is also occurring in developing countries as global capitalism spreads. The current economic recession raises valid questions about continuing affluence, however.

Alongside a higher standard of living has been a growth in the average formal **education** of the populace. The U.S. Census Bureau reported that between 1970 and 2000, when the last census data were published, the number of American adults who were high school graduates grew from 55 percent to 83 percent, and the number who were college graduates increased from 11 percent to 24 percent. The 2010 census data, when available, may change these figures. As citizens continue to become more highly educated, their expectations of life generally rise. The combination of affluence and education has formed the underpinning for a society in which some criticism of major institutions, such as business, naturally arises.

Awareness through Television, Movies, and the Internet.

Closely related to formal education is the broad and growing level of public awareness in our society. Although newspapers and magazines are read by a declining fraction of our population, more powerful media—television and movies—are accessed by virtually our entire society. Through television, the citizenry gets a profusion of information that contributes to a climate of business criticism. In recent years, especially, movies have bashed both the capitalist system and businesses. In addition, the Internet and mobile phone explosion has brought elevated levels of awareness in our country and around the world. Through e-mails, texting, blogs, and tweets, the average citizen is incredibly aware of what is going on in the world.

The prevalence and power of TV touches all socioeconomic classes. Several statistics document the extent to which our society is dependent on TV for information. According to data compiled by the ACNielsen company, the average daily time spent viewing television per household in 1950 was four and a half hours. Nielsen reports that now this figure has grown to over eight hours. A typical day for an American household now divides into three nearly equal parts: eight hours of sleep, eight hours of TV, and eight hours of work or school. Although the household average now exceeds eight hours, the average person watches over four hours per day.[14] These figures are the highest in over 50 years.[15] In the United States today, over 98 percent of homes have color TVs, and a great majority of Americans have two or more televisions. In developed countries around the world, these statistics are becoming more common. Television is indeed a pervasive and powerful medium in society.

24/7 NEWS AND INVESTIGATIVE NEWS PROGRAMS There are at least three ways in which information that leads to criticism of business appears on television. First, there are straight news shows, such as the ubiquitous 24-hour cable news channels, the evening news on the major networks, and investigative news programs. It is debatable whether or not the major news programs are treating business fairly, but in one major study conducted by Corporate Reputation Watch, senior executives identified media criticism, along with unethical behavior, as the biggest threats to a company's reputation. Reflecting on the lessons learned from high-profile cases of corporate wrongdoing, half the executives surveyed thought unethical behavior and media criticism were the biggest threats to their corporate reputations.[16] Coverage of Wall Street's complicity in the recent recession has been particularly damaging because it has called into question society's basic trust of corporate executives.

Business has to deal not only with the problems of 24/7 news coverage but also with a number of investigative news programs, such as *60 Minutes, 20/20, Dateline NBC,* and PBS's *Frontline,* that seem to delight in exposés of corporate wrongdoings or questionable practices. Whereas the straight news programs make some effort to be objective, the investigative shows are tougher on business, tending to favor stories that expose the dark side of the enterprises or their executives. These shows are enormously popular and influential, and many companies squirm when their reporters show up on their premises complete with camera crews.

PRIME-TIME TELEVISION PROGRAMS The second way in which criticisms of business appear on TV is through prime-time programs. Television's depiction of businesspeople brings to mind the scheming oilman J.R. Ewing of *Dallas,* whose backstabbing shenanigans dominated prime-time TV for years (1978–1991) before it went off the air. More recently, the popular TV reality show *The Apprentice,* featuring billionaire businessman Donald Trump, depicted aspiring business executives in often questionable roles. More often than not, the businessperson has been portrayed across the nation's television screens as smirking, scheming, cheating, and conniving "bad guys." A recent report released by the Business & Media Institute reported a study of the top 12 prime-time dramas in which 77 percent of the plots involving business were negative toward businesspeople. In this study, business characters committed almost as many serious felonies as drug dealers, child molesters, and serial killers combined. On one show, *Law & Order,* half of the felons were businesspeople.[17] Some other TV shows where this negative portrayal has been evident include *CSI, Mad Men, Damages,* and *Criminal Minds.* Any redeeming social values that business and businesspeople may have rarely show up on television. Rather, businesspeople are often cast as evil and greedy social parasites whose efforts to get more for themselves are justly condemned and usually thwarted.[18] There are many views as to why this portrayal has occurred. Some would argue that business is being characterized accurately. Others say that the television writers are dissatisfied with the direction our nation has taken and believe they have an important role in reforming American society.[19]

COMMERCIALS A third way in which television contributes to business criticism is through commercials. This may be business's own fault. To the extent that business does not honestly and fairly portray its products and services on TV, it undermines its own credibility. Commercials are a two-edged sword. On the one hand, they may sell more products and services in the short run. On the other hand, they could damage business's long-term credibility if they promote products and services deceptively. According to RealVision, an initiative to raise awareness about television's impact on society, TV today promotes excessive commercialism as well as sedentary lifestyles.[20] In three specific TV settings—news coverage, prime-time programming, and commercials— a strained environment is fostered by this "awareness" factor made available through the power and pervasiveness of television.

MOVIES Movies are also a significant source of business criticism. Hollywood seems to see corporations as powerful, profit-seeking enterprises that have no redeeming values. The Oscar-winning movie *Avatar,* along with *Up in the Air,* portrays corporations as greedy, cruel, and destructive. Michael Moore's documentary, *Capitalism: A Love Story,* slams the free enterprise system as corrupt and doomed. Other recent movies to stigmatize the business system include *The Informant, The International, Syriana,* and

Duplicity. In these movies, corporate life is depicted as amoral, at best, and possibly deadly. In 2010, the sequel to *Wall Street* was released—*Wall Street: Money Never Sleeps*—with Michael Douglas playing again the evil Gordon Gekko. Gekko is released from 14 years in prison just in time to witness the financial system's collapse and to visit his old ways. Hollywood writers seem to love advancing the "greed is good" portrayal of business, and they go out of their way to perpetuate this image of the corporate community.[21]

We should make it clear that the media are not to blame for business's problems. If it were not for the fact that the behavior of some businesses is questionable, the media would not be able to create such an environment. The media makes the public more aware of questionable practices and should be seen as only one key factor that contributes to the environment in which business now finds itself.

Revolution of Rising Expectations.   In addition to affluence, formal education, and awareness through television and the Internet, other societal trends have fostered the climate in which business criticism has occurred. Growing out of these factors has been a **revolution of rising expectations** held by many. This is defined as a belief or an attitude that each succeeding generation ought to have a standard of living higher than that of its predecessor. A recent Pew Charitable Trust study has revealed that, according to census data, today this is more of a dream than a reality. The median income for men has declined slightly over the past 20 years, but household incomes remain high due to the number of women now working full-time.[22] And, of course, the recent economic recession has moderated these rising expectations. A continuing unemployment crisis has been hitting many people very hard, and some writers have been asking if we have now reached the "end of prosperity." *The Wall Street Journal/NBC News* survey data reported in December 2009 revealed eroding confidence in the belief that the next generation will be better off than the current one. This decline in confidence continued between 2001 and 2009.[23]

If rising expectations do continue, people's hopes for major institutions, such as business, should be greater too. Building on this line of thinking, it could be argued that business criticism is evident today because society's rising expectations of business's social performance have outpaced business's ability to meet these growing expectations. To the extent that this has occurred over the past 25 years, business finds itself with a larger social problem.[24]

A **social problem** has been described as a gap between society's expectations of social conditions and the current social realities.[25] From the viewpoint of a business firm, the social problem is experienced as the gap grows between society's *expectations* of the firm's social performance and its *actual* social performance. Rising expectations typically outpace the responsiveness of institutions such as business, thus creating a constant predicament in that it is subject to criticism. Figure 1-4 illustrates the larger "social problem" that business faces today. It is depicted by the "gap" between society's expectations of business and business's actual social performance.

Although the general trend of rising expectations may continue, the revolution moderates at times when the economy is not as robust. Historically, job situations, health, family lives, and overall quality of life continue to improve, though the effect of the recession makes their future hard to predict. The persistence of social problems such as crime, poverty, homelessness, unemployment, AIDS, environmental pollution, alcohol and drug abuse, and, now, terrorism and potential pandemics such as bird flu are always there to moderate rising expectations.[26]

Entitlement Mentality.   One notable outgrowth of the revolution of rising expectations has been the development of an **entitlement mentality**. Several years ago, the

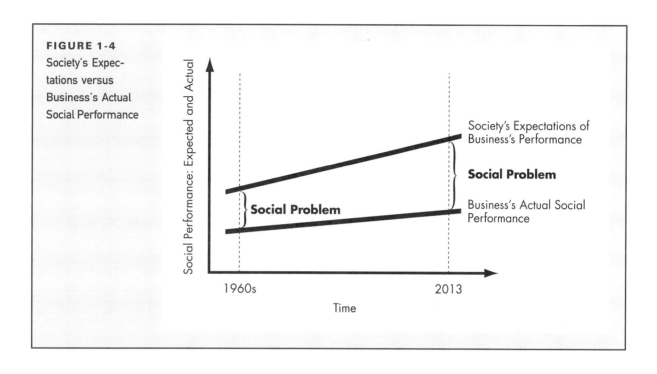

FIGURE 1-4

Society's Expectations versus Business's Actual Social Performance

Public Relations Society conducted a study of public expectations, with particular focus on public attitudes toward the philosophy of entitlement. The entitlement mentality is the general belief that someone is owed something (e.g., a job, an education, a living wage, or health care) just because she or he is a member of society. The survey was conducted on a nationwide basis, and a significant gap was found between what people thought they were entitled to have and what they actually had—a steadily improving standard of living, a guaranteed job for all those willing and able to work, and products certified as safe and not hazardous to one's health.[27]

As we are into the second decade of the 2000s, jobs, fair wages, insurance, retirement programs, and health care continue to be issues on which entitlement thinking has centered. Each of these has significant implications for business when "entitlements" are not received.

Rights Movement. The revolution of rising expectations, the entitlement mentality, and all of the factors discussed so far have contributed to what has been termed the **rights movement** that has been evident in society for several decades now. The Bill of Rights was attached to the U.S. Constitution almost as an afterthought and was virtually unused for more than a century. But in the past several decades, and at an accelerating pace, the U.S. Supreme Court has heard large numbers of cases aimed at establishing for some groups various legal rights that perhaps never occurred to the founders of our nation.[28]

Some of these rights, such as the right to privacy and the right to due process, have been perceived as generic for all citizens. However, in addition to these generalized rights, there has been activism for rights for particular groups in society. This modern movement began with the civil rights cases of the 1950s. Many groups have been inspired by the success of African-Americans and have sought progress by similar means. Thus, we have seen the protected status of minorities grow to include Hispanic Americans, Asian-Americans, Native Americans, women, the disabled, the aged, and other groups. At various levels—federal, state, and local—we have seen claims for the rights of gays, smokers, nonsmokers, obese persons, AIDS victims, convicted felons, and illegal immigrants, just to mention a few.

There seems to be no limit to the numbers of groups and individuals seeking "rights" in our society. Business, as one of society's major institutions, has been affected with an ever-expanding array of expectations as to how people want to be treated, not only as employees but also as owners, consumers, environmentally conscious citizens, and members of the community. The "rights" movement is interrelated with the special-interest society discussed earlier and sometimes follows an "entitlement" mentality among some people and within some sectors of society.

John Leo, a columnist for *U.S. News & World Report*, has argued for a moratorium on new rights.[29] He has argued that "freshly minted" rights are too common these days. Leo said that one cannot help but speculate what challenges business will face when every "goal, need, wish, or itch" is more and more framed as a right.[30]

Victimization Philosophy. It has become apparent during the past 20 years or so that there are growing numbers of individuals and groups who see themselves as having been victimized by society. The *New York* magazine featured a cover story on "The New Culture of Victimization," with the title "Don't Blame Me!"[31] *Esquire* probed what it called "A Confederacy of Complainers."[32] Charles Sykes published *A Nation of Victims: The Decay of the American Character.*[33] Sykes's thesis, with which these other observers would agree, is that the United States is fast becoming a "society of victims."

What is particularly interesting about the novel **victimization philosophy** is the widespread extent to which it is dispersing in the population. According to these writers, the victim mentality is just as likely to be seen among all groups in society—regardless of race, gender, age, or any other classification. Sykes observed that previous movements may have been seen as a "revolution of rising expectations," whereas the victimization movement might be called a "revolution of rising sensitivities" in which grievance begets grievance.

In such a society of victims, feelings rather than reason prevail, and people start perceiving that they are being unfairly "hurt" by society's institutions—government, business, and education. The philosophy of victimization is intimately related to and sometimes inseparable from the rights movement and the entitlement mentality. Taken together, these new ways of viewing one's plight—as someone else's unfairness—may pose special challenges for business managers in the future.

In summary, affluence and education, awareness through television, the revolution of rising expectations, an entitlement mentality, the rights movement, and the victimization philosophy have formed a backdrop against which criticism of business has grown and flourished. This helps explain why we have an environment that is so conducive to criticism of business. Though the U.S. economy is in its worst economic slump since World War II as this is being written, some of these same general trends are bound to continue but be moderated in the next several years. In the next two subsections, we will explore what some of the criticisms of business have been, and we will discuss some of the general responses to such criticisms.

Criticisms of Business: Use and Abuse of Power

Many criticisms have been directed toward business over the years: Business is too big, it is too powerful, it pollutes the environment and exploits people for its own gain, it takes advantage of workers and consumers, it does not tell the truth, its executives are too highly paid, and so on. If one were to identify a common thread that seems to run through all the complaints, it seems to be business's use and perceived abuse of power. This is an issue that will not go away. In a cover story article, *BusinessWeek* posed the question: "Too Much Corporate Power?" In this feature article, the magazine presented its surveys of the public regarding business power. Most Americans are willing to acknowledge that Corporate America gets much credit for the good fortunes of the country. In spite of this, 72 percent said business has too much power over too many aspects of their lives.[34] In another issue, *BusinessWeek* ran a similar cover story; this time it asked, "Is Wal-Mart Too Powerful?"[35] In Michael Moore's 2009 movie, *Capitalism: A Love Story*, the filmmaker continued his assault on business power by laying the blame for the worldwide recession on both big business and government. Whether at the general level or the level of the firm, questions about business's power continue to be raised.

Some of the points of friction between business and the public, in which corporate power is identified as partially the culprit, include such topics as corporate governance, CEO pay, investor losses, wholesale job losses, outsourcing jobs, mounting anger and frustration over health care, drug and gas prices, poor airline service, HMOs that override doctors' decisions, in-your-face marketing, e-mail spam, globalization, corporate bankrolling of politicians, sweatshops, urban sprawl, and low wages. Before discussing business power in more detail, we should note that in addition to the use or abuse of power, the major criticism seems to be that business often engages in questionable or unethical behavior with respect to its stakeholders.

What is **business power**? Business power refers to the ability or capacity to produce an effect or to bring influence to bear on a situation or people. Power, in and of itself, may be either positive or negative. In the context of business criticism, however, power typically is perceived as being abused. Business certainly does have enormous power, but whether it abuses power is an issue that needs to be carefully examined. We will not settle this issue here, but the allegation that business abuses power remains the central theme behind the details.

Levels of Power. Business power exists at and may be manifested at several different levels. Four such levels include the macrolevel, the intermediate level, the microlevel, and the individual level.[36] The *macrolevel* refers to the corporate system—Corporate America— the totality of business organizations. Power here emanates from the sheer size, resources, and dominance of the corporate system. As the corporate system has become more global, its impact has become more far reaching as well. The *intermediate level* refers to groups of corporations acting in concert in an effort to produce a desired effect—to raise prices, control markets, dominate purchasers, promote an issue, or pass or defeat legislation. Prime examples are OPEC (gas prices), airlines, cable TV companies, banks, pharmaceutical companies, and defense contractors pursuing interests they have in common. The combined effect of companies acting in concert is considerable. The *microlevel* of power is the level of the individual firm. This might refer to the exertion of power or influence by any major corporation—Google, Walmart, Microsoft, Nike, Procter & Gamble, or Johnson & Johnson, for example. The final level is the *individual level*. This refers to the individual corporate leader exerting power—for example, Andrea Jung (Avon), Steve Jobs (Apple), Jeffrey Immelt (GE), Bill Gates (Microsoft), Tiger Woods (Tigerwoods.com), or Anne Mulcahy (Xerox).

The important point here is that as one analyzes corporate power, one should think in terms of the different levels at which that power is manifested. When this is done, it is not easy to conclude whether corporate power is excessive or has been abused. Specific levels of power need to be examined before conclusions can be reached.

Spheres of Power. In addition to levels of power, there are also many different spheres or arenas in which business power may be manifested. Figure 1-5 depicts one

ETHICS IN PRACTICE CASE

Drink Specials?

While working as a waitress in a busy restaurant/bar, I observed a practice that was very common but appeared questionable. Often, in busy places of business, it is all too easy for employees to bend the rules and get away with it. Managers have so much on their hands that they have to trust their employees and, sadly, not everyone is trustworthy. In our restaurant, servers and bartenders were given a daily "spill sheet" on which they were supposed to record any alcoholic (and, especially, expensive) drinks that were accidentally spilled in the course of business that day.

When an employee is moving fast and dodging customers, spills are a natural occurrence, and the "spill sheet" was meant to take those accidents into account for the restaurant. When I began working there, I realized that at the end of the night not all of the spills on the list were genuine. Employees, typically bartenders because they had direct access, would serve free drinks to their friends all night and put the drinks on the spill sheet.

To accommodate large numbers of missing drinks, bartenders would serve their friends the same kind of beer all night and then claim a dropped case of that brand of beer. They could also claim a dropped liquor bottle and have enough to keep alcohol flowing for their friends. Other employees would also take responsibility for some of the spills to make the bartenders appear credible.

I was asked on several occasions to take responsibility for a fake "spill." In this way, employees used the spill sheet to their advantage instead of using it for its intended purpose. They would serve free drinks courtesy of "spilling" until the volume reached was just under the suspicious level. As long as a pattern was not formed, the managers never knew they were being deceived.

1. What type of ethical standards, if any, were the employees in the restaurant living by when they committed this common, but questionable, action? Is the "entitlement mentality" at work here?

2. If you were an employee and you saw this situation, would you feel it should be reported or would you keep your mouth shut and let the practice continue? If you were asked to participate and take a "spill" for the team, what would you do? Why?

3. If your manager ever confronted you about some excessive spilling, would you personally feel it was more ethical to protect the other employees or tell your manager the truth?

Contributed Anonymously

way of looking at the four levels identified and some of the spheres of power that also exist. *Economic power* and *political power* are two spheres that are referred to often, but business has other, more subtle forms of power as well. These other spheres include *social and cultural power, power over the individual, technological power,* and *environmental power.*[37]

Is the power of business excessive? Does business abuse its power? Apparently, many people think so. To provide sensible and fair answers to these questions, however, one must carefully specify which level of power is being referred to and in which sphere the power is being exercised. When this is done, it is not simple to arrive at answers that are generalizable.

Furthermore, the nature of power is such that it is sometimes wielded unintentionally. Sometimes it is consequential; that is, it is not wielded intentionally, but nevertheless exerts its influence even though no attempt is made to exercise it.[38]

Balance of Power and Responsibility.   Whether or not business abuses its power or allows its use of power to become excessive is a central issue that cuts through all the topics we will be discussing in this book. But power should not be viewed in isolation from responsibility, and this power–responsibility relationship is the foundation of calls for corporate social responsibility. The **Iron Law of Responsibility** is a concept that

FIGURE 1-5 Levels and Spheres of Corporate Power

Levels Spheres	Macrolevel (the business system)	Intermediate Level (several firms)	Microlevel (single firm)	Individual Level (single executive)
Economic				
Social/Cultural				
Individual				
Technological				
Environmental				
Political				

addresses this: "In the long run, those who do not use power in a manner which society considers responsible will tend to lose it."[39] Stated another way, whenever power and responsibility become substantially out of balance, forces will be generated to bring them into closer balance.

When power gets out of balance, a variety of forces come to bear on business to be more responsible and more responsive to the criticisms being made against it. Some of these more obvious forces include governmental actions, such as increased regulations and new laws. The investigative news media become interested in what is going on, and a whole host of special-interest groups bring pressure to bear. In the *BusinessWeek* cover story cited earlier, the point was made that "it's this power imbalance that's helping to breed the current resentment against corporations."[40]

The tobacco industry is an excellent example of an industry that has felt the brunt of efforts to address allegations of abuse of power. Complaints that the industry produces a dangerous, addictive product and markets that product to young people have been made for years. The U.S. Food and Drug Administration (FDA) tried to assert jurisdiction over cigarettes and has been trying to rein in tobacco companies through aggressive regulation. One major outcome of this effort to bring the tobacco industry under control was a $368-billion settlement, to be paid over 25 years, in which the tobacco firms settle lawsuits against them, submit to new regulations, and meet strict goals for reducing smoking in the United States. Although the industry continues to fight these measures, as it always has, it is expected that by the year 2022 tobacco's role in American society will be forever reduced.[41]

In 2002, the U.S. Congress quickly passed the Sarbanes–Oxley Act, which was designed to rein in the power and abuse that were manifested in such scandals as Enron, WorldCom, Arthur Andersen, and Tyco. Executives have been grumbling that the new law is costly, cumbersome, and redundant, but this illustrates what happens when power and responsibility get out of balance.[42] Congress passed the bill to moderate business's power and bring about greater accountability. Companies continue to lobby

Congress to amend the Sarbanes–Oxley Act to make it less strict. More recently, Congress has begun passing new laws affecting the financial services industry. Legislation targeted toward reining in credit card companies is a case in point, and this will be discussed further in later chapters.

Business Response: Concern and Changing Social Contract

Growing out of criticisms of business and the idea of the power–responsibility equation has been an increased concern on the part of business for the stakeholder environment and a changed social contract. We previously indicated that the social environment was composed of such factors as demographics, lifestyles, and social values of the society. It may also be seen as a collection of conditions, events, and trends that reflect how people think and behave and what they value. As firms have sensed that the social environment and the expectations of business are changing, they have realized that they must change, too.

One way of thinking about the business–society relationship is through the concept of **social contract**. This is a set of two-way understandings that characterize the relationship between major institutions—in our case, business and society. The social contract is changing, and this change is a direct outgrowth of the increased importance of the social environment. The social contract has been changing to reflect society's expanded expectations of business, especially in the social, ethical, and environmental realms.

The social contract between business and society, as illustrated in Figure 1-6, is partially articulated through:

1. *Laws and regulations* that society has established as the framework within which business must operate and
2. *Shared understandings* that evolve over time as to each group's expectations of the other.

Laws and regulations spell out the "rules of the game" for business. Shared understandings, on the other hand, are more subtle and create room for misunderstandings. These shared understandings reflect mutual expectations regarding each other's roles, responsibilities, and ethics. These unspoken components of the social contract represent what might be called the normative perspective on the relationship (i.e., what "ought" to be done by each party to the social contract).[43]

A parallel example to the business and society social contract may be seen in the relationship between a professor and the students in his or her class. University regulations and the course syllabus spell out the formal "laws and regulations" aspects of the

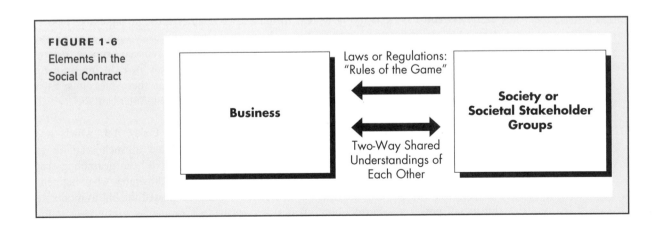

FIGURE 1-6
Elements in the
Social Contract

Business

Laws or Regulations:
"Rules of the Game"

Two-Way Shared
Understandings of
Each Other

**Society or
Societal Stakeholder
Groups**

relationship. The shared understandings address those expectations that are generally understood but not necessarily spelled out formally. An example might be "fairness." The student expects the professor to be "fair" in making assignments, in the level of work expected, in grading, and so on. Likewise, the professor expects the student to be fair in evaluating him or her on course evaluation forms, to be fair by not passing off someone else's work as his or her own, and so on.

An editorial from *BusinessWeek* on the subject of social contract summarizes well the modern era of business and society relationships:

> *Today it is clear that the terms of the contract between society and business are, in fact, changing in substantial and important ways. Business is being asked to assume broader responsibilities to society than ever before, and to serve a wider range of human values.... Inasmuch as business exists to serve society, its future will depend on the quality of management's response to the changing expectations of the public.*[44]

Another *BusinessWeek* editorial commented on the new social contract by saying, "Listen up, Corporate America. The American people are having a most serious discussion about your role in their lives." The editorial was referring to the criticisms coming out in the early 2000s about the abuse of corporate power.[45] Such a statement suggests that we will continually witness changes in the social contract between business and society.

ETHICS IN PRACTICE CASE

Donations for Profit

While working as the director of junior golf at a Nashville area golf course, I was put in charge of fund-raising. This task required me to spend numerous hours calling and visiting local businesses, seeking their donations for our end-of-the-summer golf tournament. After weeks of campaigning for money, I was pleased to have raised $3,000 for the tournament. The money was intended to be used for prizes, food, and trophies for the two-day Tournament of Champions.

I notified the golf course manager of my intentions to spend the money at a local golf store to purchase prizes for the participants. Upon hearing of my decision to spend all of the contribution money on the tournament, my manager asked me to spend only $1,500. I was confused by this request because I had encouraged various companies to contribute by telling them that their money would all be spent on the children registered in the tournament. My manager, however, told me that the golf course would pocket the other $1,500 as pure profit. He said the economy has been struggling and that the course could use any extra money to boost profits.

I was deeply angered that I had given my word to these companies and now the golf course was going to pocket half the donations. Feeling that my manager was in the wrong, I went to him again, this time with an ultimatum. Either the money was to be spent entirely on the tournament, or I would return all of the checks personally, citing my manager's plan as the reason. In response, he said that I could spend the money any way I desired, but he would appreciate it if I were frugal with the money. I spent it all.

1. Was my manager wrong in seeking to pocket half the donation money as profit? Does it make any difference that the golf course was experiencing perilous economic times? (After all, if the course goes out of business, tournaments cannot be held at all.)

2. Was I right in challenging my manager? Should I have handled this differently?

3. Do you think the companies would have felt cheated if the golf course had pocketed half their donations?

Contributed by Eric Knox

Focus of the Book

This book takes a **managerial approach** to the business and society relationship. This managerial approach emphasizes three main themes that are important to managers today: **business ethics**, **sustainability**, and **stakeholder management**. First, let us discuss the managerial approach.

Managerial Approach

Managers are practical, and they have begun to deal with social and ethical concerns in ways similar to those they have used to deal with traditional business functions—marketing, finance, operations, and so forth—in a rational, systematic, and administratively sound fashion. By viewing issues of social and ethical concern from a managerial frame of reference, managers have been able to reduce seemingly unmanageable concerns to ones that can be dealt with in a balanced and evenhanded fashion. At the same time, managers have had to integrate traditional economic and financial considerations with ethical and social considerations.

A managerial approach to the business and society relationship confronts the individual manager continuously with questions such as:

- What changes are occurring or will occur in society's expectations of business that mandate business's taking the initiative with respect to particular societal or ethical problems?
- Did business, in general, or our firm, in particular, have a role in creating these problems?
- Can we reduce broad social problems to a size that can be effectively addressed from a managerial point of view?
- What are the specific problems, alternatives for solving these problems, and implications for management's approach to dealing with social issues?
- How can we best plan and organize for responsiveness to socially related business problems?

Urgent versus Enduring Issues.   From the standpoint of urgency in managerial response, management is concerned with two broad types or classes of social issues. First, there are those issues or crises that arise instantaneously and for which management must formulate relatively quick responses. A typical example might be a protest group that shows up on management's doorstep one day, arguing vehemently that the company should withdraw its sponsorship of a violent television show scheduled to air the next week. Or a crisis could occur with respect to a company's products or services.

Second, there are issues or problems that management has time to deal with on a more long-term basis. These issues include product safety, environmental pollution, sustainability, employment discrimination, and occupational safety and health. In other words, these are enduring issues that will be of concern to society on a continuing basis and for which management must develop a thoughtful organizational response. Management must thus be concerned with both short-term and long-term capabilities for dealing with social problems and the organization's social performance.

The test of success of the managerial approach will be the extent to which leaders can improve an organization's social and ethical performance by taking a managerial approach rather than dealing with issues and crises on an ad hoc basis. Such a managerial approach will require balancing the needs of urgency with the careful response to enduring issues.

Business Ethics Theme

The managerial focus attempts to take a practical look at the social issues and expectations business faces, but ethical questions inevitably and continually come into play. **Ethics** basically refers to issues of right, wrong, fairness, and justice, and business ethics focuses on ethical issues that arise in the commercial realm. Ethical factors appear throughout our discussion because questions of right, wrong, fairness, and justice, no matter how slippery they are to deal with, permeate business's activities as it attempts to interact successfully with major stakeholder groups: employees, customers, owners, government, and the global and local communities. In light of the ethical scandals in recent years, especially the role of the financial services industry in the Wall Street collapse beginning in the fall of 2008, the ethics theme resonates as one of the most urgent dimensions of business and society relationships.

The principal task of management is not only to deal with the various stakeholder groups in an ethical fashion, but also to reconcile the conflicts of interest that occur between the organization and the stakeholder groups. Implicit in this challenge is the ethical dimension that is present in practically all business decision making where stakeholders are concerned. In addition to the challenge of treating fairly the groups with which business interacts, management faces the equally important task of creating an organizational climate in which all employees make decisions with the interests of the public, as well as those of the organization, in mind. At stake is not only the reputation of the firm but also of the business community in general.

Sustainability Theme

Over the past decade, the concept of sustainability has become one of businesses' most pressing mandates. Discussions of sustainability began with respect to the natural environment. As time has passed, however, it has become evident that it is a broader concept that applies not only to the natural environment but to the entirety of businesses' existence and processes as well, especially business's global role and development. At a fundamental level, sustainability is just about business's ability to survive and thrive over the long term.[46] The concept of sustainability is derived from the notion of sustainable development, which is a pattern of resource use that aims to meet human needs while preserving the environment so that these needs can be met not only in the present but also for future generations. The term sustainability was used by the Brundtland Commission, which coined what has become the most often-quoted definition of sustainable development as development that "meets the needs of the present without compromising the ability of future generations to meet their own needs."[47] Today, sustainability is thought to embrace environmental, economic, and social criteria, and this is the sense in which it will be used in this book. Thus, discussions of sustainability and its implications will appear in many chapters, not just in the chapter on the natural environment.

Stakeholder Management Theme

As we have suggested throughout this chapter, **stakeholders** are individuals or groups with which business interacts and who have a "stake," or vested interest, in the firm. They could be called "publics," but this term may imply that they are outside the business sphere and should be dealt with as external players rather than as integral constituents of the business and society relationship.

We consider two broad groups of stakeholders in this book—internal and external. Owners, as internal stakeholders, are considered early on. Though all chapters touch on the stakeholder management theme, Chapter 4 specifically addresses the topic of corporate governance, in which owner stakeholders are represented by boards of directors.

Spotlight on SUSTAINABILITY

What *Is* Sustainability?

- Sustainability is…providing for the needs of the present generation while not compromising the ability of future generations to meet theirs (*original definition in the U.N. Brundtland Commission Report on "Our Common Future," 1987*).
- Sustainability is…creating shareholder and social value while decreasing the environmental footprint along the value chains in which we operate (*DuPont*).
- Sustainability is generally considered to have three interdependent, coevolutionary dimensions: the economy, the society, and the natural environment (*Jean Garner Stead and W. Edward Stead,* Management for a Small Planet, *3d Ed., 2009*).
- Corporate sustainability is a business approach that creates long-term shareholder value by embracing opportunities and managing risks deriving from economic, environmental, and social developments (*3BL Media, 2009*).
- A sustainable society is one that satisfies its needs without diminishing the prospects of future generations (*Lester R. Brown, Founder and President, Worldwatch Institute*).

Later, we consider *external stakeholders*, which include government, consumers, the natural environment, and community members. Domestic and global stakeholders are major concerns. We treat government first because it represents the public. It is helpful to understand the role and workings of government to best appreciate business's relationships with other groups. Consumers may be business's most important stakeholders. Members of the community are crucial, too, and they are concerned about a variety of issues. One of the most important is the natural environment. All these issues have direct effects on the public.

The second broad grouping of stakeholders is *internal stakeholders*. Business owners are treated in our discussion of corporate governance, but then later in the book, employees are addressed as the principal group of internal stakeholders. We live in an organizational society, and many people think that their roles as employees are just as important as their roles as investors or owners. Both of these groups have legitimate legal and moral claims on the organization, and the management's task is to address their needs and balance these needs against those of the firm and of other stakeholder groups. We will develop the idea of stakeholder management more fully in Chapter 3.

Structure of the Book

The structure of this book is outlined in Figure 1-7 on page 25.

In Part 1, "Business, Society, and Stakeholders," there are three chapters. Chapter 1 provides an overview of the business and society relationship. Chapter 2 covers corporate citizenship: social responsibility, responsiveness, and performance. Chapter 3 addresses stakeholder management. These chapters provide a crucial foundation for understanding all of the discussions that follow. They provide the context for the business and society relationship.

Part 2 is titled "Corporate Governance and Strategic Management Issues." Chapter 4 covers the highly relevant topic of corporate governance, which has become more prominent during the past decade. The next two chapters address management-related topics. Chapter 5 covers strategic management and corporate public affairs. Chapter 6 addresses issues management and crisis management.

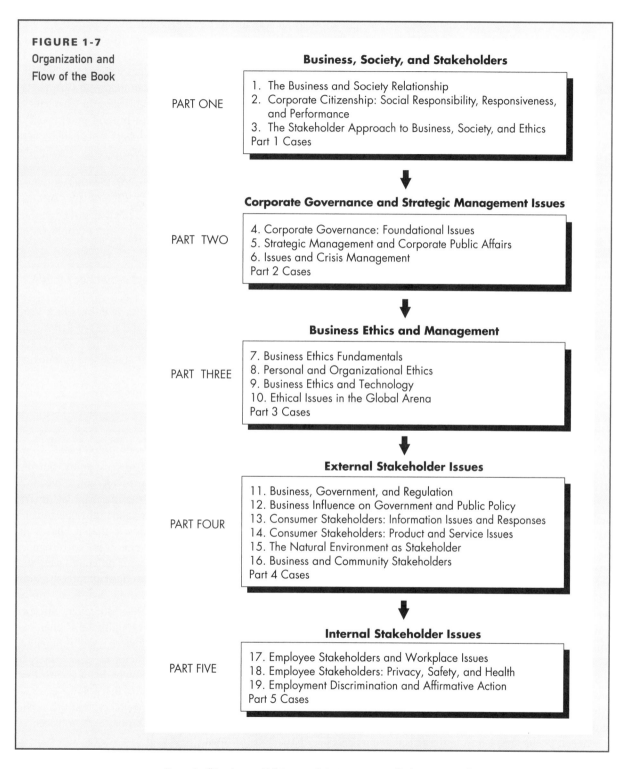

FIGURE 1-7
Organization and
Flow of the Book

Business, Society, and Stakeholders

PART ONE
1. The Business and Society Relationship
2. Corporate Citizenship: Social Responsibility, Responsiveness, and Performance
3. The Stakeholder Approach to Business, Society, and Ethics
Part 1 Cases

Corporate Governance and Strategic Management Issues

PART TWO
4. Corporate Governance: Foundational Issues
5. Strategic Management and Corporate Public Affairs
6. Issues and Crisis Management
Part 2 Cases

Business Ethics and Management

PART THREE
7. Business Ethics Fundamentals
8. Personal and Organizational Ethics
9. Business Ethics and Technology
10. Ethical Issues in the Global Arena
Part 3 Cases

External Stakeholder Issues

PART FOUR
11. Business, Government, and Regulation
12. Business Influence on Government and Public Policy
13. Consumer Stakeholders: Information Issues and Responses
14. Consumer Stakeholders: Product and Service Issues
15. The Natural Environment as Stakeholder
16. Business and Community Stakeholders
Part 4 Cases

Internal Stakeholder Issues

PART FIVE
17. Employee Stakeholders and Workplace Issues
18. Employee Stakeholders: Privacy, Safety, and Health
19. Employment Discrimination and Affirmative Action
Part 5 Cases

Part 3, "Business Ethics and Management," focuses exclusively on business ethics. Business ethics fundamentals are established in Chapter 7, and personal and organizational ethics are discussed further in Chapter 8. Chapter 9 addresses business ethics and technology. Chapter 10 treats business ethics in the global or international sphere.

Although ethical issues cut through and permeate virtually all discussions in the book, this dedicated treatment of business ethics is warranted by a need to explore in added detail the ethical dimension in management.

Part 4, "External Stakeholder Issues," deals with the major external stakeholders of business. Because government is such an active player in all the groups to follow, in Chapter 11 we consider business–government relationships and government regulations. In Chapter 12, we discuss how business endeavors to shape and influence government and public policy. Chapters 13 and 14 address consumer stakeholders. Chapter 15 addresses sustainability and the natural environment as stakeholder. Chapter 16 addresses business and community stakeholder issues, including corporate philanthropy.

Part 5, "Internal Stakeholder Issues," addresses employees as the sole stakeholders because the treatment of owner stakeholders is discussed in Part 2. Chapter 17 examines employees and major workplace issues. Chapter 18 looks carefully at the issues of employee privacy, safety, and health. In Chapter 19, we focus on the special case of employment discrimination.

Depending on the emphasis desired in the course, Part 2 could be covered in sequential order, or it could be postponed until after Part 5. Alternatively, it could be omitted if a strategic management orientation is not desired.

Taken as a whole, this book strives to take the reader through a building-block progression of basic concepts and ideas that are vital to the business and society relationship and to explore the nature of social and ethical issues and stakeholder groups with which management must interact. It considers the external and internal stakeholder groups in some depth.

Summary

The business and society relationship has faced some severe testing over the past five years. In spite of this, the pluralistic system is still at work, presenting business firms with a variety of challenges. The pluralistic business system in the United States has several advantages and some disadvantages. Within this context, business firms must deal with a multitude of stakeholders and an increasingly special-interest society. A major force that shapes the public's view of business is the criticism that business receives from a variety of sources. Factors in the social environment that have contributed to an atmosphere in which business criticism thrives include affluence, education, public awareness developed through the media (especially TV and the Internet), the revolution of rising expectations, a growing entitlement mentality, the rights movement, and a philosophy of victimization. The global recession may result in changes in business criticism and its antecedents. In addition, actual questionable practices on the part of business have made it a natural target. The ethics scandals, including Enron, post-Enron, and the Wall Street financial scandals, have perpetuated

criticisms of business. Not all firms are guilty, but the guilty attract negative attention to the entire business community. One result is that the trust and legitimacy of the entire business system is called into question.

A major criticism of business is that it abuses its power. To understand power, one needs to recognize that it may exist and operate at four different levels: the level of the entire business system, of groups of companies acting in concert, of the individual firm, and of the individual corporate executive. Moreover, business power may be manifested in several different spheres— economic, political, technological, environmental, social, and individual. It is difficult to assess whether business is actually abusing its power, but it is clear that business has enormous power and that it must exercise it carefully. Power evokes responsibility, and this is the central reason that calls for corporate responsiveness have been prevalent in recent years. The Iron Law of Responsibility calls for greater balance in business power and responsibility. These concerns have led to a changing social environment for business and a changed social contract.

Key Terms

affluence, p. 12

business, p. 6

business ethics, p. 22

business power, p. 17

economic environment, p. 8

education, p. 12

entitlement mentality, p. 14

ethics, p. 23

Iron Law of Responsibility, p. 18

macroenvironment, p. 7

managerial approach, p. 22

pluralism, p. 8

political environment, p. 8

revolution of rising expectations, p. 14

rights movement, p. 15

social contract, p. 20

social environment, p. 7

social problem, p. 14

society, p. 7

special-interest society, p. 10

stakeholder management, p. 22

stakeholders, p. 23

sustainability, p. 22

technological environment, p. 8

victimization philosophy, p. 16

Discussion Questions

1. In discussions of business and society, why is there a tendency to focus on large-rather than small- or medium-sized firms? Have the corporate ethics scandals of the first decade of the 2000s affected small- and medium-sized firms? If so, in what ways have these firms been affected?

2. What is the one greatest strength of a pluralistic society? What is the one greatest weakness? Do these characteristics work for or against business?

3. Identify and explain the major factors in the social environment that create an atmosphere in which business criticism takes place and prospers. How are the factors related to one another?

Has the revolution of rising expectations run its course? Or is it still a vital reality?

4. Give an example of each of the four levels of power discussed in this chapter. Also, give an example of each of the spheres of business power.

5. Explain in your own words the *Iron Law of Responsibility* and the *social contract.* Give an example of a shared understanding between you as a consumer or an employee and a firm with which you do business or for which you work. Is Congress justified in creating new regulations to govern the financial services industry?

2

Corporate Citizenship: Social Responsibility, Responsiveness, and Performance

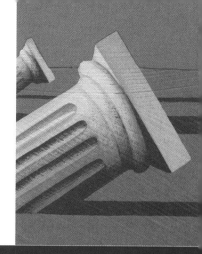

CHAPTER LEARNING OUTCOMES

After studying this chapter, you should be able to:

1. Explain how corporate social responsibility (CSR) evolved and encompasses economic, legal, ethical, and philanthropic components.

2. Provide business examples of CSR and corporate citizenship.

3. Differentiate between corporate citizenship, social responsibility, responsiveness, and performance.

4. Elaborate on the concept of corporate social performance (CSP).

5. Explain how corporate citizenship develops in stages in companies.

6. Describe the socially responsible investing movement.

For several decades now, business has been undergoing the most intense scrutiny it has ever received from the public. As a result of the many allegations being leveled against it—charges that it has little concern for the consumer, cares nothing about the deteriorating social order, has no concept of acceptable ethical behavior, and is indifferent to the problems of minorities and the environment—concerns about what responsibilities business has to society continue to be expressed. These concerns have generated an unprecedented number of pleas for corporate social responsibility (CSR). More recently, CSR has been embraced in the broader term "corporate citizenship." Concepts that have evolved from CSR include corporate social *responsiveness* and corporate social *performance*. Today, many business executives prefer the term "corporate citizenship" as an inclusive reference to social responsibility issues. Two other terms that have become popular include *corporate responsibility* (CR) and *sustainability*. In the final analysis, all these terms seem to be overlapping in their meanings. The terms are frequently used interchangeably, and a careful inspection of each is needed to understand the user's intent. We will continue to focus on CSR and will invoke the other terms when appropriate.

CSR has been a "front-burner" issue within the business community and continues to grow in importance each year. An example of this growth was the formation in 1992 of an organization called **Business for Social Responsibility (BSR)**. BSR claims to have been formed to fill an urgent need for a national business alliance that fosters socially responsible corporate policies. In 2010, BSR reported among its membership such recognizable names as Abbott Laboratories, Campbell Soup Co., Levi Strauss & Co., Timberland Company, General Electric (GE), Walmart, Mattel, Coca-Cola, UPS, Tom's of Maine, and hundreds of others. The mission statement of BSR is that it "seeks to work with business to create a just and sustainable world."[1]

In this chapter, we intend to explore several different aspects of the CSR topic and to provide some insights into what CSR means and how businesses carry it out. We dedicate an entire chapter to the CSR issue and concepts that have emerged from it because it is a core idea that underlies most of our discussions in this book.

The Corporate Social Responsibility Concept

In Chapter 1, we traced how criticisms of business have led to increased concern for the social environment and a changed social contract. Out of these developments has grown the notion of CSR. Before providing some historical perspective, let us impart an initial view of what CSR means.

An early view of CSR stated: "**Corporate social responsibility** is seriously considering the impact of the company's actions on society."[2] Another early definition was that "social responsibility…requires the individual to consider his [or her] acts in terms of a whole social system, and holds him [or her] responsible for the effects of his [or her] acts anywhere in that system."[3]

Both of these definitions provide useful insights into the idea of social responsibility that will help us appreciate some brief history. Figure 2-1 illustrates the business criticism–social response cycle, depicting how the concept of CSR grew out of the ideas introduced in Chapter 1—business criticism, the increased concern for the social environment, and the changed social contract. Figure 2-1 also shows that businesses' commitment to social responsibility has led to increased corporate *responsiveness* toward stakeholders and improved social (stakeholder) *performance*—ideas that are developed more fully in this chapter.

Some today prefer to use the term **corporate citizenship** to collectively embrace the host of concepts related to CSR. For now, a useful summary of the themes or emphases of each of the chapter title concepts helps us see the flow of ideas extended as these concepts have developed:

Corporate Citizenship Concepts

Corporate social *responsibility*—emphasizes *obligation, accountability*

Corporate social *responsiveness*—emphasizes *action, activity*

Corporate social *performance*—emphasizes *outcomes, results*

The growth of these ideas has brought about a society more satisfied with business. However, this satisfaction, despite reducing the number of factors leading to business criticism, has at the same time led to increased expectations that have resulted in more criticism. Figure 2-1 illustrates this double effect. The net result is that the overall levels of business social performance and societal satisfaction should increase with time in spite of this interplay of positive and negative factors. Should business not be responsive to societal expectations, it could conceivably enter a downward spiral, resulting in significant deterioration in the business and society relationship. The tsunami of corporate fraud scandals beginning in 2001–2002, followed by the Wall Street financial collapse beginning in 2008, has seriously called businesses' concern for society into question, and this concern continues today.

Historical Perspective on CSR

The concept of business responsibility that prevailed in the United States during most of our history was fashioned after the traditional, or classical, *economic model*. Adam

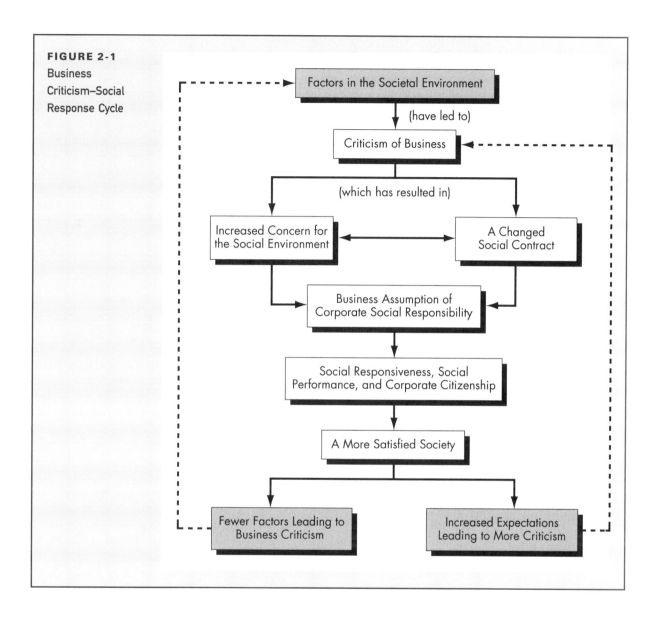

FIGURE 2-1
Business Criticism–Social Response Cycle

Smith's concept of the "invisible hand" was its major starting point. The classical view held that a society could best determine its needs and wants through the marketplace. If business is rewarded on the basis of its ability to respond to the demands of the market, the self-interested pursuit of that reward will result in society getting what it wants. Thus, the "invisible hand" of the market transforms self-interest into societal interest. Although the marketplace has done a reasonably good job in deciding what goods and services should be produced, it has not fared as well in ensuring that business always acted fairly and ethically.

Years later, when laws constraining business behavior began to proliferate, a *legal model* emerged. Society's expectations of business changed from being strictly economic in nature to encompassing issues that had been previously at business's discretion. Over time, a *social model*, followed by a *stakeholder model*, has evolved. In the stakeholder model, sustainability has become a prominent dimension.

Modification of the Economic Model

Early on, a modification of the classical economic model was seen in practice in at least three areas: philanthropy, community obligations, and paternalism.[4] History shows that businesspeople did engage in **philanthropy**—contributions to charity and other worthy causes—even during periods dominated by the traditional economic view. Voluntary **community obligations** to improve, beautify, and uplift were also evident. An early example of this was the post–Civil War cooperative effort between the railroads and the YMCA to provide community services in railroad-served areas. Although these services economically benefited the railroads, they were at the same time philanthropic in nature.[5]

During the latter part of the 19th century and into the 20th century, **paternalism** appeared in many forms. One of the most visible examples was the company town. Although business's motives for creating company towns (e.g., the Pullman, Illinois, experiment) were mixed, business had to do a considerable amount of the work in governing them. Thus, some companies took on a kind of parental, paternalistic social responsibility.[6]

The emergence of large corporations during the late 1800s played a major role in hastening movement away from the classical economic view. As society developed from the economic structure of small, powerless firms governed primarily by the marketplace to large corporations in which power was more concentrated, questions of the responsibility of business to society surfaced.[7]

Although the idea of CSR had not yet fully developed in the 1920s, managers even then had a more positive view of their role. Community service was in the forefront. The most visible example was the Community Chest movement, which received its impetus from business. This was the first large-scale endeavor in which business leaders became involved with other nongovernmental community groups for a common, nonbusiness purpose that necessitated their contribution of time and money to community welfare projects.[8] The social responsibility of business, then, had received a further broadening of its meaning.

The 1930s signaled a transition from a predominantly laissez-faire economy to a mixed economy in which business found itself one of the constituencies monitored by a more activist government. From this time well into the 1950s, business's social responsibilities grew to include employee welfare (pension and insurance plans), safety, medical care, retirement programs, and so on. These new developments were spurred both by governmental compulsion and by an enlarged concept of business responsibility.[9]

In his book *The Generous Corporation*, Neil J. Mitchell presents an interesting thesis regarding how CSR evolved.[10] According to him, American business leaders developed the ideology of CSR, particularly philanthropy, as a strategic response to the antibusiness fervor that was beginning in the late 1800s and early 1900s. The antibusiness reaction was the result of specific questionable practices, such as railroad price gouging, and public resentment of the emerging gigantic fortunes being made by late 19th-century moguls, such as John D. Rockefeller and Andrew Carnegie.[11]

As business leaders came to realize that the government had the power to intervene in the economy and, in fact, was being encouraged to do so by public opinion, there was a need for a philosophy that promoted large corporations as a force for social good. Thus, Mitchell argued, business leaders attempted to persuade those affected by business power that such power was being used appropriately. An example of this early progressive business ideology was reflected in Carnegie's 1889 essay, "The Gospel of Wealth," which asserted that business must pursue profits but that business wealth should be used for the benefit of the community. Philanthropy, therefore, became the most popular means of using corporate wealth for public benefit. A prime example of this was Carnegie's funding and building of more than 2,500 libraries.[12]

In a discussion of little-known history, Mitchell documents by specific examples how business developed this idea of the generous corporation and how it had distinct advantages: It helped business gain support from national and local governments, and it helped achieve in America a social stability that was unknown in Europe during that period. Berenbeim in his review of Mitchell's book argues that the main motive for corporate generosity in the early 1900s was essentially the same as it was in the 1990s—to keep the government at arm's length.[13]

CSR's Acceptance and Broadening of Meaning. The period from the 1950s to the present may be considered the modern era in which the concept of CSR gained considerable acceptance and broadening of meaning. During this time, the emphasis has moved from little more than a general awareness of social and moral concerns to a period in which specific issues, such as corporate governance, product safety, honesty in advertising, employee rights, affirmative action, environmental sustainability, ethical behavior, and global CSR have taken center stage. The *issue* orientation eventually gave way to the more recent focus on social performance and corporate citizenship. First, however, we can expand upon the modern view of CSR by examining a few definitions or understandings of this term that have developed in recent years.

Evolving Meanings of CSR

Let's now return to the basic question: What does CSR really mean? Up to this point, we have been operating with a rather simple definition of social responsibility:

> *Corporate social responsibility is seriously considering the impact of the company's actions on society.*

Although this definition has inherent ambiguities, most of the definitions presented by others also have limitations. A second definition is worth considering:

> *Social responsibility is the obligation of decision makers to take actions which protect and improve the welfare of society as a whole along with their own interests.*[14]

This definition suggests two active aspects of social responsibility—*protecting* and *improving*. To protect the welfare of society implies the avoidance of negative impacts on society. To improve the welfare of society implies the creation of positive benefits for society. Like the first definition, this second characterization contains several words that are perhaps unavoidably vague.

A third definition that is useful is also quite general. But, unlike the previous two, it places social responsibilities in context vis-à-vis economic and legal objectives of business:

> *The idea of social responsibility supposes that the corporation has not only economic and legal obligations, but also certain responsibilities to society which extend beyond these obligations.*[15]

This statement is attractive in that it acknowledges the importance of economic objectives (e.g., profits) side by side with legal obligations while also encompassing a broader conception of the firm's responsibilities. It is limited, however, in that it does not clarify what the certain responsibilities that extend beyond these are. Over the years, a number of different definitions or views on CSR have evolved.[16]

A Four-Part Definition of CSR

Each of the above definitions of CSR is valuable. At this point, we would like to present Carroll's four-part definition of CSR that focuses on the *types* of social responsibilities business has. This definition helps us understand the component parts that make up CSR, and it is the definition that we will build upon in this book:

> *The social responsibility of business encompasses the economic, legal, ethical, and discretionary (philanthropic) expectations that society has of organizations at a given point in time.*[17]

This four-part definition places economic and legal expectations of business in context by relating them to more socially oriented concerns. These social concerns include ethical responsibilities and philanthropic (voluntary/discretionary) responsibilities.

Economic Responsibilities.   First, business has **economic responsibilities**. It may seem odd to call an economic responsibility a social responsibility, but, in effect, this is what it is. First and foremost, the American social system calls for business to be an economic institution; that is, as an institution it should have the objective to produce goods and services that society wants and to sell them at fair prices—prices that society thinks represent the true value of the goods and services delivered and that provide business with profits sufficient to ensure its survival and growth and to reward its investors. While thinking about its economic responsibilities, business employs many management concepts that are directed toward financial effectiveness—attention to revenues, costs, investments, strategic decision making, and the host of business concepts focused on maximizing the long-term financial performance of the organization. Today, global hypercompetition in business has underscored the importance of business's economic responsibilities. Economic sustainability has become a timely topic. But economic responsibilities are not enough.

Legal Responsibilities.   Second, business has **legal responsibilities**. Just as society has sanctioned our economic system by permitting businesses to assume the productive role mentioned earlier, as a partial fulfillment of the social contract, it has also established the ground rules—the laws—under which businesses are expected to operate. Legal responsibilities reflect society's view of "codified ethics" in the sense that they embody basic notions of fair practices as established by our lawmakers. It is business's responsibility toward society to comply with these laws. It is not an accident that compliance officers now have a new role appearing on organization charts. If business does not agree with laws that have been passed or are about to be passed, however, our society has provided a mechanism by which dissenters can be heard through the political process. In the past decades, our society has witnessed a proliferation of laws and regulations striving to monitor and control business behavior. A notable *Newsweek* cover story titled "Lawsuit Hell: How Fear of Litigation Is Paralyzing Our Professions" emphasizes the burgeoning role that the legal responsibility of organizations is assuming.[18] The legal aspect of the business and society relationship will be examined further in other chapters as pertinent issues arise.

As important as legal responsibilities are, legal responsibilities do not embrace the full range of behaviors expected of business by society. On its own, law is inadequate for at least three reasons. First, the law cannot possibly address all the topics or issues that business may face. New issues continuously emerge such as e-commerce, genetically modified foods, dealing with illegal immigrants, and the use of cell phones while driving. Second, the law often lags behind more recent interpretations of what is considered appropriate behavior. For example, as technology permits more precise measurements of environmental contamination, laws based on measures made by obsolete equipment become outdated but not frequently changed. Third, laws are made by lawmakers and may reflect the personal interests and political motivations of legislators rather than appropriate ethical justifications. A wise sage once said: "Never go to see how sausages

---

ETHICS IN PRACTICE CASE

Feeling "Used"

While attending college, I spent a few years working at a used-textbook store. The majority of the books we sold were used books that we purchased from students, individuals, and used-book wholesalers. Sometimes when putting books out on the shelves, I would encounter books with phrases like "Instructor's Copy" or "Sample Copy—Not for Resale" printed on the covers. When I asked my boss about these books, he told me that they were free copies given out to instructors, but it was perfectly legal for us to sell the books because we had purchased them from another person. This made sense to me and satisfied my curiosity.

Later in the day, my boss showed me a pile of these sample-copy books and said that we take colored tape and cover up the areas that contain phrases such as "Sample Copy." When I asked why we did this, he told me that although we are legally able to sell the books, the phrases sometimes discourage customers from buying these copies although the content is identical to the standard copies. I then asked how we got these books if they were instructor copies and were not supposed to be resold.

I was told that the publishing companies send free copies of books to professors to let them read and evaluate them with the hope that they will order the book as material for their classes. We get some of these books when professors sell their sample copies to us or to a used-book wholesaler, but the majority come from individuals who go around college campuses (calling themselves *book buyers*) buying these books from professors and then selling them to a used-book store or a used-book wholesaler.

My boss also stated that because the content inside is the same, we really do not care if they are the standard copy or a sample copy and, therefore, we buy and sell these books for the same prices as standard copies.

1. Is it a socially responsible (legal? ethical?) practice for a bookstore to purchase and then resell these books that were given out as free copies?

2. Is it an ethical practice for the bookstore to conceal the fact that these books are, indeed, instructors' or sample copies?

3. Is it an ethical practice for book buyers to roam the halls of college campuses and buy these free books from professors who no longer want them?

4. Is it an ethical practice for professors to sell books that were sent to them as free sample copies?

Contributed Anonymously

---

or laws are made." It may not be a pretty picture. Although we would like to believe that our lawmakers are focusing on "what is right," political maneuvering and self-interested decisions often suggests otherwise.

Ethical Responsibilities. Because laws are essential but not adequate, **ethical responsibilities** are needed to embrace those activities and practices that are expected or prohibited by society even though they are not codified into law. Ethical responsibilities embody the full scope of norms, standards, values, and expectations that reflect what consumers, employees, shareholders, and the community regard as fair, just, and consistent with respect for or protection of stakeholders' moral rights.[19]

In one sense, changes in ethics or values precede the establishment of laws because they become the driving forces behind the initial creation of laws and regulations. For example, the civil rights, environmental, and consumer movements begun in the 1960s reflected basic alterations in societal values and thus were ethical bellwethers foreshadowing and leading to later legislation. In another sense, ethical responsibilities may be seen as embracing and reflecting newly emerging values and norms that society expects business to meet, even though they may reflect a higher standard of performance than that currently required by law. Ethical responsibilities in this sense are continually evolving. As a result, debate about their legitimacy continues. Regardless, business is expected to be responsive to newly emerging concepts of what constitutes ethical practices, such as

Whole Foods selling only those foods it considers organic, that is, ethical. In recent years, ethics issues in the global arena have complicated and extended the study of acceptable business norms and practices.

Superimposed on these ethical expectations originating from societal and stakeholder groups are the implied levels of ethical performance suggested by a consideration of the great ethical principles of moral philosophy, such as justice, rights, and utilitarianism.[20] Because ethical responsibilities are so important, we devote Part 3 of the text, composed of four chapters, to the subject. For the moment, let us think of ethical responsibilities as encompassing those decision and behavior areas in which society expects certain levels of moral or principled performance but for which it has not yet articulated or codified them into law.

Philanthropic Responsibilities.   Fourth, there are business's voluntary, discretionary, or **philanthropic responsibilities**. Though not responsibilities in the literal sense of the word, these are viewed as responsibilities because they reflect current expectations of business by the public. The amount and nature of these activities are voluntary or discretionary, guided only by business's desire to engage in social activities that are not mandated, not required by law, and not generally expected of business in an ethical sense. Nevertheless, the public has an expectation that business will "give back," and thus this category has become a part of the social contract between business and society. Such activities might include corporate giving, product and service donations, employee volunteerism, partnerships with local government and other organizations, and any other kind of voluntary involvement of the organization's resources and its employees with the community or other stakeholders.

Examples of companies fulfilling their philanthropic responsibilities, and "doing well by doing good," are many:

- Chick-fil-A, the fast-food restaurant, through the WinShape Centre® Foundation, operates foster homes for more than 120 children; sponsors a summer camp that hosts more than 1,700 campers every year, from 24 states; and has provided college scholarships for more than 16,500 students.[21]
- Chiquita, the banana producer, recycles 100 percent of the plastic bags and twine used on its farms, and it has improved working conditions by building housing and schools for its employees' families.[22]
- Timberland underwrites skills training for women working for its suppliers in China. In Bangladesh, it helps provide microloans and health services for laborers.[23]
- Thousands of companies give away money, offer services, and volunteer time to education, youth, health organizations, arts and culture, neighborhood improvement, minority affairs, and programs for the handicapped.

Although there is sometimes an ethical motivation for companies getting involved in philanthropy, more often it is considered a practical way for the company to demonstrate that it is a good corporate citizen. A major distinction between ethical and philanthropic responsibilities is that the latter typically are not *expected* in a moral or an ethical sense. Communities desire and expect business to contribute its money, facilities, and employee time to humanitarian programs or purposes, but they do not regard firms as unethical if they do not provide these services at the desired levels. Therefore, these responsibilities are more discretionary, or voluntary, on business's part, although the societal expectation that these be provided has been around for some time. This category of responsibilities is often referred to as good "corporate citizenship."

In summary, the four-part CSR definition forms a conceptualization that includes the economic, legal, ethical, and philanthropic expectations society places on organizations at

---

FIGURE 2-2 Understanding the Four Components of CSR

Type of Responsibility	Societal Expectation	Explanations
Economic	REQUIRED of business by society	*Be profitable.* Maximize sales, minimize costs. Make sound strategic decisions. Be attentive to dividend policy. Provide investors with adequate and attractive returns on their investments.
Legal	REQUIRED of business by society	*Obey all laws, adhere to all regulations.* Environmental and consumer laws. Laws protecting employees. Comply with the Sarbanes–Oxley Act. Fulfill all contractual obligations. Honor warranties and guarantees.
Ethical	EXPECTED of business by society	*Avoid questionable practices.* Respond to spirit as well as to letter of law. Assume law is a floor on behavior, operate above minimum required. Do what is right, fair, and just. Assert ethical leadership.
Philanthropic	DESIRED/EXPECTED of business by society	*Be a good corporate citizen.* Give back. Make corporate contributions. Provide programs supporting community—education, health or human services, culture and arts, and civic. Provide for community betterment. Engage in volunteerism.

---

a given point in time. Figure 2-2 summarizes the four components, society's expectation regarding each component, and explanations.

That business has accountability for each of these areas of responsibility and performance is known. This four-part definition provides us with categories within which to place the various expectations that society has of business. With each of these categories considered to be an indispensable facet of the total social responsibility of business, we have a conceptual model that more completely describes the kinds of expectations that society has of business. A major advantage of this model is its ability to accommodate those who have argued against CSR by characterizing an economic emphasis as separate from a social emphasis. This model offers these two facets along with others that collectively make up CSR.

The Pyramid of Corporate Social Responsibility. A helpful way of graphically depicting the four-part definition of CSR is envisioning a pyramid with four layers. This **Pyramid of Corporate Social Responsibility (CSR)** is shown in Figure 2-3.[24]

The pyramid portrays the four components of CSR, beginning with the basic building block of economic performance at the base. At the same time, business is expected to obey the law, because the law is society's codification of acceptable and unacceptable practices. In addition, there is business's responsibility to be ethical. At its most basic level, this is the obligation to do what is right, just, and fair and to avoid or minimize harm to stakeholders (employees, consumers, the environment, and others). Finally, business is expected to be a good corporate citizen—to fulfill its philanthropic responsibility to contribute financial and human resources to the community and to improve the quality of life.

No metaphor is perfect, and the Pyramid of CSR is no exception. It intends to illustrate that the total social responsibility of business is composed of distinct components that, when taken together, make up the whole. Although the components have been treated as separate concepts for discussion purposes, they are not mutually exclusive and are not intended to juxtapose a firm's economic responsibilities with its other responsibilities. At the same time, a consideration of the separate components helps the manager see that the different types or kinds of obligations are in constant and dynamic

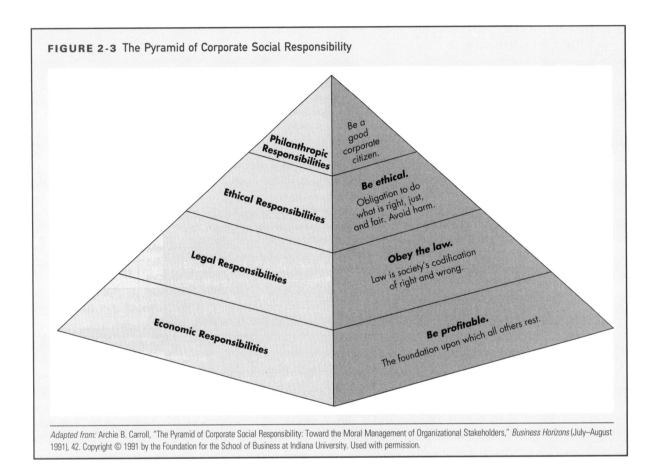

FIGURE 2-3 The Pyramid of Corporate Social Responsibility

Philanthropic Responsibilities — Be a good corporate citizen.

Ethical Responsibilities — **Be ethical.** Obligation to do what is right, just, and fair. Avoid harm.

Legal Responsibilities — **Obey the law.** Law is society's codification of right and wrong.

Economic Responsibilities — **Be profitable.** The foundation upon which all others rest.

Adapted from: Archie B. Carroll, "The Pyramid of Corporate Social Responsibility: Toward the Moral Management of Organizational Stakeholders," *Business Horizons* (July–August 1991), 42. Copyright © 1991 by the Foundation for the School of Business at Indiana University. Used with permission.

tension with one another. The most critical tensions, of course, are those between economic and legal, economic and ethical, and economic and philanthropic. Some might see this as a conflict between a firm's "concern for profits" and its "concern for society," but it is suggested here that this is an oversimplification because the two are so intertwined.

PYRAMID AS A UNIFIED WHOLE   A CSR or stakeholder perspective would focus on the total pyramid as a unified whole and on how the firm might engage in decisions, actions, policies, and practices that *simultaneously* fulfill all its component parts. This pyramid should not be interpreted to mean that business is expected to fulfill its social responsibilities in some sequential fashion, starting at the base. Rather, business is expected to fulfill all its responsibilities simultaneously.

In summary, the total social responsibility of business entails the concurrent fulfillment of the firm's economic, legal, ethical, and philanthropic responsibilities. This might be expressed in the form of an equation, as follows:

> *Economic Responsibilities + Legal Responsibilities + Ethical Responsibilities*
> *+ Philanthropic Responsibilities*
> *= Total Corporate Social Responsibility*

Stated in more practical and managerial terms, the socially responsible firm should strive to

- Make a profit.
- Obey the law.
- Be ethical.
- Be a good corporate citizen.

CSR DEFINITION AND PYRAMID ARE SUSTAINABLE STAKEHOLDER MODELS It is especially important to note that the four-part CSR definition and the Pyramid of CSR represent sustainable stakeholder models. Each of the four components of responsibility addresses different stakeholders in terms of the varying priorities in which the stakeholders are affected. Economic responsibilities most dramatically impact owners or shareholders and employees (because if the business is not financially successful, owners, and employees will be directly affected). When the economic recession hit, employees were displaced and significantly affected. Legal responsibilities are certainly crucial with respect to owners, but in today's society, the threat of litigation against businesses emanates frequently from employees and consumer stakeholders. Ethical responsibilities affect all stakeholder groups, but an examination of the ethical issues business faces today suggests that they involve consumers, employees, and the environment most frequently. Finally, philanthropic responsibilities most affect the community, but it could be reasoned that employees are next affected because some research has suggested that a company's philanthropic performance significantly affects its employees' morale. The definition and pyramid are sustainable in that they represent long-term responsibilities that overarch into future generations of stakeholders as well.

The role of stakeholders in discussions of CSR is inseparable. In fact, there have been recent calls for CSR to be redefined as corporate "stakeholder" responsibility, rather than CSR.[25] Others have suggested that CSR stand for corporate "sustainability" responsibilities. These views would be entirely consistent with the models presented in this chapter.

As we study business's major areas of social concern, as presented in various chapters in Parts 2 and 3 of the book, we will see how the model's four facets (economic, legal, ethical, and philanthropic) provide us with a useful framework for conceptualizing the issue of CSR. The social contract between business and society is, to a large extent, formulated from mutual understandings that exist in each of these areas. But it should be noted that the ethical and philanthropic categories, taken together, more accurately capture the essence of what people generally mean today when they speak of the social responsibility of business. Situating these two categories relative to the legal and economic obligations, however, keeps them in proper perspective and provides a more complete understanding of CSR.

CSR IN PRACTICE What do companies have to do to be seen as socially responsible? A study by Walker Information, a research organization, sought to discover what the general public perceived to be the activities or characteristics of socially responsible companies. Figure 2-4 summarizes what the sample said were the top 20 activities or characteristics of socially responsible companies.[26] The items in this listing are quite compatible with our discussion of CSR. Most of these characteristics would be representative of the legal, ethical, and philanthropic or discretionary components of our four-part CSR definition.

Walker Information concluded that the public thinks CSR factors impact a company's reputation just as do traditional business factors such as quality, service, and price. A related question on its survey pertained to the impact of social *irresponsibility* on firm reputation. The study found that ethical and law-abiding companies can reap rewards

FIGURE 2-4

Top 20 Activities or Characteristics of Socially Responsible Companies

- Makes products that are safe.
- Does not pollute air or water.
- Obeys the law in all aspects of business.
- Promotes honest or ethical employee behavior.
- Commits to safe workplace ethics.
- Does not use misleading or deceptive advertising.
- Upholds stated policy banning discrimination.
- Utilizes "environmentally friendly" packaging.
- Protects employees against sexual harassment.
- Recycles within company.

- Shows no past record of questionable activity.
- Responds quickly to customer problems.
- Maintains waste reduction program.
- Provides or pays portion of medical costs.
- Promotes energy conservation program.
- Helps displaced workers with placement.
- Gives money toward charitable or educational causes.
- Utilizes only biodegradable or recyclable materials.
- Employs friendly or courteous or responsive personnel.
- Tries continually to improve quality.

Source: Walker Information. Used with permission.

from CSR activities and enjoy enhanced reputations. However, those perceived to be unethical or non–law abiding can do little in the way of CSR activities to correct their images. Thus, the penalties for disobeying the law are greater than the rewards for helping society.

Arguments against and for Corporate Social Responsibility

In an effort to provide a balanced view of CSR, we will consider the arguments that traditionally have been raised against and for it.[27] We should state clearly at the outset, however, that those who argue *against* CSR are not using in their considerations the comprehensive four-part CSR definition and model presented earlier in the text. Rather, it appears that the critics are viewing CSR more narrowly—as only the organizations' efforts to pursue social goals (primarily our philanthropic category). Some critics equate CSR with only the philanthropic category.

Only very few businesspeople and academics argue against the fundamental notion of CSR today. The debate among businesspeople more often centers on the kinds and degrees of CSR and on subtle ethical questions, rather than on the basic question of whether or not business should be socially responsible or a good corporate citizen. Today, very few any longer resist CSR on the grounds of economic theory.

Arguments against CSR

Classical Economics.   Let us first look at some of the arguments that have surfaced over the years from the anti-CSR school of thought. Most notable has been the classical economic argument. This traditional view holds that management has one responsibility—to maximize the profits of its owners or shareholders. This classical economic school, led by the late Milton Friedman, argued that social issues are not the concern of businesspeople and that these problems should be resolved by the unfettered workings of the free market system.[28] Further, this view holds that if the free market cannot solve the social problem, then it falls upon government and legislation to do the job.

Friedman softens his argument somewhat by his assertion that management is "to make as much money as possible while conforming to the basic rules of society, *both those embodied in the law and those embodied in ethical customs.*"[29] When Friedman's entire statement is considered, it appears that he accepts three of the four categories of the four-part model—economic, legal, and ethical. The only category not specifically embraced in his quote is the voluntary or philanthropic category. It is clear that the economic argument views CSR more narrowly than we have depicted in our four-part model.

Business Not Equipped. This position holds that managers are oriented toward finance and operations and do not have the necessary expertise (social skills) to make social decisions.[30] Although this may have been true at one point in time, it is less true today.

Dilutes Business Purpose. Closely related to business not being equipped is a third: If managers were to pursue CSR vigorously, it would tend to dilute business's primary purpose.[31] The objection here is that CSR would put business into fields not related to its "proper aim."[32] There is virtually no practical evidence, however, that this objection has been realized.

Too Much Power Already. A fourth argument against CSR is that business already has enough power—economic, environmental, and technological—and so why should we place in its hands the opportunity to wield additional power?[33] In reality, today, business has this social power regardless of the argument. Further, this view tends to ignore the potential use of business's social power for the public good.

Global Competitiveness. Another argument that merits mention is that by encouraging business to assume social responsibilities, we might be placing it in a vulnerable position in terms of global competition. One consequence of being socially responsible is that business must internalize costs that it formerly passed on to society in the form of dirty air, unsafe products, consequences of discrimination, and so on. The increase in the costs of products caused by inclusion of social considerations in the price structure might necessitate raising the prices of products, thereby making them less competitive in international markets. The net effect might be to dissipate the country's advantages gained previously through technological advances. This argument weakens considerably when we consider the reality that social responsibility has become a global concern, not one restricted to domestic firms and operations.

The arguments presented here constitute the principal claims that have historically been made by those who oppose the CSR concept, as it once was narrowly conceived. Many of the reasons given appear appealing. Value choices as to the type of society the citizenry would like to have, at some point, become part of the total social responsibility decision. Whereas some of these objections might have had validity at one point in time, it is doubtful that most of them carry much weight today.

Arguments for CSR

Enlightened Self-Interest. The long-range self-interest view, sometimes referred to as "enlightened self-interest," holds that if business is to have a healthy climate in which to operate in the future, it must take actions now to ensure its long-term viability. The reasoning behind this view is that society's expectations are such that if business does not respond on its own, its role in society may be altered by the public—for example, through government regulation or, more dramatically, through alternative economic systems for the production and distribution of goods and services.

For managers who have a short-term orientation, it is sometimes difficult to appreciate that their rights and roles in the economic system are determined by society. Business must be responsive to society's expectations over the long term if it is to survive in its current form or in a less restrained form. This concern for the long-term viability of society is the primary driver in the current concern for sustainability, which is starting to become a synonym for CSR in the minds of many.

Warding Off Government Regulations.   One of the most practical reasons for business to be socially responsible is to ward off future government intervention and regulations. Today there are numerous areas in which government intervenes with an expensive, elaborate regulatory apparatus to fill a void left by business's inaction. To the extent that business polices itself with self-disciplined standards and guidelines, future government intervention can be somewhat forestalled. Later, we will discuss some areas in which business could have prevented intrusion and simultaneously ensured greater freedom in decision making had it imposed higher standards of behavior on itself.

Resources Available.   Two additional arguments supporting CSR deserve mention together—"Business has the resources" and "Let business try."[34] These two views maintain that because business has a reservoir of management talent, functional expertise, and capital, and because so many others have tried and failed to solve general social problems, business should be given a chance. These arguments have some merit, because there are some social problems that can be handled, in the final analysis, only by business. Examples include creating a fair workplace, providing safe products, and engaging in fair advertising. Admittedly, government can and does assume a role in these areas, but business also has responsibility for the decisions.

Proacting versus Reacting.   Another argument supporting CSR is that "proacting is better than reacting." This position holds that proacting (anticipating and initiating) is more practical and less costly than simply reacting to problems that have already occurred. Environmental pollution is a good example, particularly business's experience with attempting to clean up rivers, lakes, and other waterways that have been neglected for decades. A wiser step would have been to prevent environmental deterioration in the first place. Proaction is the basic idea that undergirds the notion of sustainable development.

Public Support.   A final argument in favor of CSR is that the public strongly supports it.[35] A *BusinessWeek*/Harris poll revealed that a stunning 95 percent of the public believes that companies should not only focus on profits for shareholders but should also be responsible toward their workers and communities, even if making things better for workers and communities requires companies to sacrifice some profits.[36]

The Business Case for CSR

After considering the pros and cons of CSR, most businesses and managers today embrace the idea. In recent years, the "business case" for CSR has been unfolding.[37] The business case reflects why businesspeople believe that CSR brings distinct benefits or advantages to their organizations and the business community. In this argument, CSR directly benefits the "bottom-line." The astute business guru, Michael Porter, perhaps the most listened to and respected consultant today in upper-level management circles and boardrooms, has pointed out how corporate and social initiatives are intertwined. According to Porter, "Today's companies ought to invest in corporate social responsibility as part of their business strategy to become more competitive." In a competitive context, "the company's social initiatives—or its philanthropy—can have great impact. Not only for the company but also for the local society."[38]

In his insightful book, *The Civil Corporation*, Simon Zadek has identified four ways in which firms respond to CSR pressures, and he holds that these form a composite business case for CSR. His four approaches are as follows:[39]

1. *Defensive approach.* This is an approach designed to alleviate pain. Companies will do what they have to do to avoid pressure that makes them incur costs.
2. *Cost–benefit approach.* This traditional approach holds that firms will undertake those activities if they can identify direct benefits that exceeds costs.
3. *Strategic approach.* In this approach, firms will recognize the changing environment and engage with CSR as part of a deliberate emergent strategy.
4. *Innovation and learning approach.* In this approach, an active engagement with CSR provides new opportunities to understand the marketplace and enhances organizational learning, which leads to competitive advantage.

Companies may vary as to why they pursue a CSR strategy, but these approaches, taken together, build a strong business rationale for the pursuit of socially responsible business. Figure 2-5 summarizes the business case (reasons and benefits) for CSR taken from two different sources.

FIGURE 2-5 The Business Case for CSR

Top 10 Reasons Companies Are Becoming More Socially Responsible:

Reason	Percentage of Respondents Agreeing
Enhanced reputation	90
Competitive advantages	75
Cost savings	73
Industry trends	62
CEO or board commitment	58
Customer demand	57
SRI demand	42
Topline growth	37
Shareholder demand	20
Access to capital	12

Benefits of Social Responsibility	
"How do you think companies benefit from fulfilling their social responsibilities?" (Please choose a maximum of three alternatives, shown here as percentages of respondents naming item.)	
A better public image or reputation	75
Greater customer loyalty	51
A more satisfied and productive workforce	37
Fewer regulatory or legal problems	37
Long-term viability in the marketplace	36
A stronger and healthier community	34
Increased revenue	6
Lower cost of capital	2
No benefit	2
Easier access to foreign markets	2

Sources: Top 10 Reasons: PricewaterhouseCoopers 2002 *Sustainability Survey Report*, reported in "Corporate America's Social Conscience," *Fortune* (May 26, 2003), S8. © PricewaterhouseCoopers LLP. Benefits of SR: The Aspen Institute, Business and Society Program, "Where Will They Lead? 2003 MBA Student Attitudes about Business & Society" (May 2003), http://www.aspenbsp.org.

ETHICS IN PRACTICE CASE

The Socially Responsible Shoe Company

When Blake Mycoskie was on a visit to Argentina in 2006, a bright idea struck him. He was wearing *alpargatas*—resilient, lightweight, canvas slip-ons—shoes typically worn by Argentinian farmworkers, during his visit to poor villages where many of the residents had no shoes at all. He formulated the plan to start a shoe company and give away a pair of shoes to some needy child or person for every shoe the company sold. This became the basic mission of his company.

Initially, Blake had to self-finance his company. He decided to name his company *Toms: Shoes for Tomorrow*. Blake is from Texas, and he likes to read books about such business success stories as those of Ted Turner, Richard Branson, and Sam Walton. He appends the following message to his e-mails: "Disclaimer: you will not win the rat race wearing Toms."

In the summer of 2006, he unveiled his first collection of Toms shoes. Stores such as American Rag and Fred Segal in Los Angeles, and Scoop in New York, started stocking his shoes. By fall, the company had sold 10,000 pairs and he was off to the Argentinian countryside, along with several volunteers, to give away 10,000 pairs of shoes. In an article in *Time* magazine, Blake was quoted as saying, "I always thought I'd spend the first half of my life making money and the

second half giving it away. I never thought I could do both at the same time."

By February 2007, Blake's company had orders from 300 stores for 41,000 of his spring and summer collection of shoes, and he had big plans to go international by entering markets in Japan, Australia, Canada, France, and Spain in the summer of 2008. The company is also planning to introduce a line of children's shoes called *Tiny Toms*. Another shoe drop is planned for Argentina, with future trips targeting Asia and Africa.

1. How would you assess Toms's CSR using the four-part CSR definition? Is the company based on the typical business case for CSR or more of an ethical or philanthropic model?

2. Do you believe Blake's twin goal of economic and social obligations is compatible in the long term and at the current level? Review the company's Web site to see additional information: http://www.tomsshoes.com/.

3. What challenges do you foresee for the company's future?

Sources: Nadia Mustafa, "A Shoe That Fits So Many Souls," *Time* (February 5, 2007), C2; "Good Guy of the Month," *The Oprah Magazine*, February 1, 2007; *Elle*, December 1, 2006, Toms Shoes Web site: http://www.toms.com/. Accessed July 5, 2010.

Corporate Social Responsiveness

We have discussed the progress of CSR, a definitional model for understanding CSR, and the arguments for and against it. It is now worthwhile to consider a related idea that has arisen over the distinction between the terms *responsibility* and *responsiveness*. **Corporate social responsiveness** is depicted as an *action-oriented* variant of CSR.

A general argument that has generated much discussion holds that the term "responsibility" is too suggestive of efforts to pinpoint accountability or obligation. Therefore, it is not dynamic enough to fully describe business's willingness and activity—apart from obligation—to respond to social demands. For example, Ackerman and Bauer criticized CSR by stating, "The connotation of 'responsibility' is that of the process of assuming an obligation. It places an emphasis on motivation rather than on performance." They go on to say, "Responding to social demands is much more than deciding what to do. There remains the management task of doing what one has decided to do, and this task is far from trivial."[40] They argue that "social responsiveness" is a more appropriate description of what is essential in the social arena.

Their point has merit. *Responsibility*, taken quite literally, does imply more of a state or condition of having assumed an obligation, whereas *responsiveness* connotes a dynamic, action-oriented condition. We should not overlook, however, that much of what business

FIGURE 2-6
Alternative Views of Corporate Social Responsiveness

Sethi's Three-Stage Schema

Sethi proposes a three-stage schema for classifying corporate behavior: social obligation, social responsibility, and social *responsiveness*. Social responsiveness suggests that what is important is that corporations be "anticipatory" and "preventive." This third stage is concerned with business's long-term role in a dynamic social system.

Frederick's CSR$_1$, CSR$_2$, and CSR$_3$

CSR$_1$ refers to the traditional, *accountability* concept of CSR. CSR$_2$ is *responsiveness* focused. It refers to the capacity of a corporation to *respond* to social pressures. It involves the literal act of responding to, or achieving, a responsive posture to society. It addresses the mechanisms, procedures, arrangements, and patterns by which business responds to social pressures. CSR$_3$ refers to corporate social rectitude, which is concerned with the moral correctness of the actions or policies taken. CSR$_3$ integrates business ethics into responsiveness.

Epstein's Process View

Responsiveness is a part of the corporate social policy process. The emphasis is on the *process* aspect of social responsiveness. It focuses on both individual and organizational processes "for determining, implementing, and evaluating the firm's capacity to anticipate, respond to, and manage the issues and problems arising from the diverse claims and expectations of internal and external stakeholders."

Sources: S. Prakash Sethi, "Dimensions of Corporate Social Performance: An Analytical Framework," *California Management Review* (Spring 1975), 58–64; William C. Frederick, "From CSR1 to CSR2: The Maturing of Business-and-Society Thought," Working Paper No. 279 (Graduate School of Business, University of Pittsburgh, 1978). See also William Frederick, *Business and Society* (Vol. 33, No. 2, August 1994), 150–164; and Edwin M. Epstein, "The Corporate Social Policy Process: Beyond Business Ethics, Corporate Social Responsibility and Corporate Social Responsiveness," *California Management Review* (Vol. 29, No. 3, 1987), 104.

has done and is doing has resulted from a particular motivation—an assumption of obligation—whether assigned by government, forced by special-interest groups, or voluntarily assumed. Perhaps business, in some instances, has failed to accept and internalize the obligation, and thus it may seem odd to refer to it as a responsibility. Nevertheless, some motivation that led to social responsiveness had to be there, even though in some cases it was not articulated to be a responsibility or an obligation. Figure 2-6 summarizes other experts' views regarding corporate social *responsiveness*.

Thus, the corporate social responsiveness dimension that has been discussed by some as an alternative focus to that of social responsibility is, in actuality, an *action phase* of management's response in the social sphere. The responsiveness orientation enables organizations to justify and apply their social responsibilities without getting bogged down in the quagmire of accountability, which can so easily happen if organizations try to derive an exact determination of what their true responsibilities are before they take any action.

In an interesting study of social responsiveness among Canadian and Finnish forestry firms, researchers concluded that the social responsiveness of a corporation will proceed through a predictable series of phases and that managers will tend to respond to the most powerful stakeholders.[41] This study demonstrates that social responsiveness is a *process* and that stakeholder *power*, in addition to a sense of responsibility, may sometimes drive the process.

Corporate Social Performance

For many years now, there has been a trend toward making the concern for social and ethical issues more and more *practical and tangible*. The responsiveness thrust was a part of this trend. It is possible to integrate these concerns into a **corporate social performance (CSP) model**. The performance focus is intended to suggest that what really matters is what companies are able to accomplish—the results or outcomes of their acceptance of social responsibility and the adoption of a responsiveness philosophy. Performance is a bottom-line concept. In developing a conceptual framework for CSP, we not only have to specify the nature (economic, legal, ethical, or philanthropic) of the responsibility, but also need to identify a particular philosophy, pattern, mode, or strategy of responsiveness. Finally, we need to identify the stakeholder issues or topical areas to which these responsibilities are manifested and applied. The issues, and especially the degree of organizational interest in the issues, are always in a state of flux. As times change, so does the emphasis on the range of social or ethical issues that business must address.

Also of interest is that businesses' concerns toward particular issues vary depending on the industry in which they exist as well as other factors. A bank, for example, is not as pressed about environmental issues as a manufacturer. Likewise, a manufacturer is considerably more concerned with the issue of environmental protection than is an insurance company.

Carroll's CSP Model

Figure 2-7 illustrates Carroll's CSP model, which brings together the three major dimensions in a graphical depiction:

1. Social responsibility categories—economic, legal, ethical, and discretionary (philanthropic).

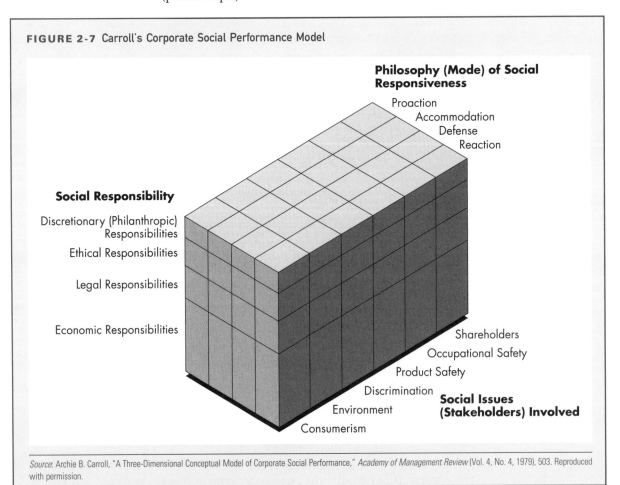

FIGURE 2-7 Carroll's Corporate Social Performance Model

Source: Archie B. Carroll, "A Three-Dimensional Conceptual Model of Corporate Social Performance," Academy of Management Review (Vol. 4, No. 4, 1979), 503. Reproduced with permission.

2. Philosophy (or mode) of social responsiveness—ranging from reaction, defense, accommodation, and proaction.
3. Social (or stakeholder) issues involved—consumers, environment, employees, and others.[42]

The first dimension of this model pertains to all that is included in our definition of social responsibility—the economic, legal, ethical, and discretionary (philanthropic) components. The second is a social responsiveness continuum or dimension. Although some writers have suggested that this is the preferable orientation when one considers social responsibility, the model in Figure 2-7 suggests that responsiveness is just one additional aspect to be addressed if CSP is to be achieved. The third dimension concerns the scope or range of social or stakeholder issues (e.g., consumerism, environment, product safety, and discrimination) that management must address in the first two dimensions.

The CSP model is intended to be useful to both academics and managers. For academics, the model is primarily a conceptual aid to understanding the distinctions among the concepts of CSR that have appeared in the literature. What was previously regarded as separate definitions of CSR are treated here as three separate aspects pertaining to CSP. The model's major use to the academic, therefore, is in helping to organize the important concepts that must be understood in an effort to clarify the CSP concept. The model is a modest but useful step toward understanding the major facets of CSP.

The conceptual model can assist managers in understanding that social responsibility is not separate and distinct from economic performance. The model integrates economic concerns into a social performance framework. In addition, it places ethical and philanthropic expectations into a rational economic and legal framework. The model can help the manager systematically think through major stakeholder issues. Although it does not provide the answer to how far the organization should go, it does provide a framework that could lead to better-managed social performance. Moreover, the model could be used as a planning and diagnostic problem-solving tool. It can assist the manager by identifying categories within which the organization and its decisions can be situated.

There have been several extensions, reformulations, or reorientations of the CSP model. Figure 2-8 summarizes some of these. Figure 2-9 depicts Wartick and Cochran's CSP model extensions, which help flesh out some important details.

Corporate Citizenship

Business practitioners and academics alike have grown fond of the term "corporate citizenship" in reference to businesses' CSR and CSP. Earlier in the chapter, we stated that corporate citizenship is a collective term embracing the concepts of *corporate social responsibility, responsiveness,* and *performance*, which have also been described earlier in the text. However, we can probe further and ask whether it has a meaning distinct from these concepts. A careful look at the concept and its literature shows that although it is a useful and attractive term, it is not distinct from the terminologies, except in the eyes of some writers who have attempted to give it a specific, narrow meaning. Nevertheless, it is a popular term and one worth exploring.

If one thinks about companies as "citizens" of the countries in which they reside, corporate citizenship just means that these companies have certain responsibilities they must fulfill in order to be perceived as good corporate citizens. One view is that "corporate citizenship is not a new concept, but one whose time has come."[43] In today's global business environment, some have argued that multinational enterprises are citizens of the world. Windsor has argued that corporate citizenship has become an important

FIGURE 2-8

Corporate Social Performance: Extensions, Reformulations, Reorientations

Wartick and Cochran's CSP Extensions

Wartick and Cochran proposed several changes/extensions to the CSP model. They proposed that the "social issues" dimension had matured into a new management field known as "social issues management." They extended the CSP model further by proposing that the three dimensions be viewed as depicting *principles* (corporate social responsibilities, reflecting a philosophical orientation), *processes* (corporate social responsiveness, reflecting an institutional orientation), and *policies* (social issues management, reflecting an organizational orientation).

Wood's Reformulated CSP Model

Wood elaborated and reformulated Carroll's model and Wartick and Cochran's extensions and set forth a reformulated model. Her definition of corporate social performance was "A business organization's configuration of principles of social responsibility, processes of social responsiveness, and policies, programs, and other observable outcomes as they relate to the firm's societal relationships." She took this definition further by proposing that each of the three components—principles, processes, and outcomes—is composed of specific elements.

Swanson's Reorientation of CSP

Swanson elaborated on the dynamic nature of the principles, processes, and outcomes reformulated by Wood. Relying on research from corporate culture, her reoriented model links CSP to the personally held values and ethics of executive managers and other employees. She proposed that the executive's sense of morality highly influences the policies and programs of environmental assessment, stakeholder management, and issues management, carried out by employees. These internal processes are means by which organizations can impact society through *economizing* (efficiently converting inputs into outputs) and *ecologizing* (forging community-minded collaborations).

Sources: Steven L. Wartick and Philip L. Cochran, "The Evolution of the Corporate Social Performance Model," *Academy of Management Review* (Vol. 10, 1985), 765–766; Donna J. Wood, "Corporate Social Performance Revisited," *Academy of Management Review* (October 1991), 691–718; D. L. Swanson, "Addressing a Theoretical Problem by Reorienting the Corporate Social Performance Model," *Academy of Management Review* (Vol. 20, No. 1, 1995), 43–64; D. L. Swanson, "Toward an Integrative Theory of Business and Society: A Research Strategy for Corporate Social Performance," *Academy of Management Review* (Vol. 24, No. 3, 1999), 596–521.

FIGURE 2-9 Wartick and Cochran's Corporate Social Performance Model Extensions

Principles	Processes	Policies
Corporate Social Responsibilities	**Corporate Social Responsiveness**	**Social Issues Management**
(1) Economic	(1) Reactive	(1) Issues Identification
(2) Legal	(2) Defensive	(2) Issues Analysis
(3) Ethical	(3) Accommodative	(3) Response Development
(4) Discretionary	(4) Proactive	
Directed at	Directed at	Directed at
(1) The Social Contract of Business	(1) The Capacity to Respond to Changing Societal Conditions	(1) Minimizing "Surprises"
(2) Business as a Moral Agent	(2) Managerial Approaches to Developing Responses	(2) Determining Effective Corporate Social Policies
Philosophical Orientation	Institutional Orientation	Organizational Orientation

Source: Steven L. Wartick and Philip L. Cochran, "The Evolution of the Corporate Social Performance Model," *Academy of Management Review* (Vol. 10, 1985), 767.

practitioner-based movement and that it conveys a sense of responsibility for social impacts or a sense of neighborliness in local communities.[44]

Broad Views

Corporate citizenship has been described by some as a broad, encompassing term that basically embraces all that is implied in the concepts of social responsibility, responsiveness, and performance. Corporate citizenship has been defined as "serving a variety of stakeholders well."[45] Fombrun proposes a broad conception. He holds that corporate citizenship is composed of a three-part view that encompasses (1) a reflection of shared moral and ethical principles, (2) a vehicle for integrating individuals into the communities in which they work, and (3) a form of enlightened self-interest that balances all stakeholders' claims and enhances a company's long-term value.[46]

Davenport's research also resulted in a broad definition of corporate citizenship that includes a commitment to ethical business behavior and balancing the needs of stakeholders, while working to protect the environment.[47] Carroll has recast his four categories of CSR as embracing the "four faces of corporate citizenship,"—economic, legal, ethical, and philanthropic. Each face, aspect, or responsibility reveals an important facet that contributes to the whole. He suggests that "just as private citizens are expected to fulfill these responsibilities, companies are as well."[48]

Narrow Views

At the narrow end of the spectrum, Altman speaks of corporate citizenship in terms of "corporate community relations." In this view, it embraces the functions through which business intentionally interacts with nonprofit organizations, citizen groups, and other stakeholders at the community level.[49] Other definitions of corporate citizenship fall between these broad and narrow perspectives, and some refer to global corporate citizenship as well, because increasingly companies are expected to conduct themselves appropriately wherever they do business.[50]

Drivers of Corporate Citizenship

A pertinent question is, "What drives companies to embrace corporate citizenship?" According to one major survey, both internal (to the companies) motivators and external pressures drive companies toward corporate citizenship.[51]

Internal motivators include:	*External pressures* include:
Traditions and values	Customers and consumers
Reputation and image	Expectations in the community
Business strategy	Laws and political pressures
Recruiting or retaining employees	

Benefits of Corporate Citizenship

The benefits of good corporate citizenship to stakeholders are readily apparent. But what are the benefits of good corporate citizenship to business itself? Following are the benefits of corporate citizenship to companies, defined broadly:[52]

- Improved employee relations (e.g., improves employee recruitment, retention, morale, loyalty, motivation, and productivity)
- Improved customer relationships (e.g., increases customer loyalty, acts as a tiebreaker for consumer purchasing, and enhances brand image)
- Improved business performance (e.g., positively impacts bottom-line returns, increases competitive advantage, and encourages cross-functional integration)

- Enhanced company's marketing efforts (e.g., helps create a positive company image, helps a company manage its reputation, supports higher prestige pricing, and enhances government affairs activities)

Stages of Corporate Citizenship

Like individual development, companies develop and grow in their maturity for dealing with corporate citizenship issues. A major contribution to how this growth occurs has been presented by Philip Mirvis and Bradley Googins at the Center for Corporate Citizenship at Boston College. The center holds that the essence of corporate citizenship is how companies deliver on their core values in a way that minimizes harm, maximizes benefits, is accountable and responsive to key stakeholders, and supports strong financial results.[53] This definition is quite compatible with the four-part definition of CSR presented earlier. They present the **stages of corporate citizenship** model to explain their points.

The development of corporate citizenship, in the center's model, reflects a stage-by-stage process in which seven dimensions (citizenship concept, strategic intent, leadership, structure, issues management, stakeholder relationships, and transparency) evolve as they move through five stages, and companies become more sophisticated in their approaches to corporate citizenship. This is a five-stage model beginning with Stage 1, which is Elementary, and growing toward Stage 5, which is Transforming.

As seen in Figure 2-10, the citizenship concept starts with an emphasis on "jobs, profits, and taxes" in Stage 1 and progresses through several emphases such as "philanthropy, environmental protection," "stakeholder management," "sustainability or triple bottom-line," and, finally, "change the game." Similarly, the other vital dimensions change orientations as they evolve through the five stages.

Another aspect of the five stages is that companies face different developmental *challenges* at each stage. Thus, in Stage 1 the challenge is to "gain credibility." As the companies grow toward Stage 5, the challenges are to build capacity, create coherence, and deepen commitment. Figure 2-11 graphically depicts the developmental challenges that trigger the movement of corporate citizenship through the five stages of growth.

Mirvis and Googins provide company examples that illustrate the various stages. GE is pictured as a company coming to the realization in Stage 1 that it must extend its emphases beyond financial success. Chiquita, Nestlé, and Shell Oil are depicted as companies becoming engaged in Stage 2. In Stage 3, Baxter International and ABB are identified as innovative companies striving to create coherence. BP's commitment to sustainability is provided as an example of Stage 4, where the theme is integration. Finally, the experiences of Unilever, widely noted for its socioeconomic investments in emerging markets, is presented as a company at Stage 5, with an emphasis on transformation in its corporate citizenship.

The stages of corporate citizenship framework effectively presents the challenges of credibility, capacity, coherence, and commitment that firms move through as they come to grips with developing more comprehensive and integrated citizenship agendas. From their work, it is apparent that corporate citizenship is not a static position but is one that progresses through different themes and challenges as firms get better and better over time.[54]

The terminology and concepts of corporate citizenship are especially attractive because they resonate so well with the business community's attempts to describe its own socially responsive activities and practices. Therefore, we can expect this concept to be around for some years to come. When we refer to CSR, social responsiveness,

FIGURE 2-10 Stages of Corporate Citizenship

Stages of Corporate Citizenship

BOSTON COLLEGE
CARROLL SCHOOL OF MANAGEMENT
Center for Corporate Citizenship

Dimensions	Stage 1: Elementary	Stage 2: Engaged	Stage 3: Innovative	Stage 4: Integrated	Stage 5: Transforming
Citizenship Concept	Jobs, Profits & Taxes	Philanthropy, Environmental Protection	Stakeholder Management	Sustainability or Triple Bottom Line	Change the Game
Strategic Intent	Legal Compliance	License to Operate	Business Case	Value Proposition	Market Creation or Social Change
Leadership	Lip Service, Out of Touch	Supporter, In the Loop	Steward, On Top of It	Champion, In Front of It	Visionary, Ahead of the Pack
Structural	Marginal: Staff Driven	Functional Ownership	Cross-Functional Coordination	Organizational Alignment	Mainstream: Business Driven
Issues Management	Defensive	Reactive, Policies	Responsive, Programs	Pro-Active, Systems	Defining
Stakeholder Relationships	Unilateral	Interactive	Mutual Influence	Partnership Alliance	Multi-Organization
Transparency	Flank Protection	Public Relations	Public Reporting	Assurance	Full Disclosure

Source: Philip Mirvis and Bradley K. Googins, *Stages of Corporate Citizenship.* A Boston: Carroll School of Management's Center for Corporate Citizenship at Boston College Monograph, 2006, p. 3. Used with permission.

and social performance, we are also embracing activities, programs, and practices that would typically fall under the purview of a firm's corporate citizenship.[55]

In addition to CSR and corporate citizenship, related concepts that have competed to become central terms in the field include *business ethics, stakeholder management, and sustainability.* These five concepts are overlapping and complementary and they each have attributes that help reveal vital dimensions of interest in the pursuit of a common core in the business and society field.[56] All of these topics will be discussed fully throughout the book.

Global Corporate Citizenship

Global CSR and **global corporate citizenship** are topics that are becoming more relevant with each passing year. As global capitalism increasingly becomes the marketplace stage for large- and medium-sized companies, the expectations that they address citizenship issues at a world level also multiply. Chapter 10 examines global business ethics in detail. Here, we state briefly that there are also challenges for global CSR and citizenship. For

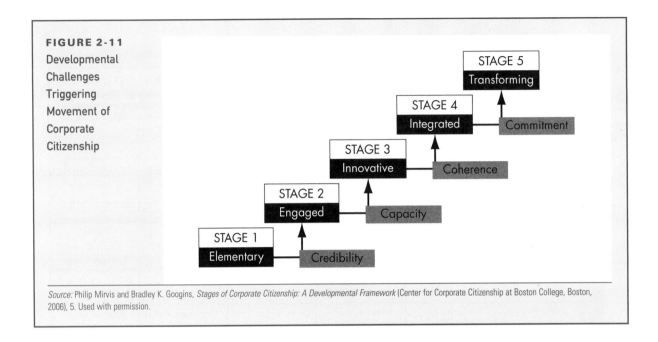

FIGURE 2-11

Developmental Challenges Triggering Movement of Corporate Citizenship

Source: Philip Mirvis and Bradley K. Googins, *Stages of Corporate Citizenship: A Developmental Framework* (Center for Corporate Citizenship at Boston College, Boston, 2006), 5. Used with permission.

the most part, these are international extensions of the concepts treated throughout this book. Because cultures have features that are both divergent and common, however, adaptations of traditional CSR and corporate citizenship concepts often are necessary.

There are two aspects of the global emphasis worthy of mention. First, U.S.-based and other multinational enterprises from countries around the world are expected to be good corporate citizens in the countries in which they are doing business. Further, they are expected to tailor as carefully as possible their citizenship initiatives to conform to the cultural environment in which they find themselves. Second, it is important to note that academics and businesspeople around the world are now doing research on and advocating CSR and corporate citizenship concepts. In fact, there has been a virtual explosion of interest in these topics, especially in the United Kingdom, Europe, and Australia/New Zealand, but also in Asia and South America. Of course, these two points are related to one another because academic interest is sparked by business interest and help to explain the growing appeal of the topic.

Two items illustrate the kind of thinking behind the idea of global corporate citizenship. First is a definition of a global business citizen presented in a recent book on the topic:

> *A global business citizen is a business enterprise (including its managers) that responsibly exercises its rights and implements its duties to individuals, stakeholders, and societies within and across national and cultural borders.*[57]

This view of a global business citizen is consistent with the discussions of this topic from a domestic perspective, but points to its expanded application across national and cultural borders. With this working definition, we can see how the citizenship concepts presented in this chapter could be naturally expanded to embrace multinational enterprises.

A second illustration of the global reach is provided by a distinction between frameworks for understanding CSR in America versus in Europe, especially the United Kingdom. This distinction illustrates how CSR around the world has a lot in common, but we must consider the specific, national contexts to fully grasp the topic. Dirk Matten and Jeremy Moon maintain that CSR is more "explicit" in America whereas it is more "implicit" in Europe. In their distinctions, they hold that explicit CSR would normally consist of voluntary, self-interest driven policies, programs, and strategies as is typical in U.S.-based understandings of CSR. By contrast, implicit CSR would embrace the entirety of a country's formal and informal institutions that assign corporations an agreed upon share of responsibility for society's concerns. Implicit CSR, such as that seen in the United Kingdom and Europe, would embrace the values, norms, and rules evident in the local culture.[58] The authors seem to be saying that CSR is more implicit, or understood, in Europe because it is more a part of the culture than in the United States. In Europe, some aspects of CSR are more or less decreed or imposed by institutions, such as government, whereas in the United States it is more voluntary, often pressured, and driven by companies' specific, explicit, actions.

In short, although CSR and corporate citizenship have much in common in terms of their applicability around the world and in diverse countries, cultural differences may also exist, which might suggest divergent or dissimilar themes depending on where business is being conducted. As the world economic stage becomes more of a common environment within which businesses function, convergence in CSR approaches seems predictable.

Business's Interest in Corporate Citizenship

Although there has been considerable academic research on the subjects of CSP and corporate citizenship over the past decades, we should stress that academics are not the only ones interested in this topic. Prominent business organizations and periodicals that report on corporate citizenship and social performance and provide awards for company social performance include *Fortune* magazine, the Conference Board, *CR* magazine, and the U.S. Chamber of Commerce. In addition, there are many other business groups with a keen interest in the topic.

Fortune's Rankings of "Most Admired" and "Least Admired" Companies

For many years now, *Fortune* magazine has conducted rankings of "America's Most Admired Companies" and has included among their "Eight Key Attributes of Reputation" the category of performance titled "Social Responsibility." The rankings are the result of a poll of more than 12,600 senior executives, outside directors, and financial analysts. In the social responsibility category, the recent most admired firms were International Paper, UPS, Starbucks, Fortune Brands, and Walt Disney.[59] In a related vein, *Fortune* also publishes "The 1000 Best Companies to Work For," on an annual basis. Most recently, the top-rated employers were Valero Energy, Microsoft, Goldman Sachs, Cisco Systems, and FedEx.[60] It is not clear what specific impact the *Fortune* rankings have on these businesses, but surely they have some positive impact on the firms' general reputations. The important point to note here, however, is that the social responsibility category is one major indicator of corporate citizenship and that it was included as a criterion of admired companies by one of the country's leading business magazines.

The Conference Board's Ron Brown Award for Corporate Leadership

The Conference Board, a business association, gives an annual award titled the "Ron Brown Award for Corporate Leadership." The award is the only presidential award to honor companies for the exemplary quality of their relationships with employees and communities. This annual award is presented to companies that have demonstrated a deep commitment to innovative initiatives that not only empower employees and communities but also advance strategic business interests. It expects that this award will promote practices that improve business performance by supporting employees and communities. The award is presented at an annual White House ceremony, amid media coverage that ensures greater public awareness of the accomplishments being honored. For company programs to be eligible, they must

- Be at the "best practice" level—distinctive, innovative, and effective.
- Have a significant, measurable impact on the people they are designed to serve.
- Offer broad potential for social and economic benefits for the U.S. society.
- Be sustainable and feasible within a business environment and mission.
- Be adaptable to other businesses and communities.

Recent recipients of the Ron Brown Award were Exelon, Northrop Grumman Corporation, and Procter & Gamble.

CR Magazine Awards

For many years, *Business Ethics* magazine published its list of Annual Business Corporate Citizenship Awards. The magazine is now called *CR, Corporate Responsibility*, and its top five winners for the year 2009 were Bristol Myers-Squibb, General Mills, IBM, Merck & Co., and HP Company. Awards are conferred for excellence in the following categories: environment, climate change, human rights, employee relations, philanthropy, financial, and lobbying.[61] Many firms today have corporate responsibility officers, and these individuals are charged with exerting CSR leadership in their respective companies.

U.S. Chamber of Commerce Corporate Citizenship Awards

Each year, through its Business Civic Leadership Center, the U.S. Chamber of Commerce awards its Corporate Citizenship Awards. These awards are designed to recognize leading business firms and their performance in the following four categories: U.S. Community Service Award, International Community Service Award, Partnership Award, and Corporate Stewardship Award. Recent award recipients include KPMG, Harris, Allstate, Coca-Cola, and Lilly.[62]

Social Performance and Financial Performance Relationship

An issue that surfaces frequently in considerations of CSR or CSP or citizenship is whether or not there is a demonstrable relationship between a firm's social responsibility or performance and its financial performance. Unfortunately, attempts to measure this relationship have typically been hampered by measurement problems. The appropriate performance criteria for measuring financial performance and social responsibility are subject to debate. Furthermore, the accurate measurement of social responsibility is difficult at best.

Over the years, many studies on the social responsibility–financial performance relationship have produced mixed results.[63] In a comprehensive meta-analysis, Orlitzky, Schmidt, and Rynes review 30 years of research on the relationship and support the conclusion that social and financial performance are positively related. The authors conclude their research by saying, "…portraying managers' choices with respect to CSP and CFP as an either/or trade-off is not justified in light of 30 years of empirical data."[64] In another recent study, Peloza has concluded that "there is a small, but positive relationship between corporate social performance and company financial performance."[65]

ETHICS IN PRACTICE CASE

Is There a Market for a Sustainable Hamburger?

According to *Forbes* magazine, Burgerville sells not only burgers but also good works. But if you don't live in Oregon or the State of Washington, you may have never heard about Burgerville, a company founded in 1961 in Vancouver, Washington. Today, there are 39 Burgerville restaurants spanning those two states.

In the 1990s, when Burgerville began losing sales of its burgers to the national chains, Chief Executive Tom Mears decided to differentiate his product, to sell "burgers with a soul." Mears, the son-in-law of the founder, decided to combine good food with good works. The company began to build its strategy around three key words: "fresh, local, and sustainable." It pursued this strategy through partnerships with local businesses, farms, and producers. In 2003, *Gourmet* magazine recognized Burgerville the home of the nation's freshest fast food.

According to the company Web site, "At Burgerville, doing business responsibly means doing business sustainably. One example of this is our commitment to purchasing 100 percent local wind power equal to the energy use of all our restaurants and corporate office." The company purchases its electricity from local windmills. Burgerville uses "sustainable agriculture," which means that their meat and produce are free from genetically modified seeds or livestock. In its cooking, the company avoids trans-fats, and once the cooking oils are used up, they are converted into biodiesel. The company buys its antibiotic- and hormone-free beef locally.

In addition to burgers, Burgerville offers a wild Coho salmon and Oregon Hazelnut Salad. Meals for children often come with seeds and gardening tools rather than the usual cheap toy offered at the national chains.

Burgerville extends its good works to its employees. The company pays 95 percent of the health insurance for its hundreds of workers. This adds $1.5 million to its annual compensation expense. To get its affordable health care, employees have to work a minimum of 20 hours a week for at least six months, a more generous arrangement than most provided by stores.

Being a good corporate citizen is expensive. Though the company won't reveal its financial bottom-line, one industry consultant estimated that its margin is closer to 10 percent compared with McDonald's 15 percent.

1. Is the world ready for a socially responsible hamburger? How much would you be willing to pay, assuming the burgers really taste good?
2. What tensions among its economic, legal, ethical, and philanthropic responsibilities do you think are most pressing to Burgerville?
3. Does Burgerville sound like a business that might work in Oregon and Washington, but maybe not elsewhere? What is the future of Burgerville?

Sources: "Fast Food: Want a Cause with That?" *Forbes* (January 8, 2007), 83. Also see the company Web site: http://burgerville.com/about-us/. Accessed July 5, 2010.

Three Perspectives on the Relationship

In understanding the research on the relationship between social and financial performance, it is important to note that there have been at least three different perspectives that have dominated these discussions and research.

Perspective 1. Perhaps the most popular view is the belief that socially responsible firms are more financially profitable. To those who advocate the concept of social performance, it is apparent why they would like to think that social performance is a driver of financial performance and, ultimately, a corporation's reputation. If it could be demonstrated that socially responsible firms, in general, are more financially successful and have better reputations, this would significantly bolster the CSP view, even in the eyes of its critics.

Perspective 1 has been studied extensively. The findings of many of the studies that have sought to demonstrate this relationship have been inconclusive. In spite of this, some studies have claimed to have successfully established this linkage. The most positive conclusion linking CSP with CFP were the two recent studies reported earlier in the text.[66]

Perspective 2.   This view, which has not been studied as extensively, argues that a firm's financial performance is a driver of its social performance. This perspective is built somewhat on the notion that social responsibility is a "fairweather" concept. That is, when times are good and companies are enjoying financial success, we witness higher levels of social performance. In their study, Preston and O'Bannon found the strongest evidence that financial performance either precedes or is contemporaneous with social performance. This evidence supports the view that social–financial performance correlations are best explained by positive synergies or by "available funding."[67]

Perspective 3.   This third perspective argues that there is an *interactive* relationship between and among social performance, financial performance, and corporate reputation. In this symbiotic view, the three major factors influence each other, and, because they are so interrelated, it is not easy to identify which factor is driving the process. Regardless of the perspective taken, each view advocates a significant role for CSP, and it is expected that researchers will continue to explore these perspectives for years to come. Figure 2-12 depicts the essentials of each of these views.

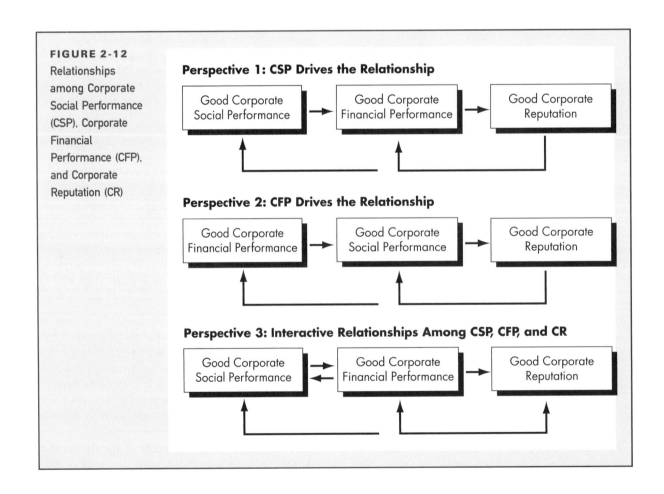

FIGURE 2-12
Relationships among Corporate Social Performance (CSP), Corporate Financial Performance (CFP), and Corporate Reputation (CR)

Perspective 1: CSP Drives the Relationship

Good Corporate Social Performance → Good Corporate Financial Performance → Good Corporate Reputation

Perspective 2: CFP Drives the Relationship

Good Corporate Financial Performance → Good Corporate Social Performance → Good Corporate Reputation

Perspective 3: Interactive Relationships Among CSP, CFP, and CR

Good Corporate Social Performance ⇄ Good Corporate Financial Performance → Good Corporate Reputation

Finally, it should be mentioned that a "contingency" view suggests that CSP should be seen as a function of the "fit" between specific strategies and structures and the nature of the social issue. According to this research, the social issue is determined by the expectational gaps between the firm and its stakeholders that occur within or between views of what is and/or ought to be, and high CSP is achieved by closing these expectational gaps with the appropriate strategy and structure.[68]

A Stakeholder–Bottom-Line Perspective

A basic premise of all these perspectives is that there is only one "bottom-line"—a corporate financial bottom-line—that addresses primarily the stockholders', or owners', investments in the firm. An alternative view is that the firm has "multiple bottom-lines" that benefit from CSP. This stakeholder–bottom-line perspective argues that the impacts or benefits of social performance cannot be fully measured or appreciated by considering only the impact on the firm's financial bottom-line.

To truly employ a stakeholder perspective, companies need to accept the multiple-bottom-line view as reflective of reality. Thus, CSP cannot be fully comprehended unless we also consider that its impacts on stakeholders, such as consumers, employees, the community, and other stakeholder groups, are recognized and measured. Research may never conclusively demonstrate a simple relationship between CSP and financial performance. If a stakeholder perspective is taken, however, it may be more straightforward to assess the impact of CSP on multiple stakeholders' bottom-lines.

The Triple Bottom-Line. A variant of the multiple-bottom-line perspective is popularly known as the "**triple bottom-line**" concept. The phrase *triple bottom-line* has been attributed to John Elkington. The concept seeks to encapsulate for business the three key spheres of **sustainability**—*economic, social,* and *environmental.* The "economic" bottom-line refers to the firm's creation of material wealth, including financial income and assets. The emphasis is on *profits.* The "social" bottom-line is about the quality of people's lives and about equity between people, communities, and nations. The emphasis is on *people.* The "environmental" bottom-line is about protection and conservation of the natural environment.[69] The emphasis is on the *planet.* It may easily be seen that these three topics are embodied in the Pyramid of CSR and represent a version of the stakeholder–bottom-line concept. At its narrowest, the term is used as a framework for measuring and reporting corporate performance in terms of economic, social, and environmental indicators. At its broadest, the concept is used to capture the whole set of values, issues, and processes that companies must address to minimize harm resulting from their activities and to create economic, social, and environmental value.[70] As a popular concept, it is a more detailed spelling out of the idea of CSP.

Corporate sustainability is the goal of the triple-bottom-line approach. The goal of sustainability is to create long-term shareholder value by taking advantage of opportunities and managing risks related to economic, environmental, and social developments. Leaders in this area try to take advantage of the market's demand for sustainable products and services while successfully reducing and avoiding sustainability costs and risks. To help achieve these goals, the Dow Jones Sustainability Indexes were created to monitor and assess the sustainability of corporations.[71] As we will observe throughout the book, the concept of sustainability overlaps considerably with other social responsibility concepts and terminology, but it has become so important in business and academic usage that it needs to be emphasized in various contexts.

Spotlight on SUSTAINABILITY

"Myths" about Sustainability

There are many misconceptions about sustainability. Often these misconceptions, or myths, serve as barriers to companies pursuing sustainable development. Myths about sustainability are eliminated when the experiences of leading companies are considered. Consultant Vijay Kanal offers insights running counter to some of these myths.

1. *Sustainability is a cost we can't afford right now.* Xerox CEO Anne Mulcahy said that being "a good corporate citizen" saved the company from bankruptcy.
2. *There's no money to be made from sustainability.* Johnson & Johnson has undertaken 80 sustainability projects since 2005 and achieved $187 million in savings with an ROI of nearly 19 percent, and rising.
3. *It's just for big companies.* Actually, smaller companies have an advantage because their competitiveness often depends on being lean, resourceful, and nimble, which sustainability makes possible.
4. *We'll be accused of greenwashing if we pursue sustainability.* Companies that set and achieve meaningful goals have the right to publicize their successes.
5. *Since we don't make things, we don't have to worry about the supply chain.* Walmart doesn't make things, but it is developing a supplier index for its thousands of suppliers to gauge the carbon impact from supplies they sell to the business.

Source: Vijay Kanal, "The Eight Biggest Myths about Sustainability in Business," November 23, 2009, GreenBiz.com, http://www. greenbiz.com/blog/2009/11/23/8-myths-about-sustainability-business?page=0%2C1. Accessed July 5, 2010.

Socially Responsible or Ethical Investing

Special-interest groups, business, the media, and academics are not alone in their interest in business's social performance. Investors are also interested. The **socially responsible or ethical investing** movement arrived on the scene in the 1970s and has continued to grow and prosper. By 2010, socially responsible investing (SRI) had matured into a comprehensive investing approach complete with social and environmental screens, shareholder activism, and community investment, accounting for over $2.7 trillion of investments in the United States, according to the Social Investment Forum.[72]

Historically, social responsibility investing can be traced back to the early 1900s, when church endowments refused to buy so-called "sin" stocks—then defined as shares in tobacco, alcohol, and gambling companies. During the Vietnam War era of the 1960s and early 1970s, antiwar investors refused to invest in defense contracting firms. In the early 1980s, universities, municipalities, and foundations sold off their shares of companies that had operations in South Africa to protest apartheid. By the 1990s, self-styled socially responsible investing came into its own.[73] In the 2000s, social investing began celebrating the fact that social or ethical investing is now part of the mainstream.

Socially conscious investments have been continuing to grow. However, managers of socially conscious funds do not use only ethical or social responsibility criteria to decide which companies to invest in. They consider a company's financial health before all else. Moreover, a growing corps of brokers, financial planners, and portfolio managers are available to help people evaluate investments for their social impacts.[74]

The concept of *social screening* is the backbone of the socially conscious investing movement. Investors seeking to put their money into socially responsible firms want to *screen out* those firms they consider to be socially irresponsible or to actively *screen in* those firms they think of as being socially responsible. Thus, there are negative social screens and positive social screens. Some of the *negative social screens* that have been used in recent years include the avoidance of investing in tobacco manufacturers, gambling casino operators, defense or weapons contractors, and firms doing business in South Africa.[75] In 1994, however, with the elimination of the official system of apartheid in South Africa, this was eliminated as a negative screen by many.

It is more difficult, and thus more challenging, to implement *positive social screens*, because they require the potential investor to make judgment calls as to what constitutes an acceptable or a strong level of social performance on social investment criteria. Criteria that may be used as either positive or negative screens, depending on the firm's performance, might include the firm's demonstrated record on issues such as equal employment opportunity and affirmative action, environmental sustainability, treatment of employees, corporate citizenship (broadly defined), and treatment of animals.

The experience of Pax World Funds, a socially responsible investor, illustrates how tricky social screening can be. When Starbucks introduced a coffee liqueur containing Jim Beam bourbon, Pax World Fund thought it had no choice but to sell its $23-million stake in Starbucks, even though it had long believed Starbucks to have a strong record of social responsibility. Pax World did divest of its Starbucks stock. In 2006, however, Pax World shareholders concluded that the company needed to eliminate its zero-tolerance policy on alcohol and gambling and they approved more flexible guidelines for the future. Under the new guidelines, the company would focus more on positive social screens, like a company's record on corporate governance, climate change, and other social issues.[76]

The financial performance of socially conscious funds shows that investors do not have to sacrifice profitability for principles. An increasing number of studies have demonstrated that socially responsible mutual funds perform competitively with non-CSR funds over time. The fast growth of socially conscious investing is the most convincing evidence that competitive returns are being achieved.[77] Over the past 20 years, the total dollars invested in SRI has grown exponentially, as has the number of institutional, professional, and individual investors involved in the field.

The Council on Economic Priorities has suggested that there are at least three reasons why there has been an upsurge in social or ethical investing:[78]

1. There is more reliable and sophisticated research on CSP than in the past.
2. Investment firms using social criteria have established a solid track record, and investors do not have to sacrifice gains for principles.
3. The socially conscious 1960s generation is now making investment decisions.

In recent years, as more and more employees are in charge of their own IRAs and 401(k)s, people have become much more sophisticated about making investment decisions than in the past. Further, more people are seeing social investments as a way in which they can exert their priorities concerning the balance of financial and social concerns.

Whether it be called social investing, ethical investing, or socially responsible investing, it is clear that social investing has "arrived" on the scene and has become a major part of the mainstream. Socially responsible investing is growing globally as well.[79] Socially conscious funds will continue to be debated in the investment community. The fact that they exist, have grown, and have prospered, however, provides evidence that the practice is a serious one and that there truly are investors in the real world who take the CSP issue quite seriously.

Summary

Corporate citizenship and corporate social responsibility, responsiveness, and performance are important and related concepts. The CSR concept has a rich history. It has grown out of many diverse views. A four-part conceptualization was presented that broadly conceives CSR as encompassing economic, legal, ethical, and philanthropic components. The four parts were also depicted as part of the Pyramid of CSR.

The concern for CSR has been expanded to include a concern for social responsiveness. The responsiveness theme suggests more of an action-oriented focus by which firms not only must address their basic obligations, but also must decide on basic strategies of responding to these obligations. A CSP model was presented that brought the responsibility and responsiveness dimensions together into a framework that also identified categories of social or stakeholder issues that must be considered. The identification of social issues has blossomed into a field now called "issues management" or "stakeholder management," which will be considered in more detail in later chapters.

The term "corporate citizenship" arrived on the scene to embrace a whole host of socially conscious activities and practices on the part of businesses. This term has become quite popular in the business community. It is not clear that the concept is distinctively different than the emphases on corporate social responsibility, responsiveness, and performance, but it is a terminology being more frequently used. A "stages of corporate citizenship" model was presented that depicted how companies progress and grow in their increasing sophistication and maturity in dealing with corporate citizenship issues.

The interest in CSR extends beyond the academic community. Business leaders are interested as well. On an annual basis, *Fortune* magazine polls executives on various dimensions of corporate performance; one major dimension is called "social responsibility." The Conference Board gives an Award for Corporate Leadership, and *CR* magazine recognizes outstanding "corporate citizens."

Finally, the socially responsible or ethical investing movement seems to be flourishing. This indicates that there is a growing body of investors who are sensitive to business's social and ethical (as well as financial) performance. Studies of the relationship between social responsibility and economic performance have not yielded consistent results, but some studies have shown a positive relationship between the two. In the final analysis, sound corporate social (stakeholder) performance is associated with a "multiple-bottom-line effect" in which a number of different stakeholder groups experience enhanced bottom-lines. The most well known of these effects is the popular "triple bottom-line," with emphases on economics (profits), society (people), and the environment (planet).

Key Terms

Business for Social Responsibility (BSR), p. 29

community obligations, p. 32

corporate citizenship, p. 30

corporate social performance (CSP) model, p. 45

corporate social responsibility, p. 30

corporate social responsiveness, p. 44

corporate sustainability, p. 57

economic responsibilities, p. 34

ethical responsibilities, p. 35

global corporate citizenship, p. 51

legal responsibilities, p. 34

paternalism, p. 32

philanthropic responsibilities, p. 36

philanthropy, p. 32

Pyramid of Corporate Social Responsibility (CSR), p. 37

socially responsible or ethical investing, p. 58

stages of corporate citizenship, p. 50

sustainability, p. 57

triple bottom-line, p. 57

Discussion Questions

1. Identify and explain the Pyramid of Corporate Social Responsibility. Provide several examples of each "layer" of the pyramid. Identify and discuss some of the tensions among the layers or components.

2. In your view, what is the single strongest argument *against* the idea of corporate social responsibility? What is the single strongest

argument *for* corporate social responsibility? Briefly explain.

3. Differentiate between corporate social responsibility and corporate social responsiveness. Give an example of each. How does corporate social performance relate to these terms? Where does corporate citizenship fit in?

4. Analyze how the triple bottom-line and the Pyramid of CSR are similar and different. Draw a schematic that shows how the two concepts relate to one another.

5. Do research on different companies and try to identify at which stage of corporate citizenship these companies reside. What are the best examples you can find of companies having achieved Stage 5 of corporate citizenship?

6. Does socially responsible or ethical investing seem to you to be a legitimate way in which the average citizen might demonstrate her or his concern for CSR? Discuss.

3

The Stakeholder Approach to Business, Society, and Ethics

CHAPTER LEARNING OUTCOMES

After studying this chapter, you should be able to:

1. Define stake and stakeholder, and describe the origins of these concepts.

2. Differentiate among the production, managerial, and stakeholder views of the firm.

3. Differentiate among the three values of the stakeholder model.

4. Explain the concept of stakeholder management.

5. Identify and describe the five major questions that capture the essence of stakeholder management.

6. Identify the three levels stakeholder management capability (SMC).

7. Describe the key principles of stakeholder management.

The business organization today, especially the modern corporation, is the institutional centerpiece of a complex society. Our society today consists of many people with a multitude of interests, expectations, and demands regarding what major organizations ought to provide to accommodate people's lives and lifestyles. We have seen business respond to the many expectations placed on it. We have seen an ever-changing social contract. We have seen many assorted legal, ethical, and philanthropic expectations and demands being met by organizations willing to change as long as the economic incentive was present and honored. What was once viewed as a specialized means of providing profit through the manufacture and distribution of goods and services has become a multipurpose social institution that many people and groups depend on for their livelihoods, prosperity, and fulfillment.

Even in recessionary times, we live in a society expecting a quality lifestyle, with more groups every day laying claims to their share of the good life. Business organizations today need to be responsive to individuals and groups they once viewed as powerless and unable to make such claims on them. We call these individuals and groups *stakeholders*. The stakeholder approach to management is an accepted framework that is constantly undergoing development, especially in the business-and-society arena. In the academic and business community, advances in stakeholder theory have illustrated the crucial development of the stakeholder concept.[1]

In terms of corporate application, a model for the "stakeholder corporation" has even been proposed. It has been argued that "stakeholder inclusion" is the key to company success in the 21st century.[2] A book titled *Stakeholder Power* presents a "winning plan for building stakeholder commitment and driving corporate growth."[3] Another titled *Redefining the Corporation: Stakeholder Management and Organizational Wealth* argues that the corporate model needs redefinition because of business size and socioeconomic power and the inadequacy of the "ownership" model and its implications.[4] Yet another, *Stakeholder Theory and Organizational Ethics*, has linked the stakeholder approach with business ethics, a topic of crucial interest in this book.[5]

An outgrowth of these developments is that it has become apparent that business organizations must address the legitimate needs and expectations of stakeholders if they want to be successful in the long run.[6] Business must also address stakeholders because it is the ethical course of action. They must also honor the stakeholders' expectations, claims, and rights. For sustainable development to become a reality, the stakeholder approach offers the best opportunity. It is for these reasons that the stakeholder concept and orientation have become central to the vocabulary and thinking in the study of business, society, and ethics.

Origins of the Stakeholder Concept

The stakeholder concept has become a key to understanding business and society relationships. The term stakeholder is a variant of the more familiar and traditional concept of *stockholders*—the investors in or owners of businesses. Just as an individual might own his or her own private house, automobile, or iPod, a stockholder owns a portion or a share of one or more businesses. Thus, a stockholder is also a type of stakeholder. However, stockholders are just one of many legitimate stakeholders that business and organizations must deal with today to be effective.

What Is the *Stake* in Stakeholder?

To appreciate the concept of stakeholders, it helps to understand the idea of a stake. A **stake** is an interest in or a share in an undertaking. If a group plans to go out to dinner and a movie for the evening, each person in the group has a stake, or interest, in the group's decision. No money has been spent yet, but each member sees his or her interests (preference, taste, priority) in the decision. A stake may also be a claim. A claim is a demand for something due or believed to be due. We can see clearly that an owner or a stockholder has an interest in and an ownership of a share of a business.

The idea of a stake can range from simply an interest in an undertaking at one extreme to a legal claim of ownership at the other. Between these extremes might be a "right" to something. It might be a legal right to certain treatment rather than a legal claim of ownership, such as that of a shareholder. Legal rights might include the right to fair treatment (e.g., not to be discriminated against) or the right to privacy (not to have one's privacy invaded or abridged). A right also might be thought of as a moral right, such as that expressed by an employee: "I've got a right not to be fired because I've worked here 30 years, and I've given this firm the best years of my life." Or a consumer might say, "I've got a right to a safe product after all I've paid for this."

As we have seen, stakes are of several different types. Figure 3-1 summarizes various categories or types of stakes.

What Is a Stakeholder?

It follows, then, that a **stakeholder** is an individual or a group that has one or more of the various kinds of stakes in the organization. Just as stakeholders may be *affected by* the actions, decisions, policies, or practices of the business firm, these stakeholders may also *affect* the organization's actions, decisions, policies, or practices. With stakeholders, therefore, there is a potential two-way interaction or exchange of influence. In short, a stakeholder may be thought of as "any individual or group who can affect or is affected

FIGURE 3-1 Types of Stakes

	An Interest	A Right	Ownership
Definitions	When a person or group will be affected by a decision, it has an interest in that decision.	(1) Legal Right: When a person or group has a legal claim to be treated in a certain way or to have a particular right protected.	When a person or group has a legal title to an asset or a property.
Examples	This plant closing will affect the community. This TV commercial demeans women, and I'm a woman. I'm concerned about the environment for future generations.	Employees expect due process, privacy; customers or creditors have certain legal rights.	"This company is mine. I founded it, and I own it," or "I own 1,000 shares of this corporation."
Definitions		(2) Moral Right: When a person or group thinks it has a moral or ethical right to be treated in a certain way or to have a particular right protected.	
Examples		Fairness, justice, equity.	

by the actions, decisions, policies, practices, or goals of the organization."[7] This definition is quite broad, but in this broad concept, the organization or decision maker is more likely to explore fully its social and ethical responsibilities than when using a narrower definition.

Who Are Business's Stakeholders?

In today's hypercompetitive, global business environment, any individuals and groups are business's stakeholders. From the business point of view, certain individuals and groups have more *legitimacy* in the eyes of the management; that is, they have a legitimate, direct interest in, or claim on, the operations of the firm. The most obvious of these groups are stockholders, employees, and customers. However, from the point of view of a highly pluralistic society, stakeholders include not only these groups, but other groups as well. These other groups include the community, competitors, suppliers, special-interest groups, the media, and society, or the public at large. Charles Holliday, former chairperson and CEO of DuPont, stated, "We have traditionally defined four stakeholder groups important to DuPont—shareholders, customers, employees, and society."[8] It has also been argued that the natural environment, nonhuman species, and future generations should be considered among business's important stakeholders.[9]

Three Views of the Firm: Production, Managerial, and Stakeholder

The advancement of the stakeholder concept parallels the growth and expansion of the business enterprise. In what has been termed the traditional **production view of the firm**, owners thought of stakeholders as only those individuals or groups that supplied resources or bought products or services.[10] Later, as we witnessed the growth of

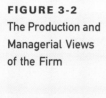

FIGURE 3-2
The Production and
Managerial Views
of the Firm

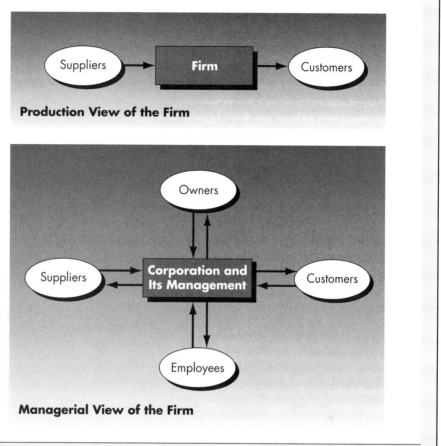

Source: From Freeman's *Strategic Management: A Stakeholder Approach,* Copyright © 1984 by R. Edward Freeman. Reprinted with permission from Pitman Publishing Company.

corporations and the resulting separation of ownership from control, business firms began to see their responsibilities toward other major constituent groups to be essential if they were to be successful. Thus, the **managerial view of the firm** emerged. Finally, as major internal and external changes occurred in business and its environment, managers were required to undergo a radical conceptual shift in how they perceived the firm and its multilateral relationships with constituent or stakeholder groups. The result was the **stakeholder view of the firm**.[11] In actual practice, however, some managers have not yet come to appreciate the need for the stakeholder view, but this is changing rapidly. Figure 3-2 depicts the evolution from the production view to the managerial view of the firm, and Figure 3-3 illustrates the stakeholder view of the firm. The stakeholder view encompasses many different individuals and groups that are embedded in the firm's internal and external environments.

In the stakeholder view of the firm, the management must perceive as stakeholders not only those groups that the management *thinks* have some stake in the firm but also those that themselves think or perceive they have a stake in the firm. This is an essential perspective that the management must take, at least until it has had a chance to weigh carefully the legitimacy of the claims and the power of various stakeholders. Of note is that each stakeholder group is composed of subgroups; for example, the government

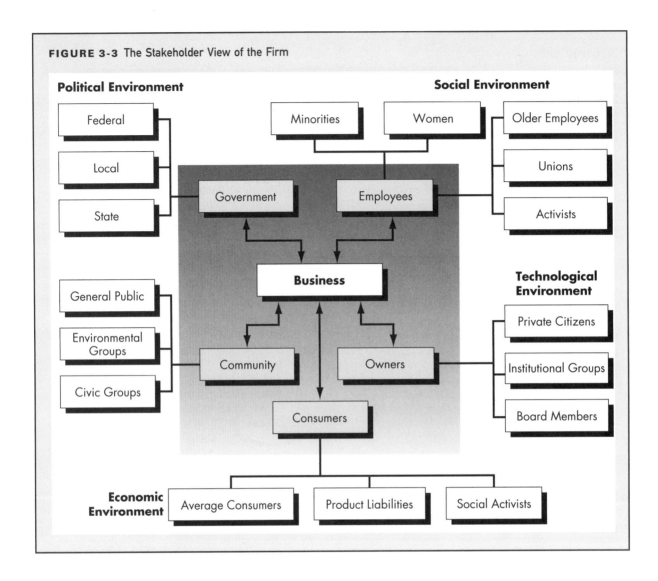

FIGURE 3-3 The Stakeholder View of the Firm

stakeholder group includes federal, state, and local government subgroups as stakeholders.

Primary and Secondary Stakeholders

A useful way to categorize stakeholders is to think of them as primary and secondary as well as social and nonsocial; thus, stakeholders may be thought of as follows:[12]

Primary social stakeholders include:

- Shareholders and investors
- Employees and managers
- Customers
- Local communities
- Suppliers and other business partners

Secondary social stakeholders include:

- Government and regulators
- Civic institutions
- Social pressure groups
- Media and academic commentators
- Trade bodies
- Competitors

Primary social stakeholders have a *direct* stake in the organization and its success and, therefore, are most influential. **Secondary social stakeholders** may be extremely influential as well, especially in affecting reputation and public standing, but their stake in the organization is more indirect. Therefore, a firm's responsibility toward secondary stakeholders may be lesser but is not avoidable. These groups may wield significant power and quite often represent legitimate public concerns that make it impossible for them to be ignored.[13]

Primary nonsocial stakeholders include:	*Secondary nonsocial* stakeholders include:
<ul><li>Natural environment</li><li>Future generations</li><li>Nonhuman species</li></ul>	<ul><li>Environmental interest groups (e.g., Friends of the Earth, Greenpeace, Rainforest Alliance)</li><li>Animal welfare organizations (e.g., People for the Ethical Treatment of Animals—PETA, American Society for the Prevention of Cruelty to Animals—ASPCA)</li></ul>

Secondary stakeholders can quickly become primary. This often occurs through the media or special-interest groups when a claim's urgency (as in a boycott or demonstration) takes precedence over its legitimacy. In today's business environment, the media have the power to instantaneously transform a stakeholder's status with its 24/7 coverage of the news. Thus, it may be useful to think of primary and secondary classes of stakeholders for discussion purposes, but we should understand how easily and quickly those categories can shift.

A Typology of Stakeholder Attributes: Legitimacy, Power, Urgency

How do managers decide which stakeholders deserve their attention? Stakeholders have attributes such as legitimacy, power, and urgency. A typology of stakeholders has been developed based on these three attributes.[14] When these three attributes are superimposed, as depicted in Figure 3-4, seven stakeholder categories may be seen.

The three attributes of legitimacy, power, and urgency help us see how stakeholders may be thought of and analyzed in these key terms. **Legitimacy** refers to the perceived validity or appropriateness of a stakeholder's claim to a stake. Therefore, owners, employees, and customers represent a high degree of legitimacy due to their explicit, formal, and direct relationships with a company. Stakeholders that are more distant from the firm, such as social activist groups, competitors, or the media, might be thought to have less legitimacy.

Power refers to the ability or capacity to produce an effect—to get something done that otherwise may not be done. Therefore, whether one has legitimacy or not, power means that the stakeholder could affect the business. For example, with the help of the media, a large, vocal, social activist group such as the People for the Ethical Treatment of Animals (PETA) could wield extraordinary power over a business firm. In recent years, PETA has been successful in influencing the practices and policies of virtually all the fast-food restaurants regarding their suppliers' treatment of chickens and cattle.

Urgency refers to the degree to which the stakeholder claim on the business calls for the business's immediate attention or response. Urgency may imply that something is critical—it really needs to get done. Or it may imply that something needs to be done immediately, or on a timely basis. A management group may perceive a union strike, a consumer boycott, or a social activist group picketing outside headquarters as urgent.

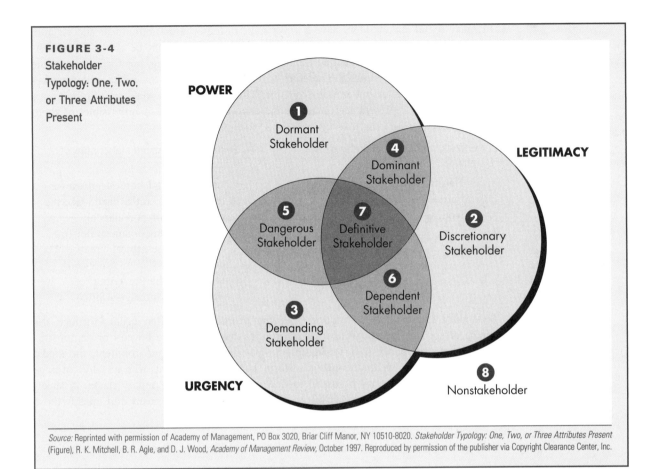

FIGURE 3-4
Stakeholder Typology: One, Two, or Three Attributes Present

POWER

① Dormant Stakeholder

④ Dominant Stakeholder

LEGITIMACY

⑤ Dangerous Stakeholder

⑦ Definitive Stakeholder

② Discretionary Stakeholder

⑥ Dependent Stakeholder

③ Demanding Stakeholder

URGENCY

⑧ Nonstakeholder

Source: Reprinted with permission of Academy of Management, PO Box 3020, Briar Cliff Manor, NY 10510-8020. *Stakeholder Typology: One, Two, or Three Attributes Present* (Figure), R. K. Mitchell, B. R. Agle, and D. J. Wood, *Academy of Management Review*, October 1997. Reproduced by permission of the publisher via Copyright Clearance Center, Inc.

Studies suggest that at least one other criterion should be considered in addition to legitimacy, power, and urgency—**proximity**.[15] The spatial distance between the organization and its stakeholders is a relevant consideration in evaluating stakeholders' importance and priority. Stakeholders that share the same physical space or are adjacent to the organization may affect and be affected by the organization. If for example, an organization is located next to a lake, river, or stream, as stakeholder, this becomes an important consideration for the natural environment. In a global example, nation states may share borders, introducing spatially related stakeholders. It is evident, therefore, that the greater the proximity, the greater the likelihood of relevant and important stakeholder relationships.[16]

An appropriate example of a stakeholder action that illustrated both power and urgency occurred in several dozen Home Depot stores around the country. In each of the stores, strange announcements began blaring from the intercom systems: *"Attention shoppers, on aisle seven you'll find mahogany ripped from the heart of the Amazon."* Shocked store managers raced through the aisles trying to apprehend the environmental activists behind the stunt. The activists had apparently gotten the access codes to the intercoms. After months of similar antics, Home Depot bowed to the demands of the environmental group and announced that it would stop selling wood from endangered forests and, instead, stock wood products certified by the Forest Stewardship Council (FSC).[17] This group was not even on Home Depot's stakeholder radar screen and then, all of a sudden, it had to capitulate to selling only FSC-certified wood.

ETHICS IN PRACTICE CASE

Are Plants Stakeholders? Do Flora Have Rights?

Scientists in Switzerland for years have created genetically modified produce, such as rice, corn, and apples. Recently, the question being raised is whether they ever stopped to think that their experiments may be humiliating to plants. A recently passed constitutional rule came into existence after the Swiss Parliament asked a panel of philosophers, geneticists, theologians, and lawyers to establish the "meaning" of a flora's dignity. The panel wrote a 22-page treatise on the "moral consideration of plants for their own sake." The document stated that vegetation has an inherent value and that it is immoral to harm plants arbitrarily. An example of this would be the "decapitation of wildflowers at the roadside without any apparent reason."

Those defending the new law state that it reflects a broader, progressive effort to protect the sanctity of living things and promote sustainability. Switzerland also granted new rights to all "social animals." For example, prospective dog owners now have to take a four-hour course on pet care before they can acquire a canine. Anglers now have to learn how to catch fish humanely. Goldfish can no longer be flushed down the toilet as a means of disposal. First, they must be anesthetized with special chemicals. One Swiss scientist recently exclaimed, "Where does it stop? Should we now defend the dignity of microbes and viruses?" In a related decision, the people of Ecuador passed a new constitution that is said to be the first to recognize ecosystem rights enforceable in a court of law. Now, the nation's rivers, forests, and air are right-bearing entities with "the right to exist, persist and regenerate."

1. Are plants stakeholders? Are they primary or secondary stakeholders? Do flora have rights?

2. Are the Swiss and Ecuadorian decisions too extreme? What are the limits of stakeholders' rights? Is this taking sustainability too far or pushing the idea to its natural limits?

3. What are the implications for business decisions of the Swiss and Ecuadorian decisions?

Sources: Gautam Naik, "Switzerland's Green Power Revolution: Ethicists Ponder Plants' Rights," *The Wall Street Journal,* October 10, 2008, A1. Human Flower Project, "Do Plants Have Rights?" http://www.humanflowerproject.com/index. php/weblog/comments/do_plants_have_rights/. Accessed June 23, 2010.

The typology of stakeholder attributes suggests that managers must attend to stakeholders on the basis of their assessment of the extent to which competing stakeholder claims reflect legitimacy, power, and urgency. Using the categories shown in Figure 3-4, therefore, the stakeholder groups represented by overlapping circles (e.g., those with two or three attributes such as Categories 4, 5, 6, and 7) are highly "salient" to the management and would likely receive priority attention.

Stakeholder Approaches

Strategic, Multifiduciary, and Synthesis Approaches

A major challenge embedded in the stakeholder approach is to determine whether it should be seen primarily as a way to *manage better* or as a way to *treat more ethically* those groups known as stakeholders. This issue may be addressed by considering the stakeholder approach used. Kenneth Goodpaster has suggested three approaches: the strategic approach, the multifiduciary approach, and the stakeholder synthesis approach.[18]

Strategic Approach. The *strategic approach* views stakeholders primarily as factors to be taken into consideration and managed while the firm pursues profits for its shareholders. In this view, managers take stakeholders into account because offended stakeholders might resist or retaliate (e.g., through political action, protest, or boycott). This approach sees stakeholders as instruments that may facilitate or impede the firm's pursuit of its strategic, business objectives; thus, it is an instrumental view.

Multifiduciary Approach.   The *multifiduciary approach* views stakeholders as more than just individuals or groups who can wield economic or legal power. This view holds that the management has a fiduciary responsibility toward stakeholders just as it has this same responsibility toward shareholders. In this approach, the management's traditional fiduciary, or trust, duty is expanded to embrace stakeholders on roughly an equal footing with shareholders. Thus, shareholders are no longer of exclusive importance as they were under the strategic approach.[19] This view broadens the idea of a fiduciary responsibility to include stockholders and other important stakeholders.

Stakeholder Synthesis Approach.   An innovative, *stakeholder synthesis approach* is preferred because it holds that business does have moral responsibilities to stakeholders but that they should not be seen as part of a fiduciary obligation. As a consequence, the management's basic fiduciary responsibility toward shareholders is kept intact, but it is also expected to be implemented within a context of ethical responsibility. This ethical responsibility is business's duty not to harm, coerce, lie, cheat, steal, and so on.[20] The result is the same in the multifiduciary and stakeholder synthesis views. However, the reasoning or rationale is different.

As we continue our discussion of stakeholder management, it should become clear that we are pursuing it from a balanced perspective, which suggests that we are integrating the strategic approach with the stakeholder synthesis approach. We should be managing strategically and morally at the same time. The stakeholder approach should not be just a better way to manage. It also should be a more ethical way to manage.

Three Values of the Stakeholder Model

In addition to the strategic, multifiduciary, and stakeholder synthesis approaches, the stakeholder model of the firm has three aspects or *values* that should be appreciated. Although interrelated, these include the descriptive, instrumental, and normative values or aspects.[21]

Descriptive Value

First, the stakeholder model has value because it is *descriptive*; that is, it provides language and concepts to describe effectively the corporation or organization in inclusive terms. The corporation is a constellation of cooperative and competitive interests possessing both instrumental and intrinsic value. Understanding organizations in this way allows us to have a fuller description or explanation of how they function. The language and terms used in stakeholder theory are useful in helping us understand organizations. As a result, we have seen stakeholder language and concepts used more and more in many fields of endeavor—business, government, politics, education, and so on.

Instrumental Value

Second, the stakeholder model has value because it is *instrumental* in that it is useful in portraying the relationship between the practice of stakeholder management and the resulting achievement of corporate performance goals. The fundamental premise here is that practicing effective stakeholder management should lead to the achievement of traditional business goals, such as profitability, stability, and growth.[22] Business school courses in strategic management often employ the instrumental model of stakeholders.

Normative Value

Third, the stakeholder model has value because it is *normative*, wherein stakeholders are seen as possessing value irrespective of their instrumental use to management. This is often considered the moral or ethical view because it emphasizes how stakeholders *should* be treated. The "principle of stakeholder fairness" is the moral underpinning, or normative justification, for the stakeholder model.[23] Thus, the normative value of stakeholder thinking is of central importance in business ethics and business and society.

In summarizing, stakeholder theory is *managerial* in the broad sense of the term in that it not only describes or predicts but also recommends attitudes, structures, and practices that constitute stakeholder management. Effective management requires simultaneous attention to the legitimate interests of all appropriate stakeholders in the creation of organizational structures and policies.[24]

Key Questions in Stakeholder Management

The managers of a business firm are responsible for establishing the firm's overall direction (its mission, strategies, goals, and policies) and ensuring implementation of these plans. As a consequence, they have some long-term responsibilities and many that are of more immediate concern. Before the stakeholder environment became as turbulent and dynamic as it now is, the managerial task was relatively straightforward because the external environment was stable. As we have transitioned to the stakeholder view of the firm, however, we see the managerial task as an inevitable consequence of the changing trends and developments described in the first two chapters.

Stakeholder management has become essential as managers have discovered the many groups that have to be addressed and relatively satisfied for the firm to meet its objectives. Without question, we still recognize the significance and necessity of profits as a return on the stockholders' investments, but now we also perceive and understand the growing claims and expectations of other stakeholder groups and the success they have had in getting what they want.

The challenge of stakeholder management, therefore, is to see to it that while the firm's primary stakeholders achieve their objectives, the other stakeholders are dealt with ethically and are also relatively satisfied. At the same time, the firm's profitability must be ensured. This is the classic "win–win" situation. The management's second-best alternative is to meet the goals of its primary stakeholders, keeping in mind the important role of its owner-investors. Without economic sustainability, all other stakeholders' interests become unresolved.

With these perspectives in mind, let us approach stakeholder management with the idea that managers can become successful stewards of their stakeholders' resources by gaining knowledge about stakeholders and using this knowledge to predict and improve their behaviors and actions. Ultimately, we should manage in such a way that we achieve our objectives ethically and effectively. Thus, the important functions of stakeholder management are to describe, to analyze, to understand, and, finally, to manage. The quest for stakeholder management embraces social, ethical, and economic considerations. Normative as well as instrumental objectives and perspectives are essential.

Five key questions are critical to capturing the essential information needed for stakeholder management:

1. *Who* are our stakeholders?
2. What are our stakeholders' *stakes*?

3. What *opportunities and challenges* do our stakeholders present to the firm?
4. What *responsibilities* (economic, legal, ethical, and philanthropic) does the firm have to its stakeholders?
5. What *strategies or actions* should the firm take to best address stakeholder challenges and opportunities?[25]

Figure 3-5 presents a schematic of the decision process outlining the five questions and key issues with respect to each.

Who Are Our Stakeholders?

To this point, we have described the likely primary and secondary stakeholder groups of a business organization. To manage them effectively, each firm and its management group must ask and answer this question: *Who are our stakeholders?* This stage is often called "stakeholder identification." To answer this question fully, management must identify not only *generic* stakeholder groups but also *specific* subgroups. A generic stakeholder group is a general or broad grouping, such as employees, shareholders, environmental groups, or consumers. Within each of these generic categories, there may be a few or many specific subgroups. Figure 3-6 illustrates some of the generic and specific stakeholder subgroups of a large organization.

McDonald's Experience.   To illustrate the process of stakeholder identification, it is helpful to consider some events in the life of the McDonald's Corporation that resulted in their broadening significantly who were considered their stakeholders. The case study begins when the social activist group PETA, which claims over two million members and supporters, decided it was dissatisfied with some of McDonald's practices and launched a billboard and bumper sticker campaign against the hamburger giant.[26] PETA, convinced that McDonald's was dragging its feet on animal welfare issues, went on the offensive. The group announced that it would put up billboards saying "The animals deserve a break today" and "McDonald's: Cruelty to Go" in Norfolk, Virginia, PETA's hometown. The ad campaign was announced when talks broke down between PETA and McDonald's on the subject of ways the company might foster animal rights issues within the fast-food industry. Using terminology introduced earlier, PETA was a secondary social or nonsocial stakeholder and, therefore, had low legitimacy. However, its power and urgency were very high as it was threatening the company with a very visible, potentially destructive campaign that was being reported by a cooperative and empathetic media.

PETA's pressure tactics continued and escalated. In the early 2000s, McDonald's announced significant changes in the requirements it was placing on its chicken and egg suppliers. Egg suppliers were required to improve the "living conditions" of their chickens. Specifically, McDonald's insisted that its suppliers no longer cage its chickens wingtip to wingtip. Suppliers were required to increase the space allotted to each hen from 48 square inches to 72 square inches per hen. They were also required to stop "forced molting," a process that increases egg production by denying hens food and water for up to two weeks.[27]

PETA then escalated its pressure tactics against the firm by distributing "*unhappy meals*" at restaurant playgrounds and outside the company's shareholder meeting venues. The kits came in boxes similar to that of Happy Meal[TM], McDonald's meal for children, but were covered instead with pictures of slaughtered animals. These also depicted a bloody, knife-wielding "Son of Ron" doll that resembled the Ronald McDonald clown, as well as toy farm animals with slashed throats. One image featured a bloody cow's head and the familiar fast-food phrase "Do you want fries with that?"[28] PETA continues to aggressively pursue McDonald's and other firms, such as Burger King and KFC, for

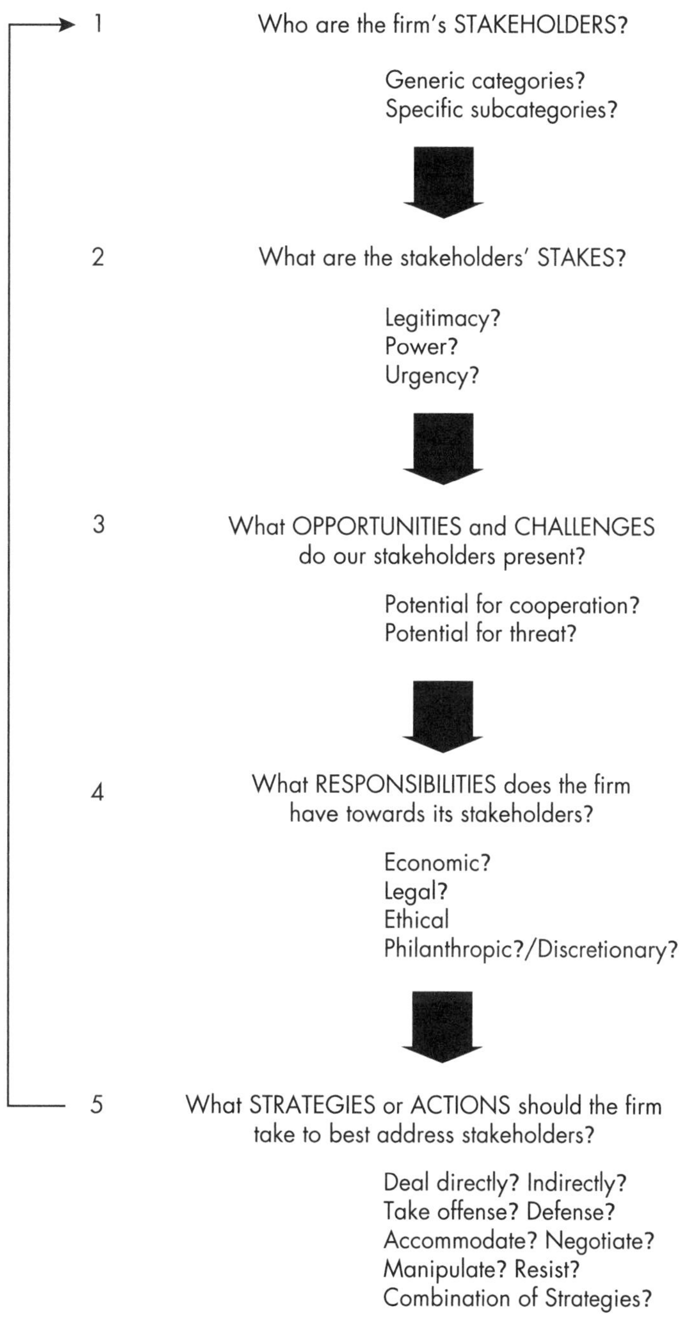

FIGURE 3-5
Stakeholder
Management: Five
Key Questions

1   Who are the firm's STAKEHOLDERS?

Generic categories?
Specific subcategories?

2   What are the stakeholders' STAKES?

Legitimacy?
Power?
Urgency?

3   What OPPORTUNITIES and CHALLENGES
do our stakeholders present?

Potential for cooperation?
Potential for threat?

4   What RESPONSIBILITIES does the firm
have towards its stakeholders?

Economic?
Legal?
Ethical
Philanthropic?/Discretionary?

5   What STRATEGIES or ACTIONS should the firm
take to best address stakeholders?

Deal directly? Indirectly?
Take offense? Defense?
Accommodate? Negotiate?
Manipulate? Resist?
Combination of Strategies?

FIGURE 3-6 Some Generic and Specific Stakeholders of a Large Firm

Owners	Employees	Governments	Customers
Trusts	Young employees	Federal	Business purchasers
Foundations	Middle-aged employees	• EPA	Government purchasers
Mutual funds	Older employees	• FTC	Educational institutions
Universities	Women	• OSHA	Global markets
Board members	Minority groups	• CPSC	Special-interest groups
Management owners	Disabled	State	Internet purchasers
Employee pension funds	Special-interest groups	Local	
Individual owners	Unions		

Community	Competitors	Social Activist Groups	
General fund-raising	Firm A	People United to Save Humanity (PUSH)	
United Way	Firm B	Rainforest Action Network (RAN)	
YMCA/YWCA	Firm C	Mothers Against Drunk Driving (MADD)	
Middle schools	Indirect competition	American Civil Liberties Union	
Elementary schools	Global competition	Consumers Union	
Residents who live close by		People for the Ethical Treatment of Animals (PETA)	
All other residents		National Rife Association	
Neighborhood associations		National Resources Defense Council	
Local media		Citizens for Health	
Chamber of Commerce			
Environments			

their chicken slaughter methods and other animal treatment issues. PETA, in other words, has become the stakeholder that refuses to go away.

As a result of this concrete example, we can see how the set of stakeholders that McDonald's had to deal with grew significantly from its traditional stakeholders to include powerful, special-interest groups such as PETA. With the cooperation of the media, especially major newspapers and magazines and TV, PETA has moved from being a secondary stakeholder to a primary stakeholder in McDonald's life.

Wool Industry under Fire.   Not only does PETA attack companies, it also takes on whole industries as well. Under pressure from PETA, many companies are beginning to ban Australian wool. PETA's complaint against Australia's $2.2 billion industry is targeted toward its use of wool from so-called mulesed merino sheep. Mulesing is a process of removing folds of skin from a sheep's hindquarters. The technique, developed over 70 years ago and named after John Mules, who devised it, is performed without anesthetics. The intention is to protect the sheep against infestation by blowflies whose eggs hatch into flesh-eating maggots while in the wool. When PETA first started lobbying against this process in 2004, most apparel makers had never heard of the process or the issue. PETA began its attacks on Benetton, the Italian company that produces sweaters. It dispatched protestors wielding signs that read "Benetton—Baaad to Sheep" to picket stores stocking the product. In New York City, PETA also put up billboards with the question "Did your sweater cause a bloody butt?" The protests worked. Benetton soon publicly came out in favor of phasing out mulesing. Other companies followed. As one European retailer observed, "who wants to be on PETA's radar screen?" More than 30 companies have signed on to the ban, including well-known ones such as Abercrombie & Fitch, Timberland, Hugo Boss, and Adidas. Meanwhile, Australia's 55,000 sheep farmers are unhappy because they believe mulesing is the best way to protect their flocks.[29]

PETA is continually moving on to new issues and making itself an important stakeholder in many other firms. PETA has been urging a city to use only humane cat control, urging help for circus animals, telling a coach to dump the use of fur, speaking out for Canadian Eskimo dogs without shelters, and taking action against deceitful "Happy Cows" ads.

These actual experiences of companies illustrate the evolving nature of the question, "Who are our stakeholders?" In actuality, stakeholder identification is an unfolding process. However, by recognizing early the potential of failure if one does not think in stakeholder terms, the value and usefulness of stakeholder thinking can be readily seen. Had McDonald's, KFC, Benetton, and other firms perceived PETA as a stakeholder with power, and some moral legitimacy, earlier on, perhaps it could have dealt with these situations more effectively. These firms should have been aware of one of the basic principles of stakeholder responsibility: "Recognize that stakeholders are real and complex people with names, faces, and values."[30]

Many businesses do not carefully identify their generic stakeholder groups, much less their specific stakeholder groups. This must be done, however, if the management is to be in a position to answer the second major question, "What are our stakeholders' stakes?"

What Are Our Stakeholders' Stakes?

Once stakeholders have been identified, the next step is to address the question: *What are our stakeholders' stakes?* Even groups in the same generic category frequently have different specific interests, concerns, perceptions of rights, and expectations. Management's challenge is to identify the nature and legitimacy of a group's stake(s) and the group's power to affect the organization. As we discussed earlier, urgency is another critical factor.

Identifying Nature or Legitimacy of a Group's Stakes.   Let's consider an example of stakeholders who possess varying stakes. Assume that we are considering corporate owners as a generic group of stakeholders and that the corporation is large, with several hundred million shares of stock outstanding. Among the ownership population are these more specific subgroups:

1. Institutional owners (trusts, foundations, churches, universities)
2. Large mutual fund organizations
3. Board of director members who own shares
4. Members of management who own shares
5. Millions of small, individual shareholders

For all these subgroups, the nature of stakeholder claims on this corporation is *ownership*. All these groups have legitimate claims—they are all owners. Because of other factors, such as power or urgency, these stakeholders may have to be dealt with differently.

Identifying the Power of a Group's Stakes.   When we examine power, we see significant differences. Which of the groups in the previous list are the most powerful?

Certainly not the small, individual investors, unless they have found a way to organize and thus wield power. The powerful stakeholders in this case are (1) the institutional owners and mutual fund organizations, because of the sheer magnitude of their investments and (2) the board and management shareholders, because of their dual roles of ownership and management (control). However, if the individual shareholders could somehow form a coalition on the basis of some interest they have in common, they could exert significant influence on management decisions. This is the day and age of dissident shareholder groups filing stockholder suits and proposing shareholder resolutions. These shareholder resolutions address issues ranging from complaints of excessive executive compensation to demands that firms improve their environmental protection policies or cease making illegal campaign contributions.

Identifying Specific Groups within a Generic Group. Let us now look at a manufacturing firm in an industry in Ohio that is faced with a generic group of environmental stakeholders. Within the generic group of environmental stakeholders might be the following specific groups:

1. Residents who live within a 25-mile radius of the plant
2. Other residents in the city
3. Residents who live in the path of the jet stream hundreds of miles away (some in Canada) who are being impacted by acid rain
4. Environmental Protection Agency (federal government)
5. Ohio's Environmental Protection Division (state government)
6. Friends of the Earth (environmental activist group)
7. Earth Liberation Front (environmental activist group)
8. Ohioans Against Smokestack Emissions (social activist group)

It would require some degree of time and care to identify the nature, legitimacy, power, and urgency of each of these specific groups. However, it could and should be done if the firm wants to get a handle on its environmental stakeholders. Furthermore, we should stress that companies have an ethical responsibility to be sensitive to legitimate stakeholder claims even if the stakeholders have no power or leverage with the management.

If we return for a moment to the fast-food and wool industry examples, we would have to conclude that PETA, as a special-interest, animal welfare group, did not have much legitimacy vis-à-vis these companies. It did claim animals' rights and treatment as a moral issue, and thus had some general legitimacy through the concerns it represented. Unfortunately for PETA, not all of the public shares its concerns or degree of concern with these issues. However, PETA had tremendous power and urgency. It was this power, wielded in the form of adverse publicity and media attention, that without a doubt played a significant role in bringing about changes in these companies' policies.

What Opportunities and Challenges Do Our Stakeholders Present?

Opportunities and challenges represent opposite sides of the coin when it comes to stakeholders. The opportunities are to build decent, productive working relationships with the stakeholders. Challenges, on the other hand, usually present themselves in such a way that the firm must handle the stakeholders acceptably or be hurt in some way—financially (short term or long term) or in terms of its public image or reputation in the community. Therefore, it is understandable why our emphasis is on challenges rather than on opportunities posed by stakeholders.

These challenges typically take the form of varying degrees of expectations, demands, or threats. In most instances, they arise because stakeholders think or believe that their needs are not being met adequately. The examples of PETA presented earlier illustrate this point. The challenges also arise when stakeholder groups think that any crisis that occurs is the responsibility of the firm or that the firm caused the crisis in some way. Examples of some stakeholder crises that illustrate this point include:[31]

- *Pepsi and Coke.* In the mid-2000s an Indian NGO (nongovernmental organization), the Centre for Science and Environment (CSE), was making life hard for these two soft drink distributors in Delhi, India. CSE tested bottles of their product and claimed they contained many times the amount of pesticides permitted by norms set by the European Union. It was even announced that the drinks would no longer be served in Indian's parliament. Both companies have continued to rebut the charges, but crises like these do not go away immediately.

- *Novartis, AG.* The Swiss drug giant, Novartis, in 2009 was attacked by aggressive animal rights groups that were stepping up their campaign against the company. The apparent issue at stake has been the drug company's use of animals in testing its products. One extreme action of the groups was to steal the ashes of the company CEO's mother from a grave site. The company also thinks the groups are behind a fire that was started at the CEO's vacation home in the Tyrol region of Austria. The company says it has taken "strong steps" to reduce its use of animal testing in recent years. A spokesperson for the company has also said that people need to understand that animal testing of drugs is required by regulatory authorities to help ensure the safety of their products for humans.

- *Boise.* A campaign to transform the entire logging industry, starting with Boise, an international distributor of office supplies and paper and an integrated manufacturer and distributor of paper, packaging, and building materials, was launched by Rainforest Action Network (RAN). At that time, Boise was one of the top loggers and distributors of old-growth forest products in the United States and a top distributor of wood products from the world's most endangered forests, including the tropical rainforests of the Amazon and the boreal forests of Canada. Boise was also the largest logger of U.S. public lands and the sole logging company to oppose the U.S. Forest Service Roadless Area Conservation Policy in court.

  As a result of RAN's campaigning, Boise implemented a domestic old-growth policy, committing to "no longer harvesting timber from old-growth forests in the United States." To catch up with public values and meet the new marketplace standards, Boise dropped its opposition to the Roadless Policy and became the first U.S. logging and distribution company to commit to "eliminate the purchase of wood products from endangered areas."[32] RAN's aggressive protection of rainforests continues to this day.[33]

If one looks at the business experiences of the recent past, including the crises mentioned here, it is evident that there is a need to think in stakeholder terms to understand fully the potential threats that businesses of all kinds face on a daily basis.

Opportunities and challenges might also be viewed in terms of *potential for cooperation* and *potential for threat*. Arguments abound that such assessments of cooperation and threat are necessary to enable managers to identify strategies for dealing with stakeholders.[34] In terms of potential for threat, managers need to consider stakeholders' relative power and its relevance to a particular issue confronting the organization. In terms of potential for cooperation, the firm needs to be sensitive to the possibility of joining forces with other stakeholders for the advantage of all parties involved. Several examples of how cooperative alliances were formed include the following.

Ross Laboratories, a division of Abbott Laboratories, was able to develop a cooperative relationship with some critics of its sales of infant formula in Third World countries. Ross and Abbott convinced these stakeholder groups (Unicef and the World Health

Organization) to join them in a program to promote infant health. Other firms, such as Nestlé, did not develop the potential to cooperate and suffered from consumer boycotts.[35] Walmart joined with one of its harshest critics, Service Employees International Union, in announcing they would join forces to press Congress to develop a system to provide low-cost health benefits for all Americans. In another example, ten major corporations banded together with environmental groups calling for a nationwide limit on carbon dioxide emissions and the creation of a market for trading allowances to emit the greenhouse gas.[36]

What Responsibilities Does a Firm Have toward Its Stakeholders?

The next logical question after identifying and understanding stakeholders' threats and opportunities is *"What responsibilities does a firm have in its relationships with all stakeholders?"* Responsibilities here may be thought of in terms of the corporate social responsibility discussion presented in Chapter 2. What economic, legal, ethical, and philanthropic responsibilities does management have toward each stakeholder? Because most of the firm's economic responsibilities are principally to itself and its shareholders, the analysis naturally turns to legal, ethical, and philanthropic questions. The most pressing threats are presented typically as legal and ethical questions. Often, opportunities are reflected in areas of philanthropy or "giving back" to the community.

It should be stressed, however, that the firm itself has an economic stake in the legal and ethical issues it faces. For example, when Johnson & Johnson (J&J) faced the Tylenol poisoning crisis, it had to decide what legal and ethical actions to take and what actions were in the firm's best economic interests. In this classic case, J&J apparently judged that recalling the tainted Tylenol products was not only the ethical choice but also one that would preserve its reputation of being concerned about consumers' health and well-being. Figure 3-7 illustrates the stakeholder responsibility matrix that management faces when assessing the firm's responsibilities to stakeholders. The matrix may be seen as a template that managers might use to systematically think through its various responsibil-

FIGURE 3-7 Stakeholder Responsibility Matrix

Stakeholders	Types of Responsibilities			
	Economic	Legal	Ethical	Philanthropic
Owners				
Customers				
Employees				
Community				
Public at Large				
Social Activist Groups				
Others				

ities. By completing each cell in the matrix, the organization has an organized way to identify and discuss its responsibilities.

What Strategies or Actions Should Management Take?

Once responsibilities have been assessed, a business must contemplate strategies and actions for addressing its stakeholders. In every decision situation, a multitude of alternative courses of action are available, and management must choose one or several that seem best. Important questions or decision choices that management has before it in dealing with stakeholders include:

- Do we deal *directly* or *indirectly* with stakeholders?
- Do we take the *offense* or the *defense* in dealing with stakeholders?
- Do we *accommodate, negotiate, manipulate,* or *resist* stakeholder overtures?
- Do we employ a *combination of the aforementioned* strategies or pursue a *singular course* of action?[37]

In actual practice, managers will need to prioritize stakeholder demands before deciding the appropriate strategy to employ.[38] In addition, strategic thinking in terms of forms of communication, degree of collaboration, development of policies or programs, and allocation of resources would need to be thought through carefully.[39] The development of specific strategies should be based on a classification of stakeholders' *potentials for cooperation and threat.* If we use these two dimensions, four stakeholder types and resultant generic strategies emerge.[40] Figure 3-8 shows these stakeholder types and corresponding strategies.

Type 1: The **Supportive** *Stakeholder.*   The supportive stakeholder is high on potential for cooperation and low on potential for threat. This is the ideal stakeholder. To a well-managed organization, supportive stakeholders might include its board of directors, managers, employees, and loyal customers. Others might be suppliers and service providers. The strategy

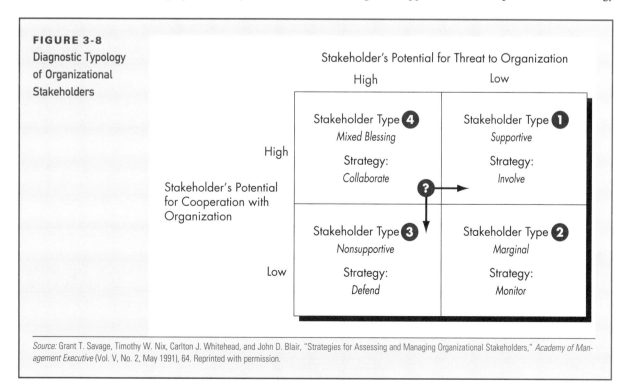

FIGURE 3-8
Diagnostic Typology of Organizational Stakeholders

Stakeholder's Potential for Threat to Organization

High   Low

Stakeholder's Potential for Cooperation with Organization

High

Stakeholder Type **4**
Mixed Blessing
Strategy:
Collaborate

Stakeholder Type **1**
Supportive
Strategy:
Involve

Low

Stakeholder Type **3**
Nonsupportive
Strategy:
Defend

Stakeholder Type **2**
Marginal
Strategy:
Monitor

Source: Grant T. Savage, Timothy W. Nix, Carlton J. Whitehead, and John D. Blair, "Strategies for Assessing and Managing Organizational Stakeholders," *Academy of Management Executive* (Vol. V, No. 2, May 1991), 64. Reprinted with permission.

here is one of involvement. An example of this might be the strategy of involving employee stakeholders through participative management or decentralization of authority.

Type 2: The **Marginal** *Stakeholder.*   The marginal stakeholder is low on both potential for threat and potential for cooperation. For large organizations, these stakeholders might include professional associations of employees, consumer interest groups, or stockholders—especially those that are not organized. The strategy here is for the organization to monitor the marginal stakeholder. Monitoring is especially called for to make sure circumstances do not change. Careful monitoring could avert later problems.

Type 3: The **Nonsupportive** *Stakeholder.*   The nonsupportive stakeholder is high on potential for threat but low on potential for cooperation. Examples of this group could include competing organizations, unions, federal or other levels of government, and the media. Special-interest groups often fall in this category. The recommended strategy here is to defend against the nonsupportive stakeholder. An example of a special-interest group that many would regard as nonsupportive is the Earth Liberation Front (ELF), a movement that originated in the Pacific Northwest. It claimed responsibility for a string of arsons in the suburbs of Los Angeles, Detroit, and Philadelphia. ELF's attacks targeted luxury homes and sports utility vehicles (SUVs), the suburban status symbols that some environmentalists regard as despoilers of the Earth. Many such radical environmental groups have been called "eco-terrorists."[41] Such organizations do not seem interested in establishing positive, or supportive, relationships with companies and industries. In the examples discussed earlier, PETA typically comes across as a nonsupportive stakeholder because of its high potential for threat.

Type 4: The **Mixed-Blessing** *Stakeholder.*   The mixed-blessing stakeholder is high on both potential for threat and potential for cooperation. Examples of this group, in a well-managed organization, might include employees who are in short supply, clients, or customers. A mixed-blessing stakeholder could become a supportive or a nonsupportive stakeholder. The recommended strategy here is to collaborate with the mixed-blessing stakeholder. By maximizing collaboration, the likelihood that this stakeholder will remain supportive is enhanced. Today, many companies regard environmental groups as mixed blessings rather than nonsupportive. These firms are turning environmentalists into allies by building alliances with them for mutual gain. These businesses are learning that by listening to the environmentalists, they can lower their energy use and save money.[42]

A summary guideline regarding these four stakeholder types might be stated in the following way:[43]

> *Managers should attempt to satisfy minimally the needs of marginal stakeholders and to satisfy maximally the needs of supportive and mixed blessing stakeholders, enhancing the latter's support for the organization.*

The four stakeholder types and recommended strategies illustrate what was referred to earlier in this chapter as the "strategic" or instrumental view of stakeholders. However, it could be argued that by taking stakeholders' needs and concerns into consideration, we are improving businesses' ethical treatment of them. We must go beyond just considering them, though. Management still has an ethical responsibility toward stakeholders that extends beyond the strategic view. We develop a fuller appreciation of what this is in Chapters 7 through 10.

Tapping Expertise of Stakeholders.   Especially with "supportive" stakeholders, but potentially with the other categories as well, it has been proposed that managers can

---

ETHICS IN PRACTICE CASE

"Taxing" Questions for This Preparer

While in college, I worked part-time for a prominent tax preparation service. I prepared customers' taxes along with about 20 other employees at different offices. Bill had been working with the service for about three seasons, but this was my first tax season. Bill was very good at tax preparation and had a pretty good reputation. The management respected him, and he seemed to do what he was asked to.

On a few occasions, I had customers come in and want to see Bill. When I explained that Bill was not at the office that day and asked if I could assist them with any questions, they would want to wait for Bill before continuing any further. This struck me as odd because all of the files are located in the office as well as on the hard drives of the firm's computers. Any employee can assist any customer, no matter who did the actual return.

When I later asked Bill about these customers, he told me that he did a few on his own time for people that couldn't afford the company's fees. This was bothersome to me because there is no telling how many times Bill had done this and how many customers he took away from the business.

1. Who are the stakeholders in this case and what are their stakes?

2. Was it unethical for Bill to be doing these taxes on his own time?

3. Was Bill actually doing the taxes on his own time or on company time when he wasn't otherwise busy?

4. Should I have told the manager the little bit of information I knew about this situation?

Contributed Anonymously

---

turn "gadflies into allies." Nonprofit special-interest groups, especially activist NGOs, hold great promise for cooperation if managements quit seeing them as "pests" and try to get them to join in the company endeavors.[44] These NGOs have resources such as legitimacy, awareness of social forces, distinct networks, and specialized technical expertise that can be tapped by companies to gain competitive advantage. Each of these can provide benefits for companies. Some of the resulting benefits are heading off trouble, helping to set industry standards, shaping legislation, foreseeing shifts in demands, and accelerating innovation. Such partnering with stakeholders requires a change in perspective and mentality. If it is done, however, the companies will be better prepared to deal with stakeholders in the future.

Effective Stakeholder Management

Effective stakeholder management requires the careful assessment of the five key questions posed in this chapter. To deal successfully with those who assert claims on the organization, managers must understand these core questions. Business has been and will continue to be subjected to careful scrutiny of its actions, practices, policies, and ethics. Stakeholder management helps deal with these issues.

Criticisms of business and calls for better corporate citizenship have been the consequences of the changes in the business–society relationship, and the stakeholder approach to viewing the organization has become one needed response. To do less is to deny the realities of business's plight in the modern world, which is increasingly global in scope, and to fail to see the kinds of adaptations that are essential if businesses are to prosper now and in the future.

Stakeholder Thinking

Stakeholder thinking is the process of always reasoning in stakeholder terms throughout the management process, and especially when organizations' decisions and actions have important implications for others. Some managers continue to think in stockholder

Spotlight on SUSTAINABILITY

Walmart's "Sustainability 360" Initiative

An excellent example of a company tapping the expertise of its stakeholders and building on cooperative stakeholder relationships is Walmart's innovative "Sustainability 360" initiative. Walmart has not only pushed its suppliers to be more concerned about the environment but it has engaged its employees, communities, and customers in its sustainability efforts. Walmart has challenged its associates and suppliers to come up with new ways to remove nonrenewable energy from products that Walmart sells. Major suppliers such as Unilever, PepsiCo, and Universal Music have provided strong support. The sustainability initiative has created new allies with groups such as Environmental Defense, which plans to work closely with Walmart, as well as with several other environmental groups.

A consulting firm developed and implemented for a consumer products distributor a strategy that included a networkwide AMP Workforce Motivation program, client team training, facility expansion planning, and support of Walmart's Sustainability 360 initiative. Cutting through corporate silos, the consultants tapped the intelligence of different senior executives. That gave them a broad-ranging perspective, which made implementation more effective.

Sources: Jayne O'Donnell, "Wal-Mart Includes Workers, Suppliers in Environment Efforts," *USA Today* (February 2, 2007), 7B. XCD Performance Consulting, "Meeting the Wal-Mart Challenge," Awareness into Action, The Sustainable Enterprise, http://www.awarenessintoaction.com/casestudies/Case-study-wal-mart-360-Sustainability-XCD-Workforce-motivation.html. Accessed June 25, 2010.

terms because it is easier. To think in stakeholder terms increases the complexity of decision making, and it is quite taxing for some managers to determine which stakeholders' claims take priority in a given situation. Despite its complexity, however, the stakeholder management view is most consistent with the environment that business faces today, and "stakeholder thinking" has become a necessary part of the successful manager's job.

In fairness, we should also note that there are criticisms and limitations of the stakeholder approach. One major criticism relates to the complexity and time-consuming nature of identifying, assessing, and responding to stakeholder claims, which constitute an extremely demanding process. Also, the ranking of stakeholder claims is no easy task. Effective stakeholder management is facilitated by a number of other useful concepts. The following concepts—stakeholder culture, stakeholder management capability, the stakeholder corporation model, and principles of stakeholder management—round out a useful approach to stakeholder management effectiveness. Each of these are considered in detail.

Developing a Stakeholder Culture

In recent years, the importance of developing a strong, values-based corporate culture has been recognized as a key to successful enterprises. Corporate culture refers to the taken-for-granted beliefs, functional guidelines, ways of doing things, priorities, and values important to managers.[45] Developing a strong **stakeholder culture** is a major factor supporting successful stakeholder management. Stakeholder culture embraces the beliefs, values, and practices that organizations have developed for addressing stakeholder issues and relationships. There are at least five categories of stakeholder cultures that reside on a continuum from little concern to great concern for stakeholders.[46]

First is *agency* culture, which basically is not concerned with others. Next are two cultures characterized by limited morality—*corporate egoist* and *instrumentalist*—which focus mostly on the firm's shareholders as the important stakeholders. These cultures focus on short-term profit maximization. Finally are two cultures that are broadly moral—*moralist* and *altruist*. Both of these cultures are morally based and provide the broadest concern for stakeholders.[47] Effective stakeholder management requires the development of a corporate culture that most broadly conceives of responsibilities to others. In the above scheme, the moralist and altruist cultures would be most compatible with stakeholder management and a stakeholder corporation.

Stakeholder Management Capability

Another way of thinking about effective stakeholder management is in terms of the extent to which the organization has developed its **stakeholder management capability (SMC)**.[48] Stakeholder management capability may reside at one of three levels of increasing sophistication.

Level 1: Rational Level

This first level simply entails the company identifying who their stakeholders are and what their stakes happen to be. This is the level that would enable management to create a stakeholder map, such as that depicted in Figure 3-3. The **rational level** is descriptive and somewhat analytical, because the legitimacy of stakes, the stakeholders' power, and urgency are identified. This represents a beginning, or early level of SMC. Most organizations have at least identified who their stakeholders are, but not all have analyzed the nature of the stakes or the stakeholders' power. This first level has also been identified as the element of *familiarization* and *comprehensiveness*, because the management operating at Level 1 is seeking to become familiar with their stakeholders and to develop a comprehensive assessment of their identification and stakes.[49]

Level 2: Process Level

At the **process level**, organizations go a step further than Level 1 and actually develop and implement approaches, procedures, policies, and practices by which the firm may scan the environment and receive pertinent information about stakeholders, which is then used for decision-making purposes. An applicable stakeholder principle here is "constantly monitoring and redesigning processes to better serve stakeholders."[50] Typical approaches at the process level include portfolio analysis processes, strategic review processes, and environmental scanning processes, which are used to assist managers in their strategic management.[51] Other approaches, such as issues management or crisis management (Chapter 6), also might be considered examples of Level 2 SMC. This second level has been described as *planning integrativeness*, because the management does focus on planning processes for stakeholders and integrating a consideration for stakeholders into organizational decision making.[52]

Level 3: Transactional Level

The **transactional level** is the highest and most developed of the three levels. This is the highest goal for stakeholder management—the extent to which managers actually engage in transactions (relationships) with stakeholders.[53] At this highest level of SMC, management must take the initiative in meeting stakeholders face to face and attempting to be responsive to their needs. The transactional level may require actual negotiations with stakeholders.[54] Level 3 is the *communication* level, which is characterized by *communication proactiveness, interactiveness, genuineness, frequency, satisfaction*, and *resource adequacy*. Resource adequacy refers to the management actually spending resources on stakeholder transactions.[55] Regarding stakeholder communications, a relevant principle is that business must "engage in intensive communication and dialogue with (all) stakeholders, not just those who are friendly."[56]

Steven Walker and Jeff Marr, in their book *Stakeholder Power: A Winning Plan for Building Stakeholder Commitment and Driving Corporate Growth*, argue that companies should compete on the basis of intangible assets—a company's priceless relationships with customers, employees, suppliers, and shareholders. Based on their own firm's 60-year history as a pioneer in corporate reputation and market research and from case studies of organizations as diverse as LensCrafters, DHL, and Edison International, the authors offer a practical model for hardwiring stakeholder management into company strategy and reaping the rewards through continuous innovation, learning, and profitable growth.[57] These ideas capture the essential nature of Level 3—the transactional level—of stakeholder management capability.

Another example of Level 3 has been the relationship established between General Motors Corporation (GM) and the Coalition for Environmentally Responsible Economies (CERES). Over a decade ago, these two organizations actually began to talk with one another, and the result was a mutually beneficial collaboration. The arrangement became a high-profile example of a growing trend within the environmental movement—that of using quiet discussions and negotiations rather than noisy protests to change corporate behavior. Though many positive outcomes have come from this improved stakeholder relationship, issues continue to arise that pose the potential for the two to be at odds with one another. Beginning in the early 2000s, for example, CERES and other environmental groups began demanding tougher governmental fuel economy standards, while automakers such as GM intensified their lobbying to keep existing rules in place, probably because of the popularity of high-fuel-consumption SUVs.[58]

Stakeholder Engagement

Recently, there has been growing interest in the topic of stakeholder engagement. **Stakeholder engagement** may be seen as an approach by which companies implement the transactional level of strategic management capability. Companies may employ different strategies in terms of the degree of engagement with their stakeholders. A ladder of stakeholder engagement, which depicts a number of steps from low engagement to high engagement, has been set forth as a continuum of engagement postures that companies might follow.[59] Lower levels of stakeholder engagement might be used for informing and explaining. Middle levels might involve token gestures of participation such as placation, consultation, and negotiation. Higher levels of stakeholder engagement might be active or responsive attempts to involve stakeholders in company decision making. At the highest level, terms such as "involvement," "collaboration," or "partnership" might be appropriate descriptions of the relationship established. An example of this highest level would be when a firm enters into a strategic alliance with a stakeholder group to seek the group's opinion in a product design that would be sensitive to the group's concerns, such as environmental impact or product safety. This was illustrated when McDonald's entered into an alliance with the Environmental Defense Fund to eliminate polystyrene packaging that was not biodegradable.[60]

This idea of stakeholder engagement is relevant to developing what Tapscott and Ticoll refer to as *The Naked Corporation*. In their book, they argue that the ten characteristics of the open enterprise, "environmental engagement" and "stakeholder engagement" are two critical factors. Environmental engagement calls for an open operating environment: sustainable ecosystems, peace, order, and good public governance. Stakeholder engagement calls for these open enterprises to put resources and effort into reviewing, managing, recasting, and strengthening relationships with stakeholders, old and new.[61] The "open enterprise" with an emphasis on "transparency" has become crucial because of the corporate scandals of the early years of the decade.

One of the latest emphases has been engaging stakeholders on sustainability. The idea here has been to involve stakeholders such as the social media, consumers, NGOs, and communities as early as possible on sustainability developments and initiatives. "Sustainability Stakeholder Engagement" conferences are now being held to facilitate this process. One of the unique aspects of these conferences has been the increasing use of social media technologies, such as Twitter, to engage stakeholders in a more timely fashion.[62]

The Stakeholder Corporation

Perhaps the ultimate form of the stakeholder approach or stakeholder management is the "**stakeholder corporation**." The primary element of this concept is **stakeholder inclusiveness**.[63]

> *In the future, development of loyal relationships with customers, employees, shareholders, and other stakeholders will become one of the most important determinants of commercial viability and business success. Increasing shareholder value will be best served if your company cultivates the support of all who may influence its importance.*

Advocates of the stakeholder corporation would embrace the idea of "**stakeholder symbiosis**," which recognizes that all stakeholders depend on each other for their success and financial well-being.[64] Executives who have a problem with this concept would probably also have trouble becoming a part of stakeholder corporations.

Principles of Stakeholder Management

On the basis of years of observation and research, a set of "**principles of stakeholder management**" has been developed for use by managers and organizations. These principles, known as "The Clarkson Principles," were named after the late Max Clarkson, a dedicated researcher on the topic of stakeholder management. The principles are intended to provide managers with guiding precepts regarding how stakeholders should be treated. Managers interested in effective stakeholder management, the transactional level of stakeholder management capability, and the stakeholder corporation, would quickly seek to use these guidelines. Figure 3-9 summarizes these principles. The key words in the principles suggest action words that reflect the kind of cooperative spirit that should be used in building stakeholder relationships: *acknowledge, monitor, listen, communicate, adopt, recognize, work, avoid, and acknowledge conflicts.*

Strategic Steps toward Successful Stakeholder Management

The global competition that characterizes business firms in the 21st century necessitates a stakeholder approach, for both effective and ethical management. The stakeholder approach requires that stakeholders be moved to the center of the management's vision. Three strategic steps may be taken that can lead today's global competitors toward the more balanced view that is needed in today's changing business environment.[65]

1. **Governing Philosophy.** *Integrating stakeholder management into the firm's governing philosophy.* Boards of directors and top management groups should move the

FIGURE 3-9 The "Clarkson Principles" of Stakeholder Management

Principle 1	Managers should **acknowledge** and actively **monitor** the concerns of all legitimate stakeholders, and should take their interests appropriately into account in decision making and operations.
Principle 2	Managers should **listen** to and openly **communicate** with stakeholders about their respective concerns and contributions, and about the risks that they assume because of their involvement with the corporation.
Principle 3	Managers should **adopt** processes and modes of behavior that are sensitive to the concerns and capabilities of each stakeholder constituency.
Principle 4	Managers should **recognize the interdependence** of efforts and rewards among stakeholders, and should attempt to achieve a fair distribution of the benefits and burdens of corporate activity among them, taking into account their respective risks and vulnerabilities.
Principle 5	Managers should **work cooperatively** with other entities, both public and private, to ensure that risks and harms arising from corporate activities are minimized and, where they cannot be avoided, appropriately compensated.
Principle 6	Managers should **avoid altogether** activities that might jeopardize inalienable human rights (e.g., the right to life) or give rise to risks that, if clearly understood, would be patently unacceptable to relevant stakeholders.
Principle 7	Managers should **acknowledge the potential conflicts** between (a) their own role as corporate stakeholders and (b) their legal and moral responsibilities for the interests of stakeholders, and should address such conflicts through open communication, appropriate reporting, incentive systems and, where necessary, third-party review.

Source: Principles of Stakeholder Management (Toronto: The Clarkson Centre for Business Ethics, Joseph L. Rotman School of Management, University of Toronto, 1999), 4.

organization from the idea of "shareholder agent" to "stakeholder trustee." Long-term shareholder value, along with sustainability, will be the objective of this transition in corporate governance.

2. **Values Statement.** *Create a stakeholder-inclusive "values statement."* Various firms have done this. J&J's is called a "credo," Microsoft's a "values statement." Microsoft emphasizes integrity and honesty, and accountability to customers, shareholders, partners, and employees. Regardless of what such a values statement is called, such a pledge reinforces the organization's commitment to stakeholders publicly.

3. **Measurement System.** *Implement a stakeholder performance measurement system.* Such a system should be auditable, integrated, and monitored as stakeholder relations are improved. Measurement is evidence of serious intent to achieve results, and such a system will motivate a sustainable commitment to the stakeholder view. One recent example of a measurement system has been Walmart's creation of a *worldwide sustainability index*. With this initiative, the company is helping create a more transparent supply chain, driving product innovation, and ultimately providing customers with information they need to assess products' sustainability.[66]

Implementation

The key to effective stakeholder management is in its *implementation*. Corporate social responsibility is made operable when companies translate their stakeholder dialogue into practice.[67] After studying three companies in detail—Cummins Engine Company, Motorola, and the Royal Dutch/Shell Group—researchers concluded that the key to effective implementation is in recognizing and using stakeholder management as a *core competence*. When this is done, at least four indicators or manifestations of successful stakeholder management will be apparent. First, stakeholder management results in *survival*. Second, there are *avoided costs*. Third, there was *continued acceptance and use* in the companies studied, implying success. Fourth, there was evidence of *expanded recognition and adoption* of stakeholder-oriented policies by other companies and consultants.[68] These indicators suggest the value and practical benefits that may be derived from the stakeholder approach. Finally, it should be noted that organizations develop learning processes over time in implementing their changing or evolving stakeholder orientations.[69]

Summary

A stakeholder is an individual or a group that claims to have one or more stakes in an organization. Stakeholders may affect the organization and, in turn, be affected by the organization's actions, policies, practices, and decisions. The stakeholder approach extends beyond the traditional production and managerial views of the firm and warrants a much broader conception of the parties involved in the organization's functioning and success. Both primary and secondary social and nonsocial stakeholders assume important roles in the eyes of management. A typology of stakeholders suggests that three attributes are especially important: legitimacy, power, and urgency.

Strategic, multifiduciary, and stakeholder synthesis approaches help us appreciate the perspectives that may be adopted with regard to stakeholders. The stakeholder synthesis approach is encouraged because it highlights the ethical responsibility business has to its stakeholders. The stakeholder view of the firm has three values: descriptive, instrumental, and normative. In a balanced perspective, managers are concerned with both goal achievement and ethical treatment of stakeholders.

Five key questions assist managers in stakeholder management: (1) Who are our stakeholders? (2) What are our stakeholders' stakes? (3) What challenges or opportunities are presented to a firm by stakeholders? (4) What responsibilities does a firm have to its stakeholders? (5) What strategies or actions should a firm take with respect to its stakeholders? Effective stakeholder management requires the assessment and appropriate response to these five questions. In addition, the use of other relevant stakeholder thinking concepts is helpful. The concept of SMC illustrates how firms can grow and mature in their approach to stakeholder management. The stakeholder corporation is a model that represents stakeholder thinking in its most advanced form. Other key ideas include stakeholder culture and stakeholder engagement.

Seven principles of stakeholder management are helpful in guiding managers toward more effective stakeholder thinking. Although the stakeholder management approach is quite complex and time consuming, it is a way of managing that is in tune with the complex environment that business organizations face today. Successful steps in stakeholder management include making stakeholders a part of the guiding philosophy, creating value statements, and developing measurement systems that monitor results. In the final analysis, implementation is the key to effective stakeholder management.

Key Terms

legitimacy, p. 67

managerial view of the firm, p. 65

power, p. 67

primary social stakeholders, p. 67

principles of stakeholder management, p. 85

process level, p. 83

production view of the firm, p. 64

proximity, p. 68

rational level, p. 83

secondary social stakeholders, p. 67

stake, p. 63

stakeholder, p. 63

stakeholder corporation, p. 85

stakeholder culture, p. 82

stakeholder engagement, p. 84

stakeholder inclusiveness, p. 85

stakeholder management capability (SMC), p. 83

stakeholder symbiosis, p. 85

stakeholder thinking, p. 81

stakeholder view of the firm, p. 65

transactional level, p. 83

urgency, p. 67

Discussion Questions

1. Explain the concepts of stake and stakeholder from your perspective as an individual. What kinds of stakes and stakeholders do you have? Discuss.

2. Explain in your own words the differences between the production, managerial, and stakeholder views of the firm.

3. Differentiate between primary and secondary social and nonsocial stakeholders in a business situation. Give examples of each.

4. How is effective stakeholder management related to sustainability and sustainable development on the part of companies?

5. How can a firm transition from Level 1 to Level 3 of stakeholder management capability (SMC)?

6. Is the stakeholder corporation a realistic model for business firms? Will stakeholder corporations become more prevalent in the 21st century? Why or why not?

Case Analysis Guidelines

The guidelines presented below have been designed to help the student analyze the cases that follow. They are not intended to be a rigid format. Each question is intended to bring out information that will be helpful in analyzing and resolving the case. Each case is different, and some parts of the guidelines may not apply in every case. Also, the student should be attentive to the questions for discussion at the end of each case. These questions should be answered in any complete case analysis. The heart of any case analysis is the recommendations that are made. The Issue/Problem Identification and Analysis/Evaluation steps should be focused on generating and defending the most effective set of recommendations possible. In all stages of the case analysis, the stakeholder, ethics, sustainability, and corporate social responsibility (CSR) concepts presented in the text should be used. The guidelines are presented in three stages, as discussed in the following sections.

ISSUE/PROBLEM IDENTIFICATION

1. **Facts and Assumptions.** What are the *central facts* of the case and the *assumptions* you are making on the basis of these facts?
2. **Major Overriding Issues/Problems.** What are the *major overriding issues* in this case? (What major questions/issues does this case address that merit(s) their/its study in this course and in connection with the chapter/material you are now covering?)
3. **Subissues and Related Issues.** What *subissues* or *related issues* are present in the case that merit consideration, discussion, and action?

ANALYSIS/EVALUATION

4. **Stakeholder Analysis.** Who are the *stakeholders* in this case, and what are their stakes? (Create a stakeholder map to depict relationships.) What *challenges/threats/ opportunities* are posed by these stakeholders? What stakeholder characteristics are at work (legitimacy, power, urgency)?
5. **CSR Analysis.** What CSRs (*economic/legal/ethical/philanthropic*) does the company have, and what exactly are the nature and extent of these responsibilities to the various stakeholders?
6. **Evaluations.** If the case involves a company's or manager's actions, evaluate what the company or manager did or did not do correctly in handling the issue affecting it. How should actions have been handled?

RECOMMENDATIONS

7. **Recommendations and Implementation.** What *recommendations* would you make in this case? If a company's or a manager's strategies or actions are involved, should they have acted the way they did? What actions *should* they have taken? What actions should the company or manager take now, and why? Be specific and include a discussion of alternatives (*right now*, *short-term*, and *long-term*). Identify and discuss any important *implementation considerations*.

Walmart: The Main Street Merchant of Doom*

The small town was in need of a hired gun. The people were tired of dealing with the local price-fixing merchant scum who ran the town like a company store. This low-life bunch of merchants held the people of the town in a death grip and were perceived by the townspeople to overcharge on every purchase. In spite of what appeared to be a case of collusion, the law was powerless to do anything. What competition there was had been effectively eliminated.

Suddenly, coming over the rise and wearing white, their hired man came riding. The women and children buzzed with excitement. The men were happy. Although his methods of getting the job done turned some people's stomachs, the local watering hole buzzed with tales of how this hired gun would change their world for the better, how someday soon they would have the benefits long afforded the big city. But, others asked, at what price?

THE MODERN VERSION OF THE "HIRED GUN"

In his final days, the man appeared to be somewhat too frail to handle the enormous job. Yet the courage and self-confidence that he instilled in his associates radiated a belief in low prices and good value for all to see. As his associates rode into town, that radiance put to rest the people's fears that things had changed. Sam's spirit, the Walmart Way, had come to town.

Sam Walton, founder, owner, and mastermind of Wal-Mart,[1] now spelled Walmart in some advertisements, passed away on April 5, 1992, leaving behind his spirit to ride herd on the colossal Walmart organization. To the consumer in the small community, his store, Walmart, was seen as a friend. On the flip side, many a small-town merchant had been the victim of Sam's blazing merchandising tactics. So what is Walmart to the communities it serves? Is Walmart the consumer's best friend, the purveyor of the free-enterprise system, the "Mother of All Discount Stores," or, conversely, is it really "The Main Street Merchant of Doom"?

---

* This case, originally prepared by William T. Rupp, University of Montevallo, was revised and updated by Archie B. Carroll, University of Georgia, in 2010.

THE MAN NAMED SAM

Samuel Moore Walton was born on March 29, 1918, near Kingfisher, Kansas. He was a strong, lean boy who learned to work hard in order to help the family. He attended the University of Missouri starting in the fall of 1936 and graduated with a degree in business administration. During his time there, he was a member of the Beta Theta Phi fraternity, was president of the senior class, played various sports, and taught what was believed to be the largest Sunday school class in the world, numbering over 1,200 Missouri students.[2]

At age 22, Sam joined JCPenney. One of his first tasks was to memorize and practice the "Penney Idea." Adopted in 1913, this credo exhorted the associate to serve the public; not to demand all the profit the traffic will bear; to pack the customer's dollar full of value, quality, and satisfaction; to continue to be trained; to reward men and women in the organization through participation in what the business produces; and to test every policy, method, and act against the question, "Does it square with what is right and just?"[3]

SAM'S FIRST STORE

In 1962, at age 44, Sam Walton opened his first Walmart store in Rogers, Arkansas. He took all the money and expertise he could gather and applied the JCPenney idea to Middle America. Sam first targeted small, underserved rural towns with populations of no more than 10,000 people. The people responded, and Walmart soon developed a core of loyal customers who loved the fast, friendly service coupled with consistently low prices. Later, Sam expanded his company into the large cities, often with numerous Walmarts spread throughout every part of the city.

THE STORE THAT SAM BUILT

By 1981, Walmart's rapid growth was evident to all and especially disturbing to Sears, JCPenney, Target, and Kmart, because Walmart had become America's largest retailer. The most telling figures were those of overhead expenses and sales per employee. The overhead expenses of Sears and Kmart ran 29 and 23 percent of sales, respectively, whereas Walmart's overhead expenses ran 16 percent of sales. At this time, the average Sears employee generated $85,000 in sales per year, whereas the average Walmart employee generated $95,000.[4]

By 2001, Walmart Stores, Inc., had become the world's largest retailer with $191 billion in sales. The company employed one million associates worldwide through nearly 3,500 facilities in the United States and more than 1,000 stores throughout nine other countries. Walmart claimed that more than 100 million customers per week visited Walmart stores. The company had four major retail divisions—Walmart Supercenters, Discount Stores, Neighborhood Markets, and Sam's Club warehouses. As it entered the 2000s, Walmart had been named "Retailer of the Century" by *Discount Store News*, made *Fortune* magazine's lists of the "Most Admired Companies in America" and the "100 Best Companies to Work For," and was ranked on *Financial Times*'s "Most Respected in the World" list.[5] By 2010, Walmart's sales had grown to $408 billion.[6]

SAM THE MOTIVATIONAL GENIUS

Sam promoted the associate—the hourly employee—to a new level of participation within the organization. He offered profit sharing, incentive bonuses, and stock options in an effort to have his Walmart associates share in the wealth. Sam, as the head cheerleader, saw his job as the chief proponent of the "Walmart Way." The Walmart Way reflected Sam's idea of the essential Walmart culture that was needed for success. Sam felt that when a customer entered Walmart in any part of the country, he or she should feel at home. Examples of the culture included "exceeding customer expectations" and "helping people make a difference." He was a proponent of the *"Ten-Foot Rule,"* which meant that if a customer came within ten feet of an associate, the associate would look the customer in the eye, greet him or her, and ask if the customer needed help.[7]

As he was growing the business, Sam, the courageous, borrowed and borrowed, sometimes just to pay other creditors. Arkansas banks that at one time had turned him down later competed with banks that Sam himself owned. Sam, the CEO, hired the best managers he could find. He let them talk him into buying an extensive computer network system. This network corporate satellite system enabled Sam to use round-the-clock inventory control and credit card sales control and provided him with information on total sales of which products where and when. This computer control center was about the size of a football field

and used a Hughes satellite for uplinking and downlinking to each store.

SAM THE MORTAL

In 1992, Sam, the mortal, died of incurable bone cancer. At age 73, Sam Walton said that if he had to do it over again, he would not change a thing. He said, "This is still the most important thing I do, going around to the stores, and I'd rather do it than anything I know of. I know I'm helping our folks when I get out to the stores. I learn a lot about who's doing good things in the office, and I also see things that need fixing, and I help fix them. Any good management person in retail has got to do what I do in order to keep his finger on what's going on. You've got to have the right chemistry and the right attitude on the part of the folks who deal with the customers."[8]

Sam, the innovator, was responsible for two early social responsibility innovations: Walmart's "Buy American" plan and its "Environmental Awareness" campaign.

SAM AND SOCIAL AWARENESS: THE "BUY AMERICAN" PLAN

Walmart's "Buy American" plan was a result of a 1984 telephone conversation with then-Arkansas Governor Bill Clinton. The program was a response to Sam's own enlightenment: He learned that Walmart was adding to the loss of American jobs by buying cheaper foreign goods. Everything Sam stood for came out of his heartfelt obligation to supply the customer with low-cost quality goods, but running counter to this inner driving force was the realization that he was responsible for the loss of American jobs. This contradiction and dilemma drove him to find a solution. His conversation with Governor Clinton inspired Sam to do something about the problem.

The goal of the Buy American plan was to support American-based manufacturers by doing business with them so that they would not go out of business. His primary method for doing this was to give the manufacturers large orders or contracts so that they could stay in business.[9]

Sam wanted other manufacturers to join him in the Buy American plan. He wrote to 3,000 American manufacturers and solicited them to sell to Walmart items that Walmart was currently buying from overseas suppliers. Walmart's competitors did not meet the challenge to "Buy American." Kmart stated that it would rather buy American-made goods but that it was looking for the best deal for the customer. Target said it was for free trade and that as the customer's representative it just wanted the best deal for the customer. Wall Street analysts responded positively, saying that Walmart's plan was possibly the beginning of a change of direction for American retailers.[10]

In February 1986, about 12 months after the Buy American plan had begun, Sam held a press conference. He showed off all the merchandise Walmart was now buying domestically. He estimated that Walmart's Buy American plan had restored 4,538 jobs to the American economy and its people.[11] The Buy American plan was one of Walmart's early efforts at corporate social responsibility.

The Buy American plan morphed over the years into the well-publicized "Made in the USA" campaign in which Walmart called customers' attention to these local products with special labels. Ironically, at some point in time, Walmart eventually abandoned this program and became one of the largest purchasers of products made overseas. In fact, the company in time became the country's largest purchaser of Chinese goods in any industry. Some say that by taking its orders abroad, Walmart forced many U.S. manufacturers out of business.[12]

SAM AND SOCIAL CONCERNS: THE "ENVIRONMENTAL AWARENESS" CAMPAIGN

As awareness of the environment was on the rise, Sam looked for a way to involve Walmart in the environmental movement. In August 1989, an ad in *The Wall Street Journal* proclaimed Walmart's "commitment to our land, air and water." Sam envisioned Walmart as a leader among American companies in the struggle to clean up the environment. John Lowne, corporate vice president and division manager for Reynolds Metals Company, stated, "Walmart's move will indeed set a precedent for the entire retail industry. I'm surprised it has taken other retailers this long to follow suit."[13]

Walmart wanted to use its tremendous buying power to aid in the implementation of the campaign. Walmart sent a booklet to manufacturers stating the following:

> At Wal-Mart we're committed to help improve our environment. Our customers are concerned about the quality of our land, air and water, and want the opportunity to do something positive. We believe it is our responsibility to step up to their challenge.[14]

In the stores, shelf tags made from 100 percent recycled paper informed customers as to the environmental friendliness of the highlighted product. As a result of these shelf tags and Walmart's advertising, customer awareness had increased, and some environmentally safe product manufacturers were reaping the rewards of increased Walmart orders. Linda Downs, administrative manager of Duraflame, California, said that Duraflame logs had been proven to burn cleaner than wood and that Walmart's campaign had helped Duraflame to deliver this message. She went on to say, "Walmart has helped drive home the message we have been trying to promote for years. They have really given us great publicity."[15]

In the *Wal-Mart Associates Handbook*, new associates were indoctrinated with the "Walmart spirit." The section on the *environment* said:

> As a responsible member of the community, Wal-Mart's commitments go beyond simply selling merchandise. With environmental concerns mounting world-wide, Wal-Mart has taken action. Home office and store associates are taking decisive steps to help the environment by making community recycling bins available on our facility parking lots. Other action plans include "Adopt-a-Highway" and "Adopt-a-Beach" programs, tree planting and community clean up and beautification. By forming a partnership with our associates, our manufacturers and our customers, we're convinced we can make the world a better place to live.[16],[17]

SAM AND THE MERCHANTS OF MAIN STREET

Not everyone was excited to see Sam and his mechanized Walmart army arrive and succeed. Small merchants across America shuddered when the winds of the "Walmart Way" began to blow. Kennedy Smith of the National Main Street Center in Washington, DC, said, "The first thing towns usually do is panic." Once Walmart comes to town, Smith says, "Downtowns will never again be the providers of basic consumer goods and services they once were."[18]

STEAMBOAT SPRINGS

Some towns learned to "just say 'no'" to Walmart's overtures. Steamboat Springs, Colorado, is one such city. Colorado newspapers called it the "Shootout at Steamboat Springs." Walmart was denied permission to build on a nine-acre parcel along U.S. Route 40. Owners of upscale shops and condos were very concerned with the image of their resort community, and Walmart, with its low-cost reputation, just did not fit. The shootout lasted for two years, and finally Walmart filed a damage suit against the city. Countersuits followed. A petition was circulated to hold a referendum on the matter. This was the shot that made Walmart blink and back down. Just before the vote, Don Shinkle, corporate affairs vice president, said, "A vote would not be good for Steamboat Springs, and it would not be good for Walmart. I truly believe Walmart is a kinder, gentler company, and, while we have the votes to win, an election would only split the town more."[19]

Iowa City

In Iowa City, Iowa (population more than 50,000), Walmart was planning an 87,000-square-foot store on the outskirts of the town. A group of citizens gathered enough signatures during a petition drive to put a referendum on the ballot to block Walmart and the city council from building the new store (the city council had approved the rezoning of the land Walmart wanted). Jim Clayton, a downtown merchant, said, "Walmart is a freight train going full steam in the opposite direction of this town's philosophy." If businesses wind up going down, Clayton says, "you lose their involvement in the community, involvement I promise you won't get with some assistant manager over at Walmart."[20] Walmart spokesperson Brenda Lockhart commented that downtown merchants can benefit from the increase in customer traffic provided "they offer superior service and aren't gouging their customers."[21] Efforts to stop Walmart and the Iowa City Council were not successful. Walmart opened its Iowa City store on November 5, 1991.

Pawhuska, Oklahoma

Meanwhile, in Pawhuska, Oklahoma, as a result of Walmart's entry in 1983 and other local factors, the local "five-and-dime," JCPenney, Western Auto, and a whole block of other stores closed their doors. Four years later, Dave Story, general manager of the local *Pawhuska Daily Journal Capital*, wrote that Walmart was a "billion-dollar parasite" and a "national retail ogre."[22]

Walmart managers have become very active in Pawhuska and surrounding communities since that time. A conversation with the editor of the Pawhuska paper, Jody Smith, and her advertising editor, Suzy Burns, revealed that Walmart sponsored the local rodeo, gave gloves to the local coat drive, and was involved with the local cerebral palsy and multiple sclerosis fund-raisers. On the other hand, Fred Wright, former owner of a TV and record store, said, "Walmart really craters a little town's downtown."[23]

Kinder, Louisiana

Consider the small town of Kinder, Louisiana (population 2,608), in 1981. On December 31, 1990, the store was closed. During the time Walmart operated in Kinder, one-third of the downtown stores closed. The downtown became three blocks of mostly run-down, red-brick buildings. The closest place to buy shoes or sewing thread was 30 miles away in Oakdale, Louisiana—at another Walmart. Moreover, Kinder lost $5,500 in annual tax revenues, which represented 10 percent of the total revenues for the city.

The tactics Walmart employed during its ten years in Kinder left a bad taste in the mouths of some small retailers. Soon after Walmart's arrival, a price war broke out between Walmart and the downtown retailers. The retailers told *The Atlanta Journal-Constitution* in November 1990, "Walmart sent employees, wearing name tags and smocks, into their stores to scribble down prices and list merchandise." Lou Pearl, owner of Kinder Jewelry and Gifts, stated that Walmart associates came to her store and noted the type of art supplies she was carrying. Shortly thereafter, Walmart began carrying the same merchandise at discount prices. Sales at Kinder Jewelry and Gifts dropped drastically, and Pearl dropped the merchandise line.[24] Within several weeks, so did Walmart. Troy Marcantel, a 29-year-old downtown clothing merchant, said it best: "What really rankled me was that they used people we have known all our lives. I still don't understand how our own people could do that to us."[25]

OPPOSITION TO WALMART GETS ORGANIZED

By the 1990s, there were dozens of organized groups actively opposing Walmart's expansion.[26] Some of these groups were and still are run by social activists dating back to the 1960s and 1970s. Instead of protesting the Vietnam War, nuclear proliferation, or the destruction of the environment, they turned their efforts to Walmart specifically and capitalism in general. One of these activists, Paul Glover, who was an antiwar organizer, defined Walmart as the epitome of capitalism, which he despises. For Glover and others, Walmart stands for "everything they dislike about American society—mindless consumerism, paved landscapes, and homogenization of community identity."[27]

BOULDER, COLORADO

In Boulder, Colorado, Walmart tried to counter these allegations by proposing a "green" store. Steven Lane, Walmart's real estate manager, said that a "green store" would be built that would be environmentally friendly, with a solar-powered sign out front and everything. His efforts were trumped by Spencer Havlick, an organizer of the first Earth Day in 1970, suggesting that the entire store be powered by solar energy. Mr. Lane did not respond.[28]

Protest organizers united against the spread of the "Walmart Way" differ from the downtown merchants in that these protesters have no financial stake. Hence, these activists are attacking on a higher plane, a philosophical plane. The accusations ring with a tone of argument that was made by other activists protesting polluting industries (e.g., the coal, nuclear, and chemical industries). These activists accuse Walmart of "strip-mining" towns and communities of their culture and values.

One possible root of this culture clash may be attributed to the unique facets of the internal corporate culture at Walmart's headquarters. This is a place where competition for the reputation as the "cheapest" is practiced. An example is the competition among employees in procuring the cheapest haircut, shoes, or necktie. Walmart is a place where playacting as a backwoods "hick" has been an acceptable behavior within the organization. Consequently, as a result of the internal culture of Walmart and the external environment, some analysts believe that a clash of priorities was inevitable as Walmart moved into larger, more urban settings.

NEW ENGLAND OPPOSITION

Some of the greatest opposition to Walmart's growth came from the New England area. This area holds great promise for Walmart because of the large population and the many underserved towns. These towns are typically underserved in three ways: in variety of product choices, in value, and in convenience. The opposition to Walmart entering these New England markets includes some high-profile names, such as Jerry Greenfield, cofounder of Ben & Jerry's Homemade ice cream, and Arthur Frommer, a well-known travel writer.[29] In addition to New England, other areas, such as resort areas, opposed Walmarts because they wanted to insulate their unique cultures from what they considered to be the offensive consumerism that is usually generated by Walmart's presence.

SPRAWL-BUSTERS

Al Norman, a lobbyist and media consultant, turned opposition to Walmart into a cottage industry. Norman publishes a monthly newsletter called *Sprawl-Busters Alert*. He has also developed a Web site (http://www.sprawl-busters.com/) that has vast information for citizens who are fighting to prevent Walmart or other "big box" stores from locating in their cities or neighborhoods. Norman achieved national attention in 1993, when he stopped Walmart from locating in his hometown of Greenfield, Massachusetts. Since then, he has appeared on *60 Minutes*, which called him "the guru of the anti-Walmart movement," and has gained widespread media attention. Today Norman continues to serve as a consultant and travels throughout the United States, helping dozens of coalitions fight Walmart. Norman has published two books: *Slam-Dunking Wal-Mart: How You Can Stop Superstore Sprawl in Your Hometown* and *The Case Against Wal-Mart*. In his books, he lays out the arguments against urban "sprawl."

On the *Sprawl-Busters* Web page, consumers around the country are given the opportunity to write in the details of their fights with Walmart. Examples in 2009–2010 included conflicts in Tuscon, Arizona; Monroeville, Pennsylvania; Ogden, Utah; and Galt, California.[30] In actuality, conflicts between Walmart and cities are taking place every day all over the country now.

Sprawl-Busters is not alone in its focused criticism of Walmart's presence in communities. Another organization, Wal-Mart Watch, has an active Web page (http://Wal-Martwatch.com/) that details what it believes to be Walmart's threat to America. Wal-Mart Watch is a joint project of The Center for Community & Corporate Ethics, a 501c3 organization devoted to studying the impact of large corporations on society.[31]

AGGRESSIVE GROWTH, A NEW CEO, AND CONTINUING CHALLENGES

For its part, Walmart has continued its aggressive diversification and growth pattern. At a retail industry convention, Lee Scott, Walmart's then CEO, was asked whether Walmart was trying to take over the world. Scott replied, "I don't think so. All we want to do is grow." But as *The Economist* magazine has asked, "How *big* can it grow?"[32] In the fall of 2008, Lee Scott announced his retirement and that beginning

---

FIGURE 1 Recent Statistics about Walmart

General Facts
- Walmart is the world's largest retailer with $405 billion in sales for the fiscal year ending January 31, 2010.
- In the United States, Walmart Stores, Inc., operates more than 4,300 facilities including Walmart supercenters, discount stores, neighborhood markets, and Sam's Club warehouses.
- Internationally, Walmart operates more than 4,000 additional stores in 15 markets worldwide, including Argentina, Brazil, Canada, Chile, China, Costa Rica, El Salvador, Guatemala, Honduras, India, Japan, Mexico, Nicaragua, the United Kingdom, and the United States.
- Walmart employs more than 2.1 million associates worldwide, including more than 1.4 million in the United States. Walmart is not only one of the largest private employers in the United States, but also the largest in Mexico and one of the largest in Canada as well.
- Walmart employs more than 257,000 African-American associates, more than 41,000 Asian and 5,900 Pacific Islander associates, more than 171,000 Hispanic associates, more than 16,000 American Indian and Alaskan Native associates, more than 869,000 women, and more than 430,000 mature associates who are 50 and older.
- In 2010, *Fortune* magazine's ranking of the world's most admired companies ranked Walmart Stores in the top ten of its 50 All Stars.

Community
- Walmart strives to be a good neighbor and to benefit the communities where it operates. In the United States, the company and the Walmart Foundation gave more than $378 million in cash and in-kind gifts in the fiscal year ending 2009.
- Walmart makes the majority of its charitable donations at the local level, where it can have the greatest and most positive impact. Walmart and its foundations gave $423 million globally in fiscal year ending 2009.
- Walmart takes pride in being a part of every community it serves.

Recent Accolades for Walmart*
2010
- 40 Best Companies for Diversity—*Black Enterprise* magazine
- 2010 Most Valuable Employers (MVE) for Military by CivilianJobs.com
- 2010 World Environment Center Gold Medal for International Corporate Achievement in Sustainable Development
- 20 Best Companies for Multicultural Women—Working Mother.com
- Ranked #1 for Retail and #9 Overall as Fast Company's "Most Innovative Companies 2010"
- Donor of the Year by Feeding America, for providing funds, vehicles, and more than 100-million pounds of food

2009
- 2009 Waste Reduction Awards Program Winner—California Integrated Waste Management Board
- President's Trophy—American Trucking Association (ATA)
- Ranked #3 out of 35 other retailers in the Q3 2009 Covalence ethical reputation index
- Ranked #1 Consumer Staples Company—Carbon Disclosure Project (CDP) 2008 report (see page 8) and scored 89 out of a possible 100
- Green Power Leadership Award for on-site generation at our California and Texas facilities—Environment Protection Agency (EPA)
- Corporate Energy Conservation, Energy and Environment Award—Aspen Institute

---

*Wal-Mart Stores, Awards and Recognitions, http://walmartstores.com/AboutUs/336.aspx. Accessed July 4, 2010.
Sources: Walmart Fact Sheets, http://walmartstores.com/pressroom/FactSheets/. Accessed June 10, 2010; "The World's Most Admired Companies," *Fortune* (March 22, 2010), 121–126; "First," *Fortune* (May 3, 2010), 27–28.

---

on February 1, 2009, Scott's groomed successor for the position, Mike Duke, would become the new CEO. Duke took over a company that had grown significantly under Scott. In Scott's final years as CEO, he had worked hard to improve the image of the company and, in spite of ongoing criticisms of the retail behemoth, had succeeded in making the company more likable. According to *The Wall Street Journal*, by 2009, Walmart's image had moved from demon to darling as a result of the strategies the company had employed. [33] Figure 1 provides some revealing current statistics about Walmart.

New Forms of Clandestine Opposition Emerge

In the summer of 2010, *The Wall Street Journal* reported that there was a new form of opposition to Walmart's growth—rival chains that had secretly funded opposition to Walmart's entrance into communities. By 2009, grocery sales had reached 51 percent of Walmart's total revenues. What *The Wall Street Journal* learned through investigative research was that in Mundelein, Illinois, a town about 20 miles northwest of Chicago with a population of about 35,000, a grocery chain with about nine stores in the area had hired Saint Consulting Group to secretly operate an anti-Walmart campaign. It was revealed that Saint had developed a specialty in fighting proposed Walmarts in communities and were using techniques it described as "black arts."[34]

Large supermarket chains such as Supervalue, Inc., Safeway, Inc., and Ahold NV retained Saint Consulting to block Walmart's entrance into communities, according to pages of Saint's documents and interviews with employees that the newspaper was able to obtain. It was reported that Saint had jokingly dubbed its staff the "Walmart killers." Supervalue's goal in retaining Saint in the Mundelein, Illinois, case was to block Walmart from competing with its nine Jewel-Osco supermarkets located within the area. City officials claimed that the efforts stalled the development of a major shopping center for three years and cost the community millions in lost sales and sales taxes.[35] It turns out that other grocery chains have employed Saint to block Walmarts in other states. Safeway hired Saint to thwart Walmart superstores in more than 30 towns in California. Earlier, in Pennsylvania, Saint had 53 projects on its books, with most of them targeted toward stopping Walmarts. These were on behalf of Giant Food Stores. According to Saint's records for the year 2007, it had lost one battle in Pennsylvania, defeated 13 projects, and delayed the remaining ones for four months to four years.[36]

The techniques used by Saint Consulting were usually clandestine. In a typical anti-Walmart project, a Saint executive would drop into the town under an assumed name and take charge of the local opposition to the store. They would flood local politicians with calls, using multiple phone lines to make it look like they were coming from different people. They would hire lawyers and traffic experts to derail the project or stall it. They would flood neighborhoods with flyers outlining the purported evils of a Walmart entering their area and the subsequent traffic and increased police calls that would follow. They would hope that the developer would back off, slow down, or drop the project altogether. They operated in secret. They deployed their strategies under assumed names and never revealed their clients' names because clients didn't want their names publicly known for fear it would draw adverse publicity or lawsuits should they be known. P. Michael Saint, founder of the consulting group, was quoted by *The Wall Street Journal* as saying that there was nothing illegal in what his company was doing and that they were protected by the First Amendment for using such secret processes to thwart the competition.[37]

Planet Walmart

The New York Times has argued that Walmart has become a nation unto itself. In fact, the newspaper stated that if Walmart were an independent nation, it would be China's eighth-largest trading partner. In terms of its low prices and impact, some economists say that the company has single-handedly cut inflation by 1 percent in some years as it has saved customers billions of dollars annually.[38] It is little wonder the newspaper calls it "The Walmartization of America."[39] Because of its number one ranking in the 2010 *Fortune* 500 listing, based on size, the magazine referred to the company as "Planet Walmart."[40]

Global Growth

In addition to domestic growth, Walmart continues its aggressive growth internationally. Today, Walmart International is a fast-growing part of Walmart's overall operations, with 4,112 stores and more than 680,000 associates in 14 countries outside the continental United States. Today, at its 2010 annual meeting, CEO Michael Duke made it clear that the company's future growth trajectory would be in distant lands. In 2009, the company's international sales exceeded $100 billion, accounting for one-fourth of the company's $405 billion in revenue. Duke made it clear that domestic growth would continue, but that the chain was committed to being "truly global." CEO Duke also made it clear that Walmart planned to emphasize mobile shopping and that it was upgrading its technology to make this happen.[41]

Political Activism

It was Walmart's desire to grow globally that caused the company to ramp up its efforts at lobbying in Washington, DC. The precipitating event was

Walmart's realization that U.S. negotiators had agreed upon a 30-store limit on retailers operating in China when it agreed to support China's entry into the World Trade Organization in the late 1990s. As a result of this realization, the company decided it had to get into lobbying even though it went against founder Sam Walton's policy of staying out of politics. Today, Walmart has a large number of lobbyists on its payroll and a number of other hired political consultants to help it. The company's political action committee grew to become the biggest corporate donor to federal parties and candidates, with more than $1 million in contributions.[42]

Millions of Supporters

In spite of its challenges, Walmart has millions of supporters. Over 100 million of Walmart's customers visit them weekly. Many consider the company to be socially responsible in addition to being a provider of thousands of jobs, low prices, and high value and service. At the end of the first decade of the new millennium, Walmart has numerous corporate citizenship initiatives at the local and national levels. Locally, Walmart stores underwrite college scholarships for high school seniors, raise funds for children's hospitals through the Children's Miracle Network Telethon, provide local fund-raisers money and workforce, and educate the public about recycling and other environmental topics with the help of "Green Coordinators."[43] In 1998, the Walton Family Charitable Support Foundation, the charitable program created by Sam Walton's family, announced what at the time was the largest ever single gift made to an American business school: $50 million to the College of Business Administration of the University of Arkansas. Helen R. Walton, the "first lady" of Walmart, said that she and her husband established the Foundation to support specific charities, including the University.[44]

Achievements

On its own Web site, Walmart touts in detail its achievements. It says the American public appreciates Walmart's community-involvement efforts and it has received many recognitions. Below are some recent honors:[45]

2010

- 2010 Most Valuable Employers (MVE) for Military by CivilianJobs.com

- Donor of the Year by Feeding America, for providing funds, vehicles, and more than 100-million pounds of food

2009

- The National Urban League honored Walmart with the 2009 Corporate Leadership Award during the organization's 53rd annual Equal Opportunity Day Awards Dinner.
- Diversity *MBA* magazine has ranked Walmart No. 2 on their 2009 "50 Out Front Companies for Diversity Leadership: Best Places for Diverse Manger to Work" list.

Today, Walmart reports on its corporate citizenship in a highly visible way. Through its Walmart Foundation, it promotes its support of education, military, hunger relief, disaster relief, and giving programs.

Walmart's Power and Impact

In spite of its achievements, article titles from recent newspapers and magazines raise questions about Walmart's power and impact. Some of these include the following:

"The Wal-Martization of America"[46]
"Is Wal-Mart Too Powerful?"[47]
"Is Wal-Mart Good for America?"[48]
"One Nation under Wal-Mart"[49]
"Wal-Mart Gives Globalization a Bad Name"[50]
"Attack of the Wal-Martyrs"[51]
"Wal-Mart's Midlife Crisis"[52]
"Planet Wal-Mart"[53]

EPILOGUE

Sam, the hired gun, learned his lessons well. The people who bought at his stores were well satisfied. The downtown merchants who survived learned to coexist with the hired gun's associates. But things would never be the same. The changes had come rapidly. The social fabric of the small town was changed forever. The larger cities continued to fight, but had only limited success.

The hired gun rode on, searching for that next town that needed to be liberated from the downtown price-fixing bad guys. The search has become more complicated as the opposition has risen, but the spirit of Sam rides on.

AN EMBATTLED WALMART: A CONTINUING STREAM OF ISSUES

Walmart's size, power, and impact on local communities is where criticism of the company began. This included the threat of putting other merchants out of business, the creation of urban sprawl, and the traffic congestion created when the company decides to locate in a particular area.

In the past few years, Walmart has begun to face other important issues. In addition to antisprawl activists and merchants, Walmart is now facing new opposition from competitors, labor unions, other activist organizations, and lawsuits. Its labor practices have been increasingly questioned. The company has been accused of paying wages so low that workers cannot live off them, making employees work "off the clock" without overtime pay, paying few or low benefits, and taking advantage of illegal immigrants. In 2004, the company was hit with a class-action lawsuit on gender discrimination against women. This class action lawsuit covers 1.6 million current and former employees, making it the largest private civil rights case in U.S. history. This case is still ongoing almost a decade later. In late 2008, Walmart agreed to pay up to $640 million to settle 63 state class-action lawsuits regarding overtime.[54]

Because these issues are so expansive and important, they are not addressed in the present case. Another case, focusing primarily on Walmart's labor practices and some of the issues outlined above, has been prepared for separate discussion. Case 32, titled "Walmart and Its Associates," may be discussed immediately following this case or deferred until a more in-depth consideration of employee stakeholders is undertaken.

QUESTIONS FOR DISCUSSION

1. What are the major issues in this case? Assess Walmart's corporate social responsibility using the four-part CSR model. Is Walmart socially responsible while it has a devastating impact on small merchants? What about its impact on communities in terms of sprawl, traffic congestion, and impact on the appearance of the environment? What responsibility, if any, does the company have to these merchants or to the communities it enters?

2. Sam Walton has been called a motivational genius. After reading this case, and with what you have observed at your local Walmart store, explain how this motivational genius empowered the employee. What is the "Walmart Way"? Explain its impact on the associate and on the community. What has happened now that Sam is no longer the motivational leader?

3. Walmart was an early leader in the area of corporate social responsibility. How do the "Buy American" program and the "Environmental Awareness" campaign illustrate this? Were these programs really early examples of corporate social responsibility or were they gimmicks to entice customers into the stores? Are the benefits of its more recent corporate citizenship programs offset by the company's detrimental impact on merchants?

4. Walmart has closed five stores in its short history. What responsibility, if any, does Walmart have to the employees who are let go? What about its loyal customers and the community?

5. Walmart continues to find severe resistance to its expansion into New England and California. From Walmart's perspective, draw the stakeholder map. Define the true goals of the opponents of Walmart. Include a consideration of the following: (a) stopping Walmart's expansion, (b) preserving the status quo (e.g., downtown community and social fabric), (c) developing a cause that will pay their bills, (d) fighting for an ideology, or (e) something else. What should Walmart do?

6. What is your assessment of competitors secretly hiring consulting firms to block Walmart's entry into new communities? Is this an ethical practice? Is this a fair trade practice with respect to competitor stakeholders?

7. As Walmart continues its expansion into the international arena, what problems or issues do you anticipate it will face? In general, what should Walmart's approach be in these other countries? Is it unethical to change another country's culture?

ENDNOTES

1. Wal-Mart Stores, Inc. (NYSE: WMT) is the legal name of the corporation. The name "Walmart," expressed as one word and without punctuation, is a trademark of the company and is used analogously to describe the company and its stores.

2. Vance H. Trimble, *Sam Walton: The Inside Story of America's Richest Man* (New York: Penguin Books, 1990), 30. Also see Bob Ortega, *In Sam We Trust* (New York: Times Business, 1998).

3. *Ibid.*, 34.

4. Janice Castro, "Mr. Sam Stuns Goliath," *Time* (February 25, 1991), 62.

5. Walmart's Web page, http://www.walmartstores .com, "Wal-Mart at a Glance."

6. "Why Wal-Mart Wants to Take the Driver's Seat," *Bloomberg Businessweek* (May 31–June 6, 2010), 17–18.

7. For up-to-date information on the Walmart culture, see http://www.walmartstores/com.

8. John Huey, "America's Most Successful Merchant," *Fortune* (September 23, 1991), 50.

9. Walmart's Web page, *Ibid.*

10. Trimble, 260.

11. *Ibid.*, 261.

12. "Made in the USA," http://www.pbs.org/itvs/store-wars/stores3.html.

13. Richard Turcsik, "A New Environment Evolves at Wal-Mart," *Supermarket News* (January 15, 1990), 10.

14. *Ibid.*, 10.

15. *Ibid.*, 11.

16. Walmart Corporation, *Walmart Associates Handbook* (July 1991), 14.

17. *Ibid.*, 14.

18. Dan Koeppel, "Wal-Mart Finds New Rivals on Main Street," *Adweek's Marketing Week* (November 10, 1990), 5.

19. Trimble, 255.

20. "Just Saying No to Wal-Mart," *Newsweek* (November 13, 1989), 65.

21. *Ibid.*, 65.

22. Karen Blumenthal, "Arrival of Discounter Tears the Civic Fabric of Small-Town Life," *The Wall Street Journal* (April 14, 1987), 1, 23.

23. *Ibid.*, 23.

24. Charles Haddad, "Wal-Mart Leaves Town 'High, Dry,'" *The Atlanta Journal-Constitution* (November 26, 1990), A4.

25. *Ibid.*, A4.

26. Bob Ortega, "Aging Activists Turn, Turn, Turn Attention to Wal-Mart Protests," *The Wall Street Journal* (October 11, 1994), A1, A8.

27. *Ibid.*, A1.

28. *Ibid.*, A8.

29. Joseph Pereira and Bob Ortega, "Once Easily Turned Away by Local Foes, Wal-Mart Gets Tough in New England," *The Wall Street Journal* (September 7, 1994), B1.

30. Sprawl-Busters, Newsflashes, http://www.sprawl-busters.com/search.php?SRCHrecent=1. Accessed June 4, 2010.

31. About Wal-Mart Watch, http://walmartwatch .com/. Accessed June 4, 2010.

32. "Special Report on Wal-Mart: How Big Can It Grow?" *The Economist* (April 17, 2004), 67–69.

33. Ann Zimmerman, "Wal-Mart's Image Moves from Demon to Darling," *The Wall Street Journal* (July 16, 2009), B1.

34. Ann Zimmerman, "Rival Chains Secretly Fund Opposition to Wal-Mart," *The Wall Street Journal* (June 7, 2010), A1.

35. *Ibid.*, A16.

36. *Ibid.*

37. *Ibid.*

38. Steven Greenhouse, "Wal-Mart, a Nation unto Itself," *The New York Times* (April 17, 2004), A15.

39. "The Wal-Martization of America," *The New York Times* (November 15, 2003), A26.

40. "First," *Fortune* (May 3, 2010), 27.

41. Stephanie Clifford and Stephanie Rosenbloom, "With a Backdrop of Glitz, Wal-Mart Stresses Its Global Growth," *The New York Times* (June 5, 2010), B3.

42. Jeanne Cummings, "Wal-Mart Opens for Business in Tough Market: Washington," *The Wall Street Journal* (March 24, 2004), A1.

43. Walmart Web page, http://www.walmartstores .com.

44. University of Arkansas Web page, http://www .uark.edu (October 6, 1998), press release.

45. Awards and Recognitions, Walmart, http://wal-martstores.com/CommunityGiving/338.aspx. Accessed June 10, 2010.

46. *The New York Times* (November 15, 2003), A26.

47. *BusinessWeek* (October 6, 2003), 100–110.

48. *The New York Times* (December 7, 2003), 1WK.

49. *Fortune* (March 3, 2003), 66–78.

50. Jeffrey E. Garten, "Wal-Mart Gives Globalization a Bad Name," *BusinessWeek* (March 8, 2004), 24.

51. Barney Gimbel, "Attack of the Wal-Martyrs," *Fortune* (December 11, 2006), 125–130.

52. Anthony Bianco, "Wal-Mart's Midlife Crisis," *BusinessWeek* (April 30, 2007), 46–56.

53. "First," *Fortune* (May 3, 2010), 27.

54. *Ibid.*

CASE 2

The Body Shop: Pursuing Social and Environmental Change*

When North American consumers are asked to describe the cosmetics industry, they often respond with words such as "glamour" and "beauty." Beginning in 1976, The Body Shop International PLC (BSI) provided a contrast to this image by selling a range of 400 products designed to "cleanse and polish the skin and hair." The product line included such items as "Honeyed Beeswax, Almond, and Jojoba Oil Cleanser" and "Carrot Facial Oil." Women's cosmetics and men's toiletries were also available. They were all produced without the use of animal testing and were packaged in plain-looking, recyclable packages.[1]

The Body Shop's primary channel of distribution was a network of over 600 franchised retail outlets in Europe, Australia, Asia, and North America.[2] The company had enjoyed annual growth rates of approximately 50 percent until 1990, when net income began to level off. The media raised few questions about this decline in performance, because the firm's social agenda and exotic product line captured most of the public's interest. Indeed, early on, The Body Shop was the poster-child company for the burgeoning corporate social responsibility (CSR) movement.

ANITA RODDICK: FOUNDER

The company's managing director and founder Anita Roddick was responsible for creating and maintaining much of the company's marketing strategy and product development.[3] Roddick believed that The Body Shop was fundamentally different from other firms in the cosmetics industry because, in her own words, "we don't claim that our products will make you look younger, we say they will only help you look your best."[4] She regularly assailed her competitors: "We loathe the cosmetics industry with a passion. It's run by men who create needs that don't exist."[5] During the 1980s, Anita Roddick became one of the richest women in the United Kingdom by challenging the well-established firms and rewriting the rules of the cosmetics industry.

HONORS AND AWARDS

Anita Roddick was greatly admired within the business community for the conviction of her beliefs and the success of her company. She received many honors and awards, including the UK Businesswoman of the Year in 1985, the British Retailer of the Year in 1989, and the Order of the British Empire.[6] The firm's customers included several celebrities, including Diana, Princess of Wales; Sting; and Bob Weir of the Grateful Dead. Ben Cohen, cofounder and chairman of Ben & Jerry's, described her as an incredibly dynamic, passionate, humorous, and intelligent individual who believes "it's the responsibility of a business to give back to the community…she understands that a business has the power to influence the world in a positive way."[7]

Roddick opened the first Body Shop store in Brighton, England, as a means of supporting her family while her husband, Gordon Roddick, was taking a year-long sabbatical in America. Gordon, a chartered accountant by trade, was using much of their savings to finance his trip. Anita Roddick had little money to open a store, much less to develop products or purchase packaging materials.[8]

FIELD EXPEDITIONS

Roddick called upon her previous experience as a resource to get started. Having been a United Nations researcher for several years in the 1960s, she had had many opportunities during field expeditions to see how men and women in Africa, Asia, and Australia used locally grown plants and extracts, such as beeswax, rice grains, almonds, bananas, and jojoba, as grooming products. She knew that these materials were inexpensive and readily obtainable. With some library research, she found several recipes, some of which were centuries old, that used these same ingredients to make cosmetics and skin cleansers. With the addition of inexpensive bottles and handwritten labels, Roddick quickly developed a line of products for sale in her first Body Shop store. She soon opened a second store in a nearby town. When Gordon Roddick returned to the United Kingdom in 1977, The Body Shop was recording sizable profits. At Anita's request, he joined the company as its chief executive officer.[9]

---

*This case was prepared by William A. Sodeman, Hawaii Pacific University, using publicly available information. It was revised by Archie B. Carroll in 2010.

EARLY STRATEGY: THE POWER TO DO GOOD

The Body Shop's early strategy grew out of the company's reliance on cost containment. Roddick was able to afford only 600 bottles when she opened her first store. Since she was looking for the cheapest packaging option, she chose urine sample bottles. Customers were offered a small discount to encourage the return of empty bottles for product refills. This offer was extended to both retail and mail-order customers.[10] The Body Shop could not afford advertising, and Roddick didn't believe in it, so she resolved to succeed without it.[11]

The Body Shop's retail stores were somewhat different from the cosmetic salons and counters familiar to shoppers in highly industrialized nations. The typical retail sales counter relied on high-pressure tactics that included promotions, makeovers, and an unspoken contract with the customer that virtually required a purchase in order for the customer to receive any advice or consultation from a sales counter employee.[12] By contrast, Body Shop employees were taught to wait for the customer to ask questions, be forthright and helpful, and not to press for sales.[13]

According to Roddick, "Businesses have the power to do good. That's why The Body Shop's Mission Statement opens with the overriding commitment, 'To dedicate our business to the pursuit of social and environmental change.' We use our stores and our products to help communicate human rights and environmental issues."[14]

EMPLOYEES AND HIRING PROCEDURES

Store employees were paid a half-day's wage every week to perform community service activities. At the company headquarters in Littlehampton, England, The Body Shop employed an anthropologist, six herbalists, and a variety of others in similar fields. There was nothing that resembled a marketing department. Husbands and wives frequently worked together and could visit their children during the workday at the on-site day-care center.[15] The company's hiring procedures included questions about the applicant's personal heroes and literary tastes, as well as their individual beliefs on certain social issues. On one occasion, Roddick was ready to hire a retail director, but refused to do so when he professed his fondness for hunting, a sport that Roddick despised because of her support for animal rights.[16]

PROSPERITY AND SOCIAL ACTIVISM

As the company prospered, Anita Roddick used her enthusiasm and growing influence on her suppliers and customers. The Body Shop began to produce products in the country of origin when it was feasible and paid the workers wages that were comparable to those in the European Community.[17] Customers were asked to sign petitions and join activist groups that The Body Shop endorsed, mostly in the areas of animal rights and environmental causes. The company said it was contributing significant portions of its earnings to these groups, including Amnesty International and People for the Ethical Treatment of Animals (PETA). Roddick was careful to choose causes that were "easy to understand"[18] and could be communicated quickly to a customer during a visit to a Body Shop store.

OPPOSITION TO ANIMAL TESTING

An example of corporate activism was The Body Shop's opposition to a practice that had become common in the cosmetics industry. Cosmetics firms were not required to perform animal testing of their products to comply with product safety and health regulations. Rather, companies voluntarily adopted animal-based testing procedures to guard against product liability lawsuits.[19]

The Body Shop was not worried about such lawsuits, because the product ingredients Roddick chose had been used safely for centuries. In addition, the older recipes had been used for many decades without incident. These circumstances led to the company's rejection of animal-based product testing. Any supplier wishing to do business with The Body Shop had to sign a statement guaranteeing that it had done no animal testing for the previous five years and would never do such testing in the future. The Body Shop used human volunteers from its own staff and the University Hospital of Wales to test new and current products under normal use. The company also volunteered to share the results of its tests on individual ingredients with other cosmetics manufacturers.[20]

Most other cosmetics firms used a variety of procedures to determine the safety of cosmetics products, with two animal-based tests becoming the standard procedures.

The Draize Test The Draize test involved dripping the substance in question, such as shampoo or a detergent paste, into the eyes of conscious, restrained rabbits and measuring the resultant damage over the course of several days. Rabbits cannot cry, which allowed researchers to complete the tests quickly.

LD50 Test Another test required researchers to force-feed large quantities of a substance to a sample of laboratory animals. The substance could be a solid (such as lipstick or shaving cream), a paste, or a liquid. The lethal dose of a substance was determined by the amount that had been ingested by an individual surviving animal when 50 percent of the sample had died; hence the name of the test, LD50.[21] Beginning in the 1970s, animal rights groups such as the Humane Society and PETA began protesting the use of these tests by the cosmetics industry. The Body Shop lent its support to these groups' efforts, labeling all animal testing as "cruel and unnecessary." By 1991, alternative procedures that involved far less cruelty to animals had already been developed, but were yet to be approved for industry use.[22]

THE BODY SHOP IN THE UNITED STATES

In the United States, The Body Shop's market share was limited by two factors. First, its prices were significantly higher than those charged for mass-marketed products in drugstores, although they were generally comparable to the prices charged for cosmetics and cleansers at department store sales counters. Second, The Body Shop was constrained by the number of stores it had opened in the United States. By 1991, only 40 stores had been opened in a dozen metropolitan areas across the country. A mail-order catalog and a telephone order line were used to supplement the American retail stores, but they were inadequate substitutes for the product sampling and advice that were readily available at The Body Shop's stores. Roddick maintained that those consumers who sampled Body Shop products became loyal customers: "Once they walk into one of our stores or buy from our catalogue, they're hooked."[23]

Going Public

The Body Shop was taken public in London in 1984, with the Roddicks owning a combined 30 percent of the outstanding stock. The firm's subsequent sales and net income figures grew during 1985–1990 from sales revenue of $15.3 and net income of $1.4 million to $137.7 and $14.7 million, respectively.[24] Without The Body Shop's monetary donations to various social causes, all of these net income figures would be higher than reported in the financial statements. Estimates of the company's annual contributions to outside organizations varied from several hundred thousand dollars to several million dollars.

Industry analysts considered The Body Shop to be a strong performer with the potential to prosper even in an economic downturn. The exotic nature of its products, such as hair conditioner made with 10 percent real bananas and a peppermint foot lotion, would attract consumers who desired affordable luxuries. Analysts regarded the public's desire for personal care products as "insatiable," especially in North America.[25] The addition of the strong emotional appeal of social issues formed the basis for one of the most successful marketing and promotional concepts in the cosmetics industry in decades.

The 20th anniversary of Earth Day, celebrated in 1990, focused media attention on many of the environmental issues that Roddick and The Body Shop regularly addressed. Further, it spurred interest in environmental issues in the commercial sector.

Competition

Several new entrants and existing competitors challenged The Body Shop in the United States and Europe. Among the largest of these firms were Estée Lauder and Revlon. The Limited had opened 50 Bath & Body Works stores, patterned after The Body Shop's outlets and located in shopping malls across the United States. In addition, an English competitor, Crabtree & Evelyn, had held a significant presence in North America and Europe since the mid-1970s.

By 1991, The Body Shop was a successful and profitable firm that had attracted a variety of well-financed competitors. The company faced a real threat from these firms because they were all well financed and had a broad range of experience in marketing cosmetics. Each of these firms was well established in the United States, yet no one firm dominated the new product segment that The Body Shop had helped create.

In addition, there were indications that the environmental concerns that attracted customers to The Body Shop might not have permanent drawing power. Roddick had vowed never to sell anything but environmentally friendly cosmetics and grooming products in her stores, but the industry was growing and changing faster than anyone had anticipated. It seemed that The Body Shop needed to take some kind of action to ensure its long-term survival.

THE BODY SHOP'S ADVERTISING CAMPAIGN

The first appearance by Anita Roddick in a U.S. television commercial was in 1993. This came as something of a surprise to long-time Body Shop customers and her competitors in the cosmetics industry. These people believed that Roddick abhorred advertising as a wasteful practice that "created" needs. The company did promote certain nonprofit groups in its stores and catalogs, including Greenpeace, PETA, and Amnesty International. However, The Body Shop had a policy of not advertising directly to consumers.[26]

AMERICAN EXPRESS AD

Roddick agreed to endorse an American Express marketing campaign that featured founders of fast-growing retail firms such as BSI and Crate & Barrel. Not coincidentally, all of the firms featured in the campaign accepted the American Express charge card as a payment method. The main message of the campaign was that customers of these stores preferred to use the American Express card and that the store founders also found the card useful in their day-to-day business.

Roddick appeared in three commercials and a series of print advertisements as part of this advertising campaign. The advertisements included Roddick's brief description of the company's purpose and sourcing practices, and used film footage and photographs of her travels in search of exotic new ingredients.

SELLING OUT?

Although the Roddick commercials received a positive response from advertising industry professionals, some long-time Body Shop customers accused Roddick of "selling out" and breaking her promise never to advertise Body Shop products. Roddick responded that the commercials promoted American Express and did not specifically promote Body Shop products. The advertisements gave The Body Shop valuable publicity in much the same way that Roddick's social activism and personal appearances had done in the past.

RUBY

In 1997, The Body Shop unveiled Ruby, a voluptuous size 18 doll created to counter media images of thin women.[27]

RODDICK'S ROLE IN THE COMPANY

When asked about her role in the company, founder Anita Roddick stated:

The purpose of a business isn't just to generate profits to create an ever-larger empire. It's to have the power to effect social change, to make the world a better place. I have always been an activist, I have always been incredibly impassioned about human rights and environmental issues. The Body Shop is simply my stage.[28]

QUESTIONS FOR DISCUSSION

1. In this case, how does The Body Shop address the four components of corporate social responsibility? In The Body Shop, what tensions among these components were at work?
2. Analyze The Body Shop's power using both levels and spheres of power discussed in Chapter 1. How do you assess the company's stated mission?
3. Does The Body Shop employ any questionable practices with respect to hiring? The Body Shop asks potential employees questions about "personal heroes" and individual beliefs. Is it ethical to ask such questions of applicants? Are such questions fair to the applicants?
4. What is your assessment of Anita Roddick's philosophy regarding the "purpose of a business"?
5. What are Anita Roddick's strengths and weaknesses as a leader? Should she stay on in a managing role or step aside and allow a more experienced person to run the marketing operations?
6. Anita Roddick claims that her firm does not advertise, yet it receives free media exposure and publicity through the social causes it champions and her personal appearances. Is this an appropriate approach for a business to follow?
7. What is your opinion of The Body Shop/American Express advertising campaign? Was it a sound business decision on Roddick's part? What does the American Express campaign imply about The Body Shop and its customers? Is this different from the image of the nonprofit organizations that The Body Shop endorses? Did Roddick commit an ethics transgression by advertising through the American Express ad that contravened her earlier statements and policy, or was this different? How should she explain herself?
8. Can a company such as The Body Shop succeed, trying to balance profitability with an obsession with social causes?

ENDNOTES

1. Catalog, The Body Shop (Fall 1990).
2. Laura Zinn, "Whales, Human Rights, Rain Forests—and the Heady Smell of Profits," *BusinessWeek* (July 15, 1991), 114.

3. *Ibid.*, 114.
4. Samuel Greengard, "Face Values," *USAir Magazine* (November 1990), 89.
5. Zinn, 114.
6. Greengard, 93.
7. *Ibid.*, 97.
8. Zinn, 115.
9. Greengard, 94.
10. *Ibid.*
11. Zinn, 114.
12. Greengard, 90.
13. Maria Koklanaris, "Trio of Retailers Finds Soap and Social Concern an Easy Sell," *The Washington Post* (April 27, 1991).
14. AnitaRoddick.com, http://www.anitaroddick.com/aboutanita.php. Accessed September 6, 2007.
15. Greengard, 90.
16. Zinn, 115.
17. The Body Shop promotional literature, 1991.
18. Zinn, 115.
19. The Body Shop promotional literature, 1991.
20. *Ibid.*
21. Peter Singer, *Animal Liberation: A New Ethics for Treatment of Animals* (New York: Avon Books, 1975), 48.
22. The Body Shop promotional literature, 1991.
23. Greengard, 89.
24. Compact Disclosure database, 1991.
25. Koklanaris.
26. The materials used in this section are based on Jennifer Conlin, "Survival of the Fittest," *Working Woman* (February 1994).
27. The Body Shop International PLC, "History," *Hoover's Online* (July 7, 2004).
28. Greengard, 97.

CASE 3

The Body Shop's Reputation Is Tarnished*

Between 1991 and 1995, The Body Shop continued to expand its operations. The company had opened 1,200 stores by early 1995.[1] Over 100 company-owned and franchised stores were operating in U.S. shopping malls and downtown shopping districts. During the period 1991–1994, sales and net income grew from $231 million and $41 million to $330 million and $47 million, respectively.

The Body Shop had moved its U.S. headquarters from Cedar Knolls, New Jersey, to a less expensive and more central location—Raleigh, North Carolina. The original location worked well when The Body Shop opened its first U.S. stores in New York City and Washington, DC, but soon proved to be a logistical problem. Roddick was frustrated that the New Jersey hires did not seem as creative or impulsive as her English staff. In retrospect, she realized that having some of her UK staff help train the first U.S. managers and employees or even setting up her headquarters in a college town such as Boulder, Colorado, or a city such as San Francisco would have been a better choice than starting from scratch in New Jersey.[2]

PROBLEMS ARISE

The Body Shop had bigger problems to deal with than the location of its national headquarters. The Limited continued to open its chain of Bath & Body Works stores on a nationwide scale. Placement of a Bath & Body Works store in a mall usually precluded The Body Shop from entering the same mall. (There were some exceptions, most notably very large shopping malls such as the Mall of America in Bloomington, Minnesota.) All of The Limited's stores, from Express and Victoria's Secret to Structure and Lerner's, were company owned. This allowed a greater degree of flexibility and speed than was the case with The Body Shop's franchising system. Further, The Limited had started grouping its stores in malls to create its own version of the department store. During the holidays, Express and Structure stores carried special selections of Bath & Body Works products to induce customer trial and develop brand awareness. The Limited's size and power as one of the major retailers in the United

---

* This case was prepared by William A. Sodeman, Hawaii Pacific University, using publicly available information. Revised by Archie B. Carroll, 2010.

States made the company a strong threat to The Body Shop's continued presence in the U.S. retail market. In an alarming move, The Limited began opening Bath & Body Works stores in the United Kingdom, which presented a direct threat to The Body Shop on the company's home soil.

CONFUSION

The similarities between The Body Shop and Bath & Body Works stores also created some confusion. Some less-observant customers of The Body Shop were bringing empty Bath & Body Works bottles to The Body Shop to be refilled because Bath & Body Works did not have its own refill policy and the products often seemed similar. The Body Shop protected its slogans, territory, and franchises with an aggressive legal strategy that included an out-of-court settlement with The Limited in 1993.[3]

COMPETITION

Other companies had successfully introduced organic or natural beauty products in discount and drugstores, a market segment that The Body Shop had completely ignored in its global operations. Traditional retailers including Woolworths and Kmart had also entered what had come to be known as the minimalist segment of the personal care products industry. Woolworths's entry was an expanded selection of organic bath and body case products in its deep-discount Rx Place chain. Kmart's line of naturalistic cosmetics was sold in over 1,800 stores.[4] Other new companies included H2O Plus, which sold its products in its own retail stores but did not make claims about animal testing as had The Body Shop and Bath & Body Works.

GOOD PRESS

The Body Shop continued to receive new accolades and to hit new heights of prosperity. Anita Roddick published her autobiography, *Body and Soul*, in late 1991. She donated her portion of the royalties to several groups, including the Unrepresented Nations and Peoples Organization, a self-governing group that spoke for Kurds, Tibetans, and Native Americans; the Medical Foundation, which treated victims of torture; and a variety of individual political prisoners. The 256-page book, which was written and designed by Roddick, Body Shop staff, and an outside group, resembled a mixture of catalog and personal memoir. Hundreds of pictures and headlines were used throughout to emphasize and clarify particular points of interest. On the final page of the book, where one would expect to see the last page of the index, is the coda of the final chapter. The last line of text, printed in large boldface letters, reads "Make no mistake about it—I'm doing this for me."[5]

MEDIA ATTENTION

Partly as a result of the book's publication, The Body Shop received a great deal of flattering media attention. *Inc.*[6] and *Working Woman*[7] ran cover stories featuring Anita Roddick. *Fortune*[8] and *BusinessWeek*[9] published shorter articles that focused on Anita Roddick and the company's performance. *Time* began its article with a story on Anita's fact-finding mission to Oman, where she obtained a perfume recipe from a local tribe only after dropping her pants and showing the Bedouin women her pubic hair. Bedouin women pluck theirs every day.[10]

BAD PRESS

In 1992, some members of the media began to criticize The Body Shop and the Roddicks. The *Financial Times* gave The Body Shop the dubious honor of headlining its 1992 list of top ten corporate losers after the price of Body Shop stock dipped from $5.20 to $2.70 during September.[11] Stock analysts had reacted to a disappointing earnings report, and the news set some minds to wonder if the company could indeed grow quickly enough to capture a leadership position in the minimalist market, or if there was a minimalist market at all.

MILLENNIUM PROJECT

Around this time, The Body Shop invested $5 million in a ten-part TV documentary series called *Millennium*. This series, which was shown around the world on television networks including PBS and the BBC, was meant to celebrate the wisdom and history of native cultures. The director quit the project during filming, accusing the Roddicks of distorting the tribal rituals depicted in the film to suit various new-age ideals.[12] The Body Shop sold a book version of *Millennium* in its stores to help promote the series and raise funds for donations.

In 1993, a British television news magazine telecast a report on The Body Shop. The show alleged that the company knowingly sourced materials from suppliers that had recently performed animal testing. The Body Shop sued the TV station and the production company for libel and won a significant financial award after a six-week court battle. Anita Roddick sat in the courtroom every day and compared the experience to confinement in a "mahogany coffin." The Body Shop won the suit and a £276,000 settlement by proving to the British court that the company had never intentionally misled consumers about the animal-testing policy, which encouraged manufacturers to give up animal testing but not claim that ingredients had never been tested on animals.[13]

JON ENTINE'S EXPOSÉ

In 1994, *Business Ethics* magazine, a well-respected U.S. publication, published a cover story on The Body Shop that built upon many of the allegations that others had presented over the years. The resulting controversy engulfed the journalist, the magazine, and The Body Shop in a new wave of controversy that threatened The Body Shop's already slow expansion into the U.S. market.

In June 1993, journalist Jon Entine had first been approached by disgruntled current and former Body Shop staffers about several of the company's practices. After overcoming his initial skepticism and doing some preliminary investigations in Littlehampton, The Body Shop's headquarters, Entine was convinced he had a sound basis on which to develop a story for his current employer, the ABC news magazine *Primetime Live*. When ABC decided not to renew the contract and to drop The Body Shop story, Entine began his own investigation, which eventually resulted in the *Business Ethics* article.[14] In the preface to the article, magazine editor and publisher Marjorie Kelly wrote:

> *Long-time readers will note that the following article represents a distinct departure from our typical editorial style. It has not been part of our mission to publish the exploits of companies that fall short of their stated social goals. But we believe the story of The Body Shop must be told, chiefly for the lessons it provides those of us who seek to promote ethical business practices. Still, we bring this story to you with mixed emotions. We have been ardent admirers of Anita Roddick and her company for many years; two years ago this month [September 1992] we featured her on our cover. But, after weeks of debate, including several conversations with Body Shop representatives, we concluded the greater good would be served by raising these issues in print. We earnestly hope this dialogue will be a constructive one.*

ENTINE'S ALLEGATIONS

In the lengthy article, Entine made several claims:[15]

- Anita Roddick had stolen the concept of The Body Shop, including the store name, recycling of bottles, store design, catalogs, and products, from a similar store she had visited in Berkeley, California, in 1971, several years before she opened her first Body Shop in Brighton in 1976.
- Roddick had not discovered exotic recipes for some of her products as she had previously claimed: Some were outdated, off-the-shelf formulas that had been used by other manufacturers, whereas others featured unusual ingredients, around which Roddick and company employees had woven fanciful tales of her travels of discovery.
- Many Body Shop products were full of petrochemicals, artificial colors and fragrances, and synthetic preservatives and contained only small amounts of naturally sourced ingredients.
- Quality control was a continuing problem with instances of mold, formaldehyde, and *E. coli* contamination reported around the world, thus requiring the use of large amounts of preservatives to give the products stable shelf lives.
- The U.S. Federal Trade Commission had launched a probe into The Body Shop's franchising practices, including deceptive financial data, unfair competition, and misleading company representation. One husband-and-wife franchising team compared the company to the Gambino crime family.
- The Body Shop's "Trade Not Aid" program was a sham, providing only a small portion of The Body Shop's raw materials while failing to fulfill the company's promises to suppliers.
- Between 1986 and 1993, The Body Shop contributed far less than the average annual pretax charitable donations for U.S. companies, according to the Council on Economic Priorities.

Entine published a similar article in a trade magazine, *Drug and Cosmetic Industry*, in February 1995.[16] In this article, he discussed The Body Shop's policies regarding animal testing, citing an internal memo from May 1992. At that time, 46.5 percent of The Body Shop's ingredients had been tested on animals by the ingredients' manufacturers, which was an increase from 34 percent the previous year. This and other practices raised new concerns about the company's slogan "Against Animal Testing" and tainted the company's 1993 victory in its libel suit against the TV program.[17]

REACTION TO ENTINE'S ARTICLE

The reaction to Entine's *Business Ethics* article was swift and furious. In June, well before the article's publication, Franklin Development and Consulting, a leading U.S.-based provider of social investment services, had sold 50,000 shares of The Body Shop because of "financial concerns."[18] With rumors spreading about the article in early August, the stock fell from $3.75 to $3.33 per share. Ben Cohen, cofounder of Ben & Jerry's and a *Business Ethics* advisory board member, severed his ties with the magazine. The U.S. and British press ran numerous pieces on the article and its allegations. These articles appeared in newspapers and magazines such as *USA Today*,[19] *The Economist*,[20] *The New York Post*,[21] and *The San Francisco Chronicle*.[22] *The London Daily Mail* secured an exclusive interview with one of the founders of the California Body Shop, who described the company's early years and how they eventually came to legal terms with the Roddicks over the rights to The Body Shop trademark.[23]

Entine was interviewed by a small newsletter, the *Corporate Crime Reporter*, in which he defended and explained his research and the article.[24] One point of interest was Entine's claim that Body Shop products were of "drugstore quality," which he based on the company's use of obsolete ingredients and formulas and a *Consumer Reports* ranking that placed Body Shop Dewberry perfume last out of 66 tested.[25] Dewberry is The Body Shop's trademark scent and is used in all of its stores as part of the "atmosphere." *Corporate Crime Reporter* also noted that another reporter, David Moberg, had brought similar allegations against The Body Shop in a separate article published the same month as Entine's.[26]

RIFT IN PROGRESSIVE COMMUNITY

In January 1995, *Utne Reader* published a forum including commentaries by Anita Roddick, Entine, Moberg, and Franklin Research founder Joan Bavaria. The forum was remarkable in the sense that it presented a structured set of responses to the charges. Editor Eric Utne noted the rift that the article had caused in the progressive business community and described how the Roddicks, Marjorie Kelly, and other parties had begun holding face-to-face meetings to mend their relationships.[27] Entine described the same meetings as "a family gathering a few days after everyone's favorite uncle was found molesting a neighbor's child. The scandal was on everyone's mind, few would openly talk about it, and most hoped that ignoring it would make it fade away. It didn't."[28] Moberg encouraged consumer watchdog groups to do their jobs more carefully, citing the case of the British group New Consumer, which had previously given The Body Shop high ratings.[29] Roddick maintained that the truth had been sacrificed in a rush to judgment but that she had managed to cope with and learn from the experience.[30]

GORDON RODDICK DEFENDS THE COMPANY

Anita Roddick has been known to ask her employees what irritates them about their store.[31] Gordon, Anita's husband, was a bit more philosophical in his approach, yet he also spoke out on issues that concerned him. After their entry into the U.S. market, the Roddicks became frustrated with the regulatory barriers they encountered. Most of the problems that The Body Shop encountered were small. However, The Body Shop had two full-time employees and one lawyer devoted exclusively to regulatory compliance in the United States. Ever the accountant, Gordon Roddick estimated that it cost The Body Shop an additional 5 percent of its revenues to do business in the United States, thus supporting his claim that the American free market economy was anything but free.[32]

Entine's *Business Ethics* article aroused Gordon to new heights of anger according to those who knew him. Body Shop lawyers had successfully persuaded *Vanity Fair* to refrain from publishing a different version of the article earlier in the year. *Vanity Fair* compensated Entine for his work, paying him $15,000 plus an additional $18,000 to cover his expenses in writing and researching the article. Entine was paid only $750 by *Business Ethics* magazine for the article.[33]

COUNTERATTACK

Early in Entine's investigation, The Body Shop had hired the international public relations firm of Hill & Knowlton (H&K) to launch a counterattack on Entine's credibility and motives. H&K vice president Frank Mankiewicz, who was a former president of National Public Radio (NPR), sent letters to ABC requesting that it drop its Body Shop story.[34] He also used his contacts at NPR to place an interview with Entine and a follow-up story that included comments from Body Shop supporters on NPR news programs such as "All Things Considered." Further attempts to intimidate *Business Ethics* magazine failed. The editor and publisher, Marjorie Kelly, knew that publishing the article was a risk, but she said she had checked and rechecked Entine's sources and was satisfied that his charges were sound. However, if The Body Shop chose to sue the magazine, she also knew that the cost of getting to the summary judgment phase of the trial could put the small magazine out of business.[35]

GORDON'S LETTER

Gordon Roddick responded to the *Business Ethics* article within a month of its publication by sending a ten-page letter on Body Shop letterhead to all *Business Ethics* magazine subscribers. In this letter, he denied many of the charges made in the article. The letter offered statements by several people that appeared to contradict their own quotations in the article. Roddick seemed to have a reasonable defense for most of Entine's allegations.

Several staff members at *Business Ethics* magazine were not pleased with the letter, which they had received in the mail because they were included as decoys on the subscriber mailing list. This is a common practice in the mailing-list industry to help prevent the misuse of subscriber addresses. The publisher of *Business Ethics* magazine could not recall authorizing the magazine's mailing-list service to rent the list to The Body Shop. It did not take long for the mailing-list company to discover that The Body Shop had obtained the magazine's subscriber list through a third party. Said Ralph Stevens, president of the mailing-list firm, "The Body Shop duped a prominent and legitimate list-brokerage company, a respected magazine, and they duped us…. If this is any indication of the way [The Body Stop does] business, of their regard for honesty and integrity, I give them a failing mark on all counts."[36] In late 1994, The Body Shop hired a business ethics expert to lead a social audit of the company.[37]

THE SITUATION AS OF 1995

By July 1995, Anita Roddick was already considering the possibility of opening Body Shop stores in Cuba, hoping to beat her competitors to that market and at the same time convert the Cubans' social revolution into a profitable yet honorable business revolution.[38] The company was also considering opening retail stores in Eastern European countries. At the same time, the media attention on the company had raised serious concerns among customers, among Body Shop supporters, and within the financial community. Since

August 1994, the company's stock price plummeted by almost 50 percent to 120p, an all-time low.

LOSSES

The Roddicks took millions of dollars in paper losses on their holdings, despite having sold a portion of their stock in July 1994.[39] The company faced increased competition from several larger firms, including Procter & Gamble, Avon, Kmart, The Limited, L'Oreal, Crabtree & Evelyn, and Marks & Spencer. Other companies, such as H2O Plus, were making progress in their efforts to open retail stores that featured products similar to those of The Body Shop. The company had hired Chiat/Day to develop advertising campaigns for worldwide use and conduct a marketing study in the United States.[40] There was at least one report that the company was looking for a U.S. advertising agency.[41] The questions that had been raised as a result of media investigations and The Body Shop's responses left some observers wondering what principles the company espoused and if the company could regain its earlier level of success.

ANITA'S FAME AS SOCIAL ACTIVIST CONTINUED

Anita Roddick continued to be recognized for her leadership on social and ethical causes. She won many awards in the mid-1990s. Among them were the following:[42]

> 1993—National Audubon Society Medal, USA
>
> 1994—Botwinick Prize in Business Ethics, USA
>
> 1994—University of Michigan's Annual Business Leadership Award, USA
>
> 1995—Women's Business Development Center's First Annual Woman Power Award, USA

QUESTIONS FOR DISCUSSION

1. During the time period of the case, how has The Body Shop continued to address the four components of corporate social responsibility?
2. What is your assessment of the Jon Entine article and critique? What is your assessment of The Body Shop's response to Entine's *Business Ethics* article? Has The Body Shop misrepresented itself to stakeholders, and if so, how?
3. Jon Entine and others have accused The Body Shop of using intimidation to stifle critics. Does this appear to be a valid criticism? Was The Body Shop justified in hiring Hill & Knowlton to conduct a public relations campaign?

4. Has The Body Shop's reputation been damaged by the incidents in this case? How might the company improve its reputation? Do you believe the steps described in this case, including the hiring of an advertising agency, will help or hinder these efforts?

5. Describe the roles you believe Gordon and Anita Roddick should play in The Body Shop's future operations. How might a stockholder, a customer, a supplier, and an employee assess the roles that the Roddicks should play?

ENDNOTES

1. Body Language—The Body Shop Web site http://www.the-body-shop.com (May 1995).

2. Anita Roddick, *Body and Soul: Profits with Principles, The Amazing Success Story of Anita Roddick & The Body Shop* (New York: Crown, 1991), 135–136.

3. Jennifer Conlin, "Survival of the Fittest," *Working Woman* (February 1994).

4. Faye Brookman, "Prototypes Debut," *Stores* (April 1994), 20–22.

5. Roddick, 1991.

6. Bo Burlingame, "This Woman Has Changed Business Forever," *Inc.* (June 1990).

7. Conlin, 29.

8. Andrew Erdman, "Body Shop Gets into Ink," *Fortune* (October 7, 1991), 166.

9. Laura Zinn, "Whales, Human Rights, Rain Forests—and the Heady Smell of Profits," *BusinessWeek* (July 15, 1991), 114–115.

10. Philip Elmer-Dewitt, "Anita the Agitator," *Times* (January 25, 1993), 52–54.

11. *Ibid.*, 54.

12. *Ibid.*, 54.

13. Conlin, 30–31.

14. Jon Entine, "Shattered Image," *Business Ethics* (October 1994), 23–28.

15. *Ibid.*

16. Jon Entine, "The Body Shop: Truth & Consequences," *Drug and Cosmetic Industry* (February 1995), 54–64.

17. *Ibid.*, 62.

18. Judith Valente, "Body Shop Shares Plunge on Reports of Sales by Funds and FTC Inquiry," *The Wall Street Journal* (August 24, 1994).

19. Ellen Neuborne, "Body Shop in a Lather over Ethics Criticism," *USA Today* (August 29, 1995), B1.

20. "Storm in a Bubble Bath," *The Economist* (September 3, 1994), 56.

21. Martin Peers, "Journalist's Probe Hits Body Shop," *New York Post* (August 25, 1994), 33.

22. Dirk Beveridge, "Uproar Threatens Body Shop Stock," *The San Francisco Chronicle* (August 25, 1994), D1.

23. Rebecca Hardy, "American Woman Recalls the Heady Days of Her Hippy Perfume Store…And a £2.3m Deal with the Roddicks," *London Daily Mail* (August 28, 1994).

24. "Interview with Jon Entine," *Corporate Crime Reporter* (September 19, 1994), 13–18.

25. *Ibid.*, 17.

26. David Moberg, "The Beauty Myth," *In These Times* (September 19–October 2, 1994).

27. Eric Utne, "Beyond the Body Shop Brouhaha," *Utne Reader* (January–February 1995), 101–102.

28. Jon Entine, "Exploiting Idealism," *Utne Reader* (January–February 1995), 108–109.

29. David Moberg, "Call in the Watchdogs!" *Utne Reader* (January–February 1995), 101–102.

30. Anita Roddick, "Who Judges the Judges?" *Utne Reader* (January–February 1995), 104.

31. Elmer-Dewitt, 52.

32. "Regulation Time: 60 Seconds with…Gordon Roddick," *Inc.* (June 1993), 16.

33. Ruth G. Davis, "The Body Shop Plays Hardball," *New York Magazine* (September 19, 1994), 16.

34. *Ibid.*

35. Maureen Clark, "Socially Responsible Business Brawl," *The Progressive* (March 1995), 14.

36. *Ibid.*

37. "Ethics Study for Body Shop," *The New York Times* (October 31, 1994), C7.

38. Conlin, 73.

39. "Stake Reduced in Body Shop," *The New York Times* (July 11, 1994), C7.

40. James Fallon, "Body Shop Regroups to Meet Competition in Crowded U.S. Arena," *Women's Wear Daily* (October 21, 1994), 1.

41. Anthony Ramirez, "Body Shop Seeks Its First U.S. Agency," *The New York Times* (June 27, 1995), D7.

42. About Dame Anita Roddick, http://www.anitaroddick.com/aboutanita.php?PHPSESSID=916ac5a4-b2eb632c07f64194e102c049. Accessed September 6, 2007.

CASE 4

The Body Shop International PLC (1998–2010)*

By 1998, The Body Shop International had grown into a multinational enterprise with almost 1,600 stores and 5,000 employees in 47 countries.[1] That year, after several years of lackluster financial performance, Anita Roddick gave the company's CEO post to a professional manager and became executive co-chairman with her husband, Gordon. Anita maintained that job titles were meaningless, anyway.[2]

Despite the change, the company's financial performance between 1995 and 1997 continued to be unimpressive:[3] Worldwide sales revenue and operating profits were $303 million and $21 million in 1995 and $377 million and $19 million, respectively, in 1997.

MORE ADVERTISING BECOMES NECESSARY

In 1995–1996, The Body Shop began to experiment with advertising in North American markets. According to one observer, the company originally thought that its brands and human rights agenda would create valuable word-of-mouth promotion among socially conscious consumers and that advertising would not be needed. The Body Shop's anti-advertising strategy largely paid off in the United Kingdom and other European nations, where human rights activism and commerce blended more seamlessly and consumers had fewer brands and retailers than in the United States. The strategy did not work effectively in the United States, where brand differentiation was crucial. In 1997, for example, The Body Shop's same-stores sales in the United States dropped 6 percent, the company's worst performance since entering the U.S. market ten years earlier.[4]

Since it has begun, U.S. advertising has been piecemeal, often targeted toward the Christmastime holiday sales push. In addition, it has been quirky. For example, Anita Roddick taped a radio spot that slammed the cosmetics industry. In the radio spot, Roddick said, "If more men and more women understood what really makes people beautiful, most cosmetic companies would be out of business."[5]

GETTING ITS ACT TOGETHER

The Body Shop seemed to be trying hard to get its act together in the U.S. market. It hired a new CEO in the fall of 1998 and created the position of vice president for promotions. These were significant moves for the company, but it would take more than advertising to turn things around. The Body Shop typically plays down product efficacy in favor of hyping product ethicality. A case in point is its Mango Body Butter, whose ingredients the company promotes as from a "woman's cooperative in Ghana." Sean Mehegan, a writer for *Brandweek*, summarized the company's dilemma this way: "How much American consumers care about such claims lies at the heart of whether The Body Shop can turn itself around here."[6]

THE BODY SHOP'S SOCIAL AUDITS

In 1994, perhaps in response to the *Business Ethics* magazine article by Jon Entine calling its integrity into question and perhaps on its own initiative, The Body Shop began an elaborate program of annual social audits examining, in particular, its environmental, social, and animal protection initiatives. Through the social audit program, which the company based on mission statements and goals in numerous social performance categories, the company established detailed social and ecological milestones for 1995–1997. In its 218-page *Values Report 1997*, the company reported its progress.[7] This lengthy, landmark document is often held out to be one of the most significant social performance reports ever prepared.

As reported in its *Values Report*, The Body Shop set policies in three areas: human and civil rights, environmental sustainability, and animal protection. In each category, the company set forth a conceptual framework for the auditing process. The auditing process in each category depended heavily on stakeholder interviews. The stakeholders who were interviewed included employees, international franchisees, customers, suppliers, shareholders, and local community/campaigning groups. The company identified the media as a potential stakeholder group for inclusion in future social auditing cycles.[8]

---

* This case was prepared by Archie B. Carroll, University of Georgia, using publicly available information.

ALLEGATIONS CONTINUE

In 1998, The Body Shop continued to face charges that could threaten its future. The company faced a flood of allegations and lawsuits by franchisees charging fraudulent presentations by the company when they bought their franchises. A number of U.S. franchisees had been angry at what they saw as unfair buyback terms if they wanted to get out of the business. There was talk of group action that could involve claims in the hundreds of millions of dollars.[9]

An example of the kind of lawsuit being filed was that of Jim White, who was asking for $32 million in damages. He was suing The Body Shop for fraud, fraudulent inducement, and inequitable treatment of franchisees. White claimed that the company offered rock-bottom buyback prices to franchisees caught in a five-year spiral of declining U.S. sales. White claimed he was offered only 20 cents on the dollar and that others were offered as low as 5 cents on the dollar.[10]

INTO THE NEW MILLENNIUM

The early 2000s continued to be tumultuous for The Body Shop. The company continued to grow, but sales and profits were not strong. As a result of poor Christmas sales in 2000, its annual profits were down 55 percent as it entered 2001. In the United Kingdom, the company found itself operating in a much more competitive marketplace than in its beginnings 25 years before. Most high street retail chains now are fielding their own "natural" cosmetics and toiletries, and price and promotional battles left the company's products more expensive than those of its rivals.[11]

CONFLICTS WITH FRANCHISEES

In September 2001, a major *Fortune* magazine article featured some of the legal difficulties The Body Shop was facing because of conflicts with franchisees. It was reported that eight U.S. Body Shop franchisees, who owned 13 locations, were accusing the parent company of impeding their business. In December 2000, this group filed a lawsuit against the company, asking for damages in the neighborhood of $2 million. One major complaint was that the company-owned stores were getting much better treatment than the franchisee-owned stores. Franchisee owners complained of the company failing to deliver them products while the company-owned stores had no problem getting products. Some franchisee owners saw this chronic out-of-stock problem as a ploy to force them to sell their franchises back for a fraction on the dollar.[12]

RODDICKS STEP ASIDE

In 2002, Anita and Gordon Roddick stepped down from their positions as co-chairs of the board of directors. Along with their friend, and early investor, Ian McGlinn, they maintained control of more than 50 percent of the company's voting rights. Anita Roddick was to remain involved in a "defined consultant role." At about this same time, the company had been in discussions with potential buyers of the company, but these talks were abandoned when offers were below what the company expected.[13] Peter Saunders, former president and CEO of The Body Shop in North America, became the CEO of the company.

Also, during 2002, The Body Shop conducted a global campaign with Greenpeace International on promoting renewable energy. The company furthered its commitment to environmental sustainability through investments in renewable energy, funding of energy-efficient projects in the developing world, and incorporating postconsumer recyclate into its packaging.[14] In 2003, the company started a global campaign to stop violence in the home. In 2003, Anita Roddick was appointed a Dame of the British Empire as part of the Queen's birthday honors.[15]

SALE TO L'ORÉAL

In mid-2006, The Body Shop was sold to France's L'Oréal. Following the sale, Peter Saunders kept his CEO title and founder Dame Anita Roddick remained on the company's board. The plan was that the company would retain its unique identify and values and continue to be based in the United Kingdom. The company would operate independently within the L'Oréal Group and would be led by its own management team, reporting directing to the CEO of L'Oréal.[16] By 2007, the company had 2,100 stores in 55 countries, and two-thirds of them are franchised.[17] It also sells its products via The Body Shop at Home, an in-home sales program in the United Kingdom, the United States, and Australia. In 2007, the company published its *Values Report 2007*, its first since it was acquired by L'Oréal. The company continues to emphasize its five core values: against animal testing, supporting community trade, activating self-esteem, defending human rights, and protecting the planet.[18]

The company continues to face stiff competition. Its top three competitors are Bath & Body Works, Estée Lauder, and Alliance Boots (the UK's number 1 retail pharmacy). But the company has dozens of other competitors including such familiar names as

Alberto-Culver, Avon, Coty, The Gap, Macy's, Mary Kay, Revlon, and Target.[19]

An article in *The Independent*, a newspaper in the United Kingdom, said in 2006 that the Body Shop's popularity plunged after the L'Oréal sale. The article argued that the sale had dented the company's reputation, and it was stated that Dame Anita Roddick had abandoned her principles by accepting the deal with L'Oréal. Roddick claimed that she would eventually give away the £130 million she made from the sale.[20]

STATUS OF COMPANY CRITICISM

Much of the targeted criticism of The Body Shop for the issues raised earlier, led in part by Jon Entine, has subsided. A review of Jon Entine's Web site, however, shows that he continues to critique The Body Shop and continues to write periodic articles and newspaper columns about the company. Entine's Web site may be accessed at http://www.jonentine.com/.

RODDICK TURNS TO PUBLISHING

Roddick published her second book, *Business as Unusual: The Triumph of Anita Roddick and the Body Shop*, in 2001. Also in 2001 she published *Take It Personally: How to Make Conscious Choices to Change the World*. She turned to writing. She explained, "I'm at the point in my life where I want to be heard." She adds, "I have knowledge and I want to pass it on."[21] In an interview with *Across the Board* magazine, Anita commented on her experiences with professional consultants and executives who are not as concerned as she is about preserving The Body Shop's values. She stated: "The hardest thing for me are the marketing people, because they focus on us as a brand and our customers as consumers. We've never called it a brand; we call it The Body Shop. In 25 years, we've never, ever, ever called a customer a consumer. Customers aren't there to consume. They're there to live, love, die, get married, have friendships—they're not put on this planet to bloody consume."[22]

In 2003 she published *A Revolution in Kindness*. Her last book, published in 2005, was *Business as Unusual: My Entrepreneurial Journey*. She continued to speak and write and raise money for social causes and even developed her own personal Web site, http://www.anitaroddick.com/index.php, where you can track everything she did during the final years of her life.

ANITA'S UNTIMELY DEATH

Quite unexpectedly, and as a shock to all, Anita Roddick died on September 10, 2007. She was 64. She died of a brain hemorrhage, according to her family. As *The New York Times* summarized, she was "a woman of fierce passions, boundless energy, unconventional idealism, and sometimes diva-like temperament."[23]

THE FUTURE UNDER L'ORÉAL AND WITHOUT ANITA

Upon the sale of The Body Shop to L'Oréal in 2006, *The Independent* (newspaper) in the United Kingdom reported that BSI's popularity had plunged after the sale. An index that tracks public perception of consumer brands found that "satisfaction" with Body Shop had slumped by almost half since the deal by its founder, Dame Anita Roddick, to sell the company to L'Oréal.[24] It is difficult to retrieve sales and profitability data for the Body Shop because these figures are embedded in L'Oréal's financial reports. According to Datamonitor report, however, 2008 sales for Body Shop were down 3.9 percent from 2007 sales. By 2009, L'Oréal was reporting that Body Shop sales had fallen by 8 percent in the last quarter of 2008. L'Oréal was quick to attribute this to the overall market downturn.[25]

In its 2009 "Living Our Values" report, The Body Shop reported that it was continuing to function as a distinct entity from L'Oréal, along with its own board and executive committee. Sophie Gasperment, chief executive, reported: "Our five core Values are as relevant today as they were when Anita first set them out—we are always looking for new ways to bring them to life. We believe that our Values are at the heart of our commercial success and they are the key to growing our business. As we go forward we will be more creative in bringing our message to customers who are searching for brands with principles that they can trust. In doing this we will deliver more positive benefits to everyone that we touch."[26] The five values to which Gasperment was referring were against animal testing, supporting community trade, activating self-esteem, defending human rights, and protecting our planet.

To demonstrate that the company was continuing to be loyal to its mission of social activism, in 2009 it announced its latest campaign titled "Stop Sex Trafficking of Children and Young People." In response to the growing trade of human trafficking, the company launched its global campaign, which it claimed had gathered support in 40 countries worldwide.[27]

When Anita Roddick sold her business to L'Oréal in 2006, she said that The Body Shop would be a "Trojan Horse." By that she meant that the ethical stance of the smaller group she founded would infiltrate the multinational.[28] Though it is not apparent that this infiltration has occurred, it does appear that the company is operating somewhat independently of L'Oréal and is striving on its own to uphold its socially oriented mission. It is not clear whether the company will be able to succeed financially, however, but it will be an interesting company to watch in the years ahead.

QUESTIONS FOR DISCUSSION

1. Did Anita Roddick betray her philosophy about advertising by beginning to advertise in U.S. markets? Did this decision have ethical implications? Or is it just a business decision?

2. Did The Body Shop's social auditing program help save the firm's reputation? Did the firm "snap back" from the damage done to its reputation in the mid-1990s?

3. Do the low buyback prices offered to U.S. franchisees reflect poor Body Shop ethics or just the economic reality of risky investments?

4. Is The Body Shop still regarded today as a socially responsible and ethical firm? Research the answer to this question and be prepared to report your findings.

5. At the end of these cases, what is your impression of Anita Roddick? Comment on her strengths and weaknesses and a businessperson and leader. Was the sale of the company to L'Oréal an indication that Roddick's philosophy had finally failed?

6. What will be the likely, longer term impact on The Body Shop's values and priorities under the leadership of L'Oréal and upon Anita Roddick's death? Is it in L'Oréal's best interests to leave the company alone and let it go in the direction Anita had provided it, or should it be brought more into the mainstream of the company?

ENDNOTES

1. "Capitalism and Cocoa Butter," *The Economist* (May 16, 1998), 66–67.

2. *Ibid.* Also see Ernest Beck, "Body Shop Founder Roddick Steps Aside as CEO," *The Wall Street Journal* (May 13, 1998), B14.

3. *Values Report 1997*, The Body Shop (October 1997), 150.

4. Sean Mehegan, "Not Tested on Humans," *Brandweek* (May 19, 1997), 54.

5. *Ibid.*

6. *Ibid.*

7. *Values Report 1997*, 7–12.

8. *Ibid.*, 10–12.

9. Jan Spooner, "Body Shop Faces U.S. Legal Fights," *Financial Mail* (London) (February 22, 1998).

10. *Ibid.*

11. Harriet Marsh, "Has the Body Shop Lost Its Direction for Good?" *Marketing* (London) (May 10, 2001), 19.

12. Carlye Adler, "The Disenfranchised," *Fortune* (September 2001), 66–72.

13. Sarah Ellison, "Body Shop's Two Founders to Step Aside; Sale Talks End," *The Wall Street Journal* (February 13, 2002), A15.

14. Company Profile: The Body Shop, 2006, http://www.thebodyshopinternational.com/NR/rdonlyres/7E8796D8-B975-4863-982E-8CDD2D6E48AD/0/TBSI_Company_profile.pdf. Accessed September 6, 2007.

15. *Ibid.*

16. *Ibid.*

17. The Body Shop International PLC, "Overview," *Hoover's Online.* Accessed September 6, 2007.

18. The Body Shop Values Report 2007, http://values-report.thebodyshop.net/index.asp?pg=111. Accessed September 6, 2007.

19. The Body Shop International PLC, "Overview," *Hoover's Online.* Accessed September 6, 2007.

20. Cahal Milmo, "UK: Body Shop's Popularity Plunges after L'Oréal Sale," *The Independent* (UK), April 10, 2006, http://www.corpwatch.org/article.php?id=13469&prinsafe=1. Accessed September 6, 2007.

21. Mike Hofman, "Anita Roddick: The Body Shop International, Established in 1976," *Inc.* (April 30, 2001), 61.

22. Matthew Budman, "Questioning Authority," *Across the Board* (January 2001), 15–16.

23. "Anita Roddick, Body Shop Founder, Dies at 64," *The New York Times* (September 12, 2007).

24. "Body Shop's Popularity Plunges after L'Oréal Deal," *The Independent*, http://www.independent.co.uk/news/uk/this-britain/body-shops-popularity-plunges-after-loreal-sale-473599.html. Accessed June 10, 2010.

25. "Body Shop Purchase Delivers a Body Blow to L'Oréal," *TimesOnline* (February 18, 2009), http://business.timesonline.co.uk/tol/business/

industry_sectors/consumer_goods/article5755471
.ece. Accessed June 10, 2010.

26. The Body Shop, "Living Our Values," The Body
Shop International, PLC *Values Report 2009*,
http://www.thebodyshop.com/_en/_ww/values-
campaigns/assets/pdf/Values_report_lowres_v2
.pdf. Accessed June 10, 2010.

27. "Sex Trafficking: The Story So Far," The Body
Shop, http://www.thebodyshop.com/_en/_ww/
values-campaigns/trafficking.aspx. Accessed June
10, 2010.

28. "Body Shop's Popularity Plunges after L'Oréal
Deal," *The Independent*.

CASE 5

The Benefit Corporation: Making a Difference while Making Money*

A new type of corporation is taking shape throughout the United States. This new corporate form is designed to aid social entrepreneurs who have found it challenging to fulfill their social good–oriented missions in traditional for-profit corporations that entail a fiduciary duty for profit maximization and shareholder primacy. The "Benefit Corporation" permits corporations to pursue stakeholder and societal welfare maximization as well as shareholder wealth maximization. A Benefit Corporation can have a broader mission that includes having a positive impact on society and that does not take a backseat to shareholder wealth maximization.

In the United States, individual states have the authority to create and charter corporations and so the benefit corporation movement is growing state by state. Maryland was the first state to pass Benefit Corporation legislation on April 13, 2010, and Vermont became the second state a month later. At this writing, New York's Benefit Corporation legislation is working through the system, and other states, such as Pennsylvania and New Jersey, are planning to introduce legislation. In addition, Oregon, Washington, and Colorado have shown interest.[1] State laws vary as states adopt this new corporate form.

The Maryland law follows the design of B-Lab, a Pennsylvania nonprofit that "unofficially" certifies socially responsible companies. In the Maryland law, entrepreneurs commit to a specific public good, and they are required to report on their for-profit ventures' contributions to that goal and permit auditing of their impact.[2]

By summer 2010, B-Lab reported that they had certified over 300 B corporations with $1.1 billion in total revenues in 54 industries. Though these companies have not yet been chartered under the Benefit Corporation legislation, because it is so new, these social entrepreneurs are virtually identical in mission with those that will be incorporated under the new legislation. In fact, some of these B corporations may very well reorganize in their states as Benefit Corporation laws are passed there.

Some of the founding B corporations included the following with their missions briefly stated:[3]

Social (k) Retirement Plans
Social (k) provides a paperless retirement platform for 401(k) and 403(b) plans with socially responsible funds.

Good Capital LLC
Good Capital is an investment firm that invests in sustainable solutions to society's most challenging problems.

Better World Books
Better World Books is a unique social enterprise—a triple bottom-line business—where creating a nursing library in Somaliland, supporting employees with profit sharing and equity ownership opportunities, and shipping book orders without damaging the environment are not just a by-product of doing business—they are the business.

White Dog Café
White Dog Café is a restaurant featuring local and sustainable foods.

GREEN and SAVE
GREEN and SAVE provides comprehensive advice for homeowners and business owners to create more environmentally friendly and energy efficient homes and buildings.

---

* This case was prepared by Ann K. Buchholtz, Rutgers University.

B-Lab's certification program has created a set of standards that helps people differentiate between good companies and good marketing according to J. Cohen Gilbert, co-founder of B-Lab. Gilbert argues that any company can market that it has a certified product even if that product represents a small fraction of its total revenue. But only certified B corporations can market that they are "certified sustainable businesses."[4] When corporations start to officially be chartered under the Benefit Corporation laws, the B-Lab certification may likely converge with the new legal arrangements.

QUESTIONS FOR DISCUSSION

1. What are the ethical issues in this case?
2. What are the advantages and disadvantages of the Benefit Corporation? Is it appropriate for businesses?
3. Would you invest in a Benefit Corporation? Is there a market for certified sustainable businesses?
4. Do you believe Benefit Corporations will be successful as for-profit ventures? Do you believe Benefit Corporations will be successful as engines of social good? Would you want to form or work for a Benefit Corporation?

5. Will the B-Lab certification become less popular when social entrepreneurs are able to adopt the new corporate form of Benefit Corporation? Or will some firms find the B-Lab certification adequate for their needs?

ENDNOTES

1. Max Abelson, "The New Be Good Business: Albany Gives Birth to New York's Benefit Corporation," *The New York Observer* (June 22, 2010), http://www.observer.com/2010/wall-street/new-be-good-business-albany-gives-birth-new-york%E2%80%99s-benefit-corporation. Accessed July 3, 2010.
2. John Tozzi, "Maryland Passes 'Benefit Corp.' Law for Social Entrepreneurs," *Bloomberg Business-Week* (April 13, 2010), http://www.businessweek.com/smallbiz/running_small_business/archives/2010/04/benefit_corp_bi.html. Accessed July 4, 2010.
3. Certified B Corporation, "Founding B Corporations," http://www.bcorporation.net/community/founders. Accessed July 10, 2010.
4. Amie Vaccaro and Celeste Reid, "Saving Money. Raising Money." Certified B-Corporation, http://www.bcorporation.net/resources/bcorp/documents/2009AP-Certification.pdf. Accessed July 10, 2010.

CASE 6

Goldman Sachs and Greece*

The year 2008 was a difficult one for even the strongest of firms. In spite of decades of success on Wall Street, Goldman Sachs failed to emerge from the financial crisis unscathed. The firm used federal assistance to survive the crisis and, along with Morgan Stanley, was forced to ask the Federal Reserve to change its status into a bank holding company. This change in status meant the last major U.S. investment banks would look more like commercial banks in the future, with the tighter regulation and increased supervision that entails.[1]

By 2009, however, Wall Street was returning to profitability with Goldman leading the way. After announcing strong quarterly earnings in April 2009, the firm said it would begin efforts to pay back its share of federal aid. The U.S. government permitted Goldman to return its federal aid in June 2009. From April 2009 to April 2010, Goldman's earnings per share rose 91 percent.

In the midst of this resurgence in profitability, Goldman faced charges of securities fraud and grilling by Congress for its activities prior to the financial crisis. The company settled an SEC civil suit that focused on a specific mortgage security and charged that the company misled investors. While no admission of wrongdoing was required, the settlement resulted in a $550 million fine and a judicial order barring the company from committing fraud in the future under U.S. security laws.[2]

At the same time, questions about Goldman's activities in Greece were being raised. Greece entered the European Union with a deficit that was larger than that allowed by the Maastricht Treaty that created the euro. Instead of reducing spending or raising revenues,

---

* This case was written by Ann K. Buchholtz, Rutgers University, in 2010.

Greece hid the true nature of its deficit through creative accounting. Goldman helped the Greek government to borrow billions and hide the loan from public view by treating it as a currency swap, something Greece did not have to disclose under European rules. This made it possible for the Greek government to remain under the European Union's deficit spending limits and join the euro.[3] As a result, the Greek government was able to continue its spending habits while putting the repercussions of that spending off into the future. In addition, Goldman arranged $15 billion of bond sales for Greece without disclosing the currency swap, thus pushing the bond price artificially higher.[4]

Other deals typically involved the country receiving cash in the present for government receipts that would arrive in the future. Greece traded away future revenues from lottery receipts, airport fees, and other sources of revenues. The lost future revenues were left off the books in spite of being liabilities. Goldman and Greece were not alone in this activity. For example, JPMorgan Chase created similar deals for Italy that enabled it to hide the financial impact of its borrowing. Greece had arrangements with other Wall Street firms as well.[5] However, the billion-dollar Goldman deal has drawn the greatest scrutiny due both to the size of the deal and to the affect of the Greek financial crisis on the European Union. The Greek debt crisis sent shockwaves through the European Union and ultimately led to a $147 EU/IMF bailout.

QUESTIONS FOR DISCUSSION

1. Did Goldman Sachs behave rightly or wrongly? German Chancellor Angela Merkel described it as a "scandal." Do you agree?
2. Goldman Sachs received hundreds of millions of dollars in return for helping the Greek government to hide the extent of its deficits, thereby maximizing shareholder wealth. Does that affect your answer to question 1?
3. Goldman Sachs was not the only firm to engage in these practices, helping countries to hide their true financial situation from their trading partners and their bondholders. If Goldman had not structured these deals, it is likely another firm would have entered and done so. Does this affect your answer to question 1?
4. These practices have been described as "legal at the time." Does that affect your answer to question 1?

ENDNOTES

1. "Goldman Sachs Group, Inc.," *The New York Times* (July 16, 2010), http://topics.nytimes.com/top/news/business/companies/goldman_sachs_group_inc/index.html. Accessed July 23, 2010.
2. *Ibid.*
3. Louise Story, Landon Thomas Jr., and Nelson D. Schwartz, "Wall Street Helped to Mask Debt Fueling Europe's Crisis," *The New York Times* (February 14, 2010), http://www.nytimes.com/2010/02/14/business/global/14debt.html. Accessed July 23, 2010.
4. Elisa Martinuzzi, "Goldman Sachs, Greece Didn't Disclose Swap Contract," *The New York Times* (February 17, 2010), http://www.businessweek.com/news/2010-02-16/goldman-sachs-greece-didn-t-disclose-swap-investors-fooled-.html. Accessed July 23, 2010.
5. Louise Story, Landon Thomas Jr., and Nelson D. Schwartz, http://www.nytimes.com/2010/02/14/business/global/14debt.html. Accessed July 23, 2010.

CASE 7

Goodbye, Indiana—Hello, Mexico: The Whirlpool Plant Closing*

In August 2009, the Whirlpool Corporation announced that it would close its Evansville, Indiana, manufacturing plant, eliminating 1,100 full-time jobs,

* The case was written by Archie B. Carroll, University of Georgia, in 2010.

and move its production to its plant in Mexico. The company had been producing refrigerators there for 54 years. The scheduled closure would take place in mid-2010. The Evansville plant primarily made top-freezer refrigerators. The company also said that its icemaker production and Refrigeration Product Development Center, which employs about 300 workers, would be relocated to a company-owned site that had not yet been determined.

WHIRLPOOL EXPLAINS DECISION

To explain its decision to close down the Indiana plant and move production to Mexico, Whirlpool representatives said the relocation was necessary to streamline operations.[1] The company also cited poor sales due to a depressed housing market to be another reason for moving its operations to Mexico.[2]

Whirlpool reported that the plant closing would cost the company $51 million—$21 million in employee termination costs, $13 million in equipment relocation costs, $5 million in asset impairment costs, and $12 million in other associated costs.[3]

EMPLOYEE REACTIONS

Employees at the plant had been hearing rumors about a possible plant closing for close to a year, but the actual announcement came as quite a shock to most of them. In fact, a wave of alarm rippled across Evansville when employees, families, and the community heard the news. On hearing the news, the president of the local union stated: "I learned about this five minutes before the employees did. I was actually devastated. I was going to retire in a few years, but now I guess I'll retire early." He went on to say, "we did whatever the company asked, but they turned around and took the company elsewhere anyway." He also noted, "It's not just a job to a lot of these people, it's their whole lives."[4]

At a town hall meeting held for the employees in August 2009, one Whirlpool employee expressed her shock and outrage: "We just found out … we had no notification." She went on to say: "It was like someone came up and kicked you in the stomach. I immediately thought about all the bills I had to pay. This was a surreal experience."[5] Though the employees had been told almost a year ahead of time that the plant would be closing, apparently many of them did not believe it and did not interpret the ensuing time between then and summer 2010 as "advance notice."

In February 2010, the union was planning a high-profile protest of the impending plant closing. Scheduled to attend the protest was AFL-CIO president Richard Trumka. In response, Whirlpool said that the protest was futile because they had already made their decision and were fully committed to shutting down the plant. A Whirlpool division vice president even sent a memo offering a fairly explicit warning to the workers that if they joined the protest they would seriously risk future employment opportunities with the company. One union official called the memo a "potentially illegal" effort to suppress speech and told

that the union was investigating whether it violated labor law rules. A writer for the Huffington Post, Sam Stein, observed the irony in a company closing a plant to send jobs abroad, threatening workers with the possibility of unemployment even after it moved.[6]

NEGATIVE RIPPLE EFFECT ON COMMUNITY

The mayor of Evansville, Jonathan Weinzapfel, gave a quick and strong announcement of opposition to the move because of its effect not only on the employees and their families, but on the broader community as well. The mayor went on to say, "also of great concern is the negative ripple effect the plant's closing will have on the local economy, impacting associated vendors, and creating more job losses." He added: "there are 40 different vendors [suppliers] throughout the area. Ten thousand people will be losing their jobs because of this—including the Goodwill Industry, the local Blind Association, and Walbash Plastics."[7]

OTHER ISSUES

In response to 1,100 jobs being sent to Mexico, one local citizen suggested that "There needs to be a bill to regulate big businesses from taking away American jobs. We need to protect American jobs and keep these American jobs in America!"[8]

Another reason why citizens of Indiana are upset over the plant closing is that Whirlpool made this decision after receiving $19 million in federal stimulus funds. In addition, the company will be the benefactor of the $296 million in federal stimulus funds being used to provide rebates to buyers to upgrade their appliances to energy-efficient models.[9]

Questions for Discussion

1. Was the Whirlpool plant closing just another "business decision," or did it carry with it social and ethical responsibilities and implications? Explain.

2. What are the legal and ethical responsibilities of Whirlpool in a plant-closing case such as the one in Evansville, Indiana?

3. In light of the federal stimulus funds that Whirlpool received, did it have a greater responsibility to make the Evansville plant sustainable? Or were the funds received totally unrelated to the plant-closing decision?

4. Was the Whirlpool division vice president's memo threatening future job opportunities an ethical practice? Was it an unfair labor practice? Explain.

5. What about the plant closing's impact on the community and related stakeholders? Did the company have any responsibility to work with the community in this decision? What should it have done and how should it have done it?

6. Should there be legislation preventing American firms from closing down and moving to less expensive parts of the world? Should NAFTA be repealed?

ENDNOTES

1. Andrew Deichler, "Lease Down (June 27–July 3): Whirlpool Finally Closes Indiana Plant," CoStar Group (June 29, 2010), http://www.costar.com/news/. Accessed July 2, 2010.

2. Sam Stein, "Whirlpool Threatens Workers: Protesting Plant Closure Risks 'Future Jobs,'" *Huffington Post* (February 24, 2010), http://www. huffingtonpost.com/2010/02/24/whirlpool-threatens-workers/. Accessed July 2, 2010.

3. "Whirlpool Discloses Indiana Plant-Closing Costs," *The City Wire* (August 31, 2009), http://www.thecitywire.com. Accessed July 2, 2010.

4. Jeanmarie Lunsford and Laura Market, "Indiana Braces for Whirpool Plant Closing," *Epoch Times* (September 5, 2009).

5. *Ibid.*

6. Stein.

7. Lunsford and Market.

8. *Ibid.*

9. "Whirlpool Taking Shots for Closing Indiana Plant," *Newton Independent* (February 23, 2010), http://www.newtonindependent.com/newton_independent/2010/02/. Accessed July 2, 2010.

CASE 8

Using Ex-Cons to Teach Business Ethics*

After the Enron scandal of 2001 and the WorldCom, Tyco, and Adelphia debacles that followed a couple of years later, the business ethics industry really started to take off. Business ethics consulting became a booming field of expertise, and those business schools that had not yet started teaching business ethics quickly created new courses to take advantage of the newly energized topic. Business schools that had ethics courses already in their curricula ramped up the number of offerings per year and started looking for innovative and interesting ways to attract students to the courses.

The early wave of ethics scandals brought about two major events that became driving forces in corporate and educational change. First, the Sarbanes–Oxley Act was passed by Congress in 2002. SOX elevated the interest in and incentives for stronger financial controls and compliance, and this led to related initiatives in the realm of business ethics. Second, the Federal Sentencing Guidelines were revised in 2004. The U.S. Sentencing Commission revised its guidelines and created a new ruling that rewarded companies for developing ethics programs and offering ethics training. The Commission passed a ruling that among the different factors to be taken into consideration when a company was accused of wrongdoing was whether or not company management had provided ethics training for its employees. If the company had not offered ethics training as part of an ethics program, the company could be more severely disciplined than if it had offered its employees such training.

On both the business school and corporate fronts, as a result, the demand for ethics training and education quickly grew in value. In partial response to this new demand, a new category of ethics education arrived on the scene—the use of ex-cons to teach business ethics via presentations in business schools.

WALT PAVLO: AN EARLY CASE STUDY

Walter A. Pavlo, Jr., had achieved many things by the time he was 40 years old. He had graduated from business school with a master's degree, worked as a manager at MCI, devised a $6 million money laundering scheme, and served two years in federal prison.

---

* This case was prepared by Archie B. Carroll, University of Georgia, using public sources.

Along the way he became divorced and unemployed, and had to move back in with his parents. As *Business-Week* reported, it was "a story that should scare any MBA straight."[1]

Walt Pavlo, a convicted white collar criminal, has been called by ABC News the "Visiting Fellow of Fraud" for his appearances on many campuses. At an appearance for a business school lecture, Pavlo claimed he was once a God-fearing student who played hard and straight. He told ABC's *Nightline* that he was taught the catechism and Ten Commandments as a child and was taught not to steal, cheat, or curse. He was taught to be honest and truthful in all that he did. Upon completion of his MBA, he got a position at MCI, the communications giant, and started working in the collections department. He became very competitive and began fretting that the next guy might be out-performing him, so he ratcheted up his efforts.[2]

Pavlo eventually became a senior manager at MCI. He was responsible for the billing and collection of almost $1 billion in monthly revenue for MCI's carrier finance division. He had a meritorious employment history. In March 1996, Pavlo and a member of his staff and an outside business associate began to carry out a fraud involving several of MCI's customers. When completed, the scheme had involved seven customers who were defrauded of $6 million over a six-month period. The money was stashed away in a Grand Cayman bank account.[3]

In explaining his going astray, Pavlo detailed how much pressure he had been under and how he was having a difficult time meeting the targets and goals that had been set for him. He told a colleague about his struggle, and the colleague said that "everybody was cheating" because "that's the way you make it." This became a pivotal moment in Pavlo's life, he reported, and that started him down the path to white collar crime.[4] After stealing the $6 million, he began to live according to his newfound means—an expensive new car, hand-tailored Italian suits, and frequent holidays—often to the Cayman Islands.

Six months into the fraud, auditors at MCI realized what he was doing and he was forced to resign. He thought the company would just write off the loss as bad debt to avoid adverse publicity, but his prayers were not answered. MCI brought in the FBI. Knowing he could not withstand a trial, Pavlo made a full confession and was sentenced to three years and five months in prison. He was required to pay recompense from any subsequent earnings for the next 27 years.

Pavlo served his time in prison, and after getting out, learned that his wife had filed for divorce. Penniless and homeless, he returned home to live with his parents but found no success in looking for work.[5]

PAVLO'S SECOND CAREER

At the end of one of his unsuccessful job interviews, Pavlo was told he did not get the job but was asked whether he could return to the company and speak to the employees about white collar crime. This was the beginning of his second career. Over the next couple of years, he spoke to the FBI, some of the nation's top accounting firms, professional societies, and numerous business schools. Pavlo was asked by ABC's *Nightline*: "You are a convicted felon and an accomplished liar. Why should anybody listen to you?"

Pavlo responded:[6]

> *Before I was a criminal or committed a criminal act, I was someone. I was someone who was on the fast track and did a lot of things right in my life. I've paid a significant price for what I've done, and I tell people that, and I educate people with a cautionary tale about what's going on out there. I'm trying to make a difference, and it's a chance for me to move on with my life and I feel good about my career, for once. For once in my life, I enjoy my work.*

THE PROS & THE CONS

The Pros & The Cons, a Web-based company offering up an array of speakers on the subjects of white collar crime, fraud, and business ethics, demonstrates how the use of ex-cons in teaching business ethics has become a profitable enterprise. In addition to Walt Pavlo, the company features several other speakers whose expertise grew out of their having spent time behind bars. Chuck Gallagher embezzled his clients' trust funds, served time in prison, and is now on the lecture circuit. Mark Morze committed an infamous fraud when he bilked banks and investors of $100 million before getting caught and serving time. Nick Wallace served six years in federal prison for bankrupting 69 savings and loan associations. Now, each of these speakers is ready and willing, for a price, to come to your business school or place of employment and share with you the secrets they learned "from behind bars." These speakers earn thousands of dollars per talk to speak to groups.[7]

OPPONENTS TO USE OF EX-CONS

Not everyone is satisfied with the idea of using ex-cons to speak to business students. Business ethicist John C. Knapp has said, "I'm disturbed that so many professors seem to be willing to invite Pavlo and other convicted felons into the classroom without verifying that their stories are true. Paying the ex-cons is rewarding them for committing a crime."[8] A reader of *BusinessWeek* chimed in: "Too bad they don't pay $2,500 to honest people who never embezzled a penny to tell students that they shouldn't be crooks."

QUESTIONS FOR DISCUSSION

1. What are the ethical issues in this case?
2. What are the advantages and disadvantages of hiring ex-cons to speak to college students on the subject of business ethics? Is it appropriate for colleges and universities to pay felons to be guest speakers?
3. What do you think you could learn from an ex-con?
4. Successful business executives who speak to students on the subject of business ethics typically do not get paid. They do this as a service. Is it wrong to pay ex-cons to speak on their illicit motives and activities?

ENDNOTES

1. Jane Porter, "Using Ex-Cons to Scare MBAs Straight," *Bloomberg Businessweek* (April 24, 2008).
2. Martin Bashir, "Walt Pavlo: The Visiting Fellow of Fraud—Ex-Corporate Criminal Makes a Good Living Talking Up Ethics," *ABC News* (January 30, 2006).
3. "Walter Walt Pavlo," The Pros & The Cons: The Only Speakers Bureau for White-Collar Criminals in the U.S., http://www.theprosandthecons.com/. Accessed July 4, 2010.
4. Bashir.
5. *Ibid.*
6. *Ibid.*
7. Christopher S. Stewart, "After Serving Time, Executives Now Serve Up Advice," *The New York Times* (June 1, 2004).
8. Quoted in Porter (2008).

CASE 9

Felony Franks: Home of the Misdemeanor Wiener*

Hot dog stands in Chicago are a dime a dozen, but entrepreneur Jim Andrews opened his new eating establishment in the summer of 2009 to some controversy. His new hot dog restaurant is named *Felony Franks*, and it serves its trademarked "misdemeanor wiener" and other jail-themed menu items through a bulletproof revolving glass window. Andrews, age 64 at the time of opening, employs only ex-cons as his employees.[1]

THEY NEED HELP: WHY NOT ME?

Though Andrews is a longtime business owner and is not an ex-con himself, his mission was to open a restaurant that would help ex-cons get back into the workforce and start new lives for themselves. Andrews had seen how hard it was for felons to find work, so when he opened Felony Franks, he hired ten ex-offenders whose crimes had ranged from drug possession to armed robbery. One of his goals was to help eliminate the stigma surrounding those who have served time in prison as they attempted to put their lives back together. Andrews said, "they need help," so "why not me?"[2] When Andrews opened his hot dog stand, he said he thought he was doing a community service. Some of his neighbors, however, thought he was the one committing a crime.[3]

Andrews is not your average hot dog slinger according to restaurant reviewer Metromix Chicago. As it turns out, this owner of the Western Avenue store founded the Rescue Foundation in 2003, a nonprofit organization that tries to help formerly incarcerated people by providing them with work and the

---

* This case was written by Archie B. Carroll, University of Georgia.

opportunity to develop business skills. Felony Franks is said to be an extension of the foundation's mission, employing only those people who have served time. For now, the restaurant is walk-up only, but there are plans for a drive-through option and may be some day indoor seating. For now, a few picnic tables are available outside.[4]

THE CLEVER, JAIL-THEMED MENU

In addition to its misdemeanor wiener and Felony Franks, the small block-building store offers a variety of jail-themed foods. Some of the cleverly titled hot dogs include the Chain Gang Chili Dog, Pardon Polish, Cell Mate Dog, and Custody Dog. One of the featured Probation Burgers is called the Warden Special. Side orders are called *Accomplices*, and include the usual round-up of condiments such as cheese sauce, pepper rings, and cheese slices. Other interesting items include Burglar Beef, Freedom Fries, and Guilty Gyros. Most of these sandwiches are priced in the $3–$6 range.[5]

When you enter the cramped store, which is framed by cinder blocks, you encounter a small space with no tables or chairs. Near the entrance, customers are presented with their mock list of Miranda rights: "You have the right to remain hungry. Anything you order can and will be used to feed you here at Felony Franks." The servers stand behind bulletproof plastic, which turns out to be standard practice in the neighborhood.[6]

The food is also served with colorful humor. When you place your order, you are "pleading your case." If you dine in, you are "serving time" (on the nearby picnic tables). If you ask for your food to go, you are "out on good behavior."

According to Andrews, the workers start at $8 an hour and can earn time-and-a-half for overtime. The profits are to be split between the charity to help ex-offenders and a profit-sharing plan for the employees. Before getting his job at Felony Franks, Lydon Walker was unemployed for over a year. The father of five said he didn't know what he would do without the job. He went on to say, "I might be back gangbanging or something or selling drugs."[7]

CRITICISM, PRAISE, FUTURE

Ever since the restaurant opened, Andrews has received both criticism and praise from his neighbors in the community. More than 70 people attended a homeowners' meeting to learn more about the project and to protest it. One concern was expressed by a Roman Catholic priest from Chicago's South Side who claimed that Andrews was exploiting the African-American men working for him.[8] Alderman Bob Fioretti argued that a "felony means time behind bars" and "we shouldn't be glorifying felonies in this day and age."[9] Fioretti also publicly denounced the business and said he would not approve a curb cut for a drive-through or sign permit.[10]

One of Andrews's workers exclaimed that he does not feel like he is being exploited. He said, "working here allows me to provide for myself and my family." This particular worker used to sell crack and served two years probation for possession of a controlled substance. He went on to say, "I've lived in this neighborhood for 15 years and there's gunfire every other day and you never hear anything about that, but all of a sudden there's all this hoopla about a hot-dog stand."[11]

Andrews thinks his business is catching on even though there are some who disapprove of the idea of a Felony Franks in their neighborhoods. He is already planning for a second location in Chicago and says he has received more than 1,600 resumes and 100 requests for franchise information.[12] Andrews says he has received a lot of support from the community. He described: "I'm trying to take a negative and turn it into a positive. And you know what? The people who will be working here will have a positive attitude. They will be taught the right way to run a business and we will work close [sic] with them so that they can better their lives."[13]

QUESTIONS FOR DISCUSSION

1. Is Felony Franks just a clever gimmick that will be a passing fad, or a worthy social entrepreneurship venture with lasting potential?
2. In dealing with ex-cons, is Andrews just deluding himself about the possible downside risks of hiring ex-felons? What are some of these risks that he should plan for?
3. Does the community have a legitimate right to complain about a Felony Franks restaurant being located there? Is Felony Franks an asset or a liability to a neighborhood?

ENDNOTES

1. Eric Horrng, "At Felony Franks, Only Ex-Cons Need Apply," *ABC News* (August 2, 2009), http://abcnews.go.com/print?id=8234771. Accessed July 2, 2010.

2. *Ibid.*

3. Julie Jargon, "Slaw and Order: Hot-Dog Stand in Chicago Triggers a Frank Debate," *The Wall Street Journal* (October 13, 2009), http://online.wsj.com/article/SB125538779820481255.html?KEY-WORDS=felony+franks. Accessed July 31, 2010.

4. "Felony Franks," Metromix Chicago, http://chicago.metromix.com/webtools/print/restaurants/burgers/felony-franks/. Accessed July 2, 2010.

5. *Ibid.*

6. Jargon.

7. Horrng.

8. Jargon.

9. *Ibid.*

10. Ashley Kohler and Charlotte Eriksen, "Felony Franks Gives Ex-Cons Second Chance," *Chicago-Storytelling* (June 21, 2010), http://chicagostorytelling.com/2010/06/21/felony-franks-gives-ex-cons. Accessed July 2, 2010.

11. Jargon.

12. *Ibid.*

13. "Ex-Cons Serve Hot Dogs at Felony Franks," UPI.com (April 24, 2009), http://www.upi.com/Odd_News/2009/04/24/Ex=cons-serve-hot-dogs-a. Accessed July 2, 2010.

PART 2

Corporate Governance and Strategic Management Issues

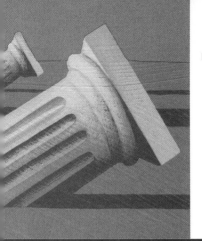

4

Corporate Governance: Foundational Issues

CHAPTER LEARNING OUTCOMES

After studying this chapter, you should be able to:

1. Link the issue of legitimacy to corporate governance.

2. Identify the best practices that boards of directors can follow.

3. Discuss the problems that have led to the recent spate of corporate scandals and the efforts that are currently underway to keep them from happening again.

4. Discuss the principal ways in which shareholder activism exerted pressure on corporate management groups to improve governance.

5. Discuss the ways in which managers relate to shareholders and the issues arising from that relationship.

6. Discuss the issue of shareholder democracy, its current state, and the trend for the future.

I n this second part of the book, we more closely examine how management has responded and should respond to the social, ethical, and stakeholder issues developed throughout this book. This chapter explores the ways in which the board and top managers govern the corporation. In Chapters 5 and 6, the view expands to look at how these social ethical and stakeholder issues fit into not only the strategic management and corporate public affairs functions of the firm but also the management of issues and crises.

The 21st century has been fraught with corporate scandals that have shaken the public's confidence in business institutions and threatened the legitimacy of business as a whole. We begin by examining the concept of legitimacy and the part that corporate governance plays in establishing the legitimacy of business. We then explore how good corporate governance can mitigate the problems created by the separation of ownership and control and examine some of the specific challenges facing those involved in corporate governance today.

Legitimacy and Corporate Governance

Corporate governance took center stage at the dawn of the 21st century. The bankruptcy of Enron, once the seventh largest company in the United States, as well as those of corporate giants WorldCom, Global Crossing, and Parmalat, sent shock waves through the corporate world. When a host of firms subsequently issued earnings restatements, investors throughout the world began wondering where they could place their trust. A few years later, the economic recession struck and investors were stunned as they watched their life savings shrivel. These worldwide events threatened more than one industry, more than one company, and more than the investors who lost great portions of their wealth. These events threatened the institution of business as a whole by calling the legitimacy of the institution of business into question. At a 2009 Harvard Business School summit designed to explore the legitimacy of business following the financial crisis, thought leaders concluded that the crisis could precipitate a general rethinking of the legitimacy of capitalism.[1]

To understand corporate governance, it is important to understand the idea of **legitimacy**. Legitimacy is a somewhat abstract concept, but it is vital in that it helps explain the importance of the relative roles of a corporation's charter, shareholders, board of directors, management, and employees—all of which are components of the modern corporate governance system. We utilize a slightly modified version of Talcott Parsons's definition of legitimacy. He argued, "organizations are legitimate to the extent that their activities are congruent with the goals and values of the social system within which they function."[2] From this definition, we may see legitimacy as a condition that prevails when there is congruence between the organization's activities and society's expectations. Thus, whereas legitimacy is a condition, **legitimation** is a dynamic process by which business seeks to perpetuate its acceptance. The dynamic process aspect should be emphasized, because society's norms and values change, and business must change if its legitimacy is to continue. It is also useful to consider legitimacy at both the micro, or company, level and the macro, or business institution, level.

At the *micro level of legitimacy*, we refer to individual business firms achieving and maintaining legitimacy by conforming to societal expectations. Companies seek legitimacy in several ways. First, a company may adapt its methods of operating to conform to what it perceives to be the prevailing standard. For example, a company may discontinue door-to-door selling if that marketing approach comes to be viewed in the public mind as a shoddy sales technique,[3] or a pharmaceutical company may discontinue offering free drug samples to medical students if this practice begins to take on the aura of a bribe. Second, a company may try to change the public's values and norms to conform to its own practices by advertising and other techniques.[4] Amazon.com was successful at this when it began marketing through the Internet.

Finally, an organization may seek to enhance its legitimacy by identifying itself with other organizations, people, values, or symbols that have a powerful legitimate base in society.[5] This occurs at several levels. At the national level, companies proudly announce appointments of celebrities, former politicians, or other famous people to managerial positions or board directorships. At the community level, the winning local football coach may be asked to endorse a company by sitting on its board or promoting its products.[6]

The *macro level of legitimacy* is the level with which we are most concerned in this chapter. The macro level refers to the corporate system—the totality of business enterprises. It is difficult to talk about the legitimacy of business in pragmatic terms at this level. American business is such a potpourri of institutions of different shapes, sizes, and industries that saying anything conclusive about it is difficult. Yet this is an important level at which business needs to be concerned about its legitimacy. What is at stake is the acceptance of the form of business as an institution in our society. William Dill has suggested that business's social (or societal) legitimacy is a fragile thing:

> *Business has evolved by initiative and experiment. It never had an overwhelmingly clear endorsement as a social institution. The idea of allowing individuals to joust with one another in pursuit of personal profit was an exciting and romantic one when it was first proposed as a way of correcting other problems in society; but over time, its ugly side and potential for abuse became apparent.*[7]

Business must now accept that it has a fragile mandate. It must realize that its legitimacy is constantly subject to ratification; and it must realize that it has no inherent right to exist. Business exists solely because society has given it that right.[8] In this sense, business is a public institution as well as a private entity.[9] When the legitimacy of business as an institution is in question, political and social factors may overshadow economic factors to change the future of the institution of business in profound ways.[10]

In comparing the micro view of legitimacy with the macro view, it is clear that, although specific business organizations try to perpetuate their own legitimacy, the corporate or business system as a whole rarely addresses the issue at all. This is unfortunate because the spectrum of powerful issues regarding business conduct clearly indicates that such institutional introspection is necessary if business is to survive and prosper. If business is to continue to justify its right to exist, we must remember the question of legitimacy and its operational ramifications.

The Purpose of Corporate Governance

The purpose of corporate governance is a direct outgrowth of the question of legitimacy. The word *governance* comes from the Greek word for steering.[11] The way in which a corporation is governed determines the direction in which it is steered. Owners of small private firms can steer the firm on their own, however, the shareholders of public firms must count on boards of directors to make certain that their companies are steered properly in their absence. For business to be legitimate and to maintain its legitimacy in the eyes of the public, it must be steered in a way that corresponds to the will of the people.

Corporate governance refers to the method by which a firm is being governed, directed, administered, or controlled and to the goals for which it is being governed. Corporate governance is concerned with the relative roles, rights, and accountability of such stakeholder groups as owners, boards of directors, managers, employees, and others who assert to be stakeholders.

Components of Corporate Governance

To appreciate fully the legitimacy and corporate governance issues, it is important that we understand the major groups that make up the corporate form of business organization, because it is only by so doing that we can appreciate how the system has failed to work according to its intended design. This chapter focuses on the Anglo-American model toward which much of the world is converging.[12] This convergence is driven largely by institutional investors who, as they invest more globally, are seeking governance mechanisms with which they are familiar and comfortable.[13]

Roles of Four Major Groups.   The four major groups we need to mention in setting the stage are the shareholders (owner-stakeholders), the board of directors, the managers, and the employees. Overarching these groups is the **charter** issued by the state, giving the corporation the right to exist and stipulating the basic terms of its existence. Figure 4-1 presents these four groups, along with the state charter, in a hierarchy of corporate governance authority.

Under American corporate law, **shareholders** are the owners of a corporation. As owners, they should have ultimate control over the corporation. This control is manifested primarily in the right to select the board of directors of the company. Generally, the degree of each shareholder's right is determined by the number of shares of stock owned. The individual who owns 100 shares of Apple Computer, for example, has 100 "votes" when electing the board of directors. By contrast, the large public pension fund that owns 10 million shares has 10 million "votes."

Because large organizations may have hundreds of thousands of shareholders, they elect a smaller group, known as the **board of directors**, to govern and oversee the management of the business. The board is responsible for ascertaining that the manager puts

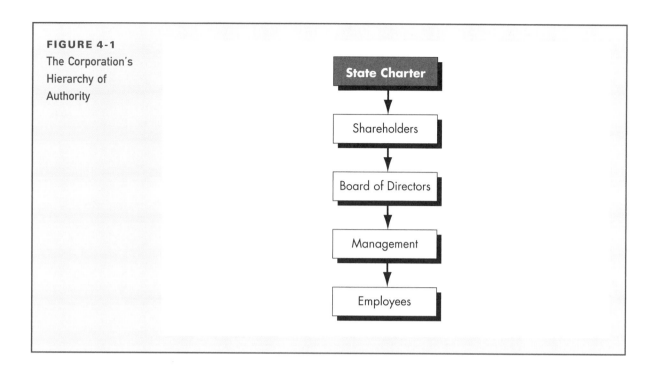

FIGURE 4-1
The Corporation's Hierarchy of Authority

State Charter

Shareholders

Board of Directors

Management

Employees

the interests of the owners (i.e., shareholders) first. The third major group in the authority hierarchy is the **management**—the group of individuals hired by the board to run the company and manage it on a daily basis. Along with the board, the top management establishes the overall policy. Middle- and lower-level managers carry out this policy and conduct the daily supervision of the operative employees. **Employees** are those hired by the company to perform the actual operational work. Managers are employees, too, but in this discussion, we use the term employees to refer to nonmanagerial employees.

Separation of Ownership from Control. The social and ethical issues that have evolved in recent years focus on the *intended* versus *actual* roles, rights, responsibilities, and accountability of these four major groups. The major condition embedded in the structure of modern corporations that has contributed to the corporate governance problem has been the **separation of ownership from control**. In the precorporate period, owners were typically the managers themselves; thus, the system worked the way it was intended, with the owners also controlling the business. Even when firms grew larger and managers were hired, often the owners were on the scene to hold the management group accountable. For example, if a company got in trouble, the Carnegies, or Mellons, or Morgans, were always there to fire the president.[14]

As the public corporation grew and stock ownership became widely dispersed, a separation of ownership from control became the prevalent condition. Figure 4-2 illustrates the precorporate and corporate periods. The dispersion of ownership into hundreds of thousands or millions of shares meant that essentially no one person or group owned enough shares to exercise control. This being the case, the most effective control that owners could exercise was the election of the board of directors to serve as their representative and watch over the management.

The problem with this evolution was that authority, power, and control rested with the group that had the most concentrated interest at stake—the management. The

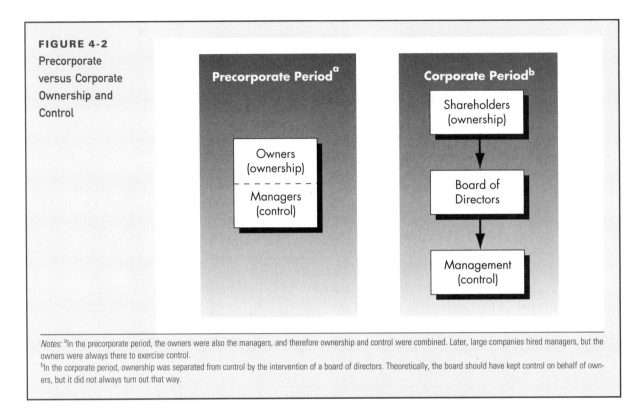

FIGURE 4-2
Precorporate versus Corporate Ownership and Control

Precorporate Period[a]

Owners (ownership)
- - - - - - -
Managers (control)

Corporate Period[b]

Shareholders (ownership)

Board of Directors

Management (control)

Notes: [a]In the precorporate period, the owners were also the managers, and therefore ownership and control were combined. Later, large companies hired managers, but the owners were always there to exercise control.
[b]In the corporate period, ownership was separated from control by the intervention of a board of directors. Theoretically, the board should have kept control on behalf of owners, but it did not always turn out that way.

corporation did not function according to its designed plan with effective authority, power, and control flowing downward from the owners. The shareholders were owners in a technical sense, but most of them perceived themselves as investors rather than owners. If you owned 100 shares of Walt Disney Co. and there were 10 million shares outstanding, you likely would see yourself as an investor rather than an owner. With just a telephone call issuing a sell order to your stockbroker, your "ownership" stake could be gone. Furthermore, with stock ownership so dispersed, no conscious, intended supervision of corporate boards was possible.

The other factors that added to management's power were the corporate laws and traditions that gave the management group control over the proxy process—the method by which the shareholders elected boards of directors. Over time, it was not difficult for management groups to create boards of directors with like-minded executives who simply collected their fees and deferred to the management on whatever it wanted. The result of this process was the opposite of what was originally intended: power, authority, and control began to flow upward from the management rather than downward from the shareholders (owners). **Agency problems** developed when the interests of the shareholders were not aligned with the interests of the manager, and the manager (who is simply a hired *agent* with the responsibility of representing the owners' best interests) began to pursue self-interest instead of the owners' best interests.

Problems in Corporate Governance

It is clear from the preceding discussion that a potential governance problem is built into the corporate system because of the separation of ownership from control. It is equally clear that the board of directors is intended to oversee management on behalf of the shareholders and with full regard for the stakeholders. However, this is where the system

Spotlight on SUSTAINABILITY

Linda Fisher, Chief Sustainability Officer for DuPont

Linda Fisher, chief sustainability officer (CSO) for the giant chemical company DuPont, describes her job as having two parts. The first part is keeping DuPont in compliance and going beyond that to reduce the company's footprint. The second is to find market opportunities that will present themselves due to society's changing needs. She describes sustainability as an evolving concept. In the 1970s, the word "sustainability" was not really used and DuPont focused on environmental compliance. In the 1980s, DuPont focused on footprint reduction and, by the 1990s, the company's focus was on energy efficiency. Now DuPont is looking at what their products might do to improve the impact of society on the environment. Will the role of the CSO be needed when sustainability becomes a societal norm? Fisher believes the sustainability concept will continue to evolve and the CSO will be needed as new waves of sustainability appear. Thomas Friedman, the columnist and author, disagrees. In the middle of a speech to DuPont's corporate officers, he turned to Fisher and said, "The goal of DuPont should be to make Linda's job a dinosaur."

Source: G. Colvin, "Linda Fisher," *Fortune* (Vol. 160, 2009), 45–50.

can break down. For corporate governance to function as it was originally intended, the board of directors must be an effective, potent body carrying out its roles and responsibilities in ascertaining that management pursue the shareholders' best interests.

With mechanisms for corporate governance in place, how could debacles like Enron and WorldCom still occur? Some of the blame must be placed on the auditors: Arthur Andersen was the auditor for Enron, WorldCom, and Global Crossing. Andersen had a built-in conflict of interest from doing both consulting and auditing for the same company. For example, Andersen earned $25 million from auditing Enron and $27 million from providing Enron with consulting services.[15] Lavish chief executive officer (CEO) paychecks and the boards who approved them also drew the ire of investors. Enron's Ken Lay made about $220 million, and Global Crossing's Gary Winnick made over $500 million prior to the bankruptcies, which left many investors with nothing.[16] Surprisingly, most of the behavior that led to these bankruptcies fell within the letter of the law. And so the response to them was geared toward changing the law, making it more difficult for firms to mislead investors. The Sarbanes–Oxley Act (SOX) of 2002, designed to tighten up the auditing process, is discussed later in this chapter.

To be fair, corporate governance is a complex process and even a well-designed board is no guarantee of success. At the start of the new century, boards had improved in many ways. More directors owned stock in the company, and boards were more likely to demand change.[17] Nevertheless, the Enron debacle occurred and subsequent legislation further increased expectations. In a post-Enron survey of corporate directors, 75 percent of respondents said they spent more time on board matters each month, and 67 percent said that meetings of the full board lasted longer.[18] In the 2008 year-end survey, 88 percent of the responding boards indicated that they evaluate board performance regularly, and 55 percent believed that those evaluations improved board performance.[19] As we discuss the failings of corporate governance in the last decade, we must keep in mind that boards share in the blame but are not responsible for all of it. They are not superheroes, and we should not expect them to be.[20]

The Need for Board Independence

Board independence from management is a crucial aspect of good governance. It is here that the difference between **inside directors** and **outside directors** becomes most pronounced. Outside directors are independent from the firm and its top managers. They can come from a variety of backgrounds (e.g., top managers of other firms, academics, former government officials) but the one thing they have in common is that they have no other substantive relationship to the firm or its CEO. In contrast, inside directors have ties of some sort to the firm. Sometimes they are top managers in the firm; at others, insiders are family members or others with a professional or personal relationship to the firm or the CEO. To varying degrees, each of these parties is "beholden" to the CEO and, therefore, might be hesitant to speak out when necessary. Another problem is managerial control of the board processes. CEOs often can control board perks, such as director compensation and committee assignments. Board members who rock the boat might find themselves left out in the cold. Since Enron imploded, changes in public policy and public opinion have led to an increase in the percentage of independent directors. However, the problem of board independence is one that will always merit attention.

Issues Surrounding Compensation

The issue of executive pay is a lightning rod for those who feel that CEOs are placing their own interests over those of their shareholders. For example, people became outraged when they heard that Wall Street firms gave out $18.2 billion as bonuses in 2008 as the economy crumbled. Two issues are at the heart of the CEO pay controversy are: (1) the extent to which CEO pay is tied to firm performance and (2) the overall size of CEO pay.

The CEO Pay–Firm Performance Relationship.   The move to tie CEO pay more closely to firm performance grew in momentum when shareholders observed CEO pay rising as firm performance fell. Many executives had received staggering salaries, even while profits were falling, workers were being laid off, and shareholder return was dropping. Shareholders were assisted in their effort to monitor CEO pay by stricter disclosure requirements from the Securities and Exchange Commission (SEC). The revised compensation disclosure rule, adopted by the SEC in 1992, was designed to provide shareholders with more information about the relationship between firm performance and CEO compensation.[21] It may have helped pay practices to be more responsive to changing economic times. The CEOs of America's 500 largest companies received a collective 38 percent pay raise in 2006 (representing about to $7.5 billion or an average $15.2 million each).[22] However, as the economy and firm profits receded, the pay of the CEOs of the 500 largest companies in the United States went down as well. They received a 15 percent collective pay cut in 2007 and an 11 percent cut for 2008.[23] According to Charles M. Elson, director of the John L. Weinberg Center for Corporate Governance at the University of Delaware, "We could begin to see a fundamental sea change in the compensation of executives."[24] Compensation research firm Equilar reported that 72 percent of the country's 100 largest companies implemented clawback provisions, requiring executives to return part of their pay under certain conditions such as malfeasance. This is up from only 17.6 percent in 2006.[25]

Efforts to strengthen the CEO pay–firm performance relationship have centered on the use of **stock options**. While they have improved the pay–performance relationship, they have also created a host of new problems. Stock options are designed to motivate the recipient to improve the value of the firm's stock. Put simply, an option allows the recipient to purchase stock in the future at the price it is today, that is, "at the money." If the stock value rises after the granting of the option, the recipient will make money. The logic behind giving CEOs stock options is that those CEOs will want to increase the value of the firm's stock so that they will be able to exercise their options, buying stock in the future at a price that is lower than its worth. Of course, this logic only works if the option is granted at the true "at the money" price. The possibility of quick gains through misrepresentation of the pricing has led to numerous abuses. The following are the ones most frequently in the news.

Stock option **backdating** occurs when the recipient is given the option of buying stock at yesterday's price, resulting in an immediate and guaranteed wealth increase. This puts the stock option "in the money" rather than "at the money," which is where an option should be granted. Of course, backdating results in an immediate gain and is not in keeping with the purpose of stock options. This is not the only stock option abuse that has been observed. Even stock options granted "at the money" can be problematic when coupled with inside knowledge that the stock price is soon going to change. **Spring-loading** is the granting of a stock option at today's price but with the inside knowledge that something good is about to happen that will improve the stock's value. **Bullet-dodging** is the delaying of a stock option grant until right after bad news. Backdating is not inherently illegal, but can be deemed so if documents were falsified to conceal the backdating. Spring-loading and bullet-dodging have been subjects of intense debate: The role of insider information in these two practices is a cause for concern. Adam Lashinsky of *Fortune* questions whether the benefits of stock options are worth the problems they create. He says, "So here's a radical proposal: Scrap the whole system. Pay employees a competitive and living wage. Pay them more when the company does well but only after shareholders have been rewarded. Do that in the form of transparent bonuses and profit-sharing plans. Outsized riches should be reserved for the company founders, not the hired help, which, let's face it, is what most executives are."[26]

Excessive CEO Pay. Concern about the size of executive compensation has been around for a long time. In ancient Greece, Plato recommended that no one in a community receive a wage higher than five times that of the lowest paid worker. Today, this issue has taken on increasing meaning as CEO salaries have skyrocketed while worker salaries have waned. Executive Excess 2009, the annual CEO compensation survey by the Institute for Policy Studies and United for a Fair Economy, reported that the ratio of CEO pay to the average worker was 319 to 1.[27] This represents a significant decline from 2000, when the gap between CEO pay and average worker pay had risen to a staggering 531 to 1. Nevertheless, it is more than seven times as large as the 42-to-1 ratio found in 1980.[28]

The **Say on Pay** movement evolved from concerns over excessive executive compensation. It began in the United Kingdom in 2002, with regulations that included the requirement to put a remuneration report to a shareholder vote at each annual meeting.[29] Soon after the United Kingdom instituted its regulations, Say on Pay requirements spread through Europe and Australia, with the Netherlands making the vote binding on the company.[30] In the United States, more than 200 shareholder proposals over the three proxy seasons between 2007 and 2009 sought Say on Pay provisions: Support for such proposals has gone up and down.[31] In 2008 and 2009, the Protection Against Executive Compensation Abuse Act, sponsored by Representative Barney Frank; the Shareholder Bill of Rights sponsored by Senator Charles Schumer; the treasury department's financial stability rules; and the SEC's expressed agenda all moved Say on Pay forward.[32] These efforts, coupled with President Obama's longstanding support for Say on Pay, makes it likely that it will be instituted in the United States in due course.

When the executive's high level of pay results from dubious practices, such as financial misconduct or the exercising of options in a questionable way, shareholders have a right to try to recover those funds, but in the past, they have lacked a mechanism for doing so. This is changing due to the increasing adoption of **clawback provisions**, which are compensation recovery mechanisms that enable a company to recoup compensation funds, typically in the event of a financial restatement or executive's misbehavior.[33] At this writing, financial reform legislation is scheduled to include "clawback" provisions to recall bonuses from financial services employees whose risky practices create problems for investors.[34]

Individual investors and other parties concerned do not have to wade through proxy statements to learn about CEO compensation. The AFL-CIO sponsors CEO PayWatch (http://www.aflcio.org/paywatch), a Web site that is an "online center for learning about the excessive salaries, bonuses and perks of the CEOs of major corporations."[35] Visitors to the Web site can enter their pay and a firm's name and find out how many years they would have to work to make what the CEO of that firm makes in one year (or how many workers are at your salary that the CEO's pay could support). They can also play "Boot the CEO," a game in which players can give the boot to greedy CEOs who are clutching bags of money. On a more serious note, the Web site provides instructions for assessing the pay of CEOs at public corporations and beginning a campaign of shareholder activism in any company.

Executive Retirement Plans and Exit Packages. Executive retirement packages have traditionally flown under the radar, escaping the notice of shareholders, employees, and the public. However, as details of some retirement packages have become public, those packages have come under increased scrutiny. The issue took center stage when former General Electric (GE) chairman and CEO Jack Welch's retirement package was disclosed during his divorce proceedings. Country club memberships, wine and laundry services, luxurious housing, and access to corporate jets were but a few of the perks that Welch had enjoyed.[36] These packages are negotiated well in advance and so they often are unrelated to performance. The $210-million exit package Robert Nardelli received following his ouster from Home Depot inflamed shareholder activists and outraged the public.[37] After Bank of America took $45 billion in federal bailout funds and became the subject of investigation by federal and state officials, outgoing CEO Ken Lewis received nearly $64 million in retirement pay and left the firm with what some compensation analysts estimate to be $125 million.[38]

Part of the public's frustration is that these CEO retirement packages stand in stark contrast to the retirement packages that workers receive. Many of today's workers do not have retirement packages, and those that do are far more likely to have the less lucrative defined contribution (that specify what will be put into the retirement fund) rather than the defined benefit plans (that specify the benefit the retiree will receive).[39] These defined contribution plans are more vulnerable to stock market fluctuations than defined benefit plans, and so the majority of workers saw their retirement funds plummet as the economic crisis hit. In September 2009, two-thirds of U.S. workers indicated that they were planning to delay their retirements because of economic factors caused by the recession.[40]

Outside Director Compensation. It was suggested earlier that there may be some link between CEO and executive compensation and board members. Therefore, it should not be surprising that directors' pay is becoming an issue, too. Paying board members is a relatively recent idea. Ninety years ago, it was illegal to pay nonexecutive board members. The logic was that because board members represented the shareholders, paying them out of the company's (i.e., shareholders') funds would be self-dealing.[41] A 1992

Korn/Ferry survey showed that board members typically spent 95 hours a year on the board. By 2000, that figure had almost doubled to 173 hours. The average director received a 23 percent increase in pay for the 82 percent increase in time spent on the job.[42] Not surprisingly, a 2003 survey by the *Corporate Board Member* magazine found that 80 percent of board members felt directors should be paid more in light of the "added responsibility of recent board governance reforms."[43] The situation seemed to have improved by 2007 when the same survey found that 73 percent of board members believed their compensation for board service was adequate.[44] However, in a clear nod to the additional requirements imposed by the Sarbanes–Oxley legislation, 66 percent of the respondents noted that the chair of the audit committee should receive additional compensation.[45]

Transparency. The SEC rules on disclosure of executive compensation are designed to address some of the more obvious problems by making the entire pay packages of top executives transparent, including those items that were hidden previously such as deferred pay, severance, accumulated pension benefits, and perks over $10,000.[46] Shareholder advocates argue that amendments to the proposed rule water down the impact of the change.[47] Nevertheless, there is general agreement that the new SEC requirements should provide greater transparency and so corporate boards have not fought the change. In a survey of board members, 88 percent of board members responded that they welcomed the new transparency requirements.[48] There is even evidence that the rules had an impact prior to implementation. Michael S. Melbinger, a compensation lawyer, tells the story of a CEO who had a contract provision that not only reimbursed all his medical expenses (including deductibles and co-pays) but also provided a **tax gross-up**, which reimbursed him for the taxes he would have to pay on his medical benefits. In contrast, employees in this company were required to cover their own medical expenses. So when the CEO realized how bad it would look that the company not only paid all his medical bills but also the taxes on that benefit, he quickly gave up that perk.[49] Tax gross-ups, such as the $11 million that AT&T CEO David Dorman received to pay the taxes on his $29-million severance, are creating shareholder resentment when brought to light.[50]

Some experts express concern that the push for transparency is actually resulting in greater opacity. There is so much information that disclosure forms can take dozens of pages. According to Brian Foley, an independent compensation consultant, "Most of us in the trade don't know whether to laugh or cry, when plowing through disclosure forms that run dozens of pages, with tables, footnotes and the kind of language that makes your hair hurt. My own test is, can I read it through or do I lose focus? I've been doing this for 30 years—if I lose focus, or can't figure something out, God help the average person."[51]

The issue of executive compensation is complex. For one, not everyone agrees that the current levels of pay are overly extravagant. Some observers argue that executives are not overpaid; they contend that CEO salaries are appropriate to their responsibilities, and that the excessive granting of stock options is clouding the data.[52] Still others argue that the efforts to curb excessive compensation are having the opposite effect. Joanne Lublin and Scott Thurm of the *Wall Street Journal* suggest that the increase in transparency has made it easier for executives to compare their pay to that of their peers, and that has led these executives to compete for higher pay. They also argue that stock options, designed to tie pay more closely to performance, have led to further abuses such as backdating and spring-loading.[53] These views run counter to the popular perception that excessive executive compensation is a simple case of greed and they illustrate the challenge of addressing this issue effectively.

The Governance Impact of the Market for Corporate Control

Mergers and acquisitions are another form of corporate governance, one that comes from outside the corporation. The expectation is that the threat of a possible takeover will motivate top managers to pursue shareholder, rather than self, interest. The merger, acquisition, and hostile takeover craze of the 1980s motivated many corporate CEOs and boards to go to great lengths to protect themselves from these takeovers. Two of the controversial practices to emerge from the hostile takeover wave were poison pills and golden parachutes. We briefly consider each of these, and see how they fit into the corporate governance problem being discussed. Then we examine the issue of insider trading.

Poison Pills.   A **poison pill** is intended to discourage or prevent a hostile takeover. They work much like their name suggests—when an acquirer tries to swallow (i.e., acquire) a company, the poison pill makes the company very difficult to ingest. Poison pills can take a variety of forms but, typically, when a hostile suitor acquires more than a certain percentage of a company's stock, the poison pill provides that other shareholders be able to purchase shares, thus diluting the suitor's holdings and making the acquisition prohibitively expensive (i.e., difficult to swallow). Poison pills have fallen out of favor, going from 2,218 such defenses in 2001 to 1,206 at the start of 2009, largely due to institutional shareholder pressure.[54]

Golden Parachutes.   A **golden parachute** is a contract in which a corporation agrees to make payments to key officers in the event of a change in the control of the corporation.[55] Advocates argue that golden parachutes provide top executives involved in takeover battles with an incentive for not fighting a shareholder wealth-maximizing takeover attempt in an effort to preserve their employment. However, a study of over 400 takeover attempts found that golden parachutes had no effect on takeover resistance.[56] Critics argue that executives are already being paid sufficiently well and that these parachutes essentially reward them for failure.[57] In a 2007 Equilar Inc. study of 137 large companies, 82 percent of the CEOs were promised exit packages if they lost their jobs following a corporate takeover, or "change in control."[58] However, new rules requiring more transparent exit packages are motivating companies to trim these plans down to less lavish terms.[59]

Insider Trading Scandals

Insider trading is the practice of obtaining critical information from inside a company and then using that information for one's own personal financial gain. A scandal began in 1986 when the SEC filed a civil complaint against Dennis B. Levine, a former managing partner of the Drexel Burnham Lambert investment banking firm, and charged him with illegally trading in 54 stocks. Levine then pleaded guilty to four criminal charges and gave up $10.6 million in illegal profits—the biggest insider trading penalty up to that point.[60] He also spent 17 months in prison.

Levine's downfall set off a chain reaction across Wall Street. His testimony led directly to the SEC's $100-million judgment against Ivan Boesky, one of Wall Street's most frenetically active individual speculators. In a consent decree, Boesky agreed to pay $100 million, which was then described as by far the largest settlement ever obtained by the SEC in an insider trading case. Boesky then fingered Martin Siegel, one of America's most respected investment bankers, at Kidder Peabody. In 1987, Boesky was sentenced to three years in prison. However, he helped prosecutors reel in the biggest fish of all— junk bond king Michael Milken. The SEC accused Milken and his employer, Drexel Burnham, of insider trading, stock manipulation, and other violations of federal securities laws. Burnham agreed in 1988 to plead guilty to six felonies, settle SEC charges, and pay a record fine of $650 million. A year later, the junk bond market crashed and Burnham filed for bankruptcy. In 1990, Milken agreed to plead guilty to six felony counts of securities fraud, market manipulation, and tax fraud. He agreed to pay a personal fine of $600 million and later was sentenced to ten years in prison.[61] He served only two years in prison before being released. In 2003, Martha Stewart was found guilty on four counts of making false statements and obstruction of justice regarding a controversial sale of ImClone Systems stock. She spent five months in prison, after which she began rebuilding her various businesses.[62] Insider trading concerns continue unabated. The 2009 statistics of United Kingdom's Financial Services Authority show suspicious trading occurring prior to nearly one-third (29.3 percent) of announced take-over attempts.[63]

Insider trading allegations cause the general public to lose faith in the stability and security financial industry. If large investors can act on information that smaller investors do not have, the playing field is not level. To prop up investor confidence, the SEC instituted disclosure rules designed to aid the small investor who historically has not had access to the information large investors hold. Regulation FD (fair disclosure) set limits on the common company practice of selective disclosure. When companies disclose meaningful information to shareholders and securities professionals, they must now do so publicly so that small investors can enjoy a more level playing field.[64]

Improving Corporate Governance

We first discuss a landmark legislative effort to improve corporate governance. SOX was passed in response to the public outcry for greater protection following the financial scandals of 2001. We then proceed to other efforts to improve corporate governance through changes in the composition, structure, and functioning of boards of directors.

Sarbanes–Oxley Act

On July 30, 2002, the **Accounting Reform and Investor Protection Act of 2002** was signed into law. Also known as the **Sarbanes–Oxley Act (aka SOX or Sarbox)**, it amends the securities laws to provide better protection to investors in public companies by improving the financial reporting of companies. According to the Senate committee report, "the issue of auditor independence is at the center of [SOX]."[65] Some of the ways the act endeavors to ensure auditor independence are by limiting the nonauditing services an auditor can provide, requiring auditing firms to rotate the auditors who work with a specific company, and making it unlawful for accounting firms to provide auditing services where conflicts of interest (as defined by the act) exist. In addition, the act enhances financial disclosure with requirements such as the reporting of off-balance-sheet transactions, the prohibiting of personal loans to executives and directors, and the requirement that auditors assess and report upon the internal controls employed by the company. Other key provisions include the requirement that audit committees have at least one financial expert, that CEOs and chief financial officers (CFOs) certify and be held responsible for financial representations of the company, and that whistle-blowers are afforded protection. Corporations must also disclose whether they have adopted a code of ethics for senior financial officers, and, if they haven't, provide an explanation for why they haven't.[66] The penalties for noncompliance with SOX are severe. A CEO or CFO who misrepresents company finances may face a fine of up to $1 million and imprisonment for up to ten years. If that misrepresentation is wilful, the fine may go up to $5 million with up to 20 years' imprisonment.[67]

After the passage of SOX, critics pointed to significant successes, while expressing concern over work that has yet to be accomplished. Some saw evidence that executives and directors were being more diligent in their reporting to shareholders but expressed concern that executives were becoming too risk averse.[68] There has been an increase in firms turning private to avoid the regulations. The cost of compliance can be as much as three times the cost prior to the act's implementation.[69] Another example of an unintended consequence is the impact SOX has had on the CFO position. The requirements of SOX made it far less attractive to sit in the CFO position. CFOs were once considered the prime stars of the executive suite, in training to be promoted to CEO. However, SOX has changed the position's focus to compliance. CFOs no longer have time to look at the big picture of corporate strategy and are thus less attractive as candidates for promotion to CEO.[70] Some observers have even expressed concern about the effectiveness of some of SOX's requirements. For example, the requirement that boards install an anonymous channel for reporting fraud may decrease the reports given to nonanonymous channels.[71] Others argue that the whistle-blower protection offered is insufficient.[72] In spite of its challenges, most firms seem to have worked their way up the learning curve. The *2008 Oversight Systems Financial Executive Report on Sarbanes–Oxley* stated that 80 percent of executives found their costs of compliance had either remained steady or declined from that of previous years.[73] Furthermore, the number of companies concerned about the morale of their employees who are responsible for compliance dropped from 24 percent in 2007 to only 13 percent in 2008.[74]

Changes in Boards of Directors

Because of the growing belief that CEOs and executive teams need to be made more accountable to shareholders and other stakeholders, boards have been undergoing a variety of changes. Here we focus on several key areas that need change as well as some of the recommendations that were set forth for improving board functioning. Figure 4-3 presents a ranked list of nine "red flags" that signal that a board member should increase his or her involvement, and the National Association of Corporate Directors' nine steps that provide a roadmap for board repair.

FIGURE 4-3 Ranking of Red Flags That Signal Board Problems and Steps to Take for Board Repair

Ranking of Red Flags	Steps to Board Repair
1. Company has to restate earnings	1. Spread risk oversight among multiple committees
2. Poor employee morale	2. Seek outside help in identifying potential risks
3. Adverse Sarbanes–Oxley 404 opinion	3. Deepen involvement in corporate strategy
4. Poor customer satisfaction track record	4. Align board size and skill mix with strategy
5. Management misses strategic performance goals	5. Revamp executive compensation
6. Company is target of employee lawsuits	6. Pick compensation committee members who will question the status quo
7. Stock price declines	7. Use independent compensation consultants
8. Quarterly financial results miss analysts' expectations	8. Evaluate CEO on grooming potential successors
9. Low corporate governance quotient rating	9. Know what matters to your investors

Sources: "What Directors Think Study 2008," Corporate Board Member http://www.boardmember.com. (This list is a result from a 2008 *Corporate Board Member* and PricewaterhouseCoopers LLP survey of 1,040 corporate directors.) Joanne S. Lublin, "Corporate Directors Give Repair Plan to Boards," *The Wall Street Journal* (March 24, 2009), B4.

Board Diversity

Prior to the 1960s, boards were composed primarily of white, male inside directors. It was not until the 1960s that pressure from Washington, Wall Street, and various stakeholder groups began to emphasize the concept of board diversity. Fifty years later, there are improvements, but board diversity is still sorely lacking. The *2008 Catalyst Census of Women Board Directors of the Fortune 500* examined the status of women on the boards of the largest public companies in the United States and they found that the news was mixed. The percent of directorships held by women in the Fortune 500 rose from 14.7 percent in 2007 to 15.2 percent in 2008; however, the number of Fortune 500 firms with no female board members rose from 59 in 2007 to 66 in 2008.[75]

The Alliance for Board Diversity conducted a study, *Women and Minorities on Fortune 100 Boards*, which also showed little progress in bringing diversity to the largest companies' boardrooms. They found that there were only very small improvements in terms of percentage of distribution for Hispanics, Asian-Americans, and minorities in general on corporate boards from 2004 to 2006. There was no change for African-Americans and a virtual stagnation for women overall on corporate boards.[76]

Problems with achieving board diversity issue are not confined to the United States. According to the 2008 Cranfield University research on FTSE100 boards, only 11.7 percent of the largest companies in the United Kingdom have women on their boards.[77] That is not very different from the 10.5 percent recorded in 2005.[78] This is slightly above the European average, which, according to the European Professional Women's Network, is about 8 percent.[79] Italy has the lowest, with fewer than 2 percent of board seats.[80]

The leader in having women on corporate boards of directors is Norway. The 500 publicly traded firms in Norway were told they would face closure if they do not meet a January 2008 deadline for achieving 40 percent female representation on their boards.[81] By 2008, every major Norwegian corporation was in compliance. The number of women on Norway's corporate board had almost quadrupled in five years.[82] By 2010, the percentage of women on publicly traded Norwegian boards was greater than 40 percent, and, even on private boards, the percentage of women had risen to more than 25 percent.[83] Not surprisingly, this dramatic shift ignited a fierce debate about the use of quotas to create change and the role of women in the workplace.[84] As of 2010, Spain and the Netherlands had passed similar laws with a 2015 deadline for compliance, the French Senate was scheduled to debate a similar bill, and Belgium, Britain, Germany, and Switzerland were considering legislation.[85]

Do diverse boards make a difference? Given the diversity of stakeholders, a diverse board is better able to hear their concerns and respond to their needs.[86] Diverse boards are also less likely to fall prey to groupthink because they would have the range of perspectives necessary to question the assumptions that drive group decisions.[87] There is some evidence of board diversity being associated with better financial performance.[88] However, a cause–effect relationship is very difficult to determine because so many factors influence the performance of a firm.

Outside Directors

Legislative, investor, and public pressure have led firms to seek a greater ratio of outside to inside board members. Outside directors are those board members who have no other relationship with the firm and its top managers; in contrast, inside directors are connected to the firm in ways other than board membership. Insiders are often top managers in the firm. However, they may also be family members of the CEO or others with a close relationship to the firm or its decision makers. Insiders might also be professionals who contract with the firm, such as lawyers or bankers. To varying degrees, each of these parties has a relationship with the CEO and, therefore, might be hesitant to speak out when necessary. Even membership in the same country club, volunteer work with the same nonprofit organization, and attendance at the same college at the same time can create board/CEO ties that lessen board member independence.

Do outside board members make a difference for both shareholders and stakeholders? As with diversity, a relationship between the proportion of outside directors and financial performance is difficult to find. For that reason, scholars have looked to more targeted measures. One study found outside directors to be associated with fewer shareholder lawsuits.[89] Regarding stakeholders, researchers found that outside directors correlated positively with dimensions of social responsibility associated with both people and product quality.[90] A recent study examined 20,000 board members from 2,080 firms and found that as board connections to the firm increased, so did earnings restatements and mergers that hurt firm performance.[91]

Outside directors are a heterogeneous group and so the impact of appointing more outside directors to boards can be expected to vary with the characteristics of the directors who are appointed, such as their expertise, their experience, and the time they have available to give to their post. Arguably, the most important characteristic for outside directors is the ability to ask difficult questions and speak truthfully about concerns, without letting ties to the firm get in the way.

Use of Board Committees

The **audit committee** is responsible for assessing the adequacy of internal control systems and the integrity of financial statements. Recent scandals, such as those to do with Enron, WorldCom, and the many companies that have subsequently needed to restate earnings, underscore the importance of a strong audit committee. In a recent survey, board members indicated that audit committee members have had the greatest increase in workload because of the added responsibilities stemming from SOX.[92] SOX mandates that the audit committee be composed entirely of independent board members and that there be at least one identified financial expert, as defined in SOX.[93] The principal responsibilities of an audit committee are as follows:[94]

1. To ensure that published financial statements are not misleading
2. To ensure that internal controls are adequate
3. To follow up on allegations of material, financial, ethical, and legal irregularities
4. To ratify the selection of the external auditor

While the audit committee has taken center stage in the current corporate governance environment, other committees still play key roles. The **nominating committee**, which should be composed of outside directors, has the responsibility of ensuring that competent, objective board members are selected. The function of the nominating committee is to nominate candidates for the board and for senior management positions. The suggested role and responsibility of this committee notwithstanding, in most companies, the CEO continues to exercise a powerful role in the selection of board members. The **compensation committee** has the responsibility of evaluating executive performance and recommending terms and conditions of employment. This committee should be composed of outside directors. Both the New York Stock Exchange (NYSE) and NASDAQ require that the compensation committee be composed of independent board members. One might ask, however, how objective these board members are when the CEO has played a significant role in their being elected to the board. Finally, each board has a **public issues committee**, or **public policy committee**. Although it is recognized that most management structures have some sort of formal mechanism for responding to public or social issues, this area is important enough to warrant a board committee that would become sensitive to these issues, provide policy leadership, and monitor the management's performance on these issues. Most major companies today have public issues committees that typically deal with such issues as affirmative action, equal employment opportunity, environmental affairs, employee health and safety, consumer affairs, political action, and other areas in which public or ethical issues are present. Debate continues over the extent to which large firms really use such committees, but the fact that they have institutionalized such concerns by way of formal corporate committees is encouraging.

The Board's Relationship with the CEO

Boards of directors have always been responsible for monitoring CEO performance and dismissing poorly performing CEOs. Historically, however, CEOs were protected from the axe that hit other employees when times got rough. This is no longer true because tough, competitive economic times; the rising vigilance of outside directors; and the increasing power of large institutional investors have had CEOs "dropping like flies."[95] As the *Christian Science Monitor* commented, "While the perks of sitting in a corner office are great, job security isn't one of them."[96]

"You have to perform or perish," according to John A. Challenger, CEO of outplacement firm Challenger, Gray & Christmas Inc. "If you don't produce immediate results, you just don't have much room to move."[97] A record number of CEOs lost their jobs in the first nine months of 2008.[98] Some analysts see the increased turnover in CEOs as a positive thing. "I take it as a good sign, because it says boards of directors are tougher on CEOs than they used to be," says Donald P. Jacobs, former dean of the Kellogg School of Business at Northwestern University.[99] Still others express their concern. Rakesh Khurana of Harvard Business School opines, "We've made this a superhero job. Boards look at the CEO as a panacea and get fixated on the idea that one single individual will solve all the company's problems."[100] Whether CEO turnover will continue to increase is unclear. There is some evidence that CEO turnover has slowed as a result of the global recession: More time must pass to know whether this is a momentary slowing or the beginning of a new trend.[101]

Board Member Liability

Concerned about increasing legal hassles emanating from stockholder, customer, and employee lawsuits, directors have been quitting board positions or refusing to accept them in the first place. In the past, courts rarely held board members personally liable in the hundreds of shareholder suits filed every year. Instead, the **business judgment rule** prevailed. The business judgment rule holds that courts should not challenge board members who act in good faith, making informed decisions that reflect the company's best interests instead of their own self-interest. The argument for the business judgment rule is that board members need to be free to take risks without fear of liability. The issue of good faith is key here because the rule was never intended to absolve board members completely from personal liability. In cases where the good faith standard was not upheld, board members have paid a hefty price.

The TransUnion Corporation case involved an agreement among the directors to sell the company for a price the owners later decided was too low. A suit was filed, and the court ordered that the board members be held personally responsible for the difference between the price the company was sold for and a later-determined "fair value" for the deal.[102] In addition to the TransUnion case, Cincinnati Gas and Electric reached a $14-million

ETHICS IN PRACTICE CASE

Monitoring the Monitors

News leaks seemed to plague Hewlett Packard. The first leaks surrounded the ouster of chairwoman and chief executive Carly Fiorina. In the midst of this internal turmoil, *The Wall Street Journal* published an article with details of closed-door board discussions about the planned management reorganization. An external legal counsel interviewed board members but did not succeed in identifying the leak. Evidence of more leaks appeared a year later as news organizations once again described the deliberations of closed-door board and senior management meetings in extensive detail. It was clear that someone from inside was leaking information. In addition to board members, reporters from such publications as the *New York Times, Wall Street Journal, BusinessWeek,* and *CNET* became targets of the ensuing investigation into ten different leaks. The methods used to try to plug these news leaks led eventually to a board shake-up, which included the departure of nonexecutive chairwoman Patricia Dunn.

Investigating board members is a difficult proposition. As the source of the potential leaks, the board could not supervise what was essentially an investigation of themselves. Neither could the employees handle the investigation because that would have put them in the untenable position of investigating their own bosses. Left with few options, HP board chairwoman Dunn turned the investigation over to a network of private investigators. According to Dunn, she could not supervise the investigation because she was a potential target. Dunn asked the head of corporate security to handle the investigation, as this was the person who handled employee investigations, but he still had conflicts of interest as an employee of the board. So the company outsourced the investigation to a network of outside investigators, telling them to conduct it within the confines of the law.

The primary source of the leaks was uncovered, but questions remained about the process of the

investigations. Although no recording or eavesdropping occurred, investigators had used a form of "pretexting" to elicit phone records. Pretexting is a way of obtaining information by disguising one's identify. In this case, investigators used pretexting to obtain phone records of not only HP board members but also reporters who covered the story. In addition, investigators followed board members and journalists and watched their homes. They also planted false messages with journalists in an effort to get them to reveal their sources inadvertently through the tracking software included in the fake messages.

1. Who should be responsible for taking action when a board member engages in problematic behavior? If the chairperson is responsible, when should he or she involve the whole board? What are the costs of early full board involvement? What are the costs of late full board involvement?

2. One complaint lodged was that HP provided board members' home phone numbers to investigators. Was this out of line? Do board members have a responsibility to provide certain basic information, or was their privacy breached when their home phone numbers were given? A board member whose phone records proved he was not involved in any leaks still resigned the board in protest that his privacy was invaded by the pretexting. Was he right?

3. The law regarding pretexting is unclear. While it is illegal when used to obtain financial records, the use of pretexting in other situations—such as the phone records in this example—was not necessarily against the law. Should it be?

4. How might things have evolved differently if the ethicality rather than the legality of the practice had been the issue? Are the two synonymous or is there a difference?

Sources: Damon Darlin, Julie Cresswell, and Eric Dash, "H.P. Chairwoman Aims Not to Be the Scapegoat," *The New York Times* (September 9, 2006), C1; Ellen Nakashima and Yuke Noguchi, "HP CEO Allowed 'Sting' of Reporter," *Washington Post* (September 21, 2006), A1.

settlement in a shareholder suit that charged directors and officers with improper disclosure concerning a nuclear power plant.[103]

The Caremark case further heightened directors' concerns about **personal liability**. Caremark, a home health care company, paid substantial civil and criminal fines for submitting false claims and making illegal payments to doctors and other health care providers. The Caremark board of directors was then sued for breach of fiduciary duties because the board members had failed in their responsibility to monitor effectively the Caremark employees who violated various state and federal laws. The Delaware Chancery Court ruled that it is the duty of the board of directors to ensure that a company has an effective reporting and monitoring system in place. If the board fails to do this, individual directors can be held personally liable for losses that are caused by their failure to meet appropriate standards.[104]

The issue of board members paying personal liability costs from their personal funds (also known as **out-of-pocket liability**) came to the forefront following the Enron and WorldCom debacles. Twelve WorldCom directors were ordered to pay $24.75 million out of their personal funds instead of drawing on their D&O insurance.[105] Ten former Enron directors agreed to pay $13 million from their personal funds.[106] In a November 2006 decision, the Delaware Supreme Court affirmed the "Caremark Standard" which states that directors can only be held liable if "1. The director utterly failed to implement any reporting or information system or controls, or 2. having implemented such a system or controls, consciously failed to monitor or oversee its operations, disabling their ability to be informed of risks or problems requiring their attention."[107] The economic meltdown raised new concerns about personal liability as directors realized they could be held personally liable when employees seek redress for the impacts of layoffs and plant closings.[108]

The Role of Shareholders

Shareholders are a varied group with a range of interests and expectations. They, however, have one aspect in common—they are the owners of the corporation. As such, they have a right to have their voices heard. Putting that right into practice, however, has presented an ongoing challenge for shareholders and managers.

Our discussion begins with an overview of the state of shareholder democracy, which relates to strengthening shareholder voice and participation in corporate governance. We then discuss shareholder activism and close with recommendations for improved shareholder relations.

Shareholder Democracy

Throughout the world, shareholders have been fighting to have their voices heard in corporate governance. This **shareholder democracy** movement stems from the lack of power shareholders have felt, particularly in board elections. In the United States, votes against board members have generally not been counted and corporations have been free to ignore shareholder resolutions.[109] Withholding a vote for a board member has typically had no impact because only the votes that were actually cast were counted.[110] Similarly, many European firms have not had one vote for each share issued.[111] Of course, the ability of shareholders to elect board members is central to the governance process because the elected board members will be governing the corporation.[112] However, pundits and scholars disagree over the value of the recommended reforms.

Proponents of shareholder democracy argue that if shareholders aren't able to select their own representatives, the board is likely to become a self-perpetuating oligarchy.[113] They contend that increased shareholder power and involvement will lead to improved firm performance.[114] Opponents counter that shareholders are not "owners" in the traditional sense of the word because they can exit their ownership relatively easily by simply selling their shares.[115] They contend that increased shareholder power will lead to inefficient and short-term-oriented decision making, as well as infighting among competing interests.[116] Irrespective of these competing views, the trend is toward increased shareholder democracy. In the United States, the Shareholder Bill of Rights Act of 2009 and the SEC amendment that would expand shareholder proxy access, giving them more power to nominate directors for election, and promote classified boards are both proposals at this writing. If adopted, they will significantly increase shareholder power.

Shareholder democracy begins with board elections and so we focus our discussion there. Three key issues that have arisen are majority vote, classified boards, and proxy access.

Majority vote is the requirement that board members be elected by a majority of votes cast. This is in contrast to the previously prevailing norm of plurality voting. With plurality voting, the board members with the greatest number of "yes" votes are elected to the available seats on the board. The "no" and withheld votes are not counted. With "plurality plus," board members who receive less than a majority of votes cast must submit their resignation; however, boards of directors have not always accepted the resignations.[117]

Classified boards are those that elect their members in staggered terms. For example, in a board of 12 members, 4 might be elected each year, and each would serve a three-year term. It would then take three years for the entire board slate to be replaced. Many shareholder activists oppose classified boards because of the time required to replace the board. Proponents of classified boards argue that board members need a longer time frame to get to make longer-term-oriented strategic decisions.

Proxy access provides shareholders with the opportunity to propose nominees for the board of directors. This has been an issue of contention for years. In the prevailing system, shareholders must file a separate ballot if they want to nominate their own candidates for director positions. This procedure is time-consuming and costly, so shareholder groups are asking for the ability to place their candidates directly on the proxy materials.

The Role of the SEC

The role of the SEC in the United States is clear; the commission is responsible for protecting investor interests. However, many critics argue that the SEC often appears more focused on the needs of business than on that of investors. In the one of the worst scandals in the SEC's 75-year history, the SEC failed to stop the Bernard Madoff ponzi scheme that cost investors around the world tens of billions of dollars. A **ponzi scheme** lures investors in with the fake promise of profit but actually pays earlier investors with later investors' money until the scheme collapses.

The SEC failed to stop Madoff in spite of having been warned of the scheme nearly a decade earlier. Harry Markopolos, an independent financial fraud investigator, provided the SEC with both the reasons and the roadmap for investigating Madoff, but they failed to stop the scheme. According to Markopolos, "I gift wrapped and delivered the largest Ponzi scheme in history to them and somehow they couldn't be bothered to conduct a thorough and proper investigation because they were too busy on matters of higher priority"[118] In addition to characterizing the regulatory agency as "financially illiterate," Markopolos considers it plagued by infighting and captive to big industry.[119] It appears that Madoff might agree. In a jailhouse interview, he said he was "astonished" that the regulators did not follow simple procedures such as checking his clearinghouse accounts when complaints surfaced.[120] The first substantive complaint the SEC received about Madoff was in 1992, 16 years before the scheme imploded.[121]

Shareholder Activism

One major reason that relations between management groups and shareholders have heated up is that shareholders have discovered the benefits of organizing and wielding power. **Shareholder activism** is not a new phenomenon. It goes back over 60 years to

1932, when Lewis Gilbert, then a young owner of ten shares, was appalled by the absence of communication between the New York-based Consolidated Gas Company's management and its owners. Supported by a family inheritance, Gilbert decided to quit his job as a newspaper reporter and "fight this silent dictatorship over other people's money." He resolved to devote himself "to the cause of the public shareholder."[122] Today, technology has made it easier for even the smallest investor to obtain information and share news, ideas, and any issues they have with the companies in which they invest.[123]

The History of Shareholder Activism

The history of shareholder activism is too detailed to report fully here, but Gilbert's efforts planted a seed that grew, albeit slowly. The major impetus for the movement came in the 1960s and early 1970s. The early shareholder activists were an unlikely conglomeration—corporate gadflies, political radicals, young lawyers, an assortment of church groups, and a group of physicians.[124] The movement grew out of a period of political and social upheaval—civil rights, the Vietnam War, pollution, and consumerism.

The watershed event for shareholder activism was Campaign GM in the early 1970s, also known as the Campaign to Make General Motors Responsible. Among those involved in this effort was, not surprisingly, Ralph Nader, who is discussed in more detail in Chapter 13. The shareholder group did not achieve all its objectives, but it won enough to demonstrate that shareholder groups could wield power if they worked at it hard enough. Two of Campaign GM's most notable early accomplishments were that (1) the company created a public policy committee of the board, composed of five outside directors, to monitor social performance and (2) GM appointed the Reverend Leon Sullivan as its first black director.[125]

One direct consequence of the success of Campaign GM was the growth of church activism. Church groups were the early mainstay of the corporate social responsibility movement and were among the first shareholder groups to adopt Campaign GM's strategy of raising social issues with corporations. Church groups began examining the relationship between their portfolios and corporate practices, such as minority hiring and companies' presence in South Africa. Church groups remain among the largest groups of institutional stockholders willing to take on the management and press for what they think is right. Many churches' activist efforts are coordinated by the Interfaith Center on Corporate Responsibility (ICCR), which coordinates the shareholder advocacy of about 275 religious orders with about $90 billion in investments. The ICCR was instrumental in convincing Kimberly-Clark to divest the cigarette paper business and pressuring PepsiCo to move out of Burma.[126]

Shareholder activists have historically been socially oriented; that is, they want to exert pressure to make the companies in which they own stock more socially responsive. While that still remains true for many, activist shareholders are now also driven by a concern for profit. Home Depot CEO Robert Nardelli was ousted following pressure from activist shareholders, most notably Ralph Whitworth, cofounder of Relational Investors.[127] The successful ouster was not Whitworth's only goal. He continued to pressure Home Depot to nominate candidates for the board election and to have input in the firm's strategic direction.[128]

The growth of shareholder activism shows no signs of abating.[129] Activist shareholders, known also as **corporate gadflies**, are no longer dismissed as nuisance and are instead viewed as credible, powerful, and a force with which to be reckoned.[130] In fact, money managers and hedge funds advertise their activist orientation in the belief that being seen as aggressive gives them an edge.[131]

Shareholder Resolutions

One of the major vehicles by which shareholder activists communicate their concerns to management groups is through the filing of **shareholder resolutions**. An example of such a resolution is, "The company should name women and minorities to the board of directors." To file a resolution, a shareholder or a shareholder group must obtain a stated number of signatures to require management to place the resolution on the proxy statement so that it can be voted on by all the shareholders. Resolutions that are defeated (fail to get majority votes) may be resubmitted provided they meet certain SEC requirements for such resubmission.

Although an individual could initiate a shareholder resolution, she or he probably would not have the resources or means to obtain the required signatures to have the resolution placed on the proxy. Thus, most resolutions are initiated by large institutional investors that own large blocks of stock or by activist groups that own few shares of stock but have significant financial backing. Foundations, religious groups, universities, and other such large shareholders are in the best position to initiate resolutions. The issues on which shareholder resolutions are filed vary widely, but they typically concern some aspect of a firm's social performance. In 2010, resolutions have addressed such issues as executive compensation, animal testing, board structure, sustainability reporting, board diversity, and climate change.[132]

Most shareholder resolutions never pass, and even those that pass are typically non-binding. So one might ask why groups pursue them. Meredith Benton, research associate with Walden Asset Management, describes why she would come to the point of wanting to put forth a resolution: "The process begins when there's an issue of concern for our clients. We look at what the issue is and how it may impact the companies in our portfolio. Once we've determined what that impact might be and believe there's a long-term business case for why one of our companies should be concerned about the issue, we approach the company. They have a couple different ways they can respond to us. They can ignore us, which happens sometimes. They can constructively engage with us and sit down with us. If they're ignoring us or strongly disagreeing with our viewpoint, we have one more option, which is the shareholder resolution."[133] Benton notes that resolutions are the most public aspect of what they do but that they actually have constructive conversations far more often.[134]

Shareholder Lawsuits

An earlier reference was made to the **shareholder lawsuit** in the TransUnion case. Shareholders sued the board of directors for approving a buyout offer that the shareholders argued should have had a higher price tag. Their suit charged that the directors had been negligent in failing to secure a third-party opinion from experienced investment bankers. The case went to trial and resulted in a $23.5-million judgment against the directors.[135] The TransUnion case may have been one of the largest successful shareholder suits at that time, but it was dwarfed by the Cendant suit, which resulted in a $ 2.83-billion class action settlement.[136]

A 2009 study by the Stanford Law School Securities Class Action Clearinghouse found that lawsuits against firms in the financial services sector dominated in 2008. A total of 210 federal securities class actions were filed, representing a 19 percent increase over the 176 filings in 2007.[137] The study goes on to say that this level of litigation activity against firms in a specific sector has not been seen since the passage of the 1995 Reform Act.[138] The **Private Securities Litigation Reform Act of 1995** was intended to rein in excessive levels of private securities litigation. The increase in the number of filings has been attributed to the financial crisis of 2008.[139]

Investor Relations

Over the years, corporate managements have neglected their owners. As share ownership has dispersed, there are several legitimate reasons why this separation has taken place. But there is also evidence that management groups have been too preoccupied with their own self-interests. In either case, corporations are beginning to realize that they have a responsibility to their shareholders that they cannot neglect further. Owners are demanding accountability, and it appears that they will be tenacious until they get it.

Public corporations have obligations to existing shareholders as well as potential shareholders. **Full disclosure** (also known as **transparency**) is one of these responsibilities. Disclosure should be made at regular and frequent intervals and should contain information that might affect the investment decisions of shareholders. This information might include the nature and activities of the business, financial and policy matters, tender offers, and special problems and opportunities in the near future and in the longer term.[140] Of paramount importance are the interests of the investing public, not the interests of the incumbent management team. Board members should avoid conflicts between personal interests and the interests of shareholders. Company executives and directors have an obligation to avoid taking personal advantage of information that is not disclosed to the investing public and to avoid any personal use of corporation assets and influence.

Another responsibility of management is to communicate with shareholders. Successful shareholder programs do exist. Berkshire Hathaway Inc. is known for attending to its shareholders, and CEO Warren Buffett is praised by shareholders in return.[141] One indication of Berkshire Hathaway's relationship with shareholders is the annual meeting. Buffett calls the annual shareholders' meeting "Woodstock weekend for capitalists." It's not unusual for shareholders to attend a minor league baseball game decked out in their forest green Berkshire Hathaway T-shirts and caps. Many wait in line to have a picture taken with Buffett or get his autograph.[142] Even in a difficult year, Buffett is honest with his shareholders. In his chairman's letter, Buffett said bluntly, "During 2008 I did some dumb things in investments."[143]

Technology has made investor relations easier to accomplish, and companies have begun to take advantage of it. Companies such as Dell Computer have set up investor relations blogs that not only share information but also give readers an opportunity to communicate with Dell executives.[144] Intel Corporation was the first company to let shareholders use the Internet to vote and submit questions to the annual meeting, and Walmart provides live Twitter and video updates from their annual meetings.[145] Herman Miller, the furniture company, has switched to virtual shareholder meetings, not only enhancing shareholder access but also saving money in the process.[146]

With good investor relations, many serious problems can be averted and those that are unavoidable are less likely to fester. If shareholders are able to make their concerns heard outside the annual meeting, they are less likely to confront managers with hostile questions when the meeting is in session. If their recommendations receive serious consideration, they are less likely to put them in the form of a formal resolution. Constructive engagement is easier for all involved.[147]

Summary

Recent events in corporate America have served to underscore the importance of good corporate governance and the legitimacy it is supposed to provide for business. To remain legitimate, corporations must be governed according to the intended and legal pattern. Governance debacles, such as the 2008 financial crisis, call not only the legitimacy of individual companies into question but also that of business as a whole.

The modern corporation involves a separation of ownership from control, which has resulted in problems with managers not always doing what the owners would rather they do. Boards of directors are responsible for ensuring that managers represent the best interests of owners, but boards sometimes lack the independence needed to monitor management effectively. This has led to serious problems in the corporate governance arena, such as excessive levels of CEO pay and a weak relationship between CEO pay and firm performance. Of course, at times an effort to solve one problem can create another. The use of stock options in CEO compensation has helped tie CEO pay to firm performance more closely, but it has resulted in skyrocketing levels of pay, as well as in the manipulation of option timing and pricing. Other issues are lavish executive retirement plans and outside director compensation. New SEC rules for transparency may have an impact on the compensation issue in the future.

In theory, the market for corporate control should also rein in CEO excesses. The threat of a takeover should motivate a CEO to represent shareholders' best interests, but the existence of poison pills can blunt the takeover threat by making it prohibitively expensive for an acquirer. Golden parachutes were designed to keep CEOs from trying to block takeover attempts, but they have not had their intended effect, and they too present a host of problems.

SOX was a landmark piece of legislation, drafted in response to the financial scandals of 2001. As with all efforts to improve corporate governance, it has held both costs and benefits. The demands of SOX have led many firms to go private to avoid the costs involved in compliance; however, evidence indicates that boards are becoming more independent, devoting more time to the governance of the firm, and not hesitating to fire a CEO who does not make the grade. Board liability has increased, and that too is a motivation behind the increased vigilance that has been observed.

Although they are the firms' owners, shareholders are too diffuse and removed from the corporation to monitor the activities of the corporation and its managers effectively. To protect their interests, shareholders have grouped together to regain their ownership power. Institutional shareholders own sufficient blocks of stock to get the ear of the firm's boards and executives. They have been using this access to effect change, and their efforts are beginning to pay off. Shareholder democracy, while still an unrealized goal, is growing as shareholders fight for greater voice in the firm's decisions. In response, firms are beginning to pay more attention to investor relations.

In many ways, corporate governance has improved. CEOs no longer enjoy job security when firm performance suffers. Corporations can no longer release false or misleading reports without threat of consequences. The growth in CEO pay has tapered off, although it remains at extremely high levels. These improvements are worthy of note, but they are insufficient to protect the legitimacy of business. Steps were taken to lessen the likelihood of another Enron occurring, but then the 2008 financial crisis occurred. Continual vigilance must be maintained if corporate governance is to realize its promise and its purpose, that of representing shareholder interests and being responsive to the needs of the many individuals and groups who have a stake in the firm.

Key Terms

Discussion Questions

1. Explain the evolution of corporate governance. What problems developed? What are the current trends?

2. What are the major criticisms of boards of directors? Which single criticism do you find to be the most important? Why?

3. Explain how governance failures such as Enron could happen. How might they be avoided?

4. Outline the major suggestions that have been set forth for improving corporate governance. In your opinion, which suggestions are the most important? Why?

5. In what ways have companies taken the initiative in becoming more responsive to owners/stakeholders? Where would you like to see more improvement? Discuss.

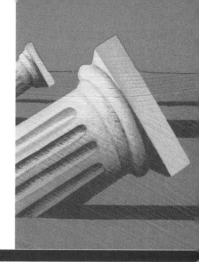

5
Strategic Management and Corporate Public Affairs

CHAPTER LEARNING OUTCOMES

After studying this chapter, you should be able to:

1. Describe the concept of corporate public policy and relate it to strategic management.

2. Articulate the four major strategy levels and explain enterprise-level strategy.

3. Explain corporate social performance reporting.

4. Identify the major activities of public affairs departments.

5. Highlight key trends with respect to the public affairs function.

6. Link public affairs with the strategic management function.

7. Indicate how public affairs may be incorporated into every manager's job.

Following on the topic of corporate governance, in this chapter and the next, we more closely examine how management has responded and should respond to the kinds of social, ethical, and stakeholder issues developed in this book. In this chapter, we provide a broad overview of how social, ethical, and public issues fit into the general **strategic management processes** of the organization. We introduce the term **corporate public policy** to describe that component of management decision making that embraces these issues. Then we discuss corporate public affairs, or public affairs management, as the formal organizational approach companies use in implementing these initiatives. The overriding goal of this chapter is to focus on planning for the turbulent social/ethical stakeholder environment, and this encompasses the strategic management process, environmental analysis, and public affairs management.

The Concept of Corporate Public Policy

The impact of the social-ethical-public-global-stakeholder environment on business organizations is becoming more pronounced each year. It is an understatement to suggest that this multifaceted environment has become tumultuous, and brief reminders of a few actual cases point out the validity of this claim quite dramatically. Ford Motor Company and its disastrous Pinto gas tank problem, Johnson & Johnson and its tainted Tylenol capsules, and Exxon's catastrophic *Valdez* oil spill are *classic* reminders of how social issues can directly affect a firm's product offerings. Scandals at such firms as Enron, WorldCom, Tyco, Adelphia, HealthSouth, and Arthur Andersen all had major impacts on firms at the general management level. More recently, the subprime mortgage meltdown, China's dairy industry scandal, and the auto industry bailout provide examples of ethical issues that have dramatic implications for top executive decision makers. In each case, public policy issues were relevant to the companies' problems.

What started as an awareness of social issues and social responsibility has matured into a focus on the management of social responsiveness and performance. Now that we have completed the first decade of the new millennium, the trend reflects a preoccupation with ethics, stakeholders, and corporate citizenship. Corporate social responsibility (CSR) is now a strategic issue with far-reaching implications for organizational purpose, direction, and functioning.

The term *corporate public policy* is an outgrowth of an earlier term, *corporate social policy*, which had been in general usage for decades. The two concepts have essentially the same meaning, but we use "corporate public policy" because it is more in keeping with terminology more recently used in business. Much of what takes place under the banner of corporate public policy is also referred to as *corporate public affairs* or *corporate citizenship* by businesses today.

Corporate Public Policy Defined

What is meant by corporate public policy?

> *Corporate public policy is a firm's posture, stance, strategy, or position regarding the public, social, global, and ethical aspects of stakeholders and corporate functioning.*

Later in the chapter, we discuss how businesses formalize this concern under the rubric of **corporate public affairs**, or public affairs management. Businesses encounter several situations daily that involve highly visible public and ethical issues, including those that are subject to intensive public debate for specific periods before they become institutionalized. Examples of such issues include sexual harassment, AIDS in the workplace, affirmative action, product safety, environmental sustainability, and employee privacy. Other issues are more basic, more enduring, and more philosophical and might include the broad role of business in society, the corporate governance question, and the relative balance of business versus government direction that is best for our society. Today, the economic meltdown and its consequences have taken center stage.

The idea behind corporate public policy is that a firm must give specific attention to issues in which basic questions of justice, fairness, ethics, or public policy reside. The dynamic stakeholder environment of the past 40 years, especially the last 10 years, has necessitated that the management employ a policy perspective to these issues. At one time, the social environment was considered a relatively constant backdrop against which the real work of business took place. Today, these issues are central, and managers at all levels must address them. Corporate public policy is the process by which management addresses these significant concerns.

Corporate Public Policy and Strategic Management

Where does corporate public policy fit into strategic management? First, let us briefly discuss strategic management. **Strategic management** refers to the overall management process that strives to identify corporate purpose and to position a firm relative to its market environment. A basic way in which the firm relates to its market environment is through the products and services it produces and the markets it chooses to participate in. It is also considered a kind of overall or comprehensive organizational governance and management by the firm's top-level executives which decides and implements an organization's sense of direction.

Top management teams must address many issues as a firm positions itself relative to its environment. The more traditional issues involve product or market decisions—the principal strategic decisions of most organizations. Other decisions relate to marketing, finance, accounting, information systems, human resources, operations, research and development, competition, and so on. Corporate public policy is that part of the overall strategic management of the organization that focuses specifically on the public, ethical, and stakeholder issues that are embedded in the decision processes of the firm. Therefore, just as a firm needs to develop policy on human resources, operations, marketing, or finance, it also must develop corporate *public* policy to address proactively the host of issues that have been discussed in and will be discussed throughout this book.

Citizens Bank of Canada is a company that concluded it needed a formal corporate public policy. As a company trying to build a strong reputation in the CSR area since opening its doors over a decade ago, the bank's management concluded that it needed more than the establishment of a few enlightened policies. It needed something that would set a systematic course and foundation for "doing well by doing good." Citizens' first step was the establishment of a document of guiding principles, called an *ethical policy*, which would steer the firm's practices toward its social and environmental commitments. To implement its policy and follow up on implementation, the bank created an "ethical policy compliance" unit.[1] The Citizens' initiatives illustrate the value of a formalized corporate public or ethics policy. In April 2008, it became the first North American–based bank to become carbon neutral, and it achieved this goal two years ahead of schedule.[2] In that same year, the bank donated $50,000 to Habitat for Humanity and one day of volunteering to nonprofit causes.[3]

Relationship of Ethics to Strategic Management

A consideration of ethics is implicit in corporate public policy discussions, but it is useful to make this relationship more explicit. Over the years, a growing number of observers have stressed this point. Early on, the emphasis was on the moral component of corporate strategy. Relevant was the leadership challenge of determining future strategy in the face of rising moral and ethical standards. Coming to terms with the morality of choice may be the most strenuous in strategic decision making, particularly stressful within the inherently amoral corporation.[4]

The focus of linking ethics and strategy was moved to the center stage in the book *Corporate Strategy and the Search for Ethics,* which argued that if business ethics were to have any meaning beyond pompous moralizing, it should be linked to business strategy. The theme was that the concept of corporate strategy can be revitalized by linking ethics to strategy. This linkage permits addressing the most pressing management issues of the day in ethical terms. The book introduces the idea of *enterprise strategy* as the one that best links these two vital notions, and this concept is examined in more detail in the next section.[5]

The concept of corporate public policy and the linkage between ethics and strategy are better understood when we think about the

1. four key levels at which strategy decisions arise and
2. steps in the strategic management process in which these decisions are embedded.

Four Key Strategy Levels

Because organizations are hierarchical, it is not surprising to find that strategic management also is hierarchical in nature; that is, the firm has several different levels at which strategic decisions are made, or the strategy process occurs. These levels range from the broadest or highest levels (where missions, visions, goals, and decisions entail higher risks and are characterized by longer time horizons, more subjective values, and greater uncertainty) to the lowest levels (where planning is done for specific functional areas and are characterized by shorter time horizons, less complex information needs, and less uncertainty). Four key strategy levels are important: (1) enterprise-level strategy, (2) corporate-level strategy, (3) business-level strategy, and (4) functional-level strategy.

Four Strategy Levels Described

Enterprise-Level Strategy.   The broadest level of strategic management is known as *societal-level strategy* or *enterprise-level strategy*. **Enterprise-level strategy** is the overarching strategy level that poses such basic questions as, "What is the role of the organization in society?" and "For what do we stand?" As will be evident from the detailed discussion later, this encompasses the development and articulation of corporate public policy and may be considered the first and most important level at which ethics and strategy are linked. Corporate governance is one of the most important topics at this level.

Corporate-Level Strategy.   **Corporate-level strategy** addresses what are often posed as the most defining business question for a firm, "In what business(es) should we be?" Thus, mergers, acquisitions, and divestitures are examples of decisions made at this level. A relevant part of corporate strategy today is the decision of whether and how to participate in global markets.

Business-Level Strategy.   **Business-level strategy** is concerned with the question, "How should we compete in a given business or industry?" Thus, a company whose products or services take it into many different businesses, industries, or markets will need a business-level strategy to define its competitive posture in each of them. A competitive strategy might address whether a product should be low cost or differentiated, as well as whether it should compete in broad or narrow markets.

Functional-Level Strategy.   **Functional-level strategy** addresses the question, "How should a firm integrate its various subfunctional activities and how should these activities be related to changes taking place in the diverse functional areas (finance, marketing, human resources, operations)?"[6] Companies today try to avoid functional silos so that they can operate in a more integrated way.

   The purpose of identifying the four strategy levels is to clarify that corporate public policy is primarily a part of enterprise-level strategy, which, in turn, is but one level of strategic decision making that occurs in organizations. In terms of its implementation, however, the other strategy levels inevitably come into play. Figure 5-1 illustrates that enterprise-level strategy is the broadest and that the other levels are narrower concepts that cascade from it.

Emphasis on Enterprise-Level Strategy

The terms *enterprise-level strategy* and *societal-level strategy* may be used interchangeably. Neither is frequently used in the business community, but both are helpful here. Although many firms address the issues enterprise-level strategy is concerned with, use of this terminology is concentrated primarily in the academic community. This terminology describes the level of strategic thinking necessary if firms are to be fully responsive to today's complex and dynamic stakeholder environment. Most organizations today

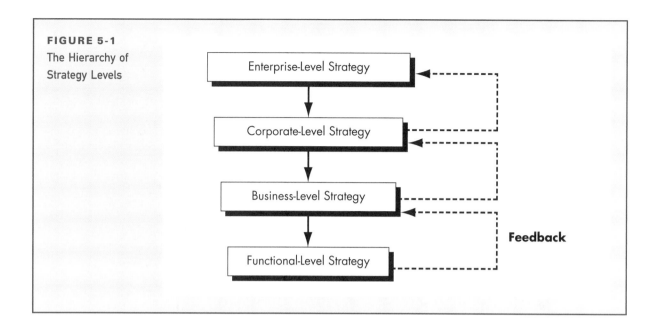

FIGURE 5-1
The Hierarchy of
Strategy Levels

convey their enterprise or societal strategy in their vision, missions, or values statements. Others embed their enterprise strategies in codes of conduct. Increasingly, these strategies are reflecting a global level of application.

Enterprise-level strategy needs to be thought of as a concept that more closely aligns "social and ethical concerns" with traditional "business concerns."[7] In setting the direction for a firm, a manager needs to understand the impact of changes in business strategy on the underlying values of the firm and the new stakeholder relations that will consequently emerge and take shape. Thus, at the enterprise level, the task of setting strategic direction involves understanding the role in society of a particular firm as a whole and its relationships to other social institutions. Important questions then become:

- What is the role of our organization in society?
- How do our stakeholders perceive our organization?
- What principles or values does our organization represent?
- What obligations do we have to society, including to the world?
- What are the broad implications for our current mix of businesses and allocation of resources?

Many firms have addressed some of these questions—perhaps only in part or in an ad hoc way. The point of enterprise-level strategy, however, is that the firm needs to address these questions intentionally, specifically, and cohesively in such a way that a corporate public policy is articulated.

How have business firms addressed these questions? What are the manifestations of enterprise-level thinking and corporate public policy? The manifestations show up in various ways in different companies, such as a firm's response when faced with public crises. Does it respond to its stakeholders in a positive, constructive, and sensitive way or in a negative, defensive, and insensitive way? Corporate decisions and actions reveal the presence or absence of soundly developed enterprise-level strategy. Companies also demonstrate the degree of thinking that has gone into public issues by the presence or absence and use or nonuse of codes of ethics, codes of conduct, mission statements,

Spotlight on SUSTAINABILITY

Enterprise-Level Strategy in Action

One of the best ways to appreciate a company's public policy or enterprise-level strategy is to examine its posture on sustainability. Wegmans, a regional U.S. supermarket chain with stores in the Mid-Atlantic region, has made a formal and effective commitment to promoting sustainability through a sustainability mission statement, a sourcing philosophy, and a sustainability coordinator.

Wegmans' mission statement begins with the Native American proverb, "We do not inherit the earth from our ancestors; we borrow it from our children." It goes on to say, "There are no simple solutions to these challenges. Still, we all have a responsibility to be aware and be accountable. We promise to take steps to protect our world for future generations—it's part of our commitment to make a difference in every community we serve."

To learn more about Wegmans' commitment to sustainability, check out its Web site: http://www.wegmans.com.

values statements, corporate creeds, vision statements, or other such policy-oriented codes and statements.

A good example of enterprise-level strategy is the corporate credo of Johnson & Johnson, shown in Figure 5-2. Note that the Johnson & Johnson credo focuses on statements of responsibility by enumerating its stakeholder groups in the following sequence: (1) doctors, nurses, patients, mothers and fathers (consumers), (2) employees, (3) communities, and (4) stockholders. The credo faced a critical test in 1982 when seven people died of cyanide poisoning after taking tainted Tylenol capsules. Then-CEO James Burke turned to the credo, which places those who use the company's products and services above all others. Rather than wasting time arguing that the company was not to blame (even though it was not), Burke promptly alerted people of the danger of the product, initiated a massive recall, and developed triple tamper-resistant packaging before returning to market. The company regained its market share within six months, supporting the last statement of the credo—that living up to the credo's principles will ultimately benefit stockholders as well as stakeholders.

Importance of Core Values.   It is crucial that firms not only have values statements that provide guidance but also that these values also "mean something." Ever since Jim Collins and Jerry Porras published *Built to Last: Successful Habits of Visionary Companies*, companies have felt they needed such statements. The authors made the case that many of the best companies adhere to a set of principles called **core values**. Core values are the deeply ingrained principles that guide all of a company's actions and decisions, and they serve as cultural cornerstones.[8] Though many companies have written publicly proclaimed values statements, many have been debased because they are not followed. To be effective, companies need to weave core values into everything they do. If a company's core values are not upheld, they become hollow or empty, such as those found at Enron, and such values statements may be doing more harm than good.

In contrast, deeply felt and strongly held values have the power to transform. A good example of that came from when Tim Cook, the man tapped to run Apple's operations in Steve Jobs' absence, was asked by investors how the company would function without Jobs. Cook's seemingly extemporaneous response created what *Fortune's* Adam Lashinsky described as a "magical moment."

FIGURE 5-2
Johnson &
Johnson Credo

Our Credo

We believe our first responsibility is to the doctors, nurses, and patients; to mothers and fathers; and to all others who use our products and services. In meeting their needs everything we do must be of high quality. We must constantly strive to reduce our costs in order to maintain reasonable prices. Customers' orders must be serviced promptly and accurately. Our suppliers and distributors must have an opportunity to make a fair profit.

We are responsible to our employees, the men and women who work with us throughout the world. Everyone must be considered as an individual. We must respect their dignity and recognize their merit. They must have a sense of security in their jobs. Compensation must be fair and adequate, and working conditions clean, orderly, and safe. We must be mindful of ways to help our employees fulfill their family responsibilities. Employees must feel free to make suggestions and complaints. There must be equal opportunity for employment, development, and advancement for those qualified. We must

provide competent management, and their actions must be just and ethical.

We are responsible to the communities in which we live and work and to the world community as well. We must be good citizens—support good works and charities and bear our fair share of taxes. We must encourage civic improvements and better health and education. We must maintain in good order the property we are privileged to use, protecting the environment and natural resources.

Our final responsibility is to our stockholders. Business must make a sound profit. We must experiment with new ideas. Research must be carried on, innovative programs developed, and mistakes paid for. New equipment must be purchased, new facilities provided, and new products launched. Reserves must be created to provide for adverse times. When we operate according to these principles, the stockholders should realize a fair return.

Johnson & Johnson

Source: Reprinted with permission from Johnson & Johnson. For more information, see http://www.jnj.com/our_company/our_credo/index.htm;jsessionid=RQUXI1 QGKCCKQCQPCCGSU0A. Accessed June 30, 2010.

We believe that we are on the face of the earth to make great products and that's not changing. We are constantly focusing on innovating. We believe in the simple not the complex. We believe that we need to own and control the primary technologies behind the products that we make, and participate only in markets where we can make a significant contribution. We believe in saying no to thousands of projects, so that we can really focus on the few that are truly important and meaningful to us. We believe in deep collaboration and cross-pollination of our groups, which allow us to innovate in a way that others cannot. And frankly, we don't settle for anything less than excellence in every group in the company, and we have the self-honesty to admit when we're wrong and the courage to change. And I think regardless of who is in what job those values are so embedded in this company that Apple will do extremely well.[9]

According to Lashinsky, Cook had been considered uncharismatic and uninspiring, but he came across in this response as "forceful, eloquent, and passionate about Apple."[10]

In what do value-based companies believe? It has been argued that three basic organizational values undergird all others: transparency, sustainability, and responsibility.[11] Transparency emphasizes the company being open and honest, especially with employees. Sustainability is about conducting today's business in a way that does not rob the future, and responsibility invokes the idea of commitment to integrity and social responsibility. A good example of a values-based business is Stonyfield Farms, a small New Hampshire yogurt company. In addition to making a profit, Stonyfield's mission is to help local dairy farmers get more money for their milk, as many had been paid less than it cost them to produce the milk. Their mission also led them to produce more organic foods for worldwide consumption.[12]

Other Manifestations of Enterprise-Level Strategic Thinking. Enterprise-level strategic thinking is manifested in other ways. It may include the extent to which firms have established board or senior management committees. Such committees might include the following: public policy or issues committees, ethics committees, governance committees, social audit committees, corporate philanthropy committees, and ad hoc committees to address specific public issues. The firm's public affairs function can also reflect enterprise-level thinking. Does the firm have an established public affairs office? To whom does the director of corporate public affairs report? What role does public affairs play in corporate-level decision making? Do public affairs managers play a formal role in the firm's strategic planning?

Another major indicator of enterprise-level strategic thinking is the extent to which the firm attempts to identify social or public issues, analyze them, and integrate them into its strategic management processes. In the final analysis, a firm will need to undergo a "**value shift**" if it is interested in integrating ethical and social considerations into its financially driven strategic plans. Such a value shift, according to Lynn Sharp Paine, would require the firm to get back to basics and adopt a different kind of management than that typically practiced by companies. She argues that superior performers of the future will be those companies that can meet both the social and financial expectations of their stakeholders,[13] a theme we seek to develop in this chapter and book. Following is a discussion of how corporate public policy is integrated into the strategic management process.

The Strategic Management Process

To understand how corporate public policy is just one part of the larger system of management decision making, it is useful to identify the major steps that make up the strategic management process. Boards and top management teams are responsible for activating the process. One conceptualization includes six steps: (1) goal formulation, (2) strategy formulation, (3) strategy evaluation, (4) strategy implementation, (5) strategic control, and (6) environmental analysis.[14] Figure 5-3 graphically portrays an expanded view of this process.

The environmental analysis component requires collection of information on trends, events, and issues that occur in the stakeholder environment, and this information is then fed into the other steps of the process. Although the tasks or steps are often discussed sequentially, they are in fact interactive and do not always occur in a neatly ordered pattern or sequence. Figure 5-3 also captures the relationship between the strategic management process and corporate public policy. Figure 5-4 illustrates Kenneth Andrews' four major components of strategy formulation and how "acknowledged obligations to society" fits into the step of strategy formulation.[15]

Strategic Corporate Social Responsibility

In recent years, the term "strategic corporate social responsibility" has captured the idea of integrating a concern for society into the strategic management processes of the

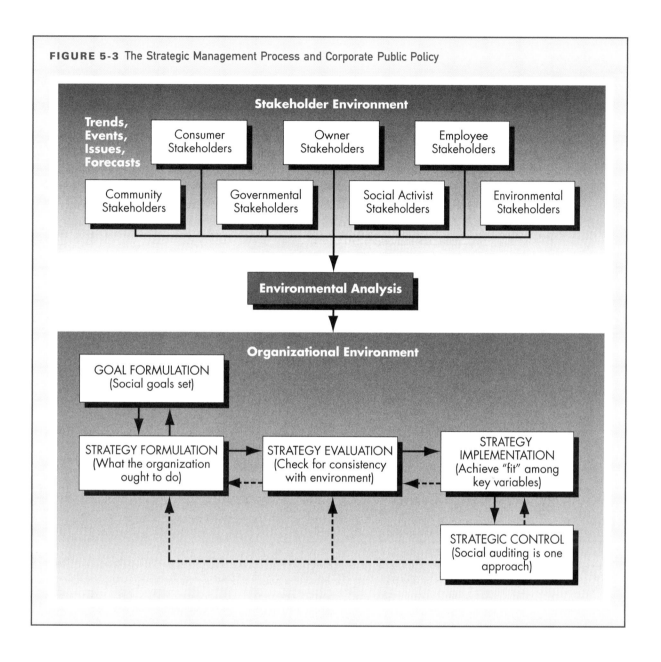

FIGURE 5-3 The Strategic Management Process and Corporate Public Policy

firm.[16] Such a perspective insures that CSR is fully integrated into the firm's strategy, mission, and vision. Strategic management also may be focused on a particular CSR topic or core value to the business firm. An example of this would be the concept of "sustainable strategic management."[17] In this concept, sustainability is focused on the "triple bottom line" as discussed earlier. In addition, this concept goes beyond the concern of the firm and argues that the survival and renewal of the greater economic system, social system, and ecosystem are important as well. Strategic CSR and sustainable strategic management reflect a firm's enterprise-level strategy discussed earlier.

The notion of strategic CSR got a huge boost when strategy expert Michael Porter began advocating the importance of the linkage between competitive advantage, a crucial strategy concept, and CSR.[18] Though Porter had been preceded by others in advocating

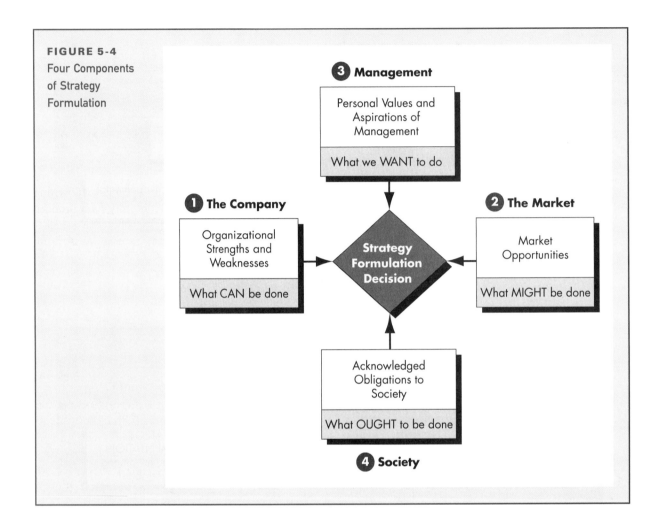

FIGURE 5-4
Four Components
of Strategy
Formulation

this linkage, the strength of his reputation has furthered the cause. He and co-author Mark Kramer argued that the interdependence between business and society takes two forms: "inside-out linkages" wherein company operations impact society, and "outside-in linkages" wherein external societal forces impact companies.[19] In order to prioritize social issues, they proceed to categorize three broad ways corporations intersect with society. First, there are "generic social issues" wherein a company's operations do not significantly impact society and the issue isn't material to the firm's long-term competitiveness. Second, there are "value chain social impacts" where a company's normal operations significantly impact society. Finally, there are "social dimensions of competitive context," wherein social issues affect the underlying drivers of a company's competitiveness.[20]

Porter and Kramer next divide these three categories into two primary modes of corporate involvement. *Responsive CSR* addresses "generic social impacts" through good corporate citizenship and "value chain social impacts" by mitigating harm from negative corporate impacts on society, whereas *strategic CSR* transforms "value chain social impacts" into activities that benefit society, while simultaneously reinforcing corporate strategy, as well as advances strategic philanthropy that leverages relevant areas of competitiveness.[21]

The aforementioned ideas are integrated into a series of steps that intend to integrate business and society strategically. These steps include:

1. Identifying the points of intersection (inside-out and outside-in).
2. Choosing which social issues to address (generic, value chain social impacts, social dimensions of competitiveness).
3. Creating a corporate social agenda (responsive versus strategic).
4. Integrating inside-out and outside-in practices (getting practices to work together).
5. Creating a social dimension to the value proposition. (The company adds a social dimension to its value proposition, thus making social impact integral to the overall strategy.)[22]

Porter and Kramer offer Whole Foods Market (WFM) as an example of this final point. The value proposition of WFM is to sell natural, organic, healthy food products to customers who passionately care about the environment. Social issues are central to WFM's mission and are implemented through sourcing approaches, commitment to the environment, and use of environment-friendly policies and practices.[23]

The Porter–Kramer framework is useful because it applies strategic thinking to both leverage positive social and environmental benefits and mitigate negative social and environmental impacts in ways that enhance competitive advantage.[24] The challenge for companies, therefore, is to find the ways in which the social dimension can be added to the basic business endeavor.

Social Auditing and Social Performance Reporting

As a management function, strategic control, the fifth step in the strategic management process, seeks to ensure that the organization stays on track and achieves its goals, missions, and strategies. Planning is not complete without control because the control function strives to keep management activities in conformance with plans.

Management control encompasses three essential steps: (1) *setting standards* against which performance may be compared, (2) *comparing* actual performance with what was planned (the standard), and (3) *taking corrective action* to bring the two into alignment, if needed.[25] A planning system will not achieve its full potential unless at the same time it monitors and assesses the firm's progress along key strategic dimensions. Furthermore, there is a need to monitor and control the "strategic momentum" by focusing on a particular strategic direction while at the same time coping with environmental turbulence and change.[26] The social audit is a planning and control approach that is worthy of discussion within the context of strategic management. Some companies actually report their social performance relative to their standards. Others just report their social or values activities and achievements.

Development of the Social Audit. In the context of corporate social performance or corporate public policy, the idea of a **social audit**, or **social performance report**, as a technique for providing planning and control has been experimented with for a number of years. Although the term *social audit* has been used to describe a wide variety of activities embracing various forms of social performance reporting, in this discussion it is defined as follows:

> *The social audit is a systematic attempt to identify, measure, monitor, and evaluate an organization's performance with respect to its social efforts, goals, and programs.*

Implicit here is the idea that some social performance planning has already taken place. And, although we refer to the social audit here as a control process, it could just as easily be thought of as a planning and control system.[27]

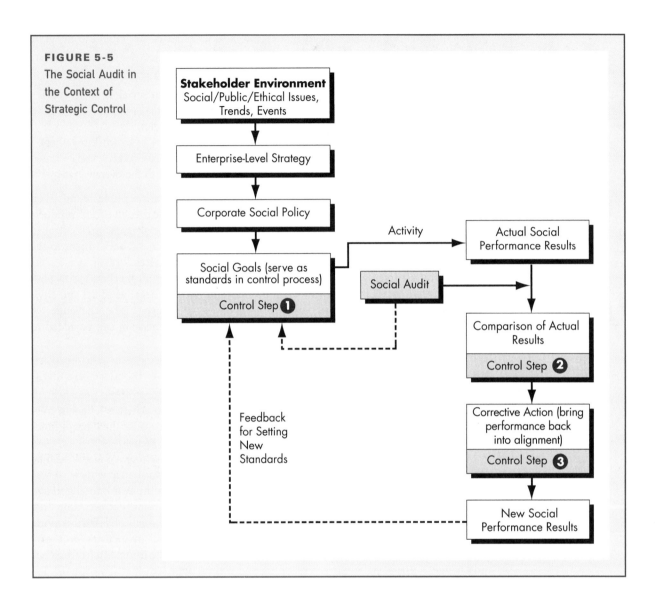

FIGURE 5-5
The Social Audit in the Context of Strategic Control

In the context of strategic control, the social audit can assume a role much like that portrayed in Figure 5-5. This figure is similar to the diagram of the strategic management process and corporate public policy shown in Figure 5-3, but it is modified somewhat to highlight social goals, corporate social performance, the social audit, and the first three steps in the strategic control process.

Corporate Social Performance Reporting

Today, all of the following terms are used to describe social performance reports issued on an annual or periodic basis by companies interested in getting their message out: *CSR reports, social performance reports, corporate citizenship reports, sustainability reports, values reports,* and so on. Most of these reports use methodologies that are less rigorous than the original idea of social audits. What these reporting processes have in common is that they make the public and stakeholders aware of their social and ethical programs, activities, and achievements. Some of the more advanced reports actually report company achievements relative to previous goals set by the management. Others just report what the company has done during the previous reporting period.

The impetus for social performance reports in recent years has come from societal and public interest groups expectations that firms report their achievements in the social responsibility and sustainability arenas. Such reports typically require monitoring and measuring progress, and this is valuable to management groups wanting to track their own progress as well as be able to report it to other interested parties. Some companies create and issue such reports because it helps their competitive positions. Social performance helps companies to manage their brands and reputations more effectively, bring coherence to their communications, and benchmark their performance.[28] Globalization is another driver for social performance reports. As more and more companies do business globally, they need to document their achievements when critics raise questions about their contributions, especially in developing countries. Companies such as Nike and Walmart have been criticized for their use of sweatshops abroad, so they have an added incentive to keep track of their social performance and issue such reports. In a recent report, GE presented data documenting its performance with respect to its supplier network and its relationship with governments in emerging markets as the company strives to cope with globalization by raising and meeting standards abroad.[29]

Ceres. The nonprofit organization Ceres (pronounced "series") just celebrated its 20th anniversary. It is a national network of investors, environmental organizations, and other public interest groups working with companies and investors to address sustainability challenges and promote social performance reporting. Because of the economic crisis, achieving a sustainable global economy is a recent interest. Ceres's mission is to integrate sustainability "into capital markets for the health of the planet and its people."[30] Because of its interests, it is little surprise that many companies today are using the terminology "sustainability reports."

A specific initiative of Ceres has been its annual award for sustainability reporting. These awards have focused attention on the concept of social performance reporting. The awards are now called the *Ceres-ACCA Awards for Sustainability Reporting*, recognizing the joint initiative with the Association of Chartered Certified Accountants (ACCA). GE Corporation won the 2009 Ceres-ACCA North American Awards for Best Sustainability Reporting. Ceres said the report "provides a complete picture of how the company's sustainability priorities are aligned with the company's strategic business priorities" and "presents these priorities in the context of emerging global challenges including climate change and energy, globalization, human rights, water scarcity, and the subprime mortgage crisis."[31]

CORPORATEREGISTER.COM The organization that keeps the most comprehensive data on social performance reports is CorporateRegister.com. CorporateRegister.com is a free directory of company-issued CSR, sustainability, and environment reports from around the world, and the site is continually updated with new reports and companies.[32] The tremendous growth in CSR reports can be seen by data collected by CorporateRegister.com. In the year 2000, 823 reports were issued, whereas in 2008, these had shot up to 3,100, showing that the number almost quadrupled in just eight years. Up until 2003, most such reports were categorized as environmental; however, since that time the two growing categories have been corporate responsibility and sustainability.[33]

GLOBAL REPORTING INITIATIVE One of the major impediments to the advancement of effective social performance reporting has been the absence of standardized measures for social reporting. Standardization is a challenge that has been undertaken by a consortium of over 300 global organizations called the **Global Reporting Initiative (GRI)**. Ceres launched the GRI in conjunction with the U.N. Environment Programme (UNEP) in 1997 with the mission of developing globally applicable guidelines for reporting on the economic, environmental, and social performance of corporations, governments, and non-governmental organizations (NGOs).[34] GRI is now considered the de-facto international standard (used by over 1,500 companies) for corporate reporting on environmental, social, and economic performance. It includes the participation of corporations, NGOs, accountancy organizations, business associations, and other worldwide stakeholders.[35]

The GRI's Sustainability Reporting Guidelines represented the first global framework for comprehensive sustainability reporting, encompassing the "triple bottom line" of economic, environmental, and social issues. In 2002, the GRI became a permanent, independent, international body with a multistakeholder governance structure. The mission of GRI is to maintain, enhance, and disseminate the guidelines through ongoing consultation and stakeholder engagement. More than 1,500 companies and organizations throughout the world issue GRI-based reports.[36]

As firms develop enterprise-level strategies and corporate public policies, the potential for social responsibility and sustainability reporting remains high. Social reporting is best appreciated not as an isolated, periodic attempt to assess social performance but rather as an *integral part* of the overall strategic management process as it described here. Because the need to improve planning and control will remain as long as the management desires to evaluate its corporate social performance, the need for approaches such

ETHICS IN PRACTICE CASE

Not Much Range for This Manager

I used to work for a golf course at their driving range. The basic responsibility of my fellow employees and me was quite simple. We took money from customers, gave them a basket of golf balls to hit, made sure the supply of golf balls was adequate, and moved the tees on the driving range so there would be decent grass for the players to hit off. It was well known that everyone, including our manager, gave away free baskets of balls to family members and, occasionally, good friends. When the golf course acquired a new golf professional, the giving away of free baskets of balls was supposed to cease.

After the new golf pro had been working for a couple of months, he realized that all, or some, of the range personnel were still giving away free baskets of balls. Our manager at the time was still giving away free balls, along with all the employees, but the golf pro was not aware of this factor. The golf pro proceeded to talk to our manager and tell him that he needed to fire the employee who continued to give away free baskets of balls.

Because the job at the range did not require much work, everyone was laidback about the job and came in a little late almost every day. Our manager, who was regularly late at least 15 to 30 minutes, set this trend. Within a week of the golf pro telling our manager to fire the employee who was giving away the free baskets, I noticed that the employee who had been working there for the longest time had been fired. Once this employee was gone, our manager wrote up a new set of rules and posted them in the office. The first rule was NO FREE BASKETS OF BALLS. NO EXCEPTIONS! When I read this new rule, I assumed the fired employee got caught by the golf pro giving away free baskets of balls. After I spoke with the fired employee, he told me that our manager fired him because of excessive tardiness.

1. Who, if anyone, in this case acted in an unethical manner? If they did, how?

2. Should I have told the golf pro the whole story? If I did, how would it affect the other employees and me?

3. Does the employee who was fired have a legal recourse to pursue further action?

Contributed Anonymously

as the social audit and social responsibility reporting will likely be with us for some time, too. The net result of continued use and refinement should be improved corporate social performance and enhanced credibility of business in the eyes of its stakeholders and the public. In terms of practice, social performance reporting has become more popular than the more complex task of social auditing. Regardless, both approaches serve much the same purpose and help keep the organization on track with its social performance goals.

Public Affairs

Public affairs and **public affairs management** are umbrella terms companies use to describe the management processes that focus on the formalization and institutionalization of corporate public policy. The public affairs function is a logical and increasingly prevalent component of the overall strategic management process. Public affairs experts argue that it has grown significantly into one of the most important parts of strategic management over the past decade and today may be seen as the strategic core business function for companies wanting to compete successfully internationally.[37]

As an overall concept, public affairs management embraces corporate public policy, discussed earlier, along with **issues and crisis management**, which is considered in more detail in Chapter 6. Indeed, many issues management and crisis management programs are housed in **public affairs departments** or intimately involve public affairs professionals. Corporate public affairs also embraces the broad areas of governmental relations and corporate communications.

We should emphasize that companies use different names to describe management's efforts to address the stakeholder environment, and they use different titles for the same functions. According to the most recent report of the Foundation for Public Affairs, the following names are often used to represent the public affairs function in companies:[38]

- Corporate Public Affairs
- Public Affairs, Policy, and Communications
- Public Policy
- Public Relations and Government Affairs
- Communications and Public Affairs
- Communications and External Affairs
- Government and Public Affairs

Public Affairs as a Part of Strategic Management

In a comprehensive management system, which this chapter describes, the overall flow of activity would be as follows: A firm engages in strategic management, part of which includes the development of enterprise-level strategy, which poses the question, "For what do we stand?" The answers to this question help the organization form a corporate public policy, which is a more specific posture on the public, social, or stakeholder environment or specific issues within this environment. Some firms call this a *public affairs strategy.*

Two important planning approaches in corporate public policy are issues management and, often, crisis management. These two planning aspects frequently derive from or are related to environmental analysis, which was mentioned earlier. Some companies embrace these processes as part of the corporate public affairs function. These processes are typically housed, from a departmental perspective, in a public affairs department. *Public affairs management* is a term that often describes all these components. Figure 5-6 helps illustrate likely relationships among these processes.

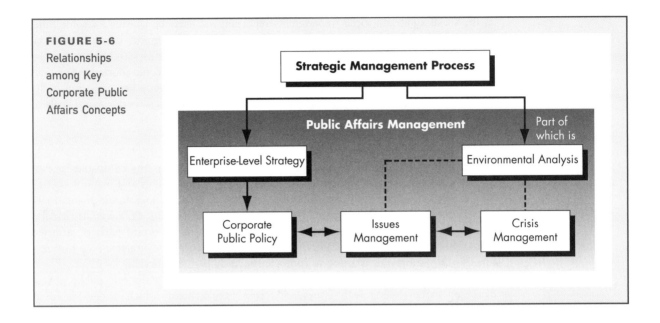

FIGURE 5-6
Relationships among Key Corporate Public Affairs Concepts

We now consider how the public affairs function has evolved in business firms, what concerns public affairs departments currently face, and how public affairs thinking might be incorporated into the operating manager's job. This last issue is crucial, because public affairs management, to be most effective, is best thought of as an indispensable part of every manager's job, not as an isolated function or department that alone is responsible for the public issues and stakeholder environment of the firm.

The Corporate Public Affairs Function Today

Public affairs blossomed in the United States because of four primary reasons: (1) the growing magnitude and impact of government; (2) the changing nature of the political system, especially its progression from a patronage orientation to an issues orientation; (3) the growing recognition by business that it was being outflanked by interests that were counter to its own on a number of policy matters; and (4) the need to be more active in politics outside the traditional community-related aspects, such as the symphony and art museums.[39]

Thus, the public affairs function as we know it today was an outgrowth of the social activism begun decades ago. Just as significant federal laws were passed in the early 1970s to address such issues as discrimination, environmental protection, occupational health and safety, and consumer safety, corporations responded with a surge of public affairs activities and creation of public affairs departments.[40]

Today, the Public Affairs Council (PAC), the leading professional organization of executives who do the public affairs work of companies, located in Washington, DC, provides the following definition of *public affairs*:

Public affairs represents an organization's efforts to monitor and manage its business environment. It combines government relations, communications, issues management and corporate citizenship strategies to influence public policy, build a strong reputation and find common ground with stakeholders.[41]

Public Affairs Activities and Functions

Public affairs as a management function progressed out of isolated company initiatives designed to handle such diverse activities as community relations, corporate philanthropy and contributions, governmental affairs, lobbying, grassroots programs, corporate responsibility, and public relations. In some firms, the public relations staff handled issues involving communication with external publics, so it is not surprising that public affairs often evolved from public relations. Part of the confusion between public relations and public affairs is traceable to the fact that some corporate public relations executives changed their titles, but not their functions, to public affairs. The key difference between public affairs and public relations is the goals of the clients. Public relations focuses on selling a product, while public affairs is designed to influence public policy.[42]

According to the PAC, the membership includes executives in such fields as:[43]

- Public Affairs
- Corporate Affairs
- External Affairs
- Government Relations
- Communications
- State Government Relations
- Community Relations, and
- Corporate Foundations

An important element of the public affairs function is the influence it has on corporate strategy and planning. If the public affairs function is to be effective in representing the "noncommercial" factors and issues affecting business decision making, it is important that public affairs has influence at the top management level. Public affairs can help to identify and prioritize issues, as well as provide input on emerging social and political trends. For public affairs to fulfill this function it is important that they have a seat at the table for corporate planning sessions.

Another way for public affairs to have an impact on top management is suggested in what has been called a "new positive model" of public affairs. In this model, the CEO of the company ought to be the company's chief public affairs officer. The idea here is that the public affairs function needs a transformation from reacting to proacting and that the best way to make this happen is to place the CEO in charge of the function.[44] This might not work as a practical reality, but the spirit of the idea is appropriate. It is an excellent idea in terms of elevating the importance of public affairs and its relationship to corporate strategy.

Useful Public Affairs Concepts

Important public affairs concepts include "looking out and looking in," "buffering and bridging," "tools and techniques," and the use of ethical guidelines for public affairs professionals. Each of these concepts is useful in terms of successful corporate public affairs.

Looking Out and Looking In

A useful perspective on the public affairs function in organizations today depicts the function as a window:

The public affairs function serves as a window: Looking out, the organization can observe the changing environment. Looking in, the stakeholders in that environment can observe, try to understand, and interact with the organization.[45]

When the public affairs function is viewed in this way, it is easy to understand how the "product" of the public affairs department is seen as the smoothing of relationships with external stakeholders and the management of company-specific issues.

Buffering and Bridging

Another important perspective on public affairs is also useful. Corporate public affairs activities can be thought of in terms of two types: activities that "buffer" the organization from the social and political environment and activities that "bridge" the organization with that environment. It has been found that as organizations experienced increased environmental uncertainty, buffering and bridging increased as well. Building bridges with external environmental uncertainty was found to be positively related to the top management's philosophy.[46] Bridging is a proactive stance that is most likely to be undertaken by companies with a stakeholder orientation.

Tools and Techniques

How do public affairs professionals get their work done? They use a mixture of tools and techniques that have been successful over the years as well as state-of-the art approaches made possible by technology and experience. Public affairs tools and techniques include the policies, practices, functions, and processes intended to fulfill public affairs objectives.[47] Among the most useful of these tools and techniques are the following:[48]

- Environmental monitoring/scanning (including issue and stakeholder management)
- Working with the grassroots
- Constituency building
- Issue advertising
- Lobbying
- Political action committees
- Corporate social audits
- Web activism
- Coalitions and alliances
- Community investment
- Stakeholder management[49]

Each of these tools and techniques has an advanced body of literature describing how they are employed by public affairs specialists to achieve their objectives.

Ethical Guidelines

A significant challenge today for public affairs professionals is to conduct their functions in an ethical fashion. As public trends push organizations toward more transparency, there are many opportunities for questionable practices, especially in such arenas as political action, government relations, and communications. Therefore, it is encouraging to know that a code of conduct or set of ethical guidelines has been established for individuals working in public affairs. These ethical guidelines are set forth in Figure 5-7. They deserve careful scrutiny.

Global Public Affairs

The global dimension of public affairs has expanded because of the following reasons: companies expanding into new markets, changes in sales in existing markets, changes in CEO priorities, changes in regulatory burden, and the acquisition of new business units.[50] To function properly, global public affairs must balance externally and internally focused activities. Externally, the central challenge is to manage the company's relations

---

FIGURE 5-7
Ethical Guidelines for Public Affairs Professionals

THE PUBLIC AFFAIRS PROFESSIONAL...

...maintains professional relationships based on honesty and reliable information, and therefore:

- represents accurately his or her organization's policies on economic and political matters to government, employees, shareholders, community interests, and others;
- serves always as a source of reliable information, discussing the varied aspects of complex public issues within the context and constraints of the advocacy role; and
- recognizes the diverse viewpoints within the public policy process, knowing that disagreement on issues is both inevitable and healthy.

...seeks to protect the integrity of the public policy process and the political system, and he or she therefore:

- publicly acknowledges his or her role as a legitimate participant in the public policy process and discloses whatever work-related information the law requires;
- knows, respects, and abides by federal and state laws that apply to lobbying and related public affairs activities; and

- knows and respects the laws governing campaign finance and other political activities, and abides by the letter and intent of those laws.

...understands the interrelation of business interests with the larger public interests, and therefore:

- endeavors to ensure that responsible and diverse external interests and views concerning the needs of society are considered within the corporate decision-making process;
- bears the responsibility for management review of public policies that may bring corporate interests into conflict with other interests;
- acknowledges dual obligations to advocate the interests of his or her employer, and to preserve the openness and integrity of the democratic process; and
- presents to his or her employer an accurate assessment of the political and social realities that may affect corporate operations.

Source: The Public Affairs Council (Washington, DC), http://pac.org/ethics/ethical-guidelines. Accessed June 30, 2010.

---

with various host countries. Requirements include understanding and meeting the host country's needs and dealing with diverse local constituencies, audiences, cultures, and governments. Internally, global public affairs programs must establish and coordinate external programs, educate company officials on public affairs techniques, and assist wherever possible the company's efforts to improve operations, activities, and image.[51]

Competencies Needed. As global public affairs continues to grow, it is useful to think in terms of competencies that are needed in the global arena. Having the following knowledge, skills, and abilities is important for successful global public affairs:[52]

- *Development of intercultural competence.* This addresses how the practice of public affairs works in different nations.
- *Knowing the impact of societal factors on public affairs.* For example, this includes state-to-state relations, level of economic development in different countries, and political ideologies.
- *Understanding local public policy institutions and processes.* This entails understanding other countries' form of government, legal systems, and political culture.
- *Nation state–specific applications of public affairs functions.* This includes knowing how community relations works and all forms of stakeholder relations.

- *Language skills.* The inability to speak multiple languages may put the public affairs professional at a disadvantage.
- *Understanding global business ethics.* Public affairs managers need to provide leadership in establishing, communicating, and maintaining ethical guidelines of companies at home and abroad.
- *Managing international consultants, alliances, and issue partners.* Sometimes specialized assistance can only come from local experts, groups, or associations.

Public Affairs Strategy

We do not discuss the issue of **public affairs strategy** extensively, but it is useful to report the findings of a major research project that was undertaken by Robert H. Miles and resulted in the classic book titled *Managing the Corporate Social Environment: A Grounded Theory*. Because little work has been done on public affairs strategy, Miles's work deserves recognition. His study focused on the insurance industry, but many of his findings are applicable to other businesses.[53]

Design of External Affairs and Corporate Social Performance

Miles studied the external affairs strategies (also called *public affairs strategies*) of major insurance firms in an effort to see what relationships existed between the strategy and design of the corporate external affairs function and corporate social performance. He found that the companies that ranked best in corporate social performance had top management philosophies that were *institution oriented*. That is, top management saw the corporation as a social institution that had a duty to adapt to a changing society and thus needed a collaborative/problem-solving external affairs strategy. The **collaborative/ problem-solving strategy** was one in which firms emphasized long-term relationships with a variety of external constituencies and broad problem-solving perspectives on the resolution of social issues affecting their businesses and industries.[54] Note how similar this is to the stakeholder management view and the bridge-building activity discussed previously.

Miles also found that the companies with the worst social performance records employed top management philosophies on the basis of the operation of the company as an independent economic franchise. Such philosophies were in sharp contrast to the institution-oriented perspectives of the best social performers. In addition, Miles found that these worst social performers employed an **individual/adversarial external affairs strategy**. In this posture, the executives denied the legitimacy of social claims on their businesses and minimized the significance of challenges they received from external critics. Therefore, they tended to be adversarial and legalistic.[55]

Business Exposure and External Affairs Design

On the subject of the external affairs units within firms, Miles found that a contingency relationship existed between what he called business exposure to the social environment and four dimensions of the external affairs design: breadth, depth, influence, and integration. High business exposure to the social environment means that the firm makes products or services that move them into the public arena because of such issues as their availability, affordability, reliability, and safety. In general, consumer products tend to be more "exposed" to the social environment than do commercial or industrial products.[56]

Breadth, depth, influence, and integration refer to dimensions of the external affairs unit that provide a measure of sophistication versus simplicity. Units that are high on

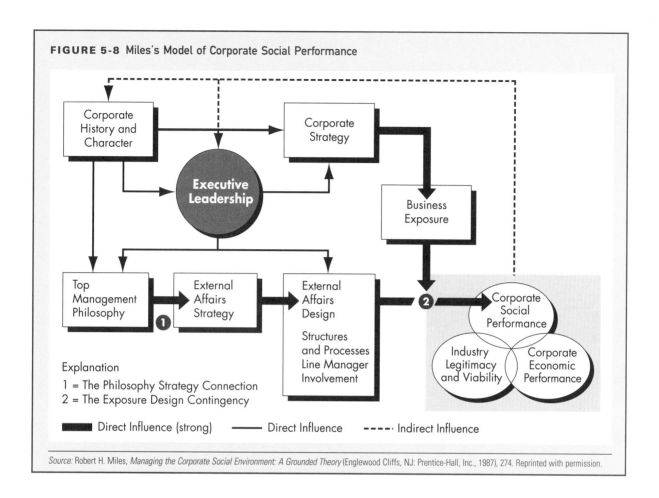

FIGURE 5-8 Miles's Model of Corporate Social Performance

Explanation

1 = The Philosophy Strategy Connection
2 = The Exposure Design Contingency

Source: Robert H. Miles, *Managing the Corporate Social Environment: A Grounded Theory* (Englewood Cliffs, NJ: Prentice-Hall, Inc., 1987), 274. Reprinted with permission.

these dimensions are sophisticated, whereas units low on these are simple. Miles found that firms with high business exposure to the social environment require more sophisticated units, whereas firms with low business exposure to the social environment could manage reasonably well with simple units.[57]

It is tempting to overgeneralize Miles's study, but we must note it as a significant finding in the realm of public affairs strategy and organizational design research. The important conclusion seems to be that a firm's corporate social performance (as well as its industry legitimacy and viability and economic performance) is a function of business exposure, top management philosophy, external affairs strategy, and external affairs design. Figure 5-8 presents Miles's theory of corporate social performance, which remains valuable today.

Other initiatives in public relations strategy include integrating public affairs into corporate strategic planning, using strategic management audits for public affairs, building a balanced performance scorecard for public affairs, managing the corporation's reputation, and using core competencies to manage performance.[58] Other key variables recognized as requiring strategic adjustments include responding to industry differences and issue life cycle challenges.[59]

Incorporating Public Affairs Thinking into All Managers' Jobs

In today's highly specialized business world, it is easy for the day-to-day operating managers to let public affairs departments worry about government affairs, community relations, issues management, PR, or any of the numerous other public affairs functions. It has been argued that organizations ought to incorporate public affairs, or what we would call *public affairs thinking*, into every operating manager's job. Operating managers are vital to a successful public affairs function, especially if they can identify the public affairs consequences of their actions, be sensitive to the concerns of external groups, act to defuse or avoid crisis situations, and know well in advance when to seek the help of the PA experts. There are no simple ways to achieve these goals, but four specific strategies may be helpful: (1) make public affairs truly relevant, (2) develop a sense of ownership of success, (3) make it easy for operating managers, and (4) show how public affairs makes a difference.[60] Each of these strategies is briefly discussed.

Make Public Affairs Relevant to All Managers

Operating managers often need help in seeing how external stakeholder factors can and do affect them. A useful mechanism is analysis of the manager's job in terms of the likely or potential impacts that her or his decisions may have on the stakeholder environment and possible developments in the environment that may affect the company or the decision maker.

- One approach toward doing this might be to list the manager's various impacts, the interested or affected strategic stakeholder groups, the potential actions of the groups, and the effects of the groups on jobs or the company.
- Another mechanism is to link achievement of the manager's goals to public affairs. A plant manager, for example, can be shown how failure to pay attention to community groups can hinder plant expansion, increased output, and product delivery. Failure to address the affected stakeholders can be shown to be related to extensive delays as these neglected groups seek media attention or pressure local officials.
- A third way is to use the language of the operating manager. Instead of using public affairs jargon, every effort should be made to employ language and terms with which the manager is familiar. Thus, terms such as *environment* to mean *local community* and *stakeholder* to mean *employees and residents* must be used cautiously, because operating managers may not respond to them.[61]
- Still another way is to demonstrate to operating managers that several operations areas are affected by public affairs issues. Some of these key areas include marketing, manufacturing, and human resources. Some of the specifics in the manufacturing arena are product safety and quality, energy conservation, water pollution, air pollution, transportation, and raw materials.

Help Managers Develop a Sense of Ownership

It is helpful for operating managers to have participated in planning and goal setting and thus to have had an opportunity to develop a sense of ownership of the public affairs endeavor. Operating managers may be formally or informally enlisted in these planning efforts. At PPG Industries, Inc., operating managers were given the responsibility for coordinating all actions concerning specific issues. As issue managers, they were asked to see to it that issue and environmental monitoring occurred, that strategy was developed, and that actions were implemented at various governmental levels.[62]

At Kroger, Inc., regional public affairs executives worked with the individual operating divisions as they were developing their business plans. A public affairs section was included in each operating division's plan, and it was the division's plan, not the public affairs department's. As a result of these efforts, the divisions began to feel that they have "ownership" of the public affairs goals in their plans.[63] This approach seemed to work much better than having public affairs executives simply impose goals or expectations on the operating units.

Make It Easy for Operating Managers

Operating managers have experience in meeting goals and timetables in their own realms. The public affairs area, however, can often appear nebulous, fuzzy, or inconclusive. Further, operating managers have neither the time for nor the interest in setting up systems or strategies for public affairs initiatives. This is where the public affairs professionals can assist them by making their tasks easier. Any procedures, data collection systems, or strategies that public affairs can supply should be used.

Training in public affairs can be helpful, too. Operating managers can better see the relevance and importance of public affairs work if carefully chosen topics are put on the agendas of their periodic training sessions. If public affairs effectiveness is to be monitored, measured, and made a part of performance evaluation systems, care must be taken to ensure that such systems are fair and straightforward, or at least understandable. If public affairs does not make a careful effort to ensure that its expectations are reasonably met, resistance, resentment, and failure will surely follow.

Show How Public Affairs Makes a Difference

Part of what professional public affairs staff members need to do is to keep track of public affairs successes in a way that operating managers can see that their specific actions or efforts have led to identifiable successes for the company. A scorecard approach, whereby operating managers can see that their efforts have helped avoid problems or prevent serious problems, is useful. The scorecard may be used to reinforce managers' efforts and to help other managers see the potential of the public affairs function. The scorecard should explicitly state the objectives that have been achieved, the problems that have been avoided, and the friends that have been made for the company.

Obviously, such a scorecard may be of a qualitative nature, but this is necessary to describe clearly what has been accomplished. Operating managers need to be shown that there are specific payoffs to be enjoyed from their public affairs efforts. It is up to the public affairs professionals to document these achievements. If no payoff is demonstrable from public affairs efforts, operating managers are likely to invest their time elsewhere.[64]

Public affairs is not just a specialized set of management functions to be performed by a designated staff. The nature of the tasks and challenges that characterize public affairs work is such that participation by operating managers is essential. It is likely that public affairs departments will continue to serve as the backbones of corporate organizations, but true effectiveness will require that operating managers be integrated into the accomplishment of these tasks. The mutual interdependence of these two groups—professionals and operating managers—will produce the best results.

Future of Corporate Public Affairs in the 21st Century

With growing worldwide sensitivity to corporate social performance and business ethics, it is easy to argue that corporate public affairs has a bright future in the 21st century. As a result of the tsunami of ethical crises in corporations in the early 2000s, public affairs specialists have an ideal opportunity to solidify their strategic roles and help to transform companies' approaches to handling business and society relationships. Three different opportunities for public affairs executives have been set forth for future consideration.[65]

First, public affairs can help develop value-based enterprises. Such enterprises actively seek out stakeholders and work cooperatively with them on social issues. An example cited was when Whirlpool reached agreements with the National Resource Defense Council, Friends of the Earth, and the Sierra Club to work together in solving energy efficiency challenges. By proactively engaging stakeholders, competitive advantages may be created.[66] Second, public affairs executives can assert themselves as thought leaders in their companies. As thought leaders, they should not just toe the company line, but actively engage academics, researchers, media, and public opinion formers, about the great issues of the day and how companies can best respond to the latest thinking about social and public issues. As public affairs executives increasingly have the ear of the top management, they are uniquely positioned to have great influence. Finally, public affairs specialists have the opportunity to seek alternative arenas of resolution as they can broaden issues to embrace global considerations while they pay close attention to domestic matters. Today, public issues migrate across geographical boundaries and political jurisdictions, and public affairs executives are in a perfect position to track these issues and employ preemptive initiatives. A case in point might be their opportunities in the global debate over genetically modified organisms that are controversial in the United Kingdom while being largely ignored in the United States.[67] In short, the public affairs function within firms is strategically positioned to wield more and better influence in the years ahead to help business build bridges between its strategic management and its corporate social performance.

Summary

Corporate public policy is a firm's posture or stance regarding the public, social, or ethical aspects of stakeholders and corporate functioning. It is a part of strategic management, particularly enterprise-level strategy. Enterprise-level strategy is the broadest, overarching level of strategy, and its focus is on the role of the organization in society. A major aspect of enterprise-level strategy is the integration of important core values into company strategy. The other strategy levels include the corporate, business, and functional levels. The strategic management process entails six stages, and a concern for social, ethical, and public issues may be seen at each stage. In the control stage, the social audit or social performance report is crucial. In recent years, social performance reports or sustainability reports have become more prevalent than social audits.

Public affairs might be described as the management function that is responsible for monitoring and interpreting a corporation's noncommercial environment and managing its response to that environment. Public affairs is intimately linked to corporate public policy, environmental analysis, issues management, and crisis management. The major functions of public affairs departments today include government relations, political action, community involvement or responsibility, issues management, global public affairs, and corporate philanthropy.

In terms of public affairs strategy, a collaborative or problem-solving one has been shown to be more effective than one that is individualistic or adversarial. Research has shown that a firm's corporate social performance, as well as its industry legitimacy, viability, and economic performance, is a function of business exposure, top management's philosophy, external affairs strategy, and external affairs design. In addition to being viewed as a staff function, public affairs is important for operating managers. Four specific strategies for incorporating public affairs into operating managers' jobs include making it relevant, developing a sense of ownership, making it easy, and showing how it can make a difference.

Public affairs executives are positioned to increase their future status and influence as they embark on such challenges as helping create values-based enterprises, exerting themselves as thought leaders in their companies, and helping seek alternative arenas of resolution as they broaden issues to embrace global considerations.

Key Terms

business-level strategy, p. 152

collaborative/problem-solving strategy, p. 168

core values, p. 154

corporate-level strategy, p. 152

corporate public affairs, p. 150

corporate public policy, p. 149

enterprise-level strategy, p. 152

functional-level strategy, p. 152

Global Reporting Initiative (GRI), p. 162

individual/adversarial external affairs strategy, p. 168

issues and crisis management, p. 163

public affairs, p. 163

public affairs departments, p. 163

public affairs management, p. 163

public affairs strategy, p. 168

social audit, p. 159

social performance report, p. 159

strategic management, p. 150

strategic management processes, p. 149

value shift, p. 156

Discussion Questions

1. Explain the relationship between corporate public policy and strategic management.

2. Which of the four strategy levels is most concerned with social, ethical, or public issues? Discuss the characteristics of this level.

3. Identify the steps involved in the strategic management process.

4. What is the difference between a social audit and a social performance report? Why are social performance reports increasing in popularity?

5. What is the difference between public relations and public affairs? Why has there been confusion regarding these two concepts?

6. Why do you think global public affairs is a major growth area? Give specific reasons for your answer.

7. Differentiate between a collaborative or problem-solving strategy and an individualistic or adversarial strategy. Which seems to be more effective in corporate public affairs?

8. What are the major ways in which public affairs might be incorporated into every manager's job? Rank them in terms of what you think their impact might be.

6

Issues and Crisis Management

CHAPTER LEARNING OUTCOMES

After studying this chapter, you should be able to:

1. Distinguish between the conventional and strategic approaches to issues management.

2. Identify and briefly explain the stages in the issues management process.

3. Describe the major components in the issues development process and some of the factors that have characterized issues management in actual practice.

4. Define a crisis and identify the four crisis stages.

5. List and discuss the major stages or steps involved in managing business crises.

I n late 2008, nearly 300 people became sick and several infants died due to tainted infant formula milk and food products; the World Health Organization declared the China dairy industry scandal as one of the largest food safety crises in recent history.[1] The crisis had several causes. Dairy farmers reacted to rising feed costs by using a lower grade of feed, which led to lower quality milk. Distributors added melamine to the milk to evade dairy standards for protein content, and dairies allowed the tainted milk to be distributed. Finally, companies such as Heinz, Mars, and Unilever unknowingly manufactured and distributed items made with the contaminated ingredients.[2] In 2009, the Peanut Corporation of America closed its doors after their deeply flawed operations created a massive salmonella outbreak in the United States: Nine people died and over 600 were sickened.[3] Over 2,000 food products were taken off the market.

The big issue for business is that of "trust." Can the public trust business? In the past few years, business has seen the trust of consumers, employees, investors, and the public erode because of issues such as these that threatened the public's safety when they become crises. Food safety is just one of many issues that raise concerns. Enron, WorldCom, Tyco, and Arthur Andersen created financial scandals that caused people to lose faith in business as an institution. That faith was further shattered in 2008 when the global financial crisis erupted. Other continuing issues, such as employee rights, sexual harassment, product safety, workplace safety, sweatshops, bribery and corruption, smoking in the workplace, and deceptive advertising, contribute to the negative opinion many people hold of business.

Of course, not all issues are caused by business. External events are sometimes unavoidable but their repercussions still need to be well managed. The World Trade Center terrorist attacks impacted business around the globe. The Haiti earthquake and Hurricane Katrina created crises for many businesses and also highlighted the need for future planning. Fears about a bird flu or an H1N1 pandemic breaking out in the world has put this issue at the top of many companies' priorities. Throughout this book, we discuss major social and ethical issues that have become controversies in the public domain. Some have been serious events or crises that continue to serve as recognizable code words for business, such as the Tylenol™ poisonings, the Union Carbide Bhopal tragedy, the Firestone/Ford tread separation controversy, and the BP *Deepwater Horizon* oil spill.

Managerial decision-making processes known as **issues management** and **crisis management** are two major ways by which business has responded to these situations. These two approaches symbolize the extent to which the environment has become turbulent and the public sensitized to business's responses to the issues that have emerged from this turbulence. In today's environment of instantaneous and global communication, no event is too small to get noticed by everyone.

In the ideal situation, issues and crises management might be seen as the natural and logical by-products of a firm's development of enterprise-level strategy and overall corporate public policy, but this has not always been the case. Some firms, for which these approaches represent first attempts to come to grips with the practical reality of a threatening external environment, have not thought seriously about public and ethical issues. When preparedness for issues and crises has occurred, however, it has typically been found that top- and middle-level managers have a higher readiness compared with employees, and thus these functions become vital leadership responsibilities.[4]

Many firms have been fortunate not to have had major crises to stun them as they did in the Johnson & Johnson (J&J) Tylenol poisonings, the Union Carbide Bhopal gas leak, the Procter & Gamble Rely tampon crisis, the Dow Corning breast implant probe, the crash of Air France's Airbus A330, or the attacks on the World Trade Center. Nevertheless, without having experienced such crises themselves, they have seen what major business crises can do to companies. Such firms should still be concerned with issues and crisis management in preparing for an uncertain future because no company is immune from the threat of a crisis.

The Relationship Between Issues Management and Crisis Management

Differentiating between issues management and crisis management is difficult, even for public relations professionals. The apparent inseparability of issues and crisis management has led issues management practitioner and expert Tony Jaques to label them "the Siamese twins of public relations."[5] As all planning processes, issues management and crisis management have many characteristics in common as well as differences, and though they are interrelated, we have chosen to treat them separately for discussion purposes. One common thread is that both processes focus on improving stakeholder management and enabling the organization to be more ethically responsive to stakeholders' expectations. Issues and crisis management, to be effective, must have an increase in the organization's responsiveness to its stakeholders as their ultimate objective.

They are also related to the extent that effective issues management may enable managements to engage in more effective crisis management; that is, through well-conducted issues management initiatives, some crises may be anticipated and avoided. Many of the crises companies face today arise out of issue categories that are being monitored and prioritized through issues management systems. In addition, effective issues management is a vital component of post-crisis management. For example, after dealing with an oil spill crisis, a company must continue to address the issue of environmental degradation.[6]

FIGURE 6-1 Issue Categories and Specific Crises Within Categories

ISSUE CATEGORIES		
Food, Beverage, and Products	**Health-Related Issues**	**Corporate Fraud and Ethics**
Crises	*Crises*	*Crises*
Peanut Corporation of America: Over 125 varieties of products recalled due to salmonella contamination (2008–2009).	H1N1: A possible flu pandemic led to crises for companies and questions of how to treat employees (2009).	Bernie Madoff: Ponzi scheme cost major foundations millions of dollars jeopardizing critical medical research (2008–2009).
Taco Bell: Outbreak of *E. coli* closed outlets nationwide (2006).	Avian flu: A possible bird flu pandemic has created a crisis environment for many businesses, including mask makers who are facing short supplies (2006–2007).	Hewlett-Packard: Boardroom information was leaked causing a governance crisis (2006).
Coca-Cola and Pepsi: Allegations that soft drinks in India contained pesticide residue (2004–2007).		Hyundai's CEO: Arrested and jailed for bribery and slush fund charges (2006).
Coca-Cola's Dasani bottled water: High levels of bromate led to recall in Great Britain (2004).	Banned dietary supplements androstenedione and ephedra by FDA: Crisis for dozens of pharmaceutical and vitamin firms (2004).	Boeing: Loses CEO and top level executive to ethics scandals (2004–2005).
Mad cow disease crisis: Outbreaks in Europe and Canada have created crises in sales and safety for meat industry (2001–2004).	Tobacco companies: Dangerous products and advertising. Allegations of addictions and death by cancer (1990s–2004).	Enron: Scandal began with off-the-books partnerships, aggressive accounting, and allegations of fraud and bankruptcy (2001–2004).
Firestone and Ford: Tire tread separation outbreak (2001–2002).	Dow Corning: Silicone breast implants alleged to lead to serious health problems (1994).	WorldCom: CEO Bernard Ebbers charged with massive accounting fraud (2003–2004).
Food Lion: Supermarket chain accused by ABC-TV's *Prime Time Live* of selling spoiled meat (1992).	Johnson & Johnson: Cyanide-tampering Tylenol poisonings (1982).	Arthur Andersen: Involvement in Enron scandal led to dissolution of firm (2002).

Figure 6-1 provides examples of major *issue* categories and specific *crises* that have occurred within these issue categories. A review of this figure should clearly illustrate the relationship between issues and crises.

Issues Management

Issues management is a process by which organizations identify issues in the stakeholder environment, analyze and prioritize those issues in terms of their relevance to the organization, plan responses to the issues, and then evaluate and monitor the results. It is helpful to think of issues management in connection with concepts introduced in the preceding chapter, such as the strategic management process, enterprise-level strategy, corporate public policy, and environmental analysis. The process of strategic management and environmental analysis requires an overall way of managerial thinking that includes economic, technological, social, and political issues. Enterprise-level strategy and corporate public policy, on the other hand, focus on public or ethical issues. Issues management, then, devolves from these broader concepts.

Two Approaches to Issues Management

Thinking about the concepts mentioned here requires us to make some distinctions. A central consideration seems to be that issues management has been thought of in two major ways: (1) narrowly, in which public, or social, issues are the primary focus, and

(2) broadly, in which strategic issues and the strategic management process are the focus of attention. Fahey has provided a useful distinction between these two approaches. He refers to (1) the **conventional approach** and (2) the **strategic management approach**.[7]

Conventional Approach (Narrowly Focused). This approach to issues management has the following characteristics:[8]

- Issues fall within the domain of public policy or public affairs management.
- Issues typically have a public policy or public affairs orientation or flavor.
- An issue is any trend, event, controversy, or public policy development that might affect the corporation.
- Issues originate in social or political or regulatory or judicial environments.

Strategic Management Approach (Broadly Inclusive). This approach to issues management has evolved in a small number of companies and is typified by the following:[9]

- Issues management is typically the responsibility of senior line management or strategic planning staff.
- Issues identification is more important than it is in the conventional approach.
- Issues management is seen as an approach to the anticipation and management of external and internal challenges to the company's strategies, plans, and assumptions.

Figure 6-2 portrays strategic issues management as depicted by H. Igor Ansoff. Note the "strategic" characteristics—threats or opportunities and strengths or weaknesses—to which we alluded in the preceding chapter.

At the risk of oversimplification, we consider the primary distinction between the two perspectives on issues management to be that the conventional approach focuses on public or social issues, whereas the strategic approach is broadly inclusive of all issues. In addition, the conventional approach can be used as a "stand-alone" decision-making process, whereas the strategic approach is intimately interconnected with the strategic management process as a whole. Another difference may be whether operating managers, strategic planners, or public affairs staff members are implementing the system. Beyond these distinctions, the two approaches have much in common.

The discussion in this chapter emphasizes the conventional approach, because this book focuses on public, social, and ethical stakeholder issues. We should point out, however, that the purpose in the preceding chapter was to convey the notion that social issues ought to be seen as just one part of the broader strategic management process. The chapter discussed environmental analysis as a broad phenomenon; here the emphasis is in social or ethical issues, although it is obvious that a consideration of these issues is embedded in a larger, more strategically focused process, such as that depicted in Figure 6-2.

Therefore, we are comfortable with both the perspectives on issues management. We should point out that the conventional approach could be perceived as a subset of the strategic approach. Much of what is said about issues management applies to issues arising from social or ethical domains or strictly business domains. In a sense, the two approaches are highly inseparable, and it is difficult for organizations to operate effectively unless they address both in some way. For our purposes, however, the conventional perspective is emphasized.

The Changing Issue Mix

The emergence in the last two decades of new "company issues management groups" and "issues managers" has been a direct outgrowth of the changing mix of issues that

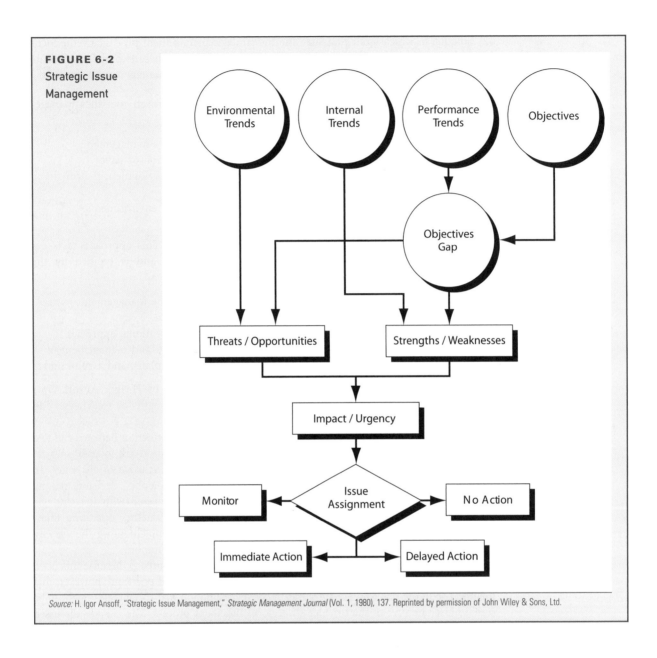

FIGURE 6-2
Strategic Issue Management

Source: H. Igor Ansoff, "Strategic Issue Management," *Strategic Management Journal* (Vol. 1, 1980), 137. Reprinted by permission of John Wiley & Sons, Ltd.

managers have had to handle. Economic and financial issues have always been an inherent part of the business process, although their complexity seems to have increased as global markets have broadened and competitiveness has become such a critical issue. The growth of technology, especially the Internet, has presented business with other issues that need to be addressed. The most dramatic growth has been in social, ethical, and political issues—all public issues that have high visibility, media appeal, and interest among special-interest stakeholder groups. We should further observe that these issues become more interrelated over time.

For most firms, social, ethical, political, and technological issues are at the same time economic issues, because firms' success in handling them frequently has a direct bearing on their financial statuses, reputations, and well-being. Over time, management groups face an escalating challenge as a changing mix of issues creates a cumulative effect.

A Portfolio Approach. Many firms get affected by so many issues that one wonders how they can deal with them all. One way is to see no connection between the issues; that is, take things on an issue-by-issue basis. An alternative is the "**portfolio approach**."[10] In this view, experience with prior issues likely influences future issues; therefore, a portfolio view is in order. Such a view provides focus and coherence to the firm's dealing with the mix of issues it faces. Issues that might show up in Royal Dutch Shell's issue portfolio, for example, might be stopping climate change, protecting biodiversity, reducing wastewater, and operating in sensitive regions. A company such as Shell might deal with hundreds of issues, but the issue portfolio helps to prioritize and provide focus for the company's resources. The nonadoption of certain issues into the portfolio does not signal neglect, but is part of a rational process of issues management in which strategic priorities are vital.[11]

Issue Definition and the Issues Management Process

Before describing the issues management process, we should briefly discuss what constitutes an issue and what assumptions we are making about issues management. An **issue** may be thought of as a matter that is in dispute between two or more parties. The dispute typically evokes debate, controversy, or differences of opinion that need to be resolved. At some point, the organization needs to make a decision on the unresolved matter, but such a decision does not mean that the issue is resolved. Once an issue becomes public and subject to public debate and high-profile media exposure, its resolution becomes increasingly more difficult. One of the features of issues, particularly those arising in the social or ethical realm, is that they are ongoing and therefore require ongoing responses.

Following are some of the characteristics of an "**emerging issue**":[12]

- The terms of the debate are not clearly defined.
- The issue deals with matters of conflicting values and interest.
- The issue does not lend itself to automatic resolution by expert knowledge.
- The issue is often stated in value-laden terms.
- Trade-offs are inherent.

The question of issue definition can be complicated because of the multiple viewpoints that come into play when an issue is considered. There are multiple stakeholders and motivations in any given management situation. Personal stakes frequently can be important factors but are often either ignored or not taken into consideration. For example, some of the affected parties may be interested in the issue from a deep personal perspective and will not compromise or give up their positions even in the face of concrete evidence that clearly refutes them.[13] Thus, the resolution of issues in organizations is not easy.

What about the assumptions we make when we choose to use issues management? It has been contended that the following assumptions are typically made:[14]

- Issues can be identified earlier, more completely, and more reliably than in the past.
- Early anticipation of issues widens the organization's range of options.
- Early anticipation permits study and understanding of the full range of issues.
- Early anticipation permits the organization to develop a positive orientation toward the issue.
- The organization will have earlier identification of stakeholders.

- The organization will be able to supply information to influential publics earlier and more positively, thus allowing them to better understand the issue.

These are not only assumptions of issues management but also benefits in that they make the organization more effective in its issues management process.

Model of the Issues Management Process. Like the strategic management process that entails a multitude of sequential and interrelated steps or stages, the issues management process has been conceptualized by many different authorities in a variety of ways. Conceptualizations of issues management have been developed by companies, academics, consultants, and associations. The issues management process discussed here has been extracted from many of the conceptualizations previously developed. This process represents the elements or stages that seem to be common to most issues management models. This process is consistent with the stakeholder orientation we have been developing and using.

Figure 6-3 presents a model of the issues management process as is discussed here. It contains *planning aspects* (identification, analysis, ranking or prioritization of issues, and formulation of responses) and *implementation aspects* (implementation of responses and evaluation, monitoring, and control of results). Although we discuss the stages in the issues management process as though they were discrete, in reality they may be interrelated and overlap one another.

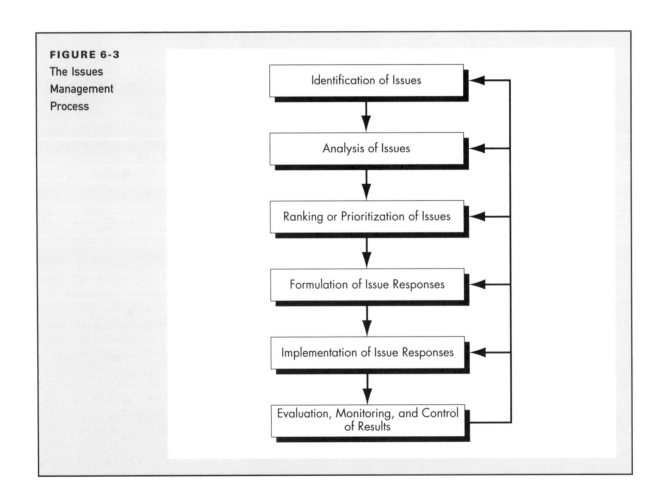

FIGURE 6-3
The Issues
Management
Process

Identification of Issues

Analysis of Issues

Ranking or Prioritization of Issues

Formulation of Issue Responses

Implementation of Issue Responses

Evaluation, Monitoring, and Control of Results

Identification of Issues. Many names have been assigned to the process of issue identification. The terms *social forecasting, futures research, environmental scanning,* and *public issues scanning* have been used at various times, and many techniques have been employed too. All of these approaches or techniques are similar, but each has its own unique characteristics. Common to all of them, however, is the need to scan the environment and identify emerging issues or trends that might later be determined to have some relevance to or impact on the organization. In recent years, examples of identified issues that may have widespread ramifications for many organizations include natural disasters (e.g., Hurricane Katrina), acts of terrorism (e.g., World Trade Center), potential pandemics (e.g., H1N1 outbreaks), and economic events (e.g., the global financial crisis).

Issue identification, in its most rudimentary form, involves the assignment to some individual in the organization the tasks of continuously scanning a variety of publications—newspapers, magazines, specialty publications, the World Wide Web, blogs—and developing a comprehensive list of issues. Often this same person, or group, is instructed to review public documents, records of congressional hearings, and other such sources of information. One result of this scanning is an internal report or a newsletter that is circulated throughout the organization. The next step in this evolution may be for the company to subscribe to a trend information service or newsletter that is prepared and published by a private individual or consulting firm that specializes in environmental or issue scanning.[15]

Two popular trend-spotting services have been (1) the author/consultant John Naisbitt, who was thrust into public recognition by his bestseller *Megatrends*, and (2) DYG, Inc., the New York-based social research firm founded by Daniel Yankelovich. DYG is a recognized leader in the field of social research and is distinguished by its expertise in the analysis and interpretation of social or cultural trends and human motivation.[16] On a fee basis, these professionals provide firms with materials they have assembled.[17] Among the services offered by such firms are newsletters, short weekly or monthly reports, telephone bulletins, and quarterly visits to discuss what the trends mean. Trend spotters do not claim clairvoyance, but they do say that they have less psychological resistance than their clients to seeing impending change.[18]

Naisbitt has claimed to be different from many trend spotters. His original approach, which has been controversial, was based on the belief that trends start with isolated local events. As Naisbitt once stated, "The really important things that happen always start somewhere in the countryside. Taken together, what's going on locally is what's going on." Thus, according to Naisbitt, it is what people are doing, not what they are saying, that provides the most reliable pictures of issues. Naisbitt has continued his identification of public issues with *Megatrends 2000: Ten New Directions for the 1990s, Global Paradox, Megatrends Asia, High Tech/High Touch,* and *Mind Set! Re-Set Your Thinking and See the Future* (2007).[19] Naisbitt's attention has now turned to China. In *China's Megatrends: The 8 Pillars of a New Society* (2010), Naisbitt and his wife, Dora, explore the dynamics underlying China's emergence as an economic power. In their words, "What we found was of much greater dimension and importance than we had expected. China is creating an entirely new social and economic system. In the next decades China will not only change the conditions of global economics, the Chinese model challenges the Western democracy as the only governing model capable of reducing poverty and providing the social and economic rights required."[20]

Though Naisbitt is the most well-known futurist, other futurists have been around for decades and have contributed to the body of knowledge that has helped issue identification. Futurist Graham T. T. Molitor, president of Public Policy Forecasting, a firm specializing in assessing political, social, and technological trends, has long been a consultant on futures research. Molitor contends that "[e]verybody is a futurist" because forecasting is inherent in the tasks of everyday life.[21] Thus by monitoring ongoing trends, individuals can do their own forecasting of the future. Molitor proposed that there are five leading forces as predictors of social change:[22]

- Leading events
- Leading authorities or advocates
- Leading literature
- Leading organizations
- Leading political jurisdictions

If these five forces are monitored closely, impending social change can be identified and, in some cases, predicted. Figure 6-4 presents Molitor's five leading forces, as well as examples that might be thought to illustrate his points. The attacks on the World Trade Center in New York and the Pentagon in Washington in 2001 and the wars in Afghanistan and Iraq have doubtlessly added the issue of "preparation for terrorism" to future lists of leading events portending significant social change. National security and business security are now vital issues for managers today. Similarly, the Global Financial Crisis has underscored the importance of corporate transparency and public affairs to managers.

Molitor estimates that he buys 1,000 books a year to add to the 30,000 books filling his personal library. He says he scans some 60 publications each day, trying to identify trends or issues that may have implications for businesses and governments. He has assembled an amazing reservoir of knowledge as he has spent four decades advising hundreds of *Fortune* 500 companies and institutions on how the world might change the next day, the next decade, even the next millennium, and how to make the most of these changes.[23]

Companies vary considerably in their willingness to spend tens or hundreds of thousands of dollars for the kinds of professional services described earlier, but some rely almost exclusively on professional services for issue identification. Others use less costly and more informal means.

Issues Selling and Buying. Though the source of all issues is the external environment, the internal perception of and managerial treatment of issues greatly affects the issue identification process. The key in issue identification is getting the people regularly confronted with issues in touch with top managers who can do something about them. This process has two aspects. First is **issue selling**. This relates to middle managers exerting upward influence in organizations as they try to attract the attention of top managers to issues salient to them and the organization.[24] In other words, they have to sell top management on the importance of the issue. The second part of this process is **issue buying**. This involves top managers adopting a more open mind-set for the issues that matter to their subordinates.[25] In short, the issue identification process is significantly affected by internal organization members and their assessments of what is salient to the organization.

Analysis of Issues. The next two steps in the issues management process (analysis and ranking of issues) are closely related. To analyze an issue means to carefully study, dissect, break down, group, or engage in any specific process that helps management better understand the nature or characteristics of the issue. An analysis requires that you look beyond the obvious manifestations of the issue and strive to learn more of its history, development, current nature, and potential for future relevance to the organization.

FIGURE 6-4 Examples of Forces Leading Social Change

Leading Forces	Examples	Public Issue Realm
Events	Salmonella outbreak	Food safety
	H1N1 flu outbreaks	Public health/safety
	Enron, WorldCom, Arthur Andersen	Corporate governance, fraud
	World Trade Center attacks	Security against terrorism
	Destruction of World Trade Center	Terrorism as public threat
	Three Mile Island/Chernobyl nuclear plant explosions	Nuclear plant safety
	Bhopal gas leak	Plant safety
	Earth Day	Environment
	Tylenol poisonings	Product tampering
	Love Canal	Toxic waste—environment
	Rely tampons	Product safety
	Ivan Boesky scandal	Insider trading abuses
	Clarence Thomas hearings	Sexual harassment
	Valdez oil spill	Environment
	Global financial crisis, subprime lending crisis	Corporate governance, regulation
Authorities/Advocates	Ralph Nader	Consumerism
	Rachel Carson	Pesticides and genetic engineering
	Rev. Martin Luther King	Civil rights
	Former Vice President Al Gore	Global warming
	General Colin Powell	Volunteerism
Literature	*Global Warming* (John Houghton)	Global warming
	Unsafe at Any Speed (Ralph Nader)	Automobile safety
	Megatrends (John Naisbitt)	Issues identification
Organizations	Friends of the Earth	Environment
	Sierra Club	Environment
	Action for Children's Television (ACT)	Children's advertising
	People for the Ethical Treatment of Animals (PETA)	Animal rights
	Mothers Against Drunk Driving (MADD)	Highway safety, alcohol abuse
Political Jurisdictions	State of Michigan—Whistle-Blower Protection Act	Employee freedom of speech
	State of Delaware	Corporate governance
	States of Connecticut, Iowa, Massachusetts, New Hampshire, Vermont	Gay Marriage

A series of key questions that focus on stakeholder groups in attempting to analyze issues has been proposed:[26]

- Who (which stakeholder) is affected by the issue?
- Who has an interest in the issue?
- Who is in a position to exert influence on the issue?
- Who has expressed opinions on the issue?
- Who ought to care about the issue?

In addition to these questions, the following key questions help with issue analysis:[27]

- Who started the ball rolling? (historical view)
- Who is now involved? (contemporary view)
- Who will get involved? (future view)

Answers to these questions place management in a better position to rank or prioritize the issues so that it will have a better sense of the urgency with which the issues need to be addressed.

Ranking or Prioritization of Issues.   Issues vary in the extent to which they matter to an organization, and so determining which issues matter most is essential in determining which ones should receive the most organizational resources, such as time and money. Of the many ways to analyze issues, the two most critical dimensions of issues are likelihood of occurrence and impact on the organization. Two essential questions are (1) *How likely is the issue to affect the organization?* and (2) *How much impact will the issue have?*[28]

Once these questions are answered, it is necessary to rank issues in some form of a hierarchy of importance or relevance to the organization. Those listed as top priority will receive the most attention and resources, while those at the bottom may even be removed from consideration because of their low likelihood or potential impact. The prioritization stage may involve a simple grouping of issues into categories ranging from the most urgent to the least important. Alternatively, a more elaborate or sophisticated scoring system may be employed.[29] Other techniques that have been used in issues identification, analysis, and prioritization include polls or surveys, expert panels, content analysis, the Delphi technique, trend extrapolation, scenario building, and the use of precursor events or bellwethers.[30] Teams of company experts are also used. For example, Baxter International, a U.S.-based health care and biotech firm, uses multidisciplinary teams because its main issues are in bioethics, and expertise in this subject cuts across a number of different knowledge-based lines of business.[31]

Earlier we described a simple issues identification process as involving an individual in the organization or a subscription to a newsletter or trend-spotting service. The analysis and ranking stages could be done by an individual, but more often, the company moves up to a next stage of formalization. This next stage involves assignment of the issues management function to a team, often as part of a public affairs department, which begins to specialize in the issues management function. This group of specialists can provide a wide range of issues management activities, depending on the commitment of the company to the process.

Several companies have created issues management units or managers to alert the management on emerging trends and controversies and to help mobilize the companies' resources to deal with them. In the past, firms such as Arco, Monsanto, and Sears have used such units. At Monsanto, an issues manager organized a committee of middle managers to help do the work. At Arco, the group monitored hundreds of publications, opinion polls, and think-tank reports. It then prepared its own daily publication called *Scan*, which summarized considerable data for over 500 company middle managers and top executives. The group tracked over 140 issues in all.[32] Today, companies such as Anheuser-Busch, BASF, Coca-Cola, ExxonMobil, IBM, Pfizer, and Shell utilize issues managers and an issues management function in their organizations.[33]

Formulation and Implementation of Responses.   Formulation and implementation of responses are two steps in the issues management process combined here for discussion purposes. We should observe that the formulation and implementation stages in the issues management process are quite similar to the corresponding stages discussed in the preceding chapter, which pertained to the strategic management process as a whole.

Formulation in this case refers to the response design process. On the basis of the analysis conducted, companies can then identify options that might be pursued in dealing with the issues, in making decisions, and in implementing those decisions. Strategy formulation refers not only to the formulation of the actions that the firm intends to take but also to the creation of the overall strategy, or degree of aggressiveness, employed in carrying out those actions. Options might include aggressive pursuit, gradual pursuit, or selective pursuit of goals, plans, processes, or programs.[34] All of these more detailed plans are part of the strategy formulation process.

Once plans for dealing with issues have been formulated, *implementation* becomes the focus. Many organizational aspects need to be addressed in the implementation process, including the clarity of the plan itself, resources needed to implement the plan, top management support, organizational structure, technical competence, and timing.[35]

Evaluation, Monitoring, and Control. These recognizable steps in the issues management process were also treated as steps in the strategic management process in Chapter 5. In the current discussion, they mean that companies should continually evaluate the results of their responses to the issues and ensure that these actions are kept on track. In particular, this stage requires careful monitoring of stakeholders' opinions. A form of stakeholder audit—something derivative of the social audit discussed in Chapter 5—might be used. The information gathered during this final stage in the issues management process is then fed back to the earlier stages in the process so that changes or adjustments might be made as needed. Evaluation information may be useful at each stage in the process.

The issues management process has been presented as a complete system. In practice, companies apply the stages across various degrees of formality or informality as needed or desired. For example, because issues management is more important in some situations than in others, some stages of the process may be truncated to meet the needs of different firms in different industries. In addition, some firms are more committed to issues management than others.

Issues Development Process

A vital attribute of issues management is that issues tend to develop according to an evolutionary pattern. This pattern might be thought of as a developmental or growth process or, as some have called it, a life cycle. The life cycle is often considered to have five stages—early, emerging, current, crisis, and dormant.[36] It is important for managers to have some appreciation of this **issues development process** so that they can recognize when an event or trend is becoming an issue and also because it might affect the strategy the firm employs in dealing with the issue. Companies may take a variety of courses of action depending on the stage of the issue in the process.

Figure 6-5 presents a simplified view of what an issue development life cycle process might look like. In the beginning, a nascent issue emerges in local newspapers, is enunciated by public interest organizations, and is detected through public opinion polling. According to a former director of corporate responsibility at Monsanto, the issue is low-key and flexible at this stage.[37] During this time, the issue may reflect a felt need, receive media coverage, and attract interest group development and growth. A typical firm may notice the issue but take no action. More issues-oriented firms may become more active in their monitoring and in their attempts to shape or help "define the issue."[38] Active firms may have the capacity to prevent issues from going any further,

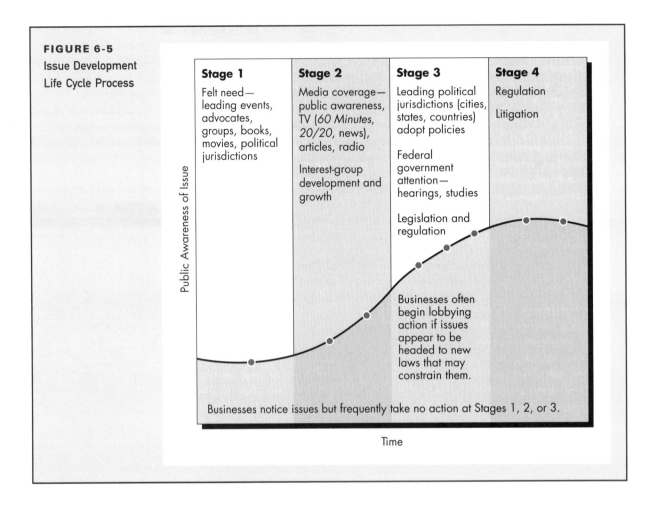

FIGURE 6-5

Issue Development Life Cycle Process

Businesses notice issues but frequently take no action at Stages 1, 2, or 3.

through either effective responses to the issues or effective lobbying. In the next stage of the cycle, national media attention and leading political jurisdictions (e.g., cities, states, or countries) may address the issue. Quite often, federal government attention is generated in the form of studies and hearings; legislation, regulation, and litigation follow. This is simply an example of a sequence. Issues vary, and so the stages in the process, especially the early stages, might occur in a different sequence or in an iterative pattern. Further, not all issues complete the process; some are resolved before they reach the stage of legislation or regulation. It is important not to oversimplify the issues development process. The paths issues follow vary with the nature of the issues and the intensity and variety of stakeholder interests and values. The complex interactions of all the variables make it unlikely issues will follow a straight line.[39]

Illustrations of Issue Development.   This evolution may be illustrated through two examples. First, consider the issue of environmental protection. The social expectation was manifested in Rachel Carson's book *Silent Spring* (1963); it became a political issue in Eugene McCarthy's political platform (1968); it resulted in legislation in 1971–1972 with the creation of the Environmental Protection Agency (EPA); and it was reflected in social control by emissions standards, pollution fines, product recalls, and environmental permits in later years. Today, the issue of sustainability can be traceable to these early roots. The second example involves product or consumer safety. The social expectation was manifested in Ralph Nader's book *Unsafe at Any Speed* (1964); it became a political issue through the National Traffic Auto Safety Act and Motor Vehicle Safety Hearings (1966); it resulted in legislation in 1966 with the passage of the Motor Vehicle Safety Act and mandatory seat belt usage laws in four states (1984); and it was reflected in social control through the ordering of seat belts in all cars (1967), defects litigation, product recalls, and driver fines. Today, product safety is an institutionalized issue that all companies must address.[40]

Issues Management in Practice

Issues management began as a way for companies to get in front of, and not simply respond to, public policy issues that could affect the organization. Howard Chase, the father of issues management, described it as "a methodology by which the private sector can get out of the unenviable position of being at the end of the crack-the-whip political line."[41] Today, issues management has become an important subset of activities performed by the public affairs departments of major corporations, and it covers not only public policy activities but also a full range of public relations and management activities.[42] A recent study found that 82 percent of companies made issues management one of the activities of their public affairs units.[43] Today, there is greater use of interdepartmental issues teams, with the public affairs department serving as coordinator and strategist but with appropriate line and staff executives charged with ultimate accountability for implementation. In practice, therefore, it can be seen that issues management does not function as a stand-alone activity but has been subsumed into a host of functions for which modern public affairs departments take responsibility.[44]

Issues management faces a serious challenge in business today. From the standpoint of the turbulence in the stakeholder environment, issues management is sorely needed. To become a permanent part of the organization, however, issues management will have to continuously prove itself. We can talk conceptually about the process with ease, but the field remains somewhat nebulous even though it is struggling to become more scientific and legitimate. Managers in the real world want results, and if issues management cannot deliver those results, it will be destined to failure as a management process. A practitioner of issues management recently warned that issues management "often attracts excessive process at the expense of real progress."[45]

Research has shown that companies that adopted issues management processes developed better overall and issue-specific reputations and had better short- and longer-term financial performance than organizations not practicing issues management.[46] By tying issues management in with stakeholder management, it was also found that the most successful companies used stakeholder integration techniques in their implementation. This means that the firms actively sought to establish close-knit ties with a broad range of external and internal stakeholders and successfully incorporated their values and interests into management decisions.[47]

From Issues Management to Crisis Management

Firms use issues management to assist them in planning for and preventing crises that then require crisis management. Effective issues management represents careful planning that may head off impending crises. This is because many crises are embedded in issues or erupt from issues that could have been anticipated and analyzed in carefully designed issues management processes. Figure 6-1 illustrated the kinds of crises that may emanate from issue categories.

An illustration of issues management anticipating and planning for crises may be seen in the example of "Wall Street West," located in the Poconos region of Northeastern Pennsylvania. Ever since the 9/11 attacks in 2001, regulators have urged the financial firms on Wall Street to build emergency backup facilities where trading can continue in the event of another terrorist attack.[48] The Poconos area is only 90 miles west of Manhattan, and is on a separate electrical grid. Thus, it may be an ideal spot for the New York financial industry to locate their backup and disaster recovery systems.

Wall Street West is a partnership of more than two dozen economic development agencies and has received funding from federal and state sources to prepare for the next disaster, should it occur.[49] In this case, the "issue" is the integrity and survival of the banking and trading system in New York, and the response has been to prepare for future "crises" by establishing this safe retreat from the metropolis outside New York City's theoretical nuclear blast zone, but close enough to be linked by high-speed data links to Wall Street.[50]

The Wall Street West example illustrates how planning for crises grows out of issues management. Issues management can serve as a form of precrisis planning as well as post-crisis management. It can help organizations anticipate and plan for possible crisis eruptions, as well as learn from past crises and the issues they raised. One of the most effective ways for keeping a crisis plan "living" is issues management.[51] Thus, we can see how issues and crisis management are different, but intimately related and difficult to separate, making the previously mentioned metaphor of conjoined twins particularly apt.

Crisis Management

Crisis management as a management concept is largely a product of the past two decades or so. This has been the era of the megacrisis: Union Carbide's Bhopal disaster, which killed over 2,000 people in India; J&J's Tylenol poisonings, which resulted in numerous deaths; and the terrifying attacks on the World Trade Center in New York, which resulted in the deaths of approximately 3,000 people. More recently, lead paint on children's toys and salmonella spread by peanut products have caused consumers alarm, as has the global economic meltdown. Other significant crises have included the following:

- Shootings at Virginia Tech raised questions about people's safety anywhere.
- Hurricanes Katrina and Rita devasted businesses and the New Orleans area and the Southeast.
- Coca-Cola and Pepsi were implicated in tainted products in India and illnesses in Belgium, France, and India.
- JetBlue's snowstorm disaster left passengers stranded for hours on the tarmac.
- Enron, WorldCom, Arthur Andersen, Tyco, and other companies accused of financial scandals and malfeasance.
- ValuJet's Flight 592 crashed in the Florida Everglades, killing all 110 people on board.
- Dow Corning was targeted in an FDA silicone breast implant probe.
- Sudafed capsules were tainted with cyanide, leading to two deaths.
- Perrier Water's benzene incident led to product recalls.
- Twenty-four customers of Luby's Cafeteria in Killeen, Texas, were shot to death during a lunch-hour massacre.
- The subprime lending crisis contributed to a global financial recession.
- Firestone and Ford were implicated in massive tire recalls due to faulty tires causing tread separations and deaths.
- Bernie Madoff's ponzi scheme defrauded thousands of investors of billions of dollars.

Spotlight on SUSTAINABILITY

Sustainable Corporations Shine in Economic Crisis

An A. T. Kearney study entitled "Green Winners: The Performance of Sustainability-Focused Companies in the Financial Crisis" analyzed 99 of the largest companies officially recognized as having a strong commitment to sustainable practice. The study defined sustainable practice as being "geared toward protecting the environment and promoting social well-being while achieving shareholder value." They found that sustainable companies outperformed their competitors by 15 percent in 16 of 18 industries from May through November 2008, with the difference representing an average of $650 million more in market capitalization per company than their competitors.

The study found that sustainability involves characteristics that help firms weather a crisis. A long-term perspective, sound risk management practices, and green innovations such as reduced waste and emissions and the use of alternate energy sources were cited as factors that gave sustainable companies a competitive edge. Recognition for their sustainability efforts may also have enabled them to differentiate themselves from their competitors.

The report concluded that "the most sustainability-focused may well emerge from the current crisis stronger than ever...recognized by investors who appreciate the true long-term value of sustainability."

Source: Robert Kropp, "Sustainable Corporations Outperform During Economic Crisis," *Social Funds* (February 16, 2009), http://www.socialfunds.com/news/article.cgi/article2628.html.

Several observers have suggested that the Tylenol poisonings in 1982 was the case that put crisis management "on the map"—it was the case that marked the beginning of the new corporate discipline known as crisis management because J&J's voluntary recall of some 31 million Tylenol bottles was the first important example of an organization assuming responsibility for its products without being pressured.[52]

It should be apparent from the list of crises presented earlier that there is a major distinction between issues management, discussed in the preceding section, and crisis management, the subject of this section. Issues typically evolve gradually over time and represent a category of concern. Issues management is a process of identifying and preparing to respond to potential issues. Crises, on the other hand, occur abruptly. They cannot always be anticipated or forecast. Some crises occur within an issue category considered, whereas many do not. Issues and crisis management are related, in that they both are concerned about organizations becoming prepared for uncertainty in the stakeholder environment.

The Nature of Crises

There are many kinds of crises. Those mentioned here have all been associated with major stakeholder groups and have achieved high-visibility status. Hurt or killed customers, hurt employees, injured stockholders, and unfair practices are the concerns of modern crisis management. Not all crises involve such public or ethical issues, but these kinds of crises almost always ensure front-page status. Major companies can be seriously damaged by such episodes, especially if the episodes are poorly handled.

What is a crisis? Dictionaries state that a **crisis** is a "turning point for better or worse," an "emotionally significant event," or a "decisive moment." We all think of crises

ETHICS IN PRACTICE CASE

Johnson & Johnson's Tylenol Response Is the Gold Standard in Crisis Management

The 1982 the Tylenol poisonings was the case that put "crisis management" into the permanent management lexicon. The facts are legendary. In the fall of 1982, a murderer added 65 mg of cyanide to some Tylenol capsules while they were on store shelves. Seven people were killed, including three persons in one family. J&J, makers of Tylenol, quickly recalled and destroyed 31 million bottles at an expense of about $100 million. James Burke, the company CEO, made numerous appearances in TV ads and in news conferences notifying consumers of the actions the company was taking. Tamper-resistant packaging was quickly introduced, and the sales of Tylenol swiftly snapped back to near precrisis sales levels. The perpetrator of this crime was never found.

Many continue to hold the Tylenol case up as the classic response to a crisis. Experts argue that 'fessing up and taking quick corrective action is the best form of crisis management. A major lesson to come out of the Tylenol crisis is that companies can take action quickly and effectively and prosper in spite of extreme adversity that befalls them.

Even today, 30 years later, J&J's response in the Tylenol scandal remains the gold standard in crisis management and is still taught in universities across the world as an outstanding example of effective crisis control.

1. Some say it was easy for J&J to take this action because the crisis did not originate within the company. Did this fact set the stage for the company's quick recovery? Would things have been different had the company been at fault?

2. How is the Tylenol case similar to or different from Ford and Firestone's linkage with dangerous tires or WorldCom, Tyco, Enron, and HealthSouth's malfeasance resulting in company leaders being accused of scheming to enrich themselves at the injury of others?

3. Was J&J really being socially responsible or were they quickly acting in their own best financial interests? Does their motivation matter?

Sources: Eric Dezenhall, "Tylenol Can't Cure All Crises," *USA Today* (March 18, 2004), 15A. Copyright © 2004 by Dezenhall Resources; Jia Lynn Yang, "Getting a Handle on a Scandal," *Fortune* (May 28, 2007), 26.

as being emotion charged, but we do not always think of them as turning points for better or for worse. The implication here is that a crisis is a decisive moment that, if managed one way, could make things worse but, if managed another way, make things better. Choice is present, and how the crisis is managed can make a difference.

From a managerial point of view, a line needs to be drawn between a problem and a crisis. Problems, of course, are common in business. A crisis, however, is not as common. A useful way to think about a crisis is as follows:

A crisis is an extreme event that may threaten your very existence. At the very least, it causes substantial injuries, deaths, and financial costs, as well as serious damage to your reputation.[53]

Another definition is also helpful in understanding the critical aspects of a crisis:

An organizational crisis is a low-probability, high-impact event that threatens the viability of the organization and is characterized by ambiguity of cause, effect, and means of resolution, as well as by a belief that decisions must be made swiftly.[54]

Consider, for a moment, the classic case wherein StarKist Foods, then a subsidiary of H.J. Heinz Co. but now a wholly owned subsidiary of the Dongwon Group, faced a management crisis. Gerald Clay was appointed general manager of the Canadian subsidiary and was given the mandate to develop a five-year business strategy for the firm. Just after his arrival in Canada, the crisis hit: The Canadian Broadcasting Corporation accused his company of shipping one million cans of rancid and decomposing tuna. Dubbed "Tuna-gate" by the media, the crisis dragged on for weeks. With guidance from Heinz, Clay chose to keep quiet, even as the Canadian prime minister ordered the tuna seized. The silence cost plenty. According to Clay's boss, "We were massacred in the press." The company, which used to have half the Canadian tuna market, watched revenues plunge by 90 percent. At one point, Clay's boss observed that the company's future was in doubt.[55] StarKist survived though they had to pull out of Canada due to the loss in market share. Tunagate was such a classic crisis management scandal, however, that it has its own entry in *Wikipedia*, the online encyclopedia.[56]

Figure 6-6 presents a "how not to do it" case in crisis management as experienced by golf star, Tiger Woods. Woods was under fire for allegations of serial infidelity that were at odds with the family-oriented image he had cultivated.

FIGURE 6-6
Crisis Management and Tiger Woods, Inc.: How Not to Do It

When Tiger Woods crashed his Cadillac Escalade into a fire hydrant and a tree in his gated Florida community, the world's media converged upon him. Allegations of serial infidelity soon arose that set the pro-golfer's personal and professional life into a tailspin. As the man behind a billion dollar financial empire and the personification of the brand it sells, Woods' personal trouble quickly developed into an organizational crisis. His management of the crisis held implications not only for him but also for the business that had been built around him.

Most crisis management experts fault his management of the crisis. Woods waited days to issue a statement, and the statement that appeared spoke only vaguely of "transgressions." Robbie Vorhaus, a crisis reputation adviser in New York, believes he should have spoken more quickly, "If you don't tell your story first, then you're letting someone else tell your story. Now he has to react and respond to what everyone else is saying." This advice is similar to the advice Woods gave in an ESPN interview when he was asked about Michael Vick's response after Vick was caught being involved in a dog-fighting ring:

If you made that big a mistake, you've got to come out and just be contrite, be honest and just tell the public that "I was wrong."

Waiting a long time got a lot of people polarized. ... If he would have come out earlier, he would've diffused a little more of it.

It has been suggested that Woods broke three basic rules of crisis management when he failed to follow his own advice:

- **Rule No. 1: Don't Wait.** After the car crash, Woods issued a statement acknowledging the accident but nothing else. Two days later, Woods issued another statement, but it was vague and the story was shaped by others in the interim.
- **Rule No. 2: Don't Run from the Truth.** Woods' first statement pleaded for privacy and claimed that "false, unfounded and malicious rumors" were circulating, giving the impression that the rumors were untrue. Three days later, he changed his story but admitted only to unspecified "transgressions."
- **Rule No. 3: Don't Hide.** Woods hid away long after the accident, leaving the women who alleged that they had relationships with him as the only voices telling the story.

Sources: Dana Mattoli, "Tiger Bungles Crisis Management 101," *The Wall Street Journal* (December 8, 2009), A31; Ryan Ballingee, "Tiger's Own Words May Be Cause for Concern About Anthony Galea," *Waggle Room* (December 18, 2009). http://www.waggleroom.com; Rachel Beck, AP Business Writer, "Commentary: Tiger Flubs Crisis Management 101," *Sporting News* (December 11, 2009), http://www.sportingnews.com.

Types of Crises.   A variety of situations leave companies vulnerable to crises. These include industrial accidents, environmental problems, union problems or strikes, product recalls, investor relations, hostile takeovers, proxy fights, rumors or media leaks, government regulatory problems, acts of terrorism, and embezzlement.[57] Other common crises include product tampering, executive kidnapping, work-related homicides, malicious rumors, and natural disasters that destroy corporate offices or information bases.[58] Since September 11, 2001, we have had to add terrorism to this list.

Crises may be grouped into seven families:[59]

- *Economic crises* (recessions, hostile takeovers, stock market crashes)
- *Physical crises* (industrial accidents, product failures, supply breakdown)
- *Personnel crises* (strikes, exodus of key employees, workplace violence)
- *Criminal crises* (product tampering, kidnappings, acts of terrorism)
- *Information crises* (theft of proprietary information, cyberattacks)
- *Reputational crises* (rumormongering or slander, logo tampering)
- *Natural disasters* (earthquakes, floods, fires)

After major crises, companies report the following outcomes: The crises escalated in intensity, were subjected to media and government scrutiny, interfered with normal business operations, and damaged the company's bottom line. For example, as a result of the horrific attacks on the World Trade Center, companies experienced major power shifts among executives as some bosses fumbled with their responsibilities and didn't handle the crisis well. Those bosses who handled the crisis well garnered more responsibility, whereas others lost responsibilities.[60]

Four Crisis Stages.   There are several ways of describing the stages through which a crisis may progress. One view is that a crisis may consist of as many as four distinct stages: (1) a **prodromal crisis stage**, (2) an **acute crisis stage**, (3) a **chronic crisis stage**, and (4) a **crisis resolution stage**.[61]

PRODROMAL CRISIS STAGE   This is the warning stage. ("Prodromal" is a medical term that refers to a previous notice or warning.) This stage could also be thought of as a symptom stage. Although it could be called a "precrisis" stage, this presupposes that one knows that a crisis is coming. Many experts suggest that a possible outbreak of avian flu would be in this stage. It is believed that crises "send out a repeated trail of early warning signals" that managers can learn to recognize.[62] Perhaps management should adopt this perspective: Watch each situation with the thought that it could be a crisis in the making. Early symptoms may be quite obvious, such as in the case where a social activist group tells the management it will boycott the company if a certain problem is not addressed. On the other hand, symptoms may be more subtle, as in the case where defect rates for a particular product a company makes start edging up over time.

ACUTE CRISIS STAGE   This is the stage at which the crisis has actually occurred, and there is no turning back. Damage has been done, and it is now up to management to handle or contain it. If the prodromal stage is the precrisis stage, the acute stage is the *actual* crisis stage. The crucial decision point at which things may get worse or better has been reached.

CHRONIC CRISIS STAGE   This is the lingering period. It may be the period of investigations, audits, or in-depth news stories. Management may see it as a period of recovery, self-analysis, or self-doubt. A survey of major companies found that crises tended to linger

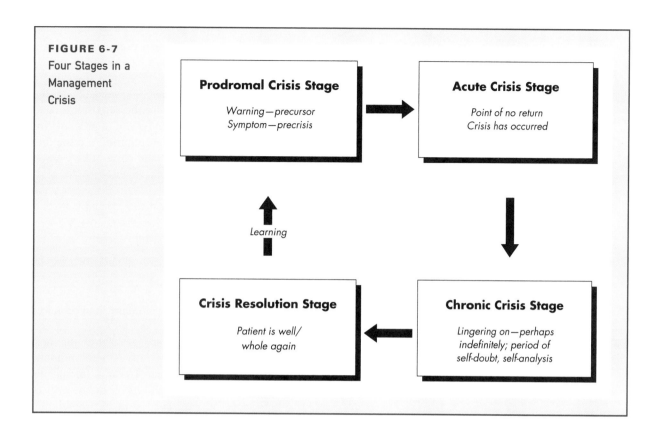

FIGURE 6-7
Four Stages in a Management Crisis

as much as two-and-a-half times longer in firms without crisis management plans than in firms with such plans.

CRISIS RESOLUTION STAGE This is the final stage—the goal of all crisis management efforts. When an early warning sign of a crisis is noted, the manager should seize control swiftly and determine the most direct and expedient route to resolution. If the warning signs are missed in the first stage, the goal is to speed up all phases and reach the final stage as soon as possible.

Figure 6-7 presents one way in which these four stages might be depicted. It should be noted that the phases may overlap and that each phase varies in intensity and duration. It is expected that management will learn from the crisis and thus will be better prepared for, and better able to handle, any future crisis.

Managing Business Crises

Five Practical Steps in Managing Crises. The following five steps, synthesized by *BusinessWeek* magazine from the actual experiences of companies going through crises, are summarized and discussed next. They are (1) identifying areas of vulnerability, (2) developing a plan for dealing with threats, (3) forming crisis teams, (4) simulating crisis drills, and (5) learning from experience.[63]

FIRST: IDENTIFYING AREAS OF VULNERABILITY In this first step, some areas of vulnerability are obvious, such as potential chemical spills, whereas others are more subtle. The key seems to be in developing a greater consciousness of how things can go wrong and get out of hand. At Heinz, after the "Tunagate" incident, a vice president set up brainstorming sessions. He said, "We're brainstorming about how we would be affected by everything from a competitor who had a serious quality problem to a scandal involving a Heinz executive."[64] A key to identifying areas of vulnerability is "recognizing the threat." The most skilled executives often fail at this stage because they are oblivious to emerging threats.[65] For example, many companies were surprised by and unprepared for the credit crisis in 2008. In contrast, AutoNation showed resilience during a crisis that devastated its industry. Years before the crisis struck, Chairman and CEO Mike Jackson considered what seemed to be unlikely scenarios. They asked themselves, What if consumers bought cars every five years instead of every three?, and What if the financing spigot turned off?[66] Recognizing low-probability but high consequence events is a challenge, but planning for them can help a company to survive major crises.[67]

Following are some ways that companies can identify areas of vulnerability:[68]

- *Scenario planning.* Create scenarios for crises that could occur over the next two years.
- *Risk analysis.* Estimate the probabilities and costs/benefits of estimated future events.
- *Incentives.* Reward managers for information sharing.
- *Networks.* Build formal coalitions to mobilize internal and external information suppliers.

SECOND: DEVELOPING A PLAN FOR DEALING WITH THREATS   A plan for dealing with the most serious crisis threats is a logical next step. One of the most crucial issues is communications planning. After a Dow Chemical railroad car derailed near Toronto, forcing the evacuation of 250,000 people, Dow Canada prepared information kits on the hazards of its products so that executives would be knowledgeable enough to respond properly if a similar crisis were to arise in the future. Dow Canada also trained executives in interviewing techniques. This effort paid off several years later when an accident caused a chemical spill into a river that supplied drinking water for several nearby towns. The company's emergency response team arrived at the site almost immediately and established a press center that distributed information about the chemicals. In addition, the company recruited a neutral expert to speak on the hazards and how to deal with them. Officials praised Dow for its handling of this crisis.[69]

Getting an entire organization trained to deal with crises is difficult and expensive, but the CEO paraphrases what a car repairman once said in a TV commercial: "You can pay now or pay a lot more later." Most of us would believe that now is infinitely better for everyone.[70]

THIRD: FORMING CRISIS TEAMS   Another step that can be taken as part of an overall planning effort is the formation of **crisis teams**. Such teams have played key roles in many well-managed disasters. A good example is the team formed at Procter & Gamble when its Rely tampon products were linked with the dreaded disease toxic shock syndrome. The team was quickly assembled, a vice president was appointed to head it, and after one week, the decision was made to remove Rely from marketplace shelves. The quick action earned the firm praise, and it paid off for P&G in the long run.

Another task in assembling crisis teams is identifying managers who can cope effectively with stress. Not every executive can handle the fast-moving, high-pressured, ambiguous decision environment that is created by a crisis, and early identification of executives who can is important. We should also note that it is not always the CEO who can best perform in such a crisis atmosphere.

Despite the careful use of crisis teams, crises can often overwhelm a carefully constructed plan. When ValuJet's Flight 592 crashed in the Florida Everglades, for example,

ValuJet flawlessly executed a three-pronged, team-based crisis management plan calling for the company to (1) show compassion, (2) take responsibility, and (3) demonstrate that the airline learned from the crisis. Experts have said that the company handled the crisis well. However, a close look at the tragedy revealed that a series of complicating factors turned the crisis into something even more difficult than a well-scripted, perfectly executed crisis management plan could handle.[71]

FOURTH: SIMULATING CRISIS DRILLS Some companies have gone so far as to run crisis drills in which highly stressful situations are simulated so that managers can "practice" what they might do in a real crisis. As a basis for conducting crisis drills and experiential exercises, a number of companies have adopted a software package known as *Crisis Plan wRiter (CPR)*. This software allows companies to centralize and maintain up-to-date crisis management information and allows company leaders to assign responsibilities to their crisis team, target key audiences, identify and monitor potential issues, and create crisis-response processes.[72]

FIFTH: LEARNING FROM EXPERIENCE The final stage in crisis management is learning from experience. At this point, managers need to ask themselves exactly what they have learned from past crises and how that knowledge can be used to advantage in the future. Part of this stage entails an assessment of the effectiveness of the firm's crisis-handling strategies and identification of areas where improvements in capabilities need to be made. Without a crisis management system of some kind in place, the organization will find itself reacting to crises after they have occurred. If learning and preparation for the future are continuous, however, the firm may engage in more proactive behavior.[73]

It is important to note that effective crisis management requires a program tailored to a firm's specific industry, business environment, and crisis management experience. Effective crisis managers will understand that there are major crisis management factors that may vary from situation to situation, such as the type of crisis (e.g., natural disaster or human induced), the phase of the crisis, the systems affected (e.g., humans, technology, or culture), and the stakeholders affected. Managers cannot eliminate crises; however, they can become keenly aware of their vulnerabilities and make concerted efforts to understand and reduce these vulnerabilities through continuous crisis management programs.[74]

Crisis Communications

An illustration of crisis management without effective communications occurred during the Jack in the Box hamburger disaster years ago. There was an outbreak of *Escherichia coli* bacteria in the Pacific Northwest area, resulting in the deaths of four children. Following this crisis, the parent company, San Diego–based Foodmaker, entered a downward spiral after lawsuits by the families of victims enraged the public and franchisees. Foodmaker did most of the right things and did them quickly. The company immediately suspended hamburger sales, recalled suspect meat from its distribution system, increased cooking time for all foods, pledged to pay for all the medical costs related to the disaster, and hired a food safety expert to design a new food-handling system. But, it forgot to do one thing: Communicate with the public, including its own employees.[75]

The company's **crisis communications** efforts were inept. It waited a week before accepting any responsibility for the tragedy, preferring to point fingers at its meat supplier and even the Washington state health officials for not explaining the state's new guidelines for cooking hamburgers at higher temperatures. The media pounced on the company. The company was blasted for years even though within itself, the company was taking proper steps to correct the problem. The company suffered severe financial losses, and it took at least six years before the company really felt it was on the road to recovery. "The crisis," as it was called around company headquarters, taught the firm an important lesson. CEO Robert Nugent was quoted later as saying "Nobody wants to deal with their worst nightmare, but we should have recognized you've got to communicate."[76]

Virtually all crisis management plans call for effective crisis communications, but they are not always effectively executed. There are a number of different stakeholder groups with whom effective communications are critical, especially the media and those immediately affected by the crisis. Many companies have failed to successfully manage their crises because of inadequate or failed communications with key stakeholder groups. Successful communications efforts are crucial to effective crisis management. It is axiomatic that *prepared* communications will be more helpful than *reactive* communications. Ten steps of crisis communication that are worth summarizing include:[77]

1. Identify your crisis communications team.
2. Identify key spokespersons who will be authorized to speak for the organization.

ETHICS IN PRACTICE CASE

Crisis Management: When to Repent? When to Defend?

When facing a crisis, especially one in which the organization is implicated, many experts on crisis management take the approach that management or the firm needs to quickly repent of its malfeasance or wrongdoing, ask for forgiveness, and promise to do better in the future. This soft approach argues for engaging in careful communications and apologizing, if necessary. This approach, it is believed, is the best route to limiting damage and restoring the public's confidence in the company and its leaders.

In a new book, *Damage Control: Why Everything You Know about Crisis Management Is Wrong* (2007), authors Eric Dezenhall and John Weber argue that this soft approach is often wrong. According to the authors, if you are facing a lawsuit, a sex scandal, a defective product, or allegations of insider trading, experts may tell you to stay positive, get your message out, and everything will be just fine. But, Dezenhall and Weber conclude, this kind of cheery talk does not help much during a real crisis, and it's easy to lose sight of your genuine priorities. If your case goes to trial, for example, you might want the public to think you're a wonderful company, but all that matters is what the jury thinks.

The authors support a political model of crisis management, which means you may have to fight back and

defend yourself. When the company has done wrong, repentance is in order. When the company has been wronged, a strong defense is recommended. The authors recommend not admitting guilt and meeting each accusation with a counter claim. They say this is how Martha Stewart turned her public image around after serving a jail sentence. In another example, they say this is how Merck, the pharmaceutical company, recovered from legal defeats and bad press as it began to portray plaintiffs as selfish opportunists. They also cite how successful the mobile phone industry was in mounting a defense against the consumer complaints that the phones were causing brain tumors. The key, they say, is determining when to be conciliatory and when to aggressively defend.

1. What are the relevant issues in this debate over the best response to a crisis?
2. Is it best to apologize, repent and move on, or stand firm and aggressively defend?
3. What is the downside risk of mounting a rigorous defense?

Sources: Eric Dezenhall and John Weber, *Damage Control: Why Everything You Know about Crisis Management Is Wrong* (New York: Portfolio Hardcover, 2007); Richard Evans, "Crisis Management for a Vindictive Age," *Financial Times* (April 24, 2007), 12.

3. Train your spokespersons.
4. Establish communications protocols.
5. Identify and know your audience.
6. Anticipate crises.
7. Assess the crisis situation.
8. Identify key messages you will communicate to key groups.
9. Decide on communications methods.
10. Be prepared to ride out the storm.

A brief elaboration on the importance of identifying key messages that will be communicated to key groups is useful (point 8). It is important that you communicate with your internal stakeholders first because rumors are often started there, and uninformed employees can do great damage to a successful crisis management effort. Internal stakeholders are your best advocates and can be supportive during a crisis. Prepare news releases that contain as much information as possible, and get this information out to all media outlets at the same time. Communicate with others in the community who have a need to know, such as public officials, disaster coordinators, stakeholders, and others. Uniformity of response is of vital importance during a crisis. Finally, have a designated "release authority" for information (point 2).[78]

The Centers for Disease Control and Prevention (CDC) states as part of its crisis communications training that the first 48 hours of a crisis are the most important. The program's mantra is reported as "be *first*, be *right*, be *credible*."[79] Being first means getting your message out first, which allows you to control its accuracy and content. If a company is late in getting its message out, the media and others will fill in the blanks, and they might include rumors, their own speculations, misunderstandings, or bias. Being right means saying and doing the right thing. This is the ethical dimension of communications. This is done after the management has gathered all the facts and understands exactly what has happened in the crisis. Being credible means being open, honest, and speaking with one consistent voice. Mixed messages from mixed sources can lead to disaster. The company's spokesperson should be sincere, be empathetic, be accountable, demonstrate competence, display expertise, and put forth consistent facts.[80] For all this to happen, of course, careful crisis communications must be a priority in the crisis plan.

Successful Crisis Management

Being Prepared for Crises. Being prepared for crises has become a primary activity in a growing number of companies. Today, most companies may be prepared for crises, but their degree of preparedness varies widely. In recent years, there is no better example of being well prepared than how well many business enterprises responded to the Hurricane Katrina disaster in 2005. They were applauded for their readiness and execution of disaster plans as the devastating hurricane hit the Southeast, especially the New Orleans and Gulf Coast regions of the country. Companies that stood out in their preparedness and assistance included Walmart and Home Depot.

These two companies had anticipated the impact of the hurricane, gotten their act together days beforehand, and implemented their plans to the benefit of thousands of affected residents. Some experts even observed that the Federal Emergency Management Agency (FEMA) and the Red Cross, both agencies whose mission it is to respond to crises, learned a lot from these companies and other such firms.[81] Because of the types of products and supplies they sell, these two companies and other big box stores always seem to play key roles in natural disasters such as hurricanes, tornadoes, and other weather-related crises. Another major company that helped the government solve transportation and communication problems was FedEx. One of FedEx's radio antennae in New Orleans became the key communication link for FEMA as it sought to establish a communication system in the area.[82]

Learning from Crises. Many corporate CEOs admitted that coping with Katrina taught them a great deal about preparing for crises and disasters. Major lessons learned included the following: take care of your employees, keep communication lines open, and get ready for the next disaster.[83] General Electric (GE) chairman and CEO Jeff Immelt described himself as "humbler and hungrier" as a result of the global recession and credit crisis that sorely tested GE.[84] In addition to the expected responses of refocusing operations and cutting costs, Immelt has looked inward, changing his management style in response to the crisis and recession. He meets more regularly and individually with his 25 top executives, pushes more decision making to lower organizational levels, and, in a move that might not come naturally to a former applied math major, he has become more comfortable with ambiguity.[85]

Sometimes being prepared for one type of crisis provides valuable learning for when other types of crises strike. A case in point was that of Childs Capital in New York City, a company that provides economic development in poor countries. The company's CEO, Donna Childs, put a disaster plan in place for business disruptions such as a subway fire, a scaffolding accident, a brownout, or some other smaller scale business disruption. She had made arrangements by developing a communications plan and a method for a continuous functioning offsite should the need arise. As a result of her crisis management for one type of disaster, she was back up and running one week after the collapse of the World Trade Center in New York. One result of her experience is that she is now giving weekly seminars on disaster preparedness and has even authored a book, *Prepare for the Worst, Plan for the Best: Disaster Preparedness and Recovery for Small Businesses.*[86]

A Successful Crisis Management Example. We conclude this chapter with an illustration of a successful crisis management case study of one company. Earlier, we presented the handling of the J&J Tylenol crisis as a success story. This success story started with the kind of phone call every company dreads—"Your product is injuring people; we're announcing it at a press conference today." Schwan's Sales Enterprises, Inc., got such a call from the Minnesota Department of Health at about noon one fateful day. The Health Department reported that it had found a statistical link between Schwan's ice cream and confirmed cases of salmonella. Thousands of people in at least 39 states became ill with salmonella after eating tainted Schwan's ice cream, potentially setting the company up for a decade's worth of litigation. Instead, in a little more than a year after the outbreak, the vast majority of claims had been handled outside the legal system through direct settlements or as part of a class action in Minneapolis.[87]

Schwan's knew that its image of the smiling man in the sunshine-yellow Schwan's truck (with a Swan on the side) busily hand-delivering ice cream to grateful consumers was one of its major assets. Before the company was sure of the Health Department's findings, it halted sales and production, shut down, and invited the state health department, the department of agriculture, and the FDA into the plant to investigate. It also notified all its sales offices nationwide. Also, within the first 24 hours of the crisis, the company set up a hotline to answer consumer questions, contacted employees and managers to staff the hotline, prepared for a product recall, and began working with its insurer.[88]

By placing consumer safety as its number one priority, Schwan's was able to resolve the crisis much more quickly than ever would have been possible without a carefully designed crisis management plan. Whether by coincidence or preparedness, the manager of public affairs and the company's general counsel had completed a review and rewriting of the company's crisis management manual just two months before the outbreak. One vital component of the plan was a crisis management team, which went to work as soon as the news came. The crisis management team quickly set up a process for handling consumers who had been affected. The team, working with its insurance company, quickly helped customers get medical treatment and their bills paid. Settlements to customers who suffered from salmonella symptoms included financial damages, medical expenses, and other costs, such as reimbursement for workdays missed.[89]

How did the ice cream get contaminated with salmonella? After a month's investigation that kept the Marshall, Minnesota, plant closed, it was determined that the ice cream mix supplied by a few vendors was the culprit. The mix of cream, sugar, and milk had been shipped in a tanker truck that had previously held raw, unpasteurized eggs that had the bacteria. Schwan's quietly sought and received legal damages from the suppliers but stayed focused on its customers throughout the crisis.

What did Schwan's learn from this crisis? Previously, Schwan's did not repasteurize its ice cream mix once the mix arrived at the Marshall plant. Within a few weeks of the outbreak, however, the company had broken ground to build its own repasteurization plant. The company also leased a dedicated fleet of tanker trucks to deliver the ice cream mix from the suppliers to the plant, set up a system for testing each shipment, and delayed shipping the final product until the test results were known. In summary, Schwan's planning, quick response, and customer-oriented strategy combined to retain customer loyalty and minimize the company's legal exposure.[90] It was a case of good, effective crisis management.

Undoubtedly, in the years to come, stories will be told of successful crisis management in the aftermath of major traumatic events in the lives of organizations and society. Sadly, preparation for acts of terrorism is now a vital national and business issue. Clearly, the events of the past few years have made crisis management a priority topic in boardrooms and among managers.

Summary

Issues management and crisis management are two key approaches by which companies may plan for the turbulent stakeholder environment. Both these approaches are frequently found housed in a company's department of public affairs. Issues management is a process by which an organization identifies issues in the stakeholder environment, analyzes and prioritizes those issues in terms of their relevance to the organization, plans responses to the issues, and then evaluates and monitors the results. There are two approaches to issues management: the conventional approach and the strategic management approach. Issues management requires knowledge of the changing mix of issues, the issues management process, the issues development process, and how companies might implement issues management in practice. Issues management serves as a bridge to crisis management.

Crisis management, like issues management, is not a panacea for organizations. In spite of well-intended efforts by management, not all crises will be resolved in the company's favor. Nevertheless, being prepared for the inevitable makes sense, especially in today's world of instantaneous global communications and obsessive media coverage. Whether thinking about the long term, the intermediate term, or the short term, managers need to be prepared to handle crises. A crisis has a number of different stages, and managing crises requires a number of key steps before, during, and after the crisis. These steps include identifying areas of vulnerability, developing a plan for dealing with threats, forming crisis teams, using crisis drills, and learning from experience. Crisis communications is critical for successful crisis management. When used in tandem, issues and crisis management can help managers fulfill their economic, legal, ethical, and philanthropic responsibilities to stakeholders.

Key Terms

acute crisis stage, p. 192

chronic crisis stage, p. 192

conventional approach, p. 177

crisis, p. 189

crisis communications, p. 195

crisis management, p. 175

crisis resolution stage, p. 192

crisis teams, p. 194

emerging issue, p. 179

issue, p. 179

issue buying, p. 182

issue selling, p. 182

issues development process, p. 185

issues management, p. 175

portfolio approach, p. 179

prodromal crisis stage, p. 192

strategic management approach, p. 177

Discussion Questions

1. Which of the major stages in the issues management process do you think is the most important? Why?

2. Following the approach indicated in Figure 6-1, identify a new issue category not listed in Figure 6-1. Identify several examples of "crises" that have occurred in recent years under each issue category.

3. Identify one example, other than those listed in Figure 6-4, of each of the leading force categories: events, authorities/advocates, literature, organizations, and political jurisdictions.

4. Identify a crisis that has occurred in your life or in the life of someone you know, and briefly explain it in terms of the four crisis stages: prodromal, acute, chronic, and resolution.

5. Do research on the impacts on business organizations of the attacks on the World Trade Center in New York and the scandals of the early to mid-2000s. What have been successful and unsuccessful examples of crisis management that have come out of this research? Is terrorism a likely crisis for which business may prepare? How does preparation for terrorism (which comes from without) compare with preparation for ethical scandals (which come from within)?

CASE 10

Chiquita: An Excruciating Dilemma between Life and Law*

AN ETHICAL DILEMMA

Assume that you are the top executive for a firm doing business in Colombia, South America. If a known terrorist group threatens to kill your employees unless you pay extortion money, should the company pay it?

If you answer "no," how would you respond to the family of an employee who is later killed by the terrorist group?

If you answer "yes," how would you respond to the family of an innocent citizen who is killed by a bomb your money funded?[1]

BACKGROUND

In many parts of the world, doing business is a dangerous proposition. Such has been the case in the country of Colombia in South America. The danger has been described in the following way: "In Colombia's notoriously lawless countryside, narco-terrorists ran roughshod over the forces of law and order—or collaborated with them in a mutual game of shakedowns, kidnappings, and murders."[2] Foreign companies that choose to do business in many parts of the world are easy targets. These companies have resources, they care about their employees, and many of them have been willing to negotiate with terrorists and just consider it one of the costs of doing business. Security in many of these countries can only be had at a price.[3]

Formerly known as United Fruit Company and then United Brands, Chiquita Brands International, based in Cincinnati, Ohio, is the type of company that faces the kind of situation described above. Today, Chiquita is a global food company that employs more than 26,000 people on six continents around the world. According to its Web site, Chiquita owns approximately 90,000 acres (36,400 hectares) and leases about 50,000 acres (20,000 hectares) of improved land, primarily in Panama, Costa Rica, Colombia, Guatemala, and Honduras. The company also grows bananas in the Ivory Coast and through joint ventures in the Philippines and Australia. For the most part, the company uses this land for growing, packing, and shipping bananas.[4]

BUYING SECURITY: PROTECTING OUR EMPLOYEES

According to CEO Fernando Aguirre, Chiquita started making payments to paramilitary groups in Colombia beginning in 1997 and extending into 2004. The payments came to a total of about $1.7 million. The company felt it was forced to make these payments because the lives of its employees were at stake.[5] During the period 2001–2004, the company was making payments to the terrorist group United Self-Defense Forces of Colombia (AUC). AUC was the group's Spanish acronym, by which the group was primarily known. A major complication during this period was that the U.S. government had declared AUC to be a specially designated terrorist organization, making it illegal to provide funds for them, and the Bush Administration had vowed to go after any company that funded terrorist groups.[6]

CHIQUITA TURNS ITSELF IN

Chiquita turned itself in and reported to the government that it had made the payments to AUC during the years indicated.

In 2007, CEO Fernando Aguirre released a public statement outlining what he called "an excruciating dilemma between life and law."[7] Following are some excerpts from his statement:

- In February 2003, senior management of Chiquita Brands International learned that protection payments the company had been making to paramilitary groups in Colombia to keep our workers safe from the violence committed by those groups were illegal under U.S. law.
- The company had operated in Colombia for nearly a century, generating 4,400 direct and an additional 8,000 indirect jobs. We contributed almost $70 million annually to the Colombian economy in the form of capital expenditures, payroll, taxes, social security, pensions, and local purchases of goods and services.

---

* This case was written by Archie B. Carroll, University of Georgia. Updated in 2010.

- But during the 1990s, it became increasingly difficult to protect our workforce. Among the hundreds of documented attacks by left- and right-wing paramilitaries were the 1995 massacre of 28 innocent Chiquita employees who were ambushed on a bus on their way to work, and the 1998 assassination of two more of our workers on a farm while their colleagues were forced to watch.
- Despite the harsh realities on the ground, the discovery that our payments were violating U.S. law created a dilemma of more than theoretical proportions for us: the company could stop making the payments, complying with the law but putting the lives of our workers in immediate jeopardy; or we could keep our workers out of harm's way while violating American law.[8]
- Each alternative was unpalatable and unacceptable. So the company decided to do what we believe any responsible citizen should do under the circumstances: We went to the U.S. Department of Justice and voluntarily disclosed the facts and the predicament. The U.S. government had no knowledge of the payments and, had we not come forward ourselves, it is entirely possible that the payments would have remained unknown to American authorities to this day.[9]

In a plea deal, the company was fined $25 million, and in September 2007 it made its first installment payment of $5 million. Chiquita's general counsel said that "this was a difficult situation for the company and that the company had to do it to protect the well-being of our employees and their families." The Department of Justice prosecutor called the payments "morally repugnant" and said that the protection payments "fueled violence everywhere else."[10]

BOARD KNOWLEDGE REVEALED

During the investigation of this incident, it was discovered that the Board of Directors of the company came to know that the questionable payments were going on. A prosecution document, according to the *Miami Herald*, presented the following timeline of events:

- 2000—Chiquita's audit committee, composed of board members, heard about the payments and took no action.
- 2002—Soon after AUC had been designated a terrorist organization, a Chiquita employee learned about this and alerted the company.

- 2003—Chiquita consulted with a Washington attorney who told the company, "Bottom line: Cannot make the payment."
- 2003—Two months later, Chiquita executives reported to the full board of directors that the company was still making payments. One board member objected and the directors agreed to make the payments known to the Department of Justice.

CHIQUITA'S SOCIAL RESPONSIBILITY INITIATIVES

An interesting description of the company's track record in the area of corporate social responsibility (CSR) makes this case particularly unusual. Jon Entine's account of Chiquita's turnaround as a company is enlightening. Apparently, Chiquita spent at least 15 years living down its longstanding reputation as a "ruthless puppeteer manipulating corrupt Latin American banana republics."[11] Once operating as United Fruit, the company began turning itself around in 1990 and remade itself into a model food distributor, complete with high environmental and ethical standards.

BETTER BANANA PROJECT

In the early 1990s, the company separated itself from its competitors by teaming up with the Rainforest Alliance on sustainability and labor standards. This became known as the Better Banana Project.[12]

Rainforest Alliance had the following to say about Chiquita's adoption of the Better Banana Project:

> Chiquita Brands International, Inc.—a global leader in banana production—today announced that it has transformed its farming practices and led the way for the banana industry. The Rainforest Alliance monitors and verifies that Chiquita's farms abide by strong environmental and social standards, which have positive impacts on rural communities and tropical landscapes. By meeting the Rainforest Alliance's standards, Chiquita has improved water quality, instituted programs for recycling and safe waste disposal, dramatically decreased agrichemical use, and improved the quality of life of workers on all its company-owned farms in Latin America.[13]

Chiquita also became well known through its publications of its corporate responsibility reports. The company issued public reports on its corporate responsibility efforts each year starting in 2000. In addition, beginning in 2003, the company issued interim updates on its corporate responsibility progress as part of our annual reports to shareholders.

Regarding its CSR initiatives and payments to terrorist groups, CEO Fernando Aguirre had the following to say:

Chiquita is completely committed to corporate responsibility and compliance. The fact that we voluntarily came forward and disclosed the payments to the paramilitaries did not simply acknowledge an illegal act, it proved our willingness to take responsibility for our actions, even when such a step comes at considerable cost.

Legal scholars, business ethicists and governmental leaders can, and should, consider the implications of the situation we faced. There are a number of questions that deserve serious discussion and debate, among them: What should a company do when faced with the excruciating conflict between a possible violation of law and protecting the lives of its workers? What is the proper public policy toward, and punishment of, companies that voluntarily reveal potentially illegal behavior to the government?[14]

In June 2004, Chiquita sold its Colombian farms at a loss of $9 million, in order to extricate itself from this difficult situation.[15]

LAWSUIT AGAINST CHIQUITA

In April 2010, three U.S. citizens who survived a five-year hostage ordeal by Colombia's notorious FARC paramilitary group, along with the family of a fourth man who was killed by FARC rebels, asserted that Chiquita owes them damages because of its payments to FARC. The three citizens were employees of defense contractor Northrop Grumman who were traveling in a plane in Colombia in 2003 when they were shot down by FARC rebels who also killed the plane's pilot and a Colombian guide who was with them. The three citizens spent five years as FARC hostages before being released in 2008.[16]

The employees' lawsuit points out that Chiquita was fined $25 million in 2007 for having paid $1.7 million to AUC, the right-wing paramilitary group that was at odds with FARC. The plaintiffs went on to say that Chiquita had paid hundreds of thousands of dollars to FARC for a decade beginning in 1989. This implied that Chiquita played both sides in the nonstop military clashes in Colombia. In its defense, Chiquita has said that it was "an extortion victim in Colombia, paying left- and right-wing groups to protect its employees, not to promote violence."[17]

The lawsuit goes on to suggest that Chiquita's connection with FARC may have been more proactive than just paying protection money. The lawsuit alleges that the company created dummy corporations and falsified its payroll records to hide its payments to FARC. The suit also claims that Chiquita used its network of local transportation contractors to transport weapons to the group.[18]

A TALE OF TWO COMPANIES

The Chiquita payment controversy has been called a "tale of two companies." One face of Chiquita comes across as a defiant, secretive multinational, with lots of resources, determined to break the law to keep its employees safe and its businesses running. The other face of Chiquita builds partnerships with groups such as Rainforest Alliance to support the Better Banana Project and issues frequent corporate social responsibility reports to keep its stakeholders pleased and informed, eventually extricating itself by turning itself in, paying a huge fine, suffering tremendous embarrassment and loss of reputational capital, and finally selling its farms to help reach closure. Which is the real Chiquita?

QUESTIONS FOR DISCUSSION

1. Go back to the ethical dilemma at the beginning of the case. Which position did you take and why? Did your position change after you read the case?

2. Was Chiquita justified in making the extortion payments to protect its employees? Was the company really between a rock and a hard place? What should it have done?

3. Using your knowledge of business ethics and global practices, what concepts, principles, or ideas from your study have a bearing on this case? Explain how some of them might have guided Chiquita toward better decisions.

4. What is your assessment of CEO Aguirre's statements? Is he sincere or just making excuses?

5. What is your analysis of the Chiquita board of directors' handling of this case? Do you think selling the farms at a loss in Colombia was the right thing to do? Why?

6. Does the lawsuit by the former Northrop Grumman employees have merit? What does this lawsuit tell you about the long-term implications of questionable dealings while doing business abroad?

7. In the "tale of two companies," which do you think is the real Chiquita and why?

ENDNOTES

1. Denis Collins, Edgewood College, Madison, Wisconsin, posed these questions in an e-mail to an International Association for Business and Society ListServ discussing the Chiquita Banana situation, on June 18, 2007. Used with permission.

2. Rushworth M. Kidder, "Ethical Bananas," *Ethics Newsline* (March 19, 2007), a publication of the Institute for Global Ethics, http://www.globalethics.org/newsline/2007/03/19/ethical-bananas/. Accessed July 12, 2010.

3. *Ibid.*

4. Chiquita, http://www.chiquitabrands.com/CompanyInfo/CompanyInfo.aspx. Accessed July 12, 2010.

5. Kidder.

6. Jane Bussey, "Chiquita Disregarded Warnings, Records Show," *The Miami Herald* (April 16, 2007).

7. *The Corporate Citizen* (April 2007), http://www.uschamber.com/bclc/resources/newsletter/2007/ chiquita_newsletter_april2007.htm. Accessed July 12, 2010.

8. *Ibid.*

9. *Ibid.*

10. Pablo Bachelet, "Chiquita Pays Fine for Supporting Colombian Terrorist Group," McClatchy Washington Bureau, McClatchy Newspapers, http://www.mcclatchydc.com/2007/09/17/v-print/ 19797/chiquita-pays-fine-for-supporting.html. Accessed July 12, 2010.

11. Jon Entine, "Chiquita Counts the Cost of Honesty," *Ethical Corporation* (May 2007), 74.

12. *Ibid.*

13. Rainforest Alliance, http://www.rainforest-alliance.org/branding.cfm?id=chiquital. Accessed July 12, 2010.

14. *The Corporate Citizen* (April 2007), http://www.uschamber.com/bclc/resources/newsletter/2007/ chiquita_newsletter_april2007.htm. Accessed July 12, 2010.

15. *Ibid.*

16. Daniel Tencer, "Lawsuit: Chiquita Fruit Company Funded Death Squads in Colombia," *The Raw Story* (April 7, 2010), http://rawstory.com/rs/2010/ 0407/chiquita-funded-death-squads-colombia/. Accessed July 12, 2010.

17. *Ibid.*

18. *Ibid.*

CASE 11

Astroturf Lobbying*

"Save Our Species Alliance," "Americans for Job Security," and "Citizens for Asbestos Reform"—the names of these organizations would lead one to believe they are composed of individual people who have organized at the grassroots level to solve a problem about which they feel deeply. However, according to a recent Public Citizen report, these organizations "are bankrolled by large corporations, industry trade associations, or ultra-wealthy individuals who have little in common

with the regular Americans they are pretending to represent."[1] The purpose of the "Save Our Species Alliance" was to make land management more industry friendly by gutting the Endangered Species Act. "Americans for Job Security" advocated for repeal of the estate tax in order to protect inherited wealth, and the "Citizens for Asbestos Reform" bases its operations in the offices of the American Insurance Association.[2]

Many other examples of this practice exist. According to *The Washington Post*, groups such as "Citizens for a Sound Economy" provide analyses that add an air of authority to corporate arguments—while often maintaining the corporate donors' anonymity."[3] The

---

* This case was written by Ann K. Buchholtz, Rutgers University. Updated in 2010.

Texas office of Public Citizen charges that "Energy Citizens," a group opposed to climate change legislation, obtains its funding primarily from the American Petroleum Institute and peoples its rallies with energy industry employees. It contends that a 2009 rally opposing greenhouse gas legislation was a "company picnic" because the only people allowed in were energy company employees who had to show IDs to attend.[4]

Organizations that falsely portray themselves to be grassroots entities are engaging in what many people call astroturf or stealth lobbying. Although astroturf lobbying occurs in a variety of arenas, the campaign for tort reform is a classic example that provides a good forum for analysis of this tactic.

THE CALA STUDY

According to a report prepared by Public Citizen and the Center for Justice and Democracy, Citizens Against Lawsuit Abuse (CALA) organizations are part of a "national corporate-backed network of front groups that receive substantial financial and strategic assistance from some of America's biggest corporations."[5] In "The CALA Files: The Secret Campaign by Big Tobacco and Other Major Industries to Take Away Your Rights," Public Citizen and the Center for Justice and Democracy argue that the goal of astroturf lobbying is to insulate corporations from having to pay a price for their reckless behavior.[6] They studied dozens of CALA groups in 18 states and found among other things that

1. Although they claim to be supported by individual donations, they are funded mostly by large corporate donors and representatives of industries that want to be shielded from lawsuits. Central to this effort is the American Tort Reform Association, a coalition of major corporations and trade associations.
2. They hide their pro-business agenda behind friendly consumer-oriented names. The intent to deceive is shown in a memo from the Tobacco Institute, "In order to be totally effective, the grassroots effort must appear to be spontaneous rather than a coordinated effort."[7]
3. According to documents made public during the tobacco litigations, tobacco companies spend millions each year to weaken tort laws through forming and funding groups such as these.
4. The CALA efforts have been successful. They have achieved passage of legislation designed to

limit consumer rights to sue manufacturers, and they have conducted successful "voter education" campaigns to unseat judges who favor expanded consumer rights and elect judges who favor limits on liability.

NOT IN MY BACKYARD

According to a report prepared by Public Citizen and Citizen Action, another leading consumer group, corporations seek tort reform only when they are the defendants. "The National Association of Manufacturers: A Study in Hypocrisy" documents a variety of cases where corporations are the plaintiffs and charges, "the same companies lobbying to restrict the legal rights of people injured or killed by defective products have unfettered access to our nation's courts as their own private playground."[8] Examples of frivolous corporate cases include the time when Exxon sued the Georgia minor league baseball team, Columbus RedStixx, for violating their trademark by having two Xs in their name and the time when Gillette sued Norelco for ads depicting nonelectric razors as "ferocious creatures."

THE VIEW FROM CALA

For their part, CALA groups say that they are not against the legal system, but that tort reform is needed to corral an out-of-control civil justice system. They don't oppose needed lawsuits, simply the frivolous excesses that abuse the system. They argue that tort litigation is costing the United States nearly 2 percent of its gross domestic product, which is twice as much as litigation costs in Europe.[9]

QUESTIONS FOR DISCUSSION

1. By searching on "CALA and lawsuit," you can find the Web sites of a variety of CALA organizations. Search their Web sites and decide whether you agree with the assessments of the CALA report. Do you find their practices to be deceptive or defensible? Do the various CALAs differ in that regard?
2. Where do you draw the line? What limits should be placed on corporate lobbying under shell grassroots organizations? Does your attitude toward "shell" lobbying groups vary with the extent to which you agree with the causes they are promoting?

3. What, if any, public policy recommendations would you make?

ENDNOTES

1. "Organizing Astroturf: Evidence Shows Bogus Grassroots Groups Hijack the Political Debate," *Public Citizen* (January 2007), http://www.cleanupwashington.org/documents/astroturf.pdf. Accessed July 24, 2010.

2. *Ibid.*

3. "Think Tanks: Corporations' Secret Weapon," *The Washington Post* (January 29, 2000), 1.

4. "Industry Astroturf Rally Against Climate Change Bill Shows Big Oil Can't Organize Real Grassroots Movement—API Throws Company Picnic, Not Town Hall Meeting, on Climate Change" (August 18, 2009), http://www.citizen.org/pressroom/pressroomredirect.cfm?ID=2946. Accessed July 24, 2010.

5. An overview of the CALA report and information on purchasing the full report are available at the Public Citizen Web site, http://www.citizen.org/pressroom/pressroomredirect.cfm?ID=481. Accessed July 22, 2010.

6. *Ibid.*

7. Robert Weissman, "The 'Lawsuit Abuse' Scam," *Multinational Monitor* (September 2000), 7.

8. *Ibid.*

9. "Putting Brakes on the Litigation Machine," *BusinessWeek* (January 29, 2001), 144.

CASE 12

The Betaseron® Decision (A)*

The U.S. Food and Drug Administration's (FDA) approval of interferon beta-1b (brand name Betaseron®) made it the first multiple sclerosis (MS) treatment to get FDA approval in 25 years. Betaseron® was developed by Berlex Laboratories, a U.S. unit of Schering AG, the German pharmaceutical company. Berlex handled the clinical development, trials, and marketing of the drug, while Chiron Corporation, a biotechnology firm based in California, manufactured it. The groundbreaking approval of Betaseron® represented not only a great opportunity for Berlex but also a dilemma. Supplies were insufficient to meet initial demand, and shortages were forecast for three years. With insufficient supplies and staggering development costs, how would Berlex allocate and price the drug?

* This case was written by Ann K. Buchholtz, Rutgers University. It was written from public sources, solely for the purpose of stimulating class discussion. All events are real. The author thanks Dr. Stephen Reingold, vice president of Research and Medical Programs at the National Multiple Sclerosis Society, and Avery Rockwell, chapter services associate of the Greater Connecticut Chapter of the Multiple Sclerosis Society, for their helpful comments. All rights reserved jointly to the author and the North American Case Research Association (NACRA). Used with permission.

THE CHALLENGE OF MULTIPLE SCLEROSIS

MS is a disease of the central nervous system that interferes with the brain's ability to control such functions as seeing, walking, and talking. The nerve fibers in the brain and spinal cord are surrounded by myelin, a fatty substance that protects the nerve fibers in the same way that insulation protects electrical wires. When the myelin insulation becomes damaged, the ability of the central nervous system to transmit nerve impulses to and from the brain becomes impaired. With MS, there are sclerosed (i.e., scarred or hardened) areas in multiple parts of the brain and spinal cord when the immune system mistakenly attacks the myelin sheath.

THE IMPACT OF MS

The symptoms of MS depend to some extent on the location and size of the sclerosis. Symptoms may include numbness, slurred speech, blurred vision, poor coordination, muscle weakness, bladder dysfunction, extreme fatigue, and paralysis. There is no way to know how the disease will progress for any individual, because the nature of the disease can change. Some people will have a relatively benign course of MS with only one or two mild attacks, nearly complete remission, and no permanent disability. Others will have a chronic progressive course resulting in severe disability. A third group displays the most typical pattern, which is periods of exacerbations, when the disease is active, and periods of remission, when the symptoms recede yet generally leave some damage. People with MS live with an exceptionally high degree of uncertainty, because their disease can change from one day to the next. Dramatic downturns as well as dramatic recoveries are not uncommon.

THE PROMISE OF BETASERON®

Interferon beta is a naturally occurring protein that regulates the body's immune system. Betaseron® is composed of interferon beta-1b that has been genetically engineered and laboratory manufactured as a recombinant product. Although other interferons (i.e., alpha and gamma) had been tested, only beta interferon had been shown, through large-scale trials, to affect MS. Because it is an immunoregulatory agent, Betaseron® was believed to combat the immune problems that make MS worse. However, the exact way in which it works was yet to be determined.

RESEARCH

In clinical studies, Betaseron® was shown to reduce the frequency and severity of exacerbations in ambulatory MS patients with a relapsing–remitting form of the disease. It did not reverse damage nor did it completely prevent exacerbations. However, Betaseron® could dramatically improve the quality of life for the person with MS. For example, people taking Betaseron® were shown to have fewer and shorter hospitalizations. Betaseron® represented the first and only drug to have an effect on the frequency of exacerbations.

ADMINISTRATION

Betaseron® is administered subcutaneously (under the skin) every other day by self-injection. To derive the most benefits from the therapy, it was important that the MS patient maintain a regular schedule of the injections. Some flu-like side effects, as well as swelling and irritation around the injection, had been noted. However, these side effects tended to decrease with time on treatment. In addition, one person who received Betaseron® committed suicide while three others attempted it. Because MS often leads to depression, there was no way to know whether the administration of Betaseron® was a factor. Last, Betaseron® was not recommended for use during pregnancy.

THE BETASERON® DILEMMA

FDA approval for Betaseron® allowed physicians to prescribe the drug to MS patients who were ambulatory and had a relapsing–remitting course of MS. An estimated one-third of the 300,000 people with MS in the United States fell into that category, resulting in a potential client base of 100,000. The expedited FDA approval process for Betaseron® took only one year instead of the customary three. As a result, Berlex was unprepared to manufacture and distribute the treatment. Chiron Corporation had been making the drug in small quantities for experimental use and did not have the manufacturing facilities to handle the expected explosion in demand. Chiron estimated that it would have enough of the drug for about 12,000–20,000 people by the end of the year. By the end of the second year, Chiron expected to be able to provide the drug to 40,000 patients. Depending on demand, it might take about three years to provide the drug to all patients who requested it. Chiron's expanded manufacturing represented the only option for Berlex, because the process required for another company to get FDA approval to manufacture the drug would take even longer.

PRICING

In addition to availability, price was a concern, because successes must fund the failures that precede them. Betaseron® represented years of expensive, risky research by highly trained scientists in modern research facilities. Furthermore, genetically engineered drugs were extremely expensive to manufacture. In the case of Betaseron®, a human interferon gene is inserted into bacteria, resulting in a genetically engineered molecule. The stringent quality controls on the procedure take time and are expensive. As a result, the price of Betaseron® was expected to be about $10,000 per year for each patient. Berlex had patent protection with Betaseron®, but competitors were working hard to bring their own treatments to the market, and so competition was certain to appear before the patent protections would expire.

Betaseron® brought great hope to people with MS and a great quandary to Berlex. How should Berlex handle the supply limitations, the distribution, and the pricing of this drug?

QUESTIONS FOR DISCUSSION

1. What are the ethical issues in this situation? Which issues must Berlex consider first when determining how to distribute Betaseron®?
2. Given the shortage of the drug, how should Berlex decide who receives it and who waits? Give a specific plan.
3. How should Berlex handle the logistics of distribution?
4. How should Berlex determine the drug's relative pricing (assume the drug costs about $12,000 per year)?
5. Who, if anyone, should be involved in the decision making?

CASE 13

Firestone and Ford: The Tire Tread Separation Tragedy*

It is often tricky to know when an ethical or social issue really begins. Does it begin before it is "recognized" or "identified" as an issue? Does it begin when an isolated manager recognizes an incident or a trend and reports it via a memo to his superiors? Does it begin once the media get hold of information and the frenzy begins? Such questions are raised in the case with the Firestone–Ford tire tread separation debacle that began dominating business news late in 2000, with implications for passenger safety that continue today. As Toyota Motor Company has recently learned, these problems garner much news and don't go away quickly.

Ask any consumer about the two most critical features of safety on their automobiles, and most will quickly respond—brakes and tires. It is not surprising, then, that the tire tread separations that began appearing on certain categories of Firestone tires, especially those associated with the Ford Explorer, caught the public's attention like few other recent product safety issues.

Was this a tire problem or an SUV problem? Was this Firestone's problem or Ford's problem? Were both companies responsible? Were government regulations administered through the National Highway Traffic Safety Administration (NHTSA) adequate to protect the public? These questions are simple to ask but difficult to answer because they are complex.[1]

Let's start where the "public" knowledge of the product dangers began to surface—with a couple of accidents reported since 1998.

TWO CRITICAL ACCIDENTS

Jessica LeAnn Taylor was a 14-year-old junior high school cheerleader on the way to a homecoming football game near her hometown of Mexia, Texas, on October 16, 1998. She was in a Ford Explorer SUV, driven by a friend of her mother's, when the tread on the left-rear Firestone ATX tire allegedly "peeled off like a banana," leading the Explorer to veer left and roll over. Jessica died in this accident.[2] In another incident, two years later, Victor Rodriguez and his family piled into the family's Ford Explorer over Labor Day weekend and prepared to visit a sick aunt at a hospital in Laredo, Texas. As Rodriguez started down Interstate 35, he was startled by a thumping sound and looked in his rearview mirror to see the tread shredding off one of his Firestone Wilderness AT tires. Rodriguez was unable to control his vehicle. It flipped, ejecting five of its passengers. Among the passengers was his ten-year-old son, Mark Anthony, who died instantly.[3]

Jessica LeAnn Taylor and Mark Anthony Rodriguez were just two of many victims in a far-reaching safety crisis that, according to some accounts, had taken the lives of close to 90 Americans by fall 2000 and had

---

* This case was written by Archie B. Carroll, University of Georgia. Updated in 2010.

"driven fear into the hearts of motorists" who had begun to think of the SUV as the ideal family car.

A KEY COURT VICTORY

Though the credit for bringing the tire safety/SUV tragedy to a head may have begun in a number of different places, one account attributes the tenacity of Jessica Taylor's family lawyer, Randy Roberts, with much of the credit. Roberts was a small-town lawyer, and when he took the case, he realized there was not much hope in taking on a corporate giant such as Firestone, a unit of Japan's Bridgestone Corporation.

As many other tire companies have successfully done in the past, Firestone ruled out a tire problem at the very outset. It and other companies have been successful in keeping lawsuits and consumer complaint data confidential, or private, saying the Taylor accident was similar to only one other with which they were familiar. The lawyer did not buy this argument, and in November 1999, he won a crucial victory from state judge Sam Bournias, who ordered Firestone to turn over any information on complaints or other lawsuits as well as employee depositions associated with these lawsuits concerning its ATX and Wilderness tires. The judge also permitted Roberts to share this information with other lawyers who were involved in similar lawsuits.[4]

OTHER LAWSUITS

Roberts discovered that other attorneys, for example, Bruce Kaster of Ocala, Florida, and Tab Turner of Little Rock, Arkansas, had been suing Firestone for much of the decade over the same type of issue. Though a trial date for his case had not been set, Roberts was one of the first to sense the broad scope of potential tire defects. At that time, he reported that there had been more than 1,100 incident reports and 57 lawsuits by February 2000.[5]

NHTSA GETS INVOLVED

By February 2000, the National Highway Traffic Safety Administration (NHTSA) had received fewer than 50 complaints over the better part of the previous decade about the suspect tires. It began to receive tips from State Farm Insurance that it was experiencing an unusually high number of insurance claims in which these tires were associated. After a report on tread separation accidents by Houston's TV station KHOU,

30 to 40 more complaints came in. At this point, NHTSA got interested. They contacted Randy Roberts, who was quite willing to help them do their research. He reported his findings about widespread complaints, and it was believed to have been a significant factor leading up to Firestone's voluntary recall of 6.5 million possibly defective tires. The voluntary recall began on August 9, 2000, and it included the Radial ATX, Radial ATXII, and certain Wilderness AT tires.[6]

By September 2000, the recall had replaced only about 2 million tires. One reason was due to a shortage of replacement tires. At about the same time, the NHTSA reported that possibly 1.4 million more tires, especially those manufactured at the Decatur, Illinois, plant, may be susceptible to the same type of tread separations.[7]

THE FINGER-POINTING BEGINS

As the bad news spread and in the absence of any good news, the finger-pointing between Bridgestone/Firestone and Ford began and continued unabated. Ford's position was best articulated by then-CEO Jacques Nasser, who stated, "this is a tire issue, not a vehicle issue." Nasser was trying to distance Ford from responsibility for the tire failures. For its part, Firestone argued that Ford's recommended lower air pressure for the tires may have contributed to the problem. Firestone said it recommended 30 PSI for the tires, whereas Ford was recommending 26 PSI for the tires.[8] It would later come out that Firestone believed the lower air pressure may have been an important contributory factor in the tire separations.

INVESTIGATIONS

The finger-pointing and squabbling between Firestone and Ford created a very murky picture of what was going on and why. The result was that both companies began to be investigated by the media and government, and the situation got worse for them both. The confusion caused Congress to begin hearings in September 2000 as top executives of both companies were summoned to Washington for testimony. At about the same time, it got worse for both as Venezuelan consumer protection officials were expected to recommend that both Ford and Firestone be charged with criminal negligence after investigating more than 60 deaths in that country that had been linked to accidents involving Ford Explorers equipped with Firestone tires.[9]

CONGRESSIONAL HEARINGS AND DISCLOSURES

In congressional hearings beginning in September 2000, Congress started grilling Bridgestone/Firestone and Ford executives about problems with their tires in the United States and abroad.[10] Congressional investigators reported on internal documents from both Firestone and Ford that the two companies were aware of the tread separation problem. The documents revealed that the companies knew something was amiss. In the unfolding paper trail, it was suggested that Firestone should have understood it had glitches at its Decatur, Illinois, plant, where some of the damaged tires had been identified as having been manufactured. A chart circulated inside the company by Firestone analysts earlier in the year had shown that nearly 60 percent of claims against the company in 1999 were for tires made during a strike that was taking place at the Decatur plant. Also, Firestone knew that two-thirds of the dollar payments it had made to settle claims involving tire separations came from the Decatur plant. On top of this, a March 12, 1999, Ford memo was disclosed that suggested that Firestone was reluctant to recall suspect tires in Saudi Arabia because doing so would require the company to notify the U.S. Department of Transportation.[11] So evidence that there was trouble was available to both the companies.

ANOTHER ACCIDENT VICTIM

After another accident victim, Lori Lazarus, heard about the big Firestone tire recall, she was very upset but not surprised. Back on Labor Day 1996, while driving home from Disney World, a Firestone tire on her Ford Explorer had shredded. Her SUV flipped into a drainage ditch, leaving her trapped. She was finally saved by passing motorists, who pulled her from the submerged vehicle. She still suffers from headaches and balance problems. The 31-year-old teacher was bitter that Ford and Firestone were just beginning to own up to their problems. She said, "They've known something was wrong for years."[12]

DAMAGE CONTROL CONTINUED

With the allegations spinning out of control, Ford and Firestone began full-blown damage control. Pressure was mounting to widen the recall. Critics wanted to know if the companies were guilty of a cover-up or just dragging their feet. Evidence continued to unfold that both companies had known about the problem for

years. Lawsuits first started occurring in 1991. Documents from those lawsuits showed that Firestone had begun reimbursing some consumers for faulty ATX tires as early as 1989. By 1997, insurance adjustors at State Farm began noticing a pattern of problems with ATX and Wilderness tires. In a few cases, they sought and received reimbursements from Firestone. State Farm said it shared its data with federal safety regulators in 1998, but an investigation into the tires was not opened up until two years later. In 1998, Ford also noticed Firestone treads unraveling on Explorers in Saudi Arabia, Asia, and South America, and in 1999 began replacing tires on nearly 50,000 foreign vehicles. Ford did not reveal to U.S. regulators its foreign recall until May 2000.[13]

PREVIOUS LAWSUITS CONCEALED

Through the judicious use of its lawyers, Firestone was able to conceal the fact that it had been sued many times before due to tire problems. How was this possible? An investigation by *U.S. News and World Report* found that Bridgestone/Firestone routinely used legal protective orders to conceal crucial data that was generated when consumers filed warranty claims with the company. The head of Trial Lawyers for Public Justice, Arthur Bryant, observed, "Deaths and serious injuries could have been prevented with these tires if manufacturers had not been able to use protective orders and court secrecy to hide the dangers." It took months for federal investigators to get access to the warranty data from Firestone. It finally became public only after Congress demanded it at the hearings in early September 2000.[14]

REPORTING NOT LEGALLY REQUIRED

Apparently, tire makers are not legally required to share potentially damaging reports with the government as other industries must do when public safety issues arise. For example, manufacturers and hospitals are required to notify the Food and Drug Administration every time a medical device such as a pacemaker is involved in an injury or death. The NHTSA has no such clout with the tire makers. The companies are required to report on themselves only if they discover a defect.

Clarence Ditlow of the Center for Auto Safety, a consumer advocacy organization, said the federal government requires manufacturers to surrender adjustment data "only in the aftermath of a tragedy."

Lawmakers have been angry about this. Transportation Secretary Rodney Slater wanted this loophole closed. He admitted the NHTSA does not have the authority to get the critical safety numbers, but it appears Congress is now getting ready to do something about this.[15] The NHTSA also claimed that it had not received adequate funding from Congress to do its work effectively.

THE CRISIS WOULD NOT GO AWAY

Throughout the fall of 2000 and early 2001, both Ford and Firestone scrambled to contain the crisis that would not go away. It was not clear which company was catching the greatest amount of heat. *Fortune* magazine called it Jacques Nasser's, Ford's then-CEO, "biggest test"—a crisis that jolts customers, suppliers, and employees and sends the company's stock reeling as it threatens the company's good name.[16] *Business-Week* referred to it as "a crisis of confidence" for Ford, as Nasser scrambled to contain the problem at Ford.[17]

Throughout most of this time, Ford was able to deflect the blame and pin most of the responsibility on the tire maker, but as investigations continued, Bridgestone/Firestone fired back. Then-Firestone Executive Vice President John Lampe said the problem was that Ford Explorers had a tendency to roll over. He pointed out that Explorers had been involved in 16,000 rollovers since the model was introduced a decade earlier and that less than 10 percent of those accidents involved tread separations of Firestone tires. Critics had been concerned about the stability of the Explorer well before Firestone announced its tire recall.[18]

FIRESTONE'S HANDLING OF THE CRISIS

For Bridgestone/Firestone, its apparent lack of savvy in handling the tire crisis seemed to make matters worse. Bridgestone president Yoichiro Kaizaki was a star in Japan. He was credited with globalizing operations and doubling profits during an earlier period. His performance in the tire crisis left a lot to be desired. His strategy was to lie low and not make public appearances. One consultant said, "This is a huge crisis, but Bridgestone and Kaizaki are handling it terribly." A former company executive said, "They just don't have a clue how to handle this." Bridgestone's apparent strategy had been to hunker down and wait for this thing to blow over. This seems to be the normal approach used in Japan. There, few managers are comfortable dealing with the press and investors. The former company executive said, "The Japanese don't understand the value of PR." Masatoshi Ono, CEO of Firestone in the United States, apparently did not perform any better than Kaizaki.[19]

OTHER FACTORS

In late 2000, representatives from Bridgestone/Firestone went into action and engaged in a lot of finger-pointing. Much of their action was to blame Ford and other factors for many of the tire problems. Some of these "other factors" included the weight of the Ford Explorer, the SUV that had figured into so many of the reported accidents and deaths. Other factors mentioned by Firestone executives were the "uneven weight distribution" on the Explorer's back axle. Firestone officials said that more weight is distributed on the left side of the Explorer, making the vehicle potentially unstable and more susceptible to a serious accident when the tires fail. Related to the weight issue, Firestone claimed that Ford recommended a tire inflation level of 26 PSI when it was calling for an inflation level of 30 PSI.[20] Ford disputed that the weight of the Explorer contributed to the tire failures.[21]

THREE OTHER FACTORS

Firestone identified three other factors it said contributed to the deadly accidents. These included unspecified "manufacturing problems" at their Decatur, Illinois, plant, the design of the tire in the shoulder area, and "customer usage." This last factor referred to the company's belief that motorists driving their vehicles at high speeds and the great amount of use to which they put the tires were contributing factors.[22]

THE LITIGATION PACKET

By early 2001, the tread separation controversy had assumed its rightful place in the long history of product litigation. In a featured article entitled "The Litigation Machine," published in *BusinessWeek*, lawyers could read about the "Firestone Tire Tread Separation" litigation packet that could be purchased from the Association of Trial Lawyers of America (ATLA). The ATLA is the powerful Washington trade group that serves as the tort bar's central brain trust. The litigation packet, all 689 pages of it, was distributed only to plaintiff lawyers. It provided a step-by-step guide to suing Bridgestone/Firestone and Ford Motor Company. After a breezy synopsis of the tire debacle, the manual proceeded to offer its lawyer-readers everything they need to get a lawsuit started.[23]

Included in the "how to sue" manual were 59 complaints from previously filed tread separation cases that, with a few minor changes to reflect local laws, could be recycled to be used anywhere in the country. Also included were a list of documents to request from Firestone, a package of useful National Highway Traffic Safety Administration documents, and a directory of informative Web sites.[24]

FIRESTONE GETS A NEW CEO

By April 2001, Firestone had a new face at the helm—John Lampe, its new CEO. The company's reputation had been badly damaged, and the company continued to fight lawsuits, but the new CEO was determined to restore credibility to the embattled company. Over the previous nine months, Firestone had recalled 6.5 million tires from Ford Explorers after some tires shredded on the highway, leading to rollovers that the NHTSA said had killed 174 people and injured 700 more. Lampe ordered Firestone's Decatur plant to change its manufacturing process and spent $50 million to upgrade several different facilities.[25]

LAMPE GOES ON DEFENSE

Lampe also went on the attack to defend his company against Ford Motor Company. Since the recall had begun, Ford placed all the blame for the Explorer rollovers on Firestone. Lampe had testified earlier that Ford had made its new Explorers too heavy to drive safely at the tire air pressure it recommended. Questions continued to be raised whether the design of the Explorer could have contributed to the crashes. According to Joan Claybrook, executive director of Public Citizen, a public advocacy group, Lampe went after Ford relentlessly. She said, "That took some guts. Very few suppliers go after the auto companies." At that time Ford was still buying one-third of its tires from Firestone and was its biggest customer, though business between the two companies was diminishing.[26]

THE CORPORATE DIVORCE

Criticism and escalating mistrust of each other led to a corporate "divorce" between Firestone and Ford in May 2001. In a May 21 meeting, it was clear the two companies were continuing to point fingers at one another and blame each other for the tire separation problems. At that emotional meeting, Lampe dropped a bombshell. He severed all ties with Ford, its largest customer. He handed Ford executives a prepared letter that said, in essence, that they would no longer do business with Ford, and then they asked to be excused from the meeting.

The letter caught Ford by surprise. Jacques Nasser recalled: "I've been around for a long time, and that's the first time I've heard anyone say they didn't want to do business with the Ford Motor Company."[27] The next day, Ford announced that it would replace 13 million Firestone tires, at a cost of $3 billion.

MAGNITUDE OF THE DIVORCE

To appreciate the magnitude of this corporate divorce, it should be noted that the two companies had had a 100-year relationship with each other. It was one of the oldest partnerships in the U.S. business history, initially forged through the personal friendships of Harvey S. Firestone and Henry Ford. Further, it was cemented by the marriage of their grandchildren William Clay Ford and Martha Parke Firestone.

Lampe later stated, "The decision I had to make to terminate our relationship with Ford was the most difficult, the most painful, decision I've ever made. But it was the only decision we could take." Ford's Nasser remained resolute. "This is a tire issue and only a tire issue," Nasser said before a congressional subcommittee. "We do not get any satisfaction from this dispute with Firestone. But we cannot and will not let them dictate when Ford Motor Company can and will act to protect our customer's safety."[28]

CLOSING OF THE DECATUR PLANT

In late June 2001, Bridgestone/Firestone announced plans to close its troubled factory in Decatur, Illinois. In terms of capacity, it was the company's third largest plant. The company decided to close the plant as it faced almost a 50 percent plunge in sales of its flagship Firestone-brand tires. The company also hoped the closure would help the company regain its financial footing and help put the tire-recall crisis behind it. Firestone also said that the Decatur plant was operating at half its capacity and was targeted because of its age and the expected cost of modernization. The

Decatur facility had been originally built as a tank factory in World War II and was converted to tire manufacturing when the company bought it in 1963.[29]

LAWSUITS AND SETTLEMENTS CONTINUED

On the lawsuit front, in August 2001, Firestone settled the first trial to come out of the Firestone tire debacle. The company agreed to pay $7.5 million to the family of a 40-year-old woman who was paralyzed and suffered brain damage in the rollover crash of a Ford Explorer. In making this settlement, the company wrapped up the first of hundreds of defective-tire lawsuits to go to trial since the recall of 6.5 million tires in August 2000. The plaintiff in this case, Dr. Joel Rodriguez, whose wife, Marisa, had suffered the injuries during a rollover crash in a Ford Explorer SUV, initially had named the Ford Motor Company as a defendant. However, Ford settled out of court before the trial for $6 million.[30] Bridgestone/Firestone had blamed the accident on the Explorer, saying that design flaws made it prone to rolling over. In settling the case, Bridgestone/Firestone admitted no liability.[31]

NASSER'S DOWNWARD SPIRAL

By fall 2001, Ford was continuing to flounder and the tire-SUV controversy was only part of the problem. The company's brand name had been sullied by the Firestone scandal, its vehicle quality ranking had plummeted, and dealers and employees had become fed up with Jacques Nasser. Though Nasser had great visions for the company, he and the company got ensnarled in events that brought them both down.

In early November 2001, Chairperson William Clay Ford, Jr., great grandson of the founder and part-time chairperson for the previous three years, fired Nasser. Bill Ford himself took over as CEO. This was a turnabout for Nasser. Just 15 months before, he was the auto industry's rising star. Some observers had compared him to a young Jack Welch. Some of his bold management innovations, however, did not endear him to his workers. One of his management initiatives was that 10 percent of all workers would receive a "C" grade on their performance evaluations; that could lead to their termination. This Darwinian HR initiative resulted in employee lawsuits. The new CEO was seen to be a healer.[32]

According to Brock Yates, editor-at-large of *Car and Driver* magazine, Nasser was a hero until the Ford Explorer/Firestone rollover squabble. From that moment on, Nasser and the company began a downward spiral that resulted in his dismissal. When you combined the severed relationship with Firestone, declining Ford product quality, and the impact of the recession, Nasser's tenure was finished.[33]

ANOTHER RECALL AND CLASS-ACTION STATUS

In October 2001, Firestone recalled an additional 3.5 million tires. It had fought the NHTSA over this additional recall for a year, but finally capitulated and agreed not to fight the recall. These tires were the Wilderness AT tires mounted on SUVs. Most of these tires were manufactured prior to 1998 and placed as original equipment on vehicles. According to Firestone, there were only about 768,000 of these tires still on the market.[34]

In late November 2001, Ford and Firestone suffered another crushing blow when U.S. District Judge Sarah Evans Barker ruled in Indianapolis that more than 500 individual lawsuits related to Explorers and Firestone and its private brand tires would be combined into a single, massive class-action lawsuit. Class-action status opens the door for millions more to join those already suing. This came as disturbing news for the automaker and tire company, both financially strapped by problems to date. According to this ruling, anyone who ever owned or leased a Ford Explorer, or had Firestone-made tires during the past 12 years, could qualify for reimbursement for economic losses from Ford or Bridgestone/Firestone. Both companies said they planned to appeal the decision.[35]

By December 2001, federal highway regulators had connected 271 deaths and hundreds of additional injuries to Firestone-Explorer accidents.[36]

EVENTS CONTINUED

In 2004, a Texas judge approved a $149 million settlement of class-action lawsuits stemming from the huge recall.[37] This settlement was only for those who were not injured or suffered property damage from the tires. The unfriendly relationship between Ford and Firestone warmed somewhat in the ensuing three years. However, Firestone did not think Ford was likely to become a customer in its U.S. market again soon. John Lampe, the CEO, said he believed that eventually Firestone will return as one of Ford's major tire suppliers at some point in time, but he wouldn't specify when.[38]

WHO OWES WHAT?

In 2001, Ford spent nearly $3 billion of its own money replacing almost 13 million Firestone tires that it said could not be trusted. To this day, some are saying that a reasonable argument could be made that Firestone owes that money to Ford. At a minimum, it has been argued that Bridgestone/Firestone owes Ford $600 million, which represents the 2.7 million Ford-replaced tires that the NHTSA formally ruled were unsafe.[39] John Lampe, in an interview in January 2004, said, "Ford's decision to do their replacement program in 2001 was their decision. They did it on their own. We were not in favor of it. Everybody knows that. We took the responsibility in 2000. They took the responsibility in 2001."[40]

DISPUTE SETTLED

In late 2006, it was reported that Bridgestone's financial results had only recently recovered from the losses related to the massive tire-recall scandal at its U.S. subsidiary, Bridgestone Firestone North America six years earlier.[41] Bridgestone paid $240 million to Ford Motor Co. in 2005 to settle its dispute in lawsuits related to the 2000–2001 recalls. The payment was intended to help cover the costs of Ford's 2001 tire replacement program. The settlement is said to have ended the dispute between the two companies.[42]

A MOVIE ON THE TRAGEDY

It was announced that a feature film was being made showing the many sides of the Ford–Firestone tire calamity. It was reported that Michael Douglas would produce and star in the film based on Adam Penenberg's book, *Tragic Indifference*.[43] The courtroom thriller was pitched as a David versus Goliath story of the lawsuit brought on by attorney Tab Turner against the Ford and Firestone corporations for negligence in connection with the SUV rollovers and defective tires. The story focused on the case of Donna Bailey, who became a quadriplegic as a result of a near-fatal accident in a Ford SUV and sought only an admission of guilt and apology from the companies.[44] The film finally was released in 2008. A *New York Times* review summary of the movie had the following to report:

> Tragic Indifference *details the landmark court case that served to expose the Ford Motor Company's willful indifference to potentially fatal flaws in the* design of their popular sport utility vehicles. When single Texas mother Donna Bailey nearly died after the SUV she was in flipped over, she was rendered paralyzed as a direct result of a flaw in Ford engineering. Attorney Tab Turner (played by Michael Douglas) represented her and sought out a public courtroom forum, which not only resulted in an enormous settlement for the crash victim, but also included a personal apology from the prolific auto manufacturer's top brass.[45]

INSIDER REVEALS LESSONS

In 2010, the Firestone and Ford debacle is still being debated. Professionals in crisis management, business ethics, and public relations are still trying to cull from this long-standing tragedy lessons that will be valuable in the future. A webcast titled "Red Alert! Ford–Firestone Insider Reveals Hard-Won Lessons and Seven Crisis Response Steps for PR in the Web 2.0 Era" was developed and presented in early 2010. In this 90-minute video, Jon Harmon uses the Ford–Firestone case study to share his hard-won crisis response lessons—and show PR professionals how they and their team can similarly master damage control in today's Web 2.0, multidimensional communications environment.[46]

QUESTIONS FOR DISCUSSION

1. What are the major and minor ethical issues involved in this case?
2. Who are the stakeholders and what are their stakes? How do legitimacy, power, and urgency factor in? Do these companies care about consumers? Discuss.
3. Conduct a CSR analysis of both Firestone and Ford. How do they measure up in fulfilling their various social responsibilities?
4. Who is at fault in the tire separation controversy? Bridgestone/Firestone? Ford Motor Company? The NHSTA?
5. Do you think Firestone had an ethical responsibility to pay Ford $3 billion (or $600 million) for the tires it replaced on its own because the company did not think they were safe?
6. Research the current status of both Bridgestone/Firestone and Ford. What has happened since the end of the case?

7. What lessons do we learn about product safety, business ethics, and issues management from this case? What lessons should Toyota Motor Company take away from this case that would help it with its recent automotive product failures and recalls?

ENDNOTES

1. "Firestone Tire Recall," "Overview of the Recall," http://www.firestone-tire-recall.com/pages/overview.html. Accessed July 13, 2010.
2. Daniel Eisenberg, "Anatomy of a Recall," *Time* (September 11, 2000), 29.
3. Keith Nauthton and Mark Hosenball, "Ford vs. Firestone," *Newsweek* (September 18, 2000), 27–28.
4. Eisenberg, 29–30.
5. *Ibid.*, 30.
6. "Bridgestone/Firestone Voluntary Tire Recall," Bridgestone/Firestone Web page, http://mirror.bridgestone-firestone.com/news/corporate/news/00809b.htm.
7. Eisenberg, 31.
8. *Ibid.*
9. Joann Muller, Jeff Green, Nicole St. Pierre, and Pamela Moore, "Firestone and Ford: The Ride Gets Bumpier," *BusinessWeek* (September 11, 2000), 42.
10. David Kiley, Earle Eldridge, and Thomas Fogarty, "Congress Seeks Details on Tire Recall Situation," *USA Today* (September 5, 2000), 8B.
11. Marianne Lavelle, "Apologies Will Not Be Accepted: Firestone Clearly Knew Something Was Amiss," *U.S. News & World Report* (September 18, 2000), 62.
12. Keith Naughton, "Spinning Out of Control," *Newsweek* (September 11, 2000), 58.
13. *Ibid.*
14. Jim Morris and Marianne Lavelle, "Secret Data Reveal Why Tires Went Bad," *U.S. News & World Report* (September 25, 2000), 42–43.
15. *Ibid.*
16. Soo-Min Oh, "Jac Nasser's Biggest Test," *Fortune* (September 18, 2000), 123–128.
17. "A Crisis of Confidence," *BusinessWeek* (September 18, 2000), 40–42.
18. Joann Muller, David Welch, and Jeff Green, "Crisis Management: Would You Buy One?" *BusinessWeek* (September 25, 2000), 46.
19. Irene Kunii and Dean Foust, "They Just Don't Know How to Handle This," *BusinessWeek* (September 18, 2000), 43.
20. Stephen Power and Timothy Aeppel, "Firestone Cites Explorer's Weight as Contributor to Tire Accidents," *The Wall Street Journal* (December 19, 2000), A4.
21. Todd Zaun, "Bridgestone Chief Repeats: Others Share Blame on Tires," *The Wall Street Journal* (December 21, 2000), A15.
22. Power and Aeppel.
23. Mike France, "The Litigation Machine," *BusinessWeek* (January 29, 2001), 114–123.
24. *Ibid.*
25. David Welch, "Meet the New Face of Firestone," *BusinessWeek* (April 30, 2001), 64–66.
26. *Ibid.*, 66.
27. Caroline Mayer and Frank Swoboda, "Anatomy of a Divorce," *The Washington Post Weekly Edition* (June 25–July 1, 2001), 17.
28. *Ibid.*
29. Timothy Aeppel and Todd Zaun, "Firestone Plans to Close Troubled Decatur Factory," *The Wall Street Journal* (June 28, 2001), A3.
30. Richard Oppel, "Bridgestone Agrees to Pay $7.5 Million in Explorer Crash," *The New York Times* (August 25, 2001).
31. "Family Settles with Firestone for $7.5 Million," *The Atlanta Journal-Constitution* (August 25, 2001), E4.
32. Keith Naughton, "Hit the Road, Jacques," *Newsweek* (November 12, 2001), 44.
33. Brock Yates, "It's Curtains for Jac the Knife," *The Wall Street Journal* (October 31, 2001), A24.
34. Nedra Pickler, "Firestone Recalls 3.5 Million More Tires," *The Washington Post* (October 4, 2001).
35. David Kiley, "Judge Expands Lawsuit vs. Ford, Firestone," *USA Today* (November 29, 2001), 3B. Also see Joseph B. White, "Suits Against Ford, Firestone Are Given Class-Action Status," *The Wall Street Journal* (November 29, 2001), B14.
36. White.
37. "Judge OKs $149 Million Firestone Settlement," *Automotive News* (March 22, 2004), 30.
38. Richard Truett, "BFS, Ford Warm Up to Each Other," *Rubber & Plastic News* (March 15, 2004).
39. Harry Stoffer, "Ford Should Collect from Firestone," *Automotive News* (April 21, 2003), 14.
40. Quoted in *Ibid.*, 14.

41. Carl Freire, "Japan's Bridgestone Reports 69 Percent Profit Drop for Jan-Sept," *Associated Press Newswires* (November 1, 2006).

42. Associated Press, "Bridgestone and Ford Settle Dispute over Defective Tires," *The New York Times* (October 13, 2005).

43. Jason Stein, "Feature Film Will Tell Ford-Firestone Story," *Automotive News* (April 26, 2004), 1.

44. "Tragic Indifference," Hollywood.com, http://www.hollywood.com/movie/Tragic_Indifference/3462877. Accessed July 13, 2010.

45. Jason Buchanan, "Tragic Indifference," *The New York Times* (2008), http://movies.nytimes.com/movie/395679/Tragic-Indifference/overview. Accessed July 13, 2010.

46. "Ford-Firestone Insider Reveals Hard-Won Lessons and Seven Crisis Response Steps for PR in the Web 2.0 Era," *Marketwire* (February 4, 2010), http://www.marketwire.com/press-release/Ford-Firestone-Insider-Reveals-Hard-Won-Lessons-Seven-Crisis-Response-Steps-PR-Web-20-1108410.htm. Accessed July 13, 2010.

CASE 14

McDonald's: The Coffee Spill Heard 'Round the World*

This case is about the most famous consumer lawsuit in the world. Everyone knows about this case, and the details involved in it are presented and debated in many different venues—classrooms, Web sites, blogs, law schools, and business schools. Regardless, it serves as one of the best platforms in the world for discussing what companies owe their consumer stakeholders and what responsibilities consumers have for their own well-being.

Now almost 20 years later, lawyers are still debating the coffee spill case. On one personal injury lawyer's blog, the following commentary was posted in 2010:

> By now we've all probably heard about the McDonald's hot coffee lawsuit wherein the victim [Stella Liebeck] recovered millions of dollars for a coffee spill in her lap. The word "frivolous" comes to mind. The reality is this. Americans are being duped by myths and falsehoods spread by insurance companies and corporations, who have spent millions of dollars to mislead the American public. The facts tell a different story. Unfortunately, the facts are no laughing matter.[1]

---
* This case was written and updated (in 2010) by Archie B. Carroll, University of Georgia.

STELLA LIEBECK

Stella Liebeck and her grandson, Chris Tiano, drove her son, Jim, to the airport 60 miles away in Albuquerque, New Mexico, on the morning of February 27, 1992. Because she had to leave home early, she and Chris missed having breakfast. Upon dropping Jim off at the airport, they proceeded to a McDonald's drive-through for breakfast. Stella, a spry, 79-year-old, retired department-store clerk, ordered a McBreakfast, and Chris parked the car so she could add cream and sugar to her coffee.[2]

What occurred next was the coffee spill that has been heard 'round the world. A coffee spill, serious burns, a lawsuit, and an eventual settlement made Stella Liebeck the "poster lady" for the bitter tort reform discussions that have dominated the news for 20 years. To this day, the case is subject to a continuing debate.

THIRD-DEGREE BURNS

According to Liebeck's testimony, she tried to get the coffee lid off. She could not find any flat surface in the car, so she put the cup between her knees and tried to get it off that way. As she tugged at the lid, scalding coffee spilled into her lap. Chris jumped from the car and tried to help her. She pulled at her sweatsuit, but the pants absorbed the coffee and held it close to her skin. She was squirming as the 170-degree coffee burned her groin, inner thigh, and buttocks. Third-degree burns were evident as she reached an emergency room. A vascular surgeon determined she had third-degree (full thickness) burns over 6 percent of her body.

HOSPITALIZATION

Following the spill, Liebeck spent eight days in the hospital and about three weeks at home recuperating under the care of her daughter, Nancy Tiano. She was then hospitalized again for skin grafts. Liebeck lost 20 pounds during the ordeal and at times was practically immobilized. Another daughter, Judy Allen, recalled that her mother was in tremendous pain both after the accident and during the skin grafts.[3]

According to a *Newsweek* report, Liebeck wrote to McDonald's in August 1994, asking them to turn down the coffee temperature. Though she was not planning to sue, her family thought she was due about $2,000 for out-of-pocket expenses, plus the lost wages of her daughter who stayed at home with her. The family reported that McDonald's offered her $800.[4]

STELLA FILES A LAWSUIT

After this, the family went looking for a lawyer and retained Reed Morgan, a Houston attorney, who had won a $30,000 settlement against McDonald's in 1988 for a woman whose spilled coffee had caused her third-degree burns. Morgan filed a lawsuit on behalf of Liebeck, charging McDonald's with "gross negligence" for selling coffee that was "unreasonably dangerous" and "defectively manufactured." Morgan asked for no less than $100,000 in compensatory damages, including pain and suffering, and triple that amount in punitive damages.

McDonald's Motion Rejected

McDonald's moved for summary dismissal of the case, defending the coffee's heat and blaming Liebeck for spilling it. According to the company, she was the "proximate cause" of the injury. With McDonald's motion rejected, a trial date was set for August 1994.

As the trial date approached, no out-of-court settlement occurred. Morgan, the attorney, said that at one point he offered to drop the case for $300,000 and was willing to settle for half that amount, but McDonald's would not budge. Days before the trial, the judge ordered the two parties to attend a mediation session. The mediator, a retired judge, recommended McDonald's settle for $225,000, using the argument that a jury would likely award that amount. Again, McDonald's resisted settlement.[5]

THE TRIAL

The trial lasted seven days, with expert witnesses dueling over technical issues, such as the temperature at which coffee causes burns. Initially, the jury was annoyed at having to hear what at first was thought to be a frivolous case about spilled coffee, but the evidence presented by the prosecution grabbed its attention. Photos of Liebeck's charred skin were introduced. A renowned burn expert testified that coffee at 170 degrees would cause second-degree burns within 3.5 seconds of hitting the skin.

THE DEFENSE HELPED LIEBECK

Defense witnesses inadvertently helped the prosecution. A quality-assurance supervisor at McDonald's testified that the company did not lower its coffee heat despite 700 burn complaints over ten years. A safety consultant argued that 700 complaints—about one in every 24 million cups sold—were basically trivial. This comment was apparently interpreted to imply that McDonald's cared more about statistics than about people. An executive for McDonald's testified that the company knew its coffee sometimes caused serious burns, but it was not planning to go beyond the tiny print warning on the cup that said, "Caution: Contents Hot!" The executive went on to say that McDonald's did not intend to change any of its coffee policies or procedures, saying, "There are more serious dangers in restaurants."

In the closing arguments, one of the defense attorneys acknowledged that the coffee was hot and that that is how customers wanted it. She went on to insist that Liebeck had only herself to blame as she was unwise to put the cup between her knees. She also noted that Liebeck failed to leap out of the bucket seat in the car after the spill, thus preventing the hot coffee from falling off her. The attorney concluded by saying that the real question in the case is how far society should go to restrict what most of us enjoy and accept.[6]

THE JURY DECIDES

The jury deliberated about four hours and reached a verdict for Liebeck. It decided on compensatory damages of $200,000, which it reduced to $160,000 after judging that 20 percent of the fault belonged to Liebeck for spilling the coffee. The jury concluded that McDonald's had engaged in willful, reckless, malicious, or wanton conduct, which is the basis for punitive damages. The jury decided upon a figure of $2.7 million in punitive damages.

Company Neglected Customers

One juror later said that the facts were overwhelmingly against the company and that the company just was not taking care of its customers. Another juror felt the huge punitive damages were intended to be a stern warning for McDonald's to wake up and realize its customers were getting burned. Another juror said he began to realize that the case was really about the callous disregard for the safety of customers.

Public opinion polls after the jury verdict were squarely on the side of McDonald's. Polls showed that a large majority of Americans—including many who usually support the little guy—were outraged at the verdict.[7] But, of course, the public did not hear all the details presented in the trial.

JUDGE REDUCES AWARD

The judge later slashed the jury award by more than 75 percent to $640,000. Liebeck appealed the reduction, and McDonald's continued fighting the award as excessive. In December 1994, it was announced that McDonald's had reached an out-of-court settlement with Liebeck, but the terms of the settlement were not disclosed due to a confidentiality provision. The settlement was reached to end appeals in the case. We will never know the final ending to this case because the parties entered into a secret settlement that has never been revealed to the public. Since this was a public case, litigated in public and subjected to extensive media reporting, some lawyers think that such secret settlements, after public trials, should not be condoned.[8]

Debate over Temperature

Coffee suddenly became a hot topic in the industry. The Specialty Coffee Association of America put coffee safety on its agenda for discussion. A spokesperson for the National Coffee Association said that McDonald's coffee conforms to industry temperature standards. A spokesperson for Mr. Coffee, the coffee-machine maker, said that if customer complaints are any indication, industry settings may be too low. Some customers like it hotter. A coffee connoisseur who imported and wholesaled coffee said that 175 degrees is probably the optimum temperature for coffee because that's when aromatics are being released. Coffee served at home is generally 135–140 degrees. McDonald's continued to say that it is serving its coffee the way customers like it. As one writer noted, the temperature of McDonald's coffee helps to explain why it sells a billion cups a year.[9]

LATER INCIDENTS

In August 2000, a Vallejo, California, woman sued McDonald's, saying she suffered second-degree burns when a handicapped employee at a drive-through window dropped a large cup of coffee in her lap. The suit charged that the handicapped employee could not grip the cardboard tray and was instead trying to balance it on top of her hands and forearms when the accident occurred in August 1999. The victim, Karen Muth, said she wanted at least $10,000 for her medical bills, pain and suffering, and "humiliation." But her lawyer, Dan Ryan, told the local newspaper that she was entitled to between $400,000 and $500,000. Attorney Ryan went on to say, "We recognize that there's an Americans with Disabilities Act, but that doesn't give them (McDonald's) the right to sacrifice the safety of their customers." It is not known how this lawsuit was settled.

Suits Go Global

It was also announced in August 2000 that British solicitors have organized 26 spill complainants into a group suit against McDonald's over the piping hot nature of its beverages. One London lawyer said, "Hot coffee, hot tea, and hot water are at the center of this case. We are alleging they are too hot." Since that time other lawsuits have been filed around the world.

Burned by a Hot Pickle

In a related turn of events, a Knoxville, Tennessee, woman, Veronica Martin, filed a lawsuit in 2000 claiming that she was permanently scarred when a hot pickle from a McDonald's hamburger fell on her chin. She claimed the burn caused her physical and mental harm. Martin sued for $110,000. Martin's husband, Darrin, also sought $15,000 because he "has been deprived of the services and consortium of his wife." According to Veronica Martin's lawsuit, the hamburger "was in a defective condition or unreasonably dangerous to the general consumer and, in particular, to her." The lawsuit went on to say, "while attempting to eat the hamburger, the pickle dropped from the hamburger onto her chin. The pickle was extremely hot and burned the chin of Veronica Martin." Martin had second-degree burns and was permanently scarred, according to the lawsuit. One report was that the McDonald's owner settled this case out of court.[10]

ISSUE WON'T GO AWAY

THE STELLA AWARDS

For over 15 years now, the coffee spill heard 'round the world continues to be a subject of heated debate. The coffee spill and subsequent trial, publicity, and resolution "prompted a tort reform storm that has barely abated."[11] One school of thought held that it represents the most frivolous lawsuit of all time. In fact, a program called the "Stella Awards" was begun to recognize each year's most outrageous lawsuit. The awards were the creation of humorist Randy Cassingham, and his summaries of award-winning cases may be found at http://www.stellaawards.com.[12] In actuality, most of the lawsuits he chronicles are far more outrageous than the coffee spill in which an elderly lady did get seriously injured. On the other hand, consumer groups are still concerned about victims of what they see as dangerous products, and they continue to assail McDonald's callous unconcern for Stella Liebeck.

In the ensuing decade and a half, lawsuits over spilt beverages have continued to come and go, but most of them have been resolved with less fanfare than Stella's case. As for S. Reed Morgan, the lawyer who successfully represented Stella Liebeck, he has handled only three cases involving beverages since Liebeck's suit. Morgan has turned down many plaintiffs, but said he is interested in such cases only if they involve third-degree burns.

ANOTHER SCALDED-GRANNY CASE

It was reported in summer of 2004 that Morgan has a new McDonald's coffee case that resembles the Liebeck case. This case involves Maxine Villegas, a grandmother in her 70s, who was a passenger in a car stopped at a drive-through, where coffee splashed on her legs and resulted in third-degree burns. In a deposition, Villegas testified coffee spilled on her legs when her sister was passing her the cup of coffee.[13]

Whether the Villegas case will turn out to be another Liebeck case or not remains to be seen. Matt Fleischer-Black, writing in *The American Lawyer*, perhaps summarized its potential well:

> *Villegas' complaint against McDonald's may generate nothing more than jokes for Jay Leno and David Letterman. Yet in light of the influence of the earlier suit, this scalded-granny case may keep a 90 million-cup-a-day industry on alert for another decade to come.*[14]

The outcome of the Villegas case has not been made public. Lawsuits of this type are often stretched out over years or get dropped with no public announcement.

A LAWSUIT IN MOSCOW

These types of lawsuits may never end. They have even gone global. In fact, a long-running case against McDonald's in Moscow was closed in 2006 by a Moscow court after the claimant withdrew her $34,000 lawsuit. Olga Kuznetsova filed a lawsuit against the company after hot coffee was spilled on her in a Russian McDonald's. Kuznetsova claimed that a swinging door hit her while she was walking out onto the restaurant's terrace with a full tray. She demanded 900,000 rubles (about $34,000) in damages. McDonald's lawyers said she had nobody to blame but herself because the paper cup carried a warning that the coffee was hot, which prompted her to go to court.[15]

QUESTIONS FOR DISCUSSION

1. What are the major issues in the Liebeck case and in the following incidents? Was the lawsuit "frivolous" as some people thought, or serious business?

2. What are McDonald's social (economic, legal, and ethical) responsibilities toward consumers in the Liebeck case and the other cases? What are consumers' responsibilities when they buy a product such as hot coffee or hot hamburgers? How does a company give consumers what they want and yet protect them at the same time?

3. What are the arguments supporting McDonald's position in the Liebeck case? What are the arguments supporting Liebeck's position?

4. If you had been a juror in the Liebeck case, which position would you most likely have supported? Why? What if you had been a juror in the pickle burn case?

5. What are the similarities and differences between the coffee burn cases and the pickle burn case? Does one represent a more serious threat to consumer harm? What should McDonald's, and other fast food restaurants, do about hot food, such as hamburgers, when consumers are injured?

6. What is your assessment of the "Stella Awards"? Is this making light of a serious problem?

7. What are the implications of these cases for future product-related lawsuits? Do we now live in a society where businesses are responsible for customers' accidents or carelessness in using products? We live in a society that is growing older. Does this fact place a special responsibility on merchants who sell products to senior citizens?

Endnotes

1. Kerckhoff Law, "McDonald's Burning Hot Coffee Lawsuit Revisited," San Diego Personal Injury Lawyers Blog, http://www.sandiegopersonalinjury-lawyersblog.com/2010/03/mcdonalds, March 30, 2010. Accessed July 22, 2010.

2. Andrea Gerlin, "A Matter of Degree: How a Jury Decided That a Coffee Spill Is Worth $2.9 Million," *The Wall Street Journal* (September 1, 1994), A1, A4.

3. Theresa Howard, "McDonald's Settles Coffee Suit in Out-of-Court Agreement," *Nation's Restaurant News* (December 12, 1994), 1.

4. Aric Press and Ginny Carroll, "Are Lawyers Burning America?" *Newsweek* (March 20, 1995), 30–35.

5. Howard, 1.

6. "Coffee-Spill Suits Meet ADA," Overlawyered.com, http://www.overlawyered.com/archives/00aug1.html.

7. Gerlin, A4.

8. "The Actual Facts about the McDonald's Coffee Case," The 'Lectric Law Library, http://www.lectlaw.com/files/cur78.htm. Accessed July 16, 2010.

9. *Ibid.*

10. Associated Press, "Couple Seeks $125,000 for Pickle Burn on Chin," *Athens Banner Herald* (October 8, 2000), 6A. Also see Associated Press, "Couple Sues over Hot Pickle Burn" (October 7, 2000), http://www.washingtonpost.com.

11. Matt Fleisher-Black, "One Lump or Two?" *The American Lawyer* (June 4, 2004).

12. "The Stella Awards for 2003," *Business Insurance* (February 16, 2004), 16. Also see "See the Funny Side of Tort," *Reactions* (December 2003), 46.

13. Fleisher-Black.

14. *Ibid.*

15. "Moscow McDonald's Coffee-Spill Case Closed," *RIA Novosti* (January 11, 2006), http://en.rian.ru/russia/20061101/55304783.html. Accessed July 16, 2010.

New Belgium Brewery: Building a Business on Sustainability*

When Jeff Lebesch and his wife, Kim Jordan, expanded from home beer brewing to commercial production in 1991, they envisioned two goals for their new company: they believed they could produce world-class beers and that they could do this while kindling social, environmental, and cultural change. By 2009 (just 18 years later), their company, New Belgium Brewing Company (NBB), had become the third largest craft brewery in the United States and the seventh largest producer in the overall industry.[1] The brewery also stood as a corporate leader in environmental sustainability, and provided a prime example of how a company could incorporate environmental concerns

* This case was prepared by Jonathan Bundy, University of Georgia.

into everyday business decisions.[2] However, as NBB entered the new decade, the company faced a number of challenges in reaching its environmental goals, many of which it could not directly control.

HISTORY OF NEW BELGIUM BREWERY

Jeff was inspired to found NBB while on a 1989 bike ride through the Belgian countryside.[3] During his trek, he perceived a lack of flavor in American beers compared to those he was drinking in Europe. When he returned home to Colorado, he set out on a quest to introduce American beer drinkers to the unique essence found in traditional Belgian brews, from the tart framboise, the light saison, and the truly one-of-a-kind trappist ales. Using his home brewing experience, Jeff was able to develop a distinctive recipe for traditional Belgian amber ale. The ale, dubbed Fat Tire in commemoration to the inspirational bike trip, became the brewery's flagship beer. By 1991, Jeff and Kim formally organized the brewery as NBB and began selling the first bottles of Fat Tire around their hometown of Fort Collins, Colorado.

Kim, serving as the businessperson of the two, engaged in the marketing and distribution operations, selling the beer to friends, neighbors, and local bars/stores. A neighbor provided the watercolors that adorn the beers' labels, a tradition that lives on today. The beers were brewed in the couple's basement, using an 8.5-barrel system (one barrel is 31 gallons), allowing for total production of 993 barrels in 1992.[4] By 2007, NBB was producing nearly 500,000 barrels, which were sold in 19 states.[5] In 1991, the company produced only two types of beer, the signature Fat Tire Amber Ale and the darker Abbey Dubbel. Today, NBB produces 18 different styles, 8 being produced year round. The brewery is still located in Fort Collins, Colorado, and all beer is produced on-site.

CORE VALUES

Unique in the founding story of NBB is the commitment to a set of values that were adopted from the beginning. Before initial production and during the planning stages of the business, Kim and Jeff developed a set of core values and beliefs by which they would guide their company. It is obvious from this set of values, listed below, that profitability is secondary to a sense of commitment and responsibility to an ideal. This responsibility is centered on two core concepts: the production of quality beer and beer culture, and a

business that can produce this beer while paying attention to environmental and social concerns. All business decisions are made according to the core values and beliefs, and everything is done with the mission "to operate a profitable company which is socially, ethically, and environmentally responsible, and that produces high quality beer true to Belgian styles."[6] This set of core values and beliefs was instituted on day one of production, even before the company had any actual employees. The values continue to live even today, unchanged from their original conception, guiding the company with 300-plus employees into the new era of craft brewing.

Our Core Values and Beliefs[7]

- *Remembering* that we are incredibly lucky to create something fine that enhances people's lives while surpassing our consumers' expectations.
- *Producing* world-class beers.
- *Promoting* beer culture and the responsible enjoyment of beer.
- *Kindling* social, environmental, and cultural change as a role model of a sustainable business.
- *Environmental stewardship*: Honoring nature at every turn of the business.
- *Cultivating* potential through learning, high involvement culture, and the pursuit of opportunities.
- *Balancing* the myriad needs of the company, our coworkers, and families.
- *Trusting* each other and committing to authentic relationships and communications.
- *Continuous*, innovative quality and efficiency improvements.
- *Having fun.*

NEW BELGIUM'S SUSTAINABILITY EFFORTS

NBB has engaged in environmentally sustainable efforts since their founding, and these efforts have served as a central concern of the organization. NBB has attempted to implement sustainable efforts in all aspects of the brewing process, focusing on the major inputs and outputs. Some of their efforts include the following.[8]

ELECTRICITY

In 1998, NBB conducted a study to analyze its carbon emissions. It was found that the single largest factor was emissions generated from its electricity consumption, emissions released by coal-fired power plants. In response, NBB owners (which included the founders and approximately 90 employees) unanimously voted to source their electricity from 100 percent renewable, carbon-free wind sources. At a premium of 57 percent on its electricity bill, NBB became the first completely wind powered brewery. In addition to the renewable sourcing, NBB has also begun an extensive energy conservation program. In 2008, the company invested $1 million in energy-sparing equipment. NBB also introduced a combination of solar PV, cogeneration, metering, and control initiatives in an attempt to become a net-zero purchaser of electricity. A further example of its efficiency and conservation efforts includes the development of a "natural draft cooling" system, which utilizes outside air for refrigeration when the temperature is below 40 degrees.

Natural Gas

NBB's top initiative to conserve natural gas is its use of a Steinecker "Merlin" brew kettle. The Merlin kettle uses an internal cone-shaped boiler designed to maximize heated surface area for the wort.[9] Instead of heating from the outside, wort is heated within the kettle, which accelerates the boiling process. In addition, the kettle is designed to minimize and capture evaporation, thus reducing waste. NBB has been able to cut its boiling time by half with the new kettle. NBB has also instituted a number of efficiencies in its bottling operations, which consumes large amounts of natural gas for sanitization. Examples of efficiencies include steam capture and heated water reuse.

Water

As stated above, the average brewery uses five gallons of water to produce one gallon of beer. NBB's ratio is only 3.8:1.[10] The majority of its water use efficiencies come from its conservation efforts.[11] The company has analyzed all of its water consumption activities and has attempted to reduce use at every stage of production. NBB also has invested in an on-site water treatment facility. Wastewater is treated in its "bio-digester" plant before being released into Fort Collins wastewater streams. NBB tries to use this processed water where it can throughout the brewery. In addition, the process creates methane, which is captured and used to cogenerate power for the brewery. NBB hopes that its efforts will help to further reduce its water-to-product ration to 3.5:1 over the next several years.

Waste and Recycling

NBB has made a number of conscious efforts to reduce input materials. It also believes in recycling; it sent only 8.5 percent of its waste to landfills in 2008.[12] The majority of its waste consists of spent grain (38,000,000 pounds in 2007), which is sold as feedstock for cattle. The remainder of its recycled waste includes a combination of glass, cardboard, and general office and industrial waste. Because NBB uses amber glass, it is difficult for them to source recycled glass for their bottles. Amber glass has to be separated from other glass to be successfully recycled, and NBB estimates that its new bottles have a recycled content of only about 10 percent. However, the company sources its bottle production locally to reduce transportation emissions and is active in advocacy for additional recycling efforts.

Carbon Emissions (Six Pack of Fat Tire Amber Ale)

In 2007, NBB partnered with The Climate Conservancy to assess the greenhouse gases emitted across the lifecycle of its signature Fat Tire Amber Ale.[13] The assessment was born from a goal to reduce the carbon footprint per barrel by 50 percent. It was found that over half of the total emissions came from "downstream" activities: distribution and retail storage. The majority of the remaining contribution comes from production and transportation of the raw inputs (barley and hops), bottles, and cardboard. Only 5 percent actually comes from brewing, with a quarter of this being the actual CO_2 found in the beer itself. Surprisingly, 26 percent of the carbon equivalent emissions come from refrigeration at retail locations, something that is completely beyond the control of NBB. By understanding where the emissions are coming from, NBB is better able to target specific initiatives to reduce its impact. Some future initiatives include trying to source more organic inputs, more recycled content in their glass and packaging, and better supplier awareness and communication. After a detailed study of the carbon footprint, NBB believes that a reduction of 25 percent in carbon equivalent emissions is a more realistic goal.

MAKING A BIGGER SPLASH

While NBB has made significant inroads in reducing the company's carbon footprint, much remains to be done. Specifically, NBB wants to make a stronger impact on the upstream (materials sourcing) and downstream (recycling) factors, factors controlled by suppliers and consumers. Beer products, by nature, involve a great deal of packaging, most of which is still ending up in landfills. NBB, as well as the entire craft brewing industry, realizes that it must do what it can to encourage more consumer recycling. One possibility is the enactment of a national "bottle bill," which would require consumers to pay a refundable deposit on glass bottles. When the consumer returns the bottle for recycling, they receive their deposit back and thus have a material incentive to recycle. The brewing and packaging industries in general do not support these kinds of bills, and many within the two industries have actively attempted to stop their passage. Opponents see the deposit as a kind of tax or price increase on the product. NBB, however, has shown an inclination for support, saying that "perhaps it is time for the domestic and craft brewers to support Bottle Bills to reduce our industry CO_2 footprint."[14] In the meantime, NBB continues to use as much recycled glass as it can.

An additional effort to impact consumer decisions to recycle relies on packaging. In an initiative begun in 2008, NBB started selling a small percentage of Fat Tire Amber Ale in lightweight 12-ounce aluminum cans.[15] Because cans weigh less than bottles, they are more efficient to transport around the country. It has been found that transporting a bottle emits 20 percent more greenhouse gases than transporting a can.[16] Consumers are also much more likely to recycle cans than bottles. Studies have shown that over half of all drinking cans are recycled and new cans generally contain more recycled content than new bottles (40 percent for cans versus 10–30 percent for bottles). However, switching from bottles to cans is easier said than done. The issue is perception; many consumers believe that the product does not taste the same out of cans compared to bottles. NBB has crafted its image around uniquely styled bottles, complete with the company's embossed logo and watercolor labels. By switching to cans, NBB would have to be willing to sacrifice this unique characteristic of the company. NBB would also be only one of a few craft brewers selling product out of cans, something that is much more commonly associated with the larger brewers. Still, NBB believes that it can sell the same quality beverage using special coating and new technology.[17]

Questions for Discussion

1. What are the ethical issues in this case?
2. What keeps other companies from having the commitment to environmental sustainability that NBB has evidenced?
3. Are you more likely to purchase a product from a company with a strong commitment to sustainability?
4. The environmental sustainability benefits of cans over bottles are well established. Should NBB make a greater commitment to cans even if it means forgoing the distinctive aspects of its bottles and the potential loss of craft beer status in customers' perceptions?
5. Are New Belgium Brewing's Core Values and Beliefs sustainable? Or will the company be forced by competition to revert to many of the traditional practices of other brewers?

Endnotes

1. Press Release, "Brewers Association Releases 2009 Top 50 Breweries List," *Brewers Association* (April 14, 2010).
2. "The Green 50: The Integrators," *Inc. Magazine* (November 1, 2006), 84.
3. Newbeligum.com, http://www.newbelgium.com/our-story. Accessed July 7, 2010.
4. Christopher Asher, Elina Bidner, and Christopher Greene, "New Belgium Brewing Company: Brewing with a Conscience," *University of Colorado, Graduate School of Public Affairs* (January 2003), 7.
5. "2007 Sustainability Report," *New Belgium Brewing Company*, 4.
6. Asher, Bidner, and Greene, 1.
7. New Belgium Brewing Company, "Company Core Values and Beliefs," http://www.newbelgium.com/our-story. Accessed July 12, 2010.
8. The data provided in this section comes from the 2007 Sustainability Report.
9. Steinnecker Marketing Pamphlet, available at http://www.krones.com/downloads/wuerzeko-chung_e.pdf.
10. "2008 Sustainability NonReport," *New Belgium Brewing Company*, http://www.newbelgium.com/blog/sustainability. Accessed July 13, 2010.
11. Asher, Bidner, and Green, 11.
12. 2008 Sustainability NonReport.
13. "The Carbon Footprint of Fat Tire Amber Ale," *The Climate Conservancy* (2007). See also Jeffery

Ball, "Six Products, Six Carbon Footprints," *The Wall Street Journal* (October 6, 2008), R1.

14. 2007 Sustainability Report, 10.

15. Steve Raabe, "New Belgium Brewing Turns to Cans," *The Denver Post* (May 15, 2008). Available at http://www.denverpost.com/commented/ci_9262005?source=commented-.

16. Brendan Koerner, "Wear Green, Drink Greenly: The Eco-Guide to Responsible Drinking," *The Slate* (March 16, 2009), http://www.slate.com/id/2186219. Accessed July 7, 2010.

17. Alissa Walker, "Ditch the Bottle? Microbreweries Say Can-Do," *Fast Company* (August 10, 2009), http://www.fastcompany.com/blog/alissa-walker/designerati/real-can-do-attitude-more-microbreweries-saying-no-bottles. Accessed July 7, 2010.

Business Ethics and Management

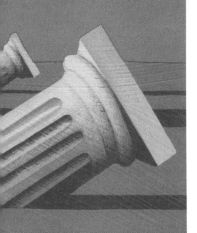

7

Business Ethics Fundamentals

CHAPTER LEARNING OUTCOMES

After studying this chapter, you should be able to:

1. Describe how the public regards business ethics.

2. Define business ethics and appreciate the complexities of making ethical judgments.

3. Explain the conventional approach to business ethics.

4. Analyze economic, legal, and ethical aspects by using a Venn model.

5. Enumerate and discuss the four important ethics questions.

6. Identify and explain three models of management ethics.

7. Describe Kohlberg's three levels of developing moral judgment.

8. Identify and discuss the elements of moral judgment.

Public interest in business ethics is at an all time high. In considering the past 30 years of business ethics, two conclusions may be drawn. First, interest in business ethics has heightened during each of the past three decades. Second, the interest in business ethics seems to have been spurred by major headline-grabbing scandals. Certainly, there has been an ebb and flow of interest on society's part, but lately this interest has grown to a preoccupation or, as some might say, an obsession. With the ethics scandal tsunami of the early 2000s, beginning with Enron, we witnessed the birth and accelerated maturation of the "ethics industry."[1] The impact of the Enron scandal was so great on business ethics that it has been dubbed the "Enron Effect."[2] The effects and lessons learned from the Enron scandal have been so colossal, that business will never be the same.

We thought we would never soon see anything like the Enron era of scandals. The Enron collapse, brought to light in 2001, ushered in an avalanche of ethics scandals that brought down WorldCom, Tyco, Arthur Andersen, and others. The magnitude of CEO greed and contempt for the law was unprecedented. Congress thought it put the problems to bed with the passage in 2002 of the Sarbanes–Oxley (SOX) Act. The legislation did bring about increased financial controls and it did strengthen the accountability of CEOs and CFOs for the veracity of financial statements. The public had a sense of relief that government regulations had once again solved their problems. Regrettably, SOX did not "fix" the problem of financial scandals among businesses, although it did improve conditions somewhat.

The public may have been lulled into a false sense of security over the next several years. And, it wasn't until the Wall Street financial scandals of 2008 that the country realized that the difficulties with corporate ethics had not been fixed. The stock market collapse in 2008 began a recession that has not been seen since the Great Depression, in terms of its effects on the world economy. It seems like we have had two business ethics "eras" in the short space of seven years, within the first decade of the 2000s. First, there was the Enron Era (2001–2008) and, in 2008, we found ourselves in the era of the Wall Street financial scandals that are not yet behind us.[3]

How have these two eras been similar and different? The headliners in the Enron Era included both companies and CEOs or CFOs. Among these were Enron (Kenneth Lay, Jeffrey Skilling, Andrew Fastow), WorldCom (Bernie Ebbers), Tyco (Dennis Kozlowski), Adelphia (John Rigas), and Global Crossing (Gary Winnick). For good measure, one could toss in HealthSouth and Martha Stewart during this era. What was unique about the Enron Era is that it included chief-level executives as the poster children for bad corporate ethics. Before Enron, many thought business ethics was a problem having to do with employees and lower- and middle-level managers; that is, the lower two-thirds of the corporate pyramid. Beginning with the Enron Era, the focus turned to the top one-third of the corporate pyramid, including negligent corporate boards.

The accusations and convictions during the Enron Era embraced a broad range of legal and ethical charges and eventual convictions. Among these were securities fraud, conspiracy to inflate profits, corrupt corporate cultures, accounting fraud, sales tax evasion, looting the company's assets, and so on. After prolonged investigations and trials, some of these chief-level executives were found guilty and were sent to prison. Ken Lay of Enron was convicted but died before he could serve his prison sentence.

The Wall Street financial scandals have ushered in a new set of corporate characters, and it has been mostly companies and not CEOs or CFOs accused of questionable dealings. The new faces in the news included Fannie Mae, Freddie Mac, Bear Stearns, Lehman Brothers, AIG, and Merrill Lynch. Some will argue that these firms did not commit ethics violations, per se, but rather made bad judgments about risk and returns. This is still being debated. At a minimum, there was widespread recklessness about risk, especially with the subprime lending crisis and exotic financial instruments that very few experts completely understood. These firms were led by the financial wizards who had become known as "the smartest guys in the room," and they should have known better. It is unethical to lend money to customers who, in your reasonable judgment, will not be able to pay it back. It is unethical to lend money without checking people's job status, income, and assets. It can be called bad risk-return calculations, but many think that is just a euphemism for the questionable business practices that were taking place. Many observers have argued that the firms got greedy and were driven by profits (and bonuses) without regard for the consequences.

Many of these corporate decision makers may not have broken laws and thus may not be prosecuted like those from the Enron Era; however, only time will tell. But, this latter scandal era has had drastically wider ramifications for the United States and the world economy, and it helped precipitate a worldwide recession. In the Enron Era, the immediate stakeholders suffered greatly, especially employees and shareholders. In the current era, the devastation has been all encompassing—the world is suffering from the economic calamity of these bad decisions. These business people have raised serious questions about trust in the financial system.

It is difficult to say what will happen next. There are some signs that economies are improving, but it may take much longer for trust in business to be restored. What the recent scandals have revealed is that the issue of business ethics has both macro and micro effects. At the macro level, the entire business system has been called into question. This is the level of big business, as an institution, maintaining its legitimacy in a complex world. At the micro level, individual companies, managers, and employees still face the continuing onslaught of ethics challenges that occur on an everyday basis. As managers, business ethics education is more focused on this latter category of ethics problems. The broad environment, which deals with business and society relationships, however, continues to be a challenging backdrop against which these daily challenges occur.

Figure 7-1 summarizes some of the major business ethics scandals that occurred beginning in 2001. The effects of some of these continue to the present day. Many of these companies and executives have claimed their innocence, and allegations and trials are at various stages of completion. Some have been convicted and sent to prison.

To gain an appreciation of the kinds of issues that are important under the rubric of business ethics, Figure 7-2 presents a brief inventory of business ethics issues compiled by the Josephson Institute of Ethics. Here we see business ethics issues categorized on the basis of stakeholder relationships. Against this backdrop, we plan to begin our business ethics discussion in this chapter and the next three chapters. This chapter

---

FIGURE 7-1 Recent Ethics Scandals: From Enron to Wall Street

Companies Implicated	Executives Implicated	Legal/Ethical Charges and Convictions
Enron	Andrew Fastow, Jeffrey Skilling, Kenneth Lay, Richard Causey, Ben Glisan, treasurer	Securities fraud, conspiracy to inflate profits, corrupt corporate culture
WorldCom	Scott Sullivan, CFO; Bernard J. Ebbers, CEO	Accounting fraud, lying, filing false financial statements
Arthur Andersen	Entire firm; David Duncan, lead auditor for Enron	Accounting fraud, criminal charges, obstruction
Tyco	Mark Schwartz, CFO; Dennis Kozlowski, CEO	Sales tax evasion, stealing through corruption, stock fraud, unauthorized bonuses and loans
Adelphia	John Rigas, sons Timothy and Michael; Michael Mulcahey; James Brown	Accounting fraud, looting the company, using it as "personal piggy bank"
Global Crossing	Gary Winnick, chairperson	Misleading "swap" transactions
Dynegy	Jamie Olis, sr. dir. tax planning; Gene S. Foster; Helen C. Sharkey, accountant	Accounting fraud
HealthSouth	Richard Scrushy, CEO	Found not guilty in company scandal, but was later convicted of bribery, conspiracy, and mail fraud
Boeing	Michael Sears, CFO; Harry Stonecipher, CEO	Unethical behavior, violating company policy, misconduct
Martha Stewart	Martha Stewart	Conspiracy, securities fraud, and obstruction of justice
Parmalat (Italy)	Calisto Tanzi, chairman and CEO, and others	Flawed corporate governance
Computer Associates	Sanjay Kumar, CEO	Pleaded guilty to fraud
Fannie Mae, Freddie Mac, Bear Stearns, Lehman Brothers, AIG, Merrill Lynch, Countrywide	Most executives were not personally accused of wrongdoing. Upper echelon executives and boards of directors were typically mentioned in list of questionable behaviors.	Recklessness, excessive risk taking, greed, bad loan decisions, governance failures, arrogance, hubris

---

FIGURE 7-2 An Inventory of Ethical Issues in Business

This checklist is designed to stimulate thought and discussion on important ethical concerns.

For each of the following issues, indicate whether ethical problems are
5 = Very serious; 4 = Serious; 3 = Not very serious; 2 = Not a problem; 1 = No opinion.
Column 1 = In the business world in general   **Column 2** = In your company

Employee–Employer Relations

_____ _____	Work ethic—giving a full day's work for a full day's pay
_____ _____	Petty theft (supplies, telephone, photocopying, etc.)
_____ _____	Cheating on expense accounts
_____ _____	Employee acceptance of gifts or favors from vendors

Employer–Employee Relations

_____ _____	Sexual or racial discrimination; sexual harassment
_____ _____	Invasions of employee privacy
_____ _____	Unsafe or unhealthy working conditions
_____ _____	Discouragement of internal criticism re: unfair, illegal, or improper activities

Company–Customer Relations

_____ _____	Unfair product pricing
_____ _____	Deceptive marketing/advertising
_____ _____	Unsafe or unhealthy products
_____ _____	Discourtesy or arrogance toward customers

Company–Shareholder Relations

_____ _____	Excessive compensation for top management
_____ _____	Self-protective management policies (golden parachutes, poison pills, greenmail)
_____ _____	Mismanagement of corporate assets or opportunities
_____ _____	Public reports and/or financial statements that distort actual performance

Company–Community/Public Interest

_____ _____	Injury to the environment
_____ _____	Undue influence on the political process through lobbying, PACs, etc.
_____ _____	Payoffs, "grease," or bribes in foreign countries
_____ _____	Doing business in countries with inhumane or anti-American policies

Source: Adapted from Josephson Institute of Ethics, *Ethics: Easier Said Than Done* (Vol. 2, No. 1, 1989).

---

introduces fundamental business ethics background and concepts. Chapter 8 considers personal and organizational ethics. Chapter 9 addresses newly emerging technology and business ethics issues. Finally, Chapter 10 turns to the international sphere as ethical issues in the global arena are discussed.

The Public's Opinion of Business Ethics

The public's view of business ethics has never been very high. Anecdotal evidence suggests that many citizens see business ethics as essentially a contradiction in terms, an oxymoron, and think that there is only a fine line between a business executive and a crook. Over the past several years, public opinion polls have revealed the public's deep concerns about the honesty and ethical standards of business and other professions. The November 2009 Gallup poll, the latest available, revealed that 38 percent of the public thought that business executives had low or very low ethics. Only 12 percent thought their ethics were very high or high, and 48 percent thought their ethics were average. Specific categories of business people had even lower ethics rankings. These included advertising practitioners, insurance sales people, stockbrokers, and car sales people.[4]

A poll of citizens as well as business people was conducted by the Marist College Institute for Public Opinion in 2009. Not surprisingly, the survey found that Americans were more likely than business executives to express a negative opinion on the course and practices of Corporate America. Other key findings included the following:[5]

- More than three-quarters of Americans, compared with 58 percent of business executives, said the moral compass of Corporate America is pointing in the wrong direction.
- A majority of Americans gave corporate America D or F grades for honesty and ethics and rated the country's business leadership as poor, while business leaders gave B and C for honesty and ethics and considered themselves as doing a fair job at leading.
- Both the public and business leaders assigned the lowest marks to the financial and investment industry. Around 53 percent of Americans and two-thirds of executives gave a grade of D or F to the sector for its honesty and ethical conduct.
- While a strong majority of Americans (75 percent) and executives (94 percent) believe that one can be successful without compromising their ethics, less than half of Americans (28 percent) and business leaders (44 percent) believe people use the same set of ethical standards in business as they do in their personal lives.
- More than 90 percent of Americans and 90 percent of executives see career advancement, personal financial gain, increasing profits, or gaining competitive advantage as the primary factors driving corporate business decisions. Only an estimated 3 in 10 Americans and executives believe that "public good" is a strong factor in the choices of corporate leaders.

Carl Anderson, a leader in commissioning the survey, was reported to have said: "Today, America faces a serious problem with a financial crisis caused in no small part by greed—the public lacks confidence in our financial system, and in much of 'corporate America.'" He went on to say, "This confidence cannot and will not be restored until American executives and companies choose to be guided by a moral compass in their business decisions. Only a strong commitment to ethical business practices on the part of executives and the companies they lead can restore America's confidence in its financial system."[6]

The public's opinion of business ethics may be reported at two levels. At a broad level is the general perception of business ethics by the public and at a narrower level are specific perceptions as to what is going on inside organizations. It is apparent from the aforementioned Marist study that there is a "trust gap" between the public and business. When asked how much they trusted various institutions in society, European and American consumers placed the large corporation at the bottom of the list in terms of trust.[7] There can be no doubt that the endless stream of ethical scandals over the past decade contributed significantly to this trust gap.

In terms of what is going on within companies, the 2009 National Business Ethics Survey (NBES) conducted by the Ethics Resource Center (ERC) had some encouraging news. The NBES was a survey of employees to determine what was going on within companies. Following are the major findings:[8]

- Ethical misconduct at work was down slightly. Fewer employees indicated they had observed misconduct on the job. In 2007, the measure was 56 percent, but it fell to 49 percent in 2009.

- Whistle-blowing had increased. In 2009, more employees said they had reported misconduct when observed. In 2007, the percentage reporting was at 58. In 2009, it had risen to 63 percent.
- Ethical cultures in organizations seemed stronger. ERC's measure of ethical culture considered ethical leadership, accountability, and values rather than rules or written ethics codes. In 2009, ERC's index of ethical culture strength increased from 53 percent to 62 percent over the two years.
- Pressure to cut corners was down. Perceived pressure by employees to commit an ethics violation declined from 10 percent in 2007 to 8 percent in 2009.
- There was one negative development though. Retaliation against those who reported misconduct appeared to increase. This was seen as a negative development in light of its detrimental effects against those seeking to bring wrongdoing to light.

The NBES researchers studied the trend lines for observed misconduct and the average monthly S&P 500 index between the years 2000 and 2009. They discovered an interesting parallel and remarkable consistency between the two measures. This important connection between workplace ethics and the larger economic business cycle led them to conclude that "when times are tough, ethics improve." By contrast, they believe that when business booms, ethics erode. They concluded from this finding that beginning in 2009, we have been experiencing an ethics bubble and that as the economy improves, misconduct may begin to rise again. Business managers need to prepare for the return of business as usual once the economy perks up. Interpreting these survey findings is tricky business. One wants to be encouraged by the improvements, but they seem to be linked to the business cycle.

The upshot of these surveys seems to be that business ethics problems continue even though some progress has been made. In spite of the ups and downs, the consensus seems to be that we have been in an era of fraud and corruption and that serious steps need to be taken to get business back on track.

As we are into the second decade of the 2000s, it appears that society is clamoring for a renewed emphasis on values, morals, and ethics and that the business ethics debate of this period is but a subset of this larger societal concern. Whether the business community will be able to close the trust gap and ratchet up its reputation to a new plateau remains to be seen. One thing is sure: There is a renewed interest in business ethics, and the proliferation of business ethics courses in colleges and universities, along with the revitalized interest on the part of the business community, paints an encouraging picture for the "ethics industry" of the future.

Are the Media Reporting Business Ethics More Vigorously?

Sometimes it is difficult to tell whether business ethics have really deteriorated or that the media is doing a more thorough job of reporting on ethics violations. There is no doubt that the media are reporting ethical problems more frequently and fervently. Spurred on by the Enron era of scandals and those of the past few years, the media have found business ethics and, indeed, ethics questions among all institutions to be subjects of growing and sustaining interest. The Martha Stewart trial took on monumental proportions as the press turned it into the proverbial media circus that most felt exceeded its merit as a business ethics issue. Many believed that the charges against Stewart were much less severe than most of the other companies and executives summarized in Figure 7-1, but because she was a high profile entertainment personality, the media coverage was nonstop. More recently, the media had a field day with the Bernie Madoff Ponzi scheme, in which he defrauded thousands of investors out of $50 billion. "Evil" Madoff got 150 years in prison for his epic fraud, and the daily reporting of his plight was a sight to behold.[9]

Of particular interest in recent years has been the in-depth investigative reporting of business ethics on such TV shows as *60 Minutes, 20/20, Dateline NBC*, and *Frontline*, as well as the growing number of such programs. Such investigations keep business ethics in the public eye and make it difficult to assess whether public opinion polls are reflecting the actual business ethics of the day or simply the reactions to the latest scandals covered on a weekly basis. In addition to TV coverage, the Internet through its Web pages and blogs, which have grown in number in recent years, and even Web sites such as YouTube.com carry detailed coverage of ethics scandals.

Is It That Society Is Actually Changing?

We would definitely make this argument here, as we did in Chapter 1. Many business managers subscribe to this belief. W. Michael Blumenthal, one-time U.S. Secretary of the Treasury and chief executive officer of the Bendix Corporation, was one of the leading advocates of this view. He argued:

> *It seems to me that the root causes of the questionable and illegal corporate activities that have come to light recently … can be traced to the sweeping changes that have taken place in our society and throughout the world and to the unwillingness of many in business to adjust to these changes.*[10]

Blumenthal went on to say, "People in business have not suddenly become immoral. What has changed are the contexts in which corporate decisions are made, the demands that are being made on business, and the nature of what is considered proper corporate conduct."[11]

Although it would be difficult to prove Blumenthal's thesis, it is an intuitively attractive one. You do not have to make a lengthy investigation of some of today's business practices to realize that a good number of what are now called unethical practices were at one time considered acceptable. Or that possibly the practices never really were acceptable to the public but that, because they were not known, they were tolerated, thus causing no moral dilemmas in the mind of the public. In spite of this analysis, one cannot help but believe that the greed by top-level business executives that has been exposed in the past decade has elevated the ethics issue to new heights. Executive lying has contributed to the problem. Though corporate governance has become better in recent years, lack of careful oversight of top-echelon executives has been a problem as well. Corporate boards, in some cases, have fallen down in their duties to monitor top-executive behavior, and one consequence has been the continuing stream of ethics scandals.

Figure 7-3 illustrates how the magnitude of the ethics problem may be more detectable today than it once was, as a result of the public's expectations of business's ethical behavior rising more rapidly than actual business ethics. Note in the figure that actual business ethics is assumed to be improving but not at the same pace as public expectations are rising. The magnitude of the current ethics problem, therefore, is seen here partially to be a function of rapidly rising societal expectations about business behavior.

Business Ethics: Meaning, Types, Approaches

Chapter 2 discusses the ethical responsibilities of business in an introductory way. We contrasted ethics with economics, law, and philanthropy. To be sure, we all have a general idea of what business ethics means, but here we would like to probe the topic more deeply. To understand business ethics, it is useful to comment on the relationship between ethics and morality.

Ethics is the discipline that deals with moral duty and obligation. Ethics can also be regarded as a set of moral principles or values. Morality is a doctrine or system of moral conduct. Moral conduct refers to that which relates to principles of right, wrong, and

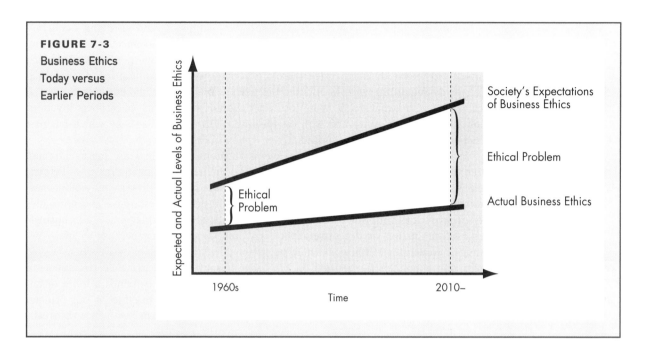

FIGURE 7-3
Business Ethics
Today versus
Earlier Periods

fairness in behavior. For the most part, then, we can think of ethics and morality as being so similar to one another that we may use the terms interchangeably to refer to the study of fairness, justice, and moral behavior in business.

Business ethics, therefore, is concerned with morality and fairness in behavior, actions, and practices that take place within a business context. Today, morality is increasingly interpreted to include the often difficult and subtle questions of fairness, justice, and equity in the work place. Business ethics is the study of practices in organizations and a quest to determine whether these practices are acceptable or not. Business ethics is also a field of study that is of interest to the public, academics, students, and managers.

Descriptive versus Normative Ethics

Two key branches of moral philosophy, or ethics, are descriptive ethics and normative ethics. It is important to distinguish between the two types because they each take a different perspective.

Descriptive ethics is concerned with describing, characterizing, and studying the morality of a people, an organization, a culture, or a society. It also compares and contrasts different moral codes, systems, practices, beliefs, and values.[12] In descriptive business ethics, therefore, our focus is on learning what *is* occurring in the realm of behavior, actions, decisions, policies, and practices of business firms, managers, or, perhaps, specific industries. The public opinion polls cited earlier give us glimpses of descriptive ethics—what people believe is going on the basis on their perceptions and understandings. Descriptive ethics focuses on "what is" the prevailing set of ethical standards in the business community, specific organizations, or on the part of specific managers. A real danger in limiting our attention to descriptive ethics is that some people may adopt the view that "if everyone is doing it," it must be acceptable. For example, if a survey reveals that 70 percent of employees are padding their expense accounts, this describes what *is* taking place, but it does not describe what *should* be taking place. Just because many are participating in this questionable activity doesn't make it an appropriate practice. This is why normative ethics is important.

Normative ethics, by contrast, is concerned with supplying and justifying a coherent moral system of thinking and judging. Normative ethics seeks to uncover, develop, and justify basic moral principles that are intended to guide behavior, actions, and decisions.[13] Normative business ethics, therefore, seeks to propose some principle or principles for distinguishing what is ethical from what is unethical in the business context. It deals more with "what ought to be" or "what should be" in terms of business practices. Normative ethics is concerned with establishing norms or standards by which business practices might be guided or judged.

Normative business ethics might be based on moral common sense (be fair, honest, truthful), or it might require critical thinking and the pursuit of different types of ethical analysis (interest based, rights based, duty based, virtue based).[14] In our study of business ethics, we need to be ever mindful of this distinction between descriptive and normative perspectives. It is tempting to observe the prevalence of a particular practice in business (e.g., discrimination or deceptive advertising) and conclude that because so many are doing it (descriptive ethics), it must be acceptable behavior. Normative ethics would insist that a practice be justified on the basis of some ethical principle, argument, or rationale before being considered acceptable. Normative ethics demands a more meaningful moral anchor than just "everyone is doing it." Normative ethics is our primary goal in this book, though we frequently compare "what ought to be" with "what is (really going on in the real world)" for purposes of comparison.

Three Major Approaches to Business Ethics

There are three major approaches to thinking about business ethics. These are as follows:

1. **Conventional approach**—based on how common society today views business ethics. The conventional approach is based on ordinary, common sense.
2. **Principles approach**—based on the use of ethics principles or guidelines to justify and direct behavior, actions, and policies.
3. **Ethical tests approach**—based on short, practical questions or "tests" to guide ethical decision making, behavior and practices.

We discuss the conventional approach to business ethics in this chapter and the other two approaches in Chapter 8.

The Conventional Approach to Business Ethics

The **conventional approach to business ethics** is essentially the kind whereby we compare a decision, practice, or policy with prevailing norms of acceptability in society. We call it the conventional approach because it is thought that this is the way conventional or general society thinks. The conventional approach relies on our use of common sense and a widely held sense of what is ethical. The major challenge of this approach is answering the questions "Whose norms do we use?" in making the ethical judgment, and "What norms are prevailing?" This approach may be depicted by highlighting the major variables to be compared with one another:

Decision, Behavior, or Practice ⟷ *Prevailing Norms of Acceptability*

There is considerable room for variability on both of these questions. With respect to whose norms are used as the basis for ethical judgments, the conventional approach would consider as legitimate those norms emanating from family, friends, religious beliefs, the local community, one's employer, law, the profession, and so on. This approach would also employ what is in one's own best self-interest as a guideline. **Ethical egoism** is an

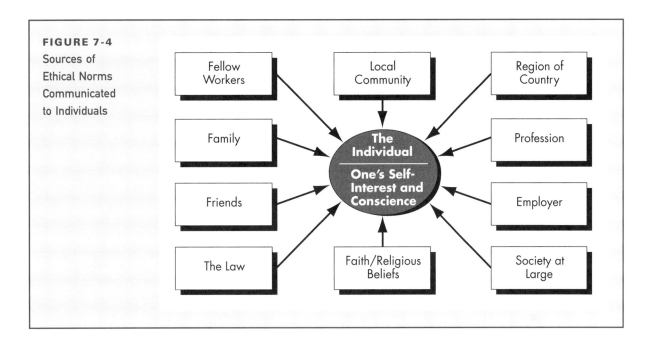

FIGURE 7-4

Sources of Ethical Norms Communicated to Individuals

ethical principle based on the idea that the individual should seek to maximize his or her own self-interests as a legitimate factor, and this belief is widely held in society. This would not preclude using other sources of ethical norms and factoring in how these might be in the individual's own self-interest.

One's conscience, or one's self-interest, would be seen by many to be a legitimate source of ethical norms. Two classic "Frank & Ernest" comic strips poke fun at the use of one's conscience. In the first, a sign on the wall reads "Tonight's Lecture: Moral Philosophy." Then it shows Frank saying to Ernest, "I'd let my conscience be my guide, but I'm in enough trouble already!" In a second comic strip, Frank says to Ernest, while they are standing at a bar, "I always use my conscience as my guide. But, fortunately, it has a terrible sense of direction." These comic strips reveal the often limiting nature of using one's conscience.

Figure 7-4 illustrates some of the sources of ethical norms that come to bear on the individual and that might be used in various circumstances, and over time, under the conventional approach. These sources compete in their influence on what constitutes the "prevailing norms of acceptability" for today.

In many circumstances, the conventional approach to ethics may be useful and applicable. What does a person do, however, if norms from one source conflict with norms from another source? Also, how can we be sure that societal norms are really appropriate or defensible? Our society's culture sends us many and often conflicting messages about what is appropriate ethical behavior. We get these messages from television, movies, books, music, and other sources in the culture.

Recently, TV shows such as *Survivor* and *The Apprentice* have run episodes in which questionable ethics have been depicted and sometimes celebrated. On *Survivor*, the participants are forever creating alliances and then breaking them in the interest of winning the game. *The Apprentice* was one of the first reality shows with a business focus. Sixteen participants competed for Donald Trump's favor as they were broken into teams to compete to become Trump's "apprentice" and go to work for $250,000 on one of Trump's projects. A number of these episodes portrayed questionable ethics passed off as business as usual. As the women's team managed Planet Hollywood for a day, they resorted to using their sexuality to increase sales. The attractive women became "The Shooter Girls" (similar to the "Hooter" girls) and tried to sell shots to the admiring men customers, using whatever tactics worked. In one scene, while participant Amy was out on the streets trying to give away coupons, she observed, "I feel like I'm pimping."[15] In other episodes, they were out on the streets of New York giving away kisses to the men who bought their products, while they flaunted their sexuality in skimpy, revealing outfits. It is just possible that an impressionable young person might see this and hundreds of other references like it and conclude that dishonesty is an acceptable standard in business.

Another example of the conflicting messages people get today from society occurs in the realm of sexual harassment in the workplace. On the one hand, today's television, movies, advertisements, and music are replete with sexual innuendo and the treatment of women and men as sex objects. This would suggest that such behavior is normal, acceptable, even desired. On the other hand, the law and the courts are stringently prohibiting sexual gestures or innuendo in the workplace. As we see in Chapter 19, it does not take much sexual innuendo to constitute a "hostile work environment" and a sex discrimination charge under Title VII of the Civil Rights Act. In this example, we see a norm that is prevalent in culture and society clashing with a norm evolving from employment law and business ethics. These examples serve to illustrate how views of ethics that are acceptable to many in conventional society would not be accepted in more rigorous forms of ethical analysis.

Ethics and the Law

We have made various references to ethics and the law. In Chapter 2, we said that ethical behavior is typically thought to reside above behavior required by the law. This is the generally accepted view of ethics. We should make it clear however, that in many respects the law and ethics overlap. To appreciate this, you need to recognize that the law embodies notions of ethics. That is, the law may be seen as a reflection of what society thinks are minimal standards of conduct and behavior. Both law and ethics have to do with what is deemed appropriate or acceptable, but law reflects society's *codified* ethics. Therefore, if a person breaks a law or violates a regulation, she or he is also behaving unethically. We should be open to the possibility, however, that in some rare cases the law may not be ethical, in which case standing up to the law might be the principled course of action. A case in point might be when Rosa Parks, a black woman, stood up to the authorities and refused to move to the back of the bus because she thought this was racial discrimination.

In spite of this frequent overlap between law and ethics, we continue to talk about desirable ethical behavior as behavior that extends beyond what is required by law. The *spirit* of the law often extends beyond the *letter* of the law. Viewed from the standpoint of minimums, we would certainly say that obedience to the law is generally regarded to be a minimum standard of ethical behavior.

There are two good business examples in which the confusion between law and ethics led to disastrous results. In one analysis, the Enron case was said to been all about the difference between the letter of the law and the spirit of the law, often regarded as ethics. Interestingly, the fraud at Enron was accompanied by obsessive and careful attention to the letter of the law. One observer stated that "the people who ran Enron did back flips and somersaults as they tried to stay within the law's lines."[16] But Ken Lay and Jeffrey Skilling apparently missed the main point of securities laws, which is that CEOs and other high-level officials should not get rich while their shareholders go broke. So, the source of all their crimes was the basic dishonesty of trying to keep Enron's stock afloat so that they could make money.[17] Their focus on the law to the neglect of ethics was a significant part of their downfall.

In another ethics scandal, involving Hewlett-Packard (HP), presented as an Ethics in Practice Case in Chapter 4, the focus on law rather than ethics became problematic. HP was experiencing leaks of information from its board meetings and started an investigation into who was leaking what information. In the process, they began to use some questionable, though possibly legal, techniques for gathering information. The company used a technique known as pretexting that employs deceit, to get phone record information from workers at phone companies. The company's lawyers had concluded that pretexting was legal, but did not pay much attention to whether the technique was ethical. A former advisor of HP's, while analyzing what went on, admitted that there was a lack of balance given to ethical considerations in the company's quest to trace the leaks from its board. The advisor went on to say that "doing it legally should not be the test; that is a given," "you have to ask what is appropriate and what is ethical" and this is where the firm failed.[18]

In addition, we should note that the law does not address all realms in which ethical questions might be raised. Thus, there are clear roles for both law and ethics to play.[19] It should be noted that research on illegal corporate behavior has been conducted for some time. Illegal corporate behavior, of course, comprises business practices that are in direct defiance of law or public policy. Research has focused on two dominant questions: (1) Why do firms behave illegally or what leads them to engage in illegal activities and (2) what are the consequences of behaving illegally?[20] We will not deal with these studies of lawbreaking in this discussion; however, we should view this body of studies and investigations as being closely aligned with our interest in business ethics because it represents a special case of business ethics (illegal behavior).

Making Ethical Judgments

When a decision is made about what is ethical (right, just, fair) using the conventional approach, there is room for variability on several counts (see Figure 7-5). Three key elements compose such a decision. First, we observe the *decision, action,* or *practice* that has taken place in the workplace setting. Second, we *compare the practice with prevailing norms of acceptability*—that is, society's or some other standard of what is acceptable or unacceptable. Third, *we must recognize that value judgments are being made* by someone as to what really occurred (the actual behavior) and what the prevailing norms of acceptability really are. This means that two different people could look at the same behavior or practice, compare it with their beliefs of what the prevailing norms are, and reach different conclusions as to whether the behavior was ethical or not. This becomes quite complex as perceptions of what is ethical inevitably lead to the difficult task of ranking different values against one another.

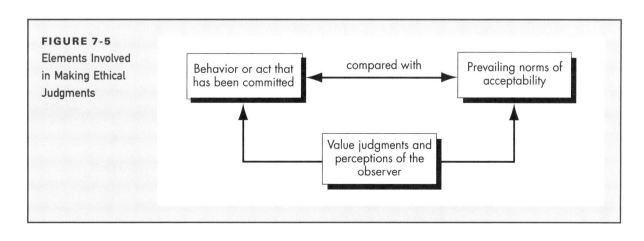

FIGURE 7-5
Elements Involved in Making Ethical Judgments

If we can put aside for a moment the fact that perceptual differences about an incident do exist, and the fact that we might differ among ourselves because of our personal values and philosophies of acceptable behavior, we are still left with the challenging task of determining society's prevailing norms of acceptability of business practice. As a whole, members of society generally agree at a very high level of abstraction that certain practices are wrong. However, the consensus tends to disintegrate as we move from general to specific situations.

Let us illustrate with a business example. We might all agree with the general belief that "You should not steal someone else's property." As a general precept, we probably would have consensus on this. But, as we look at specific situations, our consensus may tend to disappear. Is it acceptable to take home from work such things as pencils, pens, paper clips, paper, staplers, computer discs, and calculators? Is it acceptable to use the company telephone for personal long-distance calls? Is it acceptable to use company gasoline for private use or to pad expense accounts? Is it acceptable to use company computers for personal e-mail? What if everyone else is doing it?

What is interesting in these examples is that we are more likely to reach consensus in principle than in practice. Some people who would say these practices are not acceptable might privately engage in them. Furthermore, a person who would not think of shoplifting even the smallest item from a local store might take pencils and paper home from work on a regular basis. A comic strip depicting the "Born Loser" illustrates this point. In the first panel, the father admonishes his son Wilberforce in the following way: "You know how I feel about stealing. Now tomorrow I want you to return every one of those pencils to school." In the second panel, Father says to Wilberforce, "I'll bring you all the pencils you need from work." This is an example of the classic double standard, and it illustrates how actions may be perceived differently by the observer or the participant.

Thus, in the conventional approach to business ethics, determinations of what is ethical and what is not require judgments to be made on at least three counts:

1. What is the *true nature* of the practice, behavior, or decision that occurred?
2. What are society's (or business's) *prevailing norms* of acceptability?
3. What *value judgments* are being made by someone about the practice or behavior, and what are that person's *perceptions* of applicable norms?

The human factor in the situation thus introduces the problem of perception and values and makes the decision process complicated.

The conventional approach to business ethics can be valuable, because we all need to be aware of and sensitive to the total environment in which we exist. We need to be aware of how society regards ethical issues. It has limitations, however, and we need to be cognizant of these as well. The most serious danger is that of falling into an **ethical relativism** where we pick and choose which source of norms we wish to use on the basis of what will justify our current actions or maximize our freedom. A recent comic strip illustrates this point. In a courtroom, while swearing in, the witness stated, "I swear to tell the truth … *as I see it*."

In the next chapter, we argue that a principles approach is needed to augment the conventional approach. The principles approach looks at general guidelines to ethical decision making that come from moral philosophy. We also present the ethical tests approach, which is more of a practical approach.

Ethics, Economics, and Law: A Venn Model

When we focus on ethics and ethical decision making, it is useful to consider the primary forces that come into tension while making ethical judgments. In Chapter 2, these were introduced as part of the four-part definition of corporate social responsibility, and

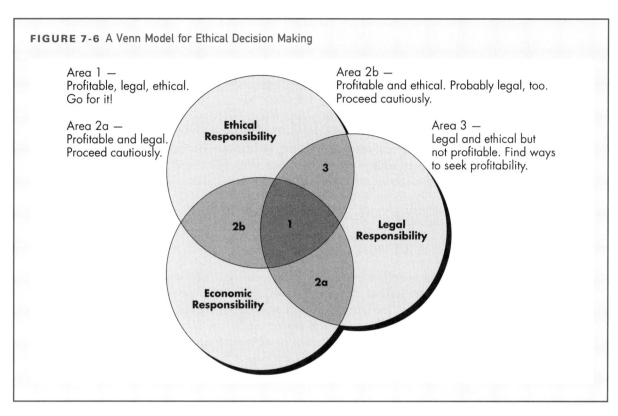

FIGURE 7-6 A Venn Model for Ethical Decision Making

Area 1 —
Profitable, legal, ethical.
Go for it!

Area 2a —
Profitable and legal.
Proceed cautiously.

Area 2b —
Profitable and ethical. Probably legal, too.
Proceed cautiously.

Area 3 —
Legal and ethical but
not profitable. Find ways
to seek profitability.

they were depicted in the Pyramid of CSR. When we discus a firm's CSR, philanthropy definitely enters the discussion. This is because philanthropic initiatives are the primary way many companies display their CSR in the community—through good and charitable works. In ethical decision making, however, we tend to set aside philanthropic expectations and focus on ethical expectations and, especially, those forces that primarily come into tension with ethics—economics (the quest for profits) and law. Thus, in most decision-making situations, ethics, economics, and law become the central variables that must be considered and balanced against each other in the quest to make wise decisions.

A firm's economic, legal, and ethical responsibilities can be depicted in a Venn diagram model illustrating how certain actions, decisions, or policies fulfill one, two, or three of these responsibility categories. Figure 7-6 presents this Venn diagram model, illustrating the overlapping potential of these three responsibility categories.

In Area 1, where the decision, action, or practice fulfills all three responsibilities, the management prescription is to "go for it"; that is, the action is profitable, in compliance with the law, and represents ethical behavior. In Area 2a, the action under consideration is profitable and legal, but its ethical status may be uncertain. The guideline here is to "proceed cautiously." In these kinds of situations, the ethics of the action needs to be carefully considered. In Area 2b, the action is profitable and ethical, but perhaps the law does not clearly address the issue or is ambiguous. If it is ethical, there is a good chance it is also legal, but the guideline again is to proceed cautiously. In Area 3, the action is legal and ethical but not profitable. Therefore, the strategy here would be to avoid this action or find ways to make it profitable. However, there may be a compelling case to take the action if it is legal and ethical and, thus, represents the right thing to do. Schwartz and Carroll have presented a three-domain approach to CSR that employs a Venn diagram format similar to that presented in Figure 7-6. They provide corporate examples to illustrate each section of the Venn diagram.[21]

By taking philanthropy out of the picture, the ethics Venn model serves as a useful template for thinking about the more immediate expectations that society has on business in a situation in which the ethical dimension plays an important role. It illustrates clearly that many business decisions boil down to trade-offs between the influences of economics, law, and ethics.

Four Important Ethics Questions

There are other ways to get at the "big picture" perspective of business ethics. One useful approach is to address four simple, but really different kinds of, questions that help us frame the business ethics challenge:[22]

1. What is?
2. What ought to be?
3. How do we get from what is to what ought to be?
4. What is our motivation in all this?

These four questions capture the core of what ethics is all about. They force an examination of *what really is* (descriptive ethics) going on in a business situation, *what ought to be* (normative ethics), how we might *close the gap* between what is and what ought to be (practical question), and what is our *motivation* for doing all this.

Before we discuss each question briefly, let us suggest that these four questions may be asked at five different levels: (1) the level of the individual (the personal level), (2) the level of the organization, (3) the level of the industry or profession, (4) the societal level, and (5) the global or international level. By asking and then answering these questions, a greater understanding and resolution of a business ethics dilemma may be achieved.

What Is?—*the Descriptive Question*

The "what is?" question forces us to identify the reality of what is actually going on in an ethical sense in business or in a specific decision or practice. Ideally, it is a factual, scientific, or descriptive question. Its purpose is to help us understand the reality of the ethical behavior we find before us in the business environment. As we discussed earlier when describing the nature of making ethical judgments, it is not always simple to state exactly what the "real" situation is. This is because we are humans and thus make mistakes when we "sense" what is happening. Also, we are conditioned by our personal beliefs, values, and biases, and these factors influence what we perceive is going on. Or, we may perceive real conditions for what they are but fail to think in terms of alternatives or in terms of "what ought to be." Think of the difficulty you might have in attempting to describe "what is" with respect to business ethics at the personal, organizational, industry/professional, societal, or global levels. Relevant questions then become:

- What are your personal ethics?
- What are your organization's ethics?
- What are the ethics practiced in your industry or profession?
- What are society's ethics?
- What global ethics are in practice today?

What Ought to Be?—*the Normative Question*

The second question is quite different from the first question and gets to the heart of ethical analysis. It is normative rather than descriptive. The "what ought to be?" question seldom gets answered directly, particularly in a managerial setting. Managers are used to identifying alternatives and choosing the best one, but seldom is this done through questions that entail moral content or the "rightness, fairness, or justice" of a decision or practice. The "ought to be" question is often viewed in terms of what management *should do* (in an ethical sense) in a given situation. Examples of this question in a business setting might be:

- How *ought* we treat our aging employees whose productivity is declining?
- How safe *ought* we make this product, knowing full well we cannot pass all the costs on to the consumer?
- How clean an environment *should* we aim for?
- *Should* we outsource certain aspects of our production to China or India even though it might mean laying off workers at home?

At a corporate planning seminar several years ago, the leader suggested that if you are the president of a large corporation, the place to start planning is with a vision of society, not with where you want to be five or ten years into the future. What kind of world do you want to have? How does your industry or your firm fit into that world? An executive cannot just walk into the office one day and say, "I had a vision last night," and expect many adherents.[23] But this does not make the question or the vision invalid. It simply suggests that we must approach the "what ought to be?" questions at a more practical level. There are plenty of issues to which this question can be applied in the everyday life of a manager. Therefore, such lofty, visionary exercises are not necessary.

How to Get from *What Is* to *What Ought to Be*—the Practical Question

This third question represents the challenge of bridging the gap between *where we are* and *where we ought to be* with respect to ethical practices. This is the practical question for

---

ETHICS IN PRACTICE CASE

Ethics in the Mailroom

To make some extra money during college, I got a part-time job in a mailroom at a rather large business. This business would send out hundreds of pieces of mail each day, all going through the mailroom. Our job as the staff of the mailroom was to package this mail to be shipped, put the proper amount of postage on it, and then take it to the post office. To put the postage on the items, we used a postage meter that was in the mailroom. The postage meter would weigh the mail and then stamp it with the correct amount of postage, and my employers would pay the postage costs in lump sums periodically throughout the year.

Occasionally my boss would run some of his personal mail along with the business mail. When I asked him if sending personal mail through the meter was basically stealing money from the company, he justified it by saying that he only used the meter to mail his bills, and he would never use it for anything over 60 cents. He also said that he had been working there

for 13 years, and he compensated for his low pay by being able to send out the occasional bill or letter. I figured that a few cents here and there would not hurt the company and looked the other way.

1. Define "what is" and "what ought to be" in this case.
2. Was my boss's practice ethical? Does working for a company for 13 years justify sending out personal mail that the company pays for?
3. Does my boss's low pay justify his using company resources to send out personal mail to compensate for the low pay? After all, isn't it just "balancing things out"?
4. Is there any reasonable way to get from "what is" to "what ought to be" without getting fired?
5. Did I do the right thing by looking the other way or should I have turned my boss in for stealing company money even though it was just a few cents here and there? What should I have done?

Contributed Anonymously

management. We may discuss idealistically where we "ought" to be in terms of our own personal ethics or the ethics of our firm, of our industry, or of society. As we move further away from the individual level, we have less control or influence over the "ought to be" question.

When faced with these challenges as depicted by our "ought to be" questions, we may find that from a practical point of view we cannot achieve our ideals. This does not mean we should not have asked the question in the first place. Our "ought to be" questions become goals or aspirations for our ethical practices. They form the normative core of business ethics. They become moral benchmarks that help us motivate and measure progress.

In all managerial situations, we are faced with this challenge of balancing what we *ought to do* with what we *must or can do*. The ideas of Leslie Weatherhead in his book, *The Will of God*, could be adapted to our discussion here. He refers to God's intentional will, circumstantial will, and ultimate will.[24] Looking at these concepts from a managerial or an ethics point of view, we might think in terms of what we *intend* to accomplish, what circumstances *permit* us to accomplish, and what we ultimately are *able* to accomplish. These ideas interject a measure of realism into our efforts to close the gap between where we are and where we want to be in a business ethics application.

This is also the stage at which managerial decision making and strategy come into play. The first step in managerial problem solving is identifying the problem (what "is"). Next comes identifying where we want to be (the "ought" question). Then comes the managerial challenge of closing the gap. "Gap analysis" sets the stage for concrete business action.

What Is Our Motivation?—a *Question of Authenticity*

Practical businesspeople do not like to dwell on this fourth question, which addresses the motivation for being ethical, because sometimes it reveals some manipulative or self-centered motive. At one level, it may not be desirable to discuss motivation, because isn't it really actions that count? If someone makes a $150 contribution to a charitable cause, is it fair to ask whether the person did it (1) because she or he really believes in the cause (altruistic motivation) or (2) because she or he just wanted a tax deduction (self-interest) or (3) wanted to "look" benevolent in the eyes of others (selfish motive)? Most of us would agree that it is better for a person to make a contribution rather than not make it, regardless of the motive.

Ideally, we would hope that people would be ethical because intrinsically they see that being ethical is a better way to live or manage. What kind of world (or organization) would most people prefer: one in which people behaved ethically because they had selfish or instrumental reasons for doing so, or a world in which people behaved ethically because they really believed in what they were doing? We will accept the former, but the latter seems more desirable and thus motivation matters. We will be better off in the long run if "right" or "fair" managerial practices are motivated by the knowledge that there is inherent value in ethical behavior.

This can be compared with the organizational situation in which managers are attempting to motivate their workers. If a manager is interested only in greater productivity and sees that being "concerned" about employees' welfare will achieve this goal, she or he had better be prepared for the fact that employees may see through the "game playing" and eventually rebel against the manager's effort. On the other hand, employees can see when management is genuinely concerned about their welfare, and they will be responsive to such well-motivated efforts. This is borne out in practice. You can examine two companies that on the surface appear to have identical human resource policies. In one company, the employees know and feel they are being manipulated. In the other company, there is confidence that management really does care.[25] In essence, the difference is one of management's authenticity of motive.

Although we would like to believe that managers are appropriately motivated in their quest for ethical business behavior and that motivations are important, we must continue to understand and accept the observation that we live in a "messy world of mixed motives." Therefore, managers do not typically have the luxury of making abstract distinctions between altruism and self-interest but must get on with the task of designing structures, systems, incentives, and processes that accommodate the "whole" employee, regardless of motivations.[26]

Three Models of Management Ethics

In attempting to understand the basic concepts of business ethics, it is useful to think in terms of key ethical models that might describe different types of management ethics found in the organizational world.[27] These models should provide some useful base points for discussion and comparison. The media have focused so much on immoral or unethical business behavior that it is easy to forget about the possibility of other ethical styles or types. For example, scant attention has been given to the distinction that may be made between those activities that are *immoral* and those that are *amoral*. Similarly, little attention has been given to contrasting these two forms of behavior with ethical or *moral* management.

Believing that there is value in discussing descriptive models, or frameworks, for purposes of clearer understanding, here we describe, compare, and contrast three models or types of ethical management:

- Immoral management
- Moral management
- Amoral management

A major goal is to develop a clearer understanding of the range of management approaches in which ethics or morality is a defining characteristic. By seeing these approaches come to life through description and example, managers will be in an improved position to assess their own ethical approaches and those of other organizational members (supervisors, subordinates, and peers). Another important objective is to identify more completely the amoral management model, which often is overlooked in the human rush to classify things as good or bad, moral or immoral. In a later section, we discuss the elements of moral judgment that must be developed if the transition to moral management is to succeed. A more detailed development of each management model is valuable in coming to understand the range of ethics that leaders may intentionally or unintentionally display. Let us consider the two extremes first—immoral and moral management—and then amoral management.

Immoral Management

Using *immoral* and *unethical* as synonyms, **immoral management** is defined as an approach that is devoid of ethical principles or precepts and at the same time implies a positive and active opposition to what is ethical. Immoral management decisions, behaviors, actions, and practices are discordant with ethical principles. This model holds that the management's motives are selfish and that it cares only or primarily about its own or its company's gains. If the management's activity is actively opposed to what is regarded as ethical, this suggests that the management understands right from wrong and yet chooses to do wrong; thus, its motives are deemed greedy or selfish. According to this model, the management's goals are profitability and organizational success at virtually any price. The management does not care about others' claims to be treated fairly or justly.

FIGURE 7-7

Characteristics of
Immoral Managers

- These managers intentionally do wrong.
- These managers are *self-centered* and *self-absorbed*.
- They care only about self or organization's profits or success.
- They actively oppose what is right, fair, or just.
- They *exhibit no concern* for stakeholders.
- These are the "bad guys."
- An ethics course probably would not help them.

What about the management's orientation toward the law, considering that law is often regarded as an embodiment of minimal ethics? Immoral management regards legal standards as barriers that the management must avoid or overcome to accomplish what it wants. Immoral managers would just as soon engage in illegal activity as in immoral or unethical activity. This point is illustrated in a recent Dilbert comic strip. Dogbert, the VP of Marketing, announces at a meeting: "It's my job to spray paint the roadkill." In panel 2 he says: "I'll use a process the experts call 'dishonesty.'" In panel 3, Dilbert concludes: "My motto is 'If it isn't immoral, it probably won't work.'"[28]

Operating Strategy of Immoral Management.   The operating strategy of immoral management is focused on exploiting opportunities for corporate or personal gain. An active opposition to what is moral would suggest that managers cut corners anywhere and everywhere it appears useful. Thus, the key operating question guiding immoral management is, "Can we make money with this action, decision, or behavior, *regardless of what it takes*?" Implicit in this question is that nothing else matters, at least not very much. Figure 7-7 summarizes some of the major characteristics of immoral managers.

Illustrative Cases of Immoral Management.   Examples of immoral management abound. Following are several that are illustrative.

ENRON   No business scandal in recent times stands out as an example of immoral management as much as Enron. Books have been written and a movie and a Broadway play have been made about the Enron scandal. The two major players in the Enron scandal were CFO Jeffrey Skilling and CEO Ken Lay, now convicted felons. Though Enron imploded in 2001, it was not until 2006 that these two individuals were brought to justice and convicted.[29] Ken Lay, founder and CEO of Enron, died on July 5, 2006, before he had a chance to serve his prison sentence that would have taken him to the end of his life.[30] The Enron scandal became so famous that it produced a British play about the financial scandal that engulfed it, and in the fall of 2009, it was announced that the play was moving to Broadway in the United States.[31]

Lay and Skilling were both convicted of securities fraud and conspiracy to inflate profits, along with a number of other charges. They used off-the-books partnerships to disguise Enron's debts, and then they lied to investors and employees about the company's disastrous financial situation while selling their own company shares.[32] In addition, Enron traders manipulated California's energy market to create phony shortages. This forced the state to borrow billions to pay off artificially inflated power bills. Voters in California were so fearful of brownouts, skyrocketing power bills, and rising state debt that they recalled Gov. Gray Davis and replaced him with Arnold Schwarzenegger.[33] In 2010, Skilling was still trying to convince the courts that he was not given a fair trial and that he should get a new trial.

Enron's collapse and eventual bankruptcy erased more than $60 billion worth of investors' stock value and left 5,600 employees jobless and facing retirements with no nest eggs.[34] In a retrospective examination of Lay's life, one writer argued that to the public, his greatest crime was in advising employees, as the firm was crashing, to keep their Enron stock, and even to buy more, while he was selling his own.[35] His lies destroyed the lives and savings of thousands. One writer summed up Enron with the following equation: "Exaggerate + spin + lie = Enron."[36] After the dust has settled, it appears that this equation was an understatement of what Lay, Skilling, and their associates did to those directly affected and to the public's trust in the business system for years to come. Lay and Skilling were clearly immoral managers.

BERNIE MADOFF Bernard Madoff perpetrated what has been called the biggest financial scandal in history, ending in his conviction at age 71, in 2009. By his own account, the amount fraudulently stolen was $50 billion, but the true amount of the losses may never be known. Using what is called a Ponzi scheme, Madoff lured investors into turning their money over to him while he led them to believe their money was safely invested and yielding large returns. The scheme claimed to be making steady, double-digit returns trading options on a share index. In reality, client funds sat in an account at JPMorgan and were only withdrawn to meet redemption requirements or to be moved to other investments. Of course, Madoff spent much of the money and used it to live a lavishly rich lifestyle all over the world. The SEC had reports on various occasions that he was swindling investors, but because of lapses in their investigations, Madoff was allowed to continue the swindle for years. When finally caught, Madoff was convicted and sentenced to 150 years in prison. The judge called the fraud "extraordinarily evil," and the sentence turned out to be the stiffest penalty ever given for a white collar crime. Hundreds of investors lost their life savings. Some of his victims included some of the world's largest banks and wealthiest people. Mr. Madoff, age 71, said he would "live with this pain, with this torment, for the rest of my life." Madoff, the immoral manager, is serving out his sentence in prison to this day.[37]

ASHLEYMADISON.COM This is a controversial Web site that has been available for several years now. AshleyMadison.com is a site that caters privately for cheating spouses. It's marketing slogan says "Life is short. Have an affair." You can register for free, and then you advertise your "availability" to other fellow cheaters. The company claims to have over a million members and counting. The site says that membership is presently around 7.5 men to every 2.5 women. After signing up for free and putting up your personal profile, normally under an assumed name, you sit back and wait for results. Ashleymadison.com is a business that has an immoral mission—facilitating married people in their quest to cheat on their spouses. Some amoral individuals might see this as an example of amorality, but in today's conventional society very few would attempt to justify this as a wholesome business. By today's standards, Ashleymadison.com would likely be seen as an example of immoral management by most people because its' mission is inherently wrong in that it promotes deception, cheating, and infidelity in marital relationships.

PROCTER & GAMBLE In another case, Procter & Gamble (P&G) admitted to corporate espionage after some of its employees had rummaged through the trashcans outside the Chicago offices of Unilever, the British-Dutch Company that makes Lipton tea, Dove soap, and several brands of shampoo. Agents of P&G retrieved about 80 pages of Unilever's confidential plans. In its defense, P&G said its agents did not violate the law, but did violate the company's own ethics policies, which prohibit rummaging through garbage to acquire information on competitors. P&G agreed to pay Unilever $10 million in the spying case and agreed to an unusual third-party audit to monitor the product development and marketing plans of the company. P&G's chairman pledged that he had taken steps to ensure that the acquired material would not be used by his company.[38] Corporate espionage of the type described here is an immoral management practice.

SURVEY RESULTS In a "Deloitte & Touche USA Ethics & Workplace" survey, respondents identified a number of questionable behaviors observed in the workplace that they thought were unacceptable. This list reveals everyday practices that would most likely correspond with the model of immoral management described earlier:[39]

- Stealing petty cash
- Cheating on expense reports
- Taking credit for another person's accomplishments
- Lying on time sheets about hours worked
- Coming into work hung over
- Telling a demeaning joke (e.g., racist)
- Taking office supplies for personal use

In this same Deloitte & Touche survey, respondents provided what they considered to be other unethical behaviors.[40] These practices would also be characterized as immoral management:

- Showing preferential treatment towards certain employees
- Taking credit for another person's accomplishments
- Rewarding employees who display wrong behaviors
- Harassing a fellow employee (e.g., verbally, sexually, racially)

All of these are examples of immoral management wherein executives' decisions or actions were self-centered, actively opposed to what is right, focused on achieving organizational success at whatever the cost, and cutting corners where it was useful. These decisions were made without regard to the possible consequences of such concerns as honesty or fairness to others. What is apparent from the Deloitte & Touche survey findings is that immoral management can occur on an everyday basis and does not need to be in the league of the megascandals such as Enron or Madoff to be unacceptable behavior.

Moral Management

At the opposite extreme from immoral management is **moral management**. Moral management conforms to the highest standards of ethical behavior or professional standards of conduct. Although it is not always crystal clear what level of ethical standards prevail, moral management strives to be ethical in terms of its focus on elevated ethical norms and professional standards of conduct, motives, goals, orientation toward the law, and general operating strategy.

In contrast to the selfish motives in immoral management, moral management aspires to succeed, but only within the confines of sound ethical precepts; that is, standards predicated on such norms as fairness, justice, respect for rights, and due process. Moral management's motives would be termed fair, balanced, or unselfish. Organizational goals continue to stress profitability, but only within the confines of legal compliance and responsiveness to ethical standards.

Moral management pursues its objectives of profitability, legality, and ethics as both required and desirable. Moral management would not pursue profits at the expense of the law and sound ethics. Indeed, the focus here would be not only on the letter of the law but on the spirit of the law as well. The law would be viewed as a minimal standard of ethical behavior, because moral management strives to operate at a level above what the law mandates.

Spotlight on SUSTAINABILITY

Ray Anderson's Epiphany

Many managers have a conversion experience before they become moral managers. In other words, they had to transition from, probably, an amoral condition to a moral style. Often this comes as a result of an epiphany, a sudden realization in understanding what they experience. A prominent example is that of Ray Anderson, former CEO of Interface Carpet, who more recently was ranked as one of the leading sustainable CEOs in business today. Anderson had a special moment occur when he was reading Paul Hawken's *Ecology of Commerce* in which he came to the conclusion that he, personally, was an environmental villain.

"It was an epiphanic spear in my heart, a life-changing moment; a new definition of success flooded my mind," he told the UK's *Guardian* newspaper about the revelation. He went on to report: "I realized I was a plunderer and it was not a legacy I wanted to leave behind. I wept."

Anderson then made it his new mission to change that legacy and proceeded to, as the *Guardian* puts it, "turn the company into a champion of environmental sustainability." By taking this courageous step, Anderson played a leadership role in getting many other companies into the conversation about sustainability. Without his ethical leadership, it is questionable when or if this would have occurred. Anderson is now a sought-after international speaker who gives nearly 100 talks each year to audiences hungry for a message about the company that is proving the business model for sustainability works.

Sources: Katherine Gustafson, "A Look at America's Most 'Sustainable' CEOs," *Tonic,* http://www.tonic.com/article/triplepundit-sustainable-ceo-contest/. Retrieved July 6, 2010. Also see "Founder and Chairman Ray Anderson Speaks on the Interface Journey and Sustainability," http://www.interfaceglobal.com/getdoc/98a03a4b-65c0-4a61-8984-bc6777b90819/Ray-Watch.aspx. Accessed July 6, 2010.

Operating Strategy of Moral Management. The operating strategy of moral management is to live by sound ethical standards, seeking out only those economic opportunities that the organization or management can pursue within the confines of ethical boundaries. The organization assumes a leadership position when ethical dilemmas arise. The central question guiding moral management's actions, decisions, and behaviors is, "Will this action, decision, behavior, or practice be fair to all stakeholders involved as well as to the organization?"

INTEGRITY STRATEGY Lynn Sharp Paine has proposed an "integrity strategy" that closely resembles the moral management model.[41] The **integrity strategy** is characterized by a conception of ethics as the driving force of an organization. Ethical values shape management's search for opportunities, the design of organizational systems, and the decision-making process. Ethical values in the integrity strategy provide a common frame of reference and serve to unify different functions, lines of business, and employee groups. Organizational ethics, in this view, helps to define what an organization is and what it stands for. Some common features of an integrity strategy include the following,[42] which are all consistent with the moral management model:

- Guiding values and commitments make sense and are clearly communicated.
- Company leaders are personally committed, credible, and willing to take action on the values they espouse.
- Espoused values are integrated into the normal channels of management decision making.

- The organization's systems and structures support and reinforce its values.
- All managers have the skills, knowledge, and competencies to make ethically sound decisions on a daily basis.

HABITS OF MORAL LEADERS Closely related to moral management is the topic of moral leadership. Carroll has set forth what he refers to as the "Seven Habits of Highly Moral Leaders."[43] Adapting the language used by Stephen Covey in his best-selling book *The Seven Habits of Highly Effective People,*[44] these qualities would need to be so common in the leader's approach that they become habitual as a leadership approach. Helping to further flesh out what constitutes a moral manager, the seven habits of highly moral leaders have been set forth as follows:

1. They (highly moral leaders) have a passion to do right.
2. They are morally proactive.
3. They consider all stakeholders.
4. They have a strong ethical character.
5. They have an obsession with fairness.
6. They undertake principled decision making.
7. They integrate ethics wisdom with management wisdom.[45]

Figure 7-8 summarizes the important characteristics of moral managers.

POSITIVE ETHICAL BEHAVIORS Drawing on the "Deloitte & Touche USA Ethics & Workplace" survey cited earlier, following are examples of positive ethical behaviors identified by the survey respondents.[46] These represent everyday ways that managers may display moral management:

- Giving proper credit where it is due
- Always being straightforward and honest when dealing with other employees
- Treating all employees equally
- Being a responsible steward of company assets (e.g., no lavish entertainment)
- Resisting pressure to act unethically
- Recognizing and rewarding ethical behavior of others
- Talking about the importance of ethics and compliance on a regular basis

Illustrative Cases of Moral Management. Several cases of moral management illustrate how this model of management is played out in actual practice.

MCCULLOCH An excellent example of moral management taking the initiative in displaying ethical leadership was provided by McCulloch Corporation, the manufacturer of

---

FIGURE 7-8
Characteristics of
Moral Managers

- These managers conform to a *high level of ethical or right behavior* (moral rectitude).
- They conform to a high level of personal and professional *standards*.
- *Ethical leadership* is commonplace—they search out where people may be hurt.
- Their goal is to succeed but only within the confines of *sound ethical precepts* (fairness, due process).

- *High integrity* is displayed in *thinking*, *speaking*, and *doing*.
- These managers embrace the letter and *spirit* of the law. Law is seen as a *minimal* ethical level. They prefer to operate *above* legal mandates.
- They possess an acute *moral sense* and *moral maturity*.
- Moral managers are the "good guys."

chainsaws. Chainsaws are notoriously dangerous. The Consumer Product Safety Commission one year estimated that there were 123,000 medically attended injuries involving chainsaws, up from 71,000 five years earlier. In spite of these statistics, the Chain Saw Manufacturers Association fought mandatory safety standards. The association claimed that the accident statistics were inflated and did not offer any justification for mandatory regulations. Manufacturers support voluntary standards, although some of them say that when chain brakes—major safety devices—are offered as an option, they do not sell. Apparently, consumers do not have adequate knowledge of the risks inherent in using chainsaws.

McCulloch became dissatisfied with the Chain Saw Manufacturers Association's refusal to support higher standards of safety and withdrew from it. Chain brakes have been standard on McCulloch saws since 1975 and are mandatory for most saws produced in Finland, Britain, and Australia. A Swedish company, Husqvarna, Inc., now installs chain brakes on saws it sells in the United States. Statistics from the Quebec Logging Association and from Sweden demonstrate that kickback-related accidents were reduced by about 80 percent after the mandatory installation of safety standards, including chain brakes.[47]

McCulloch's decision to withdraw from the CSMA is an example of moral management. After attempting and failing to persuade its association to adopt a higher ethical standard that would greatly reduce injuries, it took a courageous action and withdrew from the association. This is a prime example of moral leadership.

NAVISTAR Navistar is a diesel engine manufacturer. One of its plants is located in Huntsville, Alabama. Because of the sour economy in 2009 and 2010, the company had to cut its production from 900 engines a day to 100. The company faced imminent layoffs. Plant manager Chuck Sibley wrestled with the layoff decision and finally came up with a creative solution that saved 50 jobs. Sibley's decision was not to lay off the employees but to send them out into the community, at corporate expense, to help the needy. Their initial assignments were to help Habitat for Humanity, the Salvation Army, and CASA, all nonprofit organizations deeply involved in community volunteerism. The employees were shocked but pleasantly surprised. They will still be paid by Navistar and they will keep all their benefits. The reassignments are expected to be for three months. Plant manager Sibley argued that the company will save money because they will avoid the costs of rehiring and training. The company expects an improvement in market conditions in three months and then the plan is to bring the 50 employees back to the plant.[48] This creative solution not only saved the employees from unemployment, but helped the community in a big way as well. Only a moral manager could come up with such a win–win solution.

MERCK Another well-known case of moral management occurred when Merck & Co., the pharmaceutical firm, invested millions of dollars to develop a drug for treating "river blindness," a Third World disease that was affecting almost 18 million people. Seeing that no government or aid organization was agreeing to buy the drug, Merck pledged to supply the drug for free forever. Merck's recognition that no effective mechanism existed to distribute the drug led to its decision to go far beyond industry practice and organize a committee to oversee the drug's distribution.[49]

We should stress at this time that not all organizations now engaging in moral management have done so all along. These companies sometimes arrived at this posture after years or decades of rising consumer expectations, increased government regulations, lawsuits, and pressure from social and consumer activists. We must think of moral management, therefore, as a desirable posture that in many instances has evolved over periods of several years. If we hold management to an idealistic, 100 percent historical moral purity

ETHICS IN PRACTICE CASE

What They Don't Know Won't Hurt Them

During my last two years in college, I worked for an animal hospital in my hometown. In my time there, many animals passed away in their sleep or for unknown reasons. It was not uncommon. In these situations, our facility would offer the owners the service of an autopsy. An autopsy is a procedure in which the doctor would surgically open up the animal to check for any signs of what might have caused the animal's death.

Mrs. Johnson, a client of ours, brought in her dog that had unfortunately passed away while she was at work. Her dog was only five years old, and the owners were not aware of any health problems. No one, including the doctor, could figure out what had caused the death of Mrs. Johnson's dog. Mrs. Johnson was asked if she would give her consent for the doctor to perform an autopsy on her dog, so maybe they would be able to answer the many questions surrounding his death.

Mrs. Johnson did not want this procedure to be done; she just wanted our facility to take care of her dog's remains. The office manager at the animal hospital told the doctor she should let the vet students, who were doing their rotations at our hospital, go ahead and perform an autopsy as a learning experiment. The office manager mentioned that the owner would never know because we were in charge of the disposal, so it wouldn't be a problem.

1. Is it ethical for the doctor to allow the vet students to perform the autopsy?

2. Should the fact that the owner would never know if the autopsy was performed affect the doctor's decision?

3. What would you do in this situation? Why?

Contributed Anonymously

---

test, no management will fill the bill. Rather, we should consider moral those managements that now see the enlightened self-interest of responding in accordance with the moral management model rather than alternatives.

Amoral Management

Amoral management is not just a middle position on a continuum between immoral and moral management. Conceptually it has been positioned between the other two, but it is different in nature and kind from both, and it is of two kinds: **intentional amoral management** and **unintentional amoral management**.

Intentional Amoral Management.   Amoral managers of this type do not factor ethical considerations into their decisions, actions, and behaviors because they believe business activity resides outside the sphere to which moral judgments apply. These managers are neither moral nor immoral. They simply think that different rules apply in business than in other realms of life. Intentionally amoral managers are in a distinct minority today. At one time, however, as managers first began to think about reconciling business practices with sound ethics, some managers adopted this stance. A few intentionally amoral managers are still around, but they are a vanishing breed in today's ethically conscious world.

Unintentional Amoral Management.   Like intentionally amoral managers, unintentionally amoral managers do not think about business activity in ethical terms, but for different reasons. These managers are simply casual about, careless about, or inattentive to the fact that their decisions and actions may have negative or deleterious effects on others. These managers lack ethical perception and moral awareness. That is, they blithely go through their organizational lives not thinking that what they are doing has an ethical dimension or facet. These managers are well intentioned but are either too insensitive or too self-absorbed to consider the effects of their decisions and actions on others. These managers normally think of themselves as ethical managers, but they are frequently overlooking these unintentional, subconscious, or unconscious aspects. As it turns out, they are more amoral than moral.

UNCONSCIOUS BIASES Sometimes amoral managers may be unconscious of hidden biases that prevent them from being objective. Researchers have found that many business people go through life deluded by the illusion of objectivity. Unconscious, or implicit biases, can run contrary to our consciously held, explicit beliefs.[50] Though most managers think they are ethical, sometimes even the most well-meaning person unwittingly allows unconscious thoughts and biases to influence what appear to be objective decisions. Four sources of unintentional, or unconscious, influences include implicit forms of prejudice, bias that favors one's own group, conflict of interest, and a tendency to over claim credit.[51]

Unconscious biases were believed to be at work among accountants in some of the recent accounting scandals. Three *structural aspects* of accounting bias include ambiguity, attachment, and approval. When ambiguity exists, people tend to reach self-serving conclusions. For example, subjective interpretations of what constitutes a deductible expense may be made in a self-serving fashion. Attachment occurs when auditors, motivated to stay in their clients' good graces, approve things they might otherwise not approve. With respect to approval, external auditors may be reviewing the work of internal auditors, and self-serving biases may become even stronger when other people's biases are being endorsed or approved, especially if those judgments align with one's own biases.[52]

In addition, three aspects of human nature may amplify unconscious biases: familiarity, discounting, and escalation. With *familiarity*, it is noted that people may be more willing to harm strangers (anonymous investors) than individuals they know (clients). *Discounting* refers to the act of overlooking or minimizing decisions that may not have immediate consequences. Finally, *escalation* occurs when an accountant or businessperson allows small judgments to accumulate and become large and then she decides to cover up the unwitting mistakes through concealment. Thus, small indiscretions escalate into larger ones, and unconscious biases grow into conscious corruption.[53]

Amoral management pursues profitability as its goal but does not cognitively attend to moral issues that may be intertwined with that pursuit. If there is an ethical guide to amoral management, it would be the marketplace as constrained by law—the letter of the law, not the spirit. The amoral manager sees the law as the parameters within which business pursuits take place.

Operating Strategy of Amoral Management. The operating strategy of amoral management is not to bridle managers with excessive ethical structure but to permit free rein within the unspoken but understood tenets of the free enterprise system. Personal ethics may periodically or unintentionally enter into managerial decisions, but it does not preoccupy management. Furthermore, the impact of decisions on others is an afterthought, if it ever gets considered at all.

Amoral management represents a model of decision making in which the managers' ethical mental gears, to the extent that they are present, are stuck in neutral. The key management question guiding decision making is, "Can we make money with this action, decision, or behavior?" Note that the question does not imply an active or implicit intent to be either moral or immoral.

COMPLIANCE STRATEGY Paine has articulated a "compliance strategy" that is consistent with amoral management. The **compliance strategy**, as contrasted with her integrity

FIGURE 7-9 Characteristics of Amoral Managers	**Intentionally Amoral Managers**	**Unintentionally Amoral Managers**
	• These managers don't think ethics and business should "mix." • Business and ethics are seen as existing in *separate* spheres. Ethics is seen as too "Sunday schoolish" and not applicable to business. • These managers are a vanishing breed. There are very few managers like this left in the world.	• These managers forget to consider the *ethical dimension* of decision making. • They just don't *"think ethically."* • They may lack *ethical perception* or awareness; they have no "ethics buds" that help them sense the ethical dimension. • They are well intentioned, but morally casual or careless; may be morally *unconscious.* • Their ethical gears, if they exist, are in *neutral.*

strategy discussed earlier, is more focused on submission to the law as its driving force. The compliance strategy is lawyer driven and is oriented not toward ethics or integrity but more toward compliance with existing regulatory and criminal law. The compliance approach uses deterrence as its underlying assumption. This approach envisions managers as rational maximizers of self-interest, responsive to the personal costs and benefits of their choices, yet indifferent to the moral legitimacy of those choices.[54]

Figure 7-9 summarizes the major characteristics of amoral managers.

Illustrative Cases of Amoral Management. There are perhaps more examples of unintentionally amoral management than any other kind.

EARLY EXAMPLES When police departments first stipulated that recruits must be at least 5′9″ tall and weigh at least 180 pounds, they were making an amoral decision, because they were not considering the harmful exclusion this would impose on women and other ethnic groups who do not, on average, attain that height and weight. When companies decided to use scantily clad young women to advertise autos, men's cologne, and other products, these companies were not thinking of the degrading and demeaning characterization of women that would result from what they thought was an ethically neutral decision. When firms decided to do business in South Africa years ago, their decisions were neither moral nor immoral, but a major, unanticipated consequence of these decisions was the appearance of capitalistic (or U.S.) approval of apartheid. When Domino's initially decided to deliver pizza orders within 30 minutes or the food was free, they didn't think about how such a policy might induce their drivers to speed and, sometimes, cause auto accidents. This policy was later dropped.

NESTLÉ Nestlé's initial decision to market infant formula in Third World countries (see Chapter 10) could have been an amoral decision when it was first made. Nestlé may not have considered the detrimental effects such a seemingly innocent business decision would have on mothers and babies in a land of impure water, poverty, and illiteracy. In other words, Nestlé simply wasn't factoring ethical considerations into its decisions.

SEARS Another useful illustration of unintentionally amoral management involved the case of Sears Roebuck and Co. and its automotive service business, which spanned much of the 1990s. Paine described how consumers and attorneys general in 40 states accused the company of misleading consumers and selling them unneeded parts and services.[55] In the face of declining revenues and a shrinking market share, Sears' executives put into place new goals, quotas, and incentives for auto-center service personnel. Service employees were told to meet product-specific and service-specific quotas—sell so many brake jobs, batteries, and front-end alignments—or face consequences such as reduced working hours or transfers. Some employees spoke of the "pressure" they felt to generate business.

Although Sears' executives did not set out to defraud customers, they put into place a commission system that led to Sears' employees feeling pressure to sell products and services that consumers did not need. Soon after the complaints against Sears occurred, CEO Edward Brennan acknowledged that management had created an environment in which mistakes were made, although no intent to deceive consumers had existed. Fortunately, Sears eliminated its quota system as a partial remedy to the problem.[56]

The Sears case is a classic example of unintentionally amoral management—a well-intentioned company drifting into questionable practices because it just did not think ethically. The company simply did not think through the impacts that its strategic decisions would have on important stakeholders. Today, many companies do not think carefully about the effects employee rewards systems might have on customers and others.

Figure 7-10 provides a summary of the major characteristics of immoral, amoral, and moral management. It compares the three in terms of ethical norms, motives, goals, orientation toward the law, and operating strategy.

FIGURE 7-10 Three Approaches to Management Ethics

Organizational Characteristics		Immoral Management	Amoral Management	Moral Management
	Ethical Norms	Management decisions, actions, and behavior imply a positive and active opposition to what is moral (ethical). Decisions are discordant with accepted ethical principles. An active negation of what is moral is implied.	Management is neither moral nor immoral, but decisions lie outside the sphere to which moral judgments apply. Management activity is outside or beyond the moral order of a particular code. May imply a lack of ethical perception and moral awareness.	Management activity conforms to a standard of ethical, or right, behavior. Conforms to accepted professional standards of conduct. Ethical leadership is commonplace on the part of management.
	Motives	Selfish. Management cares only about its or the company's gains.	Well-intentioned but selfish in the sense that impact on others is not considered.	Good. Management wants to succeed but only within the confines of sound ethical precepts (fairness, justice, due process).
	Goals	Profitability and organizational success at any price.	Profitability. Other goals are not considered.	Profitability within the confines of legal obedience and ethical standards.
	Orientation Toward Law	Legal standards are barriers that management must overcome to accomplish what it wants.	Law is the ethical guide, preferably the letter of the law. The central question is what we can do legally.	Obedience toward letter and spirit of the law. Law is a minimal ethical behavior. Prefer to operate well above what law mandates.
	Strategy	Exploit opportunities for corporate gain. Cut corners when it appears useful.	Give managers free rein. Personal ethics may apply but only if managers choose. Respond to legal mandates if caught and required to do so.	Live by sound ethical standards. Assume leadership position when ethical dilemmas arise. Enlightened self-interest.

Source: Archie B. Carroll, "In Search of the Moral Manager," *Business Horizons* (March/April 1987), 8. Copyright © 1987 by the Foundation for the School of Business at Indiana University. Used with permission.

Two Hypotheses Regarding the Models of Management Morality

There are numerous other examples of amoral management, but the ones presented here should suffice to illustrate the point. A thorough study has not been conducted to ascertain precisely what proportions of managers each model represents in the total management population. However, two possible hypotheses regarding the moral management models may be set forth.

Population Hypothesis.   One hypothesis is that the distribution of the three models might approximate a normal curve, with the amoral group occupying the large middle part of the curve and the moral and immoral categories occupying the smaller tails of the curve. It is difficult to research this question. If you asked managers what they thought they were or what others thought they were, a self-serving bias would likely enter in and you would not get an accurate, unbiased picture. Another approach would be to observe management actions. This would be nearly impossible because it is not possible to observe all management actions for any sustained period. Therefore, the supposition remains a hypothesis based on one person's judgment of what is going on in the management population.

Individual Hypothesis.   Equally disturbing as the belief that the amoral management style is common among managers today is an alternative hypothesis that, within the individual manager, these three models may operate at various times and under various circumstances. That is, the average manager may be amoral most of the time but may slip into a moral or an immoral mode on occasion, based on a variety of impinging factors. Like the population hypothesis, this view cannot be empirically supported at this time, but it does provide an interesting perspective for managers to ponder. This perspective would be somewhat similar to the situational ethics argument that has been around for some time. Is the individual hypothesis more likely valid than the population hypothesis? Could it be that both may exist at the same time?

Amoral Management Is a Serious Organizational Problem.   With the exception of the major ethics scandals witnessed in the past decade, it could be argued that the more serious ethical problem in organizations today seems to be the group of well-intended managers who for one reason or another subscribe to or live out the amoral ethic. These are managers who are driven primarily by profitability or a bottom-line ethos, which regards economic success as the exclusive barometer of organizational and personal achievement. These amoral managers are basically good people, but they

FIGURE 7-11 Three Models of Management Morality and Emphases on CSR

Models of Management Morality	COMPONENTS OF THE CSR DEFINITION			
	Economic Responsibility	Legal Responsibility	Ethical Responsibility	Philanthropic Responsibility
Immoral management	XXX	X		X
Amoral management	XXX	XX	X	X
Moral management	XXX	XXX	XXX	XXX

Weighting code:
X = token consideration (appearances only)
XX = moderate consideration
XXX = significant consideration

FIGURE 7-12 The Moral Management Models and Acceptance or Rejection of Stakeholder Thinking (SHT)

Moral Management Model	Acceptance of Stakeholder Thinking (SHT)	Stakeholder Thinking Posture Embraced
Immoral management	SHT rejected: management is self-absorbed	SHT rejected, not deemed useful. Accepts profit maximization model but does not really pursue it.
Amoral management	SHT accepted: narrow view (minimum number of stakeholders considered)	Instrumental view of SHT prevails. How will it help management?
Moral management	SHT enthusiastically embraced: wider view (maximum number of stakeholders considered)	Normative view of SHT prevails. SHT is fully embraced in all decision making.

essentially see the competitive business world as ethically neutral. Until this group of managers moves toward the moral management ethic, we will continue to see businesses and other organizations criticized as they have been in the past.

To connect the three models of management morality with concepts introduced earlier, we show in Figure 7-11 how the components of corporate social responsibility (Chapter 2) would likely be viewed by managers using each of the three models of management morality.

We illustrate in Figure 7-12 how managers using the three models would probably embrace or reject the stakeholder concept or stakeholder thinking (Chapter 3). It is hoped that these suggested interrelationships among these concepts will make them easier to understand and appreciate.

Making Moral Management Actionable

The characteristics of immoral, moral, and amoral management discussed in this chapter should provide some useful benchmarks for managerial self-analysis, because self-analysis and introspection will eventually be the way in which managers will recognize the need to move from the immoral or amoral ethic to the moral ethic. Numerous others have suggested management training for business ethics. The recommendation for ethics training has great potential, but is not discussed here. Ethics training will be considered more fully in Chapter 8. However, until senior management fully embraces the concept of moral management, the transformation in organizational culture that is so essential for moral management to blossom, thrive, and flourish will not take place. Ultimately, senior management has the leadership responsibility to show the way to an ethical organizational climate by leading the transition from amoral to moral management, whether this is done by business ethics training and workshops, codes of conduct, mission/vision statements, ethics officers, tighter financial controls, more ethically sensitive decision-making processes, or leadership by example. Even if senior management does not take the lead, managers at lower levels can implement moral management on their own. It is possible for moral management to percolate upwards in the organization.

Underlying all these efforts, however, needs to be the fundamental recognition that amoral management exists and that it is an undesirable condition that can be surely, if not easily, remedied. Most notably, organizational leaders must acknowledge that amoral management is a morally vacuous condition that can be quite easily disguised as just an innocent, practical, bottom-line philosophy—something to take pride in. Amoral management is, however, and will continue to be, the bane of the management profession until it is recognized for what it really is and until managers take steps to overcome it. Most managers are not "bad guys," as they frequently are portrayed, but the idea that managerial decision making can be ethically neutral is bankrupt and not tenable in the society of the new millennium.[57] To make moral management actionable, both immoral and amoral management must be discarded.

Developing Moral Judgment

It is helpful to know something about how individuals, whether they are managers or employees, develop moral (or ethical) judgment. Perhaps if we knew more about this process, we could better understand our own behavior and the behavior of those around us and those we manage. Further, we might be able to better design reward systems for encouraging ethical behavior if we knew more about how employees and others think about ethics. A good starting point is to come to appreciate what psychologists have to say about how we as individuals develop morally. The major research on this point is **Kohlberg's levels of moral development**.[58] After this discussion, we consider other sources of a manager's values, especially those emanating from both societal sources and from within the organization itself.

Levels of Moral Development

The psychologist, Lawrence Kohlberg, has done extensive research into the topic of **moral development**. He concluded, on the basis of over 20 years of research, that there is a general sequence of three levels (each with two stages) through which individuals evolve in learning to think or develop morally. There is widespread practical usage of his levels of moral development, and this suggests a general if not unanimous consensus that it is valuable. Figure 7-13 illustrates Kohlberg's three levels and six stages. There it can be seen that as one develops morally, the focus moves from the self, to others, and then to humankind.

Level 1: Preconventional Level.   At the preconventional level of moral development, which is typically descriptive of how people behave as infants and children, the focus is mainly on the *self*. As an infant starts to grow, his or her main behavioral reactions are in response to punishments and rewards. Stage 1 is the *reaction-to-punishment stage*. If

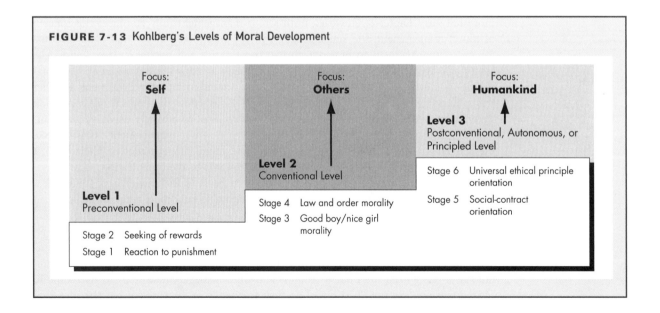

FIGURE 7-13 Kohlberg's Levels of Moral Development

Focus: **Self**

Focus: **Others**

Focus: **Humankind**

Level 3
Postconventional, Autonomous, or Principled Level

Level 2
Conventional Level

| Stage 6 | Universal ethical principle orientation |
| Stage 5 | Social-contract orientation |

Level 1
Preconventional Level

| Stage 4 | Law and order morality |
| Stage 3 | Good boy/nice girl morality |

| Stage 2 | Seeking of rewards |
| Stage 1 | Reaction to punishment |

you want a child to do something (such as stay out of the street) at a very early age, spanking or scolding is often needed. The orientation at this stage is toward avoidance of pain.

As the child gets a bit older, rewards start to work. Stage 2 is the *seeking-of-rewards stage*. The child begins to see some connection between being "good" (i.e., doing what Mom or Dad wants the child to do) and some reward that may be forthcoming. The reward may be parental praise or something tangible, such as candy, extra TV time, or a trip to the movies. At this preconventional level, children do not completely understand the moral idea of "right" and "wrong" but rather learn to behave according to the consequences—punishments or rewards—that are likely to follow.

Though we normally associate the preconventional level with the moral development of children, many adults in organizations are significantly influenced by rewards and punishments. Consequently, the preconventional level of motivation may be observed in adults as well as children and is relevant to a discussion of adult moral maturity. Like children, adults in responsible positions react to punishments (organizational sanctions) or seek rewards (approval). Ethical egoism is dominant at Level 1.

Level 2: Conventional Level.   As a person matures, she or he learns that there are *others* whose ideas or welfare ought to be considered. Initially, these others include family and friends. At the conventional level of moral development, the individual learns the importance of conforming to the conventional norms of society. This is the level at which social relationships become dominant.

The conventional level is composed of two stages. Stage 3 has been called the "*good boy/nice girl*" *morality stage*. The young person learns that there are some rewards (such as feelings of acceptance, trust, loyalty, or friendship) for living up to what is expected by family and peers, so the individual begins to conform to what is generally expected of a good son, daughter, sister, brother, friend, and so on.

Stage 4 is the *law-and-order morality stage*. Not only does the individual learn to respond to family, friends, the school, and the church, as in Stage 3, but the individual now recognizes that there are certain norms in society (in school, in the theater, in the mall, in stores, in the car, waiting in line) that are expected or needed if society is to function in an orderly fashion. Thus, the individual becomes socialized or acculturated into what being a good citizen means. These rules for living include not only the actual laws (don't run a red light, don't walk until the "Walk" light comes on) but also other, less official norms (don't break into line, be sure to tip the server, turn your cell phone off in restaurants, don't text or talk while driving). At Stage 4, the individual sees that she or he is part of a larger social system and that to function in and be accepted by this social system requires a considerable degree of acceptance of and conformity to the norms and standards of society. Therefore, many organizational members are strongly influenced by society's conventions as manifested in both Stages 3 and 4 as described.

Level 3: Postconventional, Autonomous, or Principled Level.   At this third level, which Kohlberg argues few people reach (and those who do reach it have trouble staying there), the focus moves beyond those "others" who are of immediate importance to the individual to *humankind* as a whole. At the postconventional level of moral development, the individual develops a concept of ethics that is more mature than the conventionally articulated notion. Thus, it is sometimes called the level at which moral principles become self-accepted, not because they are held by society but because the individual now perceives and embraces them as "right."

Kohlberg's third level consists of two stages that differ by whether the individual can just follow rules established by society or others, or engage in his or her own moral reasoning. Stage 5 is the *social-contract orientation*. At this stage, right action is thought of in terms of general individual rights and standards that have been critically examined and agreed upon by society as a whole. Social contracts have influence. There is a clear awareness of the relativism of personal values and a corresponding emphasis on fair processes for reaching consensus.

Stage 6 is the *universal-ethical-principle orientation*. Here the individual uses his or her thinking and conscience in accord with self-chosen ethical principles that are anticipated to be universal, comprehensive, and consistent. These universal principles (such as the Golden Rule) might be focused on such ideals as justice, human rights, and social welfare. At this stage, the individual is motivated by a commitment to universal principles or guidelines.

Kohlberg suggests that at Level 3 the individual is able to rise above the conventional level where "rightness" and "wrongness" are defined by others and societal institutions and that she or he is able to defend or justify her or his actions on some higher ethical basis. For example, in our society the law tells us we should not discriminate against minorities. A Level 2 manager might not discriminate because to do so is to violate the law and social custom. A Level 3 manager would not discriminate but might offer a different reason—for example, it is wrong to discriminate because it violates universal principles of human rights and justice. Part of the difference between Levels 2 and 3, therefore, is traceable to the motivation for the course of action taken. This takes us back to our earlier discussion of motivation as one of the important ethics questions.

The discussion to this point may have suggested that we are at Level 1 as infants, at Level 2 as youths, and, finally, at Level 3 as adults. There is some approximate correspondence between chronological age and Levels 1 and 2, but the important point should be made that Kohlberg thinks many of us as adults never get beyond Level 2. The idea of getting to Level 3 as managers or employees is desirable, because it would require us to think about people, products, and markets at a higher ethical level than that generally attained by conventional society. However, even if we never get there, Level 3 urges us to continually ask "What ought to be?" The first two levels tell us a lot about moral development that should be useful to us as managers. There are not many people who consistently operate according to Level 3 principles. Sometimes a manager or employee may dip into Level 3 on a certain issue or for a certain period of time. Sustaining that level, however, is quite challenging.

If we frame the issue in terms of the question, "Why do managers and employees behave ethically?" we might infer conclusions from Kohlberg that look like those in Figure 7-14.

Ethics of Care Alternative to Kohlberg.

One of the major criticisms of Kohlberg's research was set forth by Carol Gilligan. Gilligan argued that Kohlberg's conclusions may accurately depict the stages of moral development among men, whom he used as his research subjects, but that his findings are not generalizable to women.[59] According to Gilligan's view, men tend to deal with moral issues in terms that are impersonal, impartial, and abstract. Examples might include the principles of justice and rights that Kohlberg argues are relevant at the postconventional level. Women, on the other hand, perceive themselves to be part of a network of relationships with family and friends and thus are more focused on *relationship maintenance* and *hurt avoidance* when they confront moral issues. For women, then, morality is often more a matter of caring and showing responsibility toward those involved in their relationships than in adhering to abstract or impersonal principles, such as justice. This alternative view of ethics has been called the ethics of care.

According to Gilligan, women move in and out of three moral levels.[60] At the first level, the *self* is the sole object of concern. At the second level, the chief desire is to *establish connections and participate* in social life. In other words, maintaining relationships

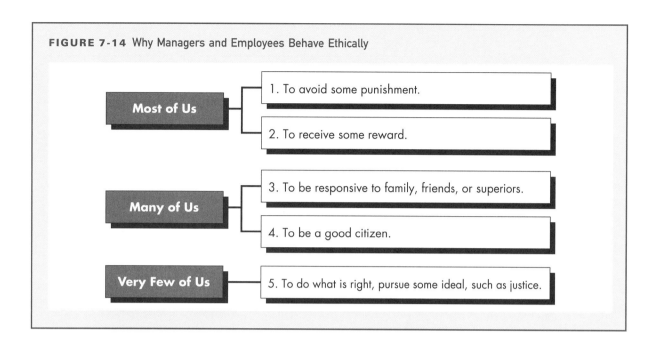

FIGURE 7-14 Why Managers and Employees Behave Ethically

Most of Us
1. To avoid some punishment.
2. To receive some reward.

Many of Us
3. To be responsive to family, friends, or superiors.
4. To be a good citizen.

Very Few of Us
5. To do what is right, pursue some ideal, such as justice.

or directing one's thoughts toward others becomes dominant. Gilligan says that this is the conventional notion of women. At the third level, women recognize their own needs and the *needs of others*—those with whom they have relationships. Gilligan goes on to say that women never settle completely at one level. As they attain moral maturity, they do more of their thinking and make more of their decisions at the third level. This level requires care for others as well as care for oneself. In this view, morality moves away from the legalistic, self-centered approach that some say characterizes traditional ethics.

Some research does not show that moral development varies by gender in the fashion described by Gilligan. However, it does support Gilligan's claim that a different perspective toward moral issues is sometimes used. Apparently, both men and women sometimes employ an impartial or impersonal moral-rules perspective and sometimes they employ a care-and-responsibility perspective. This "care perspective" is still at an early stage of research, but it is useful to know that perspectives other than those found by Kohlberg are being considered.[61] More will be said about the ethics of caring in the next chapter. In the final analysis, we need to exercise care when thinking about the applicability of Kohlberg's and Gilligan's research as well as the thousands of studies that have sought to fine tune their research. The value of this research, however, is the idea that moral development levels and stages do occur and that managers need to be aware of and sensitive to this in their approaches to dealing with people and ethics challenges in their organizations.

Different Sources of a Person's Values

In addition to considering the levels of moral development as an explanation of how and why people behave ethically, it is also useful to look at the different *sources of a manager's (employee's) values*. Ethics and values are intimately related. We referred earlier to ethics as the set of moral principles or values that drives behavior. Thus, the rightness or wrongness of behavior really turns out to be a manifestation of the ethical beliefs held by the individual. Values, on the other hand, are the individual's concepts of the relative

ETHICS IN PRACTICE CASE

Flowers versus Eyes: When Would You Have Paid?

It is human nature to think that ethical behavior is more likely provoked when a person is being observed. But what if the eyes doing the observing are not real? In an interesting experiment, some fascinating results followed. Apparently, a psychology department of a university in the United Kingdom, less than three hours from London, was experiencing a problem. Like most departments, there was a coffee station where faculty and staff could help themselves to coffee and then leave their money in the tray (approximately $1). But it was noticed by many that a number of people were helping themselves to coffee and not paying.

One of the professors came up with an idea. He initiated an experiment. For ten weeks, he and his assistants alternately taped two poster signs above the coffee station. One week, the poster displayed a picture of flowers. Another week, the poster displayed a picture of "staring eyes." They wondered whether the different posters, or pictures, would evoke different responses in terms of whether people honestly paid for their coffee.

After some weeks, the researchers noted an interesting pattern. When the "eyes poster" was displayed above the coffee station, the coffee and tea drinkers contributed 2.76 times more money than when the "flower poster" was displayed. The researchers surmised that

the sensation of "being watched," though the eyes were not real, motivated people to be more honest about paying for their coffee or tea. The originator of the idea admitted that the results were more dramatic than the slight effect expected.

Later, a police department in Birmingham, England, read a paper about the aforementioned experiment and was impressed. They decided to slap posters of staring eyes all around the city. They named their venture "We've Got Our Eyes on Criminals." Only time will tell whether the program will have the intended effect on vandalism and crime.

1. Was it unethical for the professor to conduct such an experiment on his colleagues without announcing it?

2. Are you surprised at the results?

3. Evaluate the aforementioned experiment using Kohlberg's levels of moral development. Does the experiment support or refute the results of the experiment? Would it make a difference whether the coffee drinkers were men or women?

4. Do you think the police department scheme will work? Why or why not?

Source: This case was inspired by Clive Thompson, "The Eyes of Honesty," _New York Times Magazine_ (Dec. 10, 2006), 48.

worth, utility, or importance of certain ideas. Values reflect what the individual considers important in the larger scheme of things. One's values, therefore, shape one's ethics. Because this is so, it is important to understand the many different value-shaping forces that influence employees and managers.

The increasing pluralism of the society in which we live has exposed managers to a large number of values of many different kinds, and this has resulted in ethical diversity. One way to examine the sources of a manager's values is by considering both forces that originate from _outside the organization_ to shape or influence the manager and those that emanate from _within the organization_. This, unfortunately, is not as simply done as we would like, because some sources are difficult to pinpoint. The distinction should lend some order to our discussion, however.

Sources External to the Organization: The Web of Values.　　The external sources of a person's values refer to those broad sociocultural values that have emerged in society over a long period of time. Although current events (fraud, deception, bribery) seem to affect these historic values by bringing specific ones into clearer focus at a given time, these values are rather enduring and change slowly. It has been stated that "every executive resides at the center of a web of values" and that there are five principal repositories of values influencing businesspeople. These five include religious, philosophical, cultural, legal, and professional values.[62] Each deserves brief consideration.

RELIGIOUS VALUES   Religion has long been a basic source of morality in American society, as in most societies. Religion and morality are so intertwined that William Barclay related them for definitional purposes: "Ethics is the bit of religion that tells us how we ought to behave."[63] The biblical tradition of Judeo-Christian theology forms the core for much of what Western society believes today about the importance of work, the concept of fairness, and the dignity of the individual. Other religious traditions also inform management behavior and action.

PHILOSOPHICAL VALUES   Philosophy and various philosophical systems are also external sources of the manager's values. Beginning with preachments of the ancient Greeks, philosophers have claimed to demonstrate that *reason* can provide us with principles or morals in the same way it gives us the principles of mathematics. John Locke argued that morals are mathematically demonstrable, although he never explained how.[64] Aristotle with his Golden Rule and his doctrine of the mean, Kant with his categorical imperative, Bentham with his pain and pleasure calculus, and modern-day existentialists have shown us the influence of various kinds of reasons for ethical choice. Today, the strong influence of moral relativism and postmodernism have influenced some people's values.

CULTURAL VALUES   Culture is that broad synthesis of societal norms and values emanating from everyday living. Culture has also had an impact on the manager's and employees' thinking. Modern examples of culture include music, movies, television, and the Internet. The melting-pot culture of the United States is a potpourri of norms, customs, and rules that defy summarization. In recent years, it has become difficult to summarize what messages the culture is sending people about ethics. In an influential book, *Moral Freedom: The Search for Virtue in a World of Choice*, by Alan Wolfe, the author argues that the United States, like other Western nations, is undergoing a radical revolution in morals and is now, morally speaking, a new society.[65] Wolfe thinks the traditional values that our culture has looked upon with authority (churches, families, neighborhoods, civic leaders) have lost the ability to influence people as they once did.

Wolfe goes on to say that as more and more areas of life have become democratized and open to consumer "choice," people have come to assume that they have the right to determine for themselves what it means to lead a good and virtuous life. He says that a key element in this new moral universe is nonjudgmentalism, which pushes society to suspend judgment on much immoral behavior or interpret immoral behavior as not the fault of the perpetrator. Thus, although many people may uphold the old virtues, in principle, they turn them into personal "options" in practice.[66] These trends are clearly a departure from the past, and are likely impacting the way managers perceive the world of business. Employees, likewise, share these same perspectives and this creates challenges for managers.

LEGAL VALUES   The legal system has been and continues to be one of the most powerful forces defining what is ethical and what is not for managers and employees. This is true even though ethical behavior generally is that which occurs over and above legal dictates. As stated earlier, the law represents the codification of what the society considers right and wrong or fair. Although we as members of society do not completely agree with every law in existence, there often is more consensus for law than for ethics. Law, then, "mirrors the ideas of the entire society."[67] Law represents a minimum ethic of behavior but does not encompass all the ethical standards of behavior. Law addresses only the grossest violations of society's sense of right, wrong, and fairness and thus is not adequate to describe completely all that is acceptable or unacceptable. Because it represents our official consensus ethic, however, its influence is pervasive and widely accepted.

In recent years, it has become an understatement to observe that we live in a litigious society. This trend toward suing someone to bring about justice has clearly had an impact on management decision making. Whereas the threat of litigation may make managers more careful in their treatment of stakeholders, the threat of losing tens or hundreds of millions of dollars has distorted decision making and caused many managers and companies to be running scared—never knowing exactly what is the best or fairest course of action to pursue. Therefore, it is easy to see how laws and regulations are among the most influential drivers of business ethics.[68]

PROFESSIONAL VALUES These include those emanating from professional organizations and societies that represent various jobs and positions. As such, they presumably articulate the ethical consensus of the leaders of those professions. For example, the Public Relations Society of America has a code of ethics that public relations executives have imposed on themselves as their own guide to behavior. The National Association of Realtors has created its own code of conduct. Professional values thus exert a more particularized impact on the manager than the four broader values discussed earlier.

In sum, several sources of values that are external to the organization come to bear on the manager and employees and influence their ethics. In addition to those mentioned, people are influenced by family, friends, acquaintances, and social events and current events of the day. People thus come to the workplace with personal philosophies that truly are a composite of numerous interacting values that have shaped their views of the world, of life, and of business.

Sources Internal to the Organization.   The external forces constitute the broad background or milieu against which a manager or an employee behaves or acts. There are, in addition, a number of more immediate factors that help to channel the individual's values and behavior. These values grow out of the specific organizational experience itself. These internal sources of a manager's values (within the business organization) constitute more immediate and direct influences on one's actions and decisions.

When an individual goes to work for an organization, a socialization process takes place in which the individual comes to adopt the predominant values of that organization. The individual learns rather quickly that to survive and to succeed, certain norms must be perpetuated and honored. Several of these "internal" norms that are prevalent in business organizations include:

- Respect for the authority structure
- Loyalty to bosses and the organization
- Conformity to principles and practices
- Performance counts above all else
- Results count above all else

Each of these norms may take on a major influence in a person who subordinates her or his own standard of ethics to those of the organization. In fact, research suggests that these internal sources play a much more significant role in shaping business ethics than do the host of external sources we considered first. *Respect for the authority structure, loyalty, conformity, performance*, and *results* have been historically synonymous with survival and success in business. When these influences are operating together, they form a composite "bottom-line" mentality that is remarkably influential in its impact on individual and group behavior. These values form the central motif of organizational activity and direction.

Underlying the first three norms is the focus on performance and results. This has been called the "calculus of the bottom line."[69] One does not need to study business organizations for long to recognize that the bottom line—profits—is the sacred instrumental value that seems to take precedence over all others. "Profits now" rather than later seems to be the orientation that spells success for managers and employees alike. Respect for authority, loyalty, and conformity become means to an end, although one could certainly find organizations and people who see these as legitimate ends in themselves. Only recently are some managers and organizations starting to respond to the "multiple bottom line" or "triple-bottom-line" perspective introduced in Chapter 2. From the standpoint of sustainability, managers will increasingly need to think and practice beyond that which is dictated by the short-term obsession with quarterly earnings.

Elements of Moral Judgment

A positive way to close out this chapter is to consider what it takes for moral or ethical judgment to develop. For growth in moral judgment to take place, it is necessary to appreciate the key elements involved in making moral judgments. This is a notion central to the transition from the amoral management condition to the moral management condition. Powers and Vogel have suggested that there are six major elements or capacities that are essential to making moral judgments: (1) moral imagination, (2) moral identification and ordering, (3) moral evaluation, (4) tolerance of moral disagreement and ambiguity, (5) integration of managerial and moral competence, and (6) a sense of moral obligation.[70] Each reveals an essential ingredient in developing moral judgment, which then forms the basis for personal and organizational ethics to be examined in the next chapter.

Moral Imagination

Moral imagination refers to the ability to perceive that a web of competing economic relationships is, at the same time, a web of moral or ethical relationships. Business and ethics are not separate topics but occur side by side in organizations. Those with moral imagination are able to perceive the presence of ethical issues and develop creative ways for dealing with them. Developing moral imagination means not only becoming sensitive to ethical issues in business decision making but also developing the perspective of searching out subtle places where people are likely to be harmfully affected by adverse decision making or behaviors of managers. Moral imagination requires the manager to rise above the everyday stress and confusion and carefully identify the ethical issues and values conflicts that exist in the organization or for which symptoms of problems may be present.

Moral Identification and Ordering

Moral identification and ordering refers to the ability to discern the relevance or nonrelevance of moral factors that are introduced into a decision-making situation. Are the moral issues actual or just rhetorical? The ability to see moral issues as issues that can be dealt with is at stake here. Once moral issues have been identified, they must be ranked, or ordered, just as economic or technological issues are prioritized during the decision-making process. A manager must not only develop this skill through experience but also finely hone it through repetition and the application of ethics principles. In this prioritizing process, a manager may conclude that worker safety is more important than worker privacy, though both are important qualities.

Moral Evaluation

Once issues have been identified and ordered, evaluations must be made. *Moral evaluation* is the practical, decision phase of moral judgment and entails essential skills, such as coherence and consistency that have proved to be effective principles in other contexts. What managers need to do here is to understand the importance of clear principles, develop processes for weighing ethical factors, and develop the ability to identify what the likely moral as well as economic outcomes of a decision will be. Important here is the foresight of likely consequences of different courses of action.

The real challenge in moral evaluation is to integrate the concern for others into organizational goals, purposes, and legitimacy. In the final analysis, though, the manager may not know the "right" answer or solution, although moral sensitivity has been introduced into the process.

Tolerance of Moral Disagreement and Ambiguity

An objection managers often have to ethics discussions is the amount of disagreement generated and the volume of ambiguity that must be tolerated. This must be accepted, however, because it is a natural part of ethics discussions. To be sure, managers need closure and precision in their decisions. But the situation is seldom clear in moral discussions, just as it is in many traditional and more familiar decision contexts of managers, such as introducing a new product based on limited test marketing, choosing a new executive for a key position, deciding which of a number of excellent computer systems to install, or making a strategic decision based on instincts. All of these are risky decisions, but managers have become accustomed to making them in spite of the disagreements and ambiguity that prevail among those involved in the decision or within the individual. The *tolerance of moral disagreement and ambiguity* is simply an extension of a managerial aptitude that is present in practically all decision-making situations managers face.

Integration of Managerial and Moral Competence

The *integration of managerial and moral competence* underlies all that we have been discussing. Moral issues in management do not arise in isolation from traditional business decision making but right in the middle of it. The scandals that major corporations face today did not occur independently of the companies' economic activities but were embedded in a series of decisions made at various points in time and culminated from those earlier decisions. Therefore, moral competence is an integral part of managerial competence. Managers are learning—some the hard way—that there is a significant corporate, and in many instances, personal price to pay for their amorality. The amoral manager sees ethical decisions as isolated and independent of managerial decisions and competence, but the moral manager sees every evolving decision as one in which an ethical perspective must be integrated. This kind of future-looking view is essential to sustainable organizations.

A Sense of Moral Obligation

The foundation for all the capacities we have discussed is a *sense of moral obligation* and integrity. This wisdom is the key to the process but is the most difficult to acquire. This sense requires the intuitive or learned understanding that moral threads—a concern for fairness, justice, and due process to people, groups, and communities—are woven into the fabric of managerial decision making and are the integral components that hold systems together.

These qualities are perfectly consistent with, and indeed are essential prerequisites to, the free enterprise system as we know it today. One can go back in time to Adam Smith and the foundation tenets of the free enterprise system and not find references to immoral or unethical practices as being elements needed for the system to work. The late Milton Friedman, our modern-day Adam Smith, even alluded to the importance of ethics when he stated that the purpose of business is "to make as much money as possible while conforming to the basic rules of society, both those embodied in the law and *those embodied in ethical custom*."[71] The moral manager develops a sense of moral obligation and integrity that is the glue that holds together the decision-making process in which human welfare is inevitably at stake. Indeed, the sense of moral obligation is what holds society and the business system together as a sustainable enterprise.

Figure 7-15 summarizes the six elements of moral judgment identified by Powers and Vogel as they might be perceived by amoral and moral managers. The contrast between the two perspectives should be helpful in understanding each element of moral judgment.

FIGURE 7-15 Elements of Moral Judgment in Amoral and Moral Managers

Amoral Managers	Moral Managers
Moral Imagination	
See a web of competing economic claims as just that and nothing more.	Perceive that a web of competing economic claims is simultaneously a web of moral relationships.
Are insensitive to and unaware of the hidden dimensions of where people are likely to get hurt.	Are sensitive to and hunt out the hidden dimensions of where people are likely to get hurt.
Moral Identification and Ordering	
See moral claims as squishy and not definite enough to order into hierarchies with other claims.	See which moral claims being made are relevant or irrelevant; order moral factors just as economic factors are ordered.
Moral Evaluation	
Are erratic in their application of ethics if it gets applied at all.	Are coherent and consistent in their normative reasoning.
Tolerance of Moral Disagreement and Ambiguity	
Cite ethical disagreement and ambiguity as reasons for forgetting ethics altogether.	Tolerate ethical disagreement and ambiguity while honestly acknowledging that decisions are not precise like mathematics but must finally be made nevertheless.
Integration of Managerial and Moral Competence	
See ethical decisions as isolated and independent of managerial decisions and managerial competence.	See every evolving decision as one in which a moral perspective must be integrated with a managerial one.
A Sense of Moral Obligation	
Have no sense of moral obligation and integrity that extends beyond managerial responsibility.	Have a sense of moral obligation and integrity that holds together the decision-making process in which human welfare is at stake.

Source: Archie B. Carroll, "In Search of the Moral Manager," *Business Horizons* (March/April 1987), 15. Copyright © 1987 by the Foundation for the School of Business at Indiana University. Used with permission.

Summary

Business ethics has become a serious challenge for the business community over the past several decades. The major ethics scandals of the early 2000s affected the public's trust of executives and major business institutions. The Wall Street financial scandals begun in Fall 2008 brought the public's trust of business into further question. Polls indicate that the public does not have a high regard for the ethics of business or managers. It is not easy to say whether business's ethics have declined or just seem to have done so because of increased media coverage and rising public expectations. Business ethics concerns the rightness, wrongness, and fairness of managerial behavior, and these are not easy judgments to make. Multiple norms compete to as to which standards business behavior should be compared.

The conventional approach to business ethics was introduced as an initial way in which managers might think about ethical judgments. One major problem with this approach is that it is not clear which standards or norms should be used, and thus the conventional approach is susceptible to ethical relativism. Though the conventional approach has value, the varied sources of norms informing decision making can often result in confusion.

A Venn diagram model was presented as an aid to making decisions when economics, law, and ethics expectations compete with each other and are in tension. Four important ethics questions with respect to determining the ethical course of action include (1) What is? (descriptive question), (2) What ought to be? (normative question), (3) How do we get from what is to what ought to be? (practical question), and (4) What is our motivation in this transition? (question of authenticity). Answering these questions helps one in an ethical analysis of a situation.

Three models of management ethics are (1) immoral management, (2) moral management, and (3) amoral management. Amoral management is further classified into intentional and unintentional categories. There are two hypotheses about the presence of these three moral types in the management population and in individuals themselves.

Understanding how moral judgment develops is helpful to aspiring managers. A generally accepted view is that moral judgment develops according to the pattern described by Lawrence Kohlberg. His three levels of moral development are (1) preconventional, (2) conventional, and (3) postconventional, autonomous, or principled. Some have suggested that men and women use different perspectives as they perceive and deal with moral issues. Care must be exercised in generalizing about the process of moral development.

In addition to moral maturity, managers' ethics are affected by sources of values originating from external to the organization and from sources within the organization. This latter category includes respect for the authority structure, loyalty, conformity, and a concern for financial performance and results.

Finally, six elements in developing moral judgment were presented. These six elements include (1) moral imagination, (2) moral identification and ordering, (3) moral evaluation, (4) tolerance of moral disagreement and ambiguity, (5) integration of managerial and moral competence, and (6) a sense of moral obligation. If the moral management model is to be sustained, these six elements need to be developed and successfully integrated.

Key Terms

business ethics, p. 235

compliance strategy, p. 253

conventional approach to business ethics, p. 236

descriptive ethics, p. 235

ethical egoism, p. 236

ethical relativism, p. 240

ethics, p. 234

immoral management, p. 245

integrity strategy, p. 249

intentional amoral management, p. 252

Kohlberg's levels of moral development, p. 258

moral development, p. 258

moral management, p. 248

normative ethics, p. 236

unintentional amoral management, p. 252

Discussion Questions

1. Give a definition of ethical business behavior, explain the components involved in making ethical decisions, and give an example from your personal experience of the difficulties involved in making these determinations.

2. To demonstrate that you understand the three models of management ethics—moral, immoral, and amoral—give an example, from your personal experience, of each type. Do you agree that amorality is a serious problem? Explain.

3. Give examples, from your personal experience, of Kohlberg's Levels 1, 2, and 3. If you do not think you have ever gotten to Level 3, give an example of what it might be like.

4. Compare your motivations to behave ethically with those listed in Figure 7-14. Do the reasons given in that figure agree with your personal assessment? Discuss the similarities and differences between Figure 7-14 and your personal assessment.

5. From your personal experience, give an example of a situation you have faced that would require one of the six elements of moral judgment.

8

Personal and Organizational Ethics

CHAPTER LEARNING OUTCOMES

After studying this chapter, you should be able to:

1. Understand the different levels at which business ethics may be addressed.

2. Differentiate between consequence-based and duty-based principles of ethics.

3. Enumerate and discuss principles of personal ethical decision making and ethical tests for screening ethical decisions.

4. Identify the factors affecting an organization's ethical culture and provide examples of these factors at work.

5. Describe and explain actions, strategies, or "best practices" that management may take to improve an organization's ethical climate.

The ethical issues on which managers must make decisions are numerous and varied. The news media tends to focus on the major ethical scandals involving well-known corporate names. Therefore, Bernie Madoff, Enron, WorldCom, Tyco, HealthSouth, Martha Stewart, and other such high-visibility firms attract considerable attention. As a consequence, many of the routine ethical dilemmas that managers face in medium-sized and small organizations are often overlooked.

The megascandals of the Enron era and the implicated companies during the Wall Street financial scandals are not the only issues facing the corporate world. Managers encounter day-to-day ethical dilemmas in such arenas as conflicts of interest, sexual harassment, inappropriate gifts to corporate personnel, unauthorized payments, customer dealings, evaluation of personnel, and pressure to compromise on personal standards. But often they have no experience or training in business ethics or ethical decision making to tackle such quandaries.

People today face ethical issues in a variety of settings, but our concern in this chapter is limited to personal and organizational ethics. David Callahan's highly influential book titled *The Cheating Culture: Why More Americans Are Doing Wrong to Get Ahead* talks at length about these ethical issues.[1] Callahan never clearly defines what "cheating" means, but uses its synonyms that are commonly accepted today, including *dishonest, immoral, unethical,* and *corrupt*—all of which characterize the threats we are addressing in this chapter. He argues that the instances of cheating have shot up in today's society because of four essential reasons: rising pressures on people, bigger rewards for winning, temptation, and trickle-down corruption. Each of these factors influences personal and organizational ethics and thus frames the issues that need to be addressed at these levels.

The ethical challenge in business is, indeed, a serious one, and progress on this front is vital to successful business. An ethics officer for a large corporation once said that there are three types of organizations: those that *have had* ethics problems, those that *are having* ethics problems, and those that *will have* ethics problems. Ethical issues appear through all levels of management, in many different types of jobs, and in organizations of all sizes.

A study of managers' desired leadership qualities was conducted by consultant and writer Lee Ellis, who concluded that *integrity* is the quality most sought after in leaders.[2] A retired corporate executive, now business school lecturer, Bill George, former CEO at Medtronic, has argued that we need corporate leaders with integrity.[3] But how does one get personal integrity, and as a manager, how do you instill it in your organization and create an ethical organizational climate? Following are some significant challenges: How do you keep your own personal ethics focused in such a way that you avoid immorality and amorality? What principles, concepts, or guidelines are available to help you to be ethical? What specific strategies, approaches, or best practices might be emphasized to bring about an ethical culture in your company or organization?

Ethics Issues Arise at Different Levels

As individuals and as managers, we experience ethical pressures or dilemmas in a variety of settings and at different levels, including the individual or personal level, the organizational level, the industry level, the societal level, and the global level. These levels cascade out from the individual to the global. Some observers believe that "ethics are ethics" regardless of whether they are applied at the personal or the organizational level. To some extent this is true. However, each level also introduces unique challenges. To help understand the types of decision situations that are faced at the various levels, however, it is worth considering them in terms of the types of issues that may arise in different contexts.

Personal Level

First, we all experience *personal-level* ethical challenges. These challenges include situations we face in our personal lives that are generally outside the context of our employment. Questions or dilemmas that we might face at the personal level include the following:

- Should I cheat on my income tax return by overinflating my charitable contributions?
- Should I tell the professor I need this course to graduate this semester when I really don't?
- Should I download music from the Internet although I realize it is someone else's intellectual property?
- Should I skip out on my share of the apartment rent because I'm graduating and leaving town?
- Should I connect this TV cable in my new apartment and not tell the cable company?

Wanda Johnson, a 34-year-old single mother of five from Savannah, Georgia, faced a personal-level ethical dilemma when temptation came knocking in the form of a bagful of money that contained $120,000. Johnson, a low-paid custodian at a local hospital, was on her lunch break when she witnessed the bag falling off an armored truck. She could have used the money to pay her outstanding bills. She had recently pawned her television set to procure enough cash to keep the bill collectors at bay. The bag contained small bills and nobody saw her find it. What should she do? What would you do?

Johnson later admitted that she knew she had to turn it in. After consulting with her pastor, she turned in the money to the police. Johnson reported that her religious upbringing had taught her that was the right thing to do. Later she was rewarded by the SunTrust Bank with $5,000, and was also promised an unspecified sum by EM Armored Car Service, Inc.[4] Would everyone react to this personal, ethical dilemma in the same fashion as Johnson did? We all face hundreds of such dilemmas throughout our lives.

Organizational Level

People also confront ethical issues at the *organizational level* (or firm level) in their roles as managers or employees. Many of these issues are similar to those we face personally. However, these issues carry consequences for the company's reputation and success in the community and also for the kind of ethical environment or culture that will prevail on a day-to-day basis at the office. In addition, how the issue is handled may have serious organizational consequences. Examples of issues faced at the organizational level include the following:

- Should I set high production goals for my work team to benefit the organization, even though I know it may cause them to cut corners to achieve such goals?
- Should I overreport the actual time I worked on this project, hoping to get overtime pay?
- Should I overlook the wrongdoings of my colleagues and subordinates in the interest of harmony in the company?
- Should I authorize a subordinate to violate company policy so that we can close the deal and be rewarded by month's end?
- Should I misrepresent the warranty time on some product in order to get the sale?

One August, it was revealed that months before people began dying nationwide, managers at the Bil Mar plant, a Sara Lee Corporation–owned plant in Michigan, knew they were shipping tainted hot dogs and deli meats. This was an organization-level ethical dilemma. The consumption of tainted food caused a national outbreak of listeriosis, in which 15 people were killed, 6 suffered miscarriages, and 101 got sick. Employees of the plant later revealed that several employees, as well as the management, were aware of the shipment of contaminated meat, but kept silent. According to a report, a USDA worker had told a Bil Mar employee at the time that the plant was running the risk of getting into trouble if it continued shipping contaminated foods, but the worker replied, "they would never know it was our product since [listeria] has about a two-week incubation period." Before these latest revelations, the company had pleaded guilty to a federal misdemeanor charge, paid a $200,000 fine, and made a $3 million grant to Michigan State University for food safety research.[5]

When thinking about the organizational level of ethics, the presence or absence of unethical practices goes a long way toward revealing the state of ethics that exists within that organization. To illustrate the types of unethical practices that may be evident in organizations, the results of a revealing survey conducted by the Ethics Resource Center documented what managers and employees are up against. In this survey of employees, the following were some of the types of misconduct observed and reported along with the percentage of time these items were mentioned:[6]

- Abusive or intimidating behavior toward employees (23 percent)
- Misreporting actual time or hours worked (20 percent)
- Lying to employees, customers, vendors, or the public (19 percent)

- Withholding needed information from employees, customers, vendors, or the public (18 percent)
- Discriminating on the basis of race, color, gender, age, or similar categories (13 percent)
- Stealing, theft, or related fraud (12 percent)

Each of these categories reveals the types of questionable practices that employees and managers today face in their work lives.

Industry or Profession Level

A third level at which a manager or an organization might experience business ethics issues is the *industry or profession level*. The industry might be stock brokerage, real estate, insurance, manufactured homes, financial services, telemarketing, electronics, or a host of others. Related to the industry might be the *profession*, of which an individual is a member—accounting, engineering, pharmacy, medicine, journalism, or law. Examples of questions that might pose ethical dilemmas at this level include the following:

- Is this practice that we stockbrokers have been using for years with prospective clients really fair and in their best interests?
- Is this safety standard we electrical engineers have passed really adequate for protecting the consumer in this age of do-it-yourselfers?
- Is this standard contract we mobile home sellers have adopted really in keeping with the financial disclosure laws that have recently been strengthened?
- Is it ethical for telemarketers to make cold calls to prospective clients during the dinner hour when we suspect they will be at home?

An excellent example of an industry-wide ethical problem occurred during the buildup to the Wall Street financial scandals and market collapse in 2008. The mortgage-lending industry got carried away with subprime lending. Granting home loans to individuals who could not meet their payments unless housing prices continued to rise turned out to be a questionable and unsustainable practice. The industry became infamous for its NINJA loans—*No Income, No Job, no Assets*. For the sake of keeping up with the competition, firms were granting loans just to keep up with the whirlwind competition and to collect commissions. This practice contributed significantly to the worldwide recession.

Societal and Global Levels

At the *societal and global levels*, it becomes very difficult for the individual manager to have a direct effect on business ethics. However, managers acting in concert through their companies and industries and professional associations can definitely bring about high standards and constructive changes. Because the industry, societal, and global levels are quite removed from the actual practicing manager, in this chapter we will focus our attention primarily on the personal and organizational levels. The manager's greatest impact can be felt through what he or she does personally or as a member of the management team.

An example of a major issue that companies are facing today and that has industry, societal, and global ethical implications is that of moving jobs offshore—outsourcing work to less expensive regions of the world, such as China and India. In the past few years, outsourcing has included not only manufacturing jobs but increasingly also technical and professional jobs. In a revealing *BusinessWeek* article titled "The Real Cost of Offshoring," the impact on domestic workers is documented as a considerable social issue.[7] Another societal-level ethical issue that has widespread social and ethical implications is business's support for hiring illegal immigrants.

In Chapter 10, we will deal with global ethics more specifically—a crucial topic that is increasing in importance as global capitalism comes to define our commercial world.

Personal and Managerial Ethics

In discussing personal and managerial ethics it is assumed that the individual wants to behave ethically or improve his or her ethical behavior in personal and/or managerial situations. Keep in mind that each individual is a stakeholder of someone else—a friend, a family member, an associate, or a businessperson. That "someone else" has a stake in the individual's behavior; therefore, the individual person's ethics are important to that someone else too. Our discussion here aims at those who desire to be ethical and are looking for help in doing so. All the difficulties with making ethical judgments that we discussed in the previous chapter are applicable in this discussion as well.

Personal and managerial ethics, for the most part, entails making decisions. Decision situations typically confront the individual with a conflict-of-interest situation. A conflict of interest is usually present when the individual has to choose between her or his interests and the interests of someone else or some other group (stakeholders). What it boils down to in the final analysis is answering the question, "What is the right thing to do in this situation?" In other instances, *practices* that managers and organizations employ are embedded with ethical implications. Many ongoing practices were first introduced by someone else at an earlier time, so some managers don't see that each time they continue a questionable practice, they are implicitly deciding that it is appropriate.

In answering the question about the right course of action, it often seems that individuals think about the situation briefly and then go with their instincts. There are, however, guidelines to ethical decision making that one could turn to if she or he really wants to make the best ethical decisions. What are some of these guidelines?

In Chapter 7 we indicated that there are three major approaches to ethics or ethical decision making: (1) the conventional approach, (2) the principles approach, and (3) the ethical tests approach. In that chapter, we described only the first approach, which entailed a comparison of a decision or a practice with prevailing norms of acceptability. We also discussed some of the challenges inherent in that approach. In this chapter, we will discuss the other two approaches along with other ethical concepts.

Principles Approach to Ethics

The principles approach to ethics or ethical decision making is based on the idea that managers desire to anchor their decisions on a more solid foundation than that provided by the conventional approach to ethics. The conventional approach to ethics, you may recall, depended heavily on what people thought and what the prevailing standards were at the time. Several principles of ethics have evolved over time as moral philosophers and ethicists have attempted to organize and codify their thinking and guidelines.

What Is an Ethics Principle?   From a practical point of view, a principle of business ethics is an ethical concept, guideline, or rule that, if applied when you are faced with an ethical decision or practice, will assist you in taking the ethical course.[8] Principles or guidelines have been around for centuries. The Golden Rule has been around for several millennia. In the 16th century, Miguel de Cervantes, the Spanish novelist and author of *Don Quixote*, uttered an important ethics principle that is still used today: *Honesty is the best policy.*

Types of Ethical Principles or Theories.   Moral philosophers customarily divide ethical principles or theories into two categories: teleological and deontological. **Teleological theories** focus on the *consequences* or results of the actions they produce. Utilitarianism is the major principle in this category. **Deontological theories** focus on *duties*. For example, it could be argued that managers have a duty to tell the truth when they are doing business. The ethical theory known as the *categorical imperative*, formulated by Immanuel Kant, best illustrates duty theory. The principles of rights and of justice, two major ethics theories we will discuss, seem to be nonteleological in character.[9] **Aretaic theories** are a third, less known category of ethics, put forth by Aristotle. The term comes from the Greek word *arete*, which means "goodness" (of function), "excellence" (of function), or "virtue." Aristotle saw the individual as essentially a member of a social unit and moral virtue as a behavioral habit, a character trait that is both socially and morally valued. Virtue theory is the best example of an aretaic theory.[10] Other principles, such as caring, the Golden Rule, and servant leadership, reflect concerns for duty, consequences, and virtue, or a combination of several principles.

Many different principles of ethics have been promulgated, but we must limit our discussion to those that have been regarded as most useful in business applications. Therefore, we will concentrate on the following major principles: *utilitarianism* (consequences based), *Kant's categorical imperative*, *rights*, and *justice* (duty based). In addition, we will consider the *principles of care, virtue ethics, servant leadership*, and the *Golden Rule*—views that are popular and relevant even today. The basic idea behind the principles approach is that managers may improve their ethical decision making if they factor into their proposed actions, decisions, behaviors, and practices a consideration of certain principles or concepts of ethics.

Principle of Utilitarianism. Many ethicists have held that the rightness or fairness of an action can be determined best by looking at its results or consequences. If the consequences are good, the action or decision is considered good. If the consequences are bad, the action or decision is considered wrong. The **principle of utilitarianism** is therefore a *consequential* principle, or as stated earlier, a *teleological* principle. In its simplest form, **utilitarianism** asserts: "we should always act so as to produce the greatest ratio of good to evil for everyone."[11] Another way of stating utilitarianism is to say that one should take the course of action that represents the "greatest good for the greatest number." Two of the most influential philosophers who advocated this consequential view were Jeremy Bentham (1748–1832) and John Stuart Mill (1806–1873).

The attractiveness of utilitarianism is that it forces the decision maker to think about the general welfare, or the common good. It proposes a standard outside of self-interest by which to judge the value of a course of action. To make a cost-benefit analysis is to engage in utilitarian thinking. Utilitarianism forces us to think in stakeholder terms: What would produce the greatest good in our decision, considering stakeholders such as owners, employees, customers, and others, as well as ourselves? Finally, it provides for latitude in decision making in that it does not recognize specific actions as inherently good or bad but rather allows us to fit our personal decisions to the complexities of the situation.

A weakness of utilitarianism is that it ignores actions that may be inherently wrong. A strict interpretation of utilitarianism might lead a manager to fire minorities and older workers because they "do not fit in" or to take some other drastic action that contravenes public policy and other ethics principles. In utilitarianism, by focusing on the ends (consequences) of a decision or an action, one may ignore the means (the decision or action itself). This leads to a problematic situation where one may argue that the end justifies the means, using utilitarian reasoning. Therefore, the action or decision is considered objectionable only if it leads to a lesser ratio of good to evil. Another problem with the principle of utilitarianism is that it may come into conflict with the idea of justice. Critics of utilitarianism say that the mere increase in total good is not good in and of itself because it ignores the *distribution* of good, which is also an important issue. Another stated weakness is that when using this principle, it is very difficult to formulate satisfactory rules for decision making. Therefore, utilitarianism, like most ethical principles, has its advantages and disadvantages.[12]

Kant's Categorical Imperative. Immanuel Kant's **categorical imperative** is a duty-based principle of ethics, or as stated earlier, it is a deontological principle.[13] A duty is an obligation; that is, it is an action that is morally obligatory. The duty approach to ethics refers both to the obligatory nature of particular actions and to a way of reasoning about what is right and what is wrong.[14] Kant's categorical imperative argues that a sense of duty arises from *reason* or *rational nature*, an internal source. By contrast, the *Divine Command* principle maintains that God's law is the source of duties. Thus, we can conceptualize both internal and external sources of duty.

Kant proposed three formulations in his theory or principle. The categorical imperative is best known in the following form: "Act only according to that maxim by which you can at the same time *will* that it should become a universal law." Stated another way, Kant's principle is that one should act only on rules (or maxims) that you would be willing to see everyone follow.[15] Kant's second formulation, referred to as the *principle of ends*, is "so act to treat humanity, whether in your own person or in that of any other, in every case as an *end* and never as merely a means." This has also been referred to as the *respect for persons principle*.[16] This means that each person has dignity and moral worth and should never be exploited or manipulated or merely used as a means to another end.[17]

The third formulation of the categorical imperative invokes the *principle of autonomy*. It basically holds that "every rational being is able to regard oneself as a maker of universal law. That is, we do not need an external authority—be it God, the state, our culture, or anyone else—to determine the nature of the moral law. We can discover this for ourselves."[18] Kant argues that this view is not inconsistent with Judeo-Christian beliefs, his childhood heritage, but one must go through a series of logical leaps of faith to arrive at this point.[19] Like all ethical principles, Kant's principles have strengths and weaknesses and supporters and detractors. In the final analysis, it is his emphasis on *duty*, as opposed to consequences, that merits treatment here. Further, the notion of universalizability and respect for persons are key ideas. The principles of rights and of justice, which we discuss next, seem more consistent with the duty-based perspective than with the consequences-based perspective.

Principle of Rights. One major problem with utilitarianism is that it does not handle the issue of **rights** very well. That is, utilitarianism implies that certain actions are morally right (i.e., they represent the greatest good for the greatest number) when in fact they may violate another person's rights.[20] **Moral rights** are important, justifiable claims or entitlements. They do not depend on a legal system to be valid. They are rights that we ought to have based on moral reasoning. The right to life or the right not to be killed by others is a justifiable claim in our society. The Declaration of Independence referred to the rights to life, liberty, and the pursuit of happiness. John Locke had earlier spoken of the right to property. Today we speak of human rights, some of which are **legal rights** and some moral rights.

The basic idea undergirding the **principle of rights** is that rights cannot simply be overridden by utility, but only by another, more basic or important right. Let us consider the problem of applying the principle of utilitarianism. For example, if we accept the basic right to human life, we are precluded from considering whether killing someone might produce the greatest good for the greatest number. To use a business example, if a person has the right to equal treatment (not to be discriminated against), we could not argue for discriminating against that person so as to produce more good for others.[21] However, some people would say that this is precisely what we do when we advocate affirmative action.

The principle of rights expresses morality from the point of view of the individual or group of individuals, whereas the principle of utilitarianism expresses morality in terms

FIGURE 8-1	Civil rights	Smokers' rights
Some Legal Rights	Minorities' rights	Nonsmokers' rights
and Claimed Moral	Women's rights	AIDS victims' rights
Rights in Today's	Disabled people's rights	Children's rights
Society	Older people's rights	Fetal rights
	Religious affiliation rights	Embryo rights
	Employee rights	Animals' rights
	Consumer rights	Right to burn the American flag
	Shareholder rights	Right of due process
	Privacy rights	Gay rights
	Right to life	Victims' rights
	Criminals' rights	Rights based on appearance

of the group or society as a whole. The rights view forces us in our decision making to ask what is due each individual and to promote individual welfare. It also limits the validity of appeals to numbers and to society's aggregate benefit.[22] However, a central question that is not always easy to answer is: "What constitutes a legitimate right that should be honored, and what rights or whose rights take precedence over others?"

Figure 8-1 provides an overview of many types of rights that are being claimed in our society today. Some of these are legally protected, whereas others are "claimed" as moral rights but are not legally protected. Managers are expected to be attentive to both legal and moral rights, but no clear guidelines are available to help one sort out which claimed moral rights should be protected, to what extent they should be protected, and which rights should take precedence over others. This is one of the limitations of the rights theory.

Rights may be subdivided further into two types: negative rights and positive rights.[23] **Negative right** is the right to be left alone. It is the right to think and act free from the coercion of others; for example, freedom from false imprisonment, freedom from illegal search and seizure, and freedom of speech are all forms of negative rights.[24] **Positive right** is the right to something, such as the right to food, to health care, to clean air, to a certain standard of living, or to education. In business, as in all walks of life, both negative and positive rights are played out in both legal and morally claimed forms.

In recent years, some have argued that we are in the midst of a rights revolution in which too many individuals and groups are attempting to urge society to accept their wishes or demands as rights. The proliferation of rights claims has the potential to dilute or diminish the power of more legitimate rights. If everyone's claim for special consideration is perceived as a legitimate right, the rights approach will lose its power to help management concentrate on the morally justified rights. A related problem has been the politicization of rights in recent years. As our lawmakers bestow legal or protected status upon rights claims for political reasons rather than moral reasons, managers may become blinded to which rights or whose rights really should be honored in a decision-making situation. As rights claims expand, the common core of morality may diminish, and decision makers may find it more and more difficult to balance individuals' interests with the public interest.[25]

Principle of Justice. Just as the principle of utilitarianism does not handle well the idea of rights, it does not deal effectively with the principle of justice either. One way to think about the **principle of justice** is to say that it involves the fair treatment of each person. This is why it is often called the "fairness principle." Most would accept that we have a duty to be fair to employees, consumers, and other stakeholders. But how do you decide what is fair to each person? How do you decide what is each person's due? Sometimes it is hard to say because people might be given their due according to their *type of work*, their *effort expended*, their *merit*, their *need*, and so on. Each of these criteria might be appropriate in different situations. At one time, the prevalent view was that married heads of households ought to be paid more than single males or women. Today, however, the social structure is different. Women have entered the workforce in significant numbers, some families are structured differently, and a revised concept of what is due people has changed over time. The fair action now is to pay everyone more on the basis of merit than on the basis of needs.[26]

To use the principle of justice, we must ask, "What is meant by justice?" There are several kinds of justice. **Distributive justice** refers to the distribution of benefits and burdens. **Compensatory justice** involves compensating someone for a past injustice. **Procedural justice**, or **ethical due process**, refers to fair decision-making procedures, practices, or agreements.[27]

ETHICAL DUE PROCESS Procedural justice, or ethical due process, is especially relevant to business organizations. Employees, customers, owners, and all stakeholders want to be treated fairly. They want to believe that they have been treated carefully and equally in decision situations. They want their side of the issue to be heard, and they want to believe that the managers or decision makers took all factors into consideration and weighed them carefully before making a decision. Whether the decision was who should be hired (or fired), who should get what promotion or raise, or who should get a choice assignment, employees want to know that it was fairness that prevailed and not favoritism or some other inappropriate factor. People want to know that their performance has been evaluated according to a fair process. Ethical due process, then, is simply being sure that fairness characterizes the decision-making process. It should be noted too that ethical due process is as important as, if not more so than, outcome fairness. In other words, people can live with an outcome that was not their preferred result if they believe that the method, system, or procedure used in making the decision was fair.

The term **process fairness** has also been used to describe ethical due process.[28] Three factors have been identified that help to decide whether process fairness has been achieved. First, have employees' input been included in the decision process? The more this occurs, the more fair the process is perceived to be. Second, do employees believe the decisions were made and implemented in an appropriate manner? Employees expect consistency based on accurate information. They see whether mistakes are being corrected and whether the decision-making process was transparent. Third, employees watch their managers' behavior. Do they provide explanations when asked? Do they treat others respectfully? Do they actively listen to comments being made?[29] Ethical due process, or process fairness, works effectively with all stakeholders, whether they are employees, customers, owners, or others. Everyone responds positively to being treated fairly.

RAWLS'S PRINCIPLE OF JUSTICE John Rawls, a political philosopher who died in 2002 at the age of 81, became well known for his own version of ethical due process.[30] He provided what some have referred to as a comprehensive principle of justice.[31] His theory is based on the idea that what we need first is a fair method by which we may choose the principles through which conflicts will be resolved. The two principles of justice that underlie his theory are as follows:[32]

1. Each person has an equal right to the most extensive basic liberties compatible with similar liberties for all others.

2. Social and economic inequalities are arranged so that they are both (a) reasonably expected to be to everyone's advantage and (b) attached to positions and offices open to all.

According to Rawls's first principle, each person should be treated equally. In other words, it holds that each person should enjoy equally a full array of basic liberties.[33] The second principle is more controversial. It is often misinterpreted to imply that public policy should raise as high as possible the social and economic well-being of society's worst-off individuals. It is criticized by both those who argue that the principle is too strong and those who think it is too weak. The former think that, as long as people enjoy equal opportunity, it is not a case of injustice if some people benefit from their own work, skill, ingenuity, or assumed risks. Therefore, such people are more deserving and should not be expected to produce benefits for the least advantaged. The latter group thinks that the inequalities that may result could be so great as to be clearly unjust. Therefore, the rich get richer and the poor get only a little less poor.[34]

In developing further his second principle, Rawls imagined people gathered behind a "veil of ignorance," unaware of whether they, personally, were rich or poor, talented or incompetent. He then asked what kind of society they would create. He reasoned that the rule everyone would be able to agree on would be to maximize the well-being of the worst-off person, partially out of fear that anyone could wind up at the bottom.[35] This view, of course, had its critics, and it represents an idealistic situation that could not likely be brought about.

Supporters of the principle of justice claim that it preserves the basic values—freedom, equality of opportunity, and a concern for the disadvantaged—that have become embedded in our moral beliefs. Critics object to various parts of the theory and would not subscribe to Rawls's principles at all. Utilitarians, for example, think the greatest good for the greatest number should reign supreme.

Ethics of Care. The concept of **ethics of care** or the principle of caring is being discussed just after our discussion of utilitarianism, rights, and justice because this alternative view is critical of many traditional views. Some traditional views, it has been argued, embrace a masculine approach to perceiving the world and advocate rigid rules with clear lines.[36] The "care" perspective builds on the work of Carol Gilligan, whose criticisms of Kohlberg's theory of moral development were discussed in the previous chapter. Gilligan found that women often spoke in "a different voice" that was more based on responsibility to others and on the continuity of interdependent relationships.[37]

The care perspective maintains that traditional ethics like the principles of utilitarianism and rights focus too much on the individual self and on cognitive thought processes. In the traditional view, "others" may be seen as threats, so rights become important. Resulting moral theories then tend to be legalistic or contractual.

Caring theory is founded on wholly different assumptions. Proponents who advocate this perspective view the individual person as essentially relational, not individualistic. These persons do not deny the existence of the self but hold that the self has relationships that cannot be separated from the self's existence. This caring view emphasizes the relationships' moral worth and, by extension, the responsibilities inherent in those relationships, rather than in rights, as in traditional ethics.[38]

Several writers have argued that caring theory is consistent with stakeholder theory, or the stakeholder approach, in that the focus is on a more cooperative, caring type of relationship. In this view, firms should seek to make decisions that satisfy stakeholders, leading to situations in which all parties in the relationship gain. Robbin Derry elaborates: "In the corporate environment, there is an increasing demand for business to be attentive to its many stakeholders, particularly customers and employees, in caring ways. As organizations attempt to build such relationships, they must define the responsibilities of initiating and maintaining care. The ethics of care may be able to facilitate an understanding of these responsibilities."[39]

Jeanne Liedtka, by contrast, has questioned whether organizations can care in the sense in which caring theory proposes. She contends that to care in this sense, an organization would have to care in a way that is

- Focused entirely on people, not on quality, profits, or other such ideas that today use "care talk"
- Undertaken with caring as an end, not merely as a means to an end (such as quality or profits)
- Essentially personal, in that the caring reflects caring for other individuals
- Growth enhancing for the cared-for, in that the caring moves the cared-for toward the development and use of their capacities

Liedtka takes the position that caring people could lead to a caring organization that offers new possibilities for simultaneously enhancing the effectiveness and the moral quality of organizations.[40] The principle of caring offers a different perspective to guide ethical decision making—a perspective that clearly is thought provoking and valuable.

Virtue Ethics. The major principles just discussed have been more action oriented. That is, they were designed to guide our actions and decisions. Another ethical tradition, often referred to as **virtue ethics**, merits consideration even though it is not a principle per se. Virtue ethics, rooted in the thinking of Plato and Aristotle, is a school of thought that focuses on the individual becoming imbued with virtues (e.g., honesty, fairness, truthfulness, trustworthiness, benevolence, respect, and nonmalfeasance).[41] Virtue ethics is sometimes referred to as an aretaic theory of ethics, as defined earlier in the section "Types of Ethical Principles or Theories."[42]

Virtue ethics is a system of thought that is centered in the heart of the person—the manager, the employee, the competitor, and so on. This is in contrast to the principles we have discussed, which see the heart of ethics in actions or duties. Action-oriented principles focus on *doing*. Virtue ethics emphasizes *being*. The assumption, of course, is that the actions of a virtuous person will also be virtuous. Traditional ethical principles of utilitarianism, rights, and justice focus on the question, "What should I do?" Virtue ethics focuses on the question, "What sort of person should I *be* or *become*?"[43]

Programs that have developed from the notion of virtue ethics have sometimes been called *character education*, because this particular theory emphasizes character development. Many observers think that one reason why business and society are witnessing moral decline today is that we have failed to teach our young people universal principles of good character.

VF Corporation, Josephson Institute of Ethics, and the Ethics Resource Center in Washington all have launched character education programs. It has been argued that character education is needed not only in schools but in corporations as well. Corporate well-being demands character and business leaders are a vital and necessary force for putting character back into business.[44]

Virtue ethicists have brought back to the public debate the idea that virtues are important whether they be in the education of the young or in the management training programs. Virtues such as honesty, integrity, loyalty, promise keeping, fairness, and respect for others are completely compatible with the major principles we have been discussing. The principles, combined with the virtues, form the foundation for effective ethical action and decision making. Whether the virtues are seen as character traits or as principles of decision making is not our major concern at this point. Rather, that they be used, whatever the motivation, is our central concern here. It has been strongly argued that the ethics of virtue in business is an idea whose time has arrived.[45]

Servant Leadership.   An increasingly popular approach to organizational leadership and thinking today is **servant leadership**. It is an approach to ethical leadership and decision making based on the moral principle of serving others first. Can these two roles—servant and leader—be fused in one person—a manager? What are the basic tenets of servant leadership?

Servant leadership is a model of ethical management—an approach to ethical decision making—based on the idea that serving others such as employees, customers, community, and other stakeholders is the first priority. According to Robert Greenleaf, the father of this movement, "It begins with the natural feeling that one wants to serve, to serve first." Next, a conscious choice brings one to "aspire to lead." The model manifests itself in the care taken by the leader to make sure that others' needs are being served.[46]

The modern era of servant leadership is marked primarily by the works of Robert K. Greenleaf, who spent 38 years of his career working for AT&T. Upon his retirement, he founded the Center for Applied Ethics, which was renamed the Greenleaf Center for Servant Leadership; it is housed in Indianapolis. Greenleaf's "second career" lasted until shortly before his death in 1990. During his time, he became influential in leadership circles as a thinker, writer, consultant, and speaker to many organizations.[47]

In his landmark book *Servant Leadership*, Greenleaf gives credit to the Jesus of Nazareth ministry for symbolically embodying the concept.[48] Though inspired by the teachings and life of Jesus, Greenleaf says he crystallized his idea of servant leadership after reading Hermann Hesse's short novel *Journey to the East*. In Hesse's story, a band of men take a mythical journey. The central figure in the story is Leo, who accompanies the party as the "servant" who does the menial chores, but who also sustains the men with his spirit and song. Leo is a person with extraordinary presence. All goes well until Leo disappears. Then the group falls into disarray, and their journey is abandoned. They can't make it without their servant, Leo.

The story's narrator, one of the party members, finds Leo after some years of wandering. It so happens that the narrator is taken into the Order that had sponsored the journey. There he discovers that Leo, whom he had known as "servant," was actually the titular head of the Order—its guiding spirit, a great and noble "leader." The main point Greenleaf took from this story is that the great leader is seen as servant first, and this is the key to his greatness. Leo was actually the leader all the time, but he was servant first because that was his deep internal character.

Greenleaf summarizes that the servant leader is "servant first," just as Leo was portrayed. The role begins with the natural sentiment that one first wants to serve, and then comes forth as a conscious aspiration to lead. This kind of person is distinctively different from one who is a "leader first," perhaps because of the need to gratify a power drive or acquisitiveness for material possessions. Of course, the "servant first" and the "leader first" are the two extreme types, and between them there are a number of shadings and blends that define a useful range of the notion of leadership.

Larry Spears, the former CEO of the Greenleaf Center for Servant Leadership, has deliberated on Greenleaf's original writings and has culled from these writings a set of ten key characteristics essential for the development of servant leaders. Each of these is worth listing because, collectively, they paint a portrait of servant leadership in terms of leader behaviors and characteristics. These characteristics are as follows:[49]

- Listening
- Empathy

- Healing
- Persuasion
- Awareness
- Foresight
- Conceptualization
- Commitment to the growth of people
- Stewardship
- Building community

Each of these characteristics is based on the ethical principle of putting the other person first—whether that other person is an employee, a customer, or some other important stakeholder. Some of these characteristics could be stated as virtues and some as behaviors. Thus, servant leadership embraces several of the ethical perspectives discussed earlier.

Servant leadership builds a bridge between the ideas of business ethics and those of leadership. Joanne Ciulla has observed that people follow servant leaders because they can trust them, and this invokes the ethical dimension.[50] James Autry, a top-selling leadership author, argues that servant leadership is the right way, a better way of being a manager and part of organizational life. He adds, "it will enhance productivity, encourage creativity, and benefit the bottom line."[51] It is also clear that the servant leadership principle is quite compatible with sustainability within organizations.

The Golden Rule. The **Golden Rule** merits discussion because of its popularity as a basic and strong principle of ethical living and decision making. A number of studies have found it to be the most powerful and useful to managers.[52] The Golden Rule—"Do unto others as you would have them do unto you"—is a fairly straightforward, easy-to-understand principle. Further, it guides the individual decision maker to behavior, actions, or decisions that she or he should be able to express as acceptable or not based on some direct comparisons with what she or he would consider ethical or fair.

The Golden Rule argues that if you want to be treated fairly, treat others fairly; if you want your privacy protected, respect the privacy of others. The key is impartiality. According to this principle, we are not to make an exception of ourselves. In essence, the Golden Rule personalizes business relations and brings the ideal of fairness into business deliberations.[53]

The popularity of the Golden Rule is linked to the fact that it is rooted in history and religious tradition and is among the oldest of the principles of living. Further, it is universal in the sense that it requires no specific religious belief or faith. Almost since time began, religious leaders and philosophers have advocated the Golden Rule in one form or another. It is easy to see, therefore, why Martin Luther said that the Golden Rule is a part of the "natural law," because it is a moral rule that anyone can recognize and embrace without any particular religious teaching. In three different studies, when managers or respondents were asked to rank ethical principles according to their value to them, the Golden Rule was ranked first.[54]

Leadership expert John C. Maxwell published an insightful book titled *There's No Such Thing as "Business" Ethics: There's Only One Rule for Making Decisions.* The one rule Maxwell advocates is the Golden Rule. According to Maxwell, there are four reasons why managers and all decision makers should adopt the Golden Rule.

1. The Golden Rule is accepted by most people.
2. The Golden Rule is easy to understand.
3. The Golden Rule is a win–win philosophy.
4. The Golden Rule acts as a compass when you need direction.[55]

In addition to the ethical principles and theories that we have chosen to discuss in some detail, Figure 8-2 provides a brief sketch of several ethical principles that have evolved over the years and have been advocated by different individuals or groups.

No single principle is recommended for use always. As one gets into each principle, one encounters a number of challenges with definitions, measurement, and generalizability. The more one gets into each principle, the more one realizes how difficult it would

---

FIGURE 8-2

A Brief Sketch of Ethical Principles

- **The Categorical Imperative:** Act only according to that maxim by which you can at the same time "will" that it should become a universal law. In other words, one should not adopt principles of action unless they can, without inconsistency, be adopted by everyone else.
- **The Conventionalist Ethic:** Individuals should act to further their self-interests so long as they do not violate the law. It is allowed, under this principle, to bluff (lie) and to take advantage of all legal opportunities and widespread practices and customs.
- **The Disclosure Rule:** If the full glare of examination by associates, friends, family, newspapers, television, etc. were to focus on your decision, would you remain comfortable with it? If you think you would, it probably is the right decision.
- **The Golden Rule:** Do unto others as you would have them do unto you. It includes not knowingly doing harm to others.
- **The Hedonistic Ethic:** Virtue is embodied in what each individual finds meaningful. There are no universal or absolute moral principles. If it feels good, do it.
- **The Intuition Ethic:** People are endowed with a kind of moral sense with which they can apprehend right and wrong. The solution to moral problems lies simply in what you feel or understand to be right in a given situation. You have a "gut feeling" and "fly by the seat of your pants."
- **The Market Ethic:** Selfish actions in the marketplace are virtuous because they contribute to efficient operation of the economy. Decision makers may take selfish actions and be motivated by personal gain in their business dealings. They should ask whether their actions in the market further financial self-interest. If so, the actions are ethical.
- **The Means–Ends Ethic:** Worthwhile ends justify efficient means—that is, when ends are of overriding importance or virtue, unscrupulous means may be employed to reach them.
- **The Might-Equals-Right Ethic:** Justice is defined as the interest of the stronger. What is ethical is what an individual has the strength and power to accomplish. Seize what advantage you are strong enough to take without respect to ordinary social conventions and laws.
- **The Organization Ethic:** The wills and needs of individuals should be subordinated to the greater good of the organization (be it church, state, business, military, or university). An individual should ask whether actions are consistent with organizational goals and what is good for the organization.
- **The Professional Ethic:** You should do only that which can be explained before a committee of your peers.
- **The Proportionality Principle:** I am responsible for whatever I "will" as a means or an end. If both the means and the end are good in and of themselves, I may ethically permit or risk the foreseen but unwilled side effects if, and only if, I have a proportionate reason for doing so.
- **The Revelation Ethic:** Through prayer or other appeal to transcendent beings and forces, answers are given to individual minds. The decision makers pray, meditate, or otherwise commune with a superior force or being. They are then apprised of which actions are just and unjust.
- **The Utilitarian Ethic:** Take the action that represents the greatest good for the greatest number. Determine whether the harm in an action is outweighed by the good. If the action maximizes benefit, it is the optimum course to take among alternatives that provide less benefit.

Source: T. K. Das, "Ethical Preferences Among Business Students: A Comparative Study of Fourteen Ethical Principles," *Southern Management Association* (November 13–16, 1985), 11–12. For further discussion, see T. K. Das, "How Strong Are the Ethical Preferences of Senior Business Executives?" *Journal of Business Ethics* (Vol. 56, 2005), 69–80.

ETHICS IN PRACTICE CASE

Promise versus Lie

During the spring, I worked in the billing department of a large organization as a student worker. All of the secretaries who worked in the billing department were close and would talk to each other about almost anything. One of the most talked-about topics was the office manager of the billing department and how much we would like to find another job to get away from her, because we did not like working with her. While I was working in the department, I became very close friends with the senior secretary, who worked with me in the front office.

During the same spring, my friend was offered a very prestigious job at another company. She told a few of us about having applied for the job, but she did not want us to let the office manager know about it in case she did not get it. I was her friend, so I was not going to say anything about the situation. After a few weeks of waiting, she was offered the job, which she took immediately. After confirmation about the new job, she told the office manager about it and gave two weeks' notice. All was well until the office manager came up to me one day and asked me if I had known anything about the secretary planning to leave. I was not sure what to say. I did not want to lie to the office manager, but I also did not want to break a promise I had made to a good friend. What was I to do?

1. Is this ethical dilemma at the personal level or the organizational level?
2. What ethical principles are at stake in this situation? Rights? Justice? Caring? Others?
3. What should the person who faces this ethical situation do?

Contributed by Erika Carlson-Durham

---

be for a person to use each principle consistently as a guide to decision making. On the other hand, to say that an ethical principle is imperfect is not to say that it has not raised important issues that must be addressed in personal or business decision making. The major principles and approaches we have discussed have raised to our consciousness the importance of the collective good, individual rights, caring, character, serving others first, and fairness.

In summary, the principles approach to ethics focuses on guidelines, ideas, or concepts that have been created to help people and organizations make wise, ethical decisions. Two ethical categories include the teleological (ends-based) and the deontological (duty-based). Both duty and consequences are important ethical concepts. In our discussion, we have treated the following as important components of the principles-based approach: utilitarianism, rights, justice, caring, virtue, servant leadership, and the Golden Rule. Such principles, or principle-based approaches, ought to cause us to think deeply and to reflect carefully on the ethical decisions we face in our personal and organizational lives. For the most part, these principles are rooted in moral philosophy, logic, and religion. On a more pragmatic level, we turn now to a series of ethical tests that constitute our third major approach to ethics.

Ethical Tests Approach

In addition to the ethical principles approach to guiding personal and managerial decision making, a number of practical **ethical tests** also might be set forth. Whereas the principles have almost exclusively been generated by moral philosophers, the ethical tests we discuss here have been culled from the experiences of many people. The ethical tests are more practical in orientation and do not require the depth of moral thinking that the principles do. Each simply asks a question that the decision maker should ask before taking an action. No single test is recommended as a universal answer to the question, "What action or decision should I take in this situation?" However, each person may find one or several tests that will be useful in helping to clarify the appropriate course of action in a decision situation.

To most, the notion of a test invokes the thought of questions posed that need to be answered. Indeed, each of these tests for personal ethical decision making requires the thoughtful deliberation of a central question that gets to the heart of the ethics issue. The answer to the question should help the decision maker decide whether the course of action, practice, or decision should be pursued or not. No single test is foolproof, but each should be helpful. Often, several tests can be used in conjunction with one another.

Test of Common Sense.   With this first test, the individual simply asks, "Does the action I am getting ready to take really make sense?" When you think of behavior that might have ethical implications, it is logical to consider the practical consequences. If, for example, you would surely get caught engaging in a questionable practice, the action does not pass the test of common sense. Many unethical practices have come to light when one is led to ask whether a person really used her or his common sense at all. This test has limitations. For example, if you conclude that you would not get caught engaging in a questionable practice, this test might lead you to think that the questionable practice is an acceptable course of action, when in fact it is not. In addition, there may be other commonsense aspects of the situation that you have overlooked. The test of common sense has been called the **"smell" test** by some. If a proposed course of action stinks, don't do it.

Test of One's Best Self.   Psychologists tell us that each person has a self-concept. Most people could construct a scenario of themselves *at their best*. This test requires the individual to pose the question, "Is this action or decision I'm getting ready to take compatible with my concept of myself *at my best*?" This test addresses the notion of the esteem with which we hold ourselves and the kind of person we want to be known as. Naturally, this test would not be of much value to those who do not hold themselves in high esteem. To those concerned about their esteem and reputation, however, this could be a powerful test.

Test of Making Something Public (Disclosure Rule).   The test of making something public, sometimes called the disclosure rule, is one of the most powerful tests.[56] It has been mentioned in Figure 8-2. If you are about to engage in a questionable practice or action, you might pose the following questions: "How would I feel if others knew I was doing this? How would I feel if I knew that my decisions or actions were going to be featured on the national evening news tonight for all the world to see?" This test addresses the issue of whether your action or decision can withstand public disclosure and scrutiny. How would you feel if all your friends, family, and colleagues knew you were engaging in this action? If you feel comfortable with this thought, you are probably on solid footing. If you feel uncomfortable with this thought, you might need to rethink your position.

The concept of public exposure is quite powerful. Several years ago, a poll of managers was taken asking whether the Foreign Corrupt Practices Act would stop bribes abroad. Many of the managers said it would not. When asked what would stop bribes, most managers thought that public exposure would be most effective. "If the public knew we were accepting bribes, this knowledge would have the best chance of being effective," they replied. This idea gives further testimony to the strength of the transparency movement that is permeating business today.

Test of Ventilation.   The idea of ventilation is to "expose" your proposed action to others and get their thoughts on it. This test works best if you get opinions from people who you know might not see things your way. The important point here is that you do not isolate yourself with your dilemma but seek others' views. After you have subjected your proposed course of action to other opinions, you may find that you have not been thinking clearly. In other words, ventilate—or share—your ethical quandary, rather than keeping it to yourself. Someone else may say something of value that will help you in making your decision.

Test of Purified Idea. An idea or action might be thought to be "purified"—that is, made right—when a person with authority says it is appropriate. Such a person might be a supervisor, an accountant, or a lawyer. The central question here is, "Am I thinking this action or decision is right just because someone with appropriate authority or knowledge says it is right?" If you look hard enough, you always can find a lawyer or an accountant to endorse almost any idea if it is phrased right.[57] However, neither of them is the final arbiter of what is right or wrong. Similarly, just because a superior says an action or a decision is ethical does not make it so. The decision or course of action may still be questionable or wrong even though someone else has sanctioned it with her or his approval. This is one of the most common ethical errors people make, and people must constantly be reminded that they themselves ultimately will be held accountable if the action is indefensible.[58]

Test of the Big Four. Another test of your ethical behavior is to "watch out for the big four." The Big Four are four characteristics of decision making that may lead you astray or toward the wrong course of action. The four factors are *greed, speed, laziness,* and *haziness.*[59] Greed is the drive to acquire more and more in your own self-interest. Speed refers to the tendency to rush things and cut corners because you are under the pressure of time. Laziness may lead you to take the easy course of action that requires the least amount of effort. Haziness may lead you to acting or reacting without a clear idea of what is going on. All four of these factors represent temptations that, if succumbed to, might lead to unethical behavior.[60]

Gag Test. This test was provided by a judge on the Louisiana Court of Appeals. He argued that a manager's clearest signal that a dubious decision or action is going too far is when you simply gag at the prospect of carrying it out.[61] Admittedly, this test can capture only the grossest of unethical behaviors, but there are some managers who may need such a general kind of test. Actually, this test is intended to be more humorous than serious, but a few might be helped by it. The gag test has also been called the "smell" test by some. Figure 8-3 summarizes the practical ethical guidelines that may be extracted from these ethical tests.

Use Several Tests Together. None of the previously mentioned tests alone offers a perfect way to determine whether a decision, act, or practice is ethical. If several tests are used together, especially the more powerful ones, they do provide a means of examining proposed actions before engaging in them. To repeat, this assumes that the individual really wants to do what is right and is looking for assistance. To the fundamentally unethical person, however, these tests would not be of much value.

Based on a five-year study of ethical principles and ethical tests, Phillip Lewis asserted that there is high agreement on how a decision maker should behave when faced with a moral choice. He concludes,

> *In fact, there is almost a step-by-step sequence. Notice: One should (1) look at the problem from the position of the other person(s) affected by a decision; (2) try to determine what virtuous response is expected; (3) ask (a) how it would feel for the decision to be*

FIGURE 8-3 Practical Guidelines Derived from Key Ethical Tests

Ethical Test	Practical Ethical Guideline
Common Sense	If the proposed course of action violates your "common sense," don't do it. If it doesn't pass the "smell" test, don't do it.
One's Best Self	If the proposed course of action is not consistent with your perception of yourself at your "best," don't engage in it.
Making Something Public	If you would not be comfortable with people knowing you did something, don't do it.
Ventilation	Expose your proposed course of action to others' opinions. Don't keep your ethical dilemma to yourself. Get a second opinion.
Purified Idea	Don't think that others, such as an accountant or a lawyer, can "purify" your proposed action by saying they think it is okay. You will still be held responsible.
Big Four	Don't compromise your action or decision by greed, speed, laziness, or haziness.
Gag Test	If you "gag" at the prospect of carrying out a proposed course of action, don't do it.

disclosed to a wide audience and (b) whether the decision is consistent with organizational goals; and (4) act in a way that is (a) right and just for any other person in a similar situation and (b) good for the organization.[62]

Implicit in Lewis's conclusion is evidence of stakeholder theory, virtue theory, the Golden Rule, the disclosure rule, and Rawls's principle of justice.

Managing Organizational Ethics

To this point, our discussion has centered on principles, guidelines, and approaches to personal or managerial decision making. Clearly, ethical decision making is at the heart of business ethics, and we cannot stress enough the need to sharpen decision-making skills if amorality is to be prevented and moral management is to be achieved. Now we shift our attention more to the *organizational level*, where we consider the context in which decision making occurs. Actions and practices that take place within the organization's structure, processes, culture, or climate are just as vital as decision making in bringing about ethical business practices and results. Based on his own research, Craig VanSandt has concluded, "understanding and managing an organization's ethical work climate may go a long way toward defining the difference between how a company does and what kind of organization it is."[63]

To manage ethics in an organization, a manager must appreciate that the organization's ethical climate is just one part of its overall corporate culture. When McNeil Laboratories, a subsidiary of Johnson & Johnson, voluntarily withdrew Tylenol® from the market immediately after the reports of tainted, poisoned products, some people wondered why they made this decision. An often cited response was, "It's the J & J way."[64] This statement conveys a significant message about the firm's ethical work climate or corporate culture. It also raises the question of how organizations and managers should deal with, understand, and shape business ethics through actions taken, policies established, and examples set. The organization's moral climate is a complex entity, and we can discuss only some facets of it in this section.[65]

Figure 8-4 illustrates several levels of moral climate and some of the key factors that may come to bear on the manager as he or she makes decisions. What happens in

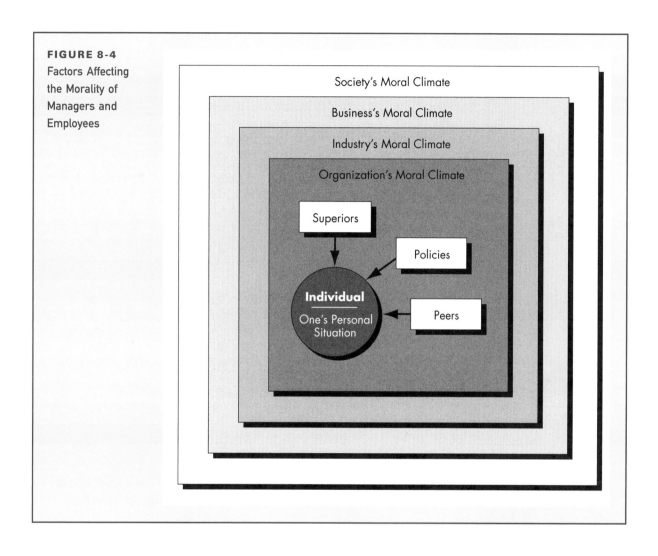

FIGURE 8-4

Factors Affecting the Morality of Managers and Employees

organizations, as Figure 8-4 depicts, is nested in industry's, business's, and society's moral climate. Our focus in this section is on the organization's moral climate. Regardless of the ethics of individuals, organizational factors prove to be powerful in shaping ethical or unethical behavior and practices. Two major questions drive the consideration of managing organizational ethics:

1. What factors contribute to ethical or unethical behavior in the organization?
2. What actions, strategies, or best practices might the management use to improve the organization's ethical climate?

Factors Affecting the Organization's Moral Climate

For managers to be in a position to create an ethical work climate, they must first understand the factors at work in the organization that influence whether or not other managers and employees behave ethically. More than a few studies have been conducted that have sought to identify and to rank the sources of ethical behavior in organizations.

One of the earliest studies on this topic involved a survey of over 1,500 *Harvard Business Review* readers (executives and managers).[66] One of the activities involved was to rank several factors that the managers thought influenced or contributed to unethical behaviors or actions. The factors found in this study, in descending order of frequency of mention, were as follows:

1. Behavior of superiors
2. The ethical practices of one's industry or profession
3. Behavior of one's peers in the organization
4. Formal organizational policy (or the lack thereof)
5. Personal financial need

A later replication of this early study was conducted using over 1,200 *Harvard Business Review* readers. One additional factor was added to the list: society's moral climate.[67] Yet another survey considered the opinions of over 1,400 managers, again asking them to rank the six factors in terms of their influence or contribution to unethical behavior.[68] Figure 8-5 summarizes the findings of these three landmark, baseline studies.

Although there is some variation in the rankings of the three studies, several findings are worthy of note:

- *Behavior of superiors* was ranked as the number one influence on unethical behavior in all three studies. In other words, the influence of bosses is real.
- *Behavior of one's peers* was ranked high in two of the three studies. People do pay attention to what their peers are doing and expecting.
- *Industry or professional ethical practices* ranked in the upper half in all three studies. These context factors are influential.
- *Personal financial need* ranked last in all three studies. But let's not assume it does not matter.

What stands out in these studies from an organizational perspective is the influence of the behavior of one's superiors and peers. Also notable about these findings is that quite often it is assumed that society's moral climate has a lot to do with managers' morality, but this factor was ranked low in the two studies in which it was considered. Apparently,

FIGURE 8-5 Factors Influencing Unethical Behavior Question: "Listed Below Are the Factors That Many Believe Influence Unethical Behavior. Rank Them in Order of Their Influence or Contribution to Unethical Behaviors or Actions by Managers."[a]

	Posner and Schmidt Study[b] (N = 1,443)	Brenner and Molander Study[c] (N = 1,227)	Baumhart Study[d] (N = 1,531)
Behavior of superiors	2.17(1)	2.15(1)	1.9(1)
Behavior of one's organizational peers	3.30(2)	3.37(4)	3.1(3)
Ethical practices of one's industry or profession	3.57(3)	3.34(3)	2.6(2)
Society's moral climate[e]	3.79(4)	4.22(5)	
Formal organizational policy (or the lack thereof)	3.84(5)	3.27(2)	3.3(4)
Personal financial need	4.09(6)	4.46(6)	4.1(5)

[a] Ranking is based on a scale of 1 (most influential) to 6 (least influential).
[b] Barry Z. Posner and Warren H. Schmidt, "Values and the American Manager: An Update," *California Management Review* (Spring 1984), 202–216.
[c] Steve Brenner and Earl Molander, "Is the Ethics of Business Changing?" *Harvard Business Review* (January/February 1977).
[d] Raymond C. Baumhart, "How Ethical Are Businessmen?" *Harvard Business Review* (July/August 1961), 6ff.
[e] This item is not included in the Baumhart study.

society's moral climate serves as a background factor that does not have a direct and immediate impact on organizational ethics. Furthermore, it is enlightening to know that personal financial need ranked so low. But we should not assume that personal needs and wants are irrelevant. What these findings suggest is that there are factors at work over which managers can exercise some discretion. Thus, we begin to see the managerial dimension of business ethics.

Pressures Exerted on Employees by Superiors. One major consequence of the behavior of superiors and peers is that pressure is placed on subordinates and/or other organizational members to achieve results, and this often requires that they compromise their ethics. In one national study of this topic, managers were asked to what extent they agreed with the following proposition: "Managers today feel under pressure to compromise personal standards to achieve company goals."[69] It is insightful to consider the management levels of the 64.4 percent of the respondents who agreed with the proposition. The results by management level were

- Top management: 50 percent agreed
- Middle management: 65 percent agreed
- Lower management: 85 percent agreed

This study revealed that the perceived pressure to compromise ethics seems to be felt most by those in lower management, followed by those in middle management. In a later study, managers were asked whether they sometimes had to compromise their personal principles to conform to organizational expectations.[70] Twenty percent of the top executives agreed, 27 percent of the middle managers agreed, and 41 percent of the lower managers agreed. In other words, the same pattern prevailed in this second study.

What is particularly insightful about these findings is the *pattern of response*. It seems that the lower a manager is in the hierarchy, the more he or she perceives pressures to engage in unethical conduct. Although there are several plausible explanations for this phenomenon, one explanation seems particularly attractive based on experience—that top-level managers do not fully understand how strongly their subordinates perceive pressures to go along with their bosses.

These varying perceptions at different levels in the managerial hierarchy suggest that higher-level managers may not be tuned in to how pressure is perceived at lower levels. A gap seems to exist between the understanding of higher managers and that of lower managers regarding the pressures that exist toward unethical behavior, especially in the lower echelons. This breakdown in understanding, or lack of sensitivity by top management to how far subordinates will go to please them, can be conducive to lower-level subordinates behaving unethically out of a real or perceived fear of reprisal, a misguided sense of loyalty, or a distorted concept of their jobs.

Another study of the sources and consequences of workplace pressure was conducted by the American Society of Chartered Life Underwriters & Chartered Financial Consultants and the Ethics Officer Association.[71] The findings of this study were consistent with those of the studies reported earlier and provided additional insights into the detrimental consequences of workplace pressure. The following were among the key findings of this study:

- The majority of workers (60 percent) felt a substantial amount of pressure on the job. More than one out of four (27 percent) felt a "great deal" of pressure.
- Nearly half of all workers (48 percent) reported that, due to pressure, they had engaged in one or more unethical and/or illegal actions during the past year. The most frequently cited misbehavior was cutting corners on quality control.

- The sources most commonly cited as contributing to workplace pressure were "balancing work and family" (52 percent), "poor internal communications" (51 percent), "work hours/workload" (51 percent), and "poor leadership" (51 percent).

The National Business Ethics Survey conducted by the Ethics Resource Center found that the percentage of employees reporting feeling pressure to compromise their standards has remained relatively constant over the past seven years.[72] In a different study, they also found some other insights regarding pressure perceived:[73]

- First-line supervisors and employees were the groups most "at risk" to feel pressure.
- Organizational transitions such as mergers, acquisitions, and restructurings are associated with increased pressure on employees to compromise organizational ethics standards.
- Employees who observe unethical actions more frequently in their organization tend to feel pressure to compromise their ethical standards.
- Employees whose organizations have in place key elements of formal ethics programs feel less pressure to compromise standards.

On an encouraging note, the Ethics Resource Center's 2009 study found that the percentage of the U.S. workforce perceiving pressure to commit wrongdoing declined by a modest 2 percent between 2007 and 2009.[74] In addition to the studies that document the extent to which managers feel pressure to perform, even if it leads to questionable activities, several actual business cases demonstrate the reality of cutting corners to achieve high production goals.

ETHICS IN PRACTICE CASE

Higher Goals, More Pressure, Lower Ethics?

Recently, I held a position as an inside sales representative for a multinational *Fortune* 500 phone company. My job was to place unsolicited phone calls to people and convince them to switch their local and long-distance calling carrier to my company. As I went through training, I was taught to "sell, sell, sell!" We were told that once we got a customer on the line, we were to not hang up unless we sold him or her a phone package.

There was also a big emphasis on meeting daily sales goals that were set by the company. As soon as I got out of training and on the phone lines, I began to encounter elderly people who had no use for the product. One day my supervisor noticed that I was not selling the product to everyone that I talked to, and she thought this was the reason I was not meeting my sales goal.

She soon asked why I did not "push" the product more. I told her that the people I was letting off the hook were too old to need anything that the company offered and that they did not even understand half of what I was talking about. She told me that I should

just sell them the product and that the customer service representatives would fix it later.

I asked my mentor what he did in these situations, to which he replied he just tells the older people that they are getting a smaller package and then "adds on" other features without them noticing. The next time I got an elderly person on the phone, I just told her to have a nice day and then I hung up.

1. What are the ethical issues facing the company and me in this case?

2. Does this illustrate personal-, organizational-, or industry-level ethical issues?

3. Should I succumb to the pressure to meet company goals in these situations?

4. Is it an ethical practice for my company to continually raise goals and expect that people in my position will just "sell" and let customer service "fix" the problems?

Contributed by Joe Popkowski

Improving the Organization's Ethical Culture

Because the behavior of managers has been identified as the most important influence on the ethical behavior of organization members, it should come as no surprise that most actions and strategies for improving the organization's ethical culture must originate from top management and other management levels as well. The process by which these kinds of initiatives have taken place is sometimes referred to as "institutionalizing ethics" into the organization.[75]

Today, the emphasis is not just on institutionalizing ethics programs. It is more on creating an ethical organizational culture or climate, one in which ethical behavior, values, and policies are displayed, promoted, and rewarded. Ethical culture has more to do with ethical leadership and values than with formal rules or codes. If ethics initiatives are not supported by the surrounding organizational culture, they have less of a chance of succeeding. One of the key findings of an earlier National Business Ethics Survey was that formal ethics and compliance programs do have an impact, but the organization's culture is more influential in producing results.[76] Organizational culture refers to shared values, beliefs, behaviors, and ways of doing things.[77] Part of the culture is driven by formal systems, but much of it is carried on by informal systems. One fact is certain: an ethical culture can be created and can survive only if it has the strong endorsement and leadership of top management, and today, this embraces the board of directors as well.

Compliance versus Ethics Orientation. An organization with a culture of ethics today is most likely a mixture of an emphasis on compliance and on such values as integrity or ethics. Early efforts of companies were to avert corporate crime. Compliance emphases took a huge step forward when the Organizational Sentencing Guidelines were introduced in 1991 and were revised in 2004 in response to the Sarbanes–Oxley Act. These guidelines began a partnership between companies and the federal government to prevent and deter corporate illegal/unethical practices.[78] They were created by the U.S. Sentencing Commission, which is an independent agency of the judicial branch of the federal government. The guidelines gave companies incentives for creating strong compliance and ethics programs. It is little wonder, then, that we have seen such programs increase in number and become vital parts of companies' corporate cultures.

Today the discussion is ongoing as to whether a **compliance orientation** or an **ethics orientation** should prevail in companies' ethics programs.[79] Historically, more emphasis has been placed on legal compliance than on ethics. Recently, much concern has been raised about the restrictiveness of a compliance focus. Several concerns articulated about the compliance focus have been identified.[80]

- First, a pure compliance focus could undermine the ways of thinking or habits of mind that are needed in ethics thinking. Ethics thinking is more philosophical or principles based, while compliance thinking is more rule bound and legalistic.
- Second, it has been argued that compliance can squeeze out ethics. An organization can become so focused on following the law that ethics considerations no longer get factored into discussions.
- Third, the issue of "false consciousness" has been raised. This means that managers may become accustomed to addressing issues in a mechanistic, rule-based way, and this may cause them to not consider tougher issues that a more ethics-focused approach might require.[81]

Because of the rule of law and growing litigation, a compliance focus cannot be eliminated. The recommended approach, however, is toward developing organizational cultures and programs that aspire to be ethics focused. The importance of both was

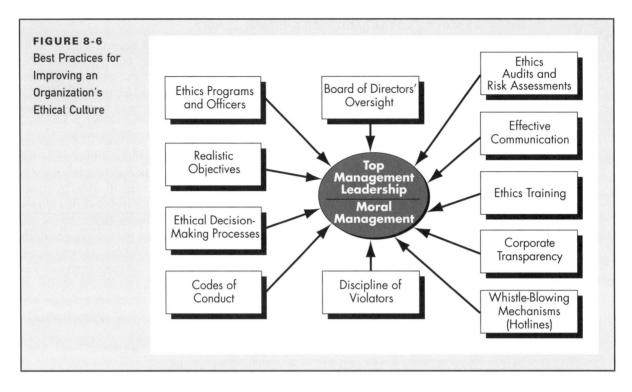

FIGURE 8-6

Best Practices for Improving an Organization's Ethical Culture

emphasized in the observation that the ethics perspective is needed to give a compliance program "soul," while compliance features may be necessary to give ethics programs more "body."[82] In short, both are essential.

In the following sections, we will consider some of the best practices that managers have concluded are vital to improving their organizations' ethical culture or climate. Figure 8-6 depicts a number of best practices for creating such an ethical organization. Top management leadership is at the hub of these initiatives, actions, or practices. Board of Director Oversight has become especially vital in the post-Enron business climate.

Top Management Leadership (Moral Management).   It has become a cliché, but this premise must be established at the outset: *the moral tone of an organization is set by top management.* A poll of communication professionals found that over half believed that top management is an organization's conscience.[83] This is because managers and employees look to their bosses at the highest levels for their cues as to what are acceptable practices. A former chairman of a major steel company stated it well: "Starting at the top, management has to set an example for all the others to follow".[84] Top management, through its capacity to set a personal example and to shape policy, is in the ideal position to provide a highly visible role model. The authority and ability to shape policy, both formal and implied, forms one of the vital aspects of the job of any leader in any organization. This aspect of becoming a moral manager has been referred to as "role modeling through visible action." Effective moral managers recognize that they live in a fishbowl and that employees are watching them for cues about what's important.[85] There are many examples of both weak and strong ethical leadership in business practice today.

WEAK ETHICAL LEADERSHIP   An example of weak ethical leadership (or role modeling) was found in one of the authors' consulting experiences in a small company, where a long-time employee was identified as having embezzled about $20,000 over a 15-year period. When the employee was approached and questioned as to why she had done

ETHICS IN PRACTICE CASE

The Anonymous CEO: Strong or Weak Ethical Leader?

John Mackey, CEO of Whole Foods, the country's No. 1 natural and organic grocery store chain, was exposed in July 2007 for having written over 1,300 anonymous postings on a Web-based Yahoo Finance stock forum between 1999 and 2006. His messages on the discussion forum bashed competitors and praised his own company.

Whole Foods is a giant firm, with 39,000 employees spread over 196 stores in the United States, Canada, and the UK. At the end of fiscal 2006, the company's gross profit margin was 35 percent, compared with 24 percent at Kroger and 29 percent at Safeway. It had sales of $5.6 billion.

Mackey, who took on the pseudonym "Rahodeb" (an anagram of Deborah, his wife), was "outed" by an FTC court filing in July 2007. The Securities and Exchange Commission began an examination of the CEO's postings to determine if he broke any laws. Interestingly, Mackey's alter ego was exposed by the FTC, which filed a lawsuit seeking to block Whole Foods' planned purchase of Wild Oats, its main competitor, on antitrust grounds.

After Mackey apologized to Whole Foods' board, the board announced it would begin an internal investigation of the matter.

In some postings, Mackey (as Rahodeb) bashed Wild Oats, criticizing their former CEO for lack of vision, while noting that it wasn't a profitable company. In a February 2005 posting, Rahodeb apparently wrote with some delight that Wild Oats was going to have to restate its earnings. Rahodeb went on to say that Oats had been misleading its investors for years and that the company was headed for shareholder litigation. He also questioned the Oats leadership regarding its competence and integrity. In spite of these comments, Whole Foods began an effort to acquire Wild Oats, its main rival, in February 2007, but the FTC was seeking to block this purchase on antitrust grounds.

In a public statement posted on Whole Foods' Web site, Mackey claimed that his anonymous postings did not reflect his or his company's policies or beliefs and that some of the views of Rahodeb did not even match his own beliefs.

A few antitrust experts say that some of Mackey's Yahoo messages could hurt his company's case and be used against him if they support the view that the health-food market is a distinct market, separate from the mainstream grocery market. The FTC was trying to argue that the health-food market was distinct and that the acquisition would increase concentration in that narrow market and drive up prices. Some experts on corporate governance and others who serve as image consultants have held that Mackey's exposure may cause the company's board to question his leadership abilities.

Mackey explained that he had made the online comments anonymously because he had fun doing it. Some of his defenders have said that his comments were never intended to disclose insider information or to move stock prices.

1. Were Mackey's actions more representative of a strong, moral leader or a weak, uncertain leader? What insights into his character are revealed by this episode? Is it ethical for a CEO to engage in such deceptions?
2. Do you see Mackey's actions as positive, negative, or indifferent in terms of setting a strong ethical tone for his company?
3. Were Mackey's deceptions just a harmless, fun activity or do they have harmful implications for Whole Foods in the future?

Sources: David Kesmodel and Jonathan Eig, "A Grocer's Brash Style Takes Unhealthy Turn," *The Wall Street Journal* (July 20, 2007), A1; Greg Farrell and Paul Davidson, "Whole Foods' CEO Was a Busy Guy Online," *USA Today* (July 12, 2007); Shelly Banjo, "For Regulars Poster on Whole Foods Board, A Dramatic Twist," *The Wall Street Journal* (July 18, 2007).

this, she explained that she thought it was all right because the president of the company had led her to believe it was okay by actions he had taken. She further explained that any time during the fall, when the leaves had fallen in his yard and he needed them raked, he would simply take company personnel off their jobs and have them do it. When he needed cash, he would take it out of the company's petty cash box or get the key to the soft drink machine and raid its coin box. When he needed stamps to mail his personal

Christmas cards, he would take them out of the company stamp box. The woman's perception was that it was all right for her to take the money because the president did it frequently. Therefore, she thought it was an acceptable practice for her as well.

STRONG ETHICAL LEADERSHIP An example of positive ethical leadership may be seen in the case of a firm that was manufacturing vacuum tubes. One day the plant manager called a hurried meeting to announce that a sample of the tubes in production had failed a critical safety test. This meant that the safety and performance of the batch of 10,000 tubes was highly questionable. The plant manager wondered out loud, "What are we going to do now?" Ethical leadership was shown by the vice president for technical operations, who looked around the room at each person and then declared in a low voice, "Scrap them!" According to a person who worked for this vice president, that act set the tone for the corporation for years, because every person present knew of situations in which faulty products had been shipped under pressures of time and budget.[86]

Each of these cases provides a vivid example of how a leader's actions and behavior communicated important messages to others in the organization. In the absence of knowing what to do, most employees look to the behavior of leaders for their cues as to what conduct is acceptable. In the second case, another crucial point is illustrated. When we speak of management providing ethical leadership, it is not just restricted to top management. Vice presidents, plant managers, supervisors, and, indeed, all managerial personnel share the responsibility for ethical leadership.

TWO PILLARS OF LEADERSHIP It has been argued that a manager's reputation for ethical leadership is founded on two pillars: perceptions of the manager both as a moral person *and* as a moral manager. Being a *moral person* requires three major attributes: traits, behaviors, and decision making. Important traits are stable personal attributes such as integrity, honesty, and trustworthiness. Critical behaviors—what you do, not what you say—include doing the right thing, showing concern for people, being open, and being personally moral. Decision making by the moral person needs to reflect a solid set of ethical values and principles. In this activity, the manager would hold to values, be objective/fair, demonstrate concern for society, and follow ethical decision rules.[87]

The concept of the second pillar, being a *moral manager*, was developed in the previous chapter. According to researchers, moral managers recognize the importance of proactively putting ethics at the forefront of their ethical agenda. This involves three major activities. First, the moral manager must engage in *role modeling* through visible action. An emphasis is placed on visible action—action that can be observed by others. Second, the moral manager *communicates about ethics and values*. This should be done in a way that explains the values that guide important actions. Third, the moral manager needs to *use rewards and discipline effectively*. This is a powerful way to send signals about desirable and undesirable conduct in the workplace.[88]

In a period in which the importance of a sound corporate culture has been strongly advocated, ethical leaders must stress the primacy of integrity and morality as vital components of the organization's culture. There are many different ways and situations in which management needs to do this. In general, management needs to create a climate of moral consciousness. In everything it does, it must stress the importance of sound ethical principles and practices.

ETHICAL LEADERSHIP CHARACTERISTICS Following are ten facets of strong ethical leadership that have been put forth as a framework for understanding what ethical leadership should mean in organizations. Ethical leaders should[89]

- Articulate and embody the purpose and values of the organization
- Focus on organizational success rather than on personal ego

- Find the best people and develop them
- Create a living conversation about ethics, values, and the creation of value for stakeholders
- Create mechanisms of dissent
- Take a charitable understanding of others' values
- Make tough calls while being imaginative
- Know the limits of the values and ethical principles they live
- Frame actions in ethical terms
- Connect the basic value proposition to stakeholder support and societal legitimacy

The leader must infuse the organization's climate with values and ethical consciousness, not just run a one-person show. This point is made vividly clear in the following observation: "Ethics programs which are seen as part of one manager's management system, and not as a part of the general organizational process, will be less likely to have a lasting role in the organization."[90] In short, ethics is more about leadership than about programs.

Effective Communication. Management also carries a profound burden in terms of providing ethical leadership in the area of effective communication. We have seen the importance of communicating through acts, principles, and organizational climate. Later we will discuss further the communication aspects of setting realistic objectives, codes of conduct, and the decision-making process. Here, however, we want to stress the importance of communication principles, techniques, and practices.

Conveying the importance of ethics through communication includes both written and verbal forms of communication. In each of these settings, management should operate according to certain key ethical principles. Candor, fidelity, and confidentiality are three very important principles. *Candor* requires that a manager be forthright, sincere, and honest in communication transactions. In addition, it requires the manager to be fair and free from prejudice and malice in the communication. *Fidelity* in communication means that the communicator should be faithful to detail, should be accurate, and should avoid deception or exaggeration. *Confidentiality* is a final principle that ought to be stressed. The ethical manager must exercise care in deciding what information she or he discloses to others. Trust can be easily shattered if the manager does not have a keen sense of what is confidential in a communication.

Ethics Programs and Ethics Officers. In recent years, many companies have begun creating **ethics programs** within their organizations. These programs frequently embrace both compliance and ethics initiatives and responsibility. Ethics programs are typically organizational units or departments that have been assigned the responsibility for ethics plans in the organization. According to national surveys conducted, ethics programs typically include the following features:[91]

- Written standards of conduct
- Ethics training
- Mechanisms to seek ethics advice or information
- Methods for reporting misconduct anonymously
- Disciplinary measures for employees who violate ethical standards
- Inclusion of ethical conduct in the evaluation of employee performance.

A key finding in business ethics research conducted by the Ethics Resource Center was that ethics programs are increasing in number and they do make a difference. The survey disclosed that the impact of ethics programs depends somewhat on the culture in which they are implemented. The study found that the more formal are the program elements, the better it is; formal programs make more of a difference in weak ethical cultures, and, once a strong culture has been established, the formal programs do not have as much impact on results.[92]

Figure 8-7 summarizes the elements that ought to exist in companies' ethics programs in order to comply with the U.S. Sentencing Commission's Organizational Guidelines. Two major benefits accrue to organizations that follow these guidelines. First, following

FIGURE 8-7

Key Elements of Effective Ethics Programs

The U.S. Sentencing Commission has identified these key elements that companies must have in their ethics programs to satisfy the commission's regulatory review. If a company has these key elements in its ethics program, it will be dealt with less harshly should violations arise. Benefits should extend beyond compliance to ethics.

Compliance Standards. Companies are expected to have established compliance standards, which are a key part of detecting and preventing violations of the law. The development of a code of conduct is an initial step in this process. A set of ethical principles that guide decision making will strengthen these standards.

High-Level Ethics Personnel. Companies must assign compliance and ethics programs to senior executives. This person, perhaps called an *ethics officer*, must have the authority, responsibility, and resources to achieve ethics goals.

Avoidance of Delegation of Undue Discretionary Authority. Companies have a responsibility to make sure they do not delegate undue discretionary authority (e.g., access to company funds, investor information, and authority to bind the company to contracts) to individuals who cannot be trusted with such authority. Someone convicted of a previous felony involving company funds would be an example. Background checks are thus becoming much more essential in screening employees.

Effective Communication. Standards and procedures must be effectively communicated. The company has a responsibility to make sure all personnel are aware of ethics codes, standards, policies, and practices. One major way to achieve this

communication is through the conduct of ethics training programs.

Systems for Monitoring, Auditing, and Reporting. Companies are expected to have systems and procedures in place for assessing compliance. This may involve a variety of monitoring and auditing systems and reporting systems as well. In other words, companies must take reasonable steps to ensure that compliance is taking place.

Enforcement. Companies are expected to have systems in place to ensure the consistent enforcement of compliance standards. The purpose here is to make sure that everyone is following standards. A high-level executive cannot be treated differently than a low-level executive.

Detecting Offenses, Preventing Future Offenses. Once an offense has been detected, several actions need to happen. If there is an actual violation of the law, the company is expected to self-report the offense and take actions to resolve the issue. The company needs to take further reasonable measures to prevent a similar offense from occurring in the future. The responsible person should be disciplined appropriately. Finally, the company is expected to accept responsibility for the offense as part of good corporate citizenship efforts.

Keeping Up with Industry Standards. Companies are expected, through ethics offices or programs, to keep up with industry practices and standards. This can be done by membership in national or local organizations. At the national level, an example would be the Ethics Officer Association (http://www.eoa.org). Many large cities also have their own such organizations. These organizations have as their major purpose the advancement of sound compliance and ethics programs.

Source: U.S. Sentencing Commission Guidelines (http://www.ussc.gov/orgguide.htm).

the guidelines mitigates severe financial and oversight penalties. Second, some prosecutors are choosing not to pursue some actions when the companies in question already have sound programs in place if they follow these guidelines.[93]

ETHICS OFFICERS Ethics programs are often headed by an **ethics officer** who is in charge of implementing the array of ethics initiatives of the organization. In some cases, the creation of ethics programs and designation of ethics officers has been in response to the Federal Sentencing Guidelines, which reduced penalties to those companies with ethics programs that were found guilty of ethics violations.[94] More recently, companies have created ethics programs and hired ethics officers because of the 2002 Sarbanes–Oxley law.

Many companies started ethics programs as an effort to centralize the coordination of ethics initiatives. Many ethics programs and ethics officers initially got started with compliance issues. Only later, in some cases, did ethics or integrity become a focal point of the programs. As suggested earlier, most ethics programs and ethics officers have major corporate responsibility for both legal compliance and ethics practices, and there is some debate as to whether they should be called compliance programs or ethics programs.[95] Major companies that do a lot of their business with the government, such as defense contractors, continue to emphasize compliance. Others strive more for a balance between compliance and ethics.

Just as ethics programs have proliferated in companies, the number of ethics officers occupying important positions in major firms has grown significantly. There are now two major professional organizations that ethics officers may join: Ethics and Compliance Officers Association (ECOA) and the Society of Corporate Compliance and Ethics (SCCE).

RAISING THE STATUS OF ETHICS OFFICERS One concern voiced by some ethics officers has been the tendency of some companies to slide the ethics officer down the organization chart so that direct access to the highest levels of organizational leadership has been decreasing. In other words, the organizational status of the ethics officer has been diminished in some organizations. Another trend has been to move the focus of the ethics officer in some organizations "downward," that is, spending little time working with or helping to manage the ethics of their superiors, but rather focusing on the ethics of lower-level organizational members, not senior management.[96] To reverse these trends, it has been recommended that the ethics office's and the ethics officers' scope of responsibilities be enlarged to embrace the total organization, including senior management. The phrase "managing ethics upward" has been developed for explaining how the ethics officers would work with their superiors.[97] In light of the rash of ethical scandals involving senior-level executives, this idea is one that has genuine value.

Two examples of how this goal might be achieved include the "bubble up" strategy and the "survey" strategy. The "bubble up" strategy would involve ethics officers using specific cases and questions that had bubbled up from the employees of the organization to meaningfully involve the senior leadership in a good faith discussion of appropriate courses of action to take. This would help senior leadership see the strong connection between their words and actions and the conduct of their employees.

The "survey" strategy would necessitate that a survey be conducted taking into consideration the entire population of employees, asking questions about their perceptions of the organization's ethical culture as well as their perceptions of senior leadership. Senior leadership could then be briefed on the findings and could then develop action plans for dealing with the results of the survey.[98] Obviously, managing ethics upward is easier to say than to do, and this would need to be handled with diplomacy. Regardless, it poses a valuable idea for getting senior-level executives more involved in the ethics programs of the company. The point has been raised by several experts that ethics officers didn't seem to help much during the Wall Street financial scandals that plunged the country into a serious recession. According to Steve Priest, president of Ethical Leadership, a consulting firm, "Many companies did little more than 'check the boxes' on ethics, abiding by the letter of the law by publishing codes of conduct, without really changing the culture of the company or tackling wider ethical issues." He went on to affirm that there is "a wide gulf between how business people define ethics and compliance and how the public sees them."[99]

As valuable as ethics programs and ethics officers are, there is a major downside danger in their existence. By holding individuals and organizational units responsible for the company's "ethics," there is some possibility that managers may come to "delegate" to these persons/units the responsibility for the firm's ethics. Ethics is everyone's job, however, and specialized units and people should not be used as a substitute for the assumption of ethical responsibility by everyone in leadership positions.

Setting Realistic Objectives.   Closely related to all ethics initiatives and programs being implemented by top management is the necessity that managers at all levels set realistic objectives or goals. A manager may quite innocently and inadvertently create a condition leading to unethical behavior on a subordinate's part. Take the case of a marketing manager setting a sales goal of a 20 percent increase for the next year when a 10 percent increase is all that could be realistically and honestly expected, even with outstanding performance. In the absence of clearly established and communicated ethical norms, it is easy to see how a subordinate might believe that she or he should go to any lengths to achieve the 20 percent goal. With the goal having been set too high, the salesperson faces a situation that is conducive to unethical behavior in order to please the superior.

Fred T. Allen, a former executive, strongly reinforced this point:

> *Top management must establish sales and profit goals that are realistic—goals that can be achieved with current business practices. Under the pressure of unrealistic goals, otherwise responsible subordinates will often take the attitude that "anything goes" in order to comply with the chief executive's target.*[100]

The point here is that there are ethical implications to even the most routine managerial decisions, such as goal setting. Managers must be keenly sensitive to the possibility of unintentionally creating situations in which others may perceive a need or an incentive to cut corners or do the wrong thing. This kind of knowledge is what justifies business ethics being a management and leadership topic.

Ethical Decision-Making Processes.   Decision making is at the heart of the management process. If there is any practice or process that is synonymous with management, it is decision making. Decision making usually entails a process of stating the problem, analyzing the problem, identifying the possible courses of action that might be taken, evaluating these courses of action, deciding on the best alternative, and then implementing the chosen course of action.

Ethical decision making is not a simple process but rather a multifaceted one that is complicated by multiple alternatives, mixed outcomes, uncertain and extended consequences, and personal implications.[101] It would be nice if a set of ethical principles was readily available for the manager to "plug in" and walk away from, with a decision to be forthcoming. However, such was not the case when we discussed principles that help personal decision making, and it is not the case when we think of organizational decision making. The ethical principles we discussed earlier are useful here, but there are no simple formulas revealing easy answers. The key here is that managers set up decision-making processes that will yield the most appropriate ethical decisions.

ETHICS SCREEN   Although it is difficult to portray graphically the process of ethical decision making, it is possible as long as we recognize that such an effort cannot totally capture reality. Figure 8-8 presents one conception of the ethical decision-making process. In this model, the individual is asked to identify the action, decision, or behavior that is being considered and then to articulate all dimensions of the proposed course of action. Next, she or he is asked to subject the course of action to what might be called an **ethics screen** which

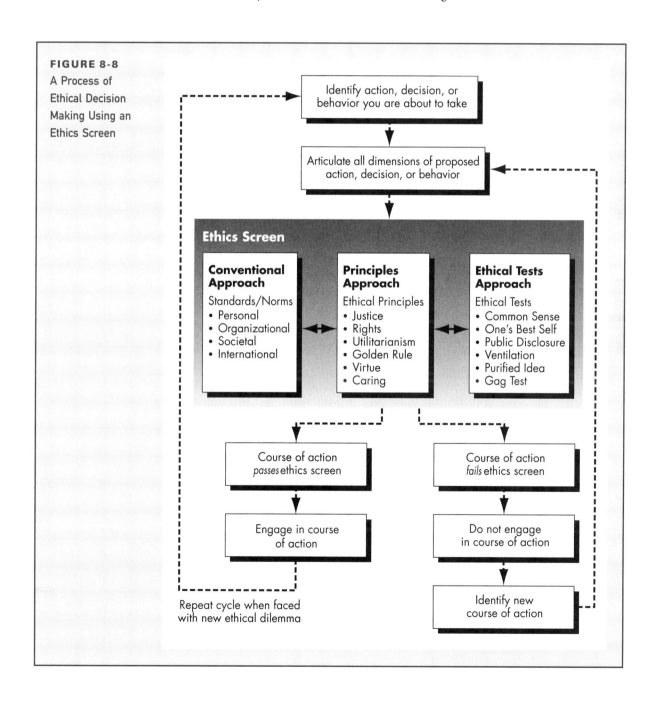

FIGURE 8-8
A Process of Ethical Decision Making Using an Ethics Screen

consists of several select standards against which the proposed course of action is to be compared. The idea is that unethical actions will be "screened out" and ethical ones will be "screened in." In the illustrated ethics screen, we reference our earlier discussion of the conventional approach (embodying societal standards/norms), the principles approach, and the ethical tests approach to ethical decision making. By using all or a combination of these ethical standards, it is expected that more ethical decisions will be made than would have been made otherwise.

In this decision-making model, it is left up to the individual to determine what mix of guidelines to use as the ethics screen. Normally, some combination of the guidelines contained in the screen would be helpful to the manager who truly is attempting to make an ethical decision. If the proposed course of action *fails* the ethics screen, the decision maker should not engage in the course of action but should consider a new decision, behavior, or action and submit it to this same process. If the proposed course of action *passes* the screen (the decision maker has determined that it would be an ethical course of action), she or he should engage in the action, decision, or behavior and then repeat the cycle only when faced with a new ethical dilemma.

Another useful approach to making ethical decisions is to systematically ask and answer a series of simple questions. It should quickly be realized that this approach is similar to the ethical tests approach presented earlier in the chapter.

ETHICS CHECK   One well-known set of questions merits mention here because of its popularity in the book *The Power of Ethical Management*.[102] The "ethics check" questions are as follows:

1. *Is it legal?* Will I be violating either civil law or company policy?
2. *Is it balanced?* Is it fair to all concerned in the short term as well as the long term? Does it promote win–win relationships?
3. *How will it make me feel about myself?* Will it make me proud? Would I feel good if my decision was published in the newspaper? Would I feel good if my family knew about it?

ETHICS QUICK TEST   Using a brief set of questions to make ethical decisions has become popular in business. For example, Texas Instruments has printed its seven-part "Ethics Quick Test" on a wallet card its employees may carry. The test's seven questions and reminders are as follows:[103]

- Is the action legal?
- Does it comply with our values?
- If you do it, will you feel bad?
- How will it look in the newspaper?
- If you know it's wrong, don't do it.
- If you're not sure, ask.
- Keep asking until you get an answer.

SEARS'S GUIDELINES   In its Code of Business Conduct, Sears, Roebuck and Co. set forth its five "Guidelines for Making Ethical Decisions," which are as follows:[104]

1. Is it *legal*?
2. Is it within Sears' *shared beliefs and policies*?
3. Is it *right/fair/appropriate*?
4. Would I want everyone *to know* about this?
5. How will I *feel about myself*?

This set of practical questions is intended to produce a process of ethical inquiry that is of immediate practical use and understanding to a group of employees and managers. Note that many of the items are similar or identical to points raised earlier in the ethical tests approach. These questions help ensure that ethical due process takes place. They cannot tell us for sure whether our decisions are ethical or not, but they can help us be sure that we are raising the appropriate issues and genuinely attempting to be ethical.

Codes of Conduct. The top management has the responsibility for establishing standards of behavior and for effectively communicating those standards to all managers and employees in the organization. One of the traditional ways by which companies and ethics officers have fulfilled this responsibility is through the use of **codes of ethics** or **codes of conduct**. According to Joan Dubinsky, ethics officer at the International Monetary Fund, "a Code of Conduct is the single most important element of your ethics and compliance program. It sets the tone and direction for the entire function. Often, the Code is a standalone document, ideally only a few pages in length. It introduces the concept of ethics and compliance and provides an overview of what you mean when you talk about ethical business conduct."[105]

Codes of conduct are a phenomenon of the past 35 years. Virtually all major corporations have them today, and the central questions in their usefulness or effectiveness revolve around the managerial policies and attitudes associated with their use.[106]

Codes of ethics vary considerably from company to company, but research suggests that the larger the company, the more likely it is to have a code of conduct. Length of the code is one attribute. Beyond length, codes of ethics vary in their focus, level of detail, thematic content, and tone.[107] Companies may also develop their codes based on geography. Levi Strauss & Co. and Caterpillar have worldwide codes of ethics. Johnson & Johnson has a worldwide credo. McDonald's has worldwide standards of best practices. Firms that operate in the domestic market have codes that reflect more local concerns.[108]

According to the Ethics Resource Center, the content of corporate codes typically addresses the following topics: employment practices; employee, client, and vendor information; public information/communications; conflicts of interest; relationships with vendors; environmental issues; ethical management practices; and political involvement.[109] Increasingly, corporate codes of conduct are addressing global issues and relationships with other firms, communities, and governments.[110]

Both successes and failures have been reported with organizational codes of conduct, but the acid test seems to be whether or not such codes actually become "living documents," not just platitudinous public relations statements that are put into a file drawer upon dissemination. Codes may not be a panacea for management, but when properly developed, administered, and communicated, they serve to raise the level of ethical behavior in the organization by clarifying what is meant by ethical conduct, encouraging moral behavior, and establishing a standard by which accountability may be measured.

A major study of the effectiveness of corporate codes found that there is a relationship between corporate codes and employee behavior in the workplace, particularly to the degree that employees perceive the codes to be implemented strongly and embedded in the organizational culture. Therefore, when codes are implemented forcefully and embedded strongly in the culture, reports of unethical employee behavior tend to be lower.[111]

WAYS OF PERCEIVING CODES A major study of corporate codes by Mark Schwartz revealed that there are a number of different ways in which employees perceive or understand codes of conduct.[112] Schwartz's research yielded eight themes or metaphors that helped to explain how codes influence behavior within organizations.

1. As a *rule book*, the code acts to clarify what behavior is expected of employees.
2. As a *signpost*, the code can lead employees to consult other individuals or corporate policies to determine the appropriateness of behavior.
3. As a *mirror*, the code provides employees with a chance to confirm whether their behavior is acceptable to the company.
4. As a *magnifying glass*, the code suggests a note of caution to be more careful or engage in greater reflection before acting.
5. As a *shield*, the code acts in a manner that allows employees to better challenge and resist unethical requests.
6. As a *smoke detector*, the code leads employees to try to convince others and warn them of their inappropriate behavior.
7. As a *fire alarm*, the code leads employees to contact the appropriate authority and report violations.
8. As a *club*, the potential enforcement of the code causes employees to comply with the code's provisions.[113]

In summary, the code metaphors provide insights into a number of ways in which codes are perceived or viewed by organizational members.

Disciplining Violators of Ethics Standards. To bring about an ethical climate that all organizational members will believe in, management must discipline violators of its accepted ethical norms and standards. A major reason the general public, and even employees in many organizations, have questioned business's sincerity in desiring a more ethical environment has been business's unwillingness to discipline violators. There are numerous cases where top management officers have behaved unethically and yet were retained in their positions. At lower levels, there have been cases of top management overlooking or failing to penalize unethical behavior of subordinates. This evidence of inaction on management's or the board's part represents implicit approval of the individual's behavior.

An organization should respond forcefully to the individual who is guilty of deliberately or flagrantly violating its code of ethics: "From the pinnacle of the corporate pyramid to its base, there can only be one course of action: dismissal. And should actual criminality be involved, there should be total cooperation with law enforcement authorities."[114]

Based on their research, Treviño, Hartman, and Brown have argued: "The moral manager consistently rewards ethical conduct and disciplines unethical conduct at all levels in the organization, and these actions serve to uphold the standards and rules."[115] The effort on the part of management has to be complete in communicating to all, by way of disciplining offenders, that unethical behavior will not be tolerated in the organization. It is management's tacit approval of violations that has seriously undermined efforts to bring about a more ethical climate in many organizational situations.

A stark example of this point was the discharge by the Boeing Company of its chief financial officer—Michael Sears—and another senior manager for engaging in unethical behavior. Sears, a 34-year veteran of the industry, had been considered to be a possible successor to then chairman and CEO Phil Condit. The company said that Mr. Sears and the other senior manager had been dismissed when they tried to conceal their alleged misconduct from a team of lawyers hired by the firm to investigate their actions. At the time of the firing, the CEO said, "When we determine there have been violations of our standards, we will act swiftly to address them, just as we have today."[116] In another similar case, Nortel Networks, North America's largest telecommunications equipment maker, fired its chief executive officer, chief financial officer, and controller for their involvement in accounting problems that had been under scrutiny. The accounting irregularities resulted in the company having to restate its earnings.[117] In the post-Enron decade, we have witnessed more and more corporate boards even taking disciplinary action with respect to CEO and top management wrongdoing.

Ethics "Hotlines" and Whistle-Blowing Mechanisms. One problem that frequently leads to the covering up of unethical acts by people in an organization is that they do not know how to respond when they observe a questionable practice. An effective ethical culture is contingent on employees having a mechanism for (and top management support of) reporting violations or "blowing the whistle" on wrongdoers. One corporate executive summarized this point as follows: "Employees must know exactly what is expected of them in the moral arena and how to respond to warped ethics."[118] According to the Ethics Resource Center's 2009 National Business Ethics Survey, whistle-blowing is up and more employees said they had reported misconduct when they observed it: 63 percent in 2009, up from 58 percent two years earlier.[119]

According to a major ethics and compliance benchmarking survey conducted by the Conference Board, 78 percent of companies had anonymous reporting systems, sometimes referred to as "hotlines." Among companies subject to Sarbanes–Oxley provisions, it was 91 percent.[120] According to a broad-based survey, employees describe various reasons for reporting or not reporting observed violations of ethics. Those who *did* report observations of misconduct gave the following justifications of their actions:[121]

- I thought it was the right thing to do (99 percent).
- I felt I could count on the support of my coworkers (76 percent).
- I believed corrective action would be taken (74 percent).
- I believed that my report would be kept confidential (71 percent).

In this same survey, employees were asked why they *did not* report observations of misconduct. These employees gave the following reasons:[122]

- I didn't believe corrective action would be taken (70 percent).
- I didn't trust that my report would be kept confidential (54 percent).
- I feared retaliation from my supervisor or manager (41 percent).
- I feared retaliation from my coworkers (30 percent).

Hotlines are the most frequent way employees blow the whistle on fraud or related infractions. Such hotlines may be telephone, Web, or e-mail based. In addition, they are typically used without alerting anyone in management about the problem ahead of time. One study tracked incidents at 500 organizations over four years and found that 65 percent of the reports were serious enough to warrant further investigation and 46 percent actually led to some type of action being taken.[123] One expert on ethics said that such anonymous tips are much more effective than internal audits at shedding light on serious problems. It should also be pointed out that even the best systems won't work if they do not have the support of top management and a corporate culture that is conducive to rooting out wrongdoing.[124]

An innovative service began operations in 2009. A group of finance and accounting professionals created a new Web-based service at http://www.zethics.com. The service asks employees and investment professionals to anonymously disclose information about the questionable business practices of their companies. In its own words, "zEthics, Inc. captures information by providing employees of publicly traded companies with a structured process to disclose questionable business practices of executives, and disseminates this information to our customers by selling annual subscriptions to our online information service." The new service is a form of public hotline in which people may report wrongdoing without having to go through their employers. Once reported, zEthics hotlines can have a downside risk, however. Ethicist Barbara Ley Toffler has argued that the hotlines may do harm. She suspects that many of the reported wrong-doings are false accusations and that if the company does not handle these issues carefully, it may do a lot of damage to morale.[125]

Business Ethics Training.   For many years, there was a debate as to whether business ethics training should be conducted. One school of thought argued that ethics is personal, already embedded within the employee or manager and, hence, not alterable or teachable. A growing school of thought argued that instruction in business ethics should be made a part of management training, executive development programs, and business school education. Today, it is accepted that business ethics training is an essential component of ethics programs.

According to a major ethics and compliance benchmarking survey conducted by the Conference Board, over 77 percent of publically traded companies try to educate their employees on the company's standards and policies through publications and training. A growing number of companies are conducting their training by way of Web-based applications.[126]

An example of a company that employs ethics training is Sun Microsystems in Santa Clara, California. According to its chief compliance officer, Sun needed to go beyond its code of conduct and its business conduct office. The company had started feeling pressure, especially after the implementation of the Sarbanes–Oxley Corporate Reform Act, which was increasingly holding executives responsible for what was going on in the company. The Sun training sessions, referred to as ethics boot camps, are becoming more important and more intense. Sun now requires all its managers across the globe to undergo ethics training. At the boot camp, one speaker is the company CEO. Other top managers and board members also address the employees. Most of the content is presented in small group settings, and the executives have to wrestle with dozens of case studies that do not clearly mention what needs to be done. Upon completion of the training courses, Sun executives and employees are given a binder that includes information on how to share with other employees what they have learned. Also, Sun now mandates all its employees to take online ethics courses, offered in eight languages. As a part of the continuous training, Sun is offering refresher courses on a regular basis and has started offering conference calls in which executives in different parts of the world can discuss the ethical dilemmas they are facing and can get feedback from others.[127]

What are the goals of ethics training? Different companies set different goals, but a typical set of goals for ethics training includes the following:

- To learn the fundamentals of business ethics.
- To learn to solve ethical dilemmas.
- To learn to identify causes of unethical behavior.
- To learn about common managerial ethical issues.
- To learn whistle-blowing criteria and risks.
- To learn to develop a code of ethics and execute an internal ethical audit.[128]

Materials and formats typically used by firms in their ethics training include the following: codes of ethics (as a training device), lectures, workshops/seminars, case studies, CDs/discussions, and articles/speeches. One major firm, Lockheed Martin, introduced some humor into its ethics training by introducing the Dilbert-inspired board game, "The Ethics Challenge," for company-wide ethics training. To play the game, players (employees) move around the board by answering "Case File" questions such as

"You've been selected for a training course in Florida, and you want to go only for the vacation." Among the answers and their respective points are "Go, but skip the sessions" (0 points), "Ask your supervisor if it would be beneficial" (5 points), and, the Dogbert answer, "Wear mouse ears to work and hum 'It's a Small World After All' all day." Sessions for the company's 185,000 employees were led by supervisors, not ethics officers. The chairman of the company kicked off the training by leading the training of those who reported to him directly.[129]

One former ethics officer of a major corporation has criticized much ethics training done by companies. He said that most of this training is being done in the form of a mandatory annual compliance exercise, typically one hour in duration. Often, it is a "check the box" exercise in that management can check off that it is completed for the year. He goes on to say that if such training is not done well, it turns out to be indistinguishable from all the other meetings employees have to attend.[130]

In terms of the effectiveness of ethics training, research has shown that exposure to lengthy programs (for example, ten weeks) resulted in significant improvements in moral development. Brief exposures to business ethics, however, yielded less encouraging results.[131]

BUSINESS ROUNDTABLE INSTITUTE FOR CORPORATE ETHICS One of the major limitations of business ethics training has been the exemption of the CEO and other top-level managers from it. This is changing. The Business Roundtable, an organization of CEOs, developed a business ethics institute targeted toward CEOs.[132] The 160 CEOs who comprise the Business Roundtable are involved. The main office for the institute is located at the Darden School at the University of Virginia. The goal of the institute is to help restore public confidence in the marketplace in light of the recent scandals in business. Through the institute, research will be conducted, courses created, and executive seminars offered on business ethics. Some skeptics wonder whether this will truly make a difference or not. Some say that CEOs are pretty set in their ways by the time they reach the pinnacle of their organizations. Optimists are withholding judgment until experience indicates whether the new institute will add value or not.[133] Regardless, it is encouraging that CEOs are finally planning to subject themselves to the same kind of training they have always wanted for their subordinates. If ethical leadership truly begins at the top, the institute should provide a useful resource for these organization leaders.

Ethics Audits and Risk Assessments. In increasing numbers, companies today are beginning to appreciate the need to follow up on their ethics initiatives and programs. Ethics audits are mechanisms or approaches by which a company may assess or evaluate its ethical climate or programs. **Ethics audits** are intended to carefully review such ethics initiatives as ethics programs, codes of conduct, hotlines, and ethics training programs. Ethics audits are similar to social audits discussed in Chapter 5. In addition, they are intended to examine other management activities that may add to or subtract from the company's initiatives. This might include management's sincerity, communication efforts, incentive and reward systems, and other activities. Ethics audits may employ written instruments, committees, and employee interviews.[134] A popular variation on the ethics audit is the **sustainability audit**. More and more companies today are employing this approach for identifying and managing sustainability issues within their organizations. The "Spotlight on Sustainability" reveals more about these.

Spurred on by the revised Federal Sentencing Guidelines, companies are increasingly designing and conducting fraud risk assessments of their operations. **Fraud risk assessments** are review processes designed to identify and monitor conditions and events that may have some bearing on the company's exposure to compliance/misconduct risk and to review company's methods for dealing with these concerns. Risk, in this context, is

ETHICS IN PRACTICE CASE

Can You Learn Business Ethics from a Convicted Crook?

In 2009, Aaron Beam, former CFO at HealthSouth Corporation in Birmingham, was released from prison. Beam was convicted for his role in the $2.7 billion accounting fraud that took place between 1996 and 2002. He made headlines when he admitted that he had cooked the books at HealthSouth Corporation, the Alabama-based provider of rehabilitation services. Beam was one of the cofounders of the business.

He was a part of the string of five CFOs who pleaded guilty to criminal charges. They all testified that CEO Richard Scrushy was behind the fraud, but through a successful defense, Scrushy's legal team got him acquitted of all the charges. Scrushy was later convicted of bribery and was sent to prison.

After selling his $3 million dream home to pay legal fees and restitution charges, Beam started living more modestly by mowing lawns for a living. But he has built himself a new career: speaking on business ethics to companies and to college students majoring in business administration. Beam thinks his personal lesson can be taught in a way that it will stick with those listening.

In his new book *HealthSouth: The Wagon to Disaster*, Beam states: "After losing possessions, serving prison time and fully coming to terms with what happened, I understand that I have committed a terrible, white-collar crime that hurt many people. Because of a lack of conviction, I will always be remembered as the guy that committed the fraud, instead of the co-founder of one of America's most successful health care companies."

Beam has been trying to turn the negative into positive by teaching college students that they are going to face these kinds of temptations every day in business.

He thinks that ethics training will help young people in these situations. He wants students and everyone to understand that there are people they will work for that will push them to commit fraud and that there are tremendous pressures on managers to do things that are inappropriate. By understanding this ahead of time, Beam hopes that when faced with similar circumstances, the students will do the right thing.

Beam thinks the whistle-blower who eventually revealed what was going on at HealthSouth was doing so because of the expectations of the Sarbanes–Oxley Act. He wished he had had the courage and wisdom to reveal the wrongdoing himself. Beam says he is now at peace with himself. His marriage survived the crisis, and he is moving on with his life. He went back to college and got a two-year certificate in turf management and runs a lawn maintenance service when he is not off speaking to college students or to companies.

1. Could you learn business ethics from a corporate felon who went to prison for doing what he is now speaking out against? Could companies benefit from his style of ethics training?

2. What do you think you could learn about business ethics from Aaron Beam? Would he have more credibility with you than a person who had never committed fraud?

3. Do you think Beam is genuine in his desire to teach others or just an opportunist now trying to make a living?

Sources: Edward Teach, "Aaron Beam, Former CFO, HealthSouth Corp., 'I should have said no.'" *CFO* (June 2009), 34–36; "Aaron Beam, Educational Speaker, Corporate Accounting Ethics," http://www.aaronbeam.net/index.html. Accessed March 17, 2010.

typically focused on the company's exposure to possible compliance, misconduct, and ethics issues. According to recent surveys, the top five subjects of ethics program risk analyses include internal policies and processes, employee awareness and understanding of compliance and ethics issues, anonymous reporting systems, disciplinary systems as prevention tools, and employee intent or incentives.[135]

In additional to providing benefits for legal reasons, the conduct of periodic risk assessments provides internal benefits to management. Some of these include the following: detecting compliance and ethics threats and permitting companies to correct problems before they occur or become worse. If problems are not detected and corrected, they may be discovered by regulators, investors, the media, or potential plaintiffs.[136]

Spotlight on SUSTAINABILITY

Sustainability Audits Becoming Popular

Sustainability audits are becoming popular today. In some instances they are done in conjunction with ethics audits. Sometimes they are done instead of ethics audits. A sustainability audit is an assessment of the environmental and/or social aspects of the workplace providing a direction for opportunities and potential risks.

Research carried out by Sustainability Training Advice Review has shown that there are a number of key building blocks that organizations seeking to become more sustainable are adopting:

1. Identification of sustainability issues within the organization
2. Sustainability performance measurement and trends
3. Stakeholder engagement, linkages, and systems thinking
4. Values and community issues
5. Change management processes toward sustainability
6. Vision and the future
7. Governance and sustainability audit

If organizations have these sustainability building blocks, this will give a good indication of how the organization is integrating sustainability thinking into its activities. The audit process will assess the extent to which the organization has a process in place to cover each of the areas identified.

Sources: Healthy Homes: Sustainability Audits, http://www.healthyhomereports.com/Healthy%20Homes%20/Sustainability_Audits.html, accessed February 2, 2010; Sustainability Audit and Review, http://www.sustainabilityconsultants.com, accessed March 17, 2010.

Corporate Transparency. One of the most recent best practices in the improvement of ethics programs is that of **transparency**. **Corporate transparency** refers to a quality, characteristic, or state in which activities, processes, practices, and decisions that take place in companies become open or visible to the outside world. A common definition of transparency is the degree to which an organization

- Provides public access to information
- Accepts responsibility for its actions
- Makes decisions more openly
- Establishes incentives for leaders to uphold these standards[137]

The opposite of transparency is **opacity**, or an opaque condition in which activities and practices remain obscure or hidden from outside scrutiny and review.

Pressures toward transparency have come both from the outside and from within companies. From the outside, various stakeholders such as consumers, environmentalists, government, and investors want to know more clearly what is going on within the organizations. The recent business scandals have served as an added outside force. Following these, the Sarbanes–Oxley Act mandated greater transparency. Transparency leads to accountability. From the inside, companies are increasingly seeing how transparency makes sense as an ethical practice. In their book *The Transparency Edge: How Credibility Can Make or Break You in Business*, Pagano and Pagano state that a transparent management approach—"what you see is what you get" code of conduct—will increase your company's credibility in the marketplace, build loyalty, and help you gain the trust and confidence of those with whom you work.[138]

Another important book on transparency is *The Naked Corporation: How the Age of Transparency Will Revolutionize Business*, by Tapscott and Ticoll. They argue that corporate transparency, today, is not optional but inevitable. They say companies should "undress for success."[139] As companies become more open enterprises, the public and other stakeholders will come to trust them more because more will be exposed to view.

A major example of the benefits of transparency is that of Chiquita Brands International, which was exposed for a variety of questionable practices such as use of pesticides despite an environmental agreement, secret control over dozens of supposedly independent banana companies, bribery, and lax security, such as use of company boats to smuggle drugs. Chiquita's reaction to this exposure was to turn the company around through a policy of corporate transparency, especially visible in its corporate social responsibility report. The report began to explain the results of external audits and employee surveys, helped the company get through bankruptcy proceedings, and helped regain public trust. We argue a point we have made previously: it all starts at the top. Open leadership is one of the strongest forces behind transparency.[140]

Board of Director Leadership and Oversight.   One would think that oversight and leadership of ethics initiatives by the boards of directors of businesses would be a "given." That has not been the case, however, in most instances.[141] The primary impetus for board involvement in and oversight of ethics programs and initiatives has been the megascandals of the past decade that have impacted many major companies. This has been coupled with the passage of the Sarbanes–Oxley Act, which has overhauled federal securities laws to improve corporate governance. We covered corporate governance in detail in Chapter 4, but here we should comment on the board's role in oversight of corporate ethics, one of the most urgent issues in recent years.

Corporate boards, like top managers, should provide strong ethical leadership. Former SEC Chair William Donaldson said that it is not enough for a company to profess a code of conduct. According to Donaldson, "the most important thing that a board of directors should do is determine the elements that must be embedded in the company's moral DNA."[142] In other words, strong leadership from the board and CEOs is still the most powerful force in improving the company's ethical culture.

Two specific areas covered in the Sarbanes–Oxley Act address the board's role in corporate ethics. First, companies are now required to make provisions for employees to report observed or suspected wrongdoing without fear of retaliation. Companies are now required to protect whistle-blowers, and criminal penalties may be issued to managers who ignore this provision. Companies are expected to have a formal policy that addresses such complaints, and the board should investigate all complaints and rectify issues as necessary.[143] The whistle-blowing mechanisms discussed earlier are now institutionalized by law. Second, the Sarbanes–Oxley Act makes it a crime to alter, destroy, conceal, cover up, or falsify any document to prevent its use in a federal government lawsuit or proceedings. This new provision came about because of the well-publicized Arthur Andersen debacle, which involved document shredding in connection with the Enron scandal. Document management initiatives have now become critical in companies, and one of the most debated areas is the handling of e-mails.[144] Sarbanes–Oxley introduced other important provisions for bringing about more effective controls and preventing fraud, but the previously mentioned items are especially important in terms of ethics oversight.

According to the ethics and compliance benchmarking survey conducted by the Conference Board, board involvement in ethics programs has risen to 96 percent of companies surveyed.[145] According to another survey of 165 company boards, it is reported that although corporate scandals and Sarbanes–Oxley have been strong forces in bringing about more board involvement in ethics, other factors have motivated it as well. In the

United States, general legal developments have increased board scrutiny of ethics programs, but in the United Kingdom, India, and Western Europe, "enhancement of reputation" has often been cited as a reason for closer board scrutiny of corporate ethics. There is also widespread enthusiasm for training board members in ethics, but such enthusiasm does not often result in action.[146]

Although we have not touched on all that can be done at the organizational level to improve or manage business ethics, the actions suggested represent best practices that can move management a long way toward improving the organization's ethical culture and climate. If management takes specific steps as suggested, many behaviors or decisions that might otherwise have been questionable have a greater chance of being in line with high ethical standards. Thus, ethics can be positively supervised, and managers do not have to treat value concerns as matters out of their influence or control. On the contrary, managers can intercede and improve the organization's ethical climate.[147]

From Moral Decisions to Moral Organizations

In the last two chapters, we have discussed ethical or moral acts, decisions, practices, managers, and organizations. Though the goal of ethics initiatives is to develop moral organizations, sometimes all we get are isolated ethical acts, decisions, or practices, or, if we are fortunate, a few moral managers. Achieving the status of moral standing is a goal, whatever the level on which it may be achieved. Sometimes all we can do is bring about ethical acts, decisions, or practices. A broader goal is to create moral managers, in the sense in which they were discussed in Chapter 7. Finally, the highest-level goal for managers may be to create moral organizations, for which many of the best practices discussed in this chapter will need to be implemented. As Kenneth Goodpaster has reminded us, "The depths of a company's *cultural* commitment to ethical values in the pursuit of economic values are a mark of corporate *moral* development."[148]

The important point here is to state that the goal of managers should be to create moral decisions, moral managers, and ultimately, moral organizations while recognizing that what we frequently observe in business is the achievement of moral standing at only one of these levels. The ideal is to create a moral organization that is fully populated by moral managers making moral decisions (and practices, policies, and behaviors), but this is seldom achieved. Figure 8-9 depicts the essential characteristics of each of these levels.

FIGURE 8-9
From Moral
Decisions to Moral
Organizations

Moral Decision(s)
Single or isolated moral acts, behaviors, policies, practices, or decisions made by a manager or managers of an organization. These are the simplest and most basic form of achieving moral status. The principles of ethical decision making presented should assist in the development of moral decisions.

Moral Manager(s)
A manager or managers who have adopted the characteristics of moral management, and this approach dominates all their decision making. These managers manifest ethical leadership and always occupy the moral high ground. Moral managers will make moral decisions via the use of ethical principles. In addition, they will learn and use the research of ethics in organizations discussed in this chapter.

Moral Organization(s)
An organization dominated by the presence of moral managers making moral decisions. Moral management has become an integral part of the culture. Moral management permeates all the organization's decisions, policies, and practices. The organization uses the best practices for achieving a moral management culture. Of special importance are moral leadership provided by board of director oversight and top management leadership.

Summary

The subject of business ethics may be addressed at several different levels: personal, organizational, industrial, societal, and international. This chapter focuses on the personal and organizational levels—the levels at which managers can have the most impact.

A number of different ethical principles serve as guides to personal decision making. Ethics principles may be categorized as teleological (ends-based), deontological (duty-based), or aretaic (virtue-based). One of the major deontological principles is the categorical imperative. Major philosophical principles of ethics include utilitarianism, rights, and justice. The Golden Rule was singled out as a particularly powerful ethical principle among various groups studied. Virtue ethics was identified as an increasingly popular concept. Servant leadership was presented as an approach to management that embraced an ethical perspective. Seven practical tests were proposed to assist the individual in making ethical decisions: the test of common sense, the test of one's best self, the test of making something public, the test of ventilation, the test of purified idea, the test of the Big Four, and the gag test.

At the organizational level, factors were discussed that affect the organization's moral culture or climate. It was argued that the behavior of one's superiors and peers and industry ethical practices were the most important influences on an organization's ethical culture. Society's moral climate and personal needs were considered to be less important. Best practices for improving the firm's ethical climate include providing leadership from management, ethics programs, and ethics officers; setting realistic objectives; infusing the decision-making process with ethical considerations; employing codes of conduct; disciplining violators; creating whistle-blowing mechanisms or hotlines; training managers in business ethics; using ethics audits and risk assessments (which may include sustainability audits); and adopting the concept of transparency and board of director oversight of ethics initiatives.

The goal of ethics initiatives is to achieve a status that may be characterized not just by isolated moral decisions but also by the presence of moral managers and the ultimate achievement of a moral organization.

Key Terms

aretaic theories, p. 276
categorical imperative, p. 277
codes of conduct, p. 303
codes of ethics, p. 303
compensatory justice, p. 279
compliance orientation, p. 293
corporate transparency, p. 309
deontological theories, p. 275
distributive justice, p. 279
ethical due process, p. 279
ethical tests, p. 285
ethics audits, p. 307
ethics of care, p. 280

ethics officer, p. 299
ethics orientation, p. 293
ethics programs, p. 297
ethics screen, p. 301
fraud risk assessments, p. 307
Golden Rule, p. 283
legal rights, p. 277
moral rights, p. 277
negative right, p. 278
opacity, p. 309
positive right, p. 278
principle of justice, p. 278
principle of rights, p. 277

principle of utilitarianism, p. 276
procedural justice, p. 279
process fairness, p. 279
rights, p. 277
servant leadership, p. 282
smell test, p. 286
sustainability audit, p. 307
teleological theories, p. 275
transparency, p. 309
utilitarianism, p. 276
virtue ethics, p. 281

Discussion Questions

1. From your personal experience, give two examples of ethical dilemmas. Give two examples of ethical dilemmas you have experienced as a member of an organization.

2. Using the examples you provided for question 1, identify one or more of the guides to personal decision making or ethical tests that you think would have helped you resolve your dilemmas. Describe how it would have helped.

3. Which is most important in ethics principles—consequences or duty? Discuss.

4. Assume that you are in your first managerial position. Identify five ways in which you might provide ethical leadership. Rank them in terms of importance, and be prepared to explain your ranking.

5. What do you think about the idea of codes of conduct? Give three reasons why an organization ought to have a code of conduct, and three reasons why an organization should not have a code of conduct. On balance, how do you regard codes of conduct?

6. A lively debate is going on in this country concerning whether business ethics can and should be taught in business schools. Do you support this argument? Substantiate your point with reasons. Can top managers and board members be taught business ethics?

7. Identify and prioritize the best practices for improving the organization's ethical climate. What are the strengths and weaknesses of each?

9

Business Ethics and Technology

CHAPTER LEARNING OUTCOMES

After studying this chapter, you should be able to:

1. Identify the role that technology plays in our business lives.

2. Gain an understanding of the technological environment and the characteristics of technology that influence business ethics and stakeholders.

3. Identify the benefits and side effects of technology in business.

4. Gain an appreciation of society's intoxication with technology and the consequences of this intoxication.

5. Learn to differentiate between information technology and biotechnology and their ethical implications for management.

6. Identify the ethical issues involved in biotechnology and present the arguments on both sides of the issues.

We live in an age dominated by advancing technology. Each new generation experiences technological advances that were not seen by previous generations. The new generation comprising young people, called the iGeneration, is said to have no "off switch" when it comes to technology. For this new group of post-Millennials, technology is said to be a "part of their DNA."[1]

Technology is how we sustain life and make it comfortable. Technology is at the core of many businesses, whether it is used to pursue new products or processes or as a means to achieve other worthwhile ends. But technology, as many have observed, is a two-edged sword. Many positive benefits flow from technological advances. By the same token, many new problems or challenges are posed by advancing technology. Futurist John Naisbitt, for example, has questioned whether advancing technology has the potential to be a "liberating" or "destructive" force in society. He has said that, at best, technology supports and improves human life, and at its worst it alienates, isolates, distorts, and destroys.[2]

In either case, technology has become such a central part of doing business in the 21st century that it cannot be ignored. Moreover, ethical issues for business and for society have arisen as a result of technological advances. Many believe that technology has developed at a speed that significantly outstrips the capacity of society, government, or business to grasp its consequences or ethics. In this chapter, we will explore some of these issues, knowing full well that other aspects will be mentioned in ensuing chapters as specific stakeholder groups are considered in more detail.

It is interesting and challenging to brainstorm about what new technologies may have in store for business. One of the current topics in technology these days is social networks. A relevant question is, what possible business applications and implications will tools such as Facebook and MySpace have? They both play a role in social networking. They provide a cyber-meeting space for people wanting to network. Tools such as Facebook provide a space where individuals can describe themselves and connect with others. It has been said that 85 percent of college students have a profile on Facebook and that the majority of them log on at least weekly.[3] Many log on numerous times a day.

But how do social networking tools connect with business? According to Albert M. Erisman, executive director of http://www.ethix.org, there are two important ways. First, social networking tools create successful, innovative businesses. Examples include Facebook, MySpace, Classmates.com, Flickr, and LinkedIn. Second, there are more direct business uses, and this is more speculative regarding the future. For example, LinkedIn.com has over 55 million members in over 200 countries and territories around the world, and the site provides a way for each individual to connect his or her network of colleagues to other networks of colleagues, enabling exponential growth for their own network. Executives from all *Fortune* 500 companies are LinkedIn members. One benefit this provides is the sharing of résumés in job searches and recruiting, and also allows connections for business opportunities in buying and selling.[4] One can only speculate what abuses of information might creep into these systems.

Another business issue in the realm of ethics and technology has been the revelation that companies are using video cameras mounted in stores to monitor our every action. We know we are being watched, but do we know how smart these technologies have become? For example, a few Macy's, CVS, and Babies 'R' Us stores have used a system called the Video Investigator. This advanced surveillance software can monitor a customer's movements and compare them between video images and recognize any type of unusual activity. If the shopper removes ten items at once from a shelf, for example, or opens a case that is normally kept closed and locked, the system alerts security guards of the activity. The system can also predict where a shoplifter is likely to hide (e.g., at the end of aisles or behind floor displays).[5] We are, indeed, being watched. Much of this is for the good. But there can be possible abuses as well.

In this chapter, we intend to explore the subject of technology and business ethics. Technology has become such an integral aspect of our work and consumer lives that special treatment of these topics is warranted. First, we will consider what technology means and some of its benefits and challenges. Second, we will briefly discuss the subject of ethics and technology. Finally, we will consider ethical issues connected with two major spheres of technology: computers and information technology, and biotechnology.

Technology and the Technological Environment

Technology means many things to many people. In this chapter, **technology** will refer to the "totality of the means employed to provide objects necessary for human sustenance and comfort." It is also seen as a scientific method used in achieving a practical purpose.[6] Technology refers to all the ways people use their inventions and discoveries to satisfy their needs and desires. Since time began, people have invented and developed tools, techniques, machines, and materials to sustain life and to improve the quality of life. Sources of power have also been discovered and developed. Taken together, these technological advances have made work easier and more productive.[7] It is little surprise that businesses have embraced and used technology as much as or more than any other sector of society.

In Chapter 1, we discussed the macroenvironment of business and how this total environment was composed of a number of significant and interrelated segments such as the social, economic, political, and technological. The **technological environment**, our current topic of concern, represents *the total set of technology-based advancements or progress taking place in society*. Pertinent aspects of this segment include new products, processes, materials, states of knowledge, and scientific advancements in both theoretical and applied senses. The rate of change and complexity of the technological environment have made it of special interest to business today. Consider the following examples. An electronic greeting card that today plays "Happy Birthday" holds more computing power than existed in the world before 1950. One of today's home video cameras wields more processing power than the old IBM 360, the wonder machine that launched the age of mainframe computers. Computers are being used to aid scientists in comprehending the secrets of matter at the atomic level and to create amazing new materials.[8] In both information technology and the burgeoning field of biotechnology, the shape of how we are living, what products we are using, and what processes we are being exposed to is changing at an accelerating pace.

Characteristics of Technology

We have moved from a world characterized by industrial technology to one dominated by information technology and biotechnology. Whatever the technological level of advancement, there are general benefits and undesirable side effects of technology, and ethical challenges inherent in technological advancements. A brief consideration of each is useful.

Benefits of Technology

Few would dispute that society has benefited greatly from technology and innovation. We live better lives today as employees, consumers, and members of the community due to technology. Technology has helped us gain control over nature and to build for ourselves a civilized life. Through the ages, technology has benefited society in four main ways.[9] First, it has increased society's production of goods and services, a benefit attributable chiefly to the business sector. Second, it has reduced the amount of labor needed to produce goods and services. Third, it not only has enabled greater production with a lesser amount of human labor, but has also made labor easier and safer. Fourth, higher standards of living have been a direct result of laborsaving technology.[10]

The benefits of technology are too vast to summarize completely. In an excellent book, *A Culture of Improvement*, Robert Friedel surveys the entire past millennium of technological advancement. He explains how we have moved from horsepower to jet engines, from Gothic vaults to skyscrapers, from Gutenberg to Google. Friedel helps us to see how society has benefited from technological innovation, but he also points out many of the flaws and entanglements that have arisen due to technology.[11]

Side Effects of Technology

Though technologies have benefited people in many ways, there have also been some unanticipated side effects too—problems or effects not anticipated before technologies were designed and implemented. One major reason for this is that technologies were often implemented before much thought was given to possible side effects, ethical problems, or downside risks. The automobile is a classic example. From the late 1800s to early 1900s, it was believed that automobiles would be more quiet and less smelly than horses. As more autos came into use, however, it quickly became obvious that roaring traffic noise exceeded the clatter of horse hoofs. Automobile exhaust became more toxic than the smell of horse manure. Fumes polluted the air with carbon monoxide and other impurities that threatened human health.[12] In addition, we experience traffic jams, shortages of gasoline, and automobile accidents—some aided by cell phone users (another recent technology)—and "road rage."

Four categories of undesirable side effects of technology should be noted. First, there is *environmental pollution*. This ranks as one of the most undesirable side effects of technology. Second, there is *depletion of natural resources*. The rapid advance of technology continually threatens the supply of natural resources. Fuel and power shortages have become a way of life. Third is the issue of *technological unemployment*. The most common form of technological unemployment occurs when machines take the place of humans, as we experienced in the automation phase of industrial development. Another form of technological unemployment is now occurring as technology-based jobs are being moved offshore to less expensive regions of the world. Fourth is the *creation of unsatisfying jobs* due to technology. Many jobs in the technological world fail to give the workers a sense of accomplishment. As jobs are broken down into smaller components, each individual worker is further removed from the finished product that might provide a greater sense of fulfillment and pride. Monotony and boredom can easily set in when jobs are significantly shaped by certain technological processes.[13]

Challenges of Technology

New technologies present many challenges to managers, organizations, and society. Foremost among these is anticipating and avoiding the unwanted side effects. Some side effects cannot be forecast or overcome, of course, but much more could be done than is currently being done. Overcoming the technological determinism that seems to be driving society today would be the right step. For example, one of the most important issues today in the realm of biotechnology is that of human cloning. It is difficult to get the scientists and researchers to slow down and talk about the possible consequences (practical and ethical) of human cloning. Many of them seem driven by the technological capacities for achieving this instead of asking the important questions concerning ethics and side effects. One expert said, "If we can clone a human, we will."

Another challenge lies in spreading the benefits of technology, which are primarily restricted to the developed world. The developing nations enjoy few of the benefits of technology enjoyed in the developed nations.[14] It is anticipated that as multinational corporations increasingly move to emerging economies for production or exploration for resources, the opportunities for technology transfer will be greatly enhanced. This is being seen, to some extent, in the case of information and medical technology jobs being moved to India and China. The challenge, however, is to move technologies to other countries in socially responsible ways.

Technology and Ethics

Technology definitely has many benefits for humankind. Our perspective at this juncture, however, is to raise the ethical questions that may be related to business development and use of technology and innovation. To do so does not mean that one is against technology. It simply means that one is concerned about the ethical use and implications of technology. Like management decision making and globalization of business, the actions of the business community with respect to technology have ethical implications that should be identified and discussed. Management's goal should be to avoid immoral and amoral practices with respect to technology and to move toward a morally sustainable management posture with respect to this potent business resource.

Spotlight on SUSTAINABILITY

Technology Meets Sustainability

It is increasingly becoming evident that technology is a vital key to sustainability and sustainable development.

Science and Innovation for Sustainability. The Forum on Science and Innovation for Sustainable Development is an attempt to sketch out the mushrooming field. Rather than looking broadly at sustainability, the forum focuses on the way in which science, innovation, and technology can be conducted and applied to meet human needs while preserving the life support systems of the planet. The forum highlights people and programs that are studying nature–society interactions and applying the resulting knowledge to create a sustainability transition around the world.

Source: http://sustsci.aaas.org/

Advancing Global Sustainability through Technology. An excellent example of technology contributing toward sustainability is the microchip. Intel represents an interesting case study. Intel began working with the Environmental Protection Agency (EPA) to proactively address its industry's impact on global climate change and help support a sustainable future. As demand for computing performance increases, so does the need for more energy-efficient platforms. Intel worked with the EPA to develop the latest ENERGY STAR computer specifications that would deliver higher energy efficiency without compromising performance.

Source: http://www.intel.com/technology/epa/?iid=SEARCH

Applying business ethics to questions involving technology is simply an extension of our discussions of business ethics up to this point. The goal of managers and businesses striving to be ethical should be to do what is right and fair, and to avoid harm. In making ethical judgments, the prevailing norms of acceptability regarding technology must be tested by the principles of fairness and justice, protection of rights, and utilitarianism. The goal should be to reconcile and build bridges over the gap between "what is" and "what ought to be."

Two Key Issues

There are two key ethical issues in the realm of technology that seem to drive everything. First is the idea of technological determinism. **Technological determinism** is the imperative that "what *can* be developed *will* be developed." When someone once asked, "why do we want to put men on the moon?" the answer was always "because we *can* put men on the moon." In other words, scientists and those who work with advanced technologies are driven to push back the frontiers of technological development without consideration of ethical issues or side effects. The second important concept is that of ethical lag. **Ethical lag** occurs when the speed of technological change far exceeds that of ethical development.[15] We will see throughout our consideration of technology and ethics that these two phenomena are present and influential.

Society's Intoxication with Technology

To emphasize the ethical dimension of technology, it is useful to note how society has become obsessed and intoxicated with technology and its power over our lives. Only by fully understanding the magnitude of this relationship society has with technology can we focus on the ethical aspects of it and the actions that should be taken. One way to appreciate what technology is doing to humankind is to consider the thoughts of John Naisbitt, Nana Naisbitt, and Douglas Philips, authors of the book *High Tech/High Touch*.[16]

In *High Tech/High Touch*, the authors call upon all members of society to understand and question the place of technology in our lives. They argue that our world has changed from a "technologically comfortable place" into a "technologically intoxicated zone." As they analyze the world, they conclude that there are six symptoms of society's intoxication with technology.[17] Some of these touch upon our character as a person, and some touch upon the ethical issues business faces with technology. The six symptoms are as follows:

1. We favor the quick fix. This is true whether it relates to nutrition or religion. As we perceive a recurring void, we search for something and we want it quickly. Technology promises to detoxify us—to simplify our complex lives, relieve our stress, and calm our nerves. However, this Band-Aid® culture of the quick fix is ultimately an empty one. We are seduced by the promise of technology.

2. We fear and worship technology. Our behavior moves us from the extremes of worship at one moment to fear the next. We accept technology, fearing that we will fall behind our competitors or coworkers. We embrace technology but then feel frustrated and annoyed when it fails to deliver.

3. We blur the distinction between what is real and what is false. When technology can transform nature, we frequently ask, "Is that real, or is that false?" "Is it authentic or simulated?"

4. We accept violence as normal. Technology has made it possible for us to package violence in the form of merchandise, often spin-offs from television or movies. This violent material is often targeted at children.

5. We love technology as a toy. As affluence finances our play, leisure tends toward diversion—something to fill the time. We live in a culture dominated by consumer technology, where leisure is often passively received. Electronic distractions busy us as we can't find anything worthwhile to do.

6. We live our lives distanced and distracted. The Internet, smart phones, and wireless technologies connect us to the world, but when is it appropriate and when is it a distraction? Technology's bells and whistles are seductive, and they distance us and distract us.

The solution to this intoxication with technology is to find the right balance. That is, we need to embrace technology that preserves our humanity and reject technology that intrudes upon it. We need to know when we should push back on technology, in our work and our lives, and when to affirm our humanity. We need to understand that technology zealots are as shortsighted as technology bashers. We need to question the place of technology in our lives.[18]

There are a number of arenas in which specific issues of business ethics and technology might be explored. Research over the past few years reveals two broad categories of issues that now merit consideration. Each is broad and deep, so we can consider them only in an introductory way in this chapter. Each, however, significantly touches business, either directly or indirectly. The two areas are computer-based **information technology** and **biotechnology**. Within each, there are hundreds to thousands of technologies that raise ethical questions. Our purpose, therefore, will be to focus on a few that give us a representative sample of ethical issues with technology.

Information Technology

Computer-based information technology, or information technology (IT), as it is most often called, touches practically all businesses and stakeholders involved in those businesses. Businesses and people both are affected by technology and are directly involved in pursuits based on technology. We will consider them both. We will discuss two broad areas in this section: *electronic commerce*, or Web-based marketing, and *computer technology in the workplace*, including telecommunications. These areas overlap significantly and are interdependent, so our separation is to lend some order to the discussion.

Electronic Commerce as a Popular Technology

Electronic commerce, often referred to as *e-commerce*, *e-business*, or *Web-based marketing*, is one of the most significant technological phenomena of our day. It primarily affects consumer stakeholders and competitors of the e-commerce firms. Most experts today are convinced that the Internet has reshaped the way business is conducted around the world. Part of this is firms selling products and services online. Beyond this, companies are integrating the Internet into every aspect of their businesses.

It is hard to track the total dollar sales business experiences via electronic commerce. It is a multiple trillion dollar business, and 90 percent of it comes from business-to-business (B2B) sales. Consumer transactions are huge and growing. The pull of e-business is powerful and companies are responding by moving their operations to the Internet. Other areas of Internet growth include knowledge management and customer relationships. Companies are spending billions of dollars linking customers, sales, and marketing over the Web, increasingly through social networking. In short, electronic commerce is a burgeoning business, and the opportunity for questionable practices arises along with this growth.

Along with the growth of electronic commerce, business ethics problems have arisen as well. One major category of problems is online scams. According to Internet Fraud Watch, con artists are taking advantage of the Internet's growth in popularity to bilk the unwary. During one recent year, for example, the top frauds over the Internet included online auctions, goods misrepresented or not delivered, fake check scams where consumers were paid with phony checks and asked to wire money back, Nigerian money offers wherein consumers were promised riches if they would allow money to be wired to their accounts, requests for payments to claim lottery winnings, and advance fee loans wherein customers were promised loans for upfront fees.[19] Other scams included credit card fraud, travel and vacation scams, pyramid schemes, and bogus investment opportunities.

Ongoing Issues in E-Commerce Ethics

Ongoing issues in e-commerce ethics include the following:[20] access, intellectual property, privacy and informed consent, protection of children, security of information, and trust. These ethical issues are not restricted to e-commerce. They also occur in brick-and-mortar businesses. The manifestations and scope of these issues, however, differ from those of traditional businesses. *Access* refers to the difference in computer access between the rich and the poor. *Intellectual property*, in e-commerce, is illustrated by the ethics of downloading music. *Privacy and informed consent* differ in e-commerce. An illustration is the novel ways companies place cookies on our computers without informed consent. In addition, firms collect online information and merge it with offline information. *Protection of children* is an important ethical issue, and it is illustrated in the issue of pornography. E-commerce makes porn more accessible than through traditional businesses. *Security* is such a major issue that even today some are reluctant to do business on the Web for fear their credit card numbers will be intercepted by someone not associated with the e-commerce business. Finally, *trust* is the basis for practically all business transactions, and it is especially crucial in e-commerce.[21]

Invasion of Privacy via Electronic Commerce

The average person encounters two forms of Internet electronic commerce: business-to-consumer (B2C) transactions and business-to-business (B2B) transactions. Most of us are quite familiar with B2C transactions when we do personal business on the Internet—buying products and services, arranging credit cards, accessing travel Web sites, and doing financial business such as personal banking. As employees, we also encounter B2B transactions, which is anticipated to be the greatest area of e-commerce growth in the coming years. One reason for this is the rapid globalization of commerce. In terms of Web-based marketing to consumers, consumer stakeholders are primarily affected by such issues as database sharing, identity theft, and invasion of privacy. Invasion of privacy is a legitimate concern in all business transactions; however, the special case of electronic commerce or Web-based marketing deserves special attention because of the ease with which data can be stored and transmitted in electronic form.

A classic illustration of a potential invasion of privacy was that of DoubleClick, Inc., the New York-based Internet advertising company that planned to share customer information with an offline marketing firm. Consumer advocates were up in arms that DoubleClick would betray such confidential information. Another example occurred when Toysmart.com, Inc. went out of business and offered its online customer list for sale, thus violating privacy agreements and understandings previously made with customers. Questions that arose from such situations included "What limits should there be on how online businesses use the information they gather about their customers?" and "What responsibility do companies have to publicly disclose such practices?"[22]

The most important ethical issue with respect to doing business over the Internet is the question of possible invasions of consumer privacy.[23] This is an ongoing topic for business executives today. According to a survey by the Conference Board, "e-business privacy issues" were among the most discussed technology issues at Conference Board meetings.[24] The consuming public is concerned as well. A survey on Internet privacy conducted by *The Wall Street Journal* and Harris Interactive revealed that 24 percent of those consumers surveyed were "very concerned" and 49 percent were "somewhat concerned" about threats to their personal privacy on the Internet. Further, about half of those surveyed indicated that concerns about privacy caused them to stop using a Web site or to forgo an online purchase.[25] Figure 9-1 summarizes some of the concerns that privacy advocates and law enforcement experts have about the Internet's threat to privacy.

Some of the technological means by which companies invade consumers' privacy include the use of cookies and spam. **Cookies** are those little identification tags that Web sites drop on our personal computer hard drives so they can recognize repeat visitors the next time we visit their Web sites.[26] Surveys show that some consumers don't know what cookies are; others are aware of them but don't take the time to block them. According to the Pew Internet & American Life Project, only 10 percent of users set their browsers to block cookies. Part of this is because over half of Internet users didn't know what a cookie was.[27]

Spam is unsolicited commercial e-mail. It is sent through "open-relays" to millions of persons. It takes a toll on Internet users' time, their resources, and the resources of Internet service providers (ISPs). A recent problem is that spammers have begun to send advertisements via text message to cell phones.[28] Many consumers interpret the receipt

---

FIGURE 9-1 Potential Threats to Privacy Posed by the Internet

Identity Theft	Someone might use the Internet to steal your identity.
Unintentionally Revealing Information	You may be unintentionally revealing information about yourself as you move through cyberspace.
Lost/Stolen Personal Information	That personal information you just provided to a Web site might be sold or stolen.
Fake Web Sites	That Web site on which you just entered your credit card number and personal information may be a fake.
Government Distribution of Information	The government may be giving out your home address, social security number, and other personal information online.
Broadcasting Information over the Internet	Companies and people who do not like you may be broadcasting your private information on the Internet.
Victim of Spying—Employer or Spouse	Your employer or spouse may be using your computer to spy on you.
Victim of Spying—Strangers	Someone you do not know may be using your computer to spy on you (e.g., hackers).
Cyberstalker	You may have a cyberstalker harassing you.

Source: Summarized from "Internet Insecurity," *Time* (July 2, 2001), 46–50. For the latest news, go to the Electronic Privacy Information Center at http://epic.org/privacy/. Accessed February 9, 2010.

---

of *spam* as an invasion of their privacy. Opening our e-mail mailboxes only to find a few dozen unsolicited ads is aggravating, at the least, and an invasion of privacy to many. Also, some companies experiment with pulsing background ads that never go away. Interestingly, dozens of companies make programs that protect our e-mail privacy, block cookies, and filter spam and porn, but very few consumers bother to use them.[29]

A serious invasion of privacy with respect to electronic commerce is the collection and use of personal information. Though non-Internet companies have engaged in this practice for years, everything seems magnified in the e-world in which we now live. None of us really knows how much personal information is collected, saved, swapped, or sold in e-commerce. Thousands of retailers, from department stores to catalog companies, collect and store personal information, from asking customers for their zip codes to collecting names, addresses, household income, and purchasing patterns through a store credit card. Retailers also share, exchange, and even sell their customer databases to other companies. In short, the average consumer has very little control over what is done with his or her personal data once it is collected.[30] A continuing concern is *identify theft* or tampering with one's financial accounts. Less serious is the inundation of marketing attempts, both online and offline, that consumers are subjected to as a result of information being distributed.

Botnet scams, one of the latest techniques by which hackers get access to personal and corporate information, are exploding in numbers. *Bots* are computers that have been compromised by hackers who are often just profit-minded crooks. A network of bots, called a *botnet*, is created by e-mails that get distributed by these compromised computers, and these are controlled by a central computer called the command-and-control server. Experts say that on any given day now, 40 percent of the 800 million computers hooked up to the Internet are infected and made a part of botnets that continue to distribute e-mail spam and malware, steal sensitive data, bombard Web sites, and spread fresh infections. As of 2009, the top five botnets were ZeuS, Koobface B, Koobface

D, Monkif-A, and Clickbot.[31] Recently, it was estimated that 73 percent of e-mails contained spam, one in 106 e-mails contained a virus, and one in 99 e-mails contained some form of a phishing attack. These numbers increase every year.

Botnets are not only the way our personal information is compromised, but they represent the greatest threat to data security for businesses and governments today.[32] In 2010, a computer-security firm disclosed that hackers in Europe and China had successfully broken into computers at more than 2,400 companies and government agencies over the previous 18 months in a coordinated global attack. Vast amounts of personal and corporate secrets were stolen. The hackers were found to be continually recruiting a botnet army by enticing users to click on contaminated Web sites or open e-mail attachments, which then installed malicious software, called malware, that was used to capture data typed into Web forms.[33]

At a personal level, many individuals are losing their privacy through the use of social networking sites such as Facebook. Cybercriminals are now accessing social networking accounts and stealing personal information. Social networks provide a rich repository of information that cybercriminals can use to fine-tune their other computer attacks. Twitter accounts are likewise vulnerable to data theft. Once stolen credentials occur, they often appear on eBay-like hacking forums where they are sold in batches of 1,000. By one account, 1,000 Facebook user names and passwords, guaranteed to be valid, were selling for up to $200. Cyber scammers can acquire e-mail addresses, contact lists, birthdates, home towns, and mothers' maiden names, which all then become useful for targeting specific victims.[34]

Government's Involvement in Internet Privacy Protection.

The federal government has gotten involved in protecting consumers' privacy, but many observers believe it is not doing enough.[35] The Financial Services Modernization Act of 1999 was the landmark legislation that permitted banks, insurers, and brokers to join forces. Under the law, it is now possible for consumers to get their credit cards, checking accounts, investments, home loans, and health insurance from one company. This is convenient for consumers. However, the law also empowered these companies to develop exceptionally detailed portraits of their customers just by merging files about their income, assets, debts, health, spending habits, and other personal data. Increasingly, this sensitive data is becoming a public commodity.[36]

Over the past several years, a number of different bills designed to protect consumer privacy on the Internet have been filed but have not yet been passed. Many of the legislators have been uncertain whether a broad privacy bill is even needed or what it should look like. Though privacy continues to be an ongoing technology issue in Congress, many lawmakers have indicated they wanted to study the issue before throwing support behind new privacy measures.[37]

The Federal Trade Commission (FTC) is the primary government agency concerned with protecting consumers' privacy today. Under the FTC Act, the commission guards against unfairness and deception. The primary legislation now governing consumers' privacy includes the Financial Services Modernization Act (Gramm–Leach–Bliley Act), concerned with financial privacy; the Fair Credit Reporting Act; and the Children's Online Privacy Protection Act.[38] Other legislation regulating consumer and employee privacy may come soon, but Congress seems preoccupied with other priorities.

Business Initiatives with Privacy Protection.

There are a number of different ways companies might strive to protect the privacy of their customers in electronic commerce.

ETHICAL LEADERSHIP First, business needs to recognize the potential ethical issues involved in electronic commerce and be committed to treating customers and all affected stakeholders in an ethical fashion. This commitment and ethical leadership undergird all other initiatives. This ethical leadership must begin with the board of directors, the CEO, and top management. Every point made in Chapter 8 about top management leadership applies to this discussion as well.

Privacy Policies Companies may take the initiative with their own carefully crafted privacy policies designed to protect customers. An example of this might be a company deciding to do more than the law requires. A company that has gone to great lengths to explain its privacy policy to customers and guests is the Walt Disney Internet Group. On its Web site, it provides its privacy policy and answers to the following types of questions:[39]

Q1. What information does this privacy policy cover?

Q2. What types of personally identifiable information do we collect about our guests?

Q3. How is your personally identifiable information used and shared?

Q4. What choices do you have about the collection, use, and sharing of your personally identifiable information?

Q5. What kinds of security measures do we take to safeguard your personally identifiable information?

Q6. How can you update your contact information and opt out choices?

One of the most significant advances in privacy policies has been made by Microsoft. Microsoft has decided to amend its privacy policies so that consumers will have greater control over what the company does with information it gathers about their online purchasing behavior. The company plans to allow certain users to decline to receive ads tailored to their Web surfing habits, and it will also sever the connections recorded between information about a computer and the Web searches carried out from that machine after about a year and a half.[40] These initiatives on the part of Microsoft are commendable, but they only scratch the surface of the issue on customer privacy.

Chief Privacy Officers An innovative approach to protecting consumers' privacy has been the increasing use of a **chief privacy officer (CPO)** in a number of major companies. Companies like American Express, Sony Corporation, Citigroup, IBM, and Facebook have appointed their own privacy chiefs.[41] One estimate is that there are now 2,000 or more such positions around the country, and their numbers may swell in the next few years.[42] In other companies, these responsibilities are falling under the administration of a chief technology officer.

It is the primary responsibility of the CPO to keep a company out of trouble, whether in a court of law or in the court of public opinion. This includes developing Internet policies, helping their companies avoid consumer litigation, creating methods of handling and resolving consumer complaints, and assessing the risk of privacy invasion of company activities and practices. Because the position is relatively new at most companies, these newly appointed individuals are still trying to figure out what they need to be doing.[43] The job is a challenging one. CPOs must balance their customers' right to privacy with the employer's need for information for financial purposes.[44] CPOs were all the rage in the early 2000s, but the economic downturn has slowed down the movement. As the economy perks back up, CPOs, once again, will likely become popular.

An ongoing debate is whether the CPOs should focus on *ethics* or *compliance*. Those in the ethics camp believe that CPOs need to be driven by integrity concerns and should proactively and strategically consider the privacy implications of their company's actions. Those in the compliance camp believe that CPOs should just focus on making sure the company stays out of trouble by not breaking the host of new laws it now faces. Some of these laws with privacy provisions include the Fair Credit Reporting Act, the Gramm–Leach–Bliley Act, and the Sarbanes–Oxley Act. As a result of limited resources, Alan F. Westin, president of Privacy & American Business, a nonprofit organization, has concluded: "Most companies have shifted from a privacy approach that would be based on proactive steps, competitive-edge orientation and customer trust building to a narrow, legal-compliance priority."[45]

CPOs also play a role in helping to ensure employee as well as consumer privacy. CPOs are relevant to the section of this chapter on the workplace and they are brought up again in Chapter 18, where employees' rights to privacy are discussed further.

DATA SECURITY One of the clearest ways companies can protect the privacy of their customers is through data security systems and practices. It turns out that data breaches are on the rise. Companies are struggling to keep customer and employee data secure. Cybercriminals are using more sophisticated techniques, including botnets, for breaking into businesses. Businesses are creating, storing, and sharing more data than ever before, and many employees simply do not understand the value of the data they work with and the countless ways that data can fall into the wrong hands. These challenges make data security extremely difficult. Companies don't lose their data; they lose the customers' and employees' data and most of these groups seem powerless to stop it. Even though 44 states have laws requiring businesses to disclose data breaches, one major study showed that these laws do not reduce the incidents. Penalties are not large enough to deter security breaches. Either government needs to create stronger incentives, or companies need to become more ethical with respect to protecting privacy.[46]

As mentioned earlier, one of the most sizeable examples of security breaches recently was uncovered in 2010 as part of a global attack that caught corporate and personal data on more than 2,400 computers. A security firm, NetWitness, disclosed that the coordinated, global assault gained access to many computers, including those of Merck & Co., Cardinal Health, and Paramount Pictures. They also broke into the computers at ten U.S. government agencies. The hackers created a botnet army that had a command center in Germany and got into corporate networks by enticing employees to click on contaminated Web sites, e-mail attachments, or ads promoting products to clean up viruses. The data breach appears to be the most far-reaching cyber attack to date. More than 75,000 computers in 196 countries were infiltrated.[47]

The large-scale cyber attack infected computers with spyware called ZeusS, which is available for free on the Internet. The way it worked was as follows. The hackers would entice employees to click on to contaminated Web sites or to open attachments. Users would open files that then installed the malicious spyware. The malware would then capture data typed into Web forms or find login information that was stored on the user's system. Then the hacker could retrieve the data from the installed software. The spyware allowed hackers to control the computers remotely.[48]

The data breaches described here point out the strong need for companies, governments, and individuals to make data security a number one priority. Companies have an ethical responsibility to protect data in spite of the lack of severe penalties for failing to do so.

Questionable Businesses and Practices. Several questionable businesses and practices have been made possible by electronic commerce and the use of the Internet. Three business categories that are viewed as questionable by many include Web-based pornography, Internet gambling, and Web-based downloading of music, movies, books, and other copyrighted digital materials. These activities raise the question of the protection of intellectual property. Pornography via the Internet is just one category of this business. The other is the production and distribution of pornography through video rental stores and through in-room videos in hotels.[49] Many ethical questions have been raised concerning this practice. The Internet porn industry has become so controversial that the U.S. Supreme Court is now hearing cases as to whether the industry is violating the Child Pornography Prevention Act of 1996 and the Communication Decency Act.

Song-swapping services made famous by the original Napster and several others continue to raise the question of the protection of intellectual property, because other people's ideas and music have been so easily acquired via the Internet. Napster made the transition to a paid subscription service in 2003; however, other music services continue to surface and call into question the system's ability to protect intellectual property.[50] In 2009, a U.S. court in Boston awarded a six-figure judgment against a Boston University student for illegally downloading and distributing 30 songs over the Internet. The $675,000 judgment, or $22,500 per track downloaded, was not the first such charge against individuals for downloading and file-sharing copyrighted music without a license, but it established once again the illegality of such activities.

For the past five years, university students in the United States have been a leading target of a litigation campaign carried out by the Recording Industry Association of America (RIAA). RIAA is the music industry trade group that has found university campuses to be hotbeds of file-sharing activity.[51] In considering this issue, one student observed that downloading was so easy and there is so much free content on the Internet that it's hard to discriminate between illegal downloading, streaming free content, and just copying something from a friend's laptop. The student went on to observe that when a product is digital, it doesn't feel like stealing. Over the past decade, peer-to-peer technology companies have transformed continuously and speedily, making it ever more complicated to police.[52] In spite of this, laws and ethics are being violated and these examples illustrate how Internet technology has threatened businesses.

Another practice that has raised questions is the use of technology to monitor consumers as they use the company's products. An example of the monitoring technology is illustrated when an individual rented a vehicle from Acme Rent-a-Car in New Haven, Connecticut, only to find out later that he was the unwitting victim of a global positioning system (GPS) device planted in the minivan he leased. The surveillance device recorded him speeding in three states at rates from 78 to 83 mph, and each violation, digitally recorded, automatically added a $150 charge to his bill.[53] The use of GPS is becoming more commonplace.

One of the most serious problems in the realm of computer scams against consumers continues to be the ongoing scam identified as **phishing**. An example of this occurred when a hacker who goes by the cyber name of Robotector sent an e-mail with the subject line "I still love you" to three million people. Within the message had been planted a small computer virus that, when executed, began to record user names and passwords each time their owner visited more than 30 online banks or payment Web sites. Then, this information was secretly e-mailed back to Robotector. This technique is called "phishing" because it lures prey (computer users) with convincing bait into revealing passwords and other private data. The Anti-Phishing Working Group, an industry association, reports that over 40,000 reports of phishing scams per month were being reported by early 2010.[54] These are just a sampling of the kinds of controversial ethical issues that arise in connection with electronic commerce.

The Workplace and Computer Technology

Whereas computer-based information technology creates ethical issues for consumer stakeholders with respect to electronic commerce and Web-based marketing, employee stakeholders also are significantly affected by technology in the workplace. We will discuss some of these issues in more detail, especially employee privacy, in Chapter 18. At this juncture, however, some brief discussion of the types of activities, technologies, and ethical issues that can arise merit consideration.

Employees generally have a positive impression of the impact of technology in the workplace. A *USA Today* poll tracked employees' attitudes toward the benefits of technology in the workplace over a recent five-year period. In four different ways, these technology users indicated increasing appreciation of the benefits of technology. They said that technology[55]

- Expands job-related knowledge
- Increases productivity during normal work hours
- Improves communication with clients and customers
- Relieves job stress

Other benefits of technology in the workplace include improved time management, expanded professional networks, development of a competitive edge, balance of work and family needs, and increased productivity during commuting time.[56]

Surveillance.   How do ethical issues arise when companies use technology in the workplace? One answer is through surveillance. **Surveillance** means companies electronically watching, monitoring, or checking up on their employees. The major ethical issue, of course, is the question of invasion of privacy. Employees are increasingly concerned about the extent to which their employers are monitoring their work-related activities and possibly their personal lives. Surveillance creates stress. Stress, in turn, may have a detrimental impact on performance or productivity. Thus, surveillance comes with attendant problems. It is useful to consider some of the technologies or ways that companies observe and monitor what their employees are doing on the job. In a revealing American Management Association study that surveyed policy changes over a five-year period, it was found that companies are increasingly keeping a closer eye on workers.[57]

In all of the following categories, companies have increased their surveillance of computers, telephone, and video over a five-year period and the trend seems to be continuing. The percentages indicate the proportion of companies now engaging in the practice and the number is growing:[58]

Computers

Monitoring Web site connections: 76 percent

Storing and reviewing employee computer files: 0 percent

Blocking access to inappropriate Web site: 65 percent

Storing and reviewing e-mail: 55 percent

Telephone

Monitoring time spent and numbers called: 43 percent

Taping phone conversations: 51 percent

Video

Video surveillance against theft: 51 percent

Video surveillance to monitor employee performance: 16 percent

Other approaches include scrutinizing social media usage and physically going undercover. Recently, 2 percent of employers said they terminated workers for content posted by employees on personal social networking sites such as Facebook and MySpace. Also, 1 percent lost their jobs due to videos posted on sites such as YouTube. A new TV show called *Undercover Boss* features CEOs actually going undercover into their companies' operations to see what all is going on that they would otherwise be unaware of.[59]

Increasingly, companies and managers are monitoring their employees using sophisticated new technologies. One CEO in California caught one of his employees in a lie when the employee phoned in sick. The boss had informed his employees that he had installed Xora, a software program that tracks workers' whereabouts by way of GPS technology on their company cell phones. When the boss logged onto the system, he found that his "sick" employee was not home in bed, but heading down the highway to Reno. When the boss phoned him, the employee could only say "you got me."[60] In another case, a supervisor was wondering about the productivity decline in one of his workers. Using software called SurfControl, he discovered that the man was spending an excessive amount of time on an innocently named Web site that he later discovered featured pornography.[61] The manager observed that what employees do at home is their business, "but what they do at work is all my business."[62] Some companies even monitor workers' access to the Internet while they are in hotel rooms when traveling. Web page requests are communicated through a Web monitoring service that can block or report access to certain sites.[63]

ETHICS IN PRACTICE CASE

Bosses Watching Employees: Are You Safe on Social Networking Sites?

Employees today should understand they are being watched—very carefully, in many instances. With the growth in the use of social networking sites such as Facebook and MySpace, some employees may begin to wonder what freedoms they actually have while using these sites on their own time. A case that has been developing in a federal court in New Jersey chronicles what can possibly happen.

In this case, managers are pitted against two employees who were caught complaining about their work while signed on to their MySpace accounts, a social networking site. The case in point tests the question of whether a manager, who managed to log on to the discussion forum, and later fired the employees who were badmouthing managers and customers, had the right to do so.

The general question is whether employees have a right to privacy in their nonwork lives and in their communications with one another while they are off work. The law is somewhat foggy. In most states, employers do not need a reason to fire nonunion workers. However,

some states, such as California, New York, and Connecticut, have laws that protect employees from discharge or dismissal while they are engaging in lawful, off-duty activities. One lawyer observed that private conversations might be covered under these statutes, but none of them specifically address social networking or blogging.

1. Do employees have a right to free speech while not at work? Do they have a right to not be monitored by their employers when they are "off the job"? Is this an ethical issue as well as a legal issue?

2. Should employees have the right to criticize their employer and managers on a social networking site? Are they violating any ethical duties they owe their employers?

3. Assuming the managers came across an incident such as that described, what actions, if any, should they take? What ethical principles should guide their actions?

Sources: Dionne Searcey, "Employers Watching Workers Online Spurs Privacy Debate," *The Wall Street Journal* (April 23, 2009), A13; Rachel King, "Companies Want to Monitor Workers on Social Networks," *BusinessWeek* (May 17, 2009).

Monitoring E-Mail and Internet Usage.   Employer monitoring of e-mail and Internet use is one of the most frequent forms of workplace surveillance. E-mail and Internet usage are frequently abused by employees and are among the most intensely checked activities. It is little wonder why employers do this. There is evidence that employees are spending more and more of their time online in such pursuits as personal e-mail, e-shopping, running their own businesses, personal communication, and visiting entertainment or social networking sites.

One major reason employers check up on their employees is that inexpensive technologies are now available that enable them to do so. Most companies today do not monitor telephone calls or postal mail as much because it is too time consuming and expensive to do so. However, companies can get software that monitors Internet usage for less than $10 per employee. Consequently, employee monitoring has been increasing at almost twice the rate of employees getting Internet access. According to one observer, "It's an example of the technology cart driving the policy horse."[64]

Availability of inexpensive technologies is helpful, but companies have other important reasons for monitoring employees' e-mail. Many of them are required to do so. The Sarbanes–Oxley Act and other regulations require publicly traded companies to archive all their e-mail messages. And, legally, employers in the private sector have full authority to monitor e-mail, provided they have created a policy and put it into place. Companies monitor e-mail to control the information that employees send through the corporate network, to make sure employees stay on task, and to see how employees are communicating with customers.[65]

A dramatic example of a company monitoring employee e-mail illustrates the kinds of ethical issues that may arise as a consequence of monitoring.

> *Man goes to Doctor for a checkup and a battery of tests. Doctor gets results and sends them via e-mail: Man has a life-threatening disease. Meanwhile, Man's company monitors his e-mail simply to ensure he uses it only for work. Technology officer reads Man's e-mail and blabs to coworkers about Man's diagnosis. Human resources gets involved. CEO gets called in, sees very expensive lawsuit looming. Health insurance company finds out about Man's problem, considers dropping coverage. Big problems for Man. Big problems for Company.*[66]

According to Joe Murphy, managing director of Interactive Integrity, the Internet has introduced enormous compliance risk and ethical issues for companies. There is the potential for sexual harassment, improper contact with competitors, use of chat rooms by people, pornography, and exchange of proprietary information over the Net by employees. Technology, therefore, has shifted the burden onto companies to monitor the workplace.[67]

In spite of the potential invasion of privacy issues, companies are monitoring employees' e-mail and Internet usage as never before. Some of the ways in which this is being done include developing policies prohibiting the Internet for personal use, using monitoring software, restricting Web site access, and restricting the hours of access.[68]

Companies are not only monitoring employee use, but taking actions as well. A recent survey of over 500 companies found the following infractions for which companies had fired employees (the figures in parentheses show the percentage of companies): e-mail misuse (26 percent), Internet misuse (26 percent), inappropriate cell phone use (6 percent), and inappropriate text messaging (3 percent).[69] In one of the most dramatic incidences to date, the CEO of the Bank of Ireland resigned from his £1-million-a-year position after he was discovered to be viewing pornographic Web sites on his company's computer. In a routine sweep of company Internet use, it was found that he had breached the company policy by viewing Web sites of what he called an "adult nature." The CEO said he felt he had to resign because the policy was his in the first place.[70]

Monitoring of employee activities has not been limited to their use of computers and the Internet. Increasingly, it is being reported that employers are monitoring employees' whereabouts and use of time through GPSs, satellite, implanting employees with microchips (with their knowledge), and hiring investigators to check up on what they are really doing at work.[71] Like all issues involving technology, there are two sides of the ethical arguments as to whether such practices are acceptable.

Biometrics. After a decade of talk, the newly emerging field of biometrics is starting to take off, especially in commercial applications. **Biometrics** is the use of body measurements, such as eye scans, fingerprints, or palm prints for determining and confirming identity. The technology of biometrics typically conjures up images of Big Brother surveillance tactics, and it has met resistance in cases where the government has wanted to use it for identification purposes. What seems to be speeding up its use, however, are commercial applications that provide assistance for consumers.[72] Resistance to government applications continues to be strong.

Only in the past several years there has been an explosion of applications in the commercial use of biometrics.[73] In several places now, consumers can scan their fingers or wave their palms over a scanner to gain access to accounts or safe deposit boxes or to make purchases. In Japan, contactless palm scanners are now being used when people want to withdraw cash from a cash point. In the Netherlands, a Dutch bank will be rolling out a system whereby customers may use their voices through voice analysis technology in a telephone banking system. Already, one can purchase laptop computers and mobile phones that come with built-in finger scanners. Other domestic applications include biometric door locks, garage locks, and safe locks. Even online services now respond to the rhythm and other characteristics of a person's typing, using a template of your "keystroke dynamics." There are flash drives that work only when activated by your thumbprint.[74] In short, biometrics is revolutionizing the way business is conducted and is expected to grow in the future.

Like most technologies, biometrics has many advantages and some possible downside risks. At the moment, the focus has not been on the legal and ethical risks associated with biometrics, but this is an issue that companies, employees, and consumers will want to watch carefully in the future. The potential abuses and invasions of privacy are many, and must be watched carefully. It is an issue that top managers and privacy officers will want to monitor closely.

Other Technology Issues in the Workplace

Surveillance extends beyond companies monitoring e-mail and Internet usage. In addition to these activities, other forms of surveillance include monitoring faxes, using video cameras in the workplace, drug testing, doing online background checks, logging photocopies, and recording phone calls. Each of these poses privacy implications that must be considered from an ethical perspective.

The world of security via computers and technology entered a new era on September 11, 2001, as a result of the terrorist attacks on the World Trade Center in New York and the Pentagon in Washington, DC. People's attitudes about privacy changed somewhat as they realized that heightened security checks are needed to guard against terrorist attacks. These added security measures have begun in public institutions (airports, government buildings, and large entertainment venues), and they are spilling over into the employment arena as companies become more cautious about their own security. There is already evidence that some use of face-recognition technology, "active" badges that track where you are, and other such technology-driven security measures have landed squarely in the workplace. There is further evidence that 9/11 spurred the development of smarter high-tech tools that are currently on the market and will in the future come to market for business use.[75]

Ethical Implications of Cell Phones and Text Messaging.

Although e-mail and the Internet most often create ethical problems in the workplace, the use of company-sponsored cell phones by employees represents one of the fastest growing technologies with increasing ethical and legal implications. To many, use of a cell phone is a private matter, but job pressures are leading more and more employees to use the phones while driving. Because companies now make cell phones available to their employees, this issue spills over into the business arena and becomes a business ethics topic. In actuality, cell phone use while driving is not a private matter, because it significantly raises the risk of harm to others on the streets.[76]

A case that dramatically brought this issue to public attention was reported in *The Wall Street Journal*. A San Francisco-based attorney was working the kind of fast-paced day that is becoming increasingly common. She was totaling her billable hours on her cell phone for her employer while driving to a scheduled 10 p.m. meeting with a client. This was typical for her—continuing to make business calls on her cell phone while driving home. This night was out of the ordinary, however. As she talked, her car swerved and struck a 15-year-old who was walking on the shoulder of the road, throwing her fatally injured body down an embankment. She later said she didn't even realize she had hit someone. She said it wasn't until morning when she was watching the news while dressing for work that she realized what she had done. She turned herself in and pleaded guilty to hit and run—a felony. The victim's family sought $30 million in damages from her employer.[77] In settlement, a jury ordered her to pay the victim's family $2 million. She also served one year in jail after pleading guilty to leaving the scene of an accident. Upon conviction, she also forfeited her license to practice law.[78] What appeared to her to be a simple, daily transaction turned into a personal and professional nightmare for her and her employer.

A trend with huge implications for employers is the growing number of employees—managers, salespeople, consultants, lawyers, ad executives, and others—who are using cell phones while driving and chalking up sales or billable hours. Hundreds of millions of people in the United States alone subscribe to wireless communication devices. Research has documented that motorists who use cell phones while driving are four times as likely to get into crashes serious enough to injure themselves or others. There are two primary problems with people using such devices while driving. First, drivers have to take their eyes off the road while driving, and second, they can become so absorbed in their conversations that their concentration is severely impaired. This jeopardizes the safety of not only the vehicle's occupants, but also that of pedestrians and other vehicles.[79]

Plaintiffs are increasingly claiming that the employer is partly to blame because it presses employees to work long hours from distant locations, often encouraging them to use cell phones without setting safety guidelines. Research is increasingly documenting the dangers of cell phone use while driving. A study by an insurance company found that chatty drivers suffered slower reaction times, took longer to stop, and missed more road signs than drivers who were legally drunk. A new term has already been coined for accidents caused by cell phone-using drivers—DWY (driving while yakking).[80]

In another major court case, a New York investment banking firm was sued for damages in federal court by the family of a motorcyclist who was killed when one of its brokers, using a car phone, ran a red light and struck him. Plaintiffs claimed that employer pressure to contact clients after hours contributed to the tragedy, and the company settled the suit for $500,000. They did not admit any wrongdoing, but wanted to avoid a jury trial.[81] Another civil case involving a car crash caused by a driver using a cell phone for business reasons was dismissed when the driver's employer agreed to pay the plaintiff $5 million.[82]

Cases such as these—linked to technology, the cell phone—should raise red flags for employers and individuals concerned about their careers. Not enough companies have the needed policies on cell phone use at this time. It appears that as high-tech tools extend the workplace into every corner of life, companies have been leaving the responsibility entirely up to the employees. These cases are tragic examples of what can happen when employees, using technology, become too distracted, pressured, or overfocused on their work.[83] Businesses are moving toward the adoption of policies against the use of cell phones while driving. One significant decision was made by the California Association of Employers when it recommended that all employers develop a cell phone policy that would require employees to pull off the road before conducting business on their cell phones.[84]

Unethical Activities by Employees Related to Technology. In most of the instances described to this point, the employer has had responsibility for the use of technology and its implications. There is another area that should be mentioned: questionable activities that are the responsibility of the employee. These activities have been aided by computer technologies. In a major study of workers, the following percentages of workers surveyed said they had engaged in the following unethical activities during the previous year:[85]

- Created a potentially dangerous situation by using new technology while driving—19 percent
- Wrongly blamed an error the employee made on a technological glitch—14 percent
- Copied the company's software for home use—13 percent
- Used office equipment to shop on the Internet for personal reasons—13 percent
- Used office equipment to network/search for another job—11 percent
- Accessed private computer files without permission—6 percent
- Used new technologies to intrude on coworkers' privacy—6 percent
- Visited porn Web sites using office equipment—5 percent

Company Actions. Companies have many options for addressing the kinds of ethical issues described to this point. A major survey of *Fortune* 500 nonmanagement employees revealed that management should define ethical computer use for employees. Options for doing this include company management making these decisions, using the Information Systems Society's code of ethics, and involving employees and users in a collaborative attempt to decide computer ethics. Only about one-half of those surveyed indicated that company guidelines were written and well known.[86] Beyond this, companies should carefully think about the ethical implications of their use of technology and integrate decisions designed to protect employees into their policies and practices, especially their codes of conduct.

The technologies discussed to this point have been computer driven. Therefore, guidelines for employee computer use would help in many of the applications described. Several professional societies also offer guidelines for computer use. The Computer Ethics Institute has set forth what it calls its "Ten Commandments of Computer Ethics." These guidelines are interesting and useful, and are summarized in Figure 9-2.

FIGURE 9-2
Ten Commandments of Computer Ethics

The Computer Ethics Institute has set forth the following ten commandments of computer ethics. These should prove useful to employees and employers alike.

- Thou shalt not use a computer to harm other people.
- Thou shalt not interfere with other people's computer work.
- Thou shalt not snoop around in other people's computer files.
- Thou shalt not use a computer to steal.
- Thou shalt not use a computer to bear false witness.

- Thou shalt not copy or use proprietary software for which you have not paid.
- Thou shalt not use other people's computer resources without authorization or proper compensation.
- Thou shalt not appropriate other people's intellectual output.
- Thou shalt think about the social consequences of the program you are designing.
- Thou shalt always use a computer in ways that ensure consideration and respect for your fellow humans.

Source: Computer Ethics Institute, Computer Professionals for Social Responsibility, "Ten Commandments of Computer Ethics," http://cpsr.org/issues/ethics/cei/. Accessed February 11, 2010.

Biotechnology

The 20th century's revolution in information technology is merging with the 21st century's revolution in biotechnology. Indeed, Walter Isaacson has labeled the 2000s as the "biotech century."[87] At this time, we are poised for the most significant breakthrough of all time—deciphering the human genome, tens of thousands of genes encoded by 3 billion chemical pairs in our DNA. Among other achievements, this accomplishment will lead to the next medical revolution, which will not only increase the natural life span of healthy human beings but will also help to conquer cancer, grow new blood vessels, block the growth of blood vessels in tumors, create new organs from stem cells, and certainly much more.[88]

The field of biotechnology carries with it significant implications for business and for business ethics, and we can only touch upon these issues here. In fact, we now have a burgeoning growth industry—the biotechnology industry. Biotechnology involves "using biology to discover, develop, manufacture, market, and sell products and services."[89] The biotech industry today consists of small entrepreneurial start-up companies funded largely by venture capitalists, along with dozens of larger, more established companies. Most of the applications of biotechnology are in health care, the pharmaceutical industry, and agriculture.[90]

Bioethics

A field called **bioethics** has emerged that deals with the ethical issues embedded in the commercial use of biotechnology. As new biotech products are developed, thorny ethical issues inevitably arise. In recent years, the question has arisen regarding the federal government's role in bioethics and stem cells. One of the actions former President George W. Bush took was to create a presidential council on bioethics. A few of the council's issues of concern include bioethics, biotechnology and public policy, cloning, genetics, neuroethics, organ transplantation, and stem cells.[91]

On the business front, some biotechnology companies have adopted the idea of bioethics to guide them in their decision making. A question that is being continually raised, however, is whether bioethical decision making is really taking place or whether the companies are using the bioethicists for public relations purposes. Companies such as Geron have pioneered the idea of a corporate bioethics advisory board. When the

Jones Institute for Reproductive Medicine began its research on human embryos, it talked up the idea of panels of bioethicists. It has been observed that many companies are savvy enough to know that the greatest single obstacle to utilizing their new technologies is the potential for public backlash.[92]

According to William Saletan, who has written extensively about bioethics, the primary tool bioethicists use is *proceduralism*. This involves elaborate protocols being established that ensure that certain classical worries, such as informed consent, are not violated. The focus, in other words, is on being sure that appropriate procedures are being followed rather than on the actual ethical content of the decisions. The worry continues, however, over whether corporate executives and scientists are deceiving their own consciences by focusing on the *how* rather than the *why*, or the *means* rather than the *end*.[93]

Both critics and supporters say that the use of bioethicists lends companies an air of credibility. The real question is, can they really be objective if they are on a company's payroll? Supporters say "yes," they function like a newspaper ombudsperson who gets paid by the paper to criticize coverage and prevent potential conflicts. Detractors say "no," there's no way around a conflict of interest if money is changing hands. A real danger is that the participation of bioethicists may be interpreted as a stamp of approval.[94]

A public policy expert has observed, "the biotech revolution has surged forward as the defining issue of this new century. On the one hand, it holds out great promise for medical advances enhancing life and health for all humankind. On the other, it raises unprecedented ethical issues." The expert goes on to conclude, "the biotech revolution is moving like a steamroller, fueled by huge potential profits, crushing everything—including moral restraint—in its path."[95] We may be too early into the biotechnology revolution to know whether this will turn out to be the case; however, it is important to raise the question of the balance between costs and benefits early on. Figure 9-3 lists several nonprofit bioethics organizations that may be found on the Web.

It is useful to consider two broad realms of biotechnology to appreciate what each represents in terms of challenges in business ethics: **genetic engineering** and **genetically modified foods (GMFs)**. Genetic engineering, primarily of humans, and genetic engineering of agricultural and food products are both part of genetic science. For discussion purposes, however, we will treat them separately. Genetic testing and profiling is another important issue that merits consideration.

Genetic Engineering

Two major areas of genetic engineering, or genetic science, seem to capture the public's imagination today. One is stem cell research, and the second is cloning. Both pose enormous and interesting challenges for business and business ethics.

Stem Cell Research. The basic building blocks that are the progenitors of all other cells were isolated in 1998 by scientists at the University of Wisconsin. These **embryonic stem cells** are the raw materials with which a human body is built. Since their isolation, stem cell research has been proliferating around the world. Though the United States has historically been the world leader in biotechnology, some experts say it has fallen behind other countries as debate over ethical implications has slowed progress.[96] According to a member of the President's Council on Bioethics, the debate over stem cell research centers on one basic moral question: the moral status of a human embryo—the product of sperm and egg—and what constitutes a human being.[97]

Stem cells come from embryos, and they may be obtained in three ways: frozen embryos, fresh embryos, or cloned embryos. Spare frozen embryos may come from fertility clinics, having been donated by infertile couples who no longer need them for

FIGURE 9-3
Web Sites of
Nonprofit Bioethics
Organizations

Bioethics is such an expansive topic that there are many different organizations, especially public action organizations, that provide information regarding specific topics via the World Wide Web. Some of these include the following:

American Society for Bioethics + Humanities (http://www.asbh.org/)

The American Society for Bioethics and Humanities (ASBH) is a professional society of more than 1,500 individuals, organizations, and institutions interested in bioethics and humanities. This Web site is intended initially to serve as a source of information about ASBH for members and prospective members. It also will serve as a resource for anyone interested in bioethics and humanities by providing a group of additional online resources and links to aid in finding other related information through the Internet.

The GE Food Alert Campaign Center (http://www.gefoodalert.org/)

This is a Web page sponsored by the Center for Food Safety. It primarily focuses on genetically engineered foods and issues related to this topic.

Do No Harm: The Coalition of Americans for Research Ethics (http://www.stemcell research.org/)

This organization is a national coalition of researchers, health care professionals, bioethicists, legal professionals, and others dedicated to the promotion of scientific research and health care that does no harm to human life.

Council for Responsible Genetics (http://www.councilforresponsiblegenetics.org/)

The council fosters debate on social, ethical, and environmental implications of new genetic technologies. The council publishes "GeneWATCH," a national bulletin on the implications of biotechnology. The site contains testimony presented to the U.S. Congress and position papers, and functions as a legislative clearinghouse.

Bioethics.net (http://www.bioethics.net/)

This Web page is quite extensive. It hosts the *American Journal of Bioethics Online* and the Center for Bioethics at the University of Pennsylvania. It has a special section on bioethics for beginners as well as a special section on cloning and genetics.

National Human Genome Research Institute (http://www.genome.gov/)

This Web site describes the Ethical, Legal, and Social Implications (ELSI) Research program. This program supports basic and applied research that identifies and analyzes the ethical, legal, and social issues surrounding human genetics research. The ELSI Research program currently is the largest federal supporter of bioethics research.

pregnancy. Most ethical guidelines recommend research only on these. Fresh embryos are those that have been specially created for research, usually in a fertility clinic. Embryos can also be created by cloning human cells. In fact, in an example of how stem cell research is outrunning public policy, a Massachusetts company used cloning technology to create human embryos that would yield the cells that might give rise to tissues that would be perfect matches for patients. This technique, known as *therapeutic cloning*, was the subject of intense debate in Congress during the early 2000s.[98] The value of stem cells is that they offer the greatest hope for developing treatments for diseases such as cancer, Alzheimer's, Parkinson's, and juvenile diabetes.[99] Further, stem cells may be grown into tissues for transplanting into patients who need them for nerve cells, bone cells, or muscle cells.[100]

President Bush (2001–2009) considered the arguments for and against the federal government funding research using stem cells. After much debate, the president decided to proceed, but cautiously. His announced decision was to allow federal government funding for research only on stem cells that had already been harvested. By 2009, a majority of Americans supported President Barack Obama's executive order doing away with the rules on federal funding of embryonic stem cell research that were in place under the Bush administration. In a 2009 Gallup Poll, 38 percent of Americans said they supported easing those restrictions and another 14 percent said they favored no restrictions at all. About four in ten Americans favored keeping the Bush restrictions or eliminating federal funding altogether.[101]

These data suggest that society is still somewhat divided over the issue. In spite of public opinion, companies and countries continue to push the issue. Companies want to develop cures for diseases and to have bragging rights about their technological superiority. This aggressive competition can lead to unethical practices, even fraud, and this is all the more reason why these issues have to be carefully watched.[102]

Most of the ethical debate over stem cell research has occurred in the public and political arenas, not business. Businesses are moving forward now even though the societal debate is not settled.[103] A real danger in the debate over the use of embryonic stem cells is the almost irresistible tendency to treat them as "property" ripe for commercial exploitation. But the interested parties are not isolated individuals. The beneficiaries are not just the sick, the aged, or the prematurely infirm. There are many stakeholders. Research universities seeking funding and prestige will benefit, as will pharmaceutical companies seeking new products and investors; the government has a stake as countries compete to market therapies for degenerative diseases.[104] The pharmaceutical industry is one of the best illustrations of how companies are already moving on research. Companies such as Johnson & Johnson, Eli Lilly, Abbott Laboratories, Schering, and Wyeth are already conducting regenerative research using adult stem cells.[105]

Cloning.   Stem cell research is well under way. Now, **cloning** continues to be in the news. Some scientists say human cloning is a distant project; however, according to some reports, a few citizens are already lining up to freeze the DNA of their dead loved ones, including pets and racehorses. Several different groups have claimed they are attempting to clone a human being.

Actually, there are at least two debates surrounding cloning and genetic science. First, there is the issue of cloning human beings. Second, there is the issue of cloning animals and plants and using genetics to identify and fight diseases. This second quest is currently the primary focus of science. But it is the fascination with duplicating human beings that arouses the most debate and fear. Surveys in the United States show very little support for human cloning. According to a 2009 Gallup Poll, 88 percent said cloning human beings was morally wrong while only 9 percent considered it morally acceptable.[106] By contrast, this same poll found that 63 percent thought cloning animals was morally wrong and 34 percent thought it was acceptable.

A variation of human cloning is known as **therapeutic cloning**. Therapeutic cloning uses the same laboratory procedures as reproductive cloning, but its aim is not procreation but rather the creation of a source of stem cells whose properties make them a possible source of replacement tissue for a wide range of degenerative diseases. Opponents of therapeutic cloning are opposed to the creation and destruction of human life for utilitarian ends. In addition, opponents fear the exploitation of women, especially in poor countries, for their eggs. On the other side of the issue, supporters want to give therapeutic cloning a chance because of its possible health advantages.[107]

Possible scenarios of therapeutic cloning have raised nightmare reactions in the minds of some. The chemicals in the human body were once estimated to be worth 89 cents. Now, however, according to the authors of a provocative, and some would say shocking, book, body parts in people and in corpses may be worth millions. In *Body Bazaar: The Market for Human Tissue in the Biotechnology Age*, Lori Andrews and Dorothy Nelkin talk optimistically about the commercialization of the human body in pursuit of new pharmaceuticals, organ transplants, and genetic research on individuals alive or dead. The book has ethicists again asking important questions: Do individuals have "rights" to their blood and tissue? Should body parts be bought and sold? Whose body is it, any-way?[108]

Andrews and Nelkin write, "whole businesses are developing around the body busi-ness. Companies have sprung up to make commercial products out of corpses' bones. Some grind up the bones into powder that, when sprinkled on broken live bones, will help them mend." They argue that body parts from the living and the dead are gold mines for pharmaceutical research. Some of the authors' writings raise provocative ethi-cal questions that business must face: Who owns the rights to a corpse? What ethical considerations need to be evaluated when a researcher seeks to do genetic testing on long-deceased individuals? What are the ethical considerations associated with the mor-bid practice of using human body parts as a means of "expression"? An exhibition that has been on tour in recent years (*Bodies: The Exhibition*) depicts corpses with plasticized body parts, with flaps of skin open to display the anatomical features of the human body. Does this practice debase the sanctity of the human body?[109] Some think so.

In an intended humorous insight into where cloning may be heading, a cartoon by Tom Toles depicted a man in an office sticking his head into the office copier; off to the side, there were cloned copies of him coming out of the machine. A sign on the wall stated, "July 2018. The ethical debate, part 2,473,561," and the question posed beneath the cartoon read: "Should employees be allowed to use the office cloning machine for personal business?"

Cloning Animals for Food.   The hottest issue on the cloning front is that of com-panies wanting to clone animals for food. Scientists and consumer experts in the United States have been debating whether the country should become the first in the world to allow food from cloned animals onto supermarket shelves. In 2007, the Food and Drug Administration (FDA) held an open period for public comment on the issue. Thousands of consumers wrote to the FDA protesting allowing cloned foods into the food supply. One consumer said the thought was "unethical, disturbing, and disgusting."[110] Scientists and companies, however, almost completely support cloning for food, indicating they see the technology as an effective, important way to produce higher quality, healthier food. Based on a final risk assessment, FDA scientists issued a report in 2008, in which it con-cluded that meat and milk from cow, pig, and goat clones and the offspring of any ani-mal clones are as safe as food we eat every day.[111] A related issue is whether food from cloned animals should be labeled as such. The FDA does not seem to think such labeling is necessary, but opponents say such labels are essential.

Opponents of cloning animals for food come from a large number of different con-sumer and scientific groups. Consumer advocate organizations such as the Center for Food Safety, Consumers Union, and the Consumer Federation of America, along with environmental and animal welfare groups, have protested the idea. They think there is inadequate data regarding the safety of such a practice and that there needs to be more review of the potential consequences of such a decision. A minority of scientists agree with the consumer groups that cloned animals should not enter the food supply.[112] This is likely to be an emotionally debated ethical issue in the months and years to come.

Genetic Testing and Profiling.   One of the most significant areas of potential ques-tionable application of biotechnology is **genetic testing**. Genetic testing has many down-side risks, especially from both a legal and an ethical perspective.[113] It is said that someday each of us will have a DNA chip that contains all our genetic information.

There are some positives associated with this. It will help each person manage his or her own personal health risks. It will also help a physician predict how well a patient will respond to various therapies. Future drugs will be developed using genetic information so that the therapy will be coupled with the DNA information. However, **genetic profiling** also provides a perfect means for identifying a person and thus raises questions of privacy and possible discrimination based on genetic factors.[114]

A decade ago, the U.S. Equal Employment Opportunity Commission (EEOC) settled its first court action challenging the use of workplace genetic testing under the Americans with Disabilities Act of 1990 (ADA). The EEOC had sought an injunction against Burlington Northern Santa Fe Railway (BNSF) to end genetic testing of employees who filed claims for work-related injuries based on Carpal Tunnel Syndrome. According to the EEOC, the company's genetic testing program was carried out without the knowledge or consent of its employees, and at least one worker was threatened with termination for failing to submit a blood sample for a genetic test.[115] Under the settlement, BNSF also agreed that it would not analyze blood it had previously obtained, nor would it retaliate against employees who opposed the testing. According to the EEOC, "Our swift action in this case allows Burlington Northern employees to continue to work free of retaliation and future invasions of privacy."[116]

In 2008, then President George Bush signed into law the Genetic Information Nondiscrimination Act (GINA) that was intended to protect Americans against discrimination based on their genetic information when it comes to health insurance and employment.[117] Its implementation took effect during 2009 and 2010. It is too early to tell how vigorously this law will be enforced and whether it will achieve its desired goals.

Genetically Modified Foods

Another major category of biotechnology that carries important and increasing ethical implications for business is that of GMFs. This is especially the case for the multibillion-dollar agribusiness industry. Many wholesalers and retailers, however, are also involved in the distribution of GMFs. GMFs are also commonly referred to as **genetically engineered foods (GEFs)**. Around the world, the percentage of major crops that were genetically engineered as of 2009 were soybeans (77 percent), cotton (49 percent), and corn (26 percent). In the United States, the figures were higher: sugar beets (95 percent), soybeans (91 percent), cotton (88 percent), and corn (85 percent).[118] It is readily apparent that most of us are consuming GMFs on a regular basis.

Extreme critics of GMFs call them "Frankenfoods," calling attention to the parallels with the mythical character Frankenstein. The world today seems to be divided into those who favor GMFs and those who fear them. Also, a significant number of consumers are simply not informed enough to know but are quick to offer their gut-reaction opinions, usually based on fear rather than facts. Because no one seems to have been "hurt" by GMFs, there is a lot of wild speculation as well as indifference at work in judging the ethics and implications of GMF.

Scant information is available to the public as to the actual safety or lack of safety of these products because field-testing continues and is seldom reported. According to the vice president for food and agriculture at the Biotechnology Industry Organization, "There is still not so much as a single, solitary sniffle or headache positively linked to their consumption."[119] According to the World Health Organization, GMFs currently available on the international market have passed risk assessments and are not likely to present risks for human health. In addition, no effects on human health have been shown as a result of the consumption of such foods by the general population in the countries where they have been approved.[120] Therefore, the debate seems to hinge on whether the perceived pros or cons of GMFs will win out as the arguments are presented and experience is gained.

According to a CBS News/*New York Times* poll, 53 percent of Americans say they won't buy food that has been genetically modified. But, as noted, it's not that easy to avoid. More than 90 percent of the U.S. soybean crop is genetically modified—had its DNA altered to increase production and withstand chemical weed killers like Roundup. Over three-quarters of all corn planted in the United States is genetically modified.[121] While most packaged and processed foods do contain genetically modified ingredients, the labels don't have to say so. Despite continuing concerns about GM foods, consumers do not support banning new uses of the technology, but rather seek an active role from regulators to ensure that new products are safe. Although a majority of respondents are uncomfortable with genetically modifying animals, the most widely favored uses are those that provide protection against disease. When asked about importation of foreign GM products, consumers demonstrated little awareness but clearly favored U.S. regulation.[122]

Though public opinion in Europe leans in opposition to GMOs, there is recent evidence that even the European Union has been approving genetically modified crops for human consumption while secretly warning about their impact on health and the environment.[123] Activist groups such as Friends of the Earth and Greenpeace have called for the immediate suspension of the use and sale of all GM foods and crops until the safety issues have been addressed.[124] European Union governments delivered a blow in 2009 to the biotechnology industry, by allowing Austria and Hungary to maintain national bans on growing genetically modified crops from Monsanto.[125] Europe's resistance to GMFs may become less important in the future as China is now the biggest investor in public biotech research in the world and they will be the first country where a major staple food of humans—rice— will be genetically engineered to resist the rice stem borer. And, in the case of China, it is not MNCs but the public sector that is leading the way.[126]

Will there be a consumer backlash against biotechnology in food production when the public becomes more familiar with it? Recently, more concern has been expressed about questionable food products, including seafood and vegetables being imported, than GMFs. It is an issue that merits continued close examination for both real and perceived reactions.

Labeling of GMFs. One of the most frequently discussed issues with respect to GMFs is the topic of labeling. Many consumer activists think that, at a minimum, foods that contain genetically engineered contents ought to be labeled as such. The Consumer Federation of America Foundation, for example, issued a report recommending mandatory labeling and other ways to improve U.S. biotech food regulations. To date, the FDA has not mandated labeling of GMFs. The FDA has created new rules wherein biotech companies would have to meet with federal regulators before putting a new product on the market, but they would not require special product labels. The FDA has been working on the new guidelines in an attempt to reassure consumers that GMFs are safe.[127]

In spite of inaction on the part of the FDA, the labeling issue will not go away. Proponents of mandatory labeling argue that the consumer has a right to full disclosure about product contents and that the consumers' right to safety argues that such knowledge should be available to them. Of special concern, the organic and natural foods market segment fears that genetically modified crops may be slipping into its products. This market segment strongly supports the Non-GMO Project.[128] The Non-GMO Project has been advocating the *Non-GMO label*, which stands for "nongenetically modified organisms." The Non-GMO Project is a nonprofit collaboration of manufacturers, retailers, processors, distributors, farmers, seed companies, and consumers. The project's shared belief is "that everyone deserves an informed choice about whether or not to consume genetically modified products and our common mission is to ensure the sustained availability of non-GMO choices."[129]

Just a few years ago, this labeling issue was unknown in the United States. Now, however, it is popping up frequently as companies attempt to take strategic advantage by promoting their products that do not contain GMOs. The Non-GMO label is now being seen on hundreds of products ranging from pasta, produce, and breakfast cereals to frozen entrees, condiments, and beverages. Industry executives believe this is a fast-growing market segment and, though labels are not mandatory, some consumer segments are attracted to this product feature.

The issues of safety and labeling of GMFs will continue. Special-interest groups on both sides of the debate continue to be active in advocating their points of view. The agribusiness industry continues to argue that the foods are safe and that mandatory testing and labeling are not necessary. The FDA does not seem inclined to impose any new requirements on producers. Consumer activists, however, have brought together environmentalists, organic farmers, chefs, and religious leaders, and they continue to make the case for rigorous safety testing and labeling.[130] To be sure, all consumer stakeholders are potentially affected by the outcome of these debates, so it is likely that this issue will be with us for some time. As the economy improves, the organic and natural foods market segment will start to grow again, and with it is likely to continue the expectation that these products will be differentiated by their non-GMO characteristic.

Summary

Business use of technology today is so dramatic that the topic merits this separate chapter. In this discussion, basic concepts such as technology and the technological environment, were introduced and defined. The benefits and side effects or hazards of technology were discussed. The symptoms of society's intoxication with technology were outlined. Questions regarding the ethics of technology were raised in two broad domains: information technology and biotechnology.

In the realm of information technology, the category with the most widespread current impact in business, topics included electronic commerce, invasion of privacy via e-commerce, government's involvement in Internet privacy invasion, and business initiatives. Questions about practices and uses of technology were raised, including particular industries such as the porn industry, Internet gambling, and Web-based downloading services. Computer technology in the workplace, one of the most significant areas of application, has been used for monitoring e-mail and employee movement, as well as Internet usage and other forms of surveillance. Questions regarding the ethics of new technologies such as cell phones were also raised. The field of biometrics merits close watch in the future.

The field of biotechnology was discussed with respect to social and ethical implications. A key topic in this sphere included the new field of bioethics. Two arenas of biotechnology were identified and discussed: that of genetic engineering, to include a discussion of stem cell research, cloning, and genetic testing and profiling, and the general domain of GMFs. It is anticipated that the debate over food safety and labeling will continue for years as different interest groups raise questions about the appropriateness and safety of GMFs and whether labels on such foods should be required.

Key Terms

bioethics, p. 334

biometrics, p. 331

biotechnology, p. 320

chief privacy officer (CPO), p. 325

cloning, p. 337

cookies, p. 322

electronic commerce, p. 321

embryonic stem cells, p. 335

ethical lag, p. 319

genetic engineering, p. 335

genetic profiling, p. 339

genetic testing, p. 338

342 Part 3 Business Ethics and Management

genetically engineered foods (GEFs), p. 339

genetically modified foods (GMFs), p. 335

information technology, p. 320

phishing, p. 327

spam, p. 322

surveillance, p. 328

technological determinism, p. 319

technological environment, p. 317

technology, p. 316

therapeutic cloning, p. 337

Discussion Questions

1. Are there any benefits or negative side effects of technology in business that have not been mentioned in this chapter? Discuss.

2. Do you agree that society is intoxicated with technology? Does this pose special problems for business with respect to the ethics of technology? Will such intoxication blind people to ethical considerations in business?

3. Do you think business is abusing its power with respect to invasion of privacy of both consumers and employees? What about surveillance? Which particular practice do you think is the most questionable?

4. Is it an exaggeration to question the ethical implications for business of cell phone and text-messaging use? Discuss both sides of this issue.

5. Do you think genetically modified foods raise a legitimate safety hazard? Should government agencies such as the FDA take more action to require safety testing? What about warning labels? Do you think warning labels would unfairly stigmatize GMFs and make consumers question their safety? Is this fair to the GMF industry?

10
Ethical Issues in the Global Arena

CHAPTER LEARNING OUTCOMES

After studying this chapter, you should be able to:

1. Differentiate between the concepts of internationalization and globalization of business.

2. Summarize the arguments for and against globalization.

3. Explain the ethical challenges of multinational corporations (MNCs) operating in the global environment.

4. Summarize the key implications of the following ethical issues: infant formula controversy, Bhopal tragedy, sweatshops and human rights abuses, and the Alien Tort Claims Act.

5. Define corruption and differentiate between bribes and grease payments, and outline the major features of the Foreign Corrupt Practices Act.

6. Describe the growing anticorruption movement and the key players in this movement.

7. Identify and discuss strategies for improving global ethics.

The rise of global business as a critical element in the world economy is one of the most important developments of the past several decades. This period has been characterized by the rapid growth of foreign direct investment by the United States, by countries in Western Europe, by Japan, and by other developing countries as well, such as China, India, and Russia. Many emerging economies are joining the mix. In the United States, domestic issues have been made immensely more complex by the escalating international growth. At the same time, the internationalization of business has created unique problems of its own. It no longer appears that international markets can be seen as opportunities that may or may not be pursued. Rather, international markets now are seen as natural extensions of an ever-expanding global marketplace that must be pursued if firms are to remain competitive. Over the past decade, there has been evidence of a backlash against global business. The attacks on the World Trade Center on September 11, 2001, the most shocking development to date, were seen by many as an attack on global capitalism, especially that practiced by the United States. This event continues in unseen ways to influence the practice of global business and its ramifications for business ethics. Across the globe, stock markets have plummeted, thereby creating the current worldwide recession that has made global commerce enormously more complicated. As economies improve, a stabilizing effect will kick in, and this recession may not be as much of a problem. However, global competition is expected to remain intense.

Peter Drucker has termed the expanded marketplace the **transnational economy**. He goes on to say that if business expects to establish and maintain leadership in one country, it must also strive to hold a leadership position in all developed markets worldwide. This helps to explain the worldwide boom in transnational investments.[1] One early definition of this transnational or global economy is as follows: trade in goods, a much smaller trade in services, the international movement of labor, and international flows of capital and information.[2] In the past decade, we have seen the globalization trend explode, and its critics continue to oppose much of it. In the United States, for example, arguments over the outsourcing of jobs and offshoring of work to less-developed countries continue to be a subject of relentless debate.

The complexity introduced by the transnational economy and the globalization of business is seen clearly when ethical issues arise. At best, business ethics is difficult when we are dealing with one culture. Once we bring two or more cultures into consideration, it gets extremely complex. Managers have to deal not only with differing customs, protocols, and ways of operating but also with differing concepts of law and standards of acceptable practices. All of this is then exacerbated by the fact that world political issues become intertwined. What might be intended as an isolated corporate attempt to bribe a foreign government official, in keeping with local custom, could explode into major international political tensions between two or more countries.

The New, New World of Global Business

We have traversed through several different eras in the internationalization of business since the post–World War II decade (1945–1955). There have been the Growth Years (1955–1970), the Troubled Years (1970–1980), and the New International Order (1980–present), according to one international business expert.[3] The new, new world of global business and business ethics can be said to have begun in the fall of 1999 with protests against global business at an annual meeting of the World Trade Organization (WTO).

Thomas Friedman, in his seminal book *The World Is Flat: A Brief History of the Twenty-First Century*, argued that there have been three great eras of globalization. Using the numbering system of the software industry, Friedman argues that Globalization 1.0 was during the period 1492–1800 and Globalization 2.0 covered 1800–2000. Globalization 3.0 began in 2000, according to Friedman, and continues today. Friedman argues that when the Internet and e-commerce became robust in the late 1990s, the world shrunk from a size small to a size tiny.[4] He argues that the availability of cheap labor and telecommunications all over the world has had the effect of creating a "flat" world. Thus, no matter where a company is physically located, it can now compete for customers who may be located anywhere in the world. Friedman argues that the driving force of this flattening process is globalization and that globalization is gaining momentum.[5]

The first strong evidence of a backlash movement against globalization occurred in the fall of 1999. At that time, the WTO was meeting in Seattle, and there were massive demonstrations and protests outpouring into the streets. The WTO talks collapsed as 50,000 protestors rioted, expressing extreme hostility and violence toward the idea of global business.[6] This backlash continued with massive demonstrations in Washington, DC, in 2000; Prague in the fall of 2000; Quebec in April 2001; Genoa during the summer of 2001; and Cancun during 2003. On a lesser scale, it continued through the G8 meeting of world leaders in Sea Island, Georgia, in the summer of 2004, though the protests were moderated. In 2006, a Time.com article discussed the backlash against globalization.[7] Today, each global meeting of the major world powers results in a strong turnout of opponents who want to use the occasion to continue their dramatic opposition to global growth.

An important defining moment in the backlash against globalization was the terrifying attacks on the World Trade Center in New York City and on the Pentagon in Washington on September 11, 2001, which had resulted in massive death and destruction. A number of observers have claimed that the hostile attacks against the twin towers of the World Trade Center represented an attack on America's leading role in global business and all it stands for. Though it is hard to know whether this is a valid interpretation, many think that it is, and in any event, this horrific incident marked a moment in time when world trade and commerce would never be the same or be seen in the same light. This treacherous act of mass murder and destruction changed global business and will continue to impact the related concerns of global business ethics and global corporate citizenship.

Perhaps the most dramatic recent series of events that perpetuated the backlash against globalization began in the United States in early 2007, when some dangerous products were imported from China. At first, tainted pet food and later a series of other potentially deadly, defective, or contaminated products including toys, tires, tooth-paste, cough syrup, and seafood have been traced to Chinese origins.[8] These incidents awakened both the United States and China to a latent crisis. If China does not rectify these problems, this will have a significant dampening effect on its exports. For the United States, and other affected countries, they must deal with the questions of product safety and regulation over imports and the issue of who is legally responsible when foreign products hurt people in the importing country.[9] Both countries have been taking initiatives to resolve these problems, but one can't help but wonder whether this might generate another wave of backlash against global trade.

To explore the topic of globalization further, it is first helpful to consider what global business really means. Second, it is useful to briefly consider some of the sentiments behind the continuing protests against globalism, because this new reality of world attitudes and questions being raised about global capitalism cannot be ignored.

Expanding Concepts of Global Business

A number of different terms are used to describe the trends in global business over the past several decades. Some of the more prominent ones include internationalization, globalization, globalism, and global capitalism. Countless businesses today have become internationalized but not necessarily globalized. **Internationalization** may be thought of as a "process by which firms increase their awareness of the influence of international activities on their future and establish and conduct transactions with firms from other countries."[10] Some of the characteristics of internationalization include exporting, acting as licensor to a foreign company, establishing joint ventures with foreign companies outside the home country, and establishing or acquiring wholly owned businesses outside the home country.[11]

By contrast, the terms **globalism** or **globalization** suggest the economic integration of the world. Globalization refers to "global economic integration of many formerly national economies into one global economy."[12] This is made possible by free trade, especially by free capital mobility, and by easy or uncontrolled migration. Whereas internationalization simply recognizes that nations increasingly rely on understandings among one another, globalization seeks the "effective erasure of national boundaries for economic purposes."[13] Though these are technical distinctions and awareness of these is helpful, in people's discussion of globalization it is not always clear whether they are using it as just another term for internationalization of business or seeing it as true global economic integration. Sometimes observers are just referring to global capitalism—the system of free movement of resources around the world. Obviously, true globalization is an extreme status that has not yet been achieved, but one that many hold as an aspiration.

According to *BusinessWeek*, globalization is a term that has come to encompass everything from "expanded trade" and "factories shifting around the world" to the "international bodies that set the rules for the global economy" (i.e., WTO, International Monetary Fund, and the World Bank).[14] For our purposes, *BusinessWeek*'s broad concept of globalism or globalization fits best. It encompasses both internationalization and trends toward globalization, and invokes the roles of the major international organizations.

What has made globalization different recently, however, is the growth of developing economies. Earlier business expanded from developed to emerging economies. Today, it flows in both directions and from one developing economy to another.[15] As the authors of a new book, *Globality*, state, business these days is all about "competing with everyone from everywhere for everything."[16] This has created a new world of hypercompetition that requires balancing growth with growth rate and the ongoing challenges of business ethics and global corporate citizenship that grow in importance.

Ongoing Backlash against Globalization

We stated earlier that there has been an evident backlash against globalization that has been most apparent since the protests in Seattle in the fall of 1999 against the activities of the WTO. The protestors at the Seattle meeting have been described in various ways. They have been identified as a peculiar meld of extreme leftists and rightists, trade unionists, radical environmentalists, and self-appointed representatives of civil society insisting on saving the poor people of developing countries from economic development.[17] They have also been described as a visible coalition between labor and environmentalists—"teamsters and turtles"—as one sign said, as well as other key constituencies, such as human rights activists.[18] In short, they are special-interest groups committed to halting the expansion of global capitalism and trade. The backlash against globalization that began in Seattle continued at a number of important, global meetings over the decade and even today remains a part of the scene at every international meeting of the world's countries.

Two later issues heightened sensitivities about globalization, especially in the United States: the trend toward the outsourcing of jobs to less-developed nations and the tenth anniversary of NAFTA.

In the past few years, no other single issue has heightened more debate over globalization in the United States than the trend toward companies moving jobs offshore. First, it was manufacturing jobs. Recently, it has been technical jobs including higher paying white-collar jobs in the information technology industry. Economists and social scientists on both sides of this issue are debating it continuously, but public opinion polls show that **outsourcing** (also called **offshoring**) jobs abroad has been unpopular, especially as unemployment has risen in the outsourcing country. Another unpopular practice is insourcing of cheap labor as manifested in the illegal alien controversy.

The second major issue to bring the subject of globalization into renewed debate was the tenth anniversary in 2004 of the **North American Free Trade Agreement (NAFTA)**. NAFTA, passed in 1994, brought under one canopy three significantly different economies—the prosperous United States, the middle-class Canada, and the striving Mexico. According to one observer, the pain of NAFTA has been felt most in the Midwest, where manufacturing jobs have been lost to Mexico and Canada, and are now being lost to China and other developing countries. It is believed that NAFTA-related job losses have been amplified by other jobs lost to globalization and that NAFTA has become the "symbol of all of that pain."[19] It is apparent that the concern over moving jobs offshore and the anniversary of NAFTA have fueled antagonism toward globalization in recent years.

The new, new world of globalization (Friedman's Globalization 3.0) is one in which the pros and cons of globalization are now back on the table for consideration and discussion. Most observers think globalization is inevitable. An opposing group thinks a form of "globophobia" has set in. The debate on globalization is likely to continue.

Globalists and Antiglobalists.   Globalization has its pros and cons. On one side we see the **globalists**, who strongly advocate open markets with private firms moving freely across the globe. They believe that investors, consumers, employees, and environmentalists are better-off due to globalization. On the other side are the **antiglobalists**, who have taken to the streets to protest the expansion and greed of corporate global enterprises. They believe that globalization is responsible for the destruction of local environments and emerging economies, abuses of human rights, the undermining of local cultures, and the sovereignty of nation-states.

The antiglobalists also decry the power of international bodies, notably the WTO, the International Monetary Fund, and the World Bank.[20] In recent years, the antiglobalists have met in their own organization, the World Social Forum, which has been called a "jamboree for NGOs, anti-capitalists, leftish intellectuals, bohemians, and bishops." The forum's main purpose is to bring together social movements from around the world to network with one another and pursue their antiglobal agenda.[21]

Figure 10-1 summarizes some of the globalists and antiglobalists views on globalization as they affect consumers, employees, the environment, developing nations, and human

FIGURE 10-1 Ethical Issues Embedded in the Pros and Cons of Globalization

Impact On:		Globalists	Antiglobalists
	Consumers	Open markets allow for free trade of goods and services, lower costs, and greater efficiency. Lower prices, greater variety of goods and services, rising living standards.	Benefits the wealthy and further impoverishes the poor. Widening wealth gap worldwide. Harmful to low-income consumers.
	Employees	Faster economic growth, higher wages, more employment, improved working conditions.	Globalism places profits above people—depressing wages, displacing workers, undermining workers' rights.
	Environment	Global capitalism means rapid economic growth, resources necessary to clean up environments, development of more efficient CO_2-reducing technologies, protection of ecosystems, pollution reduction.	Results in exploitation and destruction of ecosystems in name of corporate greed. Ignores adverse impacts on environments. More pollution, especially due to carbon dioxide. Exacerbated global warming.
	Developing Nations	Open markets and cross-border investments are keys to national economic development. Higher standards of living, better working conditions, cleaner environments.	Global capitalism, world trade bodies, world financial institutions conspire to keep developing nations in debt, destroys local economies, further impoverishes peoples.
	Human Rights	Free and open markets create cultures/institutions supporting rule of law and free expression. Spreads economic/political freedom to far corners of world (e.g., Taiwan and South Korea).	In blind pursuit of profits, global corporations ignore abuses of human rights, including political and religious oppression, false imprisonment, torture, free speech, abuses of workers, especially women and children.

Sources: Summarized from Robert Batterson and Murray Weidenbaum, *The Pros and Cons of Globalization* (St. Louis: Center for the Study of American Business, January 2001), 3–12. Also see "Pros and Cons of Globalization," http://www.buzzle.com/articles/pros-and-cons-of-globalization.html. Accessed February 22, 2010.

rights. It should be clear from these perceptions that significant ethical issues for stakeholders are embedded in globalization.

Although globalization is accepted as a reality that seems to be taking over the world; backlash against it continues today in most of the rich nations of the world. Many people in the United States and Europe view globalization as an overwhelmingly negative force, and citizens are looking to their governments to cushion the blows that have come, they believe, from their countries' trading with emerging nations.[22] *Financial Times*/Harris polls in Britain, France, the United States, and Spain revealed people were three times more likely to say that globalization was having a negative effect and not a positive effect on their countries. The opinion by executives that opening economies to freer trade is beneficial to poor and rich nations alike is not shared completely by the citizens of the rich countries.[23] In spite of the opposition and the economic meltdown that world economies have been facing since about 2008, it is expected that globalization will continue to expand in spite of the deglobalization that has been wrought by the uncertainties in the world economy.

Against this backdrop of the new, new world of business, we can consider some of the ongoing ethical challenges faced by multinational corporations as they do business in the global marketplace.

MNCs and the Global Business Environment

Multinational corporations (MNCs) operate with offices, factories, and headquarters in more than one country. They are also referred to as multinational enterprises (MNEs) and transnational corporations (TNCs). Today, most major corporations in the United States are MNCs. Not all problems of operating in a global business environment are attributable to MNCs. However, MNCs have become the symbolic heart of the problem because they represent the prototypical international business form. Fifty years ago, over half of the largest corporations in the world were based in the United States and most of them were in the manufacturing sector; this is no longer the case. Today, American MNCs are no longer dominant. MNCs from the European Union and Japan are sizable players. MNCs of developing countries continue to shoot up. Following are among the major U.S.-based MNCs: General Electric, Bank of America, JPMorgan Chase, ExxonMobil, Berkshire Hathaway, AT&T, Wal-Mart Stores, Chevron, AIG, ConocoPhillips, Citigroup, Procter & Gamble, IBM, and Wells Fargo.

Changed Scope and Nature of MNCs

Over the years, both the scope and the nature of MNCs have changed. In the early 1900s, the United Fruit Company was growing bananas in Central America and achieving a degree of notoriety for its "invasion" of Honduras. Another wave of MNCs was in the extractive industries (oil, gas, and gems). Today, financial institutions, chemical companies, pharmaceutical companies, manufacturers, and service firms represent the kinds of enterprises that may be found operating in the global business environment.

The investments of U.S.-based MNCs has been phenomenal over the past three decades or more, growing well into the hundreds of billions of dollars. Likewise, European and Asian MNCs have grown significantly during this same time period. We should also note that the most challenging situation for MNCs is when they are operating in so-called emerging nations, developing countries, or **less-developed countries (LDCs)**, where charges of exploitation, human rights violations, and abuse of power seem more plausible. These situations are ripe for charges of capitalist imperialism in struggling economies, and they are often criticized by the antiglobalists.

Underlying Challenges in a Multinational Environment

Firms face two major underlying challenges or problems as they operate in a multinational environment. One problem is that of achieving *corporate legitimacy* as the MNC seeks to be recognized and accepted in an unfamiliar society. A related problem is the fundamentally *differing philosophies* that may exist between the firm's home country and the host country in which it seeks to operate.[24] These two challenges set the stage for examining how ethical problems arise in the global environment.

Achieving Corporate Legitimacy. For an MNC to be perceived as legitimate in the eyes of a host country, it must fulfill its social responsibilities.[25] As we discussed in Chapter 2, these include economic, legal, ethical, and philanthropic responsibilities. Larger firms, in particular, are seen as outsiders, and the expectations on them are greater than on smaller, less visible firms. Further, the similarities and differences between the cultures of the two countries affect the perceived legitimacy. For example, an American firm operating in Canada is not likely to experience major problems. An American or a Western firm operating in Saudi Arabia or Turkey, by contrast, could be perceived as quite alien.[26] Differences between the values and lifestyles of managers who live in the two countries could pose serious legitimacy problems. If a host country finds the lifestyles or values of MNC managers as repugnant—as many LDCs may find the materialistic lifestyles and values of managers from advanced economies—legitimacy may be difficult to achieve.

Another, perhaps more basic, barrier to achieving legitimacy is the inherent conflict that may exist between the mission or interests of the MNC and those of the host country. The MNC seeks to *optimize globally*, while host governments seek to *optimize locally*. This may pose little difficulty for an MNC operating in a developed country, where macroeconomic or regulatory policies are sophisticated and appropriate. But it may pose serious problems in the LDCs or emerging economies, where there is often the perception that MNCs are beyond the control of local governments. In these latter situations, especially, it is not uncommon to see the local government impose various control devices, such as indigenization laws requiring majority ownership by locals, exclusion of foreign firms from certain industries, restrictions on foreign personnel, or even expropriation.[27]

Differing Philosophies between MNCs and Host Countries. Closely related to the legitimacy issue is the dilemma of MNCs that have quite different cultural or philosophical perspectives from those of their host countries. The philosophy of Western industrialized nations, and thus their MNCs, focuses on economic growth, efficiency, specialization, free trade, and comparative advantage. By contrast, many LDCs have quite different priorities. Other important objectives for them might include a more equitable income distribution or increased economic self-determination. In this context, the economically advanced nations may appear to be inherently exploitative in that their presence may perpetuate the dependency of the poorer nation.[28]

These philosophical differences build in an environment of tension that sometimes results in stringent actions being unilaterally taken by the host country. Decades ago, for example, the environment for MNCs investing in LDCs became harsh. Some of the harsh actions initiated by the host countries included outright expropriation (as occurred in the oil industry) and creeping expropriation (as occurred in the manufacturing industries when foreign subsidiaries were required to take on some local partners). Other restrictions included limits on profits repatriation.[29] As a result of the dilemmas that the MNCs have faced, it is easy to understand why business ethics expert Richard DeGeorge has argued that "First World MNCs are both the hope of the Third World and the scourge of the Third World."[30]

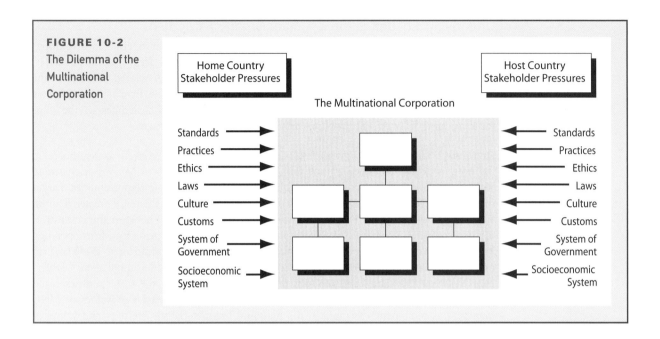

FIGURE 10-2
The Dilemma of the Multinational Corporation

Thus, MNCs often find themselves in situations where their very legitimacy to operate is in question and their philosophical perspectives may be radically different from that of their host countries. Added to this are the customary problems of operating in a foreign culture. These include different types of governments, different languages, different legal systems, diverse stakeholders, and different cultural and social values. One could well argue that ethical challenges are built into this situation. MNCs attempt to bridge the cultural gaps between two cultures; yet, as they attempt to adapt to local customs and business practices, they at times are assailed at home for not adhering to the standards, practices, laws, or ethics of their home country. Indeed, these pose ethical dilemmas for MNCs.

Figure 10-2 graphically depicts the dilemma of MNCs caught between the characteristics and expectations of their home country and those of one or more host countries. They seem to find themselves in a totally unmanageable situation, but cannot be deterred in finding working solutions.

Other MNC–Host Country Challenges

Globalization is "one of the most powerful and pervasive influences on nations, businesses, workplaces, communities, and lives…," according to Rosabeth Moss Kanter, author of *World Class: Thriving Locally in a Global Economy*.[31] Global issues are always at the forefront of CEOs' agendas. According to Richard Cavanagh, president and CEO of the Conference Board, a continuing hot topic has been "navigating the management maze of globalization."[32] As part of this, challenges facing business have been significant in the social values and ethics arenas.

There are so many issues framing the challenges between MNCs and host countries that it is almost impossible to draw limits on them. However, we must limit our focus in this chapter. Before discussing a few select ethical issues in the next section, we will first identify what a few of these broader challenges are. The fundamental issues we will touch on here include the cultural aspects of global business, business–government interactions in global operations, management and control of resources in global operations, and, finally, exploration of global markets.[33]

Facing Cultural Differences. It has been argued that the most significant reason why MNC managers fail is their inability to cope with the foreign cultural environment. Managers and companies experience culture shock when they are faced with cultures and languages that are significantly different from their own. Culture becomes one of the most critical make-or-break factors in successful multinational corporate operations. Culture, customs, language, attitudes, and institutions vary from country to country, and these differences often pose insurmountable obstacles to success for MNCs. Frequently, it is difficult to differentiate a cultural issue from an ethical issue in this environment, and this poses significant ambiguities for managers.

Business and Government Differences. Beyond the differences that stem from cultural variables, the interaction of the business and government sectors poses uncertainties for MNC executives. Depending on the region of the world and the industry under consideration, the extent of the business–government interactions may vary widely. In worldwide financial services, for example, heavy regulation was typical until the 1980s, when deregulation began in the United States and spread to other countries as well. Deregulation came fast to world banking, yet now some re-regulation is occurring.

In Europe, the government has been intimately involved in business and banking from time to time. The European Union thinks differently about the government's role in antitrust regulation than that found in the United States. Many key industries have been nationalized in Great Britain, depending on which political party is in power.[34] In the Globalization 3.0 era, multinationals are having to learn about a whole host of new business–government relationships in competing countries, especially in China, India, and Russia.

Management and Control of Global Operations. Two issues are important here. One is *organizational structure and design*, and the other is *human resource management*. MNCs must employ a multiplicity of organizational approaches in their markets. This is in significant part due to host government regulations. MNC management becomes complex when the firm licenses in Country A, has joint ventures in Country B, and countertrades in Country C. In each environment, the firm faces different organizational challenges. A second major topic is the proper use of human resources. In the arena of staffing, a question arises concerning the tactical use of home versus host country nationals. Use of each implies different costs and benefits for the firm. Other critical human resource issues include selection and training.[35] As firms globalize, another challenge is to create and enforce codes of conduct across global operations.

Exploration of Global Markets. A final topic in this section is the exploration of global markets as a vital MNC–host country challenge. Although U.S. MNCs dominated world markets for a long period of time, this is no longer the case. Today, we have a world of intense competition among firms all over the globe. In the past 20 years, there has been a remarkable resurgence, not only from Japan and the European economies but from some other countries as well (e.g., China, India, South Korea, and Latin American countries). One major issue with regard to exploration of global markets is the question of strategic alternatives that may be used by MNCs considering expansion into new foreign markets. Various strategies involving products and promotions are possible. Relevant factors in such strategic planning include the product function or need satisfied, conditions of product use, consumers' ability to buy, and communications strategy.[36]

Another major issue surrounds the pursuit of developing Third World markets, or emerging economies. Marketing concepts for Asia, Africa, and some countries in Latin America may differ markedly from those we have in the United States. This category of issue is quite important in connection with our discussion of global ethics, because LDCs pose significant temptations to MNCs to exploit and cut corners. We need to be sensitive to the long-run national interests of such countries. Three levels of sensitivity have been advocated. First, management of MNCs should be sensitive to the need to *modify or redesign products* so that they will be appropriate for their intended markets.

Second, management must be sensitive to the *impacts of products*, especially in terms of the long-term interests of non-Western markets. For example, luxury products and fundamentally labor-saving products would not necessarily be appealing under all circumstances to a development-conscious foreign government. Third, MNC managers should be sensitive to the extent to which their *products are politically vulnerable*. Products that are politically vulnerable may lead to labor agitation, public regulation (for example, price fixing and allocation quotas), nationalization, or political debates. Examples of products that in the past have led to political debates and action include sugar, salt, kerosene, gasoline, tires, and medicines.[37] A recent example is the attitude of the government of Venezuela toward the major gasoline producers.

The need to be sensitive to marketing in other countries provides an appropriate transition to our discussion of ethical issues in the global business environment. It should be clear from this discussion that ethical issues or conflicts might easily arise from cultural conditions that are not anticipated by the MNCs. Further, even though we will examine in more detail such visible issues as marketing practices, plant safety, questionable payments, and sweatshops in cheap-labor factories in developing countries, we should be ever vigilant of the fact that ethical dilemmas can also arise in such realms as operations management, financial management, risk management, labor relations, and global strategic management.

Spotlight on SUSTAINABILITY

Earth Hour: A Global Ethical Sustainability Movement

A global event called Earth Hour, which has now become an annual gesture and a combined effort by almost 5 million people in more than 100 countries, was observed successfully on March 27, 2010. The event was started in Australia in 2007 by the World Wide Fund for Nature (WWF). The organization's mission is to stop degrading Earth's natural environment and to create a low-carbon future for planet Earth.

Earth Hour is a global sustainability movement that was initiated with the hope that each year will bring about a continued celebration. The first Earth Hour was held in Australia, and after national acclaim, it gained high international interest, with more and more cities beginning to sign up for the next Earth Hour campaign.

Earth Hour has now come to be known as the world's largest global climate change initiative. The event is recognized by millions switching off their lights for one hour. Iconic buildings such as Sydney Harbour Bridge, the CN Tower in Toronto, Rome's Colosseum, India Gate, the Golden Gate Bridge in San Francisco, and many more stood in darkness in contemplation of the world's ethical responsibility to planet Earth.

Global awareness of environmental sustainability reached unprecedented levels when 192 nations took part in a historic meeting at the UN Climate Change Conference held in Copenhagen, Denmark, in December 2009.

Source: Earth Hour 2010, Infocera.com, http://www.infocera.com/Earth_Hour_2010:_a_global_sustainability_movement_organized_by_WWF_8526.htm.

Ethical Issues in the Global Business Environment

For many companies, most of the ethical problems that arise in the global environment are in the same categories as those that arise in their domestic environments. These ethical issues reside in all of the functional areas of business: production/operations, marketing, finance, accounting, and management. These issues concern the fair treatment of stakeholders—employees, customers, the community, and competitors—and involve product safety, plant safety, advertising practices, human resource management, human rights, environmental problems, business practices, and so on.

These ethical problems seem to be somewhat fewer in developed countries, but they exist there as well. The ethical challenges seem to be more acute in underdeveloped countries, LDCs, or developing countries because these countries are at earlier stages of economic development and typically do not have a legal or ethical infrastructure in place to help protect their citizenry. This situation creates an environment in which there is temptation to go with lower standards, or perhaps no standard, because few government regulations or activist groups exist to protect the stakeholders' interests. In the LDCs, the opportunities for business exploitation and the engagement in questionable practices (by developed countries' standards) are abundant.

ETHICS IN PRACTICE CASE

An Innocent Revelation?

For a couple of years, I worked as an assistant manager at a gas station in my hometown Randers, Denmark. The location of the station was perfect, which was evident by the long queues and big sales every day. The job was scheduled in such a way that the person on duty would always manage the station single-handedly, standing behind the desk, running the cash register. Every day, several thousand dollars were secured in the gas station's safe. Six people worked there—all around the age of 18.

The key to the station's safe was hidden at some place, which only the employees and the manager knew. The manager would take the money stored in the safe and deposit it at the local bank every third day, but one week this action was postponed a couple of days because of a holiday. Therefore, a large sum of money got accumulated at the station. One employee was aware of this fact and revealed it to her friends. At the same time, she agreed to tell about the place where the key was kept, and within a few days her friends broke into the station, found the key, and stole nearly $19,000.

The employee and her friends had figured out that the insurance company would pay for the manager's losses and therefore all parties would be satisfied, except for the insurance company, that, they thought, would not really be affected by the loss. They claimed, "Everybody knows how rich these insurance companies are."

However, it turned out that the insurance company did not pay, because the key was hidden in the same room where the safe was, and this apparently voided the insurance policy.

The ethical question in this story is, if you knew that no one would discover the employee's irresponsible decision to tell about the hidden key and that the insurance company would reimburse the manager, would you also have done the same thing if you had received a fairly big portion of the money? In this case, assume that the insurance company could easily afford the reimbursement, which means that all parties should be satisfied (and you would get a little richer).

1. What are the ethical issues in this case? Is it a situation unique to business in Denmark?

2. If the employee's decision to tell about the hidden key was never discovered, could her action somehow be justified as just an innocent revelation? Why or why not? Identify the ethical principles involved here.

3. Imagine that the employee's revelation was never discovered. Would you have chosen to do as she did if we assume that the manager got reimbursed? Many of us pay a lot of money in insurance premiums, so why not get a little back?

Contributed by Anders Braad

We will discuss some prominent categories of ethical issues in the global sphere to provide some appreciation of the development of these kinds of issues for business. We will discuss two classic ethical issues that have arisen with regard to questionable marketing and manufacturing safety practices. Then, we will discuss the issue of labor or human rights abuses often found in "sweatshops" (the use of cheap labor in developing countries)—a topic that has dominated international business discussions for the past decade and a half. Next, we will consider the special problems of corruption, bribery, and questionable payments. From these examples, we should be able to develop an appreciation of the kinds of ethical challenges that confront all MNCs doing business globally.

Questionable Marketing and Plant Safety Practices

A classic example of a *questionable marketing practice* is the now-infamous infant formula controversy that spanned most of the 1970s, continued into the 1980s and 1990s, and remains an issue today. The *plant safety issue* is best illustrated by examining the Union Carbide Bhopal crisis that began in 1984, continued into the 1990s, and is not completely resolved today. These issues are significant because they illustrate the endless problems companies can face as a result of mistakes made in global business ethics and how their effects can be felt for decades. It is easy to now predict that BP's oil spill in the Gulf of Mexico will be in this classic category some day as its repercussions are likely to last for decades.

Questionable Marketing: The Infant Formula Controversy.   The **infant formula controversy** is a classic example that illustrates ethical questions that can arise while doing business abroad. We will briefly reveal some basic facts about this now-classic case.[38] For decades, there was this realization among physicians working in tropical lands (many of which were LDCs) that severe health risks were posed to infants from bottle-feeding as opposed to breast-feeding. Such countries typically had neither refrigeration nor sanitary conditions. Water supplies were not pure, and therefore, powdered infant formula mixed with bacteria-infected water likely led to disease and diarrhea in the bottle-fed infant. Because people in these LDCs are typically poor, mothers tend to overdilute the powdered formula, trying to make it last longer, thus diminishing significantly the amount of nutrition the infant receives. Once a mother begins bottle-feeding, her capacity for breast-feeding quickly diminishes. Poverty also leads the mother to put less expensive substitute products such as powdered whole milk and cornstarch in the bottle. These products are not acceptable substitutes, but they save money. They are nutritionally inadequate and unsatisfactory for the baby's digestive system.

By the late 1960s, it was apparent that in LDCs there was increased bottle-feeding, decreased breast-feeding, and a dramatic increase in the numbers of malnourished and sick babies because of this. The ethical debate began when it was noted that several of the infant formula companies, aware of the conditions just described, were promoting their products and, therefore, promoting bottle-feeding in an intense way. Such marketing practices as mass advertising, billboards, radio jingles, and free samples became commonplace. These promotional devices typically portrayed the infants who used their products as healthy and robust, in sharp contrast with the reality that was brought about by the conditions mentioned.

One of the worst marketing practices entailed the use of "milk nurses"—women dressed in nurses' uniforms, walking the halls of maternity wards and urging mothers to get their babies started on formula. In reality, these women were sales representatives employed by the companies on a commission basis. Once the infants began bottle-feeding, the mothers' capacity to breast-feed diminished, and they became hooked on the formula.[39]

Although several companies were engaging in these questionable marketing practices, the Swiss conglomerate Nestlé was singled out by a Swiss social activist group in an article entitled "Nestlé Kills Babies." At about the same time, an article appeared in Great Britain entitled "The Baby Killers."[40] From this point on, a protracted controversy developed, with Nestlé and other infant formula manufacturers on one side and a host of organizations on the other side filing shareholder resolutions and lawsuits against the company. Among the groups that were actively involved in the controversy were church groups such as the National Council of Churches and its Interfaith Center on Corporate Responsibility (ICCR), UNICEF, the World Health Organization (WHO), and the Infant Formula Action Coalition (INFACT). Nestlé was singled out because it had the largest share of the world market and because it aggressively pushed sales of its infant formula in developing countries, even after the WHO developed a sales code to the contrary.[41]

In 1977, INFACT and ICCR organized and led a national boycott against Nestlé that continued for almost seven years. More than 70 American organizations representing doctors, nurses, teachers, churches, and other professionals participated in the boycott. These groups mounted an international campaign aimed at changing these objectionable marketing practices in the LDCs.[42] In 1984, after spending tens of millions of dollars resisting the boycott, Nestlé finally reached an accord with the protesters. The company agreed to make some changes in its business practices. The protesters, in return, agreed to end their boycott but to continue monitoring Nestlé's performance.[43]

The infant formula controversy continued through the 1980s and well into the 1990s. In 1991, Nestlé (which controlled more than 40 percent of the worldwide market) and American Home Products (which controlled about 15 percent of the worldwide market) announced that after decades of boycotts and controversy, they planned to discontinue the practice of providing free and low-cost formula to developing countries. With this action—its most aggressive ever—Nestlé attempted to quell the protracted criticism that it had defied WHO's marketing restrictions by dumping huge quantities of baby formula on Third World hospitals. The distribution of supply had been a lingering concern in the infant formula controversy. Until this announcement, Nestlé had supplied formula on a request basis, but over the next several years it planned to distribute formula only on a request basis to children "in need," as outlined in the WHO guidelines. The pledges by Nestlé and American Home Products, the world's two largest infant formula makers, were regarded as a watershed in the bitter infant formula controversy.[44]

The infant formula controversy illustrates the character of questionable business practices by firms pursuing what might be called normal practices were it not for the fact that they were being pursued in foreign countries where local circumstances made them suspect.[45] The infant formula controversy also illustrates the endurance of certain ethical issues, particularly in the global arena.

Later, the AIDS crisis, especially in Africa, put an unusual twist on the infant formula debate. Some now say that UNICEF, the UN agency charged with protecting children, today may be indirectly responsible for thousands of African babies being infected with the deadly AIDS virus. AIDS entered the picture since the early boycotts of Nestlé and others, and it was discovered that HIV-infected mothers could transfer the disease through breast-feeding to their own children. In response to this problem, Nestlé and formula maker Wyeth-Ayerst Labs said they stood ready to donate tons of free formula to the infected women. However, UNICEF refused to give the green light to these gifts. Nestlé claims it had gotten desperate requests from African hospitals for free formula, but the company would not act without UNICEF's approval because it did not want to renew the boycott against the company. The executive director of UNICEF, meanwhile, said that she didn't believe Nestlé and the other infant formula providers had a particular role to play in the AIDS crisis. She thinks they should just comply with the WHO code.[46]

Critics of Nestlé continued beyond the AIDS issue. For years now, the allegation has been that Nestlé is trying to market infant formula to Hispanic mothers in the United

States to boost their share of this $3 billion market. The major question seems to be whether companies such as Nestlé should market baby formula to low-income immigrant mothers, many in California, when health experts and government officials maintain that breast-feeding is healthier and saves in terms of long-term health care costs. A spokeswoman for Nestlé said that the product is being marketed with a fully bilingual label so that Hispanic mothers can make an informed choice.[47]

Even today, the International Baby Food Action Network (IBFAN) (http://www.ibfan.org/) continues to advocate safety in feeding babies and lobbies against companies that continue engaging in questionable business and marketing practices.[48] With the AIDS crisis and marketing in the United States to low-income mothers complicating the controversy, it is apparent that no quick solutions are available.

Plant Safety and the Bhopal Tragedy. The Union Carbide **Bhopal tragedy** brings into sharp focus the challenges of multinationals operating in a foreign, particularly less-developed, business environment. The legal issues surrounding this event have not yet been totally resolved and may not be for years to come in spite of earlier agreements reached. On December 3, 1984, the leakage of methyl isocyanate gas caused what many have termed the "worst industrial accident in history." The gas leak killed more than 2,000 people and injured 200,000 others. The tragedy has raised numerous legal, ethical, social, and technical questions for MNCs.[49] Observers who have studied this tragedy say the death toll and destruction are many times greater than the "official" numbers indicate. One report is that more than 3,500 were killed in the accident.[50]

Interviews with experts just after the accident revealed a belief that the responsibility for the accident had to be shared by the company and the Indian government. According to Union Carbide's own inspector, the Bhopal plant did not meet U.S. standards and had not been inspected in over two years. The Indian government allowed thousands of people to live very near the plant, and there were no evacuation procedures.[51]

Many different questions have been raised by the Bhopal disaster. Among the more important of these issues are the following:[52]

1. To what extent should MNCs maintain identical standards at home and abroad regardless of how lax laws are in the host country?
2. How advisable is it to locate a complex and dangerous plant in an area where the entire workforce is basically unskilled and uneducated, and where the populace is ignorant of the inherent risks posed by such plants?
3. How wise are laws that require plants to be staffed entirely by local employees?
4. What is the responsibility of corporations and governments in allowing the use of otherwise safe products that become dangerous because of local conditions? (This question applies to the infant formula controversy also.)
5. After reviewing all the problems, should certain kinds of plants even be located in developing nations?

At the heart of these issues is the question of differing safety standards in various parts of the world. This dilemma arose in the 1970s, when American firms continued to export drugs and pesticides that had been outlawed in the United States. Pesticides, such as DDT and others that had been associated with cancer, were shipped to and used in LDCs by farmers who may not have understood the dangers of or the cautions needed in using these products. Not surprisingly, poisonings occurred. In 1972, thousands of Iraqis died from mercury-treated grain from the United States. In 1975, many Egyptian farmers were killed and yet others became ill by a U.S.-made pesticide. Asbestos- and pesticide-manufacturing plants that violated American standards were built in several countries. These companies typically broke no laws in the host countries, but many experts are now saying that the Bhopal tragedy has taught us that companies have a moral responsibility to enforce high standards, especially in developing countries not yet ready or able to regulate these firms.[53]

One major problem that some observers say contributed to the Bhopal gas leak and, indeed, applies to MNCs generally is the requirement that firms be significantly owned by investors in the host country. Union Carbide owned only 50.9 percent of the subsidiary in Bhopal, India. It has been suggested that this situation may have reduced Union Carbide's motivation and/or capacity to ensure adequate industrial and environmental safety at its Bhopal plant, mainly by diluting the degree of parent control and reducing the flow of technical expertise into that plant. If developing countries continue to insist on a dilution of MNC control over manufacturing plants, this may also diminish the MNC's motivation and incentive to transfer environmental management and safety competence.

Another major problem highlighted by the Bhopal gas leak was the fact that the people of developing countries are often unaware of the dangers of new technology. As one expert observed, countries such as India (at the time) had not "internalized the technological culture."[54] Although the LDCs want technology because they see it as critical to their economic development, often their ability to understand and manage the new technology is in serious doubt.

The complexity and tragedy of the Bhopal gas leak case for its victims, the Indian government, and Union Carbide are attested to by the fact that this issue is unresolved even today. In 1989, Union Carbide extricated itself from relief efforts by agreeing to pay the Indian government $470 million to be divided among victims and their families. By 1993, courts had distributed only $3.1 million of this sum. The overburdened government relief programs in India have been mired in mismanagement and corruption. It has been observed that virtually every level of the relief bureaucracy in India is rife with corruption. Government officials demanded bribes from illiterate victims trying to obtain documents required for their relief money. Doctors took bribes from victims to testify in their court cases, and unscrupulous agents fished for bribes by claiming they could get victims' cases expedited on the crowded docket. Claims courts that would determine final compensation for victims were not set up until 1992—eight years after the gas leak. Lawyers and officials say it could be another 20 years before this case is settled.[55]

Dow Chemical Co. bought Union Carbide in 2001. Even today the Union Carbide tragedy continues to haunt Dow Chemical over two decades after the accident. Survivors of the accident and their supporters continue to push Dow to pay more than $1 billion in additional damages for what they claim are unmet medical bills and toxic cleanup.[56] Dow continues to argue that the $470 million settlement it paid in 1989 resolved its outstanding liabilities.[57] The company continues to argue that it never owned nor operated the Bhopal plant, which is now under the control of the state government of Madhya Pradesh, India. It says that the plant site is now owned by the state and that it is up to them to decide what to do with the property.[58]

Current Web pages (http://www.bhopal.org, http://www.bhopal.net, and http://www.bhopal.com) document that the Bhopal tragedy continues to be of deep concern even today—over 25 years after the tragedy. Like the infant formula controversy, it is an ethical issue that won't be forgotten.

The lessons from the Bhopal disaster are many and will continue to be debated. In companies around the globe, the Bhopal disaster has sparked continued controversy in the debate about operating abroad. To be sure, legal and ethical issues are central to the discussions. What is at stake, however, is not just the practices of businesses abroad but also the very question of their presence. Depending on the final outcome of the Union Carbide case, MNCs may decide that the risks of doing certain types of business abroad are just too great.

Sweatshops, Human Rights, and Labor Abuses

No issue has been more consistently evident in the global business ethics debate than the MNCs' use and abuse of women and children in cheap-labor factories in developing countries. The major players in this controversy, large corporations, have highly recognizable names—Nike, Walmart, Gap, Kmart, Reebok, J. C. Penney, and Disney, to name a few. The countries and regions of the world that have been involved are also recognizable— Southeast Asia, Pakistan, Indonesia, Honduras, Dominican Republic, Thailand, China, the Philippines, Mexico, and Vietnam. Sweatshops have not been eliminated in the United States either, but the most serious problems seem to be in the developing countries.[59]

Though **sweatshops**, characterized by child labor, low pay, poor working conditions, worker exploitation, and health and safety violations, have existed for decades, they have grown in number in the past decade as global competition has heated up and corporations have gone to the far reaches of the world to lower their costs and increase their productivity. A landmark event that brought the sweatshop issue into sharp focus was the 1996 revelation by labor rights activists that part of Walmart's Kathie Lee Collection, a line of clothes endorsed by then prominent U.S. talk-show host Kathie Lee Gifford, was made in Honduras by seamstresses slaving 20 hours a day for 31 cents an hour.

The revelation helped turn Gifford, who was unaware of where the clothes were being made or under what conditions, into an anti-sweatshop activist.[60] The Nike Corporation also became a lightning rod for social activists concerned about overseas manufacturing conditions, standards, and ethics. A major reason for this was the company's high profile and visibility, extensive advertising using athletic superstars, as well as the stark contrast between the tens of millions of dollars Nike icons Michael Jordan and Tiger Woods earned and the several dollars of daily wage rate the company's subcontractors once paid their Indonesian workers.[61]

Critics of MNC labor practices, including social activist groups, labor unions, student groups, and grassroots organizations, have been speaking out, criticizing business abusers and raising public awareness. These critics claim many businesses are exploiting children and women by paying them poverty wages, working them to exhaustion, punishing them for minor violations, violating health and safety standards, and tearing apart their families. Many of these companies counter that they offer the children and women workers a superior alternative. They say that although their wage rates are embarrassing by developed-world standards, those rates frequently equal or exceed local legal minimum wages, or average wages.

Defenders of sweatshops further say that because so many workers in LDCs work in agriculture and farming, where they make less than the average wage, the low but legal minimums in many countries put sweatshop workers among the higher-paid ones in their areas.[62] A study conducted by economists found that MNCs generally paid more, often a lot more, than the wages offered by locally owned companies. In one study, it was found that affiliates of U.S. MNCs pay a wage premium that ranges from 40 percent to 100 percent higher than the local average pay in low-income countries.[63]

Fair Labor Association (FLA).   The sweatshop issue has been so prominent in the past decade that to improve their situations or images, many criticized companies have begun working diligently to improve working conditions, further joint initiatives, establish codes of conduct or standards for themselves and their subcontractors, conduct social or ethical audits, or take other steps. In 1996, former President Clinton, with Kathie Lee Gifford, was instrumental in helping to establish the **Fair Labor Association (FLA)** (http://www.fairlabor.org), a nonprofit organization of clothing firms, unions, and human rights groups focused on the worldwide elimination of sweatshops. Participating companies make a sustained corporate commitment to the FLA to bring their entire supply chain into the FLA program. Current participating companies include Adidas Group, Follett Higher Education Group, Liz Claiborne, Inc., New Balance Athletic Shoes, Nike, Inc., Patagonia, Russell Corporation, and Tumi, Inc.

The FLA is still very active, but there have been a number of other proposals aimed at eliminating or improving sweatshops. Some call for clothing firms and their contractors to impose a code of conduct that would prohibit child labor, forced labor, and worker abuse; establish health and safety regulations; recognize workers' right to join a union; limit the workweek to 60 hours (except in exceptional business circumstances); and insist that workers be paid at least the legal minimum wage (or the "prevailing industry wage") in every country in which garments are made. Under such proposals, the garment industry would also create an association to police the agreement.

These proposals have some drawbacks, however. For example, the legal minimum wage in many developing countries is below the poverty line. In addition, the "prevailing industry wage" could prove to be a convenient escape clause. Some groups are also concerned that the task force has, in effect, sanctioned 60 hour workweeks and that it will still allow 14-year-olds to work if local laws do. Another big issue will be monitoring the agreements abroad. For example, Liz Claiborne alone has 200 contractors in over 25 countries. Furthermore, in some countries, like the Philippines, Malaysia, Thailand, and Vietnam, sweatshops go to great lengths to hide their business dealings by "fronting" businesses using false documents to "prove" they pay minimum wages and by intimidating workers to keep quiet.[64]

Social Accountability 8000 (SA8000). Another initiative to improve sweatshop conditions was created by **Social Accountability International (SAI)**. The scheme called Social Accountability 8000 or SA8000 was designed to piggyback on the ISO8000 quality-auditing system of the International Standards Organization (ISO), now used in over 57 countries and 71 industries.[65]

The SA8000 initiative involves a broad spectrum of U.S. and foreign companies, such as Avon, Sainsbury, and Toys 'R' Us, plus such labor and human rights groups as KPMG-Peat Marwick and SGS-ICS. The current standards for SA8000 may be summarized as follows:[66]

1. *Child Labor:* No workers under the age of 15; minimum lowered to 14 for countries operating under the ILO Convention 138 developing-country exception; remediation of any child found to be working.
2. *Forced Labor:* No forced labor, including prison or debt bondage labor; no lodging of deposits or identity papers by employers or outside recruiters.
3. *Health and Safety:* Provision of safe and healthy work environment; steps to prevent injuries; regular health and safety worker training; system to detect threats to health and safety; access to bathrooms and potable water.
4. *Freedom of Association and Right to Collective Bargaining:* Respect the right to form and join trade unions and bargain collectively; where law prohibits these freedoms, facilitate parallel means of association and bargaining.
5. *Discrimination:* No discrimination based on race, caste, origin, religion, disability, gender, sexual orientation, union or political affiliation, or age; no sexual harassment.
6. *Discipline:* No corporal punishment, mental or physical coercion, or verbal abuse.
7. *Working Hours:* Comply with the applicable law but, in any event, no more than 48 hours per week with at least one day off for every seven-day period; voluntary overtime paid at a premium rate and not to exceed 12 hours per week on a regular basis; overtime may be mandatory if part of a collective bargaining agreement.

8. *Compensation:* Wages paid for a standard workweek must meet the legal and industry standards and be sufficient to meet the basic need of workers and their families; no disciplinary deductions.

9. *Management Systems:* Facilities seeking to gain and maintain certification must go beyond simple compliance to integrate the standard into their management systems and practices.[67]

The SA8000 process offers companies the opportunity to be certified. To certify conformance with SA8000, every facility seeking certification must be audited. Thus auditors will visit factories and assess corporate practice on a wide range of issues and evaluate the state of a company's management systems, necessary to ensure ongoing acceptable practices. Once an organization has implemented any necessary improvements, it can earn a certificate attesting to its compliance with SA8000. This certification provides a public report of good practice to consumers, buyers, and other companies and is intended to be a significant milestone in improving workplace conditions.[68] As of September 2009, there were 2,093 certified facilities in the world, representing 64 countries, 66 industries, and 1.15 million employees.[69]

Individual Company Initiatives.   In addition to the initiatives by such industry organizations as the FLA and the SAI (SA8000), it is important to highlight some of the efforts by individual companies to address the issues surrounding sweatshops. A number of companies have developed *global outsourcing guidelines* and codes and have made important strides in attempts at self-monitoring of their production facilities in LDCs. Companies such as Nike, Levi Strauss & Co., and Gap are notable examples.[70]

In the spirit of transparency, Gap, Inc. released a 40-page report in 2004 that offered an unusual look at its factory conditions abroad. It updated this report in its 2007–2008 Social Responsibility Report. Gap's report revealed that the working conditions at many of its 3,000 factories worldwide were far from perfect. The Gap report documented a wide variety of workforce violations at plants making its clothing but revealed even worse conditions at plants vying to win Gap contracts. Some of the details revealed in the report were quite specific. The company found that 10 to 25 percent of its factories in China, Taiwan, and Saipan were using psychological coercion or verbal abuse. More than 50 percent of the factories visited in sub-Saharan Africa ran machinery without proper safety devices. As a result, the company revoked contracts with 136 factories because of severe or persistent violations. Critics of sweatshops said they were pleased with the move toward greater openness. A representative from the Interfaith Center on Corporate Responsibility in New York described the report as a "major step forward."[71] Beginning with its 2005–2006 Social Responsibility Report, Gap pledged to issue a report every two years. Its most recent report was released in 2009, which covered updates from 2007–2008.[72] Due to data gathering, the reports tend to lag by several years. Gap's strategy has motivated a number of other companies to be more forthright about their factories overseas.

Despite the best of efforts by some companies to improve factory conditions in emerging countries, there is growing evidence that some suppliers have learned how to conceal abuses and continue to get away with unacceptable practices. In a major report, *BusinessWeek* disclosed that many factories, especially in China, have learned how to "game the system" through questionable practices. Some of these practices include keeping double sets of books; scripted responses wherein managers and employees are tutored how to answer auditor's questions about hours, pay, and safety practices; and hidden production, whereby plants meet U.S. demands by secretly shifting work to subcontractors that violate pay and safety standards, but these subcontractors are hidden from the auditors.[73]

Sweatshops and labor abuses sharply contrast the "haves" and the "have-nots" of the world's nations. Consumers in developed countries have benefited greatly from the lower prices made possible by cheap labor. It remains to be seen how supportive those consumers will be when prices rise because MNCs improve wage rates and conditions in LDCs. The MNCs face a continuing and volatile ethical issue that is not likely to go away. Their profits, public image, and reputations may hinge on how well they respond. The MNCs must handle a new dimension in their age-old quest to balance shareholder profits with the desires of expanded, global stakeholders who want better corporate social performance. In the age of transparency, we should expect more revelations in the years to come.

Alien Tort Claims Act and Human Rights Violations.

Looking beyond possible human rights violations in sweatshops, claims that companies may have violated the human rights of foreign nationals may come back to haunt firms that have been accused of more serious human rights abuses. What is at stake is the U.S. courts' interpretation of an obscure piece of legislation known as the **Alien Tort Claims Act (ATCA)**. Though researchers cannot determine why Congress passed this little-known act in 1789, today it is the centerpiece of a controversy that may have widespread implications for American firms operating abroad. An interesting development has been the recent efforts to use ATCA to sue transnational companies for violations of international law in countries outside the United States. The ATCA allows foreign individuals to sue U.S. firms in U.S. courts for companies' actions abroad. If these suits succeed, the ATCA could become a powerful tool to increase corporate accountability around the globe.[74]

Current cases under adjudication in the United States are of interest to U.S.-based MNCs because they are increasingly being named as defendants in Alien Tort cases for doing business in countries with repressive governments. Some of the lawsuits allege that the companies are aiding and abetting human rights abuses of various host governments.[75] Among the ongoing representative cases have been the following:[76]

Occidental Petroleum of Los Angeles. *Relatives of people who were killed in an airstrike by the Columbian military say that the company, Occidental Petroleum, should pay them damages because its security contractor worked with the military to take out leftist terrorists accused of sabotaging Occidental's pipeline operation. In this case, the plaintiffs say the attack killed 17 unarmed civilians.*

Del Monte. *The company was sued by five union officials in Guatemala who say they were kidnapped by armed men hired by Del Monte's subsidiary and were forced to quit their jobs at a banana farm.*

Chevron. *The company fought a lawsuit filed by Nigerians who claimed Chevron should be liable for the killing of protestors by Nigerian security forces outside a refinery owned by its subsidiary. On December 1, 2008, after one month of trial proceedings, a federal jury in California handed Chevron a complete victory. The jury found that the Nigerian government, and not Chevron, was responsible for the violent end to the protest.*[77]

Geo W. Drummond, Ltd. of Alabama. *The plaintiffs in this case accused Drummond's subsidiary in Colombia of paying death squads to kill labor leaders. However, in 2007, after only four hours of deliberation, a federal jury returned a verdict in favor of Drummond, finding it was not complicit in the murders.*

There are many more cases, but the ones mentioned above illustrate the kinds of charges that can be made against the U.S. firms.

A lawyer for Drummond, Ltd. stated about its lawsuit: "I realize that there are problems in lots of different countries, but to have the U.S. courts attempt to provide remedies for all the injustices that occur in countries around the world is not a rational system."[78]

Many of the companies say that they are being unfairly targeted by liberal activists who are using the law to try to remedy the injustices of foreign governments. Many of the lawyers for these companies also say the companies are being blamed for crimes they deplore and know nothing about. The president of the National Foreign Trade Council observed that the ATCA statute is being misused and that it is being exploited by trial lawyers who have seized the law as their new "asbestos" litigation and are hoping to get rich by hitting the jackpot.[79]

If upheld in these applications, the ATCA could represent a devastating level of legal and financial liability for U.S.-based MNCs engaged in global business. Suddenly, what were once human rights ethical issues could become significant and costly legal issues. We know from the Nestlé and Bhopal cases that these crises are not quickly resolved. These are definitely cases to be carefully watched.

Corruption, Bribery, and Questionable Payments

It could easily be argued that the most frequent and severe ethical problems with respect to global business are corruption, bribes, and questionable payments. These problems are as old as history itself, but in the past decade governments around the world have escalated their attempts to eliminate them. In the United States alone, the Department of Justice (DoJ) and the Securities and Exchange Commission (SEC), both responsible for the Foreign Corrupt Practices Act prosecutions, filed a record number of cases in 2008 and 2009, the most recent years for which data were available.[80]

Corruption in global business continues to be the overarching problem. It starts with outright bribery of government officials and the giving of questionable political contributions. Beyond these, there are many other corrupt activities: the misuse of company assets for political favors, kickbacks and protection money for police, free junkets for government officials, secret price-fixing agreements, and insider dealing, just to mention a few. All of these activities have one thing in common. They are attempts to influence the outcomes of decisions wherein the nature and extent of the influence are not made public. In essence, these activities are abuses of power.[81] They undermine the system of free trade.

Though one seldom hears an official definition of corruption, such synonyms as dishonesty, sleaze, fraud, deceit, and cheating are typically assumed. Some of the definitions of corruption that have been set forth include the following:[82]

Behavior on the part of officials in the public sector, whether politicians or civil servants, in which they improperly and unlawfully enrich themselves, or those close to them, by the misuse of the public power entrusted to them. This would include embezzlement of funds, theft of corporate or public property as well as corrupt practices such as bribery, extortion or influence peddling. (Transparency International [TI])

Corruption involves behavior on the part of officials in the public and private sectors, in which they improperly and unlawfully enrich themselves and/or those close to them, or induce others to do so, by misusing the position in which they are placed. (World Bank)

Corruption comes in many forms, some petty and some grand. Though hugely lucrative to a few, corruption is incredibly damaging in terms of its effects on stakeholders. It corrodes the rule of law, the legitimacy of government, the sanctity of property rights, and incentives to invest and accumulate. Corruption also is a drag on a country's growth. One study said that Columbia's GDP would rise by about 20 percent if corruption decreased there.[83] A major problem, of course, is that those who benefit from corruption most will resist attempts to curb it, and often these are politicians who play decision-making roles.

Bribery has been the subject of continuing debate, more than any other form of corruption, and the practice merits closer examination. Simply speaking, bribery is the practice of offering something (usually money) in order to gain an illicit advantage. Bribes, of course, are illegal in most places and generally held to be unethical, but it is informative to consider the arguments that have been set forth for and against them. Some business-people continue to argue that bribery is necessary, and some countries of the world continue to assert that they are culturally obligatory or defensible.

Arguments for and against Bribery. Arguments typically given in favor of permitting bribery include the following: (1) they are necessary for profits in order to do business; (2) everybody does it—it will happen anyway; (3) it is an accepted practice in many countries—it is normal and expected; and (4) bribes are forms of commissions, taxes, or compensation for conducting business between cultures.

Arguments frequently cited against giving bribes include the following: (1) bribes are inherently wrong and cannot be accepted under any circumstances; (2) bribes are illegal in the United States and most developed nations and, therefore, unfair elsewhere; (3) one should not compromise her or his own beliefs; (4) managers should not deal with corrupt governments; (5) such demands, once started, never stop; (6) one should take a stand for honesty, morality, and ethics; (7) those receiving bribes are the only ones who benefit; (8) bribes create dependence on corrupt individuals and countries; and (9) bribes deceive stockholders and pass on costs to customers.[84]

The costs of bribes and other forms of corruption are seldom fully understood or described. Several studies suggest the economic costs of such corrupt activities. When government officials accept "speed" money or "grease payments" to issue licenses, the economic cost is 3 to 10 percent above the licensing fee. When tax collectors permit underreporting of income in exchange for a bribe, income tax revenues may be reduced by up to 50 percent. When government officials take kickbacks, goods and services may be priced 20 to 100 percent higher than they actually could have been. In addition to these direct economic costs, there are many indirect costs—demoralization and cynicism and moral revulsion against politicians and the political system. Due to bribery and corruption, politicians have been swept from office in countries such as Brazil, Italy, Japan, and Korea.[85]

The Foreign Corrupt Practices Act (FCPA). One of the first initiatives by a major government to address the problem of corruption and bribery in international business was the passage of the U.S. **Foreign Corrupt Practices Act** in 1977. Before this, many of the payments and bribes made by U.S.-based MNCs were not illegal. Even so, firms could have been engaging in illegal activities depending on whether and how the payments were reported to the Internal Revenue Service (IRS). With the passage of the FCPA, however, it became a criminal offense for a representative of an American corporation to offer or give payments to the officials of other governments for the purpose of getting or maintaining business. The FCPA specifies a series of fines and prison terms that can result if a company or management is found guilty of a violation.[86] The legislation was passed not only for legal and ethical reasons but also out of a concern for the image and reputation of the United States abroad.

The FCPA differentiates between bribes and facilitating payments, also called **grease payments**. The law does not prohibit so-called grease payments, or minor, facilitating payments to officials, for the primary purpose of getting them to do whatever they are supposed to do anyway. Such payments are commonplace in many countries. The real

ETHICS IN PRACTICE CASE

I Love My Job—Just Don't Ask How I Got It!

Last spring, one of my very close friends graduated with an MBA. She interviewed with many companies during her last semester at school. However, there was no job. After graduating, she decided to apply to other companies. At one of the companies, she got pre-selected and then selected for the final round of interviews. After the final interview was conducted, she was informed that a decision would be mailed to her within the next six weeks.

My friend's father happened to know the general manager of this company. When there was no reply for almost five weeks, he decided to speak with the general manager. The general manager checked with the human resources department and informed my friend's father that his daughter had not been short-listed and, therefore, was not being considered in the final list of applicants for a position.

About five days later, my friend's father called the general manager again, but this time for something else. He had decided to offer a bribe to the general manager, in order to get his daughter the job. Bribing high-ranking managers to secure employment is an accepted practice in my country. A sum of money was mutually agreed upon, and my friend's father personally delivered the cash to the general manager. Within the next four weeks, she was offered the management trainee position.

After working there for a month, my friend told me this whole story and how glad she was that her father had done all this for her. She loved her job and said that she couldn't have been happier anywhere else. She also told me not to mention this to anyone because it would harm her family's reputation. Bribing is an accepted practice in my country, but not out in the open.

1. Is it ethical to give or take bribes just because everybody does it and it is an accepted practice in one's country?

2. If bribery is an accepted practice, why did the friend want to keep this quiet?

3. Should employees be hired on the basis of merit or according to how much they can bribe to secure a job?

4. If you had been in my friend's place, would you have accepted the job?

Contributed by Radhika Sadanah

problem is that some forms of payments are prohibited (for example, bribes), but other payments (for example, grease payments) are not prohibited. The law is sometimes ambiguous on the distinctions between the two.[87]

To violate the FCPA, payments (other than grease payments) must be made corruptly to obtain business. This suggests some kind of *quid pro quo*. The idea of a corrupt *quid pro quo* payment to a foreign official may seem clear in the abstract, but the circumstances of the payment may easily blur the distinction between what is acceptable "grease" (e.g., payments to expedite mail pickup or delivery, to obtain a work permit, or to process paperwork) and what is illegal bribery. The safest strategy for managers to take is to be careful and to seek a legal opinion when questions arise.

Figure 10-3 presents a basic distinction, with examples, between bribes (which are prohibited) and grease (or facilitating) payments (which are not prohibited) based on the FCPA.

The FCPA was intended to have and has had a significant impact on the way American firms do business globally. A number of firms that paid bribes to foreign officials have been the subject of criminal and civil enforcement actions, resulting in large fines and, sometimes, suspension and debarment from federal procurement contracting. Sometimes their employees and officers have been imprisoned as well.[88] From 2007 to 2010, the DoJ has been cracking down on bribery abroad at an accelerating pace.[89] The consensus seems to be that the increased prosecutions have been driven by the DoJ's

FIGURE 10-3 Bribes Compared to Grease Payments

Definitions	Examples
Grease Payments	
Relatively small sums of money given for the purpose of getting minor officials to: • Do what they are supposed to be doing • Do what they are supposed to be doing faster or sooner • Do what they are supposed to be doing better than they would otherwise do	Money given to minor officials (clerks, attendants, or customs inspectors) for the purpose of expediting. This form of payment helps get goods or services through red tape or administrative bureaucracies.
Bribes	
Relatively large amounts of money given for the purpose of influencing officials to make decisions or take actions that they otherwise might not take. If the officials considered the merits of the situation only, they might take some other action.	Money given, often to high-ranking officials. Purpose is often to get these people to purchase goods or services from the bribing firm. May also be used to avoid taxes, forestall unfavorable government intervention, secure favorable treatment, and so on.

post-Enron enthusiasm and companies' increased reporting of violations under the Sarbanes–Oxley Act.[90]

The DoJ's crackdown on corrupt practices has taken a new turn in that it is now attempting to catch both U.S. and foreign-based companies. Unbeknownst to many, foreign companies whose securities are publicly traded in the United States now are also subject to the FCPA.[91] The DoJ has prosecuted over four times the number of foreign bribery cases in the past five years as in the five years before that. A primary justification for the prosecutions has been the revisions to the FCPA that extended jurisdiction to any foreign company or individual doing business in the United States.[92]

In late 2008, German engineering company Siemens AG and authorities in the United States settled a long-standing bribes-for-business case with a record $1.6 billion fine, almost 20 times higher than the largest previous penalty under the FCPA. Siemens was penalized for routinely offering bribes to win overseas contracts with the following countries—Russia, Argentina, China, and Israel. The company was said to have spent more than $1 billion in bribing government officials around the globe.[93] The United States was able to apply the FCPA to Siemens because it is now listed on the U.S. Stock Exchange. After this Siemens debacle, it was able to hire a new CEO, Peter Löscher, who had high ethical standards and made it his primary job to steer the company onto an ethical course. By 2010, the new CEO was claiming that Siemens now stands for "clean business always and everywhere."[94] Changing a corporation's ethical culture is a monumental task. Only time will tell whether he will succeed.

Many other companies have ongoing investigations of FCPA violations. As of early 2010, there were an estimated 120 pending FCPA investigations. FCPA prosecutions have exploded due to several related factors: increased penetration of U.S. companies into oil-rich countries such as Nigeria, where bribes are expected; prosecutions under the Patriot Act of 2001, which links bribing foreign officials to the advancement of terrorist activities; the Sarbanes–Oxley Act of 2002, which makes it easier to hold senior executives accountable for criminal activities of their companies; and a heightened sensitivity to violations within mergers.[95]

FIGURE 10-4
Antibribery
Provisions of the
Foreign Corrupt
Practices Act—Key
Features

- In general, the FCPA prohibits American companies from making corrupt payments to foreign officials for the purpose of obtaining or keeping business.
- The Department of Justice is the chief enforcement agency, with a coordinate role played by the Securities and Exchange Commission (SEC).
- The FCPA's antibribery provisions extend to two types of behavior: making bribes (1) directly and (2) through intermediaries.
- The FCPA applies to any individual firm, officer, director, employee, or agent of the firm and any stockholder acting on behalf of the firm.
- The person making or authorizing the payment must have a corrupt intent, and the payment must be intended to induce the recipient to misuse his or her official position to direct business wrongfully to the payer or to any other person.

- The FCPA prohibits paying, offering, promising to pay, or authorizing to pay or offer money or anything of value.
- The prohibition extends only to corrupt payments to a foreign official, a foreign political party or party official, or any candidate for foreign political office, or anyone acting in an official capacity.
- The FCPA prohibits corrupt payments through intermediaries.
- An explicit exception is made to the bribery provisions for "facilitating payments" for "routine governmental action."
- The following criminal penalties may be imposed: firms are subject to a fine of up to $2 million; officers, directors, stockholders, employees, and agents are subject to a fine of up to $100,000 and imprisonment for up to five years. Fines imposed on individuals may not be paid by the firm.

Source: "Foreign Corrupt Practices Act Antibribery Provisions," U.S. Department of Justice, http://www.osec.doc.gov/ogc/occic/fcparev.html. Accessed March 23, 2010.

Figure 10-4 summarizes some of the key features of the antibribery provisions of the FCPA.

The Growing Anticorruption Movement. As we move into the second decade of the new millennium, corruption and bribery in global business continue to be vital topics. With significant increases in global trade and competition, free markets, and democracy over the past decade, this comes as no surprise. Several powerful developments are worthy of mention. Each has contributed to what some have called a growing **anticorruption movement**.

TRANSPARENCY INTERNATIONAL An innovative special-interest group was founded in 1993—**Transparency International (TI)**—modeled after the human rights group Amnesty International. TI has established itself as the world's foremost anticorruption organization. According to its own Web site, TI is a "global civil society organization" leading the fight against corruption, bringing people together in a powerful worldwide coalition to end the devastating impact of corruption on men, women, and children around the world. TI's mission is to bring about change toward a world free of corruption.[96]

TI has defined five priorities in its fight against worldwide corruption. These include fighting corruption in (1) the private sector, (2) politics, (3) public contracting, (4) international anticorruption conventions, and (5) poverty and development. It maintains over 90 national chapters run by local activists.[97] TI has established two simple principles for businesses striving to root out corruption:

- The enterprise shall prohibit bribery in any form, whether direct or indirect.
- The enterprise shall commit to implementing a program to counter bribery.

According to TI, "These Business Principles are based on a Board commitment to fundamental values of integrity, transparency and accountability. Enterprises should aim to create and maintain a trust-based and inclusive internal culture in which bribery is not tolerated."[98]

Corruption Perception Index (CPI). One of the primary tools TI uses to combat corruption is its now-famous annual **Corruption Perception Index (CPI)**. The annual CPI has been widely credited with putting TI and the issue of corruption on the international policy agenda. The CPI ranks more than 150 countries by their perceived levels of corruption, as determined by expert assessments and opinion surveys. The result of the ranking is a list of countries in the world ranging from "highly clean" (least corrupt) to "highly corrupt."[99] In TI's 2009 rankings, the most recent available, the most "highly clean" countries included New Zealand, Denmark, Singapore, Sweden, Switzerland, Finland, the Netherlands, Australia, and Canada. The most "highly corrupt" countries included Somalia, Afghanistan, Myanmar, Sudan, Iraq, Chad, Uzbekistan, and Turkmenistan. The United States was ranked 19th from the top and the United Kingdom 17th from the top. Other rankings of interest include China, 79th from the top, and India, 84th from the top.[100]

Bribe Payers Index (BPI). In addition to the CPI, TI also publishes what it calls the **Bribe Payers Index (BPI)**. The BPI ranks leading exporting countries in terms of the degree to which international companies with their headquarters in those countries are likely to pay bribes to senior public officials in key emerging market economies. In that sense, the BPI measures the supply side of bribery in the countries where the bribes are paid. Countries are ranked on a mean score from the answers given by respondents to the following statement: "In the business sectors with which you are most familiar, please indicate how likely companies from the following countries are to pay or offer bribes to win or retain business in this country."[101] Among the 22 major exporting countries of the world, the countries that are perceived to pay more bribes include Russia, China, Mexico, India, and Italy.[102]

A new index related to the TI is the **Public Integrity Index**, the centerpiece of the Global Integrity report, issued by the Center for Public Integrity. The Global Integrity Index assesses the existence and effectiveness of anticorruption mechanisms that promote public integrity. The Public Integrity Index is a quantitative scorecard of governance practices in each country. It assesses the institutions and practices that citizens can use to hold their governments accountable to the public interest. This index does not measure corruption itself, but rather the opposite of corruption: the extent of citizens' ability to ensure their government is open and accountable. The Public Integrity Index ranks countries as strong, moderate, weak, or very weak on holding government accountable to its citizens.[103]

Undoubtedly, TI and the Center for Public Integrity hope and expect that public exposure to its corruption ratings will bring pressure to bear on countries and companies to become less corrupt.

OECD ANTIBRIBERY INITIATIVES Another major development in the growing anticorruption movement is an antibribery treaty and initiative that the 29 industrialized nations of the Organization for Economic Cooperation and Development (OECD) and five other countries agreed to in late 1997.[104] By 2009, 38 countries were subscribed to the OECD Antibribery Convention.[105] The OECD member nations agreed to ban international bribery and to ask each member nation to introduce laws patterned after the U.S. FCPA in its country. The main thrust of the treaty was to criminalize offering bribes to foreign officials who have sway over everything from government procurement contracts and infrastructure projects to privatization tenders.

The OECD Antibribery Convention to combat bribery made it a crime to offer, promise, or give a bribe to a foreign public official in order to obtain or retain international business deals. A related text effectively puts an end to the practice of according tax deductibility for bribe payments made to foreign officials. The convention commits its signatory countries, including all the world's biggest economies, to adopt common rules to punish companies and individuals who engage in bribery transactions. Today bribing a foreign public official is a crime in the 38 countries that have ratified the convention.[106]

In spite of good intentions, the OECD has been criticized for not doing enough quickly enough. It has also been criticized for dramatically failing to live up to its own governance and antisleaze standards. Even the antibribery watchdog's boss, in 2007, was accused of promoting cronies and accepting lavish pay and freebies. He defended himself by saying that attacks on him were motivated partially by his attempts to stamp out bribery in member countries.[107] The broader criticism is that the OECD antibribery signatories have failed to follow through on their plans. Implementation and execution, often problems in effective management, have been serious issues for the OECD initiatives.

It may be some years to come before the OECD Antibribery Convention is fully implemented. However, the OECD represents a significant initiative by a number of major countries in the global battle to eliminate corruption from commercial transactions.

UN CONVENTION AGAINST CORRUPTION (UNCAC) Another major initiative to combat corruption around the world was passed in 2003. The **UN Convention against Corruption (UNCAC)** was implemented in December 2005.[108] It created the opportunity to develop a global language about corruption and a coherent implementation strategy. A multitude of international anticorruption agreements already exist; however, their implementation has been uneven and only moderately successful. The UNCAC gives the global community the opportunity to address both of these weaknesses and begin establishing an effective set of benchmarks for effective anticorruption strategies.[109]

From a business perspective, UNCAC claims to hold the potential to become the global framework for combating corruption, which will pave the way for the establishment of a level playing field for all market participants. A central objective of UNCAC is to bring a higher degree of uniformity in the formulation and application of anticorruption rules across the world. For companies doing business in multiple jurisdictions, this agreement aspires to improve legal certainty and facilitate their global compliance efforts, thereby allowing them to fully compete in open markets without being exposed to extortion or unfair practices by their competitors.[110] UNCAC builds on the UN Global Compact, which presents nine principles of conduct in the areas of human rights, labor standards, and environment. Recently, a new principle of the Global Compact was adopted, the "10th Principle," which states "Businesses should work against corruption in all its forms, including extortion and bribery."[111] To date, over 140 countries have become signatories to UNCAC.[112]

INDIVIDUAL COUNTRY INITIATIVES In addition to OECD and UNCAC antibribery initiatives, some individual countries have begun antibribery campaigns on their own. Interestingly, many of the countries that have begun such campaigns are those that typically do not score very highly on business ethics surveys. A case in point was the efforts initiated in Mexico under the leadership of then President Vicente Fox. Fox appointed a new anticorruption czar. The first such czar, Francisco Barrio, a former governor of Chihuahua State in northern Mexico, was responsible for unearthing corruption and federal spending irregularities in a country with a long history of both. In a pilot undercover program, Barrio's office discovered that public servants in seven Mexican cities were charging and pocketing the equivalent of $100 apiece, in addition to regular fees, to issue driver's licenses. Barrio stated that corruption could not be eradicated in Fox's six-year term, but the government could lay the foundation for reducing it on all levels.[113] Barrio resigned in 2003 to run for Congress, and it seems that Mexico never again got back on track with its ethics improvements. The experience of Mexico tells us how hard it is to eliminate corruption when it is widespread and deeply rooted in countries like Mexico. Though the country has not been very successful in stopping corruption, some give the former president and the country credit for starting to address the issue.

Several other countries have reported attempts to clean up corruption. In Russia, President Vladimir Putin created an anticorruption coalition to start cleaning up his country. Putin admitted that Western investment would not pour into Russia without major improvements in governance and in the fight against corruption.[114] Russia, however, received an overall "Weak" rating in the 2008 Global Integrity Index, the latest available.[115] In 2009, a Swiss court ordered the confiscation of bank accounts held in connection with stolen money from Nigeria. The country is trying to shed its reputation as a repository for illegal funds. In India, the country has begun to increase transparency and is investigating alleged graft of important political officials. A readiness is beginning to appear among countries to prevent corruption, estimated at $1 trillion a year, almost equal to 5 percent of global domestic product.[116]

The best way to deal with bribes seems to be to stem the practice before it starts. A major paradox is that the very people who often benefit from illicit payments—the politicians—are the ones who must pass the laws and set the standards against bribes and corruption in the first place. Another factor is that bribes and corruption, whenever possible, need to be exposed. Public exposure, more than anything else, has the potential to bring questionable payments under control. This means that practices and channels of accountability need to be made public.[117]

The CPI and BPI should help in this regard. So should the country rankings by Global Integrity with its Public Integrity Index. Beyond these steps, managers need to see that such corruption and bribery are no longer in their best interests. Not only do bribes corrupt the economic system, but they corrupt business relationships as well and cause business decisions to be made on the basis of factors that ultimately destroy all the institutions involved. The OECD treaty and individual country efforts indicate that many countries now understand this important point. Their efforts will not totally eliminate bribery, but they do represent a significant step toward reducing bribery and bringing it under control.

We have by no means covered all the areas in which ethical problems reside in the global business environment. The topics treated have been major ones subjected to extensive public discussion. Examples of other issues that have become important recently and will probably increase in importance include the issues of international competitiveness, protectionism, industrial policy, political risk analysis, outsourcing, and antiterrorism. Also vital will be the dangers of developed countries importing dangerous products from some of the less-developed ones. These issues are of paramount significance in discussions of business's relations with international stakeholders. Other issues that include an ethical dimension are national security versus profit interests, dealing with rogue nations, the use of internal transfer prices to evade high taxes in a country, mining of the ocean floor, stealing intellectual property, and harboring of terrorists. Space does not permit us to discuss these issues in detail.

Improving Global Business Ethics

The most obvious conclusion from the discussion up to this point is that business ethics is much more complex at the global level than at the domestic level. The complexity arises from the fact that a wide variety of value systems, stakeholders, cultures, forms of government, socioeconomic conditions, and standards of ethical behavior exist throughout the world. Recognition of diverse standards of ethical behavior is important, but if we assume that firms from developed countries should operate in closer accordance with developed countries' standards than with those of LDCs, the strategy of ethical leadership in the world will indeed be a challenging one.

Because the United States and European MNCs have played such a leadership role in world affairs—usually espousing fairness and human rights—these firms have a heavy responsibility, particularly in underdeveloped countries and developing nations. The power–responsibility equation also suggests that these firms have a serious ethical responsibility in global markets. That is, the larger sense of ethical behavior and social responsiveness derives from the enormous amount of power these countries have.

In this section, we will first discuss the challenge of honoring and balancing the ethical traditions of a business's home country with those of its host country. Next, we will discuss the four recommended strategies for conducting business in foreign environments.[118] We will conclude by taking a look at some other steps companies are taking to improve their global ethics.

Balancing and Reconciling the Ethics Traditions of Home and Host Countries

One of the greatest challenges that businesses face while operating in foreign countries is achieving some kind of reconciliation and balance in honoring both the cultural and moral standards of their home and host countries. Should a business adhere to its home country's ethical standards for business practices or to the host country's ethical standards? There is no simple answer to this question. The diagram presented in Figure 10-5 frames the extreme decision choices businesses face when they consider operating globally. At one extreme, firms may engage in ethical imperialism. At the other extreme, they may employ cultural relativism. These alternatives deserve further discussion.

Ethical Imperialism.   At one extreme in Figure 10-5 is a position some have called **ethical imperialism**. This position holds that the MNC should continue to follow its home country's ethical standards even while operating in another country. Because U.S. standards for treating employees, consumers, and the natural environment are quite high relative to the standards in many LDCs, it is easy to see how managers might find this posture appealing.

As reliance on foreign factories has soared in recent years and harsh conditions have been documented by the media, an increasing number of companies, such as Levi Strauss, Nordstrom, Inc., Walmart, and Reebok, have espoused higher standards for foreign factories that cover such issues as wages, safety, and workers' rights to organize.[119] These standards more nearly approximate U.S. views on how such stakeholders ought to be treated rather than some host country's views. Such higher standards could be seen by foreign countries, however, as the United States attempting to impose its standards on the host country—thus the name "ethical imperialism" for one end of the continuum. Fortunately, the business world seems to be moving in the direction of eliminating corruption and operating according to higher ethical standards.

Cultural Relativism.   At the other extreme in Figure 10-5 is a position often called **cultural relativism**. This position is characterized by foreign direct investors such as MNCs following the host country's ethical standards. This is the posture reflected in the well-known saying "When in Rome, do as the Romans do." This position would argue that the investing MNC should set aside its home country's ethical standards and adopt the ethical standards of the host country. For example, if Saudi Arabia holds that it is illegal to hire women for most managerial positions, the investing MNC would accept and adopt this standard, even if it runs counter to its home country's standards. Or if the host country has no environmental protection laws, this position would argue that the MNC need not be sensitive to environmental standards.

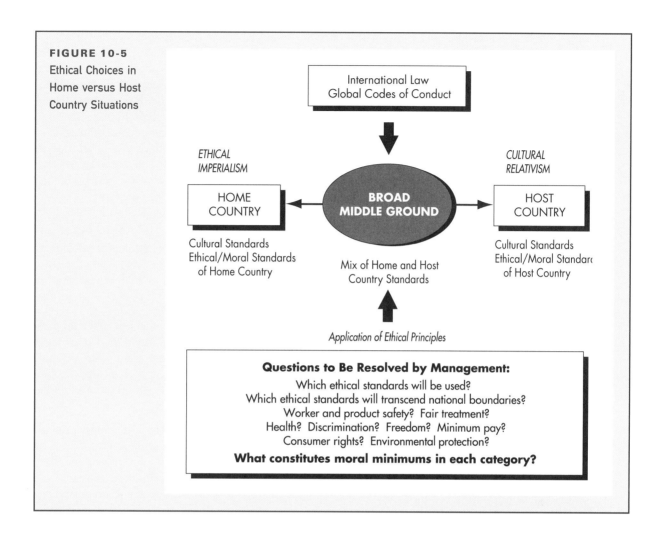

FIGURE 10-5
Ethical Choices in
Home versus Host
Country Situations

It has been argued that cultural relativism holds that no culture's ethics are better than any other's and that there are, therefore, no international rights or wrongs. If Thailand tolerates the bribery of government officials, then Thai tolerance is no worse than Japanese or German intolerance. If Switzerland does not find insider trading morally repugnant, then Swiss liberality is no worse than American restrictiveness.[120] Most ethicists find cultural relativism to be a case of moral or ethical relativism and, therefore, an unacceptable posture for MNCs to take.

Presented in Figure 10-5 is a series of questions management needs to ask to help determine its stance on home versus host country ethics. Depending on the issue (e.g., health versus minimum pay), companies may be more or less compelled to follow their home country's ethics. Key questions that must be posed and answered include the following: Which ethical standards will be used? Which ethical standards will transcend national boundaries? What constitutes moral minimums with respect to each category of ethical issue?

It may sound like a simplistic solution to say that the MNC needs to operate in some broad middle ground where a mix of home and host country ethical standards may be used. The challenge for managers will be to determine what mix of ethical standards should be used and how this decision should be made. As mentioned earlier, managers will need to ask themselves which moral standards are applicable in the situations they face. Use of ethical principles such as those articulated in the previous chapters—rights, justice, utilitarianism, and the Golden Rule—still apply. Managers will need to decide which ethical standards should transcend national boundaries and thus represent **hypernorms** (transcultural values):[121] safety? health? discrimination? freedom?

Managers will need to decide what will represent their moral minimums with respect to these and other issues. It would be nice to think that international laws and global codes of conduct will make these decisions easier. Though some are available, they may be challenging to apply. In the interim, managers will need to be guided by the ethical concepts at their disposal, possibly with help from some of the strategies to which we now turn.

Strategies for Improving Global Business Ethics

Four major strategies or categories of action that could help MNCs conduct global business while maintaining an ethical sensitivity in their practices include: (1) global codes of conduct, (2) linking ethics with global strategy, (3) suspension of business activities in certain countries, and (4) ethical impact statements and audits.[122]

Global Codes of Conduct.   Global codes of conduct seek to establish universal principles or guidelines that must be followed while doing business around the world. There are two ways of thinking about global codes of conduct. First, there are specific corporate global codes that individual companies have developed. As an added resource, the GloSecond, there are global codes or guidelines that have been developed by various international organizations. Each of these deserves some consideration.

CORPORATE GLOBAL CODES In Chapter 8, we discussed codes of conduct, and that discussion applies in the global sphere as well. While operating on the world stage, MNCs have been severely criticized for employing divergent ethical standards in different countries, thus giving the impression that they are attempting to exploit local circumstances. A growing number of MNCs, for example, Chiquita Brands International, Caterpillar Tractor, Allis Chalmers, Johnson's Wax, and Medtronic, have developed and used codes geared toward worldwide operations.[123]

One of the first and most well known of the corporate global codes was that of Caterpillar Tractor Company, issued by the chairman of the board, titled "A Code of Worldwide Business Conduct." Caterpillar has been building work machines that have been used the world over for over 80 years. The company asserts that its code sets a high standard for honesty and ethical behavior for every employee.[124] The code goes into considerable detail and has major sections that cover the following important values that Caterpillar aspires toward: integrity, excellence, teamwork, and commitment.

Other companies do not have comprehensive codes addressing their international operations but rather codes containing sections that address foreign practices. For example, in its *Standards of Business Conduct*, Northrop Grumman Corporation dedicates a whole section to the subject of "international."[125] In its "international" section, the code begins as follows:

> *Employees and consultants or agents representing the company abroad or working on international business in the United States should be aware that the company's Values and Standards of Conduct apply to them anywhere in the world. Less than strict adherence to laws and regulations that apply to the company's conduct of international business would be considered a compromise of our Values and Standards of Conduct.*[126]

The code then goes on to specifically address topics such as export controls, the FCPA, and laws of other countries.

Other companies have specific categories of ethical issues in which they address global considerations. For example, Chiquita Bananas's Code of Conduct says the following regarding *bribery and corruption:* "Chiquita policy prohibits employees from using improper, unethical, or questionable business practices while conducting business on its behalf. We abide by all international laws, treaties and regulations that forbid bribery of foreign officials, including the U.S. Foreign Corrupt Practices Act."[127]

THE GBS CODEX   Four researchers have published what they have called a Global Business Standards (GBS) Codex.[128] The **GBS Codex** was not intended to be a model code of conduct for global business, but a benchmark for companies wanting to develop their own world-class code. The researchers studied 5 well-known global codes put together by international organizations and 14 codes of the world's largest companies, and extracted the underlying ethical principles they felt the different codes had in common. The researchers found eight principles, representing worldwide ethical standards that they thought were basic to the codes studied. The eight principles identified and described standards of conduct in the following categories: *fiduciary, property, reliability, transparency, dignity, fairness, citizenship,* and *responsiveness.*[129] The researchers argued that companies that wanted to assess their current codes of conduct or to create new codes of conduct would find their eight principles useful as a standard by which comparisons could be made. It is still too early to assess the extent to which the GBS Codex has been used in practice.

Corporate codes of conduct are usually just the starting point for companies in dealing with global business ethics. The acid test is whether these codes become living documents that the companies actually use on a daily basis.

GLOBAL CODES/STANDARDS SET BY INTERNATIONAL ORGANIZATIONS   In addition to individual corporate codes, global codes or standards have been developed by a number of international organizations that they hope companies will adopt and follow. Some of these codes focus on one specific issue; many provide standards across a number of issue areas. Figure 10-6 summarizes brief information about some of the more prominent of these external standards.

Two of the most widely used global standards are the **UN Global Compact** and the **Caux Roundtable Principles**. Figure 10-7 summarizes the major specific principles in each.

Ethics and Global Strategy.   The major recommendation regarding ethics and global strategy is that the ethical dimensions of multinational corporate activity should be considered as significant inputs into top-level strategy formulation and implementation.[130] Even more broadly, corporate social policy should be integrated into strategic management.[131] At the top level of decision making in the firm, corporate strategy is established. At this level, commitments are made that will define the underlying character and identity that the organization will have. The overall moral tone of the organization and all decision making and behaviors are set at the strategic level, and management needs to ensure that social and ethical factors do not get lost in the preoccupation with market opportunities and competitive factors.

If ethics does not get factored in at the strategic formulation level, it is doubtful that it will be considered at the level of operations where strategy is being implemented. Unfortunately, much current practice has tended to treat ethics and social responsibility as residual factors. A more proactive stance is needed for dealing with ethical issues at the global level. Strategic decisions that may be influenced by ethical considerations in the global sphere include, but are not limited to, product/service decisions, plant location,

FIGURE 10-6 Global Standards or Codes of Conduct Developed by International Organizations

Codes, Standards, or Guidelines	Brief Description and Web Site
UN Global Compact	The Global Compact's operational phase was launched at UN headquarters in New York on July 26, 2000. Today, thousands of companies from all regions of the world and international labor and civil society organizations are engaged in the Global Compact, working to advance ten universal principles in the areas of *human rights, labor, the environment,* and *anticorruption.* http://www.unglobalcompact.org/
Caux Roundtable Principles	The CRT Principles for Business are a worldwide vision for ethical and responsible corporate behavior and serve as a foundation for action for business leaders worldwide. As a statement of aspirations, The CRT Principles aim to express a world standard against which business behavior can be measured. http://www.cauxroundtable.org/
Ceres Principles	The Ceres Principles are a ten-point code of corporate environmental conduct to be publicly endorsed by companies as an environmental mission statement or ethic. Imbedded in that code of conduct is the mandate to report periodically on environmental management structures and results. Over 50 companies have endorsed the Ceres Principles including 13 *Fortune* 500 firms. http://www.ceres.org/
Global Sullivan Principles	The objectives of the Global Sullivan Principles are to support economic, social, and political justice by companies where they do business; to support human rights and to encourage equal opportunity at all levels of employment, including racial and gender diversity on decision-making committees and boards; to train and advance disadvantaged workers for technical, supervisory, and management opportunities. http://www.thesullivanfoundation.org/gsp/
OECD Guidelines for Multinational Enterprises	The guidelines are recommendations addressed by governments to multinational enterprises operating in or from adhering countries. They provide voluntary principles and standards for responsible business conduct in a variety of areas including employment and industrial relations, human rights, environment, information disclosure, combating bribery, consumer interests, science and technology, competition, and taxation. http://www.oecd.org/daf/investment/guidelines
Principles for Global Corporate Responsibility: Benchmarks	The principles promote positive corporate social responsibility consistent with the responsibility to sustain the human community and all creation. The *benchmarks* state comprehensive standards and expectations fundamental to a responsible company's action. http://www.bench-marks.org/

operations policy, marketing policy and practices, and human resource management policies. More and more companies are employing departments and strategies with respect to global corporate social responsibility and global business citizenship.[132]

Levi Strauss & Co A useful illustration of ethics being factored into strategic decision making is provided by Levi Strauss & Co. Because the company operates in many countries and diverse cultures, it believes that it must take special care in selecting its contractors and the countries where its goods are produced in order to ensure that its products are being made in a manner consistent with its values and reputation. Years ago,

FIGURE 10-7 UN Global Compact and Caux Roundtable Principles

UN Global Compact Principles	Caux Roundtable Principles
Human Rights Businesses should • Principle 1: support and respect the protection of internationally proclaimed human rights and • Principle 2: make sure that they are not complicit in human rights abuses. **Labor Standards** Businesses should uphold • Principle 3: the freedom of association and the effective recognition of the right to collective bargaining, • Principle 4: the elimination of all forms of forced and compulsory labor, • Principle 5: the effective abolition of child labor, and • Principle 6: the elimination of discrimination in respect of employment and occupation. **Environment** Businesses should • Principle 7: support a precautionary approach to environmental challenges, • Principle 8: undertake initiatives to promote greater environmental responsibility, and • Principle 9: encourage the development and diffusion of environmentally friendly technologies. **Anticorruption** Businesses should • Principle 10: work against corruption in all its forms, including extortion and bribery.	1. Respect Stakeholders Beyond Shareholders 2. Contribute to Economic, Social, and Environmental Development 3. Respect the Letter and the Spirit of the Law 4. Respect Rules and Conventions 5. Support Responsible Globalization 6. Respect the Environment 7. Avoid Illicit Activities

Sources: UN Global Compact, "Ten Principles," http://www.unglobalcompact.org/AboutTheGC/TheTenPrinciples/index.html; "Principles for Responsible Business," http://www.cauxroundtable.org/index.cfm?&menuid=8.

therefore, the company developed a set of *global sourcing guidelines* that established standards its contractors must meet. As examples, their guidelines banned the use of child and prison labor. They stipulated certain environmental standards. Wages must, at minimum, comply with the law and match prevailing local practice. By factoring these ethical considerations into its strategic decisions, Levi argued that it receives important short- and long-term commercial benefits.[133] Recently, Levi Strauss took the unprecedented action of publishing on its Web site a list of all active owned-and-operated and contract factories producing the company's branded products. The company's senior vice president for Global Sourcing said, "We believe that greater transparency within the supply chain will provide additional momentum for our efforts to improve working conditions in apparel factories worldwide. Our hope is that this level of transparency will become standard across the apparel sector, fostering greater collaboration among brands in shared factories."[134] Levi Strauss & Co.'s Global Sourcing and Operating Guidelines address large, external issues that are outside the control of the company and business partner terms of engagement that apply to individual business partners and their daily operations.[135]

STARBUCKS Another example of a company integrating ethical concerns into its corporate strategies is that of Starbucks Coffee Co., the Seattle-based firm. In an innovative pilot program initiated over ten years ago, Starbucks began paying a premium above market price for coffee, with the bonus going to improve the lives of coffee workers. The initial payments were made to farms and mills in Guatemala and Costa Rica, which cofunded health care centers, farm schools, and scholarships for farm workers' children. Starbucks's incentive program was part of a larger "Framework for Action," its plan for implementing its code of conduct.[136] Starbucks began purchasing Fair Trade Certified coffee in 2000. The company has been recognized for helping grow the market for Fair Trade Certified coffee in the United States and bringing it to consumers. In 2008, Starbucks announced that it was expanding its work with Fair Trade to support small-scale farmers. In 2009, Starbucks increased its purchases to reach 40 million pounds (18 million kilograms). This makes the company the largest purchaser of Fair Trade Certified coffee in the world.[137]

Another way Starbucks integrates ethics into its corporate strategy is by setting specific goals for the future that become a part of its overall corporate policy. Its 2015 goals include the following: *ethical sourcing* (100 percent of its coffee will be responsibly grown, ethically traded); *environmental stewardship* (100 percent of its cups will be reusable or recyclable); and *community involvement* (it will commit more than 1 million community service hours each year).[138]

Suspension of Activities. An MNC may sometimes encounter unbridgeable gaps between the ethical values of its home country and those of its host country. When this occurs, and reconciliation does not appear to be in sight, the MNC should consider suspending activities in the host country. For example, years ago IBM and Coca-Cola established a precedent for this activity by suspending their activities in India because of that country's position on the extent of national ownership and control.[139] In a fight against corruption, Procter & Gamble even closed a Pampers diaper plant in Nigeria rather than pay bribes to customs inspectors.[140]

In 2006, the Ecuadorian government seized control of the operations of Occidental Petroleum prompting the U.S. government to discontinue free trade talks with the country. Officials in the United States claimed that the Ecuadorian government's confiscation of Occidental's operations broke foreign investment laws.[141] Occidental didn't have much choice but to suspend operations because of the treatment it had received. In 2007 and later, a number of companies were having difficulties operating in Venezuela. As President Hugo Chávez has been leading his country toward "21st century socialism," new rules restricting companies doing business there have been forthcoming. According to *BusinessWeek*, President Chávez forced global oil companies, phone carriers, and power companies to hand over control of key assets. He stated he has plans to nationalize the banks, hospitals, and steel companies. Foreign direct investment has plunged in Venezuela over the past couple of years.[142] Chávez's strong arm tactics have already caused two major oil companies—ExxonMobil Corp. and ConocoPhillips—to announce they are leaving the country.[143] In 2010, Google decided to move its search engine out of China because it no longer thought it to be appropriate to censor searches at the request of the Chinese government. Google is credited with a clever, strategic decision by moving its search engine to Hong Kong, which is a special administrative region that has broader free-speech protections. This decision allowed Google to adhere to its own privacy principles while also allowing the Chinese government to save face.[144]

Suspension of business in a foreign country is not a decision that can or should be taken too hastily, but it must be regarded as a viable option for those firms that desire to travel on the higher moral road of free trade. Each country is at liberty to have its own standards, but this does not mean that other country's firms must do business in that country. What does ethical leadership mean if it is not backed up by a willingness to take a moral stand when the occasion merits?

Ethical Impact Statements and Audits. MNCs need to be constantly aware of the impacts they are having on society, particularly foreign societies. One way to do this is to periodically assess the company's impacts. Companies have a variety of impacts on foreign cultures, and ethical impacts represent only a few of these. The impact statement idea derived, in part, from the practice of environmental impact statements pioneered years ago. Ethical impact statements are similar to the corporate social audit, a concept discussed in Chapter 5. Social auditing is "a systematic attempt to identify, analyze, measure (if possible), evaluate, and monitor the effect of an organization's operations on society (that is, specific social groups) and on the public well-being."[145] **Ethical impact statements** are an attempt to assess the underlying moral justifications for corporate actions and the consequent results of those actions. The information derived from these actions would permit the MNCs to modify or change their business practices if the impact statement suggested that such changes would be necessary or desirable.

One form of ethical impact assessment is some firms' attempts to monitor their compliance with their companies' global ethics codes. For example, Mattel Toy Company developed an independent audit and monitoring system for its code. Mattel's monitoring program was headed by an independent panel of commissioners who selected a percentage of the company's manufacturing facilities for annual audits. In one audit, for example, Mattel terminated its relationship with three contractor facilities for refusing to meet company-mandated safety procedures.[146] Mattel continues its auditing of compliance to its code of conduct through its Global Manufacturing Principles.[147]

In spite of the care that Mattel has used over the years, several years ago it was forced into a massive voluntary recall of 9 million toys manufactured in China. The toys apparently has been farmed out to some subcontractors who engaged in the unacceptable practices of using lead paint, which is dangerous for children, and making other toys that had hazardous magnets.[148] This contrast of high standards with poor performance demonstrates how difficult global business can sometimes be. In 2009, Mattel shifted its social responsibility independent audit program to the toy industry's ICTI CARE Process (ICP). The ICP is an approach that Mattel has long supported, and through the ICP, the toy industry is working together to address compliance issues and improvements at factories that make toys. The ICP is based on a code of ethical operating practices similar to the Global Manufacturing Principles.[149]

Companies Take Action against Corruption

A revealing study conducted by the Conference Board and the ECOA has disclosed some details on companies' recent anticorruption campaigns within their organizations. When asked what was the single most important factor in their company's decision to develop an anticorruption program, the most frequent responses were "senior management leadership and personal convictions," "bribe payments being illegal under their home country laws," the belief that "bribe payments are wrong," and the impact of "Sarbanes–Oxley Section 404."[150]

The report revealed that there were five vital steps among anticorruption programs that seemed to work best for companies:[151]

1. High-level commitment by top management
2. Detailed statements of policies and operating procedures

3. Training and discussion of policies and procedures

4. Hotlines and help lines for all organizational members

5. Investigative follow-up, reporting, and disclosure

These vital steps, when combined with the strategies for improving global business ethics discussed earlier, go a long way toward establishing a solid foundation for fighting bribery and corruption, the most insidious issues in global business ethics. The good news is that companies are now very much aware of these issues and are moving quickly to address them.

Summary

Ethical dilemmas pose difficulties, in general, for businesses, and those arising in connection with doing business in foreign lands are among the most complex. The current period is characterized by an increasing antiglobalization sentiment, and the attacks on the World Trade Center and subsequent acts of terrorism have created an uncertain global environment. A cursory examination of major issues that have arisen in global business ethics over the past several decades shows that they rank right up there with the most well-known news stories about business performance. The infant formula controversy, the Bhopal tragedy, corruption and bribery, concern about human rights and sweatshops, and the exploits of MNCs in Third World countries have all provided an opportunity for business critics to assail corporate ethics in the international sphere. These problems arise for a multiplicity of reasons, but differing cultures, value systems, forms of government, socioeconomic systems, and underhanded and ill-motivated business exploits have all been contributing factors. The possible applications of the ATCA to U.S.-based MNCs raises to a new level of urgency the actions, decisions, and policies of these firms in foreign lands.

Steps taken by the United States and other major countries to address the issues of corruption and bribery include the FCPA, the OECD Antibribery Convention, and the UNCAC. Individual country initiatives are also vital, as are the efforts of nonprofit organizations such as TI. A number of different approaches to improving global business ethics were presented. The balancing of home and host country standards were discussed with the extreme options of ethical imperialism or cultural relativism presented and contrasted. Four strategies for improving global business ethics were set forth: (1) global codes of conduct, encompassing corporate codes, the GBS Codex, and global codes created by international organizations; (2) the integration of ethical considerations into corporate strategy; (3) the option of suspending activities in the host country; and (4) the use of ethical impact statements and audits. These strategies offer some hope that global business can be better managed. A major study by the Conference Board and the ECOA indicates that companies are taking important actions against corruption within their organizations. Five vital steps being taken against corruption were presented, and these were headed up by high-level commitment by top management.

In spite of the worldwide economic recession, current trends point to a growth in business activity in the transnational economy, and though there is some evidence of a backlash against globalization, these issues will become more rather than less important in the future. Indeed, it could easily be argued that business's greatest ethical challenges in the future will be at the global level.

Key Terms

Alien Tort Claims Act (ATCA), p. 361

anticorruption movement, p. 366

antiglobalists, p. 347

Bhopal tragedy, p. 356

Bribe Payers Index (BPI), p. 367

bribery, p. 363

Caux Roundtable Principles, p. 373

corruption, p. 362

Corruption Perception Index (CPI), p. 367

cultural relativism, p. 370

ethical impact statements, p. 377

Discussion Questions

1. Drawing on the notions of moral, amoral, and immoral management introduced in Chapter 7, categorize your impressions of (a) Nestlé, in the infant formula controversy; (b) Union Carbide, in the Bhopal tragedy; and (c) Google, in moving its search engine out of China.

2. As an MNC seeks to balance and honor the ethical standards of both the home and host countries, conflicts inevitably will arise. What criteria do you think managers should consider as they try to decide whether to use home or host country ethical standards? Does it depend on the ethical issue involved? Explain.

3. Differentiate between a bribe and a grease payment. Give an example of each.

4. Conduct research, for purposes of updating the latest rankings of Transparency International and the activities of the OECD, UNCAC, and individual country initiatives. How could countries such as China, India, and Russia most effectively improve their TI rankings?

5. What are the major strategies companies might employ in improving global business ethics? What are the key steps research has shown are important to successful company anticorruption efforts?

CASE 16

To Hire or Not to Hire*

SELECTING A NEW COMPUTER ANALYST

As a manager in human resources, part of my job is to guide the process by which my company selects new employees. Recently, we selected an applicant to fill a computer analyst position. The supervising manager and a selection panel selected this applicant over a number of others based on her superior qualifications and interview.

BACKGROUND CHECK

However, a routine background check indicated that the applicant had been convicted 18 years earlier for false check writing. The application form has a section where the applicant is asked if he or she has ever been convicted of anything other than a traffic violation. In response to that question, this applicant wrote "no." When informed of this, the supervising manager stated that she would still like to hire the applicant, but asked

me for my recommendation. The job does not involve money handling.

QUESTIONS FOR DISCUSSION

1. If the applicant mistakenly thought that her record had been cleared over time and therefore did not lie intentionally, would that make any difference?
2. Should the fact that the applicant did not tell the truth on one part of the application automatically disqualify her from further consideration?
3. Should the supervising manager be allowed to hire this applicant despite the fact that the applicant lied on her application, provided the manager is willing to take the risk and assume responsibility for the applicant?
4. If the applicant freely admitted the conviction, should she still be considered for the position? Should a minor offense committed 18 years ago, when the applicant was in her early 20s, disqualify her when she is overall the most qualified applicant? What types of convictions, and how recent, should disqualify potential new hires?

* This case was prepared by Tim Timmons.

CASE 17

The Travel Billing Expense Controversy and the False Claims Act*

Early in 2000, Neal A. Roberts, an employee of PricewaterhouseCoopers LLP, the major accounting firm, learned that his employer was earning millions of dollars a year by way of a billing practice that he thought was questionable. PricewaterhouseCoopers (PwC), the accounting Goliath, had been collecting large rebates on airline tickets and other travel expenses being charged as expenses to clients of the firm. It turns out that these rebates were not being returned to the firm's clients in the form of savings, but rather, the

firm was keeping these rebates. In short, travel expenses had become a source of profits for the firm, and their unknowing clients were footing the bill.[1]

The way this was working was that the firm would bill the clients for the full price of airline tickets and other travel-related expenses, but privately, the firm negotiated discounts and rebates that they then got at the end of the year based on total amounts spent. The clients, of course, were unaware of the back-end discounts and rebates the firm was getting; therefore, they were being charged more than the firm's true out-of-pocket expenses for the items.

Roberts made a number of attempts to object to his firm's practice, but had little or mixed success. His efforts did help to generate several private lawsuits and a government investigation into PwC's rebate scheme. One case, in particular, was taking place in Texarkana,

* This case was prepared and updated in 2010 by Archie B. Carroll, University of Georgia.

Arkansas, and it resulted in the public disclosure of numerous company documents upon which the facts of the case were being publicly established. The documents revealed how a number of professional firms in accounting, consulting, and law have been turning reimbursable expenses such as airfare and hotel room expenses into profit centers for themselves.[2]

SEVERAL FIRMS INVOLVED

The lead plaintiff in this and several other cases was Warmack-Muskogee LP. Warmack-Muskogee's lawsuits were against PwC, KPMG, and Ernst & Young, so it wasn't just PwC that had been accused of these practices. These three firms had been charged with billing their clients for the full face amount of certain travel expenses, such as airline tickets, hotel rooms, and car-rental expenses, while pocketing undisclosed rebates and volume discounts they received under various contracts they had with airline, car-rental, lodging, and other travel expense–related vendors.[3] One defense these firms frequently set forth was that "everyone else is also doing it."

PwC AGREES TO SETTLEMENT

Though not admitting guilt, PwC agreed in December 2003 to a settlement estimated to be worth $54.5 million. PwC had once provided litigation-consulting services for Warmack-Muskogee. One-third of the settlement would go to the plaintiff's attorneys, and the balance would be available to current and former PwC clients in the form of cash or credits for future services.[4]

DETAILS OF THE PwC CASE

When Neal Roberts inadvertently discovered his firm's travel billing practices, he made an effort to address the problem while working within the confines of his firm. Roberts raised objections to the practice. One person responding to Roberts's concerns was Barbara Kipp, the partner in charge of PwC's ethics department. Kipp wrote an e-mail in April 2000 to another top partner in which she had said, "Al, while I appreciate the importance of managing as tight a fiscal ship as we can, I somehow feel that we are being a bit greedy here." Kipp was addressing Albert Thiess, the New York-based partner responsible for oversight of the firm's travel department.[5] Kipp also said in her e-mail that she thought the rebate policy looked like the firm was "double dipping."[6]

COMPLAINT TO ETHICS HOTLINE

Roberts was not the only partner in the firm to raise questions about the travel expense rebates. Jean Joslyn, at that time a director of the firm's health-care consulting group in Chicago, earlier wrote an e-mail in February 1999 to James F. Lennon, the firm's global-travel director. Joslyn said in her e-mail: "My question is how this rebate will be allocated back to our clients?" Lennon's reply was similar to Thiess's opinion, "We negotiate these deals, not our clients." A couple days later Joslyn, who was disturbed by the response, called the firm's ethics hotline and left a message of concern about the practice.[7]

According to the firm's documents, the ethics complaint filed by Joslyn led to a meeting in New York on March 19, 1999, in which the 14 attendees, who included members of the firm's management committee, decided that the firm would reinstate a 12.5 percent front-end discount that would lower the ticket prices to clients. What the committee did not tell Joslyn was that the total discounts, including the back-end rebates, would continue to exist and in some instances would be as high as 40 percent. This meant that PwC would continue to pocket substantial amounts on many of its expenditures.[8]

ROBERTS KEEPS PUSHING

Upon learning of the discounts and rebates the firm was keeping, Roberts sent an e-mail to a partner he was working with in Dallas on litigation consulting for the Federal Deposit Insurance Corporation. He said, "I cannot believe that such discounts exist since that would leave us open to billing fraud accusations on most government contracts and others as well."[9] Next, Roberts contacted Hilary Krane, an in-house PwC lawyer, who recommended he contact the firm's ethics department. In addition, Krane sent Roberts a copy of an earlier e-mail she had written to one of the firm's lawyers in Washington, DC, in which she had expressed her own concern about the practice. In her e-mail she expressed unease that the firm was billing government clients for plane tickets without telling them about the back-end discounts and rebates her firm was collecting.[10]

POLICY IS REVISED

By October 2000, a working group including Kipp, Krane, Thiess, and several others met and made the decision to do something. They decided to shift most of the discounts upfront so their clients could benefit from the reduced prices. Under their revised policy, PwC would seek front-end discounts of 28 percent with 8 percent rebates remaining to "cover our costs." Under this policy, the firm would still get to keep 8 percent savings. The group announced its new policy to be effective January 1, 2001, but decided there was no need to reimburse their clients for the millions they had collected previously on the earlier rebates.[11]

ROBERTS AND THE FALSE CLAIMS ACT

Roberts was still not satisfied with the firm's decision, and he continued to press the company to refund previous clients an amount equal to the back-end rebates the firm had received. By late 2000, Roberts engaged a law firm, Packard, Packard, & Johnson, of Salt Lake City, that specialized in filing False Claims lawsuits against federal contractors, such as his firm.[12]

False Claims Act

The False Claims Act is a piece of federal legislation designed to help the government ferret out fraud on the part of firms with which it does business. Under the federal False Claims Act, private citizens who know of people or companies that are defrauding the government may sue on the government's behalf and share in the proceeds of the suit. Citizens who bring these causes of actions do so under the *qui tam* provisions of the Act.[13] The *qui tam* provisions allow an individual, frequently acting in the role of a whistle-blower, to bring suit and share in the damages recovered as a result of the lawsuit. Over the past decade or more, hundreds of *qui tam* lawsuits have been filed, and these have resulted in 4 billion dollars in recoveries for the United States Treasury. The whistle-blowers who file these suits may collect between 15 percent and 30 percent of the recovered taxes and penalties, and this has resulted in more than $100 million going to them for their efforts over this time span.[14] In 2003 alone, the lawsuits filed under this Act recovered $1.5 billion.[15]

Back to Roberts's Situation

From this point on, Roberts had a financial interest in his lawsuit against his own firm. He started cooperating with investigators who began looking into the activities of his firm. During this period, Roberts reported that his pay and status at the firm were declining and he complained that he was being urged to retire early. His annual pay was cut by 50 percent, but a spokesperson for the firm said that the pay cut started before his first complaints in early 2000. He was told by partners that he was not producing enough business for the firm.

Roberts retired from PwC in May 2001. On October 1, 2001, the firm stopped taking airline rebates completely. The company started structuring all discounts as front-end price reductions that would be passed on to the clients. They also decided to charge clients $25 to $60 per ticket for "transaction" fees that are disclosed to the clients.[16] In 2005, PwC agreed to pay $41.9 million to settle the allegations that it made false claims to the U.S. government in connection with claims it made to federal agencies for travel reimbursements. Roberts was to receive an amount to be determined at a later time.[17]

Roberts and Other Claims

It turns out that on at least one other occasion in 2004, Neal Roberts, along with another man, filed charges under the False Claims Act against PwC and IBM. In this other case, the government got to collect $5.2 million from the two companies. The charges were that the companies solicited and provided improper payments on technology contracts with the government. This case was settled in 2007.[18]

Questions for Discussion

1. Identify the ethical issues in this case.
2. Who are the stakeholders and what are their stakes?
3. What is your appraisal of the ethics of the travel expense billing practices described in the case? What are the ethical arguments for and against them?
4. Did Roberts's complaint to the ethics department help or not? Did his firm seem receptive to his concerns?
5. What does the travel billing practice tell you about the *culture* of professional firms such as accountants, consultants, and lawyers? Does it make you wonder what other practices are being used in which the clients are not being informed?
6. The case ended with the company paying a huge settlement and eventually providing the discounts to the clients that Roberts and others were calling for. Is this a case of a firm's greed and self-interest

getting in the way of their sense of fairness to their customers?

7. In light of the second case that Neal Roberts was involved with, does this make you think some people may be going into business for themselves in filing false claims?

8. What is your assessment of the *qui tam* provisions of the False Claims Act? Does this provide a financial incentive for employees to want to gather "dirt" on their employers and use it for their own financial gain? What are the strengths and weaknesses of such a law?

ENDNOTES

1. Jonathan Weil, "Court Files Offer Inside Look at Pricewaterhouse Billing Clash," *The Wall Street Journal* (January 5, 2004), A1.
2. *Ibid.*
3. LuAnn Bean, "Rebates: Do the Big Four Need an Ethics Audit?" *Journal of Corporate Accounting & Finance*, (May/June 2004), 37.
4. Weil, A1.
5. Jonathan Weil, "PricewaterhouseCoopers Partners Criticized Travel Billing," *The Wall Street Journal* (September 30, 2003), C1.
6. Weil (January 5, 2004), A10.
7. *Ibid.*
8. *Ibid.*
9. *Ibid.*
10. *Ibid.*
11. *Ibid.*
12. *Ibid.*
13. The False Claims Act Resource Center, http://www.falseclaims act.com/.
14. *Ibid.* "Qui Tam Provisions of the False Claims Act."
15. "IRS May Offer Co Whistle-Blowers Share of Recovered Taxes," *The Wall Street Journal Online* (June 19, 2004), http://www.wsj.com/.
16. Weil (January 5, 2004), A10.
17. Department of Justice, Press Release, "Pricewater-housecoopers, LLP to Pay U.S. $41.9 Million to Settle False Claims Involving Claims for Travel," http://www.usdoj.gov/opa/pr/2005/July05_civ_365.htm. Accessed September 9, 2007.
18. "IBM and PriceWaterhouseCoopers to Pay U.S. More Than $5.2 Million to Settle Allegations of False Claims," Whistleblower Law Blog, August 16, 2007. Accessed June 10, 2010.

CASE 18

Phantom Expenses*

Jane Adams had just completed a sales training course with her new employer, a major small appliance manufacturer. She was assigned to work as a trainee under Ann Green, one of the firm's most productive sales reps on the East Coast. At the end of the first week, Jane and Ann were sitting in a motel room filling out their expense vouchers for the week.

INFLATING EXPENSES

Jane casually remarked to Ann that the training course had stressed the importance of filling out expense vouchers accurately. Ann immediately launched into a long explanation of how the company's expense reporting resulted in underpayment of actual costs. She claimed that all the sales reps on the East Coast made up the difference by padding their expenses under $25, which did not require receipts. A rule of thumb used was to inflate total expenses by 25 percent. When Jane questioned whether this was honest, Ann said that even if the reported expenses exceeded actual expenses, the company owed them the extra money, given the long hours and hard work they put in.

FOLLOW THE AGREED-UPON PRACTICE

Jane said that she did not believe that reporting fictitious expenses was the correct thing to do and that she

---

*This case was written by David J. Fritzsche, Penn State Great Valley. Permission to reprint granted by Arthur Andersen & Co., SC.

would simply report her actual expenses. Ann responded in an angry tone, saying that to do so would expose all the sales reps. As long as everyone cooperated, the company would not question the expense vouchers. However, if one person reported only actual expenses, the company would be likely to investigate the discrepancy and all the sales reps could lose their jobs. She appealed to Jane to follow the agreed-upon practice, stating that they would all be better off, that no one would lose his or her job, and that the company did not really need the money because it was very profitable.

QUESTIONS FOR DISCUSSION

1. What are the ethical issues in this case?
2. Given all the factors, what should Jane have done?
3. What would have been the consequences for Jane and the company if she had accurately reported her expenses? What would the consequences have been if she had inflated her expense account as Ann had urged her to do?
4. What ethical principles would be useful here?

CASE 19

Family Business*

Jane had just been hired as the head of the payroll department at R&S Electronic Service Company, a firm comprising 75 employees. She had been hired by Eddie, the general manager, who had informed her of the need for maintaining strict confidentiality regarding employee salaries and pay scales. He had also told her that he had fired the previous payroll department head for breaking that confidentiality by discussing employee salaries. She had also been formally introduced to Brad, the owner, who had told her to see him if she had any questions or problems. Both Brad and Eddie had made her feel welcome.

GREG'S HIGH COMMISSIONS

After three months of employment, Jane began to wonder why Greg, a service technician and Eddie's brother, made so much more in commissions than the other service technicians. She assumed that he must be highly qualified and must work rapidly because she had overheard Brad commending Greg on his performance on several occasions. She had also noticed Brad, Eddie, and Greg having lunch together frequently.

One day, Eddie gave Jane the stack of work tickets for the service technicians for the upcoming week. The technicians were to take whatever ticket was on top when they finished the job they were working on. After putting the tickets where they belonged, Jane remembered that she had a doctor's appointment the next morning and returned to Eddie's office to tell him she would be reporting late for work.

EDDIE SHOWS FAVORITISM

When she entered Eddie's office, she saw Eddie give Greg a separate stack of work tickets. As she stood there, Eddie told her that if she mentioned this to anyone, he would fire her. Jane was upset because she understood that Eddie was giving the easier, high-commission work to his brother. Jane also realized that Eddie had the authority to hire and fire her. Because she had been at the company for only a short time, she was still on probation. This was her first job since college. She wondered what she should do.

QUESTIONS FOR DISCUSSION

1. What are the ethical issues in this case?
2. Is a family business different from other types of businesses with respect to employee treatment?
3. What was Jane's ethical dilemma?
4. What should Jane have done? Why?

---

* This case was written by Marilyn M. Helms, University of Tennessee at Chattanooga. Permission to reprint granted by Arthur Andersen & Co., SC.

CASE 20

Should Business Hire Undocumented Workers?*

After many months of negotiations in 2007, the U.S. Senate's compromise on a comprehensive immigration bill failed to pass. The ill-fated legislation contained provisions that would have hired new border patrol agents, imposed a new system forcing employers to electronically verify the legal status of applicants and employees, established a guest worker program, and provided an avenue for legalization for the estimated 11–20 million illegal immigrants in the country at the time.[1] Politicians on both sides of the issue held strong positions regarding the proposed legislation. One group called it an "amnesty" bill and another group feared it would cost Americans jobs. Politicians of various stripes supported it because either they approved of the idea or they wanted to be sure that this burgeoning group would someday vote for them.

According to *USA Today*, the "ghost of the 1986 failure" haunted the proposal for immigration reform in 2007.[2] As background, it is useful to know that an immigration law was passed in 1986 that was supposed to deal with the then 3 million illegal immigrants who were offered legal status in exchange for tough new enforcements that were to stop the flow of undocumented workers. The 1986 plan turned out to be a sham. A system was set up in which employers had to accept just about any document a job applicant submitted to prove his or her legal status. The by-product of that system was a booming industry in phony documents and at least 12 million more illegal immigrants.[3] To many, the 1986 amnesty sparked the larger influx of unlawful immigration and showed would-be migrants that the United States was weak willed and would eventually cave in and give citizenship to illegals, thus encouraging many to breach the U.S. borders with renewed energy.[4]

OVER 20 YEARS OF UNCONTROLLED IMMIGRATION

Between 1986 and 2007, the number of illegal immigrants in the United States exploded to somewhere between 11 and 20 million. Estimates vary widely because a valid count is not possible. Using the figure of 11 million, which is the conservative guess, estimates have been made about the magnitude of this booming population. Of that population, it has been reckoned that 56 percent are from Mexico, 22 percent are from other Latin American countries, 13 percent are from Asia, and the remainder are from Europe, Canada, Africa, and elsewhere.[5]

It is little wonder how the number of illegal immigrants grew to such a huge size in the intervening 20 years. The federal government took no action to stem the tide of illegal immigrants, and many businesses discovered that the workers were willing to take almost any job at low pay. In most cases, the workers worked hard and made very few demands. As a result, it became useful to business to fill many jobs that they have said were not being filled by anyone else. Of course, that statement has been disputed. Some observers have noted that if businesses had made working conditions better and raised the wages for some of these jobs, there would have been plenty of workers. But a black market of cheap labor suppressed any wage increases.

From a societal perspective, the influx of illegal immigrants has posed many issues for tax-paying Americans who suspect the immigrants are getting a free ride. They have put pressures on local communities' social service agencies, school systems, health-care facilities, welfare systems, and, in many places, increased the crime rate. At the same time, the number of illegal immigrants has grown so large (11–20 million) that the thought of rounding them up and deporting them has not been seen as a feasible solution. Many of the illegal immigrants have now had children, and some are already third-generation illegals.

Two groups have favored amnesty for the illegal immigrants more than anyone else—the business community, who sees in them a source of cheap labor, and some politicians who are looking down the road and speculating that someday these individuals will be their supporters if they are treated favorably. The business position is of interest to us here.

THE BUSINESS STAKE

Business has one of the largest stakes in the issue of what happens to illegal immigrants. Industries ranging from agriculture to construction now depend heavily

---

* This case was prepared by Archie B. Carroll, University of Georgia, and was updated in 2010.

on immigrant labor—legal and illegal. Business wants a reliable stream of inexpensive workers and has seemed willing to hire them even if they are undocumented. Business's preference, of course, is immigration reform whereby they may hire the workers legally. It has been clearly seen, however, that in the absence of enforcement, many businesses disregard the law and hire the illegal immigrants anyway.[6]

The business community has had a number of different groups pushing for immigration reform, but they represent a few different umbrella groups with no one clearly in charge. One lobbyist observed that there are "coalitions of coalitions." Some want to allow more uneducated, entry-level-type workers who are willing to take jobs others won't take. Others want reform allowing more educated and high-tech workers into the United States. One reason the business groups cannot come together is that most of them have some issue with different parts of proposed legislation.[7]

A CASE WITH MAJOR IMPLICATIONS

A different kind of case in Georgia may be signaling a turning point for business's experience with hiring illegal aliens. A company that has depended heavily on illegal immigrants is Mohawk Industries, Inc., the $6.6 billion carpet maker in the small town of Calhoun, Georgia. Mohawk employs 32,000 workers and 4,000 of them are in and around Calhoun. This small town has been reshaped over the past decade by an enormous influx of Latinos. At one time, the company was primarily staffed by whites, but today the workforce comes mostly from Mexico and other Latin American countries. With wage rates at $7 an hour and higher, Hispanics came to make up an estimated 12 percent of the population. In 1990, the percentage was less than 1 percent.[8]

Calhoun became the center of one of the most heated debates over the hiring of illegal immigrants. In 2004, tensions between immigrants and local workers turned into a legal case that may have significant implications for companies and communities all over the United States. Four current and former workers filed a class action lawsuit against Mohawk for allegedly conspiring to depress wages by hiring illegal immigrants.[9] The workers claimed they received lower wages because of the depression on wages caused by Mohawk's actions. The federal lawsuit claimed that the company, with the help of local hiring agencies, knowingly accepted false documents, recruited illegals at the U.S.–Mexican border, and

rehired undocumented workers under different names. Mohawk denied all the allegations.[10] The company claimed that its contracts with outside employment agencies did not cause direct harm by the conduct alleged.[11]

Businesses have been watching this case closely because it was filed under the Racketeer Influenced and Corrupt Organizations Act (RICO). This 1970 law, which was originally intended to fight the Mafia, assesses triple damages against those companies found guilty of violations. RICO was amended in 1996 to allow workers to sue corporations that knowingly hire illegal workers. It turns out there are at least three similar lawsuits making their way through the legal system.[12]

Mohawk appealed the case all the way to the U.S. Supreme Court. In February 2007, the Supreme Court declined to consider an appeal by Mohawk. The court's decision allowed the case to move forward in federal court.[13] At the time, some lawyers had suggested that other potential plaintiffs around the country were considering taking action against their employers.

In April 2010, Mohawk finally settled the lawsuit with its employees, who claimed the company had depressed wages by hiring illegal aliens. The company agreed to pay $18 million to about 50,000 former and current hourly-paid employees. This was said to be the largest payout ever in this type of litigation.[14]

ENFORCEMENT STARTS TO TOUGHEN UP

Prior to the Mohawk settlement, over the past several years, states, cities, and local municipalities have started engaging in their own fights against illegal immigration because the federal government would never take action.[15] In 2007, 18 states passed 57 immigration laws. More than 25 cities and counties passed measures. Under a Green Bay, Wisconsin, ordinance, a firm could lose its business license if it hires illegal workers. In Beaufort County, South Carolina, the county passed an ordinance that says a business could have its license suspended for hiring illegal workers.[16]

Because of the defeat of the comprehensive immigration bill and the outpouring of citizen criticism against the federal government for doing nothing, a renewed initiative began taking place. In Portland, Oregon, federal agents raided a food processing plant over suspicions that the company hired and employed hundreds of illegal aliens. It also was reported that in a check of employee records at a Fresh Del Monte

Produce Company vegetable and fruit processing plant in Florida, it was found that only 48 out of 600 workers had valid Social Security numbers.[17] In Ohio, the owner of a Fairview restaurant drew a prison sentence of one year for hiring illegal aliens. He pleaded guilty to inducing, transporting, and harboring illegal aliens. He not only employed them but also provided them with housing and drove them to work at the restaurant each day. It turns out the business owner himself was in the United States illegally, and he faces deportation after serving his sentence.[18]

In August 2007, the Bush Administration said it would increase its scrutiny of and impose heftier fines on U.S. businesses that employed illegal immigrants and that it would step up enforcement despite Congress's failure to pass immigration reform legislation. According to then-Homeland Security Secretary Michael Chertoff, employers who ignored immigration laws would face an increased likelihood of criminal charges and higher financial penalties. Currently, employers are supposed to verify that their workers are in the United States legally by collecting their Social Security numbers and immigration documents. These numbers are then checked against the government's database, and employers are notified of those that do not match. Under the new rule, employers notified of a mismatch would have 90 days to confirm that the employee is in the country legally, or fire them if they were not.[19] In fiscal year 2006, the government stepped up raids of companies that used illegal labor and deported a record 185,421 individuals. The new initiative drew praises from many who have long advocated using existing laws to crack down on undocumented workers, but criticisms arose from illegal immigrant advocates and business groups.[20]

Throughout 2008 and most of 2009, increased immigration raids continued and put pressure on companies that had hired illegal workers. In a number of instances these jobs were immediately filled by American workers.[21] As the recession worsened in 2009, the depressed economy along with tougher enforcement put unprecedented stress on illegal immigrants.[22] But when President Obama took office in January 2009, he presented a different posture toward illegal immigrants. He was more inclined to support a program that gave some form of amnesty to the undocumented workers, but nothing was forthcoming. Most enforcement initiatives were continuing from the momentum started earlier or were occurring at the state and city levels.

Under the Obama Administration, illegal workers are not being rounded up via raids at factories and farms as was the case under the Bush Administration before it. The immigration raids have been replaced with a quieter enforcement strategy—auditing of employers' books. These "silent raids" involve federal agents going to employers and scouring their employment records for evidence of illegal hires. The investigations of the past used to result in the deportation of the illegal hires. The current system requires the employer to discharge illegal workers. During 2009–2010, Immigration and Customs Enforcement (ICE) conducted audits at more than 2,900 companies and levied a record $3 million in civil fines. Employers believe that the audits reached more companies than were reached in the work-site raids. In another change, ICE no longer brings criminal charges against the undocumented workers who lack legal status but otherwise have clean records. Critics of this system point out that once discovered and fired, the illegal immigrants are free to seek employment elsewhere. Thus, there is no way for this approach to purge the workers from the employment system as long as they keep moving.[23]

In spite of a lack of comprehensive immigration reform, the federal government does require that employers fill out Form I-9 for each employee, verifying that the workers are U.S. citizens. The government has even created a special program called E-Verify, which is an Internet-based, free program run by the U.S. government that compares information from an employee's Employment Eligibility Verification Form I-9 to data from U.S. government records. If the information matches, that employee is eligible to work in the United States. If there's a mismatch, E-Verify alerts the employer and the employee is allowed to work while he or she resolves the problem. The program is operated by the Department of Homeland Security (DHS) in partnership with the Social Security Administration.[24] Because the E-Verify program is free and easy to use, it makes the verification process straightforward. Employers now have fewer excuses than ever not to fulfill their obligations.

CITIES AND STATES CREATE THEIR OWN LEGISLATION

In 2010, various cities and states continued their tough enforcement against employing illegal immigrants. Under new legislation in the State of Utah, employers could be among the first in the country to face criminal charges for failing to verify their workers' immigration status.[25] In Pennsylvania, new bills would stop the hiring of illegal immigrants. Under legislation proposed by Reps. John Galloway and Daryl Metcalfe, companies that hired foreign workers who had entered the country illegally to work for lower pay and no benefits would be punished.[26] Galloway stated at a news conference: "These bills are important because they are about protecting Pennsylvania jobs." Metcalfe chimed in by saying that undocumented workers from other countries "take away the jobs of unemployed Pennsylvania construction workers" and often use state-funded health-care benefits, unemployment benefits, and public schools for which they pay no taxes to support.[27]

The most dramatic action taken by a state occurred in April 2010 in Arizona. The state of Arizona passed a sweeping law that made the failure to carry immigration documents a crime and gave the police broad power to detain anyone suspected of being in the country illegally.[28] In a Pew Research Center poll of American citizens taken in May 2010, 73 percent of those polled approved of the measure requiring people to produce documents verifying their citizenship status.[29] The Obama Administration was not happy with the new Arizona law and indicated it would urge the courts to review the law.

With 11–20 million illegal immigrants in the United States today, the resolution of this issue will not come easily. With each passing month and year, the consequences and implications of the issue accumulate and grow more urgent. The resolution will have significant implications for all sides, not only for business, but for communities, tax payers, and others waiting to enter the country legally.

Questions for Discussion

1. What are the legal and ethical issues in this case?
2. Is illegal immigration primarily an economic, legal, ethical, social, or political issue? Explain.
3. Are companies that hire illegal immigrants being socially responsible? Evaluate this practice using the Pyramid of CSR introduced in Chapter 2.
4. What are the legal and ethical arguments in favor of continuing to allow illegal immigrants to be hired by businesses? What are the legal and ethical arguments against illegal immigration? Which side do you support? Why?
5. Assess the issue of illegal immigration using a number of different ethical principles, such as the principles of rights, utilitarianism, and justice.

What does each principle have to say about the issue of illegal immigration?
6. With E-Verify making it so easy for companies to obey the law, is there any excuse for not complying with the requirements of the law?
7. What will be the consequences of the Mohawk decision? Will this deter companies from hiring illegal immigrants?
8. What is your assessment of the new Arizona law? Why do states think they need to take action on this issue rather than waiting for the federal government to act?

Endnotes

1. "The Immigration Mess," *Newsweek* (June 18, 2007), 37.
2. "Ghost of '86 Failure Haunts Bid for Immigration Reform," *USA Today* (June 22, 2007), 10A.
3. *Ibid.*
4. Nathan Thornburgh, "The Case for Amnesty," *Time* (June 18, 2007), 38–42.
5. *Newsweek.*
6. Silla Brush, "Why Business Is Running Scared," *U.S. News & World Report* (June 4, 2007), 21–22.
7. *Ibid.*
8. Brian Grow, "A Body Blow to Illegal Labor," *BusinessWeek* (March 27, 2006), 86–88.
9. *Ibid.*, 86.
10. *Ibid.*
11. "High Court Turns Down Illegal-Worker Case," MSNBC.com (February 26, 2007), http://www.msnbc.msn.com. Accessed September 11, 2007.
12. Grow (2006).
13. MSNBC.com.
14. "Mohawk Industries Settles Lawsuit after Claims They Hired Illegal Aliens to Depress Wages," *Numbers USA* (April 14, 2010), http://www.numbersusa.com/content. Accessed June 15, 2010. Also see Joe Guzzardi, "Mohawk Industries Settles RICO Illegal Aliens Class Action, Must Pay $18 Million to American Workers!" Vdare.com (April 9, 2010). Accessed June 15, 2010.
15. Emily Bazar, "Local Laws Target Immigration Ills," *USA Today* (July 12, 2007), 1A.
16. *Ibid.*
17. "Federal Agents Raid Oregon Business over Illegal Immigrants," Salem-News.com (June 13, 2007), http://salem-news.com/. Accessed September 7, 2007.
18. "Restaurant Owner Sentenced in Illegal Alien Case," *Business Courier of Cincinnati* (August 28,

2007), http://www.bizjournals.com/cincinnati/stories/2007. Accessed September 7, 2007.

19. Andy Sullivan, "U.S. Cracks Down on Employment of Illegal Immigrants," *International Business Times* (August 10, 2007), http://www.ibtimes.com/articles/2007o810/illegal-immigration.htm. Accessed September 7, 2007.

20. Eunice Moscoso, "Feds Go after Illegal Workers," *Atlanta Journal Constitution* (August 11, 2007), A1.

21. Alan Gomez, "Immigration Raids Yield Jobs for Legal Workers," *USA Today* (September 14, 2009), 4A.

22. Nathan Thornburgh/St. Helens, "Undocumented and Undeterred," *Time* (April 20, 2009), 32–36.

23. Julia Preston, "Illegal Workers Swept from Jobs in 'Silent Raids,'" *The New York Times* (July 10, 2010), A1, A12.

24. "E-Verify," Wikipedia, http://en.wikipedia.org/wiki/E-Verify. Accessed June 16, 2010.

25. Brock Vergakis, "Hiring Illegal Immigrants May Lead to Jail in Utah," *USA Today* (February 26, 2010).

26. Tom Barnes, "Bills Would Stop Hiring of Illegal Immigrants," *Pittsburgh Post-Gazette* (June 8, 2010).

27. *Ibid.*

28. Randal Archibold, "Arizona Enacts Stringent Law on Immigration," *The New York Times* (April 23, 2010), http://www.nytimes.com/2010/04/24/us/politics/24immig.html. Accessed June 16, 2010.

29. Bruce Drake, "Arizona Immigration Law: Poll Finds Broad Support," *Politics Daily* (May 2010), http://www.politicsdaily.com/2010/05/12/poll-finds-broad-support-for-arizona-immigration-law/. Accessed June 16, 2010.

CASE 21

Nike, Inc. and Sweatshops*

Jonah Peretti decided to customize his Nike shoes and visited the NikeiD Web site. The company allowed customers to personalize their Nikes with the colors of their choice and their own personal 16-character message. Peretti chose the word "sweatshop" for his Nikes.

After receiving his order, Nike informed Peretti via e-mail that the term "sweatshop" represents "inappropriate slang" and is not considered viable for print on a Nike shoe. Thus, his order was summarily rejected. Peretti e-mailed Nike, arguing that the term "sweatshop" is present in *Webster's* dictionary and could not possibly be considered inappropriate slang. Nike responded by quoting the company's rules, which state that the company can refuse to print anything on its shoes that it does not deem appropriate. Peretti replied that he was changing his previous order and would instead like to order a pair of shoes with a "color snapshot of the ten-year-old Vietnamese girl who makes my shoes." He never received a response.[1]

THE PR NIGHTMARE BEGINS

Before Nike could blink an eye, the situation turned into a public relations nightmare. Peretti forwarded the e-mail exchange to a few friends, who forwarded it to a few friends, and so forth. Within six weeks of his initial order, the story appeared in *The Wall Street Journal*, *USA Today*, and *The Village Voice*. Peretti himself appeared on *The Today Show*, and he estimates that 2 million people have seen the e-mail. At the height of the incident, Peretti was receiving 500 e-mails a day from people who had read the e-mail from as far away as Asia, Australia, Europe, and South America.[2,3]

Nike refused to admit any wrongdoing in the incident and stated that they reserved the right to refuse any order for whatever reason. Beth Gourney, a spokesperson for Nike, had the following to say regarding the incident:

---

* This case was written initially by Bryan S. Dennis, Idaho State University, and revised in 2010 by Archie B. Carroll, University of Georgia.

Clearly, he [Peretti] was attempting to stir up trouble; he has admitted it. He's not an activist. Mr. Peretti does not understand our labor policy. If he did, he would know that we do not hire children; our minimum age for hiring is 18…and we don't apologize for not putting the word "sweatshop" because our policy clearly states: "We reserve the right to cancel any order up to 24 hours after it has been submitted."[4]

Nike, Inc. is no stranger to sweatshop allegations. Ever since the mid-1990s, the company has been subject to negative press, lawsuits, and demonstrations on college campuses alleging that the firm's overseas contractors subject employees to work in inhumane conditions for low wages. As Philip Knight, the CEO and cofounder of Nike, once lamented, "The Nike product has become synonymous with slave wages, forced overtime, and arbitrary abuse."[5]

HISTORY OF NIKE, INC.

Philip Knight started his own athletic shoe distribution company in 1964. Using his Plymouth Reliant as a warehouse, he began importing and distributing track shoes from Onitsuka Company, Ltd., a Japanese manufacturer. First-year sales of $8,000 resulted in a profit of $254. After eight years, annual sales reached $2 million, and the firm employed 45 people. However, Onitsuka saw the huge potential of the American shoe market and dropped Knight's relatively small company in favor of larger, more experienced distributors. Knight was forced to start anew. However, instead of importing and distributing another firm's track shoes, he decided to design his own shoes and create his own company. The name he chose for his new company was "Nike."[6]

Nike's Use of Contract Labor

When the company began operations, Knight contracted the manufacture of Nike's shoes to two firms in Japan. Shortly thereafter, Nike began to contract with firms in Taiwan and Korea. In 1977, Nike purchased two shoe-manufacturing facilities in the United States—one in Maine, the other in New Hampshire. Eventually, the two plants became so unprofitable that the firm was forced to close them. The loss due to the write-off of the plants was approximately $10 million in a year in which the firm's total profit was $15 million. The firm had a successful IPO in 1980, eight years after the company was founded.

Nike became the largest athletic shoe company in the world.[7]

Nike does not own a single shoe or apparel factory. Instead, the firm contracts the production of its products to independently owned manufacturers. Today, practically all Nike subcontracted factories are in countries such as Indonesia, Vietnam, China, and Thailand, where the labor costs are significantly less than those in the United States. Worldwide, over 530,000 people are employed in factories that manufacture Nike products. On an earlier Web site that is no longer available, the company gave the following as a rough breakdown of the costs per shoe. With inflation ever with us, these figures increase over the years, but these data give us an idea of total costs relative to selling price:

Consumer pays:	$65
Retailer pays:	$32.50 to Nike, and then doubles the price for retail
Nike pays:	$16.25 and then doubles the price to retailers for shipping, insurance, duties, R&D, marketing, sales, administration, and profits

The $16.25 paid by the factory includes

Materials:	$10.75
Labor:	$2.43
Overhead + depreciation:	$2.10
Factory profit:	$0.97
Total costs:	$16.25[8]

Even in today's hi-tech environment, the production of athletic shoes is still a labor-intensive process. For example, for practically all athletic shoes, the upper portion of the shoe must be sewn together with the lower portion by hand. The soles must be manually glued together. Although most leaders in the industry are confident that practically the entire production process will someday be automated, it will still be years before the industry will not have to rely on human labor.

Other Firms in the Industry

Nike's use of overseas contractors is not unique in the athletic shoe and apparel industry. All other major athletic shoe manufacturers also contract with overseas manufacturers, albeit to various degrees. Athletic shoe firm New Balance Inc. is somewhat of an anomaly as it continues to operate five factories in the United States.[9]

Nike spends heavily on endorsements and advertising and pays several top athletes well over a million dollars a year in endorsement contracts. In contrast, New Balance has developed a different strategy. They do not use professional athletes to market their products. According to their "Endorsed by No One" policy, New Balance instead chooses to invest in product research and development and foregoes expensive endorsement contracts.[10]

THE SWEATSHOP MOVEMENT VERSUS NIKE

There is one pivotal event largely responsible for introducing the term "sweatshop" to the American public. In 1996, Kathie Lee Gifford, co-host of the formerly syndicated talk show "Live with Regis and Kathie Lee," endorsed her own line of clothing for Walmart. During that same year, labor rights activists disclosed that her "Kathie Lee Collection" was made in Honduras by seamstresses who earned 31 cents an hour and were sometimes required to work 20-hour days. Traditionally known for her pleasant, jovial demeanor and her love for children, Kathie Lee was outraged. She tearfully informed the public that she was unaware that her clothes were being made in so-called sweatshops and vowed to do whatever she could to promote the anti-sweatshop cause.[11]

Nike Is Accused

In a national press conference, Gifford named Michael Jordan as another celebrity who, like herself, endorsed products without knowing under what conditions the products were made. At the time, Michael Jordan was Nike's premier endorser and was reportedly under a $20 million per year contract with the firm.[12] Nike, the number-one athletic shoe brand in the world, soon found itself under attack by the rapidly growing anti-sweatshop movement.

Shortly after the Gifford story broke, Joel Joseph, chairperson of the Made in the USA Foundation,[13] accused Nike of paying underage Indonesian workers 14 cents an hour to make the company's line of Air Jordan shoes. He also claimed that the total payroll of Nike's six Indonesian subcontracted factories was less than the reported $20 million per year that Jordan received from his endorsement contract with Nike. The Made in the USA Foundation is one of the organizations that ignited the Gifford controversy and is largely financed by labor unions and U.S. apparel manufacturers that are against free trade with low-wage countries.[14]

Nike quickly pointed out that Air Jordan shoes were made in Taiwan, not Indonesia. Additionally, the company maintained that employee wages were fair and higher than the government-mandated minimum wage in all of the countries where the firm has contracted factories. The company released the following data about its wages:

Country	Minimum Monthly Wage	Average Monthly Wage at Nike Factories
Taiwan	14,124 NT$	25,609 NT$
South Korea	Won 306,030	Won 640,000
Indonesia	115,000 rupiah	239,800 rupiah
China	RMB 276	RMB 636
Thailand	2,950–3,150 baht	4,435 baht
Vietnam	331.050 VND	640.030 VND

Nike asserted that the entry-level income of an Indonesian factory worker was five times that of a farmer. The firm also claimed that an assistant line supervisor in a Chinese subcontracted factory earned more than a surgeon with 20 years of experience.[15] In response to the allegations regarding Michael Jordan's endorsement contract, Nike stated that the total wages in Indonesia were $50 million a year, which is well over what the firm pays Jordan.[16]

Nike soon faced more negative publicity. Michael Moore, the movie director whose documentary *Roger and Me* shed light on the plight of laid-off autoworkers in Flint, Michigan, and damaged the reputation of General Motors chairperson Roger Smith, interviewed Nike CEO Philip Knight for his movie *The Big One*. On camera, Knight referred to some employees at subcontracted factories as "poor little Indonesian workers." Moore's cameras also recorded the following exchange between Moore and Knight:

Moore: Twelve-year-olds working in [Indonesian] factories? That's OK with you?

Knight: They're not 12-year-olds working in factories...the minimum age is 14.

Moore: How about 14, then? Doesn't that bother you?

Knight: No.[17]

Knight, the only CEO interviewed in the movie, received harsh criticism for his comments. Nike alleged that the comments were taken out of context and were deceitful because Moore failed to include Knight's pledge to make a transition from a 14- to a 16-year-old minimum age labor force. Nike prepared its own video that included the entire interview.[18]

Thomas Nguyen, founder of Vietnam Labor Watch, inspected several of Nike's plants in Vietnam in 1998 and reported cases of worker abuse. At one factory that manufactured Nike products, a supervisor punished 56 women for wearing inappropriate work shoes by forcing them to run around the factory in the hot sun. Twelve workers fainted and were taken to the hospital. Nguyen also reported that workers were allowed only one bathroom break and two drinks of water during each eight-hour shift. Nike responded that the supervisor who was involved in the fainting incident had been suspended and that the firm had hired an independent accounting firm to look into the matters further.[19]

NIKE RESPONDS

In 1997, Nike hired former Atlanta Mayor Andrew Young, a vocal opponent of sweatshops and child labor, to review the firm's overseas labor practices. Neither party disclosed the fee that Young received for his services. Young toured 12 factories in Vietnam, Indonesia, and China, and was reportedly given unlimited access. However, he was constantly accompanied by Nike representatives during all factory tours. Furthermore, Young relied on Nike translators when communicating with factory workers.[20]

In his 75-page report, Young concluded, "Nike is doing a good job, but it can do better." He provided Nike with six recommendations for improving the working conditions at subcontracted factories. Nike immediately responded to the report and agreed to implement all six recommendations. Young did not address the issue of wages and standards of living because he felt he lacks the "academic credentials" for such a judgment.[21]

Public reaction to Young's report was mixed. Some praised Nike. However, many of Nike's opponents disregarded Young's report as biased and incomplete. One went so far as to state the report could not have been better if Nike had written it themselves and questioned Young's independence.[22,23]

In 1998, Nike hired Maria Eitel to the newly created position of vice president for corporate and social responsibility. Eitel was formerly a public relations executive for Microsoft. Her responsibilities were to oversee Nike's labor practices, environmental affairs, and involvement in the global community. Although this move was applauded by some, others were skeptical and claimed that Nike's move was nothing more than a publicity stunt.[24]

Later that same year, Philip Knight gave a speech at the National Press Club in Washington, DC, and announced six initiatives that were intended to improve the working conditions in its overseas factories. The firm chose to raise the minimum hiring age from 16 to 18 years. Nike also decided to expand its worker education program so that all workers in Nike factories would have the option to take middle and high school equivalency tests.[25] The director of Global Exchange, one of Nike's staunchest opponents, called the initiatives "significant and very positive." He also added, "we feel that the measures—if implemented—could be exciting."[26]

COLLEGE STUDENTS, ORGANIZED LABOR, AND NIKE

Colleges and universities have direct ties to the many athletic shoe and apparel companies (such as Nike, Champion, and Reebok) that contract with overseas manufacturers. Most universities receive money from athletic shoe and apparel corporations in return for outfitting the university's sports teams with the firm's products. In 1997, Nike gave $7.1 million to the University of North Carolina (UNC) for the right to outfit all of UNC's sports teams with products bearing the Nike Swoosh logo.[27] Additionally, academic institutions allow firms to manufacture apparel bearing the university's official name, colors, and insignias in return for a fee. In 1998, the University of Michigan received $5.7 million in licensing fees.[28] Most of these contract and licensing fees are allocated toward scholarships and other academic programs. Today, these practices continue and the amounts of money are much larger.

ORGANIZED LABOR

In 1995, the Union of Needletrades, Industrial and Textile Employees (UNITE) was founded. The union, a member of the AFL-CIO, was formed by the merger of the International Ladies' Garment Workers' Union and the Amalgamated Clothing and Textile Workers Union, and represented 250,000 workers in North America and Puerto Rico. Most of the union members work in the textile and apparel industry. In 1996, UNITE launched a "Stop Sweatshops" campaign after the Kathy Lee Gifford story broke to "link union, consumers, student, civil rights and women's groups in the fight against sweatshops at home and abroad."[29]

In 1997, UNITE, along with the AFL-CIO, recruited dozens of college students for summer internships. Many of the students referred to that summer as "Union Summer and it had a similar impact as Freedom Summer did for students during the civil rights movement."[30] The United Students Against Sweatshops (USAS) organization was formed the following year. It was founded and led by former UNITE summer interns.[31]

UNIVERSITY ORGANIZATIONS

The USAS established chapters at dozens of universities across the United States. Since its inception, the organization has staged a large number of campus demonstrations that are reminiscent of the 1960s. One notable demonstration occurred on the campus of UNC in 1997. Students of the Nike Awareness Campaign protested against the university's contract with Nike due to the firm's alleged sweatshop abuses. More than 100 students demanded that the university not renew its contract with Nike and rallied outside the office of the university's chancellor. More than 50 other universities, such as the University of Wisconsin and Duke, staged similar protests and sit-ins.[32]

In response to the protests at UNC, Nike invited the editor of the university's student newspaper to tour Nike's overseas contractors to examine the working conditions firsthand. Nike offered to fund the trip by pledging $15,000 toward the students' travel and accommodation costs. Ironically, Michael Jordan is an alumnus of UNC.[33]

Critics of the USAS contend that the student organization is merely a puppet of UNITE and organized labor. They cite the fact that the AFL-CIO has spent more than $3 million on internships and outreach programs with the alleged intent of interesting students in careers as union activists. The founders of the USAS are former UNITE interns. The USAS admits that UNITE has tipped off the student movement as to the whereabouts of alleged sweatshop factories. Also, in an attempt to spur campus interest in the sweatshop cause, UNITE sent two sweatshop workers on a five-campus tour. They have also coached students via phone during sit-ins and paid for regularly scheduled teleconferences between anti-sweatshop student leaders on different campuses. According to Allan Ryan, a Harvard University lawyer who has negotiated with the USAS, "[T]he students are vocal, but it's hard to get a viewpoint from them that does not reflect that of UNITE."[34]

Many students have denied allegations that they are being manipulated by organized labor and claim that they discovered the sweatshop issues on their own. Others acknowledge the assistance of organized labor but claim it is "no different from [student] civil rights activists using the NAACP in the 1960s."[35] John Sweeney, president of the AFL-CIO, claimed the role of organized labor was not one of manipulation but of motivation. Others assert that the union merely provides moral support.[36]

Regardless of the AFL-CIO's intentions, the students have had a positive impact on the promotion of organized labor's anti-sweatshop agenda over the years. According to the director of one of the several human rights groups that are providing assistance to the students,

> At this moment, the sweatshop protest is definitely being carried on the backs of university students. If a hundred students hold a protest, they get a page in The New York Times. If a hundred union people did that, they'd be locked up.[37]

In telling the world about itself, in 2010 USAS stated that it "is a grassroots organization of youth and students who believe that a powerful and dynamic labor movement will ensure greater justice for all people. We use our unique roles of students as consumers, workers, and members of the campus community to win victories that set precedents in the struggle for self-determination of working people everywhere, particularly campus workers and garment workers who make collegiate licensed apparel."[38] USAS sponsors two campaigns related to Nike's manufacturing facilities overseas: "Sweat Free Campus Campaign" and "Nike: Just Pay It."

THE FAIR LABOR ASSOCIATION AND THE WORKER RIGHTS CONSORTIUM

In 1996, a presidential task force of industry and human rights representatives was given the job of addressing the sweatshop issue. The key purpose of this task force was to develop a workplace code of conduct and a system for monitoring factories to ensure compliance. In 1998, the task force created the Fair Labor Association (FLA) to accomplish these goals. This organization was made up of consumer and human rights groups as well as footwear and apparel manufacturers. Nike was one of the first companies to join the FLA. Many other major manufacturers (Levi Strauss & Co., Liz Claiborne, Patagonia, Polo Ralph

Lauren, Reebok, Eddie Bauer, and Phillips-Van Heusen) along with hundreds of colleges and universities have also joined the FLA.[39]

FLA REQUIREMENTS

Members of the FLA must follow the principles set forth in the organization's Workplace Code of Conduct. The FLA Workplace Code of Conduct sets member standards in the following areas: forced labor, child labor, harassment or abuse, nondiscrimination, health and safety, freedom of association, wages and benefits, hours of work, and overtime compensation. Member organizations that license or contract with overseas manufacturers or suppliers are responsible for ensuring that factory employees are paid either the minimum wage as required by law or the average industry wage, whichever is higher. Additionally, the code of conduct sets limits on the number of hours employees can work, allows workers the right to collective bargaining, and forbids discrimination.[40]

Each member firm must conduct an internal audit of every manufacturing facility on a yearly basis. Furthermore, members of the FLA must disclose to the FLA the location of all subcontracted factories. This information would not be made public. The FLA uses a team of external auditors to monitor the compliance of these factories with the FLA's code of conduct. These monitoring activities consist of a combination of announced and unannounced factory visits, and results are made available to the public.[41]

THE WRC ALTERNATIVE

The USAS opposed several of the FLA's key components and created the Worker Rights Consortium (WRC) as an alternative to the FLA. The WRC asserts that the prevailing industry or legal minimum wage in some countries is too low and does not provide employees with the basic human needs they require. They proposed that factories should instead pay a higher "living wage" that takes into account the wage required to provide factory employees with enough income to afford housing, energy, nutrition, clothing, health care, education, potable water, child care, transportation, and savings. Additionally, the WRC supports public disclosure of all factory locations and the right to monitor any factory at any time. As of June 2010, 175 colleges and universities had joined the WRC and agreed to adhere to its policies.[42]

Nike, a member and supporter of the FLA, has opposed the WRC. The firm states that the concept of a living wage is impractical as "there is no common, agreed-upon definition of the living wage. Definitions range from complex mathematical formulas to vague philosophical notions." Additionally, Nike was once opposed to the WRC's proposal that the location of all factories be publicly disclosed. Nike also has claimed that the monitoring provisions set out by the WRC are unrealistic and biased toward organized labor.[43]

The University of Oregon, Philip Knight's alma mater, joined the WRC in the year 2000. Alumnus Knight had previously contributed over $50 million to the university—$30 million for academics and $20 million for athletics. Upon hearing that his alma mater had joined the WRC, Knight was shocked. He withdrew a proposed $30 million donation and stated that "the bonds of trust, which allowed me to give at a high level, have been shredded" and "there will be no further donations of any kind to the University of Oregon."[44,45]

NIKE COMES AROUND

In May 2001, Harsh Saini, Nike's corporate and social responsibility manager, acknowledged that the firm may not have handled the sweatshop issue as well as they could have and stated that Nike had not been adequately monitoring its subcontractors in overseas operations until the media and other organizations revealed the presence of sweatshops.

We were a bunch of shoe geeks who expanded so much without thinking of being socially responsible that we went from being a very big sexy brand name to suddenly becoming the poster boy for everything bad in manufacturing.

She added, "We realized that if we still wanted to be the brand of choice in 20 years, we had certain responsibilities to fulfill."[46]

OREGON REVERSES ITS DECISION

In early 2001, Oregon's state board of higher education cast doubt on the legality of the University of Oregon's WRC membership, and the university dissolved its ties with the labor organization.[47] In September of the same year, Phil Knight renewed his financial support. Although the exact amount of Knight's donation was kept confidential, it was sufficient to ensure that the $85 million expansion of the university's football stadium would go through as originally planned. In 2000, the stadium expansion plans suffered a significant setback when Knight withdrew his funding. Many of the proposed additions, such as a 12,000-seat capacity increase and 32 brand new skyboxes, could happen, largely due to Knight's pledge of financial support.[48,49]

Nike released its first corporate social responsibility report in October 2001. According to Phil Knight, "[I]n this report, Nike for the first time has assembled a comprehensive public review of our corporate responsibility practices."[50] The report cited several areas in which the firm could have done better, such as worker conditions in Indonesia and Mexico. The report, compiled by both internal auditors and outside monitors, also noted that Nike was one of only four companies that had joined a World Wildlife Fund program to reduce greenhouse admissions. Jason Mark, a spokesperson for Global Exchange, one of Nike's chief critics, praised the report and stated that Nike is "obviously responding to consumer concerns."[51]

KASKY v. NIKE, INC.

Nike's problems with fair labor issues continued on a related front. Labor activist Mark Kasky had sued Nike in 1998, arguing that Nike had engaged in false advertising when it denied that there was mistreatment of workers in Southeastern Asian factories. At issue was the question of whether Nike's defense of its practices was commercial speech or not, for which free speech protections apply. The California Supreme Court ruled that Nike's statements about labor conditions could be construed as false advertising. Nike appealed this ruling to the U.S. Supreme Court, which sent it back to the California court, without making a judgment on the free speech issue. In September 2003, Kasky and Nike settled the case for a $1.5 million donation to the FLA.[52] The settlement, however, left many questions unanswered.[53] Many feared that the risk of lawsuit would have a chilling effect, causing firms to no longer release social responsibility reports, which, unlike the SEC financial reports, are all voluntary. In 2001, Nike issued a corporate social responsibility report, but the company announced that, due to the California decision, they would not release a corporate social responsibility report in 2002–2003. Nike released a "Community Investment" report detailing its philanthropic efforts instead.[54] The company later released a corporate responsibility report in 2005–2006 and then again in 2008–2009.

CRITICS QUIET DOWN BUT DON'T GO AWAY

Nike's critics have not gone away, but they have quieted down as the company has taken steps to address many of the criticisms made over the years. Though the critics are less vocal today compared to previous periods, there is still some ongoing criticism of the company. Typical of the continuing opposition is the organization Educating for Justice (EFJ) that runs a continuing "Stop Nike Sweatshops" campaign. In 2006, EFJ planned a film titled *Sweat*. The film, as described on EFJ's Web site, describes the journey of two young Americans uncovering the story behind the statistics about Nike factory workers. Through the lens of their experiences, they claim viewers will discover the injustices of Nike's labor practices in the developing world, specifically in Indonesia, and how Nike's cutthroat, bottom-line economic decisions have a profound effect on human lives.[55] EFJ announced that the film was going to production in 2009, but in 2010, EFJ was still trying to raise money to complete the film and to release it for public viewing.[56]

One organization that remains quite active in taking Nike to task is "Team Sweat." Team Sweat identifies itself as an "international coalition of consumers, investors, and workers committed to ending the injustices in Nike's sweatshops around the world."[57] As of 2010, Team Sweat was active in the "Nike: Just Pay It" campaign that was being pushed by several anti-sweatshop organizations.

Team Sweat has claimed that Nike owes $2.2 million in severance pay to workers in Honduras when two Nike factories were closed. Team Sweat's claim was as follows:

> On Jan. 19, 2009, two Nike factories, Hugger de Honduras and Vision Tex, were closed, with severance agreements between the workers' unions and factory owners signed after the factory closures. It is 2010, still no severance has been paid, and when hounded over their exploitation of workers, Nike released a statement that they are "deeply concerned," but cannot assume any responsibility for the actions of their "subcontractors." Subcontractors, in this case, are proxies used by Nike to distance themselves from taking responsibility for the way their factory workers are treated.[58]

NIKE LATER GETS POSITIVE RECOGNITIONS

In spite of its controversial record on the issue of sweatshops and monitoring labor practices abroad, Nike has been the recipient of a variety of corporate social responsibility recognitions over the past several years. Many of these awards are for issues other than their labor practices abroad. Among the recent recognitions that Nike has received for its corporate social responsibility and sustainability practices are the following:[59]

- Nike Named as One of the 100 Best Corporate Citizens for 2010 by *Corporate Responsibility* magazine
- Nike Recognized as One of the World's Most Ethical Companies in 2010 by the Ethisphere Institute
- Nike Named in Top 10 of *Newsweek*'s 2009 Green Rankings
- Nike Named as One of 100 Most Sustainable Corporations in the World in 2009

QUESTIONS FOR DISCUSSION

1. What are the ethical and social issues in this case?
2. Why should Nike be held responsible for what happens in factories that it does not own? Does Nike have a responsibility to ensure that factory workers receive a "living wage"? Do the wage guidelines of FLA or WRC seem most appropriate to you? Why?
3. Is it ethical for Nike to pay endorsers millions while its factory employees receive a few dollars a day?
4. Is Nike's responsibility to monitor its subcontracted factories a legal, economic, social, or philanthropic responsibility? What was it ten years ago? What will it be ten years from now?
5. What could Nike have done, if anything, to prevent the damage to its corporate reputation? What steps should Nike take in the future? Is it "good business" for Nike to acknowledge its past errors and become more socially responsible?
6. What are the motivations of student organizations when they get involved in the anti-sweatshop movement? Why is their activism on some campuses but not on others?
7. Do you think Nike owes the $2.2 million in severance pay to its plants in Honduras? Or are these the responsibility of their subcontractors as they argue?
8. Nike seems to be a much more respected company today than it was back when the anti-sweatshop movement began. What has changed in Nike and the world to explain this?

ENDNOTES

1. Copy of e-mail exchange found at Department of Personal Freedom Web site, http://www.shey.net/niked.html.
2. *Ibid.*
3. ABC News Web site, http://abcnews.go.com/sections/business/DailyNews/nike010402.html.
4. *Ibid.*
5. Bien Hoa, "Job Opportunity or Exploitation," *Los Angeles Times* (April 18, 1999).
6. Philip Knight, "Global Manufacturing: The Nike Story Is Just Good Business," *Vital Speeches of the Day* 64(20): 637–640.
7. *Ibid.*
8. These data were presented on an earlier Nike Web site that is no longer available. The site was http://www.nikebiz.com/labor/faq.shtml.
9. New Balance Web site, http://www.newbalance.com/corporate/aboutus/corporate_about.php. Accessed September 21, 2007.
10. New Balance Web site, http://www.newbalance.com/.
11. David Bauman, "After the Tears, Gifford Testifies on Sweatshops—She Turns Lights, Cameras on Issue," *Seattle Times* (July 16, 1996), A3.
12. Del Jones, "Critics Tie Sweatshop Sneakers to 'Air' Jordan," *USA Today* (June 6, 1996), 1B.
13. Made in USA Foundation, http://www.madeinusa.org/. Accessed June 21, 2010.
14. *Ibid.*
15. Nike press release (June 6, 1996).
16. Del Jones, 1B.
17. Garry Trudeau, "Sneakers in Tinseltown," *Time* (April 20, 1998), 84.
18. William J. Holstein, "Casting Nike as the Bad Guy," *U.S. News & World Report* (September 22, 1997), 49.
19. Verena Dobnik, "Nike Shoe Contractor Abuses Alleged," *The Atlanta Journal-Constitution* (March 18, 1997), A14.
20. Simon Beck, "Nike in Sweat over Heat Raised by Claims of Biases Assessment," *South China Morning Post* (July 6, 1997), 2.
21. Matthew C. Quinn, "Footwear Maker's Labor Pledge Unlikely to Stamp Out Criticism," *The Atlanta Journal-Constitution* (June 25, 1997), F8.
22. G. Pascal Zachary, "Nike Tries to Quell Exploitation Charges," *The Wall Street Journal* (June 15, 1997).
23. Beck, 2.
24. Bill Richards, "Nike Hires an Executive from Microsoft for New Post Focusing on Labor Policies," *The Wall Street Journal* (January 15, 1998), B14.
25. Knight, 640.

26. Patti Bond, "Nike Promises to Improve Factory Worker Conditions," *The Atlanta Journal-Constitution* (May 13, 1998), 3B.

27. Allan Wolper, "Nike's Newspaper Temptation," *Editor & Publisher* (January 10, 1998), 8–10.

28. Gregg Krupa, "Antisweatshop Activists Score in Campaign Targeting Athletic Retailers," *Boston Globe* (April 18, 1999), F1.

29. UNITE Here, http://www.unitehere.org/. Accessed June 21, 2010.

30. Krupa, F1.

31. USAS, http://usas.org/. Accessed June 21, 2010.

32. Wolper, 8–10.

33. *Ibid.*, 8.

34. Jodie Morse, "Campus Awakening," *Time* (April 12, 1999), 77–78.

35. Krupa, F1.

36. Morse, 77–78.

37. *Ibid.*

38. USAS About Us, http://usas.org/about-us/. Accessed June 21, 2010.

39. Fair Labor Association, http://www.fairlabor.org/aboutus.html. Accessed June 21, 2010.

40. http://www.fairlabor.org/conduct. Accessed September 21, 2007.

41. *Ibid.*

42. Worker's Rights Consortium, http://www.workers-rights.org/about/. Accessed June 21, 2010.

43. Nike Web site, http://www.nikebiz.com/labor/index.shtml.

44. Philip Knight Press Release (April 24, 2000). Found at http://www.nikebiz.com/media/n_uofo.shtml.

45. Louise Lee and Aaron Bernstein, "Who Says Student Protests Don't Matter?" *BusinessWeek* (June 12, 2000), 96.

46. Ravina Shamdasani, "Soul Searching by 'Shoe Geeks' Led to Social Responsibility," *South China Morning Post* (May 17, 2001), 2.

47. Greg Bolt, "University of Oregon Ends Relationship with Antisweatshop Group," *The Register Guard* (March 6, 2001).

48. Hank Hager, "Frohnmayer: It's a Very Happy Day for Us," *Oregon Daily Emerald* (September 27, 2001).

49. Ron Bellamy, "Nike CEO to Resume Donations to University of Oregon," *The Register Guard* (September 26, 2001).

50. William McCall, "Nike Releases First Corporate Responsibility Report," *Associated Press State & Local Wire* (October 9, 2001).

51. *Ibid.*

52. Adam Liptak, "Nike Move Ends Case over Firm's Free Speech," *New York Times* (September 13, 2003).

53. For a more thorough discussion of this controversy, see David Hess and Thomas Dunfee, "The Kasky-Nike Threat to Corporate Social Reporting," *Business Ethics Quarterly* (January 2007), 5–32, and Don Mayer, "Kasky v. Nike and the Quarrelsome Question of Corporate Free Speech," *Business Ethics Quarterly* (January 2007), 65–96.

54. http://www.srimedia.com. For detailed coverage of this case and its implications, see http://www.reclaimdemocracy.org/nike/.

55. Educating for Justice, http://www.educatingforjustice.org/nikewages/sweat.html. Accessed September 21, 2007.

56. *Sweat: The Film*, http://www.sweatthefilm.org/story.htm. Accessed June 21, 2010.

57. Team Sweat, http://www.teamsweat.org/. Accessed June 21, 2010.

58. Team Sweat, "Students at Rutgers University Tell Nike to Just Pay It," March 26, 2010, http://www.teamsweat.org/?p=1355. Accessed June 21, 2010.

59. Nike: Awards and Recognitions, http://www.nikebiz.com/company_overview/awards_recognition.html. Accessed June 21, 2010.

CASE 22

DTC: The Pill-Pushing Debate*

What do Nasonex® and Flomax® have in common? They are both 2010 gold medal winners for their direct-to-consumer (DTC) advertising.[1] Although their brand name recognition does not rival that of Coca-Cola, their names are familiar to consumers across the nation. As the flag bearers of the DTC advertising efforts of the pharmaceutical industry, they are at the forefront of the DTC debate. Even the great recession did nothing to slow the rate of DTC advertising spending: In 2009, overall DTC ad spending increased by 1.9 percent to $4.51 billion, and industry experts expected the growth to continue.[2] The pill-pushing debate is one critical part of the broader issue regarding Big Pharma's marketing tactics (Case 21).

THE PROBLEM

Why debate DTC advertising? In his testimony before the Senate Commerce Subcommittee on Consumer Affairs, Dr. Sidney Wolfe, director of the Public Citizen's Health Research Group, expressed the following concern: "There is little doubt that false and misleading advertising to patients and physicians can result in prescriptions being written for drugs that are more dangerous and/or less effective than perceived by either the doctor or the patient. This can then lead to a subsequent toll of deaths and injuries that would not have occurred had safer, more effective drugs been prescribed."[3] Dr. Wolfe cites the following findings from medical studies as cause for concern:

1. Consumers rate drugs significantly more positively when ads have incomplete risk statements.
2. Consumers believe that there is prior scrutiny of DTC ads by the FTC and that DTC ads are held to a higher standard than other ads. Both of those beliefs are wrong.
3. DTC ads provide only a minimal amount of educational information.
4. When a study asked what patients would do if a doctor refused to prescribe a drug that a patient wanted because of a DTC ad, 25 percent said they would seek a prescription elsewhere; 15 percent said

they would terminate their relationship with the physician.[4]

Another concern relates to opportunity costs and the danger that DTC advertising will siphon funds from other more important purposes. A recent report from the U.S. Government Accountability Office (GAO) found that money spent on DTC advertising "increased twice as fast from 1997 through 2005 as spending on promotion to physicians or on research and development."[5] As of 2010, the United States and New Zealand remained the only two developed countries to allow the practice of DTC advertising.[6]

THE DEBATE

Consumer groups claim that one cause of the increase in health-care costs is the explosion of DTC ads and the unnecessary medication that results. The advertising seems to work. One study showed that the sales of the heavily advertised drugs increased by 32 percent compared to 14 percent for other drugs. However, proponents of DTC ads argue that they help patients. Dr. Richard Dolinar, an endocrinologist, says that the ads empower consumers, "Direct-to-consumer advertising is getting patients with diabetes into my office sooner so they can be treated."[7]

Most physicians disagree with Dr. Dolinar: 64 percent believe there should be some sort of moratorium on DTC advertising in the United States, 44 percent would approve a moratorium of two years or more, and 27 percent believe that DTC ads should be banned completely.[8] Doctors claim it makes it very difficult to prescribe the appropriate medication when a patient comes to your office already committed to the drug he or she wants the doctor to prescribe. This takes much of the diagnosis and prescribing freedom and authority out of the hands of the professionals who should be making these judgments. Dr. Kurt Stange, editor of the *Annals of Family Medicine*, described the effect of DTC ads on the patient–doctor relationship in an editorial calling for a ban of DTC ads:[9]

> *DTC ads manipulate the patient's agenda and steal precious time away from an evidence-based primary care clinician agenda that is attempting to promote healthy behavior, screen for early-stage treatable disease, and address mental health. The negative*

---

* This case was written by Ann K. Buchholtz, Rutgers University. Updated in 2010.

consequences of this manipulation of the public, the patient, the clinician, and their relationship are subtle but pervasive. An insidious adverse effect occurs in what is not done during the limited time of a visit. Discussing why the advertised drug is not the best option for a particular patient may mean that a mammogram is not ordered, an important health behavior is not discussed, a family matter is not brought up, a deeper patient concern is never articulated, and a diagnosis for which there is no drug ad is not made. The clinician is put in the role of gatekeeper for the advertised commodity rather than a gateway for prioritizing health care based on the concerns of patients and the science-based recommendations for preventive, chronic disease, mental health, and family care.

QUESTIONS FOR DISCUSSION

1. What are the ethical issues in this case?
2. Should DTC advertising be judged by the same criteria as other advertising? If not, how should it be judged differently?
3. What public policy changes would you advocate regarding DTC? Should the United States and/or New Zealand ban them?

ENDNOTES

1. http://www.dtcperspectives.com/website/Conferences/DTC-Awards/Advertising-Awards.html. Accessed July 23, 2010.
2. "Direct-to-Consumer Advertising: Review and Outlook 2010," http://www.marketresearch.com/product/display.asp?productid=2691452&xs=r.
3. Sidney M. Wolfe, "Direct-to-Consumer (DTC) Ads: Illegal, Unethical, or Both," *Public Citizen's Health Research Group Health Letter* (September 2001), 3–4.
4. *Ibid.*
5. http://www.gao.gov/htext/d0754.html. Accessed July 23, 2010.
6. "Direct-to-Consumer Advertising in the United States," http://www.sourcewatch.org.
7. Ira Teinowitz, "DTC Regulation by FDA Debated," *Advertising Age* (July 30, 2001), 6.
8. "Physicians Back DTC Ban," *MM&M* (August 2007), 26.
9. Kurt C. Stange, "Time to Ban Direct-to-Consumer Prescription Drug Marketing," *Annals of Family Medicine* (March/April 2007), 101.

CASE 23

Big Pharma's Marketing Tactics*

"Big Pharma" is the name the business press uses for the gargantuan pharmaceutical industry. Most of us are familiar with Big Business and Big Government. Now Big Pharma is in the news and has been for several years regarding its marketing, advertising, and sales tactics. As *Time* magazine recently stated, it's hard to empathize with the drug industry these days because of the high cost of our prescriptions. We either just emptied our wallets in paying for our latest prescription or just returned on a Greyhound bus from Canada, where we bought our prescriptions for less.[1] Public perceptions of the pharmaceutical industry add

to its problems. In a major poll, Big Pharma was called greedy as well as shifty, and it was found that most people do not trust the industry to disclose bad news about its products.[2]

Big Pharma has been aware that it is in for challenges to its marketing and sales tactics. Not too long ago, a major conference was held in Boston, where industry representatives discussed the sale and illegal marketing of drugs for "off label" uses that were not approved by the Food and Drug Administration (FDA). A lawyer from one of the law firms that sponsored the conference said, "Rarely has a conference been more timely."[3] Since that conference, it is uncertain how much progress has been made.

It is hard to visualize Big Pharma cowering before FDA regulators because the industry has built up an

* This case was written and revised by Archie B. Carroll, University of Georgia. Updated in 2010.

army of lobbyists in Washington, DC, to protect its interests. Public Citizen, a citizen interest group, reported that the industry had 526 lobbyists—almost one for every member of Congress. Though the public values the drugs the industry makes available for sale, increasingly, the multibillion dollar industry's social responsibilities are being questioned.[4]

THE PHARMACEUTICAL INDUSTRY

The pharmaceutical industry is one of the healthiest and wealthiest in America. According to 2009 financial data, the pharmaceutical industry was the second most profitable industry, behind only mining/crude oil production. For the top ten companies, their profits as a percentage of revenues were 19.1 percent.[5]

The top U.S. pharmaceutical companies, according to their March 2010 sales data, include the familiar names, with the most profitable at the top of the list:[6]

1. Johnson & Johnson
2. Pfizer
3. Abbott Laboratories
4. Merck
5. Wyeth
6. Bristol-Myers Squibb
7. Eli Lilly
8. Amgen
9. Genentech
10. Baxter International

Among this group, only Johnson & Johnson ranked (#4) among *Fortune*'s "most admired companies in 2010."[7] None of them appeared in the top ten most socially responsible corporations for 2010.

The pharmaceutical industry spends more on advertising than on research and development. This includes both professional and direct-to-consumer (DTC) spending by the drug makers.[8] In spite of its size and success, Big Pharma has been called into question for a number of years now for its questionable marketing, advertising, and sales techniques. The charges have included questionable advertising to consumers (DTC) (see Case 20) and dubious ethics, and a number of them have resulted in lawsuits. It seems quite amazing, actually, that the pharmaceutical industry has not been more in the spotlight than it has been.

FROM SCIENCE TO SALESMANSHIP

An overall criticism of Big Pharma is that the industry has abandoned science for salesmanship.[9] That is, the industry has become more concerned with pushing pills for whatever problem than for developing new and important drugs. An example of this was provided in the aggressive marketing by Novartis of its fourth biggest selling drug. Was this drug a lifesaver? No, it's Lamisil, a pill for toenail fungus. Yes, toenail fungus can turn a nail yellow, but apparently no one has died of this illness. On the other hand, a few people may have died taking the drug, as regulators linked the drug to at least 16 cases of liver failure, including 11 deaths. Novartis claimed most of these patients had preexisting illnesses or were on other drugs.[10]

Many patients taking Lamisil were enticed to the drug by a grotesque cartoon creature named Digger the Dermatophyte, who is a squat, yellowish character with a dumb-guy big city accent. In the TV ads, Digger lifts a toenail, creeps beneath it, and declares, "I'm not leavin'!"[11] One group calculated that Novartis spent $236 million on Lamisil ads over three years, but Novartis denies this figure. In the first run of the commercial, Digger is crushed by a giant Lamisil tablet. Regulators thought the ad so overstated the drug's benefits that the company had to pull that particular version of the ad. It has been reported that the drug cured the problem in only 38 percent of patients, but Lamisil's sales increased 19 percent after it.[12] In short, it was alleged that the industry spends a fortune on remedies to cure trivial maladies while its drug research pipelines run dry. This has been dubbed "salesmanship over science."[13] Others have called it marketing and profits coming before consumer safety and wellness.[14]

Another way pharmaceutical firms emphasize sales over science was illustrated in 2010 when the *New York Times* revealed that drug giant SmithKline Beecham had secretly compared it own diabetes drug, Avandia, to a competing medicine, Actos, which was produced by Takeda. The company discovered that their own drug was riskier, but the company spent the next 11 years trying to cover up the results. According to the *New York Times*, sales of Avandia were crucial to the company and the company failed to disclose the research so it could keep making money.[15] In short, sales trumped science. After an investigation, the FDA review panel recommended that the drug should be kept on the market.[16]

PROMOTIONS TO MED STUDENTS

Big Pharma starts its promotional techniques while the doctors are still students in medical school. There the med students have in the past received free lunches, pens, notepads, and other gifts that are given by the companies. The companies start early trying to persuade the young doctors to prescribe their products by inundating them with logo-infested products and other gifts. A number of medical students have become fed up with the practice and have resisted the free gifts and have started movements to stop the practice from occurring in the first place.

One med student, Jaya Agrawal, launched a national campaign calling on students to sign a pledge saying they would not accept drug-industry gifts. Medical students on other campuses have organized seminars and lectures on the issue. Agrawal was reminded of how difficult it would be to get everyone to think like her when she moved into an apartment she was planning to share with two other med students and noticed a Big Pharma logo on a clock in three rooms of the apartment.[17]

LAWSUITS

PRICING

The attorneys general in Ohio and Pennsylvania filed lawsuits charging fraud or deceptive sales practices against a number of companies. The State of Ohio claimed five companies provided false wholesale pricing data that led their Medicaid program to pay more than it should have for drugs. The State of Pennsylvania filed suits against Pfizer and 12 other drug makers claiming problems with pricing. They also questioned the free samples and free trips for doctors that the companies allegedly have been providing.[18] The Department of Justice spends a lot of time monitoring companies that may be collecting more from Medicare and Medicaid than they should.[19]

OFF-LABEL OFFENSES

Companies have been reportedly illegally promoting drugs for uses for which they were not approved. The result of this is that doctors may be prescribing, and patients may be using, drugs for conditions for which those medicines are not needed, are not appropriate, or might hurt patients.[20] A consideration of specific cases and specific companies reveals some of the details. Examples of this practice included Pfizer illegally prescribing Neurontin, an antiseizure drug. It is legal for doctors to prescribe FDA-approved drugs for whatever uses they see fit. However, according to the law, the drug companies are not permitted to encourage or promote their drugs for uses for which they have not been approved.[21]

Government officials claimed that Pfizer's Warner-Lambert unit pushed doctors to prescribe Neurontin for maladies ranging from migraines to social disorders even though it was not approved for such uses. The company's tactics, it was claimed, involved sending doctors on lavish trips to Florida or to the Olympics, where they received presentations on unapproved uses of the drug. The one-on-one sales tactics later used included sales pitches to doctors, the dispatching of "medical liaisons" who falsely presented themselves to be experts, and teleconferences in which the sales reps would recruit physicians to talks about off-label uses.[22] Pfizer agreed to pay $430 million in criminal fines and civil penalties, and the company's lawyers pledged that Pfizer and its units would stop promoting drugs for unauthorized purposes.[23]

Another example was the promotion of Paxil. When Eliot Spitzer was the attorney general of New York, he filed a lawsuit alleging that GlaxoSmithKline (GSK), the world's second largest drug firm, had covered up results from clinical trials of its drug, Paxil, an antidepressant. Spitzer alleged that the drug was at best ineffective in children and at worst could increase suicidal thoughts. GSK denied the charges. Spitzer charged the company with "repeated and persistent fraud" in promoting the drug.[24] Today, the company faces multiple lawsuits by patients alleging a variety of problems with the drug.[25] Since December 2009, Paxil lawsuit settlements have totaled $1 billion.[26]

The FDA and state attorneys general have been up in arms about drug companies marketing their products for "off-label" uses and continue to pursue companies for these violations.[27]

IMPROPER PAYMENTS

Sometimes the questionable marketing of drugs entails improper payments or bribes. The Securities and Exchange Commission (SEC) announced that the drug maker Schering-Plough Corporation would pay a $500,000 penalty to settle claims that one of its subsidiaries made improper payments to a Polish charity in a quest to get a Polish government health official to buy the company's products.[28]

The SEC claimed that Schering-Plough Poland donated about $76,000 to a Polish charity over a three-year period. Chudnow Castle Foundation, the charity, was headed up by a health official in the Polish government. Apparently, this information came to light while regulators were investigating several pharmaceutical companies for compliance with the U.S.

Foreign Corrupt Practices Act. The SEC charged that the payments were not accurately shown on the company's books and that the company's internal controls failed to prevent or detect them. The SEC said that the charity was legitimate, but that the company made the contributions with the expectation of boosting drug sales. In addition to paying the fine, the company also agreed to hire an independent consultant to review the company's internal control system and to ensure the firm's compliance with the Foreign Corrupt Practices Act.[29]

Johnson & Johnson is another company that has been pursued for improper payments. In its case, the improper payments were in connection with the sale of medical devices in two foreign countries. Johnson & Johnson turned itself in, and the worldwide chairperson of medical devices and diagnostics took responsibility and retired.[30] In a related case, in 2010 the company was being investigated for possible bribery in its medical device unit in Shanghai, in which it is alleged that the company bribed the deputy chief of the Chinese state FDA.[31]

PAYMENTS TO DOCTORS

Few cases more vividly illustrate the questionable marketing tactics of Big Pharma than that of the allegations against Schering-Plough. According to an investigation by the *New York Times*, Schering-Plough used the marketing tactic of making payments to doctors in exchange for their commitment to exclusively prescribe the company's medications. One doctor reported receiving an unsolicited check for $10,000 in the mail. He said it had been made out to him personally in exchange for an enclosed "consulting" agreement in which all he had to do was prescribe the company's medicines.[32]

FINANCIAL LURES

Interviews with 20 doctors, industry executives, and observers close to the investigation of Schering-Plough and other drug companies revealed a "shadowy system of financial lures" that the companies had been using to convince the physicians to favor their drugs. In the case of Schering-Plough, the tactics included paying doctors large sums of money to prescribe its drug for hepatitis C and to participate in the company's clinical trials that turned out to be thinly disguised marketing ploys that required very little on the part of the doctors. The company even barred doctors from participating in the program if they did not exhibit loyalty to the company's drugs.[33]

One doctor, a liver specialist, and eight others who were interviewed, said that the company paid them $1,000 to $1,500 per patient for prescribing Intron A, the company's hepatitis C medicine. The doctors were supposed to gather data, in exchange for the fees, and pass it on to the company. Apparently, many doctors were not diligent in recordkeeping, but the company did little. Another liver disease specialist said that the trials were "merely marketing gimmicks."[34] According to some doctors, the company would even shut off the money if one of the doctors wrote prescriptions for competing drugs, or even spoke favorably about other competing drugs. Other doctors reported being signed up for consulting services and being paid $10,000, and the only purpose was to keep them loyal to the company's products.[35] In another case, Schering-Plough had been charged with and was expected to plead guilty to federal charges that it had not provided Medicaid with the lowest drug prices and would pay a fine.[36]

In response to the allegations against the company, Schering-Plough CEO Fred Hassan reported that the violations took place before he took office. He went on to outline steps he was taking to get the company on track. This included instituting an "integrity hotline" for employees to report wrongdoing and the creation of a chief compliance officer to report directly to the CEO and the board. Hassan said that compliance has to become "part of the DNA" of a drug company.[37] Another company official said that the company has been "undergoing a company-wide transformation since the arrival of new leadership in mid-2003," which is a "commitment to quality compliance and business integrity."[38]

In 2010, Johnson & Johnson was accused of paying kickbacks to Omnicare, one of the nation's largest nursing home chains, in order to get them to prescribe certain drugs at the chain's facilities. *The Wall Street Journal* reported that the drug giant is for the first time agreeing to publish the names of the doctors to whom it has been making payments. As it turns out, Johnson & Johnson, Eli Lilly & Co., Pfizer Inc., GlaxoSmithKline PLC, Merck & Co., and Cephalon Inc. are all among the drug makers that have begun posting names of doctors, although some have been mandated under settlement terms of government probes, according to the journal.[39]

QUESTIONABLE DOCTORS

Some Big Pharma companies continue to pay doctors with questionable credentials to oversee their drug trials and contribute to marketing. One representative case was a doctor whose medical license was suspended in 1997 by the Minnesota Board of Medical Practice. *The New York Times* reported that from 1997 to 2005, this same doctor was hired by several drug firms to conduct multiple drug trials and he was paid for speaking and consulting fees as well.[40] *The New York Times*'s investigation found that 103 doctors in Minnesota, who had been disciplined by the Minnesota Board of Medical Practice, received a total of $1.7 million in payments for research and marketing services rendered.[41] Though Minnesota was the only state willing to make its records available for inspection, experts say this is a national problem.

GIFTS TO DOCTORS

In total, Big Pharma gives an estimated $19 billion worth of gifts to physicians every year. This is a practice that has worried a number of attorneys general of the states. Attorney General Anne Milgram of New Jersey summoned together a task force to consider putting limits on the gratuities given to doctors and their staffs. Milgram concluded, "Patients should be getting prescription and device recommendations based on what's best for them, not based on financial incentives doctors receive from companies."[42]

Several years ago, Bristol-Myers Squibb Co. agreed to pay more than $515 million to settle fraud allegations involving kickbacks to doctors and inflated drug prices, according to the U.S. Department of Justice. The U.S. Attorney in Boston said that Bristol agreed to settle the charges that doctors were illegally paid to motivate them to prescribe Bristol's drugs. Part of this was the company participating in various programs that included trips to luxurious resorts.[43]

Pharmaceutical companies have given meals, tickets to shows and sporting events, ski and beach vacations disguised as medical education seminars, consulting "jobs" for which the doctors do no work, and other gifts, as part of their marketing strategies, for decades. The companies expect something in return. They expect the doctors to prescribe their medicines. It is estimated that there is an army of 88,000 or more pharmaceutical reps, many of them young and beautiful, supplying the doctors and their staffs with gifts and freebies. It is argued that these gifts damage the doctors' integrity.[44]

An article published in the *New England Journal of Medicine* reported on a survey of doctors and found that 94 percent of them had some type of relationship with the drug industry. The most frequent drug-industry ties were food and drinks in the workplace (83 percent), drug samples (78 percent), payments for consulting (18 percent), payments for speaking (16 percent), reimbursement for meeting expenses (15 percent), and tickets to cultural or sporting events (7 percent).[45] The Pharmaceutical Research and Manufacturers of America (PhRMA), the main trade association of Big Pharma, did adopt a voluntary Code on Interactions with Healthcare Professionals in 2002.[46] It is widely believed, however, that the questionable marketing tactics of the industry continued. Certainly, its excessive advertising and sales-force spending lead consumers to believe that Big Pharma cares more about profits than about protecting health.[47]

BIG BUCKS, BIG PHARMA

The Media Education Foundation, a nonprofit corporation that produces and distributes educational materials observing the impact and ethics of the media industry, released a hard-hitting film, *Big Bucks, Big Pharma: Marketing Disease and Pushing Drugs*, in 2007.[48]

According to the Media Education Foundation, *Big Bucks, Big Pharma* pulled back the curtain on the multibillion dollar pharmaceutical industry to expose the insidious ways that illness is used, manipulated, and in some instances created for capital gain. Focusing on the industry's marketing practices, media scholars and health professionals helped viewers understand the ways in which DTC pharmaceutical advertising glamorizes and normalizes the use of prescription medication, and works in tandem with promotion to doctors. Combined, these industry practices have shaped how both patients and doctors understand and relate to disease and treatment.

Lobbying

Big Pharma is able to ward off most government regulations through the power of its huge lobbying force. The pharmaceutical lobby has defeated most attempts to restrain drug marketing. In September 2007, Congress passed a sweeping drug safety bill, but before it was passed, it was stripped of provisions that were intended to limit the ability of the industry to market directly to consumers. In addition, in 11 states that considered legislation to expose pharmaceutical gift-giving, the bills were either defeated or stalled.[49]

In 2010, the drug lobby showered money on its hero for the moment, Senator Harry Reid of Nevada, who was running for reelection. The drug lobby began a pro-Reid TV blitz in which Reid was praised for saving jobs and understanding that "good jobs with good benefits [mean] a better future." Voters were urged to call Reid and tell him to keep fighting for Nevada families, but "Nevada families" did not pay for the ad, the drug lobby did. Critics viewed the support of Reid by the Big Pharma lobby as payback for the health-care bill passed that he guided through the Senate.[50]

QUESTIONS FOR DISCUSSION

1. What are the ethical issues in this case?
2. Who are the primary stakeholders in these incidents?
3. Is there any justification for the marketing tactics described in the case? Which are acceptable and which are questionable?
4. What is your evaluation of giving free promotional items to med students? What are the arguments for and against such practices?
5. What ethical principles may be violated by the marketing tactics described? Do any of these ethical principles *support* the companies' actions?
6. Big Pharma needs enormous sums of money to conduct R&D and to advance its industry. Do the ends justify the means because our health is at stake?
7. What response do you think physicians should take when approached regarding some of the schemes presented in this case?
8. What does your personal research indicate is the status of the above cases or that of Big Pharma?

ENDNOTES

1. Daren Fonda and Barbara Kiviat, "Curbing the Drug Marketers," *Time* (July 5, 2004), 40–42.
2. Mark Dolliver, "People Think Big Pharma Is Shifty—In Addition, That Is, to Being Greedy," *Adweek* (May 28, 2007), 28.
3. *Ibid.*, 40.
4. Michael A. Santoro and Thomas M. Gorrie, *Ethics and the Pharmaceutical Industry* (Cambridge: Cambridge University Press, 2005).
5. *Fortune 500*, Top Industries, Most Profitable, http://money.cnn.com/magazines/fortune/global500/2009/performers/industries/profits/. Accessed July 12, 2010.
6. List of Pharmaceutical Firms, http://en.wikipedia.org/wiki/List_of_pharmaceutical_companies. Accessed July 12, 2010.
7. *Fortune*'s Most Admired Companies 2010, http://money.cnn.com/magazines/fortune/mostadmired/2010/full_list/. Accessed July 12, 2010.
8. "Big Pharma Spends More on Advertising Than Research and Development, Study Finds," January 2008, http://www.sciencedaily.com/releases/2008/01/080105140107.htm. Accessed July 12, 2010.
9. Robert Langreth and Matthew Herper, "Pill Pushers: How the Drug Industry Abandoned Science for Salesmanship," *Forbes* (May 8, 2006), 94–102.
10. *Ibid.*, 94.
11. *Ibid.*
12. *Ibid.*
13. *Ibid.*, 96.
14. Dani Veracity, "Pharmaceutical Fraud: How Big Pharma's Marketing and Profits Come before Consumer Safety and Wellness," http://www.naturalnews.com/z020345.html. Accessed July 12, 2010.
15. Gardiner Harris, "Diabetes Drug Maker Hid Test Data on Risks, Files Indicate," *The New York Times* (July 12, 2010), http://www.nytimes.com/2010/07/13/health/policy/13avandia.html?_r=1&nl=health&emc=healthupdateema2. Accessed July 13, 2010.
16. "Avandia on Trial," *The Wall Street Journal* (July 16, 2010), A16.
17. Chris Adams, "Student Doctors Protest Largess of Drug Makers," *The Wall Street Journal* (June 24, 2002), B1.
18. Monica Roman, "Pointing at Big Pharma," *BusinessWeek* (March 22, 2004), 56.
19. Arlene Weintraub, "Big Pharma: Pushing the Pills a Bit Too Hard," *BusinessWeek* (February 26, 2007).
20. Carolyn Susman, "False Marketing of Drugs Raises Red Flags," *Cox News Service* (May 25, 2004).
21. *Ibid.*
22. Lewis Krauskopf, "Pfizer Fined $430M; Guilty of Illegal Marketing of Drug," *The Record* (Bergen County, NJ, May 14, 2004), B01.
23. David Evans, "Pfizer Broke the Law by Promoting Drugs for Unapproved Uses," *Bloomberg Businessweek* (November 9, 2009), http://www.bloomberg.com/apps/news?pid=newsarchive&sid=a4yV1nYxCGoA. Accessed July 12, 2010.
24. "Business: Trials and Tribulations; Pharmaceuticals," *The Economist* (June 19, 2004), 74.

25. "Glaxo Loses Bid to Preempt Paxil Lawsuit," *Pharmalot* (February 26, 2010), http://www.pharmalot.com/2010/02/glaxo-loses-bid-to-preempt-paxil-lawsuit/. Accessed July 12, 2010.

26. Parker Waichman Alonso LLP, "Paxil Lawsuit Settlements Amount to $1 Billion So Far," Yourlawyer.com (December 14, 2009), http://www.yourlawyer.com/articles/read/17400. Accessed July 12, 2010.

27. Weintraub.

28. Judith Burns, "SEC Settles Bribery Case vs. Schering-Plough Corp.," *The Wall Street Journal* (June 9, 2004).

29. *Ibid.*

30. Weintraub.

31. Jim Edwards, "J&J's Other Headache: Foreign Bribery Probe Targets Shanghai Unit," BNET (June 25, 2010), http://industry.bnet.com/pharma/10008735/jjs-other-headache-foreign-bribery-probe-targets-shanghai-unit/. Accessed July 12, 2010.

32. Gardiner Harris, "As Doctor Writes Prescription, Drug Company Writes a Check," *The New York Times* (June 27, 2004), 1YT.

33. *Ibid.*

34. *Ibid.*

35. *Ibid.*

36. Reuters News Service, "Schering-Plough Could Plead Guilty on Pricing—NYT" (June 28, 2004).

37. Fonda and Kiviat, 41.

38. Reuters (June 28, 2004).

39. "Johnson & Johnson to Disclose Payments to Doctors," NewsInferno (July 9, 2010), http://www.newsinferno.com/archives/21870. Accessed July 12, 2010.

40. Gardiner Harris and Janet Roberts, "After Sanctions, Doctors Get Drug Company Pay," *New York Times* (June 3, 2007), A1.

41. *Ibid.*, 20.

42. Quoted in Arlene Weintraub, "Drug Marketing: Will Pharma Finally Have to Fess Up?" *BusinessWeek* (October 8, 2007).

43. Reuters News Service, "Bristol-Myers Settles U.S. Charges for $515 Million" (September 28, 2007), http://www.reuters.com/article/health-SP/idUSN2842357320071001. Accessed October 1, 2007.

44. "Gifts from Drugmakers Damage Doctors' Integrity," *USA Today* (February 8, 2006), 10A.

45. Reported in Rita Rubin, "Most Doctors Get Money, Gifts from Industry," *USA Today* (April 26, 2007), 4D. Also see "Doctors Still Chummy with Drug Sales Reps," *AARP Bulletin* (June 2007).

46. *Ibid.*

47. "Hard Times for the Hard Sell," *BusinessWeek* (February 5, 2007), 32.

48. "Big Bucks, Big Pharma: Marketing Disease and Pushing Drugs," http://www.mediaed.org/cgi-bin/commerce.cgi?preadd=action&key=224. Accessed July 13, 2010.

49. Weintraub, 36.

50. Timothy P. Carney, "Drug Lobby Showers Money on Its Hero Harry Reid," *Washington Examiner* (July 7, 2010), http://www.washingtonexaminer.com/politics/Drug-lobby-showers-money-on-its-hero-Harry-Reid-97882064.html. Accessed July 13, 2010.

CASE 24

A Moral Dilemma: Head versus Heart*

SITUATION

A 42-year-old male suddenly and unexpectedly died of a brain tumor, leaving behind a wife and a small child. During a review of his employee benefits, it was noted that although he was eligible for an additional company-sponsored life insurance plan used for plant decommissioning purposes, his name was not identified on the insurance rolls.

EVALUATION

It was determined that when the employee was promoted to supervisor three years before his death, his paperwork had been submitted to the corporate office for inclusion in the program. Coincidentally, the program was under review at the time, and the employee was not entered into the program due to administrative oversight.

LEGAL REVIEW

A legal department review determined that the program was offered to certain supervisory employees at the discretion of the company. Therefore, there was no legal obligation to pay.

_____

* This case was prepared by David A. Levigne.

DILEMMA

The death benefit was twice the employee's salary. Because the employee was not enrolled in the life insurance program, if the company were to pay any benefit, it would have to come from the general fund (paid from the business unit's annual operating budget).

TO PAY OR NOT TO PAY?

The company could argue that it must start acting like a business and use its head, not its heart. Existing company programs adequately compensate the individual's family; no additional dollars should be paid. On the other hand, it was an administrative oversight that failed to enter the employee into the program. What would you want the company to do for you if you were the one who suddenly died?

QUESTIONS FOR DISCUSSION

1. As a manager, you are steward of the company's funds. Are you willing to forgo departmental improvements and potential salary increases to honor this claim? Remember, there is no legal obligation to pay.
2. Would you feel an ethical obligated to pay? Would you be perceived as a weak manager if you do?
3. What are the ethical issues in this case?
4. What would you do? Why?

PART 4

External Stakeholder Issues

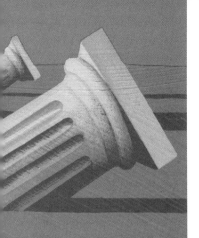

11

Business, Government, and Regulation

CHAPTER LEARNING OUTCOMES

After studying this chapter, you should be able to:

1. Articulate a brief history of the government's role in its relationship with business.

2. Appreciate the complex interactions among business, government, and the public.

3. Identify and describe the government's nonregulatory influences, especially the concepts of industrial policy and privatization.

4. Explain government regulation and identify the major reasons for regulation, the types of regulation, and issues arising out of deregulation.

5. Provide a perspective on privatization versus federalization, along with accompanying trends.

"Can governments manage more ethically than capitalism?"[1] As government involvement in business has increased, this question has taken center stage. The government tends to become involved in business after serious problems arise, and there was no shortage of problems in the early 2000s. The first decade of the 21st century has been so difficult for people and economies throughout the world that *Time* magazine dubbed it "The Decade from Hell."[2] Of course, the decade's problems were not only financial. They ranged from the natural disasters of the Asian tsunami and Hurricane Katrina to terrorist attacks and warfare. Nonetheless, from a financial perspective, the decade was a debacle, bookended by two major economic meltdowns. The decade began with the tech stock plunge and the Enron, WorldCom, and other scandals: These created a market crash that now seems mild compared with what followed at the end of the decade.[3] At the end of the decade, as *Time* noted, "a housing bubble fueled by cheap money and excessive borrowing set ablaze by derivatives, so-called financial weapons of mass destruction, put the economy on the brink of collapse. We will be sorting through the damage for years."[4] One of the key issues to sort out as that decade ends is the role of government in business, and that is the focus of this chapter. The last decade has swung the pendulum of government involvement in business from minimal intervenor to major player. The depth, scope, and direction of government's involvement in business have made the business or government relationship one of the most hotly debated issues today. The government's role, particularly in the regulation of business, has ensured its place among the major stakeholders with which business must establish an effective working relationship if it is to survive and prosper.

This increased level of government involvement in business is likely to remain for some time. The seriousness of the economic crisis revealed systemic weaknesses that have led many to call for structural change with greater protections.[5] At the same time, many worry about the impact of increased government involvement on business's innovation and growth.[6] This chapter examines the relationship between business and government, with the general public assuming an important role in the discussion as well. A central concern in this chapter is the government's role in influencing business. Exploring this relationship carefully will provide an appreciation of the complexity of the issues surrounding business or government interactions. From the prospective manager's standpoint, one needs a rudimentary understanding of the forces and factors involved in these issues before beginning to talk intelligently about strategies for dealing with them. Unfortunately, more is known about the nature of the problem than about the nature of solutions, as is common when dealing with complex social issues. The chapter discusses how business attempts to influence government and public policy.

The Pendulum of Government's Role in Business

To be certain, the government involvement pendulum has swung back and forth for years. Business has never been fond of the government's having an activist role in establishing the ground rules under which it operates. In contrast, public interest has been cyclical, going through periods when it has thought that the federal government had too much power and other periods when it has thought that government should be more activistic in its business dealings. As an exemplar of a free market economy, the United States serves as a case in point. There have been periods of strong government intervention. In 1791, while serving as Secretary of the U.S. Treasury, Alexander Hamilton pushed for tariffs to protect domestic manufacturers. The purpose was to protect fledgling industries. Then, in the 1860s, President Abraham Lincoln expanded federal powers by opening the west to settlement.[7] By the 1860s, industrialists like John D. Rockefeller dominated the steel, oil, and banking industries, swinging the pendulum back toward business autonomy.[8]

At the same time, government gave large land grants as incentives for private business to build railroads. Several railroads had grown large and strong through mergers, and people began to use them because their service was faster, cheaper, and more efficient. This resulted in a decline in the use of alternative forms of transportation, such as highways, rivers, and canals. Many railroads began to abuse their favored positions. For example, a railroad that had a monopoly on service to a particular town might have charged unfairly high rates for the service. Competitive railroads sometimes agreed among themselves to charge high but comparable rates. Higher rates were charged for shorter hauls, and preference was shown to large shippers over smaller shippers. Public criticism of what were perceived as abusive practices led to the passage of the Interstate Commerce Act of 1887, which was intended to prevent discrimination and abuses by the railroads. This act marked the beginning of extensive federal government regulation of interstate commerce. The act created the Interstate Commerce Commission, which became the first federal regulatory agency and a model for future agencies.[9]

Many large manufacturing and mining firms also began to abuse consumers during the late 1800s. Typical actions included the elimination of competition and the charging of excessively high prices. During this period, several large firms formed organizations known as *trusts*. A trust was an organization that brought all or most competitors under a common control that then permitted them to eliminate most of the remaining competitors by price-cutting, an act that forced the remaining competitors out of business. Then, the trusts would restrict production and raise prices. As a response, Congress passed the Sherman Antitrust Act (Sherman Act) in 1890, which became the first in a series of actions intended to control monopolies in various industries. The Sherman Act outlawed any contract, combination, or conspiracy in restraint of trade, and it also prohibited the monopolization of any market. In the early 1900s, the federal government used the Sherman Act to break up the Standard Oil Company, the American Tobacco Company, and several other large firms that had abused their economic power.[10]

The Clayton Antitrust Act was passed in 1914 to augment the Sherman Act. It addressed other abusive practices that had arisen. It outlawed price discrimination that gave favored buyers preference over others and forbade anticompetitive contracts, whereby a company would agree to sell only to suppliers who agreed not to sell the products of a rival competitor. The act prohibited an assortment of other anticompetitive practices. Also in 1914, Congress formed the Federal Trade Commission, which was intended to maintain free and fair competition and to protect consumers from unfair or misleading practices.[11]

Then the Great Depression led to President Franklin Roosevelt's New Deal and the creation of powerful regulatory agencies.[12] Significant legislation included the Securities Act of 1933 and the Securities and Exchange Act of 1934. These laws were aimed at curbing abuses in the stock market, stabilizing markets, and restoring investor confidence in order to prevent a second depression. Significant labor legislation during this same period signaled government involvement in a new area. Several examples were the 1926 Railway Labor Act, the 1932 Norris–LaGuardia Act, and the 1935 Wagner Act. During the New Deal period in the 1930s, government also took on a new dimension in its relationship with business, actively assuming responsibility for restoring prosperity and promoting economic growth through public works programs. In 1946, this new role of government was formalized with the passage of the Full Employment Act. Prior to the mid-1950s, most congressional legislation affecting business was economic in nature. The 1960s and 1970s continued the trend of government involvement but the concern was largely with the quality of life.[13] Several illustrations of this include the Civil Rights Act of 1964, the Water Quality Act of 1965, the Occupational Safety and Health Act of 1970, the Consumer Product Safety Act of 1972, and the Warranty Act of 1975.

The pendulum swung back when Ronald Reagan came into office in 1980. The public was growing somewhat weary of an active federal role. Throughout the 1980s, the federal government played less and less of a role, especially in terms of monitoring and regulating business. It was not without reason, therefore, that in late 1989 *Time* magazine ran a cover story entitled "Is Government Dead?"[14] The "Reagan Revolution" of an inactive federal government had left the public with a desire for government to become active again. It was against this backdrop that George Herbert Walker Bush was elected president in 1988. During the first Bush administration (1988–1992), the country witnessed a growth in the rate of federal government spending.

The Clinton administration (1992–2000) then sought a middle ground, advocating a more activist role for the government in international politics and social concerns, while launching other initiatives to control federal spending. As the economy rebounded in the early 1990s, the peace dividend bore fruit, and cost-cutting initiatives took hold, the rate of government spending slowed dramatically.[15] With the exception of the Americans with Disabilities Act of 1990, the 1990s were characterized by financial deregulation. The repeal of the Glass–Steagall Act, the Commodity Futures Modernization Act, and the revisions to the Community Reinvestment Act all created a more permissive lending environment.[16]

The George W. Bush administration came into office in 2001 on a platform of a reduced role for federal government; however, the attack on the World Trade Center changed everything.[17] Repercussions of the attack, such as the bailout of the troubled airline industry, potential relief for other distressed industries, the increase in military spending, and the federalization of airport security expanded dramatically both government spending and governmental intervention in business activities.[18] Key examples of this are the USA Patriot Act of 2001 and the Homeland Security Act. In addition, the passage of Sarbanes–Oxley Act brought stricter regulation to publicly traded businesses.

By the end of the second Bush presidency, the financial crisis prompted bailouts of the financial services and auto industries that were supported by both then-President Bush and President-elect Obama. When Barack Obama became President in 2009, the economic crisis was in full swing and government was involved in business operations at historically high levels. He continued that trend through a variety of initiatives such as efforts to institute new banking regulations and fees to recoup the bailout money, as well as plans to institute a community bank lending fund to encourage loans to small businesses. In its first 15 months, the Obama administration passed new regulations establishing credit card rules, health care reform, and consumer financial protection. At this writing, the Obama administration is focusing on financial regulatory reform.

Just as the areas in which government has chosen to initiate legislation keep changing, the multiplicity of roles that government has assumed has increased the complexity of its relationship with business. Government is not only a regulator of business that can determine the rules of the game but also a major purchaser with buying power that can affect a business or industry's likelihood of survival. It can elevate some businesses and industries while devaluing others through the setting of government policy. It can even create new businesses and industries through subsidization and privatization. The range of government roles illuminates the crucial interconnectedness between business and government and the difficulty both business and the public have in fully understanding (much less prescribing) what government's role ought to be in relation to business.

The Roles of Government and Business

We do not intend to philosophize in this chapter on the ideal role of government in relation to business, because this is outside our stakeholder frame of reference. However, we will strive for an understanding of current major issues as they pertain to this vital relationship. For effective management, government's role as a stakeholder must be understood.

The fundamental question underlying our entire discussion of business or government relationships is, "What should be the respective roles of business and government in our socioeconomic system?" This question is far easier to ask than to answer, but as we explore it, some important basic understandings begin to emerge.

The issue could be stated in a different fashion: Given all the tasks that must be accomplished to make our society work, which of these tasks should be handled by government and which by business? This poses the issue clearly, but other questions remain unanswered. If we decide, for example, that it is best to let business handle the production and distribution roles in our society, the next question becomes "How much autonomy are we willing to allow business?" If our goals were simply the production and distribution of goods and services, we would not have to constrain business severely. In modern times, however, other goals have been added to the production and distribution functions—a safe working environment for those engaging in production, equal employment opportunities, fair pay, clean air, safe products, employee rights, and so on. When we superimpose these goals on basic economic goals, the task of business becomes much more complex and challenging.

Because we do not automatically factor these more socially oriented goals into business decision making and processes, it often falls on the government to ensure that those goals that reflect social concerns be achieved. Thus, whereas the marketplace dictates

FIGURE 11-1 The Clash of Ethical Systems between Business and Government

Business Beliefs	Government Beliefs
• Individualistic ethic	• Collectivistic ethic
• Maximum concession to self-interest	• Subordination of individual goals and self-interest to group and group interests
• Minimizing the load of obligations society imposes on the individual (personal freedom)	• Maximizing the obligations assumed by the individual and discouraging self-interest
• Emphasizes inequalities of individuals	• Emphasizes equality of individuals

economic production decisions, government becomes one of the citizenry's designated representatives charged with articulating and protecting the public interest.

A Clash of Ethical Belief Systems

A clash of emphases partially forms the crux of the antagonistic relationship that has evolved between business and government over the years. Although this clash will vary between different countries and cultures, the underlying tension between business and government still holds true. This problem has been termed "a clash of ethical systems." The two ethical systems (systems of belief) are the **individualistic ethic of business** and the **collectivistic ethic of government**. Figure 11-1 summarizes the characteristics of these two philosophies.[19]

The clash of these two ethical systems partially explains why the business or government relationship is adversarial in nature. In elaborating on the adversarial nature of the business or government relationship, Neil Jacoby offered the following comments:

> *Officials of government characteristically look upon themselves as probers, inspectors, taxers, regulators, and punishers of business transgressions. Businesspeople typically view government agencies as obstacles, constraints, delayers, and impediments to economic progress, having much power to stop and little to start.*[20]

Executives continue to express frustration with government. In a 2010 McKinsey survey of executives from a range of industries and functional specialists, nearly half expressed serious frustration with government involvement in business.[21] The frustrations included concerns that regulators and policy makers do not understand the economics of their industry (41 percent), that government often blames business for society's problems (44 percent), and that it is difficult to determine the best way to work productively with government (44 percent).[22]

The business–government relationship not only continues to be adversarial but also has become more complicated in the 21st century. The goals and values of a pluralistic society continue to be complex, numerous, interrelated, and difficult to reconcile. At the same time, economic conditions compel governments around the world to take a more active role in the economy.[23] As the conflicts among diverse interest groups increase, it becomes more difficult to reconcile trade-off decisions and establish social priorities. A 2009 NBC/*Wall Street Journal* poll of adults in the United States underscores the underlying tensions in the relationship. When asked about the role of government in business following the economic crisis, 49 percent said that the government was doing too many things and 45 percent said that the government should do more.[24]

Interaction of Business, Government, and the Public

This section offers a brief overview of the influence relationships among business, government, and the public. This should be helpful in understanding both the nature of the public policy decision-making process and the current problems that characterize the business–government relationship. Figure 11-2 illustrates the pattern of these influence relationships.

One might rightly ask at this point, "Why include the public? Isn't the public represented by government?" In an ideal world, perhaps this would be true. To help us appreciate that government functions somewhat apart from the public, we depict it separately in the diagram. In addition, the public has its own unique methods of influence that we also depict separately.

Government–Business Relationship

Government influences business through regulation, taxation, and other forms of persuasion that we will consider in more detail in the next section. Business, likewise, has its approaches to influencing government, which we will deal with in Chapter 12. Lobbying, in one form or another, is business's primary means of influencing government.

Public–Government Relationship

The public uses the political processes of voting and electing officials (or removing them from office) to influence government. It also exerts its influence by forming special-interest groups (farmers, small business owners, educators, senior citizens, truckers, manufacturers, and so forth) to wield more targeted influence. Government, in turn, uses politicking, public policy formation, and other political influences to have an impact on the public.

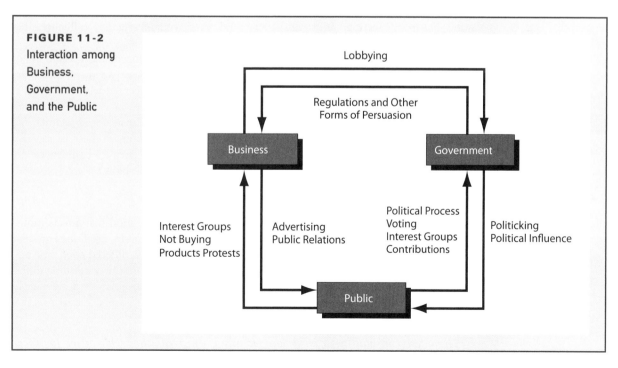

FIGURE 11-2
Interaction among Business, Government, and the Public

Business–Public Relationship

Business influences the public through advertising, public relations, and other forms of communication. The public influences business through the marketplace or by forming special-interest groups (e.g., AARP, Friends of the Earth, American Civil Liberties Union) and protest groups.

Earlier we raised the question of whether government really represents the public. This question may be stated another way: "Who determines what is in the public interest?" In our society, determining the public interest is not a simple matter. Whereas government may be the official representative of the public, we should not assume that representation occurs in a straightforward fashion. As we saw in Figure 11-2, the public takes its own initiatives both with business and with government. The three major groups, therefore, are involved in a dynamic interplay of influence processes that strive to define the current public interest.

Our central concern in this chapter is with government's role in influencing business, and we now turn our attention to that topic. Here we will begin to see more clearly how government is a major stakeholder of business. Government's official priority is in representing the public interest as it sees and interprets the public's wishes. But, like all large bureaucratic organizations, government also takes on a life of its own with its own goals and agenda.

Government's Nonregulatory Influence on Business

By recognizing that the federal government's 2011 budget was $3.8 trillion, we can begin to appreciate the magnitude of the effect government has on all institutions in society.[25] We limit our treatment to the federal government's influence on business, but we must remain mindful of the presence and influence of state and local governments as well.

Broadly speaking, we may categorize the kinds of influence government has on business as *nonregulatory* and *regulatory*. In the next section, we focus on government regulation, but in this section, let us consider the wide range of *nonregulatory* influences that government has on business.

Two major issues merit consideration before we examine some of the specific policy tools or mechanisms government uses to influence business. These two major issues are (1) industrial policy and (2) privatization. Industrial policy is concerned with the role that government plays in a national economy, and privatization zeroes in on the question of whether current public functions (e.g., public education, public transit, social security, fire service) should be turned over to the private (business) sector. Both of these issues have important implications for the business–government relationship. They are both important, because they seem to come into and out of popularity on a regular basis.

Industrial Policy

Industrial policy may be defined as "every form of state intervention that affects industry as a distinct part of the economy."[26] This very broad definition by itself does not give us enough focus to understand the concept. Industrial policy has differed over time and across countries in both its philosophy and its actions.[27] In spite of the continuing differences between countries, a global shift in approach to industrial policy is occurring. In his article, "Industrial Policy: A Dying Breed or a Re-emerging Phoenix?," Karl Aiginger notes the gradual demise of the old form of industrial policy:

> *The interest in industrial policy has recently re-emerged, although not for industrial policy as it used to be. Supporting ailing industries, subsidies, and preventing exit will*

never be completely abandoned, but they are no longer supported by policy makers, evidence, or economic theory. Fortunately, traditional industrial policy has become much more difficult thanks to trade agreements, community law and WTO.[28]

The newer form of industrial policy is exemplified by Robert Reich in his book *The Next American Frontier*, wherein he argues for a national industrial policy that attempts to identify winning (or sunrise) industries and foster their growth while redirecting resources from losing (or sunset) industries.[29] Reich's book was published when the United States lost significant ground to Japan as the world leader in industrial expansion. Many experts saw the very survival of the U.S. economy at stake in the face of subsidized foreign competition from Japan and other industrialized countries. Indeed, a trade confrontation arose between the United States and Japan over the significant trade imbalances arising out of these issues.

Today, the United States is known for preferring an industrial policy that enables regional specialization through a focus on science, technology, small firms, and industrial clusters.[30] However, the United States has always had strong reactions to any form of industrial policy because it conflicts with widely held views on the role of government in the economy.[31] During the Reagan (1980–1988) and first Bush (1988–1992) administrations, the notion of industrial policy was not looked upon with great favor. Both these administrations advocated a free market posture rather than government activism via industrial policy. President Bill Clinton, however, supported several actions that typify an active industrial policy. For example, the Clinton administration took an activist stance in promoting the Internet by creating a Framework for Global Electronic Commerce. This framework outlined key principles for supporting the evolution of electronic commerce, identified where international efforts were needed, and designated the U.S. governmental agencies responsible for leading the effort. They did this because businesses were wary of becoming involved in the then-new Internet because they were unsure of the legal environment, and they feared government intervention would stifle Internet commerce.[32]

The George W. Bush administration entered office intending to follow in the footsteps of the early Reagan and Bush administrations by adopting a free market posture and minimizing government intervention. However, the tragic events of September 11, 2001, prompted extensive new regulations in the areas of homeland security, and the Enron meltdown, as well as the other financial scandals that followed, prompted new regulations in corporate governance. That trend has continued with the Obama administration that entered office during a deep global recession. These events prompted additional investment in industrial policy in areas such as financial services and auto industry bailouts, mortgage loan intervention, and high-tech investments in non-carbon-based energies.

The trend toward stronger industrial policies is likely to continue for a while as countries work to recover from the global economic meltdown. Reich noted that the government is reshaping industries and sectors representing more than one-third of the U.S. economy, and that the percentage is likely to be even higher in Europe and Japan given their societies' greater tolerance for government intervention.[33]

Arguments for Industrial Policy

The economic meltdown of 2008 compelled governments around the world to take an active part in reviving economic growth and restoring financial stability.[34] To do this, governments have needed not only to focus on economic reform but also on ways to make government more efficient and effective.[35] The United States, with its deeply held resistance to government involvement in business, provides an opportunity to see how the pendulum of industrial policy swings back and forth.

Historically, the U.S. government has opted to minimize government involvement in business, but crises can always change that stance. The recent global financial crisis led to bailouts in the auto, banking, and insurance industries. After the September 11, 2001, terrorist attacks, the crippled airline industry requested bailouts of about $24 billion. Congress passed a bailout program of $15 billion—$5 billion in immediate cash assistance and $10 billion in loan guarantees.[36] Other affected industries soon made requests as well. There is a long history of government stepping in to rescue industries in distress. In 1971, the Lockheed Corporation received $250 million in loan guarantees from Congress. In 1976, the federal government merged seven failing Northeast railroads and then spent about $7 billion to keep the combined entity afloat. In 1979, the Chrysler Corporation received up to $1.5 billion in loan guarantees. And, in 1989, Congress addressed the Savings and Loan Crisis by closing more than 1,000 S&Ls at a cost of $124 billion.[37]

It is too early to assess the outcomes of the most recent bailouts but some government interventions have been unqualified successes. Chrysler paid off its loan seven years early, and the government received a profit of $350 million. Others, however, have been fraught with problems. The Lockheed bailout was rocky from the start. When it was revealed that Lockheed had paid foreign bribes, the government ousted two top executives and proceeded to give Lockheed activities very close scrutiny.[38] In the case of airlines, the U.S. government has made $119 million from their equity ownership in the shares of airlines like Frontier.[39] One key to success is for the government to require equity in return for aid: The U.S. government made their profit from the Chrysler bailout due to such an arrangement.[40] It would seem logical then that all government bailouts would include an equity arrangement; however, corporate lobbyists typically block the way, according to former Senator Peter Fitzgerald (R-Illinois), one of the authors of the airline bailout agreement. He said a divided airline industry made it possible for them to integrate an equity arrangement into their bailout bill.[41]

Arguments against Industrial Policy

Critics of industrial policy also have significant reasons for their views. Critics say that government interference reduces the market's efficiency and stifles innovation. How do you keep politics out of what ought to be economic decisions? Most experts do not believe the United States should focus on rescuing steel and other "sunset" industries. They argue we ought to promote emerging "sunrise" industries, such as breakthrough products in high technology.

Those who oppose industrial policy say that foreign success with it has been highly variable. As a country with a strong industrial policy, Japan provides a case in point. Japan has had as many failures as successes with its government's development agency, the Ministry of International Trade and Industry (MITI). MITI helped to build Japan's computer, semiconductor, and steel industries; however, its efforts to promote the aluminum-refining, petrochemical, shipping, and commercial aircraft industries were not successful.[42] Further, Japan's favorable industrial policies (*keiretsu*), combined with lifetime employment, are ill suited to surviving economic recessions, and the Japanese business system has produced relatively few entrepreneurial risk takers.[43]

Few observers today would argue that a strong industrial policy helps firms compete in a fast-moving global economy; in the absence of a crisis, one rarely hears the term today outside of economics. Most developed countries are not seeking to institute a strong industrial policy, if they can avoid doing so.[44] Nevertheless, government intervention in business continues, sometimes in ways that are appropriate and sometimes not. Critics charge that various interventions such as "voluntary" restrictions on imports, occasional bailouts for nearly bankrupt companies, and a wide array of subsidies, loan

---

ETHICS IN PRACTICE CASE

Incompatible Goals for the FDA

When it comes to life-saving drugs, we want both safety and speed. We want safety because a drug that cures one disease should not cause another. We want speed because the longer it takes for a life-saving drug to hit the market, the more people will die because it was not available in time to save their lives.

In the 1980s, there was a public outcry because the FDA took nearly three years to approve most drugs. With the AIDS epidemic in full swing, that meant that many people died before the drugs that would save them became available. With the help of the Congress, the FDA and the drug industry eventually worked out an arrangement in which companies would pay millions of dollars in fees in return for an FDA guarantee that drug reviews would be completed within a year, or six months for a medicine that would save lives.

The arrangement effectively addressed the problem of the time required for FDA approval; however, a new problem arose. Drug companies would not let their money pay for drug safety monitoring after the drug was on the market. As federal funding slowed, and the FDA became increasingly dependent on industry funds, the safety program diminished and speed became the watchword. The deal required that the FDA submit annual reports on review time but not on the safety of drugs that were already on the market. Managers are judged by the speed with which decisions are made. Questions about safety are seen as simply slowing down the decision process. FDA employees who speak out about safety concerns report that they are often ostracized and penalized for expressing their concerns.

1. What are the ethical issues in this case? Who are the stakeholders and what are their stakes?
2. When dealing with drugs that treat critical illnesses, how do you decide between speed and safety when enhancing one diminishes the other? On what basis are you making your decision?
3. Was it wrong for companies to help fund drug testing when it meant that life-saving drugs could be available to patients more quickly? Were the problems that arose inevitable?
4. If you were responsible for regulating pharmaceutical drugs, what changes would you make to alleviate this situation? What trade-offs would you make? What type of industrial policy would your decision be advocating? Be specific.

Source: Gardiner Harris, "Potentially Incompatible Goals at F.D.A.," *The New York Times* (June 11, 2007), Section A, 14.

---

guarantees, and special tax benefits for particular firms and industries constitute an industrial policy by default.[45] Thus, is it important to think carefully about the role of government in business so that a default industrial policy does not emerge.

Interest in the concept of industrial policy ebbs and flows, depending on which administration is in office and what is happening in the external environment. Many of the problems that started the current debate are still with us, while new problems have arisen to add further complexity to the issue. Industrial policy (whether coordinated or by default) is a powerful nonregulating approach by government to influence business that is certain to be a topic of debate for years to come.

Privatization

Privatization, generally speaking, refers to the process of "turning over to" the private sector (business) some function or service that was previously handled by some government body.[46] Privatization is an integral part of the 21st century strategies of both developed and developing countries, with the intent being able to capture both the discipline of the free market and a spirit of entrepreneurial risk-taking.[47]

Recent efforts are breaking new ground with the privatization of valuable assets instead of that of surplus and underutilized assets, as has been the focus in the past. To that end, some states have now begun to privatize their lotteries.[48] These privatization arrangements involve long-term concessions that specify clear relationships, roles, and responsibilities for the business and the government: The state continues to own the asset but gives private companies the opportunity to manage them in a way that extracts the most value.[49] Investors have paid billions for the cash flows from tolls and other user fees on such properties as the Chicago Skyway and the Indiana toll road; however, some legislators are expressing concern about possible price gouging, future infrastructure support, and the length of the leases.[50]

To understand privatization, we need to differentiate two functions government might perform: (1) producing a service and (2) providing a service.[51]

Producing versus Providing a Service. A city government would be *providing* a service if it employed a private security firm to work at the coliseum during the state basketball play-offs. This same city government would be *producing* a service if its own police force provided security at the same basketball tournament. The federal government would be providing medical care to the aged with a national Medicare program. The "production" of medical care would be coming from private physicians. The government would be providing and producing medical care if it employed its own staff of doctors, as, for example, the military does. The terminology can be very confusing, but the distinction must be made, because sometimes government provides a service (has a program for and actually pays for a service) and at other times it also produces a service (has its own employees who do it).[52]

The Privatization Debate. Proponents of privatization in both the United States and Europe suggest that the functions of entire bureaucracies need to be contracted out to the private sector. They maintain that government at all levels is involved in thousands of businesses in which it has no real comparative advantage and no basic reason for being involved. They also argue that publicly owned enterprises are less efficient and less flexible than are competitive private firms.[53] Opponents of privatization contend that there are certain activities that cannot be safely or effectively handled by the private sector. They point to the **federalization** of airport security (the return of airport security to the government sector) following the attack on the World Trade Center.

Privatization efforts are always undertaken with the hope that they will lead to improvements in efficiency and overall performance. In some cases, these hopes are realized, but in others they are not. On average, a privatized firm's performance improves, but there is considerable variance in postprivatization performance among individual firms.[54] Differences in postprivatization performance can result from differences in the ways that firms implement privatization programs as well as the nature of the program being privatized. The nature of top management, the functioning of the board, and the strategic actions the firms undertake will all contribute to the likelihood of a privatization strategy's success.[55] This was supported by the findings of a 2009 study on the efficiency and effectiveness of privatized urban transit services after 25 years of operation. They found no difference between public and private provision of services and concluded that the situation specifics are better predictors of performance than whether the service was public or private.[56]

Privatization may end up being one of the many casualties of the global economic recession. When state and local governments did not have enough money to keep up their crumbling infrastructures, they welcomed private equity firms' promises to invest billions in the infrastructure if they could privatize the operations. However, excessive optimism and high leverage led to problems. According to Dunia Wright, who heads U.S. and Europe Industry Funds Management for an Australian firm that oversees $19 billion, "Aggressive operating and financial assumptions in times when debt was cheap resulted in acquisitions that had little or no pricing discipline and didn't work for investors."[57] A public backlash is also stunting privatization efforts. Chicago mayor

Richard Daley was criticized sharply after leasing 36,000 parking meters to a Morgan Stanley-led investor group for 75 years. The new operators moved quickly to quadruple parking rates and eliminate free parking on Sundays.[58]

The two issues, industrial policy and privatization, are largely unresolved and so they continue to be discussed and debated. As we have seen, the success of these efforts is largely dependent on their context—both the environments in which they are adopted and the ways in which they are implemented. It is clear that both industrial policy and privatization will have significant implications for the business–government relationship for years to come.

We now return to our discussion of the ways in which government uses various policies and mechanisms for influencing business.

Other Nonregulatory Governmental Influences on Business

Government has a significant impact on business by virtue of the fact that it has a large payroll and is a *major employer* itself. At all levels, government employs millions of people who, as a consequence of being government employees, see things from the government's perspective. Government is also in the position of being a standard setter; for example, the eight-hour workday began in the federal government. After a decade of emphasis on the private sector, the role of government has begun to expand since the attack on the World Trade Center—bailouts of troubled industries, increased defense spending, a shift of R&D money toward defense purchases, and higher spending on the social safety net all give government a larger role in the U.S. economy.[59]

Government is one of the largest *purchasers* of goods and services produced in the private sector. Some key industries, such as aerospace, electronics, and shipbuilding, are very dependent on government purchasing. Government can exert significant influence over the private sector by its insistence that minorities be hired, depressed areas be favored, small businesses be favored, and so on. Changes in government policy can dramatically change a firm's business environment.[60] For some firms in narrow markets, such as defense, the government dominates and controls whether or not those firms have a good year—indeed, whether or not they survive at all.[61]

Government influences the behavior of business through the use of *subsidies* in a variety of ways. Generous subsidies are made available to industries such as agriculture, fishing, transportation, nuclear energy, and housing and to groups in special categories, such as minority-owned enterprises and businesses in depressed areas. Quite often these subsidies have special qualifications attached.

Government also influences business, albeit indirectly, by virtue of its *transfer payments*. Government provides money for social security, welfare, and other entitlement programs that totals hundreds of billions of dollars every year. These impacts are indirect, but they do significantly affect the market for business's goods and services.[62]

Government is a major *competitor* of business. Organizations such as the TVA compete with private suppliers of electricity; the Government Printing Office competes with private commercial publishers and printing firms; and the United States Postal Service competes with private delivery services. In areas such as health, education, recreation, and security, the competition between government and private firms runs the gamut of levels—federal, state, and local.

Government loans and *loan guarantees* are sources of influence as well. Government lends money directly to small businesses, housing providers, farmers, and energy companies. Often such loans are made at lower interest rates than those of private competitors. Loan guarantee programs, such as the one provided to Chrysler, is another way in which government's influence is felt.[63]

Spotlight on SUSTAINABILITY

Walking Their Talk at the EPA

The United States Environmental Protection Agency has undertaken an initiative to green their own operations, in keeping with the policies and procedures they promote externally. To accomplish its mission of protecting public health and the natural environment, the EPA employs approximately 24,000 people and utilizes more than 10.1 million square feet of office buildings and laboratories located across the United States. To reduce the agency's environmental footprint they are putting a range of strategies into operation, including building new, environmentally sustainable structures, improving the energy efficiency of older buildings, conserving water and energy, offsetting carbon emissions, and celebrating sustainability champions. Information on the Greening EPA initiative is available at http://www.epa.gov/greeningepa/index.htm.

Taxation, through the Internal Revenue Service, is another example of a government influence. Tax deductibility, tax incentives, depreciation policies, and tax credits are tools that are all at the disposal of the government. A critical example of the government's taxing power occurred when a "luxury tax" was added as a minor part of the government's deficit reduction package. This new luxury tax ended up virtually crippling the boat-building industry. It led to massive layoffs and adversely affected dozens of related industries. Ironically, the luxury tax resulted in lower tax revenues than those industries had produced.[64]

Monetary policy, although it is administered through the Federal Reserve System, can have a profound effect on business. Although the Federal Reserve System is technically independent of the executive branch, it often responds to presidential leadership or initiatives.

Finally, *moral suasion* is a tool of government.[65] This refers to the government's attempts, usually through the president, to "persuade" business to act in the public interest by taking or not taking a particular course of action. These public-interest appeals might include a request to roll back a price hike, show restraint on wage and salary increases, or exercise "voluntary" restraints of one kind or another. When New York Mayor Rudy Giuliani exhorted businesses to reopen, customers to return to buying, and tourists to return to New York City after the attacks on the World Trade Center, he was exerting moral suasion.

Government's Regulatory Influences on Business

In many ways, government regulation has been the most controversial issue in the business–government relationship. Government regulation has affected virtually every aspect of how business functions. It has affected the terms and conditions under which firms have competed in their respective industries. It has touched almost every business decision ranging from the production of goods and services to packaging, distribution, marketing, and service. Most people agree that some degree of regulation has been necessary to ensure that consumers and employees are treated fairly and are not exposed to unreasonable hazards and that the environment is protected. In fact, businesses have often pushed for greater regulation believing that certain regulations can give them a competitive edge.[66] However, they also think that government regulation has often been too extensive in scope, too costly, and inevitably burdensome in terms of paperwork requirements and red tape. One thing is clear, the level of regulation continues to rise.

The annual page count in the *Federal Register* is an imperfect measure of regulatory intensity but the overall upward trend tells us something about the nature of government and business; the *Federal Register* celebrated its 80th birthday in 2006. In 1936, it contained 2,355 pages; by 2005, the page count had grown more than 30-fold to a staggering 77,752 pages.[67] The upward trend seems to occur irrespective of the party in office. By 2008, the end of the George W. Bush administration, the *Federal Register* weighed in at over 80,000 pages.[68] The *Federal Register* averaged 71,578 pages for the eight years of the Clinton administration, 59,519 for the first (George H. W.) Bush administration, and 54,335 for the Reagan administration.[69]

Some analysts think the problem is worse than it has ever been. In an article entitled "America's Regulatory Mess," *The Economist* magazine suggested that an increase in political funding from business has led to increased political interference in regulatory policy. Corporate donors want results from the politicians they support.[70] Another problem is the change in the nature of the regulatory issues. According to Robert Litan of the Brookings Institution, deregulation of the trucking and airline industries involved government stepping out of the way, so industry incumbents welcomed it. Deregulation of the telecom and electrical utility industries, however, was not welcomed because regulators had to devise a form of managed competition that involved the setting of pricing, the creating of access, and so forth, which brought about elaborate rule books.[71]

Regulation: What Does It Mean?

Generally, **regulation** refers to the act of governing, directing according to rule, or bringing under the control of law or constituted authority. Although there is no universally agreed-upon definition of federal regulation, we can look to the definition of a federal regulatory agency proposed years ago by the Senate Governmental Affairs Committee.[72] It described a federal regulatory agency as one that:

1. Has decision-making authority.
2. Establishes standards or guidelines conferring benefits and imposing restrictions on business conduct.
3. Operates principally in the sphere of domestic business activity.
4. Has its head and/or members appointed by the president (generally subject to Senate confirmation).
5. Has its legal procedures generally governed by the Administrative Procedures Act.

The commerce clause of the U.S. Constitution grants to the government the legal authority to regulate. Within the confines of a regulatory agency as outlined here, the composition and functioning of regulatory agencies differ. Some are headed by an administrator and are located within an executive department—for example, the Federal Aviation Administration (FAA). Others are independent commissions composed of a chairperson and several members located outside the executive and legislative branches—such as the Interstate Commerce Commission (ICC), the Federal Communications Commission (FCC), and the Securities and Exchange Commission (SEC).[73]

Reasons for Regulation

Regulations have come about over the years for a variety of reasons. Some managers probably think that government is just sitting on the sidelines looking for reasons to butt into their business. There are several legitimate reasons why government regulation has evolved, although these same businesspeople may not entirely agree with them. For the most part, government regulation has arisen because some kind of **market failure** (failure of the free enterprise system) has occurred and government, intending to represent the public interest, has chosen to take corrective action. We should make it clear that many regulations have been created primarily because of the efforts of special-interest groups that have lobbied successfully for them. The governmental decision-making process in the United States is characterized by congressional regulatory response to the pressures of special-interest groups as well as to perceived market failures.

Four major reasons or justifications for regulations are typically offered: (1) controlling natural monopolies, (2) controlling negative externalities, (3) achieving social goals, and (4) other reasons.

Controlling Natural Monopolies.   One of the earliest circumstances in which government felt a need to regulate occurred when a natural monopoly existed. A **natural monopoly** exists in a market where the economies of scale are so great that the largest firm has the lowest costs and thus is able to drive out its competitors. Such a firm can supply the entire market more efficiently and cheaply than can several smaller firms. Local telephone service is a good example, because parallel sets of telephone wires would involve waste and duplication that would be much more costly.

Monopolies such as this may seem "natural," but when left to their own devices could restrict output and raise prices. This potential abuse justifies the regulation of monopolies. As a consequence, we see public utilities, for example, regulated by a public utility commission. This commission determines the rates that the monopolist may charge its customers.[74]

Related to the control of natural monopolies is the government's desire to intervene when it thinks companies have engaged in anticompetitive practices. A recent example of this was the Justice Department's investigation of the Microsoft Corporation case in which the company was accused of anticompetitive trade practices. The U.S. Court of Appeals in a mixed ruling overturned an initial court ruling, recommending that Microsoft be split in two. The appeals court reprimanded the judge for publicly criticizing Microsoft but upheld the finding of fact that the Windows operating system constitutes a monopoly in the PC market and that Microsoft violated the Sherman Antitrust Act with its marketing tactics. Microsoft would bundle new features into their Windows operating system as a way of breaking into new markets. They then designed their operating system so that it worked more smoothly with Microsoft products than with others—giving it a clear and, according to the courts, unfair marketing advantage.[75]

Nearly ten years after the effort to break up Microsoft began, the saga continued. In that time the Clinton administration gave way to the second Bush administration, and the attitude toward antitrust issues changed markedly. This became evident when a top antitrust official urged state prosecutors to reject a confidential antitrust complaint that Google filed alleging that Microsoft's new operating system, Vista, was designed to discourage use of Google's desktop search program.[76] Several state prosecutors indicated they believed Google's charge had merit.[77] In the end, a settlement was reached and Microsoft made requested changes to Vista.[78]

Ironically, the story continues but the players have switched sides. Many people are concerned that Google will dominate online computing services in the same way that Microsoft dominated software. Prior to being confirmed as the Obama administration's new antitrust chief, Christine Varney opined, "For me, Microsoft is so last century. They are not the problem … [Google already] has acquired a monopoly in Internet online advertising."[79] The role reversal extends to Microsoft who, many believe, has helped to stir up complaints against Google. According to Eric Goldman, director of the High Tech Law institute at the Santa Clara University School of Law in California, "Microsoft is doing a lot to try and harass Google on the antitrust front."[80]

Controlling Negative Externalities. Another important rationale for government regulation is that of controlling the **negative externalities** (or spillover effects) that result when the manufacture or use of a product gives rise to unplanned or unintended side effects on others (other than the producer or the consumer). Examples of these negative externalities are air pollution, water pollution, and improper disposal of toxic wastes. The consequence of such negative externalities is that neither the producer nor the consumer of the product directly "pays" for all the "costs" that are created by the manufacture of the product. The "costs" that must be borne by the public include an unpleasant or a foul atmosphere, illness, and the resulting health care costs. Some have called these **social costs**, because they are absorbed by society rather than incorporated into the cost of making the product.

Preventing negative externalities is enormously expensive, and few firms are willing to pay for these added costs voluntarily. This is especially true in an industry that produces an essentially undifferentiated product, such as steel, where the millions of dollars needed to protect the environment would only add to the cost of the product and provide no benefit to the purchaser. In such situations, therefore, industry incumbents may even welcome government regulation because it requires all firms competing in a given industry to operate according to the same rules. By forcing all firms to incur the costs, regulation can level the competitive playing field.

Just as companies do not voluntarily take on extra expenditures for environmental protection, individuals often behave in the same fashion. For example, automobile emissions are one of the principal forms of air pollution. But how many private individuals would voluntarily request an emissions control system if it were offered as optional equipment? In situations such as this, a government standard that requires everyone to adhere to the regulation is much more likely to address the public's concern for air pollution.[81]

Achieving Social Goals. Government not only employs regulations to address market failures and negative externalities but also seeks to use regulations to help achieve certain **social goals** it deems to be in the public interest. Some of these social goals are related to negative externalities in the sense that government is attempting to correct problems that might also be viewed as negative externalities by particular groups. An example of this might be the harmful effects of a dangerous product or the unfair treatment of minorities resulting from employment discrimination. These externalities are not as obvious as air pollution, but they are just as real.

Another important social goal of government is to keep people informed. One could argue that inadequate information is a serious problem and that government should use its regulatory powers to require firms to reveal certain kinds of information to consumers. Thus, the Consumer Product Safety Commission requires firms to warn consumers of potential product hazards through labeling requirements. Other regulatory mandates that address the issue of inadequate information include grading standards, weight and size information, truth-in-advertising requirements, product safety standards, and so on.

Other important social goals that have been addressed include preservation of national security (deregulation of oil prices to lessen dependence on imports), considerations of fairness or equity (employment discrimination laws), protection of those who provide essential services (farmers), allocation of scarce resources (gasoline rationing), and protection of consumers from excessively high price increases (natural gas regulation).[82]

Other Reasons. There are several other reasons for government regulation. One is to control **excess profits** by transferring income for the purposes of economic fairness. For example, as a result of the Arab oil embargo, oil stocks went up suddenly by a factor of ten. One argument was that the extra profits collected by these producers were somehow undeserved and the result of plain luck, not wise investment decisions. So, in situations such as this in which profits are drastically, suddenly, and perhaps undeservedly increased, some have argued for government regulation.[83]

Another commonly advanced rationale for regulation is to deal with **excessive competition**. The basic idea behind this rationale is that excessive competition will lead to prices being set at unprofitably low levels. This action will force firms out of business and ultimately will result in products that are too costly because the remaining firm will raise its prices to excessive levels, leaving the public worse off than before.[84]

Types of Regulation

Broadly speaking, government regulations address two basic types of goals, economic and social; therefore, it has become customary to identify two different types of regulation: economic regulation and social regulation.

Economic Regulation.   The classical or traditional form of regulation that dates back to the 1800s in the United States is **economic regulation**. This type of regulation is best exemplified by the old-line regulatory bodies such as the Interstate Commerce Commission (ICC), which was created in 1887 by Congress to regulate the railroad industry; the Civil Aeronautics Board (CAB), which was created in 1940; and the Federal Communications Commission (FCC), which was established in 1934 to consolidate federal regulation of interstate communications and, later, the radio, telephone, and telegraph. These regulatory bodies divide along industry lines: They regulate business behavior through the controlling and influencing economic or market variables such as prices (maximum and minimum), entry to and exit from markets, and types of services offered.[85]

In the federal regulatory budget today, the major costs of economic regulation are for (1) finance and banking (e.g., Federal Deposit Insurance Corporation and Comptroller of the Currency), (2) industry-specific regulation (e.g., Federal Communications Commission and Federal Energy Regulatory Commission), and (3) general business (e.g., Department of Commerce, Department of Justice, Securities and Exchange Commission, and Federal Trade Commission).[86]

Later we discuss deregulation, a trend that has significantly affected the old-line form of economic regulation that has dominated business–government relations for the past 100 years.

Social Regulation.   The 1960s ushered in a new form of regulation that has come to be known as **social regulation**, because its major thrust is the furtherance of societal objectives quite different from the earlier focus on markets and economic variables. While economic regulation focuses on markets, social regulation focuses on business's impacts on people. This emphasis on people addresses the needs of people in their roles as employees, consumers, and citizens.

Two major examples of social regulations having specific impacts on people as employees were (1) the Civil Rights Act of 1964, which created the Equal Employment Opportunity Commission (EEOC), and (2) the creation of the Occupational Safety and Health Administration (OSHA) in 1970. The goal of the EEOC is to provide protection against discrimination in all employment practices. The goal of OSHA is to ensure that the nation's workplaces are safe and healthy.

An example of major social regulation protecting people as consumers was the 1972 creation of the Consumer Product Safety Commission (CPSC). This body's goal is to protect the public against unreasonable risks of injury associated with consumer products. An example of a major social regulation to protect people as citizens and residents of communities was the 1970 creation of the Environmental Protection Agency (EPA).

FIGURE 11-3 Comparison of Economic and Social Regulations

	Economic Regulations	Social Regulations
Focus	Market conditions, economic variables (entry, exit, prices, services)	People in their roles as employees, consumers, and citizens
Industries Affected	Selected (railroads, aeronautics, communications)	Virtually all industries
Examples	Civil Aeronautics Board (CAB) Federal Communications Commission (FCC)	Equal Employment Opportunity Commission (EEOC) Occupational Safety and Health Administration (OSHA) Consumer Product Safety Commission (CPSC) Environmental Protection Agency (EPA)
Current Trend	Reregulation (e.g., Financial Stability Oversight Board)	Reregulation (e.g., Consumer Financial Protection Bureau)

The goal of EPA is to coordinate a variety of environmental protection efforts and to develop a unified policy at the national level.

Figure 11-3 summarizes the nature of economic versus social regulations along with pertinent examples.

Whereas economic regulation was aimed primarily at companies competing in specific industries, the newer form of social regulation addresses business practices affecting all industries. In addition, there are social regulations that are industry specific, such as the National Highway Traffic Safety Administration (automobiles) and the Food and Drug Administration (food, drugs, medical devices, and cosmetics). Figure 11-4 summarizes the major U.S. independent regulatory agencies along with their dates of establishment. In addition to these, we should remember several regulatory agencies exist within executive departments of the government. Examples of this latter category include the following:

Agency	Department
Food and Health Administration	Health and Human Services
Antitrust Division	Justice
Drug Enforcement Administration	Justice
Occupational Safety and Health Administration	Labor
Federal Highway Administration	Transportation

Government regulation represents a response to a felt need in the environment, so it is not surprising that the most recent regulations are responses to recent major environmental events, the World Trade Center attacks, the financial scandals of Enron and WorldCom, and the economic recession that began in 2008. For the former, national security has been the primary concern. In particular, the collection, protection, and dissemination of information have been impacted. In response to the latter, new economic regulations address issues of corporate accountability. Most notably, the Sarbanes–Oxley Act (SOX) set extensive new reporting procedures and requirements for firms listed on U.S. stock exchanges and instituted severe penalties for firms that fail to comply. SOX is discussed in more detail in Chapter 4.

SOX is emblematic of the dilemma of regulation. On the one hand, it is an effective response to a serious problem, the lack of investor confidence in the wake of the Enron

FIGURE 11-4 Major U.S. Regulatory Agencies

Agency	Year Established
Interstate Commerce Commission*	1887
Federal Reserve System (Board of Governors)	1913
Federal Trade Commission	1914
International Trade Commission	1916
Federal Home Loan Bank Board**	1932
Federal Deposit Insurance Corporation	1933
Farm Credit Administration	1933
Federal Communications Commission	1934
Securities and Exchange Commission	1934
National Labor Relations Board	1935
Small Business Administration	1953
Federal Maritime Commission	1961
Council on Environmental Quality	1969
Cost Accounting Standards Board	1970
Environmental Protection Agency	1970
Equal Employment Opportunity Commission	1970
National Credit Union Administration	1970
Occupational Safety and Health Review Commission	1971
Consumer Product Safety Commission	1972
Commodity Futures Trading Commission	1974
Council on Wage and Price Stability	1974
Nuclear Regulatory Commission	1974
Federal Election Commission	1975
National Transportation Safety Board	1975
Federal Energy Regulatory Commission	1977
Office of the Federal Inspector for the Alaska Natural Gas Transportation System***	1979
Transportation Security Administration	2001
Consumer Financial Protection Bureau	2010

*Terminated in 1995. Replaced by the Surface Transportation Board.

**Terminated in 1939. Functions were reassigned to various housing agencies until 1955, when it was redesignated as an independent agency. In 1989, it was abolished and responsibility for oversight of Federal Home Loan Banks was transferred to the Federal Housing Finance Board.

***Abolished by Congress in 1992 and all powers were transferred to the Secretary of Energy.

and WorldCom scandals. As with all regulation, on the other hand, however, it presents additional burdens for firms. Auditing and reporting compliance costs, for firms with revenues under $1 billion, increased 130 percent following the Act's introduction.[87] New listings of foreign firms on U.S. exchanges dropped precipitously, while a significant portion of U.S. public companies considered going private because of the cost of regulatory compliance.[88]

The Credit Card Act of 2009 provides requires credit card issuers to provide consumers with more information about their accounts and sets limits on the ways in which credit cards can increase fees. The Credit Card Act is discussed in more detail in Chapter 13. The Patient Protection and Affordable Care Act of 2010 extends health insurance to 32 million uninsured people in the United States. The Act lengthens the period in which parents can keep adult children on their insurance and eventually prohibits denial of coverage due to

ETHICS IN PRACTICE CASE

To Comply or Not to Comply with the Government Regulation

Every summer and Christmas vacation for the past four years, I have worked in the maintenance department of a paper company. While working there to help finance my college education, I have been exposed to many questionable practices. One of the most prominent problems is the adherence to safety regulations.

OSHA (Occupational Safety and Health Administration) requires that a vessel-confined-space entry permit be filled out before a person enters the confined area and that a "sniffer" (a device used to detect oxygen deficiencies and other harmful or combustible gases) be present and operational whenever a person is inside. A confined space is defined as any area without proper air ventilation and/or an area more than five feet deep. For example, tanks and pits are confined spaces.

Anytime a person enters or leaves a confined space, the person is required to place her or his initials on the entry permit. This is for the physical protection of the worker and the liability protection of the company. If workers are seen violating this policy, they can be reprimanded or fired on the spot.

In my many experiences with these confined spaces, I have observed on numerous occasions that these policies are not broken by the workers, but by the supervisors. It is their responsibility to obtain these permits and sign them, as well as obtain the use of a sniffer. Sometimes the supervisors and the workers forget that we are working in a confined space and thus forget the permit and sniffer. When someone has realized that we are in a confined space, however, the supervisors have often asked us to initial the permit at various places as if the permit had been there all along.

When we work for extended periods of time in these areas, the sniffer's batteries often go dead as well. Instead of following regulations and leaving the area until a new sniffer can be obtained, the supervisors often tell employees to stay, declaring, "The air is fine. You don't need a sniffer!"

My problem is this: Should I sign these permits when I know it is dishonest, or should I do the "right" thing and let OSHA know that this regulation is being broken time and time again? After all, I'm not even a full-time employee, so who am I to cause trouble?

1. Who are the stakeholders in this case, and what are their stakes?

2. What should I have done in this situation? Is this regulation important, or is this just more government "red tape"? Should I have just "gone along to get along" with the supervisors?

Contributed by Dale Dyals

---

preexisting conditions. Some of the Act's provisions will not take effect for a few years and attorneys general in some states are threatening to appeal its constitutionality; therefore the Act's impact will not be known fully for some time.

Issues Related to Regulation

It is important to consider some of the issues that have arisen out of the increased governmental role in regulating business. In general, managers have been concerned with what might be called "regulatory unreasonableness."[89] We could expect that business would just as soon not have to deal with these regulatory bodies; therefore, some of business's reactions are simply related to the nuisance factor of having to deal with a complex array of restrictions. However, other legitimate issues that have arisen over the past few years also need to be addressed.

To be certain, there are benefits of government regulation. Businesses treat employees more fairly and provide them with safer work environments. Consumers are able to purchase safer products and receive more information about them. Citizens from all walks of life have cleaner air to breathe and cleaner water in lakes and rivers. These benefits are real, but their exact magnitudes are difficult to measure. Costs resulting from regulation

FIGURE 11-5 Regulatory Spending in the United States

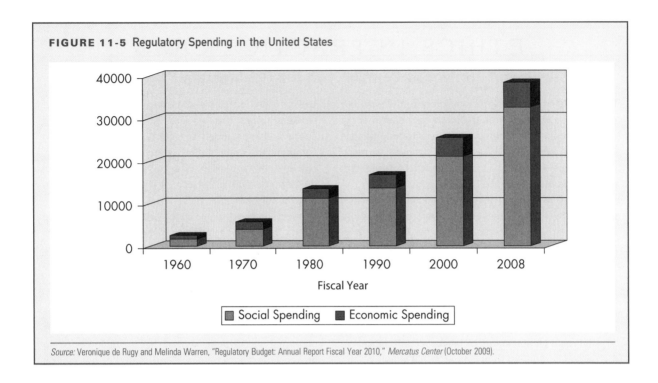

Source: Veronique de Rugy and Melinda Warren, "Regulatory Budget: Annual Report Fiscal Year 2010," *Mercatus Center* (October 2009).

also are difficult to measure. The **direct costs** of regulation are most visible when we look at the number of new agencies created, aggregate expenditures, and growth patterns of the budgets of federal agencies responsible for regulation. There were 14 major regulatory agencies prior to 1930, over two dozen in 1950, and 57 by the early 1980s. The most rapid expansion came in the 1970s.[90] Figure 11-5 shows the rise in spending for both economic and social regulation in millions of constant 2000 dollars.

In addition to the direct costs of administering the regulatory agencies, there are **indirect costs** such as forms, reports, and questionnaires that business must complete to satisfy the requirements of the regulatory agencies. These costs of government regulation are passed on to the consumer in the form of higher prices. There are also **induced costs**. The induced effects of regulation are diffuse and elusive, but they constitute some of the most powerful consequences of the regulatory process. In a real sense, then, these induced effects are also costs. Three effects are worthy of elaboration.[91]

1. *Innovation may be affected.* When corporate budgets must focus on "defensive research," certain types of innovation are less likely to take place. To the extent that firms must devote more of their scientific resources to meeting government requirements, fewer resources are available to dedicate to new product and process research and development and innovation. However, the relationship is anything but clear. A recent study showed that deregulation actually had a dramatic negative impact on public interest environmental research by public utilities whereas regulation can have a positive impact on pollution abatement research by profit maximizing firms.[92] The moral of these findings seems to be that organizations will pursue their own interests. Regulation can require firms to lower their pollution and so they can maximize their profits with greater expenditures on research to lower emissions. In contrast, utilities that once received reinforcement for doing research in the public interest may find they no longer have an incentive for that research once they begin to compete on profits.

2. *New investments in plant and equipment may be affected.* To the extent that corporate funds must be used for regulatory compliance purposes, these funds are diverted from more productive uses. Environmental and job safety requirements lessen productivity and uncertainty about future regulations diminishes motivation for introducing new products and processes.[93] Once again, the incentives will play a major part. Investments that aid the firms in complying with regulations are likely to be continued or increased, whereas those that are beyond the scope of the regulation are likely to diminish.

3. *Small business may be adversely affected.* Although it is not intentional, federal regulations can have a disproportionately adverse effect on small firms because of economies of scale. Large firms have more money, personnel, and resources with which to get the work of government done than do small firms.

Reich's advice to executives who feel the government is breathing down their necks is, "Get used to it."[94] Companies worldwide will be dealing with regulatory concerns for the foreseeable future. He notes the trend in multiple industries and cites examples. In financial services, governments in the United States, Europe, and Japan now hold equity in banks. In housing, the U.S. government is taking over a large portion of outstanding mortgage loans. The controversial bailout of insurance giant AIG made the United States a major participant in insurance markets. In the auto industry, the United States, Canada, Germany, Sweden, and Japan provided tens of billions of dollars in loans and equity. The United States, Europe, and Japan are all subsidizing non-carbon-based energy development. The United States is enacting health care reforms that will affect both the health care and pharmaceutical industries, and investing in greater broadband coverage that will affect the telecom industry.[95]

Deregulation

Quite frequently, trends and countertrends overlap with one another. Such is the case with regulation and its counterpart, **deregulation**. There are many reasons for this overlapping, but typically they include both the economic and the political. From an economic perspective, a continual striving for the balance of freedom and control for business will be best for society. From a political perspective, there is an ongoing interplay of different societal goals and means for achieving those goals. The outcome is a mix of economic and political decisions that seem to be in a constant state of flux. Thus, in the economy at any point in time, trends that appear counter to one another can coexist. These trends are the natural result of competing forces seeking some sort of balance or equilibrium.

This is how we can explain the trend toward deregulation that evolved in a highly regulated environment. Deregulation represents a counterforce aimed at keeping the economy in balance. It also represents a political philosophy that prevailed during the period of its origin and growth.

Deregulation is one kind of regulatory reform. But, because it is unique and quite unlike the regulatory reform measures discussed earlier, we treat it separately. Deregulation has taken place primarily with respect to economic regulations, and this, too, helps to explain its separate treatment.

Purpose of Deregulation

The basic idea behind deregulation has been to remove certain industries from the old-line economic regulations of the past. The purpose of this deregulation, or at least a reduced level of regulation, has been to increase competition with the expected benefits of greater efficiency, lower prices, and enhanced innovation. These goals have not been uniformly received, and it is still undecided whether deregulation works as a method of maximizing society's best interests. Figure 11-6 outlines the airline industry's experience with 25 years of deregulation.

The Changing World of Deregulation

A trend toward deregulation began in the 1980s, most notably exemplified in the financial industry, the telecommunications industry, and the transportation (trucking, airline, railroad) industry; it represented business's first major redirection in 50 years.[96] The result seemed to be a mixed bag of benefits and problems. On the benefits side, prices fell in many industries, and better service appeared in some industries along with increased numbers of competitors and innovative products and services.

Several problems arose also. Although prices fell and many competitors entered some of those industries, more and more of those competitors were unable to compete with the dominant firms. They were failing, going bankrupt, or being absorbed by the larger firms. Entry barriers into some industries were enormous and had been greatly underestimated. This has been shown to be the case in airline, trucking, railroad, and long-distance telephone service.[97] Deregulation is generally blamed for the savings and loan industry crisis, which resulted in an unprecedented $124 billion bailout by the U.S. government. Most dramatically, deregulation, specifically the repeal of the Depression-era Glass–Steagall Act that split commercial and investment banking, has been accused of causing the global recession that began in 2008.[98]

Another problem that developed was that a few firms began to dominate key industries. This trend was obvious in transportation, where the major railroad, airline, and trucking companies boosted their market shares considerably during the 1980s. The top six railroads went from about 56 percent of market share to about 90 percent during this time. The top six airlines went from about 75 percent of market share to about 85 percent. The top ten trucking firms went from about 38 percent of market share to about 58 percent. Prior to its breakup, AT&T enjoyed about an 80 percent share of the domestic market and a virtual monopoly in the huge toll-free, big business, and overseas markets.[99]

Dilemma with Deregulation

The dilemma with deregulation is how to enhance the competitive nature of the affected industries without sacrificing the applicable social regulations, that is, to allow for freer competition without lowering health and safety requirements. Unfortunately, the dog-eat-dog competition unleashed by economic deregulation can force many companies to cut corners in ways that endanger the health, safety, and/or welfare of their customers. The following two industries illustrate that challenge.

Trucking Industry.   Trucking deregulation received a big boost when George W. Bush was elected president. Duane W. Ackle and Walter P. McCormick, chairperson and president, respectively, of the American Trucking Association, became advisors to the Bush–Cheney transition team on transportation issues. These were just the first two of many trucking industry executives and lobbyists who received influential posts in the federal government since 2000. From 2000 to 2005, the trucking industry spent about $37 million on lobbying for rules that industry officials say have saved the industry billions.[100] In April 2003, the transportation department issued rules that increased the maximum allowable hours of driving from 60 to 77 over seven consecutive days and from 70 to 88 hours over eight consecutive days. Maximum daily work hours (which includes loading) were set at 14.[101]

FIGURE 11-6
The U.S. Airline Industry: First to Deregulate

October 24, 1978, was a watershed in aviation history. On that date, President Jimmy Carter signed the Airline Deregulation Act, and the world of aviation changed forever. The Civil Aeronautics Board no longer had the power to determine pricing and set the routes. The industry quickly filled with new carriers and new routes, and the country club atmosphere soon shifted to cutthroat competition. Many airlines went bankrupt or were absorbed by others. Even heavyweights like Eastern and Pan Am tottered until they both went bankrupt in 1991.

The average U.S. airfare dropped from about $140 in 1977 to $60 in 2000 (in constant 1983 dollars). As a result, the number of U.S. airline passengers nearly tripled from 220 million in 1977 to 650 million in 2000. Between 2000 and 2005, airlines lost a cumulative $35 billion. The older "legacy" carriers have slashed costs and staff to try to compete with the newer airlines such as Southwestern and JetBlue. More Americans are flying, but they are spending far less to do so. Airplanes fly at or near capacity, airports are congested, and security considerations require a much longer waiting time for passengers. All of this contributes to a diminished flying experience for the customer: Lost luggage is now one of the least of passenger concerns.

According to Bob Crandall, former CEO of American Airlines, the American airline industry is in a total state of disrepair. He blames "deplorably bad government policy" that has created three big problems. First, he says that American bankruptcy laws prevent airlines from folding when they should have their assets sold and be broken up. Second, stringent labor laws permit unions to make demands that are not consistent with the economic reality. Third, he asserts that foreign competitors have benefited from the U.S. government's inability to recognize the importance of having a strong airline industry in the United States. In addition to the problems outlined by Crandall, the airline industry faces the challenge of new regulations prompted by the attacks of 9/11. The Transportation Security Administration, part of the U.S. Department of Homeland Security, is charged with maintaining the safety of all modes of U.S. transportation.

The situation is likely to come to a head soon as an overtaxed air traffic control system stretches to its limit. The U.S. Air Transport Association expects the number of flights to increase from 45,000 in 2007 to 61,000 in 2016. In the past expansion required simply adding more equipment or hiring more controllers but the scope of the system near maximum capacity. Now, the entire system requires replacement. The Next Generation Air Transportation System uses a satellite-based navigation and surveillance system. It would make it possible to accommodate more flights and do so more safely, it would permit pilots to communicate with each other, and planes could save fuel in the process. The technology is available but the funding is not. In a deregulated industry, the challenges are great as interest groups line up to oppose major change. Private and executive aircraft do not currently contribute to the system in a way that reflects their actual usage: They do not want their user fees to rise. The closing of older air traffic control centers will mean loss of jobs for some. Regulated airfares corresponded to the distance traveled but now deregulated fares bear little resemblance to the cost of a flight for the control system. The *Economist* opined, "America was the first to deregulate, but now it's snowed under." The U.S. Congress will have some difficult decisions to make to enable the U.S. airline industry to continue to compete in an increasingly challenging environment that now includes a global recession.

Sources: Richard Newman, "Deregulation Was Good for Travelers, Hard on Airlines," *The Record, Hackensack, NJ* (December 7, 2003); "In the Land of Free Flight," *Economist* (June 16, 2007), 5–8, http://www.tsa.gov/who_we_are/what_is_tsa.shtm.

Congress provided very little scrutiny of trucking standards but the courts have been less reticent. Concerned about the relaxed standards, several safety organizations brought a lawsuit to a federal appeals court. A three-judge panel ruled that the Federal Motor Carrier Safety Administration was guilty of "ignoring its own evidence that fatigue causes many truck accidents."[102] They went on to say that "the agency admits that studies show that crash risk increases, in the agency's words, 'geometrically' after the eighth hour on duty" and questioned the legality of the "agency's passive regulatory approach."[103] The American Trucking Association supports the rules, while the Teamsters Union opposes them. The Obama administration has agreed to review the rules, but no action has yet been taken.[104]

Financial Services.   Financial services in the United States were one of the most heavily regulated industries until the passage of the Depository Institutions Deregulation and Monetary Control Act of 1980. It removed caps on deposit interest rates. Gradually, Congress then began to take apart the regulatory barriers that had been in place for decades. The Federal Deposit Insurance Improvement Act of 1991, loosened restrictions on deposit insurance premiums; the Neal–Riegle Interstate Banking Act of 1994 removed geographic restrictions on branches; and the Gramm–Leach–Bliley Act of 1999, created financial holding companies, and removed enforced separation of insurance companies and commercial and investment banks.[105] It appeared that the deregulation of financial services would continue until two events, the World Trade Center attacks and the Enron financial scandals, changed the tide.

In response, a variety of agencies within the U.S. government began to issue new financial rules and regulations; The Internal Revenue Service, the FBI, the Justice Department, the Financial Crimes Enforcement Network, and the Federal Reserve each contributed to financial service reregulation.[106] The Committee on Capital Market Regulation issued a report that claimed the U.S. share of initial public offerings (IPOs) fell from 50 percent in 2000 to 5 percent in 2005 due to "regulatory intensity." While not all observers agreed with the committee's conclusion, most concurred that the decision regarding the level at which financial services should be regulated held serious implications for the competitiveness of U.S. business in the global economy. Nevertheless, pressure for more regulation followed the economic recession that began in 2008. Most observers believe that the rescinding of the Glass–Steagall Act prompted the meltdown.[107] The Glass–Steagall Act was put in place following the Great Depression. It prevented commercial banks from becoming involved in risky trading activities. The 2008 recession motivated the Credit Card Act of 2009 and the Dodd–Frank Wall Street Reform and Consumer Protection Act. The landmark Dodd–Frank financial reform legislation created the Financial Stability Oversight Council (FSOC), which will determine which firms are critical to the financial system and thus should have higher capital requirements. It also creates the Consumer Financial Protection Bureau and allows consumers to sue credit rating agencies that recklessly overlook relevant information. The bill will not be fully implemented for years so some of its impacts are yet to be determined.[108]

Summary

Any discussion of business and society must consider the paramount role played by government. Although the two institutions have opposing systems of belief, they interconnect in their functioning in our socioeconomic system. In addition, the public assumes a major role in a complex pattern of interactions among business, government, and the public. Government exerts a host of nonregulatory influences on business. Two influences with a macro orientation include industrial policy and privatization. A more specific influence is the fact that government is a major employer, purchaser, subsidizer, competitor, financier, and persuader. These roles permit government to affect business significantly.

One of government's most controversial interventions in business is direct regulation. Government regulates business for several legitimate reasons, and in the past two decades social regulation has been more dominant than economic regulation. There are many benefits and various costs of government regulation. A response to the problems with regulation has been deregulation. However, bad experiences in key industries such as trucking, airlines, telecommunication, financial services, and utilities have caused many to wonder what the optimal mix of regulation and deregulation should be.

Key Terms

collectivistic ethic of government, p. 414

deregulation, p. 431

direct costs, p. 430

economic regulation, p. 426

excess profits, p. 425

excessive competition, p. 426

federalization, p. 420

indirect costs, p. 430

individualistic ethic of business, p. 414

induced costs, p. 430

industrial policy, p. 416

market failure, p. 423

natural monopoly, p. 424

negative externalities, p. 425

privatization, p. 419

regulation, p. 423

social costs, p. 425

social goals, p. 425

social regulation, p. 426

Discussion Questions

1. Briefly explain how business and government represent a clash of ethical systems (belief systems). With which do you find yourself identifying most? Explain. With which would most business students identify? Explain.

2. Explain why the public is treated as a separate group in the interactions among business, government, and the public. Doesn't government represent the public's interests? How should the public's interests be manifested?

3. What is regulation? Why does government see a need to regulate? Differentiate between economic and social regulation. What social regulations do you think are most important, and why? What social regulations ought to be eliminated? Explain.

4. Outline the major benefits and costs of government regulation. In general, do you think the benefits of government regulation exceed the costs? In what areas, if any, do you think the costs exceed the benefits?

5. What are the trade-offs between privatization and federalization? When would one or the other be more appropriate? What problems might you foresee?

12

Business Influence on Government and Public Policy

CHAPTER LEARNING OUTCOMES

After studying this chapter, you should be able to:

1. Describe the evolution of corporate political participation.

2. Differentiate among the different levels at which business lobbying occurs.

3. Explain the phenomenon of political action committees (PACs) in terms of their historical growth, the magnitude of their activity, and the arguments for and against them.

4. Define coalitions and describe the critical role they now assume in corporate political involvement.

5. Discuss the Bipartisan Campaign Reform Act and other issues surrounding campaign financing.

6. Outline the principal strategic approaches to political activism that firms are employing.

As our previous discussion of industrial policy showed, government is a central stakeholder of business. Government's interest, or stake, in business is broad and multifaceted, and its power is derived from its legal and moral right to represent the public in its dealings with business. Today, because of the multiple roles it plays in influencing business activity, government poses significant challenges for business owners and managers. Government not only establishes the rules of the game for business functions but also influences business in its roles as competitor, financier, purchaser, supplier, watchdog, and so on. Opportunities for business and government to cooperate in a mutual pursuit of common goals are present to some extent, but the major opportunity for business is in developing strategies for effectively working with government in such a way that businesses achieve their own objectives. In doing this, business has the responsibility of obeying the laws of the land and of being ethical in its responses to government expectations and mandates. To do otherwise raises the specter of abuse of political power. As the regulatory environment has become more intense and complex and as other changes have taken place in society, businesses have had little choice but to become more politically active, and they have are now being granted more power to do so. A 2010 Supreme Court ruling that the government should not regulate political speech, even when it comes from corporations, has strengthened business's power in political activities. The Court ruled that the government may not prohibit political spending by corporations in elections.[1]

Attempts by business to influence government are a major and accepted part of the public policy process in the United States. The active participation of interest groups striving to achieve their own objectives drives the U.S. political system. The business sector is behaving, therefore, in a normal and expected fashion when it assumes an advocacy role for its interests. Other groups, be they labor organizations, consumer groups, farmers' groups, doctors' organizations, real estate broker organizations, military groups, women's rights organizations, environmental groups, church groups, and so on, all strive to pursue their special interests with government. Today's pluralism necessitates that all of these groups seek to influence government. The public interest in this special-interest-driven process is that the system maintains some semblance of a balance of power and that the activities and practices of these organizations remain legal and ethical.

Corporate Political Participation

Political involvement is broadly defined as participation in the formulation and execution of public policy at various levels of government. As decisions about the current and future shape of society and the role of the private sector shift from the marketplace to the political arena, corporations, like all interest groups, find it imperative to increase their political involvement and activity.[2]

Historically, companies entered into debates in Washington only on an issue-by-issue basis and with no overall sense of a purpose, goal, or strategy. Companies also tended to be reactive; that is, they dealt with issues only after these became threats. This approach became obsolete as the kinds of changes we have described began to occur. Today, success in Washington is just as important as success in the marketplace. Just as business has learned that it must develop competitive strategies to succeed, it has learned that political strategies are essential as well.[3] Even a corporate giant like Microsoft had to learn to be an active and effective player.

A Lesson Learned

Microsoft opened its first lobbying office in 1995, 20 years after the founding of the company. The office had only one staff person, Jack Krumholtz, a 33-year-old lawyer with no real Washington experience and no secretary. He wasn't given a cushy office with a view of the Potomac. Instead, he had an office in the Microsoft federal sales office, across from a suburban shopping mall and seven miles from downtown DC.[4] Another lobbyist described the Microsoft command post as "Jack and his Jeep," because the Jeep was the only downtown location Krumholtz had available.[5]

After the U.S. Justice Department brought an antitrust case against Microsoft, the company began to realize its isolationist policy wasn't working. In addition to increasing its political giving, the company retained a cadre of well-connected lobbyists and public relations officials to present its case to legislators and the public.[6] A *BusinessWeek* article showed Microsoft pulling out all the stops. Krumholtz and his colleagues moved to a modern building on DuPont Circle. The in-house staff had grown to 14, and they had scores of high-powered help on retainer. They gave millions to both parties in the 2000 presidential election, hired both Bush and Gore advisers as lobbyists, and became the ninth largest "soft money" corporate donor in the United States. They ran national ad campaigns featuring a "warm and fuzzy" Bill Gates and touting their multimillion-dollar charity campaign. Think tanks that supported their interests received major donations; those that espoused views counter to theirs received nothing. They even farmed out legal work to most of the law firms in DC so that most of the lawyers in town would be constrained from working for their competitors.[7]

After years of struggling with antitrust cases both domestic and abroad, their work began to pay off. Microsoft succeeded in positioning one of its top lawyers to chair the American Bar Association's antitrust section, a group that has significant influence over the development of antitrust policy and law.[8] In addition, one of the top antitrust lawyers at a firm that represented Microsoft on several antitrust disputes became the top antitrust official at the Justice Department. In 2007, he raised eyebrows by sending a memo to state attorneys general around the United States urging them to reject a confidential Google antitrust complaint. The Justice Department under the second Bush administration sent a delegation to the EU, headed by a former Microsoft lawyer and lobbyist, which argued Microsoft's case with EU. The department has also criticized the European Commission and the Korean Fair Trade Commission for their stances on Microsoft. An appeals court overturned the court-ordered breakup of Microsoft and an agreement with the Justice Department settled the antitrust charges while still calling for more stringent oversight of the company's practices. Although Microsoft's political involvement has yielded success, the company cannot afford to relax its efforts. Anticompetitive behavior charges from the European Union and competitors such as Google continue to preoccupy the company.

Had Microsoft taken its governmental relations more seriously more quickly, the company might have avoided much of this trouble. Marshall Phelps, corporate vice president and deputy general counsel for Microsoft, said that Microsoft should have negotiated sooner with the U.S. Department of Justice. According to Phelps, the company has now learned to deal with antitrust issues but they could have saved themselves considerable difficulty. "Had Microsoft been a little quicker to give in on this, that and the other, (it) wouldn't be in the same pickle . . . one of the problems companies get into (is) when they don't realize how powerful they are and how powerful they are perceived as being."[9]

Phelps offers advice for other companies facing antitrust inquiries, "Discretion is the better part of valor, and it's better to be a bit more humble in the face of regulators because they are never going to go away. I don't care how many good lawyers you have or how much money. The regulators still win. That's just the rule. All the more reason you want to be cooperative and make the government think they won. You want to say, 'Yep, you won. We'll change our practices.'"[10] Today, Microsoft has resolved their own antitrust issues and, in an ironic twist, they are using their government relations expertise to create antitrust problems for their competitive rival Google.[11]

Microsoft learned the hard way that political involvement is not optional. In response, they continue to employ a range of activities to promote their interests. To appreciate more fully the participation of business in the process of public policy formation in the United States, it is necessary to understand the approaches that business uses to influence government stakeholders.

In this chapter, we focus only on the following major approaches: (1) lobbying, (2) political action committees (PACs), (3) coalition building, and (4) political strategy. At this point, our perspective will be largely descriptive as we seek to understand these approaches, their strengths and weaknesses, and business's successes and failures with them. At the same time, however, we must be constantly vigilant of possible abuses of power or violations of sound ethics.

Business Lobbying

Lobbying is the process of influencing public officials to promote or secure the passage or defeat of legislation. Lobbying is also used to promote the election or defeat of candidates for public office. Lobbyists are intensely self-interested. Their goals are to promote legislation that is in their organizations' interests and to defeat legislation that runs counter to that. Business interests, labor interests, ethnic and racial groups, professional organizations, and those simply pursuing ideological goals they believe to be in the public interest are lobbying at the federal, state, and local levels. Our focus is on business lobbying at the federal level, although we must remember that this process is also occurring daily at the state and local levels.

Lobbying has been defined as the professionalization of the art of persuasion.[12] Lobbying serves several purposes. It is not just a technique for gaining legislative support or institutional approval for some objective such as a policy shift, a judicial ruling, or the modification or passage of a law. Lobbying may also be directed toward the reinforcement of established policy or the defeat of proposed policy shifts. Lobbying also targets the election or defeat of national, state, and local legislators. A lobbyist may be a lawyer, a public relations specialist, a former head of a public agency, a former corporate executive, or a former elected official. In this sense, there is no typical lobbyist.[13] It is clear, however, that more and more businesses, as well as other special-interest groups, are turning to lobbyists to facilitate their involvement in the public policy process. A cartoon depicts the increasing stature of lobbyists. The teacher asks the class, "Who runs America?" She then gives her students the following choices: "the President, the Supreme Court, or Congress?" An astute class member responds, "Lobbies."[14]

Organizational Levels of Lobbying

The business community engages in lobbying at several organizational levels. At the broadest level are **umbrella organizations**, which represent the collective business interests of the United States. The best examples of umbrella organizations are the Chamber of Commerce of the United States and the National Association of Manufacturers (NAM). Out of these have grown organizations that represent some subset of business in general, such as the Business Roundtable, which was organized to represent the largest firms in America, and the National Federation of Independent Businesses (NFIB), which represents smaller firms.

At the next level are **trade associations**, which are composed of many firms in a given industry or line of business. Examples include the National Automobile Dealers Association, the National Association of Home Builders, the National Association of Realtors, and the Tobacco Institute. Finally, there are individual **company lobbying** efforts. Here, firms such as IBM, AT&T, Ford, and Delta Airlines lobby on their own behalf. Typically, companies use their own personnel, establish Washington offices for the sole purpose of lobbying, or hire professional lobbying firms or consultants located in Washington or a state capital. An example of company lobbying was given previously in Microsoft's lesson learned. Figure 12-1 depicts examples of the broad range of lobbying and political interest organizations used by businesses.

Spotlight on SUSTAINABILITY

Green Lobbying

Companies are now being judged not only on the sustainability levels in their own operations but also on the extent to which their lobbying efforts promote sustainability. In their *Guide to Greener Electronics*, Greenpeace rates electronics companies on the whether they lobby against the use of materials that damage the environment. According to Casey Harrell, Greenpeace International toxics campaigner, "Companies need to support legislative bans to ensure a consistent phase out of PVC and BFRs across all electronic products. Sony Ericsson and Apple are already calling on EU institutions to support such a ban. Other big players, such as HP and Dell—who have so far been silent—and Acer, need to ensure the ban is passed in the European Union parliament."

Source: "Greenpeace Rates Electronics Firms on Lobbying," *EnvironmentalLeader.com* (January 7, 2010), http://www. environmentalleader.com/2010/01/07/greenpeace-rates-electronics-firms-on-lobbying/.

FIGURE 12-1

Examples of the Range of Lobbying Organizations Used by Businesses

Broad Representation: Umbrella Organizations
- Chamber of Commerce of the United States
- National Association of Manufacturers (NAM)
- Business Roundtable
- National Federation of Independent Businesses (NFIB)
- State Chambers of Commerce
- City Chambers of Commerce

Midrange Representation: Trade and Professional Associations and Coalitions
- National Automobile Dealers Association
- National Association of Realtors
- American Petroleum Institute
- American Trucking Association
- National Association of Medical Equipment Suppliers
- Tobacco Institute
- Health Benefits Coalition
- United States Telecom Association

Narrow/Specific Representation: Company-Level Lobbying
- Washington and State Capital Offices
- Law Firms Specializing in Lobbying
- Public Affairs Specialists
- Political Action Committees (PACs)
- Grassroots Lobbying
- Company-Based Coalitions
- Former Government Officials

The place of organizational level lobbying has shifted in the Obama administration. According to Doug Pinkham, President of the Public Affairs Council, "The president is calling out chief executives of firms who favor or oppose his policies. This approach seems to be designed to marginalize business and trade associations that have traditionally stood between many companies and federal policy makers."[15] President Obama has held more small group meetings with CEOS and been more personally involved in the interactions, leading observers to see it as an effort to bypass umbrella organizations and trade groups.[16] Presidential advisor Valerie Jarrett sees it differently: "The chamber and other large lobbying groups in Washington have had a tradition of dominating the conversation. Our approach is to be more inclusive."[17]

We now discuss lobbying in greater detail, beginning with the use of professional lobbyists.

Professional Lobbyists. Lobbyists, sometimes derisively referred to as "influence peddlers," operate under a variety of formal titles and come from a variety of backgrounds. Officially, they are lawyers, government affairs specialists, public relations consultants, or public affairs consultants. Some are on the staffs of large trade associations based in Washington. Others represent specific companies that have Washington offices dedicated to the sole purpose of representing those companies in the capitol city. Still others are professional lobbyists who work for large law firms or consulting firms in Washington that specialize in representing clients to the lawmakers. Figure 12-2 shows the level of expenditures professional lobbyists make each year.

The Washington lobbyist is frequently a former government official. Some are former congressional staff members or former members of Congress. Others are former presidential staff assistants or other highly placed government officials. The law prohibits many of these individuals from lobbying for one year after leaving office; however, one year is a relatively short apprenticeship for people who are likely to increase their former salaries many times over. For example, after serving as chief architect of the Medicare prescription drug law, former Rep. Billy Tauzin (R-Louisiana), received a lucrative job offer to lobby for the pharmaceutical industry. Pundits suggested that he had already earned his salary when he walked in the door because the Medicare bill provided huge profits for drug makers.[18]

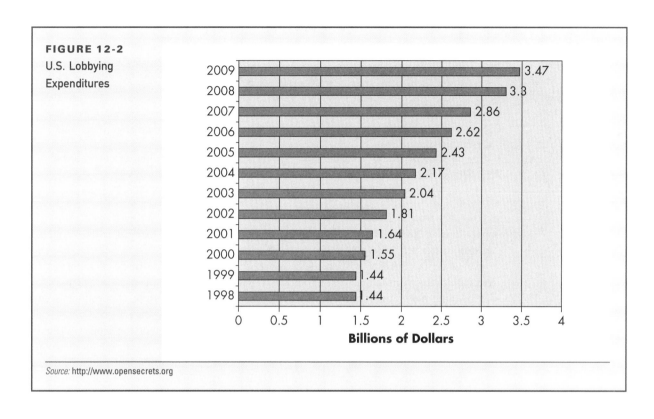

FIGURE 12-2
U.S. Lobbying
Expenditures

Source: http://www.opensecrets.org

Tauzin began his job as Chairman and CEO of the drug industry trade group, Pharmaceutical Research and Manufacturers of America (PhRMA), in January of 2005.[19] He did not register to lobby until 2006 due to a one-year waiting period mandated by the Ethics Reform Act of 1989; in the meantime, however, he was able to advise other lobbyists on how to proceed and he was able to call on his former chief of staff who joined PhRMA with him. In 2007, the House Ethics Code added a provision known as "The Tauzin Rule," which prohibited lawmakers from negotiating future employment deals while still working as representatives.[20] In 2010, Tauzin resigned his position amid criticism within the group that he was not sufficiently confrontational.[21]

The revolving door between Congress and lobbying firms has become even more pronounced in recent years. The Obama's administration's efforts to reform financial services have been met with intensive lobbying from the financial services industry. Public Citizen reported that at least 70 former Congress members and 56 former congressional aides served as Wall Street and financial industry lobbyists in 2009. These former members include Trent Lott and Bob Dole (former Senate majority leaders), Richard Gephart and Dick Armey (former House majority leaders), and Dennis Hastert (former Speaker of the House).[22] Visa, Goldman Sachs, Prudential, Citigroup, and the American Bankers Association had the most former congressional officials serving as lobbyists.[23]

The Obama administration has undertaken an effort to lessen the influence of lobbyists. Reports on the success of that initiative are mixed. Lisa Gilbert of the U.S. Public Interest Research Group says, "He's gone further than any president has on ethics and lobbying reform. In general, early evidence suggests some good has come of it."[24] Others question the success of the anti-lobbying initiatives. While it is true that the numbers of registered lobbyists has decreased, the amount of money spent on lobbying continues to increase.[25] Many argue that lobbyists are just deregistering as lobbyists and setting up

FIGURE 12-3
What Business
Lobbyists Do for
Their Clients

- Get access to key legislators (connections)
- Monitor legislation
- Establish communication channels with regulatory bodies
- Protect firms against surprise legislation
- Draft legislation, slick ad campaigns, direct-mail campaigns
- Provide issue papers on anticipated effects of legislative activity

- Communicate sentiments of association or company on key issues
- Influence outcome of legislation (promote helpful legislation, defeat harmful legislation)
- Assist companies in coalition building around issues that various groups may have in common
- Help members of Congress get reelected
- Organize grassroots efforts

operations as "arms-length strategists," because registering as a lobbyist is like "walking around with a scarlet letter."[26]

What do business lobbyists actually do? Lobbyists offer a wide range of services that include drafting legislation, creating slick advertisements and direct-mail campaigns, consulting, and, most importantly, getting access to lawmakers. Access, or connections, seems to be the central product that the new breed of lobbyist is selling—the returned phone call, the tennis game with a key legislator, or lunch with the Speaker of the House. With so many competing interests in Washington today, the opportunity to get your point across in any format is a significant advantage. Lobbyists also play the important role of showing busy legislators the virtues and pitfalls of complex legislation.[27] Figure 12-3 summarizes some of the various activities that business lobbyists accomplish for their clients.

Grassroots Lobbying. In addition to lobbying directly through the use of professional lobbyists, firms use what is called **grassroots lobbying**, which refers to the process of mobilizing the "grassroots"—individual citizens who might be most directly affected by legislative activity—to political action. Trade associations and the umbrella organizations also use grassroots lobbying actively. The better corporate grassroots lobbying programs usually arise in companies whose leaders recognize that people are a firm's most potent political resource. Although firms cannot direct or require people to become politically involved, they persuade and encourage them.

Trade associations often use grassroots support by asking their members to contact their representatives. They also organize rallies, target mail campaigns, develop instant advertisements, and use computerized phone banks.[28]

Grassroots lobbying has become one of the most frequently used and most effective techniques both for individual firms and for associations and coalitions. A few examples of successful grassroots lobbying efforts at the company level are helpful in understanding its power. During the debate over the North American Free Trade Agreement (NAFTA), Ford Motor Co. as well as other automakers tapped into a network of 32 top automobile suppliers and their employees to drum up letters and telephone calls to Capitol Hill in support of the trade pact. The company also called on its 5,000 dealers for grassroots lobbying support.[29] NAFTA was subsequently passed. In addition, credit unions across the nation employed grassroots lobbying to urge congressional support of H.R. 1151—the Credit Union Membership Access Act, which relaxed credit union membership requirements. In addition to eliciting the traditional onslaught of petitions and personal letters, thousands of credit union members lobbied their lawmakers directly on Capitol Hill.[30] These efforts undoubtedly led to the landslide vote in which the House passed the bill.

The technology revolution has ushered in **cyberadvocacy** as another form of grassroots campaigning. Computers and the Internet have made communication infinitely easier. Books and consulting services have sprung up to assist organizations in using the Internet to both amass grassroots support and enable grassroots supporters to contact their legislators. There is a danger with the use of e-mail. According to Stella Anne Harrison of the Juno Advocacy Network, "Blanket e-mail messages can be equated with spam—unwarranted and irrelevant overload of e-mail messages that can be ignored. However, targeted and specific e-mails are another matter." She recommends that advocates include their name and home address so that legislators will know they are hearing from their constituents."[31]

Grassroots lobbying can be highly effective, but the grassroots response should be genuine. Some organizations and trade associations have created fake groups that appear to be grassroots but are largely created and funded by an organization or trade association. These phony "**astroturf lobbying**," also known as **grasstops lobbying**, appear to be the result of a genuine public groundswell but are actually orchestrated and funded by professional organizations. The practice once involved the sending of hundreds of phone calls or thousands of identical postcards, letters, or e-mails that arrived on the same day and was rarely effective.[32] Fake grassroots lobbying has grown more sophisticated and is estimated to be a billion-dollar industry in Washington.[33]

For example, a group called "Americans for Technology Leadership (ATL)" funded polls that concluded the American public was not very interested in the Microsoft antitrust case. Then when 19 state attorneys general were considering what remedy to seek, ATL funded another poll that found that the public wanted their state's attorneys general to devote their attention to other issues, not the Microsoft case.[34] ATL also hired telemarketers to make unsolicited calls to people, asking them if they would send a letter to Congress to demand that Justice drop the antitrust case. The telemarketer would offer to draft and mail the letter to the person's congressperson for them—they simply needed to give permission to use their names. What was ATL? It was a group designed to develop grassroots support for Microsoft. Fully funded by Microsoft, it had few dues-paying members.[35] The Internet has now made it possible to not only create fake groups but also manufacture fake consumers. With the heavy use of listservers in a variety of arenas, corporations can now invent people to log on and record messages that show no indication of the company for which they are working.[36] Unlike openly professional lobbying, astroturf lobbying is largely unregulated.[37]

Trade Association Lobbying. In *Hidden Rivers*, the Center for Political Accountability dubbed trade associations "the Swiss bank accounts of American politics." This in-depth examination of how the nation's trade associations have become conduits for unlimited corporate political spending produced a surprising conclusion: Trade associations helped companies conceal and spend over $100 million in just one year. Of major concern is the fact that trade associations "are subject to even less disclosure than the much criticized spending of independent political committees (527s)."[38]

Lobbying at the association level is frequent today. One recent successful experience worth noting was the pharmaceutical industry's success at blocking Congress's efforts to impose price controls and allow the importation of less expensive drugs. The PhRMA spent $8.5 million to defeat the importation component of the Medicare prescription drug benefit bill. Individual companies also spent millions, including Eli Lilly & Co. ($2.2 million), Bristol–Meyers Squibb Co. ($2.6 million), and Johnson & Johnson ($2.2 million). The pharmaceutical industry as a whole spent $29 million in lobbying to scuttle importation, which was more than any other sector.[39] In a true show of the trade association's strength, the pharmaceutical industry was able to have a law passed that barred the federal government from negotiating the prices of prescription drugs supplied through Medicare.[40] The Medicare Prescription Drug Price Negotiation Act of 2010 is in process at this writing and has been referred to the House Ways and Means Committee.[41]

Industries do not always speak with one voice as has been true with the pharmaceutical industry. Trade associations sometimes find themselves in the undesirable role of battling with each other in their attempts to lobby Congress. An example of these types of battles occurred between the credit union and the banking industries regarding the scope of services supplied by credit unions. Credit unions argued that they provide services to individuals and small businesses that traditional banks shun. They contended that they should be able to expand the services they provide to this generally underserved population. Banks countered that credit unions enjoy an unfair competitive advantage by virtue of their exemptions from both taxes and the Community Reinvestment Act (CRA) obligations required of banks and thrifts. They maintained that large, multiple-employer credit unions should be subject to the same taxes, CRA rules, and safety requirements as banks. Ultimately, the House passed H.R. 1151—the Credit Union Membership Access Act, which relaxed restrictions on credit union membership.[42]

Umbrella Organizations.   The umbrella organizations are associations, too. But unlike a trade association, an umbrella organization has a broad base of membership that represents businesses in several different industries of various sizes. Historically, the two major umbrella organizations in the United States have been the Chamber of Commerce of the United States and the National Association of Manufacturers. Two other prominent organizations include the Business Roundtable and the National Federation of Independent Businesses. Each of these groups has political action as one of its central objectives.

CHAMBER OF COMMERCE OF THE UNITED STATES   The national chamber of commerce was founded in 1912 as a federation of businesses and business organizations. In addition to firms, corporations, and professional members, the chamber has thousands of local, state, and regional chambers of commerce; American chambers of commerce abroad; and several thousand trade and professional associations. Its diversity of membership shows why it is referred to as an umbrella organization.

Historically, the U.S. Chamber of Commerce had been a legislative powerhouse in its ability to influence public policy. Its power gradually waned over the years.[43] When Thomas Donohue became the chamber president, he promised to awaken the "sleeping giant, missing in action from many important battles." As president and CEO, Donohue has been credited for revitalizing the chamber in "money, members, and influence."[44] One tactic he used to great success was to dispense favors to individual businesses that might not want their company name associated with lobbying efforts. Walmart and the American Council of Life Insurers, among others, each contributed $1 million to a campaign to help elect judges known for being friendly to business.[45] Donohue is not afraid to take controversial stances. He railed at the post-Enron regulations, charging that "government agencies have gone overboard" and "accounting error should not be seen as a crime" causing the Business Roundtable to distance itself from his actions.[46] Its $145 million in 2009 lobbying expenditures dwarfed those of other individual business groups.[47]

Recently, the chamber has been at odds with the Obama administration on a variety of their initiatives. The administration has treated the chamber "with brass knuckles," causing CEOs to reconsider associating with it.[48] Presidential advisor Jarrett dismissed the organization as "old school" and acknowledged that the White House is bypassing it to work directly with CEOs.[49] In addition, the chamber is not winning friends with some of its policies. Utilities PG&E, Exelon, and PNM Resources quit the chamber over its opposition to efforts to regulate carbon emissions. The chamber's position on climate change led Apple to resign from the organization and Nike to withdraw from the board, remaining as a member to "debate climate change from within."[50]

BUSINESS ROUNDTABLE The Business Roundtable enjoys a far better relationship with the Obama White House.[51] Formed in 1972, the Business Roundtable is often regarded as an umbrella organization, although it has a restricted membership. It is an association of chief executive officers of leading corporations with a combined workforce of more than ten million employees in the United States and $3.7 trillion in revenues.[52] Previously regarded as a sleeping giant, former chair John T. Dillon and current president John Castellani turned the organization into a "lobbying juggernaut."[53] The renewed vigor has led to increased membership with Hewlett-Packard, Ford Motor, and IBM returning as members.[54]

The Business Roundtable is different from most groups, such as the U.S. Chamber of Commerce and NAM, in the extent of participation by the chief executive officers. Rather than pushing narrow issues that benefit narrow interests, the organization selects concerns based on "the impact the problem will have on the economic well-being of the nation." Working in task forces on specific issues, the Business Roundtable is committed to "advocating public policies that ensure vigorous economic growth, a dynamic global economy, and the well-trained and productive U.S. workforce essential for future competitiveness."[55] They are known for being pragmatic rather than ideological. According to Castellani, "We strive to be politically relevant, but not partisan." They neither oppose nor favor a specific approach to climate change, such as cap and trade or taxation. Instead, they provide extensive data on how different price levels would affect different companies and markets.[56]

NATIONAL ASSOCIATION OF MANUFACTURERS (NAM) NAM describes itself as "America's oldest and largest national broad-based industrial trade association."[57] Although the membership of NAM has historically been tilted toward the larger smokestack industry firms, it now includes small and medium-sized firms as well as member associations. The membership of NAM encompasses every industrial sector and all 50 U.S. states.[58] This diversity provides a challenge for NAM because their small and midsized member firms believe NAM is more concerned with the needs of the global companies than their own and the concerns of small firms often differ from those of the larger, global players.[59]

One particular point of contention is the issue of free trade. The large firms tend to be free trade advocates, a stance with which NAM agrees; however, the small firms are increasingly desirous of protection.[60] The issue came to a head during a 2007 meeting of the board. The membership of NAM had voted to fight Chinese currency manipulation because it creates an unfair situation for small U.S. firms that try to compete with Chinese firms or multinational firms operating in China.[61] The NAM board voted to go against the vote of the membership. This led to the creation of a new organization, the American Alliance for Manufacturing, based in Washington. In addition, the Michigan Tooling Association expanded and renamed itself the Tooling, Manufacturing, and Technologies Association.[62]

NATIONAL FEDERATION OF INDEPENDENT BUSINESSES (NFIB) During the end of the 20th century, the growth of small businesses came to dominate the business news. It should not be surprising, therefore, that the NFIB, as a small business association, also came into a position of power. We might think of the NFIB as an umbrella organization for smaller businesses. When *Fortune* magazine last conducted its ranking of the Power 25 Lobbying, the NFIB ranked third overall and top in business organizations for clout.[63] The NFIB has been known for being politically involved and powerful. One of the best ways to appreciate the NFIB's political power is to describe its success at grassroots lobbying.[64] The NFIB made its mark by strong and successful lobbying against former President Clinton's health care plan. They also were integral in obtaining congressional action on the inheritance tax, successful in challenging the OSHA ergonomics rule, and at the forefront of the fight to provide small business with equal access to government contracting.[65]

Part of NFIB's power stems from their ability to speak with one voice due to the homogeneity of their membership and the many issues that small businesses share because of their size. For this reason, the NFIB avoids the problems faced by the NAM and the U.S. Chamber of Commerce. However, its political activities have cost it some clout in the Obama administration. The NFIB opposed the Obama Health Care Reform agenda, as well as other administration initiatives, in much the same way as the chamber of commerce. In return, they were both excluded from an Obama White House "Jobs Summit." [66]

Coalition Building

A noteworthy and growing mechanism of political involvement in the public policy process is the creation and use of **coalitions** to influence government processes. A coalition forms when distinct groups or parties realize they have something in common that might warrant their joining forces, at least temporarily, for joint action. More often than not, an issue that various groups feel similarly about creates the opportunity for a coalition.

Coalition formation has become a standard practice for firms interested in accomplishing political goals or influencing public policy. If a company or an association wants to pass or defeat particular legislation, it needs to seek the support of any individual or organization that has a similar position on the issue.[67] Coalitions enable members to share their resources and pool their energies when they confront difficult issues. Coalitions also enable a company to push for its own agenda without necessarily having its name attached to the campaign.[68]

Because coalitions tend to form around issues, an astute political strategist could analyze past, present, and likely future coalitions so that coalition behavior could be anticipated and managed. To do this, MacMillan and Jones[69] recommend the following steps:

1. *Manage the sequence in which issues are addressed.* This kind of control can dictate priorities and emphasis and result in the proper channeling of effort to suit the organization's interests.
2. *Increase the visibility of certain issues.* By doing this, the strategist can focus attention in such a way that her or his goals are met.
3. *Unbundle issues into smaller subissues.* The strategist may be able to reach her or his goals by slowly but surely accomplishing one small step at a time. The net result may be more success for the entirety.

One high-profile example of coalition building around a specific issue is the Coalition for Security and Competitiveness. Eight leading trade associations (the Aerospace Industries Association, Association for Manufacturing Technology, Coalition for Employment through Exports, Electronic Industries Alliance, Information Technology Industry Council, National Association of Manufacturers, National Foreign Trade Council, and U.S. Chamber of Commerce) joined to lobby for modernization of the U.S. export control system in order to make it more efficient, predictable, and transparent.[70] These associations represent firms that must export goods in a time when terror concerns and global competitiveness make is increasingly difficult to use outdated methods and modalities. The goal of the proposed modernization is to protect the security of sensitive military technologies, while also maintaining technological leadership and industrial competitiveness.[71]

Political Action Committees

To this point, our discussion of lobbying has focused primarily on interpersonal contact and powers of persuasion. We now turn our attention to **political action committees (PACs)**, the principal instruments through which business uses financial resources to influence government. PACs should be thought of as one facet of lobbying. However, because they have become such an influential phenomenon, they deserve separate treatment in our discussion.

Evolution of PACs

PACs have been around for years, but their influence has been most profoundly felt in the past two decades. This is perhaps because the bottom line in politics, as well as in business, is most often measured in terms of money—who has it, how much of it, and how much power they are able to bring to bear as a result. This is the **Golden Rule of Politics**: "He who has the gold, rules."[72]

Business PACs appeared on the scene in the early 1970s as a direct result of the 1974 amendments to the Federal Election Campaign Act (FECA). Under this law, organizations of like-minded individuals (such as business, labor, and other special-interest groups) could form together and create a PAC for the purpose of raising money and donating it to candidates for public office.[73] The effect of the 2010 Supreme Court's decision on campaign financing in general and PACs in particular has not yet been felt at this writing. Essentially, the Court's ruling allows corporations and labor organizations to use treasury funds to make independent expenditures in connection with federal elections and to provide funding for campaign ads and other forms of communication. According to the Federal Elections Commission (FEC), "The ruling did not affect the ban on corporate or union contributions or the reporting requirements for independent expenditures and electioneering communications."[74] The Center for Public Integrity believes the ruling will give corporations power over unions because corporations have more money to spend.[75] At this writing, the Commission is studying the Court's opinion. Although some changes may occur, PACs are likely to remain an important part of business's involvement in elections. Figure 12-4 shows the top ten PAC contributors to federal candidates.

Arguments for PACs

Not surprisingly, those who support PACs are primarily those who collect and donate the money (e.g., the business community) and those who receive the money (many

---

FIGURE 12-4 Top Ten PAC Contributors to Candidates (2009–2010)

PAC	Total Amount ($)	Democratic Percentage	Republican Percentage
Operating Engineers Union	2,017,800	88	12
International Brotherhood of Electrical Workers	1,732,800	99	2
AT&T, Inc.	1,666,025	50	50
National Beer Wholesalers Association	1,494,000	59	41
Honeywell International	1,399,300	61	39
American Association for Justice	1,292,000	96	4
National Community Pharmacists Association	2,748,299	65	35
American Bankers Association	1,240,750	45	55
Teamsters	1,146,550	98	2
Boeing Co.	1,141,000	62	38
Lockheed Martin	1,134,700	58	42

Source: The Center for Responsive Politics, **http://www.opensecrets.org**. Based on data released by the FEC on February 21, 2010.

ETHICS IN PRACTICE CASE

Influencing Local Government

My friend runs a small Atlanta chemical company that produces alum. Alum is used for many purposes, including water purification, and the company had a contract with Fulton County for this use for many years. In all the years they had this contract, they received it through open bidding. This was the case every renewal year until this year, when they were again the low bidder. A larger company based in the North with a division in Georgia was awarded the contract, even though its bid was about 3 percent higher. This would have been acceptable had there been a quality or delivery problem in the past, but this had never been the case.

My friend met with a former county commissioner to seek advice about, and reasons for, this situation.

The commissioner believed that there was an under-the-table agreement and advised my friend to sue the county and its purchasing manager. The problem is that the contract is relatively small and the lawsuit would almost certainly cost more than the contract.

1. Is filing a lawsuit the best way for this chemical company to influence the county commission? What options does the company have?

2. Do companies now have to lobby local or other governments to get business? Do they need to make PAC contributions? Bribes or kickbacks?

3. What action should this small chemical company take?

Contributed by Jack Rood

members of Congress and candidates for office). Businesses see PACs as a positive and constructive way to participate in the political process. They see PACs as a reasonable means by which business, labor, and other interest groups may organize their giving. They argue that business giving is offset by labor giving and by the multitude of other special-interest groups that also have formed PACs.

Many of the congressional recipients of PAC contributions also advocate PACs. There is less uniformity of support among Congress than among the business community, however. One reaction from our elected officials is resentment at the suggestion that they can be bought. The larger problem seems to be the growing dependency of politicians on PAC money. In general, members of Congress seem to support the idea of PAC contributions, because their campaign financing has become increasingly dependent on it. With each passing year, however, the need for reform of PAC laws is becoming more apparent to many politicians.

Arguments against PACs

Some of the most vocal opposition to PACs and the role they are playing comes from current and past members of Congress themselves. Veteran lawmakers like Paul Simon (D-Illinois) and Bill Bradley (D-New Jersey) cited the perpetual need to chase money as a major factor in their leaving office.[76] The frustrations of many members of Congress are summed up in the comments of former senator Robert Dole (R-Kansas): "When these political action committees give money, they expect something in return other than good government. It is making it much more difficult to legislate. We may reach a point where if everybody is buying something with PAC money, we can't get anything done." He worries about differing treatment of the rich and the poor: "Poor people don't make campaign contributions. You might get a different result if there were a Poor-PAC up here."[77]

Dole's point is borne out by an article in *Money*, wherein Ann Reilly Dowd estimated the price that special-interest contributions exact on the average household. According to a Progressive Policy Institute study, U.S. taxpayers paid $47.7 billion for corporate tax breaks and subsidies, costing the average household about $483. Import quotas for sugar, textiles, and other goods totaled another $110 billion, with a total cost per household of $1,114. The average U.S. household was expected to pay $1,600 for legislation that protects corporations and the wealthy.[78] Although some of these tax breaks and subsidies are certain to be sound policy and would be implemented with or without financial motivation, Dowd raised an interesting point. Certainly many of those tax breaks, subsidies, and quotas can be traced back to the coffers of PACs.

PACs and the Vote-Buying Controversy. Many studies have been conducted to calculate correlations between PAC giving and congressional voting. The major problem is that correlations do not necessarily prove causation, but they do appear convincing, and PAC critics use these to the fullest advantage. Several political analysts have been able to conduct studies using more sophisticated statistical techniques than simple correlation. These studies have been able to control variables, such as party ideology and past voting records, in an effort to determine what independent effects the contributions have.

These studies have mixed results. Some find strong support, others find none, and a third group has mixed or marginal findings.[79] One factor may be the context of the situation, and so researchers have subsequently looked for contingencies that might explain the differences. In a recent study, Jeffrey Cohen and John Hamman explored the affect of PAC contributions on the regulation of cable television. In support of their hypotheses, they found that PAC contributions were more influential when given to House candidates than to Senate candidates. They explain it in two ways: The more frequent elections of House members make them more susceptible to campaign financing concerns, and the smaller size of the House constituencies (as opposed to the Senate constituencies) means House members have fewer interest groups with which they must contend. Similarly, they found that PAC money was more influential when issues were at the smaller interest-group level, and its importance became diluted when issues moved to the broader arena of the entire House or Senate.[80]

Although it is difficult to isolate specific PACs and specific votes, the benefits of corporate political activity are more easily determined. A recent study shows that corporate donations to political campaigns are associated with an increase in firm value of 3.5 percent.[81] The authors speculate that the increase in firm value stems from the economics benefits accruing to the companies from legislation they supported: The return is greatest for firms in the candidate's home state.[82]

PAC Effectiveness. PAC contributions appear to be most effective when certain conditions prevail.[83] These conditions include the following:

1. *When the issue is less visible.* PAC funds are more likely to be effective while the issue being debated is less visible—that is, not yet in the full glare of public and media scrutiny.
2. *During the early stages of the legislative process.* When agenda setting and subcommittee work are being done, the public, the press, and "watchdog" groups are not as attentive.
3. *When the issue is narrow, specialized, or unopposed.* PAC contributions are more effective on specialized or unopposed issues than on broad national issues.
4. *When PACs are allied.* When "PACs travel in packs" and work together, they can wield considerable power.
5. *When PACs adapt lobbying techniques to their contribution strategies.* Successful PACs also employ grassroots lobbying with contributions.

PACs and Campaign Financing

Because PAC money is easy to come by, it is clear why PACs have so much influence with their contributions. When this fact is combined with the ever-escalating sums of money that legislators need to get and stay elected, the result is quite powerful. The increasing dependency on PAC contributions is driven partly by the rising costs of becoming elected and partly by the ease of getting PAC money. According to Common Cause president and CEO Scott Harshberger, "This system is a gravy train for members of Congress—and a meal ticket for special interests, many of whom want something in return."[84]

Recent attention has focused on the way in which PAC funds are spent. Leadership PACs are a specific form of PAC with far fewer limitations on how the money may be spent. They have been around for a long time but did not come into general use until the mid-1990s when former Congressman Tom Delay (R-Texas) began to urge Republican lawmakers to make use of them. Now they are common on both sides of the aisle.[85] Leadership PACs were designed to allow those lawmakers holding safe seats to funnel money to colleagues at risk of not being reelected. Instead, they seem to be evolving into slush funds, covering such purchases as hotels, meals, flowers, jewelry, limousines, art, and even funerals.[86]

The Hard Facts about Soft Money.   The **Bipartisan Campaign Reform Act (BCRA)** is also known as McCain–Feingold for its chief sponsors, Senators John McCain (R-Arizona) and Russell Feingold (D-Wisconsin). The legislation, which went into effect on November 6, 2002, represented "the most sweeping change of the U.S. campaign finance system in a quarter century."[87] Its purpose was to remove the influence of **soft money** on candidates running for national office. Soft money is a contribution made to political parties instead of to political candidates. Soft money contributions were unregulated prior to the law and often used to run "issue ads" just before an election. In contrast, law already regulated **hard money**, donations made directly to the candidates. The BCRA banned soft money and prevented special-interest groups from airing "issue ads" in the preelection period, while raising the limits for hard money donations. This Act created a series of odd bedfellows who joined together to file lawsuits to fight it. Groups as disparate as the National Rifle Association, the American Civil Liberties Union, the U.S. Chamber of Commerce, and the AFL-CIO challenged its constitutionality in court.

Although McCain–Feingold represented a significant step forward in campaign financing, problems remain. As Republican lobbyist Ron Kaufman said, "Campaign cash is like the Pillsbury Doughboy. You push it in one place and it pops out in another."[88] In response to the legislation, Democrat and Republican strategists set up new groups to take the place of the political parties. Some worry that these groups will be less accountable than the political parties were prior to the law's inception.[89] These nonprofit organizations, known as **527s** for the section of the tax code that governs their activities, are allowed to raise and spend soft money on campaigns. The Federal Election Commission imposed limits on their use of soft money but opted not to shut them down;[90] however, the Federal Election Commission (FEC) monitors the organizations to make sure they stay within existing law by looking at how the groups word their appeals, describe themselves, and spend their money.[91] Figure 12-5 lists the top contributors to 527 organizations during the 2010 election cycle.

Another means by which firms are able to get around campaign financing reform is the act of **bundling**, the collection of individual donations that are then delivered to the candidate in a lump sum. Typically, a senior executive will host a fund-raising event and invite high-level employees to attend and donate up to the $2,000 limit. Executives may be given lucrative bonuses with the implicit understanding that they will make the maximum contribution. Bundling is not new, but it has reached new heights since McCain–Feingold. Clearly, one unintended consequence of campaign financing reform was to shift the burden for political contributions from corporations to their employees.[92]

At this writing, the Supreme Court just announced a landmark decision on campaign financing. In a 5-4 ruling in *Citizens United v. Federal Election Commission*, the court established that corporations have the same First Amendment free speech rights as

FIGURE 12-5 Top Contributors to 527 Organizations

Contributor	Total ($)
Service Employees International Union	6,635,260
Friends of America Votes	1,905,861
Operating Engineers Union	1,590,245
Laborers Union	1,135,750
United Food & Commercial Workers Union	1,027,873
American Federation of State, County and Municipal Employees	830,373
National Association of Realtors	806,357
Illinois Manufacturers Association	695,000
Sheet Metal Workers Union	663,000
Ironworkers Union	501,940
John Templeton Foundation	450,100
American Dental Association	408,327
International Brotherhood of Electrical Workers	406,648
National Democratic Club	374,281
Indiana Manufacturers Association	366,928
National Education Association	333,420
Communications Workers of America	300,050
Jon Stryker Architecture	300,000
Akonadi Foundation	260,000
Brico Fund/Time Out Enterprises	255,000

Source: http://www.opensecrets.org

individuals.[93] Supporters of campaign finance reform are upset. Senator McCain said the ruling essentially ended the campaign finance reforms he sponsored and predicted "an inundation of special-interest money into political campaigns."[94] President Obama said that the ruling "reversed a century of law to open the floodgates for special interests—including foreign corporations—to spend without limit in our elections."[95] Supporters of the decision contend that corporate power is not inherently corrupting and that the ruling rightfully opposed censorship of free speech.[96] It is too early to know the full repercussions of the ruling, but it is certain to affect the political landscape for years to come.

Strategies for Political Activism. We have discussed some of the principal approaches by which business has become politically active—lobbying, PACs, and coalitions. To be sure, there are other approaches, but these are the major ones. In our discussion, we have unavoidably made reference to the use of these approaches as part of a strategy. To develop the idea of strategy for political activism, it is important to understand that managers must not only identify useful approaches but also address when and under what conditions these various approaches should be used or would be most effective. We do not want to carry this idea too far, because it is beyond the scope of this book. On the other hand, as managers devise and execute political strategies, it is useful to see their initiatives as factors in their development of stakeholder management capabilities.

Having experienced failures and surprises in the political and social arenas, organizations are expanding their strategic vision and action by developing strategies for coping with a rapidly changing social and political environment. The purpose of political strategy is "to secure a position of advantage regarding a given regulation or piece of

ETHICS IN PRACTICE CASE

Patriotism versus Profits: What Should a Firm Do?

One way that business can influence government is to circumvent governmental mandates through creative use of loopholes. This can improve corporate profits, meeting one of business's responsibilities. But does business have any responsibility to the governments whose resources enable them to grow and prosper?

According to a report filed by Citizens for Tax Justice and Change to Win, Walmart avoided $2.3 billion in state taxes in only six years. Walmart is not alone in this strategy. Big box retailers and other companies across the country have used a variety of tactics to avoid paying taxes whenever possible. Walmart is simply the biggest of the lot, and by all accounts, the most adept at keeping costs down.

One of the techniques Walmart has used is basically to rent its stores but then pay itself the store rent. One Walmart subsidiary pays rent to a real estate investment trust (REIT), which can receive a break on taxes if it pays out dividends. Another Walmart subsidiary owns 99 percent of the REIT and thus receives the dividends tax free. This corporate tax loophole is illegal at the federal level, but states have been slower to plug it. Many have scrambled to do so. Still, as one loophole is plugged another one opens. In 2008, Walmart paid $22.6 million in cash to seven Oregonian energy projects for the right to claim $33.6 million in energy tax credits. In return, Walmart received $11 million in profit, which represents the difference between what it paid for the tax credit and the amount its taxes were reduced. These various tax-saving strategies that firms are employing have helped to lower the share of income tax that companies pay while individual income tax payments continue to rise.

1. Who are the stakeholders and how are they affected by Walmart's cost-saving strategy? Are Walmart's actions in trying to minimize income tax payments in any possible way socially responsible?

2. Do companies have a responsibility to pay a fair share of income tax to state and federal governments? Who determines what that fair share should be?

3. Where do you draw the line on tax savings by corporations? Are the aforementioned REIT strategies acceptable?

4. After receiving the bulk of U.S. government contracts to fight the wars in Afghanistan and Iraq, Halliburton relocated its operations to Dubai, a haven from U.S. taxes. Senator Leahy described this move as "the wickedest of entrepreneurial greed." Do you agree, or do you find the move acceptable?

5. Although Enron paid no taxes in 2002, they received a $278 million tax rebate on a tax break from stock options cashed in by employees. The study also found that Enron paid no taxes in four of the five years from 1996 to 2000, during which time the company collected $381 million in tax refunds. Is this socially responsible behavior?

6. U.S. law bans virtually all commerce with countries such as Iran, Syria, and Libya that have sponsored terrorists. However, three *Fortune* 500 firms—Halliburton, Conoco-Phillips, and General Electric—were identified in the report as doing business in Iran and Syria. The law contains a loophole that these firms utilized: It does not apply to any foreign or offshore subsidiary run by non-Americans.

7. What implications do these situations hold for industrial policy? What would you do if you were a CEO of one of these corporations? What changes would you make, if any, if you were a government official? Are there lines that corporations should not cross? If so, what are they?

Sources: Jesse Drucker, "Wal-Mart Cuts Taxes by Paying Rent to Itself," *The Wall Street Journal—Eastern Edition*, February 1, 2007, http://www.ctj.org; David Ivanovich, "Investigators: Enron Taxes 'Eye-Popping,'" *Houston Chronicle* (February 13, 2004); *60 Minutes* (January 25, 2004); Harry Esteve, "Walmart, Others Make Money on Oregon's Energy Tax Credits," *The Oregonian* (December 29, 2009).

legislation, to gain control of an idea or a movement and deflect it from the firm, or to deal with a local community group on an issue of importance."[97] Often such strategies are exercised in arenas beyond the regulatory/legislative scene. In pursuing political strategy, two major approaches or strategies are desirable: (1) keeping an issue off the public agenda and out of the limelight and (2) helping to define the public issue. If the company cannot do the first, which is a strategy of containment, it should strive for the second, which allows the firm to exercise some control in shaping the issue. If both of these approaches fail, the company will need to pursue a coping strategy.[98]

Summary

With the global financial meltdown, a weak economy fell into a recession, and items that were once at the forefront of the legislative agenda have been shelved to deal with issues such as joblessness and business failures. In this environment, corporate political participation has taken on renewed importance.

The 2010 Supreme Court ruling in *Citizens United v. Federal Election Commission* has changed the rules once again. In the midst of these ebbs and flows in restrictions, lobbying and corporate political contributions remain a permanent part of the political landscape. Business advocating for its interests is an important part of maintaining the balance of power needed in a pluralistic society. To maintain a true balance of power, however, businesses must advocate in a way that is both ethical and legal.

We have described several ways companies seek and pursue to influence government action by gaining access to political decision makers. While we describe these strategies individually, we should remember that politically active firms are inclined to combine various strategies.[99] Companies make PAC contributions, set up their own lobbyists in Washington offices, contract with outside lobbyists to represent their interests, and join together with like-minded organizations to push for change through trade associations and coalitions. PACs and lobbying are not separate strategies; they are part of an overall approach.[100]

Business's political activity continues to be controversial with the public. As we discussed in Chapter 1, business often receives criticism for using and abusing its power. Nowhere is this more evident than in corporate lobbying and its outcomes. The BCRA (McCain–Feingold) was a response to valid concerns that the use of soft money gave business and other advocates disproportionate power in the political process. Now the 2010 Supreme Court *Citizens United* ruling has restored some of business's power, and its repercussions are still to be felt. As new excesses develop, new regulations and rulings will come to address the problems they present. That is the ongoing "back and forth" that characterizes the political process.

Key Terms

527s, p. 450

astroturf lobbying, p. 443

Bipartisan Campaign Reform Act (BCRA), p. 450

bundling, p. 450

coalitions, p. 446

company lobbying, p. 439

cyberadvocacy, p. 442

Golden Rule of Politics, p. 447

grassroots lobbying, p. 442

grasstops lobbying, p. 443

hard money, p. 450

lobbying, p. 438

political action committees (PACs), p. 446

political involvement, p. 437

soft money, p. 450

trade associations, p. 439

umbrella organizations, p. 439

Discussion Questions

1. Explain lobbying in your own words. Describe the different levels at which lobbying takes place. Why is there a lack of unity among the umbrella organizations?

2. What is a PAC? What are the major arguments in favor of PACs? What are the major criticisms of PACs? In your opinion, are PACs a good way for business to influence the public policy process? What changes would you recommend for PACs?

3. Discuss the Bipartisan Campaign Reform Act and its likely effect on future elections. What further types of campaign financing reform would you recommend?

4. Discuss efforts by companies to circumvent governmental regulations. Is the use of legal loopholes ethical?

5. Research the Supreme Court decision on campaign financing and determine its ongoing impact. Do you agree with the decision? Would you change it if you could? If so, how?

13

Consumer Stakeholders: Information Issues and Responses

CHAPTER LEARNING OUTCOMES

After studying this chapter, you should be able to:

1. Recite the consumer's Magna Carta and explain its meaning.

2. Chronicle the evolution of the consumer movement, highlighting Ralph Nader's role.

3. Identify the major abuses of advertising and discuss specific controversial advertising issues.

4. Enumerate and discuss other product information issues that present problems for consumer stakeholders.

5. Describe the role and functions of the FTC.

6. Explain recent consumer-related legislation that has been passed.

7. Discuss the strengths and weaknesses of regulation and self-regulation of advertising and proposed consumer financial protection regulations.

As a result of the recession, businesses of all types have been fighting for the hearts and minds of consumers. By virtually all measures, consumer spending has pulled back over the past several years and consumers have become more cautious and selective about their spending on the entire gamut of products and services. Even as the economy perks up, some observers say it may be 10 to 15 years before it returns to its prerecession levels of spending. Other analysts are more optimistic. Some marketers think they are facing a new era, wherein they may be reducing stock levels, slowing down their expansion, discounting deeply and getting more creative about managing their inventories and adjusting their product lines.[1] Some think the new consumer is "down" but "not out." By all measures, however, it is clear that businesses need to be paying careful attention to customer stakeholders and especially their fair treatment.

How important are consumers as stakeholders? According to management expert Peter Drucker, there is only one valid definition of business purpose: *to create a customer*.[2] Of course, retaining customers is essential, too. In *The Loyalty Effect*, Frederick Reichheld showed that small increases in customer retention rates can lead to dramatic increases in profits.[3] Clearly, businesses must create and retain customers if they are to succeed in today's competitive marketplace. It is not surprising, therefore, that **customer relationship management (CRM)** has become an important mantra of marketing.[4] Customer relationship management is "the ability of an organization to effectively identify, acquire, foster, and retain loyal profitable customers."[5]

With CRM guiding businesses in their customer relations, one would expect consumers to be pleased, or at least satisfied, with the way they have been treated. Unfortunately, that hasn't been the case. The consumer is still "often ignored"[6] and, in practice, CRM has been said to be "an awful lot of bland talk and not a lot of action."[7] In practice, the customer care revolution is largely considered a failure.[8] A revealing survey by Customer Care Measurement and Consulting (CCMC) found that 45 percent of the individuals surveyed had a serious consumer problem or complaint in a recent year and that 60 to 70 percent of those having complaints became enraged at the way the company handled the problem.[9] It is not surprising, therefore, that 45 percent of CEOs conceded that their corporations did not deserve the loyalty of their customers.[10] According to the American Customer Satisfaction Index, consumer satisfaction in 2010 is stronger than it was before the recession; however, the index measures the satisfaction of consumers with goods and services rather than the way the customer is treated.[11] Taken together, these statistics seem to indicate that although product and service quality has improved, the treatment of customers has been weak.

As the economy is striving to come out of a serious recession, many companies have begun what has been called "the great trust offensive," where they are striving to rebuild customer confidence in their brands. Companies as diverse as Ford, American Express, and McDonald's have been revamping their marketing policies to win back the most valuable of corporate assets—their customers. This is because customer trust in business collapsed in 2009 after three years of steady growth, according to a major survey of informed citizens.[12] Companies have realized that it is critical that consumers start spending again if the economy is to bounce back.

The business and the consumer stakeholder issue is at the forefront of discussions about business and its relationships with and responsibility to the society in which it exists. Products and services are the most visible manifestations of business in society. For this reason, the whole issue deserves careful examination. We devote two chapters to it. In this chapter, we focus on the consumer movement and product information issues—most notably, advertising. In Chapter 14, we consider product and service issues, especially product safety and liability, and business's response to its consumer stakeholders.

The Consumer Movement

The basic expectations of the modern consumer movement were found in the "**consumer's Magna Carta**," or the four basic consumer rights spelled out by President John F. Kennedy in his "Special Message on Protecting the Consumer Interest."[13] Those rights included the right to safety, the right to be informed, the right to choose, and the right to be heard.

The **right to safety** concerns many products (insecticides, foods, drugs, automobiles, appliances) that are dangerous. The **right to be informed** is intimately marketing and advertising related and refers to the consumer's right to know about a product, its use, and the cautions to be exercised while using it. This right includes the whole array of marketing: advertising, warranties, labeling, and packaging. The **right to choose**, although not as great a concern today as the first two, refers to the assurance that competition is working effectively and that choices are available. The fourth, the **right to be heard**, was proposed because of many consumers' belief that they could not effectively communicate to business their desires and, especially, their grievances.[14]

Although these four basic rights do not encompass all the responsibilities that business owes to shopper stakeholders, they do capture the fundamentals of business's social responsibilities to consumers. Consumers today want "fair value" for money spent, a product that will meet "reasonable" expectations, a product (or service) with full disclosure of its specifications, a product (or service) that has been truthfully advertised, and a product that is safe and has been subjected to appropriate product safety testing. Consumers also expect that if a product is too dangerous it will be removed from the market or some other appropriate action will be taken.

For decades, there have been outcries that business has failed in these responsibilities to consumers, leaving them often neglected or mistreated.[15] The roots of consumer activism date back to 1906, when Upton Sinclair published *The Jungle*, his famous exposé of unsanitary conditions in the meatpacking industry.[16] The contemporary wave of consumer activism, however, started to build in the late 1950s, took form in the 1960s, matured in the 1970s, and continues today, although in a different form. The following definition of **consumerism** captures the essential nature of the consumer movement:

> *Consumerism is a social movement seeking to augment the rights and powers of buyers in relation to sellers.*[17]

Although the modern consumer movement is often said to have begun with the publication of Ralph Nader's criticism of General Motors in *Unsafe at Any Speed*,[18] the impetus for the movement was actually a complex combination of circumstances. The conditions necessary for bringing about a social movement of any kind were present for consumerism. These conditions are "structural conduciveness, structural strains, growth of a generalized belief, precipitating factors, mobilization for action, and social control."[19]

Figure 13-1 presents five overarching lessons that Consumers Union president Jim Guest has taken from the consumer movement.

FIGURE 13-1

Lessons from the Consumer Movement

One year after taking office as the President of Consumers Union, Jim Guest made a speech to the Consumer Federation of America's Consumer Assembly. In it, he listed five "overarching lessons" he derived from the abuses of consumer trust that had occurred in the marketplace. The following are those lessons:

1. Although the consumer movement has had a strong impact, it is still absolutely essential for achieving a fair and just marketplace for all consumers.
2. Effective public oversight is needed where
   a. corporations lack the incentives to regulate their own behavior responsibly and
   b. health, safety, and other special concerns are an issue.
3. Our product safety net and consumer protection infrastructure have serious holes. For public watchdogs to be effective, they must receive necessary resources, authority, and public support.
4. The consumer movement must intensify the fight for affordable goods and services, fair financial practices, and a fair chance at a decent standard of living. Government must provide for those who do not have a fair chance at a decent standard of living. Too many consumers still cannot afford the basic necessities.
5. In the United States, consumers must curb the wasteful overconsumption that threatens the environment.

In the closing of this talk "from one consumer organization to another," Guest described the movement as being in a time of both crisis and opportunity. Much has been achieved but there is still a very long way to go, with very serious and real problems remaining to be resolved.

Source: Remarks by Jim Guest, President, Consumers Union of U.S., Inc., "Consumers and Consumerism in America Today," *Consumer Assembly of the Consumer's Federation of America* (March 15, 2002), http://www.consumersunion.org/other/guest315.htm. Accessed July 9, 2010.

Ralph Nader's Consumerism

We cannot overemphasize Ralph Nader's contribution to the birth, growth, and nurturance of the consumer movement. Nader arrived on the scene 45 years ago, and he is still the acknowledged father of the consumer movement. The impact of Nader's auto safety exposé, *Unsafe at Any Speed,* cannot be overstated. His book not only gave rise to auto safety regulations and devices (safety belts, padded dashboards, stronger door latches, head restraints, air bags, etc.) but it also created a new era—that of the consumer. Nader, personally, was thrust into national prominence.

Nader's aforementioned book criticized the auto industry, generally, and General Motors, specifically. Nader objected to the safety of the GM Corvair, in particular. GM could not figure out what motivated Nader, so in 1966 the company hired detectives to trail and discredit him. GM denied having used women as "sex lures" as part of its investigation. However, the company did apologize to Nader at a congressional hearing and paid him $480,000 for invasion of his privacy.

Nader put his money to work and built an enormous and far-reaching consumer protection empire. His legions of zealous activists became known as "Nader's Raiders." Nader and the consumer movement were the impetus for consumer legislation being passed in the 1970s.

The 1980s, however, did not turn out to be a consumer decade. One observer noted how uncontroversial Nader had become and posited that it was not only because of the climate of the times but also because most of the significant gains that were to be made had been made.[20] In the late 1980s, however, Nader began what *BusinessWeek* dubbed his "second coming." Nader successfully campaigned to roll back car insurance rates in California and to squelch a congressional pay raise. These victories vaulted him to a prominence he had not enjoyed in years.[21] In 2000, Nader ran as the Green Party candidate for U.S. president with a campaign that focused on establishing a viable third party, attacking corporate wealth, and protecting the environment. He was unsuccessful in his goal of getting 5 percent of the total popular vote so that the Green Party would be eligible to receive federal matching funds in the 2004 presidential election. In the process, however, he raised the ire of Democrats, labor leaders, feminists, and environmentalists who characterized him as a "spoiler" who tipped the election to George W. Bush.[22] When he announced a second run for the presidency in February 2004, the Green Party disavowed him, and a poll found that two-thirds of Americans did not want him to run again.[23] He ran as a reform/populist/independent candidate and received 465,650 votes (0.38 percent).[24] This count was far fewer than the votes he received in 2000.[25]

Ralph Nader continues to be a controversial man. A 2007 documentary about Nader is entitled *An Unreasonable Man.*[26] The title came from "Maxims for Revolutionists" in George Bernard Shaw's 1903 play, *Man and Superman:*[27]

> *The reasonable man adapts himself to the world; the unreasonable one persists in trying to adapt the world to himself. Therefore all progress depends on the unreasonable man.*

Shaw was right. Nader may be an unreasonable man but he has also been the source of considerable progress for consumers. Consumer complaints did not disappear with the advent of Ralph Nader's activism; instead, they intensified. One of Nader's greatest contributions is that he made consumer complaints respectable.

Consumerism in the 21st Century

Many groups make up the loose confederation known as the consumer movement. The power held by consumers is not the result of organized group lobbying—instead, their

FIGURE 13-2

Examples of
Consumer
Problems
with Business

- The high prices of many products
- The poor quality of many products
- The failure of many companies to live up to claims made in their advertising
- Hidden fees
- The poor quality of after-sales service
- Too many products breaking or going wrong after you bring them home
- Misleading packaging or labeling
- The feeling that it is a waste of time to complain about consumer problems

because nothing substantial will be achieved
- Inadequate guarantees and warranties
- Failure of companies to handle complaints properly
- Too many products that are dangerous
- The absence of reliable information about various products and services
- Not knowing what to do if something is wrong with a product you have bought

efforts today are at the grassroots level. Grassroots activism of consumers has never been stronger. In England, a relatively small group of disgruntled consumers brought the country to a halt by protesting the price of gas. They set up blockades that emptied roads, closed schools, and caused panic buying in supermarkets. The Internet has made it easier for consumer groups to respond to issues more quickly and more forcefully. It makes it possible to not only inform consumers of concerns that have arisen but also to rally the troops to take action. This is of special concern for global companies whose interests are far flung. According to Cordelia Brabbs of *Marketing*, "Global companies find themselves under the watchful eye of their customers. If they fail to behave impeccably at all times, they risk finding their misdemeanors broadcast on a high-speed information network."[28] It is impossible to catalog them all, but Figure 13-2 lists examples of the major problems consumers have with business's products and services today.

Before we consider more closely the corporate response to the consumer movement and the consumer stakeholder, it is fruitful to analyze some of the issues that have become prominent in the business–consumer relationship and the role that the major federal regulatory bodies have assumed in addressing these issues. Broadly, we may classify the major kinds of issues into two groups: **product information** and the product itself. As stated earlier, in this chapter we focus on product information issues such as advertising, warranties, packaging, and labeling. The next chapter focuses on the product itself. Throughout our discussion of products, the reader should keep in mind that we are referring to services also.

Product Information Issues

Why have questions been raised about business's social and ethical responsibilities in the area of product information? Most consumers know the answer. Companies understandably want to portray their products in the most flattering light. However, efforts to paint a positive portrait of a product can easily cross the line into misinformation or deception regarding the product's attributes. Consumers Union (CU), an independent, nonprofit testing and information organization, exists to protect consumers' interests. They conduct independent tests of products and report their findings in their print and online editions of *Consumer Reports (CR)*.[29] "Selling It" is a segment in the print edition of *Consumer Reports*; it is designed to "memorialize the excesses in the world of marketing." Quite often the ads are contradictory. The following items are examples of the absurdities they chronicle:

- The ad implores you to "switch to Verizon high-speed internet at a super-low price that'll never go up." The ad repeats again "Guaranteed to Never Go Up." Then, when you read the fine print on the same page, it says "Rates increase after two years."[30] What part of "never go up" do they fail to understand?

- On the outside ad, CenterPoint Energy proudly exclaims: "Good News: Natural Gas Prices are Lower." But then you look inside and you find the announcement that the company has "filed to raise rates an average of $5.79 per month."[31]
- Harry & David's Dark Chocolate RASPBERRIES is what the label said. Also included on the label were pictures of the fruit. But then when you look at the list of ingredients, there are no raspberries listed in the produce. Instead, you get "infused dry apple."[32]

These cases are actual examples of the questionable and careless use of product information. It is not clear whether the firms that created the aforementioned communications were intending to deceive, but the information they provided did not match the reality of the product. Business has a legal and an ethical responsibility to provide fair and accurate information about its products or services.

The primary issue with product or service information falls in the realm of advertising. Other information-related areas include warranties or guarantees, packaging, labeling, instructions for use, and the sales techniques used by direct sellers. Information about after-sale service is also a critical issue.

Advertising Issues

The debate over the role of advertising in society has been going on for decades. Most observers have concentrated on the economic function of advertising in our market system, but opinions vary as to whether advertising is beneficial or detrimental as a business function. Critics charge that it is a wasteful and inefficient tool of business and that our current standard of living would be even higher if we could be freed from the negative influences of advertising. These critics argue that advertising raises the prices of products and services because it is an unnecessary business cost, the main effect of which is to circulate superfluous information that could be better and more cheaply provided on product information labels or by salespeople in stores. The result is that significant amounts of money are spent with no net consumer benefit.[33]

In response, others have claimed that advertising is a beneficial component of the market system and that the increases in the standard of living and consumer satisfaction may be attributed to it. They argue that, in general, advertising is an efficient means of distributing information because consumers need to know about the enormous and ever-changing array of products. From this perspective, advertising is an effective and relatively inexpensive way of informing consumers of new and improved products.[34]

Proponents of advertising argue that even uninformative advertising still tells consumers a lot. Advertising heavily, even if vaguely, helps attract shoppers to retail stores through a kind of they-must-be-doing-something-right logic. The increased customer traffic then enables the retailer to offer a wider selection of goods, raising the incentive to invest in cost-reduction technologies such as computerized inventory, modern warehouses, and quantity discounts, thus further lowering marginal costs. The advertising can promote efficiency, even if it provides no hard information, by signaling to consumers where the big-company, low-price, high-variety stores are. Economists have argued that retail juggernauts such as Walmart, Home Depot, and Best Buy have taken advantage of this phenomenon. Viewed in this way, advertising is seen as a net plus for society because it tends to lower prices and increase variety.[35]

The debate over whether advertising is a productive or wasteful business practice will undoubtedly continue. As a practical matter, however, advertising has become the lifeblood of the free enterprise system. It stimulates competition and makes available

ETHICS IN PRACTICE CASE

Where Are My Slippers?

For the past six months, I have been working as a telesales accounts manager for a manufacturer of bedroom slippers. The firm had recently opened the telesales department, on a trial basis, to reach smaller retailers whose sales volumes were not large enough to attract the attention of the regional field representatives. Traditionally, the busiest time for the firm is the period from September to December, when retailers are ordering the inventories they want to have on hand for the Christmas shopping season. Last year, the number of orders coming in was unexpectedly heavy, and the lead time needed to ship the orders was nearly a month. Unless the order was placed by the end of November, it was unlikely that the customer would have the merchandise on its shelves by Christmas.

However, the department manager encouraged us to take the late orders and promise delivery by Christmas, even though we knew that the merchandise wouldn't be delivered until early January. Most likely,

the retailers wouldn't have wanted the merchandise if they had known the actual delivery date. Our manager's reasoning for this practice was that we needed to boost our department's sales revenue to ensure that upper management saw our department as a success at the end of the trial period. In other words, our jobs could be on the line. Also, each order that we may have lost meant a smaller commission check.

1. How would you characterize the practice in which our firm engaged?

2. Were the jobs of all the people associated with the telesales department more important than ethical principles? What ethical principles are at stake?

3. Should I have followed my manager's orders and gone along with what I thought was a deceptive marketing practice? Is the practice all that bad if there is some chance we could deliver on time?

Contributed by David Alan Ostendorff

---

information that consumers can use in comparison buying. It also provides competitors with information with which to respond in a competitive way and contains a mechanism for immediate feedback in the form of sales response. So, despite its criticisms, advertising does provide social and economic benefits to consumers.

With the availability of thousands of products and their increasing complexity, the consumer today has a real need for information that is clear, accurate, and adequate. **Clear information** is that which is direct and straightforward and on which neither deception nor manipulation relies. **Accurate information** communicates truths, not half-truths. It avoids gross exaggeration and innuendo. **Adequate information** provides potential purchasers with enough information to make the best choice among the options available.[36]

Whereas providing information is one legitimate purpose of advertising in our society, another legitimate purpose is *persuasion*. Most consumers today expect that business advertises for the purpose of persuading them to buy their products or services, and they accept this as a part of the commercial system. Indeed, many people enjoy companies' attempts to come up with interesting ways to sell their products. It is commonplace for people to talk with one another about the latest appealing or entertaining advertisement they have seen. Awards are given for outstanding advertisements, as well as for those that are particularly bad. Nevertheless, there is evidence that the public may be losing its patience. A survey by Yankelovich Partners, a market research company, found that 60 percent of the survey respondents have a more negative opinion of advertising than they did previously, 61 percent believe the practice has spun out of control, and 69 percent are attracted to products that help them avoid commercials altogether.[37]

Ethical issues in advertising arise as companies step over the line in their attempts to inform and persuade consumer stakeholders. The frequently heard phrase "the seamy side of advertising" alludes to the economic and social costs that derive from advertising abuses, such as those mentioned earlier in the chapter, and of which the reader is probably able to supply ample personal examples.

Advertising Abuses.   There are at least four types of advertising abuses in which ethical issues reside. These include situations in which advertisers are ambiguous, conceal facts, exaggerate, or employ psychological appeals.[38] These four types cover most of the general criticisms leveled at advertising.

AMBIGUOUS ADVERTISING One of the more gentle ways that companies deceive is through **ambiguous advertising**, in which something about the product or service is not made clear because it is stated in a way that may mean several different things.

An ad can be made ambiguous in several ways. One way is to make a statement using **weasel words**, which leaves it to the viewer to infer the message. These are words that are inherently vague and for which the company could always claim it was not misleading the consumer. An example of a weasel word is "help." Once an advertiser uses the qualifier "help," almost anything could follow, and the company could claim that it was not intending to deceive. We see ads that claim to "help us keep young," "help prevent cavities," or "help keep our houses germ free." Think how many times you have seen expressions in advertising such as "helps stop," "helps prevent," "helps fight," "helps you feel," "helps you look," or "helps you become."[39] Other weasel words include "like," "virtually," and "up to" (e.g., stops pain "up to" eight hours—which simply means it won't stop pain for more than eight hours). The use of such words makes ads ambiguous.

Another way to make an ad ambiguous is through use of legalese, or other excessively complex and ambiguous terminology. In "Selling It," *Consumer Reports* provided the following paragraph that was included in a department store's advertising:

> *Items indicated on sale or referencing a comparative former or future price represent reductions from former or future offering prices (with or without actual sales) at Kohl's or at a competitor of the item or of comparable merchandise. Intermediate markdowns may have been taken. Clearance merchandise is excluded from entire stock categories herein.*[40]

CONCEALED FACTS A type of advertising abuse called **concealed facts** refers to the practice of not telling the whole truth or deliberately not communicating information the consumer ought to have access to in making an informed choice. Another way of stating this is to say "a fact is concealed when its availability would probably make the desire, purchase, or use of the product less likely than its absence."[41] This is a difficult area because few would argue that an advertiser is obligated to tell "everything," even if that were humanly possible. For example, a pain reliever company might claim the effectiveness of its product in superlative terms without stating that there are dozens of other products on the market that are just as effective. Or an insurance company might promote all the forms of protection that a given policy would provide without enumerating all the situations for which the policy does not provide coverage.

Ethical issues arise when a firm, through its advertisements, presents facts in such a selective way that a false belief is created. As consumers, it is up to us to be informed about factors such as competitors' products, prices, and so on. Of course, judgment is required in determining which ads have and have not created false beliefs. This makes the entire realm of deceptive advertising a challenge. At times it can be considered harmless. For example, a burrito restaurant in a college town ran a humorous newspaper ad with "FREE BEER" in large block letters; underneath in small letters were the words "will not be served." No one accused this company of unlawful deception; however, not all instances of concealed facts are considered benign. Other concealed facts often occur with respect to hidden fees or surcharges on services. Today, you have to be a sophisticated consumer willing to do timely detective work to root out the rules and policies governing fees companies charge.

An increasingly popular form of concealed advertising is **product placement**, the practice of embedding products in movies and TV shows. Critics call this "stealth advertising." Product placements are everywhere. A case in point is when Elisa and Jack of *30 Rock* fame discussed whether McDonald's McFlurry was the best dessert in the world during one of the episodes. Nonprofit activist groups have called this practice of sneaking in product pitches egregious and deceptive.[42] In a well-known example, the judges in *American Idol* (*Idol*) drink from Coke cups, and the "green room" in which contestants wait is now the "Coke Red Room."[43] More recently Vitaminwater has showed up on *Idol* after Ellen DeGeneres began appearing on the show. Ryan Seacrest tells viewers to text message their votes over AT&T Wireless and, in each episode, they somehow manage to find a new reason for the remaining contestants to sing and dance around a Ford vehicle.[44]

In a variation of product placement, termed **plot placement**, sponsors have paid to make their products integrated into the plotline of a TV show. Revlon played an important part in the plotline of ABC's *All My Children*; Avon was integrated into the plotline of NBC's *Passions*.[45] In one episode of *Biggest Loser*, the dieting contestants hiked from one Subway sandwich shop to another to get a meal as part of the contest rules. The recent product placement of the Apple iPad on *Modern Family* may have gone too far. The Dunphys went on a family mission to get Phil an iPad. At the end of the show, Phil was shown stroking his new iPad while uttering "I love you" to his new gadget.[46]

These forms of advertising are a response to the "TiVO effect." The popularity of digital video recorders (DVRs) such as TiVO has lessened the time that consumers spend watching commercials. The fact that DVRs make it easy and convenient for TV watchers to zap through commercials has advertisers looking for new ways to make customers take notice.[47] Even advertising stalwarts, like Coca-Cola with its advertising budget of more than $300 million per year, are relying less on traditional ads and more on product placement in DVDs and video games.[48]

Free Press is one of a coalition of 50 groups fighting product and plot placements. These groups have appealed to the Federal Communications Commission (FCC) to require networks to disclose such placements, but so far the FCC has passed very few regulations governing them. In their defense, the FCC says they face a delicate balancing act of protecting the public on one hand without undermining the already wobbly economics of television.[49]

EXAGGERATED CLAIMS Companies can also mislead consumers by exaggerating the benefits of their products and services. **Exaggerated claims** are claims that simply cannot be substantiated by any kind of evidence. An example of this would be a claim that a pain reliever is "50 percent stronger than aspirin" or "superior to any other on the market."

A general form of exaggeration is known as **puffery**, a euphemism for hyperbole or exaggeration that usually refers to the use of general superlatives. Is Budweiser really the "King of Beers"? Is Wheaties the "Breakfast of Champions"? Does "better ingredients" mean Papa John's has "Better Pizza"? Normally, a claim of general superiority fits squarely into puffery and is allowable. However, companies walk a fine line when engaging in puffery. They need to be certain that no direct comparison is being made.

Spotlight on SUSTAINABILITY

How Consumers View Sustainability

Two companies recently joined together to publish a report on how consumers viewed the concept of sustainability. Consumers were asked about sustainability with respect to four product areas: purchased food and beverages, household cleaning products, personal care products, and over-the-counter medications. Consumers most frequently said that sustainability meant "the ability to last over time," and "the ability to support oneself." They also linked the concept with "environmental concerns." The consumers also said that terms such as "eco-conscious" and "green" unduly limited the concept of sustainability because they do not account for the variety of economic, social, and environmental issues that real people believe are important in sustaining themselves, their communities, and society as a whole.

   The consumers surveyed went on to say that they would pay a 20 percent premium for sustainable products. To save money, many consumers today are shopping at discount stores and buying store brands that emphasize the sustainability theme.

Source: "Sustainability, Through Consumers' Eyes," http://web.ebscohost.bsu/pdf?vid=5&hid=11&sid=f9418671-7ef8.... Accessed December 3, 2009.

According to one attorney, "It is no longer enough to take comfort in making the same kinds of claims that have been made in an industry for some time. Those (marketers) making aggressive claims need to consider ways a reasonable consumer will interpret those claims, and marketers need to be able to prove every interpretation that is reasonable."[50]

   Most people are not too put off by puffery, because the claims are so general and so frequent that any consumer would know that the firm is exaggerating and simply doing what many do by claiming their product is the best. It has been argued, however, that such exaggerated product claims (1) induce people to buy things that do them no good, (2) result in loss of advertising efficiency as companies are forced to match puffery with puffery, (3) drive out good advertising, and (4) generally result in consumers losing faith in the system because they get so used to companies making claims that exceed their products' capabilities.[51] A recent study found that consumers actually have mixed reactions to puffery, and that they don't always react positively to it.[52]

PSYCHOLOGICAL APPEALS   In advertising, **psychological appeals** are those designed to persuade on the basis of human emotions and emotional needs rather than reason. There is perhaps as much reason to be concerned about ethics in this category as in any other category. One reason is that the products can seldom deliver what the ads promise (i.e., power, prestige, sex, masculinity, femininity, approval, acceptance, and other such psychological satisfactions).[53] Another reason is that psychological appeals can stir emotions in a way that is manipulative and appears designed to take advantage of the consumer's vulnerability. For example, many home security salespeople will watch the newspapers for reports of home break-ins and then call the home owner with a sales pitch for a new home security system.

   Though most advertising strives to appeal to our sight, an increasingly popular form of sensual advertising has been focusing on consumers' hearing. Neuromarketers have concluded, on the basis of research, that the most effective sounds in terms of their psychological appeals are babies giggling, cell phones vibrating, ATM machines dispensing cash, steaks sizzling on a grill, and a soda being popped and poured.[54] Whether such ploys represent unethical uses of psychological persuasion is debatable.

Specific Controversial Advertising Issues. We have considered four major kinds of deceptive advertising—ambiguous advertising, concealed facts, exaggerated claims, and psychological appeals. There are many other variations on these themes, but these are sufficient to make our point. Later in this chapter, we will discuss the FTC's attempts to keep advertising honest. But even there we will see that the whole issue of what constitutes deceptive advertising is an evolving and amorphous concept, particularly when it comes to the task of proving deception and recommending appropriate remedial action. This is why the role of business responsibility is so crucial as business honestly attempts to deal with its consumer stakeholders in a fair and truthful manner.

Let us now consider seven specific advertising issues that have become particularly controversial in recent years because of questionable ethics: comparative advertising, use of sex in advertising, advertising to children, marketing to the poor, advertising of alcoholic beverages, cigarette advertising, health and environmental claims, and ad creep.

COMPARATIVE ADVERTISING One advertising technique that has become controversial and threatens to affect advertising negatively, in general, is **comparative advertising**. This refers to the practice of directly comparing a firm's product with the product of a competitor. Some classic examples of past high-profile comparative campaigns are Coke versus Pepsi, Whopper versus Big Mac, Subway versus Quiznos, Avis versus Hertz, and Papa John's versus Pizza Hut. A recent example is the "Get a Mac" campaign. The ads feature two men, Mac and PC, standing in front of a white background. PC is in an ill-fitting jacket and tie, while Mac is in comfortable jeans. The banter between the two characters is a running comparison of the two machines. The campaign seems to have struck a nerve with the public: The Wikipedia "Get a Mac" site has a long list of spoofs that the campaign has inspired.[55] In 2009, *U.S. News & World Report* named the "Get a Mac" campaign one of the best marketing schemes in recent times.[56]

In another recent example, Domino's Pizza claimed victory in a nationwide blind taste test that pitted the Michigan-based chain against Pizza Hut and Papa John's. In the study, conducted by a large research firm, a majority of participants preferred Domino's pepperoni, sausage, and extra cheese pizzas to its main competitors' offerings. Domino's claimed the results accurately reflected consumer taste preferences, but both Pizza Hut and Papa John's immediately called them into question.[57]

Whether out of pride or general business interest, more and more companies are fighting back when they think the competition has gone too far. Companies may take their adversaries to court, before the FTC, or before voluntary associations, such as the National Advertising Division of the Council of Better Business Bureaus, that attempt to resolve these kinds of disputes. Though there can be good reasons to launch comparative ads, they sometimes come at a cost.

Several questions should be asked by those who are victims of comparative ads and by those who are contemplating using them. For example, were consumers actually asked to compare one brand with another? Was the consumers' sample representative of product users? Could the consumers in the study really discriminate between the products being compared?[58] Questions such as these are essential if companies are to develop sound research methods on which to base comparative ads. To do otherwise is to invite criticism from the public and competitors alike.

USE OF SEX IN ADVERTISING The use of sex in U.S. advertising was one of the burning ethical issues in the past. It took front stage years ago when several women's groups were offended by a series of television commercials sponsored by National Airlines. In 1971, National introduced its provocative "I'm Cheryl, Fly Me" advertising campaign. The airline followed that campaign with a commercial that showed female flight attendants looking seductively at the viewers, saying, "I'm going to fly you like you've never been flown before."[59] Today, sexual references and innuendos in advertising have become commonplace and so the issue sparks less controversy. Says consumer behavior professor Bruce Stern. "We're moving into an arena that we are becoming numb to things that would have offended us a few years ago."[60]

A recent survey conducted by Market Facts for *American Demographics* found that 31 percent of the population is offended by the use of sex in advertising. Moreover, 61 percent said they are less likely to buy a product that is sold through the use of sex in advertising, while only 26 percent are more likely.[61] Even where offense is not taken, sex does not necessarily sell. The irrelevant use of sex can take attention away from the product or service being sold.[62] Some major fashion designers have moved away from sex in their campaigns: Most notably, Abercrombie and Fitch terminated their sexually explicit catalogue not because of any offense taken but because they failed to lure customers.[63] Advertisers have responded to this change in attitudes by targeting their sexually oriented advertisements to narrower, more specific markets, "Playboy Lites" such as *Maxim, FHM,* and *Stuff* that cater primarily to teen young adult males.[64] A more recent study of the sexual content of advertising, found substantial growth in the way that men's magazine ads sexualize and objectify women: 78 percent of women in men's magazine ads were sexualized from 1993 to 2003, compared with 40 percent a decade earlier.[65]

Ads that portray young women as sex objects can have a serious impact on the physical and mental health of girls. A recent task force report from the American Psychological Association (APA) studied this issue and found that the media's sexualization of young women can lead to a lack of confidence with their bodies as well as depression, eating disorders, and low self-esteem.[66] In spite of the fact that sex in advertising is widespread today, the practice still carries serious ethical questions about its appropriateness.

ADVERTISING TO CHILDREN   A hotly debated ethical issue over the past several decades has been advertising to children, specifically on television. This practice has sometimes been called "kid-vid" advertising. A typical weekday afternoon or Saturday morning in America finds millions of kids sprawled on the floor, glued to the TV, or staring at the computer. American children watch an average of 28 hours of television per week, seeing an average of 20,000 half-a-minute commercials in the process. Given the amount of time children spend in front of the TV, it is not surprising that the content of what they see is a serious concern. The 65,000 member American Academy of Pediatrics issued a policy statement in their journal *Pediatrics.*[67] The group wants the number of ads during kid's shows cut in half with no ads for junk food in shows watched primarily by those eight years old and younger. They also recommended that ads for alcohol be limited to text and product pictures and that erectile dysfunction ads be run only after 10 p.m.[68]

Children are the consumers of the future, and so companies are eager to get their foot in the door of their spending habits. Merchandisers are trying to instill brand loyalty in the adults children will eventually become. This was taken to a new level when "Cool Shopping Barbie" had her own personal toy MasterCard, with a cash register that had the MasterCard logo, and a terminal through which Barbie could swipe her card to make a purchase. According to William F. Keenan of Creative Solutions, an advertising and marketing agency, "[If you] set the brand by age seven, they will favor the brand into adulthood. One of the smartest places to plant marketing seeds in the consumer consciousness is with kids."[69] This is particularly troubling given an APA finding that children under the age of eight do not have the cognitive development to understand persuasive intent, making them easy targets.[70] Children have proved to be receptive targets as well. A phenomenon called **age compression** or "kids getting older younger"

FIGURE 13-3
Principles of
Advertising to
Children

The following core principles underlie the Children's Advertising Review Unit's guidelines for advertising directed to children under the age of 12:

1. Advertisers have special responsibilities when advertising to children or collecting data from children online. They should take into account the limited knowledge, experience, sophistication, and maturity of the audience to which the message is directed. They should recognize that younger children have a limited capacity to evaluate the credibility of information, may not understand the persuasive intent of advertising, and may not even understand that they are being subject to advertising.

2. Advertising should be neither deceptive nor unfair, as these terms are applied under the Federal Trade Commission Act, to the children to whom it is directed.

3. Advertisers should have adequate substantiation for objective advertising claims, as those claims are reasonably interpreted by the children to whom they are directed.

4. Advertising should not stimulate children's unreasonable expectations about product quality or performance.

5. Products and content inappropriate for children should not be advertised directly to them.

6. Advertisers should avoid social stereotyping and appeals to prejudice, and are encouraged to incorporate minority and other groups in advertisements and to present positive role models whenever possible.

7. Advertisers are encouraged to capitalize on the potential of advertising to serve an educational role and influence positive personal qualities and behaviors in children, e.g., being honest and respectful of others, taking safety precautions, engaging in physical activity.

8. Although there are many influences that affect a child's personal and social development, it remains the prime responsibility of the parents to provide guidance for children. Advertisers should contribute to this parent-child relationship in a constructive manner.

Source: Self-Regulatory Program for Children's Advertising (New York: Council of Better Business Bureau, 2009), http://www.caru.org/guidelines/guidelines.pdf. Accessed July 9, 2010.

(KGOY) has marketers targeting eight and nine year olds with products once meant for teenagers. With the overabundance of ads to which they are exposed, children are tiring of toys much earlier and looking for products that they see teenagers using.[71]

The Children's Advertising Review Unit (CARU) of the Council of Better Business Bureaus was established to respond to public concerns. CARU developed "Self-Regulatory Guidelines for Children's Advertising." Figure 13-3 summarizes eight basic principles from those guidelines that are in use to this day.

The function of the CARU guidelines is to delineate those areas that need particular attention to help avoid deceptive and/or misleading advertising messages to children. The basic activity of CARU is the review and evaluation of child-directed advertising in all media. When advertising to children is found to be misleading, inaccurate, or inconsistent with the guidelines, CARU seeks changes through the voluntary cooperation of advertisers. It does not always get cooperation and sometimes the advertiser appeals to the National Advertising Review Board (NARB). For example, in 2010 CARU recommended that the Johnson & Johnson (J&J) Healthcare Products Division of McNeil–PPC discontinue advertising Listerine® Smart Rinse™ during child-directed programming. The product, manufactured in colors and flavors that may be attractive to children, was labeled, "Keep out of reach of children. If more than used for rinsing is accidentally swallowed, get medical help or contact a Poison Control Center right away." CARU said that its guidelines explicitly and unambiguously provide that advertisers should not advertise products directly to children that are labeled "Keep out of reach of children." J&J, in its defense, said that the company "appreciates CARU's finding that we did not intend to direct the challenged commercial to children under 12. We disagree with all other portions of the decision and will appeal the decision to NARB."[72] J&J later withdrew its appeal and agreed to abide by CARU's decision.

Recently, the advertising to children of products that contains sweets has become a burning issue. As the obesity epidemic among children has become widely known and debated, special interest groups have been criticizing companies for their marketing of these products to children. Now, childhood favorites such as Lucky Charms, Corn Pops, Froot Loops, and Cocoa Pebbles, and other cereals are being labeled a public health menace by the Rudd Center for Food Policy and Obesity at Yale University. The center is trying to expose the marketing tactics companies use that make kids clamor for a sugary, calorie-laden start to each day. Obesity researchers now say they have data proving that the least healthy cereals are the ones that are marketed most aggressively to children. The obesity crisis among children in the United States is now established and researchers believe that TV advertising is a significant contributing factor.

To their credit, some leading cereal makers have responded by reducing calories, fat, and sugar and increasing fiber and vitamins. Kellogg, General Mills, and Quaker's parent company, PepsiCo, are among about 12 of the largest food companies that have promised to market only "better for you" foods to kids under age 12. Skeptics are concerned because the companies themselves are deciding what constitutes "better for you" standards.[73] In the fall of 2009, a federal working group proposed that food advertising aimed at children be limited to foods that are healthful.[74]

Efforts to curb children's advertising span the globe. The European Union's directive on television regulation bans "programs that might seriously impair the development of minors" but allows unencrypted programming "that might be harmful to minors providing they are preceded by an acoustic warning or made clearly identifiable throughout their duration by means of a visual symbol."[75] The EU prohibits product placement in programming aimed at children and also does not allow words like "only" to be used to describe prices. They also forbid advertisers from persuading children to ask their parents to buy the product for them.[76] In Australia, children's advertising may not imply that the people who buy an advertised product are more generous than people who do not buy it. Mexico does not restrict the amount of children's advertising, but tobacco and alcohol advertising are prohibited. In contrast, Denmark permits the advertising of alcoholic beverages to children as long as the beverage's strength is no greater than 2.8 percent, it is not placed in a program directly aimed at children, and no children are shown drinking it.[77]

In 1990, the Children's Television Act was passed. A grassroots activist group known as Action for Children's Television claimed credit for getting this legislation passed. This act prohibited the airing of commercials about products or characters during a show about those products or characters and limited the number of commercial minutes in children's shows. Critics say the FCC created weak rules to enforce the act, thereby sending the message that it was not taking the legislation seriously. Part of the act required stations and networks to schedule educational programs for children.[78] Of course, much has changed since that act was passed. With the rise of the Internet has come a new way for firms to advertise to children. More than two-thirds of the children and teen Internet sites rely on advertising for their revenue. Banner ads were not successful in reaching children, and so these Internet sites have employed games, e-mail, and wireless technology in creative ways. For example, Candystand.com boasts a very popular golf game with Lifesaver holes.[79] The FCC has added new regulations over the last decade that address cable and Internet Web pages.

MARKETING TO THE POOR   A variety of businesses have found that significant profits can be obtained from marketing to poor people. In the subprime credit industry, businesses provide financing to high-risk borrowers at higher than interest rates. While this gives poorer people greater access to cars, credit cards, computers, and homes, it often ends with the borrower buried under a mountain of debt. The Federal Reserve reported that households earning $30,000 or less paid auto loan interest rates that were 16.8 percent higher than the rates paid by households earning more than $90,000. Several years later, the difference had risen to 56.1 percent.[80] Mortgage loans showed the same increase, with a 6.4 percent gap in 1989 to a 25.5 percent gap in 2004.[81] The past several years have been the worst ever in home mortgage foreclosures and loan defaults. Many of these have come from the subprime mortgage market where relatively poor people are lured into loans they have little hope of repaying. This has especially occurred with adjustable rate mortgages in an era of rising interest rates. Several of the deceptive marketing practices mentioned earlier have been involved in these loans: concealed facts, ambiguous advertising, and psychological appeals.

Another technique by which business profits from the poor is in the form of *payday loans*, loans that provide the borrower with an advance on his or her paycheck. As the FTC warns, these loans equal costly cash; for example, a borrower might write a personal check for $115 to borrow $100 for up to two weeks. The payday lender agrees to hold the check until the person's next payday. Then, depending on the plan, the lender deposits the check, which the borrower can redeem by paying the $115 in cash. Alternatively, the borrower can roll over the check by paying a fee to extend the loan for another two weeks. In this example, the cost of the initial loan is a $15 finance charge and 391 percent APR. If they roll over the loan three times, the finance charge would climb to $60 to borrow $100.[82] Similar tactics are used by many credit card companies, rent-to-own outfits, and used car dealers.

Tax preparation services provide another way of making money from the poor. Jackson Hewitt is one of many firms providing quick tax refund services for a fee. Advertising "Money Now," they will prepare your tax return and provide you with an advance on your refund. Low-income tax payers have access to a variety of free tax preparation services but many still use this expensive service because they do not understand the price they will pay for receiving an early refund.

BusinessWeek tells the story of a single mother with five children who was making ends meet on $8,500 a year until she was laid off. She borrowed $400 for rent and food from Advance America, a payday loan service; then she renewed the loan every two weeks, eventually paying more than $2,500 in fees before she paid it off. Two months after paying it off, she was anxious for her $4,500 tax refund and so she took out a refund-anticipation loan from Jackson Hewitt. It cost her $453 (10.4 percent) to get that short-term loan.[83] When asked about the price she paid for these loans, the young mother sounded confused, replying, "What do you call it—interest?"[84]

The issue with marketing to the poor is the vulnerability of the consumer. All consumers are vulnerable to a certain extent because business has more information about its product or service than does the consumer. However, poor people are especially vulnerable because they are likely to be less educated and thus less aware of the true price of the products or services being advertised to them. Nevertheless, businesses continue to push these products. Another vulnerable group of consumers is the elderly, and some of the same tactics are used on them that are used on the poor.

ADVERTISING OF ALCOHOLIC BEVERAGES   Special issues about advertising to adults also exist. One that became quite controversial in recent years is advertising of alcoholic beverages on television. In 1996, Seagram & Sons broke a 48-year voluntary ban on advertising hard liquor on television. The company argued that a standard serving of hard liquor contained the same amount of alcohol as beer or wine, and advertising is allowed for those products.[85] DISCUS (the Distilled Spirits Council of the United States) then rewrote its "Code of Good Practice" to allow member distillers to advertise on radio and television. The Seagram decision created a groundswell for change in all possible directions. Today, TV is a major and growing component of hard liquor advertising. In one recent year, spirits advertisers increased TV spending nearly 48 percent, despite a 2 percent cut in overall spending.[86]

Of course, hard liquor is not the only concern. Ralph Nader's Commercial Alert organization targeted Anheuser-Busch for its use of a variety of cartoon characters in its campaigns. They cited a KidCom market study that shows that the Budweiser frogs were American children's "favorite ads," just as the tobacco-smoking "Joe Camel[TM]" had been their favorite ad some years ago.[87] More recently, Anheuser-Busch has faced criticism over their new product, Spykes[TM]. The bright-colored, fruit-flavored malt beverage is sold in attractive two-ounce bottles that resemble beauty products. Critics charge that the beverage is designed to appeal to kids.[88]

Although efforts to curb advertising abuses continue, consumer advocates may find they face an uphill battle. In an online survey, advertisers were asked what they would recommend in the following scenario: "The owner of a small ad agency has an opportunity to pitch a national beer distributor on a $150 million account. He is conflicted because he believes that most alcohol advertising is irresponsible and targets young adults. Still, he realizes this could be big business. He confides in friends and colleagues, and receives mixed advice. Should he pitch the account?"[89] In response, 70.8 percent said that he should pitch the account while 21 percent said he should not pitch the account.[90]

CIGARETTE ADVERTISING No industry has been under greater attack than the cigarette industry for its products and its marketing and advertising practices. Cigarette makers are under fire from all sides. Two particularly important issues dominate the debate about cigarette advertising. First, there is the general opposition to promotion of a dangerous product. As the World Health Organization (WHO) puts it, "Cigarettes remain the only legal product that kills half of its regular users when consumed as intended by the manufacturer."[91] The second issue concerns the ethics of the tobacco industry's long-standing advertising to young people and to less-educated consumer markets.

The classic example of the latter concern was when R.J. Reynolds (RJR) was publicly taken to task by several consumer groups for its Joe Camel campaign. One frequently cited study appeared in the *Journal of the American Medical Association*. In this study, it was found that more than half the children age three to six were able to match the Joe Camel logo with a photograph of a cigarette. Six-year-olds were almost as familiar with Joe Camel as they were with a Mickey Mouse logo.[92] Perhaps one of the strongest indicators of the success of the Joe Camel ad campaign was the statistic of smoking among the youth market. From the time the Joe Camel mascot was introduced in 1987 to its discontinuation in 1997, Camel's share of the under-18 market soared from 0.5 to 33 percent, according to data supplied by a coalition of health groups. The market share among smokers age 18 to 24 increased from 4.4 to 7.9 percent. In 1997, the FTC ruled 3 to 2 that the Joe Camel ads violated the law by targeting children under 18, and asked RJR to remove the cartoon from any venue where a child might see it. RJR canceled the ad campaign.[93] Shortly after that, the government asked Philip Morris to retire the Marlboro man.[94] Although Joe Camel and the Marlboro Man are gone, the issue of advertising to young people remains.

A company worth watching today is Altria, home to Philip Morris and the popular Marlboro cigarette brand. Eventually Altria admitted, as did others in the industry, that cigarette smoking was addictive and did cause disease, but it went further and began supporting legislation that would eventually put the company under Food and Drug Administration (FDA) regulatory supervision. Some observers say that this was all a clever strategy of "societal alignment" in which Altria was striving to generate good PR by cozying up to the regulator. It was thought that this was part of a larger plan to get the FDA to approve smokeless tobacco as a less harmful alternative to cigarettes and to get the FDA to take its focus off cigarettes.[95] It has also been said that pushing smokeless tobacco is a strategy on Altria's part to dodge indoor-smoking laws, which have encouraged more smokers to quit. In recent years, Altria has been pushing smoke-free alternatives, such as Marlboro *Snus*, which come in flavors that the company hopes will invigorate sales but which critics say will be popular with youth.[96]

The Campaign for Tobacco-Free Kids, an advocacy group, has been arguing that smokeless products are gaining popularity with high school students and that this is dangerous. Some think the flavored versions are specifically targeted towards young people and getting them hooked on the addictive products. Although Altria and the industry seem to be striving to make products that are more palatable and appealing, there is still the concern that the smokeless varieties carry significant health risks. And one expert put things in perspective when he noted that for every pack of *Snus* sold in the United States, about 3,000 packs of light cigarettes are sold and these turn out to be just as addictive as regular cigarettes.[97]

The future will be somewhat determined by how the FDA decides to deal with flavored smokeless tobacco. Will the FDA support Altria and its competitors by approving the less harmful products, or will the FDA adopt a hard line towards the products. The ethical issues surrounding the promotion of tobacco products show no signs of abating and this will likely be a controversial issue into the foreseeable future.

HEALTH AND ENVIRONMENTAL CLAIMS   Advertising and labeling practices that make claims about health and environmental safety have taken on increasing importance. One reason that these issues have come to the forefront is the renewed enforcement activities of the Food and Drug Administration (FDA), the Federal Trade Commission (FTC), and state attorneys general in cracking down on misleading or unsubstantiated claims. We now live in an environmentally aware and health-conscious society, and consumers' interest in products that are healthful and protect the environment has grown significantly, and so it is not too surprising that these issues have gained so much attention.

Because health and environmental claims attract customers, marketers are tempted to tout claims that aren't really there. Nutrition bars, for example, have a $1 billion yearly market that has attracted a variety of companies. The FDA contacted 18 nutrition bar makers about their nutritional claims. The *Los Angeles Times* reported that a test of nutrition bars found that 60 percent of the bars tested failed to live up to their claims. Consumerlab.com tested 30 nutrition bars for levels of fat, sodium, and carbohydrates, among other ingredients. According to the lab, 18 of the bars were found to underreport those ingredients that dieters try to avoid; only 12 bars were found to have reported accurately. Seven bars contained two to three times the amount of sodium they reported; four bars contained more saturated fat. Half of the products tested contained more carbohydrates than their label indicated.[98]

Consumers today are undoubtedly frustrated as they scan health claims on so many products. The fronts of boxes are shouting out claims about different nutrients—sugar free, extra fiber, added vitamins, fat free, and healthy for your heart. Kellogg's even claimed that its Cocoa Krispies cereal "now helps support your child's immunity."[99] In 2009 to 2010, the FDA embarked on a quest to clean up misleading and deceptive advertising regarding the health claims of food products. The FDA has become concerned that the food claims companies are making are not backed by strong enough scientific evidence to support the claims. In one high-profile example, the FDA wrote to General Mills, maker of Cheerios, warning about its boasting for some of the cereal's health benefits. FDA went on to say, "We have determined [Cheerios] is promoted for conditions that cause it to be a drug." This resulted in late-night comedy spoofs in which it was suggested that consumers may now need a prescription to buy a box of the cereal.[100] Back in 2003, the FDA allowed qualified health claims to appear on food labels as long as the company included a disclaimer that described the reliability of the evidence supporting the claim. But the FDA has recently taken apart this policy on the theory that the disclaimers were confusing.[101] Clearly, the FDA has been taking a more activist stance regarding such health claims on food products.

Regulators in the United States and Europe recently have become more concerned about a new category of foods that are being called "functional foods." These make claims to improve your health functioning in specific ways. For example, all supermarkets today carry probiotic yogurts that claim to ease constipation, improve regularity, and fight infections. Or you might be interested in butter substitutes that declare they reduce your cholesterol, or tomato extracts that argue they can keep your skin young while warding off cancer. Sales growth of these products have been increasing fast, and Nestlé, the world's largest food company, is betting that functional foods will be a primary source of future sales growth. All this activity has caught the attention of regulators, and they are beginning to investigate whether the claims are supported or misleading.[102]

The market for more healthy food products is growing, and a few companies have been taking it upon themselves to progressively plan for the future. One highly visible example is that of PepsiCo, led by CEO Indra Nooyi. In 2010, Nooyi made it known that she wants PepsiCo to be "seen as one of the defining companies of the first half of the 21st century." She wants her company to be "a model of how to conduct business in the modern world."[103] With respect to her company's products, she wants to help customers wean off of sugar, salt, and fat. In March 2010, she unveiled a series of goals to improve the healthiness of PepsiCo products. By 2015, the company seeks to reduce the salt in its leading brands by 25 percent. By 2020, the company wants to reduce the amount of sugar in its drinks by 25 percent and the amount of saturated fat in certain snacks by 15 percent. The company recently announced it would be removing all its sugary drinks from schools around the world by 2012. Astutely, Nooyi observed that she wants to prevent the food companies from going the way of the tobacco firms.[104] Over the past two years, PepsiCo has attempted to move in these directions by hiring physicians and PhDs to help develop the new products. PepsiCo's goal is to expand its sales of healthy products at an annual growth rate of 10 percent, which is twice the company's historical average. The company also plans to push new products to undernourished people in India and other developing countries. PepsiCo's goals are ambitious but, if achieved, may set a new standard for food companies striving to be socially responsible while making money.[105]

Another major controversial advertising practice is companies claiming that their products and/or their product packages are environmentally friendly or safe. Within the past decade, many companies have been ramping up their advertising claims about the environmental friendliness of their products—that their products are "green." There have been some major indications that consumers are interested in "green" products, but the surveys reveal that it is a market niche that not all consumers are pursuing even though 44 percent of a recent survey said they thought green products were the "right things to buy." In this same December 2009 survey, 56 percent of the consumers also said green products "cost more" and 25 percent said they "should be questioned."[106]

ETHICS IN PRACTICE CASE

Should Toy Giveaways Be Banned? Who Is Responsible for Children's Health?

In a dramatic decision, the Santa Clara County, California, Board of Supervisors passed a new ordinance that will ban Happy Meal™ toys and other promotional giveaways that restaurants use to promote their high-calorie meals to children. The officials are convinced that luring kids into eating foods with high sugar, sodium, and fat by using toys as inducements will make them overweight and cause long-term health problems. The only escape from this ban will be if the restaurants can meet newly created nutritional guidelines approved by the board. The board voted 3 to 2 in favor of the ban after a contentious meeting that included testimony on both sides of the issue.

One of the board supervisors was quoted as saying, "This ordinance prevents restaurants from preying on children's love of toys" to sell high-calorie, unhealthful food. He went on to argue that "[t]his ordinance breaks the link between unhealthy food and prizes." Also in favor of the ordinance were public health administrators, parents, and doctors. Opposition included fast-food franchisees, other parents, and supporters of fast-food toys who said the promotions are frequently used to provide Christmas presents for poor children.

One physician who sees obese children on a daily basis argued that the toys are a powerful draw for children who then convince their parents to take them to the fast-food restaurants. This doctor said that parents tell them they take their children to the restaurants because of the toy giveaways. He mentioned that he has a five-year-old patient who already has type-2 diabetes.

On the other side of the issue was an owner of seven McDonald's restaurants. He argued that he and his wife work very diligently to promote healthy lifestyles for children and that they have donated to children's sports and other activities, and recently received an award for community service from the parent company.

The board agreed to postpone the implementation of the new law for 90 days to give the fast-food industry time to initiate it own voluntary program for improving the nutritional value of children's meals.

1. Who is responsible for children's health with respect to fast food? Did the board of supervisors overstep its boundaries?

2. Does this legislation block free choice for consumers?

3. What is the ethical course of action for fast-food restaurants to take in light of the childhood obesity issue and other health concerns?

Sources: Sharon Bernstein, "It's a Sad Day for Happy Meals in Santa Clara County," *Los Angeles Times* (April 28, 2010); "McDonald's Happy Meal Toys Could be Banned in California," http://www.news.com.au, accessed April 29, 2010.

The green economy is huge. It was estimated in 2010 to be $1.04 trillion and growing. This is a gigantic market segment, and the temptation for companies to promote questionable claims is strong. The major consumer challenge is the difficulty in assessing the reliability of the claims that products are environmentally friendly or safe. To offset much of the green advertising, an industry of what might be called "green watchdogs" has been growing also. Certification groups claiming to verify eco-friendly claims have arrived on the scene. Examples include Green-e, a San Francisco-based nonprofit. The Forest Stewardship Council promises to verify that the wood in your new furniture was actually harvested from a sustainably managed forest. Sustainable Travel International watches to make sure the hotel you stay at is minimizing its garbage.[107]

Other groups claiming to certify the green aspects of products include Energy Star, which is one of the best known eco-labels, evaluating energy savings, EcoLogo, which monitors 150 product categories, EPEAT (Electronic Product Assessment Tool), which covers computers and monitors, and Eco Options, which covers 3,500-plus products sold at Home Depot. Even though these groups are emerging, even some of them use looser standards than others and it is difficult knowing how much due diligence each one of them has behind their eco-seals.[108] The fact that these monitoring groups are increasing in number, however, suggests this is an issue that needs to be watched closely by consumers lest they be duped about the eco-friendliness of products they buy.

Advertisers have come on so fast and strong with their claims that there is a growing "green fatigue" developing among some consumers who are growing weary of claims. The evidence seems to be that being green is not enough. Products need to be wallet-friendly as well, especially as the economy has been trying to come out of a recession. Some marketers have noticed a green backlash among consumer attitudes. A recent Boston Consulting Group survey showed that only about one-third of consumers say that products being environmentally friendly influences their purchasing decisions.[109] Companies and advertisers will need to watch carefully the quality of their claims or a real cynicism about environmental claims may set in.

AD CREEP **Ad creep** refers to the way that advertising can increasingly be found everywhere one looks. Both produce placement and plot placement, discussed earlier, are special cases of ad creep. It is generally estimated that people see about 3,000 ads each day. According to Jim Twitchell, author of *Twenty Ads That Shook the World*, the problem of ad creep is only going to get worse. He believes that the average person is exposed to about 5,000 ads each day, and the last time one could go an entire day without seeing an ad was probably about 1915. "We're already putting them on the floor tiles in grocery stores, on worksheets in home economics classes, on video screens in shopping carts. Eventually, we could see ads on stoplights or in drinks with bubbles that will bring you a message from their sponsor."[110] Ads have also gone to places that once were not considered acceptable for advertisements. School buses, textbooks, doctors' offices, and historical monuments have all been festooned with advertisements. The traditional term for advertising that is located in nontraditional places is **ambient advertising**, but *ad creep* reflects both the way the ads have grown and the way people often feel about its creators.[111]

A variety of factors contribute to ad creep. A declining network TV audience and increased dispersion from cable and Internet outlets combine with soaring network television rates to make it difficult to blanket the population with an advertising message. The arrival of digital video recorders such as TiVo has made it easier for viewers to speed through ads without watching them. One response to ad-skipping technologies such as TiVo has been companies inserting ads into video games. Since most PCs and an increasing number of video games are connected to the Internet, it will be possible to update advertisements when required.[112]

Furthermore, ad creep generates more ad creep because people become numb to messages in traditional places and so unique new venues are sought—just to get the consumer's attention.[113] An example of the lengths advertisers go to get a person's attention can be found in Britain. A London ad agency recruited university students to wear brand logos on their foreheads for about GBP 4.20 ($6.83) an hour. The logos are temporary tattoos—wearers are allowed to shower but not rub their foreheads. John Carver, cofounder of Cunning Stunts Limited, thought up the idea as a way of getting around the many restrictions on cigarette advertising. Of course, only "suitably hip" foreheads need apply.[114]

These seven controversial advertising methods are simply the tip of the iceberg. Issues have been raised about the marketing of pharmaceutical drugs directly to patients through magazine and television ads. These ads encourage patients to ask their doctor for the prescription drug, to the frustration of doctors everywhere. Concerns have also been raised about the marketing of guns and ammunition, particularly in family stores like Walmart and Kmart. Channel One, a television station that beams educational programming to schools across the country, has been sharply criticized for its commercials, which students end up watching along with the educational programming. Audiences in movies everywhere have bemoaned the inclusion of commercials in the preview clips, as they are captive audiences, unable to change the channel. There is no end to the list of concerns about the advertising practices undertaken today. Businesspeople must tread carefully to make certain they do not cross the line where their customers become more annoyed with their practices than be attracted to their products. Further, serious ethical questions may arise about the types and placements of advertising in the future.

Warranties

From the glamorous realm of advertising, we now proceed to the less glamorous issues of warranties. **Warranties** were initially used by manufacturers to limit the length of time they were expressly responsible for products. Over time, they came to be viewed by consumers as mechanisms to protect the buyer against faulty or defective products. Most consumers have had the experience of buying a hair dryer, a stereo, a computer, a refrigerator, an automobile, a washing machine, a chain saw, or any of thousands of other products only to find that it did not work properly or did not work at all. That is when warranties and guarantees take center stage.

The law recognizes two types of warranties—implied and express. An **implied warranty** is an unspoken promise that there is nothing significantly wrong with the product and that the product can be used for the purposes intended. An **express warranty** is explicitly offered at the time of the sale. The nature of express warranties can range from advertising claims to formal certificates, and they may be oral or written.

The passage of the Magnuson–Moss Warranty Act of 1975 helped clarify the nature of warranties for consumers. It is still the basic law of the land, although the FTC has amended, clarified, and interpreted it over the years.[115] This act was aimed at clearing up a variety of misunderstandings about manufacturers' warranties—especially whether a **full warranty** was in effect or whether certain parts of the product or certain types of defects were excluded from coverage, resulting in a **limited warranty**. Also at issue was whether or not the buyer had to pay shipping charges when a product was sent to and from the factory for servicing of a defect.[116] The Warranty Act set standards for what must be contained in a warranty and the ease with which consumers must be able to understand it. If a company, for example, claims that its product has a full warranty, it must contain certain features, including repair "within a reasonable time and without charge."[117] The law holds that anything less than this unconditional assurance must be promoted as a limited warranty.

With the rise of e-commerce, warranties have become an important issue. Companies find that warranties or guarantees are essential when marketing by mail. The internationalization of commerce that has resulted from the Internet has presented new challenges. International e-commerce has been largely unregulated. Scott Nathan, an attorney who specializes in e-commerce law, explains that the "speed 'n' ease" factor heightens the warranty problems. "Because of the lack of international law governing warranties," says Nathan, "be prepared to defend the performance of your polka dot widgets in a foreign court."[118]

An issue of increasing ethical concern is **extended warranties**, service plans that lengthen the warranty period and are offered at an additional cost. Consumer advocates advise against buying most extended warranties because they often cost as much as the original item bought would eventually cost to replace. Eric Antum, editor of *Warranty*

ETHICS IN PRACTICE CASE

The "Lifetime" of a Backpack

For the past few years, I have been working at a sporting goods store that sells high-quality backpacks. One day, I was working at the customer counter, ringing up sales, and responding to queries. A man came in with a backpack that had obviously seen a great deal of life. It was torn and worn from years of heavy use. He gave it to me and said that he was returning it so that we could make good on the backpack's "Lifetime Guarantee." The backpack is of high quality and the well-known manufacturer prominently displays the guarantee in its advertising materials.

I explained to the customer that the "lifetime guarantee" does not mean that he can return the backpack after any amount of use. The guarantee is not for *his* lifetime but, instead, it is for the *lifetime of the backpack.* I then explained that, according to the manufacturer, the lifetime of a backpack is considered to be about four years.

The customer became irate. He said that the wording of the guarantee was purposely deceptive and that one shouldn't have to read the fine print, or visit the company's Web site, to determine what the guarantee really means. Then he threw the backpack in my face and stormed out, leaving his backpack behind. I thought he was being incredibly rude, so I followed him out to the parking lot to tell him so. We talked about the situation, and I explained that the information has always been available on the Web site. He questioned why he should be expected to double-check a company's Web site before buying a product. We parted cordially.

After he left, I thought about him being upset and his argument. Was the customer right? Did the wording of the guarantee deceive him? If it is a four-year warranty—why not say that? If it is deception, to what extent am I complicit? Should I warn customers about the meaning of the guarantee even if that information is likely to steer them to other products, and perhaps other stores? To whom am I most responsible?

1. Is the "lifetime guarantee" deceptive advertising?
2. Does an employee of the store have a responsibility to warn customers?
3. Does the store have a responsibility to clarify the guarantee?
4. If you were in this position, what would you do?

Contributed Anonymously

Week, explains that retailers might make only $10 on a $400 television, but will then make $50 on a $100 on extended warranty.[119] Not surprisingly, the lure of big profits has led to some hardball sales tactics.

Consumers spend billions of dollars on extended warranties.[120] They have become very popular with car purchases, perhaps because customers are keeping their cars longer. During 2009, for example, 34 percent of new-car buyers bought extended warranties. *Consumer Reports* surveyed more than 8,000 readers, and 65 percent of them said they spent significantly more for the new-car warranty than they got back in repair savings. Nevertheless, some customers view the warranties to be insurance, and they are willing to take the risk. A serious problem today are third-party vendors who are selling extended warranties on products such as autos, and some of them may go out of business when you try to collect, and some represent scams that never intend to pay off for anyone.[121]

Of course, if companies simply offer complete satisfaction, with no fine print, the warranty problem is not such a problem. Few companies accomplish this, but one that does is L.L. Bean, whose guarantee says, "Our products are guaranteed to give 100 percent satisfaction in every way. Return anything purchased from us at any time if it proves otherwise. We will replace it, refund your purchase price, or credit your credit card, as you wish. We do not want you to have anything from L.L. Bean that is not completely satisfactory."[122]

Packaging and Labeling

Abuses in the packaging and labeling areas were fairly frequent until the passage of the Federal Packaging and Labeling Act (FPLA) of 1967. The purpose of this act was to prohibit deceptive labeling of certain consumer products and to require disclosure of certain important information. This act, which is administered by the Federal Trade Commission, requires the FTC to issue regulations regarding net contents disclosures, identity of commodity, and name and place of manufacturer, packer, or distributor. Both the FTC and the Food and Drug Administration (FDA) have direct responsibilities under this act. The act authorizes additional regulations when necessary to prevent consumer deception or to facilitate value comparisons with respect to the declaration of ingredients, slack filling of packages, "downsizing" of packaging, and use of "cents off" designations. The act gives the FTC responsibility for consumer commodities. The Food and Drug Administration (FDA) administers the FPLA with respect to foods, drugs, cosmetics, and medical devices.[123] As we mentioned in an earlier section, the packaging and labeling issue is drawing renewed interest because of health and environmental claims and advertising law in specific product categories such as pharmaceuticals, tobacco, alcohol, and advertising directed at children.

Other Product Information Issues

It is difficult to catalog all the consumer issues in which product information is a key factor. Certainly, advertising, warranties, packaging, and labeling constitute the bulk of the issues. In addition to these, however, we must briefly mention several others. Sales techniques in which direct sellers use deceptive information must be mentioned. Other major laws that address information disclosure issues include the following:

1. *Equal Credit Opportunity Act*, which prohibits discrimination in the extension of consumer credit.
2. *Truth-in-Lending Act*, which requires all suppliers of consumer credit to fully disclose all credit terms and to permit a three-day right of rescission in any transaction involving a security interest in the consumer's residence (e.g., in the case of home equity loans).
3. *Fair Credit Reporting Act*, which ensures that consumer-reporting agencies provide information in a manner that is fair and equitable to the consumer.
4. *Fair Debt Collection Practices Act*, which regulates the practices of third-party debt collection agencies.

The Federal Trade Commission (FTC)

We have discussed three main areas of product information—advertising, warranties, and packaging or labeling. Both the FTC and the FDA are actively involved in these issues. It is important now to look more closely at the federal government's major instrument, the FTC, for ensuring that business lives up to its responsibilities in these areas. Actually, the FTC has broad and sweeping powers, and it delves into several other areas that we refer to throughout the book. The Consumer Product Safety Commission and the FDA are major regulatory agencies, too, but we consider them more carefully in the next chapter, where we discuss products and services more specifically.

Some brief history and evolution of the FTC will be helpful in gaining a better appreciation of government activism and its relationship to the political parties in power in Washington at various points in time. The FTC is one of the oldest federal agencies charged with the responsibility of overseeing commercial acts and practices. It was created in 1914, originally as an antitrust weapon and was broadened in 1938 to permit the agency to pursue "unfair or deceptive acts or practices in commerce."[124] In 2004, the Commission celebrated its 90th anniversary with a public symposium on its past, present, and future.[125]

Two major activities of the FTC are (1) to maintain free and fair competition in the economy and (2) to protect consumers from unfair or misleading practices. The FTC may issue cease-and-desist orders against companies it believes engage in unlawful practices. The firms must then stop such practices unless a court decision sets aside the order. The FTC also issues trade regulation guides for business and conducts a wide variety of consumer protection activities.[126] In the arena of possible deceptive advertising practices, the FTC monitors advertising and may ask advertisers for proof of their claims. If the FTC decides an ad is false or misleading, it may order the advertiser to withdraw the ad or run "corrective" advertising to inform the public that the former ads were deceptive. Advertisers also may be fined for violating an FTC order.[127]

Over the years, Congress has given the FTC enforcement responsibility in a variety of consumer-related fields, including the important Truth-in-Lending, Fair Packaging and Labeling, Fair Credit Reporting, and Equal Credit Opportunity Acts. Congress gave the FTC broad powers out of fear that any specification of a list of prohibitions might lead business to reason that it could do anything not on the list. Figure 13-4 presents information about the FTC. The FTC's Bureau of Consumer Protection has the following major divisions: advertising practices, credit practices, enforcement, marketing practices, and service industry practices.

FIGURE 13-4
About the Federal
Trade Commission

As a consumer or business person, you may be more familiar with the work of the Federal Trade Commission (FTC) than you think.

The FTC deals with issues that touch the economic life of every American. It is the only federal agency with both consumer protection and competition jurisdiction in broad sectors of the economy. The FTC pursues vigorous and effective law enforcement; advances consumers' interests by sharing its expertise with federal and state legislatures and U.S. and international government agencies; develops policy and research tools through hearings, workshops, and conferences; and creates practical and plain-language educational programs for consumers and businesses in a global marketplace with constantly changing technologies.

When the FTC was created in 1914, its purpose was to prevent unfair methods of competition in commerce as part of the battle to "bust the trusts." Over the years, Congress passed additional laws giving the agency greater authority to police anticompetitive practices. In 1938, Congress passed a broad prohibition against "unfair and deceptive acts or practices." Since then, the commission also has been directed to administer a wide variety of other consumer protection laws, including the Telemarketing Sales Rule, the Pay-Per-Call Rule, and the Equal Credit Opportunity Act. In 1975, Congress gave the FTC the authority to adopt industry-wide trade regulation rules. The FTC's work is performed by the Bureaus of Consumer Protection, Competition, and Economics. That work is aided by the Office of General Counsel and seven regional offices.

Source: http://www.ftc.gov/ftc/about.shtm. Accessed July 9, 2010.

Early Years of the FTC

The FTC actually did relatively little from 1941 to 1969, a period Thomas G. Krattenmaker called the "decades of neglect." But 1970 to 1973 were the "years of promise" for the FTC.[128] The agency became "activist" when President Richard Nixon appointed Miles Kirkpatrick chairperson. The FTC's activism continued when Michael Pertschuk became chairperson in 1977. His directorship spanned the late 1970s and early 1980s and encompassed the "kid-vid" period that we discussed earlier in this chapter. Although many of the controversial initiatives preceded his appointment, he became identified with all of them. Unfortunately, Pertschuk developed a reputation for being antibusiness. This hurt his relationship with the business community so much that he never overcame it.[129]

Succeeding Pertschuk as chairperson was James C. Miller III, appointed by President Reagan. As do so many agencies upon the election of a new administration, the FTC shifted its focus to the Reagan approach to regulation. Miller was dubbed by some in the press as Reagan's "deregulation czar," and he took the FTC off into another, less active direction. Miller characterized the FTC's activism on behalf of consumers during the 1970s as "excesses" and embarked on a course that was much more in keeping with the Reagan doctrine.[130] The same general approach to regulation continued under Miller's successor, Daniel Oliver. Miller and Oliver gained reputations as deregulators who willingly slashed the FTC's budget and staff.

The FTC Reasserts Itself in the 1990s

After almost a decade of Reagan-era deregulation that saw the FTC's workforce cut in half and its enforcement efforts greatly reduced or redirected, the FTC began reasserting itself in the early 1990s. Janet D. Steiger became its chairperson, and under Steiger the FTC came back to life. According to one observer, the FTC started looking more like the FTC of the pre-Reagan administration rather than the seemingly toothless agency it had become in the 1980s.[131]

Among the high-profile cases the FTC pursued in the 1990s, it won headlines by cracking down on Nintendo, the video-game maker, for price fixing; moving in on "900" telephone numbers for advertisements aimed at children; and accusing major colleges and Capital Cities-ABC of conspiring to limit the market for televised college football games.[132]

In another initiative, the FTC took action against shoemakers who claimed their shoes were "Made in USA" when, in fact, some were "assembled" in the United States but included some imported components and materials. This was a significant action against New Balance and Hyde Athletic Industries, who had touted the "Made in USA" claim. Although most would agree that the integrity of a "Made in USA" label is important, many agree that the increasingly global economy made 100 percent U.S. content unreachable. A spokesman for Toyota Motor Sales USA, Inc., has said, "If you applied the FTC standard to our industry, there's no such thing as an American car."[133]

In 1995, Robert Pitofsky, a specialist on trade regulation and antitrust law, became the chairperson of the FTC. Pitofsky's appointment signaled a shift in focus for the agency. Although advertising and other marketing issues were still pursued, antitrust battles moved to the front burner. In 1998, the FTC issued an antitrust complaint against Intel Corporation, alleging that the company withheld important technology information from competing vendors.[134] Pitofsky's reign as chairperson characterized one of the most activist eras of the FTC.

The FTC in the 21st Century

Timothy Muris became the new FTC chairperson in 2001. The FTC's transition from the Pitofsky to the Muris administration was characterized by continuity rather than conflict.

In an address to the American Antitrust Institute, Muris said that the areas in which he agreed with Pitofsky far outnumbered the areas in which they differed.[135] A major accomplishment of the Muris administration was the National Do-Not-Call Registry. The registry opened to consumers in 2003 and forbade telemarketers from calling consumers who sign up with the registry. The FTC also instituted a requirement that all companies placing marketing calls have their information available for consumers' caller ID systems. Consumers can then report companies that make calls in violation.[136]

In 2004, Deborah Platt Majoras was sworn in as the new chairperson of the FTC.[137] She extracted millions of dollars in settlements from firms that made misleading claims for weight loss products, but opted not to require disclosure of the existence of product placement or the sources of word-of-mouth advertising.[138] Her preference was that business self-regulate when possible and that the police action of the FTC be a court of last resort.[139] Jon Leibowitz became chairperson of the FTC in March 2009 after serving as one of its commissioners since 2004. Leibowitz has argued for a more vigorous enforcement of the FTC Act and is expected to move more aggressively on issues such as health care; advertising and marketing to children; Internet, telecom, and technology; energy; and competition enforcement beyond the Sherman Act. Under the Obama administration, it is expected that the FTC and other federal consumer protection agencies will assume a more active role than in the recent past.

Recent Consumer Legislation

Though the FTC supervises most consumer issues with respect to product and service information and advertising, and other laws have been passed that address specific issues, it is useful to briefly consider recent consumer legislation that has been passed but for which enough time has not passed to provide an in-depth analysis. One of these recent laws is the **Credit Card Act of 2009**. Another is the creation of the Consumer Financial Protection Agency passed in 2010.

Credit Card Act of 2009

For many years, consumers have been complaining about the treatment they receive from banks and credit card companies, and it came as no surprise that Congress finally passed new regulations on the industry. The *Credit Card Accountability, Responsibility, and Disclosure Act 2009* was passed by Congress and enacted in February 2010. Some of the most dramatic changes in the new law occurred in credit terms, interest rates, and fees. The legislation should lead to credit card agreements that are more transparent and with easier-to-understand terms, but possibly at a higher initial cost. Credit card issuers and analysts say the credit card reform law will make credit cards more costly for all users and less accessible for low-income families and people with bad credit. Annual fees may return with time and fewer rewards cards may be available.[140]

Some of the features of the recent bill include limitations on interest rate increases and the right to opt out of certain terms. But the opt-out provision is simply an opportunity to cancel one's credit card and then pay off the balance under the old terms of the agreement. The new law placed limitations on the use of the practice known as "universal default," which is the practice of raising interest rates on customers on the basis of their payment records with other unrelated credit issuers such as utility companies and other creditors. Credit card issuers would still be allowed to use universal default on future credit card balances provided they give at least 45 days' advance notice of the change. The new legislation features limited access to cards by young people. One must be 21 years old to get a card unless you have an adult cosigner or can demonstrate enough income to justify receiving the card. Other features include longer time periods to pay bills, clearer due dates and times, higher interest balances being paid first, limits on overlimits fees, and subprime cards for customers with poor credit. Consumers will need to realize that the new law does not protect them from everything. Card companies can still raise interest rates on future card purchases, and there is no cap on how high interest rates can go. Card issuers can continue to close accounts and cut credit limits quickly, without giving cardholders advance warning. Many banks are already finding ways around the law and introducing new fees not banned by the credit card reform law.[141] All in all, the new law improves the credit card arrangement for consumers, especially in the realm of information, but does not completely eliminate the need to be very careful about card terms before agreeing to them.

Consumer Financial Protection Agency

Throughout 2009 and 2010, momentum was building for a proposed **Consumer Financial Protection Agency (CFPA)**. In May 2010, Congress passed a comprehensive financial overhaul bill and part of that bill was the creation of a new federal regulator to both write and enforce rules protecting consumers of financial products. The CFPA was passed into law during the summer of 2010. Other stakeholder protections in the bill included additional protections for shareholders and investors.[142] The proposed agency had considerable support due to the belief by many consumers and political leaders that such an agency was needed in light of the financial misdealing and deceptions of the previous years. One aim of the bill was that it would police and write rules for financial firms' retail products such as mortgages, bank accounts, and credit cards. The proposed legislation was just one part of the Obama administration's proposed financial reforms.[143] The new protection agency, patterned in thought after the Consumer Product Safety Commission, which will be discussed in the next chapter, was a key element in financial reform legislation that had been debated in Congress. The basic motivation of the legislation had been that greedy banks had exploited naïve consumers, and this led up to the credit crisis the country has been experiencing.[144] While much of the debate has centered on banks and their role in the financial crisis, lawmakers were also concerned about how to handle other financial consumer businesses such as payday lenders, debt collectors, check-cashing businesses, title and installment lenders, and pawnbrokers.[145]

The idea for the proposed CFPA has been most often attributed to Professor Elizabeth Warren, a Harvard professor. Among other achievements, Warren had been studying families in financial trouble since about the mid-1970s. President Obama appointed her to be head of the Congressional Oversight Committee, which had the challenging task of tracking how the bailout funds had been spent. She is outspoken and has been very angry about the lack of transparency in Washington and the lack of accountability on Wall Street. Warren has argued that we regulate less important products so why not financial products? Her argument has been that we do not want lead in our paint, toxins in our water, or rat poison in our antibiotics, so why should we take chances with financial products that are of so much importance to citizens.[146]

Critics of the proposed CFPA included those who philosophically opposed more government regulation and the business community, which saw the new regulator as unnecessary. Lobbying by business associations was vigorous. The U.S. Chamber of Commerce, as well as many of the financial service firms themselves, fought the proposed agency since the beginning.[147] The American Financial Services Association, a trade group that represents consumer, auto, and small-business lenders such as GMAC, Ford Motor Credit, and AmeriCredit, tried to defeat the consumer agency proposal. The Consumer

Financial Services Association, which represents payday lenders, also argued against the proposed consumer agency. It thought the legislation would constrain credit. It argued that its industry provides almost $100 billion in short-term credit to consumers seeking to cover a check and that further restraints were not necessary.[148] In short, the majority of consumers and consumer advocacy groups were in favor of the proposed legislation, and business associations that are likely to be impacted were against the new agency. As of this writing, it was too early to tell what the eventual impact of the new agency would be.

Self-Regulation in Advertising

Cases of deceptive or unfair advertising in the United States are handled primarily by the FTC. In addition to this regulatory approach, self-regulation of advertising has become an important business response. Under the regulatory approach, advertising behavior is controlled through various governmental rules that are backed by the use of penalties. **Self-regulation**, on the other hand, refers to the control of business conduct and performance by the business itself, or business associations, rather than by government or by market forces.[149]

Types of Self-Regulation

Business self-regulation of advertising may take on various forms. One is **self-discipline**, where the firm itself controls its own advertising. Another is **pure self-regulation**, where the industry (one's peers) controls advertising. A third type is **co-opted self-regulation**, where the industry, on its own volition, involves non-industry people (e.g., consumer or public representatives) in the development, application, and enforcement of norms. A fourth type is **negotiated self-regulation**, where the industry voluntarily negotiates the development, use, and enforcement of norms with some outside body (e.g., a government department or a consumer association). Finally, a fifth type is **mandated self-regulation** (which may sound like an oxymoron), where the industry is ordered or designated by the government to develop, use, and enforce norms, whether alone or in concert with other bodies.[150]

The National Advertising Division's Program

The most prominent instance of self-regulation by business in the advertising industry is the program sponsored by the National Advertising Division (NAD) of the Council of Better Business Bureaus, Inc. The NAD and the National Advertising Review Board (NARB) were created in 1971 to help sustain high standards of truth and accuracy in national advertising, and still serves today in an effective manner. NAD only reviews national advertisements. It leaves to state and city jurisdictions the responsibility for local advertisements.

The NAD initiates investigations, determines issues, collects and evaluates data, and makes decisions as to whether an advertiser's claims are substantiated. When the NAD determines that an advertiser's claims are unsubstantiated, the advertiser is asked to undertake modification or permanent discontinuance of the advertising. If an advertiser disagrees with NAD's decision, it can file an appeal with the NARB, which has a reservoir of more than 70 men and women representing national advertisers, advertising agencies, and the public sector. The chairman of the NARB selects an impartial panel of five members for each appeal. The parties involved, including NAD, submit briefs expressing their views for discussion at an oral hearing, after which the panel issues a public report.[151] If an advertiser is unwilling to abide by the NARB panel's decision, the advertising at issue may be referred to the FTC.[152] NAD is a low-cost alternative to litigation and it reaches determinations regarding the truth and accuracy of advertising in a fair, impartial, and expeditious manner.[153]

It is useful to conclude this chapter by providing insights into how the three types of moral manager models, introduced in Chapter 7, would view consumer stakeholders. Therefore, Figure 13-5 presents a brief statement as to the likely orientations of immoral, amoral, and moral managers to this vital stakeholder group.

Summary

The issue of consumer stakeholders has come to the forefront during the recent recession. More and more, businesses are realizing that the economy is built upon consumer spending and that they need to do all they can do to get consumers spending again. Among stakeholder groups, consumers rank at the top. In a consumption-driven society, business must be especially attentive to the issues that arise in its relationships with consumers. It is a paradox that consumerism arose during the very period that the business community discovered the centrality of the marketing concept to business success. The consumer's Magna Carta includes the rights to safety, to be informed, to choose, and to be heard. Consumers, however, expect more than this, and hence the consumer movement, or consumerism, was born. Ralph Nader, considered the father of this movement, has made consumer complaining respectable. Since then, the consumer movement has been among the most active of the stakeholder categories and promises to be important in the future.

Product information issues comprise a major area in the business–consumer stakeholder relationship. Foremost among these is advertising. Many issues have arisen because of perceived advertising abuses, such as ambiguity, concealed facts, exaggerations, and psychological appeals. Specific controversial spheres have included, but are not limited to, comparative advertising, use of sex in advertising, advertising to children, marketing to the poor, advertising of alcoholic beverages, advertising of cigarettes, health and environmental claims, and ad creep. Other product information issues include warranties, packaging, and labeling. The major body for regulating product information issues has been the FTC. The FDA and the state attorneys general have become active as well. Recent legislation has included a new credit card law, and the debate has been continuing on a possible CFPA that would give consumers greater protection with financial service industry products. On its own behalf, business has initiated a variety of forms of self-regulation with respect to its product and service information, especially advertising.

Key Terms

accurate information, p. 461

ad creep, p. 474

adequate information, p. 461

age compression, p. 466

ambient advertising, p. 474

ambiguous advertising, p. 462

clear information, p. 461

comparative advertising, p. 465

concealed facts, p. 462

Consumer Financial Protection
Agency (CFPA), p. 481

consumerism, p. 457

consumer's Magna Carta, p. 456

co-opted self-regulation, p. 482

Credit Card Act of 2009, p. 480

customer relationship management
(CRM), p. 455

exaggerated claims, p. 463

express warranty, p. 475

extended warranties, p. 475

full warranty, p. 475

implied warranty, p. 475

limited warranty, p. 475

mandated self-regulation, p. 482

negotiated self-regulation, p. 482

plot placement, p. 463

product information, p. 459

product placement, p. 463

psychological appeals, p. 464

puffery, p. 463

pure self-regulation, p. 482

right to be heard, p. 456

right to be informed, p. 456

right to choose, p. 456

right to safety, p. 456

self-discipline, p. 482

self-regulation, p. 482

warranties, p. 475

weasel words, p. 462

Discussion Questions

1. In addition to the basic consumer rights expressed in the consumer's Magna Carta, what other expectations do you think consumer stakeholders have of business?

2. What is your opinion of the consumerism movement? Is it "alive and well" or is it dead? Provide evidence for your observations.

3. Give an example of a major abuse of advertising from your own observations and experiences. How do you feel about this as a consumer?

4. Has there been a need for new consumer financial products regulation? Why shouldn't consumers be left to fend for themselves with respect to consumer financial products?

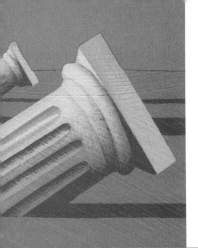

14

Consumer Stakeholders: Product and Service Issues

CHAPTER LEARNING OUTCOMES

After studying this chapter, you should be able to:

1. Describe and discuss the two major product issues—quality and safety.

2. Explain the role and functions of the Consumer Product Safety Commission and the Food and Drug Administration.

3. Enumerate and discuss the reasons for the concern about product liability and differentiate strict liability, absolute liability, and market share liability.

4. Outline business's responses to consumer stakeholders, including customer service, Total Quality Management (TQM) programs, and Six Sigma.

S am Walton, founder of Walmart, got it right when he said, "There is only one boss. The customer. And he can fire everybody in the company from the chairman on down, simply by spending his money somewhere else."

Product information is a pivotal issue between business and consumer stakeholders, but product and service issues such as quality and safety are more central to consumers' concerns. In other words, the product or service *itself* is a more compelling issue than information about it. The quest to improve product and service quality has been driven by the demands of a competitive marketplace and an increasingly sophisticated consumer base. With product safety, an additional driving force has been the threat of product liability lawsuits and the damage these can inflict upon both the balance sheet and the reputation. The marketers' challenge has been to meet these market-driven needs as well as the social and ethical expectations consumers have of them.

The Toyota Motors case provides a recent and dramatic example of the havoc that can result from product quality and safety problems. Toyota has long had a reputation for *quality*. Now that a *safety* issue has tarnished its reputation, we see the vital interconnection between the two issues. Two issues hurt Toyota when the public learned of the massive recalls of their cars following runaway acceleration problems.

First, there was the problem itself. For a company that had enjoyed a golden image and sterling reputation for many decades, it was hard to imagine how 8 million of their cars would eventually have to be recalled because of the possibility of mechanical failure (a quality and safety problem).[1] It came as such an immediate crisis that it has been called "Toyota's 'Tylenol Moment,'" in which the deaths and reports of sticking accelerators have been likened to Johnson & Johnson's (J&J) Tylenol® recalls of 1982.[2] In the Tylenol case, the parent company J&J quickly recalled the possible cyanide-laced products on a voluntary basis and came out of the crisis looking like a hero for its fast and perceived-to-be socially responsible protection of consumers. Toyota, by contrast, botched its opportunity to earn positive evaluations for its corporate responses.

The second issue was Toyota's slow response. The company had received complaints about the sticking accelerator pedals from customers in Europe beginning as early as December 2008 and started installing redesigned pedals on new vehicles there in the summer of 2009. Then, in January 2010, the company faced a pedal recall of 2.3 million cars in the United States.[3] The Toyota CEO, Akio Toyoda, eventually apologized for the company's problems, but the slow, plodding, and sometimes inept response left many consumers thinking the company had dragged its feet on an important quality and safety issue that should have been dealt with faster and better.[4] A *USA Today*/Gallup Poll conducted in late February 2010 revealed that 55 percent of consumers surveyed thought Toyota did not move quickly enough in light of the danger of their products.[5] The Toyota case illustrates vividly how a company's products can cause serious consequences for consumers and financial and reputational harm to the company that may take years to overcome. And, most relevant here, it was all because of quality and safety issues in their products.

This chapter limits the discussion to product quality and safety issues. Product quality is both a business and, increasingly, an ethical issue. In connection with safety, we consider the product liability issue and the calls for tort reform. The Consumer Product Safety Commission and the Food and Drug Administration are also discussed. Finally, business's response to consumer stakeholders regarding the issues introduced both in Chapter 13 and in this chapter is discussed.

Two Central Issues: Quality and Safety

The two central issues—quality and safety—in this chapter represent the overwhelming attention given to product and service issues over the past decade. As the Toyota example so clearly indicates, quality and safety are not separate concepts—safety is one aspect of quality. Its importance, however, merits separate attention.

The Issue of Quality

The concept of *product* quality means different things to different people. Some consumers are interested in the composition and design of a product. Others are more concerned with the product's features, functionality, and durability. All are essential aspects of quality. In general, quality is considered the totality of characteristics and features of a product and may embrace both reality and perceptions of excellence, conformance to specifications, value, and the degree to which the product meets or exceeds the consumer's expectations. With respect to *service* quality, customers are typically concerned that the service is performed the way expected or advertised, that it is completed on time, that all that was promised has been delivered, that courtesy was extended by the provider, and that the service was easily obtained and consistent from use to use. Some of these issues involve personal judgment and perception, and it can be seen how hard it often can be to judge quality.

There are several important reasons for the current obsession with product and service quality. First, a concern for quality has been driven by the average consumer household's rise in family income and consequent demand for more. With both adults often working outside the home, consumers demand a higher lifestyle. In addition, no one has surplus time to hang around repair shops or wait at home for service representatives to show up. This results in a need for products to work as they should, to be durable and long lasting, and to be easy to maintain and fix. The Internet has also made it possible for customers to communicate with other customers about their satisfaction, or dissatis-faction, with a product, and this has heightened consumers' expectations. A revealing *Time*/CNN survey showed that consumers were less interested in technical innovation and attractive designs than they were in the product's ability to function as promised, its durability, and its ease of maintenance and repair.[6] A survey of households by Walker Research found that quality ranked first, price ranked second, and service ranked third among a list of factors consumers felt impacted a firm's reputation and their own pur-chasing decisions.[7]

Closely related to rising household expectations is the global competitiveness issue. Businesses now compete in a hypercompetitive landscape in which multinational strate-gies have given way to global strategies, and the solutions that once worked no longer will.[8] As firms jockey for position in these hypercompetitive markets, they vie to attract customers by increasing the value of the product or service. Value can be a subjective calculation, but it typically refers to a comparison of the quality received for the price spent. A Sears Craftsman spark-plug wrench that sells for $24.99 is expected to be of proportionally higher quality than a spark-plug wrench sold at Walmart for $6.95. To increase value, firms try to provide higher quality than their competitors for the same price, offer the same quality at a lower price, or some combination of the two. Each time a competitor raises the quality and/or lowers the price, other competitors scramble to catch up, and the bar is raised.[9] The greater the competition, the more firms will be jockeying for position and the more often the bar will be raised. Firms that do not con-tinually improve their quality are certain to be left behind. The aforementioned story about Toyota shows how quickly, in this highly competitive atmosphere, a well-respected company can derail. Once derailed, it is difficult to catch up because of a lag in reputations. Often, consumer perceptions of quality do not catch up to actual changes in quality for years after the quality improvements have been made.[10]

Service Quality.   It should be emphasized that our discussion of quality here includes service as well as products. We have clearly become a service economy in the United States, and poor quality of service has become one of the great consumer frustrations of all time. Still there is reason for hope. The American Customer Satisfaction Index has held steady for several years and actually increased slightly in some sectors.[11] This is good news for the companies performing well because studies have shown a positive relationship between customer satisfaction and long-term stock price values.[12] It is also good news for the economy as it is striving to bounce back from a recession.

On the front line of the new economy, service—bold, fast, imaginative, and customized—is now the ultimate strategic business imperative. Consumers today often swap horror stories about poor service as a kind of ritualistic, cathartic exercise. Consider the following examples: repeated trips to the car dealer; poor installation of refrigerator ice makers, resulting in several visits from repair people; returned food to the supermarket, resulting in brusque treatment; fouled-up travel reservations; poorly installed carpeting; no clerk at the shoe department of your favorite department store—and on and on. Shoddy service comes at a price. One study showed that 54 percent of the people interviewed would lose all loyalty to a company that had rude or unhelpful staff. One in ten said they would walk away if a company did not seem to listen.[13]

Dimensions of Quality.   At least eight critical dimensions of product or service qual-ity must be understood if business is to respond strategically to this factor.[14] These include (1) performance, (2) features, (3) reliability, (4) conformance, (5) durability, (6) serviceability, (7) aesthetics, and (8) perceived quality. *Performance* refers to a pro-duct's primary operating characteristics. For an automobile, this would include such items as handling, steering, and comfort. *Features* are the "bells and whistles" of products that supplement their basic functioning. *Reliability* reflects the probability of a product malfunctioning or failing. *Conformance* is the extent to which the product or service meets established standards. *Durability* is a measure of product life. *Serviceability* refers to the speed, courtesy, competence, and ease of repair. *Aesthetics* is a subjective factor that refers to how the product looks, feels, tastes, and so on. Finally, *perceived quality* is a subjective inference that the consumer makes on the basis of a variety of tangible and intangible product characteristics. To address the issue of product or service quality, a manager must be astute enough to appreciate these different dimensions of quality and the subtle and dynamic interplays among them.

Ethical Underpinnings.   An important question is whether quality is a social or an ethical issue or just a competitive factor that business needs to emphasize to be successful in the marketplace. For many consumers, quality is seen to be something more than just a business issue. Three ethical theories based on the concept of duty that informs our understanding of the ethical dimensions of quality include (1) **contractual theory**, (2) **due care theory**, and (3) **social costs view**. The contractual theory focuses on the contractual agreement between the firm and the customer. Firms have a responsibility to comply with the terms of the sale, inform the customer about the nature of the product, avoid misrepresentation of any kind, and not coerce the customer in any way. The due care theory focuses on the relative vulnerability of the customer, who has less information and expertise than the firm, and the ethical responsibility that places on the firm. Customers must depend on the firm providing the product or service to live up to the claims about it and to exercise due care to avoid customer injury. The third view, social costs, extends beyond contractual theory and due care theory to suggest that, if a product causes harm, the firm should pay the costs of any injury, even if the firm had met the terms of the contract, exercised all due care, and taken all reasonable precautions. This perspective serves as the underpinning for strict liability and its extension into absolute liability, which is discuss later.[15]

Spotlight on SUSTAINABILITY

Sustainable Product Development Is Here to Stay

Increasingly, companies are seeking to develop sustainable products. Sustainable products are made to last for an indefinite period and have the least damaging effects on the environment. They are products providing environmental, social, and economic benefits as compared with other commercial products. An excellent example are the Levi's® Eco jeans by Levi Strauss Europe designed to tap into the consumers' interest in organic and sustainable products. Levi's also brought out a line of RECYCLED blue jeans.

DuPont is another company asserting that sustainable products are here to stay. According to its survey of consumers, 89 percent say that such products meet long-term market need. DuPont has concluded that there is broad market demand for products with an enhanced environmental profile and that the demand is coming from customers. DuPont has said that sustainable products offer the following major benefits: inherently safer materials, reduced air and water pollution, and decreased energy use.

Sources: "Levi's RECYCLED Blue Jeans," http://maidsoftampa.wordpress.com/2010/04/21/levis-recycled-blue-jeans/. Accessed May 16, 2010. DuPont, "Sustainable Products Are Here to Stay," http://www2.dupont.com/Sustainability/en_US/assets/downloads/customer_survey_fact_sheet.pdf. Accessed May 16, 2010.

The Issue of Safety

Business clearly has a duty to consumer stakeholders to sell them safe products and services. The concept of safety, in a definitional sense, means "free from harm or risk" or "secure from threat of danger, harm, or loss." In reality, however, the use of virtually any consumer product or service entails some degree of risk or some chance that harm will come to the consumer who uses the product or service. Today, it is thought to be important that even financial services do not cause damage or financial harm. It is for this reason that a Consumer Financial Product Agency is being debated in Washington. An important question that never goes away is "how safe" should a product be made? Difficult judgments about this question often thrust the issue of safety into the ethical category by many consumers.

In the 1800s, the legal view that prevailed was *caveat emptor* ("let the buyer beware"). The basic idea behind this concept was that the buyer had as much knowledge of what she or he wanted as the seller and, in any event, the marketplace would punish any violators. In the 1900s, *caveat emptor* gradually lost its favor and rationale, because it was frequently impossible for the consumer to have complete knowledge about manufactured goods.[16] Today, businesses are held responsible for all products placed on the market. Now, we have a weak version of *caveat vendor*—"let the seller take care."[17]

Through a series of legal developments as well as changing societal values, business has become significantly responsible for product safety. Court cases and legal doctrine now hold companies financially liable for harm to consumers. Yet this still does not answer the difficult question, "How safe are manufacturers obligated to make products?" It is not possible to make products totally "risk free"; experience has shown that consumers seem to have an uncanny ability to injure themselves in novel and creative ways, many of which cannot be anticipated. The challenge to management, therefore, is to make products as safe as possible while at the same time making them affordable and useful to consumers. And consumers today expect that if products are found to be unreasonably dangerous, they will be removed from market. Figure 14-1 presents the top ten ways companies can emphasize safety and avoid product recalls.

Today the public is concerned about a variety of hazards, such as the rise in genetically modified food and the dangers of living near toxic waste dumps or nuclear plants. Food and drug scares, both real and imagined, have occupied much of the public's attention. Food scares and eventual recalls occur often today. Also, consumer products such as automobiles and toys that are inherently dangerous are frequently recalled. Three separate but related recalls of automobiles by Toyota Motor Corporation occurred at the end of 2009 and early in 2010 after several vehicles experienced unintended acceleration. In 2010, Whole Food Markets voluntarily recalled Whole Catch Yellowfin Tuna Steaks

---

FIGURE 14-1

Top Ten List of Product Safety Principles

1. Build safety into product design.
2. Do product safety testing for all foreseeable hazards.
3. Keep informed about and implement latest developments in product safety.
4. Educate consumers about product safety.
5. Track and address your products' safety performance.
6. Fully investigate product safety incidents.
7. Report product safety defects promptly.
8. If a defect occurs, promptly offer a comprehensive recall plan.
9. Work with the Consumer Product Safety Council (CPSC) to make sure your recall is effective.
10. Learn from mistakes—yours and others'.

Source: Speech given by former CPSC Commissioner Ann Brown to the Defense Research Institute, a national organization of product liability attorneys, challenging industry to implement a "Top Ten List" of safety principles aimed at reducing product defects that lead to recalls.

ETHICS IN PRACTICE CASE

To Check or Not to Check the Chicken?

Over the Christmas break, I went back to work at a fast-food restaurant where I had been working since high school. The restaurant sold lots of chicken sandwiches. We were supposed to measure the temperature of the chicken every hour to make sure that it was below 40 degrees (I assume in response to the incident in which a few people died as a result of bacteria formed in warm meat). That responsibility was assigned to whoever was battering the chicken at the time. All that the person had to do was stick a thermometer in the chicken, measuring the bottom, middle, and top until the digital read stayed at a single temperature for about 10 to 15 seconds. The whole process took a few minutes at most. This information was then sent to the restaurant's home office every day.

Unfortunately, not everyone would keep up with taking the temperatures. As an assistant manager, I was responsible for making sure the temperatures were checked, but it was difficult when I had other things to do. For instance, if I were at the register, I could not leave the customers to go back and make sure the batterer was taking the temperatures. At the end of the shift, I would sometimes see a sheet of paper with few or no temperatures noted on it. The store manager would have been upset had he known that I was making up temperatures I did not know to be true, but he would have been even more upset if there had been no temperatures on the sheet at all. He would just make up the numbers himself before he sent them off to the home office, with all the temperatures, of course, below 40 degrees. I have even seen the store manager make up temperatures when he was battering chicken and had forgotten to check the temperatures on the hour.

1. What is the ethical issue in this case? Is it product quality, product safety, or deceptive practices?

2. What responsibilities does the restaurant have to consumers in this situation?

3. As an assistant manager, what should I have done about this situation?

Contributed by Jason Greene

(frozen) because of possible elevated levels of histamine that could result in symptoms that generally appear within minutes to an hour after eating the affected fish.[18] The dietary aid, Hydroxycut, was removed from the market after one death due to liver failure after using the product had been reported. Also in 2010, parents around the country were frantic as various children's and infant's medications were recalled. The recall was voluntary because the 40-some variations of liquid children's medications did not meet all quality standards. In addition, further investigation by the FDA indicated that there could be bacterial contamination within some of the affected lots.

Several years ago, many pets throughout the United States died after eating pet food tainted by contaminated wheat products from China. In just one month, 107 foods about to be imported to the United States from China were detained at the border; findings included dried apples preserved with a cancer-causing chemical, frozen catfish filled with banned antibiotics, scallops and sardines coated with moldering bacteria, and mushrooms mixed with illegal pesticides.[19] ConAgra Foods® has taken extra safety precautions since it had to recall Peter Pan Peanut Butter when a leaky roof in a Georgia manufacturing plant caused salmonella contamination.[20]

Manufacturing is a high-profile industry for which product safety is of paramount concern, as the Toyota recalls discussed earlier illustrate. Manufactured products create hazards not only because of unsafe product design but also as a result of consumers being given inadequate information regarding the hazards associated with using the products. Consequently, in product liability claims, it is not surprising to find charges based on one or more of several allegations. First may be the charge that the product was improperly manufactured, wherein the producer failed to exercise due care in the product's production, which contributed directly to the accident or injury. Second could be the charge that, though manufactured properly, the product's design could have been defective, in that alternative designs or devices, if used at the time of manufacture, may have prevented the accident. Third, that the producer failed to provide satisfactory instructions and/or warnings that could have helped avert accident or injury. Fourth, that the producer failed to foresee a reasonable and anticipated misuse of the product and warn against such misuse.[21]

To appreciate the "big picture" of dangerous products, it should be noted that the Consumer Product Safety Commission keeps track of injuries treated in hospital emergency rooms and identified the following categories of consumer products as being the most frequently associated with hospital-treated injuries (in order of prevalence):[22]

1. Sports and recreational activities and equipment
2. Home structures and construction materials
3. Home furnishings and fixtures
4. Housewares
5. Personal use items
6. Home workshop apparatus, tools, and attachments
7. Packaging and containers for household product
8. Home and family maintenance products
9. Toys
10. Space heating, cooling, and ventilation equipment

Whether we deal with consumer products (where there is potential for harm following accidents or misuse) or with food products (where not-so-visible threats to human health may exist), the field of product safety is a significant responsibility and a growing challenge for the business community. No matter how careful business is with regard to these issues, the threat of product liability lawsuits has become an industry unto itself and intimately linked with product safety discussions. Therefore, we now turn our attention to this vital topic. Product liability has become a monumental consumer issue in the United States for several reasons.

Product Liability

Though business has both an ethical and a legal responsibility to manufacture and sell safe products, in the United States, the legal responsibility has been the driving force for decades because the law entails consequences that even immoral and amoral people prefer to avoid. It should be pointed out that the legal category is based on ethical reasoning and concepts.

Reasons for Concern about Product Liability.   Product liability has become a major issue because of the sheer number of cases involving products have resulted in illness, harm, or death. The United States has been a litigious society. More than in other countries, U.S. citizens tend to file lawsuits and pursue litigation when faced with situations about which they are unhappy.

Another cause for concern is the size of the financial awards that have been given by the courts. Perhaps the path-breaking award in the product liability category was the $128.5 million awarded in 1978 in the case of a 19-year-old who at age 13 was severely injured. He was riding with a friend in a Ford Pinto that was hit from behind. The Pinto's gas tank ruptured, and the passenger compartment was filled with flames, killing his friend and causing burns over 90 percent of his body. The badly scarred teenager underwent more than 50 operations. The jury sought from Ford $666,280 for the dead driver's family and $2.8 million in compensatory damages and $125 million in punitive damages for the survivor.[23] The Pinto case was the beginning, but the awards grew after that. In 2009, there was a sizeable increase in the magnitude of the largest product liability jury awards against big businesses. There was a 52 percent increase in the total value of the top five product defect lawsuit verdicts of 2009, compared with the previous year. The verdicts seemed to point out that jurors are more inclined to take the side of their fellow citizens amidst the harm due to the economic recession, the blame for which many lay at the feet of Wall Street and big business.[24]

It has been estimated that litigation's cost to society is over $200 billion per year, more than half of which goes to legal fees and costs, some of which could be spent to hire more teachers, police officers, and fire fighters. The cost of litigation to companies has been said to represent approximately 30 percent of a stepladder's price, 50 percent of a football helmet, and 95 percent of the price of a childhood vaccine. The problem is largely confined to the United States. In a year when DuPont had nearly 5,000 personal injury lawsuits inside the United States, they had fewer than 20 outside the United States. Although half the company's sales come from overseas, 95 percent of the company's legal costs came from the United States.[25] A major study showed that the money firms pay on lawsuit settlements, damage awards, insurance lawyers and legal defense costs is money they no longer have available to spend on improvements in their processes and products. This decrease in innovation due to tort litigation carries lasting consequences for competitiveness.[26]

Since the Pinto case, multimillion-dollar lawsuits have become commonplace. Some major companies have been hit so hard by lawsuits that they have filed for protection under Chapter 11 of the federal bankruptcy law. One famous example of this is the Johns Manville Corporation, which faced an avalanche of asbestos-related lawsuits that totaled 16,500 suits demanding over $12 billion.[27] Another well-known case is that of A.H. Robins, which filed for protection after facing over 5,000 product liability lawsuits in which women charged that its Dalkon Shield, an intrauterine contraceptive device, had injured them.[28] Dow Chemical, the principal manufacturer of silicone breast implants, entered Chapter 11 in 1995.[29] The strategy continues today. W.R. Grace & Co. filed for bankruptcy protection to shield it from asbestos-related claims.[30] In 2004, however, the court tired of delays and refused to allow Grace a sixth extension of the proceedings.[31] Other companies encountering large lawsuits have included Union Carbide, with its poison gas leak in Bhopal, India; Dow Chemical, with its Agent Orange defoliant; and Bridgestone/Firestone, with its defective tires. One of the largest product liability lawsuits in history looms on the horizon. In 2010, Toyota Motor Corp. was bracing for lawsuits that could run into the billions of dollars as plaintiffs' attorneys jockeyed for position in what could become a class action lawsuit. As this writing, there were at least 75 consolidated federal suits involving Toyota's sudden acceleration problem, and the lawsuits were blaming the company for everything from diminishing the value of plaintiffs' vehicles to causing fatalities. Critics of Toyota have fretted that the massive BP oil spill in the Gulf of Mexico may overshadow the Toyota case in its magnitude.[32]

Doctrine of Strict Liability. In its most general form, the **doctrine of strict liability** holds that anyone in the value chain of a product is liable for harm caused to the user if the product as sold was unreasonably dangerous because of its defective condition. This applies to anyone involved in the design, manufacture, or sale of a defective product. Beyond manufacturing, courts have ruled against plaintiffs from a broad array of functions, such as selling, advertising, promotion, and distribution.[33] For example, the department of transportation (DOT) holds warehouses liable for violations of hazardous materials regulations even when the warehouse relied on information provided by the customer (the depositor) when documenting the shipment.[34] In other words, there is no legal defense for placing on the market a product that is dangerous to a consumer because of a known or knowable defect, unless the strict liability is imposed by a statute that allows for an argument of due diligence.[35] To prove due diligence, a company must take every possible precautionary step and follow all industry standards.

The doctrine of strict liability and the expansion of this concept in the courts have been at the heart of the litigation explosion in the United States. As mentioned previously, the social costs view of product quality underlies the concept of strict liability and its extensions. In addition, some hold the strict liability view as utilitarian; that is, society has made a determination that it is better to hold persons responsible for certain actions even without a showing of negligence because the benefits derived (e.g., safety, improved products, accountability) outweigh the burden placed on the defendant in a strict liability lawsuit. In the area of consumer product development, strict liability laws have fostered meaningful safety developments that have prevented innumerable deaths and injuries. Strict liability is not without its cost, however, and the price of consumer goods certainly reflects this cost-shifting consequence.[36]

Extensions of Strict Liability Rule.   Courts in several states and certain countries have established a standard that is much more demanding than strict liability. This concept is known as **absolute liability**. The ruling that established this concept was handed down by the New Jersey Supreme Court in *Beshada* v. *Johns Manville Corporation* (1982). The plaintiffs in the Beshada case were employees of Johns Manville and other companies who had developed asbestos-related diseases as a result of workplace exposure.[37] The court ruled in this case that a manufacturer could be held *strictly liable* for failure to warn of a product hazard, even if the hazard was scientifically unknowable at the time of manufacture and sale. Therefore, a company cannot use as its defense the claim that it did its best according to the state of the art in the industry at that time. Under this ruling, the manufacturer is liable for damages even if it had no way of knowing that the product might cause a problem later. This has led to what *The Wall Street Journal* terms the "asbestos tort blob," named for the movie *The Blob* that devours everything in its path.[38]

Although the United States has been rightly termed the litigation nation, other countries struggle with the issue as well. For example, the Supreme Court of India upheld the absolute liability of a common carrier, in this case Patel Roadways Ltd., for goods destroyed by fire. The court ruled that, in the case of damage or loss, it is not necessary for the plaintiff to establish negligence.[39] Similarly, leading charities in Great Britain have pressured the prime minister to institute a system of strict financial and legal liability before genetically modified crops can be introduced there.[40]

The absolute liability rule frequently involves cases having to do with chemicals or drugs. For example, a producer might put a drug on the market (with government approval) thinking that it is safe on the basis of current knowledge. Under the doctrine of absolute liability, the firm could be held liable for side effects or health problems that develop years, or even decades, later. The result is that a large amount of uncertainty is injected into the production process.[41] Furthermore, the company's association with the damaging product may be tenuous at best. Forty years ago, Crown Cork and Seal, Inc. (CCS), had a brief connection with Mundet Cork Company, a maker of cork-lined bottle caps. Unfortunately for CCS, Mundet also owned a small insulation company. Crown Cork's $7 million investment in Mundet led to thousands of asbestos-related claims filed against it and over $350 million in asbestos-related payments.[42] The asbestos litigation now ranks as the longest running mass tort litigation in the United States. A bill to set up an asbestos trust fund failed in 2006 even as asbestos filings were increasing.[43] More than a half million claims are expected to be filed in the coming years.[44]

Another extension of strict liability is known as **market share liability**. This concept evolved from **delayed manifestation cases**—situations in which delayed reactions to products appear years later after consumption of, or exposure to, the product.[45] Market share liability was derived from the California case in which a group of women with birth defects claimed that the defects had been caused by the drug DES, which their mothers had taken while pregnant years earlier. The women could not name the company that had made the pills their mothers had taken. But in 1980, the California Supreme Court upheld a ruling that the six drug firms that made DES would be held responsible in proportion to their market shares of DES sales unless they could prove that they had not made the actual doses the women had taken.[46] When this verdict was reached, the business press expressed alarm about the potential impact of the decision. Their concern, however, was premature. With very few exceptions, market share liability has been rejected in subsequent non-DES cases and in second-generation DES cases. DES was uniquely suited to that defense because it was a generic product, the entire industry used the same formula, and it was marketed and promoted generically by all industry members. Efforts to apply the concept to cases involving asbestos products, blood products, breast implants, DPT vaccines, polio vaccines, multipiece tire rims, lead-based paints, and benzene all failed.[47]

Product Tampering and Product Extortion. Two other concerns that have contributed to the product liability discussion are *product tampering* and *product extortion*. The most well known cases involved Tylenol in the 1980s—first in 1982, when seven Chicago people died from taking tainted Tylenol® Extra Strength capsules, and again in 1986, when cyanide-laced bottles of Tylenol were found in New York, and one woman died. James Burke, J&J chairperson at the time, characterized the case as "terrorism, pure and simple."[48] In response to these and other incidents, firms began to employ tamper-evident packaging. Although improvements in packaging have slowed the rate of pharmaceutical product tampering, they have not stopped it. Two Australian pharmaceutical manufacturers received threats from extortionists who were believed to have bought over-the-counter analgesics, poisoned them with strychnine, and returned them to the shelves. Four people were hospitalized, and nationwide product recalls cost the firms millions of dollars.[49]

Adulterated and poisoned products stretch beyond pharmaceuticals. After the 9/11 terrorist attacks, product-tampering concerns centered on anthrax and the possible ways it could be used for extortion and terror. When attorneys at Stoel Rives in Portland, Oregon, mailed 50,000 cards in envelopes with bumpy seeds, some recipients became so scared they dialed 911. Publisher's Clearinghouse mailed packages of powdered detergent to customers, causing alarm in the process.[50] Now that the furor over mail has subsided, attention has shifted to ways in which terrorists might tamper with the food supply. Since the 9/11 attacks, food companies have spent hundreds of millions of dollars to upgrade security, institute employee background checks, and install lights and video cameras.[51]

Product Liability Reform. The problems discussed up to this point have combined to generate calls from many groups for **product liability reform**, also known as **tort reform**. A tort is an act that injures someone in some way, and for which the injured person may sue the wrongdoer for damages.[52] The U.S. tort system costs Americans billions of dollars every year. The total estimated cost for a recent year was $252 billion—almost $1,000 for every person in the country. Built into the price of every product is a component to pay for liability insurance and lawsuit defense. Tort risks are the second most important factor when a company decides where to relocate or expand operations or build a new plant or introduce a new product.[53] With the recent changes in health care, many experts believe that changes in tort law are also needed as part of the process of bringing health care costs under control. However, not everyone agrees that tort reform is needed. On one side are business groups, medical associations, local and state governments, and insurance companies that want to change the system that they claim gives costly and unfair advantage to plaintiffs in liability suits. On the other side are consumer groups and trial lawyers who defend the current system as one that protects the constitutional rights of wrongfully injured parties.[54]

The business community's criticisms of the current system illustrate some of the aspects of the controversy. Currently, we have a patchwork of state laws, with the law varying significantly from state to state. The Pacific Research Institute named Vermont as the state with the worst tort system, with Rhode Island, New York, Pennsylvania, and Maryland following close behind. The states with the best-rated tort systems were Colorado, North Dakota, Ohio, and Michigan.[55] The rankings were based on 39 variables, including factors that assessed whether a state caps punitive damage awards as well as the product liability insurance loss ratio.[56]

Business wants a uniform federal code. It also argues for no punitive damages unless the plaintiff meets tougher standards of proof because meeting government standards is no defense in most states. Business thinks it should have an absolute shield against punitive damages for drugs, medical devices, and aircraft that meet government regulations. Business also wants a cap placed on how high punitive awards can be. Finally, business wants victorious plaintiffs to be able to recover damages only to the extent that defendants are liable.[57] On the other side of the issue are consumer and citizen groups and others who support the current system and say the critics of the product liability laws have exaggerated the problems. These supporters of the current system point out that some of the most infamous injuries inflicted on consumers were remedied mainly through lawsuits, not regulatory action. Examples include the Dalkon Shield, a contraceptive device that made thousands of women infertile; the Pinto's exploding gas tank; the damage to workers exposed to asbestos; tobacco cases; and many lesser-known cases.[58] According to Ralph Nader, trial lawyers are "all that is left to require wrongdoers to be held accountable."[59]

It may be possible to stem the rising tide of litigation while still being responsive to individuals with valid claims. Philip K. Howard, author of *The Collapse of the Common Good*, is a leading voice for tort reform. He helped to found Common Good, an organization devoted to reforming the legal system. Rather than advocating caps on damages, Common Good argues for a reform of the system of jurisprudence, removing education and health care claims from the court system. It would help cases through health courts that would be able to differentiate frivolous suits from those with merit. Howard argues that this would limit the overall cost of litigation to society without putting limits on the judgments awarded to those with valid claims.[60] In spite of bipartisan support, Howard is not without detractors. Ralph Nader and the Association of Trial Lawyers contend that Howard favors defendants at the expense of plaintiffs.[61]

In 2007, the Supreme Court repudiated a 1957 ruling, *Conley* v. *Gibson*, which has provided the underpinning for much of the most egregious forms of litigation. In this ruling, the Supreme Court instructed judges to not dismiss a claim except in extreme circumstances.[62] Over the next 50 years, this ruling was cited in 40,000 decisions.[63] While gratified by this decision, Philip K. Howard is concerned that it does not go far enough. He says that judges are now trained to avoid making value judgments about cases and so changing 50 years of practice will not happen easily. Figure 14-2 provides

---

FIGURE 14-2

The Double-Edged Sword of Tort Reform

The Pants with the Platinum Price Tag

A newly appointed Washington, D.C., administrative law judge, Roy L. Pearson, Jr., had five expensive Hickey Freeman suits, one for each day of the week. The pants had become uncomfortably tight so he took them for altering to a local dry cleaning service, owned by a Korean couple who came to the United States in 1992. The cleaners failed to return one pair of pants and, according to Judge Pearson, tried to pass cheaper pants off as the ones he had brought to have altered. Judge Pearson sued for $67.3 million, charging fraud because the signage in the store promised "Same Day Service" and "Satisfaction Guaranteed."

The Chemical Catch-22

Jack Cline is critically ill in an Alabama hospital: He suffers from leukemia that he claims to have contracted due to his exposure to Benzene during factory work he did years earlier. Alabama law makes it impossible for Mr. Cline to have his day in court. He could not sue when he was exposed to the benzene because it would have been too early. In Alabama, people exposed to dangerous chemicals must wait until a "manifest" injury develops. However, it was too late for him to sue when his leukemia manifested years later because Alabama has a statute of limitations that requires suits be brought within two years of exposure.

Sources: Ariel Sabar and Suevon Lee, "Judge Tries Suing Pants Off Dry Cleaner," *The New York Times* (June 13, 2007); Adam Cohen, "Editorial Observer; They Say We Have Too Many Lawsuits? Tell It to Jack Cline," *The New York Times* (January 14, 2007).

---

two examples from today's courtrooms that illustrate the range of concerns tort reform must address.

The debate over product liability reform continues. Business claims the current system is inherently inefficient, raises the costs of litigation, and imposes a hidden tax on consumers because it inhibits innovation and dampens competitiveness. Consumer groups argue that the current system has forced companies to make safer products and listen to their customers. Studies show that both sides have valid arguments. The laws have spurred some safety improvements, but they have also hampered innovation.[64] Of course, if businesses internalize the notion of product safety and take responsibility for the products and services they sell, the need for legal redress is precluded and the entire business–consumer relationship is far better served.

ETHICS IN PRACTICE CASE

The Pirated Popcorn

Last year, I worked in a local movie theater to earn money during the summer. Part of my job was to clean the theater between showings, collecting discarded cups, napkins, and popcorn tubs. I thought it was odd when my manager asked that I empty and then bring him discarded popcorn tubs that were in fairly good shape. He would then reuse them—refilling them with popcorn for unsuspecting customers.

I soon learned that the theater paid for its popcorn concession by the number of tubs it used. By reusing the tubs, the theater was able to lower its costs. However, I was fairly certain that customers would have been upset if they knew what was happening (I knew that I would be).

1. How would you characterize the practice in which the movie theater engaged? Does this practice represent fair customer service?

2. Should I have followed my manager's orders and gone along with his request? Was it really such a terrible thing to do?

There are two major government agencies that are dedicated to product safety—the Consumer Product Safety Commission and the Food and Drug Administration.

Consumer Product Safety Commission

The **Consumer Product Safety Commission (CPSC)** is an independent regulatory agency that was created by the Consumer Product Safety Act of 1972. CPSC works to reduce the risk of injuries and deaths from consumer products by[65]

1. developing voluntary standards with industry,
2. issuing and enforcing mandatory standards,
3. banning consumer products if no feasible standard would adequately protect the public,
4. obtaining the recall of products or arranging for their repair,
5. conducting research on potential product hazards, and
6. informing and educating consumers through the media, state and local governments, private organizations, and by responding to consumer inquiries.

The CPSC points with pride to the 30 percent reduction in the rates of death and injury caused by consumer products since the agency's inception.[66] Figure 14-3 presents examples of voluntary safety standards developed by the CPSC. They cover indoor air quality and hazards related to children's products, fire, or electricity.

The CPSC was created at the zenith of the consumer movement as a result of initiatives taken in the late 1960s. President Lyndon B. Johnson established a National Commission on Product Safety in 1968, and this commission recommended the creation of a permanent agency. The commission justified its recommendation by its finding that an

FIGURE 14-3 CPSC: Development of Voluntary Standards

VOLUNTARY SAFETY STANDARDS			
Indoor Air Quality Hazards	**Children's Product Hazards**	**Fire/Electrical Hazards**	**Other Hazards**
Carbon Monoxide (CO) Detectors. Includes new alarm requirements based on both CO concentration and exposure time.	Bunk Beds. Includes provisions to prevent the collapse of the mattress and its foundation, as well as provisions to prevent entrapment or strangulation in the bunk bed's structure.	National Electrical Code. Provides added GFCI protection around household sinks, requires GFCI protection for spas and hot tubs, and adds a requirement that heat tapes be safety certified.	Automatic Garage Door Openers (two revisions). Includes cautionary labeling on the risk of entrapment.
Formaldehyde in Particleboard and Formaldehyde in Hardwood and Decorative Plywood (two standards). Specifies allowable formaldehyde emissions.	Drawstrings on Children's Clothing. Four months after CPSC presented evidence of dangers to children, manufacturers voluntarily removed drawstrings from existing children's clothing and promised that new clothing would be manufactured with safer alternatives, such as Velcro and snaps.	Handheld Hair Dryers. Includes requirements for polarized plugs, cautionary labeling on the risk of use near water, and protections from electrocution when immersed, whether the unit is turned on or off.	Aboveground/ Onground Swimming Pools. Provides recommended barrier requirements (within an appendix to the standard) to prevent child drownings.

Source: U.S. Consumer Product Safety Commission, http://www.cpsc.gov.

estimated 20 million Americans were injured annually by consumer products. President Richard Nixon, who took office while the proposed agency was still being debated, supported the agency's creation, but not as one that is independent. Congress gave the agency an unusually high degree of independence and required that it open its proceedings to the public to address the often-heard criticism of regulatory agencies that they become captives of the industries they regulate. Its intent was to keep business at arm's length and to involve consumers as primary participants in the agency's decision making.[67]

Over the decades, the CPSC has experienced ups and downs and various degrees of activism as various administrations came into office. During some administrations, it was significantly bolstered in its power and budget, and during other administrations, it was downplayed and underemphasized. As with all government agencies, their directors are appointed by the presidents in office at the time and their powers are greatly affected by the budgets given them by Congress.

In 2009, President Obama appointed a new chair of the CPSC, Inez Moore Tenenbaum. She replaced the agency's controversial acting chair, Nancy Nord. Obama also promised to increase the commission to five members from three and its budget significantly. Over the past several years, the CPSC had been criticized for failing to enforce strictly product safety laws, especially those relating to lead content in children's toys. The commission's lax enforcement of these laws has been highlighted by scandals involving lead-tainted toys and other defective imports from China. Outgoing chair Nord and her board have been criticized for being too close to the companies they are supposed to regulate. The CPSC also has been criticized for its slow response to the Chinese drywall problem. For months, homeowners in many different states had complained that the drywall material emits sulfur fumes that fill homes with a "rotten eggs" odor. The drywall fumes were also linked to corroding metals in many homes, and people living with the material reported sinus and respiratory problems. A number of residents had to leave their homes because the Chinese drywall had made them unlivable, and some builders were scrambling to gut homes and replace the drywall.[68]

Since Tenenbaum became chair of the CPSC, it has become more activist and has introduced a number of new priorities including an official blog titled *OnSafety* (http://www.cpsc.gov/onsafety/) that reports the latest product safety information that consumers might need. By 2010, some of the product safety issues being closely watched by the CPSC included push toys with dangerous handles, charm bracelets with high levels of cadmium, drop-side cribs that pose hazards to sleeping infants, flammable children's sweatshirts, and children's hooded sweatshirts with drawstrings that posed a strangulation hazard. Consumers may now connect with these safety warnings on YouTube, Twitter, Flickr, Podcast, and RSS Feed, as well as the blog.[69]

The **Consumer Product Safety Improvement Act of 2008** is the most recent piece of legislation given to the CPSC for enforcement. Some of the numerous topics covered by the act include all terrain vehicles (ATVs), durable nursery products, labeling of toys and games, lead, third-party testing, and whistleblower protections.[70]

The CPSC continues to play an important role in protecting consumers from unsafe products. The CPSC remains the only clearinghouse available for consumers who have safety concerns with the more than 15,000 products under its care, and it is the only mechanism available for recalling unsafe products. Problems that continue to plague the commission include having adequate resources to do the job, having sufficient staff to address current needs, being forced to shift priorities, and the always-new challenges in a changing world marketplace. Among these latter challenges are imported products from countries that do not share U.S. safety standards and new threats posed by technology.[71]

Food and Drug Administration

The **Food and drug administration (FDA)** grew out of experiments with food safety by one man—Harvey W. Wiley—chief chemist for the agricultural department in the late 1800s. Wiley's most famous experiments involved feeding small doses of poisons to human volunteers. The substances fed to the volunteers were similar to those found in food preservatives at the time. The volunteers became known as the "Poison Squad," and their publicity generated a public awareness of the dangers of eating adulterated foods. The Food and Drugs Act of 1906 was a direct result of the publicity created by Wiley's experiments. The act was administered by Wiley's Bureau of Chemistry until 1931, when the name "Food and Drug Administration" first was used. Today, the FDA resides within the Health and Human Services Department and engages in three broad categories of activity: analysis, surveillance, and correction.

According to the FDA, the Food and Drugs Act of 1906 was the first of more than 200 laws that constitute one of the world's most comprehensive networks of public health and consumer protections. A few of the FDA's congressional milestones include the following:

- The Federal Food, Drug, and Cosmetic Act of 1938 was passed after a legally marketed toxic elixir killed 107 people, including many children. The FD&C Act completely overhauled the public health system. Among other provisions, the law authorized the FDA to demand evidence of safety for new drugs, issue standards for food, and conduct factory inspections.
- The Kefauver–Harris Amendments of 1962, which were inspired by the thalidomide tragedy in Europe (and the FDA's vigilance that prevented the drug's marketing in the United States), strengthened the rules for drug safety and required manufacturers to prove their drugs' effectiveness.
- The Medical Device Amendments of 1976 followed a U.S. Senate finding that faulty medical devices had caused 10,000 injuries, including 731 deaths. The law applied safety and effectiveness safeguards to new devices.

Today, the FDA supervises many different laws and amendments that have been passed, and regulates $1 trillion worth of products a year. It ensures the safety of all food except for meat, poultry, and some egg products; ensures the safety and effectiveness of all drugs, biological products (including blood, vaccines, and tissues for transplantation), medical devices, and animal drugs and feed; and makes sure that cosmetics and medical and consumer products that emit radiation do no harm.[72]

Figure 14-4 provides information about what the FDA does.

The FDA, like the CPSC, has been controversial over the decades, and its zeal in pursuing its mission has varied widely depending on the administration in office. On tracking its history since the 1990s, some of the major challenges the FDA faced in the first Bush administration included the AIDS epidemic, regulation of medical devices, food safety, fat substitutes, nutritional labeling, and over-the-counter drug review. In 1991, under new commissioner David Kessler, the FDA embarked on an aggressive crackdown on deceptive product labels, which created a fair amount of controversy. In early 1991, the FDA targeted two highly visible products and companies to make its point. It seized Procter & Gamble's (P&G) Citrus Hill "Fresh Choice" orange juice and, a few days later, Ragú® "Fresh Italian" pasta sauce, the nation's leading tomato sauce brand. In both cases, the FDA forced the companies to remove the term "fresh" from their products because they thought the companies were inaccurately applying that term to their products.

FIGURE 14-4

What Does the FDA Do?

The FDA is responsible for:

- protecting the public health by assuring the safety, effectiveness, and security of human and veterinary drugs, vaccines and other biological products, medical devices, our nation's food supply, cosmetics, dietary supplements, and products that give off radiation
- regulating tobacco products
- advancing the public health by helping to speed product innovations

- helping the public get the accurate, science-based information they need to use medicines and foods to improve their health

The FDA's responsibilities extend to the 50 United States, the District of Columbia, Puerto Rico, Guam, the Virgin Islands, American Samoa, and other U.S. territories and possessions.

Source: U.S. Food and Drug Administration (FDA), "What Does FDA Do?" http://www.fda.gov/AboutFDA/Basics/ucm194877.htm. Accessed May 15, 2010.

The point of the FDA was clear. It was no longer going to pursue the practice, which had become commonplace throughout the 1980s, of companies suspected of violations stretching out negotiations with the agency for years while engaging in an endless back-and-forth exchange of proposals and counterproposals. The FDA was reasserting itself as an agency planning to take swift action against violators. In addition to the two cases cited, the FDA sent warning letters to the manufacturers of Listerine®, PLAX®, and Viadent® mouthwash brands; Weight Watchers® and Kraft® brands cholesterol-free mayonnaise; and Fleischmann's® Reduced-Calorie Margarine, among other products. The agency thought that these manufacturers had made claims that misrepresented the features of their products.[73] Under Kessler's controversial leadership, the FDA aggressively and zealously pursued companies it felt were out of compliance with government regulations or were taking advantage of consumers.

In 1997, Kessler resigned and Jane Henney, vice president of research for the University of New Mexico, was nominated his successor.[74] Having served under George W. Bush and Bill Clinton, Henney enjoyed bipartisan credentials. However, her tenure as deputy to Kessler raised red flags for Senate Republicans, who found Republican Kessler overly quick to regulate and overly slow to approve treatments and devices.[75] After contentious debate, Henney was confirmed. During her tenure in office, the "abortion pill," RU486, was approved. When the Bush administration entered office, Henney handed in her protocol resignation, which was accepted shortly thereafter, effectively firing her. Although significant lobbying to retain her occurred, she was not able to duplicate the feat of Republican Kessler, who had been retained by the Democratic Clinton administration after being appointed by the first Bush administration. Observers felt that her failure to block the approval of RU486 doomed her reappointment.[76]

Mark McClellan became the head of the FDA in late 2002 but was tapped to head Medicare just 15 months later in March 2004. In his short tenure, McClellan drew praise for streamlining the approval process for new drug therapies—something at which the FDA had been quite bad.[77] Les Crawford became commissioner but only held the position for two months before he resigned abruptly. A year later, he pleaded guilty to misleading federal officials about stocks he owned in FDA-related companies. He received a three-year supervised probation, 50 hours of community service, and a $90,000 fine.[78] Andrew von Eschenbach became the commissioner in 2007.[79] In 2009, under President Obama, Margaret A. Hamburg was confirmed as commissioner.[80] In 2010, Hamburg expressed concerns over the challenges and opportunities ahead in ensuring safe food and drug imports into the United States.

Over recent years, many observers have questioned the ability of the FDA to keep the food supply safe as food imports have been rising, while the FDA's ability to police the food supply has been declining.[81] To quote a *Newsweek* article on the spate of food contamination that occurred not too long ago, "The hamstrung FDA may be unable to prevent a contamination crisis." As *Newsweek* notes, the problem has not been for lack of trying on the part of the FDA. Five years earlier, FDA officials developed an import safety plan that would have cost $100 million; their plan did not receive funding. They asked for the authority to block foods from countries repeatedly linked to contaminated products until they were able to establish their own controls; Congress did not give them the authority. A key reason for this impasse was that food manufacturers spent more than $100 million lobbying against the new regulations. Caroline Smith DeWaal of the Center for Science in the Public Interest expressed her concern: "The food supply should not be the Wild, Wild West for capitalism. If a country does not have systems in place to ensure safety, they shouldn't be able to send us food."[82] It is clear that Commissioner Hamburg will have her work cut out for her in the years ahead.

Business's Response to Consumer Stakeholders

Business's response to consumerism and consumer stakeholders has varied over the years. It has ranged from poorly conceived public relations ploys at one extreme to well-designed and implemented programs such as TQM and Six Sigma at the other. The history of business's response to consumers parallels its perceptions of the seriousness, pervasiveness, effectiveness, and longevity of the consumer movement. When the consumer movement first began, business's response was casual, perhaps symbolic, and hardly effective. Today, the consumer movement has matured, and formal interactions with consumer stakeholders have become more and more institutionalized. Business has realized that consumers today are more persistent than in the past, more assertive, and more likely to use or exhaust all appeal channels before being satisfied. Armed with considerable power, consumer activists have been a major stimulus to more sincere efforts on behalf of business to provide consumers with a forum. These efforts have included the creation of toll-free hot lines, user-friendly Web sites, and consumer service representatives. Today, virtually all successful companies have customer service programs, irrespective of whether they are selling products or services.

Customer Service Programs

Consumers today expect high-quality, safe products, and responsive customer service regarding the products and services they buy. Nothing is more frustrating than spending money on a product only to encounter after-sale problems or issues that are not quickly and easily remedied. Experts today argue that companies should strive to develop loyal customers who will always come back and that the key to customer retention is customer service. Building life-long devotion among customers takes serious commitment and hard work. It also requires that a company create a culture and employees who are motivated and committed to delivering outstanding service. P&G faced a customer relations nightmare in 2010 over its new Pampers® diapers that some consumers said caused rashes, even "chemical burns," on their children. Angry consumers even started a crusade against the company on Facebook, and P&G had a delicate line to navigate as it tried to be responsive to consumer concerns and also defend its product, which it claimed was not defective. One strategy P&G followed was to add more customer-service representatives so they could more effectively deal with irate consumers.[83]

FIGURE 14-5

Customer Service Principles and Customer-Oriented Companies

Seven Principles of Customer Service[a]

1. **Keeping your word is where it all begins**. Keeping your word builds trust. Trust is the foundation of all successful relationships.

2. **Always be honest and tell it like it is**. By being honest and telling your customers the truth, you are much more likely to get a positive response to any situation.

3. **Always think proactively, looking around the corner**. Thinking proactively when it comes to customer service boils down to addressing concerns prior to you having to hear from the customer that something needs to be done.

4. **Deal with problems as best you can yourself, never passing the buck**. The more authority employees have to address customer problems, the better it is because nothing upsets customers more than being passed from department to department.

5. **Do not argue with a customer because it is a lose/lose situation**. The best question to ask yourself is: What can be done to make the customer feel happy and cared for?

6. **Accept your mistakes, learn from them, and do not repeat them**. Accept that you have made a mistake, evaluate the situation, learn the lesson, and move on. Don't get stuck in an indefinite state of denial.

7. **Consistency is the name of the game for lasting success**. When the customer service principles discussed above are practiced consistently, customers realize over time that the integrity of how you choose to run your business is not to be compromised.

Creating a Customer-Oriented Company[b]

1. Top–down culture and commitment are essential.
2. Identify internal champions and uphold them.
3. Commit resources to the task.
4. Hire the right people.
5. Empower employees.
6. Make customer service training a priority.

---

[a]Summarized from Imran Rahman, "Seven Service Principles Guaranteed to Create Raving Fans," http://www.dreammanifesto.com/service-principles-guaranteed-create-raving-fans.html. Accessed May 13, 2010.

[b]Summarized from John Allen, "Creating a Service-Oriented Company Takes Commitment," *Houston Business Journal* (April 10, 2009), http://houston.bizjournals.com/houston/stories/2009/04/13/smallb3.html. Accessed August 11, 2010.

Companies address customer service in a variety of ways, and it is often dependent on the nature of the products or services and the competitiveness of the market that drive commitment on the part of companies. Companies provide customer service through money-back guarantees, warranties, and offices of consumer affairs in which are found customer service representatives whose full time job it is to make customers happy. The effective execution of customer service depends on a host of factors, but it is absolutely critical that top management be committed to providing a service as part of its ongoing relationship with the consumer. Management's job is to attract, maintain, and retain customers, and this requires a high degree of dedication and commitment. There are many principles that drive high-quality customer service, and many guidelines for creating a customer-oriented company. Figure 14-5 presents some key customer service principles and guidelines for developing customer-oriented companies.

Programs such as TQM and Six Sigma have become important strategic responses to product quality and safety issues. These responses merit brief consideration.

Total Quality Management Programs

Total Quality Management (TQM) has many different characteristics, but it essentially means that all of the functions of the business are blended into a holistic, integrated philosophy built around the concepts of quality, teamwork, productivity, customer understanding, and satisfaction.[84] Figure 14-6 depicts one useful view of the principles,

FIGURE 14-6 Principles, Practices, and Techniques of Total Quality Management

	Customer Focus	Continuous Improvement	Teamwork
Principles	• Paramount importance of customers • Providing products and services that fulfill customer needs; requires organization-wide focus on customers	• Consistent customer satisfaction can be attained only through relentless improvement of processes that create products and services	• Customer focus and continuous improvement are best achieved by collaboration throughout an organization as well as with customers and suppliers
Practices	• Direct customer contact • Collecting information about customer needs • Using information to design and deliver products and services	• Process analysis • Reengineering • Problem solving • Plan/do/check/act	• Search for arrangements that benefit all units involved in a process • Formation of various types of teams • Group skills training
Techniques	• Customer surveys and focus groups • Quality function deployment (translates customer information into product specifications)	• Flowcharts • Pareto analysis • Statistical process control • Fishbone diagrams	• Organizational development methods, such as the nominal group technique • Team-building methods (e.g., role clarification and group feedback)

Source: James W. Dean, Jr., and David E. Bowen, "Management Theory and Total Quality: Improving Research and Practice Through Theory Development," *Academy of Management Review* (Vol. 19, No. 3, July 1994), 395.

practices, and techniques of TQM. It should be noted that the customer, or consumer stakeholder, is the focus of the process. Efforts to show a relationship between TQM and financial performance have met with mixed results.[85] The positive impact TQM can have on safety in the workplace, in contrast, has been established.[86]

To be successful, TQM must emphasize eight key elements—Ethics, Integrity, Trust, Training, Teamwork, Leadership, Recognition, and Communication. The first three—Ethics, Integrity, and Trust—constitute the foundation on which all else is built. These three elements foster openness, fairness, and sincerity, and they create the foundation for involvement by everyone.[87]

A vital assumption and premise of TQM is that the customer is the final judge of quality. Therefore, the first part of the TQM process is to define quality in terms of customer expectations and requirements. Figure 14-7 presents several different popular definitions of quality and their strengths and weaknesses. As can be seen, quality means different things to different people, and this makes its achievement challenging.

Customer expectations and requirements are then converted to standards and specifications. Finally, the entire organization is realigned to ensure that both conformance quality (adherence to standards and specifications) and perceived quality (meeting or exceeding customer expectations) are achieved.[88] It is clear in TQM that "delighted customers" is the overarching goal of management's efforts.[89] It is important to remember that customers' perceived quality is not always the same as actual quality and so firms may have to wait for customers to realize that genuine quality improvements have been made.[90]

FIGURE 14-7 Strengths and Weaknesses of Quality Definitions

Definition	Strengths	Weaknesses
Excellence	• Strong marketing and human resource benefits • Universally recognizable—mark of uncompromising standards and high achievement	• Provides little practical guidance to practitioners • Measurement difficulties • Attributes of excellence may change dramatically and rapidly • Sufficient number of customers must be willing to pay for excellence
Value	• Concept of value incorporates multiple attributes • Focuses attention on a firm's internal efficiency and external effectiveness • Allows for comparisons across disparate objects and experiences	• Difficulty extracting individual components of value judgment • Questionable inclusiveness • Quality and value are different constructs
Conformance to Specifications	• Facilitates precise measurement • Leads to increased efficiency • Necessary for global strategy • Should force disaggregation of consumer needs • Most parsimonious and appropriate definition for some customers	• Consumers do not know or care about internal specifications • Inappropriate for services • Potentially reduces organizational adaptability • Specifications may quickly become obsolete in rapidly changing markets • Internally focused
Meeting and/or Exceeding Expectations	• Evaluates from customer's perspective • Applicable across industries • Responsive to market changes • All-encompassing definition	• Most complex definition • Difficult to measure • Customers may not know expectations • Idiosyncratic reactions • Prepurchase attitudes affect subsequent judgments • Short-term and long-term evaluations may differ • Confusion between customer service and customer satisfaction

Source: Carol A. Reeves and David A. Bednar, "Defining Quality: Alternatives and Implications," *Academy of Management Review* (Vol. 19, No. 3, July 1994), 437.

Opportunities for recognition have helped to propel quality efforts. In the United States and the rest of the industrialized world, the Malcolm Baldrige Award, ISO 9000, and the Deming Quality Award have enhanced the reputations of firms that undertake quality initiatives and complete them successfully. However, TQM became a management buzzword, and many of its slogans, such as "Getting it right the first time," became viewed as clichés. It is against this backdrop that other tools developed, such as Just in Time (JIT) and Business Process Reengineering (BPR). Many were concerned about a TQM shortcoming, as described by Phil Crosby, a leading TQM consultant: "TQM never did anything to define quality, which is conformance to standards."[91] The need for a more rigorous definition of quality was part of the appeal of Six Sigma, which is briefly described.

Six Sigma Strategy and Process

Six Sigma is a development within TQM that has become a way of life for many corporations. Six Sigma is a general heading under which is grouped a body of strategies, methodologies, and techniques. Scarcely a week goes by without a major corporation adopting Six Sigma as a way of improving quality and reducing costs.[92] Dow, DuPont, Sony, Honeywell, Nokia, GlaxoSmithKline, and Raytheon are but a few of the major corporations that have adopted the Six Sigma methodology. According to Jack Welch, former CEO of GE, "[Six Sigma—the Breakthrough Strategy] is the most important initiative GE has ever taken. . . . it is part of the genetic code of our future leadership."[93] Although some deride Six Sigma as "TQM on steroids," it has brought new commitment and energy to the quest for quality in the new millennium. It is even said to have brought "more prominence to the quality world than it has enjoyed since the glory days of the mid-1980s."[94]

Motorola first developed Six Sigma, and Allied Signal later experimented with it, but most observers believe that GE perfected it. *Sigma* is a statistical measure of variation from the mean; higher values of sigma mean fewer defects. The six-sigma level of operation is 3.4 defects per million. Most companies operate around the four-sigma level, that is, 6,000 defects per million. Corporations adopting the program must develop "black belts," that is, people specifically trained to fill sponsorship roles, provide assistance, and see the program through. They must also find "champions" at senior levels of management who are committed to shepherding the program when needed.[95]

One of Six Sigma's strengths has been the clarity of the process and the steps companies must take to adopt it. However, Six Sigma is more than a toolbox with clear instructions. The program also represents a philosophy that stresses the importance of customers as well as careful measurement. Six Sigma practitioners look for facts rather than opinions, and they believe in fixing the process rather than the product.[96] Of course, these underlying principles are the foundation of TQM and most other quality efforts.

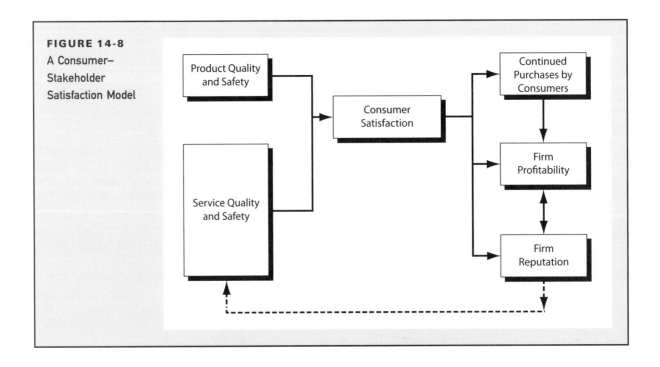

FIGURE 14-8

A Consumer–Stakeholder Satisfaction Model

The basis for all of these quality or safety approaches is the satisfaction of the consumer. Figure 14-8 outlines a **consumer stakeholder satisfaction model** that depicts how product and service quality and safety lead to consumer satisfaction and the consequences for the firm's profitability, reputation, and continued purchasing by consumers.

Summary

Consumer stakeholders have become concerned with product quality and safety, largely because businesses have failed to meet their needs reliably on these two fronts. The situation has been the same with both manufacturing and services. One major challenge has been to identify and understand all the different dimensions of the quality issue. Today, quality may mean performance, features, reliability, conformance, durability, serviceability, aesthetics, perceived quality, or some combination of these dimensions.

An extremely important legal and ethical issue has been the consumer's right to safety. Product safety has become one of the most crucial consumer issues for firms. The product liability crisis has been an outgrowth of business's lack of attention to this issue. Other factors contributing to the product liability crisis have been the number of harmful-product cases, our increasingly litigious society, the size of financial awards given by the courts, and rising insurance rates. A major consequence of these phenomena has been calls for tort reform. Product tampering and product extortion have also become safety-related issues. In recent years, the health and safety issues related to foods, drugs, and medical devices have propelled the CPSC and the FDA into prominent roles.

Companies today employ a host of different customer service programs, all of which are aimed at creating satisfied customers who will demonstrate loyalty and will return for future purchases. In addition, firms use a variety of approaches that specifically address the issue of quality, primarily in the production process, and these embrace safety as one significant feature. Quality improvement initiatives such as TQM and Six Sigma are being used systematically, but they have not solved all the problems; however, they and other techniques have the potential for addressing the problems in a significant way if they are properly formulated and implemented. In addition to these specific responses, a consumer focus and orientation needs to permeate management decision making if the concerns of consumers are to be handled effectively. In today's business environment, consumers have many choices. Consequently, companies have no alternative but to internalize the consumer focus if they are to succeed.

Key Terms

absolute liability, p. 494

Consumer Product Safety Commission (CPSC), p. 498

Consumer Product Safety Improvement Act of 2008, p. 499

consumer stakeholder satisfaction model, p. 507

contractual theory, p. 489

delayed manifestation cases, p. 495

doctrine of strict liability, p. 493

due care theory, p. 489

Food and Drug Administration (FDA), p. 500

market share liability, p. 495

product liability reform, p. 495

Six Sigma, p. 506

social costs view, p. 489

tort reform, p. 495

Total Quality Management (TQM), p. 503

Discussion Questions

1. Identify the major dimensions of quality. Give an example of a product or service in which each of these characteristics is important.

2. What ethical theories can help us to better understand the issue of quality? Discuss.

3. Identify the principal reasons why we have a product liability crisis. Have any reasons been omitted? Discuss.

4. Differentiate the doctrine of strict liability from the doctrines of absolute liability and market

share liability. What implications do these views have for the business community and for future products and services that might be offered?

5. Given the current business and consumer climate, what do you anticipate the future to be for the CPSC and the FDA? What role does politics play in your answer?

6. What is your assessment of business's response to product and service quality and safety? Have they done enough? What is missing from their approaches?

15

The Natural Environment as Stakeholder

CHAPTER LEARNING OUTCOMES

After studying this chapter, you should be able to:

1. Discuss the concept of sustainability.

2. Describe ten major natural environment issues.

3. Describe the NIMBY environmental problem.

4. Discuss the roles that business and government play in environmental issues.

5. Explain the concept of environmental ethics.

Sustainability means running the global environment— Earth Inc.—like a corporation: with depreciation, amortization and maintenance accounts. In other words, keeping the asset whole, rather than undermining your natural capital.[1]

Maurice Strong

For years, businesses conducted their operations with little concern about environmental consequences. Virtually every sector of business in every country was responsible for consuming significant amounts of materials and energy and causing waste accumulation and resource degradation. For instance, forestry firms and companies that process raw materials, such as uranium, coal, and oil, have caused major air, water, and land pollution problems in their extraction, transportation, and processing stages. Manufacturing firms, such as those in steel, petrochemicals, and paper products, have been major sources of air and water pollution. However, most major industry sectors have contributed significant levels of pollution with relatively little concern. Businesses would look the other way, simply labeling the negative consequences of their actions as *externalities*.[2] **Externalities** are side effects or by-products of actions that are not included in standard cost accounting systems.[3]

By labeling the environmental consequences as external to the process, businesses were able to both acknowledge and dismiss the problems they created. The few business environmentalism efforts that existed tended to come from two sources— compliance and efficiency.[4] Environmentalists had one approach available for getting most businesses to treat the environment with greater respect, "mandate, regulate, and litigate." Businesses would stop damaging the environment only when it became illegal and/or unprofitable to do so.[5] In some ways, those days are ending. Companies that were once infamous for the damage they did to the environment are now scrambling to lead the way in environmental initiatives. The reason for the change is simple— environmentalism is now profitable. Companies can make money not only by increasing efficiency but also by inventing entirely new businesses.[6] Nevertheless, businesses still pose hazards to the environment, as evidenced by the devastating impact of the BP oil rig explosion in 2010. As of this writing, experts are saying this may turn out to be the worst environmental disaster in U.S. history.

This chapter begins by discussing the concept of sustainability and its importance to business. It then outlines the top environmental issues facing business today. Environmental ethics begins the discussion of individual and collective responsibility for sustaining the environment. The chapter explores the role of the government and environmental interest groups in effecting change and then looks at companies that are leaders in practicing sustainable business practices. Lastly, it offers ways in which businesses can develop an environmental strategy aimed at achieving sustainability.

The Sustainability Imperative

There are many definitions of **sustainability**. For our purposes, we borrow from the Brundtland Commission (formerly the World Commission on Environment and Development [WCED]) to define sustainable business as "business that meets the needs of the present without compromising the ability of future generations to meet their own needs."[7] The focus of sustainability is the creation of a good quality of life for both current and future generations of humans and nonhumans by achieving a balance between economic prosperity, ecosystem viability, and social justice.[8] The concept is akin to walking lightly on the earth, taking only what is needed and leaving behind enough for future generations to have access to the same resources.

Sustainability is not just about cutting back and limiting waste, it is a philosophy that embraces a new type of abundance that can inspire greater levels of business creativity.[9] As the sustainability movement grows, creative business people are developing new environmentally responsible ways of doing business. For example, Paul Dolan, the former president of Fetzer Vineyards, is often referred to as the "Sustainability Guru."[10] Dolan had spent decades in the wine business by the time he became president of Fetzer Vineyards. He read *The Ecology of Commerce* by Paul Hawken just before becoming president and that book gave shape to his future plans. "It suddenly became apparent to me that sustainability was the way," said Dolan. Today, Fetzer farms all its own vineyards with certified organic practices and ranks as one of the largest growers of organic wine grapes in the world.[11] Fetzer recycles virtually all of their waste. According to Dolan, "We don't have wastebaskets anymore. When you finish a meal, you have either a paper basket, a plastic basket, a metal basket, or a scrap food basket—it's gotta fit in one of those."[12]

Dolan formed a partnership to purchase a small Mendocino County, California, winery, Parducci Cellars. Parducci became the first **carbon neutral** winery in the United States, which means that it maintains a balance between the carbon dioxide it produces and the carbon dioxide it uses.[13] It is locally owned and operated; the partners live and work there and so they have a commitment to the community that might not be felt by absentee corporate owners.[14] The vineyard's grapes are organically grown on family farms.[15] In addition, they use solar power and earth-friendly packaging to help them to achieve carbon neutrality.[16] Parducci proclaims that their practices are "right for the planet and right for the wine."[17] Dolan has written a book, *True to Our Roots: Fermenting a Business Revolution*, in which he outlines six principles of sustainable success. These are listed in Figure 15-1.

FIGURE 15-1

Six Principles of Sustainable Success

1. Your business is part of a much larger system.
2. The culture of your business is determined by the context you create for it.
3. The soul of a business is found in the hearts of its people.
4. True power is living what you know.
5. You can't predict the future, but you can create it.
6. There is a way to make an idea's time come.

Source: Paul Dolan, *True to Our Roots: Fermenting a Business Revolution* (New York: Bloomberg Press, 2003).

A Brief Introduction to the Natural Environment

Similar to other broad terms, **environment** means many things to many people—trees in the backyard, a family's favorite vacation spot, a mare and her colt in a pasture, a trout stream in the mountains, earth and the other planets and space objects in our solar system. This chapter focuses on the natural environment—specifically, what it is, why it is important, how it has become a major concern, and what businesses and other organizations have done both to and for it. It identifies what we mean when we use the term *environment* and why it has become one of the most significant societal issues of our time. The chapter also describes the variety of responses human organizations, including businesses, have developed to address this issue. Throughout the chapter, the emphasis is on two themes: that humans are a part of their natural environment and that the environment itself, as well as the issues and human responses related to it, are extremely complex, defying simple analyses.

To assist you in making business environmental decisions in the future, the chapter presents facts and figures, some of which are technical and scientific, related to environmental issues and responses. These facts and figures are included to help you understand the complexities involved in the business and public environmental issues of today. Because of the influence of business, government, and environmental interest groups and individuals, these and many other technical terms and concepts are discussed in the media and, increasingly, in business and society texts. Environmental literacy, whether for business, government, or individual decision making, requires, at minimum, some rudimentary knowledge. Without at least some basic technical information, would-be stakeholder managers abdicate their responsibility to make wise choices potentially critical to the survival of their organizations, as well as to the survival of humans and other species in the natural environment. We call your attention to Figure 15-2, which presents definitions of a few of the most important environmental terms that might be helpful to you now and in the future.

The Impact of Business on the Natural Environment

We will begin with a "top ten" list of environmental issues of today.[18] They are:

1. Climate change
2. Energy
3. Water
4. Biodiversity and land use
5. Chemicals, toxics, and heavy metals
6. Air pollution

FIGURE 15-2 Glossary of Important and Helpful Environmental Terms

Bio-Based Product	A product (other than food or feed) that is composed, in whole or in significant part, of biological products or renewable agricultural or forestry materials.
Environment	Broadly, anything that is external or internal to an entity. For humans, the environment can include external living, working, and playing spaces and natural resources, as well as internal physical, mental, and emotional states.
Carbon Footprint	The total amount of greenhouse gases a person, product, or company emits directly or indirectly.
Carbon Neutral	The maintenance of a balance between producing and using carbon dioxide.
Carrying Capacity	The volume of and intensity of use by organisms that can be sustained in a particular place and at a particular time without degrading the environment's future suitability for that use. A resource's carrying capacity has limits that need to be respected for continued use.
Entropy	A measure of disorder of energy, indicating its unavailability for recycling for the same use. Energy tends to break down into lower quality with each use. For instance, a kilowatt of electricity, once it is produced and consumed, can never be used as electricity again and, if stored, will allow far less than 1 kW to be consumed.
Ecosystem	All living and nonliving substances present in a particular place, often interacting with others.
Threshold	The point at which a particular phenomenon, previously suppressed, suddenly begins to be activated. For instance, when a population's carrying capacity threshold is exceeded, the population tends to decrease or even crash as a result of increased morbidity and mortality.
Irreversibility	The inability of humans and nature to restore environmental conditions to a previous state within relevant time frames. Human environment-related actions that appear irreversible are the destruction of a rainforest or wilderness area and the extinction of a species.

7. Waste management
8. Ozone layer depletion
9. Oceans and fisheries
10. Deforestation

Each is discussed briefly to give the reader a sense of the issue's complexity and its current status.

Climate Change

No environmental issue has been more contentious than has the subject of **climate change**, which is also known as **global warming** because scientists expect the **greenhouse effect** (i.e., the prevention of solar heat absorbed by our atmosphere from returning to space) to precipitate an unprecedented rate of warming.[19] The debate about climate change's existence has lessened dramatically due to a combination of factors, including Hurricane Katrina, a European heat wave, starving polar bears, and stronger scientific predictions.[20] Climatologists now say with some certainty that human activities are warming the earth at a dangerous level. The Intergovernmental Panel on Climate Change placed the probability that human activities are creating climate change at greater than 90 percent. Just six years earlier, the probability was determined to be 60 percent.[21] The increased confidence in their estimation stems from a longer period of data collected and a greater understanding of the climate system; those two factors have led to more reliable climate models.[22] As discussed in Chapter 12, some CEOs felt so strongly about climate change that they severed ties with the U.S. Chamber of

Commerce. Apple, PG&E, Exelon, and PNM Resources all quit the Chamber, and Nike withdrew from its board, because of the Chamber's opposition to efforts to regulate carbon emissions.[23]

The possibility of a swift and radical change in climate is so sufficiently real that the U.S. Department of Defense highlighted its implications in their 2010 *Quadrennial Review*.[24] They reported that "although they produce distinct types of challenges, climate change, energy security, and economic stability are inextricably linked."[25] They went on to say that "while climate change alone does not cause conflict, it may act as an accelerant of instability or conflict, placing a burden to respond on civilian institutions and militaries around the world."[26] The U.S. military takes climate change sufficiently seriously that the Pentagon's strategic planners have been actively developing responses to various scenarios.[27] None of these facts have had more impact, however, than the release of the movie, *An Inconvenient Truth*. Presented by former U.S. Vice President Al Gore and directed by David Guggenheim, the film won the Academy Award for best documentary and earned $49 million, making it the third-highest-grossing documentary in history. Gore released a companion book that spent 38 weeks on the *New York Times* Best Seller List, with four weeks at No. 1.[28] Skeptics denounced the movie and its accompanying book as misleading and inaccurate.[29] However, the generally positive reaction to its powerful message gave climate change a center stage from which it has not retreated.

Climate change is contentious because both the cost of addressing the issue and the cost of *not* addressing the issue are likely to be quite high.[30] Unpredictable weather, along with an increase in temperature, threatens a range of industries from agriculture to airlines to ski resorts. Natural disasters have cost insurance companies ten times more now than in the 1950s. To mitigate this risk, reinsurance companies like Swiss Re and Munich Re have lobbied for action on climate change.[31] Europe and Japan regulate greenhouse emissions now, and the United States is expected to regulate emissions in the near future. The Obama administration has declared climate change legislation as one of its goals, and Senators John Kerry (Democratic), Joseph Lieberman (Independent), and Lindsay Graham (Republican) are working together to design a bill that could gain bipartisan support.[32] The effort is nevertheless being described in the press as a "last ditch effort" and a "Hail Mary" because the many other issues confronting Congress make it an uphill battle.[33] Nevertheless, observers believe the climate change efforts will continue and that the 2010 bill will form the starting point for negotiations in 2011, if it fails to pass in 2010.[34]

Figure 15-3 shows growth in global carbon dioxide emissions, measured in million metric tons, from 1900 to 2006.

Energy

A major environmental issue is **energy inefficiency**, or the wasting of precious nonrenewable sources of energy. Nonrenewable energy sources, such as coal, oil, and natural gas, were formed millions of years ago under unique conditions of temperature, pressure, and biological phenomena (hence the term **fossil fuels**). Once these are depleted, they will be gone forever. In addition, because these fuels are not equally distributed around the world, they are the cause of significant power imbalances worldwide, with associated armed conflicts that are typically disastrous for both humans and the natural environment in general.[35] As India, China, and other fast-growth areas in the developing world increase their demand for energy, the depletion of fossil fuels is happening at a quickening pace.

Part of the answer to the nonrenewability problem is to use as little as possible of these energy sources through implementation of sound energy conservation practices.

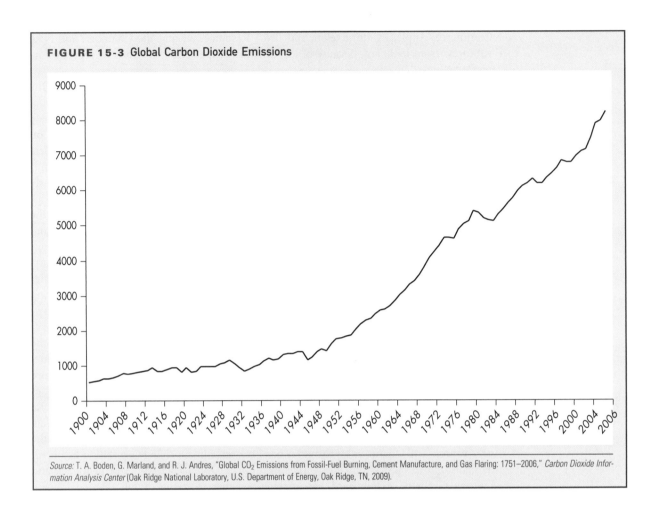

FIGURE 15-3 Global Carbon Dioxide Emissions

Source: T. A. Boden, G. Marland, and R. J. Andres, "Global CO₂ Emissions from Fossil-Fuel Burning, Cement Manufacture, and Gas Flaring: 1751–2006," *Carbon Dioxide Information Analysis Center* (Oak Ridge National Laboratory, U.S. Department of Energy, Oak Ridge, TN, 2009).

In addition, shifting to renewable energy sources, such as solar, wind, hydroelectric, and biomass, is important for both industrial and agricultural societies. Several technologies for tapping these renewable, low-polluting energy sources are becoming economically competitive with nonrenewable sources.[36] However, even though proponents argue that solar and wind power are ready for mass utilization, only 7 percent of the United States' energy supply comes from renewable sources. The remaining 93 percent comes from petroleum (37 percent), natural gas (24 percent), coal (23 percent), and nuclear energy (8 percent).[37] This may change as businesses begin to realize the economic value of sustainable practices. Walmart has put a variety of initiatives in place, including renewable energy at stores, reduced waste in packaging, and a sustainability index with which it ranks its suppliers' practices.[38] CEO Lee Green said it was for "business purposes and not for altruism," otherwise they would have scaled back during the recession.[39]

For business, the energy issue represents not only a challenge but also an opportunity. Opportunities for new businesses abound as the demand for renewable energy rises. Many states now mandate that utilities obtain a minimum percentage of their energy supply through renewable energy and companies ranging from Johnson & Johnson to Fed Ex and Starbucks have committed to buying a portion of their energy from renewable sources.[40] Analysts note that venture capital maintained investments in renewable energy in spite of the economic crisis.[41] A Cleantech Group/Deloitte LLC report found that green ventures in North America, China, Europe, and India totaled $5.6 billion through 557 deals.[42] With the money now flowing into "clean tech" funds that focus mainly on renewable sources of energy, firms are scrambling to determine how to get a piece of the pie. Not every firm will succeed in this arena but those that do stand to reap huge profits.[43]

Water

Water presents problems in both quality and quantity. The developed world has made significant progress in the quality of water—no longer are waterways so polluted that they risk catching on fire as the Cuyahoga River did in Cleveland in 1969.[44] Neverthe-less, municipal sewage, industrial wastes, urban runoff, agricultural runoff, atmospheric fallout, and overharvesting all continue to contribute to the degradation of the world's oceans and waterways. So too do dam sedimentation, deforestation, overgrazing, and overirrigation. The quality of the developing world's water quality is in far worse shape than that in the developed world. A staggering 90 to 95 percent of sewage and 70 percent of industrial waste is untreated as it flows into rivers, lakes, and the ocean.[45] More than a billion people worldwide lack clean water and the problem shows no signs of abating.[46]

Beyond the problem with pollution, experts now warn that the world is facing a "water bankruptcy."[47] The earth is a closed system with a water supply that is fixed, so as populations grow and crop irrigation increases, supplies become depleted. Pollution renders existing water unusable, further diminishing the supply. A global water crisis brought on by a combination of drought, pollution, mismanagement, and politics has thus developed.[48] No country, no matter how big, is immune from this crisis. In the United States, the giant Ogallala Aquifer, which lies under parts of eight states, is dimin-ishing dramatically due to heavy demand.[49] In China, the Yangtze River is so heavily polluted that a recent World Wildlife Fund report declared the damage to the river's eco-system to be largely irreversible.[50] The Yellow River has slowed to a trickle for much of the year, leaving nearly 400 million Chinese people, one-third of the country's popula-tion, without access to clean water.[51] In India, two-thirds of the 1.1 billion population lack clean water, and the water table drops six to ten feet each year. More than half the people in the world could be living in severely water-stressed areas by 2030 if current trends continue.[52] This water bankruptcy poses a bigger threat than the global financial crisis.[53]

Biodiversity and Land Use

An ecosystem's **biodiversity**, that is, the variation of life forms inside the system, serves as a key indicator of its health. The United Nations declared 2010 as the International Year of Biodiversity but H.E. Dr. Ali Abdussalam Treki, President of the United Nations General Assembly, found little to celebrate when he addressed the gathering. He said, "Biodiversity continues to be lost at an unprecedented rate, thus threatening the capacity of the planet to provide the required goods and services. The current rate of extinction is estimated to be 1,000 times higher than the natural rate."[54] Throughout most of time, species lived an average of one million years, with species dying out at the rate of about one species per million years. Ecosystem and habitat destruction through agricultural and urban development activities and, of course, pollution have put at risk both wildlife and beneficial plants. Excesses in individual and organizational activities are responsible for significant and tragic ecosystem and species degradation.

Another disturbing environmental issue that human populations face is land degrada-tion. Degradation includes such different multiple facets as desertification, deforestation, overgrazing, salinization, and alkalization. Soil acidification, urban sprawl, and soil seal-ing, or industrial soil contamination, are part of land degradation as well. According to

Dr. Treki, "Seventy per cent of the world's poor live in rural areas. They depend directly on biological resources for as much as 90 per cent of their needs such as food, fuel, medicine, shelter, and transportation. Over three billion people depend on marine and coastal biodiversity, while more than 1.6 billion rely on forests and non-timber forest products for their livelihoods. The degradation of habitat and the loss of biodiversity are threatening the livelihoods of more than one billion people living in dry and subhumid lands, particularly in Africa, the continent most affected by drought and desertificatication."[55] As the population of the world continues to grow, the problems created by the loss of productive soil will only increase.

Chemicals, Toxics, and Heavy Metals

The production of **toxic substances**, whether as constituents of intended products or as unwanted by-products, is an important issue because of its potential for harm. The United States Environmental Protection Agency (EPA) defines toxic substances as chemicals or compounds that may present an unreasonable threat to human health and the environment. Human exposure to toxic substances can cause a variety of health effects, including damage to the nervous system, reproductive and developmental problems, cancer, and genetic disorders.[56]

Two problems are central to the toxic substances issue. First, we are not always aware of the effects, especially the long-term and interactive effects, of exposure to the thousands of chemicals produced each year. Even in those instances where the toxicity of a chemical is known and the chemical is banned for sale in a country, such as the pesticide DDT in the United States, the substance can still be manufactured in that country and exported, only to return when products that have been exposed to these substances are imported. As we discussed in the previous chapter, strict and absolute liability doctrines hold firms to a high degree of accountability for the effects of toxic substances.

Second, toxic substances can be associated with industrial accidents, causing unforeseen widespread biological damage. The Bhopal, India, chemical plant leak; the Chernobyl nuclear power plant meltdown in the former Soviet Union; and the *Exxon Valdez* 11-million-gallon oil spill in Alaska are three well-known environmental disasters involving toxic substances. Not so well known are the 14,000 oil spills reported each year.[57] Although the *Exxon Valdez* spill covered 1,300 miles of Alaskan shoreline and was as wide as three football fields, that spill was only 53rd in the rankings of worldwide oil spills.[58] In 2010, the U.S. National Oceanic and Atmospheric Administration filed a notice of intent to prepare a supplementary environmental impact statement, noting that nearly 100 metric tons (or 23,000 gallons) of oil remain in the Prince William Sound area 20 years after the *Valdez* spill and continue to wreak havoc on the marine life in the area.[59] The BP deep-sea well in the Gulf of Mexico was permanently killed in September 2010, but not before creating the worst oil spill in U.S. history. The extent of the damage is yet unknown, but it will be far worse than the *Valdez* spill and the United States' "worst environmental disaster in decades."[60]

Air Pollution

The short- and long-term effects of both outdoor and indoor **air pollution** are wide-ranging and severe.[61] Air pollution leads to acid rain, global warming, smog, the depletion of the ozone layer are other serious conditions. It also causes serious respiratory and other illnesses, so it is not surprising that it rates high in concern according to public opinion polls.[62]

In addition to causing human health problems, ambient air pollution is also responsible for a condition called **acid rain**. Acid rain refers broadly to a mixture of wet and dry deposition (deposited material) from the atmosphere containing higher than normal amounts of nitric and sulfuric acids.[63] Both natural sources, such as volcanoes and decaying vegetation, and artificial sources, primarily emissions of sulfur dioxide and nitrogen oxides from fossil fuel combustion, can lead to acid rain.[64] Acid rain causes acidification of lakes and streams, contributes to the damage of trees at high elevations, and accelerates the decay of building materials and paints, including irreplaceable buildings and statues. Before falling to the earth, acid rain degrades visibility and harms public health.[65]

Indoor air pollution is another environmental problem that is becoming an increasing concern, because most people spend the majority of their lives indoors. Indoor air pollution has a variety of sources, including oil, gas, kerosene, coal, wood, and tobacco products, and building materials and furnishings such as asbestos-containing insulation, damp carpets, household cleaning products, and lead-based paints.[66] The immediate effects of indoor air pollution are typically short term and treatable; these include irritation of the eyes, nose, and throat, headaches, dizziness, and fatigue. However, longer-term effects that might show up years after exposure can be severely debilitating or fatal. These effects include some respiratory diseases, heart disease, and cancer.[67]

Waste Management

Reduce, Reuse, and Recycle is the waste management mantra. The first goal is to reduce the amount of waste discarded, that is, source reduction; this is the best form of waste management because in this case the waste is never generated in the first place. The next best option is to reuse containers and products—either repairing anything that is broken or giving it to someone who can repair it. Reusing is preferable to recycling because it does not require reprocessing to make the item usable again. Recycling is the third best option but still very valuable. Recycling transforms what once might have been waste into a valuable resource.

In the middle of all the dire news about environmental issues, recycling stands out as a success story. Throughout the world, recycling efforts have grown. Today Sweden recycles 90 percent of its glass and Japan recycles 86 percent of its steel.[68] The United States recycles about 20 percent of its glass, 40 percent of its paper, 50 percent of aluminum, and 60 percent of steel.[69] Business can profit greatly from the boon in recycling. By recycling, businesses are able to cut costs—producing less garbage means lower landfill fees. These efforts also present new business opportunities for the entrepreneur. The *Fortune* 100 list of fastest-growing firms includes firms that recycle scrap metal into steel.[70] Figure 15-4 shows the growth rate of per capita waste generation in the United States as it compares to the rate of recycling. Waste generation is measured in ten-pound units to facilitate comparison with the waste that was recycled. Both lines have some good news to offer. While per capita waste generation rose steadily until 2000, it has remained stable ever since. Recycling rates have continually increased.

Special consideration must be given to waste that is hazardous. Hazardous waste has properties that make it harmful or potentially harmful to human health or the environment. As defined by the EPA, the large and diverse world of hazardous waste includes liquids, solids, contained gases, or sludges.[71] Hazardous wastes can be generated by manufacturing processes, or they can simply result from discarded commercial products, such as cleaning fluids or pesticides.[72] The risk posed by these wastes creates countless causes for concern. Exposure to these wastes in the environment, whether in air, water, food, or soil, can cause cancer, birth defects, and a host of other problems.[73] Because of tightening of site controls in some areas, hazardous wastes are sometimes transported, both legally and illegally, away from their sources to sites with weaker controls.[74]

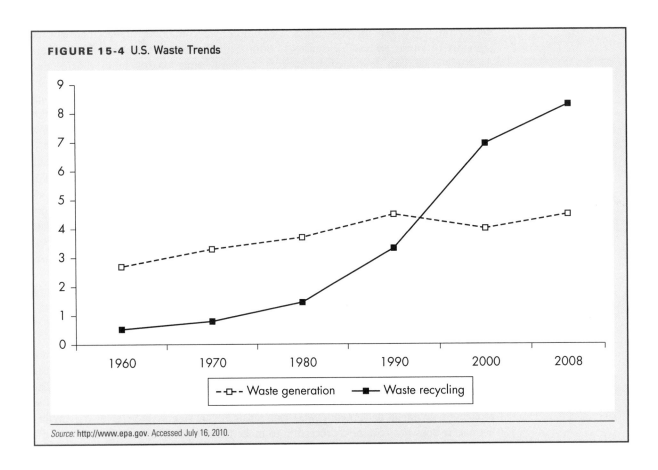

FIGURE 15-4 U.S. Waste Trends

- - □ - - Waste generation   ■ Waste recycling

Source: http://www.epa.gov. Accessed July 16, 2010.

Another concern is the toxicological effects of a number of new chemicals coming onto the market. Because they are new, we know less about their effects and the measures needed to protect human health and the environment from possible contamination.[75]

Ozone Depletion

Ozone is an oxygen-related gas that is harmful to life near the earth's surface but is vital in the stratosphere in blocking dangerous ultraviolet radiation from the sun. Over 20 years ago, NASA scientists observed a huge decrease in ozone over Antarctica. They then discovered a "hole" in the ozone layer that had grown as large as the North American continent. Their measurements showed that the flow of ultraviolet light had increased directly under the ozone hole. This phenomenon was attributed to human-produced chemicals—chlorofluorocarbons (CFCs), used in refrigeration, and halons, used in fire extinguisher systems, as well as other ozone-depleting chemicals. A thinner layer of ozone is associated with a higher rate of skin cancer and other illnesses, as well as an increase in problems with agricultural production.

The international community enacted strict controls on the use of these gasses through the 1987 United Nations Montreal Protocol. Charles Kolb, an atmospheric research specialist and president of Aerodyne, noted, "We're all feeling very proud of the fact that we identified the problem and then the international community responded."[76] However, a rift in the international community eventually formed. The Bush administration requested that an exemption be given for methyl bromide because they were concerned that U.S. strawberry farmers would not be able to compete effectively with Mexican farmers if they were unable to use that chemical.[77] Since then, however, the international community has moved in greater unison, with the Protocol having been ratified by over 190 countries. The United States was one of several countries to push for an earlier date for phasing out the ozone damaging chemicals.[78]

Although production of CFCs has been reduced, output is growing in developing countries such as China and India.[79] Great improvements have been made, but the ozone crisis is not yet over. Early estimates were too optimistic and so scientists have now revised their predictions to say that the health of the Antarctic ozone layer will not return to pre-1980 levels until 2065, 15 years later than first predicted.[80] Recently, the ozone hole grew to a record size. According to Paul Newman, atmospheric scientist at NASA's Goddard Space Flight Center, Greenbelt, Maryland, "From September 21 to 30, 2006, the average area of the ozone hole was the largest ever observed, at 10.6 million square miles."[81] Since then it has diminished slightly but not sufficiently to signify health.[82] For those interested in observing the hole in process, NASA provides "Ozone Watch" (http://ozonewatch.gsfc.nasa.gov/index.html), a Web site with pictures created from satellite images that enable observers to check on the latest status of the ozone layer over the South Pole.

Oceans and Fisheries

The EPA expresses it well by saying we all live in a **watershed**—an area that drains to a common waterway, such as a stream, lake, estuary, wetland, aquifer, or even the ocean.[83] Our actions affect the oceans and other waterways, and so far, it has not been for the better. Many of the same factors that affect fresh water have an impact on the marine environments. Each year, trillions of gallons of sewage and industrial waste are dumped into marine waters. These and other pollutants, such as oil and plastics, have been associated with significant damage to a number of coastal ecosystems, including salt marshes, mangrove swamps, estuaries, and coral reefs. The result has been local and regional shellfish bed closures, seafood-related illnesses, and reduced shoreline protection from floods and storms. Toxic and nutrient runoffs are resulting in algae blooms; trawling is destroying the sea floor; and climate change is warming the waters, causing coral reefs to die.[84]

Once it would have been inconceivable that the vast oceans would ever run short of fish to meet human needs. However, some observers believe that day may soon be coming. Recently, a team of 13 researchers in four countries studied over 50 years of global catch and other data to arrive at an unimaginable conclusion—by the middle of this century, overfishing will have destroyed the world's seafood supply.[85] Some industry experts find that prediction to be too pessimistic. While they acknowledge that a continuation of today's practices would lead to that outcome, they argue about whether increased awareness will keep the dire prediction from coming true.[86] The jury is still out, but there is something that both businesses and consumers can do to lessen the likelihood of an end to the world's seafood supply—only use or sell sustainably harvested seafood. Nearly 500 products bear the "Fish Forever" label of approval.[87] Retailers such as Red Lobster and Walmart have committed to buying only sustainably harvested seafood.[88]

The return of the Chesapeake Blue Crab bodes well for these efforts. A variety of efforts such as shortening the crabbing season, instituting a crabber license buyback program, and not permitting the raking of hibernating pregnant females from the bay floor have yielded promising results.[89] The 2010 Winter Dredge Survey estimated the blue crab population at 658 million, which was 235 percent of the 280 million found in the 2008 survey. EPA Administrator Lisa Jackson said it was "an important indicator of some improvement in the ecosystem." She also said the EPA is preparing a bay

Spotlight on SUSTAINABILITY

There's an App for That

In the midst of the economic downturn, sustainability software has become a huge growth market. More than $46 million in venture capital was invested in carbon-accounting software in 2009. With increased interest in sustainability reporting and major buyers such as Walmart requiring suppliers to show proof of sustainable practices, companies are looking for ways to improve and monitor their environmental impacts. At the same time, individuals are increasingly interested in achieving a more sustainable lifestyle. Software manufacturers have been designing apps for smart phones to make that task easier.

Greeenpeace Tissue Guide:

With a reminder that more than 400,000 trees could be saved if each family in the U.S. replaced one roll of virgin toilet paper in their home with a roll of recycled toilet paper, the Greenpeace Tissue Guide tells consumers which tissues and other paper products are green and which should be avoided.

The Find Green App:

Using the phone's GPS locater, Find Green will locate nearby businesses that specialize in sustainability and healthy living, and it will provide turn-by-turn directions to the business's location. A broad range of businesses are listed, including restaurants, yoga studios, grocery stores, and theaters. Users can specify whether the search should be for businesses in walking, biking, or driving distance from the user's location.

Seafood Watch:

This project of the Monterey Bay Aquarium strives to inform consumers about the fishing practices that are depleting fish populations, destroying habitats, and polluting the oceans. The Seafood Watch app lets consumers search for seafood and sushi so that they can make sustainable seafood choices.

Locavore:

Eating local food is not only a way to enjoy the freshest food available but also a way to reduce one's carbon footprint by minimizing transportation. Locavore identifies the foods that are currently in season, as well as those that are coming into season soon. They also provide information about the directions to local farmer's markets.

Sources: Tracy De Morsella, "Carbon Accounting Software Market Experiencing Huge Period of Growth," *FastCompany.com* (March 1, 2010), http://www.fastcompany.com/1565844/carbon-accounting-software-market-experiencing-tremendous-growth; http://www.3rdwhale.com/apps; http://www.montereybayaquarium.org/cr/SeafoodWatch/web/sfw_iphone.aspx; http://enjoymentland.com/locavore/. Accessed July 16, 2010.

restoration strategy in response to an executive order issued by President Obama that will establish limits for various pollutants. Jackson praised the efforts of Maryland and Virginia, saying they have "shown tremendous leadership in following the science and making the tough decisions that have built a strong foundation for the work ahead."[90]

Deforestation

Although humans depend on forests for building materials, fuel, medicines, chemicals, food, employment, and recreation, the world's forests can be quickly depleted by a variety of human factors. **Deforestation** adds to soil erosion problems and is a major cause of the greenhouse effect. Felled trees are no longer able to absorb carbon dioxide and are sometimes burned for land clearing and charcoal, thereby releasing rather than absorbing carbon dioxide. Moisture and nutrient ecosystem cycles can also be severely damaged in deforesting activities, negatively affecting adjacent land and water ecosystems.

Deforestation is a problem for developed and developing countries alike. A tree conservation group, American Forests, studied the financial impact of deforestation in the greater Baltimore–Washington, DC, area and assessed the economic impact of its consequences.[91] Trees slow the movement of storm water and reduce the risk of flooding. The study showed that deforestation in Baltimore–Washington resulted in a 19 percent increase in storm water flow. Replacing the storm water flow capabilities of these trees with engineered systems such as reservoirs would cost over $1 billion. The dwindling tree canopy also made it more difficult to remove approximately 9.3 million pounds of pollutants from the air. The cost of air quality control to make up for this loss would be about $24 million over 24 years.[92]

Deforestation plays a key role in global warming. Few would be able to guess which country makes the third greatest greenhouse gas emissions after China and the United States. Most would guess Germany because of its industry or Japan because of its cities and high technology. The right answer is Indonesia; it releases 3.3 billion tons of carbon dioxide a year because of deforestation.[93] Trees absorb carbon dioxide when they are alive and when they die they release it into the air. As a result, deforestation accounts for 20 percent of global carbon emissions—more than the world's trains, boats, and planes combined.[94]

Responsibility for Environmental Issues

Problems such as smog, toxic waste, and acid rain can be described as "**wicked problems**"—that is, problems with characteristics such as interconnectedness, complexity, uncertainty, ambiguity, conflict, and societal constraints. Every wicked problem seems to be a symptom of another problem.[95] Responsibility for such messy situations is difficult to affix, because solutions to wicked problems are seldom complete and final and, therefore, credit for these solutions is seldom given or taken. *Chlorofluorocarbons*, or *CFCs*, for example, were once considered safe alternatives to other, more toxic refrigerants, which is why these ozone destroyers are so ubiquitous in our society's technologies.

When no one takes responsibility, a phenomenon called the **tragedy of the commons** is likely to occur.[96] A "commons" is a plot of land available to all. When the commons is large enough to accommodate the needs of everyone, no problems occur. However, as herders continue to add animals to their herds, the carrying capacity of the commons becomes strained. It is in the self-interest of each herder to allow the animals to graze, even though the cumulative grazing will inevitably destroy the commons. The analogy of a "commons" can be applied to the environment as a whole as well as its many constituent parts. One need only look at the situation with public parks to see how unconstrained use (e.g., vehicles driving anywhere or unrestrained picking of vegetation) can damage a shared resource. As Garrett Hardin points out in his classic article on the tragedy of the commons in the environment, constraints must also be placed on the use of the commons (i.e., our environment) because in the absence of constraints, self-interest is likely to lead individuals and organizations to behave in ways that will not sustain our shared resources.[97]

Environmental Ethics

Nature itself is a polluter and destroyer. The earth's core is continually polluting many bodies of water and airsheds with a full range of toxic heavy metals. The 2010 eruption of Iceland's Eyjafjallajökull volcano melted glaciers, forcing people to flee rising floodwaters, and spewed clouds of dust into the air, snarling air traffic and stranding millions of passengers. Species have been going extinct since life evolved as, in a continuous cycle of life and death, nature acts as its own destroyer. Given this fact, what does absolute human environmental sensitivity mean? Humans must consume at least some plants and water to survive. If humans and their organizations need to pollute and destroy at least some of nature for their survival, what is the relative level of degradation that is ethical? Do nonhuman species have any "rights," and, if so, what are they, and how can they be reconciled with human rights? Concerning human rights and the environment, how do we assess the claims of indigenous cultures to the use of their respective environments? Is there any connection between the domination of humans by humans (e.g., the domination of one nation, race, or gender by another) and the domination of nature by humans? This latter question is especially central to several schools of environmental ethical thought, including social ecology, ecofeminism, and environmental justice.

Whose standards will determine what is or is not ethical? Public opinion in the United States seems to have been affected by the economic crisis. In a 2010 Gallup poll, concern about the environment had hit a 20-year low.[98] However, how much the public will do itself or insist that governments and businesses do to protect the environment is still an unanswered question. How clean do the air and water need to be, and how much is the public willing to pay to meet these standards? As in our earlier discussion of business ethics, values play a major role and can be highly variable in breadth and depth across perspectives, situations, and time.

Following the ethical models discussed in Chapters 7 and 8, we can develop a better idea of what environmental ethics is and how it can be practiced. Kohlberg's model of moral development, for instance, can be used to identify environment-related attitudes and behaviors by developmental level. At the preconventional (infant) level in environmental ethics, humans and human organizations can be perceived as being concerned only with self or with their own species and habitats. A conventional (adolescent) level might entail some appreciation of nature, but only when and where such appreciation is commonplace or "in." A postconventional (adult) environmental ethic might include more mature attitudes and behaviors that are more universal (including all species and habitats), of greater duration (including unborn generations), and more consistent (if we humans have a right to survive as a species, why don't all species have that right?).

Similarly, the moral principle of utilitarianism—the greatest good for the greatest number—could be expanded in environmental ethics to the greatest good for the greatest numbers of species and ecosystems. The Golden Rule could read, "Do unto other species as you would have them do unto you." From a virtue ethics perspective, a "Best Self" ethical test could include the question, "Is this action or decision related to the natural environment compatible not only with my concept of myself at my best but also with my concept of myself as a human representing my species at its best?"

In *Who Speaks for the Trees*, authors Sama, Welcomer, and Gerde show that integrating sustainability into a firm's philosophy is a natural extension of stakeholder theory.[99] They expand the concept of the natural environment beyond living things to the entire ecological system from which the firm obtains resources and to which it bears responsibility for the impacts, both positive and negative, that firm actions have on it. They invoke the ethic of care, discussed in Chapter 8, and explain that organizations that follow a practice of care would treat the natural environment, which they call the "silent stakeholder," with respect.[100]

The NIMBY Problem

One example of this question of responsibility is the **NIMBY**, or "Not in My Back Yard," phenomenon. This acronym, which can be found on bumper stickers and conference

---

ETHICS IN PRACTICE CASE

Going Down the Drain

I worked at a small business that used cars in their daily deliveries. To save money, the brothers who owned the business would conduct most of their own maintenance on the vehicles. As a result, they would periodically be involved in doing tune-ups, changing oil, and other such activities. One day, I noticed that the brothers would pour the old motor oil down the drain rather than take it for recycling. This troubled me because I knew how greatly old oil can add to the degradation of the environment. I brought up the subject with them and they laughed it off. They told me that, as a small business, they did not have the time or the money to be concerned with the "niceties" of life. We discussed it several times, and they made it clear they would not change their ways.

I didn't know what to do. I liked this job. The location was perfect and the people were nice (in every other way). I wanted to keep working there until I finished school. However, I felt that I shared in the responsibility for the damage caused by the oil if I knew it was happening and did nothing about it. If I reported it to someone, I knew they'd know the report came from me. What could I do?

1. Is NIMBY involved here? If so, in what way?
2. Do you share in the responsibility for negative action when you know it is happening and say nothing?
3. What would you do if you were in that position?

Contributed Anonymously

---

agendas and in newspaper articles, college courses, and many other communication vehicles, reflects human denial of responsibility for the misuse of the environment. The growth of the NIMBY attitude can be seen in the proliferation of other acronyms describing it. *NOTE* or "Not Over There Either," *BANANA* or "Build Absolutely Nothing Near Anything," and *NOPE* or "Not On Planet Earth" were all coined by observers frustrated with the human tendency to avoid assuming responsibility for societal costs.

Examples of NIMBY abound. One is the community that uses ever-increasing amounts of electricity but decides it does not want a power plant that produces electricity to locate near its homes and schools. Another is a company that generates increasing amounts of waste but is unwilling to pay the full cost of proper disposal. Recently, NIMBY attitudes almost scuttled the United States' first offshore wind farm off the coast of Cape Cod.[101] The project was approved by the Obama administration but, despite over nine years since work on the project began, still faces court tests ahead.[102] Essentially, NIMBY is an attitude or behavior set based on avoidance or denial of responsibility. When applied to the field of environmental management, NIMBY spells big trouble.

The obvious difficulty with the NIMBY syndrome is that the entities (human individuals, organizations, or both) causing environmental pollution or degradation are not identified as the sources of the problem, and therefore no action is taken to reduce the problem. The NIMBY phenomenon avoids or denies the root cause of the damage and addresses only the symptoms with an attitude of nonresponsibility characterized by an approach of "I'll create an environmental problem, but I want to have as little as possible to do with solving it." One popular cartoon characterizing the NIMBY problem pictures a stream of polluting, honking cars passing along a highway in front of a huge billboard that reads "Honk if you love the environment!"

The Role of Governments in Environmental Issues

As we mentioned earlier, governments have played major roles in environmental issues since the inception of such issues. Governments have procured, distributed, and developed habitable lands and other resources; protected, taxed, and zoned natural environment-based areas and, more recently, exercised regulatory control over how those environments could be used. This section looks at how governments in the United States have dealt with environmental challenges and then identifies what has been done in several other countries and at the international level.

Responses of Governments in the United States

Although the U.S. federal government has influenced environmental policy since at least 1899, with its permit requirement for discharge of hazardous materials into navigable waters, the major entrance of the U.S. government into environmental issues occurred in 1970 with the signing of PL 91-190, the National Environmental Policy Act (NEPA). The second section of this act spells out its purposes: "To declare a national policy which will encourage productive and enjoyable harmony between man and his environment; to promote efforts which will prevent or eliminate damage to the environment and biosphere and stimulate the health and welfare of man; and to enrich the understanding of the ecological systems and natural resources important to the Nation."[103]

In addition to establishing these broad policy goals, this legislation requires federal agencies to prepare **environmental impact statements (EISs)** for any "proposals for legislation and other major federal action significantly affecting the quality of the human environment." Environmental impact statements are reports of studies explaining and estimating the environmental impacts of questionable practices and irreversible uses of resources and proposing detailed, reasonable alternatives to these practices and uses.

Business is affected by the NEPA in several ways. First, the federal government pays private consultants to conduct tens of billions of dollars worth of EISs each year. Second, because the federal government is the largest landholder in the United States, private businesses wishing to secure licenses and permits to conduct timber, grazing, mining, and highway, dam, and nuclear construction operations likely will be parties to the preparation of EISs. Third, private businesses working under federal government contracts are typically obliged to participate in EIS preparation. Fourth, the NEPA has been used as a model by many state governments, and therefore businesses heavily involved in significant state and local government contracts are likely to be involved in the EIS process.

Also in 1970, the U.S. **Environmental Protection Agency (EPA)** was created as an independent agency to research pollution problems, aid state and local government environmental efforts, and administer many of the federal environmental laws. These laws can be categorized into three areas—air, water, and land—even though a specific problem of pollution and/or degradation, such as acid rain, often involves two or more of these categories.

Air Quality Legislation.   The key piece of federal air quality legislation, called the **Clean Air Act**, was significantly amended in 1990, and there have been smaller changes since then.[104] The overall approach of this act is similar to that used in other areas of federal regulation, such as safety and health legislation, in that standards are set and timetables for implementation are established. In the Clean Air Act, there are two kinds of standards: primary standards, which are designed to protect human health, and secondary standards, which are intended to protect property, vegetation, climate, and aesthetic values. The EPA has set primary standards (based on health effects) and secondary standards (based on environmental effects) for a variety of air pollutants, including lead, particulates, hydrocarbons, sulfur dioxide, and nitrogen oxide. Businesses that directly produce these substances, such as electric utilities, and those whose products when used cause these substances to be produced, such as automobiles, must reduce their emissions to within the set standards.[105]

The Clean Air Act introduced the concept of **emissions trading** (i.e., "**cap and trade**") to the United States. This approach is intended to reduce a particular pollutant over an entire industrial region by treating all emission sources as if they were all beneath one bubble. A business can increase its emissions of sulfur dioxide in one part of a plant or region if it reduces its sulfur dioxide pollution by as much or more in another part of the plant or region. In addition, and as an extension of this bubble analogy, businesses that reduce their emissions can trade these rights to other businesses that want to increase their emissions. Proponents of emissions credit trading hail these policies as free market environmentalism, whereas opponents ridicule them as licenses to pollute.

Although it was once highly controversial, emissions trading has become one of the fastest-growing financial services, with a London market worth about $127 billion in 2009 and expected to reach $1.4 trillion by 2020.[106] The interest in emissions trading is quite recent. In 2004, former electricity trader Louis Redshaw met with five investment banks to propose carbon dioxide trading. Only one was interested. Three years later, the situation had changed, and carbon specialists like Redshaw, 34, were among the rising stars in the London financial district. According to Redshaw, head of environmental markets at Barclay Capital, "'Carbon will be the world's biggest commodity market, and it could become the world's biggest market over all."[107]

The emissions trading system is part of the Kyoto Protocol, an international agreement that set legally binding targets and deadlines for cutting the greenhouse gas emissions of industrialized countries.[108] Few knew, however, that emissions trading would become such a thriving market. According to Chris Leeds, head of emissions trading at Merrill Lynch, carbon could become "one of the fasting-growing markets ever, with volumes comparable to credit derivatives inside of a decade."[109] In the early decade, Wall Street firms had begun investing in credit-generating projects. However, when the United States government refused to submit the Kyoto Protocol for ratification in 2001, New York lost its lead in the area.[110] According to Garth Edward of Shell Trading, "Technically, U.S. companies had the expertise. Then the Europeans really delivered."[111] Emissions trading continues to be a contentious issue in the United States. The House of Representatives passed cap and trade legislation in 2009 but it stalled in the Senate.[112] The Obama administration supports putting a price on carbon, but the climate change legislation being crafted by Senators Kerry, Lieberman, and Graham is likely to separate the cap and trade issue in order to achieve a bipartisan compromise.[113]

Water Quality Legislation.   U.S. government involvement in water quality issues has followed a pattern similar to that of air quality issues. The **Clean Water Act** (also known as the Federal Water Pollution Control Act) was passed in the early 1970s with broad environmental quality goals and an implementation system, involving both the federal and state governments, designed to attain those goals. The ultimate purpose of the Clean Water Act was to achieve water quality consistent with protection of fish, shellfish, and wildlife and with safe conditions for human recreation in and on the water. The more tangible goal was to eliminate discharges of pollutants into navigable waters, which include most U.S. rivers, streams, and lakes. These goals were to be accomplished through a pollution permit system, called the National Pollutant Discharge Elimination System, which specifies maximum permissible discharge levels, and often timetables for installation of state-of-the-art pollution control equipment. Another act—the Marine

Protection, Research, and Sanctuaries Act of 1972—sets up a similar system for control of discharges into coastal ocean waters within U.S. territory. A third water quality law administered by the EPA, the Safe Drinking Water Act of 1974, establishes maximum contaminant levels for drinking water.[114]

Land-Related Legislation.   Land pollution and degradation issues differ from air and water quality issues, because land by definition is far less fluid and therefore somewhat more visible than air and water and is more amenable to local or regional problem-solving approaches. Consequently, the U.S. federal government, in the Solid Waste Disposal Act of 1965, recognized that regional, state, and local governments should have the main responsibility for nontoxic waste management. The EPA's role in this area is limited to research and provision of technical and financial assistance to these other government levels. However, a 1976 amendment to this act, called the Resource Conservation and Recovery Act, set up a federal regulatory system for tracking and reporting the generation, transportation, and eventual disposal of hazardous wastes by businesses responsible for creating these wastes.[115]

The U.S. government has staked out a much larger role for itself in the area of toxic wastes. The 1976 **Toxic Substances Control Act** requires manufacturing and distribution businesses in the chemical industry to identify any chemicals that pose "substantial risks" of human or other natural environment harm. This act also requires chemical testing before commercialization and the possible halting of manufacture if the associated risks are unreasonable. Because there are over 70,000 chemicals already in use in the United States and more than 1,000 new chemicals introduced every year, the EPA has prioritized the substances that must be tested to focus on those that might cause cancer, birth defects, or gene mutations.[116]

The other major U.S. government activity in toxic wastes is known as **Superfund,** or, more formally, the Comprehensive Environmental Response, Compensation, and Liability Act of 1980 (CERCLA). Superfund is an effort to clean up more than 2,000 hazardous waste dumps and spills around the country, some dating back to the previous century. Funded by taxes on chemicals and petroleum, this program has established a National Priorities List to focus on the most hazardous sites, and places legal and financial responsibility for the proper remediation of these sites on the appropriate parties. In addition, CERCLA also requires that unauthorized hazardous waste spills be reported and can order those responsible to clean up the sites.[117]

One of the most important amendments to the Superfund law, the Emergency Planning and Community Right-to-Know Act of 1986, requires manufacturing companies to report to the federal government annually all of their releases into the environment of any of more than 500 toxic chemicals and chemical compounds. The EPA accumulates these reports and makes them available to the public (at http://www.epa.gov/triexplorer) with the intention that an informed public will pressure manufacturers to reduce these toxic releases.[118]

One in four Americans lives within three miles of a Superfund site.[119] Thus, it is not surprising that an outcry ensues when the Superfund suffers spending cuts. Until 1995, when the fees expired, the federal government collected money from chemical and oil companies to help fund the Superfund cleanup. Since then, a series of EPA funding cuts have squeezed the fund.[120] Since the fees expired, taxpayer costs for Superfund have risen 427 percent, leaving them with higher costs for fewer services.[121] In 2000, the number of Superfund closures dropped dramatically and has yet to recover. Furthermore, many sites are now "orphan sites," for which the money from the original polluter has been exhausted or no responsible party has been found.[122] President Obama wants to restore the Superfund tax, believing that it will add $1 billion in revenues to the 2011

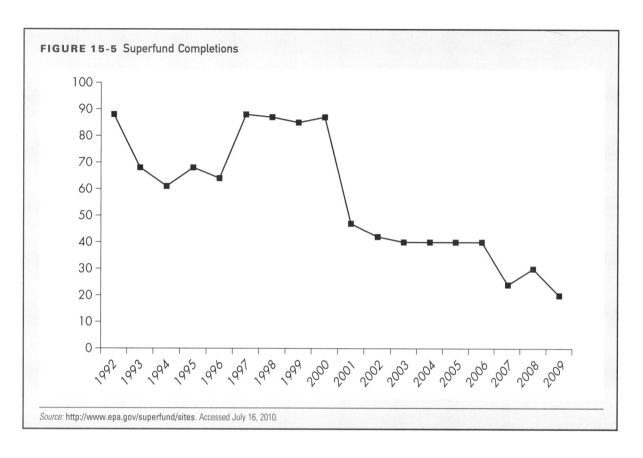

FIGURE 15-5 Superfund Completions

Source: http://www.epa.gov/superfund/sites. Accessed July 16, 2010.

budget.[123] The American Chemistry Council, the chemical industry trade group, opposes reinstatement of the Superfund Tax. They say that it makes all manufacturers pay for the crimes of a few.[124] Jeff Tittel, Director of the New Jersey Sierra Club counters, "Those who created these problems are those who should be cleaning it up, not the taxpayers."[125] In the meantime, $600 million of economic stimulus money from the Recovery Act is being spent on Superfund site cleanup.[126] Figure 15-5 shows the number of Superfund sites completed each year from 1992 to 2009.

Endangered Species. The world's species are disappearing at an alarming rate, according to the World Conservation Union, which releases an annual Red List of endangered species.[127] Their 2010 report shows that over 15,000 species are now considered threatened with extinction, over 2,300 are endangered, and over 4,300 are vulnerable.[128] "The good news," according to Russ Mittermeier, the head of Conservation International and chairperson of the World Conservation Union's primate group, "is that we still have time to save the majority of [the species], if the conservation community, governments, other organizations, and concerned individuals commit a sufficient amount of resources immediately."[129]

In the United States, responsibility for endangered species is shared by two agencies, the U.S. Interior Department's Fish and Wildlife Service and the Commerce Department's National Marine Fisheries Act. They administer the 1973 **Endangered Species Act (ESA)**. This federal law assigns the responsibility of preventing harm to species considered "endangered" (i.e., facing extinction) or "threatened" (likely to become endangered).[130] Protection of species sometimes means moving them to safe areas when their original habitats have been destroyed by human activities, but it can also mean prevention of these activities, such as mining, construction, and fishing, before such habitat deprivation occurs. This restriction of business activities can be expected to continue as the extinction rate for species climbs, resulting in sometimes intense political conflicts between business interests and environmental groups.[131]

Some environmentalists argue that the Endangered Species Act was weakened under the Bush administration.[132] They point to the fact that an average of 9.5 species has been added each year under the Bush administration, compared with 65 each year under the Clinton administration and 50 each year under the George H. W. Bush administration. Only half the acreage recommended has been designated as critical habitat, and important decision-making powers have been taken away from Fish and Wildlife Service and given to agencies with competing priorities.[133] A few weeks before President Bush left office, he issued a regulation that allowed federal agencies to forego consulting with government scientists before beginning projects that might endanger wildlife. President Obama restored the protections shortly after taking office. Environmentalists praised the restoration of protections, but business groups declared it an obstacle to projects that could move the economy forward.[134]

International Government Environmental Responses

The *United Nations Environment Programme (UNEP)* has led the way in identifying global environmental problems and in working toward their resolution. As early as 1977, UNEP was studying the ozone problem and began to lay the groundwork for the 1987 **Montreal Protocol** in which most of the CFC-producing and -consuming nations around the world agreed to a quick phase-out of these ozone-destroying substances. In 2009, the Montreal Protocol achieved universal ratification, the first United Nations treaty to do so and, by 2009, those parties to the protocol had phased out 97 percent of the Protocol-controlled chemicals.[135] Observers believe that, thanks to the Protocol, the ozone layer should return to pre-1980 levels by 2050 to 2075.[136] The ozone reduction brought by the Protocol has helped the world to avoid millions of cases of fatal skin cancer and tens of millions of cases of nonfatal skin cancer and cataracts.[137]

UNEP is also funding research and assisting in information exchange on the protection and more sustainable use of international waters. The Global Waters Assessment will examine the problems surrounding shared transboundary waters, develop scenarios on the future condition of the world's water, and analyze various policy options. UNEP is also the driving force behind efforts to initiate global sound management of hazardous chemicals. They were an integral part of the Rotterdam Convention, which requires that countries give explicit informed consent before hazardous chemicals cross their borders. UNEP also works to protect the world's biological diversity. Their efforts helped bring the elephant back from the brink of extinction.[138]

Another United Nations initiative is the **Global Compact**, already mentioned in Chapter 10. It brings thousands of companies from across the world society to support universal environmental and social principles. The Global Compact works to advance ten universal principles, three of which involve environmental issues. They are: "#7—Business should support a precautionary approach to environmental challenges, #8—Undertake initiatives to promote greater environmental responsibility, and #9—Encourage the development and diffusion of environmentally friendly technologies."[139]

The **Global Reporting Initiative (GRI)** is a collaborating center of the UNEP. GRI spearheaded the development of a sustainability reporting framework that has become the most widely used standard in the world. The reporting framework outlines the principles and indicators that organizations can use to measure and report their economic, environmental, and social performance.[140]

Other Environmental Stakeholders

Environmental Interest Groups

Perhaps no force in today's society is more responsible for the "greening" of nations around the world than are the many environmental interest groups making up what has come to be known as "the environmental movement." This collection of nonprofit membership and think-tank organizations has been credited with moving the world's governments and businesses, as well as publics, in the direction of environmental responsibility through a host of activities, including demonstrations, boycotts, public education, lobbying, and research.

The history of the environmental movement is instructive. Whereas a few U.S. groups (the National Audubon Society, the Izaak Walton League, and the Sierra Club) were formed in the early 1900s during the first green wave of the century, many of the largest national and international environmental groups, such as the Environmental Defense Fund (now called Environmental Defense), Greenpeace, and the National Resources Defense Council were created during the second environmental wave, in the late 1960s and early 1970s. Since that time, all of these groups and hundreds of other smaller, more locally focused environmental organizations have grown in size and clout. It was the century's third wave of environmentalism, beginning in the late 1980s, however, that gave many of these groups the power and legitimacy to become credible players in environmental policy making around the globe.

Environmental interest groups have been instrumental in significantly influencing business environmental policy in this third wave. For example, Environmental Defense is working with Federal Express on building a new generation of vehicles, with DuPont on developing nanotech standards, and with PHH Arval on becoming the first carbon neutral fleet.[141] Other outcomes of relationships between environmental interest groups and business stakeholders have included corporate selection of environmental group representatives for corporate boards and top management positions, mutual participation in environmental "cleanup" projects, and corporate donations of time and money to environmental groups for their environmental conservation programs. This trend toward cooperation between otherwise adversarial groups is a characteristic of the third environmental or green wave that sets this wave apart from the two previous environmental eras. That collaboration is discussed in more detail in the section on business environmentalism.

The former chair of the Sierra Club identified three types of major U.S. environmental organizations on the basis of this criterion of cooperation with business. He labeled groups characterized by confrontational behaviors as "radicals," groups that seek pragmatic reform through a combination of confrontation and cooperation as "mainstreamers," and groups that avoid confrontation and are more trusting of corporations as "accommodators."[142] As we mentioned, the differences between the types of groups are beginning to blur as business and environmental activists collaborate increasingly on shared goals. Nevertheless, it is instructive to look at some of the groups that have taken and still sometimes take a more radical approach.

One group that would fall into the radical camp is the Rainforest Action Network (RAN). RAN has been particularly successful in getting large corporations to change their ways. The ways in which RAN has accomplished their goals are described in Figure 15-6. RAN is a small organization, with a budget of only $2.4 million and a staff of just 25. Nevertheless, they have managed to garner the attention of big business in a way that the larger, more established environmental organizations have never managed. They have been described as a mosquito in a tent, "just a nuisance when it starts, but you can

---

FIGURE 15-6 The Mosquito in the Tent Strategy

Street Theater	During the holiday season, RAN carolers sang "Oil Wells" to the tune of "Jingle Bells" in front of the Citigroup headquarters on Park Avenue. RAN obtained the access code to the Home Depot intercom and announced to shoppers that they should step carefully, because the wood on Aisle 13 had been ripped from the Amazon Basin and there might be blood on the floors.
Celebrity Endorsements	The night before Citigroup's annual shareholder meeting, RAN began airing commercials showing Ed Asner, Susan Sarandon, Darryl Hannah, and Ali MacGraw cutting up their Citibank credit cards.
Coalitions	RAN doesn't go it alone. They work with other environmental organizations, socially responsible investors, liberal philanthropists, and even sympathetic insiders (which is how they got the Home Depot access code).
Internet Organizing	RAN uses the Internet to both launch their own initiatives and support those of other groups.

Sources: Marc Gunther, "The Mosquito in the Tent," *Fortune* (March 31, 2004), 158–162; Lisa Gerwitz, "It's Not Easy Being Green," *Deal.com* (March 8, 2004), 1. See also http://www.ran.org/. Accessed July 16, 2010.

---

wake up later with some serious welts."[143] Environmentalist groups believe that the threat of confrontation motivates companies to work more cooperatively with environmentalist groups. Greenpeace Research Director Kert Davies says, "What we hear over and over again, especially after a few drinks, is company people telling us, 'We wouldn't be talking to you if we weren't scared of you.'"[144]

A new category that is taking on increased importance is **ecoterrorists**. Ecoterrorists are not included under the radical designation described earlier. Radical groups favor confrontation, but ecoterrorists employ violent acts that involve real or threatened damage to people or property to attempt to achieve their goals. The FBI estimates about 1,200 acts of ecoterrorism in the United States, which have caused losses that run into millions.[145] More than 20 states have passed ecoterrorism laws that increase the penalties for vandalism, arson, and trespassing when ecoterrorism is involved.[146] At the federal level, the "Animal Enterprise Terrorism Act" of 2006 increases penalties for the use of force, violence, and threats involving animal enterprises.[147] "Operation Backfire" resulted in 11 people being charged with domestic terrorism for a five-year period of acts on behalf of the Earth Liberation Front (ELF) and the Animal Liberation Front (ALF).[148] In 2009, Marie Jeannette Mason was sentenced to serve over 21 years in federal prison and paid over $4 million in restitution for acts of arson committed on behalf of the ELF.[149]

In addition to environmental groups, businesses are paying more attention to the latest green wave because of at least three other stakeholder groups: green consumers, green employees, and green investors.

Green Consumers.   Individuals referred to as green consumers are actual and potential customers of retail firms, usually in the industrialized countries, who express preferences for products, services, and companies that are perceived to be more environment friendly than other competitive products, services, and firms. Marketing research firms in these countries have identified a range of green consumerism based on the strengths of these preferences and reported consumer purchases. "Light green" consumers are more likely to make impulsive purchase decisions, while "dark green" consumers are more likely to plan their purchases in advance.[150] Green consumers have been a sought-after segment of the market—young, well-paid, highly educated, Internet savvy, predominately female, and mostly professional or white-collar employees.[151] Experts expected an increase in green consumers as members of Generation Y (those born between 1977 and 1994) assume positions of responsibility.[152] They based this on the knowledge that nearly 100 percent of the Y generation received environmental education in school, as opposed to 19 percent of the adults in general, and were shown to be much more likely to spend money for environmentally friendly products than their parents were.[153]

In 2010, Joel Makower looked back on the 20 years since his book *The Green Consumer* and found that the predictions did not come true. He said that politicians had become more versed in environmental issues and that companies were not only increasingly engaged in environmental responsibility but that some were being truly innovative in their efforts. However, according to Makower, "One thing hasn't changed all that much: green consumers. That is, there don't seem to be that many more today than in 1990, in terms of people making significant changes to their shopping and consuming habits in ways that move markets toward greener products and services, never mind actually saving the Earth." Makower has not given up hope. In assessing the past 20 years, he concludes, "I'm not quite ready to proclaim green consumerism dead (though I can't honestly say it's ever been alive and well). There will always be a small corps of true-blue green consumers ready to vote with their dollars—at least for some products. But my 20-year-old premise—that a relative handful of committed consumers will transform companies and markets—hasn't really panned out, though I still believe it to be true."[154]

Green Employees. A second stakeholder group with which most businesses are concerned is green employees. Although the popular press has not focused as much attention on green employees as it has on green consumers, there is evidence that employees are playing a major role in promoting environmentalism at work. In addition to union and general employee environmental concerns with plant, warehouse, and office safety and health, employees in many companies have assisted management in going beyond these traditional concerns into areas such as pollution prevention, recycling, energy and environmental audits, and community environmental projects. An important survey of workers in the United Kingdom found that 69 percent welcomed green benefits from environmentally responsible employers, 14 percent would change jobs for a greener benefits package, and 35 percent believed that this would make them more loyal to the firm. In the United States, 33 percent would rather work for an environmentally sound company and more than half thought their company should do more to be eco friendly.[155]

Green Investors. Another important business stakeholder involved in environmental issues is the green investor. Similar to investors interested in advancing social causes, individuals and organizations sometimes want to put their money where their environmental values are by identifying and utilizing financial instruments that are associated with environmentally oriented companies. A growing number of mutual funds, stock and bond offerings, money market funds, and other financial instruments have included environmental components in recent years.[156] Shareholder resolutions address concerns that range from toxic emissions to recycling and waste to nuclear power plants and climate change. Climate change has emerged as one of the greatest concerns. In the 2010 proxy season, U.S. investors filed a record 95 climate change resolutions, a 40 percent increase over 2009.[157]

Spotlight on SUSTAINABILITY

Living "The Other Low-Carb Life"

Time named the Personal Carbon Footprint one of the "50 best inventions of 2009." Their reasoning was that countries never seem to be able to agree on how to reduce carbon but individuals can move forward on their own. Furthermore, the wealthy people of the world, whether from Indiana or India, produce most of the world's carbon emissions. A strategy focused on rich individuals instead of rich countries might be more effective. Many individuals have begun to make a commitment to the "carbon neutral" life by tracking and paying for the CO_2 that they spend. Carbon neutrality can be achieved through a combination of minimizing carbon emissions where possible (it is possible to book a carbon neutral flight or have carbon neutral groceries delivered to your home) and then purchasing offsets for the emissions that remain. For example, environmental consultant Guy Dauncey tallies his annual carbon spending when he tallies his taxes. He found that his personal activities caused 13.5 tons of carbon emissions. The going rate for carbon was $10 a ton, and so he made arrangements to do $135 of work for the Solar Electric Light Fund, a group that helps African villagers use solar power instead of kerosene.

The Nature Conservancy (http://www.nature.org) provides a free carbon footprint calculator that measures how many tons of carbon dioxide and greenhouse gasses are generated by the different choices an individual makes each year. They provide advice on how to evaluate carbon offset options and they offer carbon offset options, such as contributing to the Tensas River Basin Project on the Mississippi River. Their Web site also provides a range of information on global warming along with ways in which individuals can become involved in the issue.

Sources: "The 50 Best Inventions of the Year," *Time* (November 23, 2009), 57–92; Danylo Hawaleshka, "The Other Low-Carb Life," *Maclean's* (June 21, 2004), 54; http://www.nature.org. Accessed July 16, 2010.

After the *Exxon Valdez* oil spill, several environmental, labor, and social investor groups formed an organization called Ceres and developed a preamble and a set of ten policy statements called the "Valdez Principles" (later renamed the **Ceres Principles**). These principles have been advanced as models for businesses to express and practice environmental sensitivity. Excerpts from these principles are listed in Figure 15-7. Companies that have endorsed the principles include American Airlines, Bank of America, Coca-Cola, General Motors, Polaroid Corporation, and Sunoco.[158] GE Corporation won the 2009 Sustainability Award presented at the Ceres Conference.[159] In 2010, Ceres reflected on the past and looked toward the future in their "2010 Roadmap to Sustainability."[160] The emphasis is on integrating sustainability through all aspects of the organization. According to Ceres President Mindy S. Lubber, "If businesses deepen their efforts to solve social and environmental threats, it will position them to innovate and compete in the fast-changing, resource-constrained global economy. It is no longer enough for companies to have special projects or initiatives. Comprehensive sustainability strategies are expected."[161]

Business Environmentalism

Now that caring for the environment has become good business, there are countless examples of firms demonstrating that sustainable business practices can not only help the planet but also be a source of competitive advantage. We simply highlight a couple of the many companies that are proving to be responsible environmental stewards.

FIGURE 15-7
Ceres Principles

By adopting these principles, we publicly affirm our belief that corporations have a responsibility for the environment by operating in a manner that protects the earth. We believe that corporations must not compromise the ability of future generations to sustain themselves. We will update our practices constantly in light of advances in technology and new understandings in health and environmental science. In collaboration with Ceres, we will promote a dynamic process to ensure that the Principles are interpreted in a way that accommodates changing technologies and environmental realities. We intend to make consistent, measurable progress in implementing these Principles and to apply them to all aspects of our operations throughout the world.

1. **Protection of the Biosphere:** We will reduce and make continual progress toward eliminating the release of any substance that may cause environmental damage to the air, water, or earth or its inhabitants. We will safeguard all habitats affected by our operations and will protect open spaces and wilderness, while preserving biodiversity.
2. **Sustainable Use of Natural Resources:** We will make sustainable use of renewable natural resources, such as water, soils, and forests. We will conserve nonrenewable natural resources through efficient use and careful planning.
3. **Reduction and Disposal of Waste:** We will reduce and where possible eliminate waste, through source reduction and recycling. All waste will be handled and disposed of through safe and responsible methods.
4. **Energy Conservation:** We will conserve energy and improve the energy efficiency of our internal operations and of the goods and services we sell. We will make every effort to use environmentally safe and sustainable energy sources.
5. **Risk Reduction:** We will strive to minimize the environmental, health, and safety risks to our employees and the communities in which we operate through safe technologies, facilities, and operating procedures, and by being prepared for emergencies.
6. **Safe Products and Services:** We will reduce and where possible eliminate the use, manufacture, or sale of products and services that cause environmental damage or health or safety hazards. We will inform our customers of the environmental impacts of our products or services and try to correct unsafe use.
7. **Environmental Restoration:** We will promptly and responsibly correct conditions we have caused that endanger health, safety, or the environment. To the extent feasible, we will redress injuries we have caused to persons or damage we have caused to the environment and will restore the environment.
8. **Informing the Public:** We will inform in a timely manner everyone who may be affected by conditions caused by our company that might endanger health, safety, or the environment. We will regularly seek advice and counsel through dialogue with persons in communities near our facilities. We will not take any action against employees for reporting dangerous incidents or conditions to management or to appropriate authorities.
9. **Management Commitment:** We will implement these Principles and sustain a process that ensures that the Board of Directors and Chief Executive Officer are fully informed about pertinent environmental issues and are fully responsible for environmental policy. In selecting our Board of Directors, we will consider demonstrated environmental commitment as a factor.
10. **Audits and Reports:** We will conduct an annual self-evaluation of our progress in implementing these Principles. We will support the timely creation of generally accepted environmental audit procedures. We will annually complete the Ceres Report, which will be made available to the public.

Source: Ceres, http://www.ceres.org/Page.aspx?pid=416. Accessed July 16, 2010.

Patagonia

Although technically not the CEO, Patagonia founder and owner Yvon Chouinard ran away with TriplePundit.com's 2010 Most Sustainable CEO award.[162] This is not surprising because one can't discuss business sustainability without mentioning Patagonia, the outdoor lifestyle company that is said to be "arguably one of the most environmentally focused companies in the world."[163] Decades before most businesses considered the possibility of recycling, Patagonia had made it an integral part of operations.[164] The company used the mail-order catalog to send messages about the problems of overfishing and genetically modified foods. After discovering they could make their outdoor gear out of discarded plastic soda bottles, founder-owner Yvon Chouinard set about to do an environmental assessment of all their materials. He found that cotton was particularly damaging due to its dependencies on pesticides, insecticides, and defoliants. "To know this and not switch to organic cotton would be unconscionable," says Chouinard.[165] He gave his managers 18 months to make the switch. This was a difficult move in 1994, even for a founder who owned most of the company's stock. Organic cotton was rare at the time, costing 50 to 100 percent more than traditional cotton. The risk was huge because a fifth of Patagonia's products were made from cotton. Suppliers balked and the rank and file grumbled, but Chouinard said that they had to do it or the company would not sell cotton again. As often happens when companies take well-reasoned courageous stands, the risk paid off. Patagonia's cotton sales rose 25 percent and the move set up an organic cotton industry that thrives today.[166]

3M Company

In 2009, 3M was recognized by the U.S. Environmental Protection Agency and U.S. Department of Energy by winning the Sustained Excellence Award for Energy Management in recognition of continuous improvement in energy management. 3M is the only industrial company to receive this honor five years in a row.[167] The 3M Company is one of the best-known multinational companies to have adopted a long-term comprehensive, beyond-compliance, environmental policy and program. In their own words, "3M's leadership has recognized that the company's long-term success springs from the principles of sustainable development, which include: stewardship to the environment, contributions to society, and the creation of economic value."[168] Begun over 30 years ago, 3M's Pollution Prevention Pays program was a multiproduct, multiprocess approach to manufacturing. In its first year alone, through product reformulation, process modification, equipment redesign, and waste recycling, 3M prevented 73,000 tons of air emissions and 2,800 tons of sludge. They also saved more than $700 million for the company by reducing various pollutants at their sources. The company gives the credit (and financial rewards) for these environmental successes to its employees, who developed more than 4,500 subprojects under this program.[169]

The successes of 3M's environmental efforts are numerous. 3M scientists developed 3M HFEs as a CFC replacement. In just 15 years, 3M cut its volatile organic air emissions by 95 percent, its toxic releases by 94 percent, and its greenhouse gas emissions by 45 percent.[170] It's not surprising, therefore, that 3M has won awards for its environmental excellence. Thirty years ago, 3M's environmental efforts were focused on reducing emissions. Now the company is factoring environmental awareness into all stages of the product's life cycle. Its "Lifecycle Management" program is designed to minimize environmental impact from the product design to customer use and disposal. The *Corporate Responsibility Officer (CRO)* magazine (previously *Business Ethics*) described 3M as having "sustained commitment, innovation, and substantial impact in three decades of environmental stewardship."[171]

The Business Case for Sustainability

With all the pressures for financial performance in the marketplace, why would businesses devote resources to achieving sustainability? In *Green to Gold*, Daniel Esty and Andrew Winston offer three basic reasons for incorporating environmental considerations into core strategy:[172]

1. **The upside benefits**. Sustainability requires innovation and entrepreneurship that can help a firm to move ahead of competitors through new ideas, lower costs, and stronger intangibles such as trust and credibility. Companies that manage the environment carefully can even carry less risk, resulting in lower lending rates.
2. **The downside risks**. Companies that do not care for the environment run the risk of incurring society's wrath once they step over the line. Union Carbide found this out after the tragedy in Bhopal. Walmart found that even the largest of firms cannot withstand negative public reactions indefinitely.
3. **The right thing to do**. Oil giant Shell uses an acronym to explain why they do some things that on the surface appear to be costly—TINA (There Is No Alternative). Sustainability is not a luxury nor is there really a choice.[173] As the sign in Patagonia headquarters says, "There is no business to be done on a dead planet."[174]

Cost–Benefit Analysis.   Although the importance of practicing sound environmental management is clear, managers are still left with the task of deciding which projects to undertake and which to forego. **Cost–benefit analysis** has been used in other areas, especially those related to public and private capital budgeting and investment, it has also received an extraordinary amount of attention in natural environmental policy decisions. For instance, most environmental impact statements, which are required by the NEPA, have one or more cost–benefit analyses as the basis for many of the environmental decisions resulting from these studies. The idea behind cost–benefit analysis is that, in a rational planning situation, an organization wants to ensure that an environmental project is worth the investment. Costs are totaled and compared with overall benefits. If benefits are sufficiently greater than costs, the project is given the go-ahead; if not, it is shelved, revised, or scrapped. Decision makers in many dam projects, other water reclamation projects, and land development projects in the United States have utilized cost–benefit analysis to determine the value of these environment-oriented projects. Environmental groups can use cost–benefit analysis to further their agenda for change. As previously discussed, the Rainforest Action Network has been able to get large corporations to make dramatic changes in the way they do business. Essentially, they do this by changing the cost–benefit equation. By increasing the cost of environmental negligence, RAN tilts the business calculus, making it more likely that firms will find the results of a cost–benefit analysis indicate that an improvement in environmental performance is warranted.

Triple Bottom Line.   Companies around the world are adopting the **triple bottom line (TBL)** approach to reporting that covers not only economic performance but also social and environmental. The idea behind the TBL is that it will force corporations to focus not only on financial performance but also on the ways in which the company either adds to or detracts from society and the environment. A recent commentary in the *CPA Journal* suggested that U.S. firms would benefit if the SEC would require TBL reporting. Socially responsible firms would benefit from the exposure their activities would receive just as irresponsible firms would be forced to own up to their failings.[175] Although the SEC is unlikely to adopt the requirement any time soon, the voluntary use of TBL as a reporting framework continues to grow.

Business and Environmental Activist Partnerships

In the past few years, a remarkable shift in the relationship between business and environmental activists has occurred. Accommodation is replacing antagonism as the two parties begin to recognize their mutual dependence. Business needs environmental activists to both inform and validate their environmental efforts and activists need business to change the way it operates in order to protect the planet.[176]

Examples of this new partnership abound. Silicon Valley Toxic Coalition activists first communicated their concern to Dell by chaining themselves to computer monitors. They then worked with Dell on their innovative recycling program and other issues of sustainability.[177] According to Coalition founder Ted Smith, "Companies have decided it is better to invite us into the tent than have us outside picketing their keynote speeches. It's a long way from where we started."[178] When the CEOs of ten major corporations met in Washington to issue a call for mandatory carbon emission limits, the presidents of Environmental Defense and the Natural Resources Defense Council (NRDC) were at the table with them.[179]

The strangest of these new bedfellows has been the relationship between Adam Werbach, once the youngest president of the Sierra Club, and Walmart, a company he once called "a new breed of toxin."[180] Walmart has developed a variety of partnerships. Conservation International has helped them to lower energy use and Environmental Defense has opened an office in Bentonville, Arkansas, so that they can work more closely with Walmart—though they are careful to take no money from them.[181] However, the partnership between Werbach and Walmart caused a great deal of commotion.

Werbach has been a leader in the environmentalist community since he became the youngest Sierra Club president at the age of 23. His book's title, *Act Now, Apologize Later*, reflects his willingness to act decisively and deal with reactions later. In the case of Walmart, the reaction was intense. Clients of his small consulting firm, Act Now, fired him because they did not want to be associated with anyone who did business with Walmart. Old friends no longer spoke to him and strangers even threatened him.[182]

Despite the upset it has caused, both parties remained committed to this collaboration. The benefits for Walmart are clear. At a time when some observers are questioning the sincerity of their environmental initiatives, Werbach, now Global CEO of sustainability agency Saatchi & Saatchi, brings a perception of legitimacy to their efforts. For Werbach, the unprecedented scope of the opportunity was too much to resist. According to Werbach's wife Lyn, "Imagine that struggle of knowing there's an opportunity that has unprecedented reach and not taking it."[183]

Systematic Business Responses to the Environmental Challenge

Various management approaches are available for use in selecting or constructing an environmental strategy. These include management approaches that were discussed in more general terms in earlier chapters, such as crisis management, issues management, and stakeholder management. Because these topics were addressed more fully in Chapters 5 and 6, only their applicability to environmental management is discussed here.

Managers can use crisis management in the environmental area by focusing on two factors: prevention and contingency plans. As can be seen in the *Exxon Valdez* case, Exxon, Alyeska, and the federal and state governments apparently did not pay enough attention to preventing the oil spill disaster or to implementing the inadequate contingency plan to recover the oil once spilled. Although some attention had been paid to the vulnerability of the Alaskan natural environment to a small oil spill, this appears to have been understated and generally ignored. That either Exxon or Alyeska assessed its own vulnerability to a spill of any size appears doubtful. Finally, the lack of coordination between the two companies in immediately addressing the spill indicated a response plan that was only a paper tiger, never really put into practice. Had the businesses and governments followed basic crisis management principles, including vulnerability assessments and simulation drills, the outcome might have been different for both of these organizations and for Prince William Sound.

Issues management can be employed to track public interest in natural environment issues and to develop and implement plans to attempt to ensure that the scope of environmental problems is minimized and that the firm develops effective responses at each stage in the life cycles of environmental issues. Environmental issues can be developed as part of the environmental impact statement process or as part of the strategic planning macroenvironmental analysis process.

Similarly, stakeholder management applies to environmental management in that environmental stakeholders and their stakes can be identified, including the environmental public, environmental regulators, environmental groups, and various entities (human and nonhuman) across the entire natural environment. The follow-up stages of stakeholder management (i.e., planning for and interacting with stakeholders) can then be conducted so that each important environmental stakeholder is given adequate attention after it is identified.

The Future of Business: Greening and/or Growing?

The salient environmental question we all may need to address in the future: "How much is enough?" A common business and, indeed, public policy goal in most human societies has been economic growth. Typically, businesses and societies have needed increasing amounts of either materials or energy, or both, to achieve that economic growth. Limits on growth, similar to limits on human reproduction, at either the macro or micro level, have not been widely popular. One potential problem with unrestrained economic growth worldwide is that, unless technology or people change significantly within a generation, environmental problems change in degree from significant to severe.

The pressures on the environment come from many directions. World population is projected to continue to grow, creating greater demands on food and fuel resources. Large countries such as China and India are industrializing and so they will use increasing amounts of materials and energy. The already industrialized countries continue to maintain the highly consumptive lifestyles that have strained the environment already. As the name implies, the sustainability imperative is of the essence. Business no longer has the luxury of deciding whether or not to respond to it—the environment can't wait.

Summary

We began by discussing the concept of sustainability and its importance to business. We then outlined the top environmental issues facing business today. Environmental ethics began our discussion of individual and collective responsibility for sustaining the environment. We explored the role of governments and environmental interest groups in effecting change and then looked at companies that are leaders in practicing sustainable business practices. Lastly, we offered ways in which businesses can act toward achieving sustainability.

What themes are woven throughout this chapter that can be especially helpful to prospective managers? First, the natural environment is crucial for human survival and a number of complex and interconnected human-induced activities are threatening this environment. Problems such as human deforestation, pollution, and expanding populations are potentially endangering nonhuman species and ecosystems and reducing the quality of human life. Individuals and their organizations, including businesses, are directly or indirectly responsible for this situation.

Second, although there is a growing consensus about the importance of sustainability, there remain significant differences of opinion on how problems will develop in the future and what should be done to resolve them. The recent growth in partnerships between business and environmental activists is a promising sign but more changes must come. A minimum baseline of sustainability—meeting the needs of the present without compromising the ability of future generations to meet their needs—should be the bottom line for business as it moves into the future.

Key Terms

acid rain, p. 516

air pollution, p. 516

biodiversity, p. 515

cap and trade, p. 525

carbon neutral, p. 510

Ceres Principles, p. 532

Clean Air Act, p. 524

Clean Water Act, p. 525

climate change, p. 512

cost–benefit analysis, p. 535

deforestation, p. 520

ecoterrorists, p. 530

emissions trading, p. 525

Endangered Species Act (ESA), p. 527

energy inefficiency, p. 513

environment, p. 511

environmental impact statements (EISs), p. 524

Environmental Protection Agency (EPA), p. 524

externalities, p. 509

fossil fuels, p. 513

Global Compact, p. 528

Global Reporting Initiative (GRI), p. 528

global warming, p. 512

greenhouse effect, p. 512

Montreal Protocol, p. 528

NIMBY, p. 522

ozone, p. 518

Superfund, p. 526

sustainability, p. 510

toxic substances, p. 516

Toxic Substances Control Act, p. 526

tragedy of the commons, p. 521

triple bottom line (TBL), p. 535

watershed, p. 519

wicked problems, p. 521

Discussion Questions

1. What is sustainability?
2. What are several of the most important environmental issues now receiving worldwide attention?
3. What are some of the causes of environmental pollution and depletion?
4. What is the future outlook for the natural environment?
5. Who has responsibility for addressing environmental issues?
6. How can ethics be applied in response to environmental issues?
7. What are some examples of sustainable business and decision models for addressing environmental concerns?
8. Should businesses and societies continue to focus on unlimited economic growth?

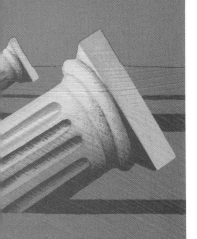

16

Business and Community Stakeholders

CHAPTER LEARNING OUTCOMES

After studying this chapter, you should be able to:

1. Identify and discuss two basic ways of business giving.

2. Discuss reasons for community involvement, various types of community projects, and management of community stakeholders.

3. Explain the pros and cons of corporate philanthropy, provide a brief history of corporate philanthropy, and explain why and to whom companies give.

4. Differentiate between strategic philanthropy, cause-related marketing, and cause branding.

5. Characterize the nature of, magnitude of, reasons for, and impacts of offshore outsourcing and business or plant closings.

6. Address steps that a business or plant might take before a decision to close is made.

7. Identify strategies that a business or plant might employ after a decision to close has been made.

The Oxford English Dictionary has over a dozen definitions of the word "community."[1] They all share an underlying theme of commonality. Communities can be joined by a shared geographic locale, a shared profession, a shared ideology, or even a shared recreational pastime. The actions of business affect a range of communities, and it is important that managers be aware of these impacts and manage in a way that respects the interests of community stakeholders. This chapter focuses typically on the business's immediate locale—the town, city, or state—in which a business resides. We should remember, however, that instant communication, speedy travel, and social networking often expand the relevant community to include the region, the nation, or even the world. From the global economic recession to terrorist bombings and disease epidemics, businesses affect and are affected by events throughout the world.

When we think of business and its community stakeholders, two major kinds of relationships come to mind. One is the positive contribution business can make to the community. Examples of these positive contributions include volunteerism, company contributions, and support of programs in education, culture, urban development, the arts, civic activities, and health and welfare endeavors. On the other hand, business can also cause harm to community stakeholders. It can pollute the environment and can put people out of work by offshore outsourcing or closing a plant. Business can abuse its power and exploit consumers and employees. When business causes harm, as with the global financial crisis, it is incumbent upon business to have a positive impact on the community. In a 2010 Bloomberg *BusinessWeek* report, Michael Porter opined, "As high unemployment, rising poverty, and dismay over corporate greed breed contempt for the capitalist market system. ... Serving the intersecting needs of business and the community is the only path to winning back respect for Corporate America."[2]

This chapter concentrates on community involvement and corporate philanthropy as community stakeholder issues. In addition, it discusses the topics of offshore outsourcing and business or plant closings as community stakeholder concerns. This discussion should provide us with an opportunity to explore both the positive and the detrimental effects that characterize business–community relationships. It begins with the positive.

In addition to being profitable, obeying the law, and being ethical, a company may create a positive impact in the community by giving in two ways: (1) donating the time and talents of its managers and employees and (2) making financial contributions. The first category, **community involvement**, manifests itself in a wide array of voluntary activities in the community. The second category involves corporate philanthropy or business giving. We should note that there is significant overlap between these two categories, because companies quite frequently donate their time and talent and give financial aid to the same general projects. First, we discuss community involvement and the various ways in which companies enhance the quality of life in their communities.

Community Involvement

Business must—not only for a healthier society but also for its own well-being—be willing to give the same serious consideration to human needs that it gives to its own needs for production and profits. The following argument for increased community involvement from the 2009 Deloitte Touche Tohmatsu Corporate Social Responsibility Report makes the case for corporate social responsibility having a positive impact on the bottom line:

> *Deloitte's commitment to the public interest goes back to the origins of our organization. Today the Deloitte Shared Values bind the people of Deloitte together across cultures, customs, and languages. Along with the Ethical Principles, of which one is "responsibility to society," these values define the way business is done in every member firm. Deloitte member firms strive to make social good a co-product of their work, alongside revenues and earnings—a business strategy that they are confident will foster their success over the long term.[3]*

Business involvement in the community represents enlightened self-interest because businesses are in a position to help themselves in the process of helping others. These dual objectives of business clearly illustrate that making profits and addressing social concerns are not mutually exclusive endeavors. Companies can develop trust and community support through making community service activities part of their identities. Through its annual "Global Day of Giving" and its generous philanthropic contributions, Eli Lilly has become a staple on Most Admired Companies lists. The 2010 *Eli Lilly Corporate Responsibility Report* drives this point home:

> *Corporate responsibility is not just a fad we have recently embraced; it is a fundamental part of who we are. We have a robust history of community involvement and believe that our obligations extend beyond the medicines we make. We seek to be a responsible employer and business partner. In addition, our company and our employees volunteer their time and skills to dozens of causes and charitable programs, strengthening the communities where we live and work.[4]*

Other rationales for business involvement in community affairs provide moral justification, beyond that of enlightened self-interest. For example, utilitarian arguments can

FIGURE 16-1

Standards of Excellence in Corporate Community Involvement

Standard 1: Leadership

My company actively and purposefully helps to define needs, set direction, and initiate meaningful change around community or societal issues.

Standard 2: Strategy

My company plans its community involvement and leverages its capacities and strengths to deliver meaningful value to society and to the business.

Standard 3: Integration

My company engages all facets of the business to contribute to and realize the benefit from community involvement.

Standard 4: Infrastructure

My company consistently provides the resources and support needed to ensure the successful execution of its community involvement strategy.

Standard 5: Performance Measurement

My company assesses the effectiveness and impact of its community involvement and uses the results for continuous improvement.

Standard 6: Communication

My company actively and openly communicates in order to inform, influence, and engage internal and external stakeholders.

Standard 7: Community Relationships

My company engages and collaborates with external stakeholders to advance its community involvement strategy.

Source: Center for Corporate Citizenship at Boston College, http://www.bcccc.net/index.cfm?pageId=2096. Accessed July 17, 2010.

support corporate giving in that improvement of the social fabric creates the greatest good for the greatest number. This need not contradict the mandates of self-interest, because the corporation is one of the community members that will benefit.[5] Although justifications for corporate involvement in the community are possible from various perspectives, one thing is clear: Business has a moral responsibility to build a relationship with the community and to be sensitive to its impacts on the world around it. The Center for Corporate Citizenship at Boston College has developed a set of seven management practices, processes, and policies that represent a global standard of excellence in community involvement. These are listed in Figure 16-1.

Volunteer Programs

One of the most pervasive examples of business involvement in communities is a volunteer program. Corporate volunteer programs reflect the resourcefulness and responsiveness of business to communities in need of increasing services. They also build employee morale: Almost two-thirds of the respondents to a recent Deloitte & Touche Volunteer IMPACT survey said they would rather work for companies that provide them with opportunities to volunteer at nonprofit organizations.[6] *The Wall Street Journal* referred to paid volunteer time as the "latest office perk" and a "hot topic at campus job fairs."[7]

There are numerous examples of corporations making a difference in communities through volunteer activities. The Longaberger Company has a longstanding commitment to the American Cancer Society to make and sell "Horizon of Hope" baskets, stuffed with breast cancer literature: The campaign has raised millions of dollars for research and education to combat breast cancer.[8] UPS has a variety of community service initiatives. Through Neighbor to Neighbor, UPS employees help to improve impoverished communities across the United States and around the world by organizing food drives, working in soup kitchens, and mentoring troubled youth. Community service is part of the Community Internship Program, UPS's senior management level development

FIGURE 16-2

Benefits of Employee Volunteerism

Benefits to the Employee

- Improves performance.
- Increases job satisfaction, attitude, and morale.
- Encourages teamwork.
- Promotes leadership and skill development.
- Improves communication between employees and their supervisors, and across departments.

Benefits to the Corporation

- Builds brand awareness and affinity.
- Strengthens trust and loyalty among consumers.
- Enhances corporate image and reputation.

- Improves employee retention.
- Increases employee productivity and loyalty.
- Provides an effective vehicle to reach strategic goals.

Benefits to the Community

- Provides skilled and talented volunteer pool, as employees devote personal and professional skills to community needs.
- Offers direct cost savings for community service organizations in saved recruiting and labor costs.
- Creates quantifiable social impact.
- Helps bring community needs into focus.

Source: VolunteerMatch, http://www.volunteermatch.org/corporations/resources/businesscase.jsp. Accessed July 17, 2010.

program, and UPS's Global Volunteer Month provides communities throughout the world with the time and talents of UPS employees. The company urges its employees to volunteer when crises occur and maintains a 20-person logistics emergency team in Asia, Europe, and the Americas. The team is trained in humanitarian relief and continues to draw a paycheck while providing skill-based support in crisis situations.[9]

Benefits from employee volunteerism extend in many directions. VolunteerMatch.org offers online support for matching nonprofit volunteers with businesses interested in civic engagement. Their list of employee volunteerism benefits derived by employees, corporations, and communities is detailed in Figure 16-2.

Managing Community Involvement

For discussion purposes, we are separating our treatment of *managing community involvement* from that of *managing corporate philanthropy*. In reality, however, this separation is impossible to achieve because there are significant overlaps between these two areas. Corporate philanthropy involves primarily the giving of financial resources. Community involvement focuses on other issues in the business–community relationship, especially the contribution of managerial and employee time and talent. This section addresses these broader community issues; a later section of this chapter deals with the more specific issue of managing corporate philanthropy.

Business Stake in the Community. When one speaks with corporate executives in the fields of community and civic affairs and examines community affairs manuals and other corporate publications, one sees a broad array of reasons why companies need to keep abreast of the issues, problems, and changes expressed as community needs. Self-interest and self-preservation provide one rationale. Companies typically have a significant physical presence in the community and so they want to protect that investment. Issues of interest to companies include zoning regulations, the threat of neighborhood deterioration, corporate property taxes, the community tax base, and the availability of an adequately trained workforce. Companies can support their communities through their daily activities in a variety of ways, including sourcing from local businesses, joining public policy debates, investing in local banks, and locating facilities in places that

FIGURE 16-3 Corporate Community Involvement: The Most Important Issues and the Most Common Methods of Addressing Them

Community Investment Issues		Community Investment Methods	
K–12 Education	71%	Volunteerism	86%
Workforce Development	68%	Cause-Related Partnerships	75%
Business Development and Growth	48%	Executive Participation in Community	71%
Higher Education	47%	Nonprofit or Community Board Participation	71%
Transportation or Public Infrastructure	38%	Cash Contributions	65%
Housing	38%	Advocacy	52%
Health and Wellness	38%	Community Advisory Panels	48%
Arts, Parks, Sports	24%	Pro Bono Work	31%
Crimes or Public Safety	22%	Donated Property or Equipment	30%
Other	19%	Community Management	28%

Source: U.S. Chamber of Commerce Survey—Summary of Findings Presented at the 2007 National Partnership Conference: Corporate Community Investment, U.S. Chamber of Commerce.

benefit community development. In addition, companies can develop community action programs that transcend daily operations. Figure 16-3 presents the results of a survey of businesses; identifying businesses' perceptions of the most important issues affecting communities as well as the methods those businesses use to address them.

Developing a Community Action Program.   The motivation for developing a **community action program** is evident when one considers the stake a firm has in the community. Likewise, the community represents a major stakeholder of business. Therefore, business has an added incentive to be systematic about its relationship with the community. First, the business must get to know the community in which it intends to become involved. The next step then is to assess the company's resources to determine what the company is best able to give. Then the company can design a community action program by matching the community needs to the resources the company has available. Finally, as with all corporate endeavors, management should monitor the performance of the community action program carefully and make adjustments where needed.

STEP ONE: KNOWING THE COMMUNITY A key to developing worthwhile community involvement programs is knowing the community in which the business resides. This is a research step that requires management to assess the characteristics of the local area. Every locale has particular characteristics that can help shape social programs of involvement. Who lives in the community? What is its ethnic composition? What is its unemployment level? Are there inner-city problems or pockets of poverty? What are other organizations doing? What are the really pressing social needs of the area? What is the community's morale?

Knowledge of community leadership is another factor. Is the leadership progressive? Is the leadership cohesive and unified, or is it fragmented? If it is fragmented, the company may have to make difficult choices about the groups with which it wants to work. If the community's current approach to social issues is well organized, "jumping on the bandwagon" may be all that is necessary. If the community's leadership is not well organized, the company may want to provide an impetus and an agenda for restructuring or revitalizing the leadership.

STEP TWO: KNOWING THE COMPANY'S RESOURCES Effective addressing of various community needs requires an inventory and assessment of the company's resources and competencies. What are the variety, mix, and range of resources—personnel, money, meeting space, equipment, and supplies? Many companies are willing to give employees time to engage in and support community projects. This involvement may be in the form of managerial assistance, technical assistance, or personnel. Wide spectra of abilities, skills, interests, potentials, and experience exist in most organizations. To put any of these resources to work, however, it is necessary to know what is available, to what extent it is available, on what terms it is available, and over what period of time it is available.

STEP THREE: SELECTING PROJECTS TO SUPPORT The selection of community projects for company involvement grows out of the matching of community stakeholders' needs with company resources. Frequently, because there are many possible matches, the company must be selective in choosing from among them. Sometimes companies develop and refine policies or guidelines to help in the selection process. These policies are extremely useful because they further delineate areas in which the company may be involved and provide perspective for channeling the organization's energies.

Policies and guidelines can go a long way toward rationalizing and systematizing business involvement in the community. Such policy statements can provide a unified focus for company efforts. Guidelines to consider include fit with the company resources (which project is most consistent with corporate resources and goals?), cost effectiveness (which project makes the best use of resources?), sustainability (will the project continue if the corporate involvement ends?), and employee preferences (with which projects would employees most want to get involved?).

An excellent example of a community project that follows these guidelines is the Ronald McDonald House Charities (RMHC) program sponsored by McDonald's Corporation. The three core programs of RMHC—the Ronald McDonald House, Ronald McDonald Family Room, and Ronald McDonald Care Mobile—are focused on helping families in need. The well-known Ronald McDonald House program provides a "home away from home" for families of seriously ill children receiving treatment at nearby hospitals. Since its inception over 35 years ago, millions of families around the world have received shelter and solace through the program.[10]

STEP FOUR: MONITORING PROJECTS Monitoring company projects involves review and control. Follow-up is necessary to ensure that the projects are being executed according to plans and on schedule. Feedback from the various steps in the process provides the information management needs to monitor progress. In later chapters, we elaborate on the managerial approach to dealing with various social issues. The guidelines previously listed, however, provide some insights into the development of business–community stakeholder relationships. As we stated earlier, community involvement is a discretionary or philanthropic activity in our corporate social performance model. The costs are significant but the potential returns, for both the corporation and the community, are great.

Corporate Philanthropy or Business Giving

The word *philanthropy* comes from the Greek *philien*, which means "to love," and *anthropos*, which means "mankind."[11] Thus the dictionary defines **philanthropy** as "a desire to help mankind as indicated by acts of charity; love of mankind."[12] One more restricted contemporary usage of the word "philanthropy" is "business giving." In this section, we concentrate on the voluntary giving of financial resources by business. One problem with the dictionary definition is that the motive for the giving is characterized as charitable, benevolent, or generous. In actual practice, it is difficult to assess the true

ETHICS IN PRACTICE CASE

Tugging the Heart or Twisting the Arm?

While working for a large corporation, I received numerous e-mails telling me of the large charitable contribution fund in which the company participates. All employees were highly encouraged to attend a town hall meeting, where other employees and managers spoke of how the fund had affected their lives and showed videos of the good work the fund had done. Top executives traveled to these town hall meetings to promote the campaign and encourage 100 percent employee participation. They told us to ask our fellow employees if they had contributed yet. They wanted to reach a goal of $1 million and believed that everyone should be able to contribute. Furthermore, all managers were expected to contribute. There was even documentation on the company's intranet Web site with guidelines for how much to give. Although the company claims all donations (or lack thereof) are anonymous and have no effect on promotions or job performance ratings, many wondered if that was entirely true. This was not the first company to strongly encourage me to contribute to its fund drive, and I doubt it will be the last.

1. Why do companies participate in charitable fund programs? Is it for societal recognition, to aid a worthy cause, or is it some combination? If different firms differ in their motivation—why might that be so?

2. Is it ethical for a company to solicit voluntary charitable contributions from employees? Can they be truly voluntary? If so, how should these campaigns be designed and implemented? Where would you draw the line?

3. If companies no longer participate in charitable fund campaigns, what would be the repercussion for the charities? Does that affect your answer?

4. If you worked in this company, what would you do? Why? If you choose to contribute, what would be your driving motivation?

Contributed by Melissa S. Magoon

motives behind businesses'—or anyone's—giving of themselves or their financial resources.

A 2009 survey of corporate giving officers by the Conference Board forecasts a drop in corporate giving due to the economic downturn, as well as a greater focus on corporate giving outcomes. The giving officers expect their philanthropy decisions to be more driven by limits on budgetary resources (56 percent) and the general economic downturn (50 percent). [13]

A Brief History of Corporate Philanthropy

Business philanthropy of one kind or another can be traced back to the 1920s when the most significant effort to "translate the new social consciousness of management into action" emerged in the form of organized corporate philanthropy.[14] Before World War I, steps had been taken toward establishing systematic, federated fund-raising for community services. The early successes of the YMCA, the War Chests, welfare federations, Community Chests, colleges and universities, and hospitals provided impetus for these groups to organize their solicitations. The business response to the opportunity to help community needs varied. At one extreme, large enterprises such as the then Bell Telephone system, with branches, offices, and subsidiaries in thousands of communities, contributed to literally thousands of civic and social organizations. Smaller firms, such as the companies in small mill towns of North Carolina, supported schools, housing projects, religious activities, and community welfare agencies with a degree of enthusiasm that exceeded most 19th-century paternalism.

From 1918 to 1929, the Community Chest movement dominated corporate giving. In the period from 1929 to 1935, there was an attempt to allow business to deduct up to 5 percent of its pretax net income for its community donations. During the years 1935 to 1945, marked by the Great Depression and World War II, business giving did not expand, but it began to grow again from 1945 to 1960. Since about 1960, corporate giving has grown to encompass a variety of initiatives. Now in the 21st century, broader social initiatives continue, but the nature of business giving has taken a turn. The corporate philanthropy watchword is now strategic philanthropy, philanthropy that benefits both society and the corporate that is giving. In the previously mentioned 2009 survey of giving officers, 47 percent expected their corporate philanthropy decisions to be driven increasingly by the closeness of the gift to business needs.[15]

A Call for Transparency in Corporate Philanthropy

A major debate has arisen over proposals for legislation that would have required companies to disclose which charities they support and how much money they give. Although companies are required to disclose the money they give through foundations because of the tax benefits derived from the foundation's tax-exempt status, companies need not disclose direct donations. This has renewed the age-old debate about the role of business in society. Proponents of disclosure contend that the money belongs to the shareholders and they alone have the right to determine where it will go. Former Representative Paul Gillmor (R-Ohio) said that he introduced legislation to require transparency because he had sat on corporate boards and observed executives distributing corporate assets to their pet charities while ignoring shareholders.

Gillmor's concern was shared by law professors such as Charles M. Elson, who argued that philanthropy often only serves to glorify corporate managers and that, unless the philanthropy clearly benefits the company, it represents a waste of corporate assets. A few nonprofits, such as the American Red Cross, also agreed that disclosure would be good public policy. Surprisingly, the National Society of Fundraising Executives even supported disclosure, arguing that it would help the image of philanthropy, which has been hurt by scandals in recent years.[16] This broad-based support notwithstanding, most corporations and nonprofits had expressed concern that disclosure would have a chilling effect on corporate donations. Their arguments include that charitable giving is a business decision, that it would provide competitors with information about a firm's strategy, that it might incite controversy with special-interest groups, and that the paperwork would become an administrative burden.[17]

The issue resurfaced in the wake of the Enron and WorldCom accounting scandals, when there were revelations about corporations giving large donations to corporate officers' pet causes. For example, Enron gave large donations to a hospital chaired by a member of its audit committee. This concern was factored into the reform legislation developed to enhance corporate accountability. The House developed a bill that included a requirement for corporations to report contributions to a nonprofit organization if any of the corporation's directors or members of their immediate family are members of that nonprofit's board. This would have applied to contributions over $10,000 made by the corporation or any officer of the corporation in the previous five years, as well as any other activity that provides a "material benefit" to the nonprofit, including lobbying.

This House bill passed, as did a Senate version, and so a conference committee met to work out the differences between the two bills. The result, of course, was the Sarbanes–Oxley Act of 2002, which did not contain the philanthropy disclosure requirements from the original House bill.[18] Gillmor reintroduced his earlier bill in February 2007 and then passed away later that year. No real closure on the issue of corporate philanthropy transparency has been achieved, and so calls for transparency in corporate giving are certain to continue.

Another issue that was added to the calls for transparency was a concern that nonprofits are being set up to get around the old campaign financing laws regarding "soft money" contributions. In a well-publicized case, the National Committee for Responsive Philanthropy (NCRP) and Common Cause filed complaints with the IRS and the House Ethics Committee that former House Majority Leader Tom DeLay (R-Texas) used a nonprofit organization for political purposes. They charged that DeLay's charity, "Celebrations for Children," provided a way for high-end donors to buy access to DeLay and other prominent politicians. According to NCRP executive director Rick Cohen, the charity evaded campaign-financing laws "through political fundraising disguised as charity." Those corporations were under no obligation to report their charitable giving, nor were they obligated to report what that giving has bought them in terms of access to politicians.[19]

Giving to the "Third Sector": The Nonprofits

According to philanthropist John D. Rockefeller III, business giving is necessary to support what has been called the **third sector**—the nonprofit sector. The first two sectors—business and government—receive support through profits and taxes. The third sector (which includes hundreds of thousands of churches, museums, hospitals, libraries, private colleges and universities, and performing arts groups) depends on philanthropy for support. Philanthropy gives these institutions the crucial margin that assures them of their most precious asset—their independence.[20]

Why Do Companies Give?   Perhaps it would be more worthwhile to know why companies give to charitable causes rather than to know how much they give. There are several ways to approach this question. We get initial insights when we consider the three categories of corporate contributions programs identified by the Committee to Encourage Corporate Philanthropy (CECP).[21] The motivations are (1) *Charitable*: community giving for which there is little or no expected benefit for the business. (2) *Community Investment*: Gifts that support long-term strategic business goals while also meeting a critical community need. (3) *Commercial*: Giving that benefits the business wherein the benefit is its primary motivation. CECP's 2009 report showed an increase in community investment giving and a decrease in commercial giving.

As economic pressures and increased international competitiveness force companies to be more careful with their earnings, we should not be surprised to see the profit motive coexisting with loftier goals in corporate contributions programs. In a subsequent section of this chapter, we illustrate how philanthropy can be "strategic," which means that corporate giving can be aligned with the firm's economic or profitability objectives.

To Whom Do Companies Give?   During the course of any budget year, companies receive numerous requests for contributions from a wide variety of applicants. Companies must then weigh both quantitative and qualitative factors to arrive at decisions regarding the recipients of their gifts. By looking at the beneficiaries of corporate contributions, we can estimate the value business places on various societal needs in the community. However, we should note that, because of the lack of transparency in corporate giving which we discuss later in the chapter, our figures for giving are simply estimates, and estimates from different sources will vary.

According to the Conference Board, the majority of business giving is distributed among four major categories of recipients in the following order of emphasis: (1) health and human services, (2) education, (3) civic and community activities, and (4) culture and the arts.[22] A very small percentage of giving went to the environment, with the recipients being environmental interest groups such as the World Wildlife Fund, the Nature Conservatory, and Greenpeace.[23] The small percentage of contributions does not mean business is unconcerned about environmental issues but that its commitment to the environment is less likely to show up in corporate philanthropy and more likely to be found in daily operations, as discussed in Chapter 15. In addition, environmental issues may end up under other categories such as community improvement. A brief discussion of each of these four categories will help explain the nature of business's involvement in philanthropy.

HEALTH AND HUMAN SERVICES Health and human services are critical to the welfare of a community, whether it is the local community in which a business operates or the global community to which we all belong. Major recipients in this category include hospitals, youth agencies, and other local health and welfare agencies. Hospitals represent an obviously important need in most communities. They receive financial support for capital investments (new buildings and equipment), operating funds, and matching employee gifts. Youth agencies include such groups as the YMCA, YWCA, Boy Scouts, Girl Scouts, and Boys and Girls Clubs. These children will grow to be attending college and moving on to employment opportunities, so it is logical for business to include youth as a prominent part of its health and welfare contributions.

Another reason that health and human services are among the largest categories of business giving is the amount donated to federated drives such as the United Way. Dating back to the Community Chest movement, business has traditionally cooperated with federated giving mechanisms. Organizations such as the United Way spend the year evaluating nonprofit programs and determining where dollars would be best spent with much of the money going to the local community. This saves businesses, particularly smaller local ones, the effort of not only trying to assess the various agencies to which they could make donations but also explaining to stakeholders why they chose one over another. Business hopes, just as the community does, that the consolidated efforts of federated drives will lend some order to the requests of major recipients in the community that business has chosen to support.

EDUCATION Most of the corporate contributions in this category have gone to higher education, that is, colleges and universities, but a growing percentage is going to K–12 programs.[24] Educational recipients include capital grants (including endowments), unrestricted operating grants, departmental and research grants, scholarships and fellowships, and employee matching gifts. Also included in this category are contributions to educational groups (e.g., the United Negro College Fund and the Council for Financial Aid to Education) and to primary and secondary schools.

As noted earlier, business has a very good reason for supporting higher education—to increase the pool of trained personnel. This has obvious credibility, because higher education institutions do form the resource base from which business fills its managerial and professional positions. K–12 institutions feed into higher education, and so strong preparation at those levels is critical to a strong professional pool down the road. In addition, many workers in the front lines will receive their education primarily from K–12 institutions, and so it is vital that they too be in a position to provide business with a strong and capable workforce.

CIVIC AND COMMUNITY ACTIVITIES This category of business giving represents a wide variety of philanthropic activities in the community. The dominant contributions in this category are those given in support of community improvement activities, environment and ecology, nonacademic research organizations (e.g., the Brookings Institution,

Spotlight on SUSTAINABILITY

Greening the Workforce

Community colleges have always been skilled at preparing two-year graduates to enter practical professions because their close ties with industry enable them to be more responsive to industry's needs. These attributes make the two-year college the perfect venue for preparing students to enter green-economy jobs. Recognizing the fit between community colleges and eco-economy job training, businesses are entering into partnerships with community colleges to prepare workers to meet their growing eco-workforce demands. For example, GE has donated a small wind turbine to Mesalands Community College in Tucumcari, NM, for their wind energy technician program and looks forward to hiring their graduates. Johnson Controls is constructing a 2,500 solar panel farm at Milwaukee Area Technical College so that students there can be trained as the photovoltaic designers and installers that Johnson Controls needs to hire. Experts predict that the expected expansion of environmental policies could increase renewable energy jobs from 9 million in 2007 to 19.5 million in 2030.

Source: Mina Kimes, "Get a Green Job in Two Years," *Fortune* (November 23, 2009), 32.

the Committee for Economic Development, and the Urban League), and neighborhood renewal.

General Mills saw the importance of community involvement when the nickname of Minneapolis went from the "City of Nice" to "Murderapolis." General Mills executives hired a consultant to analyze crime data and found that Hawthorne, just five miles from the company headquarters, was one of the city's most violent neighborhoods. They devoted thousands of employee hours and $2.5 million to ridding Hawthorne of its problems. As it turned out, the initiatives of General Mills along with a number of other prominent Minneapolis firms led to the development of a program known as Minnesota HEALS (Hope, Education, Law, and Safety) that has grown from a handful of people to dozens of corporate, community, and government groups convening to reduce violence and create hope. Today, Minneapolis is one of the leading cities in America in which business support of the community has become legendary.[25]

Also faced with a city in need of help, Prudential has focused significant philanthropic efforts on supporting the rebuilding of Newark, New Jersey, its headquarters since 1875. While it gave nearly $25 million worldwide, $6.2 million of its grants and matching gifts went directly to the city of Newark.[26] According to Gabriela Morris, President of the Prudential Foundation, "Part of your license to do business is your contract with the community.... The Prudential Foundation is 'far more concerned' with the societal impact of its programs than the business impact, and that doesn't mean you are wasting shareholder money. That reflects well on employees and the brand."[27]

CULTURE AND THE ARTS   Business support for the arts has been decreasing, and the future news is not good. Americans for the Arts predict a "dire drop" in future funding because of the global economic recession.[28] Companies faced with layoffs may feel they cannot afford to support the arts, but that outlook is short sighted. The arts provide brand recognition, ensure community development, and are key to promoting the community as a great place to live and work.[29]

The Arts and Business Council conducted a recent economic impact study of the nonprofit arts and culture industry in the United States and found good reason for business to support the arts as part of supporting the community. After surveying

156 communities and regions, representing all 50 states, they found that the nonprofit arts industry generated over one billion dollars of organization and audience expenditures in Chicago, the Greater Philadelphia area, San Francisco, and the Greater Washington, DC, area. This represents an increase of 58 percent in organization expenditures, 50 percent increase in audience expenditures, and 50 percent in overall economic activity from five years earlier. They excluded the two largest U.S. cities, New York and Los Angeles, to avoid inflating the national estimates.[30]

GIVING IN TIMES OF CRISIS In addition to the four categories previously mentioned, firms are expected to make charitable donations when crises occur in the firm's community, the nation or the world at large. We covered the general issues related to responding to a crisis in Chapter 6, noting that some firms are able to respond so well to a crisis that they can be counted on to lend a hand to others in need. For example, Walmart and Home Depot stood out in their ability to bring some relief following the devastation of Hurricane Katrina, as did Fed Ex for providing the Federal Emergency Management Agency (FEMA) with a radio antenna to set up communications. Most companies stepped up to provide contributions. Of the top 100 firms, 86 percent made donations following the disaster, while the remaining 14 percent put a link on their Web site to nonprofit organizations aiding rescue efforts.[31] This level of giving tends to follow most disasters. According to the U.S. Chamber of Commerce, U.S. businesses donated $566 million to help communities suffering from the effects of the Indian Ocean tsunami.[32]

Some observers worry that in times of crisis, corporate philanthropy becomes a zero-sum game in that contributions that go to alleviate the crisis then do not go to other causes that need them as well. Typically, giving has increased from year to year irrespective of external events; however, one statistic should give us pause. In the two weeks following the attack on the World Trade Center, corporations gave over $120 million to relief funds—an unprecedented level of corporate giving.[33] According to a survey by the *Chronicle of Corporate Philanthropy*, however, corporate giving subsequently declined.[34] Other concerns surround the possibility of donor fatigue following crises for which corporations and individuals open their checkbooks. There has been some evidence of this. In the first two weeks after the disaster, Hurricane Katrina garnered $409 million in corporate donations and the Indian Ocean tsunami received $300 million; however, after two weeks, the corporate philanthropy directed toward the Haiti earthquake was only $122 million.[35]

Managing Corporate Philanthropy

As performance pressures on business have continued and intensified, companies have had to turn their attention to managing corporate philanthropy. Early on, managers did not subject their contributions to the same kinds of rigorous analysis given to expenditures for plants and equipment, inventory, product development, marketing, and a host of other budgetary items. This began to change in the early 1980s because cutbacks in federal spending on charitable causes created an increasing need for contributions by business. At the same time, however, the economy was struggling through its worst recession in 50 years. It became increasingly clear that business had to reconcile its economic and social goals, both of which were essential.[36]

Now, with a worldwide recession at hand, the pressure on businesses to be more businesslike in their philanthropy has grown stronger. There are two aspects to this. The first is to base giving on business skills, resources, and capabilities to enhance philanthropic outcomes. The second is to focus on philanthropy that will enhance corporate profitability while also making a positive difference in the community at large. This strategic approach to philanthropy follows an ethic of enlightened self-interest and is clearly on

---

FIGURE 16-4 Critical Factors Influencing Corporate Giving Priorities

Aligning more closely with business needs	66%
Limits on budgetary resources	62%
Directions from the CEO and/or the board	51%
Strengthening the brand	35%
Costs of responding to natural disasters	23%
Being more responsive to stakeholders	18%
Changes in the workforce	10%
Other	8%
Employee needs or requests	3%
Community needs	3%
Global giving	3%

Source: Sophia A. Muirhead, "Philanthropy and Business: The Changing Agenda," *The Conference Board* (2006), 5.

---

the rise. In a recent Conference Board survey, almost half the companies responded said that the biggest change in corporate philanthropy in the previous five years was "its alignment with business objectives and corporate reputation and branding."[37] That trend will only grow as the recession makes it more necessary to align philanthropic goals with strategic priorities.[38] Figure 16-4 shows that the top four critical factors that companies consider reflect a strategic approach to corporate giving priorities. Note the dramatic difference in importance between community needs (3 percent) and business needs (66 percent).

Community Partnerships.   As a broad response to this growing need to reconcile financial and social goals, the concept of **community partnerships** evolved. A community partnership occurs when a for-profit business enters into a cooperative arrangement with a nonprofit organization for their mutual advantage. Businesses see in community partnerships the opportunity for simultaneous achievement of economic and philanthropic objectives. An example of a community partnership is the one between Home Depot and KaBOOM!®, a national nonprofit organization devoted to building community through the construction of playspaces for children. As part of their ten-year partnership, Home Depot contributes in-kind, financial, and volunteer assistance to the building of playspaces across North America with initiatives that include 1,000 Playgrounds in 1,000 Days, Operation Playground, and Racing to Play. The pair received the 2006 Golden Halo Award from the Cause Marketing Forum for their "long-term, high-impact" partnership. In 2009, Home Depot became the official sustainability partner of KaBOOM![39]

Another example of a community partnership involves the Clorox Company and the East Bay Community Foundation. Community foundations are nonprofit organizations that specialize in evaluating nonprofit organizations and responding to requests for funding. Clorox knew that the knowledge and expertise that the East Bay Community Foundation had in local nonprofit organizations would help them better manage their philanthropic funds. In turn, this would help to further their goal of improving the quality of life in Oakland, California, and its surrounding communities, the area in which Clorox is based.[40]

FIGURE 16-5 Implementation of an Effective Strategic Philanthropy Program	An effective strategic philanthropy program should incorporate the following practices: 1. Integrate philanthropy into strategic goals and company mission. 2. Connect philanthropy with other community involvement programs. 3. Budget appropriately for philanthropy. 4. Ensure effective program infrastructure.	5. Formalize policies and guidelines for funding. 6. Involve employees in philanthropy-related activities. 7. Incorporate stakeholder communication. 8. Develop long-term business–nonprofit partnerships.

Community partnerships take on many different forms. Two of the most important are strategic philanthropy and cause-related marketing. Other partnership options include sponsorships, vendor relationships, licensing agreements, and in-kind donations.[41] We consider strategic philanthropy and cause-related marketing in more detail.

Strategic Philanthropy. **Strategic philanthropy** is an approach by which corporate giving and other philanthropic endeavors of a firm are designed in a way that best fits with the firm's overall mission, goals, or objectives. This implies that the firm has some idea of what its overall strategy is and that it is able to articulate its missions, goals, or objectives. One goal of all firms is profitability. Therefore, one requirement of strategic philanthropy is to make as direct a contribution as possible to the financial goals of the firm. Philanthropy has long been thought to be in the long-range economic interest of the firm. Strategic philanthropy simply presses for a more direct or immediate contribution of philanthropy to the firm's economic success.

An important way to make philanthropy strategic is to bring contribution programs into sharper alignment with business endeavors. This means that each firm should pursue those social programs that have a direct rather than an indirect bearing on its success. Thus, a local bank should logically pursue people-oriented projects in the community in which it resides; a manufacturer might pursue programs having to do with environmental protection or technological advancement.

A third way to make philanthropy strategic is to ensure that it is well planned and managed rather than handled haphazardly and without direction. Planning implies that it has clearly delineated goals, is properly organized and staffed, and administered in accordance with certain established policies. Figure 16-5 presents *Business for Social Responsibility*'s recommendations for best practices in the implementation of a philanthropy program.

Strategic philanthropy must find the place of overlap where the philanthropy provides both social and economic benefits. In an important *Harvard Business Review* article, Michael Porter and Mark Kramer argued that few companies have effectively taken advantage of the competitive advantage corporate philanthropy can provide. They consider strategic philanthropy to be a myth—simply semantics that help companies to rationalize their contributions. To be truly strategic, philanthropy must be congruent with a company's competitive context, which consists of four interrelated elements: factor conditions, demand conditions, the context for strategy and rivalry, and related and supporting industries.[42]

FACTOR CONDITIONS These are the available inputs for productions. Porter and Kramer point to DreamWorks as an example of a company that uses strategic philanthropy to effectively improve its factor conditions. They created a program that provides training to low-income and disadvantaged youth in the skills needed to work in the entertainment industry. Of course, the societal benefits of an improved educational system are clear. While providing these social benefits, DreamWorks also enhances the labor pool from which they can draw. This not only strengthens the company but the industry as a whole as well.[43] The Clorox example of improving the community surrounding their headquarters through partnership with the community foundation also addresses factor conditions by improving the general quality of life and the local infrastructure.

DEMAND CONDITIONS These are concerned with the nature of the company's customers and the local market. Philanthropy can influence the local market's size and quality. Porter and Kramer point to Apple's long-held policy of donating computers to public schools. By introducing young people and their teachers to computers, Apple expands their market. They also increase the sophistication of their customer base, which benefits a differentiated product such as the ones Apple sells.[44] Similarly, Burger King focuses its philanthropic efforts on highly focused programs to help students, teachers, and schools.[45] This program enhances name recognition in its target population of consumers.

Whole Foods has developed a strategic philanthropy program that affects both factor and demand conditions, enabling the company to reap benefits along the length of the value chain. In the factor market, Whole Foods has designed a system for sourcing products from developing countries while maintaining product standards. It developed a strict set of criteria for its suppliers to adhere to and contracted with TransFair USA and the Rainforest Alliance, two respected third-party certifiers, to ensure the suppliers met these criteria. These certified products receive a Whole Trade logo so that customers know which products come from the developing world and meet the criteria. Its customers value these attributes and so Whole Foods' demand conditions also improve as a result of their efforts.[46]

CONTEXT FOR STRATEGY AND RIVALRY This can be influenced by strategic philanthropy. Porter and Kramer point to the many corporations that support Transparency International as examples of firms using philanthropy to create a better environment for competition. Transparency International's mission is to deter and disclose corporate corruption around the world. The organization measures and publicizes corruption while pushing for stricter codes and enforcement. By supporting Transparency International, corporations are helping to build a better competitive environment—one that rewards fair competition.[47]

RELATED AND SUPPORTING INDUSTRIES These can also be strengthened through strategic philanthropy, thereby enhancing the productivity of companies. American Express provides an excellent example of a firm that uses philanthropy to strengthen its related and supporting industries. For almost 20 years, American Express has funded travel and tourism academies in secondary schools. The program trains teachers, supports curricula, and provides both summer internships and industry mentors. A strong travel industry translates into important benefits for American Express.[48]

Now let us turn our attention to a special kind of strategic philanthropy that has become quite prevalent in recent years: cause-related marketing.

Cause-Related Marketing.   There is some debate as to whether cause-related marketing is really philanthropy. Porter and Kramer argue that it is marketing and nothing more.[49] However, because cause marketing represents a close linkage between a firm's financial objectives and corporate contributions, it is discussed here. Stated in its simplest

ETHICS IN PRACTICE CASE

Giving Back the Google Way

Google's founders, Larry Page and Sergey Brin, have never approached business in the traditional way, and their approach to corporate philanthropy is no exception. They have put together a for-profit philanthropy (Google.org) and given it a mandate to tackle poverty, disease, and global warming. As a for-profit entity, it will be responsible for paying taxes if any of its ventures shows a profit, and Google will have to pay taxes on any corporate earnings used to finance its work. The organization began operations with seed money of about $1 billion.

Dr. Larry Brilliant, executive director of Google.org, compares its for-profit status to the keys on a keyboard, "Google.org can play the entire keyboard. It can start companies, build industries, pay consultants, lobby, give money to individuals and make a profit." Because Google.org is for-profit, its funds are available to Google whenever it would want to pull them back. Some skeptics object to this, noting that Google's directors or shareholders might want to take back funds in the event of an economic downturn. They may also resent paying taxes on expenditures intended to accomplish charitable purposes.

Google.org announced that it intends to spend its money over the next 20 years. According to

Dr. Brilliant, "Poor people can't wait. Dying people can't wait for some 20-year plan. It's not what we're doing here." Google moved quickly and, within a short time, compiled a list of over 1,000 ideas, which they winnowed down to five ideas in three areas—climate change, economic development, and building an early warning system for pandemics and natural disasters.

1. Assess Google.org's decision to be a for-profit entity. Do you agree with that decision?
2. Would your opinion change if you were a shareholder of Google?
3. If Google suffers an economic downturn, should the directors and/or shareholders have the option of pulling back funds from Google.org to shore up Google's operations? Would it be right if they exercised that option?
4. Do the projects selected by Google have any relationship to the company's bottom line? Does that matter to you?
5. Would you invest in Google.org?

Sources: Katie Hafner, "Philanthropy Google's Way: Not the Usual," *The New York Times* (September 14, 2006), http://www.nytimes.com; "Face Value: Google's Guru of Giving," *The Economist* (January 19, 2008), 75.

---

form, cause-related marketing is the direct linking of a business's product or service to a specified charity. Each time a consumer uses the service or buys the product, a donation is given to the charity by the business.[50] Thus some observers refer to cause-related marketing as "quid pro quo strategic philanthropy."

The term **cause-related marketing** was coined by the American Express Company to describe a program it began in 1983 in which it agreed to contribute a penny to the restoration of the Statue of Liberty every time a customer used one of its credit cards to make a purchase. The project generated $1.7 million for the statue restoration and a substantial increase in usage of the American Express card.[51] Since that time, companies have employed this same approach to raise millions of dollars for a wide variety of local and national causes.

Recently, cause-related marketing has given way to a new concept, **cause branding**. Cause branding represents a longer-term commitment than cause marketing. It also relates more directly to the firm's line of business and the target audience. Avon Products, Inc., has become a recognized leader in cause branding. Its target audience is women, and so it has developed an array of programs to raise awareness of breast cancer, a disease that mostly affects women. The company raises money for programs that provide low-income women with education and free screening. Avon sells products featuring the pink ribbon that is worn for breast cancer awareness and then donates the proceeds from these products to nonprofit and university programs.[52]

Cause branding has become a successful marketing tool. A Cone/Roper *Cause-Related Trends Report: Evolution of Cause Branding* showed that 61 percent of consumers felt companies should make cause branding part of their regular business.[53] Moreover, 83 percent of Americans feel more positively disposed toward companies that support a cause about which they care, and 76 percent of consumers are more likely to select the more socially responsible brand when price and quality are equal. The benefits do not apply only to consumers: Employees react to cause branding as well. In companies with cause programs, 87 percent of employees indicate they feel strong loyalty, while only 67 percent feel strong loyalty in firms that do not have cause programs.[54] The findings of a recent Cone/Roper Executive Study show that cause branding strengthens internal corporate cultures and has a dramatic influence on employee pride, morale, and loyalty.[55]

Proponents of cause-related marketing argue that everyone involved in it comes out a winner. Business enhances its public image by being associated with a worthy cause and increases its sales at the same time. Nonprofit organizations get cash for their programs as well as enhanced marketing and public visibility made possible by business's expertise.

Critics of cause-related marketing fear that the needs of capitalism will overshadow the cause. These concerns cropped up in the recent promotion of the "RED™" project. The rock star Bono devised the RED project, a plan to have firms launch versions of their products that follow the RED guidelines and donate a portion of their proceeds to The Global Fund to Fight AIDS, Tuberculosis, and Malaria. None of the brands were permitted to charge a premium for RED products, but the percentage of profits to be donated was not specified.[56] *Advertising Age* created a stir by reporting that firms involved in the project had spent as much as $100 million to promote the product, while the money raised amounted to only $18 million.[57] RED spokespeople countered that the $100 million estimate was high and many observers concurred; however, they were unapologetic about the possibility that expenditures might end up larger than contributions because the project was founded on the idea that self-interest can be a method of fundraising for charity.[58] Nonprofit advocates expressed concern, however, that cause-related marketing like the RED project might crowd out philanthropic contributions if people feel that buying a RED item is a substitute for charitable giving.[59] A parody of the RED commercials on http://www.buylesscrap.org expresses the concerns of cause marketing critics and ends with an opportunity to donate directly to the nonprofit organizations designated to receive RED funds.[60]

Global Philanthropy.   The size of a company's workforce in international markets is the greatest determinant of the size of their charitable contributions to that market.[61] It should come as no surprise then that as corporate operations become increasingly globalized, so does corporate philanthropy. Firms responding to a Conference Board survey indicated that 20 percent of their philanthropic giving was international.[62] The 2010 Conference Board report on corporate philanthropy cited international development as one of the areas that will see increased funding, even in the recessionary times.[63]

Businesses want to protect the communities in which they operate, keeping them healthy and environmentally sound. Businesses also develop infrastructure to facilitate the flow of goods and services. According to Stephen Jordan of the U.S. Chamber of Commerce Business Civic Leadership Center, companies are increasing their corporate philanthropy to "create a culture of opportunity" in the developing world. He said, "Ninety-six percent of opportunity is outside our borders.... Increasingly, companies ... want to grow their customer base in emerging markets."[64]

The Loss of Jobs

We now shift our focus to the issue of job loss from offshore outsourcing and business or plant closings. In the preceding sections, we considered the ways in which business firms might have positive, constructive, and creative impacts on community stakeholders. Firms can also have detrimental impacts on communities. We see a most pervasive example of such negative effects when mass job layoffs occur because jobs are moved overseas or when a business or plant closes and its management does not carefully consider the community stakeholders affected.

The recession of the early 1980s provided a major catalyst for business and plant shutdowns. Some of the affected companies were in declining industries; some had outdated facilities or technology; some moved to less unionized regions of the country; some sought access to new markets; some were victims of the merger/acquisition frenzy; and many were victims of global competition. For most of the 1990s, plant closings were not as prevalent but offshore outsourcing became more common. As we entered the new millennium, however, an economic recession brought the problem of closings back to the forefront. The sharp decline in the technology sector resulted in the sudden closing of dotcoms and other technology-based firms. The attack on the World Trade Center put industries, such as airlines, hospitality, travel, and tourism, into distress. At the same time, offshore outsourcing emerged as a source of job loss. Finally, the recent global economic recession put a range of businesses in jeopardy and scores of people out of work. We will address the issue of offshore outsourcing first and then take a more in-depth look at business and plant closings.

Offshore Outsourcing

The word **outsourcing** refers to the relocation of business processes to a different company. **Offshore outsourcing** (or **offshoring**) refers to the relocation of businesses processes to a different country. The problems created by offshore outsourcing are not new. The concern has arisen because new technologies such as high-speed data links and the Internet have made it easier to do white-collar work overseas, where labor is cheaper. In the late 19th century, the advent of railroads had just as transforming an effect. A writer for Scribner's in 1888 said that life had changed more in the past 75 years than it had since Julius Caesar, "and the change has chiefly been made by railways."[65] Railroads destroyed industries and whole towns, in addition to jobs. There was no longer a need for icehouses or local meatpacking plants and so they closed. While new markets opened for U.S. grain, cotton farmers lost market share to cheaper Egyptian and Indian cotton. Steamboat towns faded, and struggling farmers began to resent their dependence on the wealthy railroads.[66]

Thirty years ago, concerns over offshore outsourcing focused on blue-collar occupations, primarily factory workers, and it was mostly a problem in the United States. Today it affects blue- and white-collar workers alike, and industrial nations around the globe feel its influence. The fact that white-collar workers are now losing their jobs has given the issue new momentum. Information technology workers have been particularly hard hit. A programmer who makes $11,000 in India or $8,000 in Poland and Hungary can do the work of a programmer who makes $80,000 in the United States.[67] This represents huge savings for firms dealing with global competition.

In spite of the savings involved, however, offshore outsourcing is not a panacea for companies. Some companies end up finding that the problems that develop from shipping jobs overseas outweigh the cost savings. Capital One ended a contract for a 250-person call center in New Delhi when they found that workers would boost their sales by offering unauthorized lines of credit.[68] Similarly, Dell brought a tech support center back to the United States after customers complained of thick accents and poor service.[69] Stanley Furniture moved its manufacturing facilities back to the United States after a 2008 recall of cribs made in Slovenia.[70] When GE Chairman and CEO Jeff Immelt announced plans to return some aviation parts manufacturing to the United States he referred to it as "insourcing."[71] Some companies are finding that the cost savings on labor and goods that made offshore outsourcing so attractive may not compensate for the problems with transportation costs, quality control, and intellectual property issues.[72]

As Institute for International Economics productivity expert Martin Baily notes, for the predicted benefits of offshore outsourcing to occur, people have to move into jobs that will pay them enough so that they can pay for the cheap imports.[73] Just as with business and plant closings, which we discuss later, the company has a responsibility to ascertain that offshore outsourcing is the only option. If it is, the company's responsibility then shifts to doing everything possible to minimize offshore outsourcing's negative impact on the workers involved. Manjeet Kripalani offers five best offshore outsourcing practices to consider when undertaking this profound change in operations.[74]

1. **Go offshore for the right reasons.** Make certain that you have made every effort to increase efficiency and competitiveness at home. Consider the possible backlash and make sure operations are smooth before departure. Moving a broken process overseas won't fix it.
2. **Choose your model carefully.** The decision of whether to set up your own subsidiary or contract the work out is important. Both options have pros and cons that will have different impacts on different firms.
3. **Get your people on board.** Middle managers and employees can either facilitate the move or make certain it doesn't succeed. Intensive communication efforts, careful redeployment of retained workers, and severance with retraining for those who lose their jobs are critical to garnering support.
4. **Be prepared to invest time and effort.** Setting up relationships with offshore partners and designing the transition are time-consuming processes. Careful preparation will increase the odds of a successful program.
5. **Treat your partners as equals.** Involve the offshore partners in planning and preparation. Make them feel they are part of the team and let them know that their contributions are valued.

While nothing will make offshore outsourcing easy, these practices should assist firms in making the transition as smoothly as possible.

Business and Plant Closings

There is no single reason for business and plant closings. Figure 16-6 provides a window into the extent of impact that many communities are experiencing: It is a listing of some of the plant closings that occurred in North Carolina and the reasons given for the action. Each job lost had a serious impact on the displaced worker, and each of these closings presented major challenges for the communities in which they took place. In the aggregate, these closings present a major challenge for a state as workers cannot look to the neighboring town for employment if those plants and businesses are closing, too.

Although the right to close a business or plant has long been regarded as a management prerogative, the business shutdowns of the past two decades—especially their dramatic effects—have called attention to the question of what rights and responsibilities business has in relation to employee and community stakeholders. The literature of business social responsibility and policy has documented corporate concern with the

FIGURE 16-6 Selected North Carolina Business and Plant Closings and Their Reasons

Date	Product	Jobs Lost	Reason
October 2009	Personal computers	905	Declining sales
September 2007	Furniture	521	Offshoring
January 2004	Office furniture	480	Economic conditions
January 2004	Furniture	351	Economic conditions
November 2003	Electrical switches	313	Moving jobs to Mexico
October 2003	Milling	625	Foreign competition
September 2003	Furniture	506	Foreign competition
May 2003	Auto parts	350	Moving jobs to Mexico

Sources: Mark Barrett, "Burnsville Yarn Plant Closing; 163 Workers Get Pink Slip," *Citizen-times.com* (March 1, 2004); Doug Olenick, "Dell to Shutter NC PC Plant," *This Week in Consumer Electronics* (October 12, 2009), 49; "Herndon Closing NC Plant," *Furniture Today* (September 24, 2007), 92.

detrimental impact of its actions. Indeed, business's social response patterns have borne this out. Management expert Peter Drucker suggested the following business position regarding social impacts of management decisions:

> *Because one is responsible for one's impacts, one minimizes them. The fewer impacts an institution has outside of its own specific purpose and mission, the better does it conduct itself, the more responsibly does it act, and the more acceptable a citizen, neighbor, and contributor it is.*[75]

This raises the question of whether business's responsibilities in the realm of plant closings and their impacts on employees and communities are any different from the host of responsibilities that have already been assumed in areas such as employment discrimination, employee privacy and safety, honesty in advertising, product safety, and concern for the environment. From the perspective of the employees affected, their role in plant and business closings might be considered an extension of the numerous employee rights issues.

Business essentially has two opportunities to be responsive to employee and community stakeholders in shutdown situations. It can take certain actions *before the decision* to close is made and other actions *after the decision* to close has been made.

Before the Decision to Close Is Made. Before a company makes a decision to close down, it has a responsibility to itself, its employees, and its community to thoroughly and diligently study whether the closing is the only option available. A decision to leave should be preceded by critical and realistic investigations of economic alternatives.

DIVERSIFICATION Sometimes it is possible to find other revenue streams to help the company cope with the slim margins of manufacturing. SRC Holdings was making only 2 to 3 percent a year but needed a profit of 4 percent to compete effectively. SRC chief executive John P. Stack explains, "We took our manufacturing discipline into the service sector to develop new sources of revenue.... Without creating these other businesses, we couldn't have survived. Manufacturing has very slim margins but if a company innovates the margins can be incredible."[76] In 2010, having weathered multiple economic storms, SRC took pride in being "the oldest employee-owned remanufacturer to OEM's in North America."[77]

The Wisconsin-based Menasha Corporation also drew upon its expertise in manufacturing. They developed labels embedded with computer chips that use radio frequency identification technology (RFID) with the intent of making RFID capability a business they can spin off or a service they can sell.[78] Mike Johnson, a company spokesperson, said, "It's totally new for us—an Internet I.T. play that uses intellectual capital from our manufacturing to create a new stream of revenue we can plow back into the factory."[79]

NEW OWNERSHIP After a careful study has been made, it may be concluded that finding new ownership for the plant or business is the only feasible alternative. Two basic options exist at this point: (1) find a new owner or (2) explore the possibility of employee ownership.[80] A company has an obligation to its employees and the community to try to sell the business as a going unit instead of shutting down. This is often not possible, but it is an avenue that should be explored. Quite often, the most promising new buyers of a firm are residents of the state who have a long-term stake in the community and are willing to make a strong commitment. Ideally, local organizations and the government will be able to offer incentives to companies willing to bring jobs to the areas.

For example, when the Grumman Olson facility closed in Lycoming County, Pennsylvania, several parties joined together to bring jobs back to the area. The local chamber of commerce worked with the state to develop an incentive package that included job creation tax credits and customized job training at the local college. Specialized Vehicles Corporation (SVC) bought the facility, promising to offer jobs first to the displaced workers of Grumman Olson.[81]

EMPLOYEE OWNERSHIP The idea of a company selling a plant to the employees as a way of avoiding a closedown is appealing at first glance. In the United States, over a thousand companies are **employee owned**. Most of these companies are very small. The National Center for Employee Ownership (NCEO) lists the 100 largest employee-owned companies, defined as having over 50 percent employee ownership, and, in 2010, the smallest on the list only have about 1,000 employees.[82] Although employee ownership is not a major trend in the current recessionary environment, it is instructive to understand its history and record of success and failure to appreciate fully the pros and cons of employee ownership.

Employee ownership experiences have not always been favorable.[83] In numerous cases, employees have had to take significant wage and benefit reductions to make the business profitable. Some companies, however, have met with better success. Publix Supermarkets is both employee and family owned. Employees own 31 percent of the firm, and the family of founder George W. Jenkins own most of the remaining shares.[84] Most observers credit their employee ownership with earning Publix the number one supermarket ranking on the American Customer Satisfaction Index for each of the 14 years it has been in existence. Publix employees are known for bending over backwards to please customers.[85] In 2010, Publix tops the list as the largest employee-owned company in the United States.

In a classic case of employee ownership, negotiators worked out an agreement whereby the employees of National Steel's Weirton, West Virginia, mill would purchase the mill. The new company, Weirton Steel, became what was then the nation's largest employee-owned enterprise, as well as its eighth-largest producer of steel. Experts gave the mill a surprisingly good chance of succeeding, although Weirton's workers had to take a pay cut of about 32 percent. The mill's union president argued, "Thirty-two percent less of $25 an hour is a whole lot better than 100 percent of nothing."[86]

In 1990, however, as demand sank for the steel sheet it produced, Weirton Steel found itself in the unenviable position of actually having to lay off some of its employee-owners. By 1991, Weirton had eliminated 1,000 of its 8,200 jobs, had furloughed another 200 workers, and had plans to cut 700 more jobs. After a decade as owners of the company, Weirton employees became extremely frustrated and angry that employee ownership did not guarantee them that they would not lose their jobs. One employee posed the question many were asking: "How can we be laid off if we own the company?" The reality of the situation, however, is that even an employee-owned company must take whatever actions are necessary in order to remain solvent and profitable.

One of the major pitfalls of worker ownership is that it does not rewrite the laws of capitalism—the bottom line is still the bottom line.[87] In 2004, Weirton sold its assets to the Cleveland-based International Steel Group (ISG). Weirton CEO D. Leonard Wise commented, "There's a great comfort in knowing that steelmaking will continue in Weirton.... It's quite difficult for smaller mills to survive these days. Therefore, as part of ISG, one of the nation's largest steelmakers, Weirton will have a greater chance of surviving given the worldwide consolidation of steel companies."[88] Today, following a series of mergers, ArcelorMittal Weirton Steel continues to operate as part of the largest steel-producing company in the world.[89] Given that Weirton survived and is now thriving, one could argue that the employees who purchased the mill made a good investment for their community.

Ten years after Weirton Steel learned that employee ownership is not a protection against difficult times, United Airlines found themselves in a similar situation. In 1994, United Airlines became America's largest employee-owned corporation. In one of the nastiest and most prolonged corporate battles ever, shareholders of UAL Corp., the parent of United Airlines, awarded employee groups 55 percent of the company's stock in exchange for a $4.9 billion bundle of wage and productivity concessions. U.S. labor leaders hailed this new arrangement in worker control as a model alternative to the way companies usually battle to control costs. Labor Secretary Robert Reich, whose department facilitated the deal, asserted, "If United is successful, this will be a major landmark in American business history." But the success of the new firm was by no means ensured, because the airline has been buffeted for over a decade by infighting among employee groups, repeated forays by outside potential buyers, and takeover attempts.[90] Furthermore, it still had all the problems inherent in being a legacy carrier. From the beginning, there were problems with workers who resented taking pay cuts in exchange for loans to buy 55 percent of United's common stock and flight attendants whose union opted not to join the ESOP because of concerns about the pay cuts involved and other policies. Problems began in 2000, when the airline pilots conducted a slowdown during contract negotiations. Then the machinists' union threatened to strike, and United took them to court.[91] By 2001, when the attack on the World Trade Center shook the airline industry, the ESOP had ended and United was in no better position than firms without employee-owners. In 2002, United filed for bankruptcy.[92] It emerged from bankruptcy in 2006 after paying over $335 million in fees.[93]

Some critics argue that United Airlines failed as an employee-owned enterprise because workers thought employee ownership would mean they no longer needed to be concerned about labor-management issues. Research has shown that employee ownership can provide a firm with competitive advantage; for employee ownership to work, however, it is critical that employees believe they have a part to play in leading the company. A positive ownership culture provides employees with access to information, the power to exert influence, a sense of fairness, and a feeling of ownership and entrepreneurship.[94] It should be noted, however, that the period following the World Trade Center attacks was difficult for all large airlines, and so there are limits to the inferences one can make about the impact that employee ownership had on United.

After the Decision to Close Is Made. There are a multitude of actions that a business can take once the decision has been made that a closedown or relocation is unavoidable. The overriding concern should be that the company seriously attempt to mitigate the social and economic impacts of its actions on employees and the community. Regardless of the circumstances of the move, some basic planning can help alleviate the disruptions felt by those affected. There are several actions that management can take,[95] including

- conducting a community-impact analysis;
- providing advance notice to the employees or community;
- providing transfer, relocation, and outplacement benefits;
- phasing out the business gradually; and
- helping the community attract replacement industry.

COMMUNITY-IMPACT ANALYSIS Because management is responsible for its impacts on employees and the community, a thorough community-impact analysis of a decision to close down or move is in order. The initial action should be to identify realistically those aspects of the community that would be affected by the company's plans. This entails asking questions,[96] such as:

- What groups will be affected?
- How will they be affected?
- What is the timing of initial and later effects?
- What is the magnitude of the effect?
- What is the duration of the impact?
- To what extent will the impact be diffused in the community?

Once these questions have been answered, management is better equipped to modify its plans so that negative impacts can be minimized and favorable impacts, if any, can be maximized.

ADVANCE NOTICE One of the most often discussed responsibilities in business- or plant-closing situations is the provision of advance notice to workers and communities. The national advance-notice law is called the **Worker Adjustment and Retraining Notification Act (WARN)**. WARN requires those firms employing 100 or more workers to provide 60 days' advance notice to employees before shutting down or conducting substantial layoffs. The global economic crisis has moved some states to strengthen the WARN protections. New York increased the notice to 90 days and applied the protections to firms with as few as 25 employees.[97]

Companies will sometimes try to get around the WARN requirements. A New York–based software developer was sued by its employees, who charged that the company tried to disguise mass layoffs as individual firings to avoid having to comply with the advance notice required by WARN. There is a fine line between staggering employee layoffs legally and doing it to avoid the notice requirements of WARN. Courts try to determine what employers knew at the time of the layoffs. If they deem that the employers knew they would be laying off more than 50 employees at a time, the firm is considered to be in violation of WARN. Employees who sue successfully under WARN may get back pay and benefits for up to 60 days. The penalty for not giving adequate notice is $500 per day. The only acceptable reasons for not providing a 60-day notice are (1) action being taken by the employer, which, if successful, would have postponed or eliminated the need for layoffs, (2) unforeseen business circumstances that the employer could not reasonably have foreseen, and (3) natural disasters.[98]

An investigation by the *Blade*, a newspaper from Toledo, Ohio, found that WARN often falls short of its goals. Judges threw out more than half of the 236 lawsuits filed since 1989.[99] Only about one-quarter of the more than 8,000 closings in one year were subject to WARN requirements and only about one-third of those employers subject to the requirements actually provided proper warning.[100] Since the bill's inception, legislators have tried to strengthen the law by closing loopholes and giving it some teeth. One key problem is that the Labor Department has no enforcement power over the WARN Act and so displaced employees must hire their own attorneys to hold their former employers accountable.[101]

Communication expert Hugh Braithwaite offers advice on communicating with employees being laid off.[102]

- **Be complete.** Employees will try to fill any holes in your story, and that is how rumors begin.
- **Be consistent**. Information will become muddled if the story keeps changing.
- **Inform affected employees first.** Provide a thorough "exit kit" that provides all information the employee might need to smooth their transition.
- **Inform retained employees.** Recognize that survivors have challenges too and provide ample opportunity for their questions to be asked and answered.

TRANSFER, RELOCATION, AND OUTPLACEMENT BENEFITS Enlightened companies are increasingly recognizing that the provision of separation or outplacement benefits is in the long-range best interest of all parties concerned. Everyone is better off if disruptions are minimized in the lives of the firm's management, the displaced workers, and the community. Outplacement benefits have been used for years as companies have attempted to remove redundant or marginal personnel with minimum disruption and cost to the company and maximum benefit to the individuals involved. Now these same benefits are being used in business and plant closings.

GRADUAL PHASE-OUTS Another management action that can significantly ameliorate the effects of a business shutdown is the gradual phasing out of the business. A gradual phase-out buys time for employees and the community to adjust to the new situation and to solve some of their problems.

Recently, when the semiconductor industry took a deep downturn, Sony Electronics found it necessary to close its plant in San Antonio. They let their employees go in phases as they gradually wrapped up their customer orders. Affected workers were given 60 days' notice. This did not come as a surprise because, as one worker noted, "It was fairly well-known that the company was sick for a quite a while."[103] When asked about worker reactions, one employee said, "There were a few who were upset but some of them actually requested to be included in Phase 1 (job cuts). They wanted to get their severance packages and get on with their lives."[104] Sony provided workers with severance pay based on years on the job. They also extended benefits packages, outplacement services, and job transfers, where possible, to other Sony plants in the United States. In addition, each departing worker received a DVD player.[105]

HELPING TO ATTRACT REPLACEMENT INDUSTRY The principal responsibility for attracting new industry falls on the community, but the management of the closing firm can provide cooperation and assistance. The closing company can help by providing inside information on building and equipment characteristics and capabilities, transportation options based on its experience, and contacts with other firms in its industry that may be seeking facilities. Helping the community attract replacement industry has the overwhelming advantage of rapidly replacing large numbers of lost jobs. Also, because attracted businesses tend to be smaller than those that closed, this strategy enables the community to diversify its economic base while regaining jobs.[106]

Survivors: The Forgotten Stakeholders. When job losses occur, attention is understandably placed on the workers who lose their employment and the many repercussions that loss holds for them. Their needs must come first because they bear the brunt of the impact. However, those who retain their jobs—whether they are the remaining employees at a downsized plant or the workers at a plant that survived consolidation—are in need of support as well. Even the managers who conducted the layoffs will not emerge unscathed. A recent study of managers who issued WARN notices found that they had an increase in health and sleep problems: They reported feelings of depersonalization, and a greater intent to quit, with emotional exhaustion playing a role in their difficulties.[107]

All survivors are likely to evidence a variety of negative actions, perceptions, and behaviors. These include depression, guilt, stress, uncertainty, decreased loyalty, and lower enthusiasm.[108] Firms must attend to these concerns of survivors if they are to emerge stronger after job cuts. They can do this by providing:[109]

1. Emotional support—assuring employees that they are important.
2. Directional support—communicating the direction the company is going and the employees' place in that journey.
3. Tactical support—presenting new goals and objectives for the employees.
4. Informational support—answering all questions about the layoff and future plans.

One of the most important actions a firm can take when providing informational support is to answer employees' questions clearly and completely. Michael Fox, senior vice president of Ogilvy Public Relations, has worked with firms that are conducting layoffs. He says, "You've got a good chance at preserving loyalty and lessening anxiety if you've always been pretty open and transparent with information. Tell (remaining employees) how the decision was made, the layoffs were based on performance reviews, or longevity or the loss of a big customer. If a decision seems arbitrary or unclear, it will only make resentment worse."[110] It is also important that the survivors believe the laid off employees were treated well. When United Technologies paid for a year of college courses for laid-off employees, the remaining employees felt better about staying on the job.[111]

We are only just touching the surface of the stakes and stakeholders involved in the plant-closing issue, the impacts that business closings have on employees and communities, the public's reaction to the problem, and types of corresponding actions that management might take. It is important for businesses to take positive steps to be responsive to their employees and communities. Furthermore, business closings and their adverse consequences are issues that business should continue to address in the future, lest yet another public problem culminate in new laws or another knotty regulatory apparatus.

Summary

Community stakeholders are extremely important to companies and the global economic recession has heightened the importance of business's attending to community stakeholder needs. In many ways, business can provide support in difficult times. Companies may donate the time and talents of managers and employees (volunteerism). Because business has a vital stake in the community, it engages in a variety of community projects. Community action programs are a key part of managing community involvement.

Business also contributes to community stakeholders through philanthropy. The third sector, or nonprofit sector, depends on business's support. Companies give for a variety of reasons—some altruistic, some self-interested. Major recipients of business giving include health and welfare, education, civic activities, and culture and the arts. As companies have attempted to manage their philanthropy, two major types of community partnerships have been emphasized: (1) strategic philanthropy, which seeks to improve the overall fit between corporate needs and charitable programs, and (2) cause-related marketing, which tightens the linkage between a firm's profits and its contributions. Cause-related marketing represents a unique joining of business and charity with the potential for great benefit to each.

Just as firms have beneficial effects on community stakeholders, they can have detrimental effects as well. Business or plant closings are a prime example of these detrimental effects. Loss of jobs is the primary way in which these closings is manifested. Plant closings have a pervasive influence in the sense that a multitude of community stakeholders—employees, local government, other businesses, and the general citizenry—are affected. There is no single reason why these closings occur but among the major reasons are economic conditions, consolidation of company operations, outsourcing, outmoded technology or facilities, changes in corporate strategy, and international competition.

Before management makes the decision to close a facility, it has a responsibility to itself, its employees, and the community to study thoroughly whether closing is the only or the best option. Finding a new owner for the business and pursuing the possibility of employee ownership are reasonable and desirable alternatives. After the decision to close has been made, responsible actions include community-impact analysis; giving advance notice; providing transfer, relocation, or outplacement benefits; phasing out operations gradually; and helping the community attract replacement industry. Finally, the needs of survivors must be met as the firm continues operations. Companies have an added incentive to be responsive to the business-closing issue, because state and federal governments are closely watching the manner in which firms are handling this problem.

Key Terms

cause branding, p. 555

cause-related marketing, p. 555

community action program, p. 544

community involvement, p. 541

community partnerships, p. 552

employee owned, p. 560

offshore outsourcing, p. 557

offshoring, p. 557

outsourcing, p. 557

philanthropy, p. 545

strategic philanthropy, p. 553

third sector, p. 548

Worker Adjustment and Retraining Notification Act (WARN), p. 562

Discussion Questions

1. Outline the essential steps involved in developing a community action program.
2. Explain the pros and cons of community involvement and corporate philanthropy, provide a brief history of corporate philanthropy, and explain why and to whom companies give.
3. Differentiate among community partnerships, strategic philanthropy, cause-related marketing, and cause branding. Provide an example of each not discussed in the text.
4. Identify and discuss briefly what you think are the major trade-offs that firms face as they think about offshore outsourcing, offshoring, or plant closings. When substantial layoffs are involved, what are firms' responsibilities to their employees and their communities?
5. In your opinion, why does a business have a responsibility to employees and community stakeholders in a business-closing decision? Enumerate what you think are the major reasons.

CASE 25

Coke and Pepsi in India: Issues, Ethics, and Crisis Management*

There is nothing new about multinational corporations (MNCs) facing challenges as they do business around the world, especially in developing nations or emerging markets. Royal Dutch Shell had to greatly reduce its production of oil in Nigeria due to guerrilla attacks on its pipelines. Cargill was forced to shut down its soy-processing plant in Brazil because of the claim that it was contributing to the destruction of the Amazon rainforest. Tribesmen in Botswana accused De Beers of pushing them off their land to make way for diamond mines.[1] Google was kicked out of China only to be later restored. Global business today is not for the faint hearted.

It should not come as a surprise, therefore, that MNC giants such as Coca-Cola and PepsiCo—highly visible, multibillion dollar corporations with well-known, iconic brands around the world—would encounter challenges in the creation and distribution of their products. After all, soft drinks are viewed as discretionary and sometimes luxurious products when compared to the staples of life that are often scarce in developing countries.

Whether it is called an issue, an ethics challenge, or a scandal, the situation confronting both Coke and Pepsi in India, beginning in 2003, richly illustrates the many complex and varied social challenges companies may face once they decide to embark on other country's shores. Their experiences in India may predict other issues they may eventually face elsewhere or trials other companies might face as well. With a billion-plus people and an expanding economy, and with markets stagnating in many Western countries, India, along with China and Russia, represents immense opportunities for growth for virtually all businesses. Hence, these companies cannot afford to ignore these burgeoning markets.

INITIAL ALLEGATIONS

Coke and Pepsi's serious problems in India began in 2003. In that year, India's Center for Science and Environment (CSE), an independent public interest group, made allegations that tests they had conducted revealed dangerously high levels of pesticide residue in the soft drinks being sold all over India. The director of CSE, Sunita Narain, stated that such residues can cause cancer and birth defects as well as harm nervous and immune systems if the products were consumed over long periods of time.[2] Further, CSE stated that the pesticide levels in Coke's and Pepsi's drinks were much higher than that permitted by European Union standards. On one occasion, Narain accused Pepsi and Coke of pushing products that they wouldn't dare sell at home.[3]

In addition to the alleged pesticides in the soft drinks, another special interest group, India Resource Center (IRC), accused the companies of overconsuming scarce water and polluting water sources due to its operations in India.[4] IRC dramatically criticized the companies, especially Coca-Cola, by detailing a number of different "water woes" experienced by different cities and regions of the country. IRC's allegations even more broadly accused the companies of water exploitation and of controlling natural resources, and thus communities. Examples frequently cited were the impact of Coke's operations in the communities of Kerala and Mehdiganj.[5]

In 2004, IRC continued its "Campaign to Hold Coca-Cola Accountable" by arguing that communities across India were under assault by Coke's practices. Among the continuing allegations were communities' experiencing severe water shortages around Coke's bottling plants, significant depletion of the water table, strange water tastes and smells, and pollution of groundwater as well as soil. IRC said that in one community Coke was distributing its solid waste to farmers as fertilizer and that tests conducted found cadmium and lead in the waste, thus making it toxic waste. And the accusation of high levels of pesticides continued. According to IRC, the Parliament of India banned the sale of Coca-Cola in its cafeteria.[6] Another significant event in February 2004 was the government's Joint Parliamentary Committee's "seconding" of CSE's findings.[7] In December 2004, India's Supreme Court ordered Coke and Pepsi to put warning labels on their products. This caused a serious slide in sales for the next several years.[8]

---

* This case was prepared by Archie B. Carroll, University of Georgia. Updated in 2010.

SUNITA NARAIN

One major reason that Indian consumers and politicians took seriously the allegations of both CSE and IRC was CSE's director, Sunita Narain—a well-known activist in New Delhi. Narain, now in her mid- to late-40s, was born into a family of freedom fighters whose support of Mahatma Gandhi goes back to the days when Gandhi was pushing for independence in India over 60 years ago. She took up environmental causes in high school. One major cause she adopted was to stop developers from cutting down trees. Her quest was to save India from the ravages of industrialization. She became the director of CSE in 2002.[9]

According to a *BusinessWeek* writer, Narain strongly holds forth on the topic of MNCs exploiting the natural resources of developing countries, especially India. She manifests an alarmist tone that tends toward the end-is-near level of fervency. She is skilled at getting media attention. In 2005, she won the Stockholm Water Prize, one of a number of environmental accolades she has received.[10] In addition, she has been very successful in taking advantage of India's general suspicion of huge MNCs, dating back to its tragic Bhopal gas leak in 1984.[11]

SACRED WATER

Coke and Pepsi's problems in India have been complicated by the fact that water carries much significance in India. We are often told about cultural knowledge we should have before doing business in other countries. Water is one of those issues in India. Although the country has some of the worst water in the world, due to poor sewage, pollution, and pesticide use, according to UN sources, water carries an almost-spiritual meaning to Indians. Bathing is viewed by many to be a sacred act, and tradition for some residents holds that one's death is not properly noted until one's ashes are scattered in the Ganges River. In one major poll, Indians revealed that drinking water was one of their major life activities to improve their well-being.[12] Indians' sensitivity to the subject of water has undoubtedly played a role in the public's reactions to the allegations.

COKE'S AND PEPSI'S EARLY RESPONSES

Initially, Coke and Pepsi denied the allegations of CSE and IRC, primarily through the media. It was observed that their response was limited at best as they got caught up in the technical details of the tests. Coke conducted its own tests, the conclusion of which was that their drinks met demanding European standards.[13] Over the next several years the debate continued as the companies questioned the studies and conducted studies of their own. The companies also pointed out that other beverages and foods in the Indian food supply, and indeed water, had trace pesticide levels in it, and they sought to deflect the issue in this manner.

The IRC also attacked the companies for not taking the crisis seriously. It argued that the companies were "destroying lives, livelihoods, and communities" while viewing the problems in India as "public relations" problems that they could "spin" away. They pointed out that Coca-Cola had hired a new public relations firm to help them build a new image in India, rather than addressing the real issues. According to IRC, the new CEO of Coke, Neville Isdell, immediately made a visit to India, but it was a "stealth" visit designed to avoid the heavy protests that would have met him had the trip been public. IRC also pointed out that Coke had just increased its marketing budget by a sizable amount in India. IRC then laid out the steps it felt Coke should take to effectively address its problems.[14]

PESTICIDE RESIDUE AND PARTIAL BANS

The controversy flared up again in August of 2006 when the CSE issued a new study. The new test results showed that 57 samples from 11 Coke and Pepsi brands contained pesticide residue levels 24 times higher than the maximum allowed by the Indian government. Public response was swift. Seven of India's 28 states imposed partial bans on the two companies, and the state of Kerala banned the drinks completely. Officials there ignored a later court ruling reversing the ban.[15] During 2006, the United Kingdom's Central Science Laboratory questioned the CSE findings. Coca-Cola sought a meeting with CSE that it denied. Also that year, India's Union Health Ministry rejected the CSE study as "inconclusive."[16]

THE COMPANIES RATCHET UP THEIR RESPONSES

As a result of the second major flurry of studies and allegations in 2006, both Coke and Pepsi ratcheted up their responses, sometimes acting together, sometimes taking independent action. They responded almost like different companies than they were before. Perhaps they figured this issue was not going to go away and had to be addressed more forcefully.

COKE'S RESPONSE

Coke started with a more aggressive marketing campaign. It ran three rounds of newspaper ads refuting the new study. The ads appeared in the form of a letter from more than 50 of India's company-owned and franchised Coke bottlers, claiming that their products were safe. Letters with a similar message went out to retailers and stickers were pressed onto drink coolers, declaring that Coke was "safety guaranteed." Coke also hired researchers to talk to consumers and opinion leaders to find out what exactly they believed about the allegations and what the company needed to do to convince them the allegations were false.[17]

Based on its research findings, Coke created a TV ad campaign that featured testimonials by well-respected celebrities. One of the ads featured Aamir Khan, a popular movie star, as he toured one of Coke's plants. He told the people that the product was safe and that if they wanted to see for themselves they could personally do so. In August and September 2006, over 4,000 people took him up on it and toured the plants. Opening up the plants sent the message that the company had nothing to hide, and this was very persuasive.[18] The TV ads, which were targeted toward the mass audience, were followed by giant posters with movie star Khan's picture drinking a Coke. These posters appeared in public places such as bus stops. In addition, other ads were targeted toward adult women and housewives, who make the majority of the food-purchasing decisions. One teenager was especially impressed with Khan's ads because she knew he was very selective about which movies he appeared in and that he wouldn't take a position like this if it wasn't appropriate.[19]

In a later interview, Coke's CEO Isdell said he thought the company's response during the second wave of controversy was the key reason the company began turning things around. After the 2003 episode, the company changed management in India to address many of the problems, both real and imagined. The new management team was especially concerned about how it would handle its next public relations crisis. Weeks later, in December 2006, India's Health Ministry said that both Coke's and Pepsi's beverages tested in three different labs contained little or no pesticide residue.

PEPSI'S RESPONSE

Pepsi's response was similar to Coke's. Pepsi decided to go straight to the Indian media and try to build relationships there. Company representatives met with editorial boards, presented its own data in press conferences, and also ran TV commercials. Pepsi's commercials featured the then president of PepsiCo India, Rajeev Bakshi, shown walking through a polished Pepsi laboratory.[20]

In addition, Pepsi increased its efforts to cut down on water usage in its plants. Employees in the plants were organized into teams and used Japanese-inspired *kaizens*, and suggested improvements, to bring waste under control. The company also employed lobbying of the local government.

Indra Nooyi becomes CEO   Pepsi had an advantage in rebuilding its relationships in India, because in October 2006, an Indian-born woman, Indra Nooyi, was selected to be CEO of the multinational corporation. It is not known whether Pepsi's problems in India were in any way related to her being chosen CEO, but it definitely helped. After graduating from the prestigious Indian Institute of Management, and later Yale University, Nooyi worked her way up the hierarchy at PepsiCo before being singled out for the top position.[21] She previously held positions at the Boston Consulting Group, Motorola, and ABB Group.

Prior to becoming CEO, Nooyi had a number of successes in Pepsi and became the company's chief strategist. She was said to have a perceptive business sense and an irreverent personal style. One of Nooyi's first decisions was to take a trip to India in December 2006. While there, she spoke broadly about Pepsi's programs to improve water and the environment. The Indian media loved her, beaming with pride, and covered her tour positively as she shared her own heartwarming memories of her life growing up in India. She received considerable praise. Not surprisingly, Pepsi's sales started moving upward.[22]

While all the criticism of Coke and Pepsi was going on, roughly from 2003 to 2006, both companies were pursuing corporate social responsibility (CSR) initiatives in India, many of them related to improving water resources for communities, while the conflict was center stage.

A COMMENTARY: WHAT'S GOING ON

Because of all the conflicting studies and the stridency of CSE and IRC, one has to wonder what was going on in India to cause this developing country to so severely criticize giant MNCs such as Coke and Pepsi. Many developing countries would be doing all they could to appease these companies. It was speculated by a number of different observers that what was at work was a form of backlash against huge MNCs that come into countries and consume natural resources.[23] Why were these groups so hostile toward the companies? Was it really pesticides in the water and abuse of natural resources? Or was it environmental interest groups using every opportunity to bash large corporations on issues sensitive to the people? Was it CSE and IRC strategically making an example of these two hugely successful companies and trying to put them in their place?

Late in 2006, an interesting commentary appeared in *BusinessWeek* exploring the topic of what has been going on in India with respect to Coke and Pepsi.[24] This commentary argued that the companies may have been singled out because they are foreign owned. It appears that no Indian soft drink companies were singled out for pesticide testing, though many people believe pesticide levels are even higher in Indian milk and bottled tea. It was pointed out that pesticide residues are present in most of India's groundwater, and the government has ignored or has been slow to move on the problem. The commentary went on to observe that Coke and Pepsi have together invested $2 billion in India over the years and have generated 12,500 jobs and support more than 200,000 indirectly through their purchases of Indian-made products including sugar, packing materials, and shipping services.[25]

CONTINUING PROTESTS AND RENEWED PRIORITIES AND STRATEGIES

Eventually, the open conflict settled down and sales have taken an upturn for both companies, but the issue lingers. In June 2007, the IRC continued its attacks on Coca-Cola. It accused the company of "greenwashing" its image in India.[26] The IRC staged a major protest at the new Coke Museum in Atlanta on June 30, 2007, questioning the company's human rights and environmental abuses. They erected a 20-foot banner that read "Coca-Cola Destroys Lives, Livelihoods, Communities" in front of the New World of Coke that opened in May 2007. Amit Srivastava of the IRC was quoted as saying, "This World of Coke museum is a fairy tale land and the real side of

Coke is littered with abuses." A representative of the National Alliance of People's Movements, a large coalition of grassroots movements in India, said, "The museum is a shameful attempt by the Coca-Cola Company to hide its crimes."[27]

PILING ON

The protestations by these groups apparently motivated other groups to take action against Coke. It was reported that United Students Against Sweatshops also staged a "die-in" around one of Coke's bottling facilities in India. And more than 20 colleges and universities in the United States, Canada, and the United Kingdom removed Coca-Cola from campuses because of student-led initiatives to put pressure on the company. In addition, the protests in Atlanta were endorsed by a host of groups that participated in the U.S. Social Forum.[28]

RENEWED PRIORITIES

Undaunted, Coca-Cola continues its initiatives to improve the situation in India and around the world. Coke faces water problems around the world because it is the key natural resource that goes into its products. The company now has 70 clean-water projects in 40 countries aimed at boosting local economies. It has been observed that these efforts are part of a broader strategy on the part of CEO Neville Isdell to build Coke's image as a local benefactor and a global diplomat.[29]

The criticism of Coke has been most severe in India. CEO Isdell admits that the company's experience in India has taught some humbling lessons. Isdell, who took over the company after the crisis had begun, told *The Wall Street Journal*, "It was very clear that we had not connected with the communities in the way we needed to." He indicated that the company has now made "water stewardship" a strategic priority, and in a recent 10-K securities filing, had listed a shortage of clean water as a strategic risk.[30] In August 2007, Coca-Cola India unveiled its "5-Pillar" growth strategy to strengthen its bonds with India. Coke's new strategy focuses on the pillars of People, Planet, Portfolio, Partners, and Performance. The company also announced a series of initiatives under each of the five pillars and its "Little Drops of Joy" proposal, which tries to reinforce the company's connection with stakeholders in India.[31]

Though most of the attention recently has been on Coca-Cola, it should also be noted that Pepsi has continued taking steps on a number of projects as well.

One novel initiative is that the company now gathers rainwater in excavated lakes and ponds and on the rooftops of its bottling plants in India. The company sponsors other community water projects as well.[32]

INDIAN BEVERAGE ASSOCIATION FORMED

Though Coke and Pepsi are typically fighting each another in their longstanding "cola wars," due to their mutual problems in India they formed the Indian Beverage Association (IBA) in summer of 2010. Because of continuous hostility from regulators and activist groups, the two companies decided that a joint effort to address issues might make sense.[33]

The IBA was formed to address the issues related to the government of Kerala's charge that Coke is polluting the groundwater in the state and other taxation issues that affect both companies. Their issues have been ongoing, but Kerala's government decided to form a tribunal against Coca-Cola, seeking $48 million in compensation claims for allegedly causing pollution and depleting the groundwater level there. Another important issue is the value added tax (VAT) by the Delhi government. The IBA plans to bring in other bottlers and packaging firms that have similar interests and issues in India.[34]

QUESTIONS FOR DISCUSSION

1. Identify the ongoing issues in this case with respect to issues management, crisis management, global business ethics, and stakeholder management. Rank order these in terms of their priorities for Coca-Cola and for PepsiCo.
2. Evaluate the corporate social responsibility (CSR) of Coke and Pepsi in India.
3. Are these companies ignoring their responsibilities in India, or is something else at work?
4. Why does it seem that Coke has become a larger and more frequent target than Pepsi in India? Did having an Indian-born CEO help Pepsi's case?
5. How do companies protect themselves against the nonstop allegations of special interest groups that have made them a target? Is stakeholder management an answer?
6. What should the companies have done differently in 2003 to address the water allegations? What should the company now do as it moves forward?
7. What lessons does this case present for MNCs doing business in the global marketplace?

ENDNOTES

1. "Beyond India, More Battles," *BusinessWeek* (June 11, 2007), 52.
2. Duane D. Stanford, "Coke's PR Offensive in India Pays Off," *Atlanta Journal Constitution* (December 3, 2006), D1, D9.
3. Diane Brady, "Pepsi: Repairing a Poisoned Reputation in India," *BusinessWeek* (June 11, 2007), 50.
4. Amit Srivastava, "Communities Reject Coca-Cola in India," *India Resource Center* (July 10, 2003), http://corpwatch.org.
5. *Ibid.*
6. *Ibid.*
7. "Coke and Pepsi in India—Stuck in the Middle with You," http://ethicalcorp.com/content_print.asp?Content ID=4551.
8. Stanford, D1.
9. Diane Brady, "Pepsi: Repairing a Poisoned Reputation in India," *BusinessWeek* (June 11, 2007), 46–54.
10. *Ibid.*
11. "Coke and Pepsi in India—Stuck in the Middle with You."
12. Brady, 50.
13. Stanford, D9.
14. "Campaign to Hold Coca-Cola Accountable: Coca-Cola Crisis in India," *India Resource Center* (2004), http://www.indiaresource.org/campaigns/coke/index.html.
15. Stanford, D9.
16. "Coke and Pepsi in India—Stuck in the Middle with You."
17. Stanford, D9.
18. *Ibid.*
19. *Ibid.*
20. Brady, 54.
21. *Ibid.*, 46.
22. *Ibid.*, 54.
23. *Ibid.*, 48.
24. Brian Bremner and Nandini Lakshman, with Diane Brady, "Commentary India: Behind the Scare over Pesticides in Pepsi and Coke," *BusinessWeek* (September 4, 2006), 43.
25. *Ibid.*
26. New America Media, "Coke Accused of 'Greenwashing' Its Image in India" (June 8, 2007), http://news.newamericanmedia.org/news/view_article.html?article?id=.

27. India Resource Center, "Major Protest at Coke Museum in Atlanta" (June 30, 2007), http://www.indiaresource.org/news/2007/1049.html.

28. *Ibid.*

29. Betsy McKay, "Why Coke Aims to Slake Global Thirst for Safe Water," *The Wall Street Journal* (March 15), 2007.

30. *Ibid.*

31. *Ibid.*

32. McKay.

33. Anuradha Shukla, "Coke, Pepsi Form Indian Beverage Association," *India Today* (July 6, 2010), http://indiatoday.intoday.in/site/specials/asia-cup2010/Story/104338/India/taxation-issues-bring-archrivals-coke-&-pepsi-on-same-platform.html. Accessed July 12, 2010.

34. *Ibid.*

CASE 26

The Hudson River Cleanup and GE*

One of the major challenges businesses face with respect to government regulations is that often compliance with existing regulations during an earlier period does not protect them against expensive problems that occur or come to light later. The plight of General Electric (GE) with respect to its dumping of PCBs (polychlorinated biphenyls) over 30 years ago is a classic case in point.

For decades, GE had electrical-equipment-making plants along the Hudson River in New York. During the period prior to 1977, GE discharged more than 1.3 million pounds of PCBs into a 40-mile stretch of the Hudson before the chemicals were banned in 1977. In 2001, the PCB-contaminated upper Hudson River had become the largest EPA Superfund site in the nation and is becoming the most expensive to clean up.[1]

In August 2001, the Environmental Protection Agency (EPA) circulated a draft proposal informing GE that it would have to spend hundreds of millions of dollars to clean up the PCBs that were legally dumped over a 30-year period that ended in 1977.[2] According to *BusinessWeek*, the Bush Administration and the EPA, under fire for its environmental policies, ordered GE to clean up the Hudson in what has been called the biggest environmental dredging project in U.S. history. The decision would reaffirm a plan developed in the waning days of the Clinton Administration.

A GE representative stated that the company is "disappointed in the EPA's decision," which it says, "will cause more harm than good." Environmentalists, predictably, have praised the decision, and the Sierra Club executive director called the decision a "monumental step toward protecting New Yorkers from cancer-causing PCBs."[3]

The cleanup plan became a heated and politically charged debate beginning in fall of 2001, as an investigative report detailed how environmentalists (the Greens) claimed that GE and the EPA used the terrorist attacks on the World Trade Center and Pentagon as a distraction from the priority of the planned cleanup. The Greens charged that GE and the EPA, under the leadership of EPA administrator Christine Todd Whitman, delayed the cleanup and were "negotiating in the shadow of September 11." The executive director of the Clearwater advocacy groups and spokesperson for the coalition said regarding the meetings between GE and EPA, "It smells really bad."[4]

USE OF PERFORMANCE STANDARDS

The Greens charged that a modification of the cleanup plan was in the works that would favor GE. This would be the establishment of "performance standards" to measure the effectiveness of dredging to remove the PCBs. In a change from the original Clinton Administration plan, the revised goal of the EPA would be to roll out the dredging project in stages with periodic

---

* This case was prepared by Archie B. Carroll, University of Georgia. Revised in 2010.

testing for PCBs. EPA stated: "The performance indicators being considered will include measuring PCB levels in the soil and the water column, as well as measuring the percentage of dredged material that gets re-suspended." The agency added: "Based on these objective scientific indicators, EPA will determine at each stage of the project whether it is scientifically justified to continue the cleanup. PCB levels in fish will be monitored throughout the project as well."[5]

WOULD GE BE FAVORED?

Environmentalists believed that the performance standards would be weighted in ways that would favor GE's position and would put an early lid on the project. They communicated to EPA that they did not want any standards built into the project that would offer GE an "out." Environmentalists who met with the EPA claimed they were talking to a brick wall—that their arguments were brushed off. One stated: "That office (EPA), with all due respect, seems to get its information from G.E. It's a political process being handled inside the [Washington] beltway; it's inappropriate and possibly illegal." The Greens stated they planned to start an advertising blitz hammering on its claim that terrorism was used as a cover while EPA and GE schemed a way to dilute the plan.[6]

THE HUDSON RIVER

Close to 40 miles of the half-mile-wide Hudson River is involved in the planned cleanup. It is a pastoral and wooded stretch of the river that winds in the shadows of the Adirondacks, which serve recreational activities of numerous towns and villages. At one time, these villages were thriving examples of American industrial power. Today, most of the factories, mills, and plants are closed. Like in many other industries, jobs headed south, west, across borders, or across oceans as companies tried to extricate themselves from what they saw as devastating taxes and regulations. Though not obvious to the eye, the hidden problem of hazardous waste pollution has been a significant barrier to redevelopment of the area.[7]

SUPERFUND SITE

In 1983, the upper Hudson was named a Superfund site by the EPA. This meant that GE would be held responsible by law for cleaning up the pollution resulting from years of disposal of pollutants, regardless of whether the disposal was legal at the time. John Elvin, an investigative reporter, claimed that the Hudson River is just one of 77 alleged sites to be in need of cleanup under the EPA's Superfund program. Also, it is believed that there are numerous other sites in addition to the upper Hudson River where PCBs were dumped. In addition to the Hudson River area, the chemicals were used at plants throughout the New England area.[8]

PCBs

PCBs are a large family of fire-retardant chemicals that GE once used in the production of electrical products. There are over 200 variations of the chemical, which were, for the most part, dumped legally in the years before it was determined they posed a possible cancer risk. The PCBs were oily and tarry and were disposed of as fill for roadbeds, housing developments, and other such uses. It was reported that GE often dispensed the material free to residents surrounding its factories. In various forms, the company sold or gave away what is now considered a contaminated waste product to be used as a wood preservative, fertilizer, termite inhibitor, and a component in house paints. As for directly dumped wastes, the PCBs are now said to be leaking into groundwater from landfills that GE had put caps on.[9]

PCBs AND THEIR DANGERS

According to the EPA, PCBs have been found to cause cancer and can also harm the immune, nervous, and reproductive systems of humans, fish, and wildlife. They think the chemicals are especially risky for children.[10] David Carpenter of the State University of New York's School of Public Health has been a critic of GE. According to Carpenter, all experts except those allied with GE believe PCBs to be a "probable" cause of cancer in humans. Carpenter has lashed out at GE for "deceitful and unscientific" claims that are "preposterous." Carpenter claims that PCBs are linked to reduced IQs in children, attention deficit disorder, suppressed immune systems, diabetes, and heart disease.[11]

CONTROVERSY OVER SAFETY

There is controversy over whether PCBs are dangerous or not. Like the EPA, environmental groups believe they are dangerous. A handout from the Friends of a Clean Hudson coalition states strongly: "PCBs are a class of synthetic toxic chemicals universally recognized as among the world's most potent and persistent threats to human health." On the other hand, a former GE employee who worked intimately with PCBs for 25–30 years states differently. To put it in layman's terms, he said, "You're talking about a big, fat, slippery, stable molecule that doesn't break down. That's why it was used in lubrication and cooling in the manufacturing process. It's just plain sludge, that's all."[12]

Another hazardous-waste-management expert was reported as saying: "I've been in PCBs up to my armpits. So have any number of engineers and scientists working with GE and other firms. I drank a half glass of the stuff accidentally 25 years ago. The fact is there are no reported cases of cancer traced to PCBs. This controversy is 25 percent an environmental concern and 75 percent politics in a state and towns abandoned by GE, left with no industry and a lot of trash." In spite of his views, the expert does think that GE should clean up the "hot spots" where dumping was most severe and the rest of the river should be left to heal on its own.[13]

GE'S POSITION

GE did not accept EPA's cleanup plan as a done deal. The huge, wealthy company, one of the largest in the world, cranked up a barrage of TV infomercials, radio and TV ads, and initiatives by top-tier Washington lobbyists to sway the public, media, and government. The company fielded an imposing cadre of Washington lobbyists. Among these lobbyists were former Senator George Mitchell, former House Speaker-Designate Bob Livingston, and several other prominent people.[14]

Jack Welch Chimes In

Retired former chief executive officer of GE, the legendary Jack Welch, was negotiating with regulators over this issue as far back as the 1970s. Welch summarized the company's position in a statement he made to GE stockholders while he was the CEO: "We simply do not believe that there are any adverse health effects from PCBs."[15] Today, one estimate is that GE has already spent millions of dollars fighting the proposal to clean up the river. The company contends that the proposed dredging would actually be more destructive because it will stir up PCBs buried in the mud and

recontaminate the river. Supporting GE's position, Rep. John Sweeney said that he would continue to fight the dredging plan because it would have an adverse impact on local residents.[16]

One journalist estimated that GE might end up spending as much fighting the EPA plan as it would if they just went ahead with the cleanup. This raises the obvious question as to why GE would fight the plan. According to John Elvin, investigative reporter, it is because the company thinks it is a precedent-setting case that could leave the company open to a tobacco-industry-sized settlement claim. As it turns out, this is only one of the many sites GE used legally to dispose of manufacturing by-products, and PCBs are just one of the many possibly hazardous wastes that the company had to deal with over the years. Apparently, GE used as many as 77 sites alleged to be in need of cleanup under the Superfund program.[17]

CITIZENS' AND ENVIRONMENTAL GROUPS' VIEWS

Many of the residents of the upstate area that would be most affected by a GE cleanup prefer to just leave the situation alone and let the river heal itself. A poll commissioned by GE and handled by Zogby International found that 59 percent of the residents in the region favored letting the river deal with the pollutants naturally. Another poll done by Siena College Research Institute found that 50 percent of all the residents along the entire length of the Hudson wanted the river to be left alone. On the other side of the issue, polls have shown that a large majority of the citizens want a cleanup.[18] The survey results seem to depend on which citizens are chosen to be polled.

Grassroots Opposition

There is even some grassroots opposition to EPA's dredging plan. An example is found in Citizen Environmentalists Against Sludge Encapsulation (CEASE) and Farmers Against Irresponsible Remediation (FAIR). CEASE proposed acts of civil disobedience to prevent the government from coming onto private property. According to one CEASE activist, "the downstate enviros are only interested in punishing GE at the expense of agriculture, recreation, and other economic interests in our community."[19] FAIR, for its part, asked a federal district court in Albany, New York, for a preliminary injunction blocking EPA from issuing a final decision until it provided additional information on the impact of the dredging project. But the U.S. District Court for the Northern District of New York ruled that it did not have jurisdiction over the case because the Superfund Amendments and Reauthorization Act of 1986 prohibits judicial review at this point in the case.[20]

SUPPORTERS OF THE CLEANUP

For their part, environmental groups continued to think that the cleanup is the right thing to do. Advocates of the cleanup said that the project would be a "gift from heaven" to the rustbelt towns along the Hudson River. Friends of a Clean Hudson, a coalition of 11 major environmental groups, commissioned a study in which they concluded that thousands of jobs and hundreds of millions of dollars would come into the area once the project was under way. The coalition claimed benefits that could include the creation of close to 9,000 new jobs with annual payrolls of up to $346 million. In a reaction to this report, Rep. Maurice Hinchey, whose district includes a downstate portion of the river, claimed that as a result of the dredging, "tourism will increase, the fishing industry will be revived, thousands of jobs will be created and property values will rise."[21]

According to reporter John Elvin, there are many festering grudges still held against GE. GE was once the centerpiece of the bustling and prosperous area. He contends that GE eventually left the region because of New York's antibusiness environment and that, in recent years, legislators have felt free to tax the company to their heart's content, but the company expressed its own right to pack up and leave. He maintains that many state and local officials, and some citizens, just wanted a last piece of GE's hide—a last chance to make GE pay.[22]

Only time will tell fully what will be the ramifications to GE and the contaminated Hudson River. It is obvious from all the interests involved and opinions expressed, however, that it is not totally clear what should take place in the PCB-tainted Hudson River.

WORKING TOWARD A SETTLEMENT

Companies may resist, but government agencies do not go away. Such is the case in the continuing saga of the Hudson River cleanup. In 2001, the Bush Administration ordered a full-scale dredging of a 40-mile stretch of the river. It was to be the largest environmental dredging project in history. GE has to pay the estimated $490 million charge for the cleanup and the project is expected to take about a decade, with plans for the dredging to begin in 2005.

In 2003, it was reported that the Hudson River cleanup was moving on schedule although at the time GE was withholding payments, according to environmental groups. A spokesman for Environmental Advocates, one of 13 concerned groups that formed the Friends of a Clean Hudson coalition, "contrary to dire predictions of two or three years ago, the project is on track." Critics say that GE has not been cooperative, but the company denies this evaluation of its efforts. At that time, the environmental groups graded the key players in the cleanup. The EPA got a "B" and GE got a "D."[23]

PERFORMANCE STANDARDS FINALIZED

In May 2004, the EPA finally released its final quality of life performance standards for the Hudson River cleanup.[24] By March 2004, an environmental progress report was released in which it was stated that more than 290,000 pounds of PCBs had been removed from the Hudson Falls Plant Site. GE installed a comprehensive network of collection and monitoring wells to capture PCBs in the bedrock and prevent them from reaching the river. Also in 2004, the New York State Department of Environmental Conservation (DEC) approved GE's plan to build innovative under-the-river tunnels to capture the final few ounces a day of PCBs that are thought to trickle out of the river bottom near the Hudson Falls Plant.[25]

DREDGING DELAYED, BACKROOM DEALS

According to environmental groups, GE dragged its feet in moving forward with the cleanup. Initially, dredging was to begin in 2005, but due to GE-requested delays, the start date got pushed back to 2009. Also, the Natural Resources Defense Council (NRDC), an environmental group, claimed that in 2005 the EPA rewarded GE's foot dragging by striking a backroom deal that required GE to commit only to completing the Phase 1 of the cleanup—just 10 percent of the total job.[26]

SETTLEMENT REACHED

On November 2, 2006, the federal district court signed off on the EPA–GE settlement. This agreement allowed for the dredging of the PCB-contaminated river sediments to proceed. GE continued to challenge the EPA over important details, and it continued to press a federal lawsuit challenging the EPA's authority to require GE in the future to complete Phase 2 of the cleanup. If GE gets out of the second phase, taxpayers would have to foot the bill to clean up the remaining mess, face protracted legal battles with GE to get it to complete the job, or else be forced to live with a polluted river indefinitely. Much of the upper Hudson River has already been closed to fishing. South of Troy, New York, women of childbearing age and children have been advised not to eat fish at all. And, according to the NRDC, the pollution is spreading, continuing to move downriver from Albany.[27]

PHASE 1 (2009) OF DREDGING PROJECT COMPLETED

After legal squabbling, Phase 1 of the GE dredging project began and was completed in 2009. The work spanned the period of May 15 to November 15, 2009. The task focused on removal of PCB-contaminated sediment from a six-mile stretch of the upper Hudson River. GE removed approximately 10 percent of the contamination scheduled to be dredged during the expected six-year project. During this time, the depth of contamination was found to be greater than expected due to dense logging debris.

In addition to the PCB removal, Phase 1 was intended to allow GE and EPA to evaluate project progress and to make program adjustments to improve compliance with EPA's performance standards. The standards were intended to ensure that dredging operations were done safely and with public health being protected at all times.[28]

NEXT STEPS

According to the EPA's plan, released in 2010, both EPA and GE will evaluate whether the performance standards need to be changed for Phase 2. Evaluation reports prepared by EPA and GE will be made available to the public and to an independent peer review panel for recommendations about possible changes to make the project more effective and efficient. The initial plan is that dredging for Phase 2 will begin in May of 2011.[29]

In a draft report prepared by GE, the company said that the Phase 1 dredging released almost 25 times more contaminants into the water than it had anticipated. Consequently, it spread previously buried PCBs across the river bottom, resulting in a five-fold increase in concentrations of the contaminant in fish. In early 2010, the EPA cautioned that it was much too early to say how the dredging operation might be modified.[30]

GE reported that it had spent $561 million on the project through the end of Phase 1. According to Riverkeeper, a New York clean water advocate, GE has not yet committed to perform the full scope of the dredging remediation, in particular the Phase 2 dredging. After a review of performance results of Phase 1, GE will announce whether it intends to perform Phase 2 cleanup. This, apparently, is part of the 2006 Consent Decree that GE signed with EPA.[31]

At the same time that GE has been pursuing Phase 1 of the dredging, it has had an outstanding lawsuit filed in 2000 in which it challenged the EPA Superfund law's application to the Hudson River case as unconstitutional. In June 2010, GE lost this lawsuit and its appeal to the U.S. Court of Appeals. A spokesman for the company said, "GE is evaluating the decision and reviewing its options."[32]

Progress on the Hudson River cleanup may be monitored on the EPA's Web site: http://www.epa.gov/hudson/.

QUESTIONS FOR DISCUSSION

1. What are the social and ethical issues in this case? Which are major and which are minor?
2. Who are the stakeholders and what are their stakes? Assess their legitimacy, power, and urgency.
3. Do your own research on PCBs. Do your findings clarify their status as being so hazardous they must be removed? Or are they best left where they have settled?
4. Who is responsible for the contaminated Hudson River? GE? EPA? State of New York? Local citizens? What ethical principles help to answer this question?
5. Do research on the EPA Superfund. Does it appear to be fair environmental legislation? Should a

company have to pay for something that was legal at the time they did it?

6. Toward the end of the case, it appears that GE is still not committed to the Hudson River cleanup. Does its draft report sound like it may be contending that the dredging is hurting more than helping?

7. Do research on this case and update the case facts. Has anything changed since the facts were presented that affects its resolution?

ENDNOTES

1. James L. Nash, "Compliance Not Good Enough, GE Finds Out," *Occupational Hazards* (September 2001), 47ff.

2. "Hudson River Cleanup," *Business Insurance* (August 6, 2001), 2.

3. Monica Roman, "GE's Hudson River Blues," *BusinessWeek* (August 13, 2001), 40.

4. John Elvin, "Greens Exploit Terror Against GE," *Insight* (November 19, 2001), 22–25.

5. Glenn Hess, "Hudson River Cleanup Could Cost GE About $460 Million," *Chemical Market Reporter* (August 6, 2001), 1, 29.

6. *Ibid.*, 23.

7. *Ibid.*

8. *Ibid.*, 24.

9. *Ibid.*

10. *Ibid.*, 1, 29.

11. Elvin, 25.

12. *Ibid.*, 24.

13. *Ibid.*

14. *Ibid.*, 23.

15. *Ibid.*, 25.

16. Hess, 29.

17. *Ibid.*, 24.

18. *Ibid.*

19. *Ibid.*

20. "New York Attacks Push Back Decision on Hudson Dredging," *Chemical Market Reporter* (October 1, 2001), 18.

21. Elvin, 25.

22. *Ibid.*, 22.

23. Yancey Roy, "Environmental Groups Check on Hudson River Cleanup," *Rochester Democrat and Chronicle* (February 7, 2003).

24. http://www.epa.gov/hudson/quality_life.htm#draft

25. "New York State Approves GE Plan for Hudson River Tunnel Project" (press release) (March 16, 2004), http://www.ge.com/en/company/news/hudson_tunnel.htm.

26. National Resources Defense Council, http://www.nrdc.org/water/pollution/hhudson.asp. Accessed September 27, 2007. Also see "Court Approves Hudson River Settlement," http://www.epa.gov/hudson. Accessed September 27, 2007.

27. *Ibid.*

28. Environmental Protection Agency, "Hudson River PCBs Superfund Site—Phase 1 Dredging Fact Sheet" (November 2009).

29. *Ibid.*

30. Mireya Navarro, "Adjustments Likely in Hudson River Cleanup," *The New York Times* (January 22, 2010).

31. Riverkeeper, "Hudson River PCBs," http://riverkeeper.org/campaigns/stop-polluters/pcbs/. Accessed July 22, 2010.

32. William McQuillen, "GE Loses Appeal Challenging EPA Superfund Law Over Hudson River Dredging," *Bloomberg* (June 30, 2010), http://www.bloomberg.com/news/print/2010-06-29/ge-loses-court-challenge/. Accessed July 16, 2010.

CASE 27

The BP Oil Spill and Mental Health*

When asked about the oil spill and its consequences, the response from British Petroleum (BP) typically includes the phrase, "We will make this right." On its Web page, BP says, "At BP, we have taken full responsibility for the cleanup in the Gulf."[1]

The environment pervades all aspects of people's lives, and so the wrongs that need to be righted are many. Because the environment is all-encompassing, the challenge is to determine what will make it right and what is too much to expect. One such question is generating conflict: does BP have an ethical responsibility to compensate people who have suffered mental illness problems due to the oil spill?

IMPACTS OF THE OIL SPILL ON MENTAL HEALTH

The capping of the oil spill did not put a cap on the mental health consequences of the disaster. Even as the oil slows, the mental health consequences continue to grow. "The oil spill in the Gulf carries with it a very significant risk of posttraumatic stress disorder (PTSD) and major depression, as well as other psychiatric disorders," says psychiatrist Dr. Keith Ablow.[2] Alan Levine, Louisiana Secretary of Health and Hospitals, asked the federal government for more funding with the following plea:

> Our Louisiana Spirit crisis counseling teams have already engaged and counseled more than 2,000 individuals and are reporting increases in anxiety, depression, stress, grief, excessive and earlier drinking and suicide ideation. Community-based organizations report similar findings. We know that, left untreated, these symptoms can quickly develop into behavioral health problems that lead to the breakdown of the familial structures, domestic violence, abuse and neglect.[3]

A survey found that one-third of respondents had mental health issues that stemmed from financial problems. Ten percent indicated that the spill changed their lives forever. The number of Louisiana respondents who showed signs of "probable serious mental illness" was twice as high as it was two years after Katrina. Those who were able to afford to pay for mental health services fared better. Respondents with lower income had a 32 percent greater chance of suffering from serious mental illness due to the oil spill, compared to those who made over $100,000.[4]

TO PAY OR NOT TO PAY

Independent "claims czar" Kenneth Feinberg said that the BP Oil Spill Compensation Fund, initially set up by BP at $20 billion, was not likely to pay damages for mental illness and distress. According to Feinberg, "If you start compensating purely mental anguish without a physical injury—anxiety, stress—we'll be getting millions of claims from people watching television. You have to draw the line somewhere. I think it would be highly unlikely that we would compensate mental damage, alleged damage, without a signature physical injury as well."[5] When asked if he would fund mental health damages if Congress passed a law requiring it, Feinberg replied that he would.[6]

As the administrator of the Oil Spill Compensation Fund, Feinberg is responsible for claims by individuals and businesses. Claims by governments are outside of his jurisdiction. Louisiana, Alabama, Mississippi, and Florida have all submitted requests for funding of mental health services. At this writing, BP had not responded to those requests.[7]

QUESTIONS FOR DISCUSSION

1. What are the ethical issues in this case?
2. Who are the stakeholders and how are they impacted by this situation?
3. Do you agree with Feinberg's assertion that "you have to draw the line somewhere"?
4. Do you agree with Feinberg's decision rule? His expectation that there be a signature physical injury is consistent with tort law. Does that affect your answer?
5. Feinberg does not have jurisdiction over claims by states and municipalities. Do you believe his assessment of the place of mental health damages should apply to their claims as well?

---

* This case was prepared by Ann K. Buchholtz, Rutgers University.

6. If you were responsible for determining the validity of claims, what would you do? How would you explain your reasoning? What ethical concepts or principles would guide your thinking?

ENDNOTES

1. "BP Making It Right—Highlights," http://www.bp.com/extendedsectiongenericarticle.do?categoryId=9034427&contentId=7063885. Accessed August 2, 2010.
2. Kate Daily, "In the Gulf Coast, the Spill Slows but Mental Health Concerns Continue," *Newsweek* (July 29, 2010), http://www.newsweek.com/blogs/the-human-condition/2010/07/29/in-the-gulf-coast-the-spill-slows-but-mental-health-concerns-continue.html. Accessed July 31, 2010.
3. Sasha Chavkin, "Warning of Looming Crisis, Louisiana Calls on BP to Fund Mental Health Programs," *ProPublica* (July 1, 2010), http://www.propublica.org/article/looming-crisis-louisiana-calls-on-bp-to-fund-ental-health-programs. Accessed July 31, 2010.
4. Daily.
5. Sasha Chavkin, "Mental Claims Health from Oil Spill Probably Won't Be Paid," *ProPublica* (July 27, 2010), http://www.propublica.org/article/mental-health-claims-from-oil-spill-probably-wont-be-paid. Accessed July 31, 2010.
6. *Ibid.*
7. *Ibid.*

CASE 28

Safety? What Safety?*

KIRK'S FIRST YEAR

Kirk was a bright individual who was being groomed for the controller's position in a medium-sized manufacturing firm. After his first year as assistant controller, the officers of the firm started to include him in major company functions. One day, for instance, he was asked to attend the monthly financial statement summary at a prestigious consulting firm. During the meeting, Kirk was intrigued at how the financial data he had accumulated had been transformed by the consultant into revealing charts and graphs.

NEW MANUFACTURING PLANT

Kirk was generally optimistic about the session and the company's future until the consultant started talking about the new manufacturing plant the company was adding to the current location and the per-unit costs of the chemically plated products it would produce. At that time, Bob, the president, and John, the chemical engineer, started talking about waste treatment and disposal problems. John mentioned that the current waste treatment facilities could not handle the waste products of the "ultramodern" new plant in a manner that would meet the industry's fairly high standards, although the plant would still comply with federal standards.

COST INCREASES

Kirk's boss, Henry, noted that the estimated per-unit costs would increase if the waste treatment facilities were upgraded according to recent industry standards. Industry standards were presently more stringent than federal regulations, and environmentalists were pressuring strongly for stricter regulations at the federal level. Bob mentioned that since their closest competitor did not have the waste treatment facilities that already existed at their firm, he was not in favor of any more expenditures in that area. Most managers at the meeting resoundingly agreed with Bob, and the business of the meeting proceeded to other topics.

KIRK'S DILEMMA

Kirk did not hear a word during the rest of the meeting. He kept wondering how the company could possibly have such a casual attitude toward the environment. Yet he did not know if, how, when, or with whom he should share his opinion. Soon he started reflecting on whether this firm was the right one for him.

QUESTIONS FOR DISCUSSION

1. Who are the stakeholders in this case, and what are their stakes?
2. What social responsibility does the firm have for the environment? How would you assess the firm's CSR using the four-part CSR definition presented in Chapter 2?
3. Identify the different competing "standards" at issue in this case. Which standard seems most defensible for this company considering all factors?
4. How should Kirk reconcile his own thinking with the thinking being presented by the firm's management?
5. What should Kirk do? Why?

---

* This case was written by Donald E. Tidrick, University of Texas at Austin. Permission to reprint granted by Arthur Andersen & Co., SC.

CASE 29

Something's Rotten in Hondo*

George Mackee thought of himself as bright, energetic, and with lots of potential. "So why is this happening to me?" he thought. George, with his wife, Mary, and his two children, had moved to Hondo, Texas, from El Paso four years earlier and was now the manager of the Ardnak Plastics plant in Hondo, a small plant that manufactured plastic parts for small equipment. The plant employed several hundred workers, which was a substantial portion of the population of Hondo. Ardnak Plastics Inc. had several other small plants the size of Hondo's. George had a good relationship with Bill, his boss, in Austin, Texas.

THE EMISSIONS PROBLEM

One of the problems George's plant had was that the smokestack emissions were consistently above EPA guidelines. Several months ago, George got a call from Bill, stating that the EPA had contacted him about the problem and fines would be levied. George admitted the situation was a continual problem, but because headquarters would not invest in new smokestack scrubbers, he didn't know what to do. Bill replied by saying that margins were at their limits and there was no money for new scrubbers. Besides, Bill commented, other plants were in worse shape than his and they were passing EPA standards.

A QUESTIONABLE SOLUTION

George ended the conversation by assuring Bill that he would look into the matter. He immediately started calling his contemporaries at other Ardnak plants. He found they were scheduling their heavy emissions work at night so that during the day when the EPA took their sporadic readings they were within standards. George contemplated this option even though it would result in increasing air contamination levels.

THE DOUBLE BIND

A month went by, and George still had not found a solution. The phone rang; it was Bill. Bill expressed his displeasure with the new fines for the month and reminded George that there were very few jobs out in the industry. That's when Bill dropped the whole thing into George's lap. Bill had been speaking to the Mexican government and had received assurances that no such clean air restrictions would be imposed on Ardnak if they relocated 15 miles south of Hondo in Mexico. However, Ardnak must hire Mexican workers. Bill explained that the reason for relocating would be to eliminate the EPA problems. Bill told George he had one week to decide whether to eliminate the fines by correcting the current problems or by relocating.

George knew that relocating the plant on the Mexican side would devastate the infrastructure of the city of Hondo and would continue to put contaminants into the air on the U.S. side. When he mentioned the possibility to Mary, she reinforced other concerns. She did not want him to be responsible for the loss of the jobs of their friends and extended families.

QUESTIONS FOR DISCUSSION

1. Who are the stakeholders in this situation, and what are their stakes?
2. What social responsibility, if any, does Ardnak Plastics Inc. have to the city of Hondo?
3. What are the ethical issues in this case?
4. What should George do? Why?

---

* This case was written by Geoffrey P. Lantos, Stonehill College. Permission to reprint granted by Arthur Andersen & Co., SC.

CASE 30

The High Cost of High-Tech Foods*

In September 2000, the Genetically Engineered Food Alert Coalition, a coalition of environmental and consumer groups, accused Taco Bell of using StarLink genetically modified (GM) corn in their taco shells. The FDA had approved the StarLink gene for animal (but not human) consumption. The incident prompted the recall of 300 corn-based foods and alarmed the public about the possible dangers of GM foods.[1] A recent study showed that the contamination led to a 6.8 percent decline in corn prices, and the suppression of corn prices lasted for a year.[2]

The Genetically Engineered Food Alert Coalition no longer exists, but the Institute for Agriculture and Trade Policy maintains the group's "GE Food Alert" Web site and updates it with new content. There is no shortage of new material as the debates surrounding GM food continue to grow.[3] According to David Roy of the Centre for Bioethics at the Clinical Research Institute of Montreal, the debates often produce "more heat than light." They are more emotional in nature than they are intellectual. One of the main dangers of the GM food debate is that neither side is listening to the other: Involved parties "tend to let debates become excessively polarized."[4]

SOME OF THE CURRENT ARGUMENTS

Proponents of GM foods argue that their potential risks should be judged once scientific consensus has been reached. In the meantime, they say these GM crops will feed a hungry world by multiplying per-acre yields and at the same time will reduce the need for herbicides and pesticides. GMs detractors, on the other hand, claim that possible future benefits of the technology should not outweigh present dangers. They recommend a slowdown in order that society may digest innovations of past years. They want long-term outcomes to be "clearer" before anything else is done.

* This case was prepared by Joseph G. Gerard, SUNY Institute of Technology, and Ann K. Buchholtz, Rutgers University. Updated in 2010.

SCIENTIFIC EVIDENCE

Science-based arguments contrast for both parties as well. Governments, often citing company studies, make the claim that GM crops are similar to non-GM ones and, therefore, do not pose a threat to consumers. Environmental watchdog groups, like the U.S. Public Interest Research Group, disagree. Studies claiming similarity between GM and non-GM crops, they say, are flawed and conclude nontoxicity without sufficient evidence.[5]

GOING TO EXTREMES?

Neither pole is exempt from accusations of extremist thinking. Anti-"GMers" believe that researchers and developers of new technology promise too much. In recent years, a variety of plants that produce their own pesticide—as well as herbicide-resistant seed and plants, and others with more "exotic" features—have made it to the marketplace where their benefits are lauded and their deficits seem nonexistent. But the GM food opponents ask whether the testing has been sufficiently long term to really test environmental impact. Have possible dangers for wildlife and plants that consume or ingest GM food been tested? What is the effect of that food as it moves through the food chain? Has gene flow been controlled? Some say that new reports provide evidence that studies are often too limited in both space and time to reach a conclusion.[6]

INDUSTRY'S RESPONSE

GM proponents respond that their detractors often exaggerate environmental hazards, do not substantiate their claims with scientific evidence, and are simply reacting out of fear. Those who stand by GM technology then point to examinations by government agencies "so long and rigorous that many standard foods wouldn't pass." Their field research never uncovers even a slight headache. Some even say it would be wrong to try to replicate the research.[7]

THE PROBLEM CONTINUES

In September 2006, a contaminated rice scandal bore an eerie resemblance to the StarLink situation. Greenpeace found U.S. rice on European store shelves that contained illegally genetically engineered rice. The German company Bayer was responsible for the contamination. They had ended their U.S. field trials of LL601 and LL604 over five years earlier, but some of the LL601 rice escaped the field trials and contaminated conventional U.S. rice fields.

In response to this contamination, Ebro Puleva, the world's largest rice importer, stopped the shipment of U.S. rice to Europe. LL601 rice had not been approved for human consumption when Bayer conducted their trials. When it was found that the genetically altered rice infiltrated the U.S. conventional rice crop, Bayer hastily filed an application for approval by USDA. The USDA approved LL601 for human consumption in November 2006. No other country in the world has approved LL601 for human consumption. Neither the United States nor any other country has approved LL604 for human consumption.[8]

In 2010, an estimated 10,000 peasants staged a march in Central Haiti to protest what they described as "the next earthquake for Haiti"—a donation of 475 tons of hybrid corn seeds and vegetable seeds by Monsanto. Monsanto stresses that these seeds are not genetically modified organism (GMO), but are conventional hybrids. The people of Haiti find the distinction to be unimportant because the hybrid corn does not produce seeds and is expensive to fertilize, making the people of Haiti dependent on outsiders. The issue is complex because the move comes at a time of acute need in Haiti. Nevertheless, many feel the introduction of these seeds will undermine rather than strengthen Haiti's food security. Chavannes Jean-Baptiste, leader of the peasants, describes the entry of Monsanto seeds into Haiti as "a very strong attack on small agriculture, on farmers, on biodiversity, on Creole seeds… and on what is left of our environment in Haiti."[9]

Questions for Discussion

1. What are the ethical issues in this case?
2. Do you think that either group, pro-GM or anti-GM foods, is correct while the other group is wrong? If so, what reasoning do you give for supporting the position of one group over the other? Is it possible for both to be right? What ethical concepts help you decide?
3. Is there any way to bridge the gap between these groups? If so, what would the advantages and disadvantages be?
4. If you were crafting GMO public policy, what would you recommend?
5. Do hybrid seeds represent as serious a concern as that represented by GM foods? What policy would you recommend for hybrid seeds and vegetables?

Endnotes

1. "The StarLink Fallout," *Successful Farming* (January 2001), 33–39.
2. Colin A. Carter and Aaron Smith, "Estimating the Market Effect of a Food Scare: The Case of Genetically Modified StarLink Corn," *Review of Economics & Statistics* (August 2007), 522–533.
3. http://www.gefoodalert.org/. Accessed July 20, 2010.
4. "Biotechnology and Bioethics," *MacLean's* (November 5, 2001), 38.
5. Geoffrey Lean, "Ask No Questions, Hear No Truths; Geoffrey Lean on the Scandalous Treatment of a Scientist Who Dared to Cast Doubt on the Safety of GM Foods," *The New Statesman* (September 24, 2001).
6. *Ibid.*
7. "Biotechnology and Bioethics," 38.
8. Marc Gunther, "Attack of the Mutant Rice," *Fortune* (07385587) (July 9, 2007), 20–25; "Une Contamination De Riz Par Des Ogm Est Decouverte Dans Trois Pays d'Europe," *Le Monde* (September 7, 2006), 7.
9. "10,000 Peasants March against Monsanto in Haiti; Peasant Leader to Visit US," *Trade Observatory* (June 9, 2010), http://www.tradeobservatory.org/headlines.cfm?refID=107551. Accessed July 21, 2010.

Internal Stakeholder Issues

17

Employee Stakeholders and Workplace Issues

CHAPTER LEARNING OUTCOMES

After studying this chapter, you should be able to:

1. Identify the major changes occurring in the workforce today.

2. Outline the characteristics of the new social contract between employers and employees.

3. Explain the employee rights movement and its underlying principles.

4. Describe and discuss the employment-at-will doctrine and its role in the employees' right to not be fired.

5. Discuss the right to due process and fair treatment.

6. Describe the actions companies are taking to make the workplace friendlier.

7. Elaborate on the freedom-of-speech issue and whistle-blowing.

C hanging times and the changes they bring to society's values always have an impact on the workplace. Amidst global recession, such changes become even more pronounced, and that is the case with employee stakeholders today. Although external stakeholders such as government, consumers, the environment, and the community continue to be major facets of business's concern for the social environment, considerable attention is now being paid to employee stakeholders—their status, their treatment, their rights, and their satisfaction. This should come as no surprise. For business, employees represent a significant portion of the costs incurred in doing business, and for employees, the workplace is where they spend the bulk of their daytime hours. Thus, with historic levels of worldwide unemployment, the stakes could not be higher.

The development of employee stakeholder rights has been a direct outgrowth of the kinds of social changes that have brought other societal issues into focus. The history of work has been one of steadily improving conditions for employees. Today's issues are quite unlike the old bread-and-butter concerns of higher pay, shorter hours, more job security, and better working conditions. These expectations still exist, but they have given way to other, more complex workplace trends and issues. The economic recession has accelerated the impact of issues such as pay levels, employee health care, and retirement benefits as companies try to reduce costs in order to stay competitive and employees strive to maintain their standard of living in difficult times.[1]

In the new millennium, two major themes or trends seem to characterize the modern relationship between employees and their employers: the evolution of the social contract and the expansion of employee rights. First, we will discuss the dramatic changes that have been occurring in the workplace. Prominent here will be our discussion of a newly evolving **social contract** between organizations and workers that is quite different from any such contract developed in the past. This new social contract is driven by globalization and the worldwide economic recession. Second, we will consider the continuing trend toward more expansive employee rights. These two trends are interrelated, but may seem contradictory. We will describe how the changes in the workplace have precipitated a renewal in the employee rights movement.

Because the subject of employee stakeholders and workplace issues is very extensive, we dedicate two chapters to these topics. In this chapter, we discuss some of the workplace changes that have been taking place, the emerging social contract, and the employee rights movement. Three employee rights issues, in particular, are discussed here: the right not to be fired without good cause, the right to due process and fair treatment, and the right to freedom of speech in the workplace. In Chapter 18, we will extend our discussion to the related issues of the rights of employees to privacy, safety, and health. These two chapters should be considered a continuous discussion of employee stakeholders wherein economic, legal, and ethical responsibilities are all taken into consideration.

The New Social Contract

Fifty years ago, the trend was that employees stuck to the same job in the same company for years, and those companies rewarded employees' loyalty by offering job stability, a decent wage, and good benefits.[2] Today it is estimated that a typical worker has had nine jobs by the age of 30.[3] The workforce of today is more mobile, less loyal, and more diverse. CEOs and factory workers alike know that their jobs are vulnerable, and so they have come to view themselves as free agents, bearing sole responsibility for their own careers.[4] Today's employees don't look for a promise for lifetime employment. Instead, they seek competitive pay and benefits coupled with opportunities for professional growth. They want employers who provide them with opportunities, recognize their accomplishments, and communicate openly and honestly.[5]

Employees understand that job security, compensation, and advancement depend on their contribution to the organization's mission. Changes in terminology reflect this change in attitude. What once was termed "personnel" is now called "human resources" and sometimes even "human capital." Businesses expect to leverage their human resources, just like any other resources, in a way that maximizes a firm's performance.[6] Thus, the notion of "adding value" to the organization has become a crucial factor: the bottom line is productivity. Figure 17-1 presents some of the characteristics of the old and new social contracts.

With this new social contract, loyalty is still important. Indeed, when employers treat employees with respect and consideration, they can earn employee loyalty even in (and perhaps especially in) these difficult times. Paul Savardi of Entrepreneur.com explains:

> *Employee loyalty is an earned response to the trust, respect and commitment shown to the individuals in your company.... When you demonstrate loyalty to your employees, they'll reciprocate with commitment and loyalty to your business. Remember that people don't begin their employment with you as loyal employees, but will develop loyalty over time as they're trusted, respected and appreciated by you.[7]*

The global economic recession has had some unexpected impacts on employee loyalty. The 2010 Kelly Global Workforce Index, a survey of 134,000 employees in 29 countries, found that 27 percent of respondents worldwide believe the economic recession has made them feel more loyal to their employers, 10 percent feel less loyal, and 63 percent

FIGURE 17-1 The Changing Social Contract between Employers and Employees

Old Social Contract	New Social Contract
Job security; long, stable career and employment relationships	Few tenure arrangements; jobs constantly "at risk"; employment as long as you "add value" to the organization
Lifetime careers with one employer	Fewer life careers; changing employer common; careers more dynamic
Stable positions/job assignments	Temporary project assignments
Loyalty to employer; identification	Loyalty to self and profession; diminished identification with employer
Paternalism; family-type relationships	Relationships far less warm and familial; no more parent–child relationships
Employee sense of entitlement	Personal responsibility for one's own career/job future
Stable, rising income	Pay that reflects contributions; pay for "value added"
Job-related skill training	Learning opportunities; employees in charge of their own education and updating
Focus on individual job accomplishments	Focus on team building and projects

say it made no difference.[8] In fact, 43 percent of employees say they feel "totally committed" to their current employer. The employees in North America are most "engaged," with 52 percent who say they are "totally committed" to their job. In Asia, 47 percent of employees are totally committed, and in Europe, 36 percent.[9] Oddly, recession may have engendered this level of commitment. Even employees who are not happy with their jobs and feel at the mercy of their employers are likely to feel thankful to their employers for giving them jobs when so many people are unemployed.[10] Of course, commitment and satisfaction are different. In a survey conducted in 2010, the Conference Board found that less than half the workers (45 percent) were satisfied with their work.[11] This combination of workers being dissatisfied with their jobs but still feeling grateful to have them and committed to them is expected to continue for years. In the words of *Bloomberg BusinessWeek*, "You know American workers are in bad shape when a low-paying, no-benefits job is considered a sweet deal."[12]

Even before the economic recession hit, the extreme level of global competition was affecting firms around the globe as workers began to receive an increasingly smaller portion of the economic pie. The U.S. workers' share of gross domestic product fell by 2.5 percent, German workers' share fell by 2.5 percent, and Japan went down 3 points.[13] The financial crisis exacerbated that problem with historic unemployment levels, combined by other side effects of the recession such as deteriorating working conditions and an increase in part-time work.[14] The impact of this trend differs among nations. The United States is unique in that the U.S. workers who were laid off not only lose their jobs and their incomes but also have to find a way to handle their own health benefits and retirement plans.[15] This places extreme stress on the laid-off worker, beyond the already significant stress of finding new employment. According to Peter Cappelli, director of the Center for Human Resources at the University of Pennsylvania's Wharton School, "Employers are trying to get rid of all fixed costs. First they did it with employment benefits. Now they're doing it with the jobs themselves. Everything is variable."[16] In this situation, employers have all the power and employees face all the risks.[17]

Training is vital for employees if they are to successfully navigate new waters. In this highly competitive environment, firms need workers with knowledge and the skill to leverage it. To that end, employers have instituted a wide range of training programs and tuition reimbursement programs to keep their employees at the cutting edge of the changing environment.[18] Of course, this does not help laid-off employees because the firm has no financial incentive for providing training that will enable the person to seek alternative jobs. **Outplacement**, assistance provided to laid-off employees, is an important ethical responsibility of any firm in the new environment because the duty to treat employees well does not end when they leave the firm after being laid off. Workers who are no longer associated with any firm and thus ineligible for in-house or outplacement resources need other sources of retraining—some argue that this is an example of market failure and that the government should step in to help these workers.[19]

It is difficult to say whether the new social contract is bad or good. More than anything else, it represents an adaptation to the changing world and changing business circumstances. In some respects, workers may prefer the new model. Whatever turns out to be the case, we can expect free agent employees to be more proactive about their work environments than the loyal employees of the past once were. So it is clear that employee stakeholders' expectations of fair treatment will continue to rise, and we will witness the continuing growth in the employee rights movement.

The Employee Rights Movement

In our discussion of employee rights, we will focus on employees in the private sector because of the underlying public sector–private sector dichotomy that organizations in society face. The public sector is subject to constitutional control of its power, and so government employees have more protections. In contrast, the private sector generally has not been subject to constitutional control because of the concept of **private property**, which holds that individuals and private organizations are free to use their property as they desire. As a result, private corporations historically and traditionally have not had to recognize employee rights because society honored the corporation's private property rights. The underlying issues for the private sector and its stakeholders then become why and to what extent the private property rights of business should be changed or diluted.

A brief comment on the role of labor unions is appropriate here. In general, although labor unions have been quite successful in improving the material conditions of life at work in the United States—pay, fringe benefits, and working conditions—they have not been as active in pursuing civil liberties. We must give unions credit for the gains they have made in converting what were typically regarded as management's rights or prerogatives into issues in which labor could participate. However, we should note that labor unions seem to be disappearing from the U.S. business scene. In 1953, union representation reached its highest proportion of the private employment workforce, at 36 percent.[20] By 2009, the proportion of union members in the private sector had fallen to 7.2 percent, with transportation, utilities, and construction holding the highest unionization rates.[21] Although the public sector union rate has a fivefold higher rate of 36 percent, it does not have a significant impact on the private sector employee rights we are discussing here. Compared to other countries, the U.S. unionization rate is very low, but membership statistics suggest that union membership is declining worldwide as well.[22]

The Meaning of Employee Rights

Before we consider specific employee rights issues, we should discuss briefly what we mean by **employee rights**. A lawyer might look at employee rights as claims that one can enforce in a court of law. To many economists as well, rights are only creations of

ETHICS IN PRACTICE CASE

Manager's Makeshift

It is Holland Flowers's mission to deliver fresh and innovative floral designs. To achieve this, the company hires creative university students from the local area. The company feels it is important to make every possible attempt to work around the students' schedules.

John Smith was a delivery driver for Holland Flowers and also a university student. Before accepting the position with Holland Flowers, John requested several days off the week prior to Christmas. December is a very busy time at Holland Flowers. To accommodate the increase in business, Holland Flowers hires seasonal employees. That year, the owner's son, Bob, was one of the seasonal employees. Bob was to work with John and the other drivers. The week prior to Christmas, the owner informed John that Bob was sick and unable to work. Subsequently, the owner told John he was to work that week, even though, before John was hired, they had agreed that John would be off. Reluctantly, John agreed to work.

The following night, John was downtown when he saw Bob with a drink in his hand and appearing quite healthy. John approached Bob, questioning his sickness and absence from work. Bob denied his illness, acting as if being the owner's son meant he could be off when he wanted.

John was furious, because the owner had previously stressed that Holland Flowers was built on honest working relationships. John felt that this incident went against the principles on which the company was founded. He no longer felt respect for the owner or Holland Flowers; instead, he felt lied to and betrayed. He called the owner that night and informed him of his feelings. Because the owner offered no defense, John felt he could no longer work for Holland Flowers, and he resigned.

1. Did the management of Holland Flowers behave unethically with respect to employee treatment in this case?

2. Was John right in questioning the owner's employee practices?

3. If you were John, what action would you have taken in this dilemma?

Contributed by Christopher Lockett

the law. For our purposes, we will approach employee rights from the "principle of rights" perspective, and viewed from this perspective, rights are justifiable claims that utility cannot override. While we will focus on moral employee rights, we will also consider where the law stands regarding the rights of employees. Of course, the current recessionary environment has impacted discussion of employee rights. If a right is truly a moral right, it is not contingent on business's ability to provide it. However, the deep cutbacks that arose from the recession have stimulated renewed discussion of the parameters of employee rights.

Employee rights can be positive or negative. Said differently, they can focus on achieving desired outcomes or on prohibiting unwanted outcomes. Richard Edwards has grouped employee rights into three categories based on the fact that these rights find their source in law, union contracts, or employers' promises. Rights provided by the law are called **statutory rights**. These include, for example, the rights established by the Civil Rights Act of 1964 (at a national level) or by the Massachusetts Right to Know Law (at the state level), which grant production workers the right to be notified of specific toxic substances they may be exposed to in the workplace. Union contracts, by contrast, provide workers with rights established through the process of **collective bargaining**. Examples of these rights are seniority preferences, job security mechanisms, and grievance procedures.[23]

Employer promises are the third source of employees' rights categorized by Edwards. He calls these employer grants or promises **enterprise rights**. Typical examples of such

---

FIGURE 17-2 Three Models of Management Morality and Their Orientations toward Employee Stakeholders

Model of Management Morality	Orientation toward Employee Stakeholders
Moral Management	Employees are a human resource that must be treated with dignity and respect. Employees' rights to due process, privacy, freedom of speech, and safety are maximally considered in all decisions. Management seeks fair dealings with employees. The goal is to use a leadership style, such as consultative/participative, that will result in mutual confidence and trust. Commitment is a recurring theme.
Amoral Management	Employees are treated as the law requires. Attempts to motivate focus on increasing productivity rather than satisfying employees' growing maturity needs. Employees are still seen as factors of production, but a remunerative approach is used. The organization sees self-interest in treating employees with minimal respect. Organization structure, pay incentives, and rewards are all geared toward short- and medium-term productivity.
Immoral Management	Employees are viewed as factors of production to be used, exploited, and manipulated for gain of individual manager or company. No concern is shown for employees' needs/ rights/expectations. Managers pursue a short-term focus in a coercive, controlling, and alienating environment.

---

enterprise rights might include the right to petition beyond one's immediate supervisor, the right to be free from physical intimidation, the right to a grievance or complaint system, the right to due process in discipline, the right to have express standards for personnel evaluation, the right to have one's job clearly defined, the right to a "just cause" standard for dismissal, the right to be free from nepotism and unfair favoritism, and so on.[24] Enterprise rights are provided and justified by management, and so the rationale for those rights can be as varied as the managers implementing them. They might reflect the prevailing customs and so might be necessary for the firm to be competitive. They might extend above and beyond those offered by competing firms and thus be used as a sort of recruiting tool. They may also be afforded on the basis of some normative ethical principle or reasoning (for example, "This is the way workers ought to be treated"). In this situation, the ethical principles of justice, rights, and utilitarianism, as well as notions of virtue ethics, may be the rationales.

In this connection, management may provide the employee rights as part of an effort to display moral management, as discussed in Chapter 7. To illustrate this point further, Figure 17-2 characterizes how moral managers, as well as amoral and immoral managers, might view employee stakeholders.

To summarize, employee rights may be provided on the basis of economic, legal, or ethical sources of justification. In a limited number of cases, companies even use philanthropic arguments as the bases for providing employee rights or benefits. For example, some companies provide employees with daycare facilities and other benefits on philanthropic grounds, though, of course, these benefits also help with recruitment and retention. For purposes of our discussion here, however, we will concentrate on legal and ethical bases for considering employee rights.

Following are the job-related rights that are mentioned often enough and thus merit further discussion here: (1) the *right not to be fired without good cause*, (2) the *right to due process and fair treatment*, and (3) the *right to freedom, particularly freedom of expression and freedom of speech*. In Chapter 18, we will consider the rights to privacy, safety, and health in the workplace.

The Right Not to Be Fired Without Cause

A **good cause norm**, the belief that employees should be discharged only for good reasons (i.e., just cause dismissal), prevails in the United States today. This belief persists in spite of the fact that most U.S. employees can be fired for any reason, or for no reason, as long as the firing is not discriminatory. A range of studies have shown the good cause norm to be widely held in a variety of situations, with respondents including undergraduate and graduate students as well as both blue- and white-collar workers.[25] Belief in the good cause norm stands in direct opposition to the employment-at-will doctrine, which many employers believe is their right. With employers and employees holding such contradictory views, it is easy to see why so many disputes occur, and terms like "unjust dismissals" and "wrongful discharge" have become part of our employment language.

Employment-at-Will Doctrine

The central issue in the movement to protect workers' jobs surrounds changing views of the **employment-at-will doctrine**. In the industrialized world, the United States is unique in adhering to this doctrine, based on the private property rights of the employer and the principle that the relationship between employer and employee is a voluntary one that can be terminated at any time by either party. This doctrine holds that just as employees are free to quit a company any time they choose, employers can discharge employees for any reason, or no reason, as long as they do not violate federal discrimination laws, state laws, or union contracts. What this doctrine means is that unless you are protected by a union contract (the vast majority of the workforce is not) or by one of the discrimination laws, your employer is free to let you go anytime, for any reason. This doctrine is not widely understood by the workforce. As previously mentioned, most employees in the United States believe that employment law follows a good cause norm;[26] nevertheless, most private employees in the United States are in an at-will employment relationship.[27]

This lack of awareness about at-will employment may provide the answer to a question Louis Uchitelle poses in *The Disposable American*—Why is the United States so tolerant of large-scale layoffs?[28] Uchitelle, who writes on economics for the *New York Times*, details the human costs of a system that allows employers to fire or lay off employees at will. Layoffs are traumatic events that inflict significant mental health damage. Uchitelle poses the following question to the American Psychiatric Association, "Why don't you put a warning label on layoffs?"[29]

Legal Challenges to Employment-at-Will.   Three broad categories of issues that illustrate the legal challenges that have arisen with regard to employment-at-will discharges are (1) public policy exceptions, (2) contractual actions, and (3) breach of good faith actions.[30] States vary in their adoption of exceptions to employment-at-will, creating a patchwork of employment situations around the country. Only three states, Florida, Georgia, and Rhode Island, have never adopted an exception.[31]

A major exception to the long-standing employment-at-will doctrine is known as the **public policy exception**; 43 states recognize this exception.[32] This exception protects employees from being fired because they refuse to commit crimes or because they try to take advantage of privileges to which they are entitled by law. The courts have held that management may not discharge an employee who refuses to commit an illegal act or performs a public obligation, such as serving on a jury or supplying information to the police. This exception sometimes covers whistle-blowers. We will further discuss the case of whistle-blowers later in the chapter.

Workers who believe they have contracts or implied contracts with their employers are protected in the 42 states that recognize the **implied contract exception**.[33] In some instances, the courts hold employers to promises they do not even realize they have made. For example, statements in employee handbooks or personnel manuals, job-offer letters, and even oral assurances about job security can be interpreted as implied contracts that the management is not at liberty to violate. If an employee can prove in court that the hiring manager said, "We do not fire people without a good reason," that can be enough to create an implied contract. Even the use of the term "permanent employee" to mean an employee who had worked beyond a six-month probationary period may be construed as a promise of continuous employment.

Courts have also recognized that employers should hold themselves to a standard of fairness and good faith dealings with employees. This concept is probably the broadest restraint on employment-at-will terminations. The **good faith principle** suggests that employers may run the risk of losing lawsuits to former employees if they fail to show

---

ETHICS IN PRACTICE CASE

Rowdy Recruiting

Last summer, I interned for a large company. The economy was strong, and so a large part of the company's time and money were put toward recruiting. The overwhelming majority of the company's employees were under the age of 30, and so young, energetic employees, who had recently been through the hiring process, did most of the recruiting. One Thursday night, I was asked to join a group of our employees and take a young prospect for dinner. The idea was to take the recruit out for a night on the town and entertain him on his first night in our city. The next morning he was scheduled to meet with a partner at 8 a.m. for the first of the many interviews.

At 7 p.m. sharp, we met the recruit, Mike, in the lobby of the hotel where he was staying. My first impression was that Mike was very nervous about dining with such a large group of our workers. When we arrived at the restaurant, the waiter handed us a wine list. As usual, we ordered a few bottles of wine for the table. When Mike refused our offer of a drink, my manager assured him it was okay. He consented and started in for a long night of alcohol consumption. We hopped from the restaurant to several bars in an upscale area of the city. Eventually, it was way past our bedtime, and we had all surpassed our limit. So we walked Mike back to his hotel and reminded him that we would be back to meet him bright and early in the morning.

Early Friday morning, my manager and I pushed our way through the revolving door of the hotel that we had just exited a few hours earlier. Though we were both feeling a bit hung over, we put on a smile and acted very professional. After a few minutes, the elevator door opened and Mike stumbled out. As he approached us, we noticed the lack of color in his face and wondered what kind of impression he would make in his interviews. As I reached out my hand to shake his, Mike turned his head and vomited on the floor of the hotel. After getting himself together, Mike began apologizing profusely. At that point, my manager informed Mike that he would no longer be interviewing with our company. I was shocked! All of us stayed out too late and had too much fun. Why would my manager punish Mike for something we had all done and even encouraged him to do?

1. Did the manager behave unethically with respect to treatment of the recruit? Does the fact that the recruit initially turned down the wine and the manager encouraged him to drink it affect your answer?

2. Do the rights of recruits differ from the rights of employees? If so, how?

3. If you were the manager, what action would you have taken in this situation? How would you have handled Mike? Would you have done anything to lessen the likelihood of this happening again?

Contributed Anonymously

Spotlight on SUSTAINABILITY

Employees Are Key to Sustainability

A study by the National Environmental Education Foundation (NEEF) found educating employees in environmental and sustainability (E&S) initiatives can attract and retain good talent while also increasing profitability and reducing environmental impact. The study presents a variety of case studies including eBay. eBay's green team convinced the company to build San Jose, California's largest commercial solar installation. They reduced CO_2 emissions by over 1 million pounds a year and saved well over $100,000. In a statement, Diane Wood, president of NEEF, said, "While in the past, most environmental education programs were primarily for environmental safety and health employees, many companies now realize that to achieve their sustainability goals, they need to involve the entire workforce (or all their employees).... Successful employee engagement programs motivate employees and can be an asset in recruitment and retention."

Source: Greenbiz Staff, "Why Bringing Employees on Board Helps Sustainability Projects Succeed," Greenbiz.com (February 22, 2010), http://www.greenbiz.com/news/2010/02/22/bringing-employees-board-makes-sustainability-projects-success#ixzz0pS7n8RUA.

that employees had every reasonable opportunity to improve their performance before termination. Only 20 states recognize the good faith principle.[34] As previously noted, however, the good faith principle reflects what many already believe is the responsibility of businesses toward their employees. The principle is not a problem for companies if they simply introduce fair ways of taking disciplinary measures and mechanisms for reviewing grievances that provide employees with due process. We will discuss such due-process mechanisms later in the chapter.

Moral and Managerial Challenges to Employment-at-Will.

As previously mentioned, the United States is unique in its adherence to employment-at-will and most people in the United States believe a norm of good cause applies to employment decisions, so it is not surprising that employment-at-will has been criticized on moral as well as legal grounds. The argument generally used in favor of employment-at-will is that employers invoke their property rights when they terminate an employee. In an interesting rebuttal, Werhane, Radin, and Bowie suggest that the fruits of an employee's labor are that employee's property and so property rights arguments provide an argument against the appropriateness of employment-at-will.[35]

Using the concept of employee property rights as a foundation, Werhane et al. derive three objections to employment-at-will. First they argue that employees deserve respectful treatment, which includes explaining the reasons for termination when it occurs. Second, employees do not have the option of being arbitrary or capricious with employers, and so employers should bear the same responsibility in their treatment of employees. A third issue is based on the concept of reciprocity: employees are expected to be trustworthy, loyal, and respectful in their interactions with employers, and so employers should show employees the same consideration.[36]

Employment-at-will can present managerial problems as well. We should not forget the impact that an employment-at-will environment can have on the culture of an organization. Most bad reasons for firing employees, such as discrimination, are already illegal, and managers can always fire an employee for good justifiable reasons, so employment-at-will simply protects the right of the employer to fire an employee for no reason at all. This creates an odd dynamic. Trust and loyalty are important to effective workplaces, but they are reciprocal relationships. For managers to be able to trust their employees, they must be willing to be trustworthy in return.[37]

Terminating an Employee with Care

With respect to employee termination, management needs to be aware not only of the content of the decision to terminate but also of the process for doing it. Treating employees with care is important not only to the terminated employee but also to the survivors of the process, who then know they will be treated with care if they face a similar situation. A positive corporate culture can be preserved even in difficult times with thoughtful treatment of employees. Steve Harrison offers some do's and don'ts for terminating employees in a responsible manner. The following are some specific recommendations for actions:[38]

1. *Fire employees in a private space.* Don't terminate an employee in a way that enables coworkers to see what is happening or that forces them to "walk a gauntlet" in front of them.
2. *Be mindful of employees' logistics.* How will they get closure on their projects? How will they get home that day?
3. *Preserve employees' dignity.* If you must lay off a trusted and valuable employee for economic reasons, don't confiscate IDs and cell phones immediately or cancel passwords immediately.
4. *Choreograph the notification in advance.* The purpose of the meeting should not be a surprise.
5. *Use transparent criteria for layoffs.* The rationale for terminations should be clear both to those laid off and to the survivors.

The following are some of the actions managers should *not* take when terminating employees:[39]

1. *Don't fire on a Friday.* Terminated employees would not have access to support services on weekends and so would have to cope on their own.
2. *Don't say that downsizing is finished.* It is impossible to know for sure that the downsizing has ended and being wrong about that would make subsequent layoffs more difficult for all concerned.
3. *Don't terminate an employee via e-mail.* Although this advice seems obvious, firms have done so to the detriment of employees as well as their reputations.
4. *Stick to the topic and avoid platitudes.* For example, don't say, "This is as hard for me as it is for you"—it isn't.
5. *Don't rush through the meeting.* Being willing to give a person time is a way of communicating that the person matters. Not to give the employee the time needed for the termination puts salt in the wound.

For effective stakeholder management, organizations must always consider their obligations to employee stakeholders and their rights and expectations with respect to their jobs. Companies that aspire to emulate the tenets of the moral management model will need to reexamine continuously their attitudes, perceptions, practices, and policies with respect to this issue.

The Right to Due Process and Fair Treatment

One of the most frequently proclaimed employee rights issues of the past decade has been the right to due process. Basically, **due process** is the right to receive an impartial review of one's complaints and to be dealt with fairly. In the context of the workplace, the right to due process is the right of employees to have impartial third parties review the decisions that adversely affect them. Of course, the right to not be fired without just cause would fall into this category of fair treatment; however, in this section we will expand on this concept and discuss other applications.

One major obstacle to the due-process idea is that to some extent it is a bit contrary to the employment-at-will principle discussed earlier. Due process is consistent with the democratic ideal that undergirds the universal right to fair treatment, and so one can argue that without due process, employees do not receive fair treatment in the workplace. Furthermore, the fact that the courts are gradually eroding the employment-at-will principle might serve as an indication that employment-at-will is thought to be unfair. If this is true, the due-process concept makes more sense.

Due Process

Patricia Werhane, a leading business ethicist, contends that, procedurally, due process extends beyond simple fair treatment and should state, "Every employee has a right to a public hearing, peer evaluation, outside arbitration, or some other open and mutually agreed-upon grievance procedure before being demoted, unwillingly transferred, or fired."[40] Due process can range from the expectation that the company treat employees fairly to the position that employees deserve a fair system of decision making.

Sometimes unfair treatment happens in such a subtle way that it is difficult to know that it has taken place. What do you do, for example, if your supervisor refuses to recommend you for promotion or permit you to transfer because she or he considers you to be exceptionally good at your job and doesn't want to lose you? How do you prove that a manager has given you a low performance appraisal because you resisted sexual advances? The issues over which due-process questions may arise can be quite difficult and subtle.

Due process, when formalized, is a system for ascertaining that organizational decisions have been fair.[41] As such, it aligns closely with the concept of procedural justice that we discussed in Chapter 8.[42] The following are the main requirements of a due-process system in an organization:[43]

1. It must be a procedure; it must follow rules. It must not be arbitrary.
2. It must be sufficiently visible and so well known that potential violators of employee rights and victims of abuse are aware of it.
3. It must be predictably effective.
4. It must be institutionalized—a relatively permanent fixture in the organization.
5. It must be perceived as equitable.
6. It must be easy to use.
7. It must apply to all employees.

Procedural due process is a concept derived from the 5th and 14th Amendments of the U.S. Constitution. In law, due process requires a balancing act between the interests of the government and those of the individual. In organizations, a similar balancing act occurs. The challenge is to balance the interests of the individual employee with those of the organization.[44]

Alternative Dispute Resolution

Companies can and do provide due process for their employees in several ways. The approaches described here represent some of the **alternative dispute resolution (ADR)** methods that have been employed by companies.

Common Approaches. One of the most often-used mechanisms is the **open-door policy**. This approach typically relies on a senior-level executive who asserts that her or his "door is always open" for those who think they have been treated unfairly. Alternatively, the organization might assign to an executive of the human resources department the responsibility for investigating employee grievances and either handling them or reporting them to higher management. From the employee's standpoint, the major problems with these approaches are that (1) the process is closed, (2) one person is reviewing what happened, and (3) there is a tendency in organizations for one manager to support another manager's decisions. The process is opened up somewhat by companies that use a **hearing procedure**, which permits employees to be represented by an attorney or another person, with a neutral company executive deciding the outcome based on the evidence. Similar to this approach is the use of a management *grievance committee*, which may involve multiple executives in the decision process.

The Ombudsman. An innovative due-process mechanism that has become popular for dealing with employee problems is the use of a corporate **ombudsman**, also known as *ombud* or *ombudsperson*. "Ombudsman" is a Swedish word that refers to one who investigates reported complaints and helps to achieve equitable settlements. The ombudsman approach has been used in Sweden since 1809 to curb abuses by government against individuals. In the United States, the corporate version of the ombudsman entered the scene over 35 years ago, when the Xerox Corporation named an ombudsman for its largest division. General Electric and the Boeing Vertol division of Boeing were quick to follow.[45] Today, over 200 major corporations have ombudsmen, with 50 added in the two years after the Sarbanes–Oxley (SOX) was passed.[46] SOX contains a lesser known provision that encourages employees to report wrongdoing and prohibits corporate retaliation against those employees.[47]

The ombudsman's task is quite different from that of the human resources manager. Hiring, firing, setting policy, and keeping records are all the responsibilities of the human resources department; the ombudsman does none of these.[48] In contrast he or she is formally and officially neutral and promises client confidentiality.[49] Ombuds can handle the concerns of employees who believe they have witnessed wrongdoing and do so in a way that keeps the problem from getting out of hand.[50]

The Peer Review Panel. The **peer review panel** is another due-process mechanism currently in use. Eastman Kodak has made good use of the peer review concept as it dealt with a planned workforce reduction of 4,500 to 6,000 people.[51] As Ann Reesman, former general counsel of the Equal Employment Advisory Council, put it, "The benefit of using peer review rather than some external decision maker is that the peer review panel is well-versed in the company culture and how the company operates."[52] Also, peers tend to find decisions handed down by peers to be trustworthy.[53]

The key to a successful peer review committee is to make sure that the people involved in the process are respected members of the organization. Election rather than appointment of committee members is important for participants to trust the independence of the process. Everyone involved in peer review must receive training in relevant areas such as dispute resolution, discrimination, fairness, legalities, and ethics. Representatives of both employees and management should be involved in the decision-making process.[54]

The trend toward using ADR is growing, with no end in sight. This growth is spurred partly by the time and money saved by avoiding costly litigation. KBR (formerly Kellogg Brown & Root), a Houston-based construction and engineering firm, estimates that its legal fees dropped 30 to 50 percent since employing ADR, and 70 to 80 percent of the firm's cases were settled within eight weeks (40 percent within a month). Further, the proportion of adverse settlements and the size of the judgments were no different from when they went through the court system.[55] Viewed from the "ethics of care" standpoint, alternative dispute resolution is preferable to the adversarial strategies that preceded it.[56]

Many observers expressed concern, however, that some employers were requiring new hires to sign contracts, waiving their right to sue the firm and accepting pre-dispute **mandatory arbitration** as the alternative. Arbitration is a process where a neutral party resolves a dispute between two or more parties and the resolution is binding. In mandatory arbitration, the parties must agree to arbitration prior to any dispute. Critics of this practice argue that this robs employees of their right to due process. They say that the structure of mandatory arbitration favors the organization and not the employee. Supporters contend that the arbitration process is just as fair as a jury trial while costing much less in time and money. The war against mandatory arbitration continues to wage. President Obama has signed into law bills that limit mandatory arbitration in certain circumstances, and the U.S. Congress is considering a bill that would ban mandatory arbitration in employment disputes.[57]

Freedom of Speech in the Workplace

Henry Boisvert was a testing supervisor at FMC Corporation, makers of the Bradley Fighting Vehicle. The Bradley was designed to transport soldiers around battlefields and, when necessary, "swim" through rivers and lakes. While testing the Bradley's ability to move through a pond, Boisvert found the vehicle filled with water quickly. He wrote to the Army a report of his findings, but the FMC supervisors did not send the report. When Boisvert refused to sign a falsified report of his test results, he was fired.[58]

About the same time that Boisvert was discovering the Bradley's inability to swim, Air Force Lieutenant Colonel James Burton found additional problems with the fighting machine. When hit by enemy fire, the Bradley's aluminum armor melted and filled the inside of the vehicle with poisonous fumes. After 17 years of development and $14 billion of investment for research and prototypes, the Bradley was declared unfit for warfare. Burton uncovered tests of the Bradley that were rigged by filling the gas tanks with water and the ammunition with noncombustible sand, making it impossible for the Bradley to explode. He also fought an attempt to transfer him to Alaska. Burton's insistence on speaking freely successfully forced changes in the Bradley; however, Burton was forced to take early retirement as the officers who tried to stop his investigation were promoted.[59]

Speaking truth to power is a Quaker phrase for speaking honestly and openly even when powerful parties would prefer that you keep quiet. Both Boisvert and Burton insisted on speaking truth to power and ultimately prevailed in their fights to fix the Bradley. After a 12-year legal battle, Boisvert received one of the largest damage awards ever witnessed in a federal case, well over $300 million. During the trial, evidence emerged about employees using putty to fix cracks in the machine while vehicles to be selected for random inspection were marked with "Xs" and worked on more carefully than the rest.[60] Burton's story also ends happily. Congress mandated that the Bradley be tested under the supervision of the National Academy of Sciences, using conditions that resembled true battlefield combat. As a result of these tests, the Bradley was redesigned and has been used successfully since. Burton wrote a best-selling book about his experiences, *The Pentagon Wars*, which subsequently became an HBO movie.[61] It is impossible to estimate how many soldiers' lives were saved by the courage and persistence of these two men.

Whistle-Blowing

As stated earlier, the current generation of employees has a different concept of loyalty to and acceptance of authority than that of past generations. The result is an unprecedented number of employees "blowing the whistle" on their employers. A **whistle-blower** is a former or current organization member who discloses "illegal, immoral, or illegitimate practices under the control of their employers, to persons or organizations that may be able to effect action."[62] Four key elements comprise the whistle-blowing process: the whistle-blower, the act or complaint about which the whistle-blower is concerned, the party to whom the complaint or report is made, and the organization against which the complaint is made.[63]

What is at stake is the employee's right to speak out in cases where she or he thinks the company or management is engaging in an unacceptable practice. Whistle-blowing is contrary to our cultural tradition that an employee does not question a superior's decisions and acts, especially in public. The former view held that the employee owes loyalty, obedience, and confidentiality to the corporate employer; however, the current view of employee responsibility holds that the employee has a duty not only to the employer but also to the public and to her or his own conscience. Whistle-blowing, in this latter situation, becomes an important option for the employee should management not be responsive to expressed concerns. Figure 17-3 depicts these two views of employee responsibility.

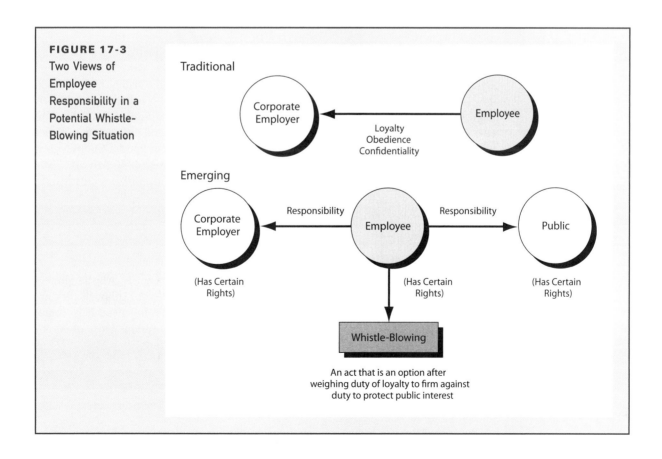

FIGURE 17-3

Two Views of Employee Responsibility in a Potential Whistle-Blowing Situation

Most whistle-blowers seem to engage in these acts out of a genuine or legitimate belief that the actions of their organizations are wrong and that they are doing the right thing by reporting them. They may have learned of the wrongful acts by being requested or coerced to participate in them, or through observation or examination of company records. The genuinely concerned employee may initially express concern to a superior or to someone else within the organization. Other potential whistle-blowers may be planning to make their reports for the purpose of striking out or retaliating against the company or a specific manager for some reason. In a survey of studies of whistle-blowers, however, Near and Miceli found the latter to be uncommon. Whistle-blowers were on average more highly paid, with higher job performance than inactive observers. They were more likely to hold supervisory or professional status, and they have both the role and responsibility to report wrongdoing and the knowledge of channels for doing so.[64]

After Enron and the scandals that followed, whistle-blowers began to receive more recognition. The *Time* Persons of the Year were three women who fit Near and Miceli's description. They named the women "the whistle-blowers": the former Enron vice president Sherron Watkins, who wrote a memo to Enron CEO Kenneth Lay, warning of improprieties in the firm's accounting methods; FBI staff attorney Colleen Riley, who told FBI director Robert Mueller about the bureau having ignored the Minneapolis field office's pleas that they investigate Zacarias Moussaoui, now convicted as a September 11 co-conspirator; and WorldCom's vice president of internal audit, Cynthia Cooper, who told the board that the company had hidden $3.8 billion in losses in falsified books.[65] According to *Time*, these women of "ordinary demeanor but exceptional guts and sense" risked their jobs, health, privacy, and sanity to bring about sea changes in their industries.[66] Some have argued that the designation of whistle-blower is incorrect because they are internal whistle-blowers. Dan Ackerman of *Forbes* writes in *The Wall Street Journal*, "A whistleblower is someone who spots a criminal inside a bank and alerts the police. That's not Sherron Watkins. What she did was write a memo to the bank robber (Mr. Lay) suggesting he was about to be caught and warning him to watch out."[67] Whatever one's opinion of the nature of their disclosures, it is hard to argue their impact on the business psyche. The media coverage of their high-profile cases is likely to have contributed to a dramatic rise in public awareness of and interest in whistle-blowing. For example, whistle-blower suits filed with the Office of Special Counsel grew from 380 in fiscal year 2001 to 555 in fiscal year 2002, an increase of 46 percent.[68] The preponderance of whistle-blower suits continues unabated, with 530 new disclosures received in 2008.[69]

Figure 17-4 depicts a checklist to be followed by whistle-blowers before blowing the whistle.

Consequences of Whistle-Blowing

What happens to employees after they blow the whistle? Unfortunately, whistle-blowers are often not rewarded for their contributions to the public interest. Although they are now more likely to get some form of protection, whistle-blowers in general have sometimes paid dearly for their actions. Although they are not fired, various types of corporate retaliation have been taken against whistle-blowers,[70] including

- More stringent criticism of work
- Less desirable work assignments
- Pressure to drop charges against the company
- Heavier workloads
- Lost perquisites (for example, telephone and parking privileges)
- Exclusion from meetings previously attended

FIGURE 17-4

A Checklist to Follow before Blowing the Whistle

The following things should be considered before you blow the whistle:

1. Is there any alternative to blowing the whistle? Make sure you have tried to remedy the problem by reporting up the normal chain of command and have had no success.

2. Does the proposed disclosure advance public interest rather than personal or political gain? Don't act out of frustration or because you feel mistreated.

3. Have you thought about the outcomes of blowing the whistle for yourself and your family? Be prepared for the possibility of disapproval from friends, family, and fellow workers.

4. Have you identified the sources of support both inside and outside the organization on which you can rely during the process? Make sure you know your legal rights and have enlisted the help of others.

5. Do you have enough evidence to support your claim? Even more evidence is needed if you plan to remain anonymous.

6. Have you identified and copied all supporting records before drawing suspicion to your concerns? Remember to keep a factual log both before and after blowing the whistle.

Sources: Department of Human Services, Victoria, Australia, **http://www.dhs.vic.gov.au/whistleblowers/checklist.htm**; *BusinessWeek* (December 16, 2002), http://www.businessweek.com/magazine/content/02_50/b3812095.htm; The Government Accountability Center, http://www.whistleblower.org/getcat.php?cid=32; Kenneth K. Humphreys, "A Checklist for Whistleblowers to Follow," *Cost Engineering* (October 2003), 14.

One person paying the price for speaking up is the whistle-blower whose courage drew worldwide attention when he made public the abuse of Iraqi detainees at Abu Ghraib Prison in Baghdad. Spec. Joseph M. Darby, a former reservist in the 372nd Military Police Company, found out about the abuse by accident when a friend gave him the pictures. He turned them over to the Army's Criminal Investigation Division anonymously. The photographs that documented this abuse shocked the world.[71]

Darby's anonymity was short lived after Defense Secretary Donald Rumsfeld spoke his name when giving congressional testimony—testimony that played on the TV as Darby was having lunch in the mess hall.[72] Fearing retaliation, Darby slept with a gun under his pillow. The army soon opted to send him home ahead of his unit for his safety.[73] Unfortunately, Darby's hometown did not prove a safe haven. The commander of the local Veterans of Foreign Wars post referred to him as a "rat" and a "traitor," and his wife, Bernadette, heard people say her husband was a "dead man" and that he was "walking around with a bull's-eye on his head."[74] Relatives from both sides of the family turned against them.[75]

The army concluded that the Darbys could not return home safely, and so they kept them on an army base with round-the-clock security guards. The Darbys have set up residence in a new town; they don't disclose the location due to ongoing safety concerns. Darby left the army and misses it. They both miss their hometown, and they know they will never go home again. When asked if he wishes it were someone other than he who had been given the pictures, Darby says, "No, because if it was someone else it might not have been reported.... Ignorance is bliss they say but to actually know what they were doing, you can't stand by and let that happen."[76]

Although whistle-blowers frequently do suffer severe consequences like the Darbys did for speaking out, other corporate actions are also possible. One encouraging episode is the case of Mark Jorgensen, who was a manager of real estate funds at Prudential Insurance Company of America.[77] Jorgensen thought he was just being an honest guy when he exposed a fraud running in his company. His world then began to fall apart. His boss, who had once been his friend, abandoned him. His colleagues at work began to shun him. Company lawyers accused him of breaking the law. Jorgensen, who was once a powerful and respected executive in the firm, began to hide out at the local library because he had been forbidden to return to his office. His long and successful career appeared to be dwindling to a pathetic end. Finally, he was fired.

Unlike most whistle-blowers, however, Jorgensen received a phone call from the company chairman, Robert Winters, who wanted to meet with Jorgensen to tell him some startling news: The company now believed him and wanted to reinstate him. Further, the company wanted to force out the boss he had accused of falsely inflating the values of funds that he managed. The turnabout was attributed to Jorgensen's persistence in fighting all odds in his quest to justify his convictions. Coming to the realization that Jorgensen had been right in his allegations all along, Prudential found itself in an unusual situation in business today—siding with the whistle-blower it had fought for months and eventually had fired. The company offered to reinstate Jorgensen in his job, but he elected instead to move on to another company. Prudential paid him a sizable amount to settle his lawsuit.[78] Although we do not read about many stories that end this way, it is encouraging to know that there are some stories that have happy endings. Speaking of endings (that may or may not be happy), Figure 17-5 chronicles Hollywood's treatment of some famous whistle-blowers.

FIGURE 17-5 Whistle-Blowers Get the Hollywood Treatment

Movie	Stars	Story	Inspiration
The Informant! (2009)	Matt Damon Scott Bakula Joel McHale	Mark Whitacre, an employee at Archer Daniels Midland (ADM), blows the whistle on the lysine price-fixing conspiracy.	This dark comedy is based on *The Informant*, a book by journalist Kurt Eichenwald.
The Insider (1999)	Russell Crowe Al Pacino Christopher Plummer	A successful scientist is fired from major tobacco company for taking a principled stand. *60 Minutes* is due to report the story, but they cave to corporate pressure.	Based on a *Vanity Fair* article, "The Man Who Knew Too Much." The movie tells the true story of Jeffrey Wigand, who was fired from Brown & Williamson tobacco company.
Silkwood (1983)	Meryl Streep (title role) Kurt Russell Cher Craig T. Nelson	Whistle-blowers try to expose unsafe practices at an Oklahoma nuclear parts factory. A worker becomes contaminated.	Based on the true story of Karen Silkwood, who was a chemical technician at the Kerr-McGee plutonium fuels production plant in Crescent, Oklahoma. As a union member and activist, she was critical of plant safety.
Serpico (1973)	Al Pacino (title role)	Frank Serpico is a nonconformist "hippie cop" in New York City who tries to report graft and corruption to his superiors. When they don't listen, he goes to *The New York Times*.	Based on Peter Maas's book, the movie tells a true story from Serpico's perspective. In the true story, another whistle-blower (David Durk) played a critical role, which is downplayed in the movie.

Government's Protection of Whistle-Blowers

Just as employees are beginning to get some protection from the courts through the public policy exception to the employment-at-will doctrine, the same is true for whistle-blowers. The federal government was one of the first organizations to attempt to protect its own whistle-blowers. A highlight of the **1978 Civil Service Reform Act** was protection for federal employees who expose illegal, corrupt, or wasteful government activities. Unfortunately, this effort has had only mixed results.[79] It is difficult to protect whistle-blowers against retaliation because so often the reprisals are subtle. An added boost for federal employees came in 1989, when Congress passed the Whistle-Blower Protection Act and the president signed it into law. The effect of this act was to reform the Merit System Protection Board and the Office of General Counsel, the two offices that protect federal employees.[80]

The **Michigan Whistle-Blowers Protection Act of 1981** became the first state law designed to protect any employee in private industry against unjust reprisals for reporting alleged violations of federal, state, or local laws to public authorities. The burden was placed on the employer to show that questionable treatment was justified on the basis of proper personnel standards or valid business reasons.[81] The Michigan Act spurred similar laws in other states; however, the National Whistleblower Center finds that all but 17 states have a patchwork of protections for whistle-blowers. As of 2010, those 17 states are Arizona, California, Connecticut, Delaware, Florida, Hawaii, Illinois, Indiana, Maine, New Hampshire, New Jersey, North Dakota, Ohio, Rhode Island, South Dakota, Tennessee, and Vermont.

Most state courts have recognized a public policy exception, and therefore whistle-blowers have some limited protection. The normal remedy for wrongful discharge of employees is reinstatement with back pay, with some sympathetic juries adding compensatory damages for physical suffering.[82] The problem with most laws intended to protect whistle-blowers is that they are quite spotty. Some state and federal laws, such as environmental, transportation, health, safety, and civil rights statutes, have provisions that protect whistle-blowers from retaliation, but relatively few states have provisions that protect private sector employees, and these provisions vary widely in their nature and protection coverage.

This crazy quilt of whistle-blower protections makes it very difficult for employees to safely shed light on corporate wrongdoing. In some states, whistle-blowers could be fired at will; in other states, they would have to sort through a bewildering assortment of statutes to determine what, if any, protection existed. However, that was supposed to change when SOX was passed.

Sarbanes–Oxley Whistle-Blower Protections

Tom Devine, Government Accounting Project (GAP) legal director, described SOX (2002) as a "lunar landing in terms of strengthening corporate responsibility to shareholders and employees alike. This is a landmark breakthrough in corporate accountability and a legal revolution for corporate freedom of speech."[83] SOX makes whistle-blowing much easier. Whistle-blowers only need to make a disclosure to a supervisor, law enforcement agency, or congressional investigator that could have a "material impact" on a company's stock price. The Labor Department then bears responsibility for investigating any complaints of the whistle-blower being terminated, demoted, or harassed.[84] The protections SOX provides include[85]

- Comprehensive coverage for all employees of publicly traded companies
- Comprehensive protection for any form of discrimination or harassment
- Any corporate conduct that could threaten shareholder value

- Timely responses through administrative investigations, temporary relief, and due process hearings
- The right to a jury trial if an administrative ruling is not received within 180 days
- Lessened burden of proof on the employee
- Compensatory damages and judicial fees
- Criminal felony penalties of up to ten years for retaliation
- Audit committees required to have procedures for responding to complaints

While acknowledging vast improvements, some critics still think that the act did not go far enough. Only employees of publicly held firms are covered, and so employees of privately held firms still have limited protection. In practice, the law still does not provide the level of protection originally intended due to a combination of aggressive defense lawyer tactics, poor judicial decisions over witness protection, and confusion among judges over SOX's intent.[86] People vary in their need to know they have protection before blowing the whistle. Figure 17-6 describes a study that looks at the differences between people who do the right thing in spite of great personal danger and others who choose to not act.

False Claims Act

A provocative piece of federal legislation that was passed to add an incentive for whistle-blowers in the public interest is the **False Claims Act (FCA)**. The act has *qui tam* (Latin shorthand for "he who sues for the king as well as himself") provisions that allow employees to blow the whistle about contractor fraud and share with the government in any financial recoveries realized by their efforts. It dates back to the Civil War, when the army wanted to find and prosecute profiteers who sold the same horse twice or sold boxes of sawdust while claiming they were guns. Citizens were permitted to sue on the

---

FIGURE 17-6
Giving Voice to Values

Developed at the Aspen Institute Business and Society Program and Yale School of Management, and housed at and supported by Babson College, *Giving Voice to Values* is an innovative curriculum development designed to help business students and practitioner to strengthen their abilities to voice their values when situations call them into conflict. The focus is not on determining what is the right thing to do, but rather on determining how to actually do it. Giving Voice to Values is designed to help students build a tool kit that will enable them to voice their values when ethical challenges arise.

Gentile cites a study of World War II rescuers that shows that moral courage can be strengthened through anticipating ethical challenges that might occur and formulating a response to them. In this study, researchers looked for commonalities among individuals who protected others from the Nazis even when they put their own lives at risk by doing so. They found that people who acted with moral courage when confronted with real danger tended to have earlier life experiences where they anticipated situations in which their values would be challenged and had a respected listener with whom they discussed how they would handle that situation. This act of practicing a response before being put in the difficult situation seemed to strengthen their subsequent ability to handle ethical challenges that occurred.

Sources: Mary C. Gentile, "Giving Voice to Values: Way of Thinking about Values in the Workplace," The Aspen Institute Center for Business Education (September 2008); Perry London, "The Rescuers: Motivational Hypotheses about Christians Who Saved Jews from the Nazis," in J. Macaulay and L. Berkowitz (eds.), *Altruism and Helping Behavior: Social Psychological Studies of Some Antecedents and Consequences* (New York: Academic Press, 1970); Douglas H. Huneke, *The Moses of Rovno* (New York: Dodd, Mead, 1985).

government's behalf and receive 50 percent of the recovery. In 1943, Congress reduced the potential payout dramatically, and so it was seldom used.[87] The act was revised in 1986 to make recoveries easier to obtain and payouts more generous, thereby encouraging whistle-blowing against government contractor fraud.[88] The 1986 act grew out of outrage in the mid-1980s over reports of fraud and abuse on the part of military contractors, such as $600 toilet seats and country club memberships billed to the government.[89]

What is particularly controversial about the FCA is the magnitude of the financial incentives that individual employees may earn as a result of their whistle-blowing efforts. The law allows individuals to be awarded as much as 15 to 25 percent of the proceeds in cases where the government joins in the action and from 25 to 30 percent of the proceeds in actions that the government does not join.[90] Even with these incentives, however, whistle-blowing is never easy, as the experiences of James Alderson illustrate.

James Alderson had been the chief financial officer of the North Valley Hospital for 17 years when Quorum, a former division of HCA, took over management of the hospital. Quorum created a second set of books and told Alderson to use these secret books to report higher-than-average expenses to the government for reimbursement. Knowing this would be both illegal and unethical, Alderson refused and five days later he was fired. After learning that other Quorum hospitals were cooking the books, too, Alderson went to Washington and talked to the U.S. Department of Justice. He took documentation with him of the false claims being filed and sued Quorum and HCA under the federal FCA.

HCA eventually paid a total of $840 million, consisting of $745 million in civil damages and $95 million in criminal penalties. They later paid another $881 million to settle all remaining fraud charges and other overpayment claims against the company. Thirteen years after Alderson was fired, the final settlement agreement between HCA and the U.S. Department of Justice was approved. The government received $1.5 billion from those payments, thanks to the efforts of Alderson and other whistle-blowers involved.[91]

There aren't many hospitals in Whitefish, Montana, so Alderson was forced to leave Whitefish to find work in hospital finance. For the next ten years, Alderson tried to earn a living while continuing to gather evidence. Federal officials had told him that he needed evidence that the practices at North Valley were widespread, and the collection of that evidence was his responsibility. Building that evidence consumed Alderson's time and money. In addition to the financial drain, Alderson had made many personal sacrifices, from missing his son's football games to not being at his mother's side when she died.[92] Alderson and his wife Connie kept a low profile. According to Connie, it was just like being in the witness protection program, "the only difference is that we weren't receiving any protection or money to keep us going."[93] Their low profile ended when the television show *60 Minutes* did a profile of Alderson. After the show aired, Alderson became a pariah in the health care industry. Says Alderson, "Even though I had a major impact in reducing health care fraud by $10 billion annually, I had one hospital CEO tell me to my face that I had ruined the industry and that I had given it a black eye."[94]

Under the FCA, Anderson received $20 million in one settlement and split $100 million with another whistle-blower in another. Alderson commented, "I won't deny that money provided an incentive, but it was only part of the motivation. What Quorum and HCA were doing was wrong, and it took me 13 years and my career to prove it. Fortunately, I received enough money from the settlement to retire."[95] However, Connie Alderson says, "Knowing what I know now and knowing how long it's been, I'm not sure I would have agreed to pursuing the case. I don't think any amount of money is going to take care of what we've been through."[96]

As of 2010, the FCA has returned over $20 billion to the federal government and the proceeds continue to grow.[97] The act continues to evolve as legislation and the courts test it. In 2003, the Supreme Court ruled unanimously that municipalities are "persons" under the FCA and can be held liable for damages and penalties from submitting a false claim to the federal government. States are considered co-sovereign, and so the court found that they are not liable under the FCA; however, municipalities are corporations, and so the court found that they should be treated like any other incorporated entity under the act.[98] Since that ruling, several states have passed their own FCA and more have plans to do so in the works.[99] In 2009, the Federal Enforcement and Recovery Act expanded the scope of the FCA by making more companies subject to FCA liability, increasing the penalty for not returning an overpayment and including nonemployees under whistle-blower protections.[100]

Management Responsiveness to Potential Whistle-Blowing Situations

Whistle-blowing situations occur after normal, less dramatic, channels of communication have failed. Ideally, employees should always feel free to open up to management about any concerns they have. Even in the best of organizations, however, people hesitate to speak up. Employee self-censorship is common.

In a recent study, workers in a leading high-technology organization were asked if they felt safe speaking up about problems in the firm. In spite of the fact that this organization had a variety of formal mechanisms as ombudsperson and grievance procedures, half the employees indicated that they did not feel safe speaking up.[101] Their overall concern was with self-preservation. They perceived a risk to speaking up that lead them to conclude, "When in doubt, keep your mouth shut."[102]

In rare instances, employees were afraid to speak out because they had experiences with managers who responded badly to past suggestions. More often, the reticent employees were simply responding to a vague perception of a threat in the work environment. Sometimes they were put off by organizational stories about people who had spoken up and then suddenly were no longer there. Typically, their silence stemmed from untested assumptions.[103]

The findings of this study have clear implications for encouraging free and open speech in the workplace. It isn't enough to remove barriers or put formal mechanisms in place. Significant change in the organizational culture must occur. The following are suggestions for how to accomplish that goal:[104]

1. Managers must be clear not to accept suggestions—they may invite them. Not all suggestions will be implemented, but it is important for managers to acknowledge each one.
2. Managers must actively and publicly refute commonly held assumptions and organizational myths that discourage communication. For example, they can counter the commonly held belief that employees should give managers suggestions in private by explaining that openly discussed ideas are likely to be useful.
3. Managers should tailor rewards so that employees share more directly in any cost savings or sales increase from ideas they offer. Tangible rewards can help employees to overcome intangible concerns.

In an ideal world, employees would automatically speak freely to managers if they saw something wrong happening or had an idea to improve operations. Unfortunately, this world is not ideal. Former Enron executive Lynn Brewer suggests that there may be "a little Enron in all of us." The problem at Enron was not "dirty secrets hidden well below the surface, but an open secret."[105] She estimates that about two-thirds of the employees at Enron were aware at some time of unethical behavior in the middle ranks, and believes if Enron employees had been asked if the company was ethical or not, 90 percent would have rated the company "highly unethical."[106] In the name of solving business problems, good people will often do bad things. It is incumbent upon managers to design organizations that enable and empower employees to come forward with information that will either stop wrongdoing or improve company operations long before whistle-blowing is needed.[107]

Summary

Employee stakeholders today are more sensitive about employee rights issues for a variety of reasons. Underlying this new concern are changes in the social contract between employers and employees that have been driven by global competition and a faltering economy. Central among the growing employee rights issues discussed in this chapter are (1) the right not to be fired without good cause, (2) the right to due process and fair treatment, and (3) the right to freedom of speech.

The basis for the argument that we may be moving toward an employee's right not to be fired is the erosion by the courts of the employment-at-will doctrine. More and more, the courts are making exceptions to this long-standing common-law principle. Three major exceptions are the public policy exception, the idea of an implied contract, and breach of good faith. Society's concept of what represents fair treatment to employees is constantly changing.

The right to due process is concerned primarily with fair treatment. Common approaches for management responding to this concern such as the open-door policy and traditional grievance procedures have been disappointing, and so newer methods such as the ombudsman approach and peer review are becoming more prevalent. Thanks to the passage of SOX, whistle-blowers in the private sector now enjoy some of the protections once accorded only to public sector employees; however, those protections have not materialized as quickly as some had hoped. Whistle-blowers still face a slew of obstacles as they seek to speak out on their concerns. Managers should be genuinely attentive to employees' rights in this realm if they wish to avert major scandals and prolonged litigation. A stakeholder approach that emphasizes ethical relationships with employees can create an organizational environment in which employees feel free to express their concerns openly, lessening the need to blow a whistle.

Key Terms

1978 Civil Service Reform Act, p. 603

alternative dispute resolution (ADR), p. 596

collective bargaining, p. 590

due process, p. 595

employee rights, p. 589

employment-at-will doctrine, p. 592

enterprise rights, p. 590

False Claims Act (FCA), p. 604

good cause norm, p. 592

good faith principle, p. 593

hearing procedure, p. 597

implied contract exception, p. 593

mandatory arbitration, p. 598

Michigan Whistle-Blowers Protection Act of 1981, p. 603

ombudsman, p. 597

open-door policy, p. 597

outplacement, p. 589

peer review panel, p. 597

private property, p. 589

public policy exception, p. 592

social contract, p. 587

statutory rights, p. 590

whistle-blower, p. 599

Discussion Questions

1. Rank the various changes that are occurring in the workplace in terms of their importance to the growth of the employee rights movement. Briefly explain your ranking.

2. Explain the employment-at-will doctrine, and describe how it is being eroded. Do you think its existence is leading to a healthy or an unhealthy

employment environment in the United States? Justify your reasoning.

3. In your own words, explain the right to due process. What are some of the major ways management is attempting to ensure due process in the workplace?

4. If you could choose only one, which form of alternative dispute resolution would be your choice as the most effective approach to employee due process? Explain.

5. How do you feel about whistle-blowing now that you have read about it? Are you now more sympathetic or less sympathetic to whistle-blowers? Explain.

6. What is your assessment of the value of the False Claims Act? What is your assessment of the value of the whistle-blower protections under the Sarbanes–Oxley Act?

18

Employee Stakeholders: Privacy, Safety, and Health

CHAPTER LEARNING OUTCOMES

After studying this chapter, you should be able to:

1. Articulate the concerns surrounding the employee's right to privacy in the workplace.

2. Identify the advantages and disadvantages of polygraphs, integrity tests, and drug testing as management instruments for decision making.

3. Discuss the right to safety and the right to know, and summarize the roles and responsibilities of OSHA.

4. Elaborate on the right to health and safety in the workplace, with particular reference to violence in the workplace, smoke-free workplaces, and family-friendly workplaces.

Besides the issues we discussed in the preceding chapter, there are several others that concern employee stakeholders. The latter are extensions of the concept of employee rights developed in Chapter 17. In this chapter, we will discuss employees' rights to privacy, safety, and a healthy work environment. As we discussed in Chapter 17, the global recession has shifted the balance of power from employees to employers. With jobs few and far between, employees may be more hesitant to ask that their rights be respected because they fear losing their jobs and not finding another. Margaret Vickers, editor-in-chief of *Employee Responsibilities and Rights Journal*, notes, "What might have been whined about by workers before their workplace morphed into the workplace-in-recession suddenly becomes acceptable to workers trying to keep their jobs."[1] In this environment, we need to be especially mindful of the rights of employees as they become increasingly vulnerable in the workplace.[2]

The right to privacy primarily addresses the psychological dimension, whereas the rights to health and safety primarily address the physical dimension. The status of an employee's right to privacy in the workplace today is ill-defined at best. Constitutional protection of privacy, such as the prohibition of unreasonable searches and seizures, applies only to the actions of government, not to those of private sector employers. From a legal standpoint, the meager amount of privacy protection that exists, as with so many employee rights, is a collection of diverse statutes that vary from issue to issue and from state to state. Hence, there is a genuine need for management groups to impose ethical thinking and standards in this increasingly important area.

Employee rights to safety and health are issues of growing intensity, too. In the United States alone, more than 5,000 employees die from traumatic injuries on the job each year, tens of thousands die from work-related diseases, and 4.6 million are seriously injured.[3] Today's workplace, whether in a manufacturing facility or in an office complex, can expose workers to a variety of hazards, risks of accidents, and occupational diseases. If normal workplace hazards were not enough, the phenomenon of violence in the workplace should cause management to pay serious attention to this threat to workplace peace and stability. Workplace violence incidents, coupled with threats from terrorism, have made safety in the workplace a major concern for employees today. Management should also be aware of the issues surrounding smoking in the workplace, as well as the need for family-friendly workplaces, with particular attention to what legal rights employees have under the Family and Medical Leave Act (FMLA).

To reiterate a point we made in the preceding chapter, the distinction between the issues discussed in that chapter and those discussed here is made for discussion purposes. With that in mind, let us continue our consideration of social and ethical issues that have become important to employee stakeholders in recent years. If managers are to be successful in dealing with employees' needs and treating them fairly as stakeholders, they must address these concerns now and in the future.

Right to Privacy in the Workplace

If your workplace were in a private space behind partitions and you knew there was no one in the outer office, would you hesitate to change into either gym clothes or more formal evening attire at the end of the day? Would you hesitate to remove some clothing to apply a prescription topical ointment when needed? If you believe you would do so, you must know about Gail Nelson, an administrative assistant who did exactly that, and then found out her employer had secretly videotaped her for months with no justification for doing so.[4]

Nelson's supervisor and coworkers knew she sometimes changed clothes in her office cubicle, an accepted practice. Her concern for privacy was such that she did so only when nobody was in the outer office, and she ensured this by listening carefully for the sound of approaching footsteps. The videotaping never revealed any illegal or unauthorized activity; nevertheless, her employer continued to do it. Furthermore, numerous employees at her workplace had viewed the videotapes. The incident came to light only when a coworker discovered it accidentally.[5] Even after appeal, the higher court upheld the legality of her employer's surveillance, saying that she did not have a reasonable expectation of privacy because other people were able to walk into the outer office.[6]

Technological developments have made surveillance simpler and less expensive—not only in public places but also in the workplace. What was once a big issue for large corporations now touches every work environment. With this growth in workplace monitoring come new ethical considerations. **Privacy in the workplace** is in flux as the implications of new technological options are considered. At this stage, the private employee has few privacy rights in (and sometimes out of) the workplace.

There are no clear legal definitions of what constitutes privacy or invasion of privacy, but everyone seems to have an opinion when one personally experiences such a situation. Most experts say that privacy means the right to keep personal affairs to oneself and to know how information about one is being used.[7] Business ethicist Patricia Werhane opts for a broader definition. She says that privacy includes (1) the right to be left alone, (2) the related right to autonomy, and (3) the claim of individuals and groups to determine for themselves when, how, and to what extent information about them is communicated to others.[8]

Defining privacy in this way, however, does not settle the issue. In today's world, achieving these ideals is extremely difficult and fraught with judgment calls about our own privacy rights versus other people's rights. This problem is exacerbated by our increasingly computerized, technological world. We gain great efficiencies from computers and new technologies, but we also pay a price. Part of that price is that information about us is stored in dozens of places, including federal agencies (the Internal Revenue Service and the Social Security Administration), state agencies (courts and motor vehicle departments), and many local departments and businesses (school systems, credit bureaus, banks, life insurance companies, and direct-mail companies).

In the realm of employee privacy, which is our central concern here, the following four important issues stand out as representative of the major workplace privacy issues:

1. Collection and use of employee information in personnel files
2. Integrity testing
3. Drug testing
4. Monitoring of employee work, behavior, conversations, and location by electronic means

Other issues also involve protection or invasion of privacy, but the four listed here account for the majority of today's concerns. Therefore, they merit separate consideration.

Collection and Use of Employee Information by Employers

The collection, use, and possible abuse of employee information is a serious public policy issue that warrants scrutiny. Today's government databases, with various agencies mixing and matching data, form a cohesive web of information on individual citizens. The **Privacy Act of 1974** set certain controls on the right of the government to collect, use, and share data about individuals. These restrictions were relaxed when the **USA Patriot Act** was signed into law in 2001 in response to the attack on the World Trade Center towers. Although many people express concern that the Patriot Act gives the government too much latitude, restrictions still remain on how the government can collect, use, and share personal data. In contrast, very few laws protect the privacy of individuals in the workplace as monitoring of employees in the workplace grows. Many privacy advocates say, "You check your privacy rights at the door when you enter the workplace."[9]

The necessity for guidelines regarding the collection of information became abundantly clear when the Equal Employment Opportunity Commission (EEOC) sued Burlington Northern Santa Fe Corporation for conducting secret genetic tests on workers who filed carpal tunnel syndrome claims. The tests came to light when one of the workers, Gary Avery, went to a mandatory medical exam as a follow-up to his successful carpal tunnel surgery. His wife, Janice, a registered nurse, became suspicious when he was asked to give seven vials of blood. She later was told that the blood was for tests to determine whether her husband had a genetic trait that made him susceptible to the syndrome.[10] Burlington Northern ended up paying $2.2 million to settle the charges.[11]

Background checks of both applicants and current employees have become a source of concern for privacy advocates. States vary in the latitude they allow employers when checking employee backgrounds, but most states, with the notable exception of California, give employers relatively free rein. The overriding principle that should guide corporate decision making with regard to the collection and use of employee information is that companies should collect only absolutely necessary information from employees and use it only in ways that are appropriate. Companies should be careful not to misuse this information by employing it for purposes for which it was not intended. Employers have a duty to treat their employee's private information with care, not releasing it to others nor allowing it to become public through careless management. Employers also have a responsibility to allow employees to correct any inaccurate information.

The requirements of the **Fair Credit Reporting Act (FCRA)** as it pertains to employers are detailed in Figure 18-1. The Federal Trade Commission (FTC) is responsible for

FIGURE 18-1
Consumer Reports Used for Employment

Employers in the United States may use consumer reports both to hire new employees and to evaluate current employees as long as they comply with the Fair Credit Reporting Act (FCRA), Sections 604, 606, and 615. Consumer reports are prepared by consumer reporting agencies (CRAs), and they contain private information about not only credit characteristics but also personal characteristics such as the applicant's or employee's character, reputation, and lifestyle. The reports may include credit payment records, driving records, criminal histories, and even interviews with neighbors, friends, or any associates. The FCRA covers only reports prepared by agencies. For example, if the employer checks references directly, the FCRA does not apply; however, verification by an employment or reference-checking agency is covered. The following are the key provisions as written by the Federal Trade Commission (FTC) to employers.

Key Provisions of the FCRA Amendments

Written Notice and Authorization. Before you can get a consumer report for employment purposes, you must notify the individual in writing—in a document consisting solely of this notice—that a report may be used. You also must get the person's written authorization before you ask a CRA for the report. (Special procedures apply to the trucking industry.)

Adverse Action Procedures. If you rely on a consumer report for an "adverse action"—denying a job application, reassigning or terminating an employee, or denying a promotion—be aware of the following:

Step 1: Before you take the adverse action, you must give the individual a pre-adverse action disclosure that includes a copy of the individual's consumer report and a copy of "A Summary of Your Rights Under the Fair Credit Reporting Act"—a document prescribed by the FTC. The CRA that furnishes the individual's report will give you the summary of consumer rights.

Step 2: After you've taken an adverse action, you must give the individual notice—orally, in writing, or electronically—that the action has been taken in an adverse action notice. It must include

- The name, address, and phone number of the CRA that supplied the report;
- A statement that the CRA that supplied the report did not make the decision to take the adverse action and cannot give specific reasons for it; and
- A notice of the individual's right to dispute the accuracy or completeness of any information the agency furnished, and his or her right to an additional free consumer report from the agency upon request within 60 days.

Certifications to Consumer Reporting Agencies. Before giving you an individual's consumer report, the CRA will require you to certify that you are in compliance with the FCRA and that you will not misuse any information in the report in violation of federal or state equal employment opportunity laws or regulations.

Source: Federal Trade Commission, "Using Consumer Reports: What Employers Need to Know," http://www.ftc.gov/bcp/edu/pubs/business/credit/bus08.shtm. Accessed May 2010.

monitoring employer use of consumer reports in the United States. Two significant loopholes exist in the protections that allow employers to bypass the FCRA. First, employers can opt to do the background checks themselves instead of using outside providers. If so, the restrictions do not apply.[12] Second, the restrictions do not apply if an adverse employment decision was made for reasons other than the contents of the background check and so employers can bypass the requirements by citing different reasons.[13] Another problem is that the FCRA does not cover the interview process and so an employer can obtain some information by simply asking. For example, a background check may not contain information on an arrest that happened more than seven years earlier. However, nothing prevents an employer from asking the employee, verbally or in writing, "Have you *ever* been arrested?"[14] In addition, if a background check is inaccurate, the employee affected can dispute its contents; however, an employer is not obligated to act upon a corrected report and reinstate a job offer.[15] The FCRA does not apply when salaries are $75,000 or more.[16]

The **Equal Employment Opportunity Commission (EEOC)** monitors employer use of background checks too, stepping in when discriminatory practices are thought to have occurred. The EEOC has ruled that the employer may not deny a person employment based on just the criminal record; instead it must factor in business necessity, the seriousness of the offense, and how long ago it occurred.[17] Two background check practices have caused the most problems for the EEOC and, by extension, the employers who are brought into court: (1) blanket no-hire policies based on criminal records or negative credit scores and (2) lack of a correlation between the information from the background check and the actual job for which the person would have been hired.[18]

Although there are still few guidelines for the collection of information in most professions, the health care industry has developed stronger guidelines for the way that collected information is handled in general, and those guidelines cover the use of medical information in employment. Medical information supplied to employers must be relevant to the job and requires the applicant's specific written consent.[19] An employer is permitted to require a pre-employment physical, but the Americans with Disabilities Act (ADA) requires that the physical be requested only *after* a job offer. We discuss the ADA later in Chapter 19. The act requires employers to protect the confidentiality of applicant and employee medical information, while also making it illegal to base employment decisions on a medical condition that does not affect the employee's ability to perform the essential functions of the job.

Background screening has become a big part of business. A Society for Human Resource Management (SHRM) survey showed that the use of background checks by personnel executives went from 51 percent to 96 percent of firms in just eight years, with two-thirds of those companies outsourcing their screening.[20] With background check usage showing no sign of abating, it is not surprising that employee screening has become a big and very profitable business.[21] Screening often goes beyond the checking of public records to include interviews with friends and associates, some of which may be disgruntled; the resulting information can contain errors or even outright lies.[22] According to industry veteran Lester Rosen, "Essentially, it's the Wild Wild West. It's an unregulated industry with easy money and not a huge emphasis on compliance or on hiring quality people to do the screening."[23] At this writing, the U.S. federal government is beginning to make moves toward shoring up the system. The EEOC is becoming increasingly active in prosecuting cases where a background check is believed to have been used in a way that had a discriminatory impact, and a bill pending in Congress would ban the use of credit reports for hiring purposes except in specific industries.[24]

Integrity Tests

Early efforts to judge a person's integrity focused on uncovering a lack of integrity, such as might be evidenced when a person lies. The notion of a "lie detector," historians tell us, is nothing new. The Bedouins of Arabia knew that certain physiological changes, triggered by guilt and fear, occurred when a person lied. The outstanding change they observed was that a liar would stop salivating. They developed a simple test in which a heated blade was passed across the tongue of a suspected liar. If innocent, the suspect would be salivating normally and the tongue would not be burned; if the person was lying, the tongue would be scorched. The ancient Chinese used dry rice powder. Someone suspected of lying was forced to keep a handful of rice powder in the mouth. If the powder was soggy when spat out, the person was telling the truth; if it was dry, the person was lying.[25]

In the invasion-of-privacy arena, few topics have generated as much controversy as the use of the **polygraph**, or lie detector, in business. The polygraph machine was developed by John Larson in 1929, although others trace it to an earlier date. It measures changes in blood pressure, respiration, and perspiration, sometimes called *galvanic skin response*. The theory behind polygraphy is that the act of lying causes stress, which in turn is manifested by observable physiological changes. The examiner, or machine operator, then interprets the subject's physiological responses to specific questions and makes inferences about whether or not the subject's answers indicate deception.[26] The **Employee Polygraph Protection Act (EPPA)** of 1988 banned most uses in the private sector of the lie detector, but it can still be used by private employers that provide security services, protection of nuclear facilities, shipment or storage of radioactive or toxic waste, public water supply facilities, public transportation, precious commodities, or propriety information. Also, employers that manufacture, distribute, or dispense controlled substances may use polygraph tests for some of their positions. Government employers are also exempt from the prohibitions on polygraph testing. The federal government may also use polygraph tests for private consultants or experts under contract to various government departments, agencies, or bureaus.[27] It is noteworthy that Aldrich Ames wrote from the prison that he passed the polygraph test with flying colors while selling U.S. secrets to Russia.[28]

The issue of lie detection is unlikely to diminish as new technologies are created. Research is progressing on the use of magnetic resonance imaging (MRI) brain scans to separate truth from fiction.[29] Other scientists are exploring the use of voice pattern technology to develop a machine to do what a polygraph once did.[30] Still others are putting their efforts into lie detector glasses that can assess truthfulness, as well as anxiety and love.[31] When these or other new technologies for lie detection develop, new protections for employees will be needed to address them. However, the ability to detect lies through technology still remains an elusive goal.[32]

As criticism grew concerning the use of lie detectors, many companies anticipated an eventual elimination of lie detector use and began experimenting with **integrity tests** (also known as *honesty tests*). Integrity tests are subjected to the same kinds of criticisms that led to severe restriction of lie detector testing. However, faced with the elimination of the polygraph, companies wanted to find a substitute, and integrity tests seemed to be a convenient alternative. Critics of integrity tests claim they are intrusive and invade privacy by the nature of their inquiries. Some critics also say that they are unreliable and that employers use them as the sole measure of the fitness of an applicant. Even when these tests are properly administered, opponents charge that employers end up rejecting many honest applicants in their efforts to screen out the dishonest ones.

Management and testing companies claim the tests are very useful in weeding out potentially dishonest applicants. They claim that each question asked has a specific purpose. They also argue that hiring by "gut feeling" is problematic, and integrity tests provide a more objective assessment.[33] There is evidence that integrity tests can have an impact. A major U.S. retailer used integrity tests in 600 of their 1,900 locations to reduce turnover and shrinkage. After one year, they saw inventory shrinkage fall by more than 35 percent in the stores that used the test, while it rose by 10 percent in the stores that did not. Even though turnover was not a goal of the test administration, they noted a 13 percent decrease in turnover at stores that did use the test and a 14 percent increase in turnover at stores that did not.[34] A large hotel chain found that integrity testing reduced worker's compensation claims significantly, more than compensating for the costs of test administration.[35]

Integrity tests are subject to the same kinds of legal and ethical hurdles that affect polygraph and drug tests. The Civil Rights Act (discussed in Chapter 19) makes it unlawful for any test to have a particularly negative impact on a protected subgroup. One integrity test, the Reid Report, has had 23 legal challenges. Administrators at Reid London House report that the EEOC or relevant state human rights agency found for each case that there was no probable cause to believe the test had disparate impact.[36] From the ADA perspective, medical examinations can be given only after a conditional offer of employment has been made. The EEOC has ruled that integrity tests are not medical examinations, and so they can be given to applicants: psychological examinations are considered medical only if they provide evidence of a mental disorder.[37] Most states apply the federal laws to selection tools. However, Massachusetts and Rhode Island have extended the polygraph statutes to integrity tests. In Massachusetts, integrity tests are against the law, while in Rhode Island they cannot be used as the primary basis for an employment decision.[38]

Although legal issues surrounding integrity tests will be resolved on a case-by-case basis, ethical issues are likely to remain. A test that will identify many of those who would behave unethically at a cost to the firm will also yield "false positives," people labeled as unethical who would have been good employees. In statistics, this is called a **type 1 error**, finding an innocent person to be guilty. In contrast, a **type 2 error** finds a guilty person to be innocent. The nature of testing is such that a decrease in one type of error leads to an increase in the other. In other words, the more strictly a test is used to rule out any person who would be guilty of unethical behavior, the more is the chance that innocent people will be judged unethical. It is important, therefore, that integrity tests be used judiciously and that they not be the primary criterion on which employment is based.

ETHICS IN PRACTICE CASE

Give Me What I Want or I'll Tell the President!

Place yourself in the role of a personnel director for a bank. It is company policy that neither personnel files nor copies of files are to leave the personnel office. The director of accounting and computer services is due to give his employees their yearly employee evaluations and has sent a memo to your secretary requesting copies of his employees' evaluations from the previous year. Your secretary shows you the memo. You are upset that the director would send such a memo to your secretary, because he should be aware of the policy concerning employee files.

So you decide to call the director and tell him that he is welcome to read the evaluations of his employees from the previous year in the personnel office. He tells you that he does not have the time to come to personnel and read the files and that he will speak to the president of the bank about this issue. The working relationship between you and the director has been addressed by the president before, and she has told the two of you that you need to be able to work out problems such as this between yourselves.

The dilemma is whether you should go against company policy in an effort to avoid another lecture from the president, and let the director take the copies of the evaluations to his office, or adhere to the bank's policy on protection of employee privacy.

1. What are the main ethical dilemmas in this situation?

2. Should you report the director's threat to step over you to the president?

3. What would you do in this situation?

Contributed by Leah Herrin

Drug Testing

Drug testing is an umbrella term intended to embrace drug and alcohol testing and employer testing for any suspected substance abuse. The issue of drug testing in the workplace has many of the same characteristics as the lie detector and integrity test issues. Companies say they need to do such testing to protect themselves and the public, but opponents claim that drug tests are not accurate and invade the employee's privacy. Concerns about drug testing center around the implications for employee privacy, the inaccuracy of tests, and the impact of drug testing on employee morale.

Quest Diagnostics, a major provider of employment-related drug-testing services, releases an annual index that shows a continued decline in positive drug tests. The most recent test, in 2009, shows an all-time low of 3.5 percent in urine tests. This represents less than one-third the 13.6 percent level of positivity recorded in 1988, the first year of measurement.[39] Hair drug tests are growing in use because hair has a longer memory than urine and is more difficult to deceive. A hair test may miss a single incident of drug use but will reflect repeated use for a period of up to 90 days. Hair tests cover fewer drugs and focus on illicit drugs.[40] Hair tests are showing a higher rate of positivity, which is consistent with Quest's experience when using them in the workplace.[41]

Arguments for Drug Testing.   Proponents of drug testing argue that the costs of drug abuse on the job are staggering. The consequences range from accidents and injuries to theft, bad decisions, and ruined lives. The greatest concern is in industries where mistakes can cost lives—for example, the railroad, airline, aerospace, nuclear power, and hazardous equipment and chemicals industries. Thus, the primary ethical argument for employers conducting drug tests is the responsibility they have to their own employees and to the general public to provide safe workplaces, secure asset protection, and safe places in which to transact business.

Arguments against Drug Testing.   Opponents of drug testing see it as both a due-process issue and an invasion-of-privacy issue. The due-process issue relates to the sometimes-questionable accuracy of drug tests. Common foods and medications can lead to a false positive, giving the appearance of drug use when the person being tested is innocent. This can create a downward spiral for that employee, causing reputational damage, lost income, and considerable expense to try to rebut the allegation of drug use.[42]

Many legitimate questions arise in the drug-testing issue. Do employers have a right to know if their employees use drugs? Are employees performing on the job satisfactorily? Obviously, some delicate balance is needed, because employers and employees alike have legitimate interests that must be protected. If companies are going to engage in some form of drug testing, they should think carefully about developing policies that not only will achieve their intended goals but also will be fair to the employees and will minimize invasions of privacy. Such a balance will not be easy to achieve but must be sought. To do otherwise will guarantee decreased employee morale, more and more lawsuits, and new government regulations.

Guidelines for Drug Testing.   If management perceives the need to conduct a drug-testing program to protect other stakeholders, it should carefully design and structure the program so that it will be minimally intrusive of employees' privacy rights. The following guidelines, reflecting the ethical aspects of drug testing, have been developed by the American College of Occupational and Environmental Medicine (ACOEM):[43]

1. Companies should have written policies and procedures, which should be applied impartially.

2. Companies should provide clear documentation of the reason for conducting drug testing (e.g., employee safety, public safety, security, etc.).

3. Any employees or applicants that will be affected should be informed in advance of the company's drug use, misuse, and testing policies, as well as their right to refuse to be tested and the consequences of refusal.

4. If testing is conducted on an unannounced and random basis, employees should be made aware of the special safety or security needs that justify this procedure.

5. All tests should be done in a uniform and impartial manner.

6. A licensed physician (MD/DO) should supervise the collection, transportation, and analysis of the specimens, as well as the reporting of results. Stringent legal, technical, and ethical requirements should be observed when reporting results.

7. A licensed and appropriately qualified physician should be designated as the medical review officer (MRO) and should evaluate positive results before a report is made to the employer.

8. An employee or applicant who tests positive should be informed of the positive results by the physician and should have the opportunity to explain and discuss the results before the employer is notified. The procedure for this should be clearly outlined.

9. Any report to the employer should provide only the information needed for work placement purposes or as required by government regulations. The employer should not be told of the specific types or levels of drug found unless required by law. A trained and qualified physician should make that report.

Guidelines shift over time, and so exceptions to these might be considered and/or new guidelines may develop. The major point is that management needs to think through its policies and their consequences very carefully when designing and conducting drug-testing programs.

State and Federal Legislation. Some states and cities have enacted laws or are considering doing so to restrict workplace drug testing. Generally, these laws restrict the scope of testing by private and public employers and establish privacy protections and procedural safeguards. Some states do not completely ban drug testing but restrict the circumstances (e.g., for reasonable cause) under which it may be used. They may also restrict drug testing to reasonable suspicion and place limits on the disciplinary actions employers may take. Other states provide discounts on worker's compensation and/or incentives of another kind to organizations that implement drug testing. This patchwork of incongruous state laws complicates drug testing for employers. The U.S. Department of Labor maintains a Web page that identifies drug-free workplace laws and policies by state.[44]

At the federal level, the **Americans with Disabilities Act (ADA)** must be considered, because the definition of disability applies to drug and alcohol addiction. The ADA prohibits companies from giving applicants medical exams before they extend those applicants' conditional offers of employment. Prehire drug tests, however, are permitted. Philadelphia employment lawyer Jonathan Segal advises employers to extend conditional offers before drug testing, because an innocent question on a drug test could easily become a medical question. He recommends conducting the drug test immediately after making the conditional offer and then waiting before beginning employment until the test results are back.[45] Employers would also be well advised to use physicians who are trained to review drug test results to evaluate claims of false positive readings.[46]

Several federal agencies have specific regulations for drug testing in organizations. The Department of Transportation's (DoT) drug and alcohol requirements are perhaps the most widely known, but other agencies, such as the Department of Defense (DoD), Department of Energy (DoE), Nuclear Regulatory Commission (NRC), and the National Aeronautics and Space Administration (NASA), also have employee drug-testing requirements.[47]

Employee Assistance Programs.   One of the most significant strategies undertaken by corporate America to deal with the growing alcohol- and drug-abuse problem in the workplace has been **Employee Assistance Programs (EAPs)**. EAPs extend into a variety of employee problem areas such as compulsive gambling, financial stress, emotional stress, marital difficulties, aging, legal problems, AIDS, and other psychological, emotional, and social difficulties. The term **broad brush EAP** describes this comprehensive model.[48] A recent major concern of EAPs has been to integrate them into the company's general health management strategy so that it can become a core strategic component.[49]

EAPs represent a positive and proactive step companies can take to deal with these serious problems. EAPs are designed to be confidential and nonpunitive, and they affirm three important propositions: (1) employees are valuable members of the organization, (2) it is better to help troubled employees than to discipline or discharge them, and (3) recovered employees are better employees. It is encouraging that in an era when employees are increasingly exerting their workplace rights, enlightened companies are offering EAPs in an effort to help solve their mutual problems. More information on EAPs can be found at the Employee Assistance Professionals Association Web site, http://www.eap-association.org.[50]

Monitoring Employees on the Job

In the old days, supervisors monitored employees' work activities by peeking over their shoulders and judging how things were going. Technology changed all that as cameras and listening devices gave way to computers and satellites as options for employee monitoring. Privacy advocates are concerned about the use of technology to gather information about workers on the job and with good reason. In its most recent survey, the American Management Association (AMA) found that the vast majority of mid- to large-sized firms participate in some type of **employee monitoring**. In some cases, the method is passive, such as installing video cameras in a lobby. However, most companies use more active means of monitoring their workers, such as recording their phone calls or voice mail, reading their computer files, monitoring e-mail or Web access, and videotaping them. Employer monitoring of employees has become the norm in businesses today. The consequence is that millions of workers are laboring under the relentless gaze of electronic supervision.

What Can Be Monitored?   According to the most recent AMA survey, 66 percent of employers monitor their employees' Web site visits in order to prevent inappropriate surfing and 65 percent block Web site connections they consider to be off-limits. The Web sites of concern to employers include adult sites, games, social networking, entertainment, shopping and auctions, sports, and external blogs. E-mail is monitored by 43 percent of companies, and 73 percent of those use technology, while 40 percent have an individual assigned to monitor and read the e-mail.[51]

As was discussed in Chapter 9, the introduction of new technologies creates new opportunities for surveillance by employers. For example, the advent of global positioning system (GPS) technology has made it possible to monitor worker location. Of course, the advent of technology works both ways. Camera phones can possibly serve as a tool that employees can use to monitor their employers. Some companies have moved to ban them from the workplace due to fear of corporate espionage.[52]

Along with many Third World countries, the United States offers few protections for the privacy of employees in the workplace. The only federal level of privacy protection in the United States is the **Electronic Communication Privacy Act (ECPA) of 1986**. The interception or unauthorized access of a wire, oral, or electronic communication is illegal under this act unless it is covered by one of the statutory exceptions or required by government compulsion. One of the statutory exceptions is the business use exception: the act does not apply if the interception or access occurs as part of the "ordinary course of business." It also does not apply if the person gives consent. An employee working for a company that has disclosed that it will monitor its employees is considered to have given implicit consent. With these broad exceptions, it is not surprising that the ECPA has been ineffective in regulating the monitoring of employees in the workplace.[53] The one clear protection is that employers may not listen to purely personal phone conversations; however, they can monitor a conversation for the time required to determine that the call is personal.[54] States have tried to enact laws to strengthen workplace privacy but with limited success, resulting in a patchwork of state laws.[55]

Efforts to enact a U.S. law specifically geared toward workplace privacy have always been stymied. Fifteen years ago, former Senator Paul Simon (D-IL) introduced the Privacy for Consumers and Workers Act. The measure would have established use limitations as well as a standard for notice and access to information. However, the bill never left its committee.[56] Former Representative Charles Canady (R-FL) and Senator Charles Schumer (D-NY) introduced the Notice of Electronic Monitoring Act (NEMA) in 2000. Efforts were under way to reach a bipartisan bill, but they came to a halt after the September 11 attack.[57] As of this writing, little more has happened on the legislative front. However, recent court cases may have implications for workplace privacy in the future. In 2010, the New Jersey Supreme Court ruled in favor of an employee whose company read e-mails that she sent to her attorney using Yahoo e-mail on the company's computer.[58] In addition, the U.S. Supreme Court heard arguments regarding whether messages sent from an employee's pager through a private communications company can be reviewed by a government employer; a decision is pending at this writing.[59]

Effects of Being Monitored. Invasion of privacy is one major consequence of employee monitoring. Another is unfair treatment. Employees working under such systems complain about stress and tension resulting from their being expected and pressured to be more productive now that their efforts can be measured. The pressure of being constantly monitored is also producing low morale and a sense of job insecurity in many places. Employees have good reason to be concerned. The most recent AMA survey found that not only do the vast majority of major U.S. companies engage in employee monitoring, but they are also now using their findings to make employment decisions: 30 percent have fired employees for misusing the Internet, and 28 percent have terminated employees for misusing e-mail.[60]

Policy Guidelines on the Issue of Privacy

During our discussion of various privacy issues, we have indicated steps that management might consider taking in an attempt to be responsive to employee stakeholders. Frederick S. Lane III, a law and technology expert and author of *The Naked Employee: How Technology Is Compromising Workplace Privacy*, offers an "Employee Privacy Bill of Rights" that sets forth guidelines for developing privacy policies and procedures that uphold the dignity of the employee.[61] To preserve employee rights, firms should

1. Obtain informed consent from employees and applicants before acquiring information about them

2. Disclose the nature of any surveillance that will occur
3. Set controls so as to avoid casual and unauthorized spread of information
4. Limit the collection and use of medical and health data to that which is relevant to the job
5. Require reasonable suspicion before doing drug tests
6. Respect and preserve the boundary between work and home

Business's concern for protection of the privacy of its employees, customers, and other stakeholders is growing. It is not surprising, therefore, that a new form of corporate executive came on the horizon. As we discussed in Chapter 9, **chief privacy officers (CPOs)** are high-ranking executives responsible for monitoring and protecting the private information held by firms. They differ from security personnel in that they determine what data should be protected while the security department determines how it will be protected. The CPO is responsible for ensuring that the privacy of individuals is respected.[62]

Workplace Safety

Workers Memorial Day was observed in the United States on April 28, 2010. That date was the 40th anniversary of both the Occupational Safety and Health Administration and the Federal Coal Mine Health and Safety Act. Sadly, it also followed the deaths of 29 coal mine workers in West Virginia, 7 refinery workers in Washington State, 4 power plant workers in Connecticut, and 11 oil platform workers off the coast of Louisiana. In his presidential proclamation, President Obama declared the day not only to be a remembrance of workers who were killed or injured but also an opportunity to renew commitment to worker safety.[63] That commitment is sorely needed because in the United States alone, more than 14 workers lose their lives every day in preventable workplace tragedies.[64]

The main law that protects the safety and health of workers in the United States is the Occupational Safety and Health Act. This act requires the Secretary of Labor to set safety and health standards that protect employees and their families. Every private employer who engages in interstate commerce is subject to the regulations promulgated under this act.[65] The federal agency responsible for overseeing the safety and health of America's workers is the **Occupational Safety and Health Administration (OSHA)**. Figure 18-2 depicts OSHA's mission.[66]

We will begin by examining the workplace safety problem and the right-to-know laws that have evolved from it. We'll then study OSHA's rocky history and its current situation. We'll lastly look at the issue of workplace violence, which is a serious concern in today's workplace. We'll then turn to the issue of smoking in the workplace and then end with a discussion of the family-friendly workplace.

The Workplace Safety Problem

Two events stand out as forerunners of the workplace safety problem. The first ranks among the landmark cases on job safety. In Elk Grove Village, Illinois, Film Recovery Systems operated out of a single plant that extracted silver from used hospital x-ray and photographic film. To extract the silver, the employees first had to dump the film into open vats of sodium cyanide and then transfer the leached remnants to another tank. Employee Stefan Golab staggered outside and collapsed, unconscious. Efforts to revive him failed, and he was soon pronounced dead from what the local medical examiner labeled "acute cyanide toxicity."[67]

FIGURE 18-2
OSHA's Mission

OSHA's Mission

OSHA's mission is to assure the safety and health of America's workers by setting and enforcing standards; providing training, outreach, and education; establishing partnerships; and encouraging continual improvement in workplace safety and health.

Our Services

OSHA and its state partners have approximately 2,100 inspectors, plus complaint discrimination investigators, engineers, physicians, educators, standards writers, and other technical and support personnel spread over more than 200 offices throughout the country. This staff establishes protective standards, enforces those standards, and reaches out to employers and employees through technical assistance and consultation programs.

The Public We Serve

Nearly every working man and woman in the nation comes under OSHA's jurisdiction (with some exceptions such as miners, transportation workers, many public employees, and the self-employed). Other users and recipients of OSHA services include occupational safety and health professionals, the academic community, lawyers, journalists, and personnel of other government entities.

Service Improvement Plan

OSHA is determined to use its limited resources effectively to stimulate management commitment and employee participation in comprehensive workplace safety and health programs.

Surveying Our Public

At OSHA, we are dedicated to improving the quality of our efforts and know that to be successful we must become an agency that is driven by commitment to public service. The first step is for OSHA to listen and respond to its customers. Accordingly, we conducted a survey to learn more about what employers and employees think of OSHA's services.

Because workplace inspections are one of OSHA's principal activities and because voluntary efforts to improve working conditions ultimately depend on strong enforcement, our survey focused primarily on the inspection process. We asked a random sample of employees and employers who had recently experienced an OSHA inspection what they thought of the inspection in particular, and of OSHA's standards and educational and other assistance activities in general.

Service Standards

We based OSHA's new standards for public service on what we learned from the survey, from meetings with employee and employer groups, and from focus group discussions with workers from many plants and industries across the country.

Our public service improvement program will be an ongoing one. We will continue to gather information on the quality of our performance in delivering services in areas not included in this year's survey, particularly in the construction sector. Next year, too, we plan to learn more about public response to our assistance and consultation programs.

Source: http://www.osha.gov/oshinfo/mission.html. Accessed July 2010.

An intensive investigation by attorneys in Cook County, Illinois, revealed a long list of incriminating details: (1) Film Recovery workers seldom wore even the most rudimentary safety equipment, (2) workers were laboring in what amounted to an industrial gas chamber, and (3) company executives played down the dangers of cyanide poisoning and removed labeling that identified it as poisonous. The prosecutors took action under an

Spotlight *on* SUSTAINABILITY

It's All Connected

Workplace safety is not always mentioned in discussions of business sustainability, but that is beginning to change. Sustainability initiatives encompass environmental, social, and economic considerations—and safety hinges on all three. The lean and green movement combines eliminating waste with respecting people and the environment. As Michael Taubitz writes, "This brings employee safety into the equation because you cannot be lean without being safe" (p. 42). A recent study of ergonomics discovered that the muscle pain and stress experienced by workers in one department of the company stemmed from root causes in another department. Furthermore, factors that were the source of the muscle pain had also affected employees in still other departments. Sustainability's focus on system-wide thinking lends itself to seeing the connections in complex systems and recognizing the resulting interactions and their consequences.

Sources: Ash M. Genaidy, Reynold Sequeira, Magda M. Rinder, and Amal D. A-Rehim, "Determinants of Business Sustainability: An Ergonomics Perspective," *Ergonomics* (March 2009), 273–301; Michael A. Taubitz, "Lean, Green, and Safe," *Professional Safety* (May 2010), 39.

Illinois homicide statute that targets anyone who knowingly commits acts that "create a strong probability of death or serious bodily harm." Three executives at Film Recovery Systems—the president, the plant manager, and the foreman—were convicted of the murder of Stefan Golab and were sentenced to 25 years in prison. This marked the first ever conviction of managers for homicide in a corporate matter such as an industrial accident.[68] The Film Recovery Systems case marked a new era in managerial responsibility for job safety. A variety of other prosecutions of managers have followed this case. What this clearly signals is not only that employees have a moral right to a safe working environment but also that managers face prosecution if they do not ensure that employees are protected.

The second event, which we also discussed in Chapter 10, was the dramatic and catastrophic poisonous gas leak at the Union Carbide plant in Bhopal, India. The death toll topped 2,000, and tens of thousands more were injured. People around the globe were startled and shocked at what the results of one major industrial accident could be. Lawsuits sought damages that quickly exceeded the net worth of the company.[69] Seven years after the leak, India's Supreme Court upheld a $470 million settlement that Union Carbide had already paid, and it lifted the immunity from criminal prosecution that it had granted the company two years after the leak occurred. The name "Union Carbide" became inextricably linked with the Bhopal Disaster. In 2001, Union Carbide became a wholly owned subsidiary of Dow Chemical.[70] Twenty-five years after the tragedy, a district court in Bhopal found seven former Union Carbide India Ltd. officials guilty of "causing death by negligence." They were sentenced to two years in prison and fined 100,000 rupees ($2,130).

Of course, not all hazards can be anticipated. The 2001 attack on the World Trade Center was a shock and surprise to the world. Shortly after the tragedy occurred, many were wondering what the impact would be on Morgan Stanley, one of the world's biggest brokerages and investment firms. The company was the largest tenant in the World Trade Center, with about 3,700 employees in the two towers. Amazingly, fewer than ten of their employees were among the missing, and only about 50 reported being injured. Company officials credit the evacuation procedures that Morgan Stanley developed after the 1993 bombing of the World Trade Center with saving so many of their employees' lives. The security staff used megaphones to keep people moving despite announcements over the building's public address system that instructed people to return to work. They moved their employees down the smoke-filled stairs (some more than 70 flights) and away from the twin towers. The earlier incident in 1993 had alerted them to their vulnerability, and they took the necessary steps to protect the health and safety of as many of their employees as possible.[71] In a world where the unexpected is to be expected, this is the type of preparedness all workplaces should emulate.

Right-to-Know Laws

Prompted by the Union Carbide tragedy in Bhopal and other, less dramatic industrial accidents, workers have demanded to know more about the thousands of chemicals and hazardous substances they are being exposed to daily in the workplace. Experts argue that employers have a duty to provide employees with information on the hazards of workplace chemicals and to make sure that workers understand what the information means in practical terms. Since the early 1980s, many states have passed **right-to-know laws** and expanded public access to this kind of information by employees and even communities. Although the states took the initiative on the right-to-know front, OSHA followed suit by creating a Hazard Communication Standard that preempted state regulations. This standard requires covered employers to identify hazardous chemicals in their workplaces and to provide employees with specified forms of information on such substances and their hazards. Specifically, manufacturers, whether they are chemical manufacturers or users of chemicals, must take certain steps to achieve compliance with the standard.[72] These steps include the following:

1. Update inventories of hazardous chemicals present in the workplace.
2. Assemble material safety data sheets (MSDSs) for all hazardous chemicals.
3. Ensure that all containers and hazardous chemicals are properly labeled.
4. Provide workers with training on the use of hazardous chemicals.
5. Prepare and maintain a written description of the company's hazard communication program.
6. Consider any problems with trade secrets that may be raised by the standard's disclosure requirements.
7. Review state requirements for hazard disclosure.

In addition to the right-to-know laws, employees have certain workplace rights with respect to safety and health on the job that OSHA provides by law. As in our discussion of the public policy exceptions to the employment-at-will doctrine in the preceding chapter, it should be clear that workers have a right to seek safety and health on the job without fear of punishment or recrimination.

The History of OSHA

From its beginning over 40 years ago, OSHA was troubled by the sheer size of its task, monitoring workplace safety and health in millions of workplaces, and the limited resources with which it was to accomplish it.

Nitpicking Rules.   In its early years, OSHA added to its troubles by promulgating rules and standards that seemed quite trivial when compared with the larger issues of health and safety. In one example, a telephone company was instructed that it could provide linemen only with "belts that have pocket tabs that extend at least 1½ inches down and 3 inches back of the inside of the circle of each D-ring for riveting on plier or tool

ETHICS IN PRACTICE CASE

How Ethical Values Vary

During my Christmas break, I was employed at ABC Company, a caulk manufactory located in a small town. Jim Wilson, who had little or no education, was employed in the shipping department at ABC. He was also trained as a blender in case someone in the Blending Department quit, went on vacation, or was fired. Luis Alberto, who was about 58 years old, was also employed at ABC Company, as a packer. Basically, a packer operates a machine that fills the cartridges with caulk, seals the tubes, and finally places either 12 or 24 ten-ounce cartridges in a box. Luis's education did not range beyond an eighth-grade level. Luis's daughter-in-law was also employed at ABC, as a chemist in the lab. She spoke up when Luis's employment situation was on the line. She even told management when it was time to consider giving Luis an increase in his earnings.

Prior to the Christmas holiday break, the hired blender quit. Knowing how hard the position was to fill, Jim was told it was a permanent position. Jim was told by his supervisor, "Jim, you can't get another job anywhere in town because you don't have a high school diploma and you can't read, so you are up the creek if you don't take this position." Nothing was mentioned to Luis about the position. Luis's daughter-in-law made sure that the supervisor kept the opening notice out of Luis's sight. Knowing the dangers of that particular job, she thought it was in his best interest not to be made aware of it. It seems as if Jim Wilson had to do all the dirty work in the plant without being able to say anything.

1. How is ethics involved in this situation at the ABC Company?

2. If ethics is involved, what procedures should be implemented?

3. What are Jim's alternatives? What should he do? Why?

4. If you observed this situation with respect to employees as stakeholders, what would you do? Why?

Contributed by Mystro Whatley

---

pockets.... There may be no more than four tool loops on any belt."[73] Such nuisance rules and standards created serious credibility problems for OSHA. Although nearly a thousand such rules were rescinded in OSHA's first decade, many times that number remained on the books.

Spotty Record.   Over the years, OSHA's record has been spotty. In the mid-1980s, injuries, illnesses, and deaths in the workplace began to climb again after several years of decline.[74] There were numerous reasons for this reversal, and not all of them could be attributed to OSHA. During the recession of the early 1980s, companies sharply reduced their spending on health and safety. With the economic recovery, many employers hired inexperienced workers, which further contributed to rising accident statistics. Further, the Reagan administration deemphasized the writing and enforcement of safety rules, and employers put greater emphasis on competitiveness, often at the expense of safety and health.[75]

A Rejuvenated OSHA.   Like so many of the federal agencies we have discussed (FTC, FDA, and CPSC), OSHA experienced a new boost of energy and enthusiasm in the post-Reagan period of the late 1980s and early 1990s. The renewed energy came at an appropriate time, because injury rates had been increasing (though part of this reported increase might have resulted from more accurate reporting). With a new administrator and an increased budget, OSHA began taking significant actions against high-visibility employers. However, OSHA continued to suffer from the budget and staff that were inadequate for the job that Congress and the public expected it to do.[76] One thing was clear: there were simply not enough inspectors to handle all businesses, and therefore a heavy responsibility fell on business for safety in the workplace. In the mid-1990s, OSHA turned to negotiated rule-making to develop standards for industry. Efforts at conciliation continued as Charles Jeffress, a former OSHA administrator who was known as an effective conciliator, took over the agency.

Questions about OSHA continued. An exposé by David Barstow of *The New York Times* painted a bleak picture. Barstow found that in a four-year period, OSHA investigated 1,242 incidents of employee death and determined the deaths occurred because the employer had "willful safety violations."[77] In 93 percent of these cases, OSHA declined to seek prosecution. Even the more than 70 of those employers who were repeat violators were rarely prosecuted. This reluctance to prosecute persisted even when the victims were teenagers, the violation caused multiple deaths, and administrative judges determined there was "willful wrongdoing."[78]

The Future of OSHA.   Early indications are that the Obama administration will adopt a tougher stance with OSHA. Following a review of 12 workplace deaths on the Las Vegas strip, and Nevada's response to these and other incidents, federal OSHA decided to conduct extensive reviews of the other state operations.[79] In 2010, OSHA created a severe violator enforcement program designed to target employers with records of continual noncompliance with more frequent inspections and higher fines.[80] Amidst global recession and with limited staffing, this tougher stance will be even more difficult to maintain. At this writing, it is too early to know if the effort will succeed.

Workplace Violence

Another issue that has become a major problem and is posing challenges to management is escalating violence in the workplace. **Workplace violence** is one of the four leading causes of death in the workplace and the leading cause of death for women.[81] It falls into two categories: (1) violence from an outside source and (2) violence stemming from coworkers. Workplace violence from coworkers cuts across all industries, while certain industries have a greater likelihood of workplace violence from the general public.[82]

In spite of the seriousness of the problem, companies are making few efforts to address it. About 5 percent of the U.S. private industry businesses that filled out a recent survey on workplace violence prevention had an incident of workplace violence within the previous 12 months. Although many of these employers reported that the incident had a negative impact on their workforce, the great majority did not change their workplace violence prevention procedures following the incident. Of even greater concern is the fact that 9 percent had no program or policy addressing workplace violence.[83]

The problem of workplace violence shows no sign of abating. Experts note that a variety of factors promote continued violence including an overall greater tolerance for violence, easily available weapons, economic stress, a difficult job market, and insufficient support systems.[84] In the United States, gun law battles are complicating an already difficult situation. Businesses have historically been able to keep guns out of the workplace with a posted sign, but gun advocates have been testing that in the courts.[85] As is often the case, companies cannot satisfy all stakeholders on this issue. Starbucks has opted not to ban guns, and so employees and some customers have mounted a petition campaign to encourage the company to changes its stance. California Pizza Kitchen opted to ban guns from its establishments, and so it is now facing a boycott by gun advocates.[86]

Who Is Affected?   Approximately 2 million U.S. workers are victims of workplace violence every year.[87] Although no workplace is immune from workplace violence, some workers are at increased risk of workplace violence from the general public. According to OSHA, the workers who are more likely to experience workplace violence include[88]

- Workers who exchange money with the public
- Workers who deliver passengers, goods, or services
- Workers who work alone or in small groups
- Workers who work late at night or very early in the morning
- Workers who work in community settings and homes where they have extensive contact with the public
- Workers who work in high-crime areas

The workers who are direct targets of the violence are not the only people affected. Not only are the family and friends of the victims impacted, but those employees in the workplace who escaped the violence also experience long-term effects. These survivors often spend years dealing with the after-effects.[89] Many fear returning to work and some never do. They will often play the event over in their minds, unable to forget what happened. Victoria Spang is a marketing director who hid in the personnel office when a client of her law firm came in with assault weapons, killing eight people and wounding six. "No one ever forgets. You'd walk by people's cubicles, and they would keep pictures of the victims up. It's a moment in life you'll always remember."[90]

Corporate image can also suffer long-term effects. The term "going postal" is a thorn in the side of the U.S. Postal Service. It became part of the lexicon after a series of post office shootings. The phrase continues even after a study commissioned by the post office found that postal workers are no more likely to commit violence than employees in other professions.[91] In fact, workplace violence can occur in the most unexpected locations. Quiet Huntsville, Alabama, was shocked when a biology professor shot three of her colleagues due to a dispute over her denial of tenure. University spokesperson Ray Garner commented, "This is a very safe campus.... This town is not accustomed to shootings and having multiple dead."[92]

Prevention.   The federal Occupational Safety and Health Act (OSHA) has a "general duty clause" that mandates employers to provide safe workplaces; however, it does not set forth specific standards or requirements addressing violence and has stated it will not try to regulate "random antisocial acts."[93] OSHA will apply the general duty clause to determine whether the violent act came from events that should have been foreseen by the company. Specifically, the company will be liable when (1) the employer neglected to keep the workplace free from a hazard, (2) the hazard was one that is generally recognized by the employer or the industry, (3) the hazard was already causing or was likely to cause serious harm, and (4) elimination or removal of the hazard was feasible.[94]

Management has both the legal and moral duty to address the problem of workplace violence. Companies have barely begun to put meaningful safety measures into place, but such measures will become more important in the future. Programs that deal with crises, and long-range efforts to bring about safer workplace environments, will be essential. Figure 18-3 lists OSHA's recommendations for what employers can do to protect their employees from workplace violence.

The Right to Health in the Workplace

As the public became more health conscious, it was not surprising that companies in the United States became much more sensitive about health issues. In efforts to control runaway health costs, which are rising at an estimated 10 percent per year, these companies took drastic steps, some of which have become controversial. Smoking is a controversial

---

FIGURE 18-3
OSHA's
Recommendations
for Preventing
Workplace
Violence

The best protection employers can offer is to establish a zero-tolerance policy toward workplace violence against or by their employees. The employer should establish a workplace violence prevention program or incorporate the information into an existing accident prevention program, employee handbook, or manual of standard operating procedures. It is critical to ensure that all employees know the policy and understand that all claims of workplace violence will be investigated and remedied promptly. In addition, employers can offer additional protections such as the following:

1. Provide safety education for employees so they know what conduct is not acceptable, what to do if they witness or are subjected to workplace violence, and how to protect themselves.
2. Secure the workplace. Where appropriate to the business, install video surveillance, extra lighting, and alarm systems and minimize access by

outsiders through identification badges, electronic keys, and guards.
3. Provide drop safes to limit the amount of cash on hand. Keep a minimal amount of cash in registers during evenings and late-night hours.
4. Equip field staff with cellular phones and hand-held alarms or noise devices, and require them to prepare a daily work plan and keep a contact person informed of their location throughout the day. Keep employer-provided vehicles properly maintained.
5. Instruct employees not to enter any location where they feel unsafe. Introduce a "buddy system" or provide an escort service or police assistance in potentially dangerous situations or at night.
6. Develop policies and procedures covering visits by home health-care providers. Address the conduct of home visits, the presence of others in the home during visits, and the worker's right to refuse to provide services in a clearly hazardous situation.

Source: Workplace Violence, OSHA Fact Sheet (2010), http://www.osha.gov/OshDoc/data_General_Facts/factsheet-workplace-violence.pdf.

---

issue related to health in the workplace and so it merits special attention. Like other issues we have examined, smoking in the workplace has employee rights, privacy, and due-process ramifications.

Smoking in the Workplace

The issue of **smoking in the workplace** began in the 1980s in the United States. The idea that smoking ought to be curtailed or restricted in the workplace is a direct result of the growing antismoking sentiment in society in general. Much of the antismoking sentiment crystallized when U.S. Surgeon General C. Everett Koop called for a smoke-free society. He proclaimed that smokers were hurting not only themselves but also the non-smoking people around them, who were being harmed by secondary, or passive, smoke in the air they breathed. Koop argued that the evidence "clearly documents that nonsmokers are placed at increased risks for developing disease as the result of exposure to environmental tobacco smoke."[95] To substantiate his point, he noted that a National Academy of Science study estimated that in one year, passive smoke was responsible for 2,400 lung cancer deaths in the United States.[96]

Evidence of the need to control smoking in the workplace continues to mount. The U.S. Environmental Protection Agency (EPA) classifies secondhand smoke involuntarily inhaled by nonsmokers from other people's cigarettes as a known human carcinogen: secondhand smoke is responsible for approximately 3,400 lung cancer deaths and an average of 46,000 heart disease deaths in adult nonsmokers annually in the United States.[97] The World Health Organization calls secondhand smoke a health hazard that kills and declares that every individual has the right to breathe smoke-free air.[98]

Worldwide, only 5.4 percent of people are protected by comprehensive national smoke-free laws, but the number of people protected is increasing each year.[99]

Corporate Responses.   Although companies did not act until considerable public sentiment against smoking had developed, they have now quickly moved to adopt policies that restrict smoking. Firms are becoming increasingly aware of the costs—higher insurance expenses and higher absenteeism—of having smokers on staff. Fifteen years ago, fewer than half of a survey's respondents said that smoking was restricted in public areas or their workspace at the office. Ten years later, a similar survey found that 92.3 percent of adults worked in places with a policy regulating smoking in public, common, or working areas.[100] Today most U.S. workplaces are smoke-free, with not only businesses but also states and localities making it a requirement.

Smoke-free workplaces provide an interesting second benefit worthy of note. Although they have been designed to protect workers from the effects of environmental tobacco smoke, there is now evidence they also support smokers in quitting. Caroline M. Fichtenberg and Stanton A. Glantz reviewed the findings of 26 studies of smoking in the workplace.[101] They found that in smoke-free workplaces, the percentage of workers who smoke drops by about 4 percent. Smokers in those workplaces reduce their smoking by about three cigarettes a day. These two effects make for a combined reduction of 29 percent in cigarette use. For the United States to achieve an equivalent reduction through taxation, the cigarette tax would have to be as high as $3 per pack. The authors also studied smoke-restricted workplaces (e.g., where a designated smoking lounge might be provided) and found the impact was muted significantly, with only about half the impact on smoking prevalence and use. Interestingly, the findings of this study have been known to the tobacco industry for some time. The authors cite tobacco industry studies with the same finding. They cite a Phillip Morris internal memo, which said, "Milder workplace restrictions have much less impact on quitting rates [than totally smoke-free workplaces] and very little impact on consumption."[102] Studies have also shown that smoke-free policies reduce heart attack hospitalizations for both smokers and nonsmokers.[103]

Weyco, Inc. has taken the smoke-free workplace issue to a new level by completely eliminating tobacco use among its workforce. Its 175 plus employees are entirely tobacco free, as are over 90 percent of the employees' spouses. They accomplished this through a gradual, and highly controversial, process. In 2003, they made a policy not to hire tobacco users, while also prohibiting smoking on campus and not allowing workers to take off-campus breaks. In 2004, they implemented voluntary testing—anyone who refused a test was fined $50 a month. In 2005, employees were told that if they refused the test or tested positive for smoking, they would lose their jobs. Random testing ensures that employees do not waiver in their nonsmoking commitment. Those who fail a random test are sent home without pay for a month to think about what they have done. If they pass the test on return, they must sign a letter agreeing to daily testing when the company wishes. A subsequent failed test results in termination. In 2006, Weyco extended its program to spouses of employees. Those with spouses who either refuse the test or fail it are fined $50 a month. Not surprisingly, Weyco's approach to the issue of smoking has raised the ire of privacy advocates who note that it would be illegal in many states.[104]

The Family-Friendly Workplace

Employees are increasingly less willing to spend every waking hour at work and are more committed to having time to spend at home with family. For example, one study found that family time was the most important work/life priority for 82 percent of men and 85 percent of women, ages 20 to 39.[105] Another found that 90 percent of working adults felt they did not spend enough time at home with their families.[106] Companies are searching for more and more ways to help employees achieve **work–life balance**, which is defined as "a state of equilibrium where the demands of a person's personal and professional life are equal."[107] However, the global economic recession has made this difficult as cost cutting has taken center stage and employees are under the added stress of securing their jobs.

The 2009 Society for Human Resource Management (SHRM) Employee Benefits Survey showed that companies are endeavoring to maintain **family-friendly** benefits while striving to reduce costs. Family-friendly benefits were largely intact except for reduced offerings in elder care referral services and adoption assistance.[108] With benefits in a general state of decline, it is unlikely that family-friendly benefits will see an employer-initiated rise before the economy turns around. Some of the most popular family-friendly benefits and the percentage of firms offering them are

1. Dependent care flexible spending accounts
2. Flextime
3. Family leave above required leave of the FMLA
4. Domestic partner benefits other than health care
5. Adoption assistance

Although not everyone thinks that companies are becoming as family friendly as they are claiming to be, it is clear that workers are talking more and more about the importance of family-friendly policies, and many leading companies are responding. With the growth in the numbers of women, single parents, and two-paycheck couples in the workforce, it seems that corporate support for families, many of whom are stressed out from their busy lives, is on the growth curve. This is further complicated by the changing nature of what constitutes a family. A recent study found that other segments of society are subject to unique work–life balance pressures but receive less support. Typically, work–life balance studies and programs have focused on employed men and women who raise their children with spouses or partners. Often forgotten are single-earner mothers and fathers, single and childless employees with significant elder-care responsibilities, grandparents raising their grandchildren, and blended families with children from both partners' other marriages.[109] In spite of the economic slump, many companies continue to offer family-friendly environments, and these have become an important part of "best places to work" surveys, which have become popular in recent years. The top five employers in the 2010 "Employee Choice Awards" were Southwest Airlines, General Mills, Slalom Consulting, Bain & Company, and McKinsey & Company. Well-known companies that typically rank high in this survey include Procter & Gamble, Kraft Foods, Google, Publix, FedEx, and Apple.[110]

It is in the context of organizations becoming more "friendly" on their own that we want to discuss a law aimed at health-related issues in the workplace—the FMLA.

Family and Medical Leave Act.   The **Family and Medical Leave Act (FMLA)** was made into law in 1993. This act was designed to make life easier for employees with family or health problems. In 2010, the law was expanded to include employees with family members on active military duty.[111] The new amendments extend "qualifying exigency leave" protections to families of active duty service members deployed abroad so that the families can have time to manage the service member's personal affairs while she or he is on active duty. In addition, family members who provide care for injured veterans can receive 26 weeks of leave.[112]

In addition to the expansions noted above, the FMLA grants employees the following rights:[113]

- An employee may take up to 12 weeks of unpaid leave in any 12-month period for the birth or adoption of a child or for the care of a child, spouse, or parent with a serious health condition that limits the employee's performance.
- Employees must be reinstated in their old jobs or be given equivalent jobs upon returning to work; the employer does not have to allow employees to accrue seniority or other benefits during the leave periods.
- Employers must provide employees with health benefits during leave periods.
- Employees are protected from retaliation in the same way as under other employment laws; an employee cannot be discriminated against for complaining to other people (even the newspapers) about an employer's family leave policy.

Employers also have rights under the FMLA.[114] These rights include the following:

- Companies with fewer than 50 workers are exempt.
- Employers may demand that employees obtain medical opinions and certifications regarding their needs for leave and may require second or third opinions.
- Employers do not have to pay employees during leave periods, but they must continue health benefits.
- If an employee and a spouse are employed at the same firm and are entitled to leave, the total leave for both may be limited to 12 weeks.

A recent study by the Department of Labor showed that the corporate views on the FMLA are mixed—generally positive but with some issues that merit concern. The good news is that the law seems to work well when employees take up to 12 weeks of unpaid leave for a close relative's sickness or the birth or adoption of a child. Problems arise when employees take unscheduled intermittent leave. In addition, defining a *serious medical condition* has been a challenge.[115]

In summary, the FMLA has not been the major problem that many envisioned, and it has accomplished much good. However, clarifying terminology is important if it is to continue to provide workers with the opportunity to fulfill their family responsibilities without sacrificing their careers. Efforts to pass additional family-friendly workplace legislation continue, but in an environment of global recession it is doubtful that major changes will occur in the near future. Efforts to streamline and clarify the FMLA are more likely to influence the direction corporate policies will take.

Summary

Critical employee stakeholder issues include the rights to privacy, safety, and health. These issues should be seen as extensions of the issues and rights outlined in Chapter 17.

With the development of new technologies, workplace privacy has increasingly become a serious issue. This wealth of available technology presents new challenges for companies as they weigh the importance of knowing their workers' activities against the importance of maintaining trust and morale. Of equal, if not more, importance to employee stakeholders are the issues of workplace safety and health. The workplace safety problem led to the creation of OSHA.

In spite of its difficulties, OSHA is still the federal government's major instrument for protecting workers on the job. State-promulgated right-to-know laws, as well as federal statutes, have been passed in recent years to provide employees with an added measure of protection, especially against harmful effects of exposure to chemicals and toxic substances. However, existing laws and regulations deal only with known problems. As the world changes, so do the threats to worker health and safety. Since the World Trade Center tragedy, the threat of terrorism has made many companies reassess operations as basic as their mail rooms. Other unexpected threats to workers' health and safety are certain to occur and will represent new challenges for managers.

Other major health issues in the current business–employee relationship are smoking and workplace violence. Smoking in the workplace raises issues of employee rights, those of both smokers and nonsmokers. Violence in the workplace is exacting a heavy toll, and businesses must be responsive. The need for employees to take family leave also impacts the work environment. Wise managers will develop policies for dealing with these issues, as well as their privacy and due-process implications.

Key Terms

Americans with Disabilities Act (ADA), p. 617

background checks, p. 611

broad brush EAP, p. 618

chief privacy officers (CPOs), p. 620

drug testing, p. 616

Electronic Communication Privacy Act (ECPA) of 1986, p. 619

Employee Assistance Programs (EAPs), p. 618

employee monitoring, p. 618

Employee Polygraph Protection Act (EPPA), p. 614

Equal Employment Opportunity Commission (EEOC), p. 613

Fair Credit Reporting Act (FCRA), p. 611

Family and Medical Leave Act (FMLA), p. 629

family-friendly, p. 629

integrity tests, p. 614

Occupational Safety and Health Administration (OSHA), p. 620

polygraph, p. 614

Privacy Act of 1974, p. 611

privacy in the workplace, p. 610

right-to-know laws, p. 623

smoking in the workplace, p. 627

type 1 error, p. 615

type 2 error, p. 615

USA Patriot Act, p. 611

work–life balance, p. 629

workplace violence, p. 625

Discussion Questions

1. In your own words, describe what privacy means and what privacy protection companies should give employees.

2. Enumerate the strengths and weaknesses of the polygraph as a management tool for decision making. What polygraph uses are legitimate? What uses of the polygraph are illegitimate?

3. What are the two major arguments for and against integrity (honesty) testing by employers? Under what circumstances could management most legitimately argue that integrity testing is necessary?

4. How has technology affected workplace privacy? What are the implications for the social contract between firms and their employees?

5. How has the World Trade Center tragedy affected workplace privacy? What are the long-term implications of that?

6. Which two of the four guidelines on the issue of privacy presented in this chapter do you think are the most important? Why?

7. Identify the privacy, health, and due-process ramifications of violence in the workplace.

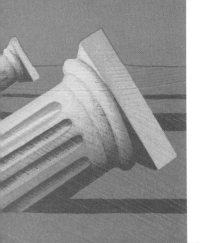

19

Employment Discrimination and Affirmative Action

CHAPTER LEARNING OUTCOMES

After studying this chapter, you should be able to:

1. Chronicle the U.S. civil rights movement and minority progress in the past 50 years.

2. Outline the essentials of the federal discrimination laws.

3. Provide two different meanings of discrimination, and give examples of how each might be committed.

4. Elaborate on issues in employment discrimination relating to race, color, national origin, sex, age, religion, sexual orientation, and disability.

5. Identify different postures with respect to affirmative action, explain the concept of reverse discrimination, and provide an overview of the Supreme Court's decisions on affirmative action.

In the two preceding chapters, we discussed employee rights issues that affect virtually everyone in the workplace. In this chapter, we focus on that group of stakeholders whose rights are protected by discrimination laws. In the United States, we have **protected groups** who have federal legal protection from discrimination based on race, color, religion, national origin, sex, age, or disability. In addition to these federal protections, 17 states have laws that protect individuals from discrimination based on sexual orientation. Many of the issues we treat in this chapter have grown out of the general belief that certain employees are likely to face discrimination because of the above-listed attributes and that they have workplace rights that ought to be protected.

Federal antidiscrimination laws date back to the U.S. Constitution—in particular, the First, Fifth, and Fourteenth Amendments, which were designed to forbid religious discrimination and deprivation of employment rights without due process. There were also the Civil Rights Acts of 1866, 1870, and 1871, which were based on these amendments. However, none of these acts was ever effective. Most authorities agree that the Civil Rights Act of 1964 was the effective beginning of the employee protection movement, particularly for those special groups that we will be discussing in this chapter.

In recessionary times, we must use the term "protected" with utmost care. It is true that the protected groups are protected from discrimination by the law. They are, however, not necessarily protected from the impacts of the global economic crisis. In the United States, young minority men are bearing a disproportionately bigger burden of the layoffs in this recession.[1] This is especially painful, as they had not earned as much as other workers prior to their layoffs.[2] This phenomenon is being felt worldwide. In Great Britain, ethnic minorities are experiencing the greatest rise in unemployment stemming from the recession,[3] and in Scotland, the percentage of women architects has dropped precipitously since the recession began.[4]

Civil rights issues among protected groups are subjects of intense debate. Although there is basic acceptance of the idea of groups' workplace rights being protected, the extent of this protection and the degree to which governmental policy should act to accelerate the infusion of protected groups into the workforce and into higher-paying jobs remain controversial topics. To explore these and related issues, we will cover the following major topics in this chapter: the civil rights movement and minority progress, federal laws that protect against employment discrimination, the meaning of discrimination, a variety of issues related to employment discrimination, and finally, affirmative action in the workplace.

The Civil Rights Movement and Minority Progress

It would take volumes to trace thoroughly the historical events that led ultimately to passage of the first significant piece of civil rights legislation in the modern period—the Civil Rights Act of 1964. The act grew out of conflict that had been apparent for years but that erupted in the 1950s and 1960s in the form of protests and boycotts.[5]

Civil Rights in the 1950s and 1960s

Behind the American dream had historically been the belief that merit rather than privilege was the means of getting ahead. Equal opportunity was supposed to be everyone's birthright. Blacks and other minorities, however, had not fully shared this American dream. In the 1950s and 1960s, the disparity between American ideals and American realities became quite pronounced and evident for minorities. Americans became aware of it, not because they suddenly awoke to the realization that equal opportunity was not available to everyone, but because of individuals who had the courage to stand up for their rights as U.S. citizens.

It began on December 1, 1955, when Mrs. Rosa Parks, a black department store worker, was arrested for refusing to yield her bus seat to a white man. Out of that previously unthinkable act grew yet another—a bus boycott by blacks. One of the leaders of the boycott was a young minister, Dr. Martin Luther King, Jr. After the bus boycott came years of demonstrations, marches, and battles with police. Television coverage depicted scenes of civil rights demonstrators being attacked by officials with cattle prods, dogs, and fire hoses. Along with the violence that grew out of confrontations between protestors and authorities came the stark awareness of the economic inequality between the races that existed in the United States at that time.[6]

Unemployment figures for blacks were double those for whites and higher still among nonwhite youth. Blacks accounted for only 10 percent of the labor force but represented 20 percent of the total unemployed and nearly 30 percent of the long-term unemployed. In 1961, only about one-half of black men worked steadily at full-time jobs compared to nearly two-thirds of white men. Against this backdrop of blacks and other minorities being denied their share in the American ideal of equal opportunity in employment, it should have been no surprise that Congress finally acted in a dramatic way in 1964 by passing the Civil Rights Act.[7]

The 1970s: The Women's Movement Begins

The women's movement began in the 1970s. Women's groups began to see that the workplace situation was little better for women than for blacks and other minorities. Despite the fact that the labor participation rate for women was growing, women were still occupying low-paying jobs. They were making some small inroads into managerial and professional jobs, but progress was very slow. Women, for the most part, were still in the lower paying "women's jobs," such as bank teller, secretary, waitress, and laundry worker.[8]

At first, in the early 1970s, blacks were making strong gains in employment and earnings. From the 1973–1975 recession, however, rampant unemployment among blacks was discouraging. By the end of the 1970s, the unemployment rate was about 12 percent for blacks, compared with 5 percent for whites.

The 1980s: Gains Are Made

In the 1980s, the circumstances of blacks and women improved, but women, in general, made greater progress in the workplace than blacks. From 1983 to 1986, the unemployment rate for all whites fell from 8.4 percent to 6.1 percent. During this same time, the unemployment rate for blacks fell from 19.5 percent to 15.1 percent. For women, it fell from 6.9 percent to 5.4 percent.[9] From these statistics we can see that unemployment represented a major problem for blacks, but not for women. Indeed, the unemployment rate for blacks remained more than twice that of whites.

During the mid- to late 1980s, inequality in the workforce remained a serious problem. Blacks continued to have lower participation rates in the workforce. Women did not face the labor participation rate problem suffered by blacks but continued to be excluded from higher-paying managerial jobs. Also problematic were pay inequities between men and women, and between whites and blacks, performing essentially the same jobs.

By the end of the 1980s, blacks had started enjoying mixed progress. Notable gains were made on the education front, but the incomes of blacks continued to trail those of whites. In 1990, nearly 80 percent of blacks aged 35 to 44 had completed four years of high school, compared with 63 percent in 1980. For the same period, 89 percent of whites completed high school, compared with 80 percent in 1980. In terms of college attendance, the rate for black females steadily increased from 24 percent in 1970 to 31 percent in 1988. For black males, the percentage attending college declined from 29 percent in 1970 to 25 percent in 1988. The poverty rate for black Americans in 1990 remained virtually the same as it had been for the past 20 years—nearly one-third.[10]

The 1990s: Some Progress, but Problems Remained

As the century drew to a close, 28 percent of blacks still lived in poverty, compared to 11 percent of whites.[11] Although 12.9 percent of the employees in private companies were African Americans, only 5.3 percent held managerial jobs.[12] Despite these problems, gains were being made at the highest levels of the corporate sector. According to Richard Parsons, then president of Time Warner and one of the United States's most powerful black executives:

> *People of color are achieving corporate positions that their parents could never have dreamed of reaching, and in unprecedented numbers. Is this trend sweeping the land? No. Are there still problems? Yes. But there's no question that the group of black leaders in business is stronger than ever.*[13]

Parsons went on to become Time Warner CEO in 2002 and Board President in 2003.[14] He resigned from Time Warner in 2008 and now serves as chairperson of the Board of Citigroup, Inc.[15]

The following incident illustrates the irony inherent in the experiences of African Americans in the workplace at the end of the 20th century. In the early 1990s, six Texaco employees filed a class-action lawsuit charging racial discrimination in hiring practices and workplace treatment. Two years later, a tape of Texaco executives surfaced that contained racial slurs directed at employees, as well as evidence that the executives were planning to shred incriminating documents and withhold information from the plaintiff's lawyers. Texaco settled the suit for $115 million.[16] When news of the tape became public, an activist friend called New York State Comptroller Carl McCall, the first African American elected to statewide office in New York, and asked him to join a picket line at the company's headquarters. McCall replied, "When you own 1 million shares of stock, you don't have to picket." McCall oversaw a public pension fund that is one of the largest in the country and one of the few funds managed by an individual rather than by a committee. He simply called then Texaco Chairperson Peter Bijur to express his concern, after which Bijur updated McCall regularly on the progress of Texaco's diversity plan.[17]

The 21st Century: New Challenges Arise While Old Problems Remain

One of the most significant issues arising in the new millennium has been the changing workforce composition. Federated Department Stores' diversity initiative covered 26 groups including seniors, the disabled, homosexuals, the devout, atheists, marrieds, and singles at the start of the new century. That represents a dramatic growth from a decade earlier when it covered only two groups, women and minorities. This proliferation of protected groups has raised concerns that the still-prevalent problem of racism will shift to the back burner. According to Lisa Willis Johnson, diversity chair for the Society of Human Resource Management (SHRM), "Race was the sacrificial lamb to launch diversity and make it palatable to corporate America."[18] Relegation of race to a back burner would be a serious mistake.[19]

As the numbers and percentages of workers protected by discrimination laws continue to increase, following current trends, civil rights issues will continue to be front-burner topics. Serious problems remain as new challenges arrive. Illegal immigration has become a politically charged topic. Complicating matters even more has been a growing sentiment against affirmative action. The challenge for business will be to assimilate an increasingly diverse workforce while adopting a posture on affirmative action that does not engender additional resentful reactions on the part of the majority. Although this was never an easy task, it has become even more challenging in a global economic recession.

An indispensable way to understand the changing public policy with respect to employment discrimination is to examine the evolution of federal laws prohibiting discrimination. Once we have a better appreciation of the legal status of protected groups, we can more completely understand the complex issues that have arisen with respect to the evolving meaning of discrimination and its relationship to related workforce issues—in particular, affirmative action.

Federal Laws Prohibiting Discrimination

This section provides an overview of the major laws that have been passed in the United States to protect workers against discrimination. We will focus our discussion on legislation at the federal level that has been created in the past 60 years. We will discuss issues arising from the various forms of discrimination in more detail later in this chapter. We should keep in mind that there are a host of state and local laws that address many of these same topics, but lack of space does not permit their consideration here. Our purpose in this section is to provide an overview of antidiscrimination laws and the major federal agencies that enforce those laws.

Title VII of the Civil Rights Act of 1964

Title VII of the Civil Rights Act of 1964, as amended, prohibits discrimination in hiring, promotion, discharge, pay, fringe benefits, and other aspects of employment on the basis of race, color, religion, sex, or national origin. It was extended to cover federal, state, and local employers and educational institutions by the Equal Employment Opportunity Act of 1972. The amendment to Title VII also gave the Equal Employment Opportunity Commission (EEOC) the authority to file suits in federal district court against employers in the private sector on behalf of individuals whose charges had not been successfully conciliated. In 1978, Title VII was amended to include the Pregnancy Discrimination Act, which requires employers to treat pregnancy and pregnancy-related medical conditions in the same manner as any other medical disability with respect to all terms and conditions of employment, including employee health benefits.[20]

Title VII also prohibits firms from retaliating against employees who file discrimination claims. In 2006, the U.S. Supreme Court strengthened the anti-retaliation provisions of Title VII. The High Court ruled that an employee can establish a retaliation claim even when they were not terminated or demoted. Any action that would "cause a worker to think twice" about lodging a discrimination complaint is sufficient (e.g., being transferred to a less desirable position at the same pay).[21] The High Court determined that lower courts had established a "jump off the page and slap you in the face" standard that was unacceptable.[22] In 2010, the U.S. Supreme Court ruled unanimously that the lawsuit clock does not begin when a biased hiring test is administered. Instead, it resets each time an employer uses the biased tests to make hiring decisions. The alternative, as Justice Scalia noted when he wrote the court's opinion, would be unending ongoing discrimination: "If an employer adopts an unlawful practice and no timely charge is brought, it can continue using the practice indefinitely, with impunity, despite ongoing disparate impact."[23]

Figure 19-1 presents an overview of Title VII's coverage.

Age Discrimination in Employment Act of 1967

This law protects workers aged 40 years and older from arbitrary age discrimination in hiring, discharge, pay, promotions, fringe benefits, and other aspects of employment. It is designed to promote employment of older people on the basis of ability rather than age and to help employers and workers find ways to meet problems arising from the impact of age on employment.

Like the provisions of Title VII, the **Age Discrimination in Employment Act (ADEA)** does not apply where age is a **bona fide occupational qualification (BFOQ)**—a qualification that might ordinarily be argued as being a basis for discrimination but for which a company can legitimately argue that it is job related and necessary. Neither does the act bar employers from differentiating among employees based on reasonable factors other than age.[24]

Equal Pay Act of 1963

As amended, this act prohibits sex discrimination in payment of wages to women and men who perform substantially equal work in the same establishment. Passage of this landmark law marked a significant milestone in helping women, who were the chief victims of unequal pay, to achieve equality in their paychecks.[25] Figure 19-2 summarizes other details of the **Equal Pay Act of 1963**.

The Equal Pay Act received a great deal of attention in 2007, when the U.S. Supreme Court heard the *Ledbetter v. Goodyear Tire & Rubber Co.* case, in which the plaintiff, Lilly Ledbetter, alleged that she had been paid less than her male counterparts but was

FIGURE 19-1
Title VII of the Civil Rights Act of 1964

EMPLOYMENT discrimination based on race, color, religion, sex, or national origin is prohibited by Title VII of the Civil Rights Act of 1964.

Title VII covers private employers, state and local governments, and educational institutions that have 15 or more employees. The federal government, private and public employment agencies, labor organizations, and joint labor–management committees for apprenticeship and training also must abide by the law.

It is illegal under Title VII to discriminate in

- Hiring and firing;
- Compensation, assignment, or classification of employees;
- Transfer, promotion, layoff, or recall;
- Job advertisements;
- Recruitment;
- Testing;
- Use of company facilities;
- Training and apprenticeship programs;
- Fringe benefits;
- Pay, retirement plans, and disability leave; or

- Other terms and conditions of employment.

Under the law, pregnancy, childbirth, and related medical conditions must be treated in the same manner as any other nonpregnancy-related illness or disability.

Title VII prohibits retaliation against a person who files a charge of discrimination, participates in an investigation, or opposes an unlawful employment practice.

Employment agencies may not discriminate in receiving, classifying, or referring applications for employment or in their job advertisements.

Labor unions may not discriminate in accepting applications for membership, classifying members, referrals, training and apprenticeship programs, and advertising for jobs. It is illegal for a labor union to cause or try to cause an employer to discriminate. It is also illegal for an employer to cause or try to cause a union to discriminate.

Source: U.S. Equal Employment Opportunity Commission, http://eeoc.gov/policy/vii.html.

FIGURE 19-2
Equal Pay Act of 1963

The **Equal Pay Act** (EPA) prohibits employers from discriminating between men and women on the basis of sex in the payment of wages where they perform substantially equal work under similar working conditions in the same establishment. The law also prohibits employers from reducing the wages of either sex to comply with the law.

A violation may exist where a different wage is paid to a predecessor or successor employee of the opposite sex. Labor organizations may not cause employers to violate the law.

Retaliation against a person who files a charge of equal pay discrimination, participates in an investigation, or opposes an unlawful employment practice also is illegal.

The law protects virtually all private employees, including executive, administrative, professional, and outside sales employees who are exempt from minimum wage and overtime laws. Most federal, state, and local government workers also are covered.

The law does not apply to pay differences based on factors other than sex, such as seniority, merit, or systems that determine wages based on the quantity or quality of items produced or processed.

Many EPA violations may be violations of Title VII of the Civil Rights Act of 1964, which also prohibits sex-based wage discrimination. Such charges may be filed under both statutes.

Source: Information for the Private Sector and State and Local Governments: EEOC (Washington: Equal Employment Opportunity Commission), 9. Also see U.S. Department of Labor, Equal Pay Act of 1963, as amended, http://www.dol.gov/oasam/regs/statutes/equal_pay_act.htm.

unaware of the discrimination until years after the decision on her pay had been made. The question at hand was whether the clock on the statute of limitations began ticking with the original pay decision or whether it was reset each time a paycheck was made.[26] The Supreme Court, controversially, decided that even if Ledbetter's employers had made a per se discriminatory decision that resulted in a lower paycheck, the statute of limitations began running from the time of that decision, and so a complaint must be filed within 180 days of the action that sets the discriminatory pay, irrespective of its ongoing impact on the employee.[27] The Lily Ledbetter Fair Pay Act of 2009 effectively undid the Court's decision, stipulating that the clock reset each time a paycheck was issued.[28]

Rehabilitation Act of 1973, Section 503

This law, as amended, prohibits job discrimination on the basis of a disability. It applies to employers holding federal contracts or subcontracts. In addition, it requires these employers to engage in affirmative action to employ the disabled, a concept we will discuss later in this chapter. Related to this act is the Vietnam Era Veterans Readjustment Assistance Act of 1974, which also prohibits discrimination and requires affirmative action among federal contractors or subcontractors.[29]

Americans with Disabilities Act of 1990

The most significant labor and employment statute to be enacted in the past 40 years was the **Americans with Disabilities Act (ADA)**. It prohibits discrimination based on physical or mental disabilities in private places of employment and public accommodation, in addition to requiring transportation systems and communication systems to facilitate access for the disabled. The ADA was modeled after the Rehabilitation Act of 1973, which applies to federal contractors and grantees.[30] The basic provisions of the ADA are detailed in Figure 19-3.

Essentially, the ADA gives individuals with disabilities civil rights protections similar to those provided to individuals on the basis of race, sex, national origin, and religion. The ADA applies not only to private employers but also to state and local governments, employment agencies, and labor unions. Employers of 15 or more employees are covered.

The ADA prohibits discrimination in all employment practices, including job application procedures, hiring, firing, advancement, compensation, training, and other terms, conditions, and privileges of employment. If a person's disability makes it difficult for him or her to function, firms are expected to make **reasonable accommodations** if the person does not represent an **undue hardship** for the firm. The act covers qualified individuals with disabilities. Qualified individuals are those who can perform the **essential functions** of the job.[31] The definition of essential function is sometimes difficult to determine. A case in point occurred with golfer Casey Martin, when he applied to the PGA for permission to ride a cart in PGA tournaments when other players were walking the course. Much controversy ensued over whether walking the golf course was an essential function of playing professional golf. The Supreme Court subsequently ruled that he could use a cart because providing the cart was a reasonable accommodation and his use of the cart would not fundamentally alter the game.

The definition of disability includes people who have physical or mental impairments that substantially limit one or more major life activities, such as seeing, hearing, speaking, walking, breathing, performing manual tasks, learning, caring for oneself, and working.[32] Uncertainty over the definition of "disability" sent the ADA to the courts for clarification. In June 1998, the Supreme Court decided that the definition of "disability"

FIGURE 19-3
The Americans with Disabilities Act

Title I of the Americans with Disabilities Act of 1990 prohibits private employers, state and local governments, employment agencies, and labor unions from discriminating against qualified individuals with disabilities in job application procedures, hiring, firing, advancement, compensation, job training, and other terms, conditions, and privileges of employment. The ADA covers employers with 15 or more employees, including state and local governments. It also applies to employment agencies and to labor organizations. The ADA's nondiscrimination standards also apply to federal sector employees under Section 501 of the Rehabilitation Act, as amended, and its implementing rules.

An individual with a disability is a person who

- Has a physical or mental impairment that substantially limits one or more major life activities;
- Has a record of such an impairment; or
- Is regarded as having such an impairment.

A qualified employee or applicant with a disability is an individual who, with or without reasonable accommodation, can perform the essential functions of the job in question. Reasonable accommodation may include, but is not limited to,

- Making existing facilities used by employees readily accessible to and usable by persons with disabilities;
- Restructuring jobs, (for parallelism) modifying work schedules, and reassigning to a vacant position;
- Acquiring or modifying equipment or devices; adjusting or modifying examinations, training materials, or policies; and providing qualified readers or interpreters.

An employer is required to make a reasonable accommodation to the known disability of a qualified applicant or employee if it would not impose an "undue hardship" on the operation of the employer's business. Reasonable accommodations are adjustments or modifications provided by an employer to enable people with disabilities to enjoy equal employment opportunities. Accommodations vary depending on the needs of the individual applicant or employee. Not all people with disabilities (or even all people with the same disability) will require the same accommodation. For example,

- A deaf applicant may need a sign language interpreter during the job interview.
- An employee with diabetes may need regularly scheduled breaks during the workday to eat properly and monitor blood sugar and insulin levels.
- A blind employee may need someone to read information posted on a bulletin board.
- An employee with cancer may need leave for radiation or chemotherapy treatments.

An employer does not have to provide a reasonable accommodation if it imposes an "undue hardship." Undue hardship is defined as an action that requires significant difficulty or expense when considered in light of factors such as an employer's size, financial resources, and the nature and structure of its operation.

An employer is not required to lower quality or production standards to make an accommodation, nor is it obligated to provide personal use items such as glasses or hearing aids.

An employer generally does not have to provide a reasonable accommodation unless an individual with a disability has asked for one. If an employer believes that a medical condition is causing a performance or conduct problem, it may discuss with the employee how to solve the problem and ask if the employee needs a reasonable accommodation. Once a reasonable accommodation is requested, the employer and the individual should discuss the individual's needs and identify the appropriate reasonable accommodation. Where more than one accommodation would work, the employer may choose the one that is less costly or is easier to provide.

It is also unlawful to retaliate against an individual for opposing employment practices that discriminate based on disability or for filing a discrimination charge, testifying, or participating in any way in an investigation, proceeding, or litigation under the ADA.

Source: EEOC Facts about the Americans with Disabilities Act (Revised September 9, 2008). Also see Department of Justice, Americans with Disabilities Act of 1990, as amended, http://www.ada.gov/pubs/ada.htm.

included both major and minor impairments. Under this ruling, the ADA applies to disabilities as diverse as HIV, diabetes, cancer, dyslexia, and bad backs.[33] In 2003, however, the EEOC issued enforcement guidance that restricts the definition of a disability. They ruled that an *impairment* is a *disability* only if it "substantially limits one or more of the employee's **major life activities**."[34] Major life activities include speaking and interacting with others, learning, thinking, concentrating, and working.[35]

The Supreme Court upheld an individual's right to sue the state under the ADA. Paraplegic and confined to a wheelchair, George Lane was ordered to appear on the second floor of a court, with no ramps or elevators. He could not climb the steps and so he crawled up the stairs to comply with the order. When he was ordered to appear in court a second time, Lane refused to crawl or be carried. He was subsequently arrested for failing to appear in court. He charged the state of Tennessee with discrimination and sued it for $100,000. When the Supreme Court upheld his right to sue, it was seen as an indication that the High Court was disinclined to let states' rights arguments prevail over civil rights.[36]

In a Louis Harris survey of corporate employers conducted five years after the act's passage, the ADA found a high level of support. These corporate executives, 81 percent of whom had modified their offices since the ADA went into effect, estimated the average cost of accommodation as $223 per disabled employee. About half of the executives (48 percent) said the ADA increased their costs a little, 82 percent reported no change in costs, and 7 percent reported that their costs increased "a lot." Most of the executives said the ADA should be strengthened or kept as it is; only 12 percent felt it should be weakened or repealed.[37] The executives' early assessment of the ADA seems to have foreseen the experience they would have with the ADA. Thirteen years after the act was passed, the American Bar Association found that employers won 94.5 percent of the ADA discrimination court cases and 78.1 percent of the administrative cases.[38]

The ADA continues to be a work in progress. The ADA Amendments Act of 2008 broadened the definition of "disability" and became effective on January 1, 2009. The bipartisan effort was designed to roll back several Supreme Court decisions that made it more difficult to qualify for disability protection. It expands the meaning of "major life activity," "substantially limits," and "regarded as." In addition, the existence of mitigating factors and a disease being episodic or in remission are no longer exclusionary factors. At this writing, the implications of the amendments are unclear as the final rules are still being written and awaiting finalization of the appointment of additional EEOC Commissioners for approval.[39]

Civil Rights Act of 1991

The primary objective of the **Civil Rights Act of 1991** was to provide increased financial damages and jury trials in cases of intentional discrimination relating to sex, religion, race, disability, and national origin. Under the original Title VII, monetary awards were limited to such items as back pay, lost benefits, and attorney fees and costs. This 1991 act permitted the awarding of both compensatory and punitive damages. In addition, charges of unintentional discrimination were more difficult for employers to defend, because the act shifted the burden of proof back to the employer.[40] Note that the act refers only to protected groups under Title VII and does not reference age or the ADEA. In 2010, this issue came to a head when the Supreme Court issued their *Gross v. FBL Financial Services, Inc.* opinion. We discuss the details in the forthcoming section on age discrimination.

The laws just discussed constitute the backbone of federal efforts to prevent employment discrimination. Several executive orders issued by the president of the United

States also prohibit discrimination. However, because these executive orders also contain provisions for affirmative action, we will discuss them during our treatment of affirmative action later in this chapter.

Equal Employment Opportunity Commission

As the major federal body created to administer and enforce job bias laws, the **Equal Employment Opportunity Commission (EEOC)** deserves special consideration. Several other federal agencies also are charged with enforcing certain aspects of the discrimination laws and executive orders, but we will restrict our discussion to the EEOC because it is the major agency.

The EEOC has five commissioners and a general counsel appointed by the president and confirmed by the Senate. The five-member commission is responsible for making equal employment opportunity policy and approving all litigation the commission undertakes. The EEOC staff receives and investigates employment discrimination charges/complaints. If the commission finds reasonable cause to believe that unlawful discrimination has occurred, its staff attempts to conciliate the charges/complaints. When conciliation is not achieved, the EEOC may file lawsuits in federal district court against employers.[41]

To provide some appreciation of the kinds of discrimination cases handled by the EEOC, Figure 19-4 presents a breakdown of the job-bias claims filed with the EEOC from 1991 to 2009. The EEOC reports that U.S. employees filed 93,277 workplace discrimination charges in 2009. That is second only to the record 95,402 charges set in 2008. For the first time, retaliation claims were at the top of the list, with 33,613 claims. Disability claims showed the greatest increase, which may be due to the ADA amendments that broadened the definition of "disabled."[42]

Like other federal regulatory bodies discussed, such as the EPA, FTC, and OSHA, the EEOC has had mixed success over the years. Its fortunes, successes, and failures have been somewhat dictated by the times, the administration in office, and the philosophy

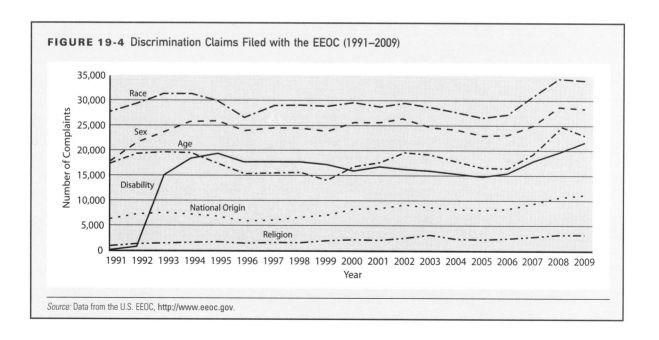

FIGURE 19-4 Discrimination Claims Filed with the EEOC (1991–2009)

Source: Data from the U.S. EEOC, http://www.eeoc.gov.

and zeal of its chairperson. During the late 1970s, the business community thought that the EEOC was on a "witch-hunt," looking for violations so it could punish business for its past wrongs.[43] In the 1980s, the Reagan administration responded to these concerns when it (1) eliminated the use of minority hiring goals and timetables used by employers to correct racial and ethnic disparities, (2) largely abandoned class-action lawsuits that relied on statistical evidence to prove widespread discrimination at large companies, and (3) yielded the EEOC's once-dominant role on civil rights initiatives to the Justice Department.[44] When former President Clinton took office in 1992, the EEOC stepped up enforcement of business discrimination laws. Among the crackdown's targets were unsettled discrimination lawsuits against major employers, polluters who dump their muck in minority neighborhoods, banks whose loan departments redline poor areas, and other forms of day-to-day discrimination.[45] Cari Dominguez, who served from 2001 to 2006, found her tenure shaped dramatically by the September 11 terrorist attacks and the need to make certain that anger against the terrorists was not misdirected as national origin discrimination toward Arab Americans.[46] Naomi Earp, EEOC vice chair, took over as the new EEOC chair in August 2006. The EEOC launched a new initiative called E-Race dedicated to "Eradicating Racism and Colorism from Employment" and tackling new technology that made it possible to discriminate in new ways, such as sorting applicants by zip codes or ethnic communities.[47] At this writing, the EEOC has just achieved full strength with the appointments of chairperson Jacqueline Berrien and two commissioners, and so it is too early to know what direction this new administration will head.[48] Although the EEOC's and the country's emphasis will shift over time, discrimination against each protected class is always present and so we will deal with each one individually.

Spotlight on SUSTAINABILITY

Are Sustainability Advocates a New Protected Class?

As head of sustainability for Grainger, one of Britain's largest property firms, Rupert Dickinson would sometimes get in conflicts with other executives at the firm. For example, when one top executive left his BlackBerry in London and ordered a staff person to fly to Ireland to bring it back to him, Dickinson believed that wasting jet fuel to return a BlackBerry and other such environmentally inappropriate actions were evidence of contempt for his sustainability beliefs. When he was later laid off, Dickinson filed suit. The judge decided that if one genuinely holds a belief in man-made climate change, and its alleged resulting moral imperatives, that can be a "philosophical belief." Grainger contends that Dickinson was let go when organizational restructuring made his position redundant. In the United Kingdom, it is unlawful to discriminate against a person on the grounds of their religious or philosophical beliefs. The case is still unfolding, but businesses are watching it carefully, believing that a finding for the plaintiff is likely to result in more workplace disputes.

Sources: Karen McVeigh, "Judge Rules Activist's Belief on Environment Akin to Religion," *guardian.co.uk* (November 9, 2009), http://www.guardian.co.uk/environment/2009/nov/03/tim-nicholson-climate-change-belief; Richard Heap, "Beyond Belief: Grainger's Former Head of Sustainability Believes His Environmental Beliefs Cost Him His Job," *Property Week* (June 5, 2009), http://www.allbusiness.com/legal/labor-employment-law-discrimination-religious/12539159-1.html.

Expanded Meanings of Employment Discrimination

Over the years, it has been left to the courts to define the word *discrimination*, because it was not defined in Title VII. Over time, it has become apparent that two specific kinds of discrimination exist: **disparate treatment** and **disparate impact**.

Disparate Treatment

Initially, the word *discrimination* meant the use of race, color, religion, sex, or national origin as a basis for treating people differently or unequally. This form of discrimination is known as unequal treatment, or disparate treatment. Examples of disparate treatment might include refusing to consider blacks for a job, paying women less than men for the same work, or supporting any decision rule with a racial or sexual premise or cause.[49] According to this simple view of discrimination, the employer could impose any criteria so long as they were imposed on all groups alike.[50] This view of discrimination equated nondiscrimination with color-blind decision making. In other words, to avoid this direct kind of discrimination, one would simply treat all groups or individuals equally, without regard for color, sex, or other characteristics.[51]

Disparate Impact

Congress later clarified that its intent in prohibiting discrimination was to eliminate practices that contributed to economic inequality. What it found was that, although companies could adhere to the disparate treatment definition of discrimination, this did not eliminate all of the discrimination that existed. For example, a company could use two neutral, color-blind criteria for selection—a high school diploma and a standardized ability test. Blacks and whites could be treated the same under the criteria, but the problem arose when it became apparent that the policy of equal treatment resulted in unequal consequences for blacks and whites. Blacks were less likely to have high school diplomas, and blacks who took the test were less likely than whites to pass it. Therefore, a second, more expanded idea of what constituted discrimination was needed.

The Supreme Court had to decide whether an action was discriminatory if it resulted in unequal consequences in the *Griggs v. Duke Power Company* case.[52] Duke Power had required that employees transferring to other departments have a high school diploma or pass a standardized intelligence test. This requirement excluded a disproportionate number of minority workers. The court noted that there were nonminorities who performed satisfactorily and achieved promotions though they did not have diplomas. The court then reached the groundbreaking conclusion that it was the consequences of an employer's actions, not its intentions, that determined whether discrimination had taken place. If any employment practice or test had an adverse or differential effect on minorities, it was a discriminatory practice. An unequal impact, or disparate impact, means that fewer minorities are included in the outcome of the test or the hiring or promotion practice than would be expected by their numerical proportion. The court also held that a policy or procedure with a disparate impact would be permissible if the employer could demonstrate that it was a business- or job-related necessity. In the *Duke Power* case, for example, a high school diploma and good scores on a general intelligence test did not have a clearly demonstrable relationship to successful performance on the job under consideration.[53]

The concept of "unequal impact" is quite significant, because it runs counter to so many traditional employment practices. For example, the minimum height and weight requirements of some police departments have unequal impact and have been struck down by courts because they tend to screen out women, people of Asian heritage, and Latinos disproportionately.[54] Several Supreme Court rulings have addressed the issue of the kind of evidence needed to document or prove discrimination. Typically, if a member of a minority group does not have a success rate at least 80 percent that of the majority group, the practice may be considered to have an adverse impact unless business necessity can be proven.[55] When this **four-fifths rule** is triggered, the firm will not necessarily be found guilty of having a disparate impact. However, it will be incumbent upon the firm to show that the selection practice is job related and necessary for the business.[56]

The issue of disparate impact is often not easily resolved. For example, the EEOC determined that a strength test given to applicants for positions in a canned meat factory had an unlawful disparate impact; the company appealed the verdict but lost.[57] The job for which the applicants were applying required them to carry 35 pounds of sausage, and lift and load it, while walking approximately four miles a day. The strength test attempted to replicate the work by having applicants carry a 35 pound bar and loading it onto other bars. A nurse observed the test and had ultimate hiring authority based on her observations. Before the company began using the test, about 50 percent of the hires were females. By the time of the verdict, that number had dropped to 8 percent. A drop from 50 percent to 8 percent is dramatic, and that was the first indication that a disparate impact might be operating. On the surface, the relationship of the test to ultimate job responsibilities appeared strong, so it became necessary to determine why the percentage of women who passed the test was so low. The key problem was that the single evaluator (the nurse) added subjectivity to the process, as evidenced by the fact that the number of women hired declined with each testing and that when women and men received similar comments on their testing forms, only men were hired.[58] As shown in Figure 19-7 on page 658, disparate impact continues to occupy the court. In 2009, the Supreme Court ruled against the City of New Haven, Connecticut's decision to not certify firefighter exam results. The City of New Haven was concerned about disparate impact because too few minorities passed the test. However, the Supreme Court found that the act of discarding the test adversely affected those who had passed the test. They noted the efforts New Haven had made to create a fair test and ruled that a test should not be considered discriminatory unless there is a strong basis in evidence.[59]

Figure 19-5 summarizes the characteristics of disparate treatment and disparate impact.

FIGURE 19-5 Two Kinds of Employment Discrimination

Definition 1 Disparate Treatment	Definition 2 Disparate Impact
Direct discrimination	Indirect discrimination
Unequal treatment	Unequal consequences or results
Decision rules with a racial/sexual premise or cause	Decision rules with racial/sexual consequences or results
Intentional discrimination	Unintentional discrimination
Prejudiced actions	Neutral, color-blind actions
Different standards for different groups	Same standards, but different consequences for different groups

Source: James Ledvinka and Vida G. Scarpello, *Federal Regulation of Personnel and Human Resources Management*, 2d ed. (Boston: PWS-Kent, 1991), 48.

Issues in Employment Discrimination

The essentials of the major federal laws on discrimination have been presented, and we have traced the evolution of the concept of discrimination. Now it is useful to discuss briefly the different issues that are related to the types of discrimination we have covered. It is also important to indicate some of the particular problems that have arisen with respect to each of the different issues.

Issues of Racial Discrimination

Although racial discrimination was one of the first forms of discrimination to attract the focus of the civil rights legislation, it still remains a major problem in workplaces in the United States and throughout the world. Although racial discrimination is always hurtful, the nature of its form and impact has been different for people of different races. The EEOC has made race and color discrimination a priority and as part of that has clarified the definition of the terms. Race discrimination includes discrimination on the basis of ancestry or physical or cultural characteristics associated with a certain race, such as skin color, hair texture or styles, or certain facial features. Forms that collect federal data on race and ethnicity in the workforce use five racial categories: American Indian or Alaska Native, Asian, black or African American, Native Hawaiian or Other Pacific Islander, and white, and one ethnicity category, Hispanic or Latino.[60]

African Americans in Corporate America. The good news is that the number of African Americans on the boards of directors rose from zero in the 1960s to 449 in 2004; however, the bad news is that the number has been decreasing since then. In 2009, the Executive Leadership Council reported that the number of African Americans holding seats on *Fortune* 500 boards decreased from 449 (8.1 percent) in 2004 to 413 (7.4 percent) in 2008.[61] According to Ancella B. Livers, executive director of the Executive Leadership Council's Institute for Leadership Development & Research, "The total number of board seats during the period declined as well, but not nearly as much as the number of seats held by African Americans. In light of current economic conditions and board reviews, there is an opportunity for companies to increase board diversity and reverse the downward trend."[62] Interestingly, the higher the company is on the *Fortune* 500 list, the more likely it is to have a diverse board.[63]

In addition to problems at the top of the hierarchy, serious problems remain in the workplace too, as evidenced by a recent case in which the EEOC obtained a $1 million settlement for a black man choked by a hangman's noose by white coworkers. That horrible incident was the culmination of a series of abuses. According to the EEOC, the company did not stop its employees from repeatedly harassing the complainant on the basis of his race and subjecting him to a hostile work environment with both verbal and physical abuse. As Senior EEOC Investigator Jeannette Leino said, "It is shocking that such egregious racial harassment still occurs in the 21st century workplace, more than 40 years after passage of the landmark Civil Rights Act."[64]

Other forms of racism are more subtle. A letter to Randy Cohen's "The Ethicist" column in *The New York Times Magazine* underscores the difficulties that remain for African Americans today, irrespective of their level of achievement. An African-American male was looking for Web programming work. When he used his first name on his resume, a name that identified his ethnicity, he received relatively few calls for interviews. He began to use his middle name on his resume, which did not signal his ethnicity, and found that he got more interview calls.[65] This man's experience underscores the challenges facing African Americans today. Even after developing professional skills and achieving a high level of education, many still cannot count on their credentials opening the same doors as they would do for other workers in the marketplace.

In spite of these obstacles, black executives have been making their mark. In 2009, Ursula Burns became the first black female *Fortune* 500 CEO when she took over the reins at Xerox.[66] This brought the total number of African-American *Fortune* 500 CEOs to five, well below the previous high of eight.[67] This is an improvement over 1995, when there were no CEOs of color, but the gains are slow.

The Case of Hispanics.   The word *Hispanic* fails to capture the diversity in this population. It is a term created by the government and was first used in the 1980 census to categorize people from Latin America or Spain. Hispanics are the only major minority group to be classified by the language they speak. They can be black (Cuba's population is 58 percent black), Asian (Peru's former President Fujimori is 100 percent Japanese), or any of a variety of races. Accordingly, many people prefer to be described as Latino (which includes people from Portugal) or as hailing from their country of origin (e.g., of Puerto Rican descent).[68]

The growth rate among Latinos in the United States is one of the most dramatic in the U.S. history. The most recent census identified a Hispanic population of 35.3 million, representing one out of eight Americans, a number greater than the entire population of Canada. This is a 58 percent increase from the 22.4 million Hispanics ten years before. For the first time, more people identify themselves as Hispanic (35.3 million) than as black (34.7 million), making Hispanics the largest minority recorded by the U.S. census. However, 1.7 million people identify themselves as partly black and partly another race, and some Hispanic people are black, so the difference in sizes of the groups is largely definitional.[69]

The Hispanic population is known for a strong work ethic. Originally centered in a few big metropolitan areas, thousands of Latinos have moved to small factory towns and suburban areas for employment. At 80 percent, workforce participation among Hispanic males is the highest of any measured group, with many becoming entrepreneurs. Those living in poverty use welfare less often than poor whites or poor blacks. In spite of this level of participation and success in the workforce, many Latinos are still working in low-wage jobs. Discrimination remains a critical problem.[70] In the most recent "National Survey of Latinos," half of the respondents said that the situation for Latinos in the United States is worse than it was a year ago. Almost one in ten of the Hispanic adults, whether native-born U.S. citizens or immigrants, report that in the past year the police or other authorities have stopped and asked them about their immigration status. Fifteen percent of Latinos said that they have had trouble in the past year finding or keeping a job and 10 percent had trouble finding or keeping housing because they are Latino.[71]

Asian Image of Model Minority.   Asian Americans have a problem that is unique to U.S. minority groups, a stereotype that may be too positive. The popular press, many pundits, and various policy makers have portrayed Asian Americans as an ideal that should be emulated by other minorities (i.e., Asian Americans are the "model minority").[72] However, scholars in various disciplines, including Asian-American studies, have refuted this characterization. They argue that aggregated data hide the impact of such critical factors as highly selective immigration policies, high numbers of hours worked, and high numbers of individuals per household. When these critics have disaggregated the data used to support the model minority characterization, they have found a bimodal distribution. One group of well-educated, higher paid Asian-American professionals does well until they reach the glass ceiling; the other group is low skilled, low paid, and generally disadvantaged.[73]

A recent study showed that although Asians comprise 4.4 percent of the U.S. population, they account for only 1.5 percent of *Fortune* 500 board members.[74] The Committee of 100, an organization of prominent Chinese Americans, commissioned the study; they note that this underrepresentation on *Fortune* 500 boards has occurred in spite of the fact that Asian Americans are wealthier and better educated than whites and other minority groups. According to Wilson Chu, a Dallas lawyer, "There's a negative perception of Asians out there. People may view them as smart people, but not as leaders."[75]

Some have argued that many of the problems of Asian Americans stem from their image as a model minority, which embraces discipline, hard work, and education. This image has a downside, because quiet achievement can be interpreted as passivity and the Asian-American professional can feel invisible in the corporation.[76] The Asian-American response to this had been to avoid confrontation and simply work harder, but groups like the Committee of 100 are working to change that. The presence of Asian Americans will continue to grow, and so their treatment in the workplace will be an issue for years to come.

Issues of Sex Discrimination

Issues surrounding sex discrimination are different from those involving race, color, and national origin. The major issues for women today include (1) getting into professional and managerial positions and out of traditional female-dominated positions, (2) achieving pay commensurate with that of men, (3) eliminating sexual harassment, and (4) being able to take maternity leave without losing their jobs. Some progress is being made on most of these fronts.

Women in Professional/Managerial Positions. Five years ago, the Catalyst Census titled their tenth annual report on women in *Fortune* 500 officer positions "Limited Progress, Challenges Persist."[77] They found a virtual standstill in the proportion of women in the top corporate officer ranks and opined it would take 40 years to achieve equality with men.[78] In 2005, eight women served as CEO of a *Fortune* 500 company. By 2010, 15 women headed *Fortune* 500 companies.

Progress is still slow as the 3 percent of *Fortune* 500 companies headed by women is disproportionately small, given the percentage of women in the population. Nevertheless, the outlook for women seems to have brightened. The Boston Consulting Group (BCG) conducted a study that led them to conclude that women will be driving the postrecession global economy.[79] They believe that a new group of women is now rising through the corporate ranks, and if these women remain on the fast track, they are poised to break the old trends. "It's nothing less than the entry of a new generation of leaders onto the world stage," according to BCG Senior Partner Michael J. Silverstein.[80] They contend that this elite group of women is more powerful than their male counterparts.[81]

Pay Equity. Pay equity can be approached from two directions: equal pay and comparable worth. Equal pay is the concept that workers doing the same job should receive the same pay, irrespective of gender. The issue of pay equity is complex, and some subgroups of women have fared better than others. In general, however, the issue of pay equity is similar to the issue described previously about the glass ceiling. Throughout the 1980s and early 1990s, the pay gap between men and women was closing gradually, from about 65 cents to every dollar earned by men in 1980 to more than 75 cents for every dollar in 1995.[82] Now, 15 years later, women are earning slightly more than 80 cents for every dollar earned by men.[83] The actual gap varies depending on who is doing the calculating and what groups are being compared. Across groups, however, there seems to be a general consensus that improvement has slowed.

Some observers have tried to explain the discrepancy by arguing that these statistics include women who lost both time and experience through extended maternity leave. However, the Bureau of Labor Statistics shows that only 5.1 percent of women take more than a week off beyond regular vacation time (for any reason), while 3.3 percent of men do the same.[84] A recent General Accounting Office (GAO) study controlled for external factors such as women working less, leaving the workforce for longer periods of time, and working at lower paying jobs. They found that women still earned significantly less than men. "After accounting for so many external factors, it seems that still, at the root of it all, men get an inherent annual bonus just for being men," said Representative Carolyn B. Maloney (D-New York).[85]

Once again, the BCG study mentioned above found a silver lining in the glacial progression of women's pay. According to Silverstein, "If you walk down the streets of Manhattan, London, or Frankfurt today, and you ask 100 single men between the ages of 25 and 39 what they make, the women will make more. The shift is statistical. Older women who tended to be paid less are retiring and a new group of younger women, who had roughly equal education and started with roughly equal wages, are rising."[86] Worldwide, women's earned income is growing faster than men's (8.1 percent versus 5.8 percent). The reasons cited are higher female earners in the developed world combined with a rise in female participation in developing countries.[87]

Comparable worth presents a controversial solution to the pay-equity problem. From this perspective, workers doing different jobs should receive the same pay if those different jobs have equal inherent worth, that is, contribute equally to the firm's performance. As previously discussed, the Equal Pay Act requires that people holding equal positions receive equal compensation. Despite the act's existence, however, the pay of men and women remains disparate, due largely to the wage effects of labor market segregation, whereby jobs traditionally held by women pay less than their requirements or contributions might indicate. The persistent disparity between men's and women's median incomes has led some legal scholars and women's advocates to recommend comparable worth.[88] Advocates of comparable worth argue that differences in seniority and education cannot explain the fact that women still earn less than men. They argue that certain jobs are paid less just because they are traditionally held by women. Opponents of comparable worth counter that it is not pragmatic to apply comparable worth to the private sector, because the private sector lacks the public sector's civil service categories, which are fixed by legislation.[89] Their arguments are supported by a study that showed that inherent job worth is a subject that is difficult to measure reliably and accurately.[90]

The only recent attempt to institute a system of comparable worth has been in one state, New York. The New York State Fair Pay Act specifically disallows a defense that inequitable wage rates match the prevailing market; this effectively creates a system consistent with comparable worth. The Fair Pay Act was passed by the State Assembly but died in a State Senate committee for the fifth year in a row due to intense business lobbying and partisan opposition.[91] In general, the concept of comparable worth is receiving little attention these days. One exception was the confirmation of Chief Justice Roberts to the Supreme Court. In a memo Roberts wrote as a young White House lawyer in the Reagan administration, he described comparable worth as "staggeringly pernicious," bringing the concept back into the media for a short while.[92]

Sexual Harassment.   Sexual harassment in the workplace is a worldwide problem with negative consequences that are pervasive and ongoing. A recent meta-analysis of sexual harassment studies found that victims of sexual harassment suffered a range of negative outcomes such as decreased job satisfaction, lower organizational commitment, withdrawal from work, poor physical and mental health, and even symptoms of posttraumatic stress disorder.[93] The study also found that the organizational climate played a part in facilitating its occurrence.[94] This trend shows no sign of abating. Another study reported that the percentage of women who reported hearing sexually inappropriate comments rose 22 percent from 2006 to 2007, but it was difficult to ascertain whether the behavior had increased or a lowering of barriers between the sexes resulted in men speaking more openly in front of women.[95]

It is difficult to document fully the extent to which **sexual harassment** has become a major issue in American business today. With the increasing number of women in the workforce, however, it is understandable why sexual harassment has become a much-debated issue. Sexual harassment has been a high-profile issue ever since 1991, when Supreme Court nominee Clarence Thomas was accused of sexual harassment by Anita Hill, a former employee of the EEOC. The country witnessed days of televised hearings over the issue, and the event created a springboard for many women to come forward and publicly claim that they had been sexually harassed by coworkers in the past. The country was divided in its opinion of whether Hill had actually been sexually harassed by Thomas ten years earlier, and Thomas was eventually confirmed to a seat on the highest court. The Thomas hearings were a watershed event for sexual harassment. The hearings catapulted sexual harassment into the limelight, just as the escape of lethal gas from the Union Carbide plant in Bhopal, India, and the massive oil spill from the *Exxon Valdez* made workplace safety and environmental issues, respectively, national concerns.

Data from the EEOC report an escalating number of sexual harassment complaints. In 1986, 2,052 complaints were filed. By 2009, there were 12,696 sexual harassment complaints, 16 percent of which were filed by males.[96] Although the number of complaints in 2009 was still high, it is a decrease from the 15,889 complaints lodged in 1997.[97] With this background, let us now consider what Title VII and the EEOC have to say about sexual harassment as a type of sex discrimination.

The EEOC defines sexual harassment in the following way:

Unwelcome sexual advances, requests for sexual favors, and other verbal or physical conduct of a sexual nature constitute sexual harassment when submission to or rejection of this conduct explicitly or implicitly affects an individual's employment, unreasonably interferes with an individual's work performance, or creates an intimidating, hostile, or offensive work environment.

Implicit in this definition are two broad types of sexual harassment. First is what has been called **quid pro quo** harassment. This is a situation where something is given or received for something else. For example, a boss may make it explicit or implicit that a sexual favor is expected if the employee wants a pay raise or a promotion. Second is what has been referred to as **hostile work environment** harassment. In this type, nothing is given or received, but the employee perceives a hostile or offensive work environment by virtue of uninvited sexually oriented behaviors or materials being present in the workplace. Examples of this might include sexual teasing or jokes or sexual materials, such as pictures or cartoons, being present in the workplace.

To clear up common misconceptions, the EEOC indicates that sexual harassment can occur in a variety of circumstances that include but are not limited to the following:[98]

- The victim as well as the harasser may be a woman or a man. The victim does not have to be of the opposite sex.
- The harasser can be the victim's supervisor, an agent of the employer, a supervisor in another area, a coworker, or a nonemployee.
- The victim does not have to be the person harassed but could be anyone affected by the offensive conduct.

FIGURE 19-6

Examples of Sexual Harassment Complaints

- Being subjected to sexually suggestive remarks and propositions
- Being sent on unnecessary errands through work areas where coworkers have an added opportunity to stare
- Being subjected to sexual innuendo and joking
- Being touched by a boss while working
- Coworkers' "remarks" about a person sexually cooperating with the boss
- Suggestive looks and gestures

- Deliberate touching and "cornering"
- Suggestive body movements
- Sexually oriented materials being circulated around the office
- Pornographic cartoons and pictures posted or present in work areas
- Pressure for dates and sexual favors
- Boss's cruelty after sexual advances are resisted
- A boss rubbing employee's back while he or she is typing

Note: It should be noted that these are "complaints." Whether each item turns out to be sexual harassment or not in the eyes of the law is determined in an official hearing or trial.

- Unlawful sexual harassment may occur without economic injury to or discharge of the victim.
- The harasser's conduct must be unwelcome.

Figure 19-6 lists the kinds of experiences about which women are typically talking when they say they have been sexually harassed.

MERITOR SAVINGS BANK V. VINSON Prior to 1986, sexual harassment was not a specific violation of federal law. In a landmark case, however, the Supreme Court ruled in 1986 in *Meritor Savings Bank v. Vinson* that sexual harassment was a violation of Title VII. In this case, the court ruled that the creation of a "hostile environment" through sexual harassment violates Title VII, even in the absence of economic harm to the employee or a demand for sexual favors in exchange for promotions, raises, or the like. Remedies made available to the victims at that time included back pay, damages for emotional stress, and attorney fees.[99] We should reiterate that sexual harassment can be committed by women against men or by individuals of the same sex.

HARRIS V. FORKLIFT SYSTEMS The stage was set for another major Supreme Court ruling (*Harris v. Forklift Systems*) in 1993 that, many were hoping, would more clearly define what constituted sexual harassment. The court agreed to hear the case of a Tennessee woman, Teresa Harris, who claimed her boss (at Forklift Systems) made sexual remarks about her clothing, asked her to retrieve coins from his pants pockets, and once joked about going to a motel "to negotiate your raise." The lower courts had thrown out her lawsuit, arguing that she had only been offended and had not suffered any "severe psychological injury."[100]

The Supreme Court overturned the lower courts and ruled that employers can be forced to pay damages even if the workers suffered no proven psychological harm. Justice Sandra Day O'Connor, who wrote the court's unanimous decision, said that employees can be awarded damages as long as their work "environment would reasonably be perceived, and is perceived, as hostile or abusive."[101]

Another key part of the Supreme Court's ruling addressed the question of "from whose perspective is sexual harassment to be judged?" Historically, the courts had used the common-law concept of a "reasonable man." An appeals court ruling had argued that the standards of a "reasonable woman" should prevail when women charged harassment. In *Harris v. Forklift Systems*, however, the Supreme Court decided that a "reasonable person" standard would prevail and that it would more appropriately focus on the conduct, not the victim.

Finally, the Supreme Court's ruling on the question of "what constitutes sexual harassment" was less than definitive. Again, Justice O'Connor wrote:

Whether an environment is "hostile" or "abusive" can be determined only by looking at all the circumstances. These may include the frequency of the discriminatory conduct; its severity; whether it is physically threatening or humiliating, or a mere offensive utterance; and whether it unreasonably interferes with an employee's work performance.[102]

TITLE IX AND SEXUAL HARASSMENT   Many people do not realize that Title IX offers protection against sexual harassment in a way that is essentially similar to Title VII. Title IX, the law that bans sex discrimination at schools receiving federal funds, is best known in its sports context for the formula that determines if schools are providing women with fair opportunities to play sports. Schools can be sued for monetary damages under Title IX for knowingly allowing sexual harassment to take place. There are four parts to the burden of proof: (1) the school must be aware of the sexual harassment, (2) the school must fail to take steps to stop it, (3) the harassment must deny access to an educational opportunity, and (4) the harassment must take place in an educational setting.[103]

The Courts.   Supreme Court rulings underscore the importance of companies' being diligent in their efforts to discourage harassing behavior. For example, the Supreme Court ruled that employers may be held liable even if they did not know about the harassment or their supervisors never carried out any threatened job actions.[104] Clearly, employers must develop comprehensive programs to protect their employees from harassment.

When businesses develop comprehensive and clear programs to prevent sexual harassment, they are legally rewarded. The Supreme Court ruled that good faith efforts to prevent and correct harassment are one prong of an "affirmative defense" companies can employ when charged with harassment. The second prong is proving the employee failed to take advantage of opportunities the firm provided for correction or prevention.[105]

In 2009, the Supreme Court expanded the scope of allowable sexual harassment claims when they ruled that employees who were fired because they cooperated with a

ETHICS IN PRACTICE CASE

Matters of the Heart

During a recent summer, I worked at the liquor store of my best friend's stepfather. Sometimes during work hours, there would be just the two of us in the store. On numerous occasions, he made sexual comments to me about my body. He would also "accidentally" brush up against the front of me. Once he called me into his office to show me graphic pictures of girls in a pornographic magazine and asked why I had not posed for one. He seemed consumed with the female anatomy. The obvious ethical question forced me to choose between my friendship with the girl I had grown up with and my self-respect, which was being severely tested at that job. A temporary hold on my ideals won out over losing the best friend I had ever had.

1. Has sexual harassment taken place in this case, or is it just my imagination?
2. What would you have done in this situation?
   a. Continued this job without confronting the owner
   b. Quit and acted as if nothing had happened
   c. Confronted the owner to see if anything changed
   d. Other (describe)

Contributed Anonymously

sexual harassment investigation could sue for retaliation. Justice David Souter, writing for the seven judge majority, said, "Nothing in the statute requires a freakish rule protecting an employee who reports discrimination on her own initiative but not one who reports the same discrimination in the same words when her boss asks a question."[106]

Pregnancy Discrimination.   For some time, maternity leave has been an issue for women. In 1987, the Supreme Court upheld a California law that granted pregnant workers four months of unpaid maternity leave and guaranteed that their jobs would be waiting for them when they returned. Justice Thurgood Marshall argued, "By taking pregnancy into account, California's statute allows women, as well as men, to have families without losing their jobs."[107]

The **Pregnancy Discrimination Act of 1978**, an amendment to Title VII, requires employers to treat pregnancy and pregnancy-related medical conditions the same way as any other medical disability with respect to all terms and conditions of employment. Until recently, however, few women have felt protected by this law. Although the EEOC had been empowered to protect women against discrimination in pregnancy, it was not until 1991 that it won a significant case that caught the public's attention. In 1991, after 13 years of litigation, the EEOC announced a $66 million settlement by which AT&T would compensate 13,000 employees for job discrimination during pregnancy. The settlement came as a result of AT&T discriminating against women by restricting their leaves beyond that permitted by law.[108] As a result of the Pregnancy Discrimination Act, the concept of maternity leave is now outdated. In fact, companies are advised to make sure they do not have "maternity leave" policies. By using the term "maternity leave," companies imply that maternity is somehow different from other temporary disabilities.[109]

Pregnancy discrimination continues to present problems. According to EEOC statistics, pregnancy discrimination charges filed over the past five years have shown a steady increase, with the total claim count rising from 3,385 in 1992 to 6,196 in 2009.[110] Some of the increase may have been due to demographics, with aging baby boomers starting families while a majority of them work. Another cause may be corporate downsizing as employers are forced to get more work out of fewer people. They may see pregnant employees as unreliable—no longer able to work long hours and, after the child is born, the first to run home when baby gets sick.[111] The Family and Medical Leave Act has helped, but pregnancy discrimination remains an important issue. In recent rulings, the lower courts have not upheld "reproductive rights" as pregnancy discrimination. This means that a man who is fired because of his partner's pregnancy is not protected.[112] In addition, the courts have ruled that a company's refusal to provide contraception under the health plan, for men or women, is not discriminatory under the Pregnancy Discrimination Act.[113]

Fetal Protection Policies.   Another form of sex discrimination was identified as the Supreme Court ruled that **fetal protection policies** constituted sex discrimination. The decisive case was *UAW v. Johnson Controls, Inc.* Johnson Controls, like a number of other major firms, developed a policy of barring women of childbearing age from working in sites in which they, and their developing fetuses, might be exposed to such harmful chemicals as lead. Johnson Controls believed it was taking an appropriate action in protecting the women and their unborn children from exposure to chemicals. Eight current and former employees and the United Auto Workers (UAW) union, who argued that the policy was discriminatory and illegal under Title VII of the Civil Rights Act, brought a class-action lawsuit against Johnson Controls. A U.S. district court ruled in the company's favor, and the Chicago-based U.S. Court of Appeals for the Seventh

Circuit affirmed that decision. The U.S. Supreme Court later reversed the appellate court, arguing that the policy was on its face discriminatory and that the company had not shown that women were more likely than men to suffer reproductive damage from lead.[114]

Even though the Supreme Court ruled that injured children, once born, would not be able to bring lawsuits against the company, several experts think it likely that such lawsuits will indeed be filed in the future. One expert said, "A mother can waive her own right to sue, but she can't waive the right of a child to bring suit. So, five or ten years down the line you might see children born with cognitive disabilities, and they could independently sue businesses." The UAW does not dispute this possibility and asserts that it should provide a major impetus for companies to make workplaces safer.[115] OSHA has identified reproductive health hazards as an area likely to experience an increase in litigation over time.[116]

A Historic Class Action. In 2010, the Ninth U.S. Circuit Court of Appeals ruled that the largest civil rights class action in history against a private employer could go forward.[117] Walmart is seeking review of the case by the Supreme Court.[118] Approximately 2 million women who have worked for Walmart are claiming that they were paid less than men in comparable positions even when they achieved higher performance ratings and had greater seniority; they were promoted less often than men to in-store management positions, and they were made to wait longer to advance.[119] The National Organization of Women (NOW) had designated Walmart as a "Merchant of Shame" for sex discrimination in pay, promotion, and compensation and exclusion of insurance coverage for women's contraception.[120]

The U.S. Chamber of Commerce filed a friend-of-the-court brief on behalf of Walmart's initial appeal arguing that the size of the class would "force employers to settle these huge claims no matter what their merit, effectively depriving them of their right to trial; and to encourage employers to adopt the kinds of quota-like policies that Title VII was enacted to prevent."[121] The court disagreed, saying, "focusing on the potential size of a punitive damage award would have the perverse effect of making it more difficult to certify a class the more egregious the defendant's conduct or the larger the defendant. Such a result hardly squares with the remedial purposes of Title VII."[122]

Other Forms of Employment Discrimination

Much of the attention surrounding employment discrimination has focused on racial and sexual discrimination. There are, however, other important forms of discrimination that represent critical issues for business today. It is important for managers to understand the many forms that discrimination can take in an increasingly diverse workforce and where courts currently stand on those issues.

Age Discrimination. A revealing survey by ExecuNet, a career networking and job search service, found that 82 percent of senior executives believed age discrimination was a serious problem in the workplace. Even more telling is the fact that 94 percent of the respondents, who were almost all in their 40s and 50s, felt that they had been the victim of age discrimination at some time. Specifically, they felt that age had taken them out of the running for a particular job.[123] This presents a serious concern as the workforce is rapidly aging and the recession has forced many older workers to remain in the workforce. In the United States, people over 65 constitute the fastest-growing worker age group, with the older age segments growing most quickly.[124] Between 2000 and 2008, the number of workers over 65 rose 25 percent, the number between 70 and

74 rose 32 percent, the number between 75 and 79 rose 38 percent, and the number over 80 rose 67 percent.[125]

The Supreme Court several years ago tackled a particularly challenging question regarding reverse age discrimination. The case stemmed from a collective bargaining agreement between General Dynamics and the UAW that allowed the company to eliminate health benefits for future retirees while grandfathering in those who were 50 years of age or older at the time of the agreement. Dennis Cline was between 40 and 50 years old when the agreement occurred, so he would not be eligible for the benefits. He joined with other employees in the same age range to bring an action before the EEOC. The EEOC's efforts to get the parties to settle informally failed, and so the employees sued General Dynamics in federal district court. The district court dismissed the case, saying that the ADEA did not protect the younger from the older. The Sixth Circuit Court of Appeals reversed the district court, saying that the ADEA prohibits discrimination against any individual because of age. General Dynamics appealed to the Supreme Court, and they agreed to hear the case because different district courts had come to different conclusions on this issue. The EEOC filed a "friend of the court" brief in favor of the employees. Ultimately, the Supreme Court reversed the Sixth Circuit Court, saying that the ADEA does not prohibit favoring the old over the young.[126]

In 2007, the EEOC revised their regulations to clarify that fact. There are some states with laws that prohibit discrimination against younger workers on the basis of age, and in those states such discrimination continues to be unlawful.[127] The revised regulations also stipulate that it is okay under the ADEA for employers to ask for date of birth or age on a job application, but the EEOC will scrutinize such applications closely to make certain the request is for permissible purposes and not those purposes prohibited by the act. Similarly, help wanted ads that request an applicant's age are not in and of themselves a violation, but the EEOC will scrutinize them closely too.[128]

In 2010, the U.S. Supreme Court raised the standard of proof for age discrimination cases in their decision regarding *Gross v. FBL Financial Services*. When Congress amended Title VII of the Civil Rights Act, it did not make a similar amendment for the ADEA and that has been a source of confusion in the courtroom since then.[129] The court's opinion in *Gross* raised the standard of proof for employees charging age discrimination by disallowing "mixed motives" defenses. In other words, employees must do more than prove age was a motivating factor. Employees must show that "but for" age, the discrimination would not have occurred.[130] At this writing, Congress is considering legislation that would supersede the *Gross* decision. Speaking in favor of that proposed legislation, EEOC Chair Jacqueline Berrien said, "The *Gross* decision was a startling departure from decades of settled precedent developed in federal district and intermediate appellate courts. It erected a new, much higher (and what will often be an insurmountable) legal hurdle for victims of age-based employment decisions. Indeed, recent case law reveals that *Gross* already is constricting the ability of older workers to vindicate their rights under the ADEA, as well as other anti-discrimination statutes."[131]

Religious Discrimination. Religious discrimination is a relatively new issue in the workplace, but it is one that is growing quickly: complaints nearly doubled in the past ten years.[132] According to Jeanne Goldberg, senior attorney adviser for the EEOC, changes in the composition of the workforce have led to changing immigration patterns that increase the number of people from parts of the world with less familiar religious beliefs and practices. "The workforce also is aging," says Goldberg. "The older people get, the more important religion becomes to them."[133]

The Workplace Religious Freedom Act (WRFA) has been introduced each year for more than a decade and is again being reviewed by the U.S. Congress.[134] Its purpose is to disallow workplace restrictions on religious expression when those restrictions are arbitrary and/or unfair. According to the act's lead sponsor, John Kerry (D-Massachusetts), "No worker should have to choose between keeping a job and keeping faith with their cherished religious beliefs."[135] Senator Orrin Hatch (R-Utah) has joined Kerry as a cosponsor in the Senate, while Carolyn McCarthy (D-New York) heads the fight for the WRFA in the House of Representatives.[136] "Federal law requires employers reasonably to accommodate employees' religious belief and practice, but courts have weakened that protection. WRFA will restore the level of protection that religious freedom deserves," says Hatch.[137] McCarthy adds, "In today's economy, people shouldn't have their jobs put at risk because they want to, say, wear a yarmulke, or have a long beard."[138]

Opposition to the act comes mainly from business groups who fear it will be burdensome.[139] Backed by a broad-based coalition of religious groups, this legislation is designed to respond to the increase in incidents of religious bias by requiring employers to do more to accommodate religious beliefs. Under current standards, employers do not have to accommodate an employee's request if it imposes more than a "de minimus," or minimal, cost on the employer. The proposed legislation would raise the definition of undue hardship to "significant difficulty," effectively raising the employer's burden of proof.[140] The proposed standards reduce the requirements for employers to make reasonable accommodation to the three areas in which most requests for accommodation fall: religious clothing, grooming, and scheduling of religious holidays. This narrowing is intended to address previous concerns that the bill was too broad.[141]

Accommodation often requires ingenuity. IBM was faced with a challenge when a newly hired Muslim woman showed up for work the first day and was told she had to have her picture taken for the employee identification badge. For Muslim women, wearing the veil is a sign of modesty, and so the new employee objected on religious grounds to showing her face. IBM officials came up with an accommodation that met the needs of all involved. She had her picture taken in a veil and that was the picture on the employee identification badge she wore each day. In addition, a woman photographer took her picture without the veil for a second badge she would carry in her bag. It was agreed that if she ever needed to show that badge she would only do so to a female security officer.[142]

Color Bias. Color bias is another issue that raises new challenges for the workplace. As part of the Civil Rights Act of 1964, discrimination based on color has been illegal for a long period of time. As a practical matter, however, color bias has been largely ignored until recently. As we mentioned previously, **color bias** is one of the focal points of the EEOC's E-Race initiative. As part of that, they have clarified the definition of color discrimination. "Even though race and color clearly overlap, they are not synonymous. Thus, color discrimination can occur between persons of different races or ethnicities, or between persons of the same race or ethnicity." Although Title VII does not define "color," the courts and the EEOC read "color" to have its commonly understood meaning—pigmentation, complexion, or skin shade or tone. Thus, color discrimination occurs when a person is discriminated against based on their lightness, darkness, or other color characteristic. Title VII prohibits race/color discrimination against all persons, including Caucasians."[143]

Most people do not realize that race and color are considered to be separate by law and both are covered by law, so many cases go unreported."[144] Nevertheless, some situations do surface. In June 2009, the EEOC sued a Puerto Rico–based furniture company for allegedly permitting a Puerto Rican store manager to harass a dark-complexioned Puerto Rican sales associate. The manager taunted him about his skin color (e.g., asking why he was "so black") and then fired him for complaining.[145]

ETHICS IN PRACTICE CASE

Workplace Training or Religious Discrimination?

For six months, I worked as a receptionist at a local doctor's office that employed about 30 people. The owner and head practitioner was a member of a religious cult. During business hours, everything seemed normal for a doctor's office of this size, but during the two-hour lunch break, all of the employees had to go upstairs and go "on course." These mandatory courses encompassed everything from communication skills to office efficiency. They were all designed by a man who founded the religious cult of which my boss was a member. Granted that they were business teachings, other staff members and I felt that these teachings were heavily weighted with religious undertones.

For example, one of the most important keys to these lessons was that you had to understand every word. After every exercise we were individually tested to make sure that we knew all of the words. Most of the words that I didn't understand could not be found in the dictionary, because they came straight from the man's religious teachings. Whenever I questioned my boss about a word, it usually led into a long discussion about the cult leader's works, and I would have to read paragraphs out of the religious teachings to "fully understand" the meaning. To me, it felt as though I was being brainwashed, and from then on I scheduled my university classes during this course time.

My dilemma was, did the doctor have the right to insist that we submit to such "teachings," which made us uncomfortable?

1. Is any form of religious discrimination or harassment taking place in this case?

2. What ethical issues arise in this case?

3. If you were faced with this dilemma, what action would you take?

Contributed by Allison Grice

Sexual Orientation and Transgender Discrimination.   Corporations have been faster than governments in instituting protections for lesbian, gay, bisexual, and transgender (LGBT) employees. As of 2009, 85 percent of the *Fortune* 500 companies include sexual orientation in their nondiscrimination policies and a majority (57 percent) provide health benefits for same-sex domestic partners.[146] The greatest growth has been in prohibition of gender identity discrimination in the *Fortune* 500. In 2000, only three companies prohibited discrimination based on gender identity, but in 2009, 35 percent had instituted gender identity discrimination protections.[147] The higher a company's *Fortune* ranking, the more likely it is to provide protections for LGBT employees. Of the *Fortune* 10, nine prohibit discrimination based on sexual orientation, eight provide partner health benefits, and six prohibit discrimination based on gender identity.[148]

Business has been generally supportive of proposed federal and state legislation that would extend LGBT protections. The Business Coalition for Workplace Fairness, composed of over 50 major corporations, is pushing for federal legislation to extend protections to both sexual orientation and gender identity. The group supports the federal Employment Non-Discrimination Act (ENDA), a bipartisan piece of federal legislation that was introduced in the U.S. House of Representatives in 2007. It passed the House, but has not progressed further as of this writing. Various versions of ENDA have been introduced in Congress every year since 1994.[149]

Gender identity, among other issues, addresses the special challenges for business of the treatment of transgender and transsexual employees. "Transgender" refers to a person who identifies with his or her opposite sex and acts accordingly. "Transsexual" refers to a person who is undergoing or has undergone sex change surgery.[150] This is not a new workplace issue. In 1993, the Washington State Supreme Court upheld Boeing Company's 1985 firing of a male software engineer who dressed in women's clothes and insisted on using the women's restroom while the sex-change operation was pending. The court ruled that discomfort with one's biological sex was not a handicap.[151] What is new is the opinion of the courts and the stance that corporations have begun to take since that day. In June 2004, the Sixth U.S. Circuit Court of Appeals (which covers Michigan, Ohio, Kentucky, and Tennessee) heard the case of a transsexual Ohio firefighter who had been fired. In the first such action by a federal court, the court ruled that Title VII of the Civil Rights Act of 1964 protects transsexuals and that the sex-stereotyping doctrine covers people who change their sex.[152] In 2010, the Eighth Circuit Court decided in favor of a motel clerk whom the company had deemed too masculine for a daytime front desk clerk position.[153] According to InsideCounsel, "The ruling confirms a legal principle that recently has gained support in circuit courts across the country: Although Title VII does not deal with sexual orientation, the statute protects individuals from discrimination for breaking gender stereotypes, the courts have found."[154]

The concept of gender identity and its legal protections continues to evolve, but the trend against gender stereotyping carries implications for future protections for various gender identity issues. InsideCounsel offers employers the following advice, "Employers across the nation should be scrutinizing their policies and practices with regard to discrimination against transgender and transsexual people as states pass laws prohibiting discrimination on the basis of gender identity and courts interpret existing civil rights laws to protect those individuals."[155]

Affirmative Action in the Workplace

Affirmative action is the taking of positive steps to hire and promote people from groups previously discriminated against. The concept of affirmative action was formally introduced to the business world in 1965, when former President Lyndon B. Johnson signed Executive Order 11246, the purpose of which was to require all firms doing business with the federal government to engage in affirmative actions to accelerate the movement of minorities into the workforce. Few people realize, however, that the federal government did not make a real commitment to affirmative action until the administration of former President Richard M. Nixon, who revived the practice of racial hiring preferences.[156] Companies today have affirmative action programs because they do business with the government, have begun the plans voluntarily, or have entered into them through collective bargaining agreements with labor unions.

The Range of Affirmative Action Postures

The meaning of affirmative action has changed since its introduction. It originally referred only to special efforts to ensure equal opportunity for members of groups that had been subject to discrimination. More recently, the term has come to refer to programs in which members of such groups are given some degree of definite preference in determining access to positions from which they were formerly excluded.[157]

Daniel Seligman identified four postures in two groupings that define the range that affirmative action may take.[158] He categorized the following affirmative action postures as "soft" or "weak":

1. *Passive nondiscrimination.* This posture involves a willingness in hiring, promotion, and pay decisions to treat the races and the sexes alike. This stance fails to recognize that past discrimination leaves many prospective employees unaware of or unprepared for present opportunities.

2. *Pure affirmative action.* This posture involves a concerted effort to enlarge the pool of applicants so that no one is excluded because of past or present discrimination. At

the point of decision to hire or promote, however, the company selects the most qualified applicant without regard to sex or race.

Postures that Seligman termed "hard" or "strong" were as follows:

3. *Affirmative action with preferential hiring.* Here, the company not only enlarges the labor pool but systematically favors minorities and women in the actual decisions as well. This could be thought of as a "soft" quota system.
4. *Hard quotas.* In this posture, the company specifies numbers or proportions of minority group members that must be hired.

Over the past 30 years, much confusion has surrounded the concept of affirmative action, because it was never clear which of the aforementioned views was being advocated by the government. In hindsight, we can now see that the government was advocating positions based on whichever posture it thought would work, or based on the particular candidate and political party in office at the time. Early on, "soft" or "weak" affirmative action (Postures 1 and 2) was advocated. It became apparent, however, that these postures were not as effective in getting the results desired. Therefore, "hard" or "strong" affirmative action (Postures 3 and 4) was later advocated. The real controversy over affirmative action began with the use of soft quotas and "preferential hiring" (Posture 3) and "hard quotas" (Posture 4). Today, when people speak of affirmative action, they are typically referring to some degree of preferential hiring, as in Postures 3 and 4. Figure 19-7 summarizes the key Supreme Court decisions on affirmative action.

FIGURE 19-7 Key Supreme Court Decisions on Affirmative Action

Year	Case	Issue	General Finding
1978	*Regents of the University of California v. Bakke*	Admission to medical school	Race deemed a legitimate factor but ruled against strict quotas
1979	*United Steelworkers v. Weber*	Admission to private employer training program (Kaiser)	Quotas acceptable if temporary and addressing a clear imbalance
1980	*Fullilove v. Klutznick*	Set asides for minority contractors	Set asides acceptable due to narrow focus and limited intent
1986	*Wygant v. Board of Education*	Layoff policy that protected minorities	Preferential layoffs unacceptable—greater injury than hiring policy
1987	*United States v. Paradise*	Hiring of state trooper in Alabama	Strict quotas accepted only because there was persistent and pervasive racism
1989	*City of Richmond v. Croson*	Construction set asides for black-owned firms	AA unconstitutional unless racial discrimination proven widespread in industry
1995	*Adarand Constructors, Inc. v. Peña*	Federal affirmative action set asides	AA must pass "strict scrutiny" test of compelling interest and narrow tailoring
1996	*Hopwood v. University of Texas Law School*	Admission to law school	Rejected legitimacy of diversity as a goal for AA
2003	*Grutter v. Bollinger*	Admission to law school	Race can be a factor (invalidates *Hopwood*)
2006	*Parents v. Seattle* and *Meredith v. Jefferson*	School integration	Unconstitutional to consider race when assigning students to schools
2009	*Ricci v. DeStefano*	Firefighter lieutenant and captain exams	Unconstitutional to discard exams due to concerns about disparate impact

The Concept of Preferential Treatment

A number of different arguments have been set forth both for and against the concept of **preferential treatment**, which undergirds affirmative action. The underlying rationale for preferential treatment is the principle of **compensatory justice**, which holds that whenever injustice is done, just compensation or reparation is owed to the injured party or parties.[159] Many people believe that groups discriminated against in the past (for example, women, blacks, Native North Americans, and Mexican Americans) should be recompensed for these injustices by positive affirmative action. Over the years, deliberate barriers were placed on opportunities for minorities—especially African Americans. These groups were prevented from participating in business, law, universities, and other desirable professions and institutions. Additionally, when official barriers were finally dropped, matters frequently did not improve. Inequalities became built into the system, and although mechanisms for screening and promotion did not intentionally discriminate against certain groups, they did favor other groups. Thus, the view that we can and should restore the balance of justice by showing preferential treatment became established as a viable option for moving more quickly toward economic equality in the workplace and in our society.[160]

The Concept of Reverse Discrimination

The principal objection to affirmative action and the reason it has become and remained controversial is that it leads to **reverse discrimination**. In 2009, the Pew Research Center conducted a survey that supported a finding that has held strong for 20 years. The public, in general, supports affirmative action when it is described as simply providing opportunities for previously disadvantaged groups. When the question is rephrased to include providing preferential treatment to minorities, the approval rate plummets by half.[161] The possibility of reverse discrimination is at the core of the controversy surrounding affirmative action.

The courts have often made it more difficult for the plaintiff to win a case of reverse discrimination by setting the standard of proof higher for the plaintiff in these cases. The EEOC has rejected that approach and adopted a policy of pursuing all forms of discrimination in the same manner. On the EEOC Web site they explain,

> *Although a plaintiff may prove a claim of discrimination through direct or circumstantial evidence, some courts take the position that if a white person relies on circumstantial evidence to establish a reverse discrimination claim, he or she must meet a heightened standard of proof. The Commission, in contrast, applies the same standard of proof to all race discrimination claims, regardless of the victim's race or the type of evidence used. In either case, the ultimate burden of persuasion remains always on the plaintiff.*[162]

In the 2009 *Ricci v. DeStefano* case, the Supreme Court found in favor of the plaintiffs, ruling that they were victims of reverse discrimination when the city threw out firefighter exams that the plaintiffs had passed. The city was concerned that too few minorities passed the test and so disparate impact litigation might ensue.

The Adarand Decision and Strict Scrutiny

The 1995 case of *Adarand Constructors Inc. v. Peña* (115 S. Ct. 2097) was a turning point in affirmative action. In this case, the Supreme Court ruled 5 to 4 that all government action based on race must meet the **strict scrutiny** standard of judicial review. Strict scrutiny has two components: the program or policy (1) must meet a compelling government interest and (2) must be tailored narrowly to meet the program or policy objectives. Although the ruling does not declare affirmative action to be unconstitutional, it sets extremely high standards for any program to pass.[163]

The effects of the Adarand decision are still being felt. An intense round of court cases followed the decision, as affirmative action programs were put to the strict scrutiny test. These cases resulted in some landmark decisions, such as *Hopwood v. The State of Texas*, in which the Fifth Circuit Court held that using race as a consideration in University of Texas Law School admissions did not pass the strict scrutiny test. In June 1995, former President Clinton issued a memorandum to all programs that use race, ethnicity, or gender as a consideration in decisions. The directive said that any program must be eliminated if it creates a quota or a preference, causes reverse discrimination, or continues after the goal of equal opportunity has been achieved. Although the Adarand decision applies to federal programs only, the private sector is feeling its effect because it sheds light on the actions the courts may take.[164] However, some argue that its application has been inconsistent and arbitrary, limiting its usefulness as a tool for assessing how the courts will respond to specific affirmative action programs.[165]

The Future of Affirmative Action

The buying power of minority groups is increasing dramatically, and that has led to an increase in business's interest in diversity programs in general and affirmative action in particular. The University of Georgia's Selig Center charts the growth of consumer groups, and their findings are instructive. Hispanic buying power has grown 307 percent, from $212 billion in 1990 to $862 billion in 2007. In comparison, the buying power of non-Hispanics in the United States grew 125 percent during the same period. Black buying power grew 167 percent during that period, compared to 134 percent for the total population. In addition, more blacks are starting their own businesses. The number of black-owned businesses increased 45 percent from 1997 to 2002, a time period in which the overall number of U.S. businesses grew by only 10 percent.[166] This growth in economic impact may be part of the reason that the public attitude toward affirmative action is becoming more positive. The Pew Research Center found that this "once contentious" issue no longer splits the nation as it once did. In 1995, 58 percent of respondents favored affirmative action; by 2007, the number had risen to 70 percent.[167] Nevertheless, resistance to affirmative action remains, as evidenced by Michigan voters who supported a ban against affirmative action after the Supreme Court upheld the right of universities to consider race in admissions.[168]

Despite the inconsistency in public opinions, business appears to be moving toward a consensus based on bottom-line considerations. Increasing minority buying power and influence is leading companies to want to undertake voluntary programs to increase the diversity in their workforce and their bottom lines. In one of life's ironies, the EEOC had to warn companies of the dangers of voluntary affirmative action. Former EEOC Chair Naomi Earp said that firms must be careful to not base employment decisions on race or any other protected category, even when the goal is greater diversity. According to Earp, customer preferences have never been an acceptable reason to discriminate in employment and reference to a global market is not sufficient justification either.[169] The legality of some diversity practices remains unsettled, and thus they may be risky. These include offering incentives for managers to achieve a diverse workforce or promoting affinity groups, formed by employees along race or gender lines.[170]

Gilbert Casellas, a former EEOC chair who now represents employers, believes that corporate diversity policies may be "outpacing the law" because companies are now eager to improve their diversity.[171] Companies know that being diverse provides them with advantages, such as recruiting a diverse and talented workforce. Companies can and should still strive to achieve workforce diversity, but they must do so in a way that follows best practices such as consistent standards and transparent practices.

Summary

This chapter addresses several subgroups of employee stakeholders whose job rights are protected by law. The United States became serious about the problem of discrimination by enacting the Civil Rights Act of 1964, which prohibited discrimination on the basis of race, color, religion, sex, or national origin. Laws covering age and disabilities were passed later. The EEOC was created to assume the major responsibility for enforcing the discrimination laws. Like other federal agencies, the EEOC has had problems. However, on balance it has done a reasonable job of monitoring the two major forms of discrimination: disparate treatment and disparate impact. Discrimination issues discussed in this chapter include issues of racial discrimination, including the plights of African Americans, Asian Americans, Hispanics, and women moving into professional/managerial positions; pay equity; comparable worth; sexual harassment; pregnancy discrimination; fetal protection policies; age discrimination; and religious discrimination. In addition, new and evolving discrimination issues such as sexual orientation, gender identity, and color bias as separate from race were discussed.

Affirmative action, the taking of positive steps to hire and promote people from groups previously discriminated against, was one of the government's answers to the problem of discrimination. Considerable controversy has surrounded the question of how far affirmative action should go. There is evidence that attitudes toward affirmative action are changing as the global economy brings a more diverse workforce and customer base. Firms should follow best practices when designing diversity programs. Sound stakeholder management requires companies to strive to be fair in their employment practices.

Key Terms

affirmative action, p. 657

Age Discrimination in Employment Act (ADEA), p. 636

Americans with Disabilities Act (ADA), p. 638

bona fide occupational qualification (BFOQ), p. 636

Civil Rights Act of 1991, p. 640

color bias, p. 655

comparable worth, p. 648

compensatory justice, p. 659

disparate impact, p. 643

disparate treatment, p. 643

Equal Employment Opportunity Commission (EEOC), p. 641

Equal Pay Act of 1963, p. 636

essential functions, p. 638

fetal protection policies, p. 652

four-fifths rule, p. 644

hostile work environment, p. 649

major life activities, p. 640

preferential treatment, p. 659

Pregnancy Discrimination Act of 1978, p. 652

protected groups, p. 632

quid pro quo, p. 649

reasonable accommodations, p. 638

reverse discrimination, p. 659

sexual harassment, p. 649

strict scrutiny, p. 659

Title VII of the Civil Rights Act of 1964, p. 636

undue hardship, p. 638

Discussion Questions

1. List the major federal discrimination laws and indicate what they prohibit. Which agency is primarily responsible for enforcing these laws?
2. Give two different definitions of discrimination, and provide an example of each.
3. What effect do you think the Americans with Disabilities Act (ADA) is having on businesses? Explain your answer.
4. Explain the dilemma of affirmative action versus reverse discrimination. Do you think the Supreme Court is headed in the right direction for handling this issue? Explain.
5. Should preferential treatment be used in university admissions? Explain your answer.

CASE 31

Walmart and Its Associates: Efficient Operator or Neglectful Employer?*

In the past decade, the primary criticism of Walmart, one of the world's largest companies, has been its impact on communities and small merchants. Anti-sprawl activists and small-town merchants, in particular, have taken issue with the company moving into their communities.[1] In *Case 1—Walmart: The Main Street Merchant of Doom*, these issues, along with Walmart's international growth and impact, were presented in some detail.

In the past few years, however, other issues concerning the company have become important as well and have begun dominating the news. In particular, Walmart's treatment of its employees has raised many issues in public and business discussions. Paradoxically, Walmart refers to its employees as "associates," a term intended to bestow a more lofty status than the term "employees."

Many people do view Walmart as an excellent provider of jobs in communities, and in spite of criticisms that have been raised, people continue to seek out employment with Walmart. Though it has high turnover, it is viewed by countless job seekers as a stable place to work, and some individuals have sought to establish careers at the company. In 2010, Walmart was ranked in the top ten "Most Admired Companies" in the annual *Fortune* magazine rankings.[2] In spite of Walmart being ranked highly for years, *Fortune* writer Jerry Useem asked, "Should we admire Walmart?" He goes on to say, "Some say it's evil. Others insist it's a model of all that's right with America. Who are we to believe?"[3] Figure 1 presents some recent corporate facts about Walmart and its associates.

Many different employee-related issues with respect to Walmart have been the focus of a great deal of news coverage in the past few years. The company has been accused of hiring too many part-time workers; offering jobs that are actually dead-end; paying low wages and poor benefits; forcing workers to work "off-the-clock," that is, to work overtime without overtime pay; and taking advantage of illegal immigrants. Over the

years, the company has also been accused of gender discrimination against women, who occupy most jobs at the company. Coupled with these allegations of employee treatment, the company, which currently is not unionized, has fought unions and unionization everywhere it locates.

LOW PAY, HARD WORK, QUESTIONABLE TREATMENT

Walmart is the nation's largest employer. It employs 2.1 million worldwide.[4] As such, it is not surprising that it has a large number of interactions with employees, and these interactions will be both positive and negative. Walmart claims to offer "good jobs, (and) good careers," but a number of employees have become vocal in recent years about their working conditions at the company. As with many retailers and service industries, Walmart is accused of offering low pay and few benefits. Many of these employees have been angered by the disparity between their low wages and the company's high profits.[5]

ONE PERSON'S EXPERIENCE

Journalist Barbara Ehrenreich, author of the best-seller *Nickel and Dimed: On (Not) Getting by in America,*" spent three weeks working at a Walmart to get insights into whether many of the claims she had heard about Walmart's treatment of employees was true. Ehrenreich claimed she'd heard stories about Walmart workers being locked in stores overnight and being asked to work extra hours without overtime pay. During her three weeks there, she said she saw one facet of the mega-retailer that most people who shop there never get to see. She remembered workers having to crouch behind racks of clothing to chat with coworkers because her department head forbade talking among workers during work hours.[6] Ehrenreich complained that it was undignified for women in their 50s to have to resort to such behavior on the job.

Further, she observed that many of the store's cheapest items were often unaffordable to the workers who sold them because of their low pay. She observed: "when you work for a company who you can't afford to buy their product, you're in trouble." She went on,

---

* This case was prepared by Archie B. Carroll, University of Georgia. Updated in 2010.

FIGURE 1 Recent Facts about Walmart

Walmart:

- Employs more than 2.1 million "associates" worldwide, more than 1.4 million in the United States alone.
- Is a *diverse* employer. It has more than 257,000 African-American associates, 41,000 Asian associates, 171,000 Hispanic associates, more than 869,000 women, and more than 430,000 associates over the age of 50.
- Employs the majority of its associates in full-time status.
- Pays a full-time hourly wage of $11.75 an hour and higher in urban areas.
- Provides insurance for 1.2 million associates and family members, making it among the nation's largest providers of private sector health insurance.
- Received the following employee-related accolades in a recent year:

2008 Employer of the Year, National Association of Governors' Committees on People with Disabilities

2008 Top Ten—Employees with a Disability, Careers and the Disabled

2008 Top Companies for Female Executives, National Association of Female Executives

2008 Best Companies for Multicultural Women, *Working Mother* magazine

2008 Diversity Elite—Top Ten (#3), Hispanic Business

2008 Top 50 Companies for Diverse Managers to Work (#3), *Diversity MBA*

2008 Top 100 Employers (#22), *The Black Collegian*

2008 Best Companies for Asian Pacific Americans, Asian Enterprise

2008 Best Diversity Companies for Hispanics, Hispanic Network

2008 40 Great Organizations for Women of Color to Work, *Women of Color* magazine

2008 Corporation of the Year, National Association of Hispanic Publications

2008 Top 35 Companies for Executive Women, National Association for Female Executives

Source: Corporate Facts, Walmart by the Numbers, March 2010, http://walmartstores.com/pressroom/factsheets/#CorporateFacts. Accessed August 1, 2010.

"Here is this store that's oriented toward the lower end of the economic spectrum, but not low enough [for its own workers]." She said on one occasion she had to go to the local food bank and she was mistaken for another Walmart worker who had just been there.[7]

Of course, some people would say that there is nothing wrong with low pay and few benefits if a business can still find workers willing to work there. After all, in a free market, this is the way the economic system works. And, indeed, one reason Walmart has been so efficient and has contributed to nationwide productivity increases is precisely because of its tight controls on labor costs. The McKinsey consulting group has said that Walmart was responsible for roughly 25 percent of the nation's productivity gains in the 1990s. Their low prices have also contributed significantly to low inflation. Financial guru Warren Buffett expressed the opinion that Walmart has contributed more than any other company to the economic vigor that is found in America.[8]

Working Off-the-Clock and Without Breaks

One of the most serious allegations of unfair treatment reported by some Walmart employees is that of being asked to "work *off*-the-clock." This means that employees are pressured to do overtime work for which they do not get paid. One employee reported that he was asked to work off-the-clock by both the store manager and the assistant manager. The allegation is that managers would wait until an employee had clocked out and then say something like, "Do me a favor. I don't have anyone coming in—could you stay here?" Before you knew it, four to five hours passed before you got away.[9] According to Walmart's *2009 Annual Report*, the company had, indeed, been the defendant in several cases containing allegations the company forced employees to work "off-the-clock" or failed to provide work breaks.[10]

In December 2008, Walmart agreed to pay up to $640 million to settle 63 suits alleging it routinely underpaid employees around the country. The settlement would close the majority of the long-running cases that the company has faced on this issue.[11]

The Pressure Is On

The company has blamed individual store and department managers for any unpaid overtime. They claim it is against company policy to not pay for overtime. However, there is evidence that managers have been under significant pressure from corporate headquarters to get more work done than can be done with the number of employees allowed. One attorney for an employee said that headquarters collect reams of data on every store and every employee and use sales figures to determine how many hours of labor it wants to allocate to each store. Then, the store managers are required to schedule fewer hours than allotted and their store performance is closely monitored on a daily basis. The store managers, in turn, put pressure on lower managers, and employees start feeling the pressure to work hours without pay. In another case, a former Walmart manager claimed that supervisors had been known to regularly delete hours from time records and even to reprimand employees who claimed overtime hours so the store could keep its labor costs under control.[12]

LABOR UNION RESISTANCE

Because of employee complaints and desires to have higher wages and more generous benefits, Walmart employees have been targeted by union organizers for decades. Walmart's huge size and number of employees allows the firm to increasingly "set the standard for wages and benefits throughout the U.S. economy."[13]

A TYPICAL "ASSOCIATE"

The experience of Jennifer McLaughlin, age 22 at the time, an employee at the Paris, Texas, Walmart is typical of many of the company's employees. Jennifer lived in a modest apartment complex with her one-year-old son and drives to the store five days a week and slips on her blue vest with "How May I Help You?" inscribed on the back. She works at a frenzied pace, often feeling there aren't enough workers to do all that has to be done. She feels stressed out; as she says, "They push you to the limit. They just want to see how much they can get away with without having to hire someone else." According to McLaughlin, she had been three years with the firm, earned less than $20,000 a year, and says, "I'm considered high paid." She continues: "The way they pay you, you cannot make it by yourself without having a second job or someone helping you, unless you've been there for 20 years or you're a manager."[14] Jennifer is the type of worker the union organizers try to get to sign a card indicating their willingness to vote for a union should a representation vote be held.

UNIONIZATION ATTEMPTS

Across the country, workers in many states have tried to get unions organized, but so far they have not had much success. According to one report, employees at more than 100 stores in 25 states, including the store in Paris, Texas, have been trying to get union representation. Walmart has tried in various ways to fight the union organizing efforts. The company has engaged in actions some of which have been judged to be in violation of federal labor laws. Walmart has been held to be in violation of the law in ten separate cases in which the National Labor Relations Board has ruled that it has engaged in illegal activities such as confiscating union literature, interrogating workers, and discharging union sympathizers.[15] According to one management consultant, Walmart will go to great lengths to keep unions out.

At the time of writing, there are no unions in any part of Walmart. Back in 2000, the meat-cutting department at a Walmart in Jacksonville, Texas, voted to join the United Food and Commercial Workers (UFCW) union, becoming the only Walmart store that had successfully unionized. The company responded quickly. Within two weeks, Walmart totally eliminated its meat-cutting departments throughout the company nationwide.[16] The company claimed it took this action as part of a strategy to have meat cut by outside vendors and supplied differently rather than as a decision to eliminate the union.

The UFCW has been most aggressively trying to unionize Walmart across the country. Several full-time union organizers have traveled the country trying to convince employees to agree to a union vote in their store. The UFCW, which represents 1.4 million workers in the grocery and retail industry, has representatives in many different cities attempting to convince workers to sign a card indicating they want a union vote held at their store. According to the National Labor Relations Board, a workplace needs 30 percent of its workers to sign cards calling for a union election to have one held. Unions often try to get 50 percent of the employees to sign a card, because they want to increase their chances of winning.[17]

SUCCESS IN UNION RESISTANCE

There are several reasons why the unions have not been successful in unionizing Walmart. First, many employees feel intimidated by the company and fear signing on with a union. They fear retaliation of some kind, and many of the employees cannot afford to lose their jobs. Second, Walmart has mastered the art and science of fighting unionization. At one point, the company had a "union avoidance program." In this program, the company, with its vast resources, will wear people down and even destroy their spirit.

One consultant said that each Walmart manager is taught to take attempts at union organizing personally and to consider that supporting a union is like slapping the supervisor in the face.[18] Walmart is considered to be a very sophisticated adversary when it comes to fighting unionization. Managers have been asked to call a 24-hour hotline if they ever see a hint of unionization taking place, and a labor team can be dispatched to a store under threat at a moment's notice.[19] Third, many Walmarts are located in southern states that do not have a history and tradition of unionization.[20] Regardless, unions in cities in the north continue, most recently in Chicago, ferociously fighting the company's plans to locate in historically union territory, but they have not had great success. These cities are hungry for jobs and cheap products, and these factors seem to win out.[21]

For its part, a Walmart spokesman says that the company is not anti-union, it is "pro-associate."[22] According to writer Karen Olsson, "Walmart has made it clear that keeping its stores union-free is as much a part of the culture as door greeters and blue aprons."[23]

USE OF UNDOCUMENTED IMMIGRANTS

Several years ago, a series of predawn raids by federal agents were conducted in which they rounded up 250 illegal immigrants working as cleaning crews in 61 Walmarts across 21 states. Although technically they were not employees of the company, the company was accused by federal officials of knowing that its contractors were using the illegal immigrants as employees. The Immigration and Customs Enforcement program claimed it has wiretaps revealing that Walmart knew contractors were using undocumented workers in their cleaning crews.[24]

Walmart continues to fight against the charges, because it reports that the company was cooperating with the government for as long as three years in federal investigations in Chicago and Pennsylvania. Walmart reports that it was led to believe that it was not a target of the investigation and that it did not sever its ties with the contractors because federal officials had asked them to leave the relationships in place during

their investigations. Walmart claimed that it was told it would be given a heads-up before any arrests were made in its stores, but that did not happen.[25]

Walmart claims that it did what it could to ensure that its contractors were hiring legal workers, both before and after the raid. Antidiscrimination provisions of the immigration code limit an employer's ability to investigate an employee's legal status, the company claimed. The company claimed that as far back as in 1996, the Immigration and Naturalization Service (INS) filed a complaint against Walmart for requiring prospective hires who were not U.S. citizens to show more verification than that required by law. The company paid a $60,000 fine and became very hesitant to ask for more assurances about the status of its contractors' employees, the company claims.[26]

ENDING RELATIONSHIPS

Walmart claimed that beginning in 2002 it began to end its relationships with outside cleaning contractors. The company concluded it could typically save money by having its own crews cleaning and polishing the floors. By October 2003, when the raid occurred, fewer than 700 stores (18 percent) were still using contractors. This was down to half of the stores that were using outside contractors in 2000. The company said it adopted a new written contract in 2002 that included stronger contractual commitment by the outside contractors that they were complying with all federal, state, and local employment laws. The company admitted that it unwittingly may have still been doing business with some of the contractors that were in violation and that their own investigations revealed they were dealing with companies with different corporate identities and names that made it difficult to eliminate suspected violators.[27]

SEX DISCRIMINATION CHARGES

The most serious employee issues Walmart continues to face are accusations of gender discrimination against women. In 2001, six women filed a gender bias lawsuit against Walmart, claiming they were discriminated against. The case, *Dukes v. Walmart*, started as an EEOC complaint by Betty Dukes, the lead plaintiff, who claimed she had been trying to get promoted from the cashier ranks for nine years.[28] In a landmark decision in June of 2004, a federal judge in San Francisco ruled that the sex discrimination lawsuit could proceed as a class-action lawsuit, affecting as many as

1.6 million current and former female employees who have worked for the company since December 26, 1998.[29] In February 2007, a federal appeals court upheld the 2004 decision that Walmart must face the class-action bias claim. Walmart appealed the decision but lost. It has been said that the company stands to lose billions of dollars should it be found guilty of sex discrimination.[30] The lawsuit, which has been called the "largest private civil rights case ever,"[31] has the potential to go on for years and doubtless will have significant repercussions for Walmart and other companies in the retail and other industries.

THE ALLEGATIONS

Lawyers for the plaintiffs presented various statistical analyses supporting their allegations of sex discrimination. They presented detailed statistical models documenting that Walmart paid their full-time female workers 5–15 percent less than full-time males doing the same jobs. The lawyers also contended that the disparities between females and males increased as employees moved up in the management ranks.[32] Plaintiffs also claimed that Walmart's 2001 payroll statistics, the year the lawsuit was filed, also revealed discriminatory patterns such as the following:

- Female workers in hourly jobs earned $1,100 less than men.
- Women managers earned $14,500 less than their male counterparts.
- 65 percent of Walmart's hourly employees were female, but two-thirds of the company's managers were men.
- On average, it took men just 2.86 years to get promoted to assistant manager, but it took women 4.38 years, despite better performance ratings.[33]

Individual cases also documented allegations of sex discrimination against the company. The case of Gretchen Adams is illustrative. Adams, the mother of four, took an hourly job at the Walmart in Stillwater, Oklahoma, in 1993. Adams was quickly promoted to manager of the deli department, where she supervised 60 workers and flew around the country training hundreds of other workers. She learned that a man she had trained was making $3,500 more than her, and she was told it was "a fluke." She witnessed other men leapfrog past her, and she never landed the job of store manager she says she was promised. Adams claimed she complained and "they told me where to go." She quit the company at the end of 2001.[34]

Other women made sworn statements that Walmart had denied them requests to be placed in a management training position leading to a salaried position, denied them jobs as support managers in favor of men who had less seniority or qualifications, gave promotions to men with less experience, and were fired for not going along with alleged acts of sexual harassment.[35]

A summary of the major allegations against Walmart includes three major areas. First, women claim they have been denied equal promotions. Second, women claim they have been paid less for the same jobs, even when they have more experience. Third, women claim they are subjected to sexist actions and gender stereotyping.[36]

DID TOP MANAGEMENT KNOW?

Lawyers for the plaintiffs are developing the argument that top managers at Walmart knew about the sex bias that was taking place in the company. The lawyers are preparing to argue that women complained to corporate executives, including then CEO Lee Scott, about pay disparities or sexism and received very little response. They also argue that information was shared with board members and that outsiders complained and got little or no response from corporate offices.[37]

THE COMPANY'S DEFENSE

Walmart has long argued that it treats its female employees fairly. The company has said that women do not apply for promotion as often as men, and this accounts for the underrepresentation of women.[38] The main argument by the company has been its opposition to the lawsuit being categorized as a class-action lawsuit. The company argued that decisions about employees are made at the individual store level and that a class-action lawsuit is too unwieldy because it thinks it should be able to present evidence defending itself against each individual plaintiff's claims and that this would not be possible in a class-action trial. Walmart claims that in a class-action lawsuit of this size, it means that store managers will not be given the opportunity to explain how they made individual compensation and promotion decisions.

The company argued in its appeal of the class-action judgment that the class was certified under laws intended to provide injunctive relief, that is, to stop a particular practice, but that the judge ruled that the class can also seek monetary damages that the company does not think applies to the case. Part of the monetary relief could be punitive damages, but for these to apply, it has to be proven that Walmart management "fostered or recklessly ignored discriminatory practices." The judge concluded that whereas the individual decisions were made at specific store locations, there was some evidence of a corporate culture of gender stereotyping that may have affected the decisions made at the store level.[39] Judge Martin Jenkins was not ruling on the merits of the case, but was simply saying there was some evidence of a corporate culture permeating the organization that may be related to the discrimination, and thus he allowed the case to move forward as a class action.

In April 2010, a federal appeals court ruled that the gender discrimination lawsuit could move forward as a class action. It has been estimated that if the company lost this lawsuit, it could cost Walmart upward of $1 billion. In addition, a loss would be a terrible blow to its reputation and much-improved corporate image.[40]

CHANGES IN LABOR PRACTICES AT WALMART

Partially as a result of criticism and bad publicity Walmart has been receiving in recent years, the company announced some changes that were planned to improve conditions for its workers. In 2004, then CEO Lee Scott outlined the changes at one of its annual shareholders' meeting in Fayetteville, Arkansas, but it may take several years before the true impact of the changes take place and are felt throughout the company.[41]

One change would include the creation of a compliance group to oversee workers' pay, hours, and breaks. The company is also testing a new program that will alert cashiers when it is time for them to take a meal break. Another change is the implementation of a new system that will require employees to sign off on any changes that are made to their time cards. The company also plans to implement software that will force managers to adhere to state employment rules regarding areas such as how late teenagers can work. While announcing these new policies, Scott mentioned several times that he was tired of the adverse publicity that the company was getting.[42]

WALMART'S CHARM OFFENSIVE

Walmart has been battered by adverse publicity in recent years and has been working to improve its image. Some of the articles aimed at the company included the following: "Attack of the Wal-Martyrs,"[43] "Bruised in Bentonville,"[44] and "The Unending Woes of Lee Scott (CEO)."[45] Its economic woes have been chronicled as "Wal-Mart's Midlife Crisis."[46] But, beginning in about 2005, the company ratcheted up its charm offensive by trying to enhance its public image. Then-CEO Lee Scott admitted the company was trying to improve its image by being more open to its critics and trying to take specific steps to improve the way the world perceived the company. He admitted that when growth was easier, they could ignore their critics, but as the share price slowed its growth, the company had to start reaching out and being more responsive to the concerns raised.[47]

SPECIFIC ACTIONS

Walmart has sought to improve its image with stakeholders on four fronts. First, in the area of outreach, the company opened offices in eight major cities in an attempt to improve community relations and be responsive to local critics. Second, the company met with several activist groups seeking to improve its environmental impact. Third, the company hired Business for Social Responsibility (BSR), the nonprofit organization, to help it establish better relations with antisweatshop advocates and to strengthen its global labor monitoring program. Fourth, the company set up quick-response teams in Washington and at its Arkansas headquarters, with the help of a public relations firm, so that it could be more responsive to public criticism.[48] It appears that Walmart has finally realized the legitimacy of the "stakeholder effect": "As companies grow and develop, some stakeholders become more important than others, and new stakeholders sometimes emerge."[49] In 2009, one writer was exclaiming how Walmart's image had moved from demon to darling, but in the world of public relations, retaining a solid corporate image is a challenging task.[50]

A NEW CEO

In 2009, CEO Lee Scott relinquished his position, and the board elected Mike Duke to be the new CEO effective February 1, 2009. Scott would remain as chairperson of the board's executive committee until 2011 and would remain active in lobbying for the company and in corporate green initiatives. Duke has a "nice guy" reputation, is very low-key, and is known to be a strategic thinker and risk taker.[51]

In 2010, Walmart continued its emphasis on sustainability and corporate philanthropy. The company unveiled an environmental labeling program for its products in a decision that some say may redefine the design and makeup of consumer goods sold around the globe.[52] And the company also announced that it planned to ramp up its donations to the nation's food banks to a total of about $2 billion over the next five years.[53]

QUESTIONS FOR DISCUSSION

1. Identify and describe the major ethical issues facing Walmart and the likely stakeholders to be affected.

2. Walmart has been said to have excessive power in its relationship with communities. How is its manifestation of power with employees similar to or different than with communities? Which is the most serious issue? Why?

3. Are many of the allegations by employees at Walmart just reflections of the changing social contract between companies and their workers? Are many of the so-called problems just the free-enterprise system at work? Discuss.

4. Regarding the various labor practices discussed in this case, do they reflect immoral or just amoral management actions?

5. Is the practice of being required to "work off-the-clock" an unethical practice or just "to be expected" in the modern world of work? After all, many salaried employees are expected to work "until the job is done" no matter how many hours it takes.

6. Is it wrong for Walmart to fight unionization? Sam Walton always felt the company should function as one big happy family and that unions were to be resisted. What is your evaluation of the union opposition?

7. Regarding the allegations of sex discrimination, does it sound like the company has been guilty of systemic discrimination?

8. If Walmart can effectively argue that women are contributors to their plight by not applying for promotions or for seeking fewer responsibilities to accommodate family priorities, should the company be held to be in violation of sex discrimination laws because the statistics reveal differences between women and men?

9. Conduct Web-based research on Walmart and update allegations and lawsuits against the company.

ENDNOTES

1. Charles Fishman, "The Wal-Mart Effect and a Decent Society: Who Knew Shopping Was So Important," *Academy of Management Perspectives* (August 2006), 6–25.

2. Anna Bernasek, "The World's Most Admired Companies," *Fortune* (March 22, 2010), 122.

3. Jerry Useem, "Should We Admire Wal-Mart?" *Fortune* (March 8, 2004), 118–120.

4. Doris Burke, "Planet Wal-Mart," *Fortune* (May 3, 2010), 27.

5. Karen Olsson, "Up Against Wal-Mart," *Mother Jones* (March/April 2003), 54–59.

6. Tammy Joyner, "Author Had Eyes Opened at Work," *Atlanta Journal Constitution* (June 27, 2004), Q1.

7. Ibid.

8. George F. Will, "Waging War on Wal-Mart," *Newsweek* (July 5, 2004), 64.

9. Olsson, 58.

10. Wal-Mart's 2009 Annual Report, 47.

11. Miguel Bustillo, "Wal-Mart to Settle 63 Suits over Wages," *The Wall Street Journal* (December 24, 2008), B1.

12. Olsson, 58.

13. Ibid., 55.

14. Ibid.

15. Ibid.

16. Ibid.

17. Cora Daniels, "Up Against the Wal-Mart," *Fortune* (May 17, 2004), 112–120.

18. Olsson, 56.

19. Daniels, 116.

20. Ibid.

21. "Unions vs. Wal-Mart: Belaboured," *The Economist* (May 29, 2010), 30–32.

22. Ibid.

23. Olsson, 58.

24. Ann Zimmerman, "After Huge Raid on Illegals, Wal-Mart Fires Back at U.S.," *The Wall Street Journal* (December 19, 2003).

25. Ibid.

26. Ibid.

27. Ibid.

28. Cora Daniels, "Women vs. Wal-Mart," *Fortune* (July 21, 2003), 79–82.

29. Ann Zimmerman, "Judge Certifies Wal-Mart Suit as Class Action," *The Wall Street Journal* (June 23, 2004), A1.

30. David Kravets, "Wal-Mart Must Face Class-Action Bias Trial: Female Workers Say Men Were Paid More," *USA Today* (February 7, 2007), 3B.

31. Stephanie Armour and Lorrie Grant, "Wal-Mart Suit Could Ripple Through Industry," *USA Today* (June 23, 2004), 4B.

32. Ann Zimmerman, "Wal-Mart Adds to Legal Team," *The Wall Street Journal* (July 1, 2004), B2.

33. Lisa Takeuchi Cullen Wilson, "Wal-Mart's Gender Gap," *Time* (July 5, 2004), 44.

34. *Ibid.*

35. Stephanie Armour, "Rife with Discrimination: Plaintiffs Describe Their Lives at Wal-Mart," *USA Today* (June 24, 2004), 3B.

36. *Ibid.*

37. Stephanie Armour, "Women Say Wal-Mart Execs Knew of Sex Bias," *USA Today* (June 25, 2004), 1B.

38. "Wal-Mart: Trial by Checkout," *The Economist* (June 26, 2004), 64.

39. Zimmerman, 2004, B2.

40. Sean Gregory, "Walmart Faces a Gender Discrimination Suit," *Time* (April 29, 2010), http://www.time.com/time/business/article/0,8599,1985549,00.html. Accessed July 31, 2010.

41. Constance L. Hays, "Wal-Mart Plans Changes to Some Labor Practices," *The New York Times* (June 5, 2004), B2.

42. *Ibid.*

43. Barney Gimbel, "Attack of the Wal-Martyrs," *Fortune* (December 11, 2006), 125–130.

44. Andy Serwer, "Bruised in Bentonville," *Fortune* (April 18, 2005), 84–106.

45. Jon Birger, "The Unending Woes of Lee Scott," *Fortune* (January 22, 2007), 118–122.

46. Anthony Bianco, "Wal-Mart's Midlife Crisis," *BusinessWeek* (April 30, 2007), 46–56.

47. Robert Berner, "Can Wal-Mart Fit into a White Hat?" *BusinessWeek* (October 3, 2005), 94–96.

48. *Ibid.*, 96.

49. R. Edward Freeman, "The Wal-Mart Effect and Business, Ethics and Society," *Academy of Management Perspectives* (August 2006), 38–43.

50. Ann Zimmerman, "Wal-Mart's Image Moves from Demon to Darling," *The Wall Street Journal* (July 16, 2009), B1.

51. Suzanne Kapner, "Changing of the Guard at Wal-Mart," *Fortune* (March 2, 2009), 69–76.

52. Miguel Bustillo, "Wal-Mart to Assign New Green Ratings," *The Wall Street Journal* (July 16, 2009), B1.

53. Associated Press, "Wal-Mart Pledges to Give Food Banks $2B over Five Years," *USA Today* (May 13, 2010), 3B.

CASE 32

The Case of the Fired Waitress*

Ruth Hatton, a waitress for a Red Lobster restaurant in Pleasant Hills, Pennsylvania, was fired from her job because she was accused of stealing a guest-comment card that had been deposited in the customer comment box by a disgruntled couple.[1] The couple, who happened to be black, had been served by Hatton and were unhappy with the treatment they perceived they got from her. At the time of her firing, Hatton, age 53, had been a 19-year veteran employee. She said, "It felt like a knife going through me."

---

* This case was prepared by Archie B. Carroll, University of Georgia.

THE INCIDENT

The couple had gone to the Red Lobster restaurant for dinner. According to Hatton, the woman had requested a well-done piece of prime rib. After she was served, she complained that the meat was fatty and undercooked. Hatton then said she politely suggested to the woman that prime rib always has fat on it. Hatton later explained, based on her experience with black customers in the working-class area in which the restaurant was located, that the customer might have gotten prime rib confused with spare rib.

Upset Customer Leaves

Upon receiving the complaint, Hatton explained that she returned the meat to the kitchen to be cooked further. When the customer continued to be displeased,

Hatton offered the couple a free dessert. The customer continued to be unhappy, doused the prime rib with steak sauce, and then pushed it away from her plate. The customer then filled out a restaurant comment card, deposited it in the customer comment box, paid her bill, and left with her husband.

INADVERTENTLY THROWN OUT

Hatton explained that she was very curious as to what the woman had written on the comment card, so she went to the hostess and asked for the key to the comment box. She said she then read the card and put it in her pocket with the intention of showing it to her supervisor, Diane Canant, later. Hatton said that Canant, the restaurant's general manager, had commented earlier that the prime rib was overcooked, not undercooked. Apparently, the restaurant had had a problem that day with the cooking equipment and was serving meat that had been cooked the previous day and so was being reheated before being served. Later, Hatton said that she had forgotten about the comment card and had inadvertently thrown it out. It also came out that it is against Red Lobster's policy to serve reheated meat, and the chain no longer serves prime rib.[2]

HATTON'S FIRING

Canant said that she fired Hatton after the angry customer complained to her and to her supervisor. Somehow, the customer had learned later that Hatton had removed the comment card from the box. Canant recalled, "The customer felt violated because her card was taken from the box and she felt that her complaint about the food had been ignored." Referring to the company's policy manual, Canant said Hatton was fired because she violated the restaurant's rule forbidding the removal of company property.

NOT A BIG DEAL

Another person to comment on the incident was the hostess, Dawn Brown, then a 17-year-old student, who had been employed by the restaurant for the summer. Dawn stated, "I didn't think it was a big deal to give her the key (to the comment box). A lot of people would come and get the key from me."[3]

THE PEER REVIEW PROCESS

Hatton felt she had been unjustly fired for this incident. Rather than filing suit against the restaurant, however, she decided to take advantage of the store's peer review process. The parent company of Red Lobster, Darden Restaurants, four years earlier had adopted a peer review program as an alternative dispute resolution mechanism. Many companies across the country have adopted the peer review method as an alternative to lengthy lawsuits and as an avenue of easing workplace tensions.

SUCCESS OF PEER REVIEW PROGRAM

Executives at Red Lobster observed that the peer review program had been "tremendously successful." It helped to keep valuable employees from unfair dismissals, and it had reduced the company's legal bills for employee disputes by $1 million annually. Close to 100 cases had been heard through the peer review process, with only ten resulting in lawsuits. Executives at the company also said that the process had reduced racial tensions. In some cases, the peer review panels have reversed decisions made by managers who had overreacted to complaints from minority customers and employees.[4]

HATTON'S PEER REVIEW PANEL

The peer review panel chosen to handle Ruth Hatton's case was a small group of Red Lobster employees from the surrounding area. The panel included a general manager, an assistant manager, a hostess, a server, and a bartender, all of whom had volunteered to serve on the panel. The peer review panel members had undergone special peer review training and were being paid their regular wages and travel expenses. The peer review panel was convened about three weeks after Hatton's firing. According to Red Lobster policy, the panel was empowered to hear testimony and to even overturn management decisions and award damages.

TESTIMONY HEARD

The panel met in a conference room at a hotel near Pittsburgh and proceeded to hear testimony from Ruth Hatton, store manager Diane Canant, and hostess Dawn Brown. The three testified as to what had happened in the incident.

Through careful deliberations, the panelists tried to balance the customer's hurt feelings with what Hatton had done and why, and with the fact that a company policy may have been violated. Initially, the panel was split along job category lines, with the hourly workers supporting Hatton and the managers supporting store management. After an hour and a half of deliberations, however, everyone was finally moving in the same direction and the panel finally came to a unanimous opinion as to what should be done.[5]

QUESTIONS FOR DISCUSSION

1. What are the ethical issues in this case from an employee's point of view? From management's point of view? From a consumer's point of view?
2. Who are the stakeholders, and what are their stakes?
3. As a peer review panel member, how would you judge this case? Do you think Hatton stole company property? Do you think the discharge should be upheld?

4. Do you think the peer review method of resolving work complaints is a desirable substitute for lawsuits? What are its strengths and weaknesses?
5. If you had been Hatton, would you be willing to turn your case over to a peer review panel like this and then be willing to live with the results?

ENDNOTES

1. Margaret A. Jacobs, "Red Lobster Tale: Peers Decide Fired Waitress's Fate," *The Wall Street Journal* (January 20, 1998), B1, B4.
2. *Ibid.*
3. *Ibid.*
4. *Ibid.*
5. *Ibid.*

CASE 33

After-Effects of After-Hours Activities: The Case of Peter Oiler*

Few people question an employer's right to control an employee's behavior on the job. However, when an employer takes action based on an employee's off-duty conduct, questions of ethics arise. More than half of all states prohibit firing based on various types of after-hours conduct.[1] Federal law prohibits firing that is discriminatory. Some cases, however, fall through those cracks. If you were the judge in the Peter Oiler lawsuit, how would you rule?

WORK HISTORY

By all accounts, Peter Oiler was an excellent employee with 20 years of experience working with Winn-Dixie. His responsibilities included driving a 50-foot truck, loading supplies from the company warehouse, driving them to Winn-Dixie stores throughout southeastern Louisiana, and unloading them. Oiler received above-average performance ratings and was promoted three times during his tenure at Winn-Dixie. He adhered to company policies in all ways, including his attire and presentation.[2] In his private time, Oiler liked to take on the persona of "Donna" at home, donning women's clothing, accessories, makeup, wigs, and fake breasts.

Though he usually stayed home, Oiler would sometimes go out as Donna with his wife and friends to restaurants, the shopping mall, or church.[3]

THE SITUATION ARISES

In 1999, Oiler had a meeting with his supervisor Greg Miles. A year earlier, Oiler had been bothered by a rumor that had been circulating that he was gay and so he asked Miles to take action against it. At the meeting, Miles asked if the rumors had subsided and Oiler said that they had. Miles asked Oiler why the rumors bothered him and Oiler said it was because he is transgender instead of gay. When Miles asked what transgender was, Oiler explained that it refers to people who have feelings about their gender that are sometimes inconsistent with their anatomical sex. Oiler added that he had no intention of ever changing his sex or living as a woman full-time.[4] He was a happily married, heterosexual man, about to celebrate his 25th wedding anniversary.

WINN-DIXIE RESPONDS

Miles said he would have to check the company policy about transgender employees. On November 1, 1999, Miles informed Oiler that a supervisor had seen Oiler dressed as a woman off-duty. Oiler said that he did sometimes dress as a woman but never on-duty. Miles responded that Oiler's activities could harm

---

* This case was prepared by Ann K. Buchholtz, Rutgers University. Updated in 2010.

Winn-Dixie's image and so the company was asking him to resign. He recommended that Oiler look for another job. Oiler said he did not want another job because he was happy at Winn-Dixie. He continued to work in his position. From November 4, 1999, to January 5, 2000, Winn-Dixie managers had five meetings with Oiler. They told him to find another job because he was about to be terminated. They said they had no problem with his work performance, but his off-duty dressing as a woman could hurt Winn-Dixie's public image. Oiler reiterated that he would not wear women's clothing at work. At the January 5, 2000, meeting, Oiler was terminated.[5]

THE AFTERMATH

Oiler sued Winn-Dixie for gender discrimination. He argued that the company fired him because he did not fit the company's gender stereotype of a man. Ken Choe, an American Civil Liberties Union attorney who represented Oiler, said, "Everyone agrees he was not terminated for anything related to his job performance. All of the cross dressing behavior occurred off the job." In September 2002, a federal judge in New Orleans ruled that transgendered people are not a protected class and so laws against sex discrimination do not apply to them.[6]

Although Oiler lost in court, he may have won the battle for public opinion. According to Oiler, "Quite a few people told me, 'You're not hurting anybody. You do your job extremely well. How can they do this?'" Oiler adds that Winn-Dixie's reaction has made other workers feel less secure. "The common theme (among former coworkers) was, 'If they can get away with this, what can they do to me?' It's got a lot of people saying, 'Where's the limit?'"[7]

ADDENDUM

At this writing, there are no federal protections for gender identity though efforts to enact the Employment Nondiscrimination Act (ENDA) continue. The purpose of this legislation is to prohibit employment discrimination on the basis of actual or perceived sexual orientation or gender identity.[8] As of 2009, 176 *Fortune* 500 firms had gender identity protections for employees in place. Winn-Dixie was not one of them.[9]

QUESTIONS FOR DISCUSSION

1. What are the ethical issues in this case?
2. Who are the stakeholders, and how are they impacted by this situation?
3. Do you agree with the federal judge's decision? If you were the judge, what would you do?
4. A recently passed ordinance in New Orleans prohibited discrimination against off-the-job cross-dressing. However, the Winn-Dixie branch that fired Oiler is located just outside that jurisdiction. Does this affect your answer to question 2?
5. For what after-hours behavior do you feel it is appropriate to terminate an employee? For what after-hours behavior is it not appropriate? Where do you draw the line, and how would you describe that line if you were developing a policy to put into an employee manual?
6. What if Peter Oiler had been a highly visible, top-level manager of the company. Would this make the company's case stronger? Or does the employee's position matter at all?

ENDNOTES

1. Carolyn Hirschman, "Off Duty, Out of Work," *HR Magazine* (February 2003), 50–56.
2. http://www.aclu.org
3. Hirschman, 50–56.
4. http://www.aclu.org
5. *Ibid.*
6. Hirschman, 52.
7. *Ibid.*, 52.
8. http://www.hrc.org/laws_and_elections/enda.asp. Accessed July 31, 2010.
9. "State of the Workplace," HRC Foundation (February 12, 2009), http://www.hrc.org/about_us/7061.htm. Accessed July 31, 2010.

CASE 34

Is Hiring on the Basis of "Looks" Discriminatory?*

According to an attractive young woman, a student at Northwestern University, the same thing happens to her every time she goes shopping at Abercrombie & Fitch (A&F). On at least three occasions, store managers have approached her and offered her a job. This young woman, Elizabeth, measures in at 5′6″ and has long blond hair. She has an attractive, stylish appearance. Elizabeth looks like she belongs in an A&F catalog.[1]

Does this happen by coincidence to her? Apparently not. A former assistant manager for A&F said that it has been, in fact, company policy that managers approach attractive people and ask them if they wanted a job. The store philosophy has been that if you have the best-looking college kids working for you, everyone would want to shop there.[2]

NOTHING NEW?

Hiring on the basis of "looks," appearance, or physical attractiveness is nothing new. Certain industries have been doing it for years. In recent years, however, it has become part of a growing trend on the part of merchants who want to project a particular image. A&F is not the only store to engage in this practice. Retail chains, such as the Gap and Benetton, take pleasure in employing attractive people, often from different backgrounds and races. Allegations against A&F, however, have been that their classic American look is narrowly defined by such traits as blond, blue-eyed, and preppy. A&F finds these workers by recruiting on certain college campuses, sororities, and fraternities.[3]

PROVOCATIVE STRATEGY

According to a CBS News report, the image of A&F has been "party-loving jocks and bare-naked ladies living fantasy lives." A&F wants its sales reps to reflect what is up on its walls—cool and seductive. Elizabeth, mentioned before, says, "the skirts are getting shorter. The tops are getting smaller. That seems to be the trend and Abercrombie is going with that."[4] A&F once had a reputation for the classical, traditional

look, but that is apparently gone now. In its place is a provocative new strategy targeted toward teens and twenties. Apparently, the more parents get outraged by their approach, the larger their sales. With more than 600 stores and annual sales in excess of $1 billion, the company has become the leading teen retailer.[5]

LAWSUITS ALLEGE DISCRIMINATION

In recent years, some discrimination experts, as well as individuals who believe they have been excluded because of looks, have been raising the question of whether hiring employees on the basis of their "looks" is discrimination of some kind. In fact, a coalition of four organizations filed an employment discrimination lawsuit against A&F. The coalition filing the lawsuit included the Mexican American Legal Defense Fund, the Asian Pacific American Legal Center, the NAACP Legal Defense and Educational Fund, and the law firm of Lieff Cabraser Heimann & Bernstein, LLP. The nine Hispanic and Asian plaintiffs to the lawsuit claimed that A&F discriminates against people of color, including Latinos, Asian Americans, and African Americans, in its hiring practices, job assignments once hired, compensation, termination, and conditions of employment.[6]

ALLEGATIONS

The young adults who comprised the plaintiff group alleged that they were qualified to work at A&F but were either not hired or terminated because of their race, color, and/or national origin. The lawsuit asserted that A&F enforces a national, corporate policy of showing preference to white people for sales positions, desirable assignments, and favorable work schedules. The lawsuit details some of the practices claimed to be illegal, including recruiting, hiring, and maintaining a disproportionately white workforce, systematically discouraging minority applicants, and refusing to hire qualified minorities for positions to work on the sales floor. The lawsuit alleges that when minorities are hired, they are channeled into less prominent positions—the stockroom, overnight shift positions, and out of the public eye.[7]

THE "A&F LOOK"

The grievance goes on to claim that the company implements its discrimination in part through a

---

* This case was written by Archie B. Carroll, University of Georgia. Updated in 2010.

detailed and meticulous "Appearance Policy" that requires all brand representatives to exhibit the "A&F look." The lawsuit maintains that the company rigorously enforces the "A&F look" by vigilant scrutiny and monitoring of its stores by managers from the region, district, and national office. In addition, as part of the monitoring policy, stores have to submit to the corporate office each quarter a picture of their brand representatives who fit the "look." Then, the corporate office selects about 15 stores' pictures and holds them up as exemplary models and distributes them throughout their national network of stores. The pictures, it alleges, are almost invariably of white, young people.[8]

Specific Complaints

A representative for the Mexican American Legal Defense and Educational Fund said, "If you look at the material they put out, they are cultivating an all-white look." He went on, "It is difficult to understand why, given that their target age demographic is even more heavily minority than the rest of the population."[9] One recent graduate of Stanford University, a Filipino American, said he applied for a position at a store at which he previously worked, but was told, "We're sorry, but we can't rehire you because there's already too many Filipinos working here."[10]

Second Lawsuit

A&F was then named in a second lawsuit alleging discriminatory practices. This lawsuit, which was seeking class-action status, was filed on behalf of a woman who alleged that her application was denied because she is an African American. This suit was filed by Jesse Jackson's Rainbow/Push Coalition and three Philadelphia-area law firms.[11] According to AbercrombieLawsuit.com, a new consolidated class-action lawsuit was formed bringing the previous two lawsuits into one consolidated suit.[12]

THE A&F POSITION HAS SUPPORTERS

Representatives from A&F say that the company does not discriminate. A&F's director of communications said that the company likes hiring sales assistants, who they call "brand representatives," who look great. He said that the brand representatives are ambassadors to the brand and the company wants them to look great, project individuality and enthusiasm, and make the store a warm and inviting place to shop.[13]

Related Opinions

Some retailers defend the approach to hiring used by A&F insofar as it attempts to identify and use brand enhancers. For example, one senior industry analyst said, "Being able to find a brand enhancer, or what I call a walking billboard, is critical. It's really important to create an environment that's enticing to the community, particularly with the younger, fashionable market. A guy wants to go hang out in a store where he can see good-looking gals."[14] A New Orleans lawyer who represents many hotels and restaurants said, "Hiring someone who is attractive isn't illegal per se. But people's views on what's attractive may be influenced by their race, their religion, their age."[15] One former sales manager for L'Oréal said that she had perceived intense pressure to hire attractive saleswomen, even if they were not competent. She said that company managers tried to force her out when she ignored a directive to fire a woman that her top manager believed was not "hot" enough.[16]

RELEVANT LAWS AND SETTLEMENT

There are no federal laws that say you cannot discriminate on the basis of appearance. It is also acceptable for employers to have certain "grooming" (appearance) guidelines. However, it is against the law to discriminate based on a number of different personal characteristics such as gender, race, age, color, disability, and other legally protected personal features. The debate arises when someone suspects they were discriminated against because of a "protected characteristic," such as color, age, national origin, and so on, but the employer claims that this was not the case. Therefore, a plaintiff wishing to challenge the legality of "appearance" discrimination somehow has to link or associate appearance to discrimination on the basis of gender, race, age, disability, or some other legally protected characteristic.[17]

The two most likely laws someone might find relevant to "appearance" discrimination would be Title VII of the Civil Rights Act and the Americans with Disabilities Act. It should be added, however, that at least one state law (District of Columbia Human Rights Act) does make it unlawful to hire on the basis of personal appearance.[18] Therefore, a careful study of federal, state, and local laws is necessary to help judge these cases.

Settlement

The class-action lawsuit described earlier was finally settled, but A&F did not admit any guilt. A federal judge in San Francisco approved the class-action settlement, and the two sides announced an agreement that calls for the company to pay $40 million to several thousand minority and female plaintiffs. A&F also agreed to hire 25 diversity recruiters and a vice president for diversity and to pursue benchmarks so that its hiring and promotion of minorities and women reflect its applicant pool.[19] The agreement also stipulates that A&F is to increase diversity, not just in hiring and promotions but also in its advertisements and catalogs, which have for many years highlighted models who were predominantly white and who seemed to have just stepped off the football field or out of fraternities or sororities.[20]

Issue Never Goes Away

In 2009, an Oklahoma teen filed suit against A&F, claiming she was told her *hijab*, a headscarf she wore in keeping with her Muslim beliefs, was not consistent with the A&F "look."[21] The Council on American Islamic Relations (CAIR) advocated this lawsuit claiming it was a violation of Title VII of the Civil Rights Act. The complaint alleged that the interviewer said that any "headgear" was prohibited by the "Look Policy," and the company refused to make an exception for the young woman to wear her *hijab* for religious reasons. In its defense, an A&F spokesperson said, "We have a strong equal opportunity employment policy and we accommodate religious beliefs and practices when possible. We are confident that the litigation of this matter will demonstrate that we followed the law in every respect."[22]

As long as the A&F "look" is part of the company's image, these issues will continue to arise. After considering the practices of A&F and other employers, several questions are left for discussion: Is it legal to make employment decisions based on "looks" or appearance? If so, under what circumstances? Is it ethical to take such actions? If so, under what circumstances? Is it unethical to deny a person a job because of his or her appearance?

Questions for Discussion

1. What are the legal and ethical issues in this case?
2. What is your evaluation of the concept of the "A&F look?" Have you personally observed this concept in practice?
3. Are the employment practices of A&F discriminatory? Are they unfair? What ethical principles or precepts guide your analysis? Since Abercrombie did not admit guilt, does the settlement bring closure to this issue of "looks" discrimination?
4. What could A&F and other retailers be doing, that they are not doing, that would make its hiring practices less controversial?
5. Where do you draw the line on A&F's hiring practices? Are there acceptable ways in which they could pursue "the look" in employment? If so, how do you determine what is acceptable and what is not?

Endnotes

1. Steven Greenhouse, "Going for the Look, but Risking Discrimination," *The New York Times* (July 13, 2003), 10YT.
2. *Ibid.*
3. *Ibid.*
4. "The Look of Abercrombie & Fitch," CBSNews.com (December 5, 2003).
5. *Ibid.*
6. "Discrimination Lawsuit Filed Against Abercrombie & Fitch Co.," Afjustice.com (2003–2004).
7. *Ibid.*
8. *Ibid.*
9. "Abercrombie & Fitch Faces Discrimination Lawsuit," *USA Today* (July 14, 2004).
10. *Ibid.*
11. "Business Brief—Abercrombie & Fitch Co: Discriminatory Hiring Practices Are Alleged in a Second Lawsuit," *The Wall Street Journal* (November 20, 2003), 1.
12. AbercrombieLawsuit.com (January 6, 2004).
13. Greenhouse, 10YT.
14. *Ibid.*
15. *Ibid.*
16. *Ibid.*
17. Gerard Panaro, "Is Hiring on the Basis of Appearance Illegal?" BankersOnline.com (July 8, 2004).
18. *Ibid.*
19. Steven Greenhouse, "Abercrombie & Fitch Bias Case Is Settled," *The New York Times* (November 17, 2004), http://www.nytimes.com/2004/11/17/national/17settle.html. Accessed October 3, 2007.
20. *Ibid.*
21. "Abercrombie & Fitch Sued over Head Scarf," CBS News (September 18, 2009), http://www.cbsnews.com/stories/2009/09/18/national/main5320868.shtml. Accessed July 23, 2010.
22. Sarah Netter and Lindsay Goldwert, "Lawsuit: Muslim Scarf Not a Part of Abercrombie & Fitch 'Look,'" ABC News/Money (September 18, 2009), http://abcnews.go.com/Business/muslim-teen-denied-abercrombie-job-hijab/story?id=8608173. Accessed August 1, 2010.

CASE 35

The Case of Judy*

Judy was paralyzed from the neck down. She required help getting out of bed, getting dressed, and getting into a motorized wheelchair. Judy says that she still has the greatest ability of all: her mind, which is as sound as ever. She says that if she can find a way to attend the university, she will get a degree in public administration and she wants to have a career in that field.

JUDY COMES TO YOU

She has come to you, a vocational counselor at the state Department of Rehabilitation, as the first step in getting the funding she needs from the state in order to

---

* This case was reprinted from Norma Carr-Ruffino, *Managing Diversity*, 4th ed. (Needham Heights, MA: Pearson Custom Publishing, 2001). Used with permission.

pursue this educational and career goal. Your responsibilities are as follows:

- *Regarding education:* to predict the possibility and probability that an applicant will actually complete the educational program he or she enters.
- *Regarding occupation:* to predict the possibility and probability that an applicant will actually get and retain a job in the proposed field.
- *Regarding funds:* to allocate scarce state funds for rehabilitation in a manner that produces the best results for persons with disabilities and for society.

QUESTIONS FOR DISCUSSION

1. Considering Judy's situation and your responsibilities, what will your decisions be? What are the potential ethical challenges in this situation?
2. What will you say to Judy?

CASE 36

The Waiter Rule: What Makes for a Good CEO?*

As the topic of corporate governance has been in the news more and more during the past several years, it is useful to reflect on what boards of directors have to do in terms of their roles and responsibilities. Acting on behalf of shareholders, one of the board's most important jobs is selection of the CEO, who will provide strategic direction for the firm, and in turn, hire the top management team. But how does a board go about hiring a CEO? Certainly, this has got to be one of the toughest jobs of selection in the business world.

In recent years, so many contentious issues have surrounded CEOs that the board's task is no small one. Many CEOs have been implicated in ethics scandals, and many of them have been criticized for what the public considers excessive compensation. Today especially, boards want to be sure they hire CEOs with high integrity and impeccable character. It is a

---

* This case was prepared by Archie B. Carroll, University of Georgia.

lofty goal and things don't always turn out the way boards wish. With a record number of CEO firings in the past five years, it is little wonder boards of directors are always seeking insights as to how to make these selection decisions.

Business people are always on the alert for guidance, for suggestions, for tips that would make their hiring more successful or run more smoothly. But if an elusive quality such as character is so important, how does one gauge a prospective CEO's or top executive's character? Or, for that matter, how can we gauge the character of any level of management? Surely, this is a vital ingredient no matter what the level of management in the organization.

SWANSON'S UNWRITTEN RULES

In a recent (2006) *USA Today* article, it was revealed that Bill Swanson, CEO of Raytheon, the defense contractor based in Waltham, Massachusetts, that has 80,000 employees and more than $22 billion in annual sales, had published a booklet containing 33 brief leadership observations.[1] The booklet was titled *Swanson's*

Unwritten Rules of Management.[2] It turns out that Raytheon has given away 300,000 copies of the booklet to members of its own organization and to virtually anyone who inquires about it. The book is filled with commonsense maxims, observations, rules, and guidelines considered to be something of a cult hit in corporate America.[3] Among the 33 guidelines or rules compiled in the booklet is one rule that Swanson has said never fails in terms of helping to assess someone's character.

THE WAITER RULE

Known as the "Waiter Rule," the observation basically says that "A person who is nice to you but rude to the waiter, or to others, is not a nice person." A number of CEOs and other corporate executives have all agreed with the Waiter Rule. They basically concur that how a privileged corporate executive treats people in subordinate roles, whether they be waiters, clerks, maids, bellmen, golf caddies, or any other service-type worker, reveals insights into the executive's character that should be taken into consideration in hiring decisions.

Office Depot CEO Steve Odland recalls that when he was working in a restaurant in Denver many years ago, he spilled a glass of purple sorbet all over the expensive white gown of an apparently important and rich woman. Though it occurred over 30 years ago, he can't get the spill out of his mind. But what struck him most was her reaction to his careless spill. The woman responded in a very kind and understanding way. She kept her composure and in a calm voice said, "It's okay. It wasn't your fault." Years later, the now-CEO of Office Depot recalls what he learned about this incident: "You can tell a lot about a person by the way he or she treats the waiter."[4]

CHARACTER REVEALED

As it turns out, just about every CEO has a waiter story to tell. The opinion they hold in common, moreover, is that the Waiter Rule is a valid way to gain insights into the character of a person, especially someone who may be in a position of authority over thousands of workers. The cofounder of Au Bon Pain, the leading urban bakery and sandwich café, Ron Shaich, became CEO of Panera Bread. He tells the story of interviewing a woman for general counsel, who was "sweet" to him but turned "amazingly rude" to the person cleaning tables. She didn't get the job.[5]

Author Bill Swanson is quoted as having written, "Watch out for people who have a situational value system, who can turn the charm on and off depending on the status of the person they are interacting with."[6] Related to this observation, Steve Odland of Office Depot has been quoted as saying, "People with situational values have situational ethics, and those are people to be avoided."[7]

QUESTIONS FOR DISCUSSION

1. Is character an essential ingredient in ethical leadership? Is it especially important in managers? In leadership, especially among CEOs, is character important? Why?

2. Do you agree with the Waiter Rule? Does it provide useful insights into who might be an ethical or unethical leader? Should corporate boards consider character when hiring someone for the top position?

3. Is using the Waiter Rule too simplistic a guideline for hiring people in important positions such as CEO?

ENDNOTES

1. Del Jones, "CEOs Vouch for Waiter Rule: Watch How People Treat Staff," USA Today (April 14, 2006), B1.
2. William H. Swanson, *Swanson's Unwritten Rules of Management* (Raytheon, 2005).
3. David Leonhardt, "Rule No. 35: Reread Rule on Integrity," *The New York Times* (May 3, 2006).
4. Jones, *Ibid.*
5. *Ibid.*
6. Quoted in Jones (2006).
7. Quoted in Jones (2006).

Case Matrix

This case matrix provides a listing of the cases in the back of the book and shows how they can accompany the text chapters. A given case may be appropriate for multiple chapters.

Chapter Number

	1	2	3	4	5	6	7	8	9	10	11	12	13	14	15	16	17	18	19
	■	■	■										■	■		■			
	■	■											■		■				
	■	■				■													
	■	■	■		■	■													
	■	■		■												■			
	■	■			■					■									
	■	■	■			■										■	■		
	■	■					■	■								■	■		
		■	■					■											
					■	■	■			■								■	
			■								■	■							
			■		■	■	■	■						■					
			■			■					■			■					
			■			■	■							■					
		■			■										■				
							■	■									■		
							■	■					■				■		
							■	■											
				■			■	■									■		■
								■		■		■					■		
						■				■							■	■	
						■					■		■						
						■				■	■		■						
			■					■											
					■	■				■				■	■	■			
	■	■				■					■	■			■	■			
		■	■			■								■	■	■			
						■	■								■				
										■					■	■			
								■	■					■	■				
							■										■		■
							■	■									■	■	■
							■	■									■		■
							■										■		■
							■										■		
				■			■	■									■		

Endnotes

Chapter 1

1. "Thirty States Back Enron Shareholders," *USA Today* (January 10, 2007), B1.
2. William Powers, "Ethics: The Good Times Do End," *Newsweek* (November 2, 2009), B8.
3. "The Perp Walk," *BusinessWeek* (January 13, 2003), 86.
4. Matthew Philips, "The Neighborhood That Wrecked the World," *Newsweek* (December 29, 2008/January 5, 2009), 16–17.
5. Niall Ferguson, "The End of Prosperity?" *Time* (October 13, 2008), 36–44.
6. Ellen Simon, "Business Year in Review: At Least You've Got Your Health," *The Atlanta Journal-Constitution* (December 26, 2008), E4.
7. Mara Der Hovanesian, "Pointing a Finger at Wall Street," *BusinessWeek* (August 11, 2008), 80.
8. Associated Press, "A New Era of Responsibility," *USA Today* (January 21, 2009), 11A.
9. Liam Fahey and V. K. Narayanan, *Macroenvironmental Analysis for Strategic Management* (St. Paul: West, 1986), 28–30.
10. *Ibid.*
11. Joseph W. McGuire, *Business and Society* (New York: McGraw-Hill, 1963), 130.
12. "Interest Groups Have a Lot at Stake in Health Care Debate," *USA Today* (November 23, 2009), 15A.
13. Greg Ip, "Not Your Father's Pay: Why Wages Today Are Weaker," *The Wall Street Journal* (May 25, 2007), A2. Also see "Income, Poverty, and Health Insurance Coverage in the U.S.: 2005," issued August 2006, http://www.census.gov/prod/2006 pubs/p60-231.pdf.
14. "Television and Health," *The Sourcebook for Teaching Science*, http://www.csun.edu/science/health/docs/tv&health.html. Accessed June 2010.
15. Cited in Geoff Colvin, "TV Is Dying? Long Live TV!" *Fortune* (February 5, 2007), 43.
16. "Executives See Unethical Behavior, Media Criticisms as Threats," *Nashville Business Journal* (June 11, 2002).
17. Timothy Lamer, "Crooks in Suits," *World* (July 29, 2006), 29.
18. Linda S. Lichter, S. Robert Lichter, and Stanley Rothman, "How Show Business Shows Business," *Public Opinion* (November 1982), 10–12.
19. Nedra West, "Business and the Soaps," *Business Forum* (Spring 1983), 4.
20. "Facts and Figures about Our TV Habits," 2010, http://www.tvturnoff.org/. Accessed June 2010.
21. Michael Medved, "Hollywood's Business-Bashing: Biting the Hand That Is You," *USA Today* (February 3, 2010), 9A.
22. Associated Press, "American Dream Gets a Reality Check," *The Huntsville Times* (May 29, 2007), B8.
23. Gerald F. Seib, "U.S. Hurting in Wallet—and Spirit," *The Wall Street Journal* (December 18, 2009), A2.
24. Robert J. Samuelson, *The Good Life and Its Discontents: The American Dream in the Age of Entitlement, 1945–1995* (New York: Times Books, 1996).
25. Neil H. Jacoby, *Corporate Power and Social Responsibility* (New York: Macmillan, 1973), 186–188.
26. Linda DeStefano, "Looking Ahead to the Year 2000: No Utopia, but Most Expect a Better Life," *The Gallup Poll Monthly* (January 1990), 21.
27. Joseph Nolan, "Business Beware: Early Warning Signs for the Eighties," *Public Opinion* (April/May 1981), 16.
28. Charlotte Low, "Someone's Rights, Another's Wrongs," *Insight* (January 26, 1987), 8.
29. John Leo, "No More Rights Turns," *U.S. News & World Report* (October 23, 1995), 34.
30. John Leo, "A Man's Got a Right to Rights," *U.S. News & World Report* (August 4, 1997), 15.
31. John Taylor, "Don't Blame Me!" *New York* (June 3, 1991).
32. Pete Hamill, "A Confederacy of Complainers," *Esquire* (July 1991).
33. Charles J. Sykes, *A Nation of Victims: The Decay of the American Character* (New York: St. Martin's Press, 1991).
34. Aaron Bernstein, "Too Much Corporate Power?" *BusinessWeek* (September 11, 2000), 144–155.
35. "Is Wal-Mart Too Powerful?" *BusinessWeek* (October 6, 2003).
36. Edwin M. Epstein, "Dimensions of Corporate Power: Part I," *California Management Review* (Winter 1973), 11.
37. *Ibid.*
38. *Ibid.*

39. Keith Davis and Robert L. Blomstrom, *Business and Its Environment* (New York: McGraw-Hill, 1966), 174–175.

40. Bernstein, 146.

41. John Carey, "The Tobacco Deal: Not So Fast," *BusinessWeek* (July 7, 1997), 34–37; Richard Lacayo, "Smoke Gets in Your Aye," *Time* (January 26, 1998), 50; Jeffrey H. Birnbaum, "Tobacco's Can of Worms," *Fortune* (July 21, 1997), 58–60; and Dwight R. Lee, "Will Government's Crusade Against Tobacco Work?" (St. Louis, MO: Center for The Study of American Business, July 1997).

42. "Honesty Is a Pricey Policy," *BusinessWeek* (October 27, 2003), 100–101.

43. Thomas Donaldson and Thomas W. Dunfee, "Toward a Unified Conception of Business Ethics: Integrative Social Contracts Theory," *Academy of Management Review* (April 1994), 252–253.

44. "The New 'Social Contract,'" *BusinessWeek* (July 3, 1971).

45. "New Economy, New Social Contract," *BusinessWeek* (September 11, 2000), 182.

46. Wayne Visser, "Sustainability," in Wayne Visser, Dirk Matten, Manfred Pohl, and Nick Tolhurst, *The A to Z of Corporate Social Responsibility*, 2007 (West Sussex, England: John Wiley & Sons), 445–446.

47. United Nations, "Sustainable Development," 1987. *Report of the World Commission on Environment and Development.* General Assembly Resolution 42/187, December 11, 1987.

Chapter 2

1. Business for Social Responsibility, "Frequently Asked Questions," http://www.bsr.org/membership/faq.cfm#23. Accessed June 24, 2010.

2. Quoted in John L. Paluszek, *Business and Society: 1976–2000* (New York: AMACOM, 1976), 1.

3. Keith Davis, "Understanding the Social Responsibility Puzzle," *Business Horizon* (Winter 1967), 45–50.

4. *Ibid.*

5. See Morrell Heald, *The Social Responsibilities of Business: Company and Community, 1900–1960* (Cleveland: Case Western Reserve University Press, 1970), 12–14.

6. James W. McKie, "Changing Views," in *Social Responsibility and the Business Predicament* (Washington, DC: The Brookings Institute, 1974), 22–23.

7. *Ibid.*, 25.

8. Heald, 119.

9. McKie, 27–28.

10. Neil J. Mitchell, *The Generous Corporation: A Political Analysis of Economic Power* (New Haven, CT: Yale University Press, 1989).

11. Ronald E. Berenbeim, "When the Corporate Conscience Was Born" (A review of Mitchell's book), *Across the Board* (October 1989), 60–62.

12. For more on Andrew Carnegie, see his biography, *Andrew Carnegie*, by David Nasaw, The Penguin Press, 2006. For a book review, see Bob Dowling, "The Robin Hood Robber Baron," *BusinessWeek* (November 27, 2006), 116.

13. Berenbeim, 62.

14. Keith Davis and Robert L., Blomstrom, *Business and Society: Environment and Responsibility*, 3d ed. (New York: McGraw-Hill, 1975), 39.

15. Joseph W. McGuire, *Business and Society* (New York: McGraw-Hill, 1963), 144.

16. For a more complete history of the CSR concept, see Archie B. Carroll, "Corporate Social Responsibility: Evolution of a Definitional Construct," *Business and Society* (Vol. 38, No. 3, September 1999), 268–295.

17. Archie B. Carroll, "A Three-Dimensional Conceptual Model of Corporate Social Performance," *Academy of Management Review* (Vol. 4, No. 4, 1979), 497–505. Also see Archie B. Carroll, "The Pyramid of Corporate Social Responsibility: Toward the Moral Management of Organizational Stakeholders," *Business Horizons* (July–August 1991), 39–48.

18. Stuart Taylor, Jr., and Evan Thomas, "Civil Wars," *Newsweek* (December 15, 2003), 43–53.

19. Archie B. Carroll, "The Pyramid of Corporate Social Responsibility: Toward the Moral Management of Organizational Stakeholders," *Business Horizons* (July–August 1991), 39–48. Also see Archie B. Carroll, "The Four Faces of Corporate Citizenship," *Business and Society Review* (Vol. 100–101, 1998), 1–7.

20. *Ibid.*

21. http://www.chick-fil-a.com/?#winshape. Accessed July 5, 2010.

22. Jennifer Alsever, "Chiquita Cleans Up Its Act," *Business 2.0* (August, 2006), 58.

23. Unmesh Kher, "Getting Smart at Being Good...Are Companies Better Off for It?" *Time, Inside Business* (January 2006), A8.

24. Carroll, *Ibid.*, 1–7.

25. R. Edward Freeman, S. Ramakrishna Velamuri, and Brian Moriarty, "Company Stakeholder Responsibility: A New Approach to CSR," *Business Roundtable Institute for Corporate Ethics Bridge Paper* (2006), 10.

26. Walker Group, "Corporate Character: It's Driving Competitive Companies: Where's It Driving Yours?" Unpublished document, 1994.

27. For further discussion, see Duane Windsor, "Corporate Social Responsibility: Cases For and Against It," in Marc J. Epstein and Kirk O. Hanson, eds., *The Accountable Corporation: Corporate Social Responsibility*, Volume 3 (Westport, CN and London: Praeger, 2006), 31–50.

28. Milton Friedman, "The Social Responsibility of Business Is to Increase Its Profits," *The New York Times* (September 1962), 126. Also see "Special Report: Milton Friedman," *The Economist* (November 25, 2006), 79.

29. *Ibid.*, 33 (emphasis added).

30. Christopher D. Stone, *Where the Law Ends* (New York: Harper Colophon Books, 1975), 77.

31. Keith Davis, "The Case For and Against Business Assumption of Social Responsibilities," *Academy of Management Journal* (June 1973), 312–322.

32. F. A. Hayek, "The Corporation in a Democratic Society: In Whose Interest Ought It and Will It Be Run?" in H. Ansoff (ed.), *Business Strategy* (Middlesex: Penguin, 1969), 225.

33. Davis, 320.

34. Davis, 316.

35. For further discussion, see Duane Windsor, "Corporate Social Responsibility: Cases For and Against," in Marc J. Epstein and Kirk O. Hanson (eds.), *The Accountable Corporation, Volume 3, Corporate Social Responsibility* (Westport, Connecticut: Praeger, 2006), 31–50.

36. Cited in Aaron Bernstein, "Too Much Corporate Power," *BusinessWeek* (September 11, 2000), 149.

37. Archie B. Carroll and Kareem M. Shabana, "The Business Case for Corporate Social Responsibility," *International Journal of Management Reviews* (2009), 1–21.

38. "CSR—A Religion with Too Many Priests," *European Business Forum* (Issue 15, Autumn 2003). Also see "Getting Smart at Being Good…" *Time Inside Business* (January 2006), A1–A38.

39. Simon Zadek, *The Civil Corporation: New New Economy of Corporate Citizenship* (London: Earthscan, 2001). See also Lance Moir, "Social Responsibility: The Changing Role of Business," Cranfield School of Management, U.K.

40. Robert Ackerman and Raymond Bauer, *Corporate Social Responsiveness: The Modern Dilemma* (Reston, VA: Reston Publishing Company, 1976), 6.

41. Juha Näsi, Salme Näsi, Nelson Phillips, and Stelios Zyglidopoulos, "The Evolution of Corporate Responsiveness," *Business and Society* (Vol. 36, No. 3, September 1997), 296–321.

42. Carroll, 1979, 502–504.

43. See special issue on "Corporate Citizenship," *Business and Society Review* (Vol. 105, No. 1, Spring 2000), edited by Barbara W. Altman and Deborah Vidaver-Cohen.

44. Duane Windsor, "Corporate Citizenship: Evolution and Interpretation," in Jörg Andriof and Malcom McIntosh (eds.), *Perspectives on Corporate Citizenship* (Sheffield, UK: Greenleaf Publishing, 2001), 39–52.

45. Samuel P. Graves, Sandra Waddock, and Marjorie Kelly, "How Do You Measure Corporate Citizenship?" *Business Ethics* (March/April 2001), 17.

46. Charles J. Fombrum, "Three Pillars of Corporate Citizenship," in Noel Tichy, Andrew McGill, and Lynda St. Clair (eds.), *Corporate Global Citizenship* (San Francisco: The New Lexington Press), 27–61.

47. Kimberly S. Davenport, *Corporate Citizenship: A Stakeholder Approach for Defining Corporate Social Performance and Identifying Measures for Assessing It*, doctoral dissertation, The Fielding Institute, Santa Barbara, CA.

48. Archie B. Carroll, "The Four Faces of Corporate Citizenship," *Business and Society Review* (100/101, 1998), 1–7.

49. Barbara W. Altman, *Corporate Community Relations in the 1990s: A Study in Transformation*, unpublished doctoral dissertation, Boston University.

50. Andreas G. Scherer and Guido Palazzo (eds.), *Handbook of Research on Global Corporate Citizenship* (Cheltenham, UK: Edward Elgar Publishing, 2008).

51. *The State of Corporate Citizenship in the U.S.: Business Perspective 2005*, Center for Corporate Citizenship at Boston College, U.S. Chamber of Commerce Center for Corporate Citizenship, and the Hitachi Foundation.

52. Archie B. Carroll, Kim Davenport, and Doug Grisaffe, "Appraising the Business Value of Corporate Citizenship: What Does the Literature Say?" Proceedings of the International Association for Business and Society, Essex Junction, VT, 2000.

53. Philip Mirvis and Bradley K. Googins, *Stages of Corporate Citizenship: A Developmental Framework* (monograph) (Boston: The Center for Corporate Citizenship at Boston College, 2006), i.

54. *Ibid.*, 1–18.

55. For more on corporate citizenship, see the special issue "Corporate Citizenship," *Business and Society Review* (Vol. 105, No. 1, Spring 2000), edited by Barbara W. Altman and Deborah Vidaver-Cohen. Also see Jorg Andriof and Malcolm McIntosh (eds.), *Perspectives on Corporate Citizenship* (London: Greenleaf Publishing, 2001). Also see Isabelle Maignan, O. C. Ferrell, and G. Tomas M. Hult, "Corporate Citizenship: Cultural Antecedents and Business Benefits," *Journal of the Academy of Marketing*

Science (Vol. 27, No. 4, Fall 1999), 455–469. Also see Malcolm McIntosh, Deborah Leipziger, Keith Jones, and Gill Coleman, *Corporate Citizenship: Successful Strategies for Responsible Companies* (London: Financial Times/Pitman Publishing), 1998.

56. Mark S. Schwartz and Archie B. Carroll, "Integrating and Unifying Competing and Complementary Frameworks: The Search for a Common Core in the Business and Society Field," *Business and Society* (Vol. 47, No. 2, June 2008), 148–186.

57. Donna J. Wood, Jeanne M. Logsdon, Patsy G. Lewellyn, and Kim Davenport, *Global Business Citizenship: A Transformative Framework for Ethics and Sustainable Capitalism* (Armonk, NY: M. E. Sharpe, 2006), 40.

58. Dirk Matten and Jeremy Moon, "Implicit and Explicit CSR: A Conceptual Framework for Understanding CSR in Europe," Research Paper Series, International Centre for Corporate Social Responsibility, Nottingham University Business School, United Kingdom, 2004, 9.

59. *Fortune*, America's Most Admired Companies, "Social Responsibility," http://cgi.money.cnn.com/tools/fortune/most_admired.jsp. Accessed June 24, 2010.

60. *Fortune* 1000 Best Companies to Work For, http://money.cnn.com/magazines/fortune/fortune500/2009/employers/. Accessed June 24, 2010.

61. CRO Magazine's 100 Best Corporate Citizens, "100 Best 2009 Methodology & Penalty Box," http://www.thecro.com/node/783. Accessed June 24, 2010.

62. Business Civic Leadership Center, U.S. Chamber of Commerce, 2008 Corporate Citizenship Award Winners, http://www.uschamber.com/bclc/awards/2008.htm. Accessed June 24, 2010.

63. See, for example, Mark Starik and Archie B. Carroll, "In Search of Beneficence: Reflections on the Connections Between Firm Social and Financial Performance," in Karen Paul (ed.), *Contemporary Issues in Business and Society in the United States and Abroad* (Lewiston, NY: The Edwin Mellen Press, 1991), 79–108; and I. M. Herremans, P. Akathaporn, and M. McInnes, "An Investigation of Corporate Social Responsibility, Reputation, and Economic Performance," *Accounting, Organizations, and Society* (Vol. 18, No. 7/8, 1993), 587–604.

64. Marc Orlitzky, Frank Schmidt, and Sara Rynes, "Corporate Social and Financial Performance: A Meta-Analysis," *Organization Studies* (Vol. 24, No. 3, 2003), 369–396. Also see Marc Orlitzky, "Payoffs to Social and Environmental Performance," *Journal of Investing* (Fall 2005), 48–51. Also see Lee E. Preston and Douglas P. O'Bannon, "The Corporate Social–Financial Performance Relationship: A Typology and Analysis," *Business and Society* (Vol. 36, No. 4, December 1997), 419–429; Sandra Waddock and Samuel Graves, "The Corporate Social Performance–Financial Performance Link," *Strategic Management Journal* (Vol. 18, No. 4, 1997), 303–319; Jennifer Griffin and John Mahon, "The Corporate Social Performance and Corporate Financial Performance Debate," *Business and Society* (Vol. 36, No. 1, March 1997), 5–31; Ronald Roman, Sefa Hayibor, and Bradley Agle, "The Relationship between Social and Financial Performance," *Business and Society* (Vol. 38, No. 1, March 1999), 121. For a reply to this study, see John Mahon and Jennifer Griffin, "Painting a Portrait: A Reply," *Business and Society* (Vol. 38, No. 1, March 1999), 126–133.

65. John Peloza, "The Challenge of Measuring Financial Impacts from Investments in Corporate Social Performance," *Journal of Management* (December 2009), 1518–1541.

66. Orlitzky, Schmidt and Rynes, 2005.

67. Preston and O'Bannon, 428.

68. Bryan Husted, "A Contingency Theory of Corporate Social Performance," *Business and Society* (Vol. 39, No. 1, March 2000), 24–48, 41.

69. Zadek, 105–114.

70. Sustainability, "Environmental, Social and Governance Goals," http://www.sustainability.com/. Accessed July 5, 2010.

71. Dow Jones Sustainability Indexes, http://www.sustainability-index.com/.

72. Social Investment Forum, "Socially Responsible Investing Facts," http://www.socialinvest.org/resources/sriguide/srifacts.cfm. Accessed June 24, 2010.

73. See, for example, Lawrence A. Armour, "Who Says Virtue Is Its Own Reward?" *Fortune* (February 16, 1998), 186–189; Thomas D. Saler, "Money & Morals," *Mutual Funds* (August 1997), 55–60; and Keith H. Hammonds, "A Portfolio with a Heart Still Needs a Brain," *BusinessWeek* (January 26, 1998), 100.

74. See Jack A. Brill and Alan Reder, *Investing from the Heart* (New York: Crown Publishers, 1992), and Patrick McVeigh, "The Best Socially Screened Mutual Funds for 1998," *Business Ethics* (January–February 1998), 15–21. See also Social Investment Forum, http://www.socialinvest.org/. Accessed July 5, 2010.

75. William A. Sodeman, *Social Investing: The Role of Corporate Social Performance in Investment Decisions,* unpublished Ph.D. dissertation, University of Georgia, 1993. See also William A. Sodeman and Archie B. Carroll, "Social Investment Firms: Their Purposes, Principles, and Investment Criteria," in International Association for Business and Society 1994 Proceedings, edited by Steven Wartick and Denis Collins, 339–344.

76. Daniel Akst, "The Give and Take of 'Socially Responsible,'" *New York Times* (October 8, 2006), 28 BU. Also see Jia Lynn Yang, "New Rules for Do-Good Funds," *Fortune* (February 5, 2007), 109–112.

77. Social Investment Forum, "Performance and Socially Responsible Investments," http://www.socialinvest.org/resources/performance.cfm. Accessed June 24, 2010.

78. Samuel B. Graves and Sandra A. Waddock, "Institutional Owners and Corporate Social Performance," *Academy of Management Journal* (Vol. 37, No. 4, August 1994), 1034–1046.

79. Social Investment Forum, http://www.socialinvest.org/resources/sriguide/srifacts.cfm. Accessed June 24, 2010.

Chapter 3

1. See, for example, Robert A. Phillips, "Stakeholder Theory and a Principle of Fairness," *Business Ethics Quarterly* (Vol. 7, No. 1, January 1997), 51–66; Sandra A. Waddock and Samuel B. Graves, "Quality of Management and Quality of Stakeholder Relations," *Business and Society* (Vol. 36, No. 3, September 1997), 250–279; James P. Walsh, "Taking Stock of Stakeholder Management," *Academy of Management Review* (Vol. 30, No. 2, 2005), 426–438; Thomas Jones and Andrew Wicks, 1999, "Convergent Stakeholder Theory," *Academy of Management Review* (20, 1999), 404–437; and Thomas Kochan and Saul Rubinstein, "Toward a Stakeholder Theory of the Firm: The Saturn Partnership," *Organizational Science* (Vol. 11, No. 4, 2000), 367–386.

2. David Wheeler and Maria Sillanpää, *The Stakeholder Corporation: A Blueprint for Maximizing Stakeholder Value* (London: Pitman Publishing, 1997).

3. Steven F. Walker and Jeffrey W. Marr, *Stakeholder Power: A Winning Plan for Building Stakeholder Commitment and Driving Corporate Growth* (Cambridge, MA: Perseus Publishing, 2001).

4. James E. Post, Lee E. Preston, and Sybille Sachs, *Redefining the Corporation: Stakeholder Management and Organizational Wealth* (Stanford: Stanford University Press, 2002).

5. Robert Phillips, *Stakeholder Theory and Organizational Ethics* (San Francisco: Berrett-Koehler Publishers, Inc., 2003).

6. Jeanne M. Logsdon, Donna J. Wood, and Lee E. Benson, "Research in Stakeholder Theory, 1997–1998: The Sloan Foundation Minigrant Project" (Toronto: The Clarkson Centre for Business Ethics, 2000).

7. This definition is similar to that of R. Edward Freeman in *Strategic Management: A Stakeholder Approach* (Boston: Pitman, 1984), 25.

8. "A Thought Leader Commentary with Charles O. Holliday, Chairman and Chief Executive Officer, DuPont," *Company Stakeholder Responsibility: A New Approach to CSR*, Business Roundtable Institute for Corporate Ethics, 2006, 12.

9. Mark Starik, "Is the Environment an Organizational Stakeholder? Naturally!" *International Association for Business and Society (IABS) 1993 Proceedings*, 466–471.

10. Freeman, 5.

11. Freeman, 24–25. Also see James E. Post, Lee E. Preston, and Sybille Sachs, *Redefining the Corporation: Stakeholder Management and Organizational Wealth* (Stanford: Stanford University Press), 2002.

12. Wheeler and Sillanpää (1997), 167.

13. *Ibid.*, 168.

14. Ronald K. Mitchell, Bradley R. Agle, and Donna J. Wood, "Toward a Theory of Stakeholder Identification and Salience: Defining the Principle of Who and What Really Counts," *Academy of Management Review* (October 1997), 853–886.

15. Mark Starik and Cathy Driscoll, "The Primordial Stakeholder: Advancing the Conceptual Consideration of Stakeholder Status for the Natural Environment," in A. J. Zakhem, D. E. Palmer, and M. L. Stoll (eds.) *Stakeholder Theory: Essential Readings in Ethical Leadership and Management* (Amherst, NY: Prometheus Books, 2007), 219–222.

16. *Ibid.*

17. Jim Carlton, "How Home Depot and Activists Joined to Cut Logging Abuse," *The Wall Street Journal* (September 26, 2000), A1.

18. Kenneth E. Goodpaster, "Business Ethics and Stakeholder Analysis," *Business Ethics Quarterly* (Vol. 1, No. 1, January 1991), 53–73.

19. *Ibid.*

20. *Ibid.*

21. Thomas Donaldson and Lee Preston, "The Stakeholder Theory of the Corporation: Concepts, Evidence, Implications," *Academy of Management Review* (Vol. 20, No. 1, 1995), 65–91.

22. *Ibid.*

23. Phillips (2003), 85–118.

24. Donaldson and Preston.

25. Parallel questions are posed with respect to corporate strategy by Ian C. MacMillan and Patricia E. Jones, *Strategy Formulation: Power and Politics* (St. Paul, MN: West, 1986), 66.

26. "Animal Rights Group Aims Ad Attack at McDonald's," *The Wall Street Journal* (August 30, 1999), B7. Also see About PETA, http://www.peta.org/about/index.asp. Accessed June 25, 2010.

27. Marcia Yablon, "Happy Hen, Happy Meal: McDonald's Chick Fix," *U.S. News & World Report* (September 4, 2000), 46.

28. *Ibid.*

29. Kerry Capell, "The Wool Industry Gets Bloodied," *BusinessWeek* (July 14 & 21, 2008), 40.

30. R. Edward Freeman, S.R. Velamuri, and Brian Moriarty, "Company Stakeholder Responsibility: A New Approach to CSR," Business Roundtable Institute for Corporate Ethics, Bridge Paper, 2006, 11.

31. "Does It Pay to Be Ethical?" *Business Ethics* (March/April 1997), 14. "What's Your Poison?" *The Economist* (August 9, 2003), 50. Web site of Rain Forest Action Network: http://www.ran.org/. Accessed June 25, 2010. Also see Jeanne Whalen, "Drug Giant Is Targeted by Attacks," *The Wall Street Journal* (August 5, 2009), 1.

32. From the Web site of Rainforest Action Network: http://ran.org/search/node/old+growth.

33. *Ibid.*

34. Grant T. Savage, Timothy W. Nix, Carlton J. Whitehead, and John D. Blair, "Strategies for Assessing and Managing Organizational Stakeholders," *Academy of Management Executive* (Vol. V, No. 2, May 1991), 61–75.

35. *Ibid.*, 64.

36. Marilyn Geewax, "Business Forges Unusual Alliances," *Atlanta Journal Constitution* (February 18, 2007), E1.

37. MacMillan and Jones, 66–70.

38. John F. Preble, "Toward a Comprehensive Model of Stakeholder Management," *Business and Society Review* (Vol. 110, No. 4, 2005), 421–423.

39. *Ibid.*, 415.

40. Savage, Nix, Whitehead, and Blair, 65.

41. Seth Hettena and Laura Wides, "Eco-Terrorists Coming Out of the Wild," *USA Today* (October 3, 2003), 22A.

42. Geewax, E7.

43. Savage, Nix, Whitehead, and Blair, 72.

44. Michael Yaziji, "Turning Gadflies into Allies," *Harvard Business Review* (February 2004), 110–115.

45. C. Geertz, *The Interpretation of Cultures: Selected Essays* (New York: Basic Books, 1973). See also, M. J. Hatch, "The Dynamics of Organizational Culture," *Academy of Management Review* (Vol. 18, 1993), 657–693.

46. Thomas M. Jones, Will Felps, and Gregory A. Bigley, "Ethical Theory and Stakeholder-Related Decisions: The Role of Stakeholder Culture," *Academy of Management Review* (Vol. 32, No. 1, 2007), 137–155.

47. *Ibid.*

48. Freeman, 53.

49. Mark Starik, "Stakeholder Management and Firm Performance: Reputation and Financial Relationships to U.S. Electric Utility Consumer-Related Strategies," unpublished Ph.D. dissertation, University of Georgia, 1990, 34.

50. Freeman, Velamur, and Moriarty (2006), 11.

51. Freeman, 64.

52. Starik (1990), 36.

53. Freeman, 69–70.

54. Freeman, Velamur, and Moriarty (2006), 11.

55. Starik (1990), 36–42.

56. Freeman, Velamur, and Moriarty (2006), 11.

57. Steven F. Walker and Jeffrey Marr, *Stakeholder Power: A Winning Plan for Building Stakeholder Commitment and Driving Corporate Growth* (Cambridge, MA: Perseus Books, 2001).

58. Jeffrey Ball, "After Long Détente, GM, Green Group Are at Odds Again," *The Wall Street Journal* (July 30, 2002), A1.

59. Andrew L. Friedman and Samantha Miles, *Stakeholders: Theory and Practice* (Oxford: Oxford University Press, 2006), 160–179.

60. *Ibid.*, 175. Also see Laura Dunham, R. Edward Freeman, and Jeanne Liedtka, "Enhancing Stakeholder Practice: A Particularized Exploration of Community," *Business Ethics Quarterly* (Vol. 16, 1, 2006), 23–42.

61. Don Tapscott and David Ticoll, *The Naked Corporation: How the Age of Transparency Will Revolutionize Business* (Free Press, 2003).

62. Perry Goldschein and Beth Bengston, "How to Engage Stakeholders on Sustainability," *GreenBiz.com* (September 17, 2009), http://www.greenbiz.com/blog/2009/09/17/how-engage-stakeholders-sustainability. Accessed June 25, 2010.

63. Wheeler and Sillanpää (1997), book cover.

64. "Stakeholder Symbiosis," *Fortune* (March 30, 1998), S2–S4, special advertising section.

65. "Measurements," *Measuring and Managing Stakeholder Relationships* (Indianapolis: WalkerInformation Global Network, 1998).

66. Walmart's Sustainability Index, http://walmartstores.com/Sustainability/9292.aspx. Accessed June 25, 2010.

67. Esben Rahbek Pedersen, "Making Corporate Social Responsibility (CSR) Operable: How Companies Translate Stakeholder Dialogue into Practice," *Business and Society Review* (Vol. 111, No. 2, 2006), 137–163.

68. James E. Post, Lee E. Preston, Sybille Sachs, "Managing the Extended Enterprise: The New Stakeholder View," *California Management Review* (Vol. 45, No. 1, Fall 2002), 22–25.

69. Marc Maurer and Sybille Sachs, "Implementing the Stakeholder View," *Journal of Corporate Citizenship* (Vol. 17, Spring 2005), 93–107.

Chapter 4

1. Curtis C. Verschoor, "Can Government Manage More Ethically Than Capitalism," *Strategic Finance* (October, 2009), 15–16 & 73.

2. Cited in Edwin M. Epstein and Dow Votaw (eds.) *Rationality, Legitimacy, Responsibility: Search for New Directions in Business and Society* (Santa Monica, CA: Goodyear Publishing Co., 1978), 72.

3. *Ibid.*, 73.

4. *Ibid.*

5. *Ibid.*

6. *Ibid.*

7. William R. Dill (ed.), *Running the American Corporation* (Englewood Cliffs, NJ: Prentice Hall, 1978), 11.

8. *Ibid.*

9. Richard C. Warren, "The Evolution of Business Legitimacy," *European Business Review* (Vol. 15, No. 3, 2003), 153–163.

10. *Ibid.*

11. "Special Report: Corporate America's Woes, Continued—Enron: One Year On," *The Economist* (November 30, 2002).

12. Ewald Engelen, "Corporate Governance, Property and Democracy: A Conceptual Critique of Shareholder Ideology," *Economy & Society* (August, 2002), 391–413; Henry Hansmann, H. and R. Kraakman, "The End of History for Corporate Law," *Georgetown Law Journal* (January, 2001), 439.

13. Christine Mallin, "Corporate Governance Developments in the U.K.," in Christine Mallin, (ed.), *Handbook on International Corporate Governance* (Northampton, MA: Edward Elgar, 2006).

14. Carl Icahn, "What Ails Corporate America—And What Should Be Done," *BusinessWeek* (October 17, 1986), 101.

15. "Special Report: Corporate America's Woes, Continued—Enron: One Year On," *The Economist* (November 30, 2002).

16. *Ibid.*

17. John A. Byrne, "The Best and Worst Boards," *BusinessWeek* (January 24, 2000), 142.

18. "What Directors Think Study 2003," Corporate Board Member, http://www.boardmember.com. Accessed June 25, 2010.

19. *Ibid.*

20. Jack Welch and Suzy Welch, "How Much Blame Do Boards Deserve?" *BusinessWeek* (January 14, 2009), http://www.businessweek.com/magazine/content/09_04/b4117102356265.htm. Accessed June 25, 2010.

21. John A. Byrne, "Executive Pay: Deliver—Or Else," *BusinessWeek* (March 27, 1995), 36–38.

22. Resource Shelf. Lists and Rankings: CEO Compensation 2007; Wall Street's Highest Earners, http://www.resourceshelf.com/2007/05/06/lists-and-rankings-ceo-compensation-2007-wall-streets-highest-earners/. Accessed June 25, 2010.

23. Scott DeCarlo and Brian Zajac, "Special Report: CEO Compensation," *Forbes.Com* (April 22, 2009), http://www.forbes.com/2009/04/22/executive-pay-ceo-leadership-compensation-best-boss-09-ceo_land.html. Accessed June 25, 2010.

24. Kathryn Jones, "Who Moved My Bonus? Executive Pay Makes a U-Turn," *The New York Times* (April 4, 2009), http://www.nytimes.com/2009/04/05/business/05comp.html. Accessed June 25, 2010.

25. David Chun, "From '06 to '09, Fortune 100 Companies Disclosing Clawbacks Jump From 17 to 72 Percent," Equilar CEO Blog (November 18, 2009), http://www.executive-compensation.com/ceo_blog/?p=240. Accessed July 11, 2010.

26. Adam Lashinsky, "Why Option Backdating Is a Big Deal," *Fortune* (July 26, 2006), http://money.cnn.com/2006/07/26/magazines/fortune/lashinsky.fortune/index.htm. Accessed July 11, 2010.

27. http://www.aflcio.org/corporatewatch/paywatch/pay/index.cfm?elink. Accessed June 2010.

28. *Ibid.*

29. Paul Hodgson, "A Brief History of Say on Pay," *Ivey Business Journal* (September/October 2009), http://www.iveybusinessjournal.com/article.asp?intArticle_ID=856. Accessed June 25, 2010.

30. *Ibid.*

31. *Ibid.*

32. *Ibid.*

33. Gretchen Morgenson, "Making Managers Pay, Literally," *The New York Times* (March 25, 2007), 1.

34. Michael O'Brien, "Financial Reform Bill Will Include Clawback Provision," The Hill.com (September 15, 2009), http://thehill.com/blogs/blog-briefing-room/news/58733-financial-reform-bill-will-include-clawback-provision. Accessed June 25, 2010.

35. ALF-CIO. Executive PayWatch, http://www.aflcio.org/paywatch. Accessed June 25, 2010.

36. John J. Sweeney, "Commentary: The Foxes Are Still Guarding the Henhouse," *Los Angeles Times* (September 19, 2003), B13.

37. "Relentless Activism," *Directorship* (January/February, 2007), 1–13.

38. Alyce Gomstin, "Why Bank of America's Ken Lewis Will Take Home More Than Peers," *ABC News Business Unit* (October 8, 2009), http://abcnews.go.com/Business/bank-america-ceo-ken-lewis-retirement-pay-higher/story?id=8775299.

39. Jordan Pfuntner, "Percent of Private Industry Workers Participating in Retirement Plans, Selected Periods, 1990–2003," *Bureau of Labor Statistics* (July 28, 2004), http://www.bls.gov/opub/cwc/cm20040720ch01.htm. Accessed June 25, 2010.

40. Catherine Rampell and Matthew Saltmarsh, "A Reluctance to Retire Means Fewer Openings," *The New York Times* (September 2, 2009), http://www.nytimes.com/2009/09/03/business/03retire.html. Accessed July 11, 2009. Jonathan Stapleton, "Two-Thirds of Workers Expect Recession to Delay Retirement Plans," *Professional Pensions* (September 24, 2009), http://www.professionalpensions.com.

41. Geoffrey Colvin, "Is the Board Too Cushy?" *Director* (February 1997), 64–65.

42. "The Fading Appeal of the Boardroom," *The Economist* (February 10, 2001), 67.

43. "What Directors Think Study 2003," Corporate Board Member, http://www.boardmember.com.

44. "What Directors Think Study 2006," Corporate Board Member, http://www.boardmember.com.

45. *Ibid.*

46. Nanette Byrnes and Jane Sasseen, "Board of Hard Knocks," *BusinessWeek* (January 22, 2007), 35–39.

47. Jeanne Sahadi, "Better Reporting on Executive Pay? Yes, But...," CNNMoney.com, http://money.cnn.com/2007/01/03/news/companies/sec_execcomp_amendrules/index.htm. Accessed June 25, 2010.

48. "What Directors Think Study 2006," Corporate Board Member, http://www.boardmember.com.

49. Byrnes and Saseen, 39.

50. J. Sassen, "When Shareholders Pay the CEO's Tax Bill." *BusinessWeek* (March 5, 2007), 34.

51. J. Schwartz, "Transparency, Lost in the Fog," *The New York Times* (April 8, 2007), 1, 6.

52. "In the Money," *The Economist* (January 20, 2007), 3–6.

53. Joann S. Lublin and Scott Thurm, "Behind Soaring Executive Pay, Decades of Failed Restraints," *The Wall Street Journal–Eastern Edition* (October 12, 2006), A1–A16.

54. Heidi N. Moore, "The Demise of Poison Pills?: Why Takeover Defenses Have Been on the Wane; Shareholders vs. Boards," *The Wall Street Journal* (February 24, 2009), C4.

55. Philip L. Cochran and Steven L. Wartick, "Golden Parachutes: Good for Management and Society?" in S. Prakash Sethi and Cecilia M. Falbe (eds.) *Business and Society: Dimensions of Conflict and Cooperation* (Lexington, MA: Lexington Books, 1987), 321.

56. Ann K. Buchholtz and Barbara A. Ribbens, "Role of Chief Executive Officers in Takeover Resistance: Effects of CEO Incentives and Individual Characteristics," *Academy of Management Journal* (June 1994), 554–579.

57. Cochran and Wartick, 325–326.

58. Phred Dvorak, "Companies Cut Holes in CEOs' Golden Parachutes: New Disclosure Rules Prompt More Criticism of Guaranteed Payouts," *The Wall Street Journal* (September 15, 2008), B4.

59. *Ibid.*

60. George Russell, "The Fall of a Wall Street Superstar," *Time* (November 24, 1986), 71.

61. James B. Stewart, "Scenes from a Scandal: The Secret World of Michael Milken and Ivan Boesky," *The Wall Street Journal* (October 2, 1991), B1.

62. Keith Naughton, "Renovating Martha Inc.," *Newsweek* (February 27, 2006), 46.

63. Brooke Masters, "US Ruling Exposes Insider Trading Divide," *Financial Times* (October 12, 2009), http://www.ft.com/cms/s/0/7f727260-b67c-11de-8a28-00144feab49a.html. Accessed July 11, 2010.

64. Christopher H. Schmitt, "The SEC Lifts the Curtain on Company Info," *BusinessWeek* (August 11, 2000).

65. Michael Schlesinger, "2002 Sarbanes–Oxley Act," *Business Entities* (November/December 2002), 42–49.

66. *Ibid.*

67. Jonathon A. Segal, "The Joy of Uncooking," *HR Magazine* (November 2002), 52–57.

68. "Leaders: Sox It to Them; American Corporate Reform," *The Economist* (August 2, 2003), 14.

69. Tom McGhee, "Public Firms Turn Private to Avoid SEC Regulations," *Knight Ridder/Tribune Business News* (October 26, 2003), 1.

70. Telis Demos, "CFO: All Pain No Gain," *Fortune* (February 5, 2007), 18–20.

71. Steven Kaplan and Joseph Schultz, "Intentions to Report Questionable Acts: An Examination of the Influence of Anonymous Reporting Channel, Internal Audit Quality, and Setting," *Journal of Business Ethics* (March 2007), 109–124.

72. Beverley H. Earle and Gerald A. Madek, "The Mirage of Whistleblower Protection Under Sarbanes-Oxley: A Proposal for Change," *American Business Law Journal* (Spring, 2007), 1–54.

73. The 5th Annual Oversight Systems Financial Executive Report on Sarbanes–Oxley, http://www.cfo.com/whitepapers/index.cfm/download/11915352. Accessed July 11, 2009.

74. *Ibid.*

75. 2008 Catalyst Census of Women Board Directors of the Fortune 500 (December 2008), http://www.catalyst.org/publication/282/2008-catalyst-census-of-women-board-directors-of-the-fortune-500. Accessed June 25, 2010.

76. New Alliance for Board Diversity Report Finds Little Change in Diversity on Corporate Boards (January 17, 2008), http://www.catalyst.org/press-release/55/new-alliance-for-board-diversity-report-finds-little-change-in-diversity-on-corporate-boards. Accessed June 25, 2010.

77. Elisabeth Marx, "Route to the Top: What Does It Take for Women to get on to FTSE 100 Boards?" (London: Heidrick & Struggles, 2009) from Ruth Sealy, Susan Vinnicombe, and Val Singh, *The Female* FTSE *Report 2008: A Decade of Delay* (Cranfiled: International Centre for Women Leaders, Cranfield School of Management, 2008).

78. Joan Warner, "Women Do Make a Difference," *Directorship* (May 2006), 14–19.

79. Stephanie Holmes, "Smashing the Glass Ceiling," *BBC News* (January 11, 2008), http://news.bbc.co.uk/2/hi/business/7176879.stm. Accessed June 25, 2010.

80. *Ibid.*

81. Warner, 14–19.

82. Holmes, http://news.bbc.co.uk/2/hi/business/7176879.stm.

83. Nicola Clark, "Getting Women into Boardrooms, by Law," *The New York Times* (January 28, 2010), http://www.nytimes.com/2010/01/28/world/europe/28iht-quota.html. Accessed June 25, 2010.

84. *Ibid.*

85. *Ibid.*

86. Thomas W. Joo, "A Trip through the Maze of 'Corporate Democracy': Shareholder Voice and Management Composition," *St. John's Law Review* (Fall, 2003), 735–767.

87. Steven A. Ramirez, "A Flaw in the Sarbanes–Oxley Reform: Can Diversity in the Boardroom Quell Corporate Corruption?" *St. John's Law Review* (Fall, 2003), 837–866.

88. Niclas L. Erhardt, James D. Werbel, and Charles B. Shrader, "Board of Director Diversity and Firm Financial Performance," *Corporate Governance: An International Review* (April 2003), 102–111.

89. Eric Helland and Michael Sykuta, "Who's Monitoring the Monitor? Do Outside Directors Protect Shareholders' Interests?" *Financial Review* (May 2005), 155–172.

90. Richard A. Johnson and Daniel W. Greening, "The Effects of Corporate Governance and Institutional Ownership Types on Corporate Social Performance," *Academy of Management Journal* (October 1999), 564–576.

91. Del Jones, "Board, CEO Ties Found among TARP Companies," *USA Today* (April 3, 2009).

92. "What Directors Think Study 2008," http://www.boardmember.com.

93. The Sarbanes–Oxley Act 2002, LegalArchiver. Org,http://www.legalarchiver.org/soa.htm. Accessed June 25, 2010.

94. Charles A. Anderson and Robert N. Anthony, *The New Corporate Directors: Insights for Board Members and Executives* (New York: John Wiley & Sons, 1986), 141.

95. Anthony Bianco and Louis Lavelle, "The CEO Trap," *BusinessWeek* (December 11, 2000), 86–92.

96. David R. Francis and Seth Stern, "Era of Shaky Job Security for the CEO," *Christian Science Monitor* (December 4, 2003), Web edition. http://www.christiansciencemonitor.com/2003/1204/p01s01-usec.html?related. Accessed June 25, 2010.

97. Nanette Byrnes and David Kiley, "Hello, You Must Be Going," *BusinessWeek* (February 12, 2007), 30–32.

98. Penny Herscher, "The Rise in CEO Turnover Is a Sign of the Times—Both Good and Bad," *The Huffington Post* (January 17, 2009), http://www.huffingtonpost.com/penny-herscher/the-rise-in-ceo-turnover_b_158736.html. Accessed June 25, 2010.

99. Anthony Bianco and Louis Lavelle, "The CEO Trap," *BusinessWeek* (December 11, 2000), 86–92.

100. *Ibid.*

101. Jane McGregor, "Same Old Faces in the C-Suite," *BusinessWeek* (September 7, 2009), 24.

102. "A Landmark Ruling That Puts Board Members in Peril," *BusinessWeek* (March 18, 1985), 56–57.

103. Laurie Baum and John A. Byrne, "The Job Nobody Wants: Outside Directors Find That the Risks and Hassles Just Aren't Worth It," *BusinessWeek* (September 8, 1986), 57.

104. Paul E. Fiorella, "Why Comply? Directors Face Heightened Personal Liability After Caremark," *Business Horizons* (July/August 1998), 49–52.

105. "Liability & Litigation," *Corporate Board* (January/February 2007), 28–29.

106. J. P. Donlon. "The Flaw of Law," *Directorship* (February 2005), 3.

107. "Liability & Litigation," 28.

108. Jennifer B. Rubin, "A View from the Bar: Directors Can Be Liable for Layoffs, Plant Closings," *Corporate Board Member* (Third Quarter 2009), http://www.boardmember.com/MagazineArticle_Details.aspx?id=3879. Accessed June 25, 2010.

109. "Ownership Matters," *The Economist* (March 11, 2006), 10.
110. Joo, 735–767.
111. "What Shareholder Democracy?" *The Economist* (March 26, 2005), 62.
112. "Who Selects, Governs," *Directorship* (May 2004), 6.
113. Dennis M. Ray, "Corporate Boards and Corporate Democracy," *Journal of Corporate Citizenship* (Winter, 2005), 93–105.
114. Lucien A. Bebchuk. "The Case for Increasing Shareholder Power," *Harvard Law Review* (January 2005), 835–914.
115. Iman Anabtawi and Lynn A. Stout, "Fiduciary Duties for Activist Shareholders," *Stanford Law Review* (February 2008), 1255–1329.
116. Lynn A. Stout, "Corporations Shouldn't Be Democracies," *The Wall Street Journal—Eastern Edition* (September 27, 2007), A17.
117. Joann S. Lublin, "Directors Lose Elections but Not Seats: Staying Power of Board Members Raises Questions about Investor Democracy," *The Wall Street Journal* (September 28, 2009), B4.
118. Allan Chernoff, "Madoff Whistleblower Blasts SEC," CNNMoney.com (February 4, 2009), http://money.cnn.com/2009/02/04/news/newsmakers/madoff_whistleblower/. Accessed June 25, 2010.
119. *Ibid.*
120. Diana B. Henriquez, "Lapses Helped Scheme, Madoff Told Investigators," *The New York Times* (October 30, 2009), A1.
121. *Ibid.*
122. Lauren Tainer, *The Origins of Shareholder Activism* (Washington, DC: Investor Responsibility Research Center, July 1983), 2.
123. Rob Curran, "Small Investor, Bigger Voice," *The Wall Street Journal* (December 3, 2009), R8.
124. *Ibid.*, 1.
125. *Ibid.*, 12–22.
126. "Religious Activists Raise Cain with Corporations," *Chicago Tribune* (June 7, 1998), Business Section, 8.
127. Charles Duhigg, "Gadflies Get Respect, and Not Just at Home Depot," *The New York Times* (January 5, 2007), 1.
128. *Ibid.*
129. Joan Warner, "Get Ready for a Red-Hot Season," *Directorship* (December 2006–January 2007), 1–27.
130. Duhigg, 2007.
131. *Ibid.*
132. Calvert, "Sustainable and Responsible Investing Calvert's Shareholder Resolutions Filed," http://www.calvert.com/sri-resolutions.html. Accessed June 25, 2010.
133. "How Shareholder Resolutions Influence Corporate Behavior," *Christian Science Monitor Daily Online Newspaper* (May 1, 2006).
134. *Ibid.*
135. Thomas J. Neff, "Liability Panic in the Board Room," *The Wall Street Journal* (November 10, 1986), 22.
136. "Shareholders Force Cendant to Change Corporate Governance by Court Order," *Investor Relations Business* (January 24, 2000), 1.
137. Cornerstone Research, "Securities Class Action Filings 2008: A Year in Review," http://securities.stanford.edu/clearinghouse_research/2008_YIR/20090106_YIR08_Full_Report.pdf. Accessed June 25, 2010.
138. *Ibid.*
139. *Ibid.*
140. "The Responsibility of a Corporation to Its Shareholders," *Criteria for Decision Making* (C. W. Post Center, Long Island University, 1979), 14.
141. Mel Duvall and Kim S. Nash, "Auditing an Oracle: Shareholders Nearly Deify Warren Buffett for the Way He Manages His Diverse Holding Company, Bershire Hathaway of Omaha," *Baseline* (August 1, 2003), 30.
142. Amy Kover, "Warren Buffett: Revivalist," *Fortune* (May 29, 2000), 58–60.
143. Carol Loomis, "Buffett's Worst Year," *Fortune* (February 18, 2009), http://money.cnn.com/2009/02/28/news/companies/buffett_worstyear.fortune/index.htm?postversion=2009022808. Accessed June 25, 2010.
144. Rob Curran, "Small Investor, Bigger Voice," *The Wall Street Journal* (December 3, 2009), R8.
145. *Ibid.*
146. *Ibid.*
147. Warner, 2007.

Chapter 5

1. Victoria Miles, "Auditing Promises: One Bank's Story," *CMA Management* (Vol. 74, No. 5, June 2000), 42–46.
2. https://www.citizensbank.ca/Personal/AboutUs/CorporateSocialResponsibility/AYearInReview/. Accessed June 30, 2010.

3. *Ibid.*

4. Kenneth R. Andrews, *The Concept of Corporate Strategy*, 3d ed. (Homewood, IL: Irwin, 1987), 68–69.

5. R. Edward Freeman and Daniel R. Gilbert, Jr., *Corporate Strategy and the Search for Ethics* (Englewood Cliffs, NJ: Prentice Hall, 1988), 20. Also see R. Edward Freeman, Daniel R. Gilbert, Jr., and Edwin Hartman, "Values and the Foundations of Strategic Management," *Journal of Business Ethics* (Vol. 7, 1988), 821–834; and Daniel R. Gilbert, Jr., "Strategy and Ethics," in *The Blackwell Encyclopedic Dictionary of Business Ethics* (Malden, MA: Blackwell Publishers Ltd., 1997), 609–611.

6. Charles W. Hofer, Edwin A. Murray, Jr., Ram Charan, and Robert A. Pitts, *Strategic Management: A Casebook in Policy and Planning*, 2d ed. (St. Paul, MN: West Publishing Co., 1984), 27–29. Also see Gary Hamel and C. K. Prahalad, *Competing for the Future* (Boston: Harvard Business School Press, 1994).

7. R. Edward Freeman, *Strategic Management: A Stakeholder Approach* (Boston: Pitman, 1984), 90.

8. James C. Collins and Jerry I. Porras, *Built to Last: Successful Habits of Visionary Companies* (HarperBusiness, 1994).

9. Adam Lashinsky, "The Cook Doctrine at Apple," *Fortune* (January 22, 2009), http://features.blogs.fortune.cnn.com/2009/01/22/the-cook-doctrine-at-apple/. Accessed June 30, 2010.

10. *Ibid.*

11. Mark Albion, *True to Yourself: Leading a Values-Based Business* (San Francisco, CA: Berrett-Koehler, 2006).

12. Kerry Hannon, "How to Build in Values in Building a Business," *USA Today* (July 31, 2006), 6B.

13. Lynn Sharp Paine, *Value Shift: Why Companies Must Merge Social and Financial Imperatives to Achieve Superior Performance* (New York: McGraw-Hill, 2003).

14. C. W. Hofer and D. E. Schendel, *Strategy Formulation: Analytical Concepts* (St. Paul: West, 1978), 52–55. Also see J. David Hunger and Thomas L. Wheelen, *Essentials of Strategic Management* (Reading, MA: Addison-Wesley, 2000).

15. Kenneth R. Andrews, *The Concept of Corporate Strategy*, 3d ed. (Homewood, IL: Irwin, 1987), 18–20.

16. William B. Werther, Jr. and David Chandler, *Strategic Corporate Social Responsibility: Stakeholders in a Global Environment* (Thousand Oaks, CA: Sage Publications), 2006.

17. W. Edward Stead and Jean Garner Stead with Mark Starik, *Sustainable Strategic Management* (Armonk, NY: M.E. Sharpe, 2004).

18. Michael E. Porter and Mark R. Kramer, "Strategy and Society: The Link Between Competitive Advantage and Corporate Social Responsibility," *Harvard Business Review* (December 2006), 80–92.

19. *Ibid.*, 84.

20. *Ibid.*, 85.

21. *Ibid.*, 85.

22. *Ibid.*, 83–90.

23. *Ibid.*, 90–91.

24. *Ibid.*

25. Archie B. Carroll, *Business and Society: Managing Corporate Social Performance* (Boston: Little, Brown, 1981), 381.

26. Peter Lorange, Michael F. Scott Morton, and Sumantra Ghoshal, *Strategic Control Systems* (St. Paul, MN: West, 1986), 1, 10. Also see Hunger and Wheelen, 161–162.

27. David H. Blake, William C. Frederick, and Mildred S. Myers, *Social Auditing: Evaluating the Impact of Corporate Programs* (New York: Praeger, 1976), 3.

28. Karen Janowski and Kathleen Gilligan, "How to Produce a Top-Notch Sustainability Report," Greenbiz.com (May 10, 2010), http://www.greenbiz.com/blog/2010/05/10/how-produce-topnotch-sustainability-report. Accessed July 14, 2010.

29. http://www.ge.com/citizenship/priorities_engagement/growth_markets.jsp. Accessed June 30, 2010.

30. Ceres Web site: http://www.ceres.org. Accessed June 30, 2010.

31. *Ibid.*

32. http://www.corporateregister.com/about.html#what. Accessed June 30, 2010.

33. http://www.corporateregister.com/charts/charts.pl. Accessed June 30, 2010.

34. http://www.ceres.org//Page.aspx?pid=435. Accessed June 30, 2010.

35. *Ibid.*

36. *Ibid.*

37. Phil Harris and Craig S. Fleisher (eds.), *The Handbook of Public Affairs* (Thousand Oaks, CA: Sage Publications, 2005), 561–562. Also see "Public Affairs at Heart of Corporate Strategy," *Corporate Public Affairs* (Vol. 16, No. 2, 2006), 1–2.

38. Foundation for Public Affairs, *The State of Corporate Public Affairs* (Washington, DC, September 2005), 29.

39. Craig S. Fleisher, "Evaluating Your Existing Public Affairs Management System," in Craig S. Fleisher (ed.), *Assessing, Managing and Maximizing Public Affairs Performance* (Washington, DC: Public Affairs Council, 1997), 4.

40. For more on the origins and development of public affairs, see John M. Holcomb, "Public Affairs in North America: US Origins and Development," in Phil Harris and Craig S. Fleisher (eds.), *The Handbook of Public Affairs* (Thousand Oaks, CA: Sage Publications, 2005), 31–49.

41. http://pac.org/faq. Accessed June 30, 2010.

42. Kassandra Hannay, "Public Affairs: A Career Worth Considering," *Public Relations Out Loud* (Spring 2010), http://www.plat-formmagazine.com/article.cfm?alias=Public-Affairs-A-Career-Worth-Considering. Accessed July 15, 2010.

43. http://pac.org/about. Accessed June 30, 2010.

44. "Corporate Public Affairs and Organizational Change: Towards a New Positive Model," *Corporate Public Affairs*, (Vol. 17, No. 1, 2007), 12.

45. James E. Post and Patricia C. Kelley, "Lessons from the Learning Curve: The Past, Present and Future of Issues Management," in Robert L. Heath and Associates, *Strategic Issues Management* (San Francisco: Jossey-Bass, 1988), 352.

46. Martin B. Meznar and Douglas Nigh, "Buffer or Bridge? Environmental and Organizational Determinants of Public Affairs Activities in American Firms," *Academy of Management Journal* (August 1995), 975–996; Martin B. Meznar, "The Organization and Structuring of Public Affairs," in Phil Harris and Craig S. Fleisher (eds.), *The Handbook of Public Affairs* (Thousand Oaks, CA: Sage Publications, 2005), 187–196.

47. Amy Showalter and Craig S. Fleisher, "The Tools and Techniques of Public Affairs," in Phil Harris and Craig S. Fleisher (eds.), *The Handbook of Public Affairs* (Thousand Oaks, CA: Sage Publications, 2005), 109–122.

48. *Ibid.*

49. Archie B. Carroll, "Stakeholder Management: Background and Advances," in Phil Harris and Craig S. Fleisher (eds.), *The Handbook of Public Affairs* (Thousand Oaks, CA: Sage Publications, 2005), 501–516.

50. Foundation for Public Affairs, *The State of Corporate Public Affairs* (Washington, DC: September 2005), 15.

51. The Public Affairs Council, "Effective Management of International Public Affairs" (Washington, DC: Public Affairs Council, April 1985), 1.

52. Craig S. Fleisher, "The Development of Competencies in International Public Affairs," *Journal of Public Affairs* (Vol. 3, No. 1, 2003), 76–82.

53. Robert H. Miles, *Managing the Corporate Social Environment: A Grounded Theory* (Englewood Cliffs, NJ: Prentice-Hall, Inc., 1987).

54. *Ibid.*, 8.

55. *Ibid.*, 9–10, 111.

56. *Ibid.*, 2–3.

57. *Ibid.*, 11, 113.

58. Fleisher (ed.) (1997), 139–196.

59. Jennifer J. Griffin, Steven N. Brenner, and Jean J. Boddewyn, "Corporate Public Affairs: Structure, Resources, and Competitive Advantage," in Marc J. Epstein and Kirk O. Hanson (eds.) *The Accountable Corporation, Volume 4: Business-Government Relations* (Westport, CT: Praeger Publishers, 2006), 132–133.

60. David H. Blake, "How to Incorporate Public Affairs into the Operating Manager's Job," *Public Affairs Review* (1984), 35.

61. *Ibid.*, 36–38.

62. *Ibid.*, 38–39.

63. Jack W. Partridge, "Making Line Managers Part of the Public Affairs Team: Innovative Ideas at Kroger," in Wesley Pederson (ed.), *Cost-Effective Management for Today's Public Affairs* (Washington, DC: Public Affairs Council, 1987), 67. Also see Fleisher (1997).

64. *Ibid.*, 40–41. Also see Craig Fleisher and Darren Mahaffy, "Building the Balanced Performance Scorecard for Public Affairs," in Fleisher (1997), 152–156.

65. Griffin, Brenner, and Boddewyn, 2006, 134–138.

66. *Ibid.*, 135–136.

67. *Ibid.*, 136–137.

Chapter 6

1. Alice M. Tybout and Michelle Roehm, "Let the Response Fit the Scandal," *Harvard Business Review* (December 2009) 82–88.

2. *Ibid.*

3. Nick Miroff and Lyndsey Layton, "Peanut Company Files for Bankruptcy Protection," *The Washington Post* (February 14, 2009), http://www.washingtonpost.com/wp-dyn/content/article/2009/02/13/AR2009021303420.html. Accessed June 29, 2010.

4. Karen L. Fowler, Nathan D. Kling, and Milan D. Larson, "Organizational Preparedness for Coping with a Major Crisis or Disaster," *Business and Society* (March 2007), 88–103.

5. Tony Jaques, "Towards a New Terminology: Optimizing the Value of Issue Management," *Journal of Communication Management* (Vol. 7, No. 2), 140–147. Cited in Tony Jaques, "Issue and Crisis Management: Quicksand in the Definitional Landscape," *Public Relations Review* (September 2009), 281.

6. Tony Jaques, "Issue Management as a Post-Crisis Discipline: Identifying and Responding to Issue Impacts Beyond the Crisis," *Journal of Public Affairs* (February 2009), 35–44.

7. Liam Fahey, "Issues Management: Two Approaches," *Strategic Planning Management* (November 1986), 81, 85–96.

8. *Ibid.*, 81.

9. *Ibid.*, 86.

10. Pursey P. M. A. R. Heugens, John F. Mahon, Steve L. Wartick, "A Portfolio Approach to Issue Adoption," *International Association for Business and Society* (2004 Annual Meeting, Jackson Hole, WY).

11. *Ibid.*

12. Joseph F. Coates, Vary T. Coates, Jennifer Jarratt, and Lisa Heinz, *Issues Management* (Mt. Airy, MD: Lomond Publications, 1986), 19–20.

13. John Mahon, "Issues Management: The Issue of Definition," *Strategic Planning Management* (November 1986), 81–82. For further discussion on what constitutes an issue, see Steven L. Wartick and John F. Mahon, "Toward a Substantive Definition of the Corporate Issue Construct," *Business & Society* (Vol. 33, No. 3, December 1994), 293–311.

14. Coates et al., 18.

15. *Ibid.*, 32.

16. See DYG's Web site at: http://www.dyg.com/about-us/dyg-inc.html. Accessed June 29, 2010.

17. Myron Magnet, "Who Needs a Trend-Spotter?" *Fortune* (December 9, 1985), 51–56. Also see Gary Hamel and C. K. Prahalad, "Seeing the Future First," *Fortune* (September 5, 1994), 64–70.

18. Magnet, 52.

19. John Naisbitt, *Megatrends 2000: Ten New Directions for the 1990s* (New York: Morrow, 1990); *Global Paradox* (New York: Avon Books, 1994); *Megatrends Asia: Eight Asian Megatrends That Are Reshaping Our World* (New York: Simon and Schuster, 1996); *High Tech/High Touch* (New York: Broadway Books, 1999); *Mind-Set! Re-Set Your Thinking and See the Future* (Collins Publishers, 2007).

20. John Naisbitt, "China's Vertical Democracy: A New Model Challenging Western Democracy," http://www.naisbitt.com/. Accessed June 29, 2010.

21. Graham T. T. Molitor, "We're All Futurists," *Vital Speeches of the Day* (November 1, 2003).

22. T. Graham Molitor, "How to Anticipate Public Policy Changes," *SAM Advanced Management Journal* (Vol. 42, No. 3, Summer 1977), 4.

23. Aimee Welch, "The New Futurists," *Insight* (January 15–22, 2001), 10–13.

24. J. E. Dutton, S. J. Ashford, R. M. O'Neill, E. Hayes, and E. E. Wierba, "Reading the Wind: How Middle Managers Assess the Context for Selling Issues to Top Managers," *Strategic Management Journal* (Vol. 18, 1997), 407–425; Jennifer A. Howard-Grenville, "Developing Issue-Selling Effectiveness over Time: Issue Selling as Resourcing," *Organization Science* (July/August 2007), 560–577.

25. Pursey P. M. A. R. Heugens, "Issues Management: Core Understandings and Scholarly Development," in Phil Harris and Craig S. Fleisher (eds.), *The Handbook of Public Affairs* (Thousand Oaks, CA: Sage Publications, 2005), 490–493.

26. William R. King, "Strategic Issue Management," in William R. King and David I. Cleland (eds.) *Strategic Planning and Management Handbook* (New York: Van Nostrand Reinhold, 1987), 259.

27. James K. Brown, *This Business of Issues: Coping with the Company's Environment* (New York: The Conference Board, 1979), 45.

28. Elizabeth Dougall, "Issues Management," *Essential Knowledge Project* (December 12, 2008), http://www.instituteforpr.org/essential_knowledge/detail/issues_management/. Accessed June 29, 2010.

29. Brown, 33.

30. Coates et al., 46.

31. Cited in Heugens, 2005, 488.

32. Earl C. Gottschalk, Jr., "Firms Hiring New Type of Manager to Study Issues, Emerging Troubles," *The Wall Street Journal* (June 10, 1982), 33, 36.

33. Heugens, 2005, 482.

34. I. C. MacMillan and P. E. Jones, "Designing Organizations to Compete," *Journal of Business Strategy* (Vol. 4, No. 4, Spring 1984), 13.

35. Roy Wernham, "Implementation: The Things That Matter," in King and Cleland, 453.

36. Dougall, 2008.

37. Gottschalk, 3.

38. Mahon, 81–82.

39. Barbara Bigelow, Liam Fahey, and John Mahon, "A Typology of Issue Evolution," *Business & Society* (Spring 1993), 28. For another useful perspective, see John F. Mahon and Sandra A. Waddock, "Strategic Issues Management: An Integration of Issue

Life Cycle Perspectives," *Business & Society* (Spring 1992), 19–32. Also see Steven L. Wartick and Robert E. Rude, "Issues Management: Fad or Function," *California Management Review* (Fall 1986), 134–140.

40. Thomas G. Marx, "Integrating Public Affairs and Strategic Planning," *California Management Review* (Fall 1986), 145.

41. W. H. Chase, "Issues and Policy," *Public Relations Quarterly* (Vol. 1, Winter 1980), 5, cited in Jaques, 2009, 282.

42. Jaques, 2009.

43. Foundation for Public Affairs, *The State of Corporate Public Affairs* (Washington, DC: Foundation for Public Affairs, 2005), 9.

44. Public Affairs Council, "Public Affairs: Its Origins, Its Present, and Its Trends," http://www.pac.org (2001).

45. Tony Jaques, "Issue Management: Process Versus Progress," *Journal of Public Affairs* (February 2006), 69–74.

46. Pursey P. M. A. R. Heugens, "Strategic Issues Management: Implications for Corporate Performance," *Business & Society* (Vol. 41, No. 4, December 2002), 456–468.

47. *Ibid.*, 459. Also see Archie B. Carroll, "Stakeholder Management: Background and Advances," in Phil Harris and Craig S. Fleisher (eds.), *The Handbook of Public Affairs* (Thousand Oaks, CA: Sage Publications, 2005), 501–516.

48. Matthew Goldstein, "Wall Street in the Poconos," *BusinessWeek* (May 21, 2007).

49. Wall Street West Web page: http://www.wallstreetwest.org/default.aspx?pageid=56, Accessed June 29, 2010.

50. Patrick McGeehan, "Pennsylvania Tries to Sell Itself as Backup for Wall Street During a Disaster," *The New York Times* (June 8, 2007), http://www.nytimes.com/2007/. Accessed June 29, 2010.

51. Kate Miller, "Issues Management: The Link Between Organization Reality and Public Perception," *Public Relations Quarterly* (Vol. 44, No. 2, Summer 1999), 5–11.

52. Ian Mitroff, with Gus Anagnos, *Managing Crises Before They Happen: What Every Executive and Manager Needs to Know about Crisis Management* (New York: AMACOM, 2001), Chapter 2.

53. Ian Mitroff, "Crisis Leadership: Seven Strategies of Strength," *Leadership Excellence* (Vol. 22, No. 1, 2005), 11.

54. Christine M. Pearson and Judith Clair, "Reframing Crisis Management," *Academy of Management Review* (Vol. 23, No. 1, 1998), 60.

55. "How Companies Are Learning to Prepare for the Worst," *BusinessWeek* (December 23, 1985), 74.

56. "Tunagate," http://en.wikipedia.org/wiki/Tunagate. Accessed June 29, 2010.

57. *Ibid.*, 68. For further discussion of types of crises, see Ian Mitroff, "Crisis Management and Environmentalism: A Natural Fit," *California Management Review* (Winter 1994), 101–113.

58. Pearson and Clair, 60.

59. Ian I. Mitroff and Mural C. Alpaslan, "Preparing for Evil," *Harvard Business Review* (April 2003), 3–9.

60. Steven Fink, *Crisis Management: Planning for the Inevitable* (New York: AMACOM, 1986), 69. Also see Sharon H. Garrison, *The Financial Impact of Corporate Events on Corporate Stakeholders* (New York: Quorem Books, 1990); and Joe Marconi, *Crisis Marketing: When Bad Things Happen to Good Companies* (Chicago: NTC Business Books, 1997). See also Carol Hymowitz, "Companies Experience Major Power Shifts as Crises Continue," *The Wall Street Journal* (October 9, 2001), B1, and Sue Shellenbarger, "Some Bosses, Fumbling in Crisis, Have Bruised Loyalty of Employees," *The Wall Street Journal* (October 17, 2001), B1.

61. Fink, 20.

62. Mitroff and Anagnos, 2001.

63. "How Companies Are Learning to Prepare for the Worst," 76.

64. *Ibid.*

65. Michael D. Watkins and Max H. Bazerman, "Predictable Surprises: The Disasters You Should Have Seen Coming," *Harvard Business Review* (March 2003), 3–10.

66. David Niles, "The Secret of Successful Planning," *Forbes* (August 3, 2009), http://www.forbes.com/2009/08/03/scenario-planning-advice-leadership-managing-planning.html. Accessed June 29, 2010.

67. *Ibid.*

68. Watkins and Bazerman (2003).

69. *BusinessWeek* (1985), 74.

70. Richard J. Mahoney, "The Anatomy of a Public Policy Crisis," *The CEO Series, Center for the Study of American Business* (May 1996), 7.

71. Greg Jaffe, "How Florida Crash Overwhelmed ValuJet's Skillful Crisis Control," *The Wall Street Journal* (June 5, 1996), S1.

72. Melissa Master, "Keyword: Crisis," *Across the Board* (September 1998), 62.

73. Ian Mitroff, Paul Shrivastava, and Firdaus Udwadia, "Effective Crisis Management," *Academy of Management Executive* (November 1987), 285.

74. Christine M. Pearson and Ian I. Mitroff, "From Crisis Prone to Crisis Prepared: A Framework for Crisis Management," *Academy of Management Executive* (Vol. 7, No. 1, February 1993), 58–59. Also see Ian Mitroff, Christine M. Pearson, and L. Katherine Harrington, *The Essential Guide to Managing Corporate Crises* (New York: Oxford University Press, 1996).

75. Robert Goff, "Coming Clean," *Forbes* (May 17, 1999), 156–160.

76. *Ibid.*

77. Johnathan L. Bernstein, "The Ten Steps of Crisis Communications" (June 4, 2001), http://www.crisisnavigator.org/ The-Ten-Steps-of-Crisis-Communications.490.0.html. Accessed June 29, 2010.

78. Richard W. Brundage, "Crisis Management—An Outline for Survival" (June 4, 2001), http://www.crisisnavigator.org/Crisis- Management-An-Outline-for-Survival.454.0.html?&no_cache=1&sword_list[]=steps. Accessed June 29, 2010.

79. Cited in Irene Rozansky, "Communicating in a Crisis," *Board Member* (March/April 2007), 2.

80. *Ibid.*

81. James C. Cooper and Kathleen Madigan, "Katrina's Impact Depends on How Business Reacts," *BusinessWeek* (September 19, 2005), 31; Justin Fox, "A Meditation on Risk: Hurricane Katrina Brought out the Worst in Washington and the Best in Business," *Fortune* (October 3, 2005), 50–61; Devin Leonard, "The Only Lifeline Was the Wal-Mart," *Fortune* (October 3, 2005), 74–80.

82. Ellen Florian Kratz, "For FedEx, It Was Time to Deliver," *Fortune* (October 3, 2005), 83–84.

83. "New Lessons to Learn," *Fortune* (October 3, 2005), 87–88.

84. Paul Glader, "GE's Immelt to Cite Lessons Learned," *The Wall Street Journal* (December 14, 2009), http://online. wsj.com/ article/SB1000142405274870-3954904574596350792489752.html.

85. *Ibid.*

86. Mike Tierney, "Disaster Planning Pushed by CEO: Business Saved Following 9/11," *Atlanta Journal Constitution* (June 2, 2007), C1.

87. Bruce Rubenstein, "Salmonella-Tainted Ice Cream: How Schwan's Recovered," Corporate Legal Times Corp., June 1998.

88. *Ibid.*

89. *Ibid.*

90. *Ibid.*

Chapter 7

1. For a history of business ethics, see Richard T. DeGeorge, "The History of Business Ethics," in Marc J. Epstein and Kirk O. Hanson (eds.), *The Accountable Corporation, Business Ethics,* Vol. 2 (Westport, CT: Praeger Publishers, 2006), 47–58.

2. Cathy Booth Thomas, "The Enron Effect," *Time* (June 5, 2006), 34–35.

3. Archie B. Carroll, "Two Scandals and the Decade Isn't Over Yet," *Athens Banner Herald* (November 14, 2009), http://www. onlineathens.com/stories/111608/bus_356090174.shtml. Accessed July 6, 2010.

4. Lydia Saad, "Honesty and Ethical Standards of Professions," http://www.gallup.com/poll/124625/honesty-ethics-poll-finds- congress-image-tarnished.aspx. Accessed July 6, 2010.

5. Reported in Elena Garcia, "Poll: Americans Give Corporate America Poor Marks for Honesty, Ethics" (March 7, 2009), http:// www.christianpost.com/article/20090307/poll-americans-give-corporate-america-poor-marks-for-honesty-ethics/index.html. Accessed July 6, 2010.

6. Quoted in *Ibid.*

7. Reported in Paul B. Brown, "In Corporations, They Don't Trust," *The New York Times* (June 9, 2007), B5.

8. Ethics Resource Center, "2009 National Business Ethics Survey," http://www.ethics.org/. Accessed July 6, 2010.

9. Robert Frank and Amir Efrati, "Evil Madoff Gets 150 Years in Epic Fraud," *The Wall Street Journal* (June 30, 2009), A1. Also see, James Bandler and Nicholas Varchaver, "How Bernie Did It," *Fortune* (May 11, 2009), 51–71.

10. Michael Blumenthal, "Business Morality Has Not Deteriorated—Society Has Changed," *The New York Times* (January 9, 1977).

11. *Ibid.*

12. Richard T. DeGeorge, *Business Ethics,* 4th ed. (New York: Prentice Hall, 1995), 20–21. See also Rogene A. Buchholz and San- dra B., *Rosenthal, Business Ethics* (Upper Saddle River, NJ: Prentice Hall, 1998), 3.

13. DeGeorge, 15.

14. Kenneth E. Goodpaster, "Business Ethics," in Patricia H. Werhane and R. Edward Freeman (eds.), *The Blackwell Dictionary of Business Ethics* (Malden, MA: Blackwell Publishers, 1997), 51–57.

15. Beth Gottfried, "The Real Thang: The Apprentice—Episode 4: Ethics Shmethics—Hollywood Gone Wild" (January 30, 2004); go to the following Web page for updates on various TV shows, including *The Apprentice*: http://www.the-trades.com/. Accessed July 6, 2010.

16. Mark Gimein, "The Skilling Trap," *BusinessWeek* (June 12, 2006), 31.

17. *Ibid.*, 32.

18. Damon Darlin, "Adviser Urges HP to Focus on Ethics over Legalities," *The New York Times* (October 4, 2006), C3.

19. For more on ethics and the law, see William A. Wines, *Ethics, Law, and Business* (Mahwah, NJ: Lawrence Erlbaum Associates, Publishers, 2006).

20. See, for example, Melissa Baucus and Janet Near, "Can Illegal Corporate Behavior Be Predicted? An Event History Analysis," *Academy of Management Journal* (Vol. 34, No. 1, 1991), 9–36; and P. L. Cochran and D. Nigh, "Illegal Corporate Behavior and the Question of Moral Agency," in William C. Frederick (ed.), *Research in Corporate Social Performance and Policy*, Vol. 9 (Greenwich, CT: JAI Press, 1987), 73–91.

21. Mark S. Schwartz and Archie B. Carroll, "Corporate Social Responsibility: A Three-Domain Approach," *Business Ethics Quarterly* (Vol. 13, Issue 4, October 2003), 503–530.

22. Otto A. Bremer, "An Approach to Questions of Ethics in Business," *Audenshaw Document No. 116* (North Hinksey, Oxford: The Hinksey Centre, Westminster College, 1983), 1–12.

23. *Ibid.*, 7.

24. Leslie Weatherhead, *The Will of God* (Nashville: Abington Press, 1944, 1972).

25. Bremer, 10–11.

26. Andrew Stark, "What's the Matter with Business Ethics?" *Harvard Business Review* (May–June 1993), 7.

27. Most of the material in this section comes from Archie B. Carroll, "In Search of the Moral Manager," *Business Horizons* (March/April 1987), 7–15. See also Archie B. Carroll, "Models of Management Morality for the New Millennium," *Business Ethics Quarterly* (Vol. 11, Issue 2, April 2001), 365–371.

28. *Dilbert* comic strip, by Scott Adams (September 15, 2007), http://www.dilbert.com. Accessed July 6, 2010.

29. Allan Sloan, "Laying Enron to Rest," *Newsweek* (June 5, 2006), 25–30.

30. "Kenneth Lay," *The Economist* (July 8, 2006), 81.

31. Dave Itzkoff, "Enron Headed to Broadway," *The New York Times* (September 29, 2009), http://artsbeat.blogs.nytimes.com/2009/09/29/enron-headed-to-broadway/. Accessed July 6, 2010.

32. Andrew Dunn, "Lay, Skilling Assets Targeted by U.S. After Guilty Verdicts" (May 26, 2006), http://Bloomberg.com. Accessed May 26, 2006.

33. Kim Clark and Marianne Lavelle, "Guilty as Charged," *U.S. News & World Report* (June 5, 2006), 44–45.

34. *Ibid.*, 45.

35. *The Economist* (July 8, 2006), 81.

36. Denis Collins, "Exaggerate + Spin + Lie = Enron," *Wisconsin State Journal* (February 5, 2006).

37. Robert Frank and Amir Efrati, "Evil Madoff Gets 150 Years in Epic Fraud," *The Wall Street Journal* (June 30, 2009), A1, A12. Also see "The Madoff Affair: A Sidekick Sings," *The Economist* (August 15, 2009), 64.

38. Julian E. Barnes, "P&G Said to Agree to Pay Unilever $10 Million in Spying Case," *The New York Times* (September 7, 2001).

39. "Deloitte & Touche USA 2007 Ethics & Workplace" survey, 2007, Deloitte Development LLC, 16.

40. *Ibid.*, 15.

41. Lynn Sharp Paine, "Managing for Organizational Integrity," *Harvard Business Review* (March–April 1994), 106–117.

42. *Ibid.*, 111–112.

43. Archie B. Carroll, "The Moral Leader: Essential for Successful Corporate Citizenship," in Jorg Andriof and Malcolm McIntosh (eds.), *Perspectives on Corporate Citizenship* (Sheffield, UK: Greenleaf Publishing Co., 2001), 139–151.

44. Stephen Covey, *The Seven Habits of Highly Effective People* (New York: Simon & Schuster, 1989).

45. Carroll (2001), *Ibid.*, 145–150.

46. "Deloitte & Touche USA 2007 Ethics & Workplace" survey, 15.

47. Ray Vicker, "Rise in Chain-Saw Injuries Spurs Demand for Safety Standards, but Industry Resists," *The Wall Street Journal* (August 23, 1982), 17.

48. Rikki Klaus, "Huntsville Company Saves 50 Jobs by Helping the Community," *WHNT News*, http://www.whnt.com/news/whnt-navistar-jobs-saved-010510,0,451836.story. Accessed July 6, 2010.

49. Business Enterprise Trust, 1994, "The Business Enterprise Trust Awards (1991 Recipients)," unpublished announcement.

50. Mahzarin R. Banaji, Max H. Bazerman, and Dolly Chugh, "How (Un) Ethical Are You?" *Harvard Business Review* (December 2003), 56–64.

51. *Ibid.*

52. Max Bazerman, George Loewenstein, and Don A. Moore, "Why Good Accountants Do Bad Audits," *Harvard Business Review* (November 2002).

53. *Ibid.*

54. Paine, 109–113.

55. *Ibid.*, 107–108.

56. *Ibid.*

57. Carroll (1987), 7–15.

58. Lawrence Kohlberg, "The Claim to Moral Adequacy of a Highest Stage of Moral Judgment," *The Journal of Philosophy* (Vol. 52, 1973), 630–646.

59. Carol Gilligan, *In a Different Voice: Psychological Theory and Women's Development* (Cambridge, MA: Harvard University Press, 1982).

60. Manuel G. Velasquez, *Business Ethics,* 3d ed. (Englewood Cliffs, NJ: Prentice Hall, 1992), 30. See also Brian K. Burton and Craig P. Dunn, "Feminist Ethics as Moral Grounding for Stakeholder Theory," *Business Ethics Quarterly* (Vol. 6, No. 2, 1996), 136–137.

61. See, for example, Robbin Derry, "Moral Reasoning in Work Related Conflicts," in William C. Frederick (ed.), *Research in Corporate Social Performance and Policy*, Vol. 9 (Greenwich, CT: JAI Press, 1987), 25–49. See also Velasquez, 30–31.

62. George A. Steiner, *Business and Society* (New York: Random House, 1975), 226.

63. William Barclay, *Ethics in a Permissive Society* (New York: Harper & Row, 1971), 13.

64. Marvin Fox, "The Theistic Bases of Ethics," in Robert Bartels (ed.), *Ethics in Business* (Columbus, OH: Bureau of Business Research, Ohio State University, 1963), 86–87.

65. Alan Wolfe, *Moral Freedom: The Search for Virtue in a World of Choice* (New York: W.W. Norton & Co., 2001).

66. John Leo, "My Morals, Myself," *U.S. News & World Report* (August 13, 2001), 10.

67. Carl D. Fulda, "The Legal Basis of Ethics," in Bartels, 43–50.

68. American Management Association, "The Ethical Enterprise: Doing the Right Things in the Right Ways, Today and Tomorrow—A Global Study of Business Ethics 2005-2015," 2006, American Management Association/Human Resource Institute, viii.

69. Carl Madden, "Forces Which Influence Ethical Behavior," in Clarence C. Walton (ed.), *The Ethics of Corporate Conduct* (Englewood Cliffs, NJ: Prentice Hall, 1977), 31–78.

70. Charles W. Powers and David Vogel, *Ethics in the Education of Business Managers* (Hastings-on-Hudson, NY: The Hastings Center, 1980), 40–45. Also see Patricia H. Werhane, *Moral Imagination and Management Decision Making* (New York: Oxford University Press, 1999).

71. Milton Friedman, "The Social Responsibility of Business Is to Increase Its Profits," *The New York Times* (September 1962), 126 [italics added].

Chapter 8

1. David Callahan, *The Cheating Culture: Why More Americans Are Doing Wrong to Get Ahead* (New York: Harcourt, Inc., 2004).

2. Lee Ellis, *Leading Talents, Leading Teams* (Chicago: Northfield Publishing, 2003), 201–204.

3. Bill George, *Authentic Leadership: Rediscovering the Secrets to Creating Lasting Value* (San Francisco: Jossey-Bass, 2003).

4. Dan Chapman, "Woman Rewarded for Act of Honesty," *The Atlanta Journal-Constitution* (September 8, 2001).

5. Jennifer Dixon, "Bosses Knew Shipped Meat Was Tainted, Workers Say," *Chicago Tribune* (August 30, 2001).

6. Ethics Resource Center, *National Business Ethics Survey 2003: How Employees View Ethics in Their Organizations* (Washington, DC: Ethics Resource Center, 2003), 28. Also see http://www.ethics.org.

7. Michael Mandel and Pete Engardio, "The Real Cost of Offshoring," *BusinessWeek* (June 18, 2007), 28–34.

8. Archie B. Carroll, "Principles of Business Ethics: Their Role in Decision Making and an Initial Consensus," *Management Decision* (Vol. 28, No. 28, 1990), 20–24.

9. John R. Boatright, *Ethics and the Conduct of Business*, 4th ed. (Upper Saddle River, NJ: Prentice Hall, 2003), 31–32.

10. Tom L. Beauchamp, *Philosophical Ethics: An Introduction to Moral Philosophy*, 3d ed. (New York: McGraw-Hill, 2001).

11. Vincent Barry, *Moral Issues in Business* (Belmont, CA: Wadsworth, 1979), 43.

12. *Ibid.*, 45–46.

13. I. Kant, *Groundwork of the Metaphysic of Morals*, trans. H. J. Paton (New York: Harper and Row, 1964).

14. Victoria S. Wike, "Duty," in Patricia H. Werhane and R. Edward Freeman (eds.), *The Blackwell Encyclopedic Dictionary of Business Ethics* (Malden, MA: Blackwell Publishers, Ltd, 1997), 180–181.

15. Boatright, 53.

16. Scott J. Reynolds and Norman E. Bowie, "A Kantian Perspective on the Characteristics of Ethics Programs," *Business Ethics Quarterly* (Vol. 14, No. 2, April 2004), 275–292.

17. Louis P. Pojman, *Ethics: Discovering Right and Wrong* (Belmont, CA: Wadsworth, 1995), 147–148.

18. *Ibid.*, 150.

19. *Ibid.*, 152–153.

20. Manuel C. Velasquez, *Business Ethics: Concepts and Cases,* 3d ed. (Englewood Cliffs, NJ: Prentice Hall, 1992), 72–73.

21. Richard T. DeGeorge, *Business Ethics,* 5th ed. (Upper Saddle River, NJ: Prentice Hall, 1999), 69–72.

22. Velasquez, 73.

23. "Rights: What Are They Anyway?" http://dspace.dial.pipex.com/town/street/pl38/rights.htm. Accessed July 18, 2007.

24. "Negative and Positive Rights," http://www.essays.cc/free_essays/e4/vak199.shtml. Accessed July 18, 2007.

25. See the following sources for a discussion of these points: David Luban, "Judicial Activism and the Concept of Rights," *Report from the Institute for Philosophy & Public Policy* (College Park, MD: University of Maryland, Winter/Spring 1994), 12–17; George F. Will, "Our Expanding Menu of Rights," *Newsweek* (December 14, 1992), 90; John Leo, "The Spread of Rights Babble," *U.S. News & World Report* (June 28, 1993), 17; and William Raspberry, "Blind Pursuit of Rights Can Endanger Civility," *The Atlanta Journal* (September 14, 1994), A14.

26. DeGeorge, 69–72.

27. *Ibid.*

28. Joel Brockner, "Why It's So Hard to Be Fair," *Harvard Business Review* (March 2006), 122–129.

29. *Ibid.*, 123.

30. "John Rawls," *The Economist* (December 7, 2002), 83.

31. John Rawls, *A Theory of Justice* (Cambridge, MA: Harvard University Press, 1971).

32. DeGeorge, 69–72.

33. Michael M. Weinstein, "Bringing Logic to Bear on Liberal Dogma," *The New York Times* (December 1, 2002), 5.

34. *Ibid.*, 72.

35. *Ibid.*, 5.

36. Dahlia Lithwick, "Women: Truly the Fairer Sex," *Newsweek* (April 20, 2009), 13.

37. Robbin Derry, "Ethics of Care," in Werhane and Freeman (1997), 254.

38. Brian K. Burton and Craig P. Dunn, "Feminist Ethics as Moral Grounding for Stakeholder Theory," *Business Ethics Quarterly* (Vol. 6, No. 2, 1996), 133–147. See also A. C. Wicks, D. R. Gilbert, and R. E. Freeman, "A Feminist Reinterpretation of the Stakeholder Concept," *Business Ethics Quarterly* (Vol. 4, 1994), 475–497.

39. Derry (1997), 256.

40. Jeanne M. Liedtka, "Feminist Morality and Competitive Reality: A Role for an Ethic of Care?" *Business Ethics Quarterly* (Vol. 6, 1996), 179–200. See also John Dobson and Judith White, "Toward the Feminine Firm," *Business Ethics Quarterly* (Vol. 5, 1995), 463–478.

41. Alasdair MacIntyre, *After Virtue* (University of Notre Dame Press, 1981). See also Louis P. Pojman, *Ethics: Discovering Right and Wrong,* 2d ed. (Belmont, CA: Wadsworth, 1995), 160–185.

42. Beauchamp, 2001.

43. Pojman, 161. See also Bill Shaw, "Sources of Virtue: The Market and the Community," *Business Ethics Quarterly* (Vol. 7, 1997), 33–50; and Dennis Moberg, "Virtuous Peers in Work Organizations," *Business Ethics Quarterly* (Vol. 7, 1997), 67–85.

44. Esther F. Schaeffer, "Character Education: A Prerequisite for Corporate Ethics," *Ethics Today* (Summer 1997), 5. Also see Josephson Institute, "Six Pillars of Character," http://charactercounts.org/sixpillars.html. Accessed January 28, 2010.

45. Oliver F. Williams and Patrick E. Murphy, "The Ethics of Virtue: A Moral Theory for Business," in Oliver F. Williams and John W. Houck (eds.), *A Virtuous Life in Business* (Lanham, MD: Rowman & Littlefield Publishers, Inc., 1992), 9–27.

46. Robert K. Greenleaf, *Servant Leadership* (New York: Paulist Press, 1977).

47. Greenleaf Center for Servant Leadership, http://www.greenleaf.org/. Accessed January 28, 2010.

48. *Ibid.*; see also Robert K. Greenleaf, *The Servant as Leader* (Indianapolis: Robert K. Greenleaf Center, 1991).

49. Larry C. Spears (ed.), *Reflections of Leadership* (New York: John Wiley & Sons, 1995), 4–7.

50. Joanne B. Ciulla (ed.), *Ethics: The Heart of Leadership* (Westport, CT: Praeger Publishers, 1998), 17.

51. James A. Autry, *The Servant Leader* (Roseville, CA: Prima Publishing, 2001), flyleaf.

52. Carroll, 22.

53. Barry, 50–51.

54. Carroll, 22.

55. John C. Maxwell, *There's No Such Thing as "Business" Ethics: There's Only One Rule for Making Decisions* (Warner Books, 2003), 24–29.

56. Gordon L. Lippett, *The Leader Looks at Ethics,* (Washington, DC: Leadership Resources, 1969), 12–13.

57. "Stiffer Rules for Business Ethics," *BusinessWeek* (March 30, 1974), 88.

58. Lippett, 12–13.

59. Eric Harvey and Scott Airitam, *Ethics 4 Everyone: The Handbook for Integrity-Based Business Practices* (Dallas, TX: The Walk the Talk Company, 2002), 31.

60. *Ibid.*, 31.

61. Frederick Andrews, "Corporate Ethics: Talks with a Trace of Robber Baron," *The New York Times* (April 18, 1977), C49–C52.

62. Phillip V. Lewis, "Ethical Principles for Decision Makers: A Longitudinal Study," *Journal of Business Ethics* (Vol. 8, 1989), 275.

63. Craig V. VanSandt, "The Relationship Between Ethical Work Climate and Moral Awareness," *Business & Society* (Vol. 42, No. 1, March 2003), 144–151.

64. Cited in John B. Cullen, Bart Victor, and Carroll Stephens, "An Ethical Weather Report: Assessing the Organization's Ethical Climate," *Organizational Dynamics* (Autumn 1989), 50.

65. For an excellent discussion, see Deborah Vidaver Cohen, "Creating and Maintaining Ethical Work Climates: Anomie in the Workplace and Implications for Managing Change," *Business Ethics Quarterly* (Vol. 3, No. 4, October 1993), 343–355. See also B. Victor and J. Cullen, "The Organizational Bases of Ethical Work Climates," *Administrative Science Quarterly* (Vol. 33, 1988), 101–125; and H. R. Smith and A. B. Carroll, "Organizational Ethics: A Stacked Deck," *Journal of Business Ethics* (Vol. 3, 1984), 95–100.

66. Raymond C. Baumhart, "How Ethical Are Businessmen?" *Harvard Business Review* (July/August 1961), 6ff.

67. Steve Brenner and Earl Molander, "Is the Ethics of Business Changing?" *Harvard Business Review* (January/February 1977).

68. Barry Z. Posner and Warren H. Schmidt, "Values and the American Manager: An Update," *California Management Review* (Spring 1984), 202–216.

69. Archie B. Carroll, "Managerial Ethics: A Post-Watergate View," *Business Horizons* (April 1975), 75–80.

70. Posner and Schmidt, 211.

71. American Society of Chartered Life Underwriters & Chartered Financial Consultants and Ethics Officer Association, "Sources and Consequences of Workplace Pressure: A Landmark Study," unpublished report (1997). See also Del Jones, "48% of Workers Admit to Unethical or Illegal Acts," *USA Today* (April 4–6, 1997), 1A–2A.

72. Ethics Resource Center, 2009 National Business Ethics Survey (Washington, DC: Ethics Resource Center, November 2009), 2.

73. Ethics Resource Center (2003), 33.

74. Ethics Resource Center, *2009 National Business Ethics Survey: Ethics in the Recession*, 36.

75. T. V. Purcell and James Weber, *Institutionalizing Corporate Ethics: A Case History, Special Study No. 71* (New York: The President's Association, American Management Association, 1979). See also James Weber, "Institutionalizing Ethics into Business Organizations: A Model and Research Agenda," *Business Ethics Quarterly* (Vol. 3, No. 4, October 1993), 419–436.

76. Ethics Resource Center, 2009 National Business Ethics Survey (Washington, DC: Ethics Resource Center, November 2009), 2.

77. T. E. Deal and A. Kennedy, *Corporate Cultures* (Reading, MA: Addison-Wesley Publishers, 1982).

78. Ronald Berenbeim, "Universal Conduct: An Ethics and Compliance Benchmarking Survey," The Conference Board, 2006, 7.

79. Archie B. Carroll, "Ethics Programs Go Beyond Compliance Strategy," *Business Ethics: Brief Readings on Vital Topics* (New York and London: Routledge Publishers, 2009), 184–185.

80. Ronald E. Berenbeim and Jeffrey M. Kaplan, "Ethics and Compliance … The Convergence of Principle- and Rule-Based Ethics Programs: An Emerging Trend," *The Conference Board, Executive Action Series*, No. 231, March 2007.

81. *Ibid.*, 2.

82. *Ibid.*, 4.

83. "The Big Picture: Ethics," *BusinessWeek* (June 19, 2006), 13.

84. L. W. Foy, "Business Ethics: A Reappraisal," *Distinguished Lecture Series, Columbia Graduate School of Business* (January 30, 1975), 2.

85. Linda Klebe Treviño, Laura Pincus Hartman, and Michael Brown, "Moral Person and Moral Manager: How Executives Develop a Reputation for Ethical Leadership," *California Management Review* (Vol. 42, No. 4, Summer 2000), 134.

86. Harvey Gittler, "Listen to the Whistle-Blowers Before It's Too Late," *The Wall Street Journal* (March 10, 1986), 16.

87. Treviño, Hartman, and Brown, 128–142.

88. *Ibid.*, 133–136.

89. R. Edward Freeman and Lisa Stewart, "Developing Ethical Leadership" (Charlottesville, VA: Business Roundtable Institute for Corporate Ethics, 2006), 3–7.

90. Steven N. Brenner, "Influences on Corporate Ethics Programs" (San Diego, CA: International Association for Business and Society, March 16–18, 1990), 7.

91. National Business Ethics Survey, 1–2.

92. *Ibid.*

93. Bruce A. Hamm, "Elements of the US Federal Sentencing Guidelines," http://www.refresher.com. Accessed April 29, 2004.

94. Susan Gaines, "Handing Out Halos," *Business Ethics* (March/April 1994), 20–24.

95. Roy J. Snell, "Should We Call It an Ethics Program or a Compliance Program?" *Journal of Health Care Compliance* (March/April 2004), 1–2.

96. Michael G. Daigneault, Jerry Guthrie, and Frank J. Navran, "Managing Ethics Upwards," in O. C. Ferrell, Sheb L. True, and Lou E. Pelton (eds.), *Rights, Relationships & Responsibilities* (Kennesaw, GA: Coles College of Business, Kennesaw State University, 2003), 61–69.

97. *Ibid.*, 65–69.

98. *Ibid.*, 67–69.

99. Claudia Parsons, "From Madoff to Merrill Lynch, 'Where Was the Ethics Officer,'" *International Herald Tribune* (January 29, 2009).

100. Fred T. Allen, "Corporate Morality: Is the Price Too High?" *The Wall Street Journal* (October 17, 1975), 16.

101. LaRue T. Hosmer, *The Ethics of Management* (Homewood, IL: Richard D. Irwin, 1987), 12–14.

102. Kenneth Blanchard and Norman Vincent Peale, *The Power of Ethical Management* (New York: Fawcett Crest, 1988), 20.

103. Texas Instruments, "Ethics Quick Test" (Texas Instruments Ethics Office), wallet card, http://www.ti.com/corp/docs/company/citizen/ethics/quicktest.shtml. Accessed February 1, 2010.

104. Sears, Roebuck and Co., Code of Business Conduct (1997), 2.

105. Joan Dubinsky, "Updating Your Corporate Code of Conduct," *Corporate Compliance Insights*, http://www.corporatecompliance-insights.com/2009/corporate-code-of-conduct-guidelines-policy-tips-writing-updating. Accessed March 17, 2010.

106. Gary Edwards, "And the Survey Said ... ," in Garone (ed.) (1994), 25.

107. Bruce R. Gaumnitz and John C. Lere, "A Classification Scheme for Codes of Business Ethics," *Journal of Business Ethics* (February 2004), 329.

108. "Codes of Ethics," by Leon V. Ryan, in Patricia Werhane and R. Edward Freeman (eds.), *The Blackwell Encyclopedic Dictionary of Business Ethics* (Malden, MA: Blackwell Publishing, 1997), 114.

109. "Common Ethics Code Provisions," http://www.ethics.org/resources/common-code-provisions.asp. Accessed July 23, 2007.

110. Cynthia Stohl, Michael Stohl, and Lucy Popova, "A New Generation of Corporate Codes of Ethics," *Journal of Business Ethics* (2009: 90), 607–622.

111. Donald L. McCabe, Linda Klebe Treviño, and Kenneth D. Butterfield, "The Influence of Collegiate and Corporate Codes of Conduct on Ethics-Related Behavior in the Workplace," *Business Ethics Quarterly* (Vol. 6, October 1996), 473.

112. Mark Schwartz, "The Nature of the Relationship Between Corporate Codes of Ethics and Behavior," *Journal of Business Ethics* (Vol. 32, 2001), 247–262.

113. *Ibid.*, 255.

114. Allen, 16.

115. Treviño, Hartman, and Brown, op. cit., 136.

116. J. Lynn Lunsford and Anne Marie Squeo, "Boeing Dismisses Two Executives for Violating Ethical Standards," *The Wall Street Journal* (November 25, 2003).

117. Ken Benson, "Nortel Fires 3 Executives Amid Accounting Inquiry," *The New York Times* (April 28, 2004).

118. Allen, 16.

119. Ethics Resource Center (2003), 12.

120. Berenbeim, 6.

121. 2003 National Business Ethics Survey, 44.

122. *Ibid.*, 43.

123. "Ethics: Phoning It In," *CFO* (February 2007), 21.

124. *Ibid.*

125. *Ibid.*, 22–23.

126. Berenbeim, 13–14.

127. Melinda Ligos, "Boot Camps on Ethics Ask the 'What Ifs?'" *The New York Times* (January 5, 2003), 12BU.

128. "Business Ethics Training," *Webucator*, http://www.webucator.com/management-training/course/business-ethics-training.cfm. Accessed February 2, 2010.

129. "At Last: Humor in Ethics Training," *Business Ethics* (May/June 1997), 10.

130. Francis J. Daly, "An Ethics Officer's Perspective," in Marc J. Epstein and Kirk O. Hanson (eds.), *The Accountable Corporation: Business Ethics,* Vol. 2 (Westport, CT: Praeger Publishers, 2006), 186.

131. Thomas M. Jones, "Can Business Ethics Be Taught? Empirical Evidence," *Business & Professional Ethics Journal* (Vol. 8, 1989), 86.

132. Business Roundtable Institute for Corporate Ethics, About the Institute, http://www.darden.virginia.edu/corporate-ethics/about.htm. Accessed February 2, 2010.

133. Katherine S. Mangan, "Business Schools and Company CEOs to Create Ethics Center," *Chronicle of Higher Education* (January 30, 2004), A9. Also see Louis Lavelle and Amy Borrus, "Ethics 101 for CEOs," *BusinessWeek* (January 26, 2004), 88.

134. Michael Metzger, Dan R. Dalton, and John W. Hill, "The Organization of Ethics and the Ethics of Organizations: The Case for Expanded Organizational Ethics Audits," *Business Ethics Quarterly* (Vol. 3, No. 1, January, 1993), 27–43. Also see Thomas Petzinger, Jr., "This Auditing Team Wants You to Create a Moral Organization," *The Wall Street Journal* (January 19, 1996), B1.

135. Ronald E. Berenbeim, "Ethics Programs and Practices: A 20-Year Retrospective," *Executive Action Series*, The Conference Board, No. 207, September 2006, 5.

136. Marcia Narine, "Conducting a Risk Assessment—One Approach," Risk Assessments and Compliance Program Benchmarking, The Conference Board, Webcast, V-0060-05-CH, November 2, 2005.

137. Ethics Resource Center, 2009 National Business Ethics Survey 20–21.

138. Barbara Pagano and Elizabeth Pagano, *The Transparency Edge: How Credibility Can Make or Break You in Business* (New York: McGraw Hill Trade, 2003).

139. Don Tapscott and David Ticoll, *The Naked Corporation: How the Age of Transparency Will Revolutionize Business* (New York: Free Press, 2003).

140. Janice Brand, "Book Review: The Naked Corporation," *Darwin Magazine* (May 4, 2004), http://www.darwinmag.com/read/writeon/column.html.

141. Archie B. Carroll, "Slack Corporate Governance Costs Us All," *Business Ethics: Brief Readings on Vital Topics* (New York and London: Routledge Publishers, 2009), 86–87.

142. Quoted in Curtis C. Verschoor, "Unethical Workplace Is Still with Us," *Strategic Finance* (April 2004), 16.

143. William Atkinson, "Sarbanes–Oxley Act: Not Just for Corporations," *Public Power Magazine* (March–April 2004).

144. *Ibid.*

145. Berenbeim, 5.

146. The Conference Board Press Release, "Boards of Directors Getting More Involved in Companies" Ethics Programs," *PR Newswire* (March 4, 2004).

147. W. Edward Stead, Dan L. Worrell, and Jean Garner Stead, "An Integrative Model for Understanding and Managing Ethical Behavior in Business Organizations," *Journal of Business Ethics* (Vol. 9, 1990), 223–242. See also Robert D. Gatewood and Archie B. Carroll, "Assessment of Ethical Performance of Organization Members: A Conceptual Framework," *Academy of Management Review* (Vol. 16, No. 4, 1991), 667–690.

148. Kenneth E. Goodpaster, "Examining the Conscience of the Corporation," in Marc J. Epstein and Kirk O. Hanson (eds.), *The Accountable Corporation: Business Ethics,* Vol. 2 (Westport Connecticut: Praeger Publishers, 2006), 102.

Chapter 9

1. Sharon Jayson, "iGeneration Has No Off Switch," *USA Today* (February 10, 2010), 1D.

2. John Naisbitt, Nana Naisbitt, and Douglas Phillips, *High Tech/High Touch: Technology and Our Search for Meaning* (Nicholas Brealey Publishing Co, 1999).

3. Albert M. Erisman, "Social Networking for Business," http://www.ethix.org/article.php3?id=377. Accessed July 28, 2007.

4. *Ibid.*

5. Elizabeth Woyke, "Attention Shoplifters: With $30 Billion in Theft, There's a Revolution in Surveillance Systems," *BusinessWeek* (September 11, 2006), 46.

6. *Webster's Ninth New Collegiate Dictionary* (Springfield, MA: Merriam-Webster, Inc., 1983), 1211.

7. "Technology," *The World Book Encyclopedia* (Chicago: World Book, Inc., 1988), 76.

8. Richard L. Daft, *Management,* 5th ed. (New York: The Dryden Press, 2000), 75.

9. "Technology," 77–78.

10. *Ibid.,* 78–79.

11. Robert Friedel, *A Culture of Improvement: Technology and the Western Millennium* (Cambridge, MA: MIT Press, 2007). Also see the review of this book, Adam Keiper, "The March of Machines," June 7, 2007, http://www.wsj.online. Accessed July 28, 2007.

12. Friedel, 79.

13. *Ibid.,* 80.

14. *Ibid.,* 80–81.

15. Beverly Kracher and Cynthia L. Corritore, "Is There a Special E-Commerce Ethics?" *Business Ethics Quarterly* (Vol. 14, Issue 1, January 2004), 77.

16. Naisbitt, Naisbitt, and Phillips.

17. John Naisbitt, "High Tech, High Touch," *Executive Excellence* (Vol. 16, No. 12, December 1999), 5ff.

18. *Ibid.* Also see Stephen Goode, "Naisbitt Questions the Future of Technology," *Insight* (June 11, 2001), 37–38.

19. NCL Fraud Center, http://www.fraud.org/internet/2007internet.pdf. Accessed February 9, 2010.

20. Kracher and Corritore, 71–94.

21. *Ibid.,* 78–82.

22. "Putting the Ethics in E-Business," *Computerworld* (Vol. 34, No. 45, November 6, 2000), 81ff.

23. To appreciate the different issues in which privacy arises, go to the Web site of Privacy Rights Clearinghouse: http://www.privacyrights.org/ar/Privacy-IssuesList.htm. Accessed July 30, 2007.

24. "Executives Note Hot Business Topics," *USA Today* (July 26, 2001), 1B.

25. "Exposure in Cyberspace," *The Wall Street Journal* (March 21, 2001), B1.

26. The EPIC Cookies Page: http://epic.org/privacy/internet/cookies/. Accessed February 9, 2010.

27. "Privacy Options Are a Blur," *USA Today* (April 10, 2001), 3D.
28. SPAM—Unsolicited Commercial Email, http://epic.org/privacy/junk_mail/spam/. Accessed February 9, 2010.
29. *Ibid.*
30. Donna De Marco, "What's in a Name?" *Insight* (July 30, 2001), 30–31.
31. Byron Acohido, "An Invitation to Crime," *USA Today* (March 4, 2010), 2A.
32. Bryon Acohido and Jon Swartz, "Botnet Scams Are Exploding," *USA Today* (March 17, 2008), 1B–2B.
33. Siobhan Gorman, "Hackers Mount New Strike," *The Wall Street Journal* (February 18, 2010), A3.
34. Acohido, 1A–2A.
35. Roger Grimes, "Privacy protection: The Government Is No Help," *InfoWorld* (June 16, 2006), http://www.infoworld.com/article/06/06/16/79260_25OPsecadvise_1.html. Accessed March 19, 2010.
36. Mike France, "Why Privacy Notices Are a Sham," *BusinessWeek* (June 18, 2001), 82–83. Also see Federal Trade Commission, Privacy Initiatives, http://www.ftc.gov/privacy/privacyinitiatives/glbact.html. Accessed July 30, 2007.
37. Jason Anders, "Congress Is Wasting No Time in Effort to Address Major Issues Raised by Web," *The Wall Street Journal* (February 27, 2001), B13C.
38. Federal Trade Commission, Privacy Initiatives, http://www.ftc.gov/privacy/index.html. Accessed February 9, 2010.
39. Walt Disney Internet Group, Privacy Policy, http://disney.go.com/corporate/privacy/pp_wdig.html. Accessed February 9, 2010.
40. Aaron Ricadela, "Microsoft: Privacy Champion?" *BusinessWeek Online*, http://www.BusinessWeek.com Online, July 24, 2007, 1. Accessed August 10, 2007. Microsoft's Online Privacy Policy may be viewed at http://privacy.microsoft.com/en-us/fullnotice.mspx. Accessed February 9, 2010.
41. Michelle Kessler, "Position of Privacy Officer Coming into Public Eye," *USA Today* (November 30, 2000), 1B.
42. Jared Sandberg, "The Privacy Officer," *The Wall Street Journal* (July 16, 2001), R10. Also see Steve Ulfelder, "CPOs: Hot or Not?" *Computerworld* (March 15, 2004), 40.
43. Cara Garretson, "Why Your Company Needs a Chief Privacy Officer," *Network World* (May 28, 2007), 20.
44. *Ibid.*
45. Ulfelder, 40.
46. Ben Worthen, "Data Breaches Are on the Rise with Businesses Rarely Penalized," *The Wall Street Journal* (September 9, 2008), B9.
47. Gorman, A3.
48. *Ibid.*
49. Timothy Egan, "Technology Sent Wall Street into Market for Pornography," *The Wall Street Journal* (October 23, 2000), A1, A20.
50. Jefferson Graham, "As Napster Shuts, Others Carry the Tune," *USA Today* (July 12, 2001), 3D.
51. Nazanin Lankarani, "A Push in Law School to Reform Copyright," *The New York Times* (December 1, 2009), http://www.nytimes.com/2009/12/02/business/global/02iht-riedmedia.html?scp=3&sq=illegal%20downloading%202009&st=Search. Accessed February 10, 2010.
52. *Ibid.*
53. Margaret Carlson, "Someone to Watch over Me," *Time* (July 16, 2001).
54. Jeremy Wagstaff, "Gone Phishing: Web Scam Takes Dangerous Turn," *Wall Street Journal Europe* (May 28, 2004), A5. Also see Anti-Phishing Working Group, http://www.antiphishing.org/. Accessed February 10, 2010.
55. Darryl Haralson and Sam Ward, "Technology's Positive Impact," *USA Today* (October 22, 2001), 1B.
56. Amanda Mujica, Edward Petry, and Dianne Vickery, "A Future of Technology and Ethics," *Business and Society Review* (Vol. 104, No. 3, 1999), 279–290.
57. Stephanie Armour, "Employers Look Closely at What Workers Do on the Job," *USA Today* (November 8, 2006), 1B–2B. Also see, "Big Brother Is Watching," *CFO* (August 2007), 16.
58. *Ibid.*, 2B. Survey was of 526 companies.
59. Laura Petrecca, "Feel Like Someone's Watching? You're Right," *USA Today* (March 17, 2010), 1B–2B.
60. Kristina Dell and Lisa Takeuchi Cullen, "Snooping Bosses," *Time* (September 11, 2006), 62.
61. *Ibid.*
62. *Ibid.*
63. "Employers Spying on Staff: Big Brother Bosses," *The Economist* (September 12, 2009), 71.
64. Janet Kornblum, "The Boss Is Tracking Moves of a Third of Online Workers," *USA Today* (July 10, 2001), 3D.
65. Matt Villano, "The Risk Is All Yours in Office E-Mail," *The New York Times* (March 4, 2007), 17BU.
66. John Galvin, "The New Business Ethics: Cheating, Lying, Stealing—Technology Makes It Easy, Get Used to It," http://Smartbusinessmag.com (June 2000), 86.
67. *Ibid.*, 88.
68. "Keeping Tabs on Employees Online," *BusinessWeek* (February 19, 2001), 16.
69. Petrecca, 2010, 1B.

70. Gary Duncan, "Bank Chief Caught Out by Routine Surveillance," *The Times* (May 31, 2004), 19.

71. Armour, 2006, *Ibid.*

72. "Biometrics Gets Down to Business," *The Economist Technology Quarterly* (December 2, 2006), 21–22.

73. "Biometrics: Wobbly ID," *The Economist* (April 2, 2009).

74. *Ibid.*

75. Aaron Pressman, "Homeland Security 2.0," *BusinessWeek* (January 22, 2007), 73.

76. Insurance Information Institute, "Cellphones and Driving," http://www.iii.org/media/hottopics/insurance/cellphones/. Accessed February 11, 2010.

77. Sue Shellenbargar, "Should Employers Play a Role in Safe Use of Cellphones in Cars?" *The Wall Street Journal* (July 18, 2001), B1.

78. "Jane Wagner," Zoominfo, http://www.zoominfo.com/people/Wagner_Jane_16402535.aspx. Accessed February 11, 2010.

79. "Cell Phones and Driving," Insurance Information Institute (August 2007), http://www.iii.org/media/hottopics/insurance/cellphones/. Accessed August 13, 2007. Also see Archie B. Carroll, "Ethical Companies Curb Phone Use While Driving," *Athens Banner Herald* (October 31, 2009).

80. Trish Worron, "Cellphones Don't Ring My Chimes," *The Toronto Star* (January 2004).

81. Shellenbargar, B1.

82. "Cell Phones and Driving," August 2007.

83. *Ibid.*

84. *Ibid.*

85. Mujica, Petry, and Vickery, 286.

86. Thomas Hilton, "Information System Ethics: A Practitioner Survey," *Journal of Business Ethics* (December 2000), 279–284.

87. Walter Isaacson, "The Biotech Century," *Time* (January 11, 1999), 42–43.

88. *Ibid.*

89. Alison Taunton-Rigby, "Bioethics: The New Frontier" (Waltham, MA: The Sears Lectureship in Business Ethics, Center for Business Ethics, Bentley College, April 19, 2000), 7.

90. *Ibid.*, 7–8.

91. The President's Council on Bioethics, http://www.bioethics.gov/. Accessed March 19, 2010.

92. "Bioethics: Wanna Buy a Bioethicist?" *Christianity Today* (October 1, 2001), 32–33.

93. *Ibid.*

94. Nell Boyce, "And Now, Ethics for Sale," *U.S. News & World Report* (July 30, 2001), 18–19.

95. Charles Colson, "The New Tyranny: Biotechnology Threatens to Turn Humanity into Raw Material," *Christianity Today* (October 1, 2001), 128.

96. Kerry Capell, "At Risk: A Golden Opportunity in Biotech," *BusinessWeek* (September 10, 2001), 85–87.

97. John Heys, "University Hosts Forum on Ethics of Stem Cell Research," *Knight Ridder Tribune Business News* (March 4, 2004), 1.

98. Sheryl Gay Stolberg, "Company Using Cloning to Yield Stem Cells," *The New York Times* (July 13, 2001).

99. Tim Friend, "The Stem Cell Hard Sell," *USA Today* (July 17, 2001), 6D.

100. Rick Weiss, "Which Life Matters More?" *The Washington Post National Weekly Edition* (July 23–29, 2001), 31.

101. Lymari Morales, "Majority of Americans Likely Support Stem Cell Decision," *Gallup Poll* (March 9, 2009), http://www.gallup.com/poll/116485/majority-americans-likely-support-stem-cell-decision.aspx. Accessed February 16, 2010.

102. "Value Conflicts in Stem-Cell Research: Governments Struggle with Bioethical Issues," *The Futurist* (January–February 2007), 8–9.

103. Alice Park, "The Quest Resumes," *Time* (February 9, 2009), 36–43.

104. Kenneth Woodward, "A Question of Life or Death," *Newsweek* (July 9, 2001), 31.

105. Arlene Weintraub, "Biotech Frontier: Repairing the Engines of Life," *BusinessWeek* (May 24, 2004), 99–106.

106. "Cloning," *Gallup Poll* (May 2009), http://www.gallup.com/poll/6028/cloning.aspx. Accessed February 16, 2010.

107. "Pregnant Pause," *The Economist* (January 22, 2004).

108. Quoted in Elizabeth M. Whelan, "Biomedical Prostitution?" *Insight* (May 28, 2001), 27.

109. *Ibid.* Also see Bodies: The Exhibition, http://www.bodiestheexhibition.com/bodies.html. Accessed August 17, 2007.

110. Pallavi Gogoi, "Cloning: Scientists vs. Consumers," *BusinessWeek Online* (May 7, 2007), 31.

111. Food and Drug Administration, "Animal Cloning," http://www.fda.gov/animalveterinary/safetyhealth/animalcloning/default.htm. Accessed February 16, 2010.

112. Gogoi, 31.

113. Anne Kates Smith, "The Downside of Genetic Testing," *Kiplinger's Personal Finance* (May 2008), 13–14.

114. Taunton-Rigby, 18–19.

115. "Genetic Discrimination," *Multinational Monitor* (May 2001), 30.

116. "EEOC Settles Genetics Suit with Burlington Northern," *The Wall Street Journal* (April 19, 2001), B10.

117. "Genetic Information Nondiscrimination Act of 2008 (GINA)," http://www.genome.gov/24519851. Accessed February 16, 2010.

118. Elizabeth Weise, "Technology Creates a Standoff on Farms: Genetically Modified Crops Catch on in USA," *USA Today* (March 17, 2010), 1D.

119. L. Val Giddings, "No: These Crops Pass Multiple Tests Before Approval and Are a Boon to the World's Hungry," *Insight* (August 6, 2001), 43.

120. World Health Organization, "Genetically Modified Foods," http://www.who.int/foodsafety/publications/biotech/20questions/en/. Accessed February 16, 2010.

121. CBS Evening News, "Figuring Out What's in Your Food" (May 11, 2008), http://www.cbsnews.com/stories/2008/05/11/eveningnews/main4086518.shtml. Accessed February 16, 2010.

122. *Ibid.*

123. James Sturke, "EU Commission Admitted GM Food Uncertainty," *Guardian Unlimited* (April 6, 2006), http://www.guardian.co.uk/eu/story/0,,1756138,00.html#article_continue. Accessed August 14, 2007.

124. *Ibid.*

125. James Kanter, "Europe to Allow Two Bans on Genetically Altered Crops," *The New York Times* (March 2, 2009), http://www.nytimes.com/2009/03/03/business/worldbusiness/03biotech.html. Accessed February 16, 2010.

126. Weise, 2010, 2D.

127. "FDA Developing GM Food Guidelines; New Rules Fall Short of Label Requests," *Chemical Market Reporter* (January 22, 2001), 13. See a summary of the current government perspective at Biotechnology Industry Association, "Summary of Government Regulations," http://bio.org/foodag/action/reg.asp. Accessed February 17, 2010.

128. William Neuman, "Biotech-Free, Mostly," *The New York Times* (August 29, 2009), B1.

129. Non-GMO Project, http://www.nongmoproject.org/. Accessed February 16, 2010.

130. For an interesting discussion of the environmentalists' viewpoint, see Jonathan Rauch, "Will Frankenfood Save the Planet?" *The Atlantic Monthly* (October 2003), 103–108.

Chapter 10

1. Peter F. Drucker, "The Transnational Economy," *The Wall Street Journal* (August 25, 1987), 38. See also Tammie S. Pinkston and Archie B. Carroll, "Corporate Citizenship Perspectives and Foreign Direct Investment in the U.S.," *Journal of Business Ethics* (Vol. 13, 1994), 157–169.

2. Paul Krugman, cited in Alan Farnham, "Global—Or Just Globaloney?" *Fortune* (June 27, 1994), 97–98.

3. Richard D. Robinson, "Background Concepts and Philosophy of International Business from World War II to the Present," in William A. Dymsza and Robert G. Vambery (eds.), *International Business Knowledge: Managing International Functions in the 1990s* (New York: Praeger, 1987), 3–4.

4. Thomas L. Friedman, *The World Is Flat: A Brief History of the Twenty-First Century* (Farrar, Straus & Giroux, 2005, 2006).

5. *Ibid.*

6. "The Meaning of Seattle," *Multinational Monitor* (December 1999), 5. See also Ernesto Zedillo, "Globaphobia," *Forbes* (March 19, 2001), 49.

7. Michael Elliott, "A Backlash Against Globalization," *Time.com* (March 20, 2006), http://www.time.com/time/magazine/article/0,9171,501060327-1174760,00.html. Accessed August 15, 2007.

8. "China's Shoddy Standards Threaten U.S. Consumers," *USA Today* (July 10, 2007), 11A.

9. Roger Parloff, "China's Newest Export: Lawsuits," *Fortune* (July 23, 2007), 48.

10. Paul Beamish, Allen Morrison, Philip Rosenzweig, and Andrew Inkpen, *International Management: Text and Cases* (Boston: Irwin McGraw Hill, 2000), 3.

11. *Ibid.*, 3.

12. Herman E. Daly, "Globalization and Its Discontents," *Philosophy & Public Policy Quarterly* (Vol. 21, No. 2/3, Spring/Summer 2001), 17.

13. *Ibid.*, 17.

14. "Backlash Behind the Anxiety over Globalization," *BusinessWeek* (April 24, 2000), 38.

15. "A Bigger World: A Special Report on Globalization," *The Economist* (September 20, 2008), 3.

16. Hal Sirkin, Jim Hemerling, and Arindam Bhattacharya, *Globality: Competing with Everyone from Everywhere for Everything* (Boston Consulting Group, 2008).

17. Ernesto Zedillo, "Globaphobia," *Forbes* (March 19, 2001), 49.

18. *Ibid.*; "The Meaning of Seattle," 5.

19. Tim Weiner, "Free Trade Accord at Age 10: The Growing Pains Are Clear," *The New York Times* (December 27, 2003), A1.

20. Robert Batterson and Murray Weidenbaum, *The Pros and Cons of Globalization* (St. Louis: Center for the Study of American Business, January 2001), i.

21. "The World Social Forum: Dear Capitalists, Admit You Got It Wrong," *The Economist* (February 7, 2009), 53–54.

22. Chris Giles, "Globalization Backlash in Rich Nations," *Financial Times FT.Com* (July 22, 2007), http://www.ft.com/cms/s/2a735dd0-3873-11dc-bca9-0000779fd2ac.html. Accessed August 15, 2007.

23. *Ibid.*

24. John Garland and Richard N. Farmer, *International Dimensions of Business Policy and Strategy,* 2d ed. (Boston: Kent Publishing Company, 1990), 166–173.

25. Anupama Mohan, "Global Corporate Social Responsibilities Management in MNCs," *Journal of Business Strategies* (Spring 2006), 9–32.

26. *Ibid.,* 167–168.

27. *Ibid.,* 169.

28. *Ibid.,* 172.

29. *Ibid.*

30. "Ethical Dilemmas of the Multinational Enterprise," *Business Ethics Report, Highlights of Bentley College's Sixth National Conference of Business Ethics* (Waltham, MA: The Center for Business Ethics at Bentley College, October 10 and 11, 1985), 3. See also Richard T. DeGeorge, *Competing with Integrity in International Business* (New York: Oxford University Press, 1993).

31. Rosabeth Moss Kanter, *World Class: Thriving Locally in the Global Economy* (New York: Simon & Schuster, 1995).

32. Michael L. Wheeler, "Global Diversity: Reality, Opportunity, and Challenge," *BusinessWeek* (December 1, 1997), special section.

33. James C. Baker, John C. Ryans, Jr., and Donald G. Howard, *International Business Classics* (Lexington, MA: Lexington Books, 1988), 73–367.

34. *Ibid.,* 127–138.

35. *Ibid.,* 245–246.

36. *Ibid.,* 314–315.

37. Richard D. Robinson, "The Challenge of the Underdeveloped National Market," in Baker, Ryans, and Howard, 347–356.

38. James E. Post, "Assessing the Nestlé Boycott: Corporate Accountability and Human Rights," *California Management Review* (Winter 1985), 115–116.

39. *Ibid.,* 116–117.

40. Rogene A. Buchholz, William D. Evans, and Robert Q. Wagley, *Management Response to Public Issues* (Englewood Cliffs, NJ: Prentice Hall, 1985), 80.

41. *Ibid.,* 81–82.

42. Oliver Williams, "Who Cast the First Stone?" *Harvard Business Review* (September–October, 1984), 155.

43. "Nestlé's Costly Accord," *Newsweek* (February 6, 1984), 52.

44. Alix M. Freedman, "Nestlé to Restrict Low-Cost Supplies of Baby Food to Developing Nations" and "American Home Infant-Formula Giveaway to End," *The Wall Street Journal* (February 4, 1991), B1.

45. For further discussion, see S. Prakash Sethi, *Multinational Corporations and the Impact of Public Advocacy on Corporate Strategy: Nestlé and the Infant Formula Case* (Boston: Kluwer Academic, 1994).

46. Alix M. Freedman and Steve Stecklow, "As UNICEF Battles Baby-Formula Makers, African Infants Sicken, " *The Wall Street Journal* (December 5, 2000).

47. Miriam Jordan, "Nestle Markets Baby Formula to Hispanic Mothers in U.S.," *The Wall Street Journal* (March 4, 2004), B1.

48. The International Baby Food Action Network, http://www.ibfan.org/index-ibfan.html. Accessed March 1, 2010.

49. Stuart Diamond, "The Disaster in Bhopal: Lessons for the Future," *The New York Times* (February 5, 1985), 1. See also Russell Mokhiber, "Bhopal," *Corporate Crime and Violence* (San Francisco: Sierra Club Books, 1988), 86–96.

50. Deepti Ramesh and Ian Young, "Tata Boss Proposes Cleanup of Bhopal Site; Survivors Protest," *Chemical Week* (January 17, 2007), 13.

51. Stuart Diamond, "Disaster in India Sharpens Debate on Doing Business in Third World," *The New York Times* (December 16, 1984), 1.

52. *Ibid.*

53. *Ibid.*

54. Thomas M. Gladwin and Ingo Walter, "Bhopal and the Multinational," *The Wall Street Journal* (January 16, 1985), 1.

55. Molly Moore, "In Bhopal, a Relentless Cloud of Despair," *The Washington Post National Weekly Edition* (October 4–10, 1993), 17.

56. Jim Carlton and Thaddeus Herrick, "Bhopal Haunts Dow Chemical," *The Wall Street Journal* (May 8, 2003), B3.

57. David Bogoslaw, "Dow Chem Face Hldr Proposal on Bhopal Risk at Annual Mtg," *The Wall Street Journal* (May 13, 2004). Matt Kovac, "Dow Chemical: Shareholder Resolutions a Reality of Life," *ICIS Chemical Business Americas* (April 30-May 6, 2007), 10. Accessed August 16, 2007. "Dow Chemical: Liable for Bhopal?" *BusinessWeek* (June 9, 2008), 61–62.

58. Ramesh and Young. Also see http://www.dow.com/commitments/debates/bhopal/. Accessed March 23, 2010.

59. Mark Clifford, Michael Shari, and Linda Himelstein, "Pangs of Conscience: Sweatshops Haunt U.S. Consumers," *Business-Week* (July 29, 1996), 46–47. See also Keith B. Richburg and Anne Swardson, "Sweatshops or Economic Development?" *The Washington Post National Weekly Edition* (August 5–11, 1996), 19.

60. "Stamping Out Sweatshops," *The Economist* (April 19, 1997), 28–29.

61. Clifford, Shari, and Himelstein, 46.

62. *Ibid.*

63. Ronald Baily, "Sweatshops Forever," *Reason* (February 2004), 12–13.

64. *Ibid.*

65. Social Accountability International, http://www.sa-intl.org/. Accessed March 21, 2010.

66. SA8000 Standards, http://www.sa-intl.org/index.cfm?fuseaction=Page.viewPage&pageId=937&parentID= 479&nodeID=1. Accessed March 21, 2010.

67. Details may be found at http://www.sa-intl.org/index.cfm?fuseaction=Page.viewPage&pageId=473. Accessed August 17, 2007.

68. SA 8000 Certification, http://www.sa-intl.org/index.cfm?fuseaction=Page.viewPage&pageId=617&parentID=473. Accessed March 21, 2010.

69. SA 8000 Certified Facilities Summary, http://www.saasaccreditation.org/certfacilitieslist.htm. Accessed March 21, 2010.

70. Laura P. Hartman, Denis G. Arnold, Richard E. Wokutch (eds.), *Rising Above Sweatshops: Innovative Approaches to Global Labor Challenges* (Westport, CT: Praeger Publishers, 2003).

71. Amy Merrick, "Gap Offers Unusual Look at Factory Conditions," *The Wall Street Journal* (May 12, 2004), A1.

72. Gap, Inc., Social Responsibility Report, http://www.gapinc.com/public/SocialResponsibility/socialres.shtml. Accessed March 21, 2010.

73. Dexter Roberts, Pete Engardio, Aaron Bernstein, Stanley Holmes, and Xiang Ji, "Secrets, Lies, and Sweatshops" (cover story), *BusinessWeek* (November 27, 2006), 50–58.

74. "Alien Tort Claims Act," *Global Policy Forum*, http://www.globalpolicy.org/intljustice/atca/atcaindx.htm. Also see "Alien Tort Claims," *International Law Update* (Vol. 13, April 2007), 66–67.

75. Warren Richey, "When Can Foreigners Sue in U.S. Courts?" *Christian Science Monitor* (March 30, 2004).

76. Alan Gomez, "Foreign Workers Sue U.S. Companies under Old Law; Lawsuits Allege Violations of 1789 Statute," *USA Today* (April 2, 2007), 2A.

77. Alien Tort Claims Act, http://www.kelleydrye.com/resource_center/global_litigation_usa/20090126/01. Accessed March 21, 2010.

78. *Ibid.*

79. *Ibid.*

80. Gibson Dunn, "2009 Year End FCPA Update" (January 4, 2010), http://www.gibsondunn.com/publications/Pages/2009Year-EndFCPAUpdate.aspx. Accessed March 23, 2010.

81. Bruce Lloyd, "Bribery, Corruption and Accountability," *Insights on Global Ethics* (Vol. 4, No. 8, September 1994), 5.

82. "Corruption Definitions," *Zero Tolerance for Corruption*, http://www.anticorruption.info/other_defs.php. Accessed March 23, 2010.

83. "Fighting Corruption," *The Economist* (April 29, 2004).

84. Ian I. Mitroff and Ralph H. Kilmann, "Teaching Managers to Do Policy Analysis: The Case of Corporate Bribery," *California Management Review* (Fall 1977), 50–52.

85. "The Destructive Costs of Greasing Palms," *BusinessWeek* (December 6, 1993), 133–138. See also Henry W. Lane and Donald G. Simpson, "Bribery in International Business: Whose Problem Is It?" (Reading 12) in H. W. Lane, J. J. DiStefano, and M. L. Maznevski (eds.), *International Management Behavior*, 4th ed. (Oxford: Blackwell Publishers, 2000), 469–487.

86. "Foreign Corrupt Practices Act," *Department of Justice*, http://www.justice.gov/criminal/fraud/fcpa/. Accessed March 23, 2010.

87. Garland and Farmer, 183.

88. Lay Person's Guide to the FCPA, http://www.justice.gov/criminal/fraud/docs/dojdocb.html. Accessed March 23, 2010.

89. Gibson Dunn.

90. *Ibid.*

91. Paul Berger, Erin Sheehy, Kenya Davis, and Bruce Yannett, "Is That a bribe?" *International Financial Law Review* (April 2007), 76–78.

92. Emma Schwartz, "Hiking the Cost of Bribery," *U.S. News & World Report* (August 13, 2007), 31.

93. Mike Esterl and David Crawford, "Siemens to Pay Huge Fine in Bribery Inquiry," *The Wall Street Journal* (December 15, 2008), B1; Siri Schubert and T. Christian Miller, "Siemens: Where Bribery Was Just a Line Item, *The New York Times* (December 21, 2008), BU 1.

94. "CEOs Moral Compass Steers Siemens," *USA Today* (February 15, 2010), 3B.

95. Michael Perlis and Wren Chais, "Commentary: Investigating the FCPA," *Forbes* (December 8, 2009), http://www.forbes.com/2009/12/08/foreign-corrupt-practices-act-opinions-contributors-michael-perlis-wrenn-chais.html. Accessed March 25, 2010.

96. "What Is Transparency International?" http://www.transparency.org/about_us. Accessed March 25, 2010.

97. TI's Global Priorities, http://www.transparency.org/global_priorities. Accessed March 25, 2010.

98. "Business Principles for Countering Bribery," http://www.transparency.org/global_priorities/private_sector/business_principles. Accessed March 25, 2010.

99. TI's Corruption Perception Index, http://www.transparency.org/policy_research/surveys_indices/cpi. Accessed August 18, 2007.

100. TI's Corruption Perception Index, http://www.transparency.org/policy_research/surveys_indices/cpi/2009/cpi_2009_table. Accessed March 25, 2010.

101. Transparency International, http://www.transparency.org/policy_research/surveys_indices/bpi/bpi_2008. Accessed March 25, 2010.

102. TI's Bribe Payer's Index, http://www.transparency.org/policy_research/surveys_indices/bpi. Accessed March 25, 2010.

103. Global Integrity, http://www.globalintegrity.org/aboutus/index.cfm. Accessed March 25, 2010.

104. Paul Deveney, "34 Nations Sign Accord to End Bribery in Deals," *The Wall Street Journal* (December 18, 1997), A16.

105. "The OECD Antibribery Convention, http://www.oecd.org/topic/0,3373,en_2649_34859_1_1_1_1_37447,00.html. Accessed March 25, 2010.

106. http://www.oecd.org/topic/0,3373,en_2649_34857_1_1_1_1_37447,00.html. Accessed March 25, 2010.

107. Sam Fleming, "OECD Chief's Fury over Sleaze Claim," *Daily Mail* (London) (April 21, 2007), 68.

108. United Nations Convention Against Corruption, http://www.unodc.org/unodc/en/crime_convention_ corruption.html. Accessed August 22, 2007.

109. UN Office on Drugs and Crime, http://www.unodc.org/unodc/corruption.html. Accessed August 22, 2007.

110. UN Convention against Corruption, http://www.unodc.org/unodc/en/treaties/CAC/signatories.html. Accessed March 25, 2010.

111. UN Global Compact, http://www.unglobalcompact.org/AboutTheGC/TheTenPrinciples/principle10.html. Accessed March 25, 2010.

112. UN Convention against Corruption.

113. Susan Ferriss, "Chihuahua Watchdog: Anti-Corruption Czar in Mexico Has Hands Full," *The Atlanta Journal-Constitution* (September 23, 2001), B6.

114. Paul Starobin and Catherine Belton, "Cleanup Time: The Kremlin Is Launching a Major Attack on Corruption," *BusinessWeek* (January 14, 2002), 46–47.

115. Global Integrity Country Reports: Russia, http://report.globalintegrity.org/Russia/2008. Accessed March 25, 2010.

116. Perlis and Chais.

117. Lloyd, 5.

118. Gene R. Laczniak and Jacob Naor, "Global Ethics: Wrestling with the Corporate Conscience," *Business* (July–September 1985), 3–10.

119. G. Pascal Zachary, "Levi Tries to Make Sure Contract Plants in Asia Treat People Well," *The Wall Street Journal* (July 28, 1994), A1.

120. Tom Donaldson, "Global Business Must Mind Its Morals," *The New York Times* (February 13, 1994), F-11. See also Tom Donaldson, "Ethics Away from Home," *Harvard Business Review* (September–October, 1996).

121. Tom Donaldson and Thomas W. Dunfee, "When Ethics Travel: The Promise and Peril of Global Business Ethics," *California Management Review* (Vol. 41, No. 4, Summer 1999), 48–49.

122. Laczniak and Naor, 3–10.

123. *Ibid.*, 7.

124. Caterpillar Worldwide Code of Conduct, http://www.cat.com/code-of-conduct. Accessed March 29, 2010.

125. Northrop Grumman, Standards of Business Conduct, http://www.northropgrumman.com/corporate-responsibility/ethics/assets/noc_standards_conduct.pdf. Accessed March 29, 2010.

126. *Ibid.*

127. Chiquita Code of Conduct, http://www.chiquitabrands.com/content/ChiquitaCode.FINAL.pdf. Accessed March 29, 2010.

128. Lynn Paine, Rohit Deshpandé, Joshua Margolis, and Kim Eric Bettcher, "Up to Code: Does Your Company's Conduct Meet World-Class Standards?" *Harvard Business Review* (December 2005), 122–133.

129. *Ibid.*

130. Laczniak and Naor, 7–8.

131. Archie B. Carroll, Frank Hoy, and John Hall, "The Integration of Corporate Social Policy into Strategic Management," in S. Prakash Sethi and Cecilia M. Falbe (eds.), *Business and Society: Dimensions of Conflict and Cooperation* (Lexington, MA: Lexington Books, 1987), 449–470.

132. Donna J. Wood, Jeanne M. Logsdon, Patsy G. Lewellyn, and Kim Davenport, *Global Business Citizenship: A Transformative Framework for Ethics and Sustainable Capitalism* (Armonk, NY: M.E Sharpe), 2006.

133. Robert D. Haas, "Ethics in the Trenches," *Across the Board* (May 1994), 12–13.
134. Quoted in CSRWire.com, http://www.csrwire.com/News/4529.html. Accessed August 21, 2007.
135. Levi Strauss & Co., *Global Sourcing and Operating Guidelines*, http://www.levistrauss.com/Downloads/GSOG.pdf. Accessed March 29, 2010.
136. "Starbucks Pays Premium Price to Benefit Workers," *Business Ethics* (March/April 1998), 9.
137. "Starbucks and Fair Trade," http://www.starbucks.com/sharedplanet/ethicalInternal.aspx?story=fairTrade. Accessed March 29, 2010.
138. Starbucks, "Our Responsibility," http://www.starbucks.com/sharedplanet/ourresponsibilityinternal.aspx?story=globalreporting. Accessed March 30, 2010.
139. Laczniak and Naor, 8.
140. "The Short Arm of the Law," *The Economist* (March 2, 2002), 63–65.
141. "Ecuador Seizes Oxy," *Multinational Monitor* (May/June 2006), 4.
142. Geri Smith, "Venezuela: A Love-Hate Relationship with Chavez," *BusinessWeek* (June 25, 2007), 42–46.
143. Stanley Reed, "The Problem's Not Peak Oil, It's Politics," *BusinessWeek* (July 9 and 16, 2007), 41–42.
144. L. Gordon Crovitz, "Google's Search Result: Hong Kong," *The Wall Street Journal* (March 29, 2010), A21.
145. David H. Blake, William C. Frederick, and Mildred S. Myers, *Social Auditing: Evaluating the Impact of Corporate Programs* (New York: Praeger, 1976), 3.
146. Mattel press release (November 20, 1997).
147. Mattel, "Responsible Manufacturing," http://corporate.mattel.com/about-us/corporate-responsibility.aspx. Accessed March 30, 2010.
148. MSNBC, "Mattel Issues New Massive China Toy Recall" (August 14, 2007), http://www.msnbc.msn.com/id/20254745/. Accessed August 21, 2007.
149. Mattel, "Responsible Manufacturing," http://corporate.mattel.com/about-us/corporate-responsibility.aspx#ResponsibleManufacturing. Accessed March 29, 2010.
150. Ronald E. Berenbeim, *Resisting Corruption: How Company Programs Are Changing, Research Report R-1397-06-RR* (New York: The Conference Board, 2006).
151. *Ibid.*

Chapter 11

1. Curtis J. Verschoor, "Can Government Manage More Ethically Than Capitalism?" *Strategic Finance* (October 2009), 15–16, 63.
2. Andy Serwer, "The '00s: Goodbye (at Last) to the Decade from Hell," *Time* (November 24, 2009), http://www.time.com/time/nation/article/0,8599,1942834,00.html. Accessed July 8, 2010.
3. *Ibid.*
4. *Ibid.*
5. Verschoor, 15.
6. *Ibid.*
7. Bob Davis, Damian Paletta, and Rebecca Smith, "Sour Economy Spurs Government to Grab a Bigger Oversight Role," *The Wall Street Journal* (July 25, 2008), A12.
8. *Ibid.*
9. "Antitrust Laws," *The World Book Encyclopedia,* Vol. 1 (Chicago: World Book, 1988), 560. See also "The Interstate Commerce Act" (Vol. 10), 352–353.
10. *Ibid.*
11. *Ibid.*
12. *Ibid.*
13. Alfred L. Seelye, "Societal Change and Business-Government Relationships," *MSU Business Topics* (Autumn 1975), 5–6.
14. "Is Government Dead?" *Time* (October 23, 1989).
15. Michael J. Mandel, "Rethinking the Economy," *BusinessWeek* (October 1, 2001), 28–33.
16. "25 People to Blame for the Financial Crisis," *Time* (November 24, 2009), http://www.time.com/time/specials/packages/article/0,28804,1877351_1877350_1877322,00.html. Accessed July 8, 2010.
17. Paul Magnusson, "Suddenly, Washington's Wallet Is Open," *BusinessWeek* (October 1, 2001), 34.
18. Mandel, 30.
19. L. Earle Birdsell, "Business and Government: The Walls Between," in Neil H. Jacoby (ed.), *The Business–Government Relationship: A Reassessment* (Santa Monica, CA: Goodyear, 1975), 32–34.
20. Jacoby, 167.
21. McKinsey & Company, "McKinsey Global Survey," *McKinsey Quarterly* (January 2010), 7.

22. *Ibid.*
23. Nancy Killefer, "The New Business of Government," *McKinsey Quarterly* (Issue 3, 2009), 7.
24. Naftali Bendavid, "Rage at Government for Doing Too Much and Not Enough," *The Wall Street Journal* (October 13, 2009), A5.
25. Lori Montgomery and Michael A. Fletcher, "Obama Budget Calls for New Spending to Lower Unemployment, Help Middle Class," *The Washington Post* (February 2, 2010), http://www.washingtonpost.com/wp-dyn/content/article/2010/02/01/AR2010020100981.html. Accessed July 8, 2010.
26. James Foreman-Peck and Giovanni Frederico, *European Industrial Policy: The Twentieth-Century Experience* (Oxford University Press, 1999).
27. Karl Aiginger, "Industrial Policy: A Dying Breed or a Re-emerging Phoenix?" *Journal of Industry, Competition & Trade* (December 2007), 297–323.
28. *Ibid.*
29. Robert B. Reich, *The Next American Frontier* (New York: Penguin Books, 1983).
30. Christian H. M. Ketels, "Industrial Policy in the United States," *Journal of Industry, Competition & Trade* (December 2007), 147–167.
31. *Ibid.*
32. Anonymous, "The Clinton Administration's Framework for Global Electronic Commerce: Executive Summary (July 1, 1997)," *Business America* (Vol. 119, No. 1, January 1998), 5–6.
33. Robert B. Reich, "Government in Your Business," *Harvard Business Review* (July–August, 2009), 94–99.
34. Killefer, 7.
35. *Ibid.*
36. Magnusson, 34.
37. Michael Arndt, "What Kind of Rescue?" *BusinessWeek* (October 1, 2001), 36–37.
38. *Ibid.*
39. Jon Birger, "The Bailout Bounty," *Fortune* (March 5, 2007), 24–26.
40. *Ibid.*
41. *Ibid.*
42. Monroe W. Karmin, "Industrial Policy: What Is It? Do We Need One?" *U.S. News & World Report* (October 3, 1983), 47.
43. Hiroyuki Tezuka, "Success as the Source of Failure? Competition and Cooperation in the Japanese Economy," *Sloan Management Review* (Vol. 38, No. 2, March 1997), 83–93.
44. Jeffrey Kutler, "Financial Industrial Policy," *Security Industry News* (April 30, 2007), http://www.securitiesindustry.com/issues/20070429/20313-1.html. Accessed July 8, 2010.
45. Ira C. Magaziner and Robert B. Reich, *Minding America's Business: The Decline and Rise of the American Economy* (New York: Vintage Books, 1983), 255.
46. Ted Kolderie, "What Do We Mean by Privatization?" (St. Louis: Center for the Study of American Business, Washington University, May 1986), 2–5.
47. Shaker A. Zahra, R. Duane Ireland, Isabel Gutierrez, and Michael A. Hitt, "Privatization and Entrepreneurial Transformation: Emerging Issues and a Future Research Agenda," *Academy of Management Review* (July 2000), 509–524.
48. Geoffrey Segal, "Several States Consider Privatizing Their Lotteries," *The Reason Foundation* (February 23, 2007), http://reason.org/news/show/several-states-consider-privat. Accessed August 4, 2010.
49. *Ibid.*
50. Eamon Javers, "Roadblocks Ahead for Investors?" *BusinessWeek* (June 25, 2007), 12.
51. Kolderie, 2–5.
52. *Ibid.*, 3–5.
53. Steve Coll, "Retooling Europe," *The Washington Post National Weekly Edition* (August 22–28, 1994), 6–7.
54. Alvaro Cuervo and Bélen Villalonga, "Explaining the Variance in the Performance Effects of Privatization," *Academy of Management Review* (July 2000), 581–590.
55. *Ibid.*, 581–590.
56. Suzanne Leland and Olga Smirnova, "Reassessing Privatization Strategies 25 Years Later: Revisiting Perry and Babitsky's Comparative Performance Study of Urban Bus Transit Services," *Public Administration Review* (September/October 2009), 855–867.
57. Jason Keller and Jonathan Keehner, "Privatize This!" *BusinessWeek* (March 15, 2010), 54–56.
58. *Ibid.*
59. Mandel, 30.
60. Richard Reed, David J. Lemak, and W. Andrew Hesser, "Cleaning Up after the Cold War: Management and Social Issues," *Academy of Management Review* (Vol. 22, No. 3, July 1997), 614–642.
61. Murray L. Weidenbaum, *Business, Government and the Public,* 3d ed. (Englewood Cliffs, NJ: Prentice Hall, 1986), 5–6.

62. *Ibid.*, 6–8.

63. *Ibid.*

64. Alan Keyes, "Why 'Good Government' Isn't Enough," *Imprimis* (Vol. 21, No. 10, October 1992), 2.

65. *Ibid.*, 10–11.

66. Eric Lipton and Gardiner Harris, "In Turnaround, Industries Push for Regulations after Efforts to Block Them," *The New York Times* (September 16, 2007), A1, 13.

67. "Happy Birthday Federal Register," The Mercatus Institute, http://mercatus.org/media_clipping/happy-birthday-federal-register. Accessed August 4, 2010.

68. *Federal Register,* "Federal Register Pages Published Annually," http://www.llsdc.org/attachments/wysiwyg/544/fed-reg-pages.pdf.

69. Susan E. Dudley, "The Bush Administration Regulatory Record," *Regulation* (Winter 2004–2005), 4–11.

70. "America's Regulatory Mess," *The Economist* (July 26, 2003), 57–58.

71. *Ibid.*

72. *Congressional Quarterly's Federal Regulatory Directory,* 5th ed. (1985–1986), 2.

73. *Ibid.*, 2–3.

74. *Ibid.*, 9.

75. "Microsoft: Time to Change," *BusinessWeek* (July 16, 2001), 100.

76. Stephen Labaton, "Microsoft Finds a Legal Defender in Justice Department," *The New York Times* (June 10, 2007), http://www.nytimes.com.

77. *Ibid.*

78. Stephan Labaton, "Antitrust Complaints Prompt Changes to Vista," *The New York Times* (June 19, 2007), http://www.nytimes.com/2007/06/19/technology/20softcnd.html.

79. James Rowley, "Antitrust Pick Varney Saw Google as Next Microsoft," *Bloomberg.com* (February 17, 2009), http://www.bloomberg.com/apps/news?pid=email&sid=aG9B5.J3Bl1w. Accessed August 4, 2010.

80. Thomas Catan and Jessica E. Vascellaro, "Google, Microsoft Spar on Antitrust," *The Wall Street Journal* (March 1, 2010), http://online.wsj.com/article/SB10001424052748703510204575086534063777758.html?KEYWORDS=Varney+google. Accessed July 8, 2010.

81. *Congressional Quarterly's Federal Regulatory Directory*, 10–11.

82. *Ibid.*, 12.

83. Stephen Breyer, *Regulation and Its Reform* (Cambridge, MA: Harvard University Press, 1982), 21–22.

84. *Ibid.*, 31–32.

85. Weidenbaum, 178–179.

86. Melinda Warren, "Federal Regulatory Spending Reaches a New Height: An Analysis of the Budget of the U.S. Government for the Year 2001" (St. Louis, Missouri: Center for the Study of American Business, June 2000); derived from the budget of the U.S. government.

87. Jeff Thain, "Sarbanes–Oxley: Is the Price Too High? *The Wall Street Journal* (May 27, 2004), A20.

88. *Ibid.*

89. Graham K. Wilson, *Business and Politics: A Comparative Introduction* (Chatham, NJ: Chatham House, 1985), 39.

90. Murray L. Weidenbaum, *Costs of Regulation and Benefits of Reform* (St. Louis: Center for the Study of American Business, Washington University, November 1980), 3. See also Murray Weidenbaum and Melinda Warren, *It's Time to Cut Government Regulations* (St. Louis: Center for the Study of American Business, Washington University, February 1995).

91. *Ibid.*, 12–14.

92. Paroma Sanyal, "The Effect of Deregulation on Environmental Research by Electric Utilities," *Journal of Regulatory Economics* (June 2007), 335–353.

93. *Ibid.*, 12.

94. Reich, 98.

95. *Ibid.*, 94–99.

96. "Deregulating America," *BusinessWeek* (November 28, 1983), 80–89.

97. "Is Deregulation Working?" *BusinessWeek* (December 22, 1986), 50–55.

98. Alison Vekshin, "U.S. Senators Propose Reinstating Glass–Steagall Act," *Bloomberg.com* (December 16, 2009), http://www.bloomberg.com/apps/news?pid=20601103&sid=aQfRyxBZs5uc. Accessed July 8, 2010.

99. *Ibid.*, 52.

100. Stephen Labaton, "As Trucking Rules Are Eased, a Debate on Safety Intensifies," *The New York Times* (December 3, 2006), 1, 30.

101. *Ibid.*

102. *Ibid.*, 30.

103. *Ibid.*, 30.

104. Dave Harmon, "Obama Administration to Review Truckers' Hours of Service Rules Yet Again," *Purchasing* (October 29, 2009).

105. "Financial Deregulation," Chapter 21, *Cato Handbook for Congress: Policy Recommendations for the 108th Congress* (2003), http://www.cato.org/pubs/handbook/hb108/hb108-21.pdf. Accessed July 8, 2010.

106. Richard W. Rahn, "Regulatory Malpractice," *The Cato Institute* (March 27, 2004), http://www.cato.org/pub_display.php?pub_id=2587.

107. Vekshin, 2009.

108. David Lawder, "Timeline: Long Road to Implement Financial Reform Bill," *Reuters.com* (July 21, 2010), http://www.reuters.com/article/idUSTRE66K49320100721. Accessed August 4, 2010.

Chapter 12

1. Adam Liptak, "Justices 5-4, Reject Corporate Spending Limit," *The New York Times* (January 22, 2010), http://www.nytimes.com/2010/01/22/us/politics/22scotus.html. Accessed July 8, 2010.

2. S. Prakash Sethi, "Corporate Political Activism," *California Management Review* (Spring 1982), 32.

3. David B. Yoffie and Sigrid Bergenstein, "Creating Political Advantage: The Rise of the Corporate Political Entrepreneur," *California Management Review* (Fall 1985), 124. See also John F. Mahon, "Corporate Political Strategy," *Business in the Contemporary World* (Autumn 1989), 50–62.

4. Jeffrey H. Birnbaum, "Microsoft's Capital Offense," *Fortune* (February 2, 1998), 84–86.

5. Dan Carney, "Microsoft's All-Out Counterattack," *BusinessWeek* (May 15, 2000), 103–106.

6. Hanna Rosin, "Mining Microsoft," *New Republic* (June 8, 1998), 12–13. See also Birnbaum, 84–86.

7. Carney, 103–106.

8. Ted Bridis, "Microsoft Lawyer to Be on Antitrust Panel," http://www.findlaw.com (February 5, 2004).

9. Candace Lombardi, "Microsoft to Google: Take an Antitrust Lesson from Us; The Software Maker's Deputy General Counsel Says It's Learned Its Lesson in Dealing with Regulators. Is Google Listening?" http://CNET.com (June 28, 2007).

10. *Ibid.*

11. Thomas Catan and Jessica E. Vascellaro, "Google, Microsoft Spar on Antitrust," *The Wall Street Journal* (March 1, 2010).

12. H. R. Mahood, *Interest Group Politics in America* (Englewood Cliffs, NJ: Prentice Hall, 1990), 52.

13. *Ibid.*, 53–54.

14. Dick Lochner, editorial cartoon, *U.S. News & World Report* (September 19, 1983), 63.

15. Doug Pinkham, "CEOs Only Please," *Public Affairs Perspective* (November 18, 2009), http://pac.org/blog/ceos-only-please. Accessed July 8, 2010.

16. David J. Lynch, "Change Puts U.S. Chamber on the Spot," *USA Today* (November 12, 2009), http://www.usatoday.com/money/companies/2009-11-11-Chamber11_cv_N.htm. Accessed July 8, 2010.

17. *Ibid.*

18. "The Glint of the Revolving Door," *The New York Times* (February 5, 2004).

19. M. Asif Ismail, "Spending on Lobbying Thrives: Drug and Health Products Industries Invest $182 Million to Influence Legislation," *Center for Public Integrity Report* (April 1, 2007), http://www.publicintegrity.org/rx/report.aspx?aid=823. Accessed July 8, 2010.

20. David Kirkpatrick and Duff Wilson, "Health Reform in Limbo: Top Drug Lobbyist Quits," *The New York Times* (February 12, 2010), http://www.nytimes.com/2010/02/12/health/policy/12pharma.html. Accessed July 8, 2010.

21. *Ibid.*

22. Erich Lichtblau, "Lawmakers Regulate Banks, Then Flock to Them," *The New York Times* (April 13, 2010), http://www.nytimes.com/2010/04/14/business/14lobby.html. Accessed July 8, 2010.

23. *Ibid.*

24. Dan Eggen, "Success of President Obama's Crackdown on Lobbying Questioned," *Washington Post* (February 14, 2010), http://www.washingtonpost.com/wp-dyn/content/article/2010/02/13/AR2010021301186.html. Accessed July 8, 2010.

25. *Ibid.*

26. Theo Francis and Steve Levine, "Don't Call Them Lobbyists," *BusinessWeek* (August, 10, 2009), 43–44.

27. Evan Thomas, "Peddling Influence," *Time* (March 3, 1986), 27.

28. Jane M. Keffer and Ronald Paul Hill, "An Ethical Approach to Lobbying Activities of Businesses in the United States," *Journal of Business Ethics* (September 1997), 1371–1379.

29. Peter H. Stone, "Learning from Nader," *National Journal* (June 11, 1994), 1342–1344.

30. Kristin Gilpatrick, "Sound Your Horn," *Credit Union Management* (May 1998), 10–11.

31. Stella Anne Harrison, "The Internet, Cyberadvocacy, and Citizen Communication," *Vital Speeches of the Day* (June 21, 2001).

32. Jeffrey H. Birnbaum, "Washington's Power 25," *Fortune* (December 8, 1997), 145–158.

33. Daniel Stone, "The Browning of Grassroots," *Newsweek* (August 20, 2009), http://www.newsweek.com/id/212934. Accessed July 8, 2010.

34. Carney, 103–106.

35. Dan Carney and Richard S. Dunham, "Outreach, Microsoft Style," *BusinessWeek* (July 23, 2001), 47.

36. George Monbiot, "The Fake Persuaders: Corporations Are Inventing People to Rubbish Their Opponents on the Internet," *The Guardian* (May 14, 2002).

37. Stone.

38. Center for Political Accountability, "Hidden Rivers (2006): How Trade Associations Conceal Corporate Political Spending, Its Threat to Companies, and What Shareholders Can Do," http://www.politicalaccountability.net/index.php?ht=display/ ContentDetails/i/1025. Accessed July 2010.

39. "Drug Firms Spend Millions to Battle Importation Plan," *The Wall Street Journal* (October 13, 2003), A15.

40. Ismail.

41. H.R. Medicare Prescription Drug Price 4752: Negotiation Act of 2010, http://www.govtrack.us/congress/bill.xpd?bill=h111-4752. Accessed July 8, 2010.

42. Jeffrey Marshall, "Credit Union Battleground Shifts," *US Banker* (April 1998), 10–11. See also Jill Wechsler, "Employers, Healthcare Industry Lash Back at White House, Congress," *Managed Healthcare* (February 1998), 8.

43. Nancy E. Roman, "Chamber of Commerce Hires New Lobbyists to Counter Unions," *Washington Times—National Weekly Edition* (January 11, 1998), 10. See also Douglas Harbrecht, "Chamber of Commerce Battle Cry—Kill All the Lawyers," *BusinessWeek* (March 2, 1998), 53.

44. John D. Schulz, "Leading the Charge," *Traffic World* (June 16, 2003), 1.

45. Robert Lenzner and Matthew Miller, "Buying Justice," *Forbes* (July 21, 2003), 64.

46. Richard S. Dunham, Amy Borrus, and Aaron Pressman, "A Pro-Business Pit Bull Sets Some Teeth on Edge," *BusinessWeek* (April 25, 2005), 49.

47. "Lobbying Hit Record $3.5 Billion in 2009," *USA Today* (February 12, 2010), http://content.usatoday.com/communities/onpolitics/post/2010/02/lobbying-hit-record-35-billion-in-2009/1. Accessed July 8, 2010.

48. Kimberly A. Strassel, "Business Fights Back," *The Wall Street Journal* (October 24–25, 2009), A13.

49. *Ibid.*

50. Jane Sasseen, "Who Speaks for Business?" *BusinessWeek* (October 19, 2009), 22–24.

51. *Ibid.*

52. Business Roundtable Web site, http://www.businessroundtable.org.

53. Louis Jacobson, "The Roundtable's Turnaround," *National Journal* (June 28, 2003), 2120.

54. *Ibid.*

55. Business Roundtable Web site, http://www.businessroundtable.org. Accessed July 8, 2010.

56. Sasseen, 22–24.

57. National Association of Manufacturers Web site, http://www.nam.org/preview/. Accessed July 8, 2010.

58. *Ibid.*

59. Timothy Aeppel, "Manufacturer's Group Comes to Capitol Hill to Gain Support," *The Wall Street Journal* (February 12, 2004), A9.

60. *Ibid.*

61. "Trade Issues Cause Schism between NAM and American Manufacturers," *Manufacturing Business Technology* (April 2007), 14.

62. *Ibid.*

63. Jeffrey H. Birnbaum, "Washington's Power 25," *Fortune* (May 28, 2001), 95.

64. Susan Headden, "The Little Lobby That Could," *U.S. News & World Report* (September 12, 1994), 45–48.

65. National Federation of Independent Business Web site, http://www.nfib.com. Accessed July 8, 2010.

66. Kara Rowland, "Critics Not Invited to White House Jobs Summit," *Washington Times* (December 2, 2009), http://www.washingtontimes.com/news/2009/dec/02/obama-policy-critics-not-invited-to-jobs-summit/. Accessed July 8, 2010.

67. Gerald D. Keim, "Foundations of a Political Strategy for Business," *California Management Review* (Spring 1981), 45.

68. For examples of collaboration, see the following articles: Anonymous, "Employers Seek Court Review of OSHA Compliance Program," *Business Insurance* (January 26, 1998), 1–2; John S. McClenahon, "The Dragon and the Bull (Market)," *Industry Week* (September 1, 1997), 82–86; Steven Brostoff, "Employers Back GOP Push for Medicare Market Reforms," *National Underwriter* (October 23, 1995), 33; the Health Benefits Coalition 2001 Web site, http://www.hbcweb.com. Accessed July 8, 2010.

69. Ian C. MacMillan and Patricia E. Jones, *Strategy Formulation: Power and Politics*, 2d ed. (St. Paul, MN: West, 1986), 68.

70. "Competitiveness Problems," *Manufacturing Engineering* (May 2007), 36–38.

71. The Coalition for Security and Competitiveness Web site, http://www.securityandcompetitiveness.org/. Accessed July 8, 2010.

72. Larry J. Sabato, "PAC-Man Goes to Washington," *Across the Board* (October 1984), 16.

73. Federal Election Commission Web site, http://www.fec.gov.

74. Federal Election Commission, "The FEC and the Federal Campaign Finance Law," http://www.fec.gov/pages/brochures/fecfeca.shtml (updated January 2010).

75. Josh Israel and Aaron Mehta, "Citizens United Ruling Could Tilt Playing Field against Labor, toward Corporations," *Center for Public Integrity* (January 27, 2010), http://www.publicintegrity.org/articles/entry/1920/. Accessed July 8, 2010.

76. Ann Reilly Dowd, "Look Who's Cashing In on Congress," *Money* (December 1997), 128–138.

77. *Ibid.*

78. *Ibid.*

79. Frank R. Baumgartner and Beth L. Leech, *Basic Interests: The Importance of Interest Groups in Politics and Political Science* (Chicago: University of Chicago Press, 1995), cited in Jeffrey E. Cohen and John A. Hamman, "Interest Group PAC Contributions and the 1992 Regulation of Cable Television," *The Social Science Journal* (2003), 357–369.

80. Cohen and Hamman, 357–369.

81. Daniel Fisher and William P. Barrett, "All Follow the Money," *Forbes* (April 16, 2007), 48; Michael J. Cooper, Huseyin Gulen, and Alexei V. Ovtchinnikov, "Corporate Political Contributions and Stock Returns" (January 23, 2007). Available at SSRN: http://ssrn.com/abstract=940790. Accessed July 8, 2010.

82. *Ibid.*

83. Sabato, 23.

84. "Incumbents Enjoy Huge Fundraising Advantage" (November 14, 2000, press release), http://commoncause.org. Accessed July 8, 2010.

85. Brody Mullins, "Lawmakers Tap Pac Money to Pay Wide Array of Bills," *The Wall Street Journal—Eastern Edition* (November 2, 2006), A1–A8.

86. *Ibid.*

87. OpenSecrets.org Center for Responsive Politics, http://www.opensecrets.org. Accessed July 8, 2010.

88. Jeffrey H. Birnbaum, "The New Soft Money: Campaign Finance Reform Didn't Kill Big Political Donations, It Just Changed the Rules of the Game," *Fortune* (October 27, 2003).

89. Alan Murray, "Political Capital: Forget Theory—Finance Law Fails to Work in Practice," *The Wall Street Journal* (December 23, 2003), A4.

90. Jeanne Cummings, "U.S. Limits Advocacy Groups but Stops Short of Tougher Rules," *The Wall Street Journal* (February 19, 2004), A4.

91. Matthew Mosk, "FEC to Police '527' Groups' Campaign Activities," *Washington Post* (February 2, 2007), A13.

92. Caren Chesler, "Buttonholed! Are Wall Street Employees Pressured by Bosses to Give?" *Investment Dealer's Digest* (February 2, 2004).

93. Warren Richey and Linda Feldmann, "Supreme Court's Campaign Finance Ruling: Just the Facts," *Christian Science Monitor* (February 2, 2010), http://www.csmonitor.com/USA/Justice/2010/0202/Supreme-Court-s-campaign-finance-ruling-just-the-facts. Accessed August 8, 2010.

94. *Ibid.*

95. Associated Press, "White House Stands Ground on High Court Criticism," *The New York Times* (March 14, 2010), http://www.nytimes.com/aponline/2010/03/14/us/politics/AP-US-White-House-Supreme-Court.html?ref=us. Accessed July 8, 2010.

96. Richey and Feldmann.

97. John F. Mahon, "Corporate Political Strategy," *Business in the Contemporary World* (Autumn 1989), 50–62.

98. *Ibid.*

99. Douglas A. Schuler, Kathleen Rehbein, and Roxy D. Cramer, "Pursuing Strategic Advantage through Political Means: A Multivariate Approach," *Academy of Management Journal* (August 2002), 659–672.

100. *Ibid.*

Chapter 13

1. Jena McGregor, "The Hard Sell," *BusinessWeek* (October 26, 2009), 43–50.

2. Peter F. Drucker, *Management: Tasks, Responsibilities, Practices* (New York: Harper & Row, 1973), 61.

3. Frederick F. Reichheld, *The Loyalty Effect* (Cambridge, MA: Harvard Business School Press, 1996).

4. Russell S. Winer, "A Framework for Customer Relationship Management," *California Management Review* (Summer 2001), 89–105.

5. "The Customer Is Often Ignored," *Marketing Week* (September 27, 2001), 3.

6. Camilla Ballesteros, "Don't Talk About CRM; Do It," *Marketing Week* (September 27, 2001), 49.

7. *Ibid.*

8. Scott M. Broetzmann, "Why the Customer Care Revolution Has Failed: How Companies Misuse the Telephone when Responding to Customers" (May 31, 2006), http://www.tmcnet.com/news/2006/04/18/1581418.htm. Accessed August 9, 2010.

9. Don Oldenburg, "Seller Beware: Customers Are Mad as Hell," *Washington Post* (September 9, 2003), C10.

10. Strativity Group, Inc., Worldwide Survey of 165 Executives, March–November 2003, cited in *BusinessWeek* (March 8, 2004), 14.

11. American Customer Satisfaction Index, "Customer Satisfaction Resilient—Essential for Economic Recovery According to ACSI" (February 16, 2010), http://www.theacsi.org/images/stories/images/news/Q409_press_release.pdf. Accessed July 8, 2010.

12. David Kiley and Burt Helm, "100 Best Global Brands: The Great Trust Offensive," *BusinessWeek* (September 28, 2009), 38–42.

13. Robert J. Holloway and Robert S. Hancock, *Marketing in a Changing Environment,* 2d ed. (New York: John Wiley & Sons, 1973), 558–565.

14. *Ibid.,* 565–566.

15. Robert O. Herrmann, "Consumerism: Its Goals, Organizations, and Future," *Journal of Marketing* (October 1970), 55–60.

16. Ruth Simon, "You're Losing Your Consumer Rights," *Money* (Vol. 25, No. 3, 1996), 100–111.

17. Philip Kotler, "What Consumerism Means for Marketers," *Harvard Business Review* (May–June 1972), 48–57.

18. Ralph Nader, *Unsafe at Any Speed* (New York: Grossman Publishers, 1965).

19. Kotler, 50. Kotler states that these conditions were proposed by Neil J. Smelser, *Theory of Collective Behavior* (New York: The Free Press, 1963).

20. Robert J. Samuelson, "The Aging of Ralph Nader," *Newsweek* (December 16, 1985), 57.

21. Rich Thomas, "Safe at This Speed," *BusinessWeek* (August 22, 1994), 40; Douglas Harbrecht and Ronald Grover, "The Second Coming of Ralph Nader," *BusinessWeek* (March 6, 1989), 28.

22. Paul Magnusson, "The Punishing Price of Nader's Passion," *BusinessWeek* (November 20, 2000), 44.

23. Gary Fields, "Leading the News: Nader to Run for President Again; Democrats Fear a Reprise of 2000," *The Wall Street Journal* (February 23, 2003), A3.

24. Federal Election Commission, "2004 Election Results," http://www.fec.gov/pubrec/fe2004/tables.pdf. Accessed July 8, 2010.

25. Scott Shane, "The 2004 Election: The Independent; Nader Is Left with Fewer Votes, and Friends, after '04 Race," *The New York Times* (November 6, 2004).

26. http://www.anunreasonableman.com/. Accessed July 8, 2010.

27. "Bernard Shaw: Collected Plays with Their Prefaces." Vol. 2, ed. Dan H. Laurence (London: Max Reinhardt, The Bodley Head, 1971), 489–733.

28. Cordelia Brabbs, "Web Fuels Consumer Activism," *Marketing* (September 21, 2000), 23.

29. http://www.consumerreports.org/cro/index.htm

30. "Never Say Never," http://www.ConsumerReports.org (September 2009), 63.

31. "So You'll Pay…More," http://www.ConsumerReports.org (February 2010), 63.

32. "A Raspberry for Apple Candy," http://www.ConsumerReports.org (October 2009), 63.

33. William Leiss, Stephen Kline, and Sut Jhally, *Social Communication in Advertising* (Toronto: Methuen, 1986), 13.

34. *Ibid.*

35. Rob Norton, "How Uninformative Advertising Tells Consumers Quite a Bit," *Fortune* (December 26, 1994), 37.

36. William Shaw and Vincent Barry, *Moral Issues in Business,* 11th ed. (Belmont, CA: Wadsworth, 2009), 389–414.

37. Stuart Elliott, "A Survey of Consumer Atttitudes Reveals the Depth of the Challenge That the Agencies Face," *The New York Times* (April 14, 2004), C8.

38. Shaw and Barry, *Ibid.*

39. *Ibid.,* 404.

40. "Selling It," *Consumer Reports* (October 2001), 63.

41. Shaw and Barry, *Ibid.*

42. Tom Lowry and Burt Helm, "Blasting Away at Product Placement," *BusinessWeek* (October 26, 2009), 60.

43. Dean Foust and Brian Grow, "Coke: Wooing the TV Generation," *BusinessWeek Online* (March 1, 2004).

44. Brian Levin, "American Idol's Launch of Text Voting Shows Mobile Voting Can Survive, Wireless Business and Technology" (January 1, 2000), http://wireless.sys-con.com/node/41214. Accessed August 9, 2011. Also see http://www.americanidol.com/videos/view/?vid=608. Accessed July 8, 2010.

45. Joe Flint and Emily Nelson, "All My Children Gets Revlon Twist—First Came Product Placement Now TV 'Plot Placement' Yields ABC a Big Ad Buy," *The Wall Street Journal* (March 15, 2002); Leslie Ryan, "Passions Product Pitch; NBC, Avon Weave New Cosmetics Line into Soap Opera's Story," *Television Week* (July 28, 2003).

46. Ingela Ratledge, "Modern Product Placement," *TVGuideMagazine.com* (April 12, 2010).

47. Ronald Grover, Tom Lowry, Gerry Khermouch, Cliff Edwards, and Dean Foust, "Can Mad. Ave. Make Zap-Proof Ads?" *BusinessWeek* (February 2, 2004), 36–37.

48. *Ibid.*

49. Lowry and Helm, 2009, 60.

50. James Heckman, "Puffery Claims No Longer So Easy to Make," *Marketing News* (February 14, 2000), 6.

51. Eli P. Cox, "Deflating the Puffer," *MSU Business Topics* (Summer 1973), 29.

52. "Consumers Have Mixed Reactions to Puffery in Advertising" (January 19, 2010), http://www.physorg.com/news183128214. html. Accessed July 8, 2010.

53. Shaw and Barry.

54. Jeffrey Kluger, "Now Hear This," *Time* (March 1, 2010).

55. Get a Mac, http://en.wikipedia.org/wiki/Get_a_Mac. Accessed July 8, 2010.

56. Nicole Martinelli, "Get a Mac Campaign Named One of the Best Marketing Jobs Ever" (January 15, 2009), http://www.cultof-mac.com/get-a-mac-campaign-named-one-of-best-marketing-jobs-ever/7091. Accessed July 8, 2010.

57. "Papa John's Attack Ads Aren't Just for Politicians" (March 11, 2010), http://www.jordanmelnick.com/taxonomy/term/90. Accessed July 8, 2010.

58. Bruce Buchanan, "Can You Pass the Comparative Ad Challenge?" *Harvard Business Review* (July–August 1985), 106.

59. *Time* (June 24, 1974), 76.

60. Hillary Chura, "Spirited Sex; Alcohol Ads Ratchet Up the Sex to Woo Jaded Customers," *Advertising Age* (July 9, 2001), 1.

61. John Fetto, "Where's the Lovin'?" *American Demographics* (February 2001), 10–11.

62. Herbert Jack Rotfeld, "Misplaced Marketing Gardening, Pizza, Tacos, Truck Parts and Fake Jewelry: Misuse and Misdirection of Sex in Advertising," *Journal of Consumer Marketing* (Vol. 20, No. 3, 2003), 189–191.

63. Jacob Bernstein, "Fashion's Miss Modesty: Designers Drop Raunchy in Favor of the Demure," *WWD: Women's Wear Daily* (February 13, 2004), 1–2.

64. Tom Reichert and Jacqueline Lambiase (eds.), "Sex in Consumer Culture: The Erotic Content of Media and Marketing" (Mahwah, NJ: L. Erlbaum Associates, 2006).

65. http://www.uga.edu/columns/060410/profile.html

66. http://www.apa.org/releases/sexualization.html

67. Ira Teinowitz, "Pediatricians Call for Ad Restrictions," *Television Week* (December 4, 2006), 8.

68. *Ibid.*

69. "Barbie Gets Her First Credit Card," *Credit Card Management* (January 1998), 6–8.

70. American Psychological Association, http://www.apa.org. Accessed July 8, 2010.

71. Jayne O' Donnell, "As Kids Get Savvy, Marketers Move the Age Scale," http://www.usatoday.com/money/advertising/2007-04-11-tween-usat_N.htm. Accessed July 8, 2010.

72. "CARU Recommends that J&J Discontinue Advertising," http://www.caru.org/news/2010/5151PR.pdf. Accessed July 8, 2010.

73. Bonnie Rochman, "Sweet Spot: New Data on How the Least Healthy Cereals Do the Most Marketing," *Time* (November 2, 2009), 55–56.

74. Ilan Brat and Jared Favole, "Food Makers Warned on Claims," *The Wall Street Journal* (March 4, 2010), D2.

75. Bob Jenkins, "Much Ado about Ads," *License!* (November 2006), 72–75.

76. *Ibid.*

77. *Ibid.*

78. Ellen Edwards, "Television's Problem Child," *The Washington Post National Weekly Edition* (June 20–26, 1994), 22.

79. Ellen Neuborne, "For Kids on the Web, It's an Ad, Ad, Ad, Ad World," *BusinessWeek* (August 13, 2001), 108–109.

80. Brian Grow and Keith Epstein, "The Poverty Business," *BusinessWeek* (May 21, 2007), 57–67.

81. *Ibid.*

82. http://www.ftc.gov/bcp/conline/pubs/alerts/pdayalrt.shtm

83. Grow and Epstein, 62.

84. *Ibid.*

85. Kirk Davidson, "Look for Abundance of Opposition to TV Ads," *Marketing News* (January 6, 1997), 26–28.

86. Jeremy Mullman, "The Booze Tube: Spirits Biz Pours Ad Bucks into TV," *Advertising Age* (July 17, 2006), 3–29.

87. http://www.commercialalert.org

88. http://www.newsday.com/news/local/longisland/ny-usdrin065160180apr06,0,3966732.story?track=rss

89. Michael Applebaum, "Ethical Journalists, Shyster Admen? All's Right in the World," *Brandweek* (February 14, 2005), 30.

90. *Ibid.*

91. WHO, " Regulation Urgently Needed to Control Growing List of Deadly Tobacco Products" (May 30, 2006), http://www.who.int/mediacentre/news/releases/2006/pr28/en/index.html. Accessed July 8, 2010.

92. Eben Shapiro, "FTC Staff Recommends Ban of Joe Camel Campaign," *The Wall Street Journal* (August 11, 1993), B1.

93. Ira Teinowitz, "FTC's Camel Case Hinges on Ad's Power Over Kids," *Advertising Age* (June 2, 1997), 4, 45.

94. Judann Pollack and Ira Teinowitz, "With Joe Camel Out, Government Wants the Marlboro Man Down," *Advertising Age* (July 14, 1997), 3, 34.

95. Duff Wilson and Julie Creswell, "Where There's No Smoke, Altria Hopes There's Fire," *The New York Times* (January 31, 2010), BU 1.

96. *Ibid.*

97. *Ibid.*, 5.

98. Benedict Carey, "Nutritional Analysis of Bars Reveals Discrepancies," *Los Angeles Times* (November 5, 2001), S2.

99. "Food Labels Provide More Confusion Than Clarity," *USA Today* (November 3, 2009), 8A.

100. Scott Gottlieb, "The FDA Takes on Cheerios," *The Wall Street Journal* (March 2, 2010), A23.

101. *Ibid.*

102. "Regulating Health Food: The Proof Is in the Pudding," *The Economist* (October 31, 2009), 17–18.

103. "Pepsi Gets a Makeover: Taking the Challenge," *The Economist* (March 27, 2010), 67.

104. *Ibid.*

105. "Pepsi Brings in the Health Police," *Bloomberg Business* (January 25, 2020), 50–51.

106. "What Consumers Think about Green Products," *USA Today* (December 3, 2009), 1B.

107. "The Green Watchdogs," *Smartmoney* (April 2010).

108. *Ibid.*

109. Megan Basham, "Green Fatigue," *World* (March 27, 2010), 59–60.

110. Charles Pappas, "Ad Nauseum," *Advertising Age* (July 10, 2000), 16–18.

111. Carrie McLaren, "Ad Creep," *Print* (November/December 2000), 102–107.

112. "Inserting Advertisements into Video Games Holds Much Promise," *The Economist* (June 9, 2007), 73–74.

113. *Ibid.*

114. Erin White, "Ad Agency Aims to Turn Heads into Billboards," *The Wall Street Journal* (February 11, 2003).

115. "A Businessperson's Guide to Federal Warranty Law," *Federal Trade Commission*, http://www.ftc.gov/bcp/edu/pubs/business/adv/bus01.shtm. Accessed July 8, 2010.

116. "The Guesswork on Warranties," *BusinessWeek* (July 15, 1975), 51; "Marketing: Anti-Lemon Aid," *Time* (February, 1976), 76.

117. *Ibid.*

118. Amy Zuckerman, "Order in the Courts?" *World Trade* (September 2001), 26–28.

119. "Stores Make Big Profits on Warranties You Don't Need. Here's a Look at Some of the Hooey You Shouldn't Heed," *Consumer Reports Buying Guide* (2007), 8.

120. *Ibid.*

121. Neal Templin, "Please Spare Me the Extended Warranty," *The Wall Street Journal* (October 14, 2009), D1.

122. http://www.llbean.com. Accessed July 8, 2010.

123. "Fair Packaging and Labeling Act," *Federal Trade Commission*, http://www.ftc.gov/os/statutes/fpla/outline.shtm. Accessed July 8, 2010.

124. "The Escalating Struggle Between the FTC and Business," *BusinessWeek* (December 13, 1976), 52.

125. FTC, "Federal Trade Commission: A History," http://ftc.gov/ftc/history/ftchistory.htm. Accessed July 8, 2010.

126. "Federal Trade Commission," http://www.ftc.gov/ftc/about.shtm. Accessed July 8, 2010.

127. *Ibid.*

128. Thomas G. Krattenmaker, "The Federal Trade Commission and Consumer Protection," *California Management Review* (Summer 1976), 94–95.

129. Susan J. Tolchin and Martin Tolchin, *Dismantling America: The Rush to Deregulate* (Boston: Houghton-Mifflin, 1983), 147–149.

130. James C. Miller III, "Revamping the Federal Trade Commission" (St. Louis: Center for the Study of American Business, December 1984), 3.

131. Mark Potts, "What's Gotten into the FTC?" *The Washington Post National Weekly Edition* (June 17–23, 1991), 32.

132. *Ibid.*

133. Michael Oneal, "Does New Balance Have an American Soul?" *BusinessWeek* (December 12, 1994), 86–87.

134. Detailed information on FTC activities is available on the FTC's Web site at http://www.ftc.gov. Accessed July 8, 2010.

135. *Ibid.*

136. *Ibid.*

137. Mark Taylor, "Antitrust Watchdog," *Modern Healthcare* (June 26, 2006), 28–30.

138. Jim Edwards, "FTC Chief Majoras Offers a (Laissez) Faire Deal," *Brandweek* (February 5, 2007), 9.

139. *Ibid.*

140. "What the New Credit Card Law Means for You," *CreditCards.com*, http://www.creditcards.com/credit-card-news/help/what-the-new-credit-card-rules-mean-6000.php. Accessed July 8, 2010.

141. *Ibid.*

142. Sewell Chan, "Finding the Way to the Final Bill," *The New York Times* (May 22, 2010), B1, B6.

143. "America's Consumer-Protection Bill: Sizzling Away," *The Economist* (October 24, 2009), 85–86.

144. "First, Slap Limits on Bank Leverage," *Bloomberg Businessweek* (March 22, 29, 2010), 26–27.

145. Sewell Chan, "Consumer Groups Urge Regulation of Nonbank Financial Institutions," *The New York Times* (March 6, 2010), B3.

146. Julia Baird, "Voice of the Middle Class: Why Wall Street Hates Elizabeth Warren," *Newsweek* (March 22, 2010), 20.

147. Bob Herbert, "Derailing Help for Consumers," *The New York Times* (March 27, 2010), A17.

148. Chan, 2010, *Ibid.*

149. John F. Pickering and D. C. Cousins, *The Economic Implications of Codes of Practice* (Manchester, England: University of Manchester Institute of Science and Technology, Department of Management Sciences, 1980), 17. Also see J. J. Boddewyn, "Advertising Self-Regulation: Private Government and Agent of Public Policy," *Journal of Public Policy and Marketing* (1985), 129.

150. *Ibid.*, 135.

151. Better Business Bureau, http://www.bbb.org. Accessed July 8, 2010.

152. Edwards, 9.

153. National Advertising Division, http://www.nadreview.org/AboutNAD.aspx. Accessed July 8, 2010.

Chapter 14

1. Alan Ohnsman, Jeff Green, and Kae Inoue, "The Humbling of Toyota," *Bloomberg BusinessWeek* (March 22, 29, 2010), 33–36.

2. "Toyota's 'Tylenol Moment,'" *Newsweek* (February 15, 2010), 12.

3. James Kanter, Micheline Maynard, and Hiroko Tabuchi, "Toyota's Pattern Is Slow Response on Safety Issues," *The New York Times* (February 7, 2010), 1.

4. David Welch, "Oh, What a (Hideous) Feeling," *Bloomberg BusinessWeek* (February 15, 2010), 21–22.

5. "55% say Toyota Dragged Its Feet," *USA Today* (March 2, 2010), 1B.

6. Janice Castro, "Making It Better," *Time* (November 13, 1989), 78–80. See also "Quality: How to Make It Pay," *BusinessWeek* (August 8, 1994), 54ff.

7. Walker Research, "Reputation and Social Performance Assessment Study" (Indianapolis: Walker Research, August 1994), 17.

8. Michael Harvey, Milorad M. Novicevic, and Timothy Kiessling, "Hypercompetition and the Future of Global Management in the Twenty-First Century," *Thunderbird International Review* (September/October 2001), 599–616.

9. Rajaram Veliyath and Elizabeth Fitzgerald, "Firm Capabilities, Business Strategies, Customer Preferences, and Hypercompetitive Arenas," *Competitiveness Review* (Vol. 10, 2000), 56–82.

10. Debanjan Mitra and Peter N. Golder, "Quality Is in the Eye of the Beholder," *Harvard Business Review* (April 2007) 26–28.

11. "ACSI Quarterly Scores," *American Customer Satisfaction Index*, http://www.theacsi.org/index.php?option=com_content&task=view&id=203&Itemid=214. Accessed May 6, 2010.

12. Christopher W. Hart, "Beating the Market with Customer Satisfaction," *Harvard Business Review* (March 2007), 30–32.

13. "Customers Turned Off by Poor Service Levels," *Marketing Week* (March 5, 1998), 11.

14. David A. Garvin, "Competing on the Eight Dimensions of Quality," *Harvard Business Review* (November–December 1987), 101–109.

15. Manuel G. Velasquez, *Business Ethics: Concepts and Cases* (Upper Saddle River, NJ: Prentice Hall, 2002), 335–344.

16. Yair Aharoni, *The No Risk Society* (Chatham, NJ: Chatham House Publishers, 1981), 62–63.

17. Velasquez, 348.

18. U.S. Food and Drug Administration, http://www.fda.gov/safety/recalls/ucm207477.htm. Accessed May 13, 2010.

19. Rick Weiss, "Tainted Chinese Imports Common," *The Washington Post* (May 20, 2007), A01.

20. *Ibid.*

21. E. Patrick McGuire, "Product Liability: Evolution and Reform" (New York: The Conference Board, 1989), 6.

22. "2003 Annual Report of the Consumer Products Safety Commission," http://www.cpsc.gov. Accessed July 17, 2010.

23. "Ford's $128.5 Million Headache," *Time* (February 10, 1978), 65.

24. "Product Liability Lawsuits Up in 2009," http://www.youhavealawyer.com/blog/2010/01/12/product-liability-lawsuit-verdicts-up/. Accessed May 13, 2010.

25. Earnest W. Deavenport, Jr., "Profound Opportunities: Profound Threats," *Vital Speeches of the Day* (May 1, 1997), 428–430.

26. Kara Sissell, "Study Tallies Tort Litigation's Effect on Innovation," *Chemical Week* (April 4, 2007), 43.

27. Andrew Hacker, "The Asbestos Nightmare," *Fortune* (January 20, 1986), 121.

28. Francine Schwadel, "Robins and Plaintiffs Face Uncertain Future," *The Wall Street Journal* (August 23, 1985), 4.

29. David J. Morrow, "Implant Maker Reaches Accord on Damage Suits," *The New York Times* (July 9, 1998), A1.

30. Kristine Henry, "Fails to Hurt Grace Much," *The Sun* (July 26, 2001), 2C.

31. Soma Biswas, "No Grace for Grace," *The Deal.com* (March 24, 2004), 1.

32. Dionne Searcey, "Lawyers Preen in Toyota Case," *The Wall Street Journal* (May 14, 2010), B4.

33. Fred W. Morgan and Karl A. Boedecker, "A Historical View of Strict Liability for Product-Related Injuries," *Journal of Macromarketing* (Spring 1996), 103–117.

34. Ann Christopher, "Avoiding a Hazardous Violation," *Warehousing Management* (August 2001), 20.

35. Kerry Powell, "Liability Language: Know the Difference Between Strict and Absolute," *On-Site* (March 2004), 46.

36. Curt Ward, "What Is Strict Liability?" http://www.buteralaw.com/newsletters.asp?c=47&id=366. Accessed May 13, 2010.

37. Terry Morehead Dworkin and Mary Jane Sheffet, "Product Liability in the 1980s," *Journal of Public Policy and Marketing* (1985), 71.

38. "The Asbestos Blob, Cont.," *The Wall Street Journal* (April 6, 2004), A16.

39. "Business Line: India Supreme Court Ruling on Damage Liability of Common Carrier," *Businessline* (June 30, 2000), 1.

40. "Charities Appeal to Blair to Stop Use of GM Crops in Britain," *Third Sector* (March 10, 2004), 2.

41. Roger Leroy Miller, "Drawing Limits on Liability," *The Wall Street Journal* (April 4, 1984), 28.

42. Natalie Kosteini, "Top Court Reverses Crown Asbestos Ruling," *Philadelphia Business Journal* (February 23, 2004).

43. Steven T. Taylor, "While the Asbestos Trust Fund May Be Dead (for Now), Litigation in This Area Is Alive and Well," *Of Counsel* (December 2006), 1–15.

44. *Ibid.*

45. Dworkin and Sheffet, 69.

46. Clemens P. Work, "Product Safety: A New Hot Potato for Congress," *U.S. News & World Report* (June 14, 1982), 62.

47. Edward J. Schoen, Margaret M. Hogan, and Joseph S. Falcheck, "An Examination of the Legal and Ethical Public Policy Consideration Underlying DES Market Share Liability," *Journal of Business Ethics* (Vol. 24, 2000), 141–163.

48. "Tampering with Buyers' Confidence," *U.S. News & World Report* (March 3, 1986), 46.

49. Damien Thomlinson, "Drug Extortion Highlights Risks," *Business Insurance* (June 26, 2000), 33–37.

50. Dean Foust, Brian Grow, and Sheridan Prasso, "Evolution of the Envelope," *BusinessWeek* (November 5, 2000), 14.

51. Thomas Lee, "Food Service Is on Front Line of Terror War," *St. Louis Post-Dispatch* (September 23, 2002), 8.

52. "Tort," *The Lectric Law Library's Lexicon*, http://www.lectlaw.com/def2/t032.htm. Accessed May 13, 2010.

53. "Tort Reform in the States" (April 15, 2010), *The Heritage Foundation*, http://www.heritage.org/Research/Lecture/Tort-Reform-in-the-States-Protecting-Consumers-and-Enhancing-Economic-Growth. Accessed May 13, 2010.

54. Peter Waldman and Eileen White, "Battle Rages over Damages, Insurance Rates: States Are Debating Sweeping Changes in Tort Laws," *The Wall Street Journal* (April 15, 1986), 5; See also R. J. Samuelson, "Lawyer Heaven," *The Washington Post National Weekly Edition* (June 27–July 3, 1994), 28.

55. Robert Vosper, "Tortuous States," *InsideCounsel* (July 2006), 17.

56. *Ibid.*

57. Michele Galen, "The Class Action Against Product Liability Laws," *BusinessWeek* (July 29, 1997), 74.

58. Richard D. Haley, "Don't Let the Rogues off the Hook," *ENR* (May 4, 1998), 89; Robert Kuttner, "How Tort Reform Will Hurt Consumers," *San Diego Union Tribune* (June 24, 1994), B7. See also Jerry Phillips, "Attacks on the Legal System: Fallacy of Tort Reform Arguments," *Trial* (February 1992), 106–110.

59. Stuart Taylor and Evan Thomas, "Civil Wars," *Newsweek* (December 15, 2003), 47.

60. "Health Care Reform," *Common Good*, http://commongood.org/learn.html. Accessed May 15, 2010.

61. Taylor and Thomas, 42–53. Philip K. Howard, *The Collapse of the Common Good: How America's Lawsuit Culture Undermines Our Freedom* (New York: Ballantine, 2002).

62. Philip K. Howard, "Conley R.I.P." *The New York Sun* (June 4, 2007).

63. *Ibid.*

64. "The Defects in Product-Liability Laws," *BusinessWeek* (July 29, 1991), 88.

65. Information about the Consumer Product Safety Commission is available at the CPSC Web site: http://www.cpsc.gov. Accessed July 17, 2010.

66. "2000 Annual Report to Congress," *Consumer Product Safety Commission*, http://www.cpsc.gov. Accessed July 17, 2010.

67. "Consumer Product Safety Commission," *Federal Regulatory Directory*, 6th ed. (Washington, DC: Congressional Quarterly, 1990), 46–47.

68. "Obama Names New CPSC Commissioner," *NewsInferno.com* (May 6, 2009), http://www.newsinferno.com/archives/5939. Accessed May 15, 2010.

69. OnSafety, http://www.cpsc.gov/onsafety/. Accessed May 15, 2010.

70. Consumer Product Safety Improvement Act of 2008, http://www.cpsc.gov/about/cpsia/cpsia.html. Accessed May 15, 2010.

71. "Congress, CPSC Debate Resources, Budget," The House Committee on Appropriations Subcommittee on Financial Services and General Government hearing about the CPSC on February 28, 2007, http://blogs.consumerreports.org/safety/2007/03/congress_cpsc_d.html. Accessed July 17, 2010.

72. U.S. Food and Drug Administration (FDA), "Regulations," http://www.fda.gov/RegulatoryInformation/Legislation/default.htm. Accessed May 15, 2010.

73. Malcolm Gladwell, "A Fresh Approach at the FDA," *The Washington Post Weekly Edition* (May 13–19, 1991), 32.

74. "Woman in the News: Jean Ellen Henney: For FDA an Old Hand," *The New York Times* (June 24, 1998), A16.

75. Richard S. Dunham, "New Trials at the FDA," *BusinessWeek* (June 1, 1998), 50.

76. James G. Dickinson, "Henney Fired, RU-486 Approved Torpedoed Retention," *Medical Marketing and Media* (March 2001), 32.

77. Sara Calabro, "Reshuffle Won't Disrupt FDA, Pitt Says," *PRWeek* (March 8, 2004), 4.

78. Dennis Murray, "Former Commissioner to Pay Big Fine," *Medical Economics* (April 6, 2007), 21.

79. Jill Wechsler, "Von Eschenbach Confirmed as FDA Commissioner," *Pharmaceutical Technology* (January 2007), 20–26.

80. U.S. FDA, Commissioner's Page, http://www.fda.gov/AboutFDA/CommissionersPage/default.htm. Accessed May 15, 2010.

81. John Carey, "How Safe Is the Food Supply?" *BusinessWeek* (May 21, 2007), 40.

82. *Ibid.*, 42.

83. Ellen Byron, "Diaper Gripes Grow Louder for P&G," *The Wall Street Journal* (May 14, 2010), B1.

84. K. Ishikawa, *What Is Total Quality Control?* (Milwaukee, WI: Quality Press, 1985).

85. Victor B. Wayhan and Erica L. Balderson, "TQM and Financial Performance: What Has Empirical Research Discovered?" *Total Quality Management & Business Excellence* (May 2007), 403–412; Victor B. Wayhan and Erica L. Balderson, "TQM and Financial Performance: A Research Standard," *Total Quality Management & Business Excellence* (May 2007), 393–401.

86. I. Salaheldin Salaheldin and Zain Mohamed, "How Quality Control Circles Enhance Work Safety: A Case Study," *TQM Magazine* (2007), 229–244.

87. "The Eight Elements of TQM," *Six Sigma*, http://www.isixsigma.com/index.php?option=com_k2&view=item&id=1333:the-eight-elements-of-tqm&Itemid=155. Accessed May 25, 2010.

88. Lawrence A. Crosby, "Measuring Customer Satisfaction," in E. E. Scheuing and W. F. Christopher (eds.), *The Service Quality Handbook* (New York: AMACOM, 1993), 392.

89. A. Blanton Godfrey and E. G. Kammerer, "Service Quality vs. Manufacturing Quality: Five Myths Exploded," *The Service Quality Handbook*, 5.

90. Debanjan Mitra and Peter N. Golder, "Quality Is in the Eye of the Beholder," *Harvard Business Review* (April 2007), 26–28.

91. Ron Basu, "Six Sigma to Fit Sigma," *IIE Solutions* (July 2001), 28–33.

92. Michael Hammer and Jeff Godling, "Putting Six Sigma in Perspective," *Quality* (October 2001), 58–62.

93. SSA&Company (formerly The Six Sigma Academy) Web site, http://www.ssaandco.com/. Accessed July 17, 2010.

94. Hammer and Godling, 58.

95. Basu, 28–33.

96. *Ibid.*

Chapter 15

1. Michael de Pencier, "Interview with Maurice Strong," *Corporate Knights: The Canadian Magazine for Responsible Business* (June 4, 2003), http://static.corporateknights.ca/Maurice_Strong.pdf. Accessed July 16, 2010.

2. Paul R. Ehrlich, Anne H. Ehrlich, and Gretchen C. Daily, *The Stork and the Plow: The Equity Answer to the Human Dilemma* (New Haven, CT: Yale University Press, 1997), 24.

3. Full cost accounting (FCA) has been developed more recently to account for externalities and other tradeoffs of business processes.

4. Marc Gunther, "Going Green," *Fortune* (April 2, 2007), 44.

5. *Ibid.*, 44.

6. *Ibid.*

7. "Report of the World Commission on Environment and Development," http://www.un.org/documents/ga/res/42/ares42-187.htm. Accessed July 16, 2010.

8. W. Edward Stead and Jean Garner Stead with Mark Starik, *Sustainable Strategic Management* (Armonk, NY: M. E. Sharpe, Inc., 2004).

9. William McDonough and Michael Braungart, *Cradle to Cradle: Remaking the Way We Make Things* (New York: North Point Press, 2002).

10. David Eddy, "Sustainability Guru," *American Fruit Grower* (June 2004), 10.

11. *Ibid.*

12. Marjorie Kelly, "Using Conversation to Change the World," *Business Ethics* (Winter 2003), 21.

13. http://www.parducci.com

14. *Ibid.*

15. *Ibid.*

16. *Ibid.*

17. http://www.mendocino.winecountry.com/

18. Daniel C. Esty and Andrew S. Winston, *Green to Gold: How Smart Companies Use Environmental Strategy to Innovate, Create Value, and Build Competitive Advantage* (New Haven, CT: Yale University Press, 2006).

19. William Collins, Robert Colman, James Haywood, Martin R. Manning, and Philip Mote, "The Physical Science Behind Climate Change," *Scientific American* (August 2007), 64–71.
20. "Cleaning Up (Cover Story)," *Economist* (June 2, 2007), 3–4.
21. Collins et al., 64–71.
22. *Ibid.*
23. Jane Sasseen, "Who Speaks for Business?" *BusinessWeek* (October 19, 2009), 22–24.
24. The Department of Defense, *The Quadrennial Defense Review Report* (February 2010), http://www.defense.gov/QDR/QDR%20as%20of%2029JAN10%201600.pdf#page=107.
25. *Ibid.*, 84.
26. *Ibid.*, 85.
27. David Stipp, "Climate Collapse: The Pentagon's Weather Nightmare," *Fortune* (January 26, 2004).
28. "An Inconvenient Truth Publisher Rodale Congratulates Former Vice President Al Gore on His Oscar," *Business Wire* (February 26, 2007), http://www.allbusiness.com/services/business-services/4529904-1.html.
29. William J. Broad, "From a Rapt Audience, a Call to Cool the Hype," *The New York Times* (March 13, 2007), http://www.nytimes.com/2007/03/13/science/13gore.html. Accessed August 16, 2010.
30. Esty and Wilson.
31. *Ibid.*
32. Steve Hargreaves, "Climate Change's Hail Mary," *CNNMoney.com* (March 17, 2010), http://money.cnn.com/2010/03/17/news/economy/cap_and_hybrid/. Accessed July 16, 2010.
33. *Ibid.*
34. *Ibid.*
35. "How a Market Heats Up," *Fortune* (May 29, 2006), 74–75.
36. Wolfram Krewitt, Sonja Simon, Wina Graus, Sven Teske, Arthouros Zervos, and Oliver Schafer, "The 2°C Scenario: A Sustainable World Energy Perspective," *Energy Policy* (October 2007), 4969–4980.
37. DOE/EIA (July 2009), Energy Information Administration/Renewable Energy Consumption and Electricity Preliminary Statistics, 2008, http://www.eia.doe.gov/cneaf/alternate/page/renew_energy_consump/rea_prereport.html. Accessed July 16, 2010.
38. Martin LaMonica, "Walmart Chairman: Go Green for Money, Not Image," *CNET News* (April 12, 2010), http://news.cnet.com/8301-11128_3-20002313-54.html. Accessed July 16, 2010.
39. *Ibid.*
40. Esty and Winston.
41. "Venture Capital Didn't Abandon Renewable Energy Despite Crisis," *EcoSeed* (January 13, 2010), http://www.ecoseed.org/en/general-green-news/features/in-depth/5848-Venture-capital-didn%E2%80%99t-abandon-renewable-energy-despite-crisis. Accessed July 16, 2010.
42. *Ibid.*
43. Esty and Winston.
44. *Ibid.*
45. *Ibid.*
46. Mary Carmichael, Sarah Schafer, and Sudip Mazumdar, "Troubled Waters," *Newsweek* (June 4, 2007), 52–56.
47. Geoffrey Lean, "Water Crisis Now Bigger Threat Than Financial Crisis," *The Independent* (March 15, 2009), http://www.independent.co.uk/environment/climate-change/water-scarcity-now-bigger-threat-than-financial-crisis-1645358.html. Accessed July 16, 2010.
48. Carmichael, Schafer, and Mazumdar, 52–56.
49. Esty and Winston.
50. Carmichael, Schafer, and Mazumdar, 52–56.
51. *Ibid.*
52. Lean, 2009.
53. *Ibid.*
54. "Message by H.E. Dr. Ali Abdussalam Treki, President of the United Nations General Assembly," http://www.cbd.int/doc/speech/2009/sp-2009-11-09-iyb-welcome-unga-treki-en.pdf. Accessed July 16, 2010.
55. *Ibid.*
56. "Pollutants/Toxics: Toxic Substances," http://www.epa.gov/ebtpages/polltoxicsubstances.html. Accessed July 16, 2010.
57. "Responding to Oil Spills" (2001), http://www.epa.gov. Accessed July 16, 2010.
58. "Ten Years After the Spill," *Newsweek* (March 29, 1999).
59. "Intent to Prepare a Supplemental Environmental Impact Statement on the Exxon Valdez Oil Spill Trustee Council's Restoration Efforts," http://www.fakr.noaa.gov/notice/75fr3706.pdf. Accessed July 16, 2010.
60. Cain Burdeau and Holbrook Mohr, "Gulf Coast Oil Spill Could Eclipse Exxon Valdez," *The Washington Post* (April 30, 2010), http://www.businessweek.com/ap/financialnews/D9FD13700.html. Accessed August 16, 2010.

61. "Air Pollution Effects," http://www.epa.gov/ebtpages/airairpollutioneffects.html. Accessed July 16, 2010.

62. Mark Dolliver, "Environmental Worries Will Never Be Extinct," *Adweek* (March 26, 2007), 35.

63. "What Is Acid Rain," http://www.epa.gov/acidrain/what/index.html. Accessed July 16, 2010.

64. *Ibid.*

65. *Ibid.*

66. "Why Should You Be Concerned about Air Pollution?" http://www.epa.gov/air/caa/peg/concern.html. Accessed July 16, 2010.

67. *Ibid.*

68. Esty and Winston.

69. *Ibid.*

70. *Ibid.*

71. "Wastes," http://www.epa.gov/epawaste/index.htm. Accessed July 16, 2010.

72. *Ibid.*

73. *Ibid.*

74. Alex Kirby, "It's a Waste," http://www.unep.org/OurPlanet/imgversn/104/kirby.html. Accessed July 16, 2010.

75. *Ibid.*

76. R. Cooke, "Scientists Report Gains in Protecting Ozone Layer May Be Paying Off," *Seattle Times* (March 4, 2001), A13.

77. Jeffrey Frankel, "Bush's Spectacular Failure," *The International Economy* (Spring 2004), 22–28.

78. "EPA: HCFCs Set for an Early Ban," *ICIS Chemical Business* (March 26, 2007), 32.

79. *Ibid.*

80. Liz White, "Ozone Crisis Not Over," *Urethanes Technology* (Dec/Jan 2007), 20.

81. "Earth-Shattering Ozone Record," *R&D Magazine* (December 2006), 7.

82. Ozone Hole Watch, http://ozonewatch.gsfc.nasa.gov/meteorology/annual_data.html. Accessed July 16, 2010.

83. http://www.epa.gov. Accessed July 16, 2010.

84. E. Linden, "Condition Critical," *Time—Special Edition on How to Save the Earth* (Spring 2000), 18–24.

85. Unmesh Kher, Kristina Dell, and Kathleen Kingsbury, "Oceans of Nothing," *Time* (November 13, 2006), 56–57.

86. *Ibid.*

87. Unmesh Kher, "Oceans of Nothing," *Time* (November 5, 2006), http://www.time.com/time/magazine/article/0,9171,1555121,00.html. Accessed August 16, 2010.

88. Kher, Dell, and Kingsbury, 56–57.

89. Alex Dominguez, "Officials: Bay Blue Crab Population up 60 Percent," *Bloomberg BusinessWeek* (April 14, 2010, http://www.businessweek.com/ap/financialnews/D9F32J280.htm. Accessed July 16, 2010.

90. *Ibid.*

91. "What Tree Loss Costs," *The Futurist* (August/September 1999).

92. *Ibid.*

93. Bryan Walsh, Zamira Loebis, and Jason Tedjasukmana, "Getting Credit for Saving Trees," *Time* (July 23, 2007), 58–60.

94. *Ibid.*

95. David C. Wagman, "Wicked Problems," *Power Engineering* (May 2006), 5.

96. Garrett Hardin, "The Tragedy of the Commons," *Science* (Vol. 162, 1968), 1243–1248.

97. *Ibid.*

98. Wendy Koch, "Poll: Worries about Environment Hit Low," *USA Today* (March 17, 2010), http://www.usatoday.com/news/nation/environment/2010-03-16-environment_N.htm. Accessed July 16, 2010.

99. Linda M. Sama, Stephanie A. Welcomer, and Virginia W. Gerde, "Who Speaks for the Trees? Invoking an Ethic of Care to Give Voice to the Silent Stakeholder," in S. Sharma and M. Starik (eds.), *Stakeholders, the Environment and Society* (Cheltenham, UK: Edward Elgar, 2004), 140–165.

100. *Ibid.*

101. Katharine Q. Seelye, "Big Wind Farm Off Cape Cod Gets Approval," *The New York Times* (April 29, 2010), http://www.nytimes.com/2010/04/29/science/earth/29wind.html?scp=2&sq=cape%20cod%20wind%20farm&st=cse. Accessed July 16, 2010.

102. *Ibid.*

103. Public Law 91-190 (1969), 42 U.S.C. Section 4331 et seq.

104. http://www.epa.gov/air/caa/

105. http://www.epa.gov/air/caa/peg/understand.html

106. Ben German, "Carbon Emissions Market Could Reach $1.4 Trillion in 2020," *The Hill* (January 18, 2010), http://thehill.com/blogs/e2-wire/677-e2-wire/76637-global-carbon-market-could-reach-14-trillion-in-2010-report. Accessed July 16, 2010.

107. *Ibid.*

108. "Kyoto Protocol," http://unfccc.int/kyoto_protocol/items/2830.php.

109. James Kanter, "In London's Financial World, Carbon Trading Is the Next Big Thing," *New York Times* (July 6, 2007), http://www.nytimes.com. Accessed July 16, 2010.

110. *Ibid.*

111. *Ibid.*

112. Steve Holland, "Obama: Cap and Trade May Be Separate in Senate Bill," *Reuters* (February 1, 2010), http://www.reuters.com/article/idUSTRE6115V820100202. Accessed July 16, 2010.

113. *Ibid.*

114. T. McAdams, *Law, Business & Society*, 3rd. Ed. (Homewood, IL: Irwin, 1992), 784–787, http://www.epa.gov. Accessed July 16, 2010.

115. http://www.epa.gov/history/topics/rcra/index.htm. Accessed August 16, 2010.

116. *Ibid.*

117. http://www.epa.gov/superfund/about.htm. Accessed July 16, 2010.

118. http://www.epa.gov/superfund/contacts/infocenter/epcra.htm. Accessed July 16, 2010.

119. http://www.epa.gov/superfund/25anniversary/index.htm. Accessed July 16, 2010.

120. Steven Averett, "Bush Seeks EPA Cut," *Waste Age* (March 2006), 24.

121. http://www.pirg.org. Accessed July 16, 2010.

122. John M. Broder, "Without Superfund Tax, Stimulus Aids Cleanups," *The New York Times* (April 25, 2009), http://www.nytimes.com/2009/04/26/science/earth/26superfund.html. Accessed July 16, 2010.

123. *Ibid.*

124. *Ibid.*

125. *Ibid.*

126. *Ibid.*

127. IUCN 2010. *IUCN Red List of Threatened Species. Version 2010.1.* http://www.iucnredlist.org/. Accessed July 16, 2010.

128. *Ibid.*

129. *Ibid.*

130. http://www.epa.gov/lawsregs/laws/esa.html. Accessed August 16, 2010.

131. *Ibid.*

132. Juliet Eilperin, "Endangered Species Act Sapped?" *The Washington Post* (July 4, 2004), A1.

133. *Ibid.*

134. Suzanne Goldenberg, "Obama Reverses Bush Decision on Endangered Species Act," *The Guardian* (March 3, 2009), http://www.guardian.co.uk/environment/2009/mar/03/obama-bush-endangered-species-act-us. Accessed July 16, 2010.

135. http://ozone.unep.org/Publications/MP_Key_Achievements-E.pdf. Accessed July 16, 2010.

136. *Ibid.*

137. *Ibid.*

138. http://unep.org. Accessed July 16, 2010.

139. http://www.unglobalcompact.org/AboutTheGC/TheTenPrinciples/humanRights.html. Accessed August 16, 2010.

140. http://www.globalreporting.org/Home. Accessed August 16, 2010.

141. http://www.environmentaldefense.org/partnership_project.cfm?projectID=31. Accessed July 16, 2010.

142. M. E. Kriz, "Shades of Green," *National Journal* (July 28, 1990).

143. Mark Gunther, "The Mosquito in the Tent," *Fortune* (March 31, 2004), 158–162; Lisa Gerwitz, "It's Not Easy Being Green," *Deal.com* (March 8, 2004), 1.

144. Sharon Begley, "Good Cop/Bad Cop Goes Green," *Newsweek* (May 4, 2009), 49.

145. "Terrorists by Any Name," *The Wall Street Journal* (January 26, 2006), 11.

146. Karen Charman, "The U.S. Goes on Green Alert," *OnEarth* (Fall 2003), 8.

147. "Eco-Terrorism," http://epw.senate.gov/public/index.cfm?FuseAction=Issues.View&Issue_id=5cb5b9b1-802a-23ad-463d-0a3d4a72465a. Accessed July 16, 2010.

148. "Eco-Terror Indictments," http://www.fbi.gov/page2/jan06/elf012006.htm. Accessed July 16, 2010.

149. "Michigan State University Eco-Terrorist Sentenced in Arson Case," http://checkbiotech.org/node/24475. Accessed July 16, 2010.

150. "'Light Green' Consumers Differ from 'Dark Green' Consumers," *Environmentalleader.com* (October 21, 2009), http://www.environmentalleader.com/2009/10/21/light-green-consumers-differ-from-dark-green-consumers/. Accessed July 16, 2010.

151. R. Gardyn, "Saving the Earth, One Click at a Time," *American Demographic* (January 2001), 30–33.

152. *Ibid.*

153. *Ibid.*

154. Joel Makower, "The Green Consumer, 1990–2010," *Greenbiz.com* (March 29, 2010), http://www.greenbiz.com/blog/2010/03/29/green-consumer-1990-2010. Accessed July 16, 2010.

155. Josephine Rossi, "Show Them the Green," *T+D* (June 2007), 12–13.

156. Barnaby J. Feder, "Funds Want Oil Companies to Report on Climate," *The New York Times* (February 27, 2004), C3.

157. http://www.ceres.org/Page.aspx?pid=1221. Accessed July 16, 2010.

158. http://www.ceres.org/page.aspx?pid=705. Accessed July 16, 2010.

159. http://www.environmentalleader.com/2009/04/10/ge-wins-award-for-best-sustainability-reporting/. Accessed July 16, 2010.

160. http://www.ceres.org/Ceresroadmap. Accessed July 16, 2010.

161. Peyton Fleming, "A Race Toward Sustainability—and Profits: New Report Delivers Powerful Message and Roadmap for Companies," *20 Ceres Years* (March 11, 2010), http://www.ceres.org/Page.aspx?pid=1227. Accessed July 16, 2010.

162. http://www.triplepundit.com/2010/01/top-ten-sustainable-ceos/. Accessed July 16, 2010.

163. Esty and Winston, 25.

164. Susan Casey, "Éminence Green," *Fortune* (April 2, 2007), 62–70.

165. *Ibid*, 67.

166. *Ibid.*

167. http://solutions.3m.com/wps/portal/3M/en_US/global/sustainability/s/recognition/. Accessed July 16, 2010.

168. http://solutions.3m.com/wps/portal/3M/en_US/global/sustainability/s/vision-strategy/ceo-statement/. Accessed July 16, 2010.

169. *3M's Pollution Prevention Pays: An Initiative for a Cleaner Tomorrow* (St. Paul, MN: 3M Company, 1991).

170. http://solutions.3m.com/wps/portal/3M/en_US/global/sustainability/s/performance-indicators/environment/eco-efficiency-results/. Accessed July 16, 2010.

171. http://www.thecro.com/awards_winners. Accessed August 16, 2010.

172. Esty and Wilson.

173. *Ibid.*

174. Casey, 64.

175. Daniel Tschopp, "It's Time for Triple Bottom Line Reporting," *The CPA Journal* (December 2003), 11.

176. John Carey and Michael Arndt, "Hugging the Tree-Huggers," *BusinessWeek* (March 12, 2007), 66–68.

177. *Ibid.*; Dell's recycling program and other initiatives are profiled in their 2006 Sustainability Report, http://www.dell.com. Accessed July 16, 2010.

178. *Ibid.*, 66.

179. *Ibid.*

180. Danielle Sacks, "Working with the Enemy," *Fast Company* (September 2007), 74–81.

181. Carey and Arndt, 66–68; Sacks, 74–81.

182. Sacks, 74–81.

183. *Ibid*, 79.

Chapter 16

1. *Oxford English Dictionary* (Revised March 2010), http://dictionary.oed.com/. Accessed July 17, 2010.

2. "Michael Porter on Inner City Business," *Bloomberg Businessweek* (May 27, 2010), http://www.businessweek.com/smallbiz/content/may2010/sb20100526_383016.htm.

3. "2009 Deloitte Touche Tohmatsu Corporate Responsibility Report" (Revised March 31, 2010), http://www.deloitte.com/assets/Dcom-Global/Local%20Assets/Documents/dtt_2009_DTT_CR_Report_261009.pdf. Accessed July 17, 2010.

4. http://www.lilly.com/responsibility/. Accessed July 17, 2010.

5. Bill Shaw and Frederick Post, "A Moral Basis for Corporate Philanthropy," *Journal of Business Ethics* (October 1993), 745–751.

6. "Deloitte Volunteer IMPACT Research," http://www.deloitte.com/view/en_US/us/About/Community-Involvement/f0d3264f0b0fb110VgnVCM100000 ba42f00aRCRD.htm. Accessed July 17, 2010.

7. Sarah E. Needleman, "The Latest Office Perk: Getting Paid to Volunteer," *The Wall Street Journal* (April 29, 2008), D1.

8. Longaberger Horizon of Hope, Amercian Cancer Society, "Our Story," http://www.horizonofhope.com/OurStory09.html.

9. Jayne O'Donnell, "UPS Workers Head to Haiti to Provide Relief," *USA Today* (January 25, 2010), 48.

10. Ronald McDonald House of Charities, "Small Gestures," http://www.rmhc.com (2010). Accessed July 17, 2010.

11. Cecily Railborn, Antoinette Green, Lyudmila Todorova, Toni Trapani, and Wilborne E. Watson, "Corporate Philanthropy: When Is Giving Effective," *The Journal of Corporate Accounting and Finance* (November/December 2003), 47–54.

12. *Webster's New World Dictionary* (Cleveland: World Publishing Company, 1964), 1098.

13. Carolyn Cavicchio, "Economy Will Change Corporate Philanthropy," *The Nonprofit Advisor* (April 2009), 9.

14. Morrell Heald, *The Social Responsibilities of Business: Company and Community 1900–1960* (Cleveland: Case Western Reserve University Press, 1970), 112.

15. Cavicchio, 9.

16. Adam Bryant, "Companies Oppose Disclosure of Details on Gifts to Charity," *The New York Times* (April 3, 1998), A1.

17. *Ibid.*

18. OMB Watch, "Corporate Disclosure Bill Goes to President Without Philanthropy Disclosure Requirements" (July 26, 2002), http://www.ombwatch.org. Accessed July 17, 2010.

19. OMB Watcher, "More Complaints Filed Against Congressman DeLay" (April 5, 2004), press release (November 20, 2003), National Committee for Responsive Philanthropy.
20. John D. Rockfeller III, "In Defense of Philanthropy," *Business and Society Review* (Spring 1978), 26–29.
21. Giving in Numbers 2009, *Committee to Encourage Corporate Philanthropy*, http://www.corporatephilanthropy.org/pdfs/giving_in_numbers/GivinginNumbers2009.pdf.
22. Sophia A. Muirhead, "The 2006 Corporate Contributions Report," The Conference Board (2006).
23. *Ibid.*
24. The Conference Board, "Corporate Giving Priorities and Challenges in 2007," *Executive Action Series* (June 2007).
25. Wilfred Bockelman, *Culture of Corporate Citizenship: Minnesota's Business Legacy for the Global Future* (Lakeville, MN: Galde Press, Inc., 2000), 15–16.
26. "Reflecting Responding Rebuilding in Newark," Prudential Community Resources 2008 Supplement.
27. Dennis Schaal, "Prudent, Feisty and Unapologetic," *Corporate Responsibility Magazine* (March 19, 2008), http://www.thecro.com/node/644. Accessed July 17, 2010.
28. Bob Diddlebock, "To Give or Not to Give," *Time* (May 11, 2009), 10.
29. *Ibid.*
30. http://www.artsusa.org/information_services/research/services/economic_impact/default.asp. Accessed August 19, 2010.
31. Karen E. Mishra, "Help or Hype: Symbolic or Behavioral Communication during Hurricane Katrina," *Public Relations Review* (November 2006), 358–366.
32. Elizabeth Kelleher, "U.S. Companies Step Up the Business of Giving Overseas," http://www.america.gov/st/develop-english/2006/April/20060411182239berehellek0.1802027.html.
33. Louis Lavelle, "Giving as Never Before," *BusinessWeek* (October 1, 2001), 10.
34. Ian Wilhelm, "Corporate Giving Takes a Dip," *Chronicle of Philanthropy* (July 24, 2003).
35. "Corporate Kindness," *Newsweek* (February 15, 2010), 14.
36. James J. Chrisman and Archie B. Carroll, "Corporate Responsibility: Reconciling Economic and Social Goals," *Sloan Management Review* (Winter 1984), 59–65.
37. Sophia A. Muirhead, "Philanthropy and Business: The Changing Agenda," *The Conference Board* (2006), 5.
38. Carolyn Cavicchio, "The 2010 Philanthropy Agenda: Is the Pressure Easing?" *The Conference Board* (March 2010).
39. KaBOOM!, "KaBOOM! Partner: Home Depot," http://kaboom.org/about_kaboom/sponsors_partners/meet_our_partners/kaboom_partner_home_depot. Accessed July 17, 2010.
40. The Clorox Company Corporate Social Responsibility, "The Clorox Company Foundation," http://www.thecloroxcompany.com/community/history.html.
41. Richard Steckel and Robin Simons, *Doing Best by Doing Good* (New York: Dutton Publishers, 1992).
42. Michael Porter and Mark Kramer, "The Competitive Advantage of Corporate Philanthropy," *Harvard Business Review* (December 2002), 56–69.
43. *Ibid.*
44. *Ibid.*
45. http://www.bk.com/en/us/company-info/corporate-responsibility/people.html. Accessed August 19, 2010.
46. Jenny McTaggart, "Whole Foods Steps Up Sourcing Standards," *Progressive Grocer* (April 15, 2007), 12–13.
47. Porter and Kramer, 56–69.
48. *Ibid.*
49. *Ibid.*
50. Patricia Caesar, "Cause-Related Marketing: The New Face of Corporate Philanthropy," *Business and Society Review* (Fall 1986), 16.
51. Martin Gottlieb, "Cashing In on a Higher Cause," *The New York Times* (July 6, 1986), 6-F.
52. Michelle Wirth Fellman, "Cause Marketing Takes a Strategic Turn," *Marketing News* (April 26, 1999), 4–8.
53. Peggy Bernstein, "Philanthropy, Reputation Go Hand in Hand," *PR News* (January 17, 2000), 1–8.
54. 1999 Cone/Roper Cause-Related Trends Report.
55. Public Service Advertising Research Center, http://www.psaresearch.com. Accessed July 17, 2010.
56. David Benady, "Paved with Good Intentions (Cover Story)," *Marketing Week* (March 15, 2007), 24–25.
57. Mya Frazier, "Costly Red Campaign Reaps Meager $18m (Cover Story)," *Advertising Age* (March 5, 2007), 1–43.
58. Benady, 24–25.
59. *Ibid.*
60. *Ibid.*
61. The Conference Board.
62. Muirhead.
63. Carolyn Cavicchio, "The 2010 Philanthropy Agenda: Is the Pressure Easing?" The Conference Board (March 2010).

64. Kelleher, 2006. Accessed September 27, 2010.
65. Bob Davis, "Wealth of Nations: Finding Lessons of Outsourcing in Four Historical Tales," *The Wall Street Journal* (March 29, 2004), A1.
66. *Ibid.*
67. Dale Kasler, "Outsourcing Reaps Winners, Losers in U.S. Economy," *The Sacramento Bee* (April 26, 2004).
68. Brad Stone, "Should I Stay or Should I Go," *Newsweek* (April 19, 2004), 52–53.
69. *Ibid.*
70. Sarah Kabourek, "Back in the USA," *Fortune* (September 28, 2009), 30.
71. *Ibid.*
72. *Ibid.*
73. Jodie T. Allen, "Maybe We Could All Deliver Pizza," *The Washington Post* (March 7, 2004), B1.
74. Manjeet Kripalani, "Five Offshore Practices That Pay Off," *BusinessWeek* (January 30, 2006), 60–61.
75. Peter F. Drucker, *Management: Tasks, Responsibilities, Practices* (New York: Harper & Row, 1974), 327–328.
76. Susan Diesenhouse, "To Save Factories, Owners Diversify," *The New York Times* (November 30, 2003), 5.
77. SRC, "We Work with OEMs," http://www.srcholdings.com/. Accessed July 17, 2010.
78. Diesenhouse, 5.
79. *Ibid.*
80. Archie B. Carroll, "When Business Closes Down: Social Responsibilities and Management Actions," *California Management Review* (Winter 1984), 131.
81. Vincent J. Matteo, "The Chamber View," *Williamsport Sun-Gazette* (July 7, 2003), 2.
82. Corey Rosen, "The Employee Ownership Update," *The National Center for Employee Ownership* (June 1, 2010), http://www.nceo.org/main/column.php/id/366. Accessed July 17, 2010.
83. Terri Minsky, "Gripes of Rath: Workers Who Bought Iowa Slaughterhouse Regret That They Did," *The Wall Street Journal* (December 2, 1981), 1.
84. "The Opposite of Wal-Mart," *Economist* (May 5, 2007), 79.
85. *Ibid.*
86. "A Steel Town's Fight for Life," *Newsweek* (March 28, 1983), 49.
87. Maria Mallary, "How Can We Be Laid Off if We Own the Company?" *BusinessWeek* (September 9, 1991), 66.
88. ArcelorMittal Weirton Inc., "Weirton Steel to Sell Assets to ISG Following Judge's Decision," Weirton Steel press announcement (April 22, 2004), http://www.weirton.com.
89. *ArcelorMittal Annual Report*, http://www.arcelormittal.com/rls/data/upl/638-17-0-ArcelorMittalAnnualReport2009.pdf. Accessed August 19, 2010.
90. Kenneth Labich, "Will United Fly?" *Fortune* (August 22, 1994), 70–78.
91. Suzanne Cohen, "United Airlines ESOP Woes," *Risk Management* (June 2001), 9.
92. Greg Schneider, "Owner Role Always Tense for United Employees," *The Washington Post* (December 10, 2002), E1.
93. "United's Bankruptcy Tab: $335 Million-Plus in Fees," *USA Today* (October 3, 2006), http://www.usatoday.com/travel/news/2006-03-10-ual-bankruptcy-fees_x.htm. Accessed July 17, 2010.
94. Cohen, 9.
95. Carroll, 132.
96. Grover Starling, *The Changing Environment of Business* (Boston: Kent, 1980), 319–320.
97. Emily Thornton, "The Hidden Peril of Layoffs," *BusinessWeek* (March 2, 2009), 52–53.
98. Loretta W. Prencipe, "Impending Layoffs Need Warning," *Info World* (April 9, 2001), 15.
99. James Drew and Steve Eder, "Without Warning: Flaws, Loopholes Deny Employees Protection Mandated by WARN Act," *The Blade* (July 15, 2007), http://www.toledoblade.com. Accessed July 17, 2010.
100. *Ibid.*
101. James Drew and Steve Eder, "Different Workers Face the Same Problem with the WARN Act," *The Blade* (July 17, 2007), http://www.toledoblade.com. Accessed July 17, 2010.
102. Kelly M. Butler, "Going above and beyond Advance WARNing," *Employee Benefit News* (February 2009), 7.
103. Greg Jefferson, "Sony Lays Off 120 Workers, Moves Closer to Closing San Antonio Plant," *San Antonio Express-News* (August 8, 2003), 1.
104. *Ibid.*
105. *Ibid.*
106. Cornell University Workshop Report, 28–30.
107. Leon Grunberg, Sarah Moore, and Edward S. Greenberg, "Managers' Reactions to Implementing Layoffs: Relationship to Health Problems and Withdrawal Behaviors," *Human Resource Management* (Summer 2006), 159–178.
108. Suzanne M. Behr and Margaret A. White, "Layoff Survivor Sickness," *Executive Excellence* (November 2003), 18.

109. *Ibid.*
110. "Survivor Guilt: How the Corporate Ax Affects Remaining Employees," *PR News* (March 12, 2001), 1.
111. *Ibid.*

Chapter 17

1. Phred Dvorak and Scott Thurm, "Slump Prods Firms to Seek New Compact with Workers," *The Wall Street Journal* (October 20, 2009), A18.
2. Diane Lewis, "Out in the Field: Workplace Want Loyal Workers? Then Help Them Grow," *Boston Globe* (July 15, 2001), H2.
3. Michelle Conlin, "Job Security, No. Tall Latte, Yes," *BusinessWeek* (April 2, 2001), 62–64.
4. *Ibid.*
5. Lewis, H2.
6. John Challenger, "Establishing Rules for the New Workplace," *USA Today Magazine* (November 2002), 30–34.
7. Paul B. Brown, "Keeping Good Employees when You Can't Pay Them More," *The New York Times* (August 18, 2009), http://www.nytimes.com/2009/08/18/business/smallbusiness/18toolkit.html?scp=17&sq=company%20loyalty&st=cse.
8. "Employee Loyalty Rises during Global Economic Recession, Kelly International Workforce Survey Finds," *Kelly Services* (March 8, 2010), http://www.easyir.com/easyir/customrel.do?easyirid=95BBA2C450798961 &version=live&prid=591880 &releasejsp=custom_123.
9. *Ibid.*
10. David Lazarus, "As Labor Day Nears, Workers Are Just Thankful to Have a Job," *Los Angeles Times* (September 6, 2009), http://articles.latimes.com/2009/sep/06/business/fi-lazarus6.
11. Peter Coy, Michelle Conlin, and Moira Herbst, "The Disposable Worker," *BusinessWeek* (January 7, 2010), http://www.businessweek.com/magazine/content/10_03/b4163032935448.htm.
12. *Ibid.*
13. Denise M. Rousseau and Rosemary Batt, "Global Competition's Perfect Storm: Why Business and Labor Cannot Solve Their Problems Alone," *Academy of Management Perspectives* (May 2007), 16–23.
14. "Global Employment Trends," *International Labour Office* (January 26, 2010), http://www.ilo.org/empelm/what/pubs/lang–en/docName–WCMS_120471/index.htm.
15. *Ibid.*
16. Coy, Conlin, and Herbst, http://www.businessweek.com/magazine/content/10_03/b4163032935448.htm.
17. *Ibid.*
18. Challenger, 30–34.
19. Louis Uchitelle, J. T. Battenberg III, and Thomas Kochan, "Employer-Employee Social Contracts: Fashioning a New Compact for Workers," *Academy of Management Perspectives* (May 2007), 5–16.
20. Leo Troy, *The End of Unionism: An Appraisal* (St. Louis: Center for the Study of American Business, Washington University, September 1994), 1–2.
21. "Union Members—2009," *Bureau of Labor Statistics News Release* (January 22, 2010), http://www.bls.gov/news.release/pdf/union2.pdf.
22. Catherine Rampell, "Trade Unions' Decline Around the World," *The New York Times* (November 5, 2009), http://economix.blogs.nytimes.com/2009/11/05/trade-unions-around-the-world/.
23. Richard Edwards, *Rights at Work* (Washington, DC: The Brookings Institution, 1993), 25–26.
24. *Ibid.*, 33–35.
25. Mark V. Roehling, "The 'Good Cause Norm' in Employment Relations: Empirical Evidence and Policy Implications," *Employee Responsibility and Rights Journal* (September 2002), 91–104.
26. Ellen Dannin, "Why At-Will Employment Is Bad for Employers and Just Cause Is Good for Them," *Labor Law Journal* (Spring 2007), 5–16.
27. Tara J. Radin and Patricia H. Werhane, "Employment-At-Will, Employee Rights, and Future Directions for Employment," *Business Ethics Quarterly* (April 2003), 113–130.
28. Louis Uchitelle, *The Disposable American* (New York: Knopf, 2006).
29. Uchitelle, Battenberg, and Kochan, 7.
30. David H. Autor, John J. Donohue III, and Stewart J. Schwab, "The Employment Consequences of Wrongful-Discharge Laws: Large, Small, or None at All?" *American Economic Review* (May 2004), 440–446.
31. "Employment at Will Exceptions by State," *National Conference of State Legislatures* (April 2008), http://www.ncsl.org/default.aspx?tabid=13339.
32. *Ibid.*
33. *Ibid.*
34. *Ibid.*

35. Patricia H. Werhane, Tara J. Radin, and Norman E. Bowie, *Employment and Employee Rights* (Malden, MA: Blackwell Publishing, 2004).

36. *Ibid.*

37. Dannin, 5–16.

38. Steve Harrison, *The Manager's Book of Decencies: How Small Gestures Build Great Companies* (Columbus, OH: McGraw-Hill, 2007).

39. *Ibid.*

40. Patricia H. Werhane, *Persons, Rights and Corporations* (Englewood Cliffs, NJ: Prentice Hall, 1985), 110.

41. William M. Haraway, "Employee Grievance Programs: Understanding the Nexus between Workplace Justice, Organizational Legitimacy and Successful Organizations," *Public Personnel Management* (Winter 2005), 329–342.

42. Richard A. Posthuma, "Procedural Due Process and Procedural Justice in the Workplace: A Comparison and Analysis," *Public Personnel Management* (Summer 2003), 181.

43. David W. Ewing, *Freedom Inside the Organization: Bringing Civil Liberties to the Workplace* (New York: McGraw-Hill, 1977), 11.

44. Posthuma, 181–195.

45. "Where Ombudsmen Work Out," *BusinessWeek* (May 3, 1976), 114–116.

46. Allen Church, "Ombudsmen Ease Governance Compliance," *Claims* (December 2004), 63–65.

47. Jonathan A. Segal, "The Joy of Uncooking," *HR Magazine* (November 2002), 52–57.

48. Carolyn Hirschman, "Someone to Listen," *HR Magazine* (January 2003), 46–50.

49. *Ibid.*

50. *Ibid.*, 46–51.

51. Margaret M. Clark, "Jury of Their Peers," *HR Magazine* (January 2004), 54.

52. *Ibid.*

53. *Ibid.*

54. "Peer-Review Policy Provides Protection," *Credit Union Directors Newsletter* (April, 2004), 7–8.

55. Kay O. Wilburn, "Employment Disputes: Solving Them Out of Court," *Management Review* (March 1998), 17–21. Marc Lampe, "Mediation as an Ethical Adjunct of Stakeholder Theory," *Journal of Business Ethics* (May 2001), 165–173.

56. Marc Lampe, "Mediation as an Ethical Adjunct of Stakeholder Theory," *Journal of Business Ethics* (May 2001), 165–173.

57. Jon Hyman, "Congress Employment Law Agenda: 7 Bills to Watch Closely," *HR Specialist* (March 2010), 7.

58. Lee Gomes, "A Whistle-Blower Finds Jackpot at the End of His Quest," *The Wall Street Journal* (April 27, 1998), B1.

59. Robert P. Lawrence, "Go Ahead, Laugh at Army's Expense," *The San Diego Union-Tribune* (February 27, 1998), E12.

60. Gomes, B1.

61. Lawrence, E12.

62. Marcia P. Miceli and Janet P. Near, *Blowing the Whistle: The Organizational and Legal Implications for Companies and Employees* (New York: Lexington Books, 1992), 15.

63. Janet P. Near and Marcia P. Miceli, "The Whistle-Blowing Process and Its Outcomes: A Preliminary Model" (Columbus, OH: The Ohio State University, College of Administrative Science, Working Paper Series 83–55, September, 1983), 2. See also Miceli and Near, 15.

64. Janet P. Near and Marcia P. Miceli, "Whistleblowing—Myth and Reality," *Journal of Management* (1996 Special Issue), 507–526.

65. Richard Layco and Amanda Ripley, "Persons of the Year," *Time* (December 30, 2002), 32.

66. *Ibid.*

67. Dan Ackerman, "Whistleblower?" *The Wall Street Journal* (December 24, 2002), A10.

68. Amelia Gruber, "Whistleblower Volume Rises," *Government Executive* (September 2003), 16.

69. "Annual Report to Congress: Fiscal Year 2008," *Office of the Special Counsel*, http://www.osc.gov/documents/reports/ar-2008.pdf.

70. Janet P. Near, Marcia P. Miceli, and Tamila C. Jensen, "Variables Associated with the Whistle-Blowing Process" (Columbus, OH: The Ohio State University, College of Administrative Science, Working Paper Series 83–11, March 1983), 5.

71. Elizabeth Williamson, "One Soldier's Unlikely Act," *The Washington Post* (May 6, 2004), A16.

72. http://www.cbsnews.com/stories/2006/12/07/60minutes

73. Nat Hentoff, "The Abandoned Abu Ghiraib Whistleblower," *Jewish World Review* (December 26, 2006), http://www.jewishworldreview.com.

74. *Ibid.*

75. http://www.cbsnews.com/stories/2006/12/07/60minutes

76. *Ibid.*

77. Kurt Eichenwald, "He Told. He Suffered. Now He's a Hero," *The New York Times* (May 29, 1994), 1-F.

78. *Ibid.*

79. Joann S. Lublin, "Watchdog Has Hard Time Hearing Whistles," *The Wall Street Journal* (October 17, 1980), 30.

80. Ana Radelat, "When Blowing the Whistle Ruins Your Life," *Public Citizen* (September/October 1991), 16–20.

81. Alan F. Westin, "Michigan's Law to Protect the Whistle Blowers," *The Wall Street Journal* (April 13, 1981), 18. Also see Daniel P. Westman, *Whistle Blowing: The Law of Retaliatory Discharge* (Washington, DC: The Bureau of National Affairs, 1991); Robert L. Brady, "Blowing the Whistle," *HR Focus* (February 1996), 20.

82. Michael W. Sculnick, "Disciplinary Whistle-Blowers," *Employment Relations Today* (Fall 1986), 194.

83. http://www.whistleblower.org

84. Paula Dwyer, Dan Carney, Amy Borrus, Lorraine Woellert, and Christophe Palmeri, "Year of the Whistleblower," *BusinessWeek* (December 16, 2002), 106–110.

85. http://www.whistleblower.org

86. "Protections Still Lacking for SOX Whistleblowing," *HR Focus* (July 2007), 2.

87. Todd Wilkinson, "After Eight Years, an Insider Gets His Reward," *Christian Science Monitor* (July 24, 2001), 1.

88. Miceli and Near, 247.

89. Andrew W. Singer, "The Whistle-Blower: Patriot or Bounty Hunter?" *Across the Board* (November 1992), 16–22.

90. Alfred G. Feliu, *Primer on Individual Employee Rights* (Washington, DC: The Bureau of National Affairs, Inc., 1992), 194–195.

91. Grover L. Porter, "Whistleblowers: A Rare Breed," *Strategic Finance* (August 2003), 51–53.

92. Kurt Eichenwald, "He Blew the Whistle, and Health Giants Quaked," *The New York Times* (October 18, 1998), 1.

93. Porter, 52.

94. *Ibid.*, 53.

95. *Ibid.*

96. *Ibid.*

97. http://www.taf.org/top20.htm

98. http://journalism.medill.northwestern.edu/docket

99. http://www.corporatecrimereporter.com/falseclaimsact012406.htm

100. Melissa Klein Aguilar, "Reach, Scope of False Claims Act Only Gets Bigger," *Compliance Week* (December 2009), 21.

101. James R. Detert and Amy C. Edmondson, "Why Employees Are Afraid to Speak," *Harvard Business Review* (May 2007), 23–25.

102. *Ibid.*, 24.

103. *Ibid.*, 23–25.

104. *Ibid.*

105. Lynn Brewer, "Is There a Little Bit of Enron in All of Us?" *Journal for Quality & Participation* (Spring 2007), 26.

106. *Ibid.*

107. *Ibid.*

Chapter 18

1. Margaret H. Vickers, "The 'Workplace-During-Recession' Reminding Us of Employee Rights and Responsibilities," *Employee Responsibilities and Rights Journal* (March 2009), 3–6.

2. *Ibid.*

3. David Michaels, "Transparency at Work: Making Your Workplace a Safer Workplace," *FDCH Regulatory Intelligence Database* (April 29, 2010).

4. "NWI Surveillance Bill Enacted—Additional Efforts Underway," *Workrights News* (Fall-Winter 2005/2006).

5. *Ibid.*

6. http://www.epic.org/privacy/nelson/

7. "Big Brother, Inc., May Be Closer Than You Think," *BusinessWeek* (February 9, 1987), 84.

8. Patricia H. Werhane, *Persons, Rights, and Corporations* (Englewood Cliffs, NJ: Prentice Hall, 1985), 118.

9. http://www.privacyrights.org/ar/Privacy-IssuesList.htm#D (updated March 2007).

10. Steve Bates, "Science Friction," *HR Magazine* (July 2001), 34–44.

11. Joanne Wojcik, "Wired into Workplace Privacy," *Business Insurance* (September 15, 2003), 28.

12. http://www.privacyrights.org, "Fact Sheet 16: Employment Background Checks" (updated April 2010).

13. *Ibid.*

14. http://www.privacyrights.org/fs/FS16c-FAQ-BkgChk-060928.htm#5 (2006–2010).

15. *Ibid.*

16. *Ibid.*
17. *Ibid.*
18. Jim Giuliana, "Recruiting: EEOC Warns About Background Checks," *HR Morning* (January 6, 2010), http://www.hrmorning.com/recruiting-eeoc-warns-about-background-checks/.
19. http://www.privacyrights.org/fs/FS16c-FAQ-BkgChk-060928.htm#5 (2006–2010).
20. Chad Terhune, "The Trouble with Background Checks," *BusinessWeek* (June 9, 2008), 54–57.
21. *Ibid.*
22. *Ibid.*
23. *Ibid.*, 56.
24. "Feds Turning Up Heat on HR Background Checks," *Employment Law* (May 2010), 1–5.
25. Kenneth F. Englade, "The Business of the Polygraph," *Across the Board* (October 1982), 21–22.
26. James H. Coil III and Barbara Jo Call, "Congress Targets Employers' Use of Polygraphs," *Employment Relations Today* (Spring 1986), 23.
27. David E. Terpstra, R. Bryan Kethley, Richard T. Foley, and Wanthanee Limpaphayom, "The Nature of Litigation Surrounding Five Screening Devices," *Public Personnel Management* (Spring 2000), 43–54.
28. Diana Ray, "Can They Fool the Polygraph?" *Insight* (July 2–9, 2001), 18–19.
29. Philip Ross, "Mind Readers," *Scientific American* (September 2003), 74.
30. Linda Stern, "We Know You're Lying," *Newsweek* (November 17, 2003), E4.
31. R. Colin Johnson, "Lie-Detector Glasses Offer Peek at Future of Security," *Electronic Engineering* (January 19, 2004), 1.
32. Nick Barron, "Honest to Goodness," *SC Magazine: For IT Security Professionals* (June/July 2009), 17.
33. Gregory M. Lousig-Nont, "Seven Deadly Hiring Mistakes," *Supervision* (April 2003), 18–19.
34. David W. Arnold and John W. Jones, "Who the Devil's Applying Now?" *Security Management* (March 2002), 85–88.
35. Michael Sturman and David Sherwyn, "The Utility of Integrity Testing for Reducing Worker's Compensation Costs," *Cornell Hospital Quarterly* (November 2009), 432–445.
36. Arnold and Jones, 85–88.
37. *Ibid.*
38. Sturman and Sherwyn, 423–445.
39. http://ir.questdiagnostics.com/phoenix.zhtml?c=82068&p=irol-newsArticle&ID=1357770&highlight= positivity. Accessed June 6, 2010.
40. *Ibid.*
41. *Ibid.*
42. Marc D. Greenwood, "FALSE Positives," *Fire Chief* (April 2003), 48–53.
43. ACOEM, "Ethical Aspects of Drug Testing," http://www.acoem.org/guidelines.aspx?id=722 (updated January 28, 2006).
44. http://www.dol.gov/asp/programs/drugs/said/StateLaws.asp
45. Jane Easter Bahls, "Dealing with Drugs: Keep It Legal," *HR Magazine* (March 1998), 104–116.
46. "ADA Claim Fails to Disturb Refusal to Hire Based on Positive Test Results," *Venulex Legal Summary* (2009) 1–3.
47. http://www.dol.gov/elaws/asp/drugfree/drugs/regulation.htm
48. Eileen Smith, "How to Choose the Right EAP for Your Employee," *Employee Benefit News* (November 1, 2000).
49. Sean Fogarty, "EAPs New Role: A Core Strategic Element," *Employee Benefits Advisor* (April 2010), 40–46.
50. *Ibid.*
51. http://press.amanet.org/press-releases/177/2007-electronic-monitoring-surveillance-survey/
52. John P. Mello, Jr., "Camera Phones a Flashpoint of Concern," *Boston Works* (April 11, 2004), G7.
53. Nancy J. King, "Electronic Monitoring to Promote National Security Impacts Workplace Privacy," *Employee Responsibilities and Rights Journal* (September 2003), 127–147.
54. *Ibid.*
55. http://www.epic.org/privacy/workplace
56. *Ibid.*
57. http://www.workrights.org
58. *New Jersey Supreme Court Rules in Favor of Employee Privacy* (March 30, 2010), http://epic.org/privacy/workplace/#news.
59. *Ibid.*
60. http://press.amanet.org/press-releases/177/2007-electronic-monitoring-surveillance-survey/
61. Frederick S. Lane, III, *The Naked Employee* (New York: AMACOM, 2003).
62. Cara Garretson, "Why Your Company Needs a Chief Privacy Officer," *Network World* (May 28, 2007), 20.
63. Presidential Proclamation–Workers Memorial Day, http://www.whitehouse.gov/the-press-office/presidential-proclamation-workers-memorial-day.

64. http://osha.gov/pls/oshaweb/owadisp.show_document?p_table=SPEECHES&p_id=2155

65. The Legal Information Institute, http://www.law.cornell.edu/topics/workplace_safety.html.

66. http://www.osha.gov

67. Joseph P. Kahn, "When Bad Management Becomes Criminal," *Inc.* (March 1987), 47.

68. David R. Spiegel, "Enforcing Safety Laws Locally," *The New York Times* (March 23, 1986), 11F.

69. "Union Carbide Fights for Its Life," *BusinessWeek* (December 24, 1984), 52–56.

70. http://www.unioncarbide.com/about/index.htm (2010).

71. "By the Numbers Operation at Morgan Stanley Finds Its Human Side," *The New York Times* (September 16, 2001), section 3, 8; "War on Terrorism: The Victims—Snapshot of the Briton Who Became an American Hero, Seconds Before Death," *The Independent* (September 27, 2001), 3.

72. http://www.osha.gov/pls/oshaweb/owadisp.show_document?p_table=FACT_SHEETS&p_id=151

73. "OSHA's Nitpicking Rules Die," *Athens Banner Herald* (November 24, 1978), 5.

74. Robert L. Simison, "Job Deaths and Injuries Seem to Be Increasing after Years of Decline," *The Wall Street Journal* (March 18, 1986), 1, 25.

75. *Ibid.*, 1.

76. Scott Bronstein, "They Treated Us Like Dogs, Say Workers at Plant Where 25 Died," *The Atlanta Journal* (September 5, 1991), A6.

77. David Barstow, "U.S. Rarely Seeks Charges for Deaths in Workplace," *The New York Times* (December 22, 2003), A1.

78. *Ibid.*

79. Alexandra Berzon, "OSHA Boosts Oversight of State Safety Agencies," *The Wall Street Journal* (March 29, 2010), A4.

80. J.J., "OSHA Toughens Penalties," *Chemical and Engineering News* (May 3, 2010), 29.

81. Cole A. Wist and Hugh C. Thatcher, "Workplace Violence: An American Secret," *Labor Employment and Law* (Winter 2010), 6.

82. *Ibid.*

83. "Survey Finds Problems with Employer Workplace Violence Prevention Efforts (Cover Story)," *Safety Compliance Letter* (May 1, 2007), 1–6.

84. Wist and Thatcher, 6.

85. "Workplace Violence: New Regulation, Threats and Best Practices," *Security Director's Report* (May 2010), 1–11.

86. *Ibid.*

87. "Workplace Violence," *OSHA Fact Sheet* (2010), http://www.osha.gov.

88. *Ibid.*

89. Stephanie Armour, "Companies, Survivors Suffer Years after Violence at Work," *USA Today* (July 9, 2003), 3A.

90. *Ibid.*, 3A.

91. *Ibid.*

92. Sarah Wheaton and Shaila Dewan, "Professor Said to Be Charged after 3 Are Killed in Alabama," *The New York Times* (February 12, 2010), http://www.nytimes.com/2010/02/13/us/13alabama.html.

93. Wist and Thatcher, 6.

94. *Ibid.*

95. Otto Friedrich, "Where There's Smoke," *Time* (February 23, 1987), 23.

96. Lois Therrien, "Warning: In More and More Places, Smoking Causes Fines," *BusinessWeek* (December 29, 1986), 40.

97. http://www.epa.gov/smokefree/healtheffects.html (updated April 30, 2007).

98. Christian Nordqvist, "Second Hand Smoke Kills Says World Health Organization," *Medical News Today* (May 31, 2010), http://www.medicalnewstoday.com/articles/190429.php.

99. *Ibid.*

100. Alison Stein Wellner, "Editor's Note: Smoke Signals," *Forecast* (January 2001), 12.

101. Caroline M. Fichtenberg and Stanton A. Glantz, "Effect of Smoke-Free Workplaces on Smoking Behaviour: Systematic Review," *British Medical Journal* (July 2002), 188–194.

102. *Ibid.*, 191.

103. "Study Shows Smoke Free Policies Cut Hospitalization Costs," *HR Magazine* (May 2009), 29.

104. http://www.workrights.org

105. Nancy R. Lockwood, "Work/Life Balance: Challenges and Solutions," *HR Magazine* (June 2003), S1.

106. *Ibid.*

107. *Ibid.*

108. "Employee Benefits Down Slightly in 2009," *Society for Human Resource Management* (June 29, 2009), http://www.shrm.org/about/pressroom/PressReleases/Pages/EmployeeBenefits2009.aspx.

109. Saroj Parasuraman and Jeffrey Greenhaus, "Toward Reducing Some Critical Gaps in Work-Family Research," *Human Resource Management Review* (Autumn 2002), 299–312.

110. "Best Places to Work 2010," *Glassdoor.com*, http://www.glassdoor.com/Best-Places-to-Work-LST_KQ0,19.htm. Accessed June 7, 2010.
111. "Military Expansions in FMLA Are Now Law," *HR Focus* (January 2010), 2.
112. *Ibid.*
113. http://fmlaonline.com/
114. *Ibid.*
115. Mark Schoeff, "Department of Labor Study Reveals FMLA Challenges," *Workforce Management* (July 23, 2007), 8–10.

Chapter 19

1. Zachary Karabell, "We Are Not in This Together," *Newsweek* (April 20, 2009), 30–32.
2. *Ibid.*
3. "Ethnic Minorities Badly Hit by Recession," *Equal Opportunities Review* (February 2010), 4.
4. Will Hurst and Sian Griffiths, "Scots Back President's Concerns over Women," *Building Design* (October 16, 2009), 6.
5. William F. Glueck and James Ledvinka, "Equal Employment Opportunity Programs," in William F. Glueck, *Personnel: A Diagnostic Approach,* rev. ed. (Dallas, TX: Business Publications, 1978), 593–633.
6. *Ibid.*, 597–599.
7. "Equal Opportunity: A Scorecard," *Dun's Review* (November 1979), 107.
8. *Ibid.*, 108.
9. *The World Almanac and Book of Facts 1987* (New York: World Almanac, 1986), 129.
10. McKay Jenkins, "Despite Education Gains, Blacks Still Trailing Whites in Income," *The Atlanta Journal* (September 20, 1991), A16.
11. Isabelle dePomereau, "United States: Why Black Financial Progress Is Running into Speed Bumps," *The Christian Science Monitor* (February 4, 1998), 5.
12. "Black Hole," *The Economist* (November 16, 1996), 67–68.
13. Roy S. Johnson, "The New Black Power," *Fortune* (August 4, 1997), 47.
14. http://www.timewarner.com/corp/management/corp_executives/bio/parsons_richard.html (August, 2007).
15. http://people.forbes.com/profile/richard-d-parsons/19731
16. Johnson, 47.
17. Eileen P. Gunn, "The Money Men," *Fortune* (August 4, 1997), 75.
18. Cora Daniels, "Too Diverse for Our Own Good," *Fortune* (July 9, 2001), 116.
19. Aaron Bernstein, "Racism in the Workplace," *BusinessWeek* (July 30, 2001), 64–67.
20. EEOC, "Title VII: Enforces Job Rights" (Washington, DC: The U.S. Equal Employment Opportunity Commission, Office of Communications, October 1988), 1.
21. Gerald L. Maatman, Jr., "Supreme Court Rulings Score a Worker Trifecta," *Business Insurance* (October 16, 2006), 26.
22. *Ibid.*
23. "Supreme Court: Title VII Deadline Clock Resets with Each New Biased Decision," *The HR Specialist* (June 2010), http://www.thehrspecialist.com/32469/Supreme_Court__Title_VII_deadline_clock_resets_with_each_new_biased_decision.hr?cat=.
24. EEOC, "Age Discrimination Is Against the Law" (Washington, DC: The U.S. Equal Employment Opportunity Commission, Office of Communications, April 1988), 1.
25. EEOC, "Equal Work, Equal Pay" (Washington, DC: The U.S. Equal Employment Opportunity Commission, Office of Communications, October 1988), 1.
26. Harold M. Brody and Alexander Grodan, "The Effect of the Fair Pay Act on Disparate-Impact Cases," *Employment Relations Today* (Winter 2010), 73–78.
27. "A Backpay Bonanza," *The Wall Street Journal* (August 2, 2007), A10.
28. Sheryl Gay Stolberg, "Obama Signs Equal Pay Legislation," *The New York Times* (January 29, 2009), http://www.nytimes.com/2009/01/30/us/politics/30ledbetter-web.html.
29. EEOC, "Equal Employment Opportunity Is the Law" (Washington, DC: The U.S. Equal Employment Opportunity Commission, Office of Communications 1986), 1.
30. Henry H. Perritt, Jr., *Americans with Disabilities Act Handbook* (New York: John Wiley & Sons, 1990), vii.
31. U.S. Department of Justice, Office on the Americans with Disabilities Act, *The Americans with Disabilities Act: Questions and Answers* (Washington, DC: Government Printing Office, 1991), 1. Also see "Disabilities Act to Cover 500,000 More Firms," *The Atlanta Journal* (July 25, 1994), E1.
32. *Ibid.*

33. Ron Lent, "Employers Usually Win Disability Cases," *Journal of Commerce* (July 9, 1998), 5A.

34. Karen E. Saul, "EEOC Issues ADA Guidance," *Credit Union Magazine* (August 2003), 82.

35. *Ibid.*

36. Warren Richey, "Court Boosts Civil Rights Law for Disabled," *The Christian Science Monitor* (May 18, 2004), 1.

37. Jay Matthews, "Most Corporate Leaders Support Disabilities Act; Poll Reveals Little Increase in Actual Hiring," *The Washington Post* (July 14, 1995), B3.

38. Daily Record Staff, "Survey Finds Employers Prevail 94.5 Percent of Time in Discrimination Cases," *Daily Record* (July 3, 2003), 1.

39. "ADA Amendments Act Update: Issues HR Professionals Must Know," *HR Focus* (May 2010), 12–15.

40. John D. Rapoport and Brian L. P. Zevnik, *The Employee Strikes Back* (New York: Collier Books, 1994), 233–234.

41. http://www.eeoc.gov

42. "Employees Still Filing Job-Discrimination Complaints in Near-Record Numbers," *HR Specialist* (February 2010), 8.

43. Bob Tarmarkin, "Is Equal Opportunity Turning into a Witch Hunt?" *Forbes* (May 29, 1978), 29–31.

44. Bill McAllister, "Civil Rights: What Happened at the EEOC when Thomas Was There?" *The Washington Post Weekly Edition* (September 16–22, 1991), 31.

45. "Quiet Crackdown: The Quarry—Corporate Civil Rights Violators," *BusinessWeek* (September 26, 1994), 52.

46. Kathy Gurchiek, "Former EEOC Chair Proud of Her Battle against Bias," *HR Magazine* (October 20, 2006), 29–32.

47. "EEOC Campaign Takes Aim at Race, Color Bias," *Workforce Management* (March 12, 2007), 10.

48. Morgan D. Hodgson and Sandra Sanders, "EEOC Finally at Full Strength," *Employment Relations Today* (Spring 2010), 61–72.

49. James Ledvinka, *Federal Regulation of Personnel and Human Resource Management* (Boston: Kent, 1982), 37. Also see W. N. Outten, R. J. Rabin, and L. R. Lipman, *The Rights of Employees and Union Members* (Carbondale, IL: Southern Illinois University Press, 1994), chapter VIII, 154–156.

50. Glueck and Ledvinka, 304.

51. Ledvinka, 37–38.

52. *Griggs v. Duke Power Company*, 401 U.S. 424, 1971.

53. Theodore Purcell, "Minorities, Management of and Equal Employment Opportunity," in L. R. Bittel (ed.), *Encyclopedia of Professional Management* (New York: McGraw-Hill, 1978), 744–745.

54. *Smith v. City of East Cleveland*, 502 F. 2d 492, 1975.

55. Mary-Kathryn Zachary, "Discrimination without Intent," *Supervision* (May 2003), 23–26.

56. *Ibid.*

57. Maria Greco Danaher, "Strength Test Falls," *HR Magazine* (February 2007), 115–116.

58. *Ibid.*

59. Kathy DeAngelo, "Title VII's Conflicting 'Twin Pillars' in Ricci v. DeStefano, 129 S. Ct. 2658 (2009)," *Harvard Journal of Law and Public Policy* (Winter 2010), 73–78.

60. http://eeoc.gov/policy/docs/qanda_race_color.html (2010).

61. "African Americans Lost Ground on Fortune 500 Boards: Blacks Remain Seriously Underrepresented," *Executive Leadership Council* (July 17, 2009), http://www.elcinfo.com/BoardCensus.php.

62. *Ibid.*

63. *Ibid.*

64. http://www.eeoc.gov/press/3-21-06.html

65. Randy Cohen, "The Ethicist, You Name It," *New York Times Magazine* (May 30, 2004), 16.

66. Latif Lewis, "Xerox Welcomes Ursula Burns, First Black Female CEO of Fortune 500 Company," *DailyFinance.com* (May 22, 2009), http://www.dailyfinance.com/story/company-news/xerox-welcomes-ursula-burns-first-black-female-ceo-of-fortune-5/1553732/.

67. http://www.blackentrepreneurprofile.com/fortune-500-ceos/

68. Marie Arana, "The Elusive Hispanic/Latino Identity," *Nieman Reports* (Summer 2001), 8–9.

69. Michael Barone, "The Many Faces of America," *U.S. News & World Report* (March 19, 2001), 18. See also Thomas P. Edsall, "Census a Clarion Call for Democrats, GOP," *The Washington Post* (July 8, 2001), A5.

70. *Ibid.*

71. Mark Hugo and Susan Minushkin, "2008 National Survey of Latinos: Hispanics See Their Situation in U.S. Deteriorating; Oppose Key Immigration Enforcement Measures," *Pew Hispanic Center* (September 18, 2008), http://pewhispanic.org/reports/report.php?ReportID=93.

72. Anthony Ramirez, "America's Super Minority," *Fortune* (November 24, 1986), 148–164.

73. Cliff Cheng, "Are Asian-American Employees a Model Minority or Just a Minority?" *Journal of Applied Behavioral Science* (September 1997), 277–290. See also Joyce Taing, "The Model Minority Revisited," *Journal of Applied Behavioral Science* (September 1997), 291–315. Some popular press articles have also questioned the model minority characterization of Asian

Americans. For examples, see James Walsh, "The Perils of Success," *Time* (Fall 1993), 55–56, and Chris Peacock, "The Asian-American Success Myth," *Utne Reader* (March 1988), 22–23.

74. http://www.committee100.org/initiatives/initiative_corporate.htm

75. Karl Schoenberger, "Asian Americans Underrepresented on Corporate Boards, Group Says," *San Jose Mercury News* (April 1, 2004), 1.

76. Sun Wei and William Starosta, "Perceptions of Minority Invisibility among Asian American Professionals," *Howard Journal of Communications* (April–June 2006), 119–142.

77. 2005 Catalyst Census of Women Corporate Officers and Top Earners of the *Fortune* 500, http://www.catalyst.org.

78. *Ibid.*

79. Rana Foroohar and Susan H. Greenberg, "Working Women Are Poised to Become the Biggest Economic Engine the World Has Ever Known," *Newsweek* (November 2, 2009), B3–B5.

80. *Ibid.*, B4.

81. *Ibid.*

82. David Leonhardt, "Scant Progress on Closing Gap in Women's Pay," *The New York Times* (December 24, 2006), 1.

83. "The Gender Wage Gap: 2009," *Institute for Women's Policy Research* (Updated March 2010), http://www.iwpr.org/pdf/C350.pdf.

84. Victor D. Infante, "Why Woman Still Earn Less Than Men," *WorkForce* (April 2001), 31.

85. "Women Earn 20% Less Than Men, GAO Finds; Decision to Leave Jobs for Longer Periods Does Not Account for Disparity," *The Washington Post* (November 21, 2003), E4.

86. Faroohar and Greenberg, B4.

87. *Ibid.*

88. Laura Pincus and Bill Shaw, "Comparable Worth: An Economic and Ethical Analysis," *Journal of Business Ethics* (April 1998), 455–470.

89. Cathy Trost, "Pay Equity, Born in Public Sector, Emerges as an Issue in Private Firms," *The Wall Street Journal* (July 8, 1985), 15.

90. E. Jane Arnault, Louis Gordon, Douglas H. Jones, and G. Michael Phillips, "An Experimental Study of Job Evaluation and Comparable Worth," *Industrial and Labor Relations Review* (July 2001), 806–815.

91. Joel P. Rudin and Kimble Byrd, "U.S. Pay Equity Legislation: Sheep in Wolves' Clothing," *Employee Responsibilities and Rights Journal* (December 2003), 183–190.

92. Linda Chavez, "Comparable Worth," *The Wall Street Journal—Eastern Edition* (August 24, 2005), A10.

93. Chelsea R. Willness, Piers Steel, and Kibeom Lee, "A Meta-Analysis of the Antecedents and Consequences of Workplace Sexual Harassment," *Personnel Psychology* (Spring 2007), 127–162.

94. *Ibid.*

95. Christopher Farrell, "Is the Workplace Getting Raunchier?" *BusinessWeek* (March 17, 2008), 19.

96. http://www.eeoc.gov

97. *Ibid.*

98. *Ibid.*

99. Marilyn Machlowitz and David Machlowitz, "Hug by the Boss Could Lead to a Slap from the Judge," *The Wall Street Journal* (September 25, 1986), 20.

100. "Ruling to Define Sex Harassment in the Workplace," *The Atlanta Journal* (March 2, 1993), A4.

101. Lisa Genasci, "What Does High Court's Harassment Ruling Mean?" *Athens Banner-Herald* (November 10, 1993), 21.

102. Quoted in *Ibid.*

103. Erik Brady, "Colorado Scandal Could Hit Home to Other Colleges," *USA Today* (May 26, 2004), http://www.usatoday.com.

104. Susan B. Garland, "Finally, a Corporate Tip Sheet on Sexual Harassment," *BusinessWeek* (July 13, 1998), 39.

105. Anita Cava, "Sexual Harassment Claims: New Framework for Employers," *Business and Economic Review* (July–September 2001), 13–16; Ted Meyer and Linda Schoonmaker, "Employers Must Think Outside the Sexual Harassment Box," *Texas Lawyer* (February 12, 2001), 36.

106. Adam Liptak, "Court Expands Ability to Sue in Sexual Harassment Investigations," *The New York Times* (January 26, 2009).

107. Beth Brophy, "Supreme Court Gives Motherhood Its Legal Due," *U.S. News & World Report* (January 26, 1987), 12.

108. Isabel Wilkerson, "AT&T Settles Bias Suit for $66 Million," *The New York Times* (July 18, 1991), A16.

109. Gillian Flynn, "Watch Out for Pregnancy Discrimination," *Workforce* (November 2002), 84.

110. http://www.eeoc.gov

111. Mary Lord, "Pregnant—and Now without a Job," *U.S. News & World Report* (January 23, 1995), 66.

112. "Pregnancy Discrimination Act Does Not Protect Male Fired Due to His Partner's Pregnancy; No Protection for 'Reproductive Rights,'" *Fair Employment Practices Guidelines* (July 1, 2007), 1–4.

113. *Ibid.*

114. "Under a Civil Rights Cloud, Fetal Protection Looks Dismal," *Insight* (April 15, 1991), 40–41.

115. *Ibid.*

116. http://www.osha.gov/SLTC/reproductivehazards/(2010).

117. Jonathan Birchali, "Walmart to Seek Lawsuit Review," *Financial Times* (April 27, 2010), http://www.ft.com/cms/s/0/44370374-5162-11df-bed9-00144feab49a.html.

118. *Ibid.*

119. Allen Smith, "Certification of Largest Civil Rights Class OK'd," *HR Magazine* (March 2007), 26–34.

120. http://www.now.org

121. Smith, 34.

122. *Ibid.*

123. Anne Fisher, "Older, Wiser, Job-Hunting," *Fortune* (February 9, 2004), 46.

124. Carole Fleck, "No Rest for the Weary," *AARP Bulletin* (September 2009), 18–20.

125. *Ibid.*

126. Jeffrey J. Kros, "Age Discrimination Law Narrowed," *Workspan* (May 2004), 78–80.

127. Judy Greenwald, "Ruling Spurs EEOC to Revise Age-Bias Regs," *Business Insurance* (July 16, 2007), 6.

128. *Ibid.*

129. Meng Ouyang, "A Look at Disparate Law Treatment after Gross v. FBL Financial Services, Inc.," *Employee Relations Law Journal* (Spring 2010), 61–71.

130. *Ibid.*

131. Statement of Jacqueline A. Berrien, Chair U.S. Equal Employment Opportunity Commission, before the Committee on Health, Education, Labor and Pensions, United States Senate (May 6, 2010), http://www.eeoc.gov/eeoc/events/berrien_protecting_older_workers.cfm.

132. http://eeoc.gov/eeoc/statistics/enforcement/religion.cfm17 (2010).

133. Neal Lerner, "Employers Attempt to Balance Work and Religion; Complaints Alleging Religious Discrimination Have Jumped 75 Percent in the Past Decade," *The Christian Science Monitor* (April 12, 2004), 14.

134. Lauren E. Bohn, "Workplace Religious Freedom Bill Finds Renewed Interest," *PEW Forum on Religion and Public Life* (May 3, 2010), http://pewforum.org/Religion-News/Workplace-religious-freedom-bill-finds-revived-interest.aspx.

135. John Elvin, "Does Religion Belong in the Workplace?" *Insight on the News* (October 28–November 10, 2003), 16.

136. *Ibid.*

137. *Ibid.*

138. *Ibid.*

139. *Ibid.*

140. *Ibid.*

141. *Ibid.*

142. Kelley Holland, "When Religious Needs Test Company Policy," *The New York Times* (February 25, 2007), 17.

143. http://www.eeoc.gov/eeoc/publications/fs-race.cfm (2010).

144. Marjorie Valbrun, "EEOC Sees Rise in Intrarace Complaints of Color Bias," *The Wall Street Journal* (August 7, 2003), B1.

145. http://www.eeoc.gov/eeoc/initiatives/e-race/caselist.cfm#color (2010).

146. LGBT Equality at the Fortune 500 (February 12, 2009), http://www.hrc.org/issues/fortune500.htm.

147. *Ibid.*

148. *Ibid.*

149. *Ibid.*

150. Jennifer Hamilton, "Supreme Court to Hear Transgender, Transsexual Case," *Pacific Business News* (February 27, 2004), 5.

151. "Labor Letter: Transexual Employees," *The Wall Street Journal* (April 13, 1993), A1.

152. "HRC Lauds Federal Court Ruling Asserting Protection for Transsexual Employees Under Existing Law," *Human Rights Campaign Press Release* (June 1, 2004), http://www.hrc.org.

153. Christopher Danzig, "Gender Stereotyping Leads to Title VII Claim," *Inside Counsel* (April 2010), 63–64.

154. *Ibid.*

155. Dave Wieczorek, "Transsexual Employee's Title VII Claim Goes Forward," *InsideCounsel* (May 2006), 77–79.

156. David L. Chappell, "If Affirmative Action Fails … What Then?" *The New York Times* (May 8, 2004), B7; Terry H. Anderson, *The Pursuit of Fairness: A History of Affirmative Action* (New York: Oxford University Press, May 2004).

157. Thomas Nagel, "A Defense of Affirmative Action," *Report from the Center for Philosophy and Public Policy* (College Park, MD: University of Maryland, Fall 1981), 6–9.

158. Daniel Seligman, "How 'Equal Opportunity' Turned into Employment Quotas," *Fortune* (March 1973), 160–168.

159. Tom L. Beauchamp and Norman E. Bowie (eds.), *Ethical Theory and Business,* 2d ed. (Englewood Cliffs, NJ: Prentice Hall, 1983), 477–478.

160. *Ibid.*, 478.
161. "Public Backs Affirmative Action but Not Minority Hiring Preferences," *PEW Research Center Publications* (June 2, 2009), http://pewresearch.org/pubs/1240/sotomayor-supreme-court-affirmative-action-minority-preferences.
162. http://pewresearch.org/pubs/1240/sotomayor-supreme-court-affirmative-action-minority-preferences
163. Mitchell F. Rice and Maurice Mongkuo, "Did Adarand Kill Minority Set-Asides?" *Public Administration Review* (January/February 1998), 82–86.
164. *Ibid.*
165. Norma M. Riccucci, "Moving Away from a Strict Scrutiny Standard for Affirmative Action," *American Review of Public Administration* (2007), 123–141.
166. http://www.terry.uga.edu/news/releases/2006/buying_power_study.html
167. http://pewresearch.org/pubs/434/trends-in-political-values-and-core-attitudes-1987-2007
168. Madison J. Gray, "Nationwide Attack on Affirmative Action," *Black Enterprise* (February 2007), 29.
169. "Voluntary Diversity Plans Can Lead to Risk," *HR Focus* (June 2007), 2.
170. *Ibid.*
171. *Ibid.*, 2.

Name Index

Subject Index

Page numbers in italics refer to figures.